Economic Development

Revised Edition

Economic Development

PROBLEMS, PRINCIPLES, AND POLICIES

Revised Edition

Benjamin Higgins

Professeur titulaire
des sciences économiques,
Université de Montréal

W · W · NORTON & COMPANY · INC · *New York*

Library of Congress Catalog Card No. 67-11081

ISBN 0 393 09714 5

PRINTED IN THE UNITED STATES OF AMERICA

5 6 7 8 9 0

TO THOSE WHO TAUGHT ME MOST

Alvin Hansen

Herbert Heaton   Lionel Robbins

Arthur Marget   Paul Rosenstein-Rodan

Contents

—————————————— PART 4 ——————————————

Theories of Underdevelopment

—————————————— PART 5 ——————————————

Policies

—————————————— PART 6 ——————————————

Case Studies

—————————————— PART 7 ——————————————

Afterword

Preface to the Revised Edition

Over seven years have passed since the first edition of this book was written. In a field as fast moving as economic development, the rate of obsolescence of ideas is high; a revision is long overdue. Meanwhile, courses in economic development have become firmly entrenched in the curricula of our universities, and the need for comprehensive textbooks is more apparent than it was seven years ago. Thus, while the level of discussion is not substantially changed, and while—I hope—some sparks of originality may still appear here and there, this new edition is conceived as more of a textbook and less of a treatise than the original one.

As far as my own approach to the subject matter is concerned, four sets of experience have been of paramount importance in shaping the revision. First, as I hoped it would, my move from MIT to Texas involved some shift of interest, with respect to field work and discussion, from Asia and the Middle East to Latin America. I have been privileged to undertake two missions for AID in Brazil and to make shorter visits, under United Nations and AID auspices, to Chile, Argentina, and Mexico; and any social scientist at the University of Texas is more or less continuously aware of Latin American problems. Not that I have escaped Asia and the Middle East altogether; I have undertaken missions to Ceylon, Libya, Egypt, and the Lebanon as well. An assignment from OECD has acquainted me with Greek development problems. These new field experiences are reflected in the revision, especially in the case studies.

Second, I have been involved in a number of expert groups and training seminars, organized by OECD or one or another of the UN specialized agencies, concerned with social development, particularly education, and with social aspects of economic development. These experiences have resulted in a considerable expansion of my discussion of these topics, together with substantial rewriting of the sections concerned with social aspects of economic development. In particular, the economics of education, scarcely mentioned in the first edition, is accorded a chapter of its own.

Third, I have participated in a number of meetings on techniques of planning economic development. As a consequence, the chapter on planning has been entirely rewritten and now takes a viewpoint totally different from the original.

Fourth, I have undertaken in the meantime a book for the MIT Center for International Studies on foreign aid and stabilization policy, an evaluation for OECD of the impact of technical assistance in Greece, and another evaluation mission for the UN in Libya. These experiences have resulted in a substantial revision of the sections on foreign aid and international stabilization policy.

These personal experiences reflect fairly accurately, it seems to me, what has been happening in the field as a whole. The last few years have seen a resurgence of interest in Latin America, not only among development economists but among social scientists as a group, among politicians and statesmen, and among the general public. The Alliance for Progress was born during these years. There has also been a general move toward a more interdisciplinary approach to development problems, with a widening and deepening of interest in the political, sociocultural, and psychological aspects of development. It is recognized now that simple transfer of the more advanced technology of the richer countries, even if accompanied by significant capital inflow as well, is not enough. In addition it is necessary to create a whole range of skills—labor skills, agricultural skills, scientific and technical skills, managerial and entrepreneurial skills. Some would argue that it is also necessary to inculcate certain attitudes, values, and incentives. This heightened interest in "the human factor" has found its most striking expression in the incredible rate of growth of the literature on "investment in human resources," or the economics of education; but it also appears in the efforts of economists to analyze sociological, anthropological, psychological, and political factors in development, and in the efforts of sociologists, anthropologists, psychologists, and political scientists to analyze economic development.

There has not been any dramatic progress in the general theory of economic development. The lack of "breakthrough" in this respect has been no surprise to this writer. The chief barrier to economic development is still our ignorance of the process, and we face a long period of painful accumulation of the relevant empirical knowledge before general theory can be much improved. However, there have been two or three significant attempts at new theoretical formulations, and these are dealt with in the section on theories of underdevelopment.

Our empirical knowledge has been significantly strengthened in seven years. There has also been a marked improvement in the techniques of planning and programming. Unfortunately, our ability to plan—given the basic knowledge—has outrun our knowledge of the development process; that is, we know quite well how to handle the relevant data so as to arrive at the appropriate decisions regarding the scale and composition of a development program, but we seldom have all the data we want to put into our programming models. In some cases we are not altogether sure which are the relevant data.

The first edition prompted a considerable number of reactions, in letters to myself or the publisher and in reviews in professional journals. On the whole the readers and reviewers of the first edition were kind; their criticisms were mainly of a constructive nature. I have tried to take account of all this constructive criticism in the present volume. Inevitably, some of the comments conflicted with each other. Many observers suggested that the book was too long while praising its comprehensiveness and complaining that the treatment of certain favorite topics was much too short. Chapters picked for special praise by some were damned by others. Where such conflicting opinions have been expressed, I have followed the majority, used my own judgment, or done what I wanted to do in the first place.

On the whole the reactions to the manner in which the history of thought was presented were favorable, and I have left this section largely unchanged. I have added some pages on the Malthusian population theory. When writing the first edition I deliberately left out all mention of this theory, expressly because it is the one thing everyone associates with Malthus, and I wanted to draw attention to his two-sector analysis of underdeveloped countries, which seemed to me more important. I have since realized, however, that if one puts together the analysis of underdevelopment in the Principles and the theory of population explosion of the Essay and interprets the material generously (as Paul Rosenstein-Rodan taught me to do years ago) one has virtually all the elements of the contemporary theory of underdevelopment. In revising this section I have brought out this point. I have also heeded the complaints that my treatment of Harrod was too long and too complicated for a book on underdeveloped countries, and have noted Hans Singer's protest against my completely ignoring Lord Keynes.

Since history does not change as rapidly as contemporary theory, I have changed Part III on Lessons of History relatively little. However, it has been necessary to take account of Walt Rostow's book and the storm of controversy to which it has given rise. In Part IV, apart from the expanded and modified treatment of sociological factors mentioned above and the addition of discussions of new general theories, I have responded to the protests of my geographer friends that my treatment of environmental factors was far too slim. They have acquainted me with the considerable literature that has grown up in recent years on geographic aspects of development and I have given some space to this literature. Also, I feel that the argument concerning the terms of trade and economic growth can be stated in more definitive terms now than was the case seven years ago. I have dropped the rather complicated analysis of Dr. Atallah, not because my regard for this analysis has declined, but because it is material that is virtually impossible to summarize and a bit too complex for a textbook.

In the discussion of policy the main changes are revision of the section on foreign aid, the addition of two chapters on programming education and other aspects of social development, another chapter on urbanization and physical planning, and a complete rewriting of the chapter on planning. To offset the addition of new material in an already long book, I have dropped a good deal of discussion which was not specifically related to problems of underdeveloped countries.

The most difficult decision related to the case material. A number of reviewers of the first edition complained about the division of the case material between the beginning and the end of the book. Upon reflection, I came to agree with them. But where to put it? There is something to be said for arousing the curiosity of the students by describing problems of particular countries early in the book; there is also something to be said for analyzing the experience of these countries after some tools of analysis have been provided. My decision was to put all the case material in one section and leave it to individual instructors (or readers) to decide where this case material can best be introduced. Perhaps it would be desirable to refer to it at several points in reading other parts of the book.

I have also changed the list of countries. In writing the first edition, I felt constrained to limit the case materials to those countries where I had personal experience, supported, in the case of India and Italy, by the enormous amount of work going on around me at MIT in the India and Italy projects. This time, however, I have included countries of obvious importance, even when I have had no intensive experience of my own in them, notably Japan. I felt it desirable to include one Socialist country, and made use of material on Cuba prepared originally for another purpose, in collaboration with Professor Eastin Nelson. Finally, in view of the growing interest in experiments in regional planning I have added a chapter on Greece.

I hesitated for some time regarding the inclusion of Libya. In one sense Libya has lost its interest since petroleum was discovered; it is no longer a model of a desperately resource-poor country. A second mission to Libya, however, convinced me that the sudden transition from a resource-poor to a resource-rich country was of great interest in itself. I have therefore left Libya in but changed the treatment.

I regret the absence of case material for African countries south of the Sahara. An ill-timed attack of amoebic hepatitis—one of the occupational hazards of the development economist—upset my plans for acquiring first-hand knowledge of that vast and important area. I hope to rectify this shortcoming for the third edition.

In general, in revising the case material, I have moved in the direction of dealing in each country with the special features of its problems, and of the efforts to solve them, which give it a peculiar interest. In other words, I have not tried to provide comprehensive reviews of all aspects of development problems and policies in each of these countries. Rather, I have been selective, and have tried to bring out different points for each of the countries covered.

Most of the work for this edition was done at the University of Texas, and I should like to express my gratitude to my colleagues and the administration at that University for their tolerance of the erratic ways of the development economist. I should also like to thank Chancellor Jones and his excellent staff at the East-West Center of the University of Hawaii, where my sojourn as Senior Specialist helped greatly in advancing this and other projects.

Benjamin Higgins

Acknowledgments

Acknowledgments are due to the following publishers and journals for permission to utilize or draw upon earlier publications by the author: *The American Economic Review; The Canadian Journal of Economics and Political Science; The Economic Journal; The Economic Record; Ekonomi dan Keuangan Indonesia; Economic Development and Cultural Change;* the Institute of Pacific Relations; *Land Economics;* the Melbourne University Press; *Philippines Economic Journal; Social Research;* the United Nations; and *World Politics.*

Acknowledgments are due to the following authors and publishers for permission to quote: John H. Adler, *Absorptive Capacity,* The Brookings Institution; G. C. Allen and A. G. Donnithorne, *Western Enterprise in Indonesia and Malaya,* Macmillan & Co., Ltd.; M. K. Atallah, *The Long-term Movement of the Terms of Trade between Agricultural and Industrial Products,* Netherlands Economics Institute; P. Bauer and B. S. Yamey, *The Economics of Underdeveloped Countries,* University of Chicago Press; J. H. Boeke, *Economics and Economic Policy of Dual Societies,* Institute of Pacific Relations; R. V. Clemence and F. S. Doody, *The Schumpeterian System,* Addison-Wesley Press; Charles J. Erasmus, *Man Takes Control,* University of Minnesota Press; *Employment Objectives in Economic Development,* International Labour Office, Geneva; S. H. Frankel, *The Economic Impact on Underdeveloped Societies,* Oxford University Press; Clifford Geertz, *Peddlers and Princes,* University of Chicago Press; Norton Ginsberg (ed.), *Essays on Geography and Economic Development,* University of Chicago, Department of Geography; A. O. Hirschman, *The Strategy of Economic Development,* Yale University Press; B. F. Hoselitz (ed.), *The Progress of Underdeveloped Areas,* University of Chicago Press; Leo Huberman and Paul Sweezy,

xv

Cuba: Anatomy of a Revolution, Monthly Review Press; Harold A. Innis, *The Fur Trade in Canada*, University of Toronto Press; D. H. K. Lee, *Climate and Economic Development in the Tropics*, Harper & Row, Publishers, Inc. for the Council on Foreign Relations; R. Lekachman (ed.), *National Policy for Economic Welfare at Home and Abroad*, Doubleday & Company, Inc.; H. Leibenstein, *Economic Backwardness and Economic Growth*, University of California Press and John Wiley & Sons, Inc.; W. A. Lewis, The Theory of Economic Growth, Richard D. Irwin, Inc.; D. C. McClelland, *The Achieving Society*, D. Van Nostrand Company, Inc.; W. Malenbaum, *East and West in India's Development*, National Planning Association; R. Malthus, *Principles of Political Economy*, Augustus Kelly; G. M. Meier and R. E. Baldwin, *Economic Development: Theory, History, and Policy*, John Wiley & Sons, Inc.; Walter C. Neale, *India: The Search for Unity, Democracy, and Progress*, D. Van Nostrand Company, Inc.; D. Novak and R. Lekachman, *Development and Society*, St. Martin's Press; W. W. Rostow, *The Stages of Economic Growth*, Cambridge University Press; J. Schumpeter, *Business Cycles*, McGraw-Hill Book Company, Inc.; D. Seers, *Cuba: The Economic and Social Revolution*, The University of North Carolina Press; Miyohei Shinohara, *Growth Cycles in the Japanese Empire; Social Aspects of Economic Development in Latin America*, UNESCO; J. J. Spengler and O. D. Duncan, *Demographic Analysis* and *Population Theory and Policy*, Richard D. Irwin, Inc.; John Vaizey, *The Economics of Education*, The Macmillan Company; R. Vernon (ed.), *Public Policy and Private Enterprise in Mexico*, Harvard University Press; H. F. Williamson and J. Buttrick, *Economic Development: Principles and Patterns*, Prentice-Hall, Inc.; W. S. Woytinsky, *World Population and Production*, The Twentieth Century Fund, Inc.

Acknowledgments are also due to the following journals and authors for permission to quote: *The American Economic Review*, R. Eckaus, R. R. Nelson, H. Singer; *Economic Development and Cultural Change*, Phyllis Deane; *The Economic Journal*, H. Myint; *Foreign Affairs*, John Kenneth Galbraith, *The Manchester School of Economic and Social Studies*, W. A. Lewis; *Oxford Economic Papers*, H. Myint; *The Quarterly Journal of Economics*, R. Solow; *Regional Science*, Mary Megee; *Tempo*, Easton Nelson.

The sources of various tables used throughout the text and in the statistical appendix are provided with the tables.

PART I | Introduction: the Problem

1 | The Worldwide War against Poverty

The poor are a part of the necessary furniture of the earth, a sort of perpetual gymnasium where the rich can practice virtue when they are so inclined.

A man can be neither a saint, nor a lover, nor a poet, unless he has comparatively recently had something to eat.

I give you the toast of the Royal Economic Society, of economics and economists, who are the trustees not of civilization, but of the possibility of civilization.

If morals have any meaning at all, they must entail that the hungry are fed, the naked clothed, the homeless sheltered, and all the sons of men given some little share in the world's great patrimony of knowledge and opportunity, of health and hope.

These four quotations illustrate the "revolution of rising expectations" that has embroiled the people of our day, in underdeveloped and advanced countries alike. The first, from the *Discorsi Politici* of Francesco Giucciardini, was written early in the sixteenth century, in a period of relative economic and social stagnation. It suggests no hope that poverty should be abolished, or even that income distribution could be much altered. The second is from the Reverend Philip H. Wicksteed, a leading neoclassical economist, and was written at the turn of this century. Here there is no longer an inevitable division into rich and poor. It implies that to have a share in civilization one must first be granted the basic necessities. The third is Lord Keynes in 1945, not long before his death; it expresses the view of the twentieth-century liberal and humanist, who believes in progress as a normal state of affairs if only reason is allowed to prevail, and who recognizes economic development as the necessary foundation for other forms of advancement of mankind. The fourth, from Lady Barbara Ward Jackson in this decade, reflects the new sense of urgency and the new determination to abolish poverty from the face of the earth.

Rich Lands and Poor

The concept of "rich" and "poor" extends today to nations as well as to individuals and groups; the rich nations are committed to the practice of virtue, not just in the sense of sharing their wealth with the poor ones, but in the much more ambitious sense of helping the poor nations to raise their productivity and incomes so that they may one day join the ranks of the rich. So far, only limited progress has been made. The international distribution of income among countries remains much more unequal than is typical of income distribution among individuals in particular countries, and this inequality continues to grow. As may be seen from Table 1–1,

TABLE 1–1

The Distribution of World Income

Region	Share of Population			Percentage Share of Income		
	1860	1913	1960	1860	1913	1960
North America	3.1	6.3	8.0	14.8	34.3	37.4
Oceania	0.1	0.4	0.5	0.5	1.4	1.0
Europe	19.0	19.7	16.2	39.1	35.0	14.0
Latin America	3.3	6.3	8.0	4.0	4.1	6.3
Soviet Union	6.8	8.7	8.6	4.0	7.4	17.4
Far East	2.3	3.9	5.1	1.4	1.8	1.3
China	40.2	32.5	27.1	19.8	8.0	7.3
Japan	2.9	3.2	3.7	1.6	1.5	2.5
Southeast Asia	22.3	20.3	22.7	11.8	6.9	2.6

SOURCE: Adapted from L. J. Zimmerman, *Poor Lands, Rich Lands: The Widening Gap* (New York, 1965), pp. 35–37.

North America's share in world income has risen from 14.8 per cent to 37.4 per cent in the course of a century, whereas the population grew only from 3.1 per cent to 8.0 per cent. The Soviet Union shows a spectacular gain since 1913, as does Japan. No other region shows improvement in relative income per capita. Oceania (Australia and New Zealand) in 1860 had a share of income five times its share of population; in 1913 the income was still three and a half times the population share, but in 1960 it was only double, reflecting the relative stagnation of these economies after

World War I. Even Europe has suffered a much greater decline in share of world income than in share of world population. The Asian countries (except Japan) and Latin America all show a deterioration of their relative position in distribution of world income. Worst of all is Southeast Asia, where the share of world population has remained almost unchanged over the century, whereas the share of world income has fallen from 11.8 per cent to 2.6 per cent.

Put in another way, in the century following 1860 the share of the quarter of the world's population living in the world's richest countries increased from 58 per cent to 72 per cent; the share of the next richest quarter rose from 15.5 per cent to 19 per cent; the share of the next quarter fell from 14 per cent to 7 per cent, and the share of the quarter of the population living in the poorest countries dropped from 12.5 per cent to a mere 3 per cent.

Unfortunately, the new concern with the problems of poor countries has yet to produce any narrowing of the gap between them and the rich countries. On the contrary, as may be seen from Table 1–2, the gap in per

TABLE 1–2

Current Growth Rates of Income and of Population, Averages for Developed and Less-Developed Countries

Per cent growth rates per year	AC's*	UDC's
Of income	4.4	4.7
Of population	1.3	2.4
Of income per capita	3.1	2.3
GNP per capita	$1,828	$400–480
Growth of GNP per capita, in dollars per year	$57	$9–11

* AC = Advanced countries; UDC's = underdeveloped countries.
SOURCE: Theodore Morgan, "Economic Planning-Points of Success and Failure," *The Philippine Economic Journal*, Second Semester, 1965, p. 404.

capita incomes between economically advanced countries as a group (AC's) and the underdeveloped countries as a group (UDC's) is still growing rapidly. Because of the much higher rates of population growth in poor countries taken together, even the percentage increase in per capita incomes is lower than in rich countries, despite a higher rate of growth of national income as a whole.

Poverty is the ultimate concern of economics and economists. Because pockets of poverty remain even in the richest of countries, including the United States and Canada, it is well that some economists should continue to interest themselves in the problems of economically advanced countries. But with the achievement of "affluence" in the more industrialized countries and with the recognition that we all live in one world, our fates irrevocably intertwined, it is natural that the major effort of economists since World War II should have been directed toward the appalling problems of countries where the majority of people are still poor. These are the countries labeled "underdeveloped."

The Campaign

Economists are far from being alone in this effort. Alleviation of the mass poverty that still prevails in most countries has become a worldwide campaign in which virtually every nation—rich or poor—is involved. It is one venture in which the Communist countries and the industrialized countries of the West join hands—not, of course, without some rivalry in selling to the developing countries their own brand of economic and political systems. Nonetheless, the international war on poverty has brought a degree of international cooperation undreamed of a generation ago. Robert L. Heilbroner goes so far as to call this gigantic multi-national effort "the first real act in world history" which "towers over any previous enterprise of man." [1] Barbara Ward says bluntly that "we live in the most catastrophically revolutionary age that men have ever faced." [2]

The "revolution of rising expectations" and the united international effort to deal with it have given rise to a battery of new institutions since World War II. The International Bank for Reconstruction and Development and its International Development Association provide loan and grant capital to the governments of underdeveloped countries. The International Finance Corporation, another subsidiary of the Bank, provides funds for private investment in underdeveloped areas. The Technical Operations Agency, the Food and Agriculture Organization, the International Labor Organization, the World Health Organization, UNESCO, other UN Specialized Agencies, and the Ford Foundation provide technical assistance. The United States has its own program of technical and capital assistance through the Agency for International Development. The United States Export-Import Bank, although originally established for other purposes, has in recent years allocated the bulk of its funds for loans to underdeveloped areas. Australia, Canada, and Great Britain are providing capital and technical assistance to Commonwealth countries, and to some others as well, through the Colombo Plan Organization. Japan, France, Germany, and other West European countries also have bilateral aid programs and are joined with the United States, the United Kingdom, and Canada in a "donors' club" through the Organization for Economic Cooperation and Development.

Since 1956 Russia has become an increasingly strong competitor of the Western countries in providing technical and capital assistance. Russian assistance has been concentrated in the "uncommitted" countries of Africa, Asia, and the Middle East. As a consequence, economic aid to these countries has become a major instrument in the Cold War.[3]

No set of institutions, unfortunately, can help very much unless the people who man them know what they are doing. A major obstacle to

[1] Robert L. Heilbroner, *The Great Ascent* (New York and Evanston, 1963), p. 17.
[2] Barbara Ward, *The Rich Nations and the Poor Nations* (New York, 1962), p. 13.
[3] Foreign aid programs are discussed more extensively in Part 5.

economic development is still plain ignorance. The disheartening truth is
that no aspect of human knowledge is completely irrelevant to the process
of development. Eugene R. Black, who had a unique opportunity to study
the problem of underdevelopment during his fourteen years as President
of the International Bank for Reconstruction and Development, said in
1960:

Few subjects have received more intensive study in recent years than the subject of economic development. The disciplines of all the social sciences have
been brought to bear, and a whole new body of literature has resulted. To
digest and order this body of literature would require a philosopher, widely
schooled in academic economics, with a good command of history, who held
a degree in civil engineering, with geography and anthropology as minor subjects, and who had taken a post-graduate course in modern social psychology.[4]

Those of us who live in the advanced countries of Europe, North
America, and Australasia might find Mr. Black's lament excessively
gloomy. Many of us have come to take progress for granted and to be
resentful of any slowing down of progress through unemployment, inflation, balance of payments difficulties, or other "temporary" interruptions
to steady economic advance. Isn't there some simple lesson to be learned
from the experience of the now rich nations which can readily be applied
to the poor ones?

The answer is clearly "no." If it were possible to chart per capita income for all the countries now belonging to the United Nations, starting
with the beginning of human history and ending with World War II, the
charts would show long periods of dreary stagnation, interrupted by short
spurts of economic progress in a few countries. One historian of the ancient world has argued that the wealth of ancient Rome was not surpassed
in Europe or the United States until the nineteenth and twentieth centuries.[5] The rapid and essentially continuous rise in per capita income in
Europe, North America, and Australasia during the past two and a half
centuries, which many of us in the Western world have come to regard as
"normal," would appear as a phenomenon unique in history. Perhaps, as
some economic historians insist, this remarkable rise in productivity, confined to so small a share of world population for so short a period, was
"more than industrial and less than revolution"; but certainly the difference in *degree* between the rise in general living standards in those countries at that time, and any economic development that has yet occurred
elsewhere is so great as to constitute a difference in kind. Stagnation is the
rule; economic development is the exception that requires explanation.

Certainly understanding of the economics and politics (and perhaps the
social psychology and the ethics) of development must be more widespread in both underdeveloped and advanced countries if we are to realize

[4] Eugene R. Black, *The Diplomacy of Economic Development and Other Papers*
(New York, 1963), p. 3.
[5] M. I. Rostovtzeff, quoted in L. J. Zimmerman, *Poor Lands, Rich Lands: The
Widening Gap* (New York, 1965), p. 9.

our brave hopes of wiping poverty off the face of the earth. This book is designed to make some small contribution to the extension of such knowledge.

What Is an Underdeveloped Country?

The enormous variety of economic and social conditions found in countries classified as "underdeveloped" may be illustrated from the author's own experience. The Balinese village of Ubud has a population of perhaps 5,000 people, but it is known as an art center even in that particularly artistic region of Bali. It has an art school and gallery, a school of music and dance, and several exquisite temples. The cultural life centers around the *kratan* (palace) of the *Tjokorda Agung* (Sultan), but few households are without a painter, a sculptor, a musician, or a dancer. It is a rare evening when there is no performance of theater, music, or dance in the neighborhood. Art forms tend to follow the classical framework but are highly inventive and dynamic within that framework. For example, the author was privileged to be present at the invention of a woodwind trio, which sounded like Bach but was actually, as a Dutch musicologist explained, a high-grade "jam session." This small village has two full *gamelans,* roughly equivalent to having two full symphony orchestras. So keen was the rivalry between these two orchestras that the Dutch musicologist refused to go to rehearsals in North Ubud, for fear of offending his friends in South Ubud.

Is this, then, an underdeveloped country, this lovely island where people can provide themselves with food, clothing, and shelter with about twenty hours' work a week, and devote the rest of their time to their religion and their arts?

From the roof garden of a skyscraper hotel in São Paulo one can see in every direction elegant office and apartment buildings in the modern Brazilian style, covering a substantially greater area than Manhattan, soaring skyward. On the streets below smartly dressed people proceed in limousines to concerts and the opera, to superb restaurants and sophisticated nightclubs. With binoculars one might make out the road to Santos, lined on either side with huge modern factories. Is *this* an underdeveloped country?

In a remote desert village in the Fezzan no women between the ages of fifteen and fifty were to be seen; they were hidden in the women's quarters of the straggling whitewashed mud huts, in strict *purdah.* Children with grossly bloated stomachs gave mute evidence of the starvation level at which they lived. The filmed eyes, typical of trachoma, were to be seen everywhere. The children had wearied of slapping at flies that refused to stay away; their eyes were ringed with black as the flies sought what moisture they could find in that desert country. Surely, *this* was an underdeveloped country.

In Recife, one can drive from a charming nineteenth-century hotel, with a view over a triangular plaza, past the modern skyscrapers and seventeenth-century Dutch houses, to the outskirts of town. Here are shacktowns, with people swarming among the stilts on which their wretched one-room huts were built to keep them out of the mud which was the only land available for them. Here again are the bloated stomachs and the telltale signs of deficiency diseases; here women rummage in the mud in the hope of finding a few tiny shrimp or at least some grubs. Surely, this, too, is underdevelopment.

Calcutta. A sprawling city of six million people. Thousands of people on the streets, many of them beggars. An old man lies motionless on the sidewalk; he is dying of starvation. Some softhearted person has put a chunk of bread beside him, but by now he is too weak to reach for it. The crowds pass him by, knowing that there are hundreds of others in the same predicament at that same moment and that there is little they, as individuals, can do to help.

Bucolic idylls, rural squalor and misery; urban elegance, urban starvation; these and other contrasts are to be found among, and even within, the countries we label "underdeveloped." What, if anything, is the common denominator that allows us to lump them together and contrast them with the "economically advanced" countries?

Stressing the great variety of conditions in developing countries, Eugene Black says:

That vast stretch of the planet, extending eastward from Latin America, through Africa and the Middle East, to South and Southeast Asia, which we have come to call the underdeveloped world, is an area of great diversity. Here can be found virtually every race and creed which exists on earth, every kind of geographical environment and climate, and communities in widely differing stages of development. If most people are poor in the material things of life, there is in much of this area a wealth of resources waiting to be tapped. If the land in some places is dangerously over-crowded, in other places it could support two or three times the present population, even without much economic advance. These parts of the world would seem to defy useful generalizations.[6]

This diversity has prompted the noted United Nations economist Hans Singer to say that an underdeveloped country is like a giraffe; it is difficult to describe, but you always know it when you see one.

The Income Criterion

Basically the term "underdeveloped" is a policy one; a country becomes classified as underdeveloped if it so declares itself by applying for foreign aid and if the donor countries confirm its status by providing assistance. Looking at Appendix Table 1 and considering the countries listed from this point of view, we would draw a dividing line between underdeveloped and advanced countries somewhere between $500 and $600 for gross national products per capita—or, let us say, at about one-fifth to one-quarter of the per capita GNP of the United States. There would be some doubtful cases. Venezuela, with a per capita income above that of Italy or Ireland, would be regarded by many people—both in Venezuela and in

---

[6] Black, *op. cit.*, p. 6.

advanced countries—as capable of financing its own development by "sowing its petroleum." Yet half the people of Venezuela are malnourished according to World Health Organization standards, and levels of health and education are low. As recently as 1964, Venezuela received loans from the World Bank. Argentina has higher general levels of health, nutrition, and education than Venezuela, but its per capita income is substantially lower. Japan has joined the "donors club" as a member of the Organization for Economic Cooperation and Development (OECD) and is providing foreign aid on a substantial scale; yet its per capita income is lower than that in some countries universally classified as underdeveloped. The United States recently decided that Lebanon was capable of financing its own development and suspended a capital assistance program in that country. The same decision was made some years earlier in the case of Greece. Yet both of these countries continue to receive assistance from other donors, and their per capita incomes are still low. Italy and Israel are both donors and recipients of international assistance. Mainland China is one of the poorest countries of all, yet China has been a donor country on occasion.

A definition of "underdevelopment" that runs in terms of governmental action regarding foreign aid is intellectually unsatisfactory and sometimes ambiguous. It is also clear that per capita income will not suffice as the sole criterion of the level of development; otherwise we would have to place Kuwait and Qtar among the most advanced of countries. About all we can say is that countries are likely to be regarded as "underdeveloped" if they have per capita incomes below $500 (or $600) per year; to make the income criterion a bit more dynamic, we could say that countries with per capita incomes less than one-fifth (or one-quarter) of the United States level are likely to be considered underdeveloped.

Problems of Measurement

More serious than the arbitrariness of the dividing line is the sheer difficulty of translating per capita incomes into United States dollars. Obviously, the Togoland figure of $55 cannot mean that the average standard of living was equivalent to what an American would suffer with an income of $55 per year. The regional planning authorities of the Canadian province of Quebec have found that $2,500 is a minimal family income for mere subsistence in that part of the world. The United Nations outlines some of the difficulties faced in making estimates of this kind.[7]

In this connexion it is understandable that improvement in the quality of the estimates of national product has been generally more difficult and slower in the less developed countries than in the more widely industrialized countries of the world where as a rule, adequate statistical systems have evolved over the years. A problem of particular importance confronting the less developed countries in estimating their national product arises from the existence of a substantial nonmonetized economy. Where only a part of the total output

[7] United Nations, *Per-capita National Product of Fifty-five Countries: 1952–54*, Statistical Papers Series E, No. 4 (New York, 1957), p. 4.

of goods and services of a country is traded at the market it is necessary for national income purposes to estimate that part which is produced outside the monetary sphere. This area of estimation is indeed subject to a wide margin of error since the extent of such activities is known in a very approximate manner only. . . . The use of exchange rates for expressing estimates of national product in a common currency unit is subject to a number of serious shortcomings, both theoretical and statistical, which have been described in various studies. The main criticism is directed at the fact that this method oversimplifies a complex problem of evaluating in a common currency unit the total output of goods and services of different countries. It is contended that approximately correct results can be obtained by this method only where there exists an equivalence between the prevailing exchange rates and the relationship of internal prices. This equivalence is unlikely to be achieved for most countries today in view of the prevalent use of exchange controls and quantitative restrictions on trade.

Within broad categories, the figures in Appendix Table 1 are probably meaningful for relative levels of income. Thus it probably makes sense to say that average incomes in the Philippines are two and a half times as high as in India, or that incomes in the Argentine are a bit higher than in Ireland, and that United States incomes are some 30 per cent higher than Canadian. On the other hand, to say that in the United States incomes are more than forty times as high as they are in Burma has little real meaning.

What Underdeveloped Countries Are Not

It may bring us closer to a definition of underdevelopment if we clear away some misconceptions. First of all, very few of them are "undeveloped" in the sense that no development has ever taken place. Virtually all underdeveloped countries have at least one large city, and some have several, in which the architecture, the transportation, the boulevards, the bars, nightclubs, and restaurants, and even the technology seem much the same as in Europe or North America. Most of these countries have factories, power plants, and mines operating on a large scale with the most modern techniques available. Many of them have large-scale, land-and-capital-intensive commercial agriculture utilizing highly scientific methods. By definition an underdeveloped country is one in which a small proportion of the population is employed in this modern sector; but it is not necessarily a country in which no substantial amount of investment and technological progress has ever taken place.

Second, underdeveloped countries as a class are not stagnant. On the contrary, some countries commonly considered underdeveloped have recorded postwar growth rates far higher than were achieved earlier by the countries now labeled "advanced." During the fifties the star performers in the world were Japan, Venezuela, Communist China, West Germany, the Soviet Union, Greece, Turkey, Yugoslavia, Italy, and the Philippines. Of these, West Germany, the Soviet Union and Japan do not qualify today as "underdeveloped" countries. On the other hand, not all underdeveloped countries are high growth countries by any means; some, like India and

Peru, have growth rates below those of most advanced countries, especially in terms of per capita income. A few, like Indonesia, pre-Castro Cuba, Argentina, and Chile have been stagnant or worse.

As the world was not created with rich and poor countries, clearly there must have been a time when rich countries as a whole grew faster than poor countries as a whole. Looking at Table 1–3, we see that during the

TABLE 1-3

Percentage Changes in Per Capita Incomes, 1860–1960

Country	Annual percentage change		
	1860–1913	1913–1960	1860–1960
North America	1.65	1.41	1.54
Oceania	0.52	1.25	0.84
Northwest Europe	1.31	1.34	1.33
Soviet Union	1.00	3.72	2.26
Southeast Europe	1.14	1.59	1.35
Latin America	0.89	1.55	1.20
Japan	1.54	2.59	2.03
Far East	1.12	0.63	0.89
Southeast Asia	0.52	0.16	0.38
China	0.13	1.83	0.92
Total	1.52	1.52	1.52

SOURCE: Adapted from L. J. Zimmerman, *Poor Lands, Rich Lands: The Widening Gap* (New York, 1965), p. 34.

entire period from 1860 to 1913 only Japan enjoyed increases in per capita income as great as those of North America and northwestern Europe. From 1913 to 1960, however, China, Latin America, and southeastern Europe as well as Japan grew faster than the rich regions.

Third, underdeveloped countries as a group cannot be described as "overpopulated" or even densely populated. Population densities are indeed high in some underdeveloped countries, such as Ceylon, India, Taiwan, and El Salvador. But in the Congo, Mexico, Chile, Brazil, and other very poor countries, population densities are lower than in the United States, let alone France or the United Kingdom (Table 1–4).

Fourth, underdeveloped countries are not "export economies." It is true that exports from Ceylon amount to some 40 per cent of gross national product, but in Brazil exports are only 6 or 7 per cent of gross national product.

Fifth, they are not, as a class, countries with food deficiencies. Burma, Thailand, and Vietnam are all net rice exporters. In many underdeveloped countries, large segments of the population are undernourished, but in some (Turkey, Argentina, Uruguay, and Greece, for example) the caloric intake is not too far below the American average.

"Some Are But Some Are Not"

That there are great differences among underdeveloped countries in terms of almost any conceivable single index of development is already

TABLE 1–4
Population Growth and Density

Area	Percentage of annual rate of increase, 1958–63	Population density, 1963*
Africa:		
Cape Verde Islands	2.6	54
Dem. Republic of Congo	2.2	6
Gambia	2.8	5
Libya	3.7	1
Mauritius	3.1	376
Portuguese Guinea	1.1	15
Southern Rhodesia	3.3	10
Swaziland	2.8	16
Union of South Africa	2.4	14
North America:		
Canada	2.0	2
United States	1.6	20
Central America:		
Costa Rica	4.5	27
El Salvador	3.2	127
Guatemala	3.2	38
Mexico	3.2	19
South America:		
Argentina	1.6	8
Brazil	3.1	9
Chile	2.3	11
Colombia	2.2	13
Paraguay	2.4	5
Venezuela	3.4	9
Asia:		
Burma	2.1	35
Ceylon	2.5	162
India	2.3	151
Indonesia	2.3	67
Iran	2.4	13
Israel	3.5	115
Japan	0.9	259
Malaya	3.2	58
Nepal	1.8	69
Pakistan	2.1	104
Philippines	3.2	101
Taiwan	3.5	325
Europe:		
France	1.3	87
Ireland	−0.1	40
Italy	0.6	168
United Kingdom	0.7	221
Australia	2.1	1

* Per square kilometer.
SOURCE: United Nations, *Demographic Yearbook, 1964* (New York, 1965).

apparent. Although most underdeveloped countries conform to a certain norm when judged by some criteria, when judged by others they diverge from the norm in a manner that seems unrelated to their general level of development as indicated by per capita income. One of these criteria is rate of population growth. Most of the countries with which we are concerned have population growth rates that are high in comparison with North America, northwestern Europe, or Australasia. Yet Burma, Pakistan, Nepal, Portuguese Guinea, Argentina, Colombia, and Japan all have population growth rates as low as or lower than those of Canada and Australia (Table 1–4). Similarly, if we consider major regions of the world, it is clear that both birth rates and death rates are above the world average in Asia, Africa, and Latin America, and are below the average in North America and Europe (Table 1–5). Yet Ceylon has a death rate lower than England's and so do China, Mexico, Israel, Japan, and a number of Caribbean and Pacific countries.

Typologies and "Levels of Living"

Faced with the great differences among underdeveloped countries and the inadequacy of any single criterion for spotting them, some writers have resorted to typologies based on composite indices of "levels of living." The United Nations Statistical Office has suggested a composite index including health, food consumption and nutrition, education, employment and conditions of work, housing, social security, clothing, recreation, and human freedoms. These components differ in character. The first six are fairly easily quantified in a manner permitting international comparisons. Health, for example, can be measured by death rates, life expectancy, infant mortality, and the like. Education can be measured by literacy and the proportion of the relevant age-groups completing primary, secondary, and university education. The last three, on the other hand, are difficult to translate into figures that will have essentially the same meaning for all countries. Clothing requirements vary greatly with climate; tastes in recreation vary, and facilities are consequently more expensive in some countries than in others (beaches in Bali are free, horse-racing in Bangkok is expensive). Freedom is even more difficult to express statistically.

Father Roger Vekemans, Director of the Bellarmino Center for Research and Social Action, in Santiago, has developed a similar admixture of economic and socio-cultural measures to classify Latin American countries by level of development. His basic table is reproduced as Appendix Table 2. A glance at this table shows why per capita income alone is an unsatisfactory measure of economic and social welfare. Venezuela has much the highest per capita income in Latin America, yet it ranks low on the other economic indices, including calorie intake, is very low on the industrialization scale measured as proportion of labor force engaged outside of agriculture, and is near the bottom on some education and health indices. On these grounds, Professor Vekemans excludes Venezuela from the elite "Group VI," comprising the three southernmost countries. Cuba ranked fifth in per capita income but was a "seventh-class" country in

TABLE 1–5

Population, 1963, and Annual Birth, Death, and Population Growth Rates,*
by Regions, 1958–1963

World and regions	Population midyear 1963, in millions	Birth rates	Death rates	Population growth rates in per cent
World	3,160	34	16	1.8
Africa	294	46	23	2.3
Western Africa	93	54	28	2.6
Eastern Africa	80	43	23	2.0
Northern Africa	72	44	19	2.5
Middle Africa	30	40	25	1.5
Southern Africa	19	41	18	2.3
America	439	32	12	2.2
Northern America	208	24	9	1.6
Latin America	231	40	14	2.7
Tropical South America	123	43	15	2.8
Middle America (mainland)	51	43	13	3.0
Temperate South America	35	29	10	1.9
Caribbean	22	38	17	2.1
Asia	1,748	38	20	1.8
East Asia	828	33	19	1.4
Mainland region	682	35	21	1.4
Japan	96	17	7	1.0
Other East Asia	50	38	14	2.4
South Asia	920	42	20	2.2
Middle South Asia	621	42	21	2.1
South East Asia	236	42	18	2.4
South West Asia	63	42	18	2.4
Europe	437	19	10	0.9
Western Europe	140	18	11	1.2
Southern Europe	120	21	9	0.8
Eastern Europe	99	18	10	0.7
Northern Europe	78	18	11	0.6
Oceania	16.8	27	11	2.1
Australia and New Zealand	13.5	23	9	2.0
Melanesia	2.3	43	23	2.0
Polynesia and Micronesia	1.0	47	12	3.5
USSR	225	24	7	1.6

* Rates are annual average for 1958–1963; birth and death rates are per 1,000 population; population growth is the per cent rate, calculated by compound interest formula.

SOURCE: United Nations, *Demographic Yearbook, 1964* (New York, 1965).

power consumption, tenth-class (the bottom of the scale) in industrialization, and ninth-class in secondary school enrollment. Panama and Costa Rica have much lower incomes, but because of fairly good performance on other indices, they end up in the same group as Venezuela and Cuba. Usually discrepancies between a country's ranking in terms of per capita income and in terms of other measures of the level of living reflect a highly unequal distribution of income, low standards of public service, or both. A country with high income widely diffused among all groups in the society and with high standards for public services will not have low figures for caloric intake, electricity consumption, radios, education and health, or housing.

Some of these "extra" indices add a great deal more information than others. Most of them are already in the national income figure, directly or indirectly; if their market value is less than their true "social" value, it would be possible to assign to them a "shadow" or "accounting" price above the market price for purposes of national accounting. It is possible, for example, that education and health are "worth more" than they cost; if so, and if we know what they are "worth," we can assign higher values to them in measuring national income. Cement consumption may tell more about rate of growth (new construction) than level of development; both cement consumption and electricity consumption are really indicators of the degree of industrialization, already covered by the occupational structure and the income figures themselves. Newspaper consumption overlaps with urbanization, literacy, and other education indices, but it may also give some insight into political participation, as does the number of radio sets. The number of cinema seats tells something about recreation and communications, but not much—it may be a "proxy variable" for urbanization. Health might better be measured by results than by inputs of doctors, hospital beds, etc.

One obvious difficulty with such composite indices is that the components are cross correlated. Per capita consumption of electricity and of cement are so closely related to the level and growth of per capita income that adding them to the index gives little additional information. Another weakness is that the political and cultural data would have to be interpreted differently in different settings. In Brazil, for example, the number of Indians and Negroes tells little about the degree of cultural integration because of Brazil's extraordinary success as a melting pot; and in Asia or Africa different figures would be needed and would require quite different interpretations.

Basic Characteristics of Underdeveloped Countries

Let us go back to the beginning. Our arch enemy (as economists) is poverty; we are particularly interested in a certain set of countries labeled "underdeveloped" because they are poor in a way that other countries are not. Let us say that any country should be considered underdeveloped if more than half of its population lives in poverty. Poverty itself is an ambiguous term, and the concept of poverty changes with the times; but let us define poverty as a level of living that provides no margin—above the food, clothing, and shelter essential for health—for simple luxuries ("frugal comfort," in the language of the Australian Commonwealth Arbitration Court), recreation, education, and provision for sickness, old age, and temporary loss of income. "Poverty" is thus defined for legal purposes in a number of countries, and it could be determined by this yardstick within a reasonably narrow range in any country.

Our problem is then reduced to finding the figures that will provide an approximation to a measure of the incidence of poverty in various countries. The level of per capita income is a start, but it does not tell us enough. We need to know something about the distribution of income, including the impact on disposable income of government intervention in the form of taxation and expenditures on public services. Few of the countries in which we are interested have data on income distribution, so we must use "proxy variables." Of these, the most useful are the structure of employment, regional differences in income, levels of education, and standards of nutrition. Other data that might be considered are those relating to public health and communications, employment, unemployment, and underemployment.

Occupational Structure

Colin Clark [8] demonstrated as long ago as 1935 that economic progress tends to be accompanied by a decline in the proportion of the labor force in agriculture and an increase in the proportion in manufacturing and services. Since then, it has become increasingly clear that transferring people from low-productivity agriculture to high-productivity jobs in the secondary and tertiary sectors has been a major, if not the major, source of economic growth in the past. As may readily be seen from Table 1–6, no country that could be considered advanced has more than one-third of its labor force engaged in agriculture. Indeed the correlation between level of per capita income and share of the labor force employed outside of agriculture is extremely high.[9]

Moreover, the countries that have most of their labor force in agriculture are also relatively inefficient in the agricultural sector. That statement holds even in terms of yields per acre or per hectare (see Statistical Appendix Tables). When one considers how capital-and-land-intensive is North American, European, and Australasian agriculture and how labor-intensive is Asian, African, and some Latin American agriculture, it is clear that differences in man-year productivity are even more dramatic. In fact, as may be seen from Tables 1–7 and 1–7a, it is precisely in agriculture (where most of the population is engaged) that the underdeveloped countries are most at a disadvantage in comparison with the advanced countries. Clearly we are on the track of something more than a characteristic of underdeveloped countries here; we have a clue to the cause of widespread poverty.

Technological Dualism

One of the most striking features of developing countries is what has been called "technological dualism": the division of the economy into two distinct and radically different sectors, one technologically advanced and

---

[8] Colin Clark, *The Conditions of Economic Progress* (London, 1935).

[9] L. J. Zimmerman, *op. cit.*, p. 47.

Professor L. J. Zimmerman obtains the following equation:

$$\log y = 0.202x + 1.3235 \qquad (R = 0.92)$$

where y is per capita income and x is the percentage of total employment in non-agrarian activities.

TABLE 1-6

Population Engaged in Agricultural Occupations
in Specified Countries

Continent and countries	Percentage in agriculture		Per capita GNP, 1961*
	1930–44	1945–62	
Europe:			
France	36	26	1,203
Great Britain	6	5	1,345
Ireland	49	40	570
Italy	48	26	623
Yugoslavia	..	..	306
North America:			
Canada	26	11	2,040
United States	19	7	2,790
Latin America:			
Argentina	..	20	533
Brazil	67	58	268
Chile	35	28	348
Colombia	72	54	287
Costa Rica	63	55	278
El Salvador	75	60	191
Guatemala	71	68	184
Mexico	65	54	297
Paraguay	..	54	129
Uruguay	..	14	449
Venezuela	50	32	644
Asia:			
Ceylon	..	53	123
China (Taiwan)	..	50	116
India	66	70	70
Indonesia	66	72	99
Israel (Jewish pop.)	..	13	733
Japan	48	40	383
Malaya	61	58	368
Philippines	73	58	188
Africa:			
Congo	..	84	103
Egypt (UAR)	71	57	150
Nyasaland	..	92	161
Rhodesia	..	77	161
Oceania:			
Australia	19	13	1,475
New Zealand	23	14	1,470

* Expressed in U.S. dollars.
SOURCE: Food and Agriculture Organization, *Statistical Yearbook*: Rosenstein-Rodan, *Review of Economics and Statistics.*

TABLE 1–7

Production per Laborer in the Primary, Secondary,
and Tertiary Sectors (about 1953)

Economic geographic area	Productivity per laborer in dollars		
	Primary sector	Secondary sector	Tertiary sector
North America	2,860	5,530	5,200
Oceania	4,150	2,360	2,430
Northwest Europe	1,040	1,700	1,590
Southeast Europe	310	1,280	720
Latin America	360	1,120	1,480
Japan	400	1,100	1,020
Near East	280	690	680
Southeast Asia	170	370	380

TABLE 1–7a

Production per Laborer in the Primary and Tertiary
Sectors, as Percentage of the Secondary Sector

Economic geographic area	Primary sector	Tertiary sector
North America	54	97
Northwest Europe	62	94
Southeast Europe	24	56
Latin America	33	132
Japan	33	92
Near East	41	99
Southeast Asia	40	101

SOURCE: L. J. Zimmerman, *op. cit.*, p. 49.

the other technologically retarded. Typically, in the advanced or "modern" sector is found the petroleum industry (where it exists), other mining, large-scale manufacturing, large-scale, mechanized plantation agriculture, and the transport, finance, insurance, trading, and other services associated with these activities. In the retarded or "traditional" sector is found peasant agriculture, handicrafts or cottage industry and very small-scale industry, and once again the services related to these undertakings. In the modern sector the typical operation—including plantations—is capital-intensive, and the form of organization is frequently the corporation, simply because of the capital requirements involved. Thus, the oil companies, tin mines, or tea and rubber plantations in developing countries often sell their shares on all the world's leading capital markets. The technology is usually as advanced as modern science can make it. Productivity per man-hour or per man-month is accordingly high—as high as or higher than in the advanced countries. In the traditional sector, techniques are themselves traditional, sometimes centuries old, highly labor-intensive. Productivity is correspondingly low.

Underdeveloped countries, in other words, are not countries in which no development has taken place at all. If one looks at the percentage rate of growth of the modern sector alone, which frequently produces for the world market as well as raising capital in the world market, it is often very impressive. But somehow or other, the underdeveloped countries have failed to draw a large proportion of the labor force into this modern sector. Almost by definition, an underdeveloped country is one in which the bulk of the population is compelled to seek a livelihood in the traditional sector, where productivity is low, and the people are consequently poor. Clearly, there is a relationship between the technological dualism that characterizes developing countries and the fact that the bulk of the population in these countries is engaged in agriculture.

Regional Dualism

Regional dualism is also a common characteristic of underdeveloped countries. Professor Gunnar Myrdal, looking at European experience, was perhaps the first to suggest that underdeveloped countries are characterized by large and increasing gaps in productivity and income among major regions, and advanced countries by small and diminishing ones.[10] So general and so important is the phenomenon of regional disintegration that it can serve almost as a definition and a measure of underdevelopment. The correlation between the degree of regional integration and the level of economic and social development, whether measured in terms of the degree of maturity in the occupational structure, in terms of per capita income, or in social and political terms, is very high. Even small developing countries such as Ceylon, Greece, and Guatemala have rich and poor, leading and lagging regions. In bigger countries such as Brazil, Mexico, Indonesia, and Pakistan, and in middle-sized countries such as Italy and Egypt, the regional contrasts are dramatic.

Economic growth of any country involves rich and poor, leading and lagging regions. Healthy growth, however, seems to require that the poor or lagging regions be converted into leading ones before too much time has gone by—as has been repeatedly the case in the United States. Otherwise the agglomerative pull of the leading regions may become so strong that lagging rgions become chronically poor, as is the case in the Mexican south or in the Siamese or Brazilian northeast.

The problem seems to be especially acute when sectors and regions overlap as they do in many underdeveloped countries. Then regional dualism becomes a reflection of technological dualism. In many cases, the leading sector is identified not merely with a region but with a few cities. Latin American countries are already substantially urbanized and are rapidly become more so. Asian cities have grown fantastically since 1940. The agglomerative pull of the capital cities is particularly strong, but in some cases (such as São Paulo, Monterrey, Chiang Mai, Medellín, and

[10] The suggestion arose originally out of studies within Europe, conducted under Myrdal's direction by the UN Economic Commission for Europe. The idea has since been expounded in several of Myrdal's writings, including *Economic Theory and Under-developed Regions* (London, 1957).

Bombay) there are commercial, financial, and industrial centers in addition to the capital city that show rapid rates of growth.

Under conditions of technological dualism it is possible to have very substantial investment in the modern sector and quite satisfactory increases in per capita income in that sector, without making any dent in the problem of poverty in the traditional sector and region. That is precisely the situation in Brazil, Mexico, and Thailand today. Impressive though it is, the investment taking place in the modern sector does not provide new employment opportunities at a rate high enough to permit even a *relative* decline in the proportion of population living in the traditional sector and region, let alone to permit an absolute decline in population of that region, which may prove necessary for a solution to the problem of poverty there.

In the worst cases the lagging sectors and regions are associated with less highly developed social groups as well. In these cases, moving people from low-productivity occupations to more highly productive ones is not only a matter of moving them from one part of the country to another; it is also a matter of moving them from one socio-cultural framework to another. For a Brazilian peasant in the northeast or a Mexican peasant in the south, both the geographic and cultural distances that many people must move to obtain jobs in the progressing sector of the society may be very great indeed. Once technological and sociological dualism set in together, a "feedback" mechanism tends to appear for the simple reason that the pattern of emigration tends to dilute the quality of the population—without sufficiently reducing its quantity. The best educated, best trained, most progressive, most ambitious men and women will be the ones who will leave the lagging region for the progressive one. Thus the lagging region is denuded of the very qualities that are needed to reconstruct it and reverse the trend, launching a process that will narrow the gaps in productivity and income. Meanwhile, at the other end of the migratory route, underdeveloped countries suffer from urban congestion, slums, and urban underemployment.

Education

The attainment of higher levels of education is such a universal goal of underdeveloped countries that it would be legitimate to ascribe a high weight to education as such in the measurement of the level of development. In the ultimate philosophical sense, participation in the modern world and awareness of the range of satisfactions available, both of which may be attained through education, might be regarded as major aspects of development. In addition, however, generally high levels of education are an indication that incomes are reasonably high and equitably distributed, or that the standard of public services is high, or both. There are a few countries, such as Ceylon, where educational standards are quite high while income is low, but these are exceptions to the rule. Generally speaking, levels of education correlate closely with other indices of development. This close correlation is hardly surprising; for one thing, improved education tends to bring higher levels of productivity; for another, people tend to spend a larger share of income on education as incomes rise (income elasticity of demand for education is high) and as countries get richer they want to and can afford to spend more on education.

This being the case, do indicators of "human resource development" provide information that is not already provided by figures of per capita income? The answer is clearly "yes." Looking at Tables 1–8 and 1–8a,

TABLE 1–8

Countries Grouped by Levels of Human Resource Development
According to Composite Index

Level I—Underdeveloped		Level III—Semi-advanced	
0.3	Niger	33.0	Mexico
0.75	Ethiopia	35.1	Thailand
1.2	Nyasaland	35.2	India
1.55	Somalia	35.5	Cuba
1.9	Afghanistan	39.6	Spain
1.9	Saudi Arabia	40.0	South Africa
2.2	Tanganyika	40.1	Egypt
2.6	Ivory Coast	40.8	Portugal
2.95	Northern Rhodesia	47.3	Costa Rica
3.55	Congo	47.7	Venezuela
4.1	Liberia	48.5	Greece
4.75	Kenya	51.2	Chile
4.95	Nigeria	53.9	Hungary
5.3	Haiti	53.9	Taiwan
5.45	Senegal	55.0	South Korea
5.45	Uganda	56.8	Italy
7.55	Sudan	60.3	Yugoslavia
		66.5	Poland
Level II—Partially developed		68.9	Czechoslovakia
10.7	Guatemala	69.8	Uruguay
10.7	Indonesia	73.8	Norway
10.85	Libya		
14.2	Burma	Level IV—Advanced	
14.5	Dominican Republic	77.1	Denmark
14.8	Bolivia	79.2	Sweden
15.25	Tunisia	82.0	Argentina
17.3	Iran	84.9	Israel
19.5	China (mainland)	85.8	West Germany
20.9	Brazil	88.7	Finland
22.6	Columbia	92.9	USSR
22.7	Paraguay	101.6	Canada
23.15	Ghana	107.8	France
23.65	Malaya	111.4	Japan
24.3	Lebanon	121.6	United Kingdom
24.4	Ecuador	123.6	Belgium
25.2	Pakistan	133.7	Netherlands
26.8	Jamaica	137.7	Australia
27.2	Turkey	147.3	New Zealand
30.2	Peru	261.3	United States
31.2	Iraq		

TABLE 1–8a

Indicators of Human Resource and Economic Development:
Arithmetic Means by Levels of Human Resource Development*
(rounded to nearest digit)

Indicator	Level I 17 countries	Level II 21 countries	Level III 21 countries	Level IV 16 countries
Composite index (secondary and higher education)	3	21	50	115
GNP per capita, US dollars	$85	$182	$380	$1,100
Per cent active population in agriculture	83	65	52	23
Teachers (first and second levels) per 10,000 population	17	38	53	80
Scientists and engineers per 10,000 population	0.6	3	25	42
Physicians and dentists per 10,000 population	0.5	3	8	15
First-level enrollment ratio (unadjusted)	22	42	62	73
First and second level enrollment (adjusted)	20	45	66	89
Second level enrollment ratio (adjusted)	2.7	12	27	59
Third level enrollment ratio (unadjusted)	0.15	1.6	5	11
Per cent enrolled in scientific and technical faculties	24	28	26	28
Per cent enrolled in humanities, fine arts, and law faculties	34	39	33	32
Public expenditures on education as per cent of national income	3.7	2.1	3.1	4.2
Per cent in age group, 5–14 inc.	24	24	22	18

* Sources in addition to special UNESCO tabulations: *Basic Facts and Figures*, *1961* (Paris: UNESCO, 1962); Norton Ginsburg (ed.), *Atlas of Economic Development* (Chicago, 1961); and Mikoto Usui and E. E. Hagen, *World Income, 1957* Center for International Studies, M.I.T., November, 1959.

SOURCE: F. Harbison and C. A. Myers, *Education, Manpower, and Economic Growth* (New York, 1963).

taken from Harbison and Myers' pioneering work, we see that in terms of broad categories of countries the rank correlation between indicators of human resource development and indicators of economic development is perfect, except for public expenditures on education as a percentage of national income; and this indicator is a bit misleading because 3.7 per cent of $84 is less than 2.1 per cent of $182. That is, the per capita outlays on education do correlate perfectly with the level of per capita income. Also, the relative roles of private education should be considered. When we look at individual countries, however, there are some surprises, some results that could not be anticipated by looking at the usual economic indicators alone. Thus among the "advanced" countries, Japan, with a much lower level of per capita income, ranks above both France and Canada in terms of Harbison and Myers' "composite index" of secondary and higher education, and Argentina ranks above Denmark and Sweden. Among partially developed countries, again, one would hardly have expected from income figures that Pakistan and Peru would rank above Brazil.

The same conclusion is borne out by the figures for Asian countries shown in Tables 1–9 and 1–9a. Ceylon, although fifth in per capita income, is first in percentage of GNP spent on education by the public authorities. With 87 per cent of the primary-school-age children in school, Ceylon is nonetheless only fifth in rank on this criterion, the Philippines and South Korea being slightly ahead of her and Taiwan and Japan well ahead. When it comes to secondary school students, only Japan does better than Ceylon. But at the university level, Ceylon drops to 13th place among the seventeen countries. Similarly, Ceylon ranks high in numbers of first- and second-level teachers but rather low in numbers of engineers, physicians, and dentists. Japan, on the other hand, is first among Asian countries on all indicators except proportion of GNP spent on public education. These figures suggest a need to attack the education problem vigorously at all levels if high levels of productivity and income are to be achieved.

On the whole, it appears that it is well worth while having a look at education statistics when appraising the level of development of various countries.

Employment and Unemployment

It is clear that unemployment is a problem in developing countries in a way that it is not in advanced ones, but it is not so clear what the difference is, and it is still less clear that the employment problem is a separate characteristic of underdeveloped countries and not just another symptom of the characteristics already noted above. The magnitude of the problem is certainly greater in developing countries than in advanced ones. Today no government in a high-income country would dare present to the electorate a long-range economic program in which it simply admitted defeat on the employment front. Yet the Indian Third Five-Year Plan does just that; despite the impressive increase in the ratio of investment to income entailed in the series of three Five-Year Plans (from 5 per cent to 14 per cent), the government expects the level of unemployment to be just as high at the end of the Third Five-Year Plan as it was at the beginning. Ceylon's Ten-Year Perspective Plan makes reduction in unemployment the major goal of development policy; yet in ten years of accelerated investment it would do little more than cut unemployment in half. Very few underdeveloped countries can foresee full employment within the next decade, even with investment ratios that would bring rates of increase in per capita income substantially higher than in North America.

There is also a difference in causation of unemployment between advanced and developing countries. Serious unemployment in industrialized countries has beeen associated during the past century with recessions and depressions, and these in turn have been traced to a deficiency of effective demand. This kind of unemployment occurs in less-developed countries but is not the major employment problem. True, we have also learned since World War II that even highly industrialized countries can have creeping inflation and unemployment—even increasing unemployment—simultaneously. Inflation is supposed to reflect an excess of effective demand; obviously one cannot have an excess and a deficiency of effective demand simultaneously in the economy as a whole. To explain simultaneous inflation and unemployment in advanced countries, we are forced to consider intersectoral and interregional relationships and structural problems in a fashion that brings us far toward the type of analysis formerly reserved for developing countries. Yet there is a difference in degree so great as to constitute almost a difference in kind; the unemployment that occurs in advanced countries when there is no deficiency of effective demand is relatively minor. In less-developed countries it can be substantial, when underemployment is included. Conversely, rates of open unemployment, in the sense of people with no jobs at all who are seeking work, tend to be considerably lower in developing countries than they have been during depressions in advanced ones.

Defining and measuring underemployment is no easy task, and we shall return to it later. In general, it means the number of people working less than a "normal" working week—in some sense—and seeking additional work. Table 1–10 shows estimates for four Asian countries. It is apparent that all of these figures, except the International Labor Organization (ILO) estimate for West Pakistan, are very high in comparison with figures of underemployment for advanced countries. Those working less than a "normal" workweek but not seeking additional work, of which there are usually even greater numbers in developing countries, are sometimes referred to as "disguised unemployed," or, more accurately, those in low-productivity employment. Other characteristics of the employment problem in developing countries are a very large volume of seasonal unemployment, and (particularly in arid countries) unemployment generated from the supply side through drought or other causes of crop failure.

Thus the employment problem in the less-developed countries is more serious in its volume and tenacity than it is in advanced countries today and somewhat different in its causation. However, the employment problem is very largely a reflection of the large proportion of the labor force in agriculture and of the related phenomena of technological and regional dualism. Although underemployment is not absent from the cities, in terms of numbers it is mainly a rural problem. Its basic cause is the concentration of capital formation in the modern sector (and rich region), so that employment creation fails to keep pace with the growth of the labor force. So-called disguised unemployment, or low productivity resulting from acceptance of a short working week, is also the result of concentration of investment in the capital-intensive sector together with a social organization that shares income by sharing work. Seasonal unemployment occurs in agriculture in all countries, but it is more serious in the less-developed

TABLE 1-9
Per Capita Income and Indicators of Educational Development

	Japan	Malaya	Iran	China (Taiwan)	Ceylon	Philippines	Cambodia	Korea, Rep. of	Thailand	Vietnam, Rep. of	India	Pakistan	Burma	Afghanistan	Indonesia	Laos	Nepal
Per capita income U.S. dollars (1963)*	508	280	174	142	124	123	112	99	96	89	78	73	62	60	50	…	…
Indicators of educational development																	
Enrollment ratios																	
First level	99.8	83	44	98	87	88	55	88	75	55	57	34	48	10	38	27	14
Second level	82	24	12	32	40	31	6	28	14	13	23	11	10	1	11	2	6
Third level	12.1	1.0	1.9	6.1	0.9	5.7	0.3	5.6	2.5	1.8	3.5	0.9	1.1	0.3	1.8	0.3	…
Proportion of enrollments at vocational schools to population, 13–17 years (per cent)†	13.1	1.0	0.5	7.8	…	3.1	0.3	7.7	2.8	…	0.7	0.2	…	…	1.9	…	0.1
Proportion of students at third level in natural sciences, engineering, and agriculture to population, 18–22 years (per cent)‡	1.9	…	0.3	1.9	…	1.2	0.03	1.6	0.2	…	0.9	0.5	…	…	0.3	…	…

TABLE 1-9 (continued)

	Japan	Malaya	Iran	China (Taiwan)	Ceylon	Philippines	Cambodia	Korea, Rep. of	Thailand	Vietnam, Rep. of	India	Pakistan	Burma	Afghanistan	Indonesia	Laos	Nepal
Stock of high-level manpower per 100,000 of population§ Teachers at first and second level	84	68	28	61	72	55	29	39	51	23	31	23	22	5	29	15	8
Engineers	35.3	2.6	3.8	20.1	0.9	5.0	...	...	.03	...	3.4	...	0.3	...	...	...	0.1
Physicians and dentists	14.3	...	3.1	7.4	2.4	1.7	0.4	3.5	1.4	0.4	2.0	1.2¶	0.8	0.3	0.3	0.2	0.1
Per cent literate adults (15 years and over)#	98	47	13	54	68	72	31	89	68	...	24	19	58	3	43	18	5
Per cent of GNP spent on public education by public authorities§	4.6	3.5	3.3	2.8	5.3	2.7	3.7	4.1	2.5	1.8	1.6	1.8	2.1	1.1	1.3	2.7	...

* Estimates prepared by ECAFE secretariat. Income data in general relate to net national product at factor cost: for Afghanistan and Malaya gross national product at market prices and for Cambodia gross domestic product at market prices.
† Calculated from *United Nations Demographic Year Book 1963* and *UNESCO Statistical Yearbook 1963*.
‡ Calculated from *United Nations Demographic Yearbook 1963* and *UNESCO Statistical Yearbook 1963*; enrollment estimates for Indonesia and Iran were derived from country reports of UNESCO Planning Teams.
§ *Educational Situation in Asia. Past Trends and Present Status*, May, 1965.
¶ Physicians only.
# *UNESCO Statistical Yearbook 1963* and *Educational Situation in Asia. Past Trends and Present Status*, May, 1965.
SOURCE: Economic Commission for Asia and the Far East, *Economic Survey of Asia and the Far East, 1965*, p. 90.

TABLE 1–9a

Ranking of Asian ECAFE Countries by Per Capita Income and Indicators of Educational Development

	Japan	Malaya	Iran	China (Taiwan)	Ceylon	Philippines	Cambodia	Korea Rep. of	Thailand	Vietnam Rep. of	India	Pakistan	Burma	Afghanistan	Indonesia	Laos	Nepal
	1	2	3	4	5	6	7	8	9	10	11	12	13	14	15		
Per capita income	1	2	3	4	5	6	7	8	9	10	11	12	13	14	15	..	..
Indicators of educational development																	
Enrollment ratios																	
First level	1	6	13	2	5	3	10	3	7	10	8	14	12	17	9	15	16
Second level	1	6	10	3	2	4	14	5	8	9	7	11	13	17	11	16	14
Third level	1	11	7	2	12	3	13	4	6	8	5	12	10	13	8	13	..
Proportion of enrollments at vocational schools to population, 13–17 years	1	7	9	2	..	4	10	3	5	..	8	11	..	..	6	..	12
Proportion of students at third level in natural sciences, engineering and agriculture to population, 18–22 years	1	..	7	1	..	4	10	3	9	..	5	6	..	..	7	..	..
Stock of high-level manpower per 100,000 of population																	
Teachers at first and second level	1	3	11	4	2	5	9	7	6	12	8	12	14	17	9	15	16
Engineers	1	6	4	2	7	3	..	..	8	..	5	..	8	..	..	..	10
Physicians and dentists	1	..	4	2	5	7	11	3	8	11	6	9	10	13	13	15	16
Per cent literate adults (15 years and over)	1	8	14	7	4	3	10	2	4	..	11	12	6	16	9	13	15
Per cent of GNP spent on public education by public authorities	2	5	6	7	1	8	4	3	10	12	14	12	11	16	15	8	..

source: Economic Commission for Asia and the Far East, *Economic Survey of Asia and the Far East, 1965*, p. 91.

TABLE 1–10

Selected ECAFE Countries: Measurements of Underemployment

	Degree of underemployment (per cent)
1. *India*	
(a) National Sample Survey, Round 14 (July 1958–June 1959)*	14.7
(b) National Sample Survey, Round 16 (July 1960–June 1961)†	10.7
2. *Pakistan*	
(a) Survey conducted by the International Labor Organization, Expanded Program for Technical Assistance 1955‡	
East Pakistan	17.0
West Pakistan	4.7
(b) M. Habibullah, Dacca University, 1962§	25.0
3. *Philippines*	
The Philippines Statistical Survey of Households, 1963¶	12.4
4. *Indonesia*	
ILO, Expanded Program for Technical Assistance, 1958#	33.0

* National Sample Survey, India, has conducted a series of sample surveys over a number of years to measure unemployment and underemployment. The measure of underemployment is based on the number of gainfully employed persons who reported availability for work. This included persons working up to fifty-six hours a week. The reference period was a week, during a period of two months. The year was divided into six two-monthly periods and inquiry was made in each of these six periods. The figure relates to rural areas only.

† The same as Round 14, with revised terminological changes of activity status.

‡ Interviewing in West Pakistan was done between 15 August and 15 October and in East Pakistan between 15 September and 15 November. The survey covered only eight weeks of the year and does not represent the situation for the whole year. The degree of underemployment is defined as percentage of persons working less than twenty-six hours a week (or roughly half a regular working week of fifty hours) of the total number at work during the reference period. Family workers working less than fifteen hours a week are excluded from the labor force. The figure relates to both rural and urban areas.

§ M. Habibullah: *The Pattern of Agricultural Unemployment:* A Case Study of an East Pakistan Village (Dacca, 1962). Weekly interviews were made over the whole year, supplemented by continuous observation by interviewers living in the village. The supply of man-days available was defined in terms of hours of work with eight hours a day as standard, so that adjustment for overtime work was made. The degree of underemployment was measured by the percentage of the total supply of man-days for which no work was available. In this estimate supply of man-days does not include women and children.

¶ The reference period was a week and the survey is conducted for three-quarters of the year. Unpaid family workers are included in the labor force. The degree of underemployment is measured by the percentage of persons working less than forty hours a week during the reference period and wanting additional work to the total number of persons at work. The figure measures underemployment for both agricultural and nonagricultural workers. The figure for agriculture alone was higher at 13.7 per cent.

The investigation was carried out in the agricultural peak and slack seasons. Per-

countries because agricultural productivity is low and because a large proportion of the labor force is engaged in the agricultural sector. Similarly, drought and other causes of crop failure bring additional unemployment to farmers (and processors of agricultural products) anywhere they occur, but are less disastrous when only a small proportion of the labor force is affected and general levels of productivity are high.

Our conclusion might be that when the other characteristics of underdevelopment are present, one need hardly look at the employment situation before classifying a country as underdeveloped; one can be virtually certain that the employment situation will follow the general pattern. But if other data are lacking or if the country seems to be a borderline case in terms of other criteria, employment statistics can provide very useful additional information. Certainly data on employment and unemployment are among the most important in the formulation of policies, plans, and programs.

Other Social Indicators

We have already noted that other social indicators, such as measures of health and nutrition, correlate closely with the level of per capita income. Tables 1–11 and 1–11a show the results of a survey of the United Nations Department of Social Affairs. These tables contain no surprises. Generally speaking, one gains little additional information about the level of economic and social development by adding such series to a composite index. However, in individual cases (such as the Venezuelan one) such indicators may help to detect situations in which most of the people are living in conditions associated with poverty despite high average levels of income, because of inequitable income distribution and inadequate public services.

Backward, Underdeveloped, Developing

In United Nations circles the terms "developing" or "less developed" are replacing the less-polite expression "underdeveloped" and the still more impolite label "backward." The trouble with the term "developing" is that it is frequently a blatant misnomer for some of the countries with which we are concerned; it would apply more accurately to countries such as Russia and West Germany which obviously do not belong among the countries with the characteristics indicated above. The term "less developed" is really meaningless; all other countries are "less developed"

---

sons under twelve years of age were not considered part of the labor force. The supply of labor was worked out at 305 working days in a year and seven hours a day for a labor force determined by the number of persons of over twelve years of age at work during the peak season. The number of hours actually worked was measured at peak and slack seasons. The difference as a percentage of supply of man-days measured the degree of underemployment. The estimate of the supply of man-days, however, does not take into account the willingness of the persons to work for the stipulated number of hours per day or number of days per year. Underemployment in urban areas was 2.8 per cent.

SOURCE: Economic Commission for Asia and the Far East, *Economic Survey of Asia and the Far East*, 1965, chap. 2.

TABLE 1–11

Average Levels under Selected Economic and Social Indicators
of Countries Grouped by National Income

	Per capita income groups					
	I $1,000 & over	II $575– 1,000	III $350– 575	IV $200– 350	V $100– 200	VI under $100
1. Per capita national income (1956–58 average in dollars)	1,366	760	431	269	161	72
2. Per capita energy consumption in kilograms of coal equivalent (1956–58 average)	3,900	2,710	1,861	536	265	114
3. Expectation of life (1955–58 average)	70.6	67.7	65.4	57.4	50.0	41.7
4. Infant mortality rate (1955–58 average)	24.9	41.9	56.8	97.2	131.1	180.0
5. Number of inhabitants per physician (latest year reported)	885	944	1,724	3,132	5,185	13,450
6. Percentage of population literate; 15 years and over (estimated circa 1950)	98	94	81	70	51	29
7. School enrollment ratio (latest year reported)	91	84	75	60	48	37
8. Per capita calorie consumption (latest year reported)	3,153	2,944	2,920	2,510	2,240	2,070
9. Starchy staples as percentage of total calories consumed	45	53	60	74	70	77
10. Percentage of male labor force in agriculture (estimated mid-1956)	17	21	35	53	64	74
11. Level of urbanization around 1955	43	39	35	26	14	9
12. Percentage of national income originating in agriculture (latest year)	11.4	10.9	15.3	29.9	33.4	40.8

SOURCE: United Nations, *Report on the World Social Situation* (New York, 1961), p. 41.

than the United States. It is a pity that we do not have in English a term equivalent to the German *Entwickelungsländer*—literally "development countries"—meaning simply those countries about whose low level of development people both within the country and in the advanced "donor" countries are concerned. Because we do not, it seems better to stick to the term "underdeveloped," remembering that it is a technical term to summarize the characteristics outlined in the previous section. We shall, however, continue to use the words "developing" or "less developed" as synonyms for "underdeveloped."

TABLE 1–11a

Coefficients of Rank Correlation*

Per capita national income and energy consumption	0.90
Per capita national income and infant mortality†	−0.84
Per capita national income and school enrollment	0.84
Per capita national income and calorie consumption	0.80
Per capita national income and starchy staples†	−0.86
Energy consumption and infant mortality†	−0.69
Energy consumption and school enrollment	0.76
Urbanization and infant mortality†	−0.69
Urbanization and school enrollment	0.71
Urbanization and starchy staples†	−0.66
Urbanization and calorie consumption	0.69
Infant mortality and school enrollment†	−0.67
Infant mortality and number of inhabitants per physician	0.43
Infant mortality and calorie consumption†	−0.81
Literacy and school enrollment	0.78
Male labor force in agriculture and infant mortality	0.86
Male labor force in agriculture and energy consumption	−0.89
Male labor force in agriculture and school enrollment†	−0.81

* It should be noted that the number of countries included in each calculation is not identical. Where the correlation includes infant mortality, only countries with data officially reported as complete are included. It might be expected that, if the countries with estimated infant mortality rates were included, the correlation with per capita national income would be less close. In fact, it is slightly closer (0.87 instead of 0.84). The same situation is found with correlations of infant mortality with energy consumption and school enrollment. On the other hand, an examination of some twenty low-income countries, mainly in Africa, shows a correlation between per capita energy consumption and school enrollment ratio of only 0.20. It is quite possible that the correlations would show substantial differences if countries were selected from different income ranges, or from different regions.

† Infant mortality rates, number of inhabitants per physician, starchy staples as per cent of total calories and percentage of male labor force in agriculture involve negative correlations—except where they are correlated with each other—since they are inverse measures of development in the sectors concerned (e.g., the infant mortality rate is an inverse measure of health). Where correlations of the infant mortality rate or of other of these rates are discussed in the text, it will be understood that the inverse of the measure in question is meant.

SOURCE: United Nations, *Report on the World Social Situation* (New York, 1961), p. 42.

Conclusions

We are concerned, therefore, with countries in which more than half of the population lives in poverty, lacking any secure margin above basic food, clothing, and shelter for education and health, for recreation, for "frugal comfort," and for the forms of communication that constitute participation in the modern world. By and large, these will be countries with per capita incomes below $600 per year. However, there may be cases in which average incomes are higher than this figure but the country is nonetheless underdeveloped because income distribution is unusually inequitable or public services are at an unusually low level or both; and conceivably some country may have a per capita income slightly below this figure and yet not be underdeveloped because income is evenly spread throughout the population. Underdeveloped countries will typically have more than one-third of their labor force engaged in agriculture, and will be characterized by both technological and regional dualism. Their levels of education will usually be low. Chronic underemployment and low-productivity employment associated with a short working week will prevail. There will also be a high volume of seasonal unemployment and sometimes unemployment resulting from crop failures as well. As a rule, standards of health and nutrition will also be low.

As everything else tends to correlate closely with per capita income, if we are to rely on a single indicator of the level of development, per capita income is the most revealing, even with its imperfections. Indeed, if we had Pareto curves of disposable income, showing not only the level but the pattern of distribution of income, including the impact of taxes and transfer payments on disposable income, we could probably dispense with other indicators. Lacking such data, it is helpful to look at the "proxy variables" already listed.

By the same token we shall mean by "economic development" a discernible rise in total and per capita income (emigration is not really development) widely diffused among occupational groups and among regions and continuing for at least two generations. Fluctuations may take place around a long-run trend, but a rise in income for a decade or two followed by relapse into chronic stagnation over longer periods (such as seems to have taken place in Indonesia) would not constitute development. The process will be accompanied by structural change, narrowing gaps in productivity among sectors and regions, and improved education and health.

2 The Population Explosion

Per capita income by itself is an imperfect measure of the level of development, but economic progress in underdeveloped countries requires rising per capita incomes no matter what the values and tastes of the society. Whether top priority is attached to Bibles or beer, the Koran or the kitchen, leisure or lentils, rising average incomes are the means of obtaining more of whatever the people in any society want. In no country now considered underdeveloped can the problem of poverty be solved entirely by simple redistribution of present income among individuals, groups, regions, or uses. Much as such redistribution would help in some cases, in underdeveloped countries merely redividing the pie is not enough; it is also essential that the pie grow faster than the population.

This being the case, we are led immediately to an obvious but fundamental proposition of simple arithmetic: the higher the rate of population growth—other things being equal—the more difficult the problem of launching and sustaining a process of economic development. We make no moral judgment, and at this stage we suggest no policy conclusions. In a later chapter on population policy we will consider the possibility that population pressure may have encouraged economic development in some countries in the past and may still do so in a few cases today. But it is an elementary fact that the over-all task of economic development is greatly complicated by the current high rate of population growth. Not entirely by accident, the awakening of international consciousness of and conscience concerning the poverty in which the majority of the world's people still lives coincides with the highest rate of population growth the world as a whole has ever known. The acceleration of the rise in human numbers is so marked as to warrant the term "population explosion."

Population Growth and Capital Requirements

Before reviewing the main facts, let us proceed one step beyond the tautology, "the higher the rate of population growth, the higher must be the rate of growth of national income to outrun it." Let us suppose that in some mythical underdeveloped country—let's call it Esperanza—the incremental capital-output ratio (ICOR for short) is 3:1. That is, to produce a permanent increase in income of one million, we need a permanent addition to the stock of capital of three million. This figure is not taken at random; it is fairly typical of "middle-class" countries, with per capita incomes between $200 and $400 per year, seeking to raise incomes by further industrialization.

This relationship can also be expressed in the form $\Delta Q/\Delta Y$ or $I/\Delta Y$, where Q is the stock of capital, I is the net addition to the stock of capital or investment, and Y is income. Let us suppose first that the population in Esperanza is growing by 1 per cent per year. To keep per capita income constant, we must raise income at the same rate. Thus $\Delta Y/Y \times 100$ will be one; I/Y must be three times that amount, or 3 per cent of national income. To achieve an annual growth of per capita income of 3 per cent, so as to double income each generation, investment must be 9 per cent of national income. Most developing countries are capable of generating a savings and investment ratio of 9 per cent of national income. If we aim at doubling per capita income in one decade, as Japan has done, the annual growth of per capita income must be 7 per cent and net investment must be 21 per cent of national income, a level beyond the capacity of many, if not most, developing countries.

Now let us suppose that Esperanza has a dramatically successful public health campaign; death rates drop sharply and the rate of population growth rises to 3 per cent. Now we need an investment ratio of 9 per cent just to prevent per capita income from falling. To double per capita income in a generation now requires an annual net investment of 27 per cent of national income; what seemed easily attainable before may now seem impossible. And to double per capita income in one decade we would need a net investment of 63 per cent of national income, a level far higher than any country has ever attained.

Much of the discussion of the population explosion has centered around the possibility of feeding the world's population in the more remote future, or even of finding "standing room" for all. Such discussion may prove to be alarmist. Meanwhile, however, there can be little doubt that the unprecedented rate of world population growth magnifies the task of abolishing poverty from the face of the earth.

The Main Facts

The first fundamental fact is that the current population explosion is something essentially new. There was a spurt of population growth in

Europe during the early decades of the Industrial Revolution, and individual countries in Asia experienced high rates of population growth in the nineteenth century. Taking the world as a whole throughout human history, there is justification for drawing the curve of population with a sharp break around 1750 and accelerating growth ever since, with a slight slowing down just before World War II and a marked speeding up since. In Chart 2-1, if the Old Stone Age were in scale, the chart would have to extend thirty-five feet to the left. It took hundreds of thousands of years for the world population to reach three billion, but if current rates of growh continue, the second three billion will be added in just forty years. The population explosion, in other words, is partly a matter of high current rates of growth and partly a matter of an already greatly expanded base.

Novelty of the Demographic Situation

Demographers, biologists, and others have recently resorted to lurid language to drive home the fact that the recent demographic situation is something new in human history. Thus, Sir Julian Huxley writes:[1]

The world's present rate of population increase is something phenomenal. It is about fifty million a year, and increasing every year, both for simple arithmetic reasons and because the compound interest rate of increase is still itself increasing. That means the equivalent of one good sized town every 24 hours—a hundred and forty thousand odd. If you like to think of it in terms of minutes, it is the equivalent of ten baseball teams complete with coach every minute. And yet there are people who have so little quantitative sense that they talk of getting rid of our surplus population by sending them off to other planets!

Professor Philip M. Hauser writes in similar vein:[2]

Although the first complete census of mankind has yet to be taken, it is possible to reconstruct, with reasonable accuracy, the history of world population growth. This history may be encapsulated in the following estimates of the population of the earth: at the end of the Neolithic period in Europe (8,000 to 7,000 B.C.) perhaps 10 million; at the beginning of the Christian era 200 to 300 million; at the beginning of the modern era (1650) 500 million; in 1950, 2.5 billion.

These four numbers constitute a measurement of one of the most dramatic aspects of man's existence on the globe, and they explain the purple language of the demographer in describing the changes in the rate of population growth during the modern era as a "demographic revolution" or "population explosion."

Table 2–1 gives various estimates for the growth of world population, by major regions, from 1650 to 1960. It will be noted that the absolute growth in numbers between 1920 and 1960 exceeded the increase for the entire 250 years between 1650 and 1900.

[1] Sir Julian Huxley, "The Impending Crisis," in Larry K. Y. Ng (ed.), *The Population Crisis* (Bloomington, Ind., 1965), p. 5.
[2] Philip M. Hauser, "Demographic Dimensions of World Politics," in Ng, *op. cit.*, p. 59.

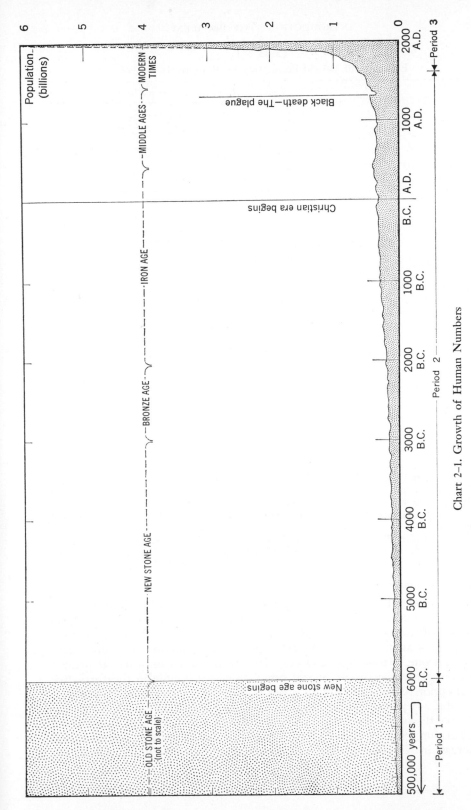

Chart 2-1. Growth of Human Numbers

SOURCE: Larry K. Y. Ng (ed.), *The Population Crisis* (Bloomington, Ind., 1965), p. 26.

TABLE 2–1

Estimates of World Population by Regions, 1650–1960

Source of estimates and date	Estimated population in millions							
	World	Africa	Northern America*	Latin America†	Asia (excl. USSR)†‡	Europe and Asiatic USSR‡	Oceania	Area of European Settlement§
Willcox:								
1650	470	100	1	7	257	103	2	113
1750	694	100	1	10	437	144	2	157
1800	919	100	6	23	595	193	2	224
1850	1,091	100	26	33	656	274	2	335
1900	1,571	141	81	63	857	423	6	573
Carr-Saunders:								
1650	545	100	1	12	327	103	2	118
1750	728	95	1	11	475	144	2	158
1800	906	90	6	19	597	192	2	219
1850	1,171	95	26	33	741	274	2	335
1900	1,608	120	81	63	915	423	6	573
United Nations:								
1920	1,810	140	117	91	966	487	9	704
1930	2,013	155	135	109	1,072	532	10	786
1940	2,246	172	146	131	1,212	573	11	861
1950	2,495	200	167	163	1,376	576	13	919
1960	2,972	244	200	207	1,665	641	16	1,064

* United States, Canada, Alaska, St. Pierre and Miquelon.
† Central and South America and Caribbean Islands.
‡ Estimates for Asia and Europe in Willcox's and Carr-Saunders' series have been adjusted so as to include the population of the Asiatic USSR with that of Europe.
§ Includes northern America, Latin America, Europe and the Asiatic USSR and Oceania.
SOURCE: United Nations, *The Determinants and Consequences of Population Trends*, 1953. Larry K. Y. Ng (ed.), *The Population Crisis* (Bloomington, Ind., 1965), p. 34.

Projections into the Future

When current trends are projected some distance into the future, the picture becomes even more alarming. Table 2–2 shows world population from 1650 to 1930, with projections to 1975 and 2010. Whereas it may have taken as much as 1,650 years for world population to double after the year one, it took only 200 years to double the second time. If present rates of growth continue, world population will double in the forty-five years prior to 1975 and double again only thirty-five years after that.

Table 2–3 presents projections to the year 2000, broken down by major areas of the world. Between 1950 and 2000, over half the growth of world population will take place in Asia if current trends continue. The estimated increase in Asia alone will be almost equal to the entire world population

TABLE 2–2
Estimated Population of the World and the
Number of Years Required for It to Double

Year (A.D.)	Population (billions)	Number of years to Double
1	0.25 (?)	1650 (?)
1650	0.50	200
1850	1.1	80
1930	2.0	45
1975	4.0	35
2010	8.0	?

SOURCE: Harold F. Dorn "World Population Growth,"
in Philip M. Hauser (ed.), *The Population Dilemma*
(Englewood Cliffs, N.J., 1963), p. 10.

TABLE 2–3
Population Growth in the Twentieth Century

Year	Developed*	Underdeveloped		
		Population (in millions†)		
		Total	Asia‡	Latin America	Africa
1900	554	996	813	63	120
1925	700	1,207	961	99	147
1950	838	1,659	1,297	163	199
1975	1,115	2,741	2,107	303	331
2000	1,448	5,459	4,145	651	663
		Per cent increase			
1900–1925	26.4	21.2	18.2	57.1	22.5
1925–1950	19.7	37.4	35.0	64.6	35.4
1950–1975	33.0	65.2	62.5	85.9	66.3
1975–2000	29.9	99.2	96.7	114.8	100.3
		Per cent of earth's total			
1900	35.7	64.3	52.4	4.1	7.7
1925	36.7	63.3	50.4	5.2	7.7
1950	33.6	66.4	51.9	6.5	8.0
1975	28.9	71.1	54.6	7.9	8.6
2000	21.0	79.0	60.0	9.4	9.6

* Including Europe, USSR, northern America, Australia, New Zealand, and Japan.
† Enumerated or estimated, 1900–1950; projected, 1975 and 2000, high estimates.
‡ Excluding the Asian portion of the USSR and Japan.
SOURCE (with modifications): United Nations Department of Economic and Social
Affairs, *The Future Growth of World Population*. Table 5, p. 23, Population Studies
No. 28. New York, 1958. Larry K. Y. Ng (ed.), *The Population Crisis* (Bloomington,
Ind., 1965), p. 35.

in 1960. The increase in numbers will be somewhat greater in Africa than in Latin America; both of these areas will have more population growth than Europe, and more than three times as much as North America.

The share of the developed countries in world population would fall from nearly 37 per cent in 1925 to 21 per cent in 2000; during the same period the share of Asia would have risen to 60 per cent, Latin America to 9.4 per cent, and Africa to 9.6 per cent. The total population of under-developed countries that must somehow be provided with rising levels of living will have grown from one billion in 1900 to almost five and a half billion in 2000.

If one wants to be still more fanciful and project current rates of popu-lation growth for 800 years—not a long time in human history—then indeed we end up with "standing room only"; one square foot per person.

The Causes

Much the most important cause of the population explosion is the dramatic improvement in public health. It used to be thought that low levels of per capita income and high death rates inevitably went together. There is still an inverse correlation between death rates and incomes for all countries taken together, but the correlation has less and less significance as time goes by. Diligent application of modern medical science can lower death rates even in poor countries to the levels typical of rich ones. The most frequently cited case is that of Ceylon. In that country, public health expenditures of $2 per head—mostly for residual spraying with DDT to eliminate malaria—cut death rates by 40 per cent in a single year and by 75 per cent over a single decade. The death rate now is below that of some European countries, and life expectancy has doubled in one generation. In Turkey, too, malaria control reduced death rates from 28 per thousand to 10 per thousand between 1941 and 1947. In western Europe it took several decades to achieve comparable reductions in death rates.

In the advanced countries of North America, Europe, and Australia, rising fertility rates have contributed to the population explosion, espe-cially during the forties and early fifties. Larger families became fashion-able for a while in these countries, a new form of "conspicuous consump-tion." In the developing countries, the picture is mixed, as may be seen from Appendix Table 5; but for developing countries as a group, in-creased fertility has not been a major factor in the spurt of population growth. Some Latin American countries have experienced slight increases in birth rates, some Asian countries slight decreases. These changes are minor in comparison to the fall in death rates.

Growth Potential

Developing countries where rates of population growth are relatively low, such as the Middle African countries of Table 1–5, are for the most part countries where the revolution in public health has not yet taken place, rather than countries where birth rates are low. If death rates in these countries are cut in half, as they may well be when public health campaigns are launched, rates of population growth could double. In short, developing countries with currently low rates of population growth are countries of potentially high population growth. Japan is an exception to this rule; it has a very low death rate and a very low birth rate as well, giving a low current rate of population growth.

We have already seen that not all underdeveloped countries face population pressure in the same degree; there is a wide variation in current rates of population growth. Between 1958 and 1963, East Asia had rates of population growth just equal to the world average. Middle Africa was below the world average, temperate South America just above it, and Central America far above it. But recent rates of population growth do not tell the whole story. The level and density of population are also important. As far as prognosis is concerned, a growth rate of 2 per cent as a consequence of a 4 per cent birth rate and a 2 per cent death rate has very different implications from one resulting from a 3 per cent birth rate and a 1 per cent death rate. For in the latter case the death rate is already about as low as it can go, and acceleration of population growth through further improvements in public health is just about impossible. In the former case, on the other hand, death rates can be cut in half and the rate of population growth can be raised still higher. In predicting natality, age distribution counts; obviously a population heavily concentrated in the age bracket between fifteen and forty is more likely to have high birth rates in the next few years than one with heavier concentrations in the lower or higher age brackets.

Demographers have developed a concept of "population types" that permits them to classify countries into "low-growth potential," "high-growth potential," and "transitional" on the basis of all the relevant demographic data. Countries tend to go through phases with respect to their demographic patterns. Thus we see from Table 2–4 that in countries classified as low-growth potential, the rates of growth between 1920 and 1950 were not markedly different from those in countries of high-growth potential. But when we look at the differences in birth and death rates, and take into account age distributions as well, it is apparent that the countries in Asia and Africa have a much higher growth potential than other countries in the world. There are, of course, differences from country to country not shown here; but most of the underdeveloped countries in the world are still in the high-growth potential group. Latin America as a whole, however, falls into the "transitional" classification. There death rates are already low, and many demographers would expect fertility rates to drop in due course, following the pattern that has been set in the past by Europe and the New World.

Some demographers doubt whether the high-growth potential countries can be expected to follow the same demographic patterns as the advanced countries did. These were still high-growth potential up to the end of the eighteenth century, although natality in western Europe was never so high as in present-day Asia and Africa, and mortality seems to have been somewhat lower and thus had less far to drop. The declines in both death rates

TABLE 2-4

World Population, Growth Rates, Birth Rates, and Death Rates

Area	1950 Population, in millions	Annual increase 1920-50 per thousand	Annual rates, 1946-48, per thousand			Annual rates, 1936-38, per thousand		
			Birth	Death	Natural increase	Birth	Death	Natural increase
World	2,406	9	35-37	22-25	11-14	34-38	24-27	8-13
Low-growth potential (type I):	486	9	.....	.....	10	.....	.....	5
Northwest central Europe	215	6	19	12	7	17	13	4
North America	166	13	25	10	15	17	11	6
South Europe	92	9	23	12	11	23	16	7
Oceania	13	14	28	12	16	20	11	9
High-growth potential (type II):	1,387	8	.....	.....	12	.....	.....	7-13
Far East*	670	5	40-45	30-38	7-13	40-45	30-35	7-13
South-central Asia	442	11	40-45	25-30	12-18	40-45	30-35	7-13
Africa	199	13	40-45	25-30	12-18	40-45	30-35	7-13
Near East	75	10	40-45	30-35	7-13	40-45	30-35	7-13
Transitional (type III):	533	11	.....	.....	15	.....	.....	13-17
Soviet Union and eastern Europe	287	7	28	18	10	30-34	17-21	11-15
Latin America	162	19	40	17	23	40-45	20-25	17-23
Japan	84	14	31	15	16	28	17	11

* Excluding Japan.
SOURCE: United Nations, *Demographic Yearbook*, 1957.

and birth rates came slowly. Joseph J. Spengler summarizes the process as follows:[3]

In the course of the nineteenth and twentieth centuries, populations situated in the European sphere of civilization which were subjected to the pressures of industrialization and urbanization underwent a number of transformations: (1) Age-specific fertility and mortality, together with crude natality, declined below eighteenth-century levels, often to less than half. (2) The age structure changed (the relative number of younger persons diminishing while that of older persons increased) and this change eventually re-enforced the impact upon natality of the forces making for a decline in age-specific fertility. (3) Intragroup differences in fertility for a time were intensified, since at first fertility declined relatively more in such groups as urban dwellers, professional families and the better educated. Then the factors making for family limitation became sufficiently diffused so that the diverging fertility pattern gave place to a converging one, and a comparatively stable pattern of small differences was again in process of being established. (4) Because the per capita demand for farm produce was comparatively constant, (i.e., both price and income inelastic), improvements in agricultural methods caused the rural population to decline relatively and then absolutely. The associated drift of the population to towns and cities was accentuated by the development of urban and industrial employments, until today the number of potential emigrants in rural situations in most industrially developed countries is very small. (5) Because populations grew at different rates in different countries and because the multiplication of economic opportunities proceeded more rapidly in some countries than in others, the nineteenth and early twentieth century witnessed considerable international migration. This was finally halted by restrictive legislation and a narrowing of differences between prospects at home and prospects abroad, as envisaged by potential migrants.

In other words, in the Western world economic development came first, and the initial declines in death rates reflected mainly improved economic conditions. The impact of medical science on death rates came considerably later. In the now underdeveloped countries, on the other hand, dramatic declines in death rates are being produced by medical science *before* any substantial economic development has taken place. The Ceylonese case is the most spectacular for so short a period, but the same sort of thing has been happening in many underdeveloped countries. Malaria, "the world's most potent single cause of sickness, invalidism, and death," is on the wane in a good number of these countries, and other diseases are also being brought under control. Dr. Kingsley Davis points out that "the drop in the death rate has tended to go much further without

[3] Joseph J. Spengler, "Demographic Patterns," in H. F. Williamson and J. A. Buttrick, *Economic Development: Principles and Patterns* (New York, 1954), pp. 90–91. Spengler adds:
"It is easy to exaggerate the role of migration. Around 1850 the annual number of emigrants from Europe formed about 0.1 per cent of the European population and, at the emigration peak around 1905–15, only 0.3 per cent. In the decades 1880–90 and 1900–10, immigration increased the poulation of the United States only about 0.9 and 0.7 per cent, respectively."

a significant decline in the birth rate than was the case in the West."[4] Consequently, a good many of these countries are now expanding their populations at figures close to 30 per thousand, considered to be the "biological maximum."

The Lag Between the Drop in Death Rates and the Drop in Birth Rates

As a matter of pure arithmetic it is evident that the extent to which the population explosion gathers momentum in any country depends on the length of time between the initial drop in death rates and the subsequent drop in birth rates—if any. The European spurt of population in the eighteenth and nineteenth centuries was restrained in comparison with the present population explosion in developing countries, not only because the drop in death rates was less rapid and less dramatic, but also because it was followed after a few generations by a still sharper fall in birth rates. Except for Japan this sharp drop in birth rates has yet to appear in developing countries, even in cases such as Indonesia where the drop in death rates began over a century ago. "The great and rapid success of death-control now occurring in many tropical areas, unmatched by equally effective birth-control, leads to explosive increases in population."[5]

Demographers describe the pattern of population growth in western Europe as a "population cycle" with four stages: a high-fluctuating stage with both death rates and birth rates at a high level and a slow but irregular increase in population; an early-expanding stage with rapidly falling death rates and constant birth rates; a late-expanding stage with falling birth rates; and a low-fluctuating stage with both birth rates and death rates low. Chart 2–2 illustrates this cycle for the "typical" example of England and Wales.

By-products of the Population Explosion

The unprecedented growth of population has side effects that further complicate the problem of raising the levels of living in poor countries. One of these is the increasing youthfulness of a rapidly rising population, and the consequent decline in the ratio of active to inactive population. In themselves, high birth rates and falling death rates bring an increase in family size and a higher ratio of children to adults. In addition, improved public health tends to have particularly marked effects on infant mortality. For the world as a whole, infant mortality has fallen in the course of a few generations from about 200 per thousand to about 30 per thousand; "six babies are saved out of every seven who would have died two centuries

[4] Kingsley Davis, "The Amazing Decline of Mortality in Underdeveloped Areas," *American Economic Review, Papers and Proceedings*, XLVI, (May, 1956), p. 314.
[5] Political and Economic Planning, *World Population and Resources* (London, 1962), p. 12.

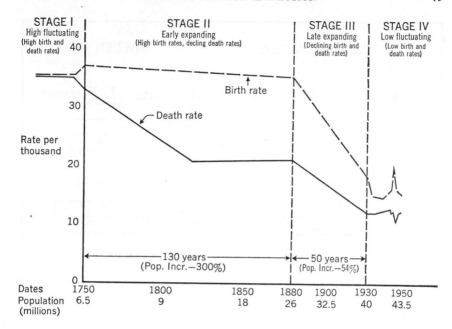

Chart 2-2. The Population Cycle, England and Wales
SOURCE: Political and Economic Planning, *World Population and Resources* (London, 1955 [1962]), p. 10.

ago."[6] In some developing countries, infant mortality has dropped from even higher levels and has taken only decades instead of centuries. The net result is that in the now developing countries each adult has to support a larger number of children than was the case when the now advanced countries were in the early stages of industrialization. Whereas the now advanced countries have a maximum of 25 to 30 per cent of their population below the age of fifteen (the age at which people are usually considered to enter the active labor force), the underdeveloped countries have 40 to 45 per cent of their population in the "inactive" age group zero to fifteen. For some time to come, the "inactive" group will continue to increase more rapidly than the "active" group in developing countries.

Chart 2-3 illustrates graphically the difference in age structure of a country where both death rates and birth rates are low (Sweden) and one where birth rates are high and death rates still fairly high (Costa Rica).

For much the same reasons an initial spurt in population growth is almost certain to become cumulative. Today's children are tomorrow's parents; a large proportion of population below the age of fifteen now means a larger proportion in the most fertile age groups during the next few years. "A decline in age specific mortality rates prior to childbearing

[6] Political and Economic Planning, *op. cit.*, p. 5.

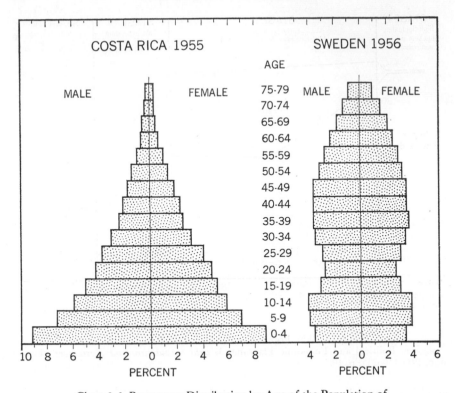

Chart 2–3. Percentage Distribution by Age of the Population of
Costa Rica in 1955 and of the Population of Sweden in 1956
SOURCE: Harold F. Dorn, "World Population Growth," in Philip M. Hauser (ed.),
The Population Dilemma (Englewood Cliffs, N.J., 1963), p. 23.

ages has the same demographic effect as an increase in the birth rate."[7]

Effect on Savings

We have seen above that in its simplest form the problem of economic
development is one of saving and investing enough to produce a flow of
income that will grow faster than the population. The population explosion not only increases the ratio of savings and investment needed to
guarantee rising per capita incomes; it also aggravates the difficulty of
saving:

High fertility can depress private savings in two ways: (1) by reducing the
volume of savings by individual families when such savings are an important
component of the national total; (2) by increasing the proportion of national
income that must accrue to non-savers if standards of consumption play any
part in determining the earnings of low-income families.

[7] Harold F. Dorn, "World Population Growth," in Philip M. Hauser (ed.), *The
Population Dilemma* (Englewood Cliffs, N.J., 1963), p. 23.

When it is the government rather than individual entrepreneurs that provides a large proportion of national investment, fertility affects the level of investment through its effect on the capacity of the government to raise money through taxation. . . . For any given level of deprivation that it is prepared to impose (the government) can raise more taxes from a low fertility population than from a high fertility population with the same national income and the same number of adults in each.[8]

Effect on the Pattern of Investment

Large families and a growing proportion of young people also complicate the problem of raising per capita income by shifting investment in the direction of relatively capital-intensive projects, particularly education and housing. Quite apart from the importance of education and training in raising productivity, the elimination of illiteracy and the provision of universal primary school education are high priority objectives in their own rights in most developing countries. Some indication of what the population explosion means for education requirements is provided by Table 2–5. Education yields high returns in the long run, as we shall see below; but it is a form of investment with a particularly long gestation period, and the immediate impact of a "big push" in education

TABLE 2–5
Children Aged 5 to 14 (Elementary School Ages), 1960 and 1975

Country	Numbers (in thousands)		Increase	
	1960–63	1975–78	Amount (in thousands)	Per cent
India	100,100	150,300	50,200	50.1
Pakistan	24,323	38,752	14,429	59.3
Indonesia	21,363	34,666	13,303	62.3
Mainland China	182,800	292,700	109,900	60.1
Japan	20,242	13,300	−6,942	−34.3

Youth Aged 15 to 19, 1960 and 1975

Country	Numbers (in thousands)		Increase	
	1960–63	1975–78	Amount (in thousands)	Per cent
India	41,500	60,000	18,500	44.6
Pakistan	9,517	15,035	5,518	58.0
Indonesia	8,416	14,275	5,859	69.6
Mainland China	62,000	113,500	51,500	83.1
Japan	9,552	7,251	−2,301	−24.1

SOURCE: Irene B. Taeuber, "Asian Populations: The Critical Decades," in Philip M. Hauser (ed.), The Population Dilemma (Englewood Cliffs, N.J., 1963), pp. 84–85.

[8] Ansley J. Coale, "Population and Economic Development," in Philip M. Hauser (ed.), op. cit., pp. 54–55.

is the diversion of some of the most productive resources—educated and trained people—from the production of other goods and services to the classroom. In developing countries outside the tropics, where school buildings must meet the requirements of substantial variations in climate, the rapid growth of a school-age population also imposes a severe strain on the construction industry.

The increasing number and size of families also add greatly to the housing problem; and housing, at least in the cities, is also a relatively capital-intensive investment. The appalling implications of the housing problem have been dramatically drawn by Eugene R. Black in an address to the U.N. Economic and Social Council:[9]

Some calculations have been made about the cost of providing houses in India during the next generation, if the population continues to grow at its present rate of about 2% a year. If you disregard the cost of rural housing, on the somewhat optimistic assumption that it can be carried out entirely with local materials and labor, then you still have to pay for the homes of nearly 200 million extra people who, it is expected, will be living in India's cities 25 years hence. Making full allowance for the fact that many of the extra persons will be children needing not new houses, but simply more space in existing households, a sober estimate of the cost suggests that in the thirty years between 1956 and 1986 a total investment in housing of the order of 118 billion rupees, or roughly $25 billion, will be needed. If you find a figure like that difficult to grasp, I may say that it is well over four times the total lent by the World Bank in all countries since it started business 15 years ago. Put another way, it is more than 30 times the initial resources of the International Development Association—and those resources are supposed to cover IDA's first five years of operations.

It is in this context that the "baby boom" of advanced countries is most directly related to the problem of underdevelopment. The "devastating torrent of babies," as Lord Robbins once called it, is now flooding the schools and universities of advanced countries. The strain on educational and housing facilities with the rapid growth of the school-age population and increased rate of family formation makes heavy demands on the capital formation and human skills of advanced countries. It reduces accordingly the amount of capital and technical assistance to developing countries that is politically and administratively feasible.

Effect on Employment and Unemployment

In Chapter 1 we saw that among the common characteristics of underdeveloped countries are unemployment, underemployment, and low-productivity employment, sometimes called "disguised unemployment." Many economic development plans include an employment objective as an end in itself, recognizing that there may be some conflict between the goal of raising per capita income and the goal of providing more employment. Maximizing employment requires choice of labor-intensive tech-

[9] Eugene R. Black, "Address to the Economic and Social Council of the United Nations," in Larry K. Y. Ng (ed.), *op. cit.*, pp. 42–43.

niques and labor-intensive products; maximizing income in some cases may require the converse.

The population explosion makes it just that much more difficult to raise employment and per capita income together, for a large and growing proportion of the population in the zero-to-fifteen-year-old age group now means a large and growing proportion in the fifteen-to-twenty-year-old age group a few years hence. In other words it means a swelling stream of entrants into the labor force, and therefore a labor force that grows even more rapidly than the total population. Future drops in birth rates "will have no effect whatsoever on the size of the labor force for 15 years, and only a very minor effect for three decades."[10] The amount of capital formation needed to provide jobs will grow accordingly. Moreover, with an increasing share of total capital formation absorbed into education and housing where the capital-job ratio is relatively high, the amount left over to provide jobs elsewhere in the economy is correspondingly reduced.

Feeding the Population

In view of the universally accepted objective of bringing substantial improvements in general levels of living to underdeveloped countries in the next few decades, it is disturbing that the question of feeding the world population should be seriously considered. If there is doubt about our ability to provide food for the world's population, there must be still more doubt about our ability to provide food plus all the other components of a high level of living. Yet the issue is one that is being seriously debated. Indeed the Food and Agricultural Organization of the United Nations, after fifteen years of concentrated efforts to raise agricultural productivity in developing countries, felt in 1961 that the food prospect had reached crisis proportions, and embarked on its Freedom from Hunger Campaign.

More than 1.5 billion people in the world are undernourished or malnourished to begin with; world food production must be raised by some 25 per cent merely to eliminate existing deficiences. It is not just a matter of total calories. "When the staple food provides over 80 percent of the total it is in a position to dictate the total value of he whole diet. If the staple food is low in protein (e.g., cassava) or is over-refined (e.g., highly milled cereals), malnutrition is then inevitable. Such diets are usually found in parts of the world where the total calories are also inadequate. Possibly three-quarters of the world's population is badly fed in one or the other of these ways, or from a shortage of calories."[11] Most of these people are in Asia, but Africa, Latin America, and even Europe have among them hundreds of thousands of underfed people.

[10] Gunnar Myrdal, "The United Nations, Agriculture, and the World Economic Revolution," *Journal of Farm Economics*, November, 1965.

[11] Political and Economic Planning, *op. cit.*, p. 27. It should be noted that these figures refer to 1952. As the Food and Agricultural Organization is the source of data in both cases, a comparison with the 1962 statement suggests some improvement during the intervening decade.

When the expected increase in population is also taken into account, the magnitude of the food problem becomes truly staggering. The Food and Agriculture Organization itself states the problem in these terms:[12]

World food supplies must be trebled by the turn of the century if world population, which is expected to double and to exceed 6,000 million by then, is to have enough to eat. At present it is estimated that 300 to 500 million people out of 3,000 million in the world are underfed and that up to one half of the world population—perhaps even more—suffer from hunger or malnutrition.

It is against this grim background that the Freedom from Hunger Campaign launched by the Food and Agriculture Organization of the United Nations (FAO) needs to be viewed. The magnitude of the problem and the continuing inadequacy of food production in the "hungry regions" of the world present a challenge to all who think in terms of a better and peaceful world. Such a world is impossible in the present circumstances.

Unfortunately, the biggest increases in population will take place precisely in the regions where nutrition is least adequate. In order to take care of the increased population, without any improvement in levels of nutrition, food supplies must increase by 150 per cent in the low-calorie countries and by about 120 per cent in the world as a whole.

Cannot food-surplus countries like the United States, Canada, and Australia meet the world requirements through "Food for Peace" and similar food-aid programs? Not very easily; by 1980, to meet the increase in numbers and provide a modest rise of per capita consumption of 10 per cent, grain production would have to be *raised* by almost as much as the present total output of North America and western Europe combined. Even if the grain were there, it would take an enormous increase in shipping facilities to get it to the hungry people.

Hopefully, modern science, including food technology, can find ways of expanding food production to meet requirements despite population growth. The question, however, is not whether or not we face mass starvation, but rather, what is the cost, in terms of other objectives, of providing basic necessities for all? A distinguished geographer points out that all the good land is already occupied; only about 25 per cent of the earth's land surface, he says, is suitable for food production and for human life generally. Thus, expanding food production means mainly increasing yields; in his view, if population growth continues at current rates, "the future points to trouble—deep trouble, for in the great world food supply is no match for population."[13] Some scientists are much more optimistic, pointing to the possibilities of increased yields through use of tracer elements, eating plankton from the sea, etc.

[12] Food and Agriculture Organization, *Six Billions to Feed* (Rome, 1962).
[13] C. Langdon White, "Geography and the World's Population," in Larry K. Y. Ng (ed.), *op. cit.*, pp. 18–19.

Conclusions

However we appraise the race between the agricultural scientists and food technologists on the one hand and population on the other, one thing is clear: we have waited until very late in the day to launch an all-out attack on world poverty. As the renowned demographer Irene B. Taeuber puts it:[14]

Thus Asia begins its modernization, not with the 250 million people of 1650, or the 650 million people of 1850, but the 1.5 billion people of today (1960). The tragedy of the period of European expansion for Asian countries inheres in this simple fact. Populations multiplied again and again; once empty lands were filled, and once occupied lands were occupied even more densely. But economies remained primarily subsistence agriculture, people remained illiterate, and living and values alike remained traditional. Birth rates remained at the high levels appropriate to ancestral-oriented cultures where the succession of sons was essential and life was precarious. Social, economic and demographic transformations that might have come slowly over centuries must come swiftly over decades if the good and the reasonably long lives that are the aspirations of Asian peoples become realities.

Professor Gunnar Myrdal, former Director General of the Economic Commission for Europe and one of the world's leading economists—and no alarmist—concluded his address to the Thirteenth Conference of the Food and Agricultural Organization with these sobering words.[15]

I fear that we are becoming accustomed to living on happily and attending to the business of the day while not giving much thought to the possibility or probability of the unthinkable ahead of us. To this category I reckon the outcome of the atomic armament race and the less publicized preparation for biological and chemical warfare. . . . To this category of unthinkably menacing calamities belongs also the gathering food crisis. . . . Social catatrophies are different from the certainty of death for the individual, as they can and should be averted. And if we do not use foresight and take measures against them, we all perish and there will be no posterity.

Eugene Black, who was a Wall Street financier before becoming President of the World Bank, is not a man given to extravagant statements. Yet, in addressing the Economic and Social Council in 1961, he felt obliged to say:[16]

I must be blunt. Population growth threatens to nullify all our efforts to raise living standards in many of the poorer countries. We are coming to a situation

[14] Irene B. Taeuber, "Asian Populations. The Critical Decades," in Larry K. Y. Ng (ed.), *op. cit.* p. 79.
[15] Gunnar Myrdal, *The 1965 McDougall Lecture*, Stockholm (Institute for International Economic Studies), November 22, 1965.
[16] Eugene R. Black, Address to the Economic and Social Council of the United Nations, in Larry K. Y. Ng (ed.), *op. cit.* p. 140.

in which the optimist will be the man who thinks that present living standards can be maintained. The pessimist will not look even for that. Unless population growth can be restrained, we may have to abandon for a generation our hopes of economic progress in the crowded lands of Asia and the Middle East.

Achieving the brave hopes set forth in Chapter 1 will be no simple task. The worldwide war on poverty is one that will both merit and require the total wisdom and best efforts of all mankind—social scientists and natural scientists, engineers and technicians, politicians and statesmen, the managers and the managed, and workers in both field and factory.

The chief obstacle to economic development is still ignorance. But something has been learned about the nature of the development process. Much was known even before World War II, and the concentrated effort since has added greatly to our store of knowledge. A great deal remains to be learned, but persistent and universal application of principles already established could accelerate the rate of economic development enough to make the difference between success or failure. In an earlier publication this writer coined the outrageously mixed metaphor, "The road to development is paved with vicious circles."[17] But as Albert O. Hirschman has pointed out, some circles are more vicious than others.[18] The task of the analyst is to discover which of these vicious circles are the basic causes of the others, which can more readily be broken into, and which can be converted into feedback mechanisms contributing to sustained economic growth. Let us therefore turn to the principles of economic development.

[17] Benjamin Higgins, "Financing Economic Development," *International Conciliation*, 1955.
[18] Albert O. Hirschman, *The Strategy of Economic Development* (New Haven, 1958).

PART II | General Theories

3 | The Classical Theory of Capitalist Development: Growth and Stagnation

The economists of the late eighteenth and early nineteenth centuries were very much concerned with the conditions for economic progress. This was the period of the "Industrial Revolution" in Europe. The Classical economists and Karl Marx lived through the period of take-off into sustained growth; Marx and Mill saw peak rates of growth attained in Europe. The observations of these economists regarding the nature and causes of economic progress are, therefore, of considerable interest.

Europe in 1750 differed from Asia and Africa in 1950, as we shall explain in some detail below. Nevertheless, the most dramatic examples of take-off into sustained and cumulative growth are to be found in eighteenth- and nineteenth-century Europe. Economic development of the New World was of course equally spectacular, but it was in part a transplanting of the development of Europe, and it was relatively easy because of the unusually favorable resource-population pattern. What happened in those countries in that period is what we want to happen in Asia, Africa, and Latin America now. Consequently, it is important to find out what the best thinkers of that period regarded as responsible for the current economic growth and what they considered was required to keep it going. The "best thinkers" of the Classical and Marxist schools brought to bear some of the most powerful minds ever to be directed toward questions of economics. Without examining their development theories, we can have no assurance that subsequent work in this field is any more penetrating than theirs, particularly since the field was almost totally neglected between 1870 and 1935. At the very least, any points of agreement in eighteenth- and nineteenth-century theories of growth are well worth our attention.

Since we are interested in basic ideas which may be still relevant today, and in isolating points of agreement and disagreement, we shall treat the literature somewhat differently from the usual history of economic thought. In the first place, we shall be generous in interpreting ideas, translating them into basic functional relationships, and closing up any open ends in the analytical systems. Moreover, we shall translate these ideas into a common contemporary terminology. Not only does this approach help us to evaluate what they had to say, it also makes it easier to see the real points of difference and agreement.

For the most part—despite the controversies that took place within it— we will treat the Classical school as a unit. We shall refer to some differences among members of the school only at the end of this chapter, especially differences between Malthus and the others. Finally, since we want to present the best of the ideas of the Classical school, we shall concentrate on the writings of Adam Smith, Malthus, and Mill rather than those of Ricardo, Senior, and others. To be sure, Ricardo's system was in many respects tighter logically than those of his contemporaries, but his greater rigor was the result of a higher degree of abstraction. More important for us, he was much less interested in economic development than he was in the theory of value and distribution. Schumpeter has gone so far as to state that Ricardo "all but identifies economics with the theory of distribution, implying that he had little or nothing to say about—to use his language— 'the laws which regulate total output'."[1] For this reason Schumpeter considered Ricardian analysis as "a detour."[2] This evaluation may be too harsh when considering Ricardo's position in the history of economic thought as a whole, but it is true where the theory of growth is concerned.

A strong case can be made for including Marx in the Classical school. As Schumpeter says, the Marxist system is "part and parcel of that period's general economics."[3] The basic theories of production and value are much the same in Classical and Marxist models, as is the explanation of the process of economic growth. Even the theory of distribution is not really so very different. Nevertheless, there are good grounds for treating the Classical and Marxist models separately. First, the Marxist prognosis regarding capitalism is quite different from that of the Classical school. Second, Marx paid more explicit attention to interrelations among sectors in the economy, and the sectors he distinguished were different from those emphasized by the Classicists. Third, Marx had a stronger sense of history and of cultural variations than most of his contemporaries. Fourth, there is a more clear-cut suggestion that we cannot rely on "psychological individualism" (generalizing from the behavior of individual workers, capitalists, and landlords), but must conduct our analysis of economic development in terms of groups (classes). Accordingly, we shall confine this chapter to the essential features of the Classical theory of growth, and devote the next chapter to the Marxist model.

[1] Joseph A. Schumpeter, *History of Economic Analysis* (New York, 1954), pp. 568–69.
[2] *Ibid.*, p. 474.
[3] *Ibid.*, pp. 383–85.

The Classical Model

For the Classical economists, the development of capitalist economies was a race between technological progress and population growth, a race in which technological progress would be in the lead for some time but which would end in a dead heat, or stagnation. Technological progress, in turn, depended on capital accumulation, which would permit increasing mechanization and greater division of labor. And the rate of capital accumulation depended on the level and trend of profits.

In order to give form to our presentation and to facilitate comparison with other models, let us translate the basic propositions of the Classical theory of growth into a series of mutually consistent and interacting propositions—or, in mathematical terms, into a set of simultaneous equations, with equal numbers of equations and unknowns, so that the system is soluble or "determinate."

Proposition 1: The Production Function

Smith, Malthus, and Mill all had it quite clearly in mind that total output, O, depended on the size of the labor force, L, the stock of capital, Q, the amount of land available—which we shall denote by K, to mean supply of known resources—and the level of technique, T. Using the common symbol f to mean "function of" or "depends upon," we can then write,

$$O = f(L, K, Q, T) \tag{1}$$

Repeating this proposition in words for those who find equations a hindrance rather than a help, total output depends on the size of the labor force, the supply of land (or known and economically useful resources), the stock of capital, the proportions in which these factors of production are combined, and the level of technology.

We are perhaps being overgenerous to the Classicists in translating "land" into "supply of known and economically useful resources." Clearly, it is not the area of the country alone, or even the amount of arable land and its fertility that determines output but the total supply of natural resources. In this context "supply" includes only resources currently known to exist and to be economically useful; it does not include resources yet to be discovered or useful only after some future change in technology. Perhaps no member of the Classical school would have denied that only in this sense can "land" be treated as a distinct factor of production along with capital and labor, but much of their discussion was couched in terms of the total area of agricultural land as such. Later on we shall want to use "land" to mean "supply of known and economically useful resources," and we shall denote it by the symbol K—we cannot use L for more than one variable in our system. So let us be generous and introduce it in this sense into the Classical model. Perhaps, after all, they included resource discoveries as part of technological progress, so that at any point of time the supply of land could be treated as fixed.

On the other hand, we may be a little unfair to the Classicists in not including entrepreneurship explicitly in our system. By "entrepreneurship" is meant the function of seeing investment and production opportunities; organizing an enterprise to undertake a new production process; raising capital, hiring labor, arranging for a supply of raw materials, finding a site, and combining these factors of production into a going concern; introducing new techniques and commodities, discovering new sources of natural resources; and selecting top managers for day-to-day operations. As we shall see in Chapter 5, the entrepreneur in this sense plays the vital role in Schumpeter's theory of growth. Of course the Classical economists were aware of the importance of the entrepreneurial function, but they did not make it a strategic part of their system, and they did not make the crucial distinction between entrepreneurship and management.[4] So we omit the entrepreneur until we come to Schumpeter's model.

Most Classicists probably thought of the production function as "linear and homogeneous"; that is, they would have expected that if the quantities used of all factors of production were doubled at once, output would double. Adam Smith might have made the case for increasing returns to scale; doubling all factors would increase the opportunities for division of labor. But they would have regarded such propositions as rather uninteresting, because in their view, it would have been nonsense to talk about doubling the supply of land. Any country has so much land, and that is that. It would not be nonsense, however, to talk of doubling the supply of known and economically useful resources over some period—which is the important difference between "land" as we shall use the term and "land" as the Classicists seemed to use it. It is a little inelegant to include all resource discoveries as a form of technological progress, as we must do with the Classical definitions; in any case, they did not seem to regard resource discoveries as an important source of progress. Perhaps for nineteenth-century England they were right, but for a *general* theory we would not want to treat the supply of natural resources—or even arable land—as fixed.

For the Classicists, then, the key cross section of the production function was the one showing what happens to output when land is fixed and the labor supply is increased. This cross section is shown by the solid line in Figure 3–1, which shows the usual four phases: increasing marginal returns, decreasing marginal returns, decreasing average returns, and decreasing total returns. It is also clear that the Classicists thought Europe was in the third phase, in which an increase in the amount of labor employed on the land would bring some increase in output, but would reduce output *per capita*, and so well beyond the second phase, where each additional unit of labor would add less to total output than the last one, although still increasing *per capita* output. In symbols, we can write

$$\frac{\delta f}{\delta L} \cdot \frac{dL}{dt} > 0 \qquad \frac{\delta^2 f}{\delta L^2} \cdot \frac{d^2 L}{dt^2} < 0 \qquad \text{and} \qquad \frac{d}{dL}\left(\frac{O}{L}\right) < 0 \qquad (1a)$$

which says just what we have said in the last sentence.[5]

---

[4] *Ibid.*, pp. 554–56.

[5] The symbols δ and d mean "rate of increase in." Thus dL/dt is the rate of growth in the labor force through time, etc.

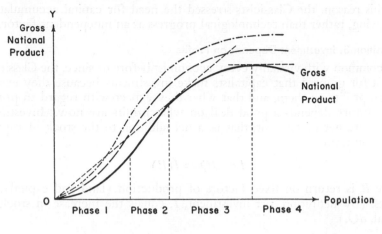

Figure 3–1

Now, the solid curve in Figure 3–1 shows what happens if the amount of labor is increased while the land utilized is fixed and nothing else happens either. If additional capital is accumulated, the curve will have the same general shape but will be higher, as indicated by the dotted curves in Figure 3–1. Each successive curve shows the effect of using a larger stock of capital together with the fixed amount of land and varying amounts of labor.

Proposition 2: Capital Accumulation Permits Technological Progress

This consideration brings us to the second basic proposition. The Classical economists seemed to think that there was always a plentiful supply of better techniques and new commodities to be introduced, but they considered that the rate at which these opportunities could be exploited was limited by the flow of capital for new investment. It would be too much to say that their analysis precluded altogether the possibility that new techniques might be capital saving after being introduced; conceivably the capital-output ratio might be lower, once the new improvement was in operation. But the Classicists did not give much weight to this possibility. They thought that, on balance, new net saving was needed to permit society to take advantage of the steady advance of technology; reinvestment of depreciation reserves would not be enough. For them, the whole process of technological progress was capital absorbing, whatever may have been the nature of inventions. (We shall have more to say about this question later.) In symbols, then, our second equation is

$$T = T(I) \tag{2}$$

which means, the level of technique depends on the level of investment.

For this reason, the Classicists stressed the need for capital accumulation and saving, rather than technological progress as an independent factor.

Proposition 3: Investment Depends on Profits

In common with virtually every economist before or since, the Classicists took it for granted that capitalists make investments because they expect to earn profits on them, and that what they expect with regard to profits in the future depends a good deal on what profits are now.[6] Investment means here net investment, that is, a net addition to the stock of capital. So we can write

$$I = dQ = I(R) \qquad (3)$$

where R is return on fixed factors of production (land and capital), or profits. (By definition, net investment, I, equals the increase in stock of capital, dQ.)

Proposition 4: Profits Depend on Labor Supply and the Level of Technique

Of course, the whole nexus of economic events has an effect on profits, and any simple proposition regarding determination of profits is bound to be an abstraction from reality. Since some things are a good deal more important than others in determining the level of profits, one is justified in concentrating on those things, at least to begin with.

For the Classical school, profits were the outcome of the same race mentioned at the beginning of this section. As population grew, diminishing returns would be encountered in agriculture, raising labor costs (manhour costs of food) and reducing profits. But offsetting this tendency was historically *increasing* returns, especially in industry, through improvements in technique. Which force is more powerful is a question of fact, not of pure theory, and varies from country to country and from time to time in the same country. Most of the Classicists felt that technological progress was winning for the time being, in their own country (England), but that it could not win for very much longer. Our fourth equation, then, is

$$R = R(T, L) \qquad (4)$$

That is, the level of profits depends on the level of technique and the size of the labor force.

The labor force and the population were generally conceived to vary together. Of course the Classical economists could ignore neither the existence of unemployment nor variations in the amount of unemployment, especially in the decades following the Napoleonic Wars. But on the whole they regarded unemployment as an aberration, at least in a growing economy, and felt that population growth and employment must move together. Thus population growth always brought a decline in per capita output, *unless* offset by technological progress.

---

[6] Malthus, however, attached considerable importance to the whole "climate" for investment, as well as actual profits.

We already have some indication of the circularity of their argument. The level of technique depends on the level of investment, investment depends on profits, and profits depend partly on the level of technique. This circularity is no accident or oversight; it is precisely what the Classicists—and most later economists—have wished to stress; in economic development nothing succeeds like success, and nothing fails like failure. We can express this circularity by substituting Equations (3) and (4) in Equation (2), which gives us

$$T = T(I) = T[I(R)] = T\{I[R(T, L)]\} \qquad (4a)$$

Thus a rapid rate of technological advance will tend to call forth a level of investment that will permit the rapid technological advance to continue, but the reverse is also true. Do we already have a clue to the difference in performance of advanced and underdeveloped countries? Perhaps; but let us go on with the Classical system.

Proposition 5: The Size of the Labor Force Depends on the Size of the Wages Bill

Few of the basic propositions of the Classical school have been so vehemently attacked as the "iron law of wages." The general idea is that the rate of population growth depends on how much money (working capital) is available to pay wages. If the total wages fund is increased and real average rates rise above the subsistence level, larger number of working-class children can survive to become members of the labor force. There are no checks on the size of working-class families except the amount of wages available to them and the number of children that can subsist on those wages. Thus there is a constant tendency for real wage rates to return to the subsistence level. An increase in wages paid may bring a temporary improvement in living standards, but this improvement will soon be swamped in an increased rate of population growth.

Sometimes the Classicists seemed to be thinking of subsistence wages as a true physiological minimum, below which children literally could not survive; sometimes they seemed to think rather of an "accustomed normal" living standard, not far above the physical subsistence level, which working-class families would not endanger by having more children. In terms of a systematic model, it does not matter much which explanation is given. In either case, a temporary increase in real wage rates would be squeezed out by accelerated population growth.

This argument often seems far-fetched to people living in advanced countries today, but it probably gave a fairly accurate description of what happened in Europe in the late eighteenth and early nineteenth centuries. It also seems to be true of peasant societies in Asian, African, and some Latin American countries today. Of course we do not know a great deal about the complex psychological, sociological, biological, and technical factors which enter into family size. We can, however, say a few things about it. First, improved standards of public health and nutrition permit a more rapid rate of population growth. Second, every society, from primitive African or Australian tribes through ancient Egypt, Greece, and Rome to modern societies, has practiced population control in some form and to some degree. Third, the technical efficiency of the methods used has varied enormously, even within the same society. Fourth, limitation of family size is practiced only if there seems to be some good reason for it— some vision of a better life if the number of children is restricted. As Professor Myrdal has put it, these facts mean that if people have a very strong desire to keep family size down, they will do so, even if they must resort to infanticide, abortion, complicated and prolonged initiation rites to delay marriage, or similarly crude or brutal devices. If people want larger families, and if the means are available to support them and health standards are high, population growth will attain high levels. And if most people are rather indifferent about family size, because they cannot see that their way of life will be very different with four children or eight, population growth is still likely to reach fairly high levels, so long as health and nutritional standards permit it.

In Europe in the eighteenth century, and in Asia, Africa, and Latin America in recent decades, health and nutrition were improving, while most people could not visualize a significantly higher standard of living to be achieved by acceptable and available means of limiting family size. Thus they were probably rather indifferent about family planning. When wage rates rose, more children could be brought to maturity without impinging on the customary living standards of the working class, and consequently population growth could increase. There was no strong incentive for limiting family size, and no cheap and convenient ways of family planning were available. Under these conditions, the Classical theory of population makes good sense.

We shall have more to say about population growth later; meanwhile we can write the equation for this proposition as

$$L = L(W) \tag{5}$$

Proposition 6: The Wages Bill Depends on the Level of Investment

The Classical school thought of capital—or at least part of it—as consisting of a "wages fund," an amount of money available for hiring labor. This wages fund was built up by saving and put into effective use through investment. Except for Malthus, who showed a high degree of sophistication in this respect, the Classicists tended to think that savings found their way into investment more or less automatically. Thus the wages bill could be increased only by net (savings and) investment, and our sixth equation is

$$W = W(I) \tag{6}$$

Closing the System

We now have all the "operational" equations of the Classical system, that is, all propositions expressing fundamental causal relationships. But so far we have listed seven variables and have only six equations; the system is indeterminate. We can close the system by adding an identity, *total output equals profits plus wages*, or

$$O = R + W \tag{7}$$

We can interpret this equation in either of two ways. If we define profits as we have done above, to include returns on fixed factors of production, including land as well as capital, the equation expresses an identity by definition. The total national income is equal to the total cost or value of all goods or services produced, and this amount is divided between workers and others.

If we want to be more purely Classical, we can think of it in another way, taking account of the somewhat fancy Classical theory of rent. According to the Classical school, value is equal to labor cost of production on "marginal" or no-rent land. Included in this labor cost is the cost of "embodied labor" tied up in capital; so value includes a return to capital as well as to labor. Price is value in money terms. Thus if we think of O as equal to pq, price times quantity of all goods and services, it will be equivalent to the total wages bill plus the total return to capital. If landlords succeed in getting rent, it is because workers or capitalists get less than their actual contribution to the value of output—which is exactly what the Classical economists wanted to imply. As a matter of social ethics they may have had a case; but as a matter of general theory this treatment of rent is a bit of a nuisance. So let us stick to the first interpretation.

We now have a determinate system with seven equations and seven unknowns. If we like, we can add an eighth variable, w, to mean the minimum wage rate, which is a constant, and then add an eighth equation expressing a long-run equilibrium condition,

$$W = wL \tag{8}$$

Summary

Let us now put together our interpretation of the Classical system and have a look at it:

$$O = f(L, K, Q, T) \tag{1}$$
$$T = T(I) \tag{2}$$
$$I = dQ = I(R) \tag{3}$$
$$R = R(T, L) \tag{4}$$
$$L = L(W) \tag{5}$$
$$W = W(I) \tag{6}$$
$$O = R + W \tag{7}$$

And in long-run equilibrium, we have also

$$W = wL \tag{8}$$

The circularity that we noticed above is even more apparent when we have the whole system before us. We can break into the circular flow anywhere and show how the system will evolve under various conditions, but let us start with profits as the prime mover of the capitalist system.

We could write schematically, $dR \to dI \to dQ \to dT$, $dW \to dL \to dR$. That is, an increase in profits brings an increase in investment, and so an addition to the stock of capital, which permits capitalists to take advantage of the steady flow of improved techniques and also raises the wages fund; that brings an accelerated population growth, which causes decreasing returns to labor on the land, raising labor costs and reducing profits. We could, of course, go on: reduced profits mean reduced investment, retarded technological progress, a diminished wages fund, and slowing down of population growth.

If we want to be a bit more sophisticated, we could make investment a function of the change in profits rather than the level of profits; thus capital accumulation would take place only if profits increase, and capital decumulation occurs when profits fall.

Figure 3–2 presents a diagrammatic summary of the Classical theory of growth. We cannot, of course, present seven or eight variables in one diagram; since we have at best three dimensions, we must pick the variables that tell us most. Moreover, the whole process of growth takes place in time; time is the variable with respect to which all the variables in our equations must be differentiated to get a picture of the growth process. So we are left with two other variables to be shown directly in the diagram. We have chosen to treat population and total production as the key variables; after all, what we are ultimately interested in is the trend of per capita output. The other variables must be treated implicitly, in terms of the circular flow outlined in the equations above. For example, we treat technological progress as depending only on the rate of capital accumulation, and we show variations in both, implicitly, by the change in total output with a given population as time goes by.

We begin at $t = O$, with a stock of capital and a technology which gives us the relationship between labor force and output shown in the curve O_0. Let us suppose that actual population is P_0 and output is at the point GNP_0, in the phase of diminishing average returns on this curve. Profits are earned and some investment takes place, permitting technological progress and increased wage payments. Thus as time goes by we move onto a new curve, O_1, with a higher output than before for any *given* labor force on the fixed amount of land. Meanwhile, of course, the population has also grown, so that at time $t = 1$ our actual position is GNP_1. And so on.

This movement through time has a clearly defined shape. According to the Classical school, when population is relatively small, returns on land will be high, perhaps even increasing; but as population grows we encounter more and more rapidly diminishing returns. Technological progress takes place at a *steady* rate, provided enough capital is forthcoming to exploit opportunities for improvement to the full. Thus in an advanced or "mature" economy, diminishing returns to land, and the consequent rise in labor costs, will outrun effective technological progress. Profits will fall. Then investment drops, technological progress is retarded, the wages fund ceases to grow, and so population also ceases to grow. In the Classical model, the end result of capitalist development is stagnation.

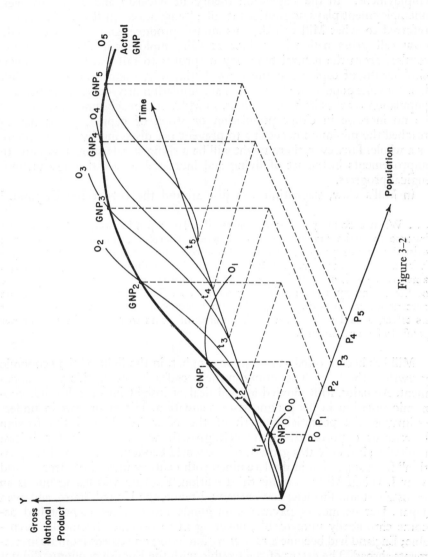

Figure 3-2

Thus the Classical concept of the "stationary state"—which for the Classical school was a historical phase and not just an analytical model—was essentially a concept of a mature economy. Adam Smith saw that the "stationary state" might be one in which wealth would be "very great," but nevertheless one in which "there would be a constant scarcity of employment." In the stagnation theory of Ricardo and Mill, however, unemployment plays no significant role; "stagnation" in Ricardo's analysis referred to what Mill called gross annual produce, and what we would now call gross national product at full employment. The stagnation resulted from the natural tendency of profits to fall and the consequent choking off of capital accumulation. Ultimately, stagnation would result in a constant population; but capital accumulation may cease "long before" population reaches its highest point. In Mill's stationary state, there would be no increase in either population or stock of capital, profit having reached the minimum necessary to prevent net dissaving by the economy as a whole. However, there might still be a rising standard of living due to improvements in the art of living and increased leisure through technological progress.

In Mill's view, stagnation was just around the corner for England: [7]

. . . When a country has long possessed a large production, and a large net income to make savings from, and when, therefore, the means have long existed of making a great annual addition to capital; it is one of the characteristics of such a country, that the rate of profit is habitually within, as it were, a hands' breadth of the minimum, and the country therefore on the very verge of the stationary state. [As for England] . . . The mere continuance of the present annual increase in capital if no circumstance occurred to counteract its effect, would suffice in a small number of years to reduce the rate of net profit to [the minimum].

Mill has been scoffed at as a poor prophet, in the light of the economic growth of the English economy in the decades following this pronouncement. Actually, Mill showed a good deal of insight into the English economic situation in his prognosis of stagnation. His error was in underestimating the potential growth of the New World and the foreign investment opportunities that such growth would provide for British capitalists; but only this growth of the world economy prevented "stagnation" from appearing in the late nineteenth century instead of after World War I. When Mill wrote his third edition, England was losing out as an industrialist and financier to Germany, France, the United States, and even Japan. Her balance of payments on goods and services account had become chronically unfavorable, never again to become chronically favorable; England had become a *rentier* nation living on returns from its investments abroad. The extent of the trouble with the English economy did not become apparent, however, until World War I reduced this *rentier* income from abroad.

[7] J. S. Mill, *Principles of Political Economy*, Book IV, chap. IV (3d ed., London, 1852).

The Malthus Version

We cannot leave our discussion of the Classical theory of development without drawing attention to its refinements in the Malthus version. For although the general theory of Malthus is described by the model presented above, certain features of his theory make it particularly enlightening both for an understanding of the requirements for steady growth in advanced countries and for the launching of development in underdeveloped countries.

To begin with, Malthus showed more appreciation than most of his contemporaries of the importance of a distinct and systematic theory of growth. Book I of his *Principles of Political Economy* [8] was concerned with value and distribution, Book II with "The Progress of Wealth." This book opens with the following statement: [9]

There is scarcely any inquiry more curious, or, from its importance, more worthy of our attention, than that which traces the causes which practically check the progress of wealth in different countries, and stop it, or make it proceed very slowly, while the power of production remains comparatively undiminished, or at least would furnish the means of a great and abundant increase of produce and population.

He defines the *problem* of development as explaining any difference between potential gross national product ("power of producing riches") and actual gross national product ("actual riches").

There is nothing automatic about economic growth, Malthus warns. To say that population growth by itself is enough to bring economic advance is absurd. In the first place, population growth—despite the strength of the psychological and physiological forces tending to bring it about—is an *end product* of the whole economic process; "an increase of population cannot take place without a proportionate or nearly proportionate increase of wealth." As evidence that the natural tendency toward population growth is no guarantee that either population or income will grow, he cites such "underdeveloped" countries as Spain, Portugal, Hungary, Turkey, "together with nearly the whole of Asia and Africa, and the greatest part of America." [10]

Secondly, mere increases in numbers do not provide a stimulus to economic expansion; population growth encourages development only if it brings an increase in effective demand. "A man whose only possession is his labor has, or has not, an effective demand for produce according as his labor is, or is not, in demand by those who have the disposal of produce." [11] And the demand for labor, in turn, depends on the rate of capital accumulation.

[8] The first edition of Malthus' *Principles* appeared in 1820, the second in 1836. (Page references are to the Augustus Kelly reprint of the second edition; New York, 1951.)

[9] *Ibid.*, p. 309.

[10] *Ibid.*, p. 314.

[11] *Ibid.*, pp. 311–12.

In elaborating his theory of effective demand and its relation to savings and investment, Malthus anticipated some of the basic ideas of such modern writers as Keynes and Kalecki. He flatly repudiated "Say's law," which said in effect that supply creates its own demand and that savings are just a demand for capital goods. Saving, in the sense of planned or *ex ante* saving, or abstinence, means not consuming; and not consuming in itself brings a decline in effective demand, profits, and investment.

Malthus drew attention to a circularity of a kind quite different from the one spelled out by the other Classicists, which has been restated more systematically by Kalecki and others in our own day. Going back to Equation (7) above, we have national income (or output) equal to profits plus wages. Let us rewrite the equation,

$$R = O - W \qquad\qquad (7a)$$

Now workers, as a class, are too poor to save. They spend all their income on consumption. Let us denote workers' consumption as C_w. Capitalists, however, do save; these savings create income in so far as they are invested. So we may write, substituting in Equation (7a)

$$R = (I + C_c + C_w) - C_w = I + C_c \qquad\qquad (7b)$$

That is, national income or output is generated by investment, capitalists' consumption, and workers' consumption. Profits are national income less wages; wages equal workers' consumption—and so profits are equal to investment plus capitalists' consumption. Thus abstinence on the part of capitalists, far from accelerating economic growth, will, in itself, retard it.[12]

Malthus does not, of course, deny the need for saving and investment for economic growth. But he suggests a concept of "optimum propensity to save." Up to a certain point saving is needed to finance (without inflation) the investment for which profitable opportunities exist. Beyond that point, however, saving will reduce consumer spending to such an extent that investment too will be discouraged.[13] High rates of growth do not occur with high levels of *ex ante* savings (abstinence) on the part of the upper-income groups, but with high levels of *ex post* (realized) savings and investment, which are in large degree the result of growth, and do not require reductions in consumer spending: [14]

. . . The fortune of a country, though necessarily made more slow, is made in the same way as the fortunes of individuals in trade are generally made—by savings, certainly; but by savings which are furnished by increased gains, and by no means involve a diminished expenditure on objects of luxury and enjoyment. . . . The amount of capital in this country is immense, and it certainly received very great additions during the last forty years but on looking back, few traces are to be found of a diminishing expenditure in the shape of revenue.

[12] This argument is made in effect in *ibid.*, pp. 311, 361.
[13] *Ibid.*, pp. 326–29.
[14] *Ibid.*, p. 367.

Thus Malthus had the picture of an advanced economy enjoying steady growth, with consumption, investment, and *ex post* (realized) savings expanding together.

Malthus also demonstrated a number of random insights into the factors which may retard a take-off into sustained economic growth. He attached considerable importance to backward-sloping supply curves of effort—both for workers and managers—in the explanation of the underdeveloped condition of such countries as Mexico and Ireland. He denied that the indolence characterizing underdeveloped countries could be explained by the tropical climate; the scene in the Cordilleras, where the climates "seem to be the finest in the world," is "not essentially different" from that of the "lower regions of New Spain." [15] The problem, as he saw it, was rather a matter of absence of incentives. He suggested that broadening international trade could help a good deal to straighten out these supply curves, by providing incentives for additional expenditure of effort, until an economy could get "over the hump" to the point where its own production was sufficiently varied to provide all the incentive needed for further growth.[16]

... The peasant, who might be induced to labor an additional number of hours for tea or tobacco, might prefer indolence to a new coat. ... And the trader or merchant, who would continue his business in order to be able to drink and give his guests claret and champagne, might think an addition of homely commodities by no means worth the trouble of so much constant attention.

Meanwhile anything that can be done to widen the market and permit more division of labor by internal measures is well worthwhile; and improved transport is one such measure.[17]

... It has never, I believe, occurred, that the better distribution of the commodities of a country occasioned by improved facilities of communication has failed to increase the value as well as the quantity of the whole produce.

Malthus also noted the phenomenon which Colin Clark has stressed in our own day; economic development entails structural change of a sort which diminishes the relative importance of agriculture in the economy.[18] He argued that technological progress tends to increase employment [19] and that tapering-off of the growth of income and output causes unemployment.[20] He suggested land reform as one means of expanding output.[21]

More important for us than any of these insights, however, was Malthus' anticipation of the theory of "dualism" as applied to underdeveloped countries. We shall see below that our understanding of the problem of underdevelopment can be greatly increased by breaking up the economy

[15] *Ibid.*, p. 338.
[16] *Ibid.*, p. 354.
[17] *Ibid.*, p. 362.
[18] *Ibid.*, p. 334.
[19] *Ibid.*, p. 352.
[20] *Ibid.*, p. 312.
[21] *Ibid.*, p. 373.

into sectors and studying interactions among them; even a two-sector model is a great advance over a single-sector model. A charitable interpretation of the Classical theory of growth can convert it into such a two-sector model, but the intersectoral analysis emerges more clearly in Malthus' writings than in those of other members of the Classical school.

Malthus envisaged the economy as consisting of two major sectors: one industrial, one agricultural. Technological progress he regarded as a phenomenon confined to the industrial sector—in advanced countries, at any rate. "Increasing returns" was a property of this sector, and unmitigated diminishing returns was the primary characteristic of the agricultural sector. If we think of nineteenth-century England, this picture was probably a good approximation to reality. The first wave of agricultural progress, undertaken by the "improving landlords," had helped to set the stage for the Industrial Revolution, but it was pretty well over when Malthus was writing; and the "industrial revolution" in agriculture itself (mechanization) did not set in until later. The good land was already occupied and no major resource discoveries were taking place. Meanwhile, striking progress was evident in power, manufacturing, and transport.

The Malthusian picture of economic development seems to have been one in which capital was invested in agriculture until all the arable land was brought into cultivation, stocked, and improved; after that there were no more opportunities for profitable investment in that sector, and investment opportunities existed only in the industrial sector. Diminishing returns to increased employment on the land could be avoided only if technological progress in the industrial sector was rapid enough, and if enough investment took place, to absorb most of the population growth in the industrial sector and to reduce the cost of living of workers on the land, permitting reductions in their corn (goods) wage rates.[22]

For those who like equations, we might express this relationship as follows. Let us assume once again that the rate of technological progress in the industrial sector depends only on the amount of capital available for utilizing the steady flow of improvements. Malthus explicitly recognized the possibility of unemployment arising from inadequate investment, so the level of industrial employment can also be treated as a function of investment. Thus we can regard industrial output as depending solely on the amount of capital invested in the industrial sector:

$$O_i = a \cdot Q_i \tag{9}$$

where O_i is the output of the industrial sector, Q_i is the amount of capital in the industrial sector, and $1/a$ is the capital-output ratio for the sector. Differentiating with respect to time,

$$\frac{dO_i}{dt} = a \cdot \frac{dQ_i}{dt} + Q_i \cdot \frac{da}{dt} \tag{9a}$$

If technological progress is "neutral" so that the capital-output ratio can be considered a constant, the second term drops out and the trend of

[22] See especially *ibid.*, pp. 278, 284.

industrial output through time depends only on the rate of capital accumulation (investment) in the industrial sector. The rate of investment in turn depends on the level of profits, as we already know; and in this model, the rate of profits will depend on the wage rate (which in turn depends on the cost of producing wage goods, especially foodstuffs) and effective demand, which depends on capitalists' consumption and investment.

In the agricultural sector the situation is different. There are no investment opportunities in the agricultural sector of a "mature" economy, and in underdeveloped countries capital is needed only to increase the effective supply of improved land. So we may write,

$$O_a = f(L_a, K) \qquad (10)$$

That is, agricultural output depends only on the supply of labor to the agricultural sector and the stock of improved land. Through time the change in agricultural output is

$$\frac{dO_a}{dt} = \frac{\delta f}{\delta L_a} \cdot \frac{dL_a}{dt} + \frac{\delta f}{\delta K} \cdot \frac{dK}{dt} \qquad (10a)$$

In a mature economy, K is constant, so the second term drops out. We are then left only with the first term to explain the trend in agricultural output. Now the first half of that term, $\delta f/\delta L_a$, is the marginal productivity of agricultural labor, which will be positive but diminishing. The second part, dL_a/dt, is the rate of growth of the agricultural labor force. It will increase until net investment in agriculture disappears, because agricultural profits have dropped too low, as a result of falling output per man-year as agricultural employment increases.

The kind of interaction between these two sectors which leads to the stationary state (stagnation) in mature economies has been outlined above. Malthus also, however, makes some suggestions about sectoral interaction in underdeveloped areas, which help to explain why they remain underdeveloped. First, he points out that each sector constitutes the market for the output of the other sector (in the absence of international trade). Thus failure of either sector to expand acts as a drag on the growth of the other; "balanced growth" is necessary if we are to have growth at all. The development of the industrial sector of underdeveloped countries is limited by the poverty of the agricultural sector. Speaking of Latin American countries, Malthus writes:

Except in the neighborhood of the mines and near the great towns, the effective demand for produce is not such as to induce the great proprietors to bring their immense tracts of land properly into cultivation: and the population, which, as we have seen, presses hard at times against the limits of subsistence, evidently exceeds in general the demand for labor, or the number of persons which the country can employ with regularity and constancy in the actual state of its agriculture and manufactures.

The continuing poverty of the peasant agriculture sector does not arise from scarcity of fertile land; poverty persists because large landowners have no incentive for more intensive cultivation with the present limita-

tions of the market, whereas the peasants lack the capital that would be
needed for efficient cultivation, which alone would permit them to pay
enough to induce landlords to rent some of their land: [23]

In the midst of an abundance of fertile land, it appears that the natives are
often very scantily supplied with it. They would gladly cultivate portions of
the extensive districts held by the great proprietors, and could not fail of thus
deriving an ample subsistence for themselves and their families; but in the
actual state of the demand for produce in many parts of the country, and in
the actual state of the ignorance and indolence of the natives, such tenants
might not be able to pay a rent equal to what the land would yield in its
uncultivated state, and in this case they would seldom be allowed to intrude
upon domains; and thus lands which might be made capable of supporting
thousands of people, may be left to support a few hundreds of cattle.

Thus the industrial sector (including large-scale agriculture) remains
limited in total size. Because of its land-and-capital-intensive nature it provides employment for relatively few people. The bulk of the population,
meanwhile, lives in poverty by means of labor-intensive peasant agriculture which provides no effective demand for further growth.
In other words, there is an "indivisibility" with respect to demand; a
certain minimum level of effective demand is necessary before cumulative
growth can set in.[24]

Without sufficient foreign commerce to give value to the raw produce of
the land; and before the general introduction of manufacturers had opened
channels for domestic industry, the demands of the great proprietors for labor
would be very soon supplied; and beyond this, the laboring classes would have
nothing to give them for the use of their lands.

With no alluring use of increased income to tempt them to greater efforts,
the landlord-capitalists find themselves on the backward-sloping portions
of their supply curves. The concentration of land ownership deprives the
peasants of any incentives they might have for raising output through
greater efforts.[25]

And under these circumstances, if a comparative deficiency of commerce
and manufactures, which great inequality of property tends rather to perpetuate
rather than to correct, prevents the growth of that demand for labor and
produce, which can alone remedy the discouragement to population occasioned
by this inequality, it is obvious that Spanish America may remain for ages
thinly peopled and poor, compared with her natural resources. And so, in fact,
she has remained.

And so she remains today, over a century later. As Malthus said then, so
now, although "the increase of population and wealth has been considerable, particularly of late years, yet altogether it has been far short of what

23 *Ibid.*, p. 341.
24 *Ibid.*, p. 342.
25 *Ibid.*, p. 343.

it would have been, even under a Spanish government," if appropriate development policies had been pursued.

Malthus on the Population Explosion

Malthus is better known for his *Essay on the Principle of Population* than for his *Principles of Political Economy*. Indeed, so close is the association of the name of Malthus with the concept of population pressure, that the more significant two-sector analysis of underdevelopment outlined above has been largely neglected. As Professor M. Blaug points out in his introduction to a recent edition of the *Essay*, the tremendous interest engendered by the Malthusian population theory can be explained at least partially by "population explosion" in the last two decades of the eighteenth century. Dr. Blaug adds, "Every schoolboy at the turn of the twentieth century could prove that Malthus had gone wrong by underestimating the potentialities of technical progress." [26] By the same token, the renewed interest in population pressure in developing countries has resulted in a resurgence of popularity of the Malthusian theory.

Malthus wrote the *Essay* at the age of 32, before he wrote the *Principles*, and seven years before he married. He never thoroughly integrated his population theory with the theory of underdevelopment, but there can be no doubt that he was constantly aware of population growth and its implications for development of underdeveloped countries. The sixth and last edition of the Essay in Malthus' lifetime was published in 1826, some years after the first edition of the *Principles*. If we do Malthus the service of coordinating for him his population theory with his theory of underdevelopment, virtually all of the ideas regarding technological dualism and the population explosion, presented in Chapter 14 below, will prove to have been anticipated by him.

Malthus begins his *Essay* by saying that any research on social progress must begin by investigating the factors that have impeded progress in the past, and then proceed to a consideration of "the probability of the total or partial removal of these causes in the future." To investigate "all factors influencing human happiness," he adds, "is beyond the powers of any single person. . . ." Malthus was well aware that every society ever known has practiced family planning in some manner and to some degree. There is yet to exist, he maintained, a society in which the potential of population growth has been left to exercise itself to the full: [27]

Whether the law of marriage be instituted, or not, the dictate of nature and virtue seems to be an early attachment to one woman; and where there were no impediments of any kind in the way of a union to which such an attachment would lead, and no causes of depopulation afterwards, the increase of the human species would be evidently much greater than any increase which has been hitherto known.

[26] M. Blaug, Introduction; Thomas R. Malthus, *An Essay on the Principle of Population, or A View of Its Past and Present Effects on Human Happiness with an Inquiry into our Prospects Respecting the Future Removal or Mitigation of the Evils Which It Occasions*, (Homewood, Ill., 1963), p. ix.

[27] Thomas R. Malthus, *op. cit.*, p. 3.

Malthus had a high regard for love. "Perhaps there is scarcely a man," he wrote, "who has once experienced the genuine delight of virtuous love, however great his intellectual pleasures may have been, who does not look back to that period as the sunny spot of his whole life, where his imagination likes most to bask, which he recollects and contemplates with the fondest regret, in which he would wish to live over again." He takes Godwin to task—with some justice—for saying, "Strip the commerce of the sexes of all its attendant circumstances, and it would be greatly despised." Malthus replies, "He might as well say to a man who admires trees, strip them of their spreading branches and lovely foliage, and what beauty can you see in a bare pole?" It is "the symmetry of person, the vivacity, the voluptuous 'softness of temper, the affectionate kindness of feeling, the imagination and wit' of a woman, which excites the passion of love, and not the mere distinction of being a female."

Malthus also anticipated Freud in some measure, recognizing that sexuality pervades the whole of human behavior. It would be a mistake, he maintained, to imagine that "the passion between the sexes" is influential only "when the immediate gratification of it is in contemplation." The whole pattern and plan of human life, he insists, are "connected in a considerable degree with the prospect of the gratification of this passion and with the support of children arising from it." [28]

Malthus envisaged a process of increasing population pressure on the land, not unlike what has in fact taken place in many underdeveloped countries today. Once all the fertile land is occupied, further increases in food production depend on agricultural improvement. But the natural tendency is for the fertility of the soil to decrease, not increase, whereas population, given an adequate food supply, would continue to expand indefinitely. Perhaps, he says, it would be possible to double the agricultural output of Great Britain in the next twenty-five years. It is impossible to imagine that in the next twenty-five years agricultural production could be quadrupled. Yet, a quadrupling of population is to be expected. As for the United Kingdom itself, some relief could be found through emigration. However, "taking the whole earth, instead of this island, emigration would of course be excluded; and, supposing the present population equaled to a thousand million, the human specie would increase as the numbers 1, 2, 4, 8, 16, 32, 64, 128, 256, and subsistence as 1, 2, 3, 4, 5, 6, 7, 8, 9." Here we have the "law" most frequently associated with Malthus: the geometric growth of population and the arithmetic growth of means of subsistence.

Malthus then proceeds to consider the various checks to population growth. The ultimate check, of course, is lack of food. The immediate check consists "in all those customs, and in all those diseases, which seem to be generated by a scarcity of the means of subsistence." These checks may be divided into the "preventive" and the "positive" checks. In so far as the preventive check is voluntary it is peculiar to mankind. Essentially, it consists of restraint; and "if this restraint do not produce vice, it is

[28] *Ibid.*, p. 61

undoubtedly the least evil that can arise from the principle of population."

The positive checks "include every cause, whether arising from vice or misery, which in any degree contributes to shorten the natural duration of human life." These include unwholesome occupations, severe labor and exposure to the seasons, and extreme poverty, bad nursing of children, great towns, and "the whole train of common diseases and epidemics, wars, plague, and famine."

Restraint from marriage, if it is not accompanied by "irregular gratifications," is "moral restraint." But "promiscuous intercourse, unnatural passions, violations of the marriage bed, and improper arts to conceal the consequences of irregular connections, are preventive checks that clearly come under the head of vice." [29]

The great bulk of the *Essay* consists of armchair anthropology, designed to provide factual support for his theory. His "law" regarding arithmetic growth of food supply and geometric growth of population is based on a kind of empirical observation from afar—the only kind of empirical research possible for a gentleman living in England in the early nineteenth century. However, he makes use of such literature as he could find to make observations on checks to population among such diverse societies as that of the American Indians, and those of the South Pacific islands, North and South Siberia, Hindustan and Tibet, China and Japan, the ancient Greeks and Romans, and contemporary Europe.

His poor opinion of colonial administration in Latin America becomes evident once again. No settlements, he says, could have been worse managed than those in Mexico, Peru, and Quito. The tyranny, superstition, and vices of the mother country were introduced, exorbitant taxes were exacted, arbitrary restrictions were imposed on trade, and the governors were corrupt. Nonetheless, he says, the population grew. The same is true of Brazil, governed "with almost equal tyranny" by the Portuguese. But in the United States, for which Malthus had much admiration, the rate of population growth was much greater.

When we add this theory of the population explosion to the two-sector model outlined above, the continuing poverty in underdeveloped countries is amply explained. For the population growth continues, in spite of everything, as long as the food supply permits a mere subsistence level of existence. As the industrial sector does not expand enough to absorb a large share in the increase in population, population pressure on the land continues to increase, and per capita productivity and income in the traditional rural sector fall.

[29] It is interesting to note that Malthus apparently believed that those who engaged in promiscuity would somehow avoid having children. It may be, however, that he had in mind nothing more sophisticated than abortion. He speaks later of the American Indians, stating that "the libertinage which generally prevails among the women before marriage, with the habit of procuring abortions, must necessarily render them more unfit for bearing children afterwards." As evidence he cites the practice among the Natchez of swapping wives unless they have children, indicating that many marriages are unfruitful.

4

The Marxist Model: Growth and Collapse

Karl Marx is one of those influential thinkers about whom much more has been written than he himself ever wrote. As the prophet of doom for capitalism and chief saint in the Communist hierarchy he is revered by hundreds of millions of people and reviled by other hundreds of millions. Because of the continuing importance of his ideas in shaping policies in Russia, China, and other Communist countries, and in determining the programs of Communist parties the world over, some knowledge of Marxist thought is essential if we wish to understand what is going on in the world.

Here, however, our purpose is quite different. We shall make no attempt to evaluate the Marxist system as a whole, but will do for that just what we have done for the Classical school: isolate the key propositions of its pure theory of economic development. Of course, Marx's theory of development was the core of his system, and because so few people can be detached about this system, our highly condensed presentation of his theory of development is unlikely to please. We cannot deal thoroughly with the Marxist literature. Yet no book on economic development with any pretensions to generality can ignore the Marxist theory. For, as Schumpeter says: [1]

Based upon a diagnosis of the social situation of the 1840's and 1850's that was ideologically vitiated at its roots, hopelessly wrong in its prophecy of ever-

---

[1]Joseph Schumpeter, *History of Economic Analysis*, p. 573. See also his *Capitalism, Socialism, and Democracy* (3d ed.; New York, 1950), p. 21, for a eulogy of Marx as "a very learned man."

increasing mass misery, inadequately substantiated both factually and analytically, Marx's performance is yet the most powerful of all. In his general schema of thought, development was not what it was with all the other economists of that period, an appendix to economic statics, but the central theme. And he concentrated his analytic powers on the task of showing how the economic progress, changing by itself by virtue of its own inherent logic, incessantly changes the social framework—the whole society in fact.

Marx never underestimated the capacity of the capitalist system for economic expansion. Indeed, in this respect he was perhaps more optimistic in his prognosis for capitalist development than Malthus or Mill. True, he expected capitalism to break down, but for sociological reasons, not because of stagnation, and only after a very high degree of development had been attained. To quote Schumpeter once more: [2]

. . . nobody—not even the most ardent of optimists with whom Marx had this point in common—had then a fuller conception of the size and power of the capitalist engine of the future. With a quaint touch of teleology Marx said repeatedly that it is the "historical task" or "privilege" of capitalist society to create a productive apparatus that will be adequate for the requirements of a higher form of human civilization.

We are interested, then, in the basic elements of the Marxist theory of capitalist development and breakdown. We shall proceed as in the previous chapter, by stating the basic propositions and translating them into a set of simultaneous equations. Some of the propositions and equations are the same as those of the Classical school, from which Marx derived them in the first place; these propositions need not be elaborated again. Also, we hope that by now even those readers who have little previous experience with the use of symbols will have acquired the basic idea, so that we need not delay quite so often to translate symbols back into words.

Proposition 1: The Production Function

The Marxist ideas about the production function were the same as those of the Classical school, so we can use the same basic equation:

$$O = f(L, K, Q, T) \qquad (1)$$

Marx laid a good deal more stress on technological progress as the "motor" of capitalist growth, and by the same token, assigned a more important role to the entrepreneur. He saw more clearly than his predecessors—and most of his contemporaries—that there is a two-way relationship between investment and technological progress. Certainly investment is needed to take advantage of technological progress, but technological progress also provides the opportunities for profitable investment.

A second difference is that we must now mean by L the labor force actually employed. Marx incorporated the analysis of unemployment into

[2] *Ibid.*, p. 573.

his system, and population and employment cannot be treated as varying together in the Marxist system.

Marx also had a clearer picture of the interactions between development overseas and development in Europe; he thought of England and her colonies, or France and hers, as two sectors of a single economy, administered from the metropolitan country in the interests of the capitalists of that country. Like the Classicists, he regarded the supply of land (natural resources) in Europe as essentially fixed, and he considered Europe to be in the stage of decreasing average returns to labor on the land. But he saw more distinctly than they that foreign trade and investment offered a means of escaping these diminishing returns. His followers built on this insight in developing the Marxist theory of "imperialism" and "colonial wars."[3]

Proposition 2: Technological Progress Depends on Investment

As we have already noted, in the Marxist system this proposition could be stated either way around; but in order to stress points of agreement, we shall write Equation (2) of the Marxist system in the same form as Equation (2) of the Classical system:

$$T = T(I) \qquad\qquad (2)$$

Proposition 3: Investment Depends on the Rate of Profits

Although the Marxist theory of investment resembled that of the Classical school, it was a bit more refined. The Classicists tended to think of profits as a category of income, accruing to capitalists, and providing funds for savings and investment. Marx thought of investment as depending, not merely on the size of capitalists' income, but on the rate of return on capital. Using R' to mean this rate of return,

$$I = I(R') \qquad\qquad (3)$$

Marx himself used the term "surplus value," but surplus value was really what we have previously called profits, or the difference between total national income and the wages bill. He thought of capital as being divided into two parts. The first part is "variable capital," or working capital, which really boils down to payrolls, and which we will accordingly denote by W.[4] The second part is "constant capital," the stock of capital goods including inventories, which we shall continue to denote by Q.

---

[3] *Ibid.*, p. 49.

[4] In translating the Marxist concepts into contemporary terms, we are following Joan Robinson, *Essay on Marxian Economics* (London, 1942). It is perhaps worth emphasizing in passing that the Marxist concept of surplus value was not the difference between (the wages bill) and (the marginal productivity of labor) times (number of units of labor employed). It was simply the difference between national product and the wages bill. Throughout most of his analysis, Marx assumed pure competition; prices were equal to marginal labor cost and workers were paid according to their marginal productivity.

**Proposition 4: The Rate of Profits Is the Ratio of Profits
to Payrolls Plus Capital Costs**

Instead of the fourth proposition of the Classical school, we can now substitute an identity or definition to which Marx attached great importance:

$$R' = \frac{O - W}{W + Q'} = \frac{R}{W + Q'} \tag{4}$$

Q' means capital goods and inventories currently used up in producing O. Here Q' can be regarded as having a fixed relation to both Q and O. Thus the rate of return, R', is really a rate of return on turnover; and it is profits in this sense that Marx considered to determine investment.

Now Marx had definite ideas about the historical relationships of these variables in a capitalist economy. Like the Classicists, he regarded technological progress as being labor saving and capital absorbing—as it seemed to be in nineteenth-century Europe. Consequently there was, according to Marx, a tendency for the ratio of "constant capital to variable capital" to rise; or as we would say now, a tendency for capital costs to rise relative to labor costs, or for capital per worker to rise. He seemed to regard the capital-output ratio, as well as the capital-labor ratio, as rising through time. The advantage in new techniques came only from saving labor. The great implications of these tendencies are apparent from a glance at Equation (4); unless they are accompanied by an increased spread between national product or income and the wages bill (increased "exploitation of the working class"), the increase in capital per worker must result in a fall in the rate of profit. By this process, rather than through diminishing returns to labor on the land, Marx explained the tendency of profits to fall.

Proposition 5: Wages Depend on the Level of Investment

The fifth equation takes the same form as in the Classical system, although now it has a somewhat different meaning. For in the Marxist system, the wages bill will depend on the level of employment as well as on the wage rate.

$$W = W(I) \tag{5}$$

Proposition 6: Employment Depends on the Level of Investment

Employment as well as wages depends on the level of investment. For Marx, however, innovation was essentially a labor-saving device (although he apparently did not think enough labor could be displaced by innovation to prevent the rate of profit from falling). Accordingly he put a good deal of emphasis on technological unemployment. An investment boom would tend to increase employment while it lasted, but each addition to the stock of capital would tend to swell the "reserve army" of technologically displaced workers. Employment rises only if investment goes up relative to the existing stock of capital. Thus we may write:

$$L = L(I/Q) \tag{6}$$

Proposition 7: Consumption Depends on the Wages Bill

We have seen that Malthus had already pointed out the danger that underconsumption might slow down economic growth; he had recognized that in a closed economy one productive sector constitutes the market for the other. Marx also stressed intersectoral relationships, but he conducted his analysis in terms of capital goods and consumers' goods sectors, rather than of industrial and agricultural sectors. These two kinds of sectoral breakdown are, of course, closely related but are not identical. Whereas Malthus emphasized capitalists' consumption and investment as providing the market for the industrial sector, Marx argued that investment cannot be profitable unless consumption increases enough to absorb the increased output of final products, and that however luxuriously capitalists may live, it is the workers who provide most of the market for consumers' goods. We may therefore write as our seventh equation,

$$C = C(W) \tag{7}$$

Proposition 8: Profits Depend on the Level of Technology and the Level of Consumer Spending

Equation (4) is really an identity, and does not express a functional (causal) relationship. What determines the level of profits—the spread between gross national product or income and the amount paid out in wages? As in the Classical system, the level of technique is a major factor; technological progress is tantamount to the introduction of labor-saving devices, and so permits a given output to be produced with less labor. With wages steady at the subsistence level, an increase in man-year productivity permits an increase in profits. Unfortunately for the capitalists, there is a "contradiction" here—according to Marx. For workers do most of the consuming, and reducing labor costs of production will not raise profits if it lowers worker spending; the output must be sold if profits are to be made. So the profits-determining equation in the Marxist system takes the form,

$$R = R(T, C) \tag{8}$$

It should be remembered, however, that Marx stressed the *rate* of profit (rate of return on capital) rather than the aggregate amount of profit as the factor determining capitalist behavior. It is the rate of profit, not the amount of profits, that must fall in the Marxist system. Thus what happens to R is important primarily for its effect on R' in Equation (4).

Closing the System. Three Identities

We shall have to exercise a bit more ingenuity to close the Marxist system than was necessary for the Classical one. We have, of course, the same identity as in the Classical model,

$$O = R + W \tag{9}$$

and since Marx makes more of the division of the economy into capital goods and consumers' goods sectors, we can add

$$O = C + I \qquad (10)$$

Finally, we can treat current capital costs as bearing a fixed relation to the stock of capital, which we shall denote by u to mean "user cost," the added cost of using capital to produce goods and services rather than just holding it. We shall assume that u is given. Then with Equation (11),

$$Q' = u \cdot Q \qquad (11)$$

we have eleven equations and eleven unknowns.

Summary

Let us now bring the system together:

$$
\begin{aligned}
O &= f(L, K, Q, T) & (1) \\
T &= T(I) & (2) \\
I &= I(R') & (3) \\
R' &= \frac{O - W}{W + Q'} = \frac{R}{W + Q'} & (4) \\
W &= W(I) & (5) \\
L &= L(I/Q) & (6) \\
C &= C(W) & (7) \\
R &= R(T, C) & (8)
\end{aligned}
$$

and the three identities:

$$
\begin{aligned}
O &= R + W & (9) \\
O &= C + I & (10) \\
Q' &= u \cdot Q & (11)
\end{aligned}
$$

If we put this system side by side with the Classical model, we see both similarities and differences. Equations (1), (2), and (5) are the same in both systems. Equation (6) looks the same, but in the Classical system the L refers to the total labor force, which is thought to vary directly with the total population, whereas in the Marxist system it means labor actually employed. The consumption function, Equation (7), is crucial to the Marxist system, but plays no important role in the Classical system, except for Malthus, who would have written it differently. In Equation (3) of the Marxist system, investment depends on the *rate* of profit rather than on the level of profits, thus bringing into the system the "drag" imposed on new investment by the stock of capital already accumulated. Equation (10) of the Marxist system is really implicit in the Classical system as well, but it plays no great role in the latter, because the division of the economy into capital goods and consumers' goods sectors is less important in the Classical analysis. As we shall see more clearly below, Equation (4) of the Marxist system contains the kernel of his theory of breakdown.

The difference in the form of the profits-determining equation is of particular interest. Both Marx and the Classicists recognized improvements in technique as the one factor that could stave off for any length of time the natural tendency for profits to fall; but where the Classicists regarded population pressure as the cause of diminishing returns, rising labor costs, and falling profits, Marx stressed the "contradiction" that maintaining profits requires reducing the wages bill relative to gross national product, whereas success in doing so reduces workers' purchasing power, so that part of the output goes unsold, reducing profits after all. Marx did not believe that the working class tended naturally to reproduce on such a scale as forever to bring wages back down to the subsistence level; he regarded this Malthusian doctrine as "a libel on the human race." Even today, orthodox Marxists deny that population pressure can occur in a communist country; until recently the Chinese government leaders, well-trained Marxists that they are, have been extremely reluctant to admit that China, with its 650 million people, was, or could become, overpopulated. In the Marxist view, mass poverty is to be explained only by capitalist exploitation. It cannot continue in a communist society, whatever the level and rate of growth of the population.

The System in Operation

It is clear that the Marxist system has all the circularities of the Classical one, and a few of its own besides. With the Marxist, as with the Classical system, we could break into the circular flow anywhere and deduce from our set of relationships how the system will operate. Since Marx had his own very strong views as to how the system must evolve historically, we may follow him a bit further.

As already noted, Marx considered technological change the prime mover of the whole system. The technology of each era in a country's development determines not only the economic situation, but also the "style" of the whole society. As Engels put it in his Preface to *The Communist Manifesto,*

In every historical epoch the prevailing mode of economic production and exchange, and the social organization necessarily following from it, form the basis upon which is built up, and from which alone can be explained, the political and intellectual history of that epoch.

For Marx, capitalism is merely one of a series of stages in the evolution of society toward the socialist state, which is the inevitable final form of economic, social, and political organization. Each stage of social evolution, with its characteristic technology and "style," breeds its particular kind of class struggle which leads to its breakdown and the emergence of the next, higher form of social organization. Thus feudalism arose out of primitive communism, but feudalism led to a struggle between serfs and feudal lords, out of which arose a class of emancipated serfs who became merchants and launched the first phase of capitalism. Capitalism brings a very high stage of technological advance. But capitalism leads eventually to a bitter class struggle between workers and capitalists, from which the workers will emerge victorious and establish the "dictatorship of the proletariat." This transitional phase will lead gradually to the full-fledged socialist (communist) society. Poverty will disappear. The state will "wither away," as a superfluous institution in a society without conflict. Each will contribute to national income according to his abilities and receive from it according to his needs.

In order to see how this prognosis for capitalism arises from the Marxist analytical framework, let us break into the system at Equation (4), which is the crucial one for the Marxist theory. It will help us to see the full significance of this equation, if we break up the wages bill into employment, L, and the wage rate, w, and if we break up total output into employment and output per man, o. We then have, substituting in Equation (4),

$$R' = \frac{L \cdot o - L \cdot w}{W + Q'} \qquad \text{or} \qquad R' = \frac{L(o - w)}{W + Q'} \qquad (4a)$$

Now we can see the pincers in which the capitalists are caught. In order to survive the competitive race, they must be continually introducing improved techniques, which means accumulating capital, using more capital-intensive and less labor-intensive techniques. But the result is that Q, and so Q', increases relative to output. Under the circumstances, the only way to maintain R' is to increase the spread between o and w.

This end may be achieved in several ways. First, the wage rate can be cut to the subsistence level $\overline{w}$ and kept there—it cannot go lower. Second, more labor-saving devices can be introduced, raising o, while wages are held at or near $\overline{w}$. The trouble with this device, of course, is that (according to Marx) it can only be done by further increases in Q and Q'. Technological progress is a treadmill for capitalists—they must run ever faster just to stand still, for technological progress must always keep one step ahead of the rate of capital accumulation. However, labor-saving innovations help in another way; they displace workers, adding to the "industrial reserve army" of unemployed. Chronic technological unemployment weakens the bargaining power of workers, who are always competing for jobs against their unemployed brethren, thus making it easier for the capitalists to keep wages down to the subsistence level. Third, through the "stretch-out," hours can be increased and work speeded up without raising wages, thus again raising o without increasing w. Fourth, monopoly positions can be strengthened, to raise prices without raising wages.

All these devices for maintaining profits prove self-defeating. In the short run, they give rise to economic fluctuations. In the long run, they lead to revolution and the disappearance of the capitalist system.

The Theory of Economic Fluctuations

The Marxian theory of business cycles is scattered throughout his writings, and it takes a somewhat charitable interpretation of his *obiter dicta* on this subject to make them into a tight and systematic theory. Nevertheless, to Marx must go the credit for an early attempt at an explanation of the recurring cycles of prosperity and depression that mark the development of capitalist societies. Moreover, he anticipated some basic ideas of contemporary theories of fluctuations.

Marx really had three different business cycle theories. The simplest stressed the disproportionalities in rates of expansion of different industries in an "unplanned" economy, where investment decisions are made by hosts of independent entrepreneurs. In the course of a boom, some industries turn out to be overextended because the output of complementary goods has not kept pace with them. Put in such terms, this theory of Marx is very similar to the later theory of Spiethoff. But if we lay primary emphasis on unbalanced expansion of the capital goods sector on the one hand and the consumers' goods sector on the other, as Marx seemed to do at points, we approach some of the more modern theories that are built around the savings-investment relationship, such as the "over-investment theory" of Professor F. A. von Hayek.

The second theory is closer to Keynes or Kalecki than to Hayek and explains the collapse of the boom in terms of the "shift to profits" and consequent underconsumption. The boom starts with innovation, which brings a temporary increase in profits which Marx called "superprofits" to indicate their transitory character and to distinguish them from true "surplus value," which is a more enduring spread between wages and output. The appearance of these superprofits, however, encourages an increase in investment. But this very gain of the capitalists at the expense of the workers proves the undoing of the boom; for capitalists tend to save a large proportion of increases in their incomes, in contrast to workers who spend any increase in income on consumption and who, by the same token, must reduce their consumption to the extent of any drop in their incomes. Monopolization fails for the same reason; capitalists tend to "price themselves out of the market." Thus investment in the boom fails to generate the purchasing power needed to absorb the increase in output of final products. Goods go unsold and profits drop again. Investment falls and depression ensues.

The third theory is less clearly stated than the other two, and at first blush, seems inconsistent with the second theory. For in this variant, the crisis emerges because the investment undertaken in the boom temporarily creates full employment and brings a temporary increase in wages. In such an inflationary boom, the innovations are not enough to maintain an increased spread between o and w; and since capital is being accumulated, the rate of profit must fall, leading to reduced investment and depression. In this model the shift to profits does not occur, and there is no clear reason why consumer spending should not be high enough to clear the market.

The apparent inconsistency between the second and third theories persists in the literature of today; underconsumption, the squeeze on profits through wage increases, and the drag on new investment through the increase in the stock of capital, all have their place in contemporary theories. One way of reconciling these two views is to say that either sequence may occur. "Weak booms" end, before full employment is reached and significant wage increases appear, through the shift to profits and underconsumption. "Strong booms" may survive the initial under-consumption and create inflationary conditions in which wage increases occur; these booms expire because of the squeeze on profits and the accumulation of capital.

Thus in the Marxist system economic fluctuations consist mainly of occasional booms, launched by investment undertaken to introduce new labor-saving techniques, which temporarily carry the economy above the trend line. But sooner or later, and usually sooner, the economy sinks back to its long-run trend, with its inevitable tendency for the rate of profits to fall. This trend toward a growing gap between potential and actual output shows up as deeper and deeper depressions, shorter and weaker booms.

Now everything the capitalists do to maintain profits in the face of this trend increases "the misery of the working class." The increasing tendency toward monopoly has another effect that helps to pave the way for revolution; it leads to the disappearance of the middle class. In the late stages of "high capitalism," capitalists become desperate indeed. Encountering increasing resistance at home, they turn to colonies for more ready exploitation of labor. Colonies also provide sources of cheap raw materials, new outlets for investment, and new markets in which monopoly positions can be established for the sale of final products. So valuable are these colonies in staving off the collapse of capitalism that the advanced capitalist countries fight imperialist wars for their possession.

All in vain. At best, these desperate measures of desperate men can bring only temporary respite. The rate of profits continues to decline, and capitalists cannot resist turning the screws on workers a bit more in the effort to save their way of life. Eventually the workers can stand it no longer; by sheer strength of numbers, they overthrow the system through revolution.

Conclusions: An Appraisal

As indicated above, any appraisal of Marx is likely to displease more people than it pleases; it will have too little vilification for some and too little veneration for others. But let us try, nonetheless, remembering that we are reviewing the earlier literature for the light it may throw on the development problems of today.

Obviously, Marx was a bad prophet. He was right, of course, in predicting the spread of communism, but both the establishment of communist societies and their subsequent evolution have taken forms very different from those envisaged by Marx. In particular, the countries that have gone Communist have not been those in which capitalist development has been most advanced but those in which it has lagged. For in the advanced capitalist countries workers have become increasingly prosperous rather than more miserable, and the middle class, far from disappearing, has grown until it dominates society. And in the Communist countries, poverty has been slow in disappearing and there are no signs of the state's "withering away."

We cannot attempt here to explain all the reasons for Marx's failure as a prophet; we are concerned only with his analytical framework as a means of explaining economic growth. One obvious mistake was in not foreseeing the rise of powerful trade unions; but it may be questioned whether trade unions would have become so strong if the competitive position of unorganized labor had not become increasingly favorable in the first place. Let us note only two fundamental analytical errors. First, Marx did not see that innovations can be capital saving as well as labor saving. If capital-output ratios fall through improved techniques, as they frequently do, the rate of profit can rise even though wages rise too. Second, Marx was trapped by the labor theory of value which he took over from the Classical school. By measuring everything in terms of man-hours, he attached a quite wrong significance to a fall in the rate of profits in terms of man-hours. He did not see that a rise in man-hour productivity and in real wage rates can be accompanied by a rise in money profits (and real profits), even though profits in terms of man-hours may fall as man-hours become more valuable. And what really counts for capitalists is their actual income, not the number of man-hours' worth of labor a given amount of profit will buy. In other words, Marx did not foresee a process of economic development in which technological progress brings such increases in productivity and total output that both wages and profits can rise together.

On the other hand, Marx introduced certain ideas into the theory of economic development that have been there ever since. Virtually every writer on the subject since Marx has incorporated into his system the basic idea that technological progress is the mainspring of economic growth, and that innovation is the main function of the entrepreneur. By the same token investment decisions and capital accumulation are the core of most modern theories of growth, and in all theories these decisions are related somehow to the rate of return on capital. Another fundamental idea is that economic development under capitalism tends to take the form of fluctuations; economic growth is a destabilizing phenomenon. In particular, as Marx showed, stable growth requires maintenance of the proper balance between investment and consumption, and thus between savings and investment. Marx also pointed to the relationship between the savings-investment relationship on the one hand and the distribution of income on the other, a relationship that has remained a fundamental feature of growth theories ever since. He indicated the slenderness of the tightrope which an economy must walk for steady growth—wages either too high or too low relative to output can choke off investment and cause depression. This "damned if you do and damned if you don't" character of the boom has also remained a recognized feature of any complete analysis of cycles and trends. Marx also made employment and unemployment a major variable in the system.

These are sizable bricks for the construction of a theory of growth, even if Marx's own structure collapsed because some of its pillars were faulty. So far as the problem of steady growth in advanced capitalist countries is concerned, Marx's main contribution, apart from these bricks, was in putting capitalism in its historical setting, which helps a good deal in evaluating its past and its future.

So far as its pure economics is concerned, Marx's system is less directly applicable to problems of underdeveloped countries than that of Malthus. Marx did not really think of underdevelopment as an enduring state; underdeveloped countries were simply precapitalist ones, which, unfortunately, would have to go through the capitalist phase before they could attain the Elysian Fields of communism. His exclusion of the possibility of population pressure is a severe handicap in trying to apply his system to most underdeveloped countries. Perhaps just because he did not believe population pressure possible he also missed the fundamental feature of "dualism"; he did not see that technological progress might be confined to one sector of an economy while leaving the rest of the economy virtually untouched.

The Marxist sociological and political theory, however, provides some clues to the economic history of underdeveloped countries. It suggests to us that we look at power relations among social classes and see whether these relations are of a sort that imposes barriers to spontaneous growth. It suggests that we should look for an explanation of colonial policies in the economic conditions of the home countries, rather than economic conditions in the colonies themselves. It suggests, too, that part of the explanation of underdevelopment in the former colonies might be traced to these policies. As we shall see in more detail below—for reasons not fully explained by Marx himself—in some underdeveloped countries conditions occurred rather like those Marx predicted for advanced ones: labor was indeed exploited; wages were indeed kept close to subsistence levels; a "reserve army" of chronic unemployment did in fact exist; the class structure was sharply defined and a middle class virtually non-existent; in some cases there is even evidence of "increasing misery." That such conditions could result in revolution of one sort or another few people would deny.

We must be wary of the pitfalls in the Marxist system, but for all its errors, the Marxist theory of economic development has much to contribute to an understanding of development or the lack of it.

5 Unstable Growth: Schumpeter

With the work of Joseph Schumpeter we move into the twentieth century. The basic ideas of his theory of economic growth were presented in his *Theory of Economic Development*, first published in German in 1911. He continued to elaborate his analysis of capitalist development throughout his brilliant career.[1] The most complete statement of it, however, was contained in his *Business Cycles,* published in 1939. It is on this version that we shall draw most heavily in presenting the skeleton of his system.

Apart from his genius and prodigious capacity for work, Schumpeter had a breadth of experience which was unusual for economists of his generation, and which gives particular interest to his pronouncements on the factors involved in economic development. Here is a man who in the course of his career was Finance Minister of a Socialist government in Austria, professor of economics in Bonn and Tokyo, and from 1927 until his untimely death in 1950, professor of economics at Harvard University. Thus Schumpeter studied the economic scene closely over a period of four decades, during which he lived in four countries and three continents.

---

[1] Richard V. Clemence and Francis S. Doody, *The Schumpeterian System* (Cambridge, Mass., 1950), p. 1. "The Schumpeterian System occupies a remarkable place in the history of economic thought. Almost from the beginning of his work on the theories of interest and of business cycles Professor Schumpeter saw a vision of a distinctly capitalist process taking place in historic time. His youthful vision, first reduced to a comprehensive model in 1911, has since been elaborated and refined, but it has been altered in no essential respect to the present day. Such extraordinary consistency is almost unique in our science, and it is by no means a proof of virtue. What it rather suggests is that tests be made of the hypothesis that the model withstands critical attack. That is what we propose to do in this book."

Few economists of his generation had so wholehearted an admiration for the capitalist system as Schumpeter. He was not one of those who believed that the capitalist machine produces high rates of economic growth which offset the attendant social evils; Schumpeter heartily enjoyed and endorsed the society and civilization produced by "pure" capitalism as well. He preferred the relatively uninhibited and undemocratic capitalism, accompanied by a high level of cultural attainment, which prevailed in Europe before World War I, to the modified capitalism that has developed since. Even the semifeudal capitalism of prewar Japan struck a responsive chord in Schumpeter.

What his real political position was few people really knew. A few years before his death, in a speech to an organization of French Canadian employers in Montreal, he said bluntly that the way to stem the tide of socialism was to organize the corporative state under the guidance of the Roman Catholic Church.[2] It would be quite wrong to conclude from these random remarks that he had fascist leanings. At the same time, no one can doubt that he considered the existence of a sharply defined class structure a small price to pay for the continued economic and social progress which he believed unbridled capitalism brings.

We are not concerned here with the personal or political views of this

[2] "L'Avenir du Capitalisme," in *Comment Sauvegarder l'Entreprise Privée* (Montreal, 1946).

In his address to the American Economic Association in 1949, Schumpeter made the following statement: "Familiar facts of our own trade-union practice suggest that a development toward some form of guild socialism is not entirely off the cards. And other familiar facts suggest that observable tendencies or some of them may be compatible with forms of social reorganization that are not socialist at all, at least not in the sense which has been adopted for this paper. For instance, a reorganization of society on the lines of the encyclical *Quadragesimo anno*, though presumably possible only in Catholic societies or in societies where the position of the Catholic Church is sufficiently strong, no doubt provides an alternative to socialism that would avoid the "omnipotent State."

In the same address he said: "It would spell complete misunderstanding of my argument if you thought that I 'disapprove' or wish to criticize any of these [New Deal] policies. Nor am I one of those who label all or some of them 'socialist.' Some have been espoused, even in the eighteenth century, by conservative or even autocratic rulers; others have been on the programs of conservative parties and have been carried by them long before New Deal days. All I wish to emphasize is the fact that we have traveled far indeed from the principles of laissez-faire capitalism and the further fact that it is possible so to develop and regulate capitalistic institutions as to condition the working of private enterprise in a manner that differs but little from genuinely socialist planning. . . . Having discovered this possibility of a *laborist capitalism* they go on to conclude that *this* capitalism may survive indefinitely, at least under certain favorable conditions. This may be so but it does not amount to a denial of my thesis. Capitalism does not merely mean that the housewife may influence production by her choice between peas and beans; nor that the youngster may choose whether he wants to work in a factory or on a farm; nor that plant managers have some voice in deciding what and how to produce it. It means a scheme of values, an attitude toward life, a civilization—the civilization of inequality and of the family fortune. This civilization is rapidly passing away, however. Let us rejoice or else lament the fact as much as everyone of us likes; but do not let us shut our eyes to it." Joseph Schumpeter, "The March into Socialism," *American Economic Review Papers and Proceedings*, XL (1950), pp. 447, 449–50.

brilliant, vigorous, charming, fascinating, and enigmatic personality. As with the economists already discussed, we are concerned only with his analytical framework and its usefulness for attacking the growth problems of underdeveloped and advanced countries today. These comments on Schumpeter's tastes and views are made for but one reason: Schumpeter's intellectual debt to Marx was greater than his debt to any other figure in the history of economic thought, and it is important to understand that a man may levy upon the Marxist system and still hate communism. Schumpeter's dislike of collectivism extended to a profound distaste even for capitalism in harness or the welfare state.

Much as he admired the capitalist system, however, Schumpeter shared the gloomy prognosis of the Classical school and of Marx. He believed that capitalism will eventually stagnate and break down. This prospect was for him saddening indeed, especially since, in his view, the breakdown would come only from the lack of appreciation of what capitalism can do and the conditions which it needs in order to prosper. According to Schumpeter, not the failures of capitalism, but its very success, would lead eventually to the slaughter of the goose that lays the golden eggs. But we anticipate; let us review his system in the same manner as we have reviewed the Classical and Marxist systems, and see how he reaches this pessimistic conclusion.[3]

Proposition 1: The Production Function

Schumpeter had the same general concept of the production function as did Marx and the Classical school. We can therefore use the same Equation (1) once again:

$$O = f(L, K, Q, T) \tag{1}$$

Proposition 2: Savings Depend on Wages, Profits and the Interest Rate

Schumpeter defines saving as "saving up" for future consumption or for investment. With this definition, workers as well as capitalists are able to save, and both will save more as their incomes rise. However, Schumpeter retained in his system the neo-classical proposition that savings tend to increase with the interest rate. The *proportion* of a given wage or profit income that will be saved will increase as the interest rate goes up. Thus we may write for our second equation

$$S = S(W, R, r) \tag{2}$$

[3] Although Schumpeter's prognosis was certainly pessimistic for someone admiring capitalism and disliking socialism as much as Schumpeter did, he vehemently denied that his attitude was "defeatist." "The report that a given ship is sinking is not defeatist," he insisted. "Only the spirit in which this report is received can be defeatist: the crew can sit down and drink. But it can also rush to the pumps. . . . What normal man will refuse to defend his life merely because he is quite convinced that sooner or later he will have to die anyway." *Capitalism, Socialism, and Democracy* (3d ed.; New York, 1950), p. xi. Similarly, he wrote, "If a doctor predicts that his patient will die presently, this does not mean that he desires it. One may hate socialism or at least look upon it with cool criticism and yet foresee its advent. Many conservatives did and do" (*ibid.*, p. 61).

Proposition 3: Total Investment May Be Subdivided into Induced Investment and Autonomous Investment

One of Schumpeter's important contributions was a distinction between two kinds of investment: investment which is stimulated by recent increases in output, income, sales, or profits which we shall call "induced investment," I_i; and investment which is brought forth by such long-run considerations as technological change, which we shall call "autonomous investment," I_A. So far as our third equation is concerned, then, we have an identity,

$$I = I_i + I_A \tag{3}$$

Proposition 4: Induced Investment Depends on the Level of Profits and the Interest Rate

The factors determining induced investment might be expressed in various ways, but Schumpeter laid particular stress on the relationship between profits, R, and the interest rate, r. In this respect, too, he followed the neoclassical tradition. Induced investment tends to rise as current profits rise and to fall as the interest rate goes up; the gap between profits and the interest rate is of primary importance in determining induced investment. However, the more capital has already been accumulated, the bigger must be the excess of profits over interest to induce more investment. We may therefore write

$$I_i = I(R, r, Q) \tag{4}$$

$$\frac{\delta I_i}{\delta R} > 0 \qquad \frac{\delta I_i}{\delta r} < 0 \qquad \frac{\delta I_i}{\delta Q} < 0$$

Proposition 5: Autonomous Investment Depends on Resource Discovery and Technological Progress

In his insistence that the most important part of private investment is determined by long-run factors, not directly related to recent changes in income, output, sales, and profits, Schumpeter made his major contribution to the theory of investment. He laid particular stress on what he called "innovation" as the mainspring of autonomous investment. What he meant by "innovation," however, might be regarded either as technological progress or resource discovery (or both), defining these terms broadly. He thought of innovation in general as any change in the production function which would bring an increase in output. "Any doing things differently," he said, which increases the productivity of the bundle of factors of production available (including resources given in the economy but not yet discovered) is an innovation. He listed five major forms of innovation:[4]

Development in our sense is then defined by the carrying out of new combinations.

This concept covers the following five cases: (1) the introduction of a new good—that is, one with which consumers are not yet familiar—or of a new

[4] Schumpeter, *The Theory of Economic Development*, p. 66.

quality of a good. (2) The introduction of a new method of production, that is, one not yet tested by experience in the branch of manufacture concerned, which need by no means be founded upon a discovery scientifically new, and can also exist in a new way of handling a commodity commercially. (3) The opening of a new market, that is, a market into which the particular branch of manufacture of the country in question has not previously entered, whether or not this market has existed before. (4) The conquest of a new source of supply of raw materials, or half-manufactured goods, again irrespective of whether this source already exists or whether it has first to be created. (5) The carrying out of the new organization of any industry, like the creation of a monopoly position (for example through trustification) or the breaking up of a monopoly position.

We shall use the term K to mean the rate of resource discovery through time, dK/dt, and T to mean the rate of technological progress through time, dT/dt. We then have the following relationship:[5]

$$I_A = I_a(K, T) \qquad (5)$$

Readers already familiar with the Keynes-Hansen theory of development, in which population growth plays a prominent role as a stimulant to autonomous investment, may wonder why population growth is not included in Equation (5) of our model of the Schumpeter system. It seems more faithful to Schumpeter's own views on the subject to omit population growth. Schumpeter did not deny that population growth, under some circumstances, may bring forth long-run investment, or that a tapering-off of population growth might result in a drop in investment if not offset by other factors.[6] But he clearly did not attach much weight to population growth as an economic force; he chose to regard it as an "external factor" rather than as an integral part of his system.[7] He readily

---

[5] Autonomous investment, as well as induced investment, may be retarded by capital accumulation, although the relationship is presumably somewhat less powerful. Also, even autonomous investment may depend somewhat on the level of output. Thus we could write, instead of Equation (5),

$$I_A = \lambda(O) + \phi(K, T) - \psi(Q)$$

But since in the long run O and Q move closely together and have opposite effects on investment, we can safely drop the first and third terms.

[6] See especially his *Business Cycles*, pp. 1035–1036.

[7] Two quotations will serve to illustrate his attitude toward the population growth factor: "Changes in numbers and age distributions due to other causes than migration sometimes are in fact external factors or consequences of external factors, such as wars. Sometimes they are not, as we may see from the cyclical component in marriage rates. But as it is impossible to accept a minimum-of-existence theory of wages—which it would be necessary to do in order to make the relation between the rate of change of population and economic situations stringent—and as nativity and mortality display substantive independence of economic fluctuations—however much their historic changes have to do with the ulterior cultural effects of the working of the capitalist machine—it has seemed best to class them with external factors. . . .

"Our reason for listing variations in population among external factors was that there is no unique relation between them and variations in the flow of commodities. Hence, it seemed convenient for our purpose, although it would be inadequate for others, to look upon an increase in population as an environmental change condition in certain phenomena. Moreover, it could be demonstrated by familiar cases (India and China) that mere increase in population does not *bring about* any of those phe-

admitted that population growth, like saving, can lead to *growth* of the economy, but he made a distinction between growth and development. True *development* requires qualitative change:[8]

> By "development," therefore, we shall understand only such changes in economic life as are not forced upon it from without but arise by its own initiative from within. . . . Nor will the mere growth of the economy, as shown by the growth of population and wealth, be designated here as a process of development. For it calls forth no qualitatively new phenomena, but only processes of adaptation of the same kind as the changes in the natural data. Since we wish to direct our attention to other phenomena, we shall regard such increases as changes in data.

Propositions 6 and 7: Technological Progress and the Rate of Resource Discovery (Innovations) Depend on the Supply of Entrepreneurs

The stress on the leading role of the entrepreneur in economic development under capitalism is the main feature of the Schumpeter system. As we saw in the previous chapter, Marx also considered the entrepreneurial function important, but he did not isolate it for special emphasis in the same degree as Schumpeter did.

The entrepreneur is the man who sees the opportunity for introducing a new technique or a new commodity, an improved organization, or for the development of newly discovered resources. He raises the money to launch a new enterprise, assembles the factors of production, chooses top managers, and sets the organization going. He need not be a "capitalist"— he may not provide any funds of his own. He may not be a day-to-day manager. Nor is he usually an inventor or explorer. Inventions or discoveries by themselves have little economic effect, Schumpeter argues. He instances the Montgolfier balloon, which caused considerable wonderment when invented, but had little effect on economic life. The Patent Registry is filled with files of patent applications for inventions that never see the light of day. For inventions or resource discoveries to be significant, someone with the special talent for seeing their economic potential and bringing them into use must come along. That man is the entrepreneur.

We may therefore write, using E to mean the rate of increase in the

---

nomena which presuppose either a certain density or a certain rate of increase in population except a fall in real income per head. Finally, it occurs so continuously as to be capable of current absorption. Short-time variations in marriage rates are obviously the reflex of business fluctuations and do not cause them." (*Business Cycles*, pp. 10, 74.)

[8] Schumpeter, *The Theory of Economic Development*, p. 63.

Clemence and Doody paraphrase Schumpeter on this point as follows: "Growth is defined as changes in population, and in total savings and accumulations of households and firms respectively, corrected for variations in the purchasing power of the monetary unit. Growth has so far been excluded from the system on the ground that changes in population and in saving can be currently absorbed without giving rise to cyclical fluctuations. Cycles can be understood without Growth, but not vice versa, and the quantitative importance of Growth, especially of saving, is due to the process of capitalist development. Such saving, of course, may be used to finance innovation, although not without effects on economic contours, such as those of price levels" (*op. cit.*, p. 15).

supply of entrepreneurs, dE/dt, *and* $K(dk/dt)$ for the rate of resource discovery,

$$T = T(E) \text{ and } K = K(E) \qquad (6 \text{ and } 7)$$

Admittedly, the supply of entrepreneurship is not an easy thing to measure; but in Schumpeter's system the supply of entrepreneurship is the ultimate determining factor of the rate of economic growth, so we must give it a place of honor in our system of equations.

Proposition 8: The Supply of Entrepreneurs Depends on the Rate of Profits and the Social Climate

Like Marx, Schumpeter lays considerable stress on sociological factors, and some of these are not easily reduced to simple mathematical expressions. This stricture applies to Schumpeter's concept of the "social climate," a complex phenomenon reflecting the whole social, political, and socio-psychological atmosphere within which entrepreneurs must operate. It would include the social values of a particular country at a particular time, the class structure, the educational system, and the like. It would certainly include the attitude of society toward business success, and the nature and extent of the prestige and other social rewards, apart from profits, which accompany business success in the society. A particularly important factor in "climate" is the entrepreneur's understanding of the "rules of the game," the conditions under which he must operate. Sudden changes in the rules of the game are particularly deleterious to an increasing flow of enterprise.

With apologies for its inadequacy, we shall use the symbol χ to stand for the whole matter of "climate." We then have, as the determinant of a society's entrepreneurial resources,

$$E = E(R,\chi) \qquad (8)$$

Proposition 9: Gross National Product Depends on the Relationship between Savings and Investment and the Supermultiplier

These words are probably not those which Schumpeter would have chosen to state this proposition; but they express the fundamental relationship which was recognized by Schumpeter, as well as by Marx before him and by most of Schumpeter's contemporaries and juniors. An excess of investment over voluntary savings, financed by credit creation, will raise gross national product (in money terms) by an amount which will be some multiple of the original gap between investment and saving. Conversely, an excess of voluntary savings over investment will reduce gross national product, in value terms, by some multiple of the original gap. We can therefore write[9]

$$\triangle O = k(I - S) \qquad (9)$$

[9] It is useful to differentiate this particular equation with respect to time. We can then write

$$\frac{dO}{dt} = K \left(\frac{dI}{dt} - \frac{dS}{dt} \right)$$

That is, the rate of change in gross national product through time will be some multiple of the gap between the rate of growth in investment and the rate of growth to time in voluntary savings.

Proposition 10: The Wages Bill Depends on the Level of Investment

Schumpeter carried over into his system the proposition, common both to the Classical school and to Marx, that wage incomes tend to increase with investment, and vice versa. We may therefore write once more,

$$W = W(I) \tag{10}$$

Proposition 11: The "Social Climate" Is Reflected by the Distribution of Income

In order to close the system, we have to stretch a bit. We have already noted that Schumpeter's concept of "climate" is a very complex and subtle affair. However, it is clear from some of his later writings that he considered income distribution to be a good "thermometer" of the general climate. Any development tending to squeeze profits, such as growing strength of trade unions, progressive income taxes, social welfare programs, or any other government intervention designed to limit profits or to redistribute income, is tantamount to deterioration of the climate. Thus Schumpeter explained the depth and duration of the Great Depression of the 1930's in terms of the labor legislation, social security, public works spending, progressive tax structure, public utilities regulation, and other "New Deal" policies introduced in the middle and late 1930's. These constituted a change in the "rules of the game" so drastic as to discourage enterprise and thus retard investment. All these forms of government intervention have a direct short-run impact on the relationship between wages and profits (after taxes). The ratio of profits to wages is a mere shorthand expression for all the factors influencing "climate," but it is a convenient shorthand, so we will write

$$\chi = \chi(R/W) \tag{11}$$

Proposition 12: An Identity: Gross National Product Equals Profits Plus Wages

To close the system we can resort once more to the now familiar identity and write

$$O = R + W \tag{12}$$

We now have twelve equations and twelve unknowns and can turn to an analysis of the operation of this system as Schumpeter viewed it.

Scope of the System

The Schumpeter analysis may be regarded as wide or narrow in scope, depending on what one expects from a theory of economic development. Schumpeter himself had this to say of his theory:[10]

Economic development is so far simply the object of economic history, which in turn is merely a part of universal history, only separated from the rest for purposes of exposition. Because of this fundamental dependence of the economic aspect of things on everything else, it is not possible to explain *economic* change by previous *economic* conditions alone. For the economic state

[10] Schumpeter, *The Theory of Economic Development*, p. 58.

of a people does not emerge simply from the preceding economic conditions, but only from the preceding total situation.

This statement certainly makes Schumpeter's aim sound ambitious enough. On the other hand, as Clemence and Doody point out in their appraisal:[11]

In comparison with the systems of such scholars as Toynbee and Spengler, the Schumpeterian System has very modest dimensions. No effort is made to achieve a synthesis of world history or even of the history of Western civilization. On the contrary, the whole analysis is concerned with the economic aspects of capitalist society, and most of the resources of modern economics are brought to bear on the comparatively narrow problem of the economic process of the capitalist era. Not only economics, but other social sciences as well are drawn upon heavily in the attempt to develop a model of this process. The important question, however, is not what resources are utilized but what results are achieved, and the present study is part of an effort to find out.

In general, the scope of Schumpeter's system is about as broad as that of the Classical school, and a bit less broad than that of Marx. Schumpeter does not try to provide a systematic explanation of changes in non-economic data; but in explaining changes in economic data he draws on a wide range of sociological, psychological, political, and technological factors.

Operation of the System

Schumpeter starts his analysis with an economy in stationary equilibrium, characterized by a "circular flow" which forever repeats itself. This stationary equilibrium is described by Clemence and Doody as follows:[12]

The Pure Model has as its basis an economic system in general equilibrium. All economic activity in the model is essentially repetitive, following the course of familiar routine, and the model may thus be regarded as a circular flow of economic life. Every firm in the system is in perfect competitive equilibrium, with its costs, consisting of wages and rents, exactly equal to its receipts. Prices everywhere are equated to average costs; profits are zero; profit opportunities are nonexistent; interest rates are zero; and there is no involuntary unemployment of resources. Every household, like every firm, is in full long-run equilibrium, with receipts equal to expenditures, and with a budgetary pattern that cannot, under the existing circumstances, be advantageously altered.

The essence of development is a *discontinuous* disturbance of this circular flow:[13]

Development in our sense is a distinct phenomenon, entirely foreign to what may be observed in the circular flow or in the tendency towards equilibrium. It is spontaneous and discontinuous change in the channels of the flow, disturbance of equilibrium, which forever alters and displaces the equilibrium state previously existing. Our theory of development is nothing but a treatment of this phenomenon and the processes incident to it.

[11] Clemence and Doody, *op. cit.*, p. 2.
[12] *Ibid.*, p. 9.
[13] Schumpeter, *Theory of Economic Development*, p. 64.

The discontinuous disturbance comes in the form of an innovation. The innovation entails the construction of new plant and equipment. It may do so in any of three different ways. First, it may hasten the replacement of existing plant and equipment by rendering it obsolete. Second, it may create an expectation of high monopoly profits for the first firm in the new field and thus raise the "marginal efficiency" (expected yield, after allowance for risk) of capital in general, leading to an increase in total net investment. Third, it may produce a new product that seems so attractive that people are willing to cut into their savings to have it, thus raising the propensity to consume and making additional plant and equipment profitable and necessary. Schumpeter himself stresses the second of these types of expansionary process. He also argues "as if" the construction of new plant and equipment was undertaken by New Firms, and points out that historically there is no lack of realism in such an argument; most of the major innovations—such as the railways and steamships of the nineteenth century, and the automobiles, chemicals, and electric power of the twentieth—have in fact been developed mainly by new firms.

Schumpeter also argues that the development of the new firms is usually associated with the rise to business leadership of New Men, and here too he points to history to substantiate his argument. This part of Schumpeter's theory is very important, if it is true, for it means that unless business leadership is forthcoming to build up new firms for the exploitation of innovations, capitalist economies may suffer more or less chronic depression. As we have seen, enterprise of the sort basic to economic expansion, according to Schumpeter, is something different from the genius of the inventor, or the efficiency of the executive of a going concern, or the willingness to risk one's own capital in new enterprises. It consists mainly of seeing and seizing the opportunity for development of a New Firm; historically, it has been this kind of special skill that has been most handsomely rewarded in capitalist economies.

Once the innovator has demonstrated the profitability of his venture, followers will enter the field in "clusters." The original innovator will of course try to maintain his monopoly position. In the past, he has seldom had complete success in this regard. Today, when a growing proportion of inventions comes from the research departments of existing firms, it is easier for monopolies to protect their positions, and to prevent any "cluster" of would-be followers from entering a new field of production. By the same token, the expansionary force of an innovation is diminished.

The development of the new industry is followed by the adaptation of old industries to the changed pattern of demand. The development of railroads entailed the construction of new towns, relocation of old industries, expansion of the iron and steel industry, and so forth. The development of the automobile industry brought with it the move to the suburbs, the construction of highways, the development of new recreation centers, enormous expansion of the petroleum and rubber industries, and so on. A "big" innovation like railroads or automobiles can generate a huge wave of new investment, through its direct and indirect effects on the economy.

Schumpeter, like most other analysts of economic fluctuations, assumes that the wave of new investment is financed largely by new credit created by the banks. In other words, the investment is assumed to be financed by monetary expansion rather than by an increase in current (*ex ante*) savings, so that new investment produces a spread between investment and *ex ante* savings and generates an upswing. This assumption is, of course, perfectly realistic.

When the "gestation" period is over, and the new plants are completed, the rate of investment drops to the level necessary for replacement only; net investment ceases. Obviously, the operation of a railway involves less current investment than its construction. Moreover, once the new plants are in operation there will be a new and increased flow of consumers' goods onto the market; this factor in itself would tend to reduce prices. The tendency for prices to fall is enhanced by contraction of the money supply; as the new firms begin to sell their product, they come into possession of a "stream of receipts," which enables them to reduce their indebtedness to the banks. Reducing debt means simply the cancellation of deposits, and consequently the money supply contracts. With increasing supplies of goods on the market and a decreasing supply of money to buy them, prices naturally tend to fall. Some firms make windfall losses as a result of this unforeseen drop in prices. Commercial failures increase. Aggregate profits decline. Expectations become gloomy, and the impulse for innovation itself dries up. Depression ensues.

It will be noted that the validity of Schumpeter's theory as an explanation of economic fluctuations depends on the "swarming" of innovations in "clusters" in the early stages of the upswing, when the economy is still close to an equilibrium position. Perhaps no feature of Schumpeter's theory has been so frequently subjected to attack as this one. To the present writer, however, this feature of the Schumpeterian system seems acceptable enough. Two similar opinions might be cited in support of this view:[14]

1. Why is innovating activity most favored by equilibrium? A comparison of the difficulties and risks of innovation at different stages of the two-phase cycle shows a heavy balance in favor of this situation. The stability of business conditions, as well as the complete absence of profits, is more conducive to innovation than any other stage of the cycle could be. Since the risk of failure is at a minimum, and the pressure to innovate at a maximum, we should expect that innovating activity, under capitalist arrangements, would be extraordinarily great.

2. The standard criticism which has been raised against Professor Schumpeter's theory of the business cycle is concerned with the "clustering" of innovations at certain periods of time. The explanation sought by the critics was either in terms of the social psychology of innovations, i.e., that one successful innovation encourages others (a point which Professor Schumpeter himself makes, cf. Vol. i, p. 100, which, however, is not of decisive importance for the theory), or in terms of a clustering in time of technological inventions. These explanations being refuted, the theory was easily rejected. But all this is quite irrelevant. Professor Schumpeter's theory does not rest upon either of these points. The clustering is a consequence of the changing risk of failure. Whatever the time

[14] Clemence and Doody, *op. cit.*, p. 54; Oscar Lange, review of Joseph Schumpeter *Business Cycles*, in *Review of Economic Statistics*, November, 1941, p. 192.

shape of the supply of new inventions, new plans of organization, etc., or of entrepreneurial skill, the actual introduction of innovations will be "bunched" at periods of neighborhood of equilibrium when the risk of failure is the smallest; and as an intensification of the rate of innovation disequilibrates the economy and increases the risk of failure, this rate must slacken again. Thus we can dismiss the standard criticism; the clustering is explained quite satisfactorily in Professor Schumpeter's theory.

Although Schumpeter's theory is not in itself a complete theory of business cycles, it contains elements which must be included in any complete theory. In particular, his analysis of innovations is still the best explanation of how an upswing gets started. Certainly he has made an important contribution to the theory of development by his systematic exposition of the thesis suggested by Marx that capitalist development tends to proceed by leaps, bounds, and falls rather than by a smooth and steady progression. But another aspect of Schumpeter's theory of fluctuations is more troublesome from our standpoint.

Whereas in his original presentation he talked of only one kind of cycle, in his *Business Cycles* he talked of three: the "Kitchin" cycle of three to four years duration; the "Juglar" cycle of seven to eleven years; and the "Kondratieff" cycle of fifty to fifty-five years (in each case the name given the cycle is that of the economist who first provided statistical evidence of its existence and attempted an explanation of it). We are not troubled by Schumpeter's using the same theory to explain all three cycles, although that has bothered some of his critics. It is entirely feasible that the impact of such major innovations as steam or electricity should be felt over long periods and the impact of minor innovations like tubeless tires over short ones, although it is not clear why their impact should be spread over precisely the periods designated by Schumpeter. What does bother us is that, whereas the Kitchin and Juglar cycles appear clearly in the data, the very existence of the Kondratieff cycle is debatable. First, there are very few countries for which reliable time series are available for a couple of centuries—and even a two-century-long time series covers only four Kondratieff cycles, which is not a large sample. Secondly, the "long wave" seems to show up in some time series and not in others. It is fairly clear in prices but it does not appear in figures of total output or employment. It is clear enough that during long periods, such as 1825–50 and 1870–90 in the United Kingdom, or 1870–90 and 1929–40 in the United States, a lot of people talked about "depression." The "Great Depression" of the 1930's and the depression of the 1830's and 1840's show some striking similarities; these were depressions in any language. The so-called "great depression" of the 1870's and 1880's, on the other hand, was a period in which total output went merrily on up throughout. Professor Rostow, who has certainly given the matter as careful study as anyone, finds little evidence of such a cycle in his study of nineteenth-century Britain.

The matter is of some importance for development policy. For if cycles exist in which for twenty-five years a prosperity and expansion phase, interrupted only by the shorter cycles, can be followed by an equally long period of general depression and contraction, it becomes necessary to distinguish the true long-run trend from the movements in the Kondratieff cycle, as well as in the short-run cycle, in order to evaluate the results of a development program. And to do that we would have to know a great deal more about the nature and causes of the Kondratieff cycle than we do. It is also important to know whether there are any cures for the "long wave," and if so what. If a country launches its development program in the downswing of a Kondratieff cycle, it will be very hard to generate enthusiasm for the program by saying that although income is not currently rising, it is rising *relative* to what it would have done without the development program, and that in another twenty-five years or so, when the Kondratieff upturn appears, a rapid rate of increase in per capita income can be confidently expected.

Schumpeter's Theory of Trend

Schumpeter's pure theory is a contribution to the analysis of business cycles rather than to the analysis of economic development. It seems likely that Schumpeter himself became aware of this fact in the course of his career. His great two-volume book published in 1939 is a further elaboration of the ideas in his 1911 *Theory of Economic Development;* it is significant that the title of the later work was changed to *Business Cycles: A Theoretical, Historical, and Statistical Analysis of the Capitalist Process.* Schumpeter's main point was precisely that the capitalist process is necessarily cyclical. He did not provide any systematic explanation of trends; indeed, he treated the trend as a statistical concept—a line drawn through the inflection points of a curve showing the pattern of business cycles. But what determines whether that trend is upward, downward, or horizontal? On this question Schumpeter had little to offer but insights and observations, and although these were very helpful in themselves, they do not really constitute a "theory" of economic development.

Let us summarize the system as outlined above:

$$O = f(L, K, Q, T) \tag{1}$$
$$S = S(W, R, r) \tag{2}$$
$$I = I_i + I_A \tag{3}$$
$$I_i = I(R, r, Q) \tag{4}$$
$$I_A = I_a(K, T) \tag{5}$$
$$T = T(E) \tag{6}$$
$$K = K(E) \tag{7}$$
$$E = E(R, \chi) \tag{8}$$
$$O = k(I - S) \tag{9}$$
$$W = W(I) \tag{10}$$
$$\chi = \chi(R/W) \tag{11}$$
$$O = R + W \tag{12}$$

When we compare this set of equations, summarizing the Schumpeter system, with those summarizing the Classical or the Marxist system, we note three major differences.

First is the introduction of the interest rate as a determinant of savings. Not every economist would regard this feature of the system as a great advantage, since the relationship of savings to the level of interest rates is none too clear. Second is the separation of autonomous from induced investment and the isolation of "innovations" as the factor influencing autonomous investment; many economists consider this feature Schumpeter's major contribution to the theory of development. Third is the emphasis on entrepreneurship as the vital force in the whole economy. This feature was and remains the most distinctive aspect of Schumpeter's system, and it is this feature that has found its way most frequently into later theories of growth.

But what are we to say about it? What determines the supply of entrepreneurship? Without answers to this question, we still do not know why an economy grows, stagnates, or collapses; and Schumpeter does not provide very satisfactory answers. It all resolves itself into the vague concept of "climate" for the rise of the New Men who will do the job of establishing New Firms and making the economy grow.

We have only three indications of what Schumpeter regarded as the essence of this all-important matter of "climate": a more or less offhand remark in his earlier book, some statements about the psychological make-up of entrepreneurs, and his explanation of the Great Depression. The remark is[15]

The more life becomes rationalised, levelled, democratised, and the more transient become the relations of the individual to concrete people (especially in the family circle) and to concrete things (to a concrete factory or to an ancestral home), the more many of the motives enumerated in the second chapter lose their importance and the more the entrepreneur's grip on profit loses its power. To this process the progressive "automatisation" of development runs parallel, and it also tends to weaken the significance of the entrepreneurial function.

The entrepreneur is, among other things, a social deviant:[16]

The third point consists in the reaction of the social environment against one who wishes to do something new. This reaction may manifest itself first of all in the existence of legal or political impediments. But neglecting this, any deviating conduct by a member of a social group is condemned, though in greatly varying degrees according as the social group is used to such conduct or not. Even a deviation from social custom in such things as dress or manners arouses opposition, and of course all the more so in the graver cases. This opposition is stronger in primitive stages of culture than in others, but it is never absent. Even mere astonishment at the deviation, even merely noticing it, exercises a pressure on the individual. The manifestation of condemnation may at once bring noticeable consequences in its train. It may even come to social ostracism and finally to physical prevention or to direct attack. Neither the fact that progressive differentiation weakens this opposition—especially as the most important cause of the weakening is the very development which we wish to explain—nor the further fact that the social opposition operates under certain circum-

---

[15] Schumpeter, *The Theory of Economic Development*, p. 155.
[16] *Ibid.*, p. 89.

stances and upon many individuals as a stimulus, changes anything in principle in the significance of it. Surmounting this opposition is always a special kind of task which does not exist in the customary course of life, a task which also requires a special kind of conduct.

He is also egocentric, untraditional, and ambitious:[17]

The typical entrepreneur is more self-centered than other types, because he relies less than they do on tradition and connection and because his characteristic task—theoretically as well as historically—consists precisely in breaking up old, and creating new, tradition. Although this applied primarily to his economic action, it also extends to the moral, cultural, and social consequences of it. It is, of course, no mere coincidence that the period of the rise of the entrepreneur type also gave birth to Utilitarianism. . . .

First of all, there is the dream and the will to found a private kingdom, usually, though not necessarily, also a dynasty. The modern world really does not know any such positions, but what may be attained by industrial or commercial success is still the nearest approach to medieval lordship possible to modern man. . . .

Then there is the will to conquer; the impulse to fight, to prove oneself superior to others, to succeed for the sake, not of the fruits of success, but of success itself. From this aspect, economic action becomes akin to sport—there are financial races, or rather boxing-matches. . . .

Finally, there is the joy of creating, of getting things done, or simply of exercising one's energy and ingenuity.

Schumpeter's ideas about the breakdown of capitalism are perhaps most clearly stated in the final chapter of his *Business Cycles,* where he discusses the "stagnation thesis" in relation to the Great Depression of the 1930's. This theory, which is the subject of Chapter 7, states in essence that the length and depth of the Great Depression was to be explained in terms of vanishing investment opportunity, because of declining rates of population growth, disappearance of the frontier, and a tendency for innovations to become capital saving. Schumpeter does not deny the logical validity of the stagnation thesis:[18]

The validity of that theory is not denied on the grounds that its basic proposition is wrong. . . . Capitalism is essentially a process of (indigenous) economic change. Without that change or, more precisely, that kind of change which we have called evolution, capitalist society cannot exist, because the economic functions and, with the functions the economic bases of its leading strata—of the strata which work the capitalist engine—would crumble if it ceased: without innovations, no entrepreneurs; without entrepreneurial achievement, no capitalist returns and no capitalist propulsion. . . . The atmosphere of industrial revolutions—of "progress"—is the only one in which capitalism can survive. In this sense stabilized capitalism is a contradiction in terms.

He also accepts "the companion proposition that investment opportunity in this sense may, and in fact is quite likely to, vanish sometime in the future." He even adds "an element of his own." The mechanization of progress may "produce effects similar to those which cessation of tech-

[17] *Ibid.,* pp. 91–93.
[18] Schumpeter, *Business Cycles,* p. 1033.

nological progress would have. Even now the private entrepreneur is not nearly so important a figure as he has been in the past. We have moreover noticed the implications of chemical and other developments which may result in making innovation capital saving or at least less capital absorbing than, say, it has been in the railroad age." He considers the argument regarding population growth to be "inadequately formulated," but agrees that "provision for an indefinite family future is of central importance in the scheme of bourgeois motivation, and much driving power may be eliminated by childlessness."

However, he flatly denies that such a theory is an explanation of the Great Depression. A particularly deep and long depression was to be expected at that time anyhow, he maintains, in terms of his own theory of long waves. Even the "disappointnig Juglar" of 1933–37, which ended in a new downswing long before full employment was restored, is in part to be explained in terms of his general theory: "It did not differ in character from the comparable Juglar prosperities of the preceding Kondratieff downgrades, and therefore does not indicate any fundamental change in the working of the capitalist organism."[19] However, he does feel that more was involved in the Great Depression, and particularly in the disappointing Juglar, than the general nature of interacting Kondratieff and Juglar cycles: to wit, the deterioration of the climate for entrepreneurial activity. For "Capitalism produces by its mere working a social atmosphere—a moral code, if the reader prefers—that is hostile to it, and this atmosphere, in turn, produces policies which do not allow it to function."[20] Moreover, there is no "equilibrating apparatus" to guarantee that this atmosphere will not appear before "the capitalist process will have really spent its force or be spending it." In the United States of the 1930's, he suggests, this atmosphere appeared too soon.

As evidence of this hostile climate, he cites first the burden of direct taxation since 1932. He attaches more importance to the income, corporation, and estate taxes than to some of the newer taxes, such as undistributed profits and capital gains taxes, but he agrees that such "changes in the rules" were inimical to entrepreneurial activity. The tax on payrolls for financing the social security program was also of some significance. In addition, "labor policies reduced investment opportunity—besides employment per unit of output—mainly by forcing up wage rates."[21] His general analysis leads him to expect that "developments in the field of public utilities would be a leading factor of the current, as they had been in the preceding Juglar." The failure of this expectation to be fulfilled he explains in terms of the increasing activity of the federal and municipal governments in this field. The reappearance of "the big stick" with respect to monopoly was another discouraging factor. Finally, "the personnel and methods by which and the spirit in which" the New Deal measures were administered were "much more important than anything contained in any enactment."

[19] *Ibid.*, p. 1037.
[20] *Ibid.*, p. 1038.
[21] *Ibid.*, p. 1042.

Thus Schumpeter's theory of economic growth (as distinct from his theory of economic fluctuations) has a large element of tautology in it, making it difficult to test empirically. It is not set up as a "refutable hypothesis." Economic growth occurs when the social climate is conducive to the appearance of a sufficient flow of New Men, but the only real way to test whether the social climate is appropriate, is to see whether the New Men are in fact appearing; that is, whether there is economic growth. If vigorous economic growth appears, the social climate is appropriate; when there is no vigorous economic growth, the social climate is by definition inimical to it.

In general, the climate is appropriate when entrepreneurial success is amply rewarded, and where there are good—but not too good—chances of success. If entrepreneurs are to be social deviants, the society must oppose them in some degree, accepting them only after they have proved their success. In contrast to Marx, who thought of "capitalists" as a "class" almost in the sense of caste, a group to which workers could not aspire, an essential aspect of Schumpeter's vigorous capitalist development is rapid circulation of the elite. Success in the innovational process must lead also to the top of the social ladder—if not for oneself, then at least for one's son or grandson—as it did in nineteenth-century Europe.[22]

Accepting the Schumpeter theory of growth raises an interesting question: what can be expected from a society in which entrepreneurs are no longer deviants, since collective entrepreneurial activity is regarded as the most acceptable form of endeavor. Can an economy of "organization men," safe and secure in their junior executive or trade-union positions, produce a rate of economic expansion as rapid as was obtained under unbridled capitalism, in which entrepreneurial activity was highly regarded only when spectacularly successful?

Schumpeter certainly thought not. In his address to the American Economic Association in 1949 (published posthumously) he said:[23]

The very success of the business class in developing the productive powers of its country and the very fact that this success has created a new standard of life for all classes has paradoxically undermined the social and political position of the same business class whose economic function, though not obsolete, tends to become obsolescent and amenable to bureaucratization. . . . The concentration of the business class on the tasks of the factory and the office was instrumental in creating a political system and an intellectual class the structure and interests of which developed an attitude of independence from, and eventually of hostility to, the interests of large-scale business. The latter is becoming increasingly incapable of defending itself against raids that are, in the short run, highly profitable to other classes.

[22] One factor that Schumpeter seems to have missed is the importance of the frontier in the circulation of the elite. A major difference between the "open society" of the United States, and the more stratified society of Australia, with its accompanying emphasis on the role of government and social welfare, is that in Australia the same opportunities for rising to the top of the economic ladder, and thus to the top of the social ladder, by "going West" did not prevail. We shall have more to say of this matter in the next chapter.

[23] *American Economic Review Papers and Proceedings*, XL (May, 1950), p. 449.

Similarly, in his *Capitalism, Socialism, and Democracy* he wrote:[24]

This social function (of entrepreneurship) is already losing importance . . . it is much easier now than it has been in the past to do things that lie outside the familiar routine—innovation itself is being reduced to routine. Technological progress is increasingly becoming the business of teams of trained specialists . . . personality and will power must count for less in environments which have become accustomed to economic change . . . social and technological change undermined and eventually destroyed the function and position of [the warrior knight]. Now a similar social process—in the last analysis the same social process —undermines the role and, along with the role, the social position of the capitalist entrepreneur.

In concluding this chapter, let us say one word about the relationship of the Schumpeter theory to the problems of underdeveloped areas. Tautological though the theory may be, there can be little doubt of its relevance. The lack of adequate entrepreneurship is one of the most frequently cited obstacles to take-off in such countries, as we shall see in Chapter 12. It also appears true that the relatively small entrepreneurial group in such countries frequently consists of a deviant class: the Chinese in Southeast Asia, the Hindus in East Bengal, the Jews in Libya, the Indians in Africa, and so on. Schumpeter's theory also raises doubts about the possibilities of successful development in countries which *start* with a climate inimical to entrepreneurship, as is the case in many of the underdeveloped countries. The "socialist" intent of many of these countries has been announced. Such "New Deal" legislation as social security programs, high and progressive income tax rates, labor legislation, and the like have been introduced in many underdeveloped countries in the years following World War II, with levels of income and stocks of capital that are only a tiny fraction of those of the United States in the 1930's. It may be possible for the entrepreneurial function to be performed by government agencies instead of by private individuals, but the Schumpeter theory would throw some doubt on this possibility.

[24] Schumpeter, *Capitalism, Socialism, and Democracy* (3d ed.: New York, 1950), pp. 132–133.

6 | Requirements for Steady Growth I: Harrod, Domar

The publication of Keynes' *General Theory of Employment, Interest, and Money* in 1936 was followed by a spate of theories relating to the requirements for steady growth. These theories, essentially elaborations and refinements of the Keynesian system, were directed toward problems of advanced countries. When they were conceived, the problem of "secular stagnation" or chronic unemployment was still very much in people's minds. However, they were sufficiently general and symmetrical to be useful in dealing with problems of inflationary pressure during World War II. This same generality makes them valid, with appropriate modifications of the underlying empirical assumptions, in underdeveloped countries as well. They do not, however, tell us much about how to launch a process of development where it does not exist.

In this chapter and the next we present two of these theories, one formulated by R. F. Harrod of Oxford and the other by Alvin H. Hansen of Harvard. These two are chosen from the many because they seem to be particularly enlightening when applied to the problem of underdevelopment.

Growth versus Development

Some writers, including the famous French economist François Perroux, have sought to distinguish "growth" from "development." Fundamentally, growth consists of rising national and per capita real income; development entails a good deal more—structural change, technological advance, resource discovery, and closing sectoral and regional gaps, as indicated in

Chapter 1. The problem of maintaining steady growth where it is already occurring is complex enough, as we shall see; but it is simple in comparison to the problem of launching and sustaining development in an under-developed country. It may be questioned whether high rates of growth can be maintained for very long without development as well—a question soon to be faced in practical form in countries so advanced that structural change is nearing its end and sectoral and regional differences are already small. Conceptually, however, it is possible for an economy to grow without developing; indeed India seems to have done just that in the early postwar years. Development without growth is a little harder to imagine. Of the two theories of steady growth to be presented here, it will be noted that Hansen's contains elements of a true development theory, whereas Harrod's is a more pure theory of growth.

The Harrod Model

In contrast to much of the recent literature on "dynamics," Harrod's essay *Towards a Dynamic Economics* has the main attributes of a truly dynamic theory. Harrod concentrates upon the explanation of secular *trends;* he insists that it is precisely this explanation of trends that is the distinguishing characteristic of *dynamic* economics. Comparative statics, he argues, are still statics; more than imperfect foresight, or imperfect knowledge, or mere change, or presence of expectations, or lags and frictions, or "dating" of variables is needed to take us into the realm of economic dynamics. Even trade cycle theory is not dynamic if it merely explains fluctuations around a constant trend. Only a theory explaining secular changes in the volume of output may validly claim to be called dynamic. Harrod's theory is directed toward an explanation of the secular causes of unemployment and inflation, and of the factors determining the optimum and the actual rate of capital accumulation. Although clearly distinct from theories of equilibrium or of comparative statics, Harrod's theory is nevertheless related to them, and it uses those concepts and tools of equilibrium theory and comparative statics that are serviceable in analyzing secular trends. Accordingly, his work provides a foundation upon which it should ultimately be possible to build, brick by brick, an imposing structure of dynamic analysis. Harrod considers the building of such a structure the major task facing economists today: [1]

The idea which underlies these lectures is that sooner or later we shall be faced once more with the problem of stagnation, and that it is to this problem that economists should devote their main attention.

On the basis of his analysis Harrod concludes that advanced countries will soon confront the problem of a chronic deflationary gap (and by inference that underdeveloped countries will continue to be handicapped by a chronic inflationary gap) unless appropriate policies are pursued.

In our exposition of the Harrod theory, we shall deviate from the pattern

[1] R. F. Harrod, *Towards a Dynamic Economics* (London, 1948), p. v.

of the earlier chapters in one respect. Harrod's presentation is tight and terse, and he uses his own equations. We shall not, therefore, translate his system into a set of simultaneous equations. We shall only translate Harrod's symbols into our own.

The three "fundamental elements" in his system are (1) manpower, (2) output per head, (3) quantity of capital available. The second of these presumably breaks down into (a) level of technique, (b) supplies of known resources; but Harrod discusses changes in output per head solely in terms of "inventions."

A "neutral" stream of inventions is one that leaves the ratio of required capital to output ("capital coefficient") unchanged. A "capital-saving" stream of inventions would reduce the capital coefficient, a "labor-saving" stream of inventions would increase it. Thus "labor-saving" inventions are defined as capital-absorbing inventions. Surely an invention could reduce the ratio of labor to output, without raising the ratio of capital to output. This definition also raises the question, which occurs periodically in the course of Harrod's analysis, as to whether he really means inventions when he uses the word, or whether he means innovations. An invention may be capital saving once in place, but the innovation based on it may neverthe- less be capital absorbing during the gestation period. What is needed for a growing offset to savings is not a stream of *inventions* that is capital ab- sorbing in the *engineering* sense, but a stream of *innovations* that is capital absorbing in the economic sense.[2] Harrod, unfortunately, fails to make this important distinction. He seems to be talking mainly about inventions, which, he says, may very well be more or less neutral in reality,[3] but at times his arguments make sense only if cast in terms of innovations.

"Capital requirements" are the proportion of income that must be saved and invested to maintain a given rate of increase in income, with a given rate and type of technological progress, and a given rate of popula- tion growth. A simplifying assumption that underlies the discussion of capital requirements, which Harrod does not make explicit, is that the labor force and the body of consumers grow in the same proportion; that is, that the ratio of labor force to population and of consuming units to population does not change. Only then would it be true, for example, that capital requirements with no technological advance and no change in in- terest rates would equal "the increase of population in a period regarded as a fraction of the total income multiplied by the capital coefficient." [4]

More generally, his concept of capital requirements, C_r, could be trans- lated as follows. Let I_r be required net savings and investment, Y be na- tional income, and p (for period of investment) be the "capital coefficient." Then [5]

[2] Benjamin Higgins, "Concepts and Criteria of Secular Stagnation," in *Income, Employment, and Public Policy: Essays in Honor of Alvin Hansen* (New York, 1948).

[3] Harrod, *op. cit.*, p. 28.

[4] *Ibid.*, p. 22.

[5] If L is population and T is level of technique, t is time and Q_r is quantity of capital required for a given level of output, then

$$Q_r = R(L, T) \quad \text{where} \quad L = L(t) \quad \text{and} \quad T = T(t)$$

$$I_r = \frac{\Delta Y}{Y} \cdot p \quad \text{and} \quad C_r = \frac{I_r}{\Delta Y}$$

In an economy with a growing population and no technological progress, capital requirements will increase proportionately to the population. So also, Harrod argues, will "hump" savings (saving to meet specific future needs) and 'corporate' savings. Consequently, if there is "inheritance" saving (saving to build up an estate) to begin with, and all capital requirements are to be met, "inheritance" saving must also grow proportionately to income; that is, it must grow in total volume enough to keep the average per capita inheritance constant. Of course, total savings may tend to grow faster than capital requirements, leading to a condition of chronic excess savings and a need for falling interest rates, even in an economy with a growing population; but the need for a falling interest rate is clearly much greater in a stationary state than in one with a growing population.

Harrod's basic equation is $GC = s$: where G is the growth during a unit of time, $\Delta Y/Y$; C is net capital accumulation in the period (including goods in process and stocks), divided by the increase in output in the period, $I/\Delta Y$; and s is the average propensity to save,[6] S/Y. Thus the equation is really a restatement of the truism that *ex post* savings equals *ex post* investment; it could be written:

$$\frac{\Delta Y}{Y} \cdot \frac{I}{\Delta Y} = \frac{S}{Y} \quad \text{or} \quad \frac{I}{Y} = \frac{S}{Y} \quad \text{or} \quad I = S$$

Harrod's second fundamental equation, $G_w C_r = s$, expresses the equilibrium conditions for a steady advance. G_w, the "warranted rate of growth," is the value of $\Delta Y/Y$ that barely satisfies entrepreneurs; C_r, the "capital requirements," is the value of $I/\Delta Y$ that is needed to sustain the warranted rate of growth.[7] It will be noted that s is the same in both equations. Thus in dynamic equilibrium (stable value of $\Delta Y/Y$), $G_w C_r = GC$; the actual, or *ex post* value of I/Y, equals the equilibrium value, which is a subjective phenomenon. Moreover, G must equal G_w and C must equal C_r. For if G exceeds G_w, then C will be below C_r; that is, entrepreneurs will consider the amount of capital accumulation inadequate to sustain the increase in total output and will increase their orders for capital goods (and conversely). But then G will depart still further from G_w in the next period, and a cumulative movement away from equilibrium will set in. Thus: "Around the line of advance which, if adhered to, would alone give satis-

---

Then, ignoring cross-derivatives, which would in any case be very small,

$$Ir = \frac{dQr}{dt} = \frac{\delta Qr}{\delta L} \cdot \frac{dL}{dt} + \frac{\delta Qr}{\delta T} \cdot \frac{dT}{dt}$$

L is here defined in terms of output per capita.

[6] These symbols are used in the usual sense: Y is national income, I is net investment, and S is net savings. Since Harrod has preempted C for another use in this chapter, we shall denote consumption by C_n.

[7] If inventions are "neutral," C_r will also be the new capital required to sustain the increase in consumption that consumers want, as a result of the increase in their incomes during the period.

faction, centrifugal forces are at work, causing the system to depart further and further from the required line of advance." [8]

There are two possible interpretations of Harrod's argument that if G exceeds G_w, C must be below C_r, and vice versa. If $G_w C_r = GC = s$ by assumption, then the proposition follows by mere arithmetic. Harrod's presentation, however, suggests that he thinks $G_w C_r$ *must* equal GC for economic and definitional reasons, in much the same way that *ex post* savings *must* equal *ex post* investment. It is hard to see that such is the case. It is clear enough that G and C must vary inversely with a given I/Y or C. But why should the equilibrium ratio of (*ex post*) savings and investment to income (i.e., the ratio that satisfies entrepreneurs, or $G_w C_r =$ equilibrium $\frac{I = S}{Y}$) be continuously equal to the *actual* ratio of savings and investment to income (GC, or *actual* $\frac{I = S}{Y}$)?

Harrod's main argument does not depend upon the equality of GC and $G_w C_r$ anyhow. It depends rather on the acceleration principle (or better, on the "relation"). For if G exceeds G_w, what this really means is that the rate of increase in total spending is greater than is necessary to call forth the current rate of investment, and consequently investment will increase. By definition, if the rate of investment is above the equilibrium level, C_r is below C. Such a situation would be inconsistent with an excess of GC (actual $I/Y = S/Y$) over $G_w C_r$ (equilibrium $I/Y = S/Y$), since investment cannot be simultaneously above and below the equilibrium level; but it would be quite consistent with an excess of $G_w C_r$ over GC. That is, $C - C_r$ may exceed $G_w - G$; entrepreneurs may consider actual investment low, not only relative to the actual rate of increase in consumer spending, but also relative to the level of income. In this case there would be a double incentive to increase investment in the next period. The movement away from equilibrium when $G > G_w$, and *in addition* $GC < G_w C_r$, will be greater than if $G > G_w$ but $GC = G_w C_r$.

Harrod anticipates the criticism that his formulation gives too much weight to the acceleration principle, and he suggests that the criticism could be met by rewriting the first equation $GC = s - k$, where k is investment not due to the current increase in orders for output. It is not quite clear how much investment is meant to go into k and how much into C. C would presumably not include primary investment induced by innovations—let us say, building of automobile factories in the early stages of the automobile long wave, or "Kondratieff." But would the petroleum refineries, rubber plantations, and roadside restaurants brought into being by the automobile Kondratieff go into C or into k? Harrod says k will include "capital outlay which no one expects to see justified or not justified in a fairly short period." [9] How long is that? As will appear below, it is not a matter of indifference how investment is distributed between C and k.

Another problem arises in connection with C and C_r. The "relation" usually expresses the extent to which investment increases as a consequence

[8] Harrod, *op. cit.*, p. 86.
[9] *Ibid.*, p. 79.

of increases in demand for the final products of plant and equipment of a given type. For the "relation" to operate in the economy as a whole (without any change in the period of investment, which is not closely related to rates of consumption, and which Harrod excludes from this part of his analysis), there must be a change in the rate of consumer spending. The relation might be expressed as $I = r \cdot dC_n$. Harrod argues throughout as though an increase in income necessarily entailed an increase in consumption, and also as though an increase in investment would always bring with it an increase in consumption. Why else would the increase in investment, $C_r \Delta Y$, resulting from an excess of G over G_w (excess of C_r over C) carry the system *further* from equilibrium?

Harrod's point is, it will be remembered, that the greater investment brought about by $C_r > C$ will raise G still further above G_w. In the context of his argument, this proposition must mean that the increase in investment in the next period will bring with it an increase in the rate of expansion of consumer spending $\Delta C_n / C_n$. Now, if the increased investment is deficit financed, it is quite likely that the increase in rate of expansion of consumption that accompanies an increase in investment, $\dfrac{d}{dI}\left(\dfrac{dC_n}{C_n}\right)$, will be positive; for then the multiplier will operate on the increase in I and so raise consumer spending substantially. But in most of Harrod's argument, savings and investment are always equal; if entrepreneurs consider their investment too low, they also consider their saving too low. An increase in investment financed by an equal and simultaneous increase in saving will not raise income at all, and consumption will actually fall. In this event, investment in period 2 will be too high, rather than still too low, and will be reduced rather than raised in period 3, and so on. The initial excess of G over G_w would in this case set up a series of damped fluctuations, and in the absence of a new disturbance, the system would tend toward a new equilibrium with the actual $\dfrac{I = S}{Y}$ equal to the equilibrium $\dfrac{I = S}{Y}$, and so with $G = G_w$ and $GC = G_w C_r$.

The manner in which new investment is financed is crucial to Harrod's analysis. Unless he can demonstrate beyond a shadow of doubt that it is *impossible* for enough of an increase in investment to be financed by new savings to make $\dfrac{d}{dI}\left(\dfrac{dC_n}{C}\right)$ zero or negative, he can argue that an initial divergence of G and G_w may start a cumulative movement; but he cannot argue that it must start a cumulative movement.

Harrod's third fundamental equation is $G_n C_r$ may or may not be equal to s; here G_n is the "natural rate of growth" or "that steady rate of advance determined by fundamental conditions." [10] What G_n really seems to be is the rate of increase in output at full employment, given the rate of population increase and the rate of technological progress. A better term would have been "potential rate of growth"; there is nothing very natural about full employment. It will be noted that, whereas Harrod seems to feel

[10] Harrod, *op. cit.*, p. 87.

that G_wC_r *must* equal GC, he stresses the possibility that G_nC_r may not equal GC, by making G_nC_r equal, or not equal, to s.

With the introduction of G_n, Harrod is able to develop a theory of increasing underemployment for advanced economies. If G_w exceeds G_n (as it well may when population growth tapers off, or the rate of improvement in technique or discovery of new resources tapers off), G will also tend to lie below G_w, C will be chronically above C_r, and the economy will be chronically depressed. (After all, G can exceed G_n only in the recovery phase of the cycle.) Conversely, in a rapidly expanding economy (where population growth, or technological progress, or geographic expansion is at a high level) there will be a chronic excess of G_n over G_w, and also of G over G_w, and thus a chronic excess of C_r over C, and a perpetual tendency for inflationary boom to develop. We might call economies of the former type "deflationary gap" economies and of the latter type, "inflationary gap" economies. We shall have something to say later on as to whether or not underdeveloped countries are, by definition, "inflationary gap" countries as well. Harrod's general conclusion about the "virtue of saving" should surprise no one; it is a "good thing" in an "inflationary gap" economy, and a "bad thing" in a "deflationary gap" economy.

The causal relation between G_w and s is one of many problems that could have been made clearer by an elaboration of the central concept, G_w. The term "warranted rate of growth" is not a very happy one for what Harrod seems to have in mind. Nor is "the line of entrepreneurial contentment" [11] a very clear-cut definition of G_w. In his *Economic Journal* article of March, 1939, he defines G_w as "that rate of growth which if it occurs, will leave all parties satisfied that they have produced neither more nor less than the right amount"; it is the rate that "will put them in the frame of mind which will cause them to give such orders as will maintain the same rate of growth." Thus G_w is subjective, but not, apparently, *ex ante*; it is the rate of growth that makes entrepreneurs satisfied with what has happened, rather than a plan for the future.[12]

Although reference to the article makes Harrod's concept of G_w a bit clearer, it still does not tell us what Harrod thinks are the determinants of G_w; and what determines G_w is obviously all-important, for C_r depends on G_w; it is, indeed, defined in terms of G_w. G and C cannot be changed except as a result of entrepreneurial decisions, and these decisions depend on G_w. Thus what happens in Harrod's dynamic economy depends ultimately on G_w. Harrod nowhere presents an analysis of the determinants of G_w, but in the course of his discussion he does indicate the following relationships:

G_w varies (1) inversely with C_r (capital requirements); (2) directly with s (the average propensity to save); (3) inversely with the volume of public works; (4) inversely with the volume of investment, that is, inde-

[11] *Ibid.*, p. 88.
[12] Harrod also explains in his article that he uses "the unprofessional term warranted instead of equilibrium," because the equilibrium is a "highly unstable one." Stable or unstable, the term "equilibrium" conveys more meaning than "warranted."

pendent of the current rate of growth, k; (5) directly with the rate of interest r (since k and C_r vary inversely with r, and s probably varies directly with r).

The first of these relationships is arithmetic. Given s, G_w must vary inversely with C_r, just as G varies inversely with C. There are no clues to entrepreneurial behavior here. The second relationship has already been discussed; it, too, seems to be a matter of definition rather than of business behavior. Relationships (3) and (4) really amount to the same thing. Public works are one kind of investment that need not depend solely on the current rate of growth of income and that may, therefore, be included in k. Since $G_w C_r = s - k$, by definition, any increase in k must, other things being equal, be accompanied by a reduction in G_w. The fifth relationship is a product of several others:

1. s varies directly with r, and since G_w varies directly with s, G_w varies directly with r.

2. k varies inversely with r, G_w varies inversely with k, and therefore, G_w varies directly with r.

3. C_r varies inversely with r, G_w varies inversely with C_r, and therefore, G_w varies directly with r.

The relationship between s and r is a true causal relationship; $s(r)$ is a savings function with psychological meaning: savings depend on the interest rate. The same is true of the $k(r)$ function, which is really the marginal efficiency of capital schedule: investment depends on the rate of interest. The $C_r(r)$ function is the period of investment, which also has meaningful content: as the interest rate falls, the capital-output ratio will be increased. But $G_w(r)$ has no meaning of its own whatsoever; given the other relationships, the dG_w/dr is given by definition. Thus not one of these G_w relationships is a truly causal one, with meaning in terms of entrepreneurial behavior.

Finally, Harrod adds two refinements. If d represents the fraction of income needed for capital involved in lengthening the production process ("deepening"), then $G_w C_r = s - d$. If inventions are capital saving, d is negative, and the equilibrium rate of growth is enhanced. Thus any tendency toward chronic underemployment resulting from $G_w > G_n$ will be aggravated by capital-saving inventions. Harrod thinks falling interest rates might tend to lengthen the period of production and so keep d positive.

In his fourth chapter, "The Foreign Balance," Harrod points out that when we move to an open economy, the appropriate equations are $GC = s - b$ and $G_w C_r = s - b$, where b is the foreign balance. The equation expresses what is already well known: in a country with chronic underemployment, $G_w > G_n$, a favorable balance of trade on goods and services account helps to reduce the deflationary gap—and conversely for countries with a chronic inflationary gap.

Application to Underdeveloped Areas

Harrod himself did not apply his system to the problems of underdeveloped countries, but that fact should not prevent us from doing so.

First, let us note that there is nothing in Harrod's equations to assure us that the line of "steady growth" is the trend of gross national income with full employment and no inflation. Perhaps entrepreneurs will be content with a rate of investment and increase in national income involving chronic or even increasing unemployment, or a steadily rising price level. Intuition may tell us that they will not, but we cannot be sure until we have studied the question carefully. The trend of gross national income or production with full employment and no inflation is what Harrod calls—unfortunately—the natural rate of growth, G_n; what we would prefer to call the potential rate of growth. It will depend on the rate of population growth, the rate of resource discovery, the rate of technological progress, and on the rate of capital accumulation (which in the long run depends a good deal on the other growth factors). So we have the third fundamental equation,

$$G_n C_r =, \neq s \qquad (3)$$

That is, the rate of capital accumulation needed to finance the natural rate of growth may or may not be equal to the actual rate of saving—even in dynamic equilibrium.

Let us consider first a truly stagnant underdeveloped economy. High birth rates are offset by equally high death rates, there is no technological progress and no resource discovery, no capital accumulation, and no net savings. Such an economy is not an absurd abstraction from reality; in Africa one can find cases closely approximating these conditions—or could at the end of World War II. Will the economy suffer from chronic inflation? The answer is no; it will not suffer from anything but poverty, and it will not enjoy much either. For in this case the natural rate of growth is zero, and so, whatever the incremental capital-output ratio, capital requirements are also zero. Thus,

$G_n C_r = s = 0$ and since there is no growth $GC = 0$

We must also have under these conditions $G_w C_r = 0$. For if, for example, $G_w C_r$ were positive—meaning that only a positive rate of growth would keep entrepreneurs content—either s is also positive and growth is actually taking place, or stagnation does not represent an equilibrium position. The actual rate of growth, G, would be less than the warranted rate, G_w, and the actual (zero) rate of capital accumulation would still be too much to suit entrepreneurs. Capital accumulation would fall below zero, the rate of growth would become negative (income would fall) making entrepreneurs still more unhappy, and so on. Thus in our model stagnation represents "steady growth" at a zero rate, or dynamic equilibrium.

Now let us suppose that some *ex post* saving is taking place, with nothing else changed. We now have $GC = s > 0$; if it is to continue $G_w C_r$ is also positive. But $G_n C_r$ is still zero. How can savings and investment take place? The answer is, through chronic inflation. And if the rate of inflation is just sufficient to keep entrepreneurs content, it can go on indefinitely. Of course, a steady rate of inflation is a phenomenon almost unheard of in history; at some point, it tends to become cumulative. When it does, G will exceed G_w and C will be below C_r, so that still more investment will take place and hyperinflation will set in. All we can say is that an economy with no long-run growth factors to encourage savings and investment is unlikely to have them.

Next, let us introduce population growth, but let us still assume that there is no resource discovery and no technological progress. This model would also approximate certain underdeveloped countries of the real world. Now in such countries population growth is not a stimulus to investment, for reasons that will become clearer in Part 3. There is already a superabundance of unskilled labor, and mere population growth does not permit further capital accumulation without diminishing returns to capital. Nor does population growth raise effective demand, since the increased population merely shares the existing income. Under these conditions, the introduction of population growth has no effect on the actual rate of growth, and no very clear effect on the warranted rate of growth. It looks as though we will still have

$$GC = G_wC_r = s = 0$$

But now the natural rate of growth is positive; if the increased population were employed, output would increase. $G_nC_r > 0$. Thus under these conditions we have stagnation in income, output, and prices, with growing unemployment and falling per capita income.

Let us be a little more kind to our suffering economy, and suppose that prices of its exports rise. In the Harrod equations, this will mean an increase in G, and G will now exceed G_w. Consequently, C_r will exceed C, and investment will increase. Investment will raise G further and encourage still more investment. Unless all this investment is financed by savings from the beginning, or unless it puts to work men and resources which were previously unemployed—both rather unlikely events—the result will be cumulative inflation. We have not helped our economy much after all.

Let us try something else. We will launch a development plan, undertaking some public investment projects, encouraging exploration to raise the rate of resource discovery, and arranging for technical assistance to raise the rate of technological progress. In so doing we ought to stimulate some autonomous private investment as well, provided we have a few Schumpeterian entrepreneurs around. Now all this autonomous investment, public and private, is lumped together by Harrod in his innocent-looking little k. We now have, in dynamic equilibrium,

$$GC = G_wC_r = s - k$$

We have presumably raised G_n, if our plan is successful. But we are still not sure about G, at least in the short run. Suppose the entire development program, public and private, is financed by an increase in saving, so that $s - k$ just equals our previous s. In that case G need not rise; the increased investment is just offset by reduced consumption. In this case there is no particular reason why anything should happen until the new investment bears fruit. What happens then does not show directly in Harrod's equations; for the immediate effect will be a fall in prices just offsetting the increased flow of goods with the flow of money income unchanged. What happens to the all-important warranted rate of growth?

It may fall at the outset. Remember that only induced investment is covered in the left-hand side of Harrod's equations. So if Schumpeter is right, and successful innovation leads to a "cluster of followers" quite apart from what happens to current sales, it means that entrepreneurs regard the current rate of growth as enough, under the changed conditions, to warrant increased investment. Of course, the increased investment will raise G still further above G_w; we will have a boom on our hands, probably an inflationary one at that, since it is unlikely that *ex ante* savings will keep pace with investment throughout the expansion process. When the investment projects mature and new goods are thrown on the market, the rate of increase in money income is likely to slow down; G_w will then exceed G, investment will fall, and we shall have a slump. Thus we end up with a Schumpeterian cycle translated into Harrod's terms.

A second possibility is that G_w remains unchanged. In this case we shall have no initial boom—since G is unchanged—but only the slump when the increased output hits the market. It is unlikely, however, that execution of the development plan will have no secondary effects whatever, and we need not take this case too seriously.

A third possibility, also rather unlikely, is that G_w will rise. If the development program consists mainly of public enterprise and involves a great deal of intervention in the conduct of private enterprise, entrepreneurs may feel that only an increase in the rate of growth would warrant continued investment at current rates. In this case—since G does not rise immediately on our assumption that the whole program is financed by savings at the beginning—the slump comes immediately and becomes cumulative.

Now let us relax our rather artificial assumption that the whole development program is financed by savings at the outset, and let us suppose that the government engages in deficit financing and that some of the private investment is financed by credit.

In this case G, the actual rate of growth, will rise. At the same time C, the actual rate of induced investment, will fall; that is, scarce resources will be bid away from the induced investment sector to the autonomous investment sector, denoted by k. On the reasoning of the earlier models, we can expect G_w to fall: the development program should bring forth some "Schumpeterian" investment, not related to current rates of growth of output. Thus G will exceed G_w, C_r will be greater than C—and inflation will set in.

This application of the Harrod analysis to the conditions of underdeveloped countries does not demonstrate the absolute inevitability of "chronic" inflation in such countries. It does *not* show that in the absence of positive policies to prevent it, prices must always have an upward trend. Indeed, we have seen that under some conditions, which could easily arise in underdeveloped countries, there could even be cumulative deflation. More likely is just plain stagnation. But the analysis does suggest that underdeveloped countries are hypersensitive to forces causing inflation. Relatively small absolute changes in the rate of growth or capital accumulation can constitute big percentage changes, for the simple reason that *initial* rates of growth and capital accumulation are low. Divergence between actual and equilibrium rates of change can therefore arise easily, leading to cumulative movements away from equilibrium, at least until parameters change or until "ceilings" and "floors" are hit. In development-minded countries, these divergences are more likely to be on the inflationary than on the deflationary side.

Thus we see that Harrod's analytical framework can be applied to almost any situation that may exist. In a way, this flexibility is its weakness as well as its strength; his analysis is *too* general. What we badly need are facts, so that we could decide which model best fits the conditions of typical underdeveloped countries. Harrod's analysis does not provide many facts; indeed, it does not even provide us with functional (causal) relationships, which would at least tell us the direction in which other things change if, for example, the government undertakes a program of developmental investment or other changes in strategic variables occur.

Of his fundamental equation, $GC = s$, Harrod says, "I should like to think that it might serve as a target for frequent attack, like Fisher's famous truism, $MV = PT$." This is, in a way, a modest enough hope. Fisher's equation of exchange proved rather sterile; it isolated some important quantities for analysis, but told us nothing of the functional relationships among them or of the functional relationships determining their magnitudes. Some economists might even argue that until the significant *causal* relationships of Keynesian and neo-Keynesian economics were discovered, the Fisher equation did more harm than good, leading to overemphasis of the quantity theory of money. It seems likely that Harrod's hope will be fulfilled, and that his fundamental equations will be attacked on much the same grounds. They, too, merely isolate some significant quantities for analysis but fail to set forth the fundamental functional relationships among them and the causal relations that determine their magnitude.

The Domar Variant

The literature on economic growth contains frequent references to the "Harrod-Domar" model. Professor Evsey D. Domar of the Massachusetts Institute of Technology, presented a model, seemingly similar in form to Harrod's, that he discovered independently and at about the same time. In fact, however, the implications of the Domar model are not identical with those of Harrod's theory; Domar identifies additional or supplementary requirements for steady growth. Harrod, as we have seen, was concerned with conditions that would keep entrepreneurs content with their investment plans so that they would repeat in each period the investment decisions of earlier periods. Domar was concerned with the income growth required for full utilization of a growing capital stock, with full

employment and stable prices. As already noted, there is no *a priori* reason
for these two sets of requirements to be the same.

The Domar Model[13]

The basic Domar model includes the following terms: Y_d is the level of
national income (effective demand) at full employment and with constant
prices. Y_s is the level of effective supply, or the value of total output with
full employment and full use of capacity. I is investment, K the stock of
real capital, α the marginal propensity to save, and σ is the incremental
output-capital ratio, relating increases in income to net investment. We
then have the following equations:

$$\text{level of effective demand} \ldots Y_d = \frac{I}{\alpha} \tag{1}$$

$$\text{level of productive capacity} \ldots Y_s = \sigma K \tag{2}$$

$$\text{equilibrium condition} \ldots Y_d = Y_s \text{ or } \frac{I}{\alpha} = \sigma K \tag{3}$$

$$\text{increment of demand} \ldots \Delta Y_d = \frac{\Delta I}{\alpha} \tag{4}$$

$$\text{increment of capacity} \ldots \Delta Y_s = \sigma \Delta K = \sigma I \tag{5}$$

$$\text{equilibrium condition} \ldots \Delta Y_d = \Delta Y_s \text{ or } \frac{\Delta I}{\alpha} = \sigma I \tag{6}$$

$$\text{growth rate of investment} \ldots r = \frac{\Delta I}{I} = \alpha \sigma \tag{7}$$

Thus,

$$\text{growth rate of demand} \ldots \frac{\Delta Y_d}{Y_d} = \frac{\Delta I/\alpha}{Y_d} = \frac{\Delta I/\alpha}{I/\alpha} = \frac{\Delta I}{I} = \alpha \sigma \tag{8}$$

Basically, then, steady growth in the Domar model requires investment
to grow at the same percentage rate as income, and this rate must be equal
to $\alpha\sigma$. All this assumes, of course, that both α and σ are constant. The
economy must meet the conditions of Equation (3) to achieve full employ-
ment and the conditions of Equation (6) to maintain it. The double-edged
nature of investment is made clear by this model. Investment increases
productive capacity but guarantees only a given level of income and
effective demand (Equation 1). In order to generate an increase in effective
demand to offset a rise in productive capacity, investment itself must
increase.

Kenneth Kurihara points out the fundamental limitation of the Domar
model when applied to underdeveloped countries.[14] Even if all the conditions for steady growth set forth in this model are met, the unemployment,
underemployment, and disguised unemployment (low-productivity employment) that plague underdeveloped countries could still be on a large
scale; meeting Domar's conditions only guarantees that there will be no

[13] Evsey D. Domar, *Essays in the Theory of Economic Growth* (New York, 1957).
The presentation here follows closely Kenneth Kurihara, *The Keynesian Theory of
Economic Development* (London, 1959), chap. iv.
[14] Kenneth K. Kurihara, *op. cit.*, pp. 70–71.

unemployment resulting purely from a deficiency of effective demand. Also, of course, the growth of income could be "steady" at a very low percentage rate, implying constant or even falling per capita incomes in the face of population growth.

Daniel Hamberg demonstrates mathematically what is really apparent intuitively: the Domar and Harrod models become identical if, in Harrod's terms, $G_w = G_n$.[15] That is, if the economy is on the full-employment, full-capacity path and this is what entrepreneurs like, then both Domar's and Harrod's conditions will be met if income and investment continue to grow at the same constant rate, equal to G_n. But there is no assurance that such will be the case. True, entrepreneurs may not be happy forever with growing excess capacity or swelling inventories, or even with a chronic excess of orders over capacity production, but they can be content for a long time with chronic inflation, chronic underemployment, or both. In advanced countries, perhaps, many businessmen are good Keynesians, and identify their own prosperity with a high level of employment in the economy as a whole. In underdeveloped countries, this identification is much less common.

It is worth noting in passing that the conditions laid down by Harrod and Domar are by no means the only ones that must be met for steady growth. If wages are too high in relation to prices, profits are squeezed, investment falls, and with it income and employment. If wages are too low in relation to prices, there is a "shift to profits," the propensity to consume falls, investment follows, and income and employment fall again. Other distortions of the price structure can also bring trouble. If interest rates are temporarily too low in relation to wage rates, investment may be excessively concentrated in capital-intensive projects and techniques, building up a structure of capital that will prove to have too high a capital-output ratio and so be unprofitable when interest rates rise again. Anticipations regarding prices, wages, profits, etc., must be fulfilled, or else wind-fall losses and gains must precisely offset each other and factors of production must be completely mobile. *Ex ante* (planned) and *ex post* investment must both exceed *ex ante* savings by a constant percentage amount. Technologicial progress and resource discovery must be steady and neutral, population growth must be constant. Indeed when all the ways in which "lapses from steady growth" may occur are taken into account, it is a wonder that recent growth in industrialized countries has been as steady as it has been.

[15] Daniel Hamberg, *Economic Growth and Instability* (New York, 1956), pp. 64–73.

7

Requirements for Steady Growth II: Hansen

Few economic theories have aroused such a storm of protest, or have been so thoroughly and so widely misunderstood, as Alvin Hansen's theory of "economic maturity" or "secular stagnation." The reason is not far to seek; because of the time at which this theory was developed, it was subject to all the passions aroused by the Great Depression and the New Deal. To the more staunch advocates of the free private enterprise economy, the stagnation thesis seemed to offer more serious challenge to the efficiency of that system than the business cycles theories of the 1920's and early 1930's, which regarded economic fluctuations as mere "lapses from full employment" and inflationary booms. These theories suggested that fluctuations were largely the result of misbehavior of the banking system and subject to control by monetary policy. The Hansen thesis went further. It maintained that, in the absence of appropriate monetary and fiscal policy, advanced capitalist countries are subject to chronic and increasing underemployment. It called for government intervention of a more continuous nature than did the prevailing concept of business cycles. Thus it raised more serious doubts as to the efficiency of private enterprise under conditions of laissez faire.

Moreover, because the thesis was advanced during the second Roosevelt administration, at a time when Professor Hansen himself was a high-ranking "brain truster," the theory became linked in the minds of the public with "New Deal economics" in general. The intensity of political feeling aroused by the New Deal was transferred in some measure to the stagnation thesis. When George Terborgh wrote a counterattack in popular vein, it was declared a "must" for businessmen's reading by the

National Association of Manufacturers, was summarized in *Fortune*, was enthusiastically reviewed in *The New York Times* and elsewhere, and was hailed in some quarters as an effective debunking of all that is lumped together as "New Deal economics." [1]

Terborgh labeled those who accepted the Hansen thesis "stagnationists" and "professional pessimists." As we shall see, however, the Hansen theory of economic development is actually the most optimistic of those discussed in this book. The Classical school believed that capitalist development would end in stagnation. Marx and Schumpeter thought that it would end in complete breakdown. The import of Harrod's theory is that maintaining full employment without inflation is extremely difficult in a capitalist society, and that cumulative movements away from equilibrium are always around the corner. Hansen, in contrast, presented the bright vision of a stable yet growing capitalist economy and argued only that the achievement of such an economy required appropriate monetary and fiscal policies.

In the light of the Harrod-Domar analysis, perhaps Hansen's picture was *too* optimistic; that is another matter. But when Hansen was writing, the "new era" psychology had not yet been forgotten; there were still people who felt that the "natural" thing was steady growth with full employment, and to these people Hansen's writing seemed a serious challenge. Thus Shields and Woodward, writing as recently as 1945, insisted that "the general condition over the years was one of prosperity interrupted infrequently by brief periods of adjustment." [2]

Now that thirty years have passed and the policies Hansen recommended have been adopted by most countries in the Western world, one should be able to review his theories more dispassionately than was possible when they were first presented. We shall devote this chapter to such a review; and in addition to considering once again the implications of the theory for advanced countries, we shall endeavor to apply it to the problems of underdeveloped countries as well.

The Essence of the Theory

The main contributions of the Hansen thesis to a general theory of economic development are as follows:

1. Providing a more complete theory of autonomous (long-run) investment.

2. Recognition that chronic and growing gaps between potential gross national product (with constant prices) and actual gross national product can arise from acceleration or deceleration of the growth rates of basic factors influencing autonomous investment.

3. Putting empirical content into his model by applying it to a particular country at a particular time.

Let us consider these contributions in that order. We shall first present

---

[1] George Terborgh, *The Bogey of Economic Maturity* (Chicago, 1945).

[2] Murray Shields and Donald B. Woodward, *Prosperity, We Can Have It If We Want It* (New York, 1945), p. 112.

the bare bones of this theory in the form of simple equations and then go on to consider the causal relations implied in those equations.

Let us write $O_a = k \cdot I_a$, where O_a stands for actual output (gross national product or income at constant prices), I_a for total net investment, and k for the Keynesian multiplier. Dividing investment into its major components and spelling out the multiplier formula, we have:

$$O_a = \frac{1}{dS/dO_a + d\tau/dO_a} \cdot \left(I_i(\dot{O}_a) + I_g + I_A(\dot{L}, \dot{K}, \dot{T}) \right) \qquad (1)$$

Here S is saving; τ is taxes; $\dot{O}_a$ is dO_a/dt, or the variation in gross national income through time; I_i is induced investment; I_g is government investment; I_A is autonomous investment; $\dot{L}$ is dL/dt, the rate of population growth; $\dot{K}$ is dK/dt, the rate of resource discovery; and $\dot{T}$ is dT/dt, the rate of technological progress.

Using O_p for potential output (gross national product at full employment) we have also

$$O_p = f(L, K, Q, T) \qquad (2)$$

This equation expresses the now familiar production function that has appeared in most of the systems outlined above, except that here L, K, Q, and T stand for the supplies of labor, resources, capital equipment, and technology available, rather than the amounts actually used in production.

We want now to express these two sets of relationships in terms of variations through time. To keep the equations simple, let us assume that both the marginal propensity to save and the marginal propensity to pay taxes are constant through time, in the absence of deliberate government actions to change them. Using G for the combined "growth effects" on autonomous investment of population growth, resource discovery, and technological progress,

$$\frac{dO_a}{dt} = \frac{I}{dS/dO + d\tau/dO} \cdot \left(\frac{\Delta I_i}{\Delta O_a} \cdot \frac{d^2O_a}{dt^2} + \frac{dI_g}{dt} + \frac{\Delta I_a}{\Delta G} \cdot \frac{d^2G}{dt^2} \right) \qquad (1a)$$

Thus the trend of actual gross national product through time will depend partly on the marginal propensity to save and the marginal propensity to pay taxes—the higher either of these, the lower the rate of economic growth, other things being equal. It will also depend partly on the level of induced investment, but induced investment varies in turn with the rate of increase in national income. If national income is constant, induced investment will not appear at all; and if the rate of growth of national income is constant, induced investment will remain at a constant level. Thus induced investment comes into the picture only as an aggravating or amplifying force when something else happens. The volume of government investment, of course, is a matter of policy decision. As we have set up the model, the really dynamic factor is autonomous investment, which depends on the rate of population growth, the rate of resource discovery, and the rate of technological progress. If the combined effects of these are constant, autonomous investment will be constant. If then government investment is also constant, gross national product will rise at a constant rate and induced investment will also be constant.

The rate of increase of potential output through time will be,

$$\frac{dO_p}{dt} = \frac{\delta f}{\delta L} \cdot \frac{dL}{dt} + \frac{\delta f}{\delta K} \cdot \frac{dK}{dt} + \frac{\delta f}{\delta Q} \cdot \frac{dQ}{dt} + \frac{\delta f}{\delta T} \cdot \frac{dT}{dt} \qquad (2a)$$

That is, the growth of potential output will depend only on the rates at which the size of the labor force, the supply of known resources, the stock of capital, and the level of technique rise.

Now let us postulate the conditions which Hansen argued characterized the American economy in the 1920's and 1930's: population growth tapered off; the frontier disappeared and the rate of resource discovery slowed down, while the rate of technological progress remained more or less unchanged. Under these conditions, the combined effect of the growth factors, G, must fall; in Equation (1a), d^2G/dt^2 becomes negative. With government investment, I_g, constant (and even falling after 1929), the actual level of gross national product must fall; and once that happens, induced investment, I_i, becomes negative as well, aggravating the downswing. Meanwhile, however, the labor force, the supply of known resources, the level of technique continued to rise. Even the stock of capital rose, except in the very worst years of the Depression; net investment fell from 1929 to 1933, but was positive in most interwar years. Thus *potential* output continued to rise throughout the whole period. The result was a growing gap between actual and potential gross national product, which appeared in the form of increasing unemployment and excess capacity after 1929.

It should be noted that in Hansen's view only the drop in induced investment was an ordinary cyclical phenomenon. The drop in autonomous investment was a secular affair, a reaction to much longer-run trends. Whether Hansen thought of the interwar years as the trough of a Kondratieff wave, as Schumpeter did, or something longer-run still, is not altogether clear; some of his writing suggests the former, some the latter.[3] The question of the duration of the tendency toward increasing underemployment, of course, rests on the duration of basic causal factors, viz., the declining rate of population growth and the declining rate of resource discovery. We shall return to these questions of fact below.

Meanwhile, let us note that the major policy implications of the Hansen thesis are already apparent from our two simple equations. The government can do three things to offset the tendency for private investment to fall, and thus for national income to drop and unemployment to appear: it can increase public investment; it can reduce taxes, thus raising the multiplier; or it can redistribute income from savers to spenders, thus reducing

---

[3] His Presidential Address to the American Economic Association (*American Economic Review*, Supplement, March, 1939) and his *Full Recovery or Stagnation* (New York, 1938) suggest the latter thesis; his *Fiscal Policy and Business Cycles* (New York, 1941) the former one. Hansen's stagnation theory is largely an oral tradition; in reply to a direct question, Hansen once told the author that he was thinking of long waves.

the marginal propensity to save and raising the multiplier in that way. A complete policy for maintenance of steady growth might involve a judicious admixture of all three of these measures.

Aggravating Factors: Capital-saving Innovations

In our efforts to keep the equations simple, we temporarily ignored some of the components of the Hansen thesis, concentrating on its essential features. For example, we have treated the parameter I_A as though it were constant through time; that is, we have assumed implicitly that a given rate of population growth, resource discovery, and technological progress would always bring forth the same level of autonomous investment. The response of autonomous investment to the growth factors might itself vary through time, however, and Hansen argued that it does. There is a tendency, he maintained, for innovations to become increasingly capital saving as time goes by. If so, the response of investment to technological progress becomes weaker and weaker; in terms of Equation (1a), $\delta I_A / \delta T$ is itself falling through time. This factor in itself would tend to produce a falling level of (money) income, and so unemployment, if everything else, including the savings function, remained unchanged.

Thus far, we have slurred over the distinction between money income and real income. If money income is Y and the price level is P, then $Y = PO_a$ and $P = Y/O_a$. Once we have made this distinction, we must replace the left-hand side O_a with Y in Equation (1), for what the factors in that equation determine is the money income generated. We must also use Y instead of O_a in the multiplier formula. The question then arises as to whether or not we should also replace O_a with Y as the determinant of induced investment. If entrepreneurs are subject to the "money illusion," and tend to think that things are getting better when their money profits rise even if the purchasing power of their profits does not increase, we probably should. If there is a significant lag of costs behind prices, so that even real profits rise with expansion of money incomes, we certainly must replace O_a with Y. With this change, a tendency toward capital-saving innovation becomes a retarding factor in economic growth in another way; for it means that the capital-output ratio falls through time. A given level of investment, while generating the same amount of money income as before, produces a bigger increase in output than before. Thus there is chronic pressure on the price level (other things being equal) and a constant level of autonomous investment will be associated with ever lower levels of induced investment.

The "Great New Industries" Argument

Hansen also suggested that recent trends in the nature of technological progress weaken the response of investment to a given rate of technological progress. In the nineteenth century, he pointed out, innovations took the form of "great new industries," such as railroads, iron and steel, electricity, and the automobile. These innovations transformed not only economic organization but also daily life, leading to large-scale supplementary investment in related fields: new cities and towns, suburbs, cinemas, rural electrification, roads and highways, etc. In Schumpeter's terms, innovations of this type, especially in energy and transport, bring forth particularly large "clusters of followers." In the twentieth century, on the other hand, innovations have consisted more in improved techniques for producing the same final products, or of new and improved consumer durables such as radio, television, air-conditioning, etc. These innovations do not bring forth the same volume of secondary investment that "great new industries" do and they bring a high rate of obsolescence into the field of capital equipment, making higher prospective rates of return necessary if investment is to take place.

We might note in passing two related trends which might weaken the response of investment to technological progress. Domar has suggested that the growth of monopoly and institutionalization of research have retarded innovation.[4] In other words, with a given rate of scientific progress, or a given flow of inventions, the rate of introduction of new techniques, or innovation, is slowed down by monopolistic control over research and its application. Obsolescence has become a major threat to the profitability of enterprise, and monopolists tend to delay introduction of new techniques in order to earn additional returns on past investment, unless total costs with the new technique are lower than operating costs with the old ones. With pure competition and freedom of entry, new firms would introduce the new techniques if total costs with them were lower than total costs, including overhead, with the old ones. Second, if Schumpeter is right about the deterioration of the social climate for entrepreneurship, a given rate of scientific progress (or of resource discovery) would bring forth a smaller volume of investment as an economy matures.

Aggravating Factors: The Loss of the "Frontier Spirit"

Although not spelled out or put into systematic form, Hansen's writings suggest another and more intriguing idea about the effect of "the closing of the frontier": the disappearance of the frontier is not just a matter of the tapering off of the rate of resource discovery; it also weakens the spirit of adventure in the field of business. The possibility of "going West, young man" to areas where the soil was fertile and mineral resources abundant, kept alive a venturesome entrepreneurial spirit throughout the century and a half of this country's most rapid expansion. The many cases of successful enterprises growing up with frontier communities gave rise to the "log cabin to riches" folklore of the United States and encouraged a generally optimistic attitude toward new commercial, industrial, and agricultural ventures. In the twentieth century, such opportunities for watching a new business grow with a frontier community were disappearing, and "young men" became more cautious in their attitude toward risk-taking.

[4] Evsey D. Domar, "Investment, Losses and Monopolies," in *Income, Employment, and Public Policy: Essays in Honor of Alvin Hansen* (New York, 1948).

In terms of our equations, then, the "disappearance of the frontier" would show up not only as a drop in K (the rate of discovery of new resources), but also a drop in the parameters dI_a/dK, and dI_a/dT, and dI_a/dL—that is, as a weakening of the response to given rates of resource discovery, technological progress, and population growth.

A Rising Propensity to Save?

As we have seen above, it is not necessary for the propensity to save to rise in order for the Hansen thesis to hold. It is only necessary for *ex ante* (planned) savings to continue rising with income, while at some point, investment drops because of the weakening of long-run growth forces. It is equally clear, however, that the tendency toward increasing underemployment will be stronger if *in addition* there is a secular trend toward a higher ratio of savings to income. Hansen has suggested that such a trend does in fact exist because of the increased "institutionalization" of savings. Corporations have relied increasingly on self-finance, rather than distributing profits in dividends and then appealing to the capital market for the funds needed for expansion. At the same time, increasing shares of personal savings have taken the form of such contractual obligations as insurance premiums, contributions to pension funds, and the like. One result is that the share of total income saved tends to rise through time. Another is that savings are less responsive to short-run fluctuations in income than they were when most savings were generated by periodic decisions of individuals not to spend all their current income.

Yet Hansen has also pointed out an "upward drift in the propensity to consume" in the United States national income data for the interwar period. How could the share of income saved rise if the share spent for consumption rose through the same period? The answer is that the two statements refer to quite different concepts. The contention that there is a tendency toward a rising propensity to save refers to the long-run *ex ante* savings function. This function shows how savings and consumption would change if income rose steadily but nothing else changed. In Figure 7–1, the long-run consumption function at time 1 is $C(Y)_t$. Some years later, this function has fallen to $C(Y)_{t+n}$, reflecting the rise in the long-run *ex ante* savings function with the "institutionalization" of saving. The amount of (actual or realized) *ex post* saving and consumption, however, depends not only on *ex ante* saving and consumption plans but also on the actual level of investment (public and private). The two together will determine the *actual* level of national income, and thus the *actual* level of savings and consumption. Moreover, the level of actual current consumption depends not only on current income, but also on the level of income reached in the last cyclical peak. When incomes rise, standards of living are adjusted to a higher level, after a lag; when incomes drop, an effort is made for some time to maintain these new standards of living. Thus when incomes fall, savings are squeezed out; the more incomes that fall, the more savings are squeezed out. The extent to which savings are squeezed out is reduced by the inflexibility introduced on the savings side by "institutional-ization," but the *net* effect is still an increase in the ratio of consumption to income when income drops.

Now the period 1919–35, during which the "upward drift in the consumption function" manifested itself, was one of particularly dramatic fluctuations in income. There were sharp drops in income between 1920 and 1922, between 1929 and 1933, and between 1937 and 1938. Thus this period was one in which the "squeezing out of savings" took place with a vengeance. The result is that the *data* of consumption and income—which by definition are *ex post* or realized positions—record the "upward drift," despite the *downward* drift of the long-run *ex ante* consumption function. In terms of Figure 7–1, the short-run consumption functions (dotted lines)

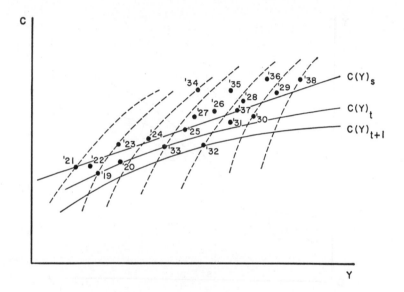

Figure 7–1

shift in such a way that, in conjunction with the actual fluctuations in income, they yield a scatter-diagram of consumption-income points that can be fitted by the straight line $C(Y)_s$, the statistical long-run consumption function. This curve actually lies above the initial long-run consumption function $C(Y)_t$. Thus the "upward drift in the consumption function" is the *result* of the particular depth and duration of the Great Depression, resulting partly from a rising trend in the *ex ante* propensity to save! This part of the Hansen thesis is thus an application to the theory of trend of a proposition now generally accepted with respect to economic fluctuations: the *effort* to save more, unless offset by higher investment, will result in the society's *actually* saving less.

Logical Validity of the Hansen Thesis

If the relationships postulated by Hansen exist, and if the variables have behaved as he says they have, there can of course be no question that his thesis of "increasing underemployment" in industrialized countries is right. If government policy were "neutral" the pattern of economic development would look like that in Figure 7–2. Once the long-run rate of economic growth generated by autonomous investment begins to taper off, economic fluctuations will take place around a trend of actual gross national product that falls farther and farther below the trend of potential (full employment) gross national product.

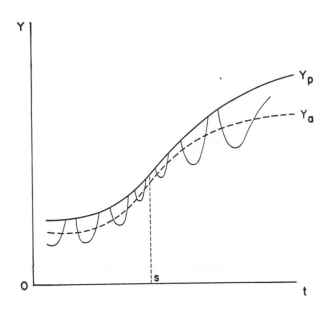

Figure 7–2 (Hansen)

In this diagram the curve Y_p is the trend of "potential income," that is, the trend of national income at full employment and with constant prices. The curve Y_a is the trend of actual gross national income at constant prices, around which economic fluctuations take place, as indicated by the dotted lines.[5]

---

[5] As indicated in my note on "The Concept of Secular Stagnation" (*American Economic Review*, March, 1950), "the trend of national income at full employment without inflation" is by no means a simple idea: " 'Inflation' in this context cannot mean any rise in the general price level; it must mean a rise that takes place (or continues) *after* full employment is reached. Such a definition of 'inflation' is clear

Strictly speaking, there are three trend curves in Hansen's concept: GNP at full employment, the historical trend, and the historical trend as it would be under "a policy of mid-nineteenth century laissez-faire." [6] The actual historical trend of the average level of GNP over cycles as a whole is in no small measure the product of fiscal policy, especially during war and immediate postwar periods. There is good reason to suppose that the Hansen thesis refers to a growing gap between GNP at full employment and the trend that would exist under a policy of complete fiscal neutrality. Whether this latter curve would lie above or below the historical trend is not certain. Fiscal policy has tended in the past to accentuate both upswings and downswings.[7] Economic expansion over long periods, such as the period of "railroadization," has usually been supported by government subsidies of one sort or another, but some booms appear to have been prematurely checked by deflationary monetary and fiscal policy. On the whole, it seems likely that the *trend* would not have been much different under a completely laissez faire fiscal policy; but this is one of the many questions surrounding the stagnation thesis that needs more thorough study.[8]

Hansen has little to say about the trend of national income at full employment. His thesis would be quite compatible with an increasing, con-

---

enough, but hides certain difficulties. If the points on the Y_p curve represent the levels of gross national income at which full employment is reached in the upswing, the only relevant points on the trend curve are those which lie on cyclical upswings; when national income goes through the trend curve in a downswing, full employment will not prevail. If the Y_p curve is defined as the trend of gross national income at full employment, with prices just high enough to yield full employment, the question arises as to just how high that would be. It is possible—perhaps even likely—that if full employment is reached when prices are rising, only a continually rising price level would maintain full employment. On the other hand, if full employment is reached after a period of fairly stable prices, as in 1929, it is conceivable that full employment could be maintained with a price level falling as techniques improve.

"The first interpretation is, I think, what most economists mean when they speak of 'full employment without inflation' as a goal of economic policy. If the war had ended just when full employment was reached late in 1941, the goal would have been to maintain full employment without a further rise in the general price level. Few economists indeed would oppose a limited price rise during an approach to full employment from a position of unemployment, if the price rise could be checked as soon as full employment was reached. The present situation is more complicated; what does full employment 'without inflation' mean today? It doesn't mean reducing prices to the 1941 level while maintaining full employment, although most economists would probably favour some 'disinflation' if it did not threaten full employment. The main question is, presumably, whether the distortion of the price-cost structure during the *past* inflation can be more easily cured by reducing prices that are too high, or by raising incomes that are too low.

"These ambiguities in the concept of 'full employment without inflation' are a strong argument for defining 'potential income' in real terms."

[6] Alvin Hansen, "Some Notes on Terborgh's *The Bogey of Economic Maturity*," *Review of Economic Statistics*, February, 1946, p. 13.

[7] Cf. Benjamin Higgins, *Public Investment and Full Employment* (Montreal, 1946), Part V.

[8] The nature of the underlying trend will affect the amplitude and duration of cycles, thus affecting in turn the statistical trend. See Benjamin Higgins, "Interaction of Cycles and Trends," *The Economic Journal*, December, 1955.

stant, or declining rate of growth of potential national income, provided the gap was present and growing. No doubt the implication in his discussion is that the rate of growth of potential, as well as actual, national income must eventually taper off. Indeed, no other hypothesis is reasonable. Given declining population growth and disappearing frontiers, it would take an ever-increasing rate of technological progress to keep the growth of national income at full employment from slowing down; and population and known supplies of mineral resources cannot be increased at a constant (percentage) rate indefinitely, if only because of purely spatial limitations.[9]

In order to distinguish the Hansen prognosis from those discussed above, we might translate the Classical, Marxist, and Schumpeterian views of capitalist development into a similar form. Although thinkers of the Classical school (particularly Malthus) were not unaware that unemployment might appear in a stagnant society, they were not primarily concerned with the gap between potential and actual income. For them, potential income itself would stagnate when both population growth and capital accumulation were choked off by the drop in profits and investment. Thus the Classical prognosis would look like Figure 7–3, which is simply one cross section of the three-dimensional Figure 3–2.

With Marx, until the downfall of capitalism through the revolution of the working classes, the picture of capitalist growth would be that of Figure 7–4. Here, too, a gap appears between the trend of potential gross national income and the trend of actual gross national income, but this gap is the product solely of increasing amplitude of cycles. Since national income in real terms cannot rise above the full employment level, increasing amplitude of fluctuations in real terms means increasingly severe downswings, which bring the trend of actual income farther and farther below the trend of potential national income.

Figure 7–5 is the Schumpeter version. The curve Y_a represents the trend of actual income at *current* prices, if the behavior of the system conforms to Schumpeter's "two-phase cycles," consisting of inflationary boom and return to equilibrium. Actually, of course, Schumpeter's theory included the dip below full employment levels, as a result of secondary and tertiary factors. It is not quite clear from Schumpeter's own writings whether he thought of the waning of entrepreneurial spirit as producing a gap between actual and potential income, or as checking the growth of actual income, in the fashion of the Classical school. Most of his writings suggest that it

---

[9] For a discussion of physical and technological limits to a constant rate of growth of national product, see M. King Hubbert, "Economic Transition and Its Human Consequences," *Advanced Management*, July–September, 1941, pp. 99, 100. He points out that for the percentage rate of increase in production from 1820 to 1910 (when the rate began to fall) to have been maintained, production in 1929 would have had to be 1.5 times its actual level, and in 1941 it would have had to be double its actual level; and he concludes "that any such exponential expansion . . . is a distinctly temporary state of affairs and that this phase must be followed by a long-time period of levelling off or decline." Any exponential expansion approaches infinite absolute growth at some point and is, therefore, an economic impossibility.

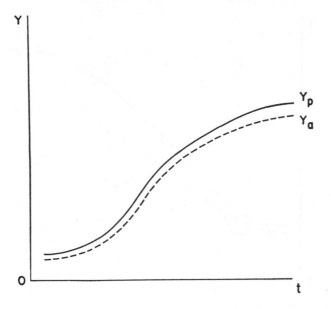

Figure 7–3 (Classics)

was the former that he had in mind. With the disappearance of the innovating entrepreneur, it would be the upswings that would get weaker and
weaker, so that the trend—which Schumpeter drew through the inflection
points, it will be remembered—would gradually flatten out. Figure 7–6
represents the Keynesian version of "unemployment equilibrium." There
is chronic underemployment, but it is not necessarily growing.

Thus we see that the distinguishing feature of Hansen's prognosis is
increasing underemployment as economies mature, in the absence of government action to raise the propensity to consume or to fill the gap with
public investment. This situation can occur without actual stagnation of
either the trend of potential gross national income or the trend of actual
gross national income, with or without intervention by the government.
Accordingly, it seems better to refer to the Hansen thesis as a theory of
increasing underdevelopment, rather than as a theory of stagnation. In
Figure 7–2, what Hansen called "stagnation" sets in at point s; yet neither
the actual nor the potential trend shows actual stagnation at that point. It
is probably less misleading to spell out the description of this situation; it
is one of the declining rates of growth and increasing underemployment.

Although Hansen's thesis has been bitterly attacked, the criticism has
not taken the form of challenging its logical validity, given the existence
of an autonomous investment function in the form Hansen postulated, and
assuming that the historical behavior of the strategic variables has been
what he said it was. Criticism has centered mainly on the latter aspect of
the Hansen thesis; most of his opponents have argued that his thesis does

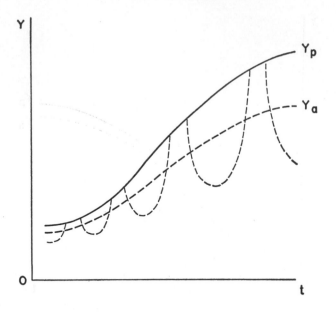

Figure 7–4 (Marx)

not explain the timing of the Great Depression. We shall have a word about these criticisms later.

A few critics, however, have challenged the validity of the long-run investment function itself. Clearly, for our purposes it is the latter criticisms that are important. Although the explanation of the Great Depression is not without interest for a general theory of economic development, it is not our primary concern. On the other hand, if Hansen's autonomous investment function holds good, it is an important tool of analysis of economic growth in advanced and underdeveloped countries alike. Accordingly, we turn now to an examination of the autonomous investment function.

The Autonomous Investment Function

As has been indicated in the earlier chapters, virtually all writers on economic development, from Adam Smith on, have recognized the importance of resource discovery and technological progress as factors in economic expansion. The Classical school regarded population growth as a drag on expansion, whereas Marx and Schumpeter tended to treat it as an exogenous factor. Thus of the components of Hansen's autonomous investment function, it is the relationship between long-run investment and population growth that is most original. Accordingly, let us begin our discussion of this function with the relationship between population

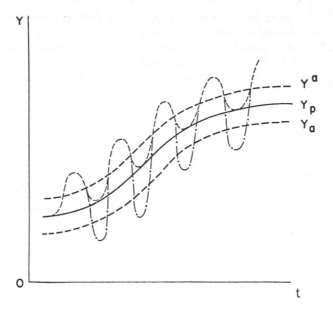

Figure 7-5 (Schumpeter)

growth and long-run investment.

Population growth affects investment in two main ways. First, a growing population provides a growing labor force. So long as population growth keep pace with capital accumulation, the marginal productivity of capital will, in the absence of other influences, remain constant; but when population growth falls off, capital accumulation must also fall off, if, apart from other influences, the marginal productivity of capital is not to decline. Second, a growing population provides an increasing demand for goods and services. The correlation between long-run increases of population and of consumption is so high that one can be more or less substituted for the other; and consequently the "acceleration principle" argument, which states that a mere drop in the rate of increase in consumption may cause an absolute decline in investment, can be applied with minor modifications to population.

The early discussion of population growth and investment failed to distinguish adequately between percentage and absolute rates of growth; and although this confusion has now been largely eliminated [10] there is still insufficient clarification as to which is more important and as to which is relevant to what arguments. Speaking generally, the absolute rate of

[10] *Vide* Hans A. Adler, "Absolute or Relative Rate of Decline in Population Growth?" *Quarterly Journal of Economics*, August, 1945; and Alvin Hansen, "Some Notes on Terborgh's *The Bogey of Economic Maturity*," *Review of Economic Statistics*, February, 1946, pp. 13–15.

growth is the more important concept, and a falling percentage rate of increase is significant mainly as a harbinger of a later drop in the absolute increase. So far as population as a source of labor is concerned, the percentage rate of increase is important only if it is necessary to maintain a certain percentage increase in quantity of capital in order to offset a

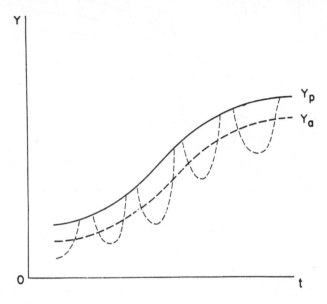

Figure 7–6 (Keynes)

given percentage increase in the volume of savings. However, this situation would be the real one to the extent that the volume of business saving in any year tends to equal a certain percentage of existing plant and equipment and, therefore, to rise at a cumulative rate. For the acceleration principle aspect of the argument, the absolute rate of increase is clearly more important.

Hansen's critics have not denied that in a country which starts its expansion with a scarcity of labor, population growth permits a more rapid rate of capital accumulation, without a drop in profits, than would be possible without population growth. The attack has concentrated more on the second part of the argument. Why must an increase in population carry with it an increasing effective demand for final products? What assurance is there that the increased numbers will be provided with additional income? Or conversely, if population growth is slowed down, why should not the rate of increase in per capita spending go up, so that the expansion of final demand remains the same?

Hansen's own argument was cast, not in terms of the effect of population growth on effective demand in general, but in terms of its effect on certain types of demand which seem particularly closely related to population growth:

It is not difficult to see [he argues] that a country experiencing a rapid increase in population requires a vast capital outlay in order to provide housing, transportation and all the facilities necessary for modern methods of living such as municipal utilities and the like. The enormous capital outlays of the nineteenth century were, of course, in the first instance conditioned by new technological developments, but they were determined also by the vast growth of population.

Hansen estimates that during the nineteenth century, the growth of population accounted for nearly half the outlay of new capital.

The surface plausibility of the argument seems greater if one thinks of a relationship between population growth and housing, transportation facilities, public utilities, and the like, than if one thinks of demand for goods and services in general. Certainly investors in these fields do think a good deal in terms of levels of population and potential rates of population growth. Actually, the same questions arise here as in the case of goods and services in general. What assurance is there that greater numbers of people will have proportionally increased incomes to spend on housing, transport, and the like? Or conversely, if population growth tapers off, why should people not have bigger houses, better transport facilities, and improved public services?

There is, of course, the possibility that people will spend their incomes differently if population is growing rapidly than they will if it is growing slowly, and that the pattern of spending with high rates of population growth is more stimulating to investment than the pattern which accompanies a low rate of population growth. At one point, Hansen does put his argument in those terms: [11]

Now the rate of population growth must necessarily play an important role in determining the character of the output; in other words, the composition of the flow of final goods. Thus a rapidly growing population will demand a much larger per capita volume of new residential building construction than will a stationary population. A stationary population with its larger proportion of old people may perhaps demand more personal services; and the composition of consumer demand will have an important influence on the quantity of capital required. The demand for housing calls for large capital outlays, while the demand for personal services can be met without making large investment expenditures. It is therefore not unlikely that a shift from a rapidly growing population to a stationary or declining one may so alter the composition of the final flow of consumption goods that the ratio of capital to output as a whole will tend to decline.

We would seem to be on more solid ground when the argument is put in these terms, but two questions of fact remain. Is it true that, as family size diminishes and the proportion of older people in the population rises, the demand for housing, transport facilities, and the like goes down while

[11] Alvin H. Hansen, "Progress and Declining Population," *The American Economic Review*, Vol. XXIX, No. 1, Part I (March, 1939), p. 7.

the demand for services goes up? And is it true that the capital-output ratio is lower for services than for housing, public utilities, and the like?

Efforts to test this part of the Hansen thesis empirically have not been very successful. For one thing, the relationship between investment and population growth is hard to isolate. There is, of course, no question that population growth in the United States has been highly correlated with the growth of investment, consumer spending, and national income. If we take the Kuznets data of national income for overlapping decades, and correlate either the level of national income or consumer spending with the level of population, the correlation coefficient for the period 1870–1929 is above .99 in both cases. In the case of investment the correlation with population growth for the period 1870–1919 is again in the neighborhood of .99. Because of the sharp drop in net investment during the 1919–21 depression, and the complete collapse of net investment during the Great Depression of the thirties, the correlation is of course considerably less high if one takes the whole period from 1870–1933.

The difficulty with these figures, as a test of the Hansen argument regarding the relation of investment to population growth, is precisely that population growth does correlate so highly with so many other economic variables. In an economy expanding as rapidly and as steadily as the American one did between 1870 and 1929, high correlations among major aggregate variables are bound to arise. It is very hard to determine causal relationships from such statistical correlations.

The critics of the Hansen thesis have accordingly tried to test the role of population growth in investment in other ways. For example, Fellner [12] endeavors to test the population aspect of the Hansen thesis by examining the relationship of population growth to the consumption function. This approach is unsatisfactory on several counts. First, the Hansen argument regarding population growth is not dependent upon upward shifts of the consumption function—although of course any tendency for the average or marginal propensity to consume to rise with population would strengthen Hansen's argument. Second there is the usual difficulty in historical statistical analysis that the historical relationship between income and consumption is the product of many factors, of which population growth is only one. Third, as we have shown above, the apparent stability of the (marginal) propensity to consume over the long run does not preclude the possibility that the historical relationship is the product of upward shifts in the function. Finally, the "over-all historical consumption function" shows absolute increases in income greater than the absolute increases in consumption over most periods. That is, investment also grew, and the growth of population may have been responsible for the growth of investment, without which the whole historical consumption function would have been different. Indeed, Fellner's figure 16, based on the Kuznets data, actually shows a very close relation between population growth and capital formation. If the "abnormal" World War I period is left out, the scatter can be well fitted by a very steep curve that is convex

[12] W. Fellner, *Monetary Policy and Full Employment* (Berkeley, Calif., 1946), Part II.

downward, suggesting that investment rises more than proportionately to population. The curve is so steep, however, as to suggest that factors other than population growth were dominant in the expansion of investment.

George Terborgh endeavored to test this part of the Hansen theory by comparing rates of population growth and rates of increase in per capita output of various countries in various periods. Since he finds no evidence that countries with high rates of population growth have had a more rapid rise in per capita production than countries with slow population growth, he dismisses the Hansen thesis on these grounds. As any statistician knows, however, the absence of such correlation in historical cases proves nothing in regard to the lack or presence of causal relationships. The countries and periods he compares are so varied that they do not come even close to isolating the effects of population growth on per capita output from all the other factors which were operative. In any case, to test the Hansen thesis Terborgh should have correlated investment with population growth rather than per capita output. Terborgh recognizes this fact but says that we need not worry about what happens to investment so long as production increases. This may be valid, but it is quite irrelevant to the problem of designing empirical tests of the Hansen argument with respect to population growth.

The truth in Hansen's population theory would seem to be something as follows. In Europe during the Industrial Revolution, and in the United States from the very beginnings of European settlement until the present day, population was small relative to resources, and the labor force was limited relative to the demand for labor. Population was chronically below optimum, in the strict sense that per capita output could have been raised by a simple increase in the population and in the labor force. Under these conditions, and with resource discovery and technological progress contributing to the maintenance of high rates of investment, the growth of population was accompanied by higher incomes and higher spending. Moreover, given the "lumpiness" of capital and the need for production at some minimal scale for effective use of some improved techniques, the very growth of the economy with population growth permitted more rapid technological progress. For this reason, entrepreneurs came to associate population growth with an expanding market, particularly for such highly durable consumer goods as housing, transport facilities, and public utilities. Indeed, forecasts of population growth became a major consideration in determining the scale of investment in such fields. For this reason, investment has in fact been highly correlated with population growth in advanced countries, and no doubt will continue to be so for some time to come, unless and until it becomes apparent to entrepreneurs that the relationship between consumer spending in these fields and population growth has broken down.

Resource Discovery and the Frontier

Few people indeed would deny that resource discoveries provide opportunities for investment. Hansen, however, had something more in mind than the rate of resource discovery in a purely quantitative sense. He argued that resource discovery in the *special* form of opening up a geographic frontier has particularly stimulating effects on private investment.[13] If we are to test this thesis, either in terms of the relationship between investment and frontier development, or in terms of the timing of the "disappearance of the frontier," we need a concept of "geographic frontier" more precise than Hansen's "discovery and development of new territory and new resources." [14] Moreover, when is a territory "new"? When it is entirely unpopulated, or when population per square mile is below a certain figure, or when the inhabitants do not practice the most modern techniques, or when its natural resources are not completely known? The mere presence of "unoccupied territory"—that is, land upon which no one is employed [15]—clearly does not constitute a frontier in the economic sense, if it is worth no one's while to employ someone to do something with it or on it. Yet growth of population in one part of a country may at some stage make it worthwhile to exploit previously unoccupied territory. Similarly, an innovation may make some previously worthless resource highly useful (witness atomic energy and known but untouched uranium deposits) and so make it worthwhile to move people into a region formerly unoccupied. A reduction in transportation costs, or cheaper power, may also result in development of known resources formerly left idle. Development of new territory is clearly one of the incidental effects of population growth and of some kinds of innovation. A shift in demand may also open up new territory.

Many tenable concepts of "geographic frontier" suggest themselves; but it seems most useful to define a *geographic* frontier as an area within which there are increasing returns to both labor and capital with existing technical knowledge, population, and tastes. An area within which increasing returns would appear only with a change in techniques, population, or tastes might be called an *economic* frontier. Thus, "economic frontiers" become "geographic frontiers" as a result of dynamic changes. The frontier might be said to have "disappeared" when the point of di-

[13] Adequate investment outlets are necessary to sustain full employment and a satisfactory income level. But investment outlets are more difficult to find in a nonexpanding economy. We are living in a period which is, in several important respects, distinctly different from the nineteenth century. It was one thing to find adequate investment outlets in a century quite unique in the world's history—a century with vast, rich areas inviting occupation and large capital outlays on housing, manufacturing, and transportation equipment. In such an expanding economy, investment outlets were easy to find and indeed the main difficulty was a shortage of capital and manpower. Now all this has changed and we are confronted with an economy with no large, rich areas to be occupied anywhere in the entire globe (see Isaiah Bowman, ed., *Limits of Land Settlement*, New York, 1937) and with a practically stationary population in the industrial countries. Cf. Hansen, *Full Recovery or Stagnation* (New York, 1938), pp. 312–13.

[14] American Co-ordinating Committee for International Studies, "A Report to the Tenth International Studies Conference," Paris, June 18–July 3, 1937.

[15] An alternative definition of "unoccupied" territory would be land for which no legal ownership has been established; but for economic analysis this definition seems less convenient, and Hansen himself has rejected it. "Some Notes on Terborgh's *The Bogey of Economic Maturity*," *Review of Economic Statistics*, February, 1946, p. 15.

minishing average returns to labor and/or capital has been reached; and might be said to "begin disappearing" when the point of diminishing marginal returns to labor and/or capital has been reached.

As used in the Hansen thesis, however, the concept of "frontier" is a relative one. The existence of a "new" area into which labor and capital are being moved implies the existence of an "old" area from which labor and capital come; and the "opening up of a frontier" involves movement of labor and capital. Increasing returns to labor and capital is a necessary, but not a sufficient, condition for an area to be a geographic frontier; in the nineteenth century, England as well as America would have fulfilled this condition. For a region to constitute a geographic frontier, therefore, one of the following additional conditions must be present as well:

1. It may be an area where the most advanced *known* techniques are not utilized.

2. It may be an area where the marginal productivity of labor and/or capital is less high than in other countries, because the ratio of labor and/or capital to natural resources is lower than in other countries.

3. It may be an area capable of absorbing capital, population, and goods without an equal return flow to other countries, that is, a country able and willing to have an import surplus. (This condition may be a characteristic of all frontier economies, rather than a separate criterion.)

4. A frontier might be said to exist if migration of labor and capital into a "new" area will raise the marginal productivity of labor and capital in the "mature" economy, without raising it above the level in the "new" territory.

A less tangible factor which may nevertheless play some role is "frontier psychology." In economic terms, this factor would consist of a relatively low level of liquidity—and safety—preference, or a relatively high marginal efficiency of capital, for any given set of objective conditions.

These definitions also make it possible to distinguish the development of a frontier from mere migration of industry. If investment of labor and capital in the "new" area is accompanied by a decline in the amount of labor and capital utilized in the "old" area (either in a particular field or in the whole economy of the area), there has been a migration of industry (either in a particular field or in the whole economy). Migration of industry may nevertheless result in temporary increase in *current* investment in the "old" and "new" areas combined, because the fixed plant of the old area cannot be moved to the new one. When the movement into a "new" area results in a rise in the amount of labor and capital utilized in the "old" area, the increment constitutes the development of a frontier. Thus by definition, the opening of a frontier results in an increase in investment in the new and old economies combined.

The importance of the distinction between the geographic and economic frontiers as here defined can hardly be exaggerated. In countries where a geographic frontier exists, there is now, with present knowledge, techniques, and tastes, a supply of fertile agricultural land and mineral resources to be exploited. In terms of the production function, the existence of a geographic frontier has the same effects on the marginal efficiency of capital as population growth; that is, it keeps capital always relatively scarce, and returns on new investment relatively high. Neither industrial nor agricultural investment runs into a bottleneck with respect to natural resources. The existence of a geographic frontier also keeps labor scarce, even in agriculture, a factor of enormous import in the comparison of advanced with underdeveloped economies, as we shall see below. And this was the situation that existed in the United States from the beginning of European settlement until the late nineteenth century, if not later.

Quite different was the case of Europe in the nineteenth century, with the fertile soil already under cultivation, and with the mineral resources that were important with the then *existing* techniques already discovered. The Classical school was right to worry about diminishing returns to increased supplies of labor on the given supply of land; scarcity of foodstuffs and raw materials was truly a barrier to capital accumulation, which was broken only by the development of the New World and the expansion of world trade.

Quite different, too, is the case of countries like Indonesia. Many Indonesians are convinced that there are more natural resources to be discovered, but nobody knows where they are. Moreover, the present distribution of population reflects accurately the relative fertility of the soil. In the Philippines, too, past response to population pressure has been to bring more land under cultivation, so as to maintain customary ratios of labor to land with traditional techniques; but now the point is being reached where this sort of "widening" of capital in agriculture is no longer possible without resorting to inferior land. The "geographic frontier" is disappearing, leaving only a dubious "economic frontier," provided that techniques or tastes change, or something else happens.

In the United States, frontier development, as well as population growth, correlates highly with general economic expansion, whether measured in terms of investment or in terms of consumption or gross national product. In a generally growing economy such correlations are bound to appear. As an approximation to a quantitative measure of frontier development, we might use "westward movement" as shown by the center of population. When we plot the degree of west longitude of the center of population between 1790 and 1950 on the vertical axis and the year on the horizontal axis, we get an almost perfect growth curve. The inflection point occurs in 1850 at about 81 degrees west; "marginal westward movement," which we take as an approximation to "marginal rate of frontier development," reached its peak at that time. The "average rate of westward movement" or "average rate of frontier development" was at its height toward the end of the nineteenth century, with the center of population at about 88 degrees west longitude. Despite variations over time, both private investment and national income follow much the same growth pattern, when the "trend" is separated out from cyclical fluctuations.

In terms of westward movement, investment, and income, one other country would show much the same pattern of development: Canada, the country which has achieved the *second* highest standard of living. No other country enjoyed the continual presence of a geographic frontier throughout the century and a half of its most rapid growth.

In one respect, however, the American case is absolutely unique. For the westward movement does not tell the whole story of frontier development in the United States; there have been movements north and south from the center as well. Texas and the Pacific Northwest served as geographic frontiers after the westward movement of the center of population had virtually ceased. The relative stability of the center in this century does not reflect lack of population movement, but rather the diffusion of new resource development north and south, and even east and west, of this center. No other country can match the remarkable spread of urban growth throughout its entire area, in wave after successive wave, that has occurred in the United States. In Canada, urban development has been confined to a narrow strip within a few hundred miles of the United States border, and only two great cities have been created there. Australian frontier development built no cities away from the coast. In Europe, the major cities have grown up side by side over several centuries; there has been no progressive opening up of new frontiers, followed by urban growth, such as has occurred in this country. The story of Chicago, Detroit, Kansas City, St. Louis, Dallas, Houston, and Los Angeles is a purely American story. It is surely not unreasonable to suppose that this continuous opening up of new areas and the concomitant urban growth has been a major factor, both in providing investment opportunities and in keeping alive the "log cabin to riches" folklore and the enterprising spirit that goes with it.[16]

The contrast between American and Australian frontier development is of particular interest. Dr. Carter Goodrich was among the first to recognize that the relative lack of venturesome entrepreneurship in Australia, and the accompanying relative stagnation after 1924, can be traced in part to the absence of a "poor man's frontier," of the kind that prevailed in Canada or the United States, and an accompanying absence of westward movement.[17] The acquisition of huge tracts of land by "rich squatters"

[16] For an account of the role of the frontier in American history, see Frederick Jackson Turner, *The Frontier in American History* (New York, 1920) and *The Significance of Sections in American History* (New York, 1932). For an analysis of Turner's and other frontier theories, see F. L. Paxson, *History of the American Frontier 1763–1893* (Boston, 1924). A brief review of these theories and an application to Australia can be found in Fred Alexander, *Moving Frontiers* (Melbourne, 1947).

[17] Carter Goodrich, "The Australian and American Labor Movements," *The Economic Record*, November, 1928. For a generation after 1924 man-year productivity in Australia stagnated relative both to previous trends in Australia and in comparison with other young countries. The role of the "big man's frontier" in producing a mid-nineteenth century Australian society "in terms of a few flockmakers, bankers, and merchants, and a numerous peon class," and the thesis that "Australia owes much of its collectivism to the fact that its frontier was hospitable to the large man," instead of to the small man, as in the United States, are spelled out in Brian Fitzpatrick, *The British Empire in Australia: An Economic History* (Melbourne, 1941).

South African frontier development seems to have been intermediate between the Australian and American cases, but somewhat closer to the Australian than to the American pattern. See S. Daniel Neumark, *Economic Influences on the South African Frontier 1652–1836* (Stanford, Calif., 1957).

created employment opportunities in the suburbs of Melbourne and Sydney, but not in the center of the country. Development of the center resulted in population growth on the fringe, not in the center. Clearly, it requires a different sort of attitude to set up a grocery in a suburb of Sydney than to move hundreds of miles to the westward and launch a new enterprise in a strange raw territory. Moreover, the opportunity to start a small business and watch it grow into a large one as the city grew around you was confined to a few coastal centers. The "log cabin to riches" legend had less meaning in Australia than in the United States.

But if a frontier in the Canadian or American sense was lacking in Australia, its absence is still more striking in the case of most underdeveloped areas. For centuries, such economic development as took place brought no obvious movement in the center of population. Nothing remotely resembling the westward movements in the United States and Canada, or even the movements from country areas to cities in nineteenth-century England, has taken place in most underdeveloped areas. Consequently, no "frontier spirit" is to be found in these countries.[18] Is it not possible that venturesome entrepreneurship, inculcated by generations of steady movement to new territories, may extend also to the frontiers of technology? May there not be a relationship between the lack of interest in movement to new territories and the lack of interest in the introduction of new techniques?

Application to Underdeveloped Areas

When Hansen's theory was developed, he, like Harrod, was concerned primarily with problems of advanced countries. Accordingly, he did not attempt an application of his theory to underdeveloped countries. But as with Harrod, so with Hansen we are free to make that application and see what enlightenment can be gained thereby.

In applying the Hansen system, however, we must begin by making changes in the equations to take account of differences in the institutional and sociological framework between advanced and underdeveloped countries; in this sense, because it is specified more completely, Hansen's theory is less "general" than Harrod's.

The Investment Function

The most significant change we must make relates to the role of population growth. There is a sharp contrast in the effects of population growth under conditions in which population is kept continuously below optimum because development starts with a low population base, as it did in the now advanced countries, and its effects where development starts with population far above optimum. As we have seen earlier, where increases in population bring increases in per capita output, merely because labor is a relatively scarce factor, population growth has a favorable effect on investment in a number of ways. The increase in scale of the economy, and the

[18] North Sumatra and some of the larger Latin American countries may be exceptions to this rule. See the case study of Brazil that follows.

growth of the market, not only provide increasing demand for housing, transport facilities, public utilities, and the like, but permit the use of better and already known techniques. (The selection of better techniques from among those that are already known should be not confused with technological progress, viz., the introduction of superior but hitherto unknown techniques.) It also means that optimal proportions can be maintained between labor and other factors of production, particularly capital, as capital accumulates. Where populations are already above optimum levels, however, where lack of savings rather than lack of effective demand limits investment, and where an addition to the labor supply would lower per capita output and income even if the additional workers were fully employed, population growth is a drag on economic development. It may prevent per capita income from increasing, or even lower per capita income, thus aggravating the difficulty of saving (and investing) enough to generate expansion.

We shall see more clearly below that in the conditions of underdeveloped countries population growth often adds to underemployment rather than to income. Accordingly, entrepreneurs have no reason to associate population growth, particularly in rural areas, with increased demand. Moreover in village communities, housing, irrigation systems, roads, and the like are often provided on a self-help or mutual-aid basis, so that growth of rural population does not lead to any increase in *monetary* investment, but only to a direct "widening" of capital, so long as more land and other natural resources are available.

Hansen was concerned with investment as a generator of money income. Later, when we are concerned with capital-output ratios and the impact of capital accumulation on real income, we shall find it expedient to reintroduce L into the investment function. At the moment, however, we shall drop the term L from our monetary investment equation and rewrite it in the form:

$$I = I_g + I_i(\dot{Y}) + I_A (\dot{K}, \dot{T}) \tag{1}$$

This alteration is the only one we need make in the actual form of the equation, but there will also be differences in the value of some of the variables. For one thing, for reasons which will become apparent below, we can expect $\delta I_A/\delta K \cdot d^2K/dt^2$ (increases in autonomous investment due to acceleration of resource discovery) to be lower in most of the present underdeveloped countries than it was in the advanced countries at the beginning of their industrialization. Considerable resource discovery has already taken place in most underdeveloped countries, and there is little reason to suppose that the *rate* of resource discovery will rise significantly in the future as compared with the last century. True geographic frontiers exist in very few of these countries. As stated above, the distribution of population reflects quite accurately the relative fertility of the soil, and all known mineral deposits have been under development for some time. Few of the underdeveloped countries present the opportunity of moving from the now occupied areas to land *still richer* in agricultural and mineral resources, an opportunity that existed in the New World between, say,

1750 and 1900. And without internal migration the "frontier spirit" will not accompany resource discovery.

On the other hand, there may be some hope that the $\delta I_A/\delta T \cdot d^2T/dt^2$ (increases in autonomous investment through acceleration of technological progress) will be higher in underdeveloped countries than it ever was in advanced ones, at least for some time. During the "catching up period," while underdeveloped countries are applying known techniques which have been developed in advanced countries, but for which the necessary capital has not hitherto been available, a very rapid rate of technological progress may be generated. There are limitations even here, as we shall see. The techniques which have been most successful in advanced countries are considerably less suited to conditions in underdeveloped ones. But even with this limitation, a significant rate of technological progress should be obtainable.

It is also possible that the parameter I_A (the relationship between autonomous investment and given rates of growth) will increase through time, as the supply of New Men in underdeveloped countries increases, as objective and subjective security is improved, and greater political stability is achieved.

Finally, it is likely that I_i, the parameter relating induced investment to changes in income, will be particularly high and perhaps rising in underdeveloped countries. When inventory accumulation is included in investment, as it should be if we are considering the possibilities of steady growth in underdeveloped countries, we must take account of the readiness of entrepreneurs in underdeveloped countries to speculate on price rises through the accumulation of stock. As entrepreneurs increase in numbers and become more sophisticated, their response to changes in income may be even stronger than it is now.

The Savings Function

In order to take account of all the factors operative in underdeveloped countries, the form of the savings function should also be changed. We could write $S = S(O_a, r, p)$, where r is the interest rate and p is the rate of time preference. In discussing the long-run savings function in advanced countries, we ignored the effects of interest rate and of time preference. There were good reasons for doing so. In the first place, there is considerable evidence that interest rates play a minor role in determining the volume of savings in advanced countries. However that may be, with interest rates as low as they are in advanced countries, any long-run trend toward still lower interest rates cannot have very much effect. Thus the $\delta S/\delta r$ is small, dr/dt is small, and $\delta S/\delta r \cdot dr/dt$ is very small indeed. In underdeveloped countries, however, effective interest rates are sometimes extremely high. Therefore, there is a good possibility that the trend dr/dt may be of quantitative importance. Also, although savings may not alter very much where most savings are institutionalized and interest rates are in any case low, where personal savings play a more important role, and effective interest rates may be in excess of 40 per cent per year, reduction of interest rates may indeed have an effect on savings. Thus $\delta S/\delta r \cdot dr/dt$

(the response of savings to declining interest rates) in underdeveloped countries may be quantitatively significant.

On the other hand, $\delta S/\delta p \cdot dp/dt$ (the response of savings to diminishing time preference) may also be significant, and would tend to move in the opposite direction. There is ample evidence of a high rate of time preference in underdeveloped countries, particularly in the village communities where families will borrow several months' income in order to have an appropriate feast on the occasion of a wedding, funeral, or circumcision. As economies mature and people become more sophisticated, they tend to take more interest in the future—or so Harrod argues—and consequently the rate of time preference drops. On this score one could expect a rising trend in the proportion of income saved. Thus as we move through time, the saving schedule will tend to shift upwards, because of the decline in time preference. Savings will also tend to increase through a movement along the schedule to higher levels of income. There will be one offsetting factor, the drop in interest rates. Taking all these factors together, we can probably expect some increase in the ratio of savings to income, and perhaps also in the ratio of increases in savings to increases in income, in the early phases of economic development. In terms of our equations, this would mean that the multiplier would tend to fall in the first phase of economic growth.

Implications for Steady Growth

Does all this add up to "chronic inflation" in underdeveloped countries, as the other side of the coin of chronic increasing underemployment in advanced countries? Not necessarily; stagnation is another possibility. Looking again at Equation (1), in many underdeveloped countries both K and T are low and are not increasing rapidly. That is, the rates of technological progress and resource discovery are not particularly high, and are not noticeably rising. Autonomous investment is on a very low level. Public investment is also low, because of limited tax and borrowing capacity of the government. Thus national income is not rising very rapidly either and induced investment will be close to zero. With low levels of income, the average and marginal propensity to save are also low. The multiplier is high, but there is nothing to multiply. The result is an economy which stagnates with levels of per capita income close to the subsistence level.

What is certainly true, however, is that in such a society any event favoring growth immediately creates inflationary pressure. If, for example, public investment for development purposes increases, income will rise; induced investment will come into play, and the high multiplier will begin to operate. Output cannot possibly keep pace with the increase in money income that will be generated, and inflation is the only possible result.

The same sequence will ensue if something happens to raise the rate of resource discovery or technological progress so that autonomous private investment increases suddenly. Since development plans are designed primarily to raise the public investment in development projects and to encourage autonomous investment for development purposes, it is apparent that under the conditions prevailing in underdeveloped countries, the undertaking of a development program will almost inevitably create severe inflationary pressure. The very fact that the rates of resource discovery and technological progress are low in percentage terms, and that both autonomous investment and government investment are small percentages of national income, means that a rather small *absolute* increase in any of these variables can constitute a very large *percentage* increase. Yet the percentage increase in the actual supplies of the resources, labor, and technique, will still be small in the short run. Consequently, the increase in output will also be small in percentage terms, particularly during the gestation period of the new development projects.

Thus although inflation need not be "chronic" if nothing is done to accelerate the rate of economic growth in underdeveloped countries, it is always endemic, and it becomes epidemic whenever vigorous action is taken to increase the rate of economic growth.

8

Summary
and Synthesis
of General Theories
# of Development

The years since World War II have seen a return of interest to the problem that attracted most of the attention of economists, and much of the attention of statesmen, in the late eighteenth and early nineteenth centuries: how to assure continually rising standards of living? Currently, this problem is discussed under the heading, "economic development." The term is recent, the basic concept as old as economics. Fundamentally, it means rising per capita incomes. In an effort to make the concept a little more precise, however, we now define it as "a discernible rise in total and in per capita income, widely diffused throughout occupational and income groups, continuing for at least two generations, and becoming cumulative."

An underdeveloped country, then, is one in which this process has not taken place during the last two centuries and where, accordingly, per capita income is still low. "Low" is a relative term and any division between "low" and "high" incomes is necessarily arbitrary. We have chosen the figure of $600 per capita. This choice is designed to include all those countries that are underdeveloped in a policy sense; that is, countries "with announced goals and policies with regard to economic development and which are regarded as candidates for technical and capital assistance under the foreign aid programs of the United States and other advanced Western countries." Such countries have per capita incomes estimated at under $50 to about $600 per year.

There are, of course, significant differences among countries falling into this classification. Obviously, the problem of economic development is more pressing where per capita incomes are below $100 per year than it is where incomes are between $300 and $600. Some underdeveloped countries are resource-poor, some are relatively resource-rich. Some have low but rising incomes; some are both poor and stagnant. But all are alike in considering it important to discover ways to launch and sustain, or to sustain where already launched, a process of continually rising standards of living.

This part of the book has been devoted to a review of general theories of economic development from Adam Smith and Malthus to Harrod and Hansen. In closing, we shall endeavor to pin down major points of agreement in general theories of economic growth and to evaluate this body of knowledge as a basis for policy in underdeveloped countries.

Similarities and Differences

In summarizing the theories outlined in the previous chapters, it may be useful to turn once again to our equations, which permit us to show similarities and differences in schematic forms. First of all, there are three equations and two identities which run through all the theories:

$$\text{the production function} \ldots O = f(L, K, Q, T) \qquad (1)$$
$$\text{the technical progress function} \ldots \dot{T} = T(I) \qquad (2)$$
$$\text{the investment function} \ldots I = dQ = I(R) \qquad (3)$$
$$\text{and two identities} \ldots O = C + I \qquad (4)$$
$$O = R + W \qquad (5)$$

One equation is common to Marx and the Classics:

$$\text{the wages-bill function} \ldots W = W(I) \qquad (6)$$

Three equations are important in the Classical system but not in the others:

$$\text{the population growth function} \ldots L = L(W) \qquad (7)$$
$$\text{the profits function} \ldots R = R(T, L) \qquad (8)$$
$$\text{the iron law of wages} \ldots W = wL \qquad (9)$$

Population growth and consequent diminishing returns to labor on the land play a less significant role in the other theories than in the Classical one. These nine equations close the Classical system, since we have specified eight variables, w, the subsistence level of wages, being given.

In their theories of profit, Malthus, Marx, and the "moderns" (Schumpeter, Harrod, and Hansen) differ from the Classics. They recognize the importance of technological progress (and resource discovery) as a creator of profit opportunities, but they also recognize the importance of effective demand and the drag on profit rates and investment of the existing stock of capital. They also stress the relationship between income, effective demand, profits, and investment. Marx considered wages particularly important as a generator of consumer spending. The others are aware that the propensity to consume out of wages may be higher than the propensity to consume out of profits, but would consider both income streams important in determining effective demand. Thus we have instead of the Classical Equation (8),

the profits function . . . $R = R(T, C, Q)$ (8)

and the demand function . . . $C = C_1(W) + C_2(R)$ (9)

The moderns have been more concerned than the nineteenth-century economists with the determination of money income and the whole savings-investment relationship. This concern adds two equations:

definition of savings . . . $S = Y - C$ (10)

the multiplier equation . . . $Y = k \cdot I = \dfrac{1}{dS/dY} \cdot I$

and $\Delta Y = \dfrac{1}{dS/dY} \Delta I$ (11)

The moderns introduced a distinction between induced and autonomous investment, and for policy purposes, found it useful to separate out government investment as well. They stressed technological progress and resource discoveries as generators of autonomous investment. Hansen and Harrod also emphasized population growth; Schumpeter was more ambivalent about it. Induced investment in turn depends on changes in income (or its major components). This analysis adds three equations:

$$I = I_A + I_i + I_g \qquad\qquad (12)$$
$$I_a = I_A(K, T, L) \qquad\qquad (13)$$
$$I_i = I_i(Y) \qquad\qquad\qquad (14)$$

These equations close the "modern" system.

Harrod adds an important new factor—or rather, brings it out into the open—in the form of the capital-output ratio. We can express it $Q = r \cdot O$. Later we shall want to use an output-capital ratio which is the reciprocal of this: [1] $O = a \cdot Q$.

Where does all this lead us?

---

[1] We might note in passing that the "moderns" determine the distribution of income between wages and profits through the production function. With an appropriate definition of the factors of production,

$$O = \frac{\delta f}{\delta L} \cdot L + \frac{\delta f}{\delta Q} \cdot Q$$

That is, total output is the sum of (marginal productivity of labor times number of units of labor employed) plus (marginal productivity of capital times number of units of capital). Under pure competition,

$$\frac{W}{L} = \frac{\delta f}{\delta L} \qquad \text{and} \qquad \frac{R}{Q} = \frac{\delta f}{\delta Q}$$

The wage rate equals marginal productivity of labor, the rate of profit the marginal productivity of capital (fixed factors). Thus

$$W = \frac{\delta f}{\delta L} \cdot L \qquad \text{and} \qquad R = \frac{\delta f}{\delta Q} \cdot Q$$

Each factor of production derives from national income what it "contributes" to it. Under monopoly conditions this relationship breaks down and the outcome depends on bargaining power.

Application to Underdeveloped Areas

First of all, let us note that even the relationships in the "agreed" system tell us some useful things about development policy. Look at the production function, for example. Even so simple a statement as this provides guidance as to the proximate causes of higher standards of living. Without capital accumulation, resource discovery, population growth, or technological progress, increases in output are impossible. When the form of the production function is specified on the basis of empirical knowledge, the equation tells us also that the level of production depends not only on the quantities of factors of production and the degree of technological advance but also on the proportions in which the factors are combined— a very important consideration. In other words, for every "factor endowment," there is an optimal combination of factors of production. One of the purposes of development planning is to find this combination and see to it that it is maintained.

Among the writers discussed, there is, moreover, substantial agreement concerning the relative importance of the factors in the production function and the interrelations among them. In all these theories, pride of place is given to *technological progress,* the introduction of new techniques which raise the productivity of available resources, especially labor. The Industrial Revolution of the eighteenth and nineteenth centuries was essentially a period of remarkably rapid introduction of new machines, new materials, new sources of power, and new processes. In the advanced countries, this process of "innovation" continues at a high rate, productivity continues to increase, and *per capita* incomes continue to rise. Speaking generally, the highly developed countries are also developing most rapidly—one of the many bits of evidence that economic progress is largely a matter of getting started.

The key figure in this process of technological advance is the entrepreneur. He is the man who sees the opportunity for introducing the new commodity, technique, raw material, or machine, and brings together the necessary capital, management, labor, and materials to do it. He may not be, and historically has usually not been, the scientific inventor; his skills are less scientific than organizational. His skills are also different from those of the salaried manager, who takes over an enterprise *after* it has been launched. In any society, the rate of technological progress, and so of economic development, depends greatly on the number and ability of entrepreneurs available to it. But a few entrepreneurs may go a long way in promoting economic expansion. In the now advanced countries, once a leader has shown the way—to steam power, or electricity, or better textile machinery, or automobiles, or airplanes, or whatever—a "cluster of followers" has joined the parade in search of profits, power, or public weal.

The acquisition of new manual, managerial, and professional skills is virtually inseparable from resource discovery and technological change. Economic development can scarcely occur without some improvement of skills, and learning more productive ways of operating rarely takes place without the use of new techniques or the discovery of new resources. Learning to use the *same* tools and the *same* materials more efficiently has seldom brought substantial increases in productivity; it has never been the mainspring of economic growth. It is hard to think of any improvement of skill, in and of itself, that did have revolutionary economic effects. This statement is not meant to belittle acquisition of skills as a factor in economic development; in the present underdeveloped countries, improving skills is exceedingly important. But it is also important to remember that improvement of skills does not take place in a vacuum; for the most part, it means using better tools or better materials. No degree of skill can make a sickle as effective as a well-handled scythe; no amount of training will enable the man with a scythe to cut as much hay as the man with a reaper.

Thus capital accumulation is the very core of economic development. Whether in a predominately private enterprise system like the American, or in a communistic system like the Russian or the Chinese, economic development cannot take place without capital accumulation: the construction of irrigation systems, use of fertilizers and better seeds or livestock, land reclamation, building dams, bridges, or factories with machines in them, roads, railways, and airports, ships, and harbors—all the "produced means of further production" associated with high levels of productivity. Many underdeveloped countries have a particularly pressing need for "social capital"—equipment used by society at large, rather than by particular enterprises, such as transport facilities, public utilities, schools, and hospitals. But the process of building up the necessary stock of capital equipment has an inescapable financial counterpart—in private enterprise and communist systems alike. Either a part of national income must be saved or paid in taxes to pay for the purchase or production of capital goods, or the necessary funds must be borrowed abroad.

Can capital accumulation take place without technological progress? Society could just go on building more transport facilities, more sources of power, more factories, of the same sort; this process is sometimes called "widening" of capital, in contrast with "deepening," which implies use of more capital-intensive techniques. None of the theories of development outlined above expected progress from "widening" alone. In all of them, capital accumulation and technological progress go hand in hand. Capital accumulation is *possible* without technological improvement, but technological improvement is virtually impossible without prior capital accumulation. For the most part, the most efficient techniques require heavy investment for their introduction, even if they reduce capital costs per unit of output once they are installed and operating. All these theories imply that no nation that is unwilling either to save and pay taxes, or to borrow abroad, will enjoy the fruits of the most advanced techniques.

Equation (2) of the "agreed" system thus becomes a crucial one. Once we recognize that technological improvements of all kinds—including improvements in labor and managerial skills—require investment for their *introduction*, whether or not the innovations prove capital saving when in place, we need not dwell upon whether capital accumulation is as important as technological progress, or whether an underdeveloped country can get out of its rut through technical improvements alone and avoid the harsh necessity of saving more or borrowing abroad. The process of technological progress is inseparably linked with the process of capital accumulation. True, an advanced economy that has already accumulated a large stock of capital, and which generates a continuous flow of capital-saving innovations, may be able to maintain a respectable rate of economic growth without net savings and investment, merely by reinvesting depreciation allowances in ever more efficient equipment and organization. But this possibility offers little comfort to underdeveloped countries, since they cannot take advantage of it until the stock of capital and the level of technique have already been raised far above existing levels.

The third equation of the "agreed" system also tells us something important: if the process of capital accumulation (and thus of improving technology) is to be left to private initiative, it must be profitable—at least as profitable, after appropriate discounting for differences in safety and liquidity of assets, as it is in advanced countries. The point is axiomatic and should also be obvious; but as we shall see in Chapter 26 below, it is a point ignored by the governments of many, if not most, underdeveloped countries. For many underdeveloped countries still rely heavily on private investment in their development planning, while imposing severe limitations on its profitability and introducing measures which reduce the safety and liquidity of assets.

The point is made more strongly in the Schumpeter analysis. In his view neither capital accumulation nor technical progress will reach high levels through private initiative unless the social, political, and economic "climate" is one conducive to the appearance of a large and growing supply of entrepreneurs. Few indeed of the underdeveloped countries have made serious efforts to create such a climate.

Economists of all periods have agreed on three other points arising from analysis of the interactions among the causal relations expressed in the equations. First, all theories of economic development imply a tendency for capitalist economies to stop growing after an advanced stage of development has been reached. Hansen and his followers suggest ways in which this tendency can be offset in a "mixed" economy. Harrod and Schumpeter are less optimistic but would certainly recommend the effort. Second, all are agreed that growth or acceleration of growth tends to bring instability (although the Classical school made little of this point). *Steady* growth is very difficult, perhaps impossible, to attain, although here, too, Hansen and his followers are more optimistic than most economists who have analyzed the problem, contending that the right combination of monetary and fiscal policy can do much to eliminate instability in the economy while sustaining growth. Third, although with varying emphasis, all the economists discussed in this part agree that expansion of international trade and investment provides an "escape valve" from stagnation in advanced countries and helps to bring the transition from stagnation to expansion in underdeveloped ones. The size of the market is treated as a major factor in determining potential growth rates. In Malthus' exposition this concept is stated in terms of "balanced growth": in a closed economy the growth of one sector is limited by the size of the other(s). These limitations can be overcome by expansion of foreign trade, which brings an effective increase in the size of the market for one or more sectors in the economy.

Of these three propositions, only the second is of much use in approaching the problems of underdeveloped countries. The governments or peoples of underdeveloped countries are unlikely to eschew economic development for fear that, having achieved the levels of income of the United States or the United Kingdom, they may need an ingenious set of policy measures to assure further advance. Only if the causes of stagnation in advanced countries were similar to the causes of stagnation in underdeveloped ones would this facet of development theory be of great importance in underdeveloped countries today. At first glance the relationship between the two kinds of stagnation seems rather remote; stagnation in advanced countries results mainly from a tendency for *ex ante* savings to exceed investment at high levels of employment. Stagnation in underdeveloped countries results from low levels of investment *and* of *ex ante* savings at *any* level of employment. Policies designed to cure the first sort of stagnation are unlikely to cure the second, as we shall see more clearly in Part V. The third proposition seems irrelevant to the present underdeveloped countries. Many of these have experienced substantial inflow of foreign capital and impressive expansion of foreign trade, without any apparent increase in the average incomes of the domestic population. This seeming paradox is the subject of Chapters 13 and 14.

The relationship between growth and instability, however, is one for the governments and peoples of underdeveloped countries to ponder. Our preliminary efforts to apply the modern theories of fluctuations to underdeveloped countries suggest that, once launched, ambitious programs of economic development are almost certain to be inflationary in their original impact; if inflation is checked after it starts, the outcome is likely to be a series of fluctuations. On the other hand, insistence that development must not have any destabilizing effects may hamper economic growth. The problem confronting underdeveloped countries, then, is to determine the maximum rate of growth consistent with stability—or the maximum degree of stability consistent with acceptable rates of growth—and to choose the combination of growth and stability that best meets their aims and wishes. This problem, too, is dealt with in Part V.

Population Growth

The Classical economists, generalizing from what they saw in Europe at the time, were prepared to treat population growth as a function of workers' incomes. People arrived in the world with both hands and mouths, but because of limitations on the supply of land they tended to eat more during their lifetime than they added to output, barring technological progress to increase their productivity. This analysis suggests a concept of "optimal size of population" which would maximize per capita output at any point of time. The Classicists thought this level of population had already been surpassed in Europe. Marxists have argued that population growth may be a problem for capitalist societies, where capital accumulation depends on profits, but not for a socialist society.

The treatment of population growth by the "moderns" differs in two respects. First, they have been much more reluctant to say just what determines the rate of population growth. By the time they were writing, it was clear that increasing wage incomes did not always bring more rapid increases in population. The importance of death rates as well as birth rates, the obvious fact that people could limit the size of their families if they wished to do so, and the role of migration impressed economists with the complexity of the factors determining rates of population growth in particular societies at particular times. Thus the "moderns" have tended to treat population growth as "exogenous"—outside the system—so far as its causation is concerned. On the other hand, Hansen and others have treated population growth as an endogenous factor—inside the system—in the determination of autonomous investment. It is not just a question of whether hands or mouths prove bigger in economic terms; the rate of capital accumulation itself depends on the rate of increase in the population. This theory suggests a concept of "optimal rate of population growth" in addition to the concept of optimal size of population. Taking account of the impact of population growth on investment, there would be some rate of population growth which would maximize the rate of increase in per capita output. It would be a somewhat complex affair, depending on the rate at which the optimal *size* of population, in terms of the production function, increased with the stock of capital, the precise quantitative effect of population growth on investment, both directly and through pushing people into frontier areas, and on the initial values of all the factors in the production function. There would be *some* rate of population growth, however, at which all the favorable effects on output would be more than offset by the increased numbers of people to share in it.

In both these "modern" aspects, the treatment of population growth is unsatisfactory as a basis for analyzing the problem of underdevelopment. As pointed out in Chapter 7, the relationship between population growth and autonomous investment breaks down when the labor supply is already redundant and there is no assurance that greater numbers will mean an increase in effective demand. In underdeveloped countries there may be nothing for extra hands to do and nothing to put into extra mouths that is not snatched from other mouths. The population may already be above optimum and the optimal rate of growth may even be negative. Nor can we be content to treat the causes of population growth as "exogenous" when we are concerned with raising per capita output and income. If we are to be sure that our policy recommendations will succeed in this respect, we *must* have some idea about what is going to happen to the rate of population growth.

Yet we must agree with the "moderns" that the Classical theory of population growth was too simple. Here is one respect, then, in which a theory of development that is to serve as a guide to policy in underdeveloped countries must differ from those outlined in Part II.

The distinction between autonomous and induced investment, and the isolation of resource discovery and innovations as the major factors in stimulating autonomous investment in underdeveloped countries are useful additions to our store of knowledge. Once it is recognized that *increasing rates* of resource discovery or technological progress are needed to raise autonomous investment, any easy optimism about prospects of launching growth from this direction should be dispelled.

The reintroduction into the discussion of growth of the capital-output ratio, as a consequence of the contributions of Harrod and Domar and others, is also useful—especially when the relation between capital accumulation, technological progress, resource discovery, and acquisition of skills is recognized. The capital-output ratio—and particularly the incremental capital-output ratio relating investment to increases in output—is a factor that must enter into any serious attempt at development planning. It is a slippery concept when used in plan preparation, as we shall see in Chapter 18. But it is none the less important for that.

Synthesis of General Theories

Let us now attempt a simple synthesis of all the aspects of these general theories that seem to be useful as a guide to policy in underdeveloped countries. Let us write

$$O = a \cdot Q \qquad (1)$$

Here a is an output-capital ratio; O is total output, and Q is the stock (quantity) of capital as before. Most of the literature refers to a capital-output ratio, and particularly to an incremental capital-output ratio relating increases in output to additions to the stock of capital. If the value of a is independent of the level of O and Q, it is the reciprocal of the incremental capital-output ratio. Then

$$\Delta O = a \cdot \Delta Q + \Delta a \cdot Q \qquad (1a)$$
$$= a \cdot I + \Delta a \cdot Q \qquad (1b)$$

(The symbol Δ, as before, means simply "change in.") This formulation is an improvement over the production function in showing that investment and so investment decisions are the hard core of the development process, while at the same time recognizing that there are ways of using an existing stock of capital more effectively so as to raise output.

To get closer to the decision-making process, we can break up investment into its three major parts: government investment, I_g, determined directly by the plan; induced private investment, I_i, brought forth by recent changes in income, effective demand, profits, etc.; and autonomous private investment, I_A, stimulated by long-run growth factors:

$$I = I_g + I_i + I_A(\dot{L}, \dot{K}, \dot{T}) \qquad (2)$$

For our present purposes we can simplify this equation in two ways. First, we can ignore induced investment in an initial approximation. Only if significantly high rates of increase in current income and demand are achieved will induced investment be quantitatively significant; in other words, if short-lived inflationary booms are avoided, induced investment will become significant only if development plans are successful. We must look to the other two kinds of investment for the *generation* of rising incomes. Second, as we have seen, few underdeveloped countries can regard population growth as a stimulus to long-run investment, since in most such countries population is already above optimum. Growth of the total size of the labor force is not needed to permit capital accumulation without a departure from the optimal ratio of labor to capital, nor does it carry with it increased effective demand for housing, transport, public utilities, etc., as it does in advanced countries. Thus we can use a simplified equation:

$$I = I_g + I_A(\dot{K}, \dot{T}) \tag{2a}$$

Substituting in (1b),

$$\Delta O = \Delta a \cdot Q + a_1 \cdot I_g + a_2 \cdot I_A(\dot{K}, \dot{T}) \tag{3}$$

This formulation tells us a good deal about the content and purpose of a development plan. An effective plan must be designed to do the following things:

1. Increase government investment, at least to the point at which opportunities for private investment are maximized. Over a very wide range public investment can provide the impulse to increased private investment. When government investment reaches a level at which it is competing for scarce resources with private enterprise, it may still be worth expanding if the stimulating effects on the rate of resource discovery and technological progress lead to a net increase in private investment nonetheless, or if it raises the output-capital ratio so as to more than offset any net drop in private investment. The methods of financing government investment should be of a sort that will not discourage private investment or result in less effective use of existing capital.

2. Increase the rate of resource discovery and technological progress. In part this objective can be obtained through government expenditures on geological surveys, research, transport facilities, etc. In part it involves providing incentives to private exploration and development through tax policy, foreign exchange policy, land policy, patents, etc.

3. Raise the parameter I_A; that is, encourage a higher level of private investment with the *existing* rate of resource discovery and technological progress. This might be done by training indigenous managers, entrepreneurs, and technicians; by reducing effective rates of interest and making credit more readily available; by encouraging a "long view" through promotion of confidence, assuring physical security, insurance schemes, etc.; by improved foreign exchange policy; and by improving the climate for foreign investment.

4. To raise the output-capital ratio (reduce the incremental capital-output ratio). This can be done by training managers and workers, inducing improved factor-proportions, improving the product mix, introducing capital-saving innovations, etc.

Equation (3) has the added advantage of indicating that the capital-output ratio is likely to be different for different sectors of the economy, and that the aggregate ratio will, therefore, depend on the sectoral allocation of total investment.

We could go further, introduce different incremental capital-output ratios for each type of investment, and also distinguish between the industrial and agricultural sectors. There would be still further advantages in introducing distributed lags, to take account of differences in gestation periods of investment in various sectors. We would then end up with something like this for each sector:

$$O_t - O_{t-1} = (a_t - a_{t-1}) \cdot Q_{t-1} + a_1 I_i (O_{t-1} - O_{t-2}) + a_2 I_{gt-3} + a_3 I_A (\dot{K}, \dot{T})_{t-4} \tag{4}$$

Here the t subscripts refer to time periods: t is the present income-period (quarter, let's say), $t-1$ is the previous quarter, $t-2$ is the quarter before that, and so on.

If we are concerned with financing the development program without inflation, we might also make use of "financial equations" derived from the Hansen theory. To make the analysis more realistic, let us take account of the marginal propensity to import, dF/dY, the marginal propensity to pay taxes, dT/dY, and the impact of the development plan on exports, in addition to variables in the simpler version of this equation presented in Chapter 6. We then have:

$$\Delta Y = \frac{1}{\Delta S/\Delta Y + \Delta F/\Delta Y + \Delta T/\Delta Y} \cdot \Delta (I_g + I_A + I_i + X)$$

We know also that $P = Y/O$, P being the general price level, O here standing for physical output. If the price level is to be stable, output must increase enough to offset the increase in money income. We already have

$$\Delta O = a \cdot (I_g + I_A + I_i)$$

So we can readily calculate the increase in output from the data in the plan. Comparing the increase in output with the increase in money income that will be generated by the development program with *existing* tax rates, monetary policies, etc., we can decide how much we must raise taxes and savings to prevent undesirable inflation. We can also calculate the impact on the balance of payments, having both the increase in exports and the increase in imports.

We shall return to these matters in Part V and consider them in more detail. Our purpose here is only to indicate what can be done with the sort of theory outlined in this part. Clearly, theories that enable us to do this sort of planning are very helpful. Just as clearly, however, these theories do *not* tell us how to turn a poor and stagnant economy into an expanding one with hope of becoming truly prosperous. They do not even tell us how underdeveloped countries got that way; and we cannot hope to devise policies to produce growth until we know why some countries have grown and others have not.

It would be pleasant indeed if we had available a theory of economic development general enough to serve as a basis for policy in countries at all stages of economic advance and with all types of economic system. But we do not. Professor Kuznets put the situation this way: [2]

Can we hope to formulate a theory of economic growth that would indicate the factors in the development of the more industrially advanced nations and thus illuminate the problem of their possible secular stagnation; to frame the factors so that a testable analysis of obstacles to economic growth of underdeveloped nations and hence a basis for intelligent development policy become possible; to consider the operation of these factors under a system of free enterprise, as well as within the authoritarian system, so that their interplay and potentialities in both become clear; and to distinguish the factors that make for peaceful and for warlike behavior, so that the bearing of each on economic growth can be clearly perceived? To put the question in this way is to predetermine a negative answer—provided that by a theory we mean a statement of testable relations among empirically identifiable factors, such relations and factors having been found relatively invariant under diverse conditions in time and space. Such a theory of economic growth of nations may never be within our reach. But one can safely assert that we do not have it now; and what is more important, are not yet ready for it. The very concern about economic growth is recent; and it is hardly an exaggeration to say that for almost a hundred years, since the mid-nineteenth century, when the economic theories of the long run of the Classical and Marxian schools had already been formulated, there has been no significant theoretical work in this field, excepting the various attempts to revise Marxian theory in the light of subsequent events.

We might do well, then, to abandon the search for a truly "general" theory at this stage, and content ourselves with a quest for a "special" theory of *under*development. Such a theory would be tailor-made for the institutional, technological, sociological, and psychological conditions common to underdeveloped countries. Part 4 is devoted to the quest for such a theory. But before returning to theory, there are two other things we can usefully do. First, we can review ideas concerning the historical causes of growth in the now advanced countries. Secondly, we should look more closely at the underdeveloped countries. What are the significant differences between them and the advanced countries—now, and as they were when the latter began their periods of sustained growth? The next two chapters deal with these questions.

[2] Simon Kuznets, "Toward a Theory of Economic Growth," in Simon Kuznets, *Economic Growth and Structure* (New York, 1965), pp. 4–5.

PART III Lessons of History

9 | Historical Theories of the Rise of Capitalism

Economic historians have devoted a good deal of thought and documentary research to the acceleration of economic development in Europe after 1500, which culminated in the Industrial Revolution of the eighteenth and nineteenth centuries. This process of marked acceleration of economic growth has been labeled "the rise of capitalism." Although there is no reason to expect the presently poor countries to follow exactly the same path, it is nonetheless interesting to consider the general theories of the "rise of capitalism" which have come out of these historical studies. They may point to some prerequisites for economic growth which are just as necessary in underdeveloped countries today as they were in the now industrialized countries two or three centuries ago. At their least useful, such theories should indicate some important differences between advanced countries, when their accelerated growth began, and underdeveloped countries today.

The "Rise of Capitalism"

Much historical research has been directed to the question of the date and causes of the beginning of capitalism. When did it arise, and why?

Marx

Karl Marx recognized the existence of a "sporadic" capitalism in the Mediterranean cities of the fourteenth and fifteenth centuries but dated the "era" of capitalism from the sixteenth century. He interpreted the "rise" of capitalism as a successful struggle of the "capitalist class" against the feudal lords and the guild-masters. The basis of its rise was the exploitation of subservient labor. Through enclosures and the breakup of feudalism "a mass of free proletarians was hurled on the labour market." The old nobility was devoured by wars. Cruel legislation failed to stop the movement. This process of forcible expropriation gained new impetus from the Reformation and "hurled" the inmates of the monasteries "into the proletariat." The agricultural people were driven from their homes and then maltreated into a condition and discipline suitable for wage labor. The capitalist class rose out of the class of independent farmers and landlords who exploited labor, and benefited by rising prices. Hand in hand with the breakup of the manor and the expropriation of the peasants went the destruction of domestic industry and the concentration of control of manufacture into the hands of individual capitalists, who gained all the profits. The Middle Ages contributed two kinds of capital: usurers' capital and merchants' capital. Until the breakdown of feudalism, this capital was prevented from being converted into industrial capital. Exploitation of colonies, slave trade, and monopolies also added to the capital accumulation.[1]

Sombart

Werner Sombart considered "capitalism" as an idealized "type" of economic organization, which characterizes a very definite historical period. This "type" of organization developed from 1500 to 1760, was at its height from 1760 until August, 1914, and is now on the decline. The capitalistic "type" of economy has certain characteristics:

1. Technical progress is "typical" of capitalism; in the precapitalistic period technique was stable, bound by custom and tradition.

2. Economic freedom—laissez faire—is also typical of capitalism. Freed from precapitalistic control by guilds, municipal authority, manorial customs and traditions, enterprise was able to make quick use of new improvements, of investment opportunities, etc.

3. Capitalism has its own "spirit," which did not exist previously. It is an unshackled, accumulating, profit-seeking spirit, careless of social consequences and communal relationships.

Sombart was even more emphatic than Marx in his distinction between the Middle Ages and the period following the beginning of the sixteenth century. The medieval organization was not only acapitalistic but was incapable of producing a store of capital. In this essentially localized handicraft economy, it was difficult enough to obtain a bare subsistence, let alone accumulate capital. Capitalism developed mainly out of the operation of the properties of the feudal lords, and from the increased holdings of urban properties.[2]

Later research has shown that many features of capitalism are to be found in medieval economic organization, particularly in commerce, and that commerce was much more important in providing funds for invest-

[1] Karl Marx, *Capital: a Critical Analysis of Capital Production*, ed., Friedrich Engels (London, 1887).
[2] Werner Sombart, *Der Moderne Kapitalismus*, (Leipzig, 1927).

ment than was landholding. Indeed, there is evidence that the commercial capitalists were able to displace the feudal landlords in economic and political control.[3] However, in showing the relation between the rise of the state and of capitalism, Sombart does give a partial explanation. State finance offered one of the best ways for commercial capitalists to increase their wealth, witness the Medici, Fuggers, and other great trading families. Church finance, too, was an important factor in the development of financial institutions, for the heavy taxes imposed by the Popes necessitated the development of both transfer mechanisms and of credit.[4]

The Weber-Tawney Thesis

Max Weber's explanation of the "rise of capitalism" is at once most fascinating and most controversial. The reason for capitalistic development in the sixteenth century is that the Reformation provided the proper philosophical and ethical setting for the "capitalist spirit" to flourish. The impulse to acquisition is common to all times and all places, but Roman Catholicism held in check the pursuit of profit and the accumulation of wealth which characterize capitalism. The problem is not the advent of capitalistic activity but the appearance of the sober bourgeois society in which capitalism reached its apex. Even contemporary society gives us a clue to the rise of this middle-class society, Weber argued, for in countries of mixed religion, we find a dominance of Protestants among entrepreneurs, owners of capital, and high-grade labor. It was also true that the more highly developed districts were those which gave most support to the Reformation, finding its creed more suitable to aggressive and progressive ways of life. The spirit of capitalism is typified by Benjamin Franklin's "philosophy of avarice." Acquisition of wealth becomes an end in itself. In the Middle Ages, such ideas were considered as the lowest kind of avarice; after the Reformation, such conduct became highly respectable. At the beginning of modern times, it was not the existing entrepreneurs who represented the capitalistic spirit, for they were bound by traditionalism: fixed profits, limited interest rates, just wages, and just prices. It was in the lower middle class that the spirit was strongest. This spirit, and not new streams of money, stimulated the rise of capitalism. The chief reward for making money was the feeling of having done the job well.

This concept is to be found in Luther's doctrines under the name of the "calling," the idea that each individual is "called" to do a certain job and to do it as well as possible. The highest form of moral conduct is the fulfillment of duty in worldly affairs. The ideal of monastic asceticism was extended to worldly life; one should not indulge in luxury. Yet Luther was opposed to monopoly and to usury, and cannot be regarded as the apostle of capitalism. The real enemy of Catholicism was Calvinism. In order to become one of the "chosen," one must work hard and spend

[3] H. Sieveking, "Die Kapitalistische Entwicklung in den italienische Städten des Mittelalters," *Vierteljahrshefte für Sozial und Wirtschaftsgeschichte*, Vol. VII, 1909.
[4] Cf. J. Strieder, "Origin and Evolution of Early European Capitalism," *Journal of Economic and Business History*, November, 1929; F. Scheville, *History of Florence from the Foundation of the City through the Renaissance* (New York, 1936).

little. One must accept one's lot as part of God's scheme. The intensity of worldly activity alone dispels doubts as to one's being among the "elect." Pietism was a similar doctrine of predestination which influenced the ascetic movement. Methodism was an Anglo-Saxon movement corresponding to Pietism. In practice, the reasoning of the Baptist sects becomes equivalent to Calvinism.

The net result was to justify the pursuit of wealth, provided that happened to be one's "calling." Poverty was not required, but the pursuit of riches must not lead one to reckless enjoyment. Profits are as holy as wages, and interest is not wrong unless wrung from the poor. The cardinal sin is idleness. As for laborers, only when they were poor did they remain obedient to God, but remaining obedient they attained eternal happiness in another world. Thus the Reformation gave to the entrepreneur and to the capitalist a clear conscience to pursue profits to the best of their ability. In condemning expenditure, it provided the basis for capital accumulation. The profits of this era were not absorbed into the life of a new nobility but were reinvested. On the other hand, the new spirit justified a marked class distinction and forbade open dissatisfaction on the part of oppressed labor.[5]

This explanation of the rise of capitalism was introduced to English readers by R. H. Tawney.[6] Although essentially the same as Weber's, his treatment is more general and develops the thesis in relation to its historical setting. Like Weber, Tawney points out that the Catholic Church opposed usury and emphasized the sin of avarice. The outbursts of commercial activity in the fifteenth century made the older teaching an economic anachronism. (It will be noted that Tawney is more inclined than Weber to say that the Reformation stimulated a movement already under way.) Catholic teaching was an effective barrier to capitalistic development despite its neglect in practice. Tawney attributes less positive, and more negative, influence to Luther than does Weber. Luther, he says, was opposed to the accumulation of wealth, usury, monopoly, high prices, speculation, and the luxury trade with the East. But Calvin's teaching was most characteristic and most influential of the new doctrines. He saw economic life with the eyes of a peasant, and recognized frankly the need for capital, credit and banking, and large-scale commerce and finance. Thrift, diligence, sobriety, and frugality are the Christian virtues, and profits and interest are not necessarily evil gains.

Perhaps the most forceful critic of the Weber-Tawney thesis is H. M. Robertson. He regards his *Aspects of the Rise of Economic Individualism* as a "more realistic treatment," historical rather than sociological. The capitalist, he says, is and always has been a purely secular creature who sees no reason for religion to meddle in his business affairs. Men do not need to be "called" to the pursuit of riches. Weber's philological interpretation of "calling" is unfounded, and there is no essential difference between Catholics and Puritans on this point. The true interpretation of "calling" savors little of capitalism. Secondly, the *Erwerbsprinzip* is not

[5] Max Weber, *The Protestant Ethic and the Spirit of Capitalism* (New York, 1930).
[6] R. H. Tawney, *Religion and the Rise of Capitalism* (New York, 1926).

new; society has been acquisitive for thousands of years. There was plenty of capitalism in the Middle Ages. If we look to Scotland, a stronghold of Calvinism, we find not an advanced but a lagging development of capitalism. As for usury, its approval was no part of the Protestant creed; the literature is full of condemnation of it. In practice, Calvin's own attitude toward interest and that of the Catholic Church were essentially the same. (One could add here that the Catholic Church itself did much to foster capitalism.) As the bases of capitalism, Robertson emphasizes the rise of the nationalist state, the Machiavellian philosophy, and in particular, the "price revolution" following the discoveries.

It is clear that much of Robertson's criticism is justified, but he goes rather too far in his nihilism with respect to the Reformation. It is fairly generally agreed today that the Protestant ethic was one element in the acceleration of capitalistic development.[7] The relationship between predominant religion and per capita income is too close for religion to be dismissed out of hand as a factor in *past* economic history. If we refer to Appendix Table 1, we can see that the six countries with the highest *per capita* incomes in 1961 were Christian and Protestant. Of the twenty-two countries with per capital incomes over $600 per year (the "developed" countries in our definition), all but seven are predominantly Protestant, the others (except Israel) are predominantly Roman Catholic. Those with per capita incomes between $250 and $600 are mainly Roman Catholic; those between $100 and $250 are mainly Roman Catholic and Moslem; those below $100 are mainly Hindu, Buddhist, and pagan. We can reach no conclusions about causes and effects on the basis of these facts, but the facts are worth pondering—along with other facts. For in other parts of the world than Europe, quite different religions have produced the spirit of enterprise. Professor Walt W. Rostow, discussing the role of entrepreneurship in the acceleration of economic growth, writes: [8]

In this connection it is increasingly conventional for economists to pay their respects to the Protestant ethic.[9] The historian should not be ungrateful for this light on the grey horizon of formal growth models. But the known cases of economic growth which theory must seek to explain take us beyond the orbit of Protestantism. In a world where Samurai, Parsees, Jews, North Italians, Turkish, Russian, and Chinese Civil Servants (as well as Huguenots, Scotsmen and British North-countrymen) have played the role of a leading élite in economic growth John Calvin should not be made to bear quite this weight. More fundamentally, allusion to a positive scale of religious or other values conducive to profit-maximising activities is an insufficient sociological basis for this important phenomenon. What appears to be required for the emergence

[7] A contemporary critic of Weber is P. C. G. Walker, "Capitalism and the Reformation," *Economic History Review*, November, 1937. He objects to Weber's method of using qualitative rather than quantitative criteria. Moreover, such an investigation cannot take the Reformation as a datum; it must inquire into the causes that lay behind it. He rightly criticizes the emphasis upon the post-sixteenth-century history of capitalism. He follows Roberston in emphasizing the price revolution.

[8] W. W. Rostow, "The Take-off into Self-sustained Growth," *The Economic Journal*, March, 1956.

[9] See, for example, N. Kaldor, "Economic Growth and Cyclical Fluctuations," *Economic Journal*, March, 1954, p. 67.

of such élites is not merely an appropriate value system but two further conditions: first, the new élite must feel itself denied the conventional routes to prestige and power by the traditional less acquisitive society of which it is a part; second, the traditional society must be sufficiently flexible (or weak) to permit its members to seek material advance (or political power) as a route upwards alternative to conformity.

In this chapter we are concerned with general theories arising from the study of economic history rather than with economic history proper. To present the history of early modern Europe and the Industrial Revolution that emerged from it would require a book in itself. However, we should note two important points before moving on to other historical explanations of the upsurge of economic development in Europe. First, other things besides the Reformation happened in the sixteenth century. Some of these are discussed below. Others, which may have been equally important—such as the rise of the national state, the new wave of scientific progress during the Renaissance, and the liberal policies of Antwerp as the new financial center of Europe—are not. Second, the Reformation itself had economic effects more direct than those entailed in the change in ideology it introduced. The dissolution of the abbeys and the confiscation and sale of Church properties transferred capital from less enterprising to more enterprising owners. The persecuted Protestants who immigrated into England, West Germany, and Holland brought with them technical skills, scientific knowledge, and managerial talents. Later religious persecution contributed to the development of the New World, and thus indirectly to the development of Europe itself. The impact on ideology may have been an important aspect of the Reformation, but it was certainly not the only one influencing economic history.[10]

The Crusades and Commercial Expansion

Those who associate the "rise of capitalism" with the development of medieval commerce tend to stress the Crusades as a series of events leading to rapid progress. These basically religious movements had as their chief results the colonization of unsettled Continental districts, the opening of new Mediterranean markets and ports, the development of the European luxury trade with the Near East, the introduction of new commodities and new techniques into Europe, improved navigation and ships, better-organized capital and foreign exchange markets, the beginning of the absorption of the old feudal aristocracy by the new commercial capitalists, the economic development of the Italian cities. Indeed, if one wants to risk picking a single cause for the "rise of capitalism," the Crusades would seem to be the choice, for out of the commercial capitalism of the Middle Ages and the capital accumulation that it made possible grew the industrial capitalism of later periods.[11] Of course, one may fall prey to the *post hoc, ergo propter hoc* fallacy in this connection.

[10] See, for example, Herbert Heaton, *Economic History of Europe* (New York, 1948), chaps. XI–XX, and the literature there cited.
[11] Since the Crusades are dealt with by almost every author who discusses the development of medieval commerce and finance no specific reference is given.

Capitalistic Agriculture: Enclosures and the Black Death

In so far as the development of capitalism is synonymous with the decay of feudalism,[12] the causes of the breakup of the manor are likewise causes of the rise of capitalism. Since the enclosures replaced serfdom with a free labor class to some extent, and since the commutation of labor service for money rents replaced serfdom with more or less free enterprise farming for profit, there can be no doubt that the decay of feudalism was a stimulus to capitalistic development.

The growth of the towns was in part a result of the breakup of the manor, but towns were growing up before the enclosures set in and their growth was also a cause of the decline of feudalism. The existence of an artisan and an entrepreneurial class who did not work land to supply their wants for food, clothing, and raw materials directly meant that markets existed for exports from the manors located near the towns. Exporting involved specialization of agricultural output, and specialization is the antithesis of feudalism. The growth of towns stimulated farming for profit rather than farming for consumption.

The growth of towns had another effect through increasing the demand for labor and thus raising wages. This tendency led to the freeing of serfs, and many not freed ran away to take advantage of higher industrial wages.

Another impetus to agricultural specialization was the growth of commerce after the Crusades, and again after the discoveries. These events meant new markets, new commodities, better navigation. The manors could export not only to towns but to other countries. The introduction of new agricultural methods into Europe also made specialization more profitable.

Although there has been some debate on the subject, there can be little doubt that the Black Death accelerated the movement.[13] The immediate effect of the plague and the depopulation resulting from it was an increase in relative supply of and a decrease of demand for commodities, so that prices fell tremendously. Rather than sell livestock and equipment at such prices, landlords sought to acquire more land. This immediate effect was followed by a great reduction in output due to labor scarcity, and prices rose precipitously. This factor made the acquisition of land desirable to expand output and to profit from the high prices. Because of the rise in wage rates, however, it was desirable to replace labor-intensive industries with land-intensive activities such as sheep farming. Here was another reason for enlarging landholdings. The seizure of land was made easier by the frequent arrears in rents due to lack of manpower to obtain the necessary production. The landlords were glad to free villeins because, in face of the high costs and prices, it was too expensive to permit them to go on using the land, at the rents fixed in their leases.

[12] This is the contention of Marx, as we have seen, and Walker's definition amounts to the same thing.
[13] Cf. Ephraim Lipson, *Economic History of England* (London, 1937–43), Vol. I, pp. 82ff.; H. Robbins, "A Comparison of the Effects of the Black Death on the Economic Organization of France and England," *Journal of Political Economy*, August, 1928.

There is little evidence of the "struggle" between feudal lord and commercial capitalist that Marx emphasizes, unless the competition for labor can be called a "struggle." It is not true that all the labor freed was forced off the land by the nobility; in many cases, the villeins were glad to be freed to accept the higher industrial wages. Yet Marx is right in suggesting that feudalism had outlived its usefulness. Indeed, the main reason for its disappearance was its sheer inefficiency and the opportunity for profit in better methods.

Enclosures were accompanied by the concentration of ownership of land into fewer hands. Scattered strips were amalgamated into more workable plots, arable land was converted into pasture, and the commons were appropriated for production. These tendencies were present before the Black Death but are more noticeable afterward. Sheep farming was the most important agricultural industry, and yielded large profits.

Thus in the period from the thirteenth to the sixteenth centuries, and even afterward, we notice a gradual transition from farming for consumption to more specialized and more efficient farming for profit, which is one feature of capitalism.

The Discoveries and the "Price Revolution"

Those, like Henri Sée, who place the period of the "rise of capitalism" at a later date, usually stress the new geographical discoveries, and the consequent inflow of precious metals, as causes. The most important of these discoveries were the Cape route to the Orient (da Gama, 1498), the North American continent (Columbus, 1492), Brazil (Cabral, 1500), and Magellan's circumnavigation of the globe (1522). Hamilton, while admitting the significance of other factors such as the rise of the national state and improvements in agriculture, regards these discoveries as the great cause of capitalistic development.[14] The effects, according to him, were:

1. Improved shipping: the effect was similar to the effect upon aviation of the trans-Atlantic flights. Bigger and better ships and new navigation instruments were developed.

2. New techniques: the widening of the market facilitated division of labor and led to technological improvements.

3. The influx of new goods from America and the Orient, including the slave trade.

4. Emigration, which relieved population pressure, provided new raw materials, and markets for finished goods.

5. Guild organization, unable to deal with new problems, crumbled and gave way to the capitalistic employer.

6. The vast influx of gold and silver: this last factor was most important. During the fourteenth and fifteenth centuries, expanding output led to declining prices, which acted as a deterrent to expansion. The gold and silver which came first to Spain and Portugal was distributed throughout Europe through the Ricardian specie-flow mechanism. Prices quadrupled,

[14] E. J. Hamilton, *American Treasure and the Price Revolution in Spain, 1501–1650* (Cambridge, Mass., 1934).

wages and rents lagged, giving an incentive to speculation, capital building, promotion of new industries, etc. Tremendous profits were made from the Oriental goods without need to sell an equal value of European goods to the Orient. It thus broadened the area of trade, and provided sources for new profits. Without it, the "unfavorable" trade with the Orient could not have been continued. Much of the metal coming from America ended in the Orient.

It should be pointed out that the mere possession of precious metals cannot, in and of itself, provide an incentive to economic development. The countries richest in "treasure" have not always been the most economically advanced. Not the general price level, but the relation between the price of consumers' and of capital goods, determines the amount of new investment. It is profit inflation, due to a lag in costs, that encourages expansion.

In the appendix on mercantilism in his *General Theory*, Keynes provides another rationale for the relation between the "price revolution" and the rise of capitalism. The important aspect of the gold inflow, Keynes argues, was not so much its effect on prices as its effects on liquidity and bank reserves. In a monetary system where the volume of bank credit depends on the size of the nation's reserves of precious metals, the influx of these metals results in low interest rates and "easy money." The volume of private investment and the consequent rate of economic growth is accordingly maintained on a relatively high level.

Did Capitalism "Rise" or Evolve?

Of late some economic historians have become fond of spiking all historical theories about the "rise" of capitalism in one period or another, contending that most of the features attributed to capitalism by Sombart, for example, can be found in the Middle Ages as well. Capitalism, commerical, financial, and industrial, has evolved gradually over several centuries. Some skeptics among historians have contended that one ought not to speak of a "rise of capitalism" at all, or at least not as a phenomenon characteristic of any one period or resulting from any one constellation of events. There has been some degree of capitalism in all civilizations, and the features which constitute the present economic organization have been added gradually and one by one. Nor has the trend been one of continual progress. Features of modern capitalism have existed in one period, have been abandoned in the next, and then reintroduced—investment banking in Venice, for example. One can speak of a "rise of capitalism" only in the sense that economic development has been somewhat more rapid or more marked in some periods than in others. There is, so to speak, a change in the *third* derivative of the function showing the rate of increase in *per capita* output through time.

Commercial Capitalism

In the period following the Crusades, these skeptics point out, a highly organized international trade existed in Europe. The area to develop first was the Mediterranean. Although Italian cities took the lead, Spanish cities, such as Barcelona, and French cities like Marseilles were not far behind. The Mediterranean trade was with North Africa and the Near East and consisted largely of luxury goods. Ships were quite large, capable of handling respectable cargoes. The organization was capitalistic, capital being provided mainly through the *commenda* and *societas* arrangements and often obtained through issuing shares. Ships were sometimes state-owned. Almost contemporaneous with the early development of the Mediterranean trade was the development of the north-to-south trade. This trade took place through the organization of fairs, such as that of Champagne, or of Antwerp, Lyons, Avignon, Bruges, Brussels, as well as those of Genoa, Venice, Barcelona, etc. In the conduct of this trade there was considerable division of labor among wholesalers, retailers, financiers, etc. The purely northern trade between Scandinavia and England, England and The Netherlands, Scandinavia and France, etc., was dominated by the Hanseatic League. The important members of the Hanse, like the great Italian traders, were true capitalists earning large profits; they were often able to become nobles on the proceeds of their financial success. They controlled the peasants and labor and exerted political influence.

The period following the great discoveries at the turn of the fifteenth and sixteenth centuries and up to the eighteenth century is often called the era of "commercial revolution." This term does not give an accurate picture of the period, excluding as it does industrial and agricultural developments and indicating a change more rapid and more violent than actually took place. Yet certain trends can be discerned which begin in the late fifteenth century and continue through the sixteenth and seventeenth centuries. First, there was an enormous expansion in European commerce, both domestic and international. France, England, and Holland began to rival Italy and Spain as trading countries.

The influence of the discoveries on this expansion can be over-emphasized, and the old trade routes were not abandoned. New ones were added, however, bringing new commodities and new markets. There was a relative decline in the importance of the Italian cities and the Hanseatic League in control of international trade. The new routes made the position of the Italian cities less advantageous; the loss of fishing trade and the rise of national states made the Hanseatic League less powerful. Yet the Italian cities continued to dominate the luxury trade until well into the seventeenth century, and many of the Hanse towns continued to be important economic centers. The Commercial Revolution finished the overturn of medieval organization, with its guilds, its manors, and town control of foreign trade. Considerable technical progress occurred in the field of navigation. Ships were built larger and faster, with more decks and more masts and a combination of square-rigged and lateen sails. Knowledge of currents and winds was enlarged. The science of astronomy advanced; the compass and astrolabe made possible more efficient navigation on long voyages. Maps and charts were improved, lighthouses built, and harbors cleared. These developments in the field of commerce constitute a part of the development of "capitalism"—so the skeptics maintain.

Financial Capitalism

Contrary to Sombart, says this group of critics, the development of finance in the Middle Ages had many characteristics that we are inclined to regard as "modern." [15] The most highly developed capital markets were in the Mediterranean cities and in the Netherlands. Commerce was financed to a very large extent by borrowed capital. Capital might be provided under the various *commenda* arrangements, through the *societas*, or even through the *sea loan*. Straightforward loans on personal or commercial security were also made. Often shares were sold to raise capital for ships or cargoes. In Italy and in Spain banks of deposit existed, and payments were made by bank transfers. In certain periods these banks also made loans. Foreign exchange transactions were carried on both as a means of making loans and to transfer capital. The operation of the fairs involved a great deal of sales credit, as did also the transaction of local business. Public finance involved the issue of government securities, state banks, huge international loans, etc. The great financial houses like the Bardi, Peruzzi, Medici, etc., rivaled the Rothschilds and Morgans and Rockefellers of modern times.

The fifteenth and sixteenth centuries, so far as financial capitalism was concerned, were characterized by the spread of these methods of finance to other parts of Europe, notably Germany and England. It might be more accurate to say the development of these financial methods in these countries, since in England, at least, much use was made of credit in the Middle Ages. In the sixteenth century, however, England developed its own class of big capitalists, such as Gresham. In Germany, great houses like the Fuggers became internationally significant in the fifteenth century and were at their height in the early sixteenth century. In England, the development was continued after the sixteenth century, her relative importance increasing. During the sixteenth century, Antwerp was the most important international financial center, overshadowing the Italian cities of Venice and Genoa. The public control of banking made strides in the fifteenth and sixteenth centuries. The legal attitude toward credit operations underwent some revision in this period, particularly in England and the northern part of the Continent. Financial capitalism was perhaps more highly developed in Europe up to 1600 than any other form of capitalism.

In this period there occurred the first modern crisis, based not upon famine nor plague nor invasion but upon overextension of credit. The break came in 1556, and the panic reached its height in 1559. The depression in the financial market continued for several years afterward, and the capitalistic development of Europe was retarded as a result. The basis of the credit inflation was Spanish war finance, with the Fuggers and other large houses making huge loans to the King. Antwerp was glutted with obligations of the Spanish Crown. Gresham noticed signs of disturbance

[15] See for example André Sayous, " 'Der Moderne Kapitalismus' de Werner Sombart et Genes aux XII et XIII Siecles," *Revue d'Histoire Economique et Sociale*, XVIII (1930), p. 427.

as early as 1553.[16] In France, both King and Cardinal were borrowing constantly. In addition to these public loans, an inestimable amount of private credit was extended by merchants, financiers, and bankers. In 1557, the war between France and Spain broke out. Philip was advised by the Church to repudiate, but he refunded and consolidated for fear of losing his credit altogether. Short-term loans were converted into perpetual *rentes*. Security values fell accordingly. On the date set for payment, only a small part of the interest owed was paid, and the King announced the flotation of a new loan. The market was unable to stand such a strain; both France and Spain became bankrupt and were forced into peace. The "wars of religion" completed the collapse of the international capital market.[17] Thus the financial crisis, which is a characteristic of the capitalistic system, makes its appearance in the sixteenth century. When did "capitalism" arise?

Industrial Capitalism and Urbanism

Some economic historians have maintained that the rise of industrial capitalism coincided with the decay of feudalism and the growth of the towns. If the rise of towns were a mere transplanting of cottage industry from the manor to a town there would be no basis for such a statement. But in fact the growth of towns involved a change in ownership. The cottage workers no longer owned raw materials and products. The raw materials were supplied either by customers or by merchants who bought the raw materials and sold the finished product for a profit. Such merchants were capitalists, and such artisans were dependent workers, hired fore piece-rate wages. Such a change is more significant than the growth of factories as such, for factories existed in ancient times with slave labor. Weber mentions various kinds of factory organizations in the Middle Ages: mills, ovens, breweries, iron foundries. With few exceptions, however, such organizations were operated in a communal rather than a capitalistic manner. The independent craftsman, the cottage worker, and the putting-out system were still predominant. Lipson tells us that as late as the sixteenth century the town craftsmen were forbidden to work at their craft during harvest, in order to be available for work on the manors. True there were large workshops, particularly in the textile industry, during the sixteenth century. But one must distinguish between increased use of machinery and division of labor and a mere collection of workers under one roof. Technical specialization was still relatively rare in the sixteenth century. Yet mere size does have some significance; some sixteenth-century

[16] "This Bourse of Antwerp is strange. One day there is plenty of money, and the next one, because there are so many good takers and deliverers that if one will not act, another will. Fugger and Jasper Schetz are bare of money and no good can be done with them at present, as the Emperor owes about 300,000 livres." (See William B. Turnbull, *Callendar of State Papers of the Reign of Queen Mary, 1553–1558,* Foreign Series No. 104, London, 1861.)

[17] Henri Hauser, "The European Financial Crisis of 1559," *Journal of Economic and Business History,* 1930, pp. 241–55.

manufacturers did rise to considerable prominence and contribute to the accumulation of capital. The trend toward the factory system is discernible in the sixteenth century, and even in the fifteenth, as is shown by legislation against large-scale production and the use of machinery. Yet the rise of industrial capitalism is a feature of later centuries.

Technical progress in industry is also not a phenomenon which is limited to the period following 1600, this group of historians insists. One of the earliest and most important advances was the use of water power in place of man or animal power; this opened up many new possibilities in manufacturing. Opposition to the introduction of water power began in the thirteenth century and was largely overcome in the early fifteenth century. The commercial expansion following the discoveries opened up new markets, created new demands, and gave a stimulus to technical progress. Certain new industries grew up: gunpowder mills, cannon foundries, alum and copperas factories, sugar refineries, saltpeter works. Plants were set up involving investments far greater than individual craftsmen or guilds could provide. More important than these new industries were the improvements in old industries. Better methods in mining and production of metals were introduced even before the sixteenth century: drains, pumps, ventilation, etc., in mining and the blast furnace, water-driven hammers, standardization of metal products, machine-drawn wires, etc., in metallurgy. The substitution of coal for wood and charcoal for heating was important in view of the diminishing lumber supply. The sixteenth century saw an acceleration of such technological progress. The advantage of calcining iron ore before smelting it was discovered. William Lee invented the stocking frame. The production of salt from sea water involved large plants. Cranes and pulleys made possible the moving of heavier weights in construction and manufacturing. The finishing of textiles—dyeing, fulling, and calendaring—was much improved and done on a large scale. Thus it is clear that so far as technical improvement is concerned the eighteenth century was more "capitalistic" than the sixteenth only in the sense that the pace was more rapid and the inventions more striking.[18]

Entrepreneurship

Nor can "capitalism" be dated from the seventeenth or eighteenth centuries in terms of appearance of entrepreneurs, say the skeptics. Even in the Middle Ages there was a distinct entrepreneurial class in commerce and in finance. During the sixteenth century, if not earlier, the industrial entrepreneur appears. To what extent the development of an entrepreneurial class is dependent upon freedom of enterprise is perhaps debatable. Yet there seems to be some support for the contention that the exhausting struggle between Emperor and Pope in the Middle Ages left the cities free to develop under the domination of merchant capitalists. It is at least worth asking, therefore, whether the rise of the national state and the breakdown

[18] Cf. especially J. U. Nef, "The Progress of Technology and the Growth of Large-Scale Industry in Great Britain, 1540–1640," *Economic History Review*, October, 1934.

of town control contributed substantially to the rise of an entrepreneurial class and the growth of capitalism.

There can be no doubt that town and guild administration involved a complicated and lengthy set of rules for trade and commerce. Severe penalties were imposed for the infraction of rules concerning standards, quality, fraud, adulteration, etc. Particularly important were the laws against forestalling, regrating, and engrossing. An attempt was made to prevent monopolization. The conditions of buying and selling, prices, wages, and hours, were determined by law. It would seem that entrepreneurs hemmed in by such restrictions would be discouraged and pine away into insignificance, but it is doubtful whether the rules were enforced. The impossibility of enforcing the rules against forestalling, etc., led to price fixing. But although prices were fixed, quantity and quality of commodities varied, so that the *de facto* prices actually fluctuated. The large revenue collected from fines imposed for infringement of rules indicated that the rules were not kept and that it paid to break them. It is possible, therefore, that town and guild regulation was not such an impediment to capitalistic development as it may appear at first glance.

When, on the other hand, we turn to the state control and mercantilism that succeeded "town policy," we do not find much relaxation of the administrative regulation of the economy. In practice, mercantilism involved much more than the control of exports, imports, and the foreign exchanges. As always, it was found that intervention in one part of the economy required intervention in others. Control of foreign exchanges necessitated control of the capital market. Regulation of imports and exports meant interference with particular businesses. Bullionist policy was extended to emigration and immigration. There were other types of interference not directly related to mercantilism, such as wage regulation and the legislation against large-scale and machine industry already mentioned.

On the whole, it seems probable that the rise of the national state made commerce and industry somewhat more free within and between towns of a particular country, even if town customs taxes and regulations did not immediately disappear. Also, if one regards monopoly as typical of capitalism, the mercantilist policy aided the development of capitalism, for the creation of monopolies was a feature of this period. The granting of monopolies to creditors of the state was a medieval practice, but the monopolies of the early modern world were more lucrative and contributed more to the accumulation of capital.

Rostow's Stages of Economic Growth

The work of economic historians in the last few decades, pushing back the beginning of "the rise of capitalism," is essentially a reaction against the too facile explanation of the Industrial Revolution in terms of a series of inventions in the eighteenth and early nineteenth centuries—the cotton gin, the spinning jenny, steam, the coking process. The difficulty with this sort of research, of course, is that it tends toward agnosticism. If we find evidence of commercial, financial, and even industrial capitalism in the sixteenth century, how do we explain the marked acceleration of economic growth in the eighteenth and nineteenth centuries? To say that there was no fundamental difference between economic organization and activity in the eighteenth century and in the seventeenth or sixteenth is clearly no help.

Recently, an eminent economic historian, who is also well versed in economic theory and a specialist on economic development, has been bold enough to set forth a new synthesis of historical knowledge about the beginnings of economic growth. Professor Walt W. Rostow characterizes his famous book in these words:

> This book presents an economic historian's way of generalizing the sweep of modern history. The form of this generalization is a set of stages-of-growth. I have come gradually to the view that it is possible and, for certain limited purposes, it is useful to break down the story of each national economy—and sometimes the story of regions—according to this set of stages. They constitute, in the end, both a theory about economic growth and a more general, if still highly partial, theory about modern history as a whole.[19]

The five stages are the traditional society, establishing the preconditions for take-off, the take-off, the drive to maturity, and the age of high mass consumption.

Rostow has little to say about the traditional society. He defines it as a society "whose structure is developed with limited production functions, based on pre-Newtonian science and technology, and on pre-Newtonian attitudes towards the physical world." [20] Because productivity is limited, the people are obliged to devote a high proportion of their resources to agriculture. The social structure is hierarchical with little scope for vertical mobility.

It is hard to see how one could identify a traditional society in terms other than its level of economic development. As Rostow himself admits, "To place these infinitely various, changing societies in a single category, on the ground that they all share the ceiling on the productivity of their economic techniques, is to say very little indeed." Essentially, however, the traditional society is one in which the preconditions for take-off have not yet been established; if we can determine precisely what the preconditions are, we can also distinguish traditional societies as those where the preconditions have not yet appeared.

The Preconditions for Take-off

The preconditions for take-off were first developed, Rostow argues, in western Europe in the late seventeenth and early eighteenth centuries, as modern science began to be applied to both agriculture and industry. He adds, however, that ". . . all that lies behind the break-up of the Middle Ages is relevant to the creation of the preconditions for take-off in West-

[19] W. W. Rostow, *The Stages of Economic Growth: A Non-Communist Manifesto* (Cambridge, 1961), p. 1. (Henceforth W. W. Rostow, *Stages, op. cit.*)
[20] *Ibid.,* p. 4.

ern Europe," thus greatly complicating the problem of discerning the appearance of preconditions in other countries. He distinguishes two cases: a "general" case covering most of Europe, Asia, the Middle East, and Africa, and a second case covering "the small group of nations that were, in a sense, 'born free.' " The second group includes the United States, Australia, New Zealand, Canada, "and perhaps a few others."

These countries are distinguished from the others by being "created out of a Britain already far along in the transitional process." Moreover, they were founded by social groups—usually one type of nonconformist or another—who were "at the margin of the dynamic transitional process slowly going forward within Britain."

Like most economic historians, Rostow makes a bow to the entrepreneur, and his entrepreneur is not very different from the Schumpeterian one. To get the rate of investment up, some men in the society must be able to manipulate and apply modern science and introduce useful cost-reducing inventions. Some others must take the risk of converting inventions into innovations, actually creating productive enterprises, and others still must take the risk of providing the financial backing. He also hints that the presence of entrepreneurs may not be enough; there must also be an interest in modernization on the part of the "effective political coalition." Both the will and the ability to create "an urban-based modern society" must be present.

THE "LEADING SECTOR" DOCTRINE

In discussing the preconditions, Rostow also outlines his "leading sector" theory. As presented in his original book, the theory is not much different from the well-known "staples" theory of Professor Harold Innis regarding Canadian development.[21] There has first to be an increase in productivity in the primary sector, usually in food production, but wool, cotton, or silk, or timber or rubber—or in the case of the Middle East, oil—may also play the role of leading sector. In any case, the preconditions are likely to be established somewhere within the primary sector.

In his presentation to the meeting of the International Economic Association at Konstanz, which was devoted to his thesis, Rostow concentrated on his leading sector doctrine, posing the question: "Why does the intro-

[21] "The economic history of Canada has been dominated by the discrepancy between the center and the margin of western civilization. Energy has been directed towards the exploitation of staple products and the tendency has become cumulative. . . . Large-scale production of raw materials was encouraged by improvement of techniques of production, of marketing, and of transport as well as by improvement in the manufacture of the finished product. . . . Agriculture, industry, transportation, trade, finance, and governmental activities tend to become subordinate to the production of the staple for a more highly specialized manufacturing community. . . . Canada remained British in spite of free trade and chiefly because she continued as an exporter of staples to a progressively industrialized mother country."
Harold A. Innis, *The Fur Trade in Canada* (New Haven, 1930), p. 388. It should be noted that the Innis theory was applied to "regions of recent settlement" trading with more advanced regions. See also Douglass North, "Location Theory and Regional Economic Growth," *Journal of Political Economy*, June, 1955, and *The Economic Growth of the United States, 1790–1860* (Englewood Cliffs, N.J., 1961).

duction of modern technology tend to assume the form of a series of leading sectors?" [22] The question itself seems a rather curious one. One might better ask: "Why should one expect technological progress to affect the whole economy simultaneously and proportionately, given the history of scientific advance, which itself has been sporadic and concentrated in one sector after another?" Still more relevant questions would be: "How can one create leading sectors where they do not exist?" and "How can one assure that innovation in one sector will spread to the rest of the economy?" Rostow states, correctly enough, that "the state becomes dependent then, on the recurrent coming into the capital stock of new technology and new production functions (including new land or raw material supplies) which, by imparting rapid growth to a limited number of sectors, manage to keep the average level of growth relatively steady against the inevitable erosion imposed by the passage of time on the momentum of individual sectors." [23]

In other words, to have economic growth there must be leading sectors, and they must lead—in the sense of having net spread effects to the rest of the economy. No one could deny the validity of this argument, but it adds little to our knowledge of the development process.

Borrowing from Schumpeter and Perroux, Rostow goes on to introduce a concept of "clusters of sectors" similar to Schumpeter's "clusters of followers" and also to Perroux's concept of "pôles de croissance." Anticipating one of the criticisms of his doctrine, he also raises the question, "Just how self-sustained is self-sustained growth?" The fact of deceleration itself, he points out, shows that growth is not automatic. On the contrary, to sustain a high average rate of growth a society "must engage in an endless struggle against deceleration." In this sense, therefore, sustained growth requires the *repetition* of the take-off process. But if economic growth consists of a *series* of take-offs, it is hard to see how Rostow's stages can be maintained rigorously.

The population increase, he says, in discussing linkages between leading sectors and other factors, is only obliquely linked to the leading sectors of take-off; and it is not linked in any simple or systematic way. [24] This statement taken literally is correct, but it rather underemphasizes the relationship between take-off and the population explosion. The simple fact is that in virtually every country where industrialization has begun, the rate of population growth has also increased, not because of any direct tie between industrialization and population growth, but rather because the general circumstances that give rise to an industrial revolution are also circumstances in which public health and law and order are improved.

Rostow also makes the point that an increase in agricultural productivity and production is an essential part of the whole process. Historically agriculture has not been a leading sector in most countries, but it provides

[22] W. W. Rostow (ed.), *The Economics of Take-Off into Sustained Growth*, Proceedings of a Conference held by the International Economic Association (London and New York, 1963). (Henceforth, W. W. Rostow, *Economics, op. cit.*)
[23] *Ibid.*, p. 3.
[24] *Ibid.*, p. 11.

necessary inputs into a leading sector. That is, agriculture has not been a leading sector in terms of national income and total employment, but it has sometimes been a leading sector for exports, as in the case of Australia or Canada.

Rostow also makes the interesting point that a highly favorable population-resource balance, of the kind enjoyed in the United States, Canada, and Argentina in the early phases of their development, may actually delay industrialization through concentration on "staples." He points out that "take-off has nearly always been preceded by improvements in transportation and other forms of social overhead capital." Here he comes close to Colin Clark's recipe for economic development, which consists of first raising agricultural productivity and then improving transport facilities, after which industrialization is supposed to take place more or less automatically.

OTHER "PRECONDITIONS"

Rostow makes a bow toward "reactive nationalism"—reaction against intrusions from more advanced nations—as "a most important and powerful motive force in the transition from traditional to modern societies." He then proceeds to ask, "Why Britain?" Why should the take-off not have appeared in France, Holland, or even the United States? The French, he says, "were too rough with their Protestants." The Dutch on the other hand "became too committed to finance and trade, without an adequate manufacturing base." These statements come uncomfortably close to saying, "The take-off came first in Britain because Britain had the necessary conditions for take-off before other countries." In the United States, the trouble was that the country was too *rich;* the natural resources were such that there was no need for people to turn to manufacturing—and manufacturing was the leading sector at that time. One is reminded here of Toynbee's "challenge and response" theory of the advance of civilization; the "challenge" must be serious enough to evoke "response," but not so serious as to lead to defeatism, apathy, and decay.

The Take-off

The take-off, says Rostow, "is the interval when the old blocks and resistances to steady growth are finally overcome. The forces making for economic progress, which yielded limited bursts and enclaves of modern activity, expand and come to dominate the society. Growth becomes its normal condition." The main feature of the take-off is an increase in the ratio of savings and investment to national income from perhaps 5 per cent to 10 per cent or more. Where the requirement for social overhead capital is heavy, it may require an investment ratio higher than 5 per cent to generate take-off. Usually, Rostow says, the beginning of take-off can be traced to some particular sharp stimulus. However, it seems that the stimulus need not be so sharp after all; for what is essential "is not the form of stimulus but the fact that the prior development of the society and its economy result in a positive, sustained and self-reinforcing response to it." [25] This statement makes it sound as though almost any stimulus will do

[25] *Ibid.,* p. 37.

provided only that the preconditions have already been established.

In addition to the rise in the rate of productive investment from 5 per cent or less to 10 per cent or more, two other features characterize the take-off: the development of one or more substantial manufacturing sectors with a high rate of growth, and the existence or quick emergence of a political, social, and institutional framework to exploit the impulses to expansion in the modern sector. "This view of take-off is, then," Rostow says, "a return to a rather old fashioned way of looking at economic development. The take-off is defined as an industrial revolution."

The take-off period is pinned down to an interval of about twenty years for a number of countries. Thus for Great Britain, Rostow assigns the years 1783–1802, for France 1830–1860, for United States 1843–1860, for Japan 1878–1900, for Canada 1896–1914, and for India 1952 up to the present time.

The Drive to Maturity

The take-off is followed by "a long interval of sustained if fluctuating progress" with 10 to 20 per cent of the national income steadily invested, "permitting output regularly to outstrip the increase in population." Rostow calls this interval the "drive to maturity," and "maturity" is generally obtained some sixty years after take-off. The dates assigned for achievement of maturity are 1850 for Great Britain, 1900 for the United States, 1910 for France, 1940 for Japan, and 1950 for Canada. Thus the interval between take-off and achievement of "maturity" varies from one country to another.

What happens during this long interval between take-off and maturity is none too clear from Rostow's discussion. In particular, the difference between his "take-off" and his "drive to maturity" is not easily stated. We have already seen that almost any stimulus will do once preconditions are established; and during the drive to maturity, with preconditions established, other stimuli appear to keep the process going. The process seems to be essentially the same as take-off itself, "with new leading sectors gathering momentum to supplant the older leading sectors." After the railroad take-off in the third quarter of the nineteenth century we have steel, new ships, chemicals, electricity, and the like. Thus "the drive to maturity" really seems to be a sort of "striptease stage," during which the economy just goes on taking off and taking off.

It should be noted that "maturity" in Rostow's sense is a far cry from the concept of "economic maturity" developed by Alvin Hansen and others, in which the economy faces stagnation because of the tendency to save more out of very high levels of income than can be invested profitably. The economy does not cease to grow with the achievement of maturity; on the contrary, it continues until the final stage of "high mass consumption" is reached. This stage of development from "maturity" to "high mass consumption" is apparently the longest of all. It has taken a century since "maturity" for the United States to achieve high mass consumption, and no other country has yet achieved it, although Great Britain experienced its "take-off" as early as 1850. The mature economy in Rostow's terminology is simply one in which structural change no longer takes place at a rapid rate. "The economy, focused during the take-off around a relatively narrow complex of industry and technology, has extended its range into more refined and technologically often more complex processes." Here, however, questions of fact arise; it does not seem that the rate of structural change in the United Kingdom slowed down markedly after 1850; and certainly the United Kingdom in 1850 was far indeed from what the present writer has termed a "climax economy" in which the process of luring people out of agriculture into the industrial and services sector has come to an end, and the structure of employment is much the same in all parts of the country.

The Take-off into Sustained Controversy

Rostow's colleagues have done him an honor accorded to very few economists; they have written more about him than he has written himself. In this respect, at least, the author of the Non-Communist Manifesto resembles the author of the Communist Manifesto.

In an article under the above title, Professor Henry Rosovsky reviews the meeting of the International Economic Association devoted to Rostow and the book arising out of that conference.[26] Based on the papers published in this volume, Rosovsky says, there are four possible answers to the question "What do you think of Rostow's take-off theory?" These answers (and the economists giving them) are: (1) Don't like it (Kuznets, Habakkuk, and Deane, Marczewski, Gerschenkron, and Solow); (2) Quite positively approve (Hoffman, Tsuru, Leibenstein, Boserup, Cairncross, Berrill, and Landes); (3) Very positively approve (Rostow); (4) Don't much care but was glad to have attended the conference (North, Fischer, Bulhoẽs, and Cootner).

Rosovsky finds no pattern in this alignment. It is not, for example, that the historians approve and the theorists disapprove, or that economists interested in Europe approve and those interested in developing countries do not. Nor is the attitude toward the Rostow theory "determined by the level of economic aggregation one feels is useful in the analysis of economic growth." Rostow himself, Rosovsky maintains, provides both an aggregate and a sectoral version of his theory.

The criticism of Rostow's thesis may be divided into three categories: first, those which apply to all stage theories; secondly, those which apply to the particular stage theory of Rostow; and thirdly, those which question the facts.

The general criticism of stage theories was well put by Professor Simon Kuznets in his contribution to the Konstanz Conference. If the major differences between modern and non-modern growth are recognized, says Kuznets, and if the cumulative character of growth is taken as a matter of definition, it is all too easy to suggest stages: [27]

[26] Henry Rosovsky, "The Take-off into Sustained Controversy," *Journal of Economic History*, March, 1965, pp. 271–275. The book is W. W. Rostow, *Economics, op. cit.*
[27] Simon Kuznets, "Notes on the Take-Off," in W. W. Rostow, *Economics, op. cit.*, p. 23.

Since modern economic growth presumably has roots in the past, a non-modern economic stage and a stage of preparation are clearly suggested: and we could easily divide the latter into several "phases"—initial preparatory phase; middle preparatory phase; final preparatory phase. Then since again by definition modern economic growth is not attained in a few years, we can discuss the early or emergence period, the middle stage, maturity [biological analogy], post-maturity, and so on.

Rosovsky points out that Rostow's theoretical weaknesses are shared by all other brands of stage theory, and he asks, "Why is it that economic historians cannot seem to abandon this (frequently discredited) type of reasoning?" Prof. Rosovsky answers his own question: "We cannot do justice to history by sweeping only with a single broom, and we yearn for periodization to create order in our minds. Considerations such as these must have driven Rostow back to stage theory and any practicing economic historian will sympathize even though he may not approve." [28]

With regard to Rostow's specific stage theory, it is apparent that a major prerequisite for its acceptance is that it must be conceptually possible to prove it wrong. To prove it wrong (that is, for it to be stated as a reputable hypothesis) the stages must be definable and presentable in terms other than economic development itself. This requirement is particularly true of the "traditional society." For the implication of Rostow's theory (or at least of his central formulation of it) is that once a society leaves the "traditional" stage and establishes the prerequisites for take-off, the economy will move more or less automatically through each of the succeeding stages until high mass consumption is reached. This statement is even more true if the Rostow theory is to become a basis for policy. For example, if the theory were taken seriously, we would not allocate foreign aid to countries where the preconditions already are present, because those countries are assured sustained economic development without it; rather, we would use foreign aid to establish preconditions where they are absent.

How do we recognize the traditional society? Rostow's own characterization of it—limited production functions, pre-Newtonian science and technology, belief that the external world is subject to a few knowable laws, and a high proportion of resources devoted to agriculture because of the limitations on productivity—these are really definitions of underdevelopment rather than an analysis of causes. How would one recognize "pre-Newtonian science and technology?" Clearly, the failure of the Javanese peasant to adapt the techniques of rice production of the state of Texas—sowing seeds from aircraft, reaping with harvesting machines, and the like—does not reflect lack of contact with modern technology, but rather the fact that his farm is less than two acres and that his capital is almost non-existent. Moreover, this definition of the traditional society

[28] Prof. Rosovsky believes that there is more hope in theories of long waves:
"There are (perhaps one could almost say 'there were') doubts about the reality of long swings, but they cannot persist in the face of increasing evidence on their behalf. With these long swings we can look at shorter segments of economic history with greater understanding, without having to subscribe to an international law of development, or to an ascent from lower to even higher economic stages." Rosovsky, *op. cit.*, p. 275.

completely ignores the dualistic character of the great majority of the developing economies. There is nothing "pre-Newtonian" about the plantation, mining, petroleum, and manufacturing sectors of Indonesia, the Philippines, or Brazil. Are we to say that these countries have no development problems?

Rostow himself is ambivalent about the continuity of development once preconditions are established. He speaks of the tendency for development to bog down and the need for continuous effort. It follows directly from the fact of deceleration, he says, that growth is not automatic. In order to sustain a high average rate of growth a society must "engage in an endless struggle against deceleration. . . . In this sense sustained growth requires the repetition of the take-off process." But if economic growth is a continuous series of take-offs, how does one discern the initial take-off phase? This question relates to another. Rostow's dating of phases for various countries leaves long gaps between take-off and maturity, and further gaps between maturity and high mass consumption. What happens in between? If the "drive to maturity" ends with maturity, why has it taken Great Britain more than a century after reaching maturity to achieve high mass consumption?

Kuznets, in his critique, lays down some minimum requirements for any stage theory that is to be taken seriously: a given stage must display empirically testable characteristics common to all or to an important group of units experiencing modern economic growth; the characteristics of a given stage must be distinctive, in that in combination they are unique to that stage; the analytical relations to the preceding stage must be indicated —that is, the processes in the preceding stage which completed it and make the next stage "highly probable" must be identified; the analytical relation to the succeeding stage must be indicated; and the universe for which the generality of common and distinctive characteristics is claimed must be indicated clearly.

Specific Criticisms of the Rostow Theory

Apart from attacks directed at stage theories in general, there have been attacks on the specific theoretical model underlying Rostow's particular version of the stages of economic growth. As mentioned, Rosovsky points out that there are at least two theories in Rostow's volume, one an aggregate version, the other a sectoral version of the take-off. "Instead of an intelligible pattern," Rosovsky says, "one finds quite a mish-mash."

Kuznets points out that Rostow's stages are considerably blurred. Much of what Rostow would attribute to the take-off, Kuznets argues, has already occurred in the preconditions stage. The traditional stage presumably does not see a rise in the investment ratio from 5 to 10 per cent; yet the agricultural revolution which Rostow assigns to the preconditions stage, and the building up of the infrastructure also assigned to the preconditions stage, in themselves involve substantial increases in investment. Indeed, according to Rostow, "The essence of the transition can be described legitimately as a rise in the rate of investment to a level which regularly, substantially, and perceptibly outstrips population growth."

Kuznets accordingly says, "One wonders whether the three specifically stated characteristics of take-off could not be found in the preconditions stage."

Kuznets feels that the dividing line between take-off and the following stage of self-sustained growth is also blurred. The only characteristics pertinent to the take-off and not to the next stage are the rise in the investment ratio to something over 10 per cent and the implicit acceleration of the growth of income. "But are we to assume," Kuznets asks, "that both the rate of investment and the rate of growth of product (total and per capita) level off at the high values attained at the end of the take-off stage?" The stage of self-sustained growth following the take-off, says Kuznets, "is somewhat of a puzzle. Is it self-sustained in a sense that it is *not* during the take-off and any earlier phase?" There is nothing in the Rostow theory to suggest that societies are likely to relapse to the stage of traditional societies once a take-off has occurred, although he does refer in his Konstanz lecture to the need for repeated efforts. Surely, however, Rostow is not arguing that repeated efforts and innovations are needed to achieve self-sustained growth, but that no effort is needed after that stage is reached? "Obviously," says Kuznets,[29]

The term is an analogy rather than a clearly specified property or characteristic; and for this reason alone should be avoided. In one sense any growth is self-sustained: It means an irreversible rise to a higher level of economic performance that may make it easier to find results for further growth. . . . In another sense any growth is self-limiting: the rise to a higher level may mean a reduction in incentive, pressure upon scarce irreproducible resources, and, perhaps most important, the strengthening of entrenched interests that are likely to resist growth in competing sectors.

In conclusion, Kuznets says, with respect to the theoretical framework of the Rostow model,[30]

Given this fuzziness in the limiting of the take-off stage and in formulation of its distinctive characteristics; given the distinctiveness only in the statistical level of the rate of productive investment (and the implicit rate of growth), there is no solid ground upon which to discuss Prof. Rostow's view of the analytical relation between the take-off stage and the preceding and succeeding stages.

Professor Gerschenkron takes Rostow to task for defining stages mainly in terms of growth rates of national income and share of investment. "He discusses them," says Gerschenkron, "as though reliable information and such magnitudes were readily available." But even if complete and reliable data were available, Gerschenkron maintains, it would still be doubtful whether national income figures would indicate the inception of a new process of growth. According to his findings, in Europe, at least, the more backward the country is on the eve of its "great spurt," the higher was the proportion of population in the agricultural sector and the greater the concentration of growth in the relatively small industrial sector. "Under these conditions," Gerschenkron writes, "a good deal of time must elapse

[29] Simon Kuznets, in W. W. Rostow, *Economics, op. cit.*, p. 39.
[30] *Ibid.*, p. 27.

before even a very rapid growth in the small area can affect national income as a whole." Gerschenkron would prefer to rely on a kink in the curve of industrial output itself as an indicator of the launching of his "great spurt," with the continuation of the spurt through a period of international depression without marked decline in the rate of growth as a secondary piece of evidence. However, Gerschenkron is unwilling to divide economic history into neat stages, partly because the situation constituting a "great spurt" can recur at several points in the economic history of a particular country.[31]

Professor Robert Solow, speaking for the economic theorists, chided Rostow for his failure to specify the theoretical model that he was testing with his historical data. In saying that "the take-off" is a distinct stage, he asks, does Rostow mean merely that when a certain level of strategic variables has been reached a new stage has also been reached, or are stages to be defined in terms of momentum or rates of change? It may also mean a change in the parameters—in the "fundamental laws governing economic life." Solow feels that the failure to include the role of expansion of foreign trade was another serious weakness in the model.

Solow also pointed to the inadequacy of the Rostow model in dealing with the technological dualism that characterizes most of the developing countries. It seems clear that interactions between agricultural and industrial sectors are at the core of the development process, especially in the transition from a poor and stagnant country to a rapidly developing one; yet the Rostow model provides no explicit analysis of these interactions. Indeed, Solow argued, Rostow really did not have a model at all, in the sense of "a set of behavior rules or statements connecting the movements of one economic variable with other economic and non-economic variables." The terminology and description of the Rostow model are evocative, but the model has "little or no analytical content." Consequently, discussion of it would not be cast in terms of the validity of the theoretical model, but rather would have "to concentrate mainly on such questions as 'Did Ruritania experience a take-off?' and 'Exactly when did Ruritania experience take-off?' "[32]

Still another problem in testing the Rostow thesis was the paucity of data. Long period quantitative data are available for only some fifteen countries. Under the circumstances there is no choice but to do the best one can with the data of these countries; but one must be cautious in translating the results of examination of these cases into an empirical law.

The Facts

Rostow's facts have also been challenged. With regard to the investment portion, Kuznets maintains, the data for Great Britain do not indicate any take-off at all, but rather a slow and relatively steady acceleration throughout the whole period from 1770 to 1914. The same is true of the national

[31] Alex Gerschenkron, "The Early Phases of Industrialization in Russia: Afterthoughts and Counterthoughts," in W. W. Rostow, *Economics, op. cit.*, pp. 151–169.

[32] Robert Solow, quoted in D. C. Haque, "Summary Record of the Debate," in W. W. Rostow, *Economics, op. cit.*, p. 472.

income data for Britain. Much the same is true of Germany. The investment proportion increased only 60 per cent in the 20 years dated by Rostow as the take-off, and took six decades to double. In Sweden it took eight decades for the investment proportion to double. In Japan there was no significant increase in the investment ratio until after World War I, and there is no evidence of perceptible acceleration in the rate of growth of either total or per capita income.

Professors Habakkuk and Deane deal with the British case in much more detail. They point out that the acceleration following 1740 is at least as marked as that following 1780, the date assigned to the beginning of take-off by Rostow.[33] "If we are looking for the critical threshold beyond which growth became more or less automatic," these authors ask, "is it not as reasonable to see it in the 1740's when, for the first time in English history, population began to expand continuously without being checked by an output barrier?"[34] They also find much more continuity in technological change in the British case than Rostow suggests. They find no evidence that the industries that Rostow claims ignited the Industrial Revolution had much effect on investment by the beginning of the nineteenth century. The big impact came considerably later. If there was an important breakthrough during the last decade of the eighteenth century, it was in the expansion of international trade rather than in technology. In their concluding paragraph, they write:[35]

In the end it seems that the most striking characteristic of the first take-off was its gradualness. Professor Neff has traced the process of industrialization back to the sixteenth century. The sustained rise in the rate of total in output probably dates back to the 1740's. If the 1780's be taken as the starting point for the revolutionary changes in industrial techniques and organization then it took about a century for the long-term rate of growth in average rural incomes (measured over 30 year periods) to rise from about 1 per cent per annum to just over 2 per cent per annum. . . . The evidence suggests a long steady climb, inspired by periodic bursts of energy or enterprise and lagging seriously only in the twentieth-century interwar period.

That Rostow is not always sure of his facts is indicated by his reference to Canada, where he says that the "contemporary mature Canada contains the still lagging province of Quebec." This statement would suggest that Quebec has a level of technological advance, a structure of employment, and a level of per capita income substantially different from that of the rest of the country. In fact, however, the Province of Quebec is more advanced than Canada as a whole in terms of structure of output and employment, has never lagged far behind the neighboring leading region of Ontario in this respect, has never for long grown less rapidly in either manufacturing or agriculture, and is currently the most rapidly expanding region in the country. It is true that per capita incomes in Quebec are some

[33] H. J. Habakkuk and Phyllis Deane, "The Take-off in Britain," in W. W. Rostow, *Economics, op. cit.*, pp. 63–82.
[34] *Ibid.*, p. 68.
[35] *Ibid.*, p. 82.

15 per cent below the Canadian average, but they are not nearly as far below as in the lagging region of the Maritime Provinces.

Conclusions on Rostow's Stages

In characterizing his own theory, Rostow says: "These stages are not merely descriptive. They are not merely a way of generalizing certain factual observations about the sequence of development of modern society. They have an inner logic and continuity. They have an analytical bone structure rooted in a dynamic theory of production." [36] In summary, he writes: "The period of pre-conditions is the time in the life of a society when the traditional structure is undermined piecemeal while important dimensions of the old system remain. Just before and during the take-off the new modern elements, values and objectives obtain a definite break-through; and they come to control the society's institutions; and then, having made their point, with their opponents in retreat or disarray, they drive to carry the process of modernization to its logical conclusion." Unfortunately, this entire summary statement is a series of tautologies.

In his reply to his critics, Rostow suggests that economic growth may be too complex to be reduced to theoretical models simple enough to satisfy economic theorists. Economic theory, he says, has great power over a limited range. "It may not be able to function in the world of organized complexity which growth analysis, at its best, is bound to be." The circularity of Professor Rostow's reasoning appears again here, however: [37]

For a society to absorb new production functions, in ways which generate the spread effects on which the take-off depends, requires massive prior change away from the pattern of the traditional society. Before take-off can occur there must be changes in the economy's infrastructure, working force, agriculture, and foreign exchange earning or borrowing capacity. There must also be "changes in rules of behavior," particularly in the form of emergence of a minimal initial group of entrepreneurs.

Once again, it appears that Rostow says little more than that for a take-off to occur, the conditions for take-off must be present.

One thing, however, is clear; no matter how critical Rostow's colleagues may be of his system, his terminology is here to stay. The expressions, "the take-off" and "self-sustained growth," are thoroughly entrenched in the literature, and will continue to be used by development economists, including the present writer.

We must admit to a sense of disappointment at what the economic historian has to offer by way of explanation of how economic development did take place in the now advanced countries.[38] We have added very

---

[36] W. W. Rostow, *Stages, op. cit.,* pp. 12–13.

[37] W. W. Rostow, *Economics, op. cit.,* p. xxv.

[38] It seems that economic history must be rewritten with each advance in economic theory. Arthur Lewis has put the situation well: "Every economist goes through a phase where he is dissatisfied with the deductive basis of economic theory, and feels sure that a much better insight into economic processes could be obtained by studying the facts of history. The instinct is sound; yet the enthusiasms of this phase

little to the list of strategic variables included in our synthesis of general theories: the importance of capital formation; the vital role of technological progress and the entrepreneurial function; the widening of the market and expansion of international trade as a means of widening markets; the necessity of structural change, with a relative decline of the agricultural sector at the same time that agricultural productivity rises. All this we knew from our survey of general theory. One hint in the historical analysis, however, is worth recording for future consideration when we turn to the problems of underdeveloped countries today: the Black Death not only gave European countries a respite from population pressure but drastically changed the factor-proportion situation. Labor became scarce even in agriculture, and a shift to more land-and-capital-intensive techniques became profitable to landowners. The expansion of world trade, coming conveniently at the same time, provided growing markets for the product of the new extensive agriculture, and by another strikingly convenient coincidence, the growth of manufactures provided employment for peasants forced off the land by enclosures, or lured to the burgeoning cities by opportunities for self-advancement there.

---

seldom survive any serious attempt to get to grips with the facts of history. This is because there are very few facts in the relevant senses. We mean by this, in the first instance, that it is only for a very few countries and for very recent periods that any adequate quantity of historical records exists; and even when there are plenty of records we cannot always be certain exactly what happened. We mean also, more significantly, that the 'facts' which would interest the theorist are not what happened but why it happened; and while history may record what happened, it is seldom able to record why it happened. . . . Most economic historians explain economic events in terms of the economic theories current at the time of writing . . . and a new crop of economic theories is liable to be followed by a new crop of historical articles rewriting history in terms of the new theory." (*The Theory of Economic Growth*, p. 15.)

10 Economic Development: Past and Present

In the preceding chapter we put this question: "What were the major causes of the rise of capitalism?" Another way to learn from history is to ask: "What are the differences between the present situation of underdeveloped countries and the situation in the now advanced countries at the time of their take-off into sustained economic growth?" Such a comparison may help us to appreciate the dimensions of the task now facing underdeveloped countries as they try to reach higher standards of living. Even a superficial examination of the economic history of the Western world between 1700 and 1950 reveals an extraordinary conjunctrue of factors favorable to economic growth. Was this conjuncture a historical accident, an accident that cannot be reproduced by acts of policy?

This chapter is addressed to these questions. For purposes of analysis—and recognizing the arbitrary nature of any such distinction—the various factors are divided among economic, political, sociological, and technological categories.

Economic Factors

In Part II, we saw that all theories of economic development, from Adam Smith to Hansen, relate increases in per capita income to four major factors: capital accumulation, population growth, discoveries of new resources, and technological progress. These four factors are interrelated in various ways; indeed, theories of economic development differ mainly with regard to the nature of these interrelationships. Let us examine conditions affecting these four factors in the now advanced countries, during the period of their most rapid growth, and compare those with conditions affecting them in the now underdeveloped countries.

Our review of development theories showed that the effect of capital accumulation on development is ambivalent. Each act of net investment raises national income but retards further net investment. Other things being equal, profits tend to decline as the stock of capital grows. For continued economic expansion to occur, one or more of the other three factors must operate favorably, so as to produce a steady rate of capital accumulation.

In the now advanced countries, net savings and investment during the periods of rapid growth averaged between 10 and 20 per cent of national income. In most, but not all the now underdeveloped countries, net savings and investment run between 5 and 10 per cent of the national income. Here is one of the many vicious circles encountered in any study of the problem of economic development. A high level of national income results in a high level of savings and investment, and consequently, in a rapid rate of economic growth. Underdeveloped countries in general have such low incomes that any substantial volume of savings and investment out of existing income is extremely difficult. To a large degree, the problem of economic growth is a problem of "getting over the hump" to the point where levels of per capita income are high enough to permit sufficient net savings and investment to guarantee continued expansion.

It has been suggested that significant increases in *per capita* income can be achieved without much capital investment.[1] Our own view is that opportunities for raising *per capita* output in a fashion requiring little *per capita* investment should certainly be seized, but that opportunities for this type of development project are not sufficient in themselves to get the underdeveloped countries "over the hump"—unless a new technology, suited to the factor endowment of these underdeveloped countries, can be discovered. This new technology, which would be labor absorbing and capital saving, would have to apply over a much wider range of economic activity than the road-building, irrigation, and similar projects proposed for the purpose of absorbing disguised unemployment and raising productivity without much investment.[2]

In this chapter, where we are concerned with a comparison of what did happen in the now advanced countries with what might happen in the now underdeveloped ones, we need make only two observations: first, the "trigger mechanism" of the Industrial Revolution did not consist of such projects as building roads and undertaking irrigation projects, with disguised unemployed labor utilizing known techniques, but rather of technical advance occurring more or less simultaneously over a wide field; second, at least some of the underdeveloped countries have transport facilities and irrigation systems in a relatively advanced state. There seems no way but

[1] Cf. James Duesenberry, "Some Aspects of the Theory of Economic Development," *Explorations in Entrepreneurial History*, December, 1950; Ragnar Nurkse, *Problems of Capital Formation in Underdeveloped Countries* (New York, 1953); and International Labor Office, *Report of the Director-General* (Geneva, 1953), pp. 37–48.

[2] Problems relating to the choice of technology are discussed further in Chap. 18.

to increase the flow of savings and investment if the less developed countries wish to enjoy high standards of living.

Population Growth

It is useful to distinguish among four types of population situation.
First, population may be less than optimum, in the strict technical sense
that *per capita* income could be raised merely by increasing the size of the
population, with no changes in other strategic variables. Second, *per capita*
income may not rise with increasing population alone, but a feasible development program might create a situation in which population growth
would have a favorable effect on *per capita* income. Third, the marginal
productivity of labor (and thus of population increases) may be positive,
although *per capita* income would fall with rising population, despite any
measures that could be taken as part of any feasible development program.
Fourth, the situation may be one in which the marginal productivity of
labor is zero or negative, and will remain so despite the development
program.

Some of the now advanced countries, such as Canada, are still in the first
category. More important, almost all the advanced countries were in this
category *at the beginning* of their periods of most rapid growth. The
Industrial Revolution began at a time when European populations were
very small. With technological progress, resource discoveries, and expanding world markets, the level of the optimum population became steadily
higher, so that actual population remained below optimum throughout
most of the period of rapid growth.

Some of the Latin American countries appear to be in the second
category; a rise in population by itself might not raise per capita income,
but appropriate and feasible development plans could create a situation in
which population growth would have a favorable effect on *per capita*
income. Unfortunately, most of the Middle Eastern and Asian countries
(with the possible exceptions of Burma, Indochina, and Malaya) are in
the third, or even in the fourth, category.

There is, therefore, a discontinuity in the growth function with respect
to population increases. Where population grows in a country with less
than optimal population, that growth provides an additional stimulus to
expansion, by encouraging investment in housing, transport, public utilities, and the like, and by permitting optimal capital-labor ratios to be
maintained as capital accumulates. But where populations are already above
optimum levels, further increases act only as a drag on economic development, preventing any rise in per capita income, or even lowering per
capita income, and thus aggravating the difficulty of saving and investing
enough to generate expansion. Moreover, the population growth of underdeveloped countries takes a very wasteful form. The combination of high
birth rates and high death rates means that a large proportion of the
population consists of unproductive children, many of whom will not live
long enough to repay the community's investment in them.

In short, the now advanced countries had their take-off before their
population explosion, whereas many of the now underdeveloped countries

have had their population explosion before a take-off. Moreover, European rates of population growth were never so high as they are in some under-developed countries today.

Perhaps the most important consequence of this difference in sequence is the contrast in levels of per capita income at the time of actual or at-tempted take-off. We saw in Chapter 1 that any international comparison of income levels is precarious; it becomes still more precarious when current incomes in some countries are compared with incomes in another country two centuries ago. Nevertheless, the estimates made by Phyllis Deane (Table 10–1) suggest, when allowance is made for subsequent changes in price levels, that incomes in England in the eighteenth century were closer to those of Argentina or Chile today than to those of India or Burma today. Obviously, it is easier to save and invest enough to meet the requirements for take-off out of an average income of $300 than out of an average of $100.

The relatively high incomes in Europe before the Industrial Revolution reflect another factor of great importance—a factor facilitated, and

TABLE 10–1

Contemporary Estimates of the National Income of the
United Kingdom in the Nineteenth Century

Year and deriva-tion of national income estimates	Population, in millions	Average money national income, £	Domestic exports as percentage national income	Estimate of trend in average real incomes 1800 = 100
1800 (Pitt, Beeke, Bell)	15.7	19	13	100
1812 (Colquhoun)	18.4	22	10	94
1822 (Lowe)	21.3	17	10	114
1831 (Pebrer)	24.1	23	7	174
1836 (Mulhall)	25.4	24	8	168
1841 (Spackman)	26.8	21	11	145
1846 (Smee)	28.0	21	10	160
1851 (Levi)	27.4	23	13	193
1860 (Mulhall)	28.8	33	14	234
1867 (Levi, Baxter)	30.4	28	21	205
1870 (Mulhall)	31.3	31	22	222
1879–80 (Levi)	34.3	35	18	274
1880 (Mulhall)	34.6	33	19	278
1882–83 (Levi)	35.2	36	21	296
1883 (Giffen)	35.5	36	18	307
1886 (Mulhall)	36.3	34	18	326
1889 (Mulhall)	37.2	35	19	342
1895 (Mulhall)	39.2	36	16	402
1902 (Giffen)	41.9	42	16	405

SOURCE: Phyllis Deane, "The Industrial Revolution and Economic Growth: The Evidence of Early British National Income Estimates," *Economic Development and Cultural Change*, Vol. V, No. 2, January, 1957.

indeed encouraged, by the lack of population pressure. In Europe a long period of agricultural improvement, tending toward more extensive agriculture, preceded the Industrial Revolution. Industrialization in turn permitted a second wave of agricultural improvement in the form of mechanization. As we shall see in more detail in Chapter 14, some underdeveloped countries have had considerable industrialization while agricultural producitivity lagged further and further behind. This low productivity in agriculture is largely a result of population pressure and consequent division of landholdings into tiny splinters.

Simon Kuznets emphasizes six major differences between underdeveloped countries today and the now advanced countries when they began their industrialization: (1) the *present* level of per capita product in the underdeveloped countries in their pre-industrial phase (well above $200 at 1952–54 prices) is much lower than it was in the now advanced countries, with the single exception of Japan; (2) the supply of land per capita is much smaller in developing countries today than it was in the present advanced countries when they began their industrialization; (3) agricultural productivity in developing countries today is probably lower than it was in advanced countries in the past; (4) the inequality in the distribution of income is wider today than in the past, but not in a way that favors accumulation of productive capital; (5) the social and political structure of the low-income countries today is a much greater barrier than it was in the past; (6) most of the present-day underdeveloped countries are launching development after a long period of colonial status, whereas the European countries began industrialization after a long period of political independence.[3]

No expert can suggest any simple short-run policy to meet this situation. The happy circumstance in which economic expansion took place at a time when populations were below optimum, so that population growth was a favorable factor in the development picture, cannot be reproduced in most of the now underdeveloped countries, except by drastic measures introduced in the social, economic, and technical fields all at once.

Discovery of New Natural Resources

We have seen that the discovery of new natural resources, or the opening up of frontiers, plays a prominent role in recent theories of economic development. Yet all these theories imply, if they do not explicitly state, that resource discovery in itself is not enough to produce economic growth; an *increasing rate* of resource discovery is required.[4] In so far as resource discovery is a factor influencing past and present

---

[3] Simon Kuznets, *Economic Growth and Structure: Selected Essays* (New York, 1965), pp. 177–78.

[4] See, for example: Benjamin Higgins, "The Theory of Increasing Under-Employment," *The Economic Journal*, June, 1950; Evsey Domar, "Capital Expansion, Rate of Growth, and Employment," *The American Economic Review*, March, 1947; and "Investment, Losses, and Monopoly," in *Income, Employment, and Public Policy: Essays in Honor of Alvin Hansen* (New York, 1948); R. F. Harrod, *Towards A Dynamic Economics* (London, 1948); and Burton Keirstead, *The Theory of Economic Change* (Toronto, 1948).

levels of investment, a constant rate of discovery is needed merely to prevent a *decline* in investment, and thus in employment and output. This consideration is an important one, since most underdeveloped countries have enjoyed substantial rates of resource discovery in the past. In the former colonial areas especially, considerable time, effort, ingenuity, and capital have been devoted to discovery and development of new natural resources. In these areas, producing a rate of resource discovery *more rapid* than that which has taken place in the past will be no easy task.

The problem is complicated by the fact that most underdeveloped areas do not have "frontiers" in the sense that they existed in the New World in the nineteenth century, or even in the sense that they existed in Europe in the eighteenth century. The peoples of the present underdeveloped areas do not have the opportunity of moving to virgin land that is richer than the land now occupied. In most underdeveloped countries, the present distribution of population reflects very accurately the distribution of known resources, including soil fertility. In Libya, for example, moving from the settled areas means moving out into the Sahara. In Indonesia, the areas selected for transmigration, in order to relieve population pressure in Java and provide opportunities for technically improved agriculture, were far indeed from being easily accessible, virgin, and rich. Some were cut-over areas, once intensively cultivated, later abandoned, and now covered with useless *alang-alang* grass which is both hard and costly to remove. The rest was jungle, virgin perhaps, but extremely difficult and expensive to clear. Moreover, the soil in these areas was less fertile than the rich volcanic soils of Java, from which the settlers are to come. In neither of these countries, therefore—and in few other underdeveloped countries—do people have the opportunity of moving to areas *still richer* in known natural resources than those they formerly occupied.

The outlook with respect to mineral resources is less clear, since surveys are not complete. On the other hand, colonial powers have spent much energy and money in searching for mineral resources. In general, in those countries where exploration has been at all successful, past investment in resource development has been high. To discover enough new natural resources to generate *still higher* levels of developmental investment than occurred in the past will be a difficult task.

Apart from the influence on investment through the production function and through presentation of new market opportunities, we have seen that the frontier, as it existed in Canada or the United States, was an important growth factor through the inculcation of a "frontier spirit." The possibility of "moving West" to areas where the land was fertile and mineral resources abundant kept alive a venturesome entrepreneurial spirit throughout a century and a half. We have seen that the absence of such a frontier is one factor in the difference between Australian experience and that of countries of English background in the New World. But if the frontier in the Canadian or American sense was lacking in Australia, its absence is still more striking in the case of most underdeveloped areas. For centuries, such economic development as took place brought no obvious movement in the centroid of population. Nothing remotely resembling the westward movements in the United States and Canada, or even the movements from country areas to cities in nineteenth-century England has taken place in most underdeveloped areas. Consequently, no "frontier spirit" of venturesome entrepreneurship is to be found in these countries.

Technological Progress

The theories of economic development outlined above generally lay primary stress on technological progress. Here too, it is worth remembering that in most of these theories, it is an *increase in the rate* of technological progress, rather than the mere existence of technological advance, which produces economic expansion. Few underdeveloped countries indeed have been without substantial improvements in technique in the past. The problem is not merely one of introducing some degree of improvement in techniques, it is a matter of raising the *rate* of technological progress.

The outlook in this connection is certainly more favorable than in the case of resource discoveries or population growth. The level of techniques is low in the rural sector of underdeveloped areas where the large proportion of the population is occupied. During the "catching-up period," while the level of techniques in these sectors is approaching that of the advanced countries—or of the more advanced industrial sector in the same countries—the rate of technological progress might be very high indeed. Once this catching-up period is over, the problem of *increasing* the rate of technological progress still further will be serious indeed, but this problem need not worry us for some time.

Nevertheless, there are problems with regard to increasing the rate of technological progress in underdeveloped countries. A high rate of technological advance requires both inventions and innovations; that is, it requires that new techniques be not only discovered but also brought into use. Our discussion of Schumpeter's theory emphasized the introduction of inventions into use, or innovation, as the very essence of entrepreneurship. Unfortunately, most underdeveloped countries have limited indigenous entrepreneurship. In Europe before the Industrial Revolution, the ideological changes accompanying the Reformation created attitudes favorable to enterprise. The entrepreneurial spirit was enhanced by the opportunities presented by the enclosure movement, the discoveries, and the expansion of world trade. In contrast to this upsurge of enterprise is the feudal attitude toward commerce and industry which still prevails in many underdeveloped countries. In some of these countries today, as in Europe generations ago, the gentleman does not sullly his hands in trade. The educated man should be a doctor, a lawyer, a university professor, possibly an engineer, or best of all, a government official. He who becomes a mere businessman is a species of failure. Nor is innovation respected and rewarded in most of these societies.

True, the government may replace private enterprise as innovator. But as Singer has pointed out,[5] government enterprise has disadvantages for

[5] H. W. Singer, "Obstacles to Economic Development," *Social Research,* Spring, 1953.

development of underdeveloped countries. Most underdeveloped areas are very short of trained people at top levels of government. If these people concentrate on development problems, they may neglect the regular duties of government. The result will be bad administration, which is one of the main barriers to economic development. As Singer indicates, we are confronted here with another of the vicious circles so frequently encountered in this field. It takes good administrators to improve administration. Moreover, Singer argues, it is disadvantageous for economic development policy to be mixed up with nationalism and with local politics.

The Indonesian scene provides illustrations of the effect of nationalism in retarding enterprise. The Indonesian government recognizes the importance for Indonesian development of the complex of power and industrial projects constituting the Asahan Valley Program. The launching of this program, however, is blocked by the inability of the Indonesian government to finance and manage such large-scale undertakings itself, and by the reluctance of strong nationalist groups to see natural resources in the hands of foreigners.

The Philippines provides an example of the injurious effects of political control over development activities. There is lip service to the need for a development program, and the planning techniques are quite sophisticated. But the measures really necessary to solve the country's economic problem—an effective tax system, change in the structure of production, land reform, increased government responsibility—have run contrary to the interest of the politically powerful group which has a big stake in maintaining the *status quo*.

There are other economic problems connected with the generation of a high rate of technological progress. Rapid technological progress requires not only entrepreneurship of the Schumpeterian type, but also managerial, technical, and labor skills. Unfortunately, the underdeveloped countries are short of all these. If technological progress consists merely of adapting techniques or introducing commodities already known in the West, there are further disadvantages. Although this process may permit a high rate of technological advance at first, the "leverage effects" may be low. The "geographic multiplier effects" will be felt very largely outside the country, rather than inside it, as was the case where new techniques were developed in the same country as that in which it was applied. If the top management and technicians are brought in from abroad—and it is difficult to imagine how Western techniques could be introduced rapidly otherwise —the process may not become cumulative or self-sustaining, since an indigenous class of top managers and technicians may not develop quickly. Most underdeveloped countries have balance of payments problems, and the importation of capital equipment, in order to take advantage of superior techniques of the Western world, may result in a temporary deterioration of this balance that can be ill-afforded. The advanced countries now have a virtual monopoly of scientific and industrial research, and this research is not directed toward the special problems and the factor endowment of underdeveloped countries. Finally, modern technology brings rapid obsolescence, which only advanced countries with a high ratio of savings and investment to income, can afford.

Despite these limitations, it is a rapid rate of technological progress that offers most hope of economic development of underdeveloped areas.

Importance of Conjuncture of Economic Factors

The extraordinary advance of Europe during the Industrial Revolution, and of the New World in the nineteenth and twentieth centuries, was the result of a favorable *conjuncture* of all these economic forces. Population grew from levels below optimum, so that population growth constituted a further stimulus to expansion. Population growth was accompanied by migration to areas even richer in natural resources than those which were left behind. These two factors were accompanied by a rapid rate of technological progress, which encouraged search for other types of resources and brought new population movements. Population growth also provided additional demand for the new products and for increased output, and it prevented capital accumulation from outrunning the labor supply. Together with resource discoveries, the growing labor force prevented diminishing rates of profit.

Achieving a rapid rate of technological progress in underdeveloped countries is not impossible despite the barriers. What does seem virtually impossible is the achievement of the same *favorable conjuncture of all the economic factors* which was enjoyed by the Western world during its period of most rapid economic progress.

Political Factors

Political as well as economic factors combined to create an atmosphere conducive to economic development of the Western world in the eighteenth and nineteenth centuries. These favorable factors may be divided into two main categories: the politics of the technically superior country during the period and the politics of the relatively underdeveloped areas at the same time.

Politics of Technically Superior Countries

During the eighteenth century, economic development was largely a matter of developing new industries and areas within the geographic area subject to control by the government concerned. The political advantages of this sort of development are too obvious to need stressing here. It will be more fruitful to compare the politics of the technically superior countries during the nineteenth century, when the United States, Canada, Australia, and the New World generally enjoyed rapid growth, with the politics of the technically superior countries today. During the eighteenth and nineteenth centuries, the technically superior countries were the United Kingdom, France, Holland, and Germany. For our purposes, however, we can concentrate our attention on the United Kingdom, as the dominant power in that period. Similarly, the technically superior countries today are the United States and Canada, and possibly Australia, the United Kingdom, Holland, Switzerland, Sweden, Germany, France, and Russia; but we can usefully concentrate on the policies of the United

States because of its overwhelming importance in the world economy.

Let us first consider foreign trade policy. During most of the period under consideration, the United Kingdom followed a policy of free trade. There were, of course, good reasons for this policy line. The United Kingdom enjoyed virtually a monopoly position with respect to the sale of its manufactured goods, and a monopsony position in the purchase abroad of agricultural raw materials and foodstuffs. Perhaps because its monopoly-and-monopsony position is somewhat less secure, the United States has followed a high tariff policy rather than a free trade policy. Difficulties in marketing their output of raw materials and foodstuffs, because of the high tariff policy pursued by the United States, operate as a retarding influence on the economic development of the now under-developed areas.

The United Kingdom was also a heavy importer. After 1825, its balance of trade in commodities became unfavorable. From 1873 on, its balance of trade in goods and services combined was unfavorable: Great Britain financed its trade deficit from the large amounts of interest and profits earned on its heavy investment abroad.[6] Not only was its balance of trade unfavorable, but the volume of British imports was high relative to national income, probably averaging some 25 per cent. The United States, by contrast, not only has a high tariff but has consistently maintained favorable balances of trade in recent years. Moreover, its imports are a very small fraction of gross national income, averaging less than 5 per cent. Relative to the scale of its own economy and of the present-day world economy, the United States is providing a much less advantageous market for the products of underdeveloped areas, with respect both to the balance and to the volume of trade, and perhaps with respect to the terms of trade as well.

A similar contrast appears with respect to foreign investment. Professor Cairncross estimated over a decade ago that if the United States were to lend abroad on a scale equivalent in terms of *per capita* real income to that of the United Kingdom during the nineteenth century, the United States would have had, even in 1952, 600 billion dollars of foreign investments, on which it would have earned 30 billion dollars a year.[7] In other terms, to match the flow of capital from the United Kingdom in the nineteenth century, relative to its *per capita* real income, the United States would have to carry out the entire Marshall Plan twice every year! The scale of foreign aid and investment would need to be increased tenfold. Today, of course, these figures would have to be raised again. There was no "chronic shortage of sterling" during the period of rapid growth of the United States, Canada, and Australia, but there has been a "chronic shortage of dollars" through much of the period since World War II.

It has been suggested that the large scale of British foreign investment in the nineteenth century, although dictated largely by private economic

---

[6] Cf. A. E. Kahn, *Great Britain in the World Economy* (New York, 1946), especially chap. VIII.

[7] A. K. Cairncross, *Home and Foreign Investment, 1870–1913* (Cambridge, 1953), p. 3.

interests, was consistent with domestic government policy. The French Revolution instilled a deep-seated fear in Britain's elite, and a feeling that the masses deserved—or might insist upon—more consideration than they had received in the past. There was, therefore, a wish in high places to obtain cheap food. Frontier developments using British capital made cheaper food possible. Thus apart from the immediate economic interest in developing underdeveloped countries through large-scale foreign investment, there was a more subtle political purpose.

Finally, the technically superior countries were able to enforce stability in underdeveloped areas. Originally the "underdeveloped areas" were within their own borders. Later, colonies assumed paramount importance. Later still, the United States and the Dominions became major recipients of foreign investment. Perhaps it was less easy for the United Kingdom to police investments in the Dominions than in its colonies, and less easy in colonies than within its own borders; but the superior military force of the United Kingdom was one factor in promoting confidence among investors. In the underdeveloped countries today, even a slight suggestion that Western powers are trying to exercise physical control may cause serious trouble for foreign investors. In Indonesia in 1952, the technically superior country (the United States) found itself unable even to obtain a Mutual Security Administration agreement which included military aid—a single example of the difficulty the technically superior country faces in dealing with the underdeveloped areas today.

During the nineteenth century the technically superior countries confronted no major political challenge in underdeveloped areas. The United Kingdom, France, Holland, and Germany, might have been rivals but they had a common interest in maintaining political stability in such areas. Today, one set of powers has a distinct interest in fomenting unrest in those areas. Efforts of the technically superior country to enforce stability may drive underdeveloped countries into the enemy camp. This fact naturally affects the attitudes of potential investors in the technically superior countries, whether private or governmental, toward investment in the now less developed areas.[8]

Politics of Underdeveloped Areas

In sharp contrast to the current situation in underdeveloped areas, in the New World during the eighteenth and nineteenth centuries nationalism seldom took a form antipathetic to foreign capital. Even in the United States, which won its independence from the British Empire through a revolution, nationalist feeling imposed no serious obstacles to a large and continuous flow of British capital into the country. In colonies, and even in areas which were not legally colonies at all, forced labor and expropriation of property played their roles in economic development, as Bronfenbrenner has pointed out.[9]

How different is the current situation in the underdeveloped countries,

[8] These matters are treated more fully in a subsequent discussion.
[9] Cf. Martin Bronfenbrenner, "The High Cost of Economic Development," *Land Economics*, May, 1953, pp. 98–99.

ECONOMIC DEVELOPMENT: PAST AND PRESENT

most of which are now sovereign nations. Far from being able to force labor or expropriate property, the foreign investor is more apt to find himself at the mercy of powerful trade unions backed by government arbitration boards, and threatened with outright expropriation of his property, or import and immigration restrictions and foreign exchange controls which are tantamount to expropriation. In many underdeveloped countries today, risks of unpredictable and injurious government action, often based on nationalist sentiment, are added to the normal risks attendant upon investment abroad.

Moreover, in the New World of the eighteenth and nineteenth centuries development was undertaken mainly by and with people from the investing countries themselves. As Cairncross has demonstrated, capital and labor flowed together from the Old World to the New.[10] The emigrants who provided the management and the labor force for foreign undertakings spoke the same language and represented the same culture as those providing the capital. The situation naturally led to a higher degree of confidence in foreign investment than can be expected where governments insist on use of nationals of a culture alien to the investor, as they do in many of the present underdeveloped areas. For similar reasons, search for new natural resources by foreign capitalists was more attractive in the New World in the eighteenth and nineteenth centuries than it is in most underdeveloped areas today. Then there were no problems with regard to transfers of profits when earned, or with regard to personal and corporation income taxes, visas for managerial and technical personnel, land leases, and the like. These same conditions facilitated a higher rate of technological progress, since the movement of capital was usually accompanied by a transfer of skills and of technical knowledge.

Another aspect of the internal policies of the underdeveloped areas which is inimical to rapid development is insistence on early introduction of a full-fledged welfare state. In the now advanced countries, the welfare state appeared only after generations of industrialization. In the present underdeveloped areas, the usual policy seems to reverse this process. Most of these countries want the blessings of the welfare state today, complete with old age pensions, unemployment insurance, family allowances, health insurance, forty-hour week, and all the trimmings. Similarly, trade unions became powerful in the now advanced countries only after considerable industrial development had taken place. The statistics are none too good, but it seems likely that the material standard of living of European wage earners *declined* in the first stages of the Industrial Revolution. In terms of actual welfare, industrial slum dwellers in eighteenth-century England were almost certainly worse off than the peasants who were their forebears—and perhaps worse off than the Indonesian *tani* today. Many of the now underdeveloped areas, on the other hand, are encouraging the development of trade unionism in advance of industrialization. In some countries the trade unions, backed by governmental arbitration boards, are demanding higher wages, shorter hours, and "fringe benefits" which do

---

[10] Cairncross, *op. cit.*, especially chaps. III and VIII.

not reflect any commensurate rise in man-hour productivity. Especially where the employer is a foreigner, trade-union members are nationals, and nationalist sentiments run high because of recent release from colonialism, governments are hard put to it to support employers against trade unions, even where economic development is adversely affected by crippling demands. Too few of the trade-union leaders of underdeveloped countries have learned the hard lesson that a higher standard of living for labor as a group requires higher productivity of labor as a group.

Finally, as Hansen has suggested, the fiscal systems of most Western countries in the early stages of industrial development were such as to redistribute income from poor to rich.[11] Taxes consisted almost entirely of customs and excise duties, which fell relatively heavily on the poor, who spent most of their incomes for consumers' goods. Income and inheritance taxes were unknown. Government expenditures, on the other hand, were of a type benefiting mainly the upper-income groups: interest on government bonds, subsidies to private enterprise, transport facilities, and the like. However reprehensible these fiscal systems may have been from the social viewpoint, they added to the flow of savings and investment, and thus accelerated economic development. Most underdeveloped countries today want exactly the opposite kind of fiscal system, with progressive income and inheritance taxes and social security expenditures, designed to improve the distribution of income and wealth. Laudable as these policies are on social grounds, they tend in themselves to reduce the flow of savings and investment and so to retard economic growth.

Sociological Factors

Sociological, as well as economic and political, factors coincided to favor rapid economic growth of the Western world in the eighteenth and nineteenth centuries. There is a whole literature purporting to show how the Reformation raised the propensity to save. The byword of Puritanism was "make what you can, but save what you can." This attitude helped produce a flow of savings sufficient to finance the introduction of new commodities and new techniques brought by the Industrial Revolution. This attitude is lacking in most of the underdeveloped countries today. Not only are these countries poor, so that large volumes of savings entail real sacrifices, but even among the higher-income groups, both the propensity to consume and the propensity to import are high. Especially in urban centers, one sees desire to emulate the Western nations with regard to consumption; hence, unless policy is specifically designed to prevent it, a large share of increases in income tends to be spent on imports. An initial increase in income fails to produce significant increases in savings, and it leads to a deterioration of the balance of payments unless prevented from

[11] Alvin Hansen, *Fiscal Policy and Business Cycles* (New York, 1941), Chaps. VI and IX. We have seen that in the Philippines a tax structure that is rather regressive in its actual effects has not resulted in a high ratio of private investment to national income. Perhaps Weber was right—the "Protestant ethic" may be needed to convert unequal income distribution into a high propensity to save.

doing so by policy. Thus, initial increases in income generated by development are likely to be dissipated in higher levels of consumer spending. The people of underdeveloped areas are more eager to consume the goods of the Western world, than they are to duplicate the saving and the quantity and quality of work which have produced the higher standard of living in the West.

A second contrast, which need not be labored for economic historians, is that between present efforts in underdeveloped areas to achieve geographic and occupational shifts on a voluntary basis with the drastic effects of the enclosures in Europe. However painful may have been the social impact of the enclosures, they were a very effective device for moving people out of agriculture into urban industry. The attachment to the village way of life in many of the underdeveloped areas makes it more difficult to achieve the industrialization which is necessary for high standards of living.

Another sociological factor is the difference between incentives in a society organized around the undivided family and those in a society based on the immediate-family unit. The rapid expansion of the European economies in the eighteenth century and of some New World economies in the nineteenth was based on a social system organized around immediate-family units. Whatever the merits or demerits of this system from other points of view, it offered effective economic incentives. The social unit concerned in a choice between income and leisure, between consumption and saving, between more children and a higher living standard, was the social unit that derived the immediate benefit from it. If a man worked overtime for extra pay, his own immediate family benefited from his decision. If he decided to limit his family, he could be reasonably sure that he could provide a better life for the children he did have. If he saved money, it was his own children who benefited from his sacrifice.

In the extended family system prevalent among underdeveloped countries, this consistency between the decision-making social unit and the benefiting social unit may not exist. The man who works harder than others may merely find himself taking care of a larger number of distant relatives, while his own children benefit little from his extra effort. If he limits the number of his own children, he may only be obliged to take care of a larger number of nephews and cousins. His savings may be regarded as at the disposal of the extended family unit as a whole, rather than for his own wife and children alone. Under these conditions, the incentive to work harder or longer, to save, and to practice birth control are obviously much diluted. Either the social organization must change, or the basic choices must be presented in a different fashion, so that the social unit that makes the decision will itself derive any benefit that accrues from it.

A final sociological factor is the "backward-sloping supply curves" of effort and risk-taking in underdeveloped countries. Nearly all observers of individual behavior in these countries point to the difficulty of encouraging additional effort, or additional risk-taking, by the promise of higher money income. One need not agree with Boeke that the people of underdeveloped areas are fundamentally different in their motivation from those of advanced countries to believe that stagnation is self-reinforcing.[12] At whatever level stagnation sets in, it has the effect of converting upward-sloping supply curves of effort and risk-taking into backward-sloping curves. To have an incentive to work harder or better, or to take additional risks with one's capital, one must have a clear picture of the use to which additional income is to be put. A strong "spirit of emulation," or a high "demonstration effect," occurs only where some people actually show that additional effort or risk-taking pays off. "Keeping up with the Joneses" is a dynamic force only when one sees the Joneses move to a higher standard of living. If life in the village has been much the same for generations, and if no one in the village has before him the picture of people moving to ever higher standards of living through their own efforts or their own willingness to risk capital, expending additional effort, or accepting additional risk, will seem rather absurd. Here is still another of the vicious circles so common in the field of development in under-developed areas: a progressive society inculcates attitudes and provides incentives favorable to economic growth; a stagnant one does not.

This analysis only appears inconsistent with the foregoing argument concerning the high marginal propensity to import. If national income rises for some extraneous reason, such as increasing export prices, people will wish to spend a large share of the increased income on imported semi-luxuries. But the villagers see no easy way of raising their incomes through their own efforts or initiative, because they do not have before their eyes enough examples of people succeeding in doing so. Thus their wish for imported semiluxuries provides no effective incentive for additional effort or risk-taking. Still another vicious circle: the "spirit of emulation" is necessary to provide incentives to harder and better work and increased enterprise, but if that spirit takes the form of a wish for imported semi-luxuries, it aggravates balance of payments problems.

Technological Factors

Finally, technological factors were more favorable to development in the Western world during the eighteenth and nineteenth centuries than they are in the underdeveloped countries today. The simplest of these technological factors is the extent of the resource endowment. If one compares the United States or Canada with Libya or East Pakistan in terms of per capita resource endowment the contrast is apparent. In countries like Indonesia, where there is great diversity of resources, the contrast is less clear; some observers have spoken of Indonesia as a country "rich in natural resources." Closer examination of the Indonesian position in terms of the extent and quality of resources in relation to its population of 105 million people suggests that, although Indonesia is certainly better off than many of the underdeveloped areas, it is far indeed from being as well endowed with natural resources as most of the now advanced countries.

[12] J. H. Boeke, *Economics and Economic Policy of Dual Societies* (New York, 1953), especially pp. 39–41, 36–52, and 100–112. Boeke's theory is analyzed in Chap. 12 below. See also Wilbert E. Moore, *Industrialization and Labor* (Ithaca, N.Y., 1951).

Moreover, in the underdeveloped countries the present factor endowment, in terms of proportions in which land, labor, and capital are available, is a drag on development. The very essence of economic development is a fall in the ratio of agricultural employment to total employment. But the proportions in which factors of production are available in underdeveloped areas favor agriculture against industry: labor is abundant, even redundant, land is relatively limited; capital is very scarce. In agriculture, relatively good results can be obtained by labor-intensive techniques, with much labor and little capital applied to available land. Industrialization with known techniques requires a much higher capital-labor ratio.

Some recent analysis suggests that the techniques which would maximize total value output in underdeveloped countries, even assuming that enough capital was available to introduce them, would not provide full employment. Here is a dilemma: unemployment is a serious social phenomenon; yet maximum value product is needed, not only to raise standards of living at the moment, but in order to permit a ratio of savings and investment to income which would generate continued economic growth.

Unfortunately, technological research has been carried on mainly in countries where labor is a relatively scarce factor. Technological progress is regarded as a synonym for labor-saving devices. Little scientific endeavor has been directed toward raising production in countries where capital is scarce and labor abundant, and where consequently, labor-saving devices make little sense. No advanced technology has yet been discovered which is suited to the factor-proportions of underdeveloped countries. Perhaps such a technology does not exist; but it is important to find out. Meanwhile, the lack of technological advance adapted to their factor-proportions is a serious obstacle to development of underdeveloped areas—an obstacle that scarcely existed in the Western world during its Industrial Revolution.

A related technical problem is the apparent discontinuity in the production function with respect to capital supply. Certain types of production process are inefficient unless carried on at a minimum scale which is itself large in terms of capital requirements. For example, one of the most hopeful projects on the horizon in Indonesia is the complex of power, aluminum, fertilizer, and related industries constituting the Asahan program. A project of this kind runs into hundreds of millions of dollars, yet it is not worth undertaking on a small scale.

Moreover, evidence is accumulating to suggest that raising *per capita* income by a given percentage amount requires a larger percentage addition to the stock of capital in underdeveloped countries than it does in advanced countries. This difference reflects partly the extremely high capital cost involved in providing social capital, such as housing, community facilities, public utilities, and transport, as industrialization takes place. Even in agriculture, however, the incremental capital-output ratio may be very high where land reform is necessary, involving shifts to new types of agriculture, or where expansion requires land reclamation, jungle clearance, and the like. Here is still another vicious circle. Advanced countries can add to their *per capita* income with a smaller (percentage) sacrifice of current income than can underdeveloped countries.

Capital-saving inventions have been suggested as a solution to this problem. However, it is essential to distinguish between capital-saving inventions and capital-saving innovations. Probably most inventions are capital saving, in the sense that they reduce the capital required per unit of output, once the new plant is in place. In this sense, it seems likely that even the steam railroad was a capital-saving invention; capital required per ton-mile of freight carried is probably less on a modern railway than it was with horses and wagons. However, capital-saving inventions of this type do not help very much, if the capital requirements for *introducing* them are beyond the means of underdeveloped countries. In other words, the *installation* of a new technique that may ultimately be capital saving may require very large amounts of capital indeed. Even capital-saving inventions are easier for advanced countries to introduce than for underdeveloped ones. Where a great deal of capital has already been accumulated, capital-saving inventions can be introduced by using existing replacement funds. Where the capital stock is low, however, replacement funds will be insufficient for major innovations, even if they consist in introduction of capital-saving inventions. What underdeveloped countries need is not merely capital-saving inventions in this sense but means of raising productivity without increasing the current rate of total investment, *even temporarily*. Clearly, the technical requirements of this sort of innovation are much more severe than for capital-saving inventions of the usual sort.

There is also a problem of scale, or a discontinuity, on the side of demand. As Rosenstein-Rodan has pointed out, the establishment of a shoe factory may prove unprofitable in an underdeveloped country, since so small a share of the income created by investment in a shoe factory will return to the producer of shoes.[13] Only large-scale expansion, consisting of development of a few industries of very large scale or of a great many small scale industries, will raise income sufficiently to generate significant increases in demand for all commodities.

Moreover, there is reason to suspect that a collection of small industries has lower "leverage effects" than a single large one involving the same initial amount of total investment. The construction of a railway, opening up new territory, facilitating population movements, and making necessary the development of new communities, is likely to have a greater aggregate effect on investment than a collection of shoe factories, textile plants, and the like, even if the initial investment is equally large in both cases. Again we are confronted with a vicious circle. It is difficult to industrialize without the increases in income which would provide the demand for increased output of industrial goods, but such increases in income are difficult to achieve without industrialization.

In those underdeveloped countries that rely heavily on exports of the traditional plantation staples still another technological problem arises. Most of these industries involve a combination of highly mechanized

[13] P. N. Rosenstein-Rodan, "Problems of Industrialization of Eastern and South-Eastern Europe," *The Economic Journal*, June, 1943.

processing operations with labor-intensive agricultural operations, a combination which puts the plantation industries in an extremely awkward position. The large amount of capital required in the processing plants means that these plants must operate close to capacity if they are to be profitable. But operating *plants* to capacity requires the operation of *plantations* to capacity. Full use of the productive capacity of the plantations would require cultivation of all the land previously conceded to these estates, and the employment of a full labor force working effectively for a full week of at least forty hours. With losses of productive land through destruction, squatters, expropriation, blights, disease, and inadequate maintenance, the output of many plantations is no longer sufficient to keep the plants operating at capacity. In addition, the effective working week on many plantations is considerably less than what is required. Finally, in direct contrast to the process that took place in other countries during their period of rapid economic advance, growing strength of labor organization and consequent increases in wage rates are preceding, instead of following, increases in labor productivity.

The question is, therefore, whether the productivity of labor can be raised as fast as wage rates, so as to prevent labor costs from rising to a point where the whole operation becomes unprofitable. Certainly, much can be done to improve labor skills, and much more to increase the quantity and quality of effort expended. However, increases in labor productivity from this side will require a long and difficult process of training, not only to improve skills but to increase the sense of social obligation on the part of workers, and to bring an understanding of the relationship of their own efforts to their standard of living. As replanting takes place, higher-yield and disease-resistant strains can be introduced; but this, too, is a slow process, and one that will raise output per hectare considerably more than output per man-hour. The scope for technological progress in the sense of mechanization, or introduction of labor-saving devices, appears to be limited in most plantation industries, although the problem merits further study. The necessity of careful selection in picking and cutting, the importance of skilled tapping, the need to utilize land to the full, and the like, restrict the degree to which labor can be replaced by equipment on the plantations themselves. Meanwhile, no such limitations to technological progress and cost reduction occur in the production of substitute materials through synthetic processes, such as the manufacture of synthetic rubber, nylon fibers, mineral oils, and the like.

An Impossible Task?

In our whole review of strategic factors in economic growth, we have discovered only one with respect to which the now underdeveloped areas have a comparative advantage over the Western world of the eighteenth and nineteenth centuries. All underdeveloped countries have a large sector of their economies, in which the majority of their people are occupied, with levels of technique and skill far below that of the advanced countries or of the more advanced sector of their own economies. There is accordingly an opportunity for a high rate of technological progress, through the application of the most advanced technical knowledge available to the underdeveloped sector.

Even this advantage, however, is doubtful; the equipment and technical skills that have been so effective in raising levels of productivity in the West are largely inappropriate to the factor-proportions of underdeveloped countries. Almost without exception, the technical advances of the Western world have been designed to replace labor with machinery. In countries where capital is scarce and labor redundant, such labor-saving devices cannot add so much to the productivity of the economy as a whole. Even if labor-saving devices can raise the total value of output in underdeveloped countries, they may do so at the cost of adding to the pool of disguised unemployment. In every other respect, the now underdeveloped countries seem to be at a disadvantage as compared to Europe and the New World at the beginning of their periods of rapid economic development.

Must our conclusion be that the task of developing the now underdeveloped areas is an impossible one? My own answer to this question is no: if both the underdeveloped countries and the advanced countries agree on the necessity of economic development of underdeveloped areas; if they understand what is required to obtain this development and recognize the magnitude of the task; and if they accept it nevertheless. The first condition seems to be met. As for the second condition, increasing the understanding of the nature and magnitude of the development problem is the major purpose of this book. Considerable progress has already been made toward a general theory of underdevelopment and we turn now to a consideration of the literature on this subject.

PART **IV** | Theories of
Underdevelopment

11 | Environmental Determinism

A glance at the map (page 211) will reveal the striking geographic concentration of economic development. The advanced countries are confined to North America, Australasia, and northwest Europe. Except for Venezuela, the countries of intermediate development are all in temperate zones: Argentina, Uruguay, Chile, and southern Brazil; the Union of South Africa; eastern Europe; and Japan. In short, virtually all underdeveloped countries are either too hot or too cold. The lack of development in icy and resource-poor countries, such as Greenland, is easy enough to understand. The great majority of the less-developed countries, however, are in the tropics, and no tropical country has as yet graduated into the ranks of advanced countries. Venezuela is the only tropical country to reach even the "intermediate" stage of development, but, as noted in Chapter 1, its oil wealth has not brought a high level of welfare to the majority of the people.

Faced with facts like these it is necessary to ask, "Is the level of development determined by the physical environment?" The question can be broken down into three major aspects of the physical environment: soil, climate, and natural resources in general.

Tropical Soils

To the uninitiated, the apparently lush vegetation of the tropical jungle bespeaks a rich, fertile soil. Too often, unfortunately, the reverse is the case. Dr. Karl J. Pelzer, Professor of Geography at Yale University, puts the matter thus: [1]

Ever since the first European explorers beheld the luxuriant plant growth of the tropical rain forest, observers coming from the mid-latitudes have drawn the faulty conclusion that the rain forest is an indicator of high soil fertility. This myth of the extraordinary fertility of the tropics, as the cause of the apparently endless stretches of magnificent forest growth in the basins of the Amazon and the Congo and on such Southeast Asian islands as Kalimantan (Borneo) and Sumatra, refuses to die. Although it is true that some luxuriant tropical rain forests grow on truly fertile soils, actually, all too often tropical forests stand on extremely impoverished soils.

Luxuriant vegetation is not necessarily an indication of rich soil. On the contrary, "tropical soils are poorer and more fragile than those of temperate regions." [2] The virgin jungle demands scarcely anything from the soil, because organic matter fallen from the trees provides its own humus. But "clearing causes unpleasant surprises, for, instead of deep humus, sand is found, and the forest may have greatest difficulty in growing up again once man's exploitation has exposed the underlying soil." The relatively poor soil is an important factor in the low yields per acre in Asian and African countries, and for the same reasons, the shifting, slash-and-burn agriculture common in underdeveloped countries is particularly disastrous. Once cleared, the vegetation does not revert to its original state. Such agriculture is inefficient in terms of productivity per acre, and the prevalence of such agriculture is one reason for low density of population.

There are several other reasons why agricultural productivity may be expected to be low in the tropics, where so many of the underdeveloped countries are, in whole or in part. First, the monocultures common to these countries are prone to disease and pests. Second, the use of fertilizer is a good deal more complicated than in the temperate zones. Third, livestock is less productive.

Of the relationship of monoculture to the incidence of diseases and pests, Dr. Douglas H. K. Lee writes: [3]

It matters little whether the agent be a microbe, an insect, a larger animal, or a plant form; the principle remains the same: pure stands invite disease. . . . Under tropical conditions such infestations could easily become widespread epidemics with disastrous results. Blights which have thus affected the cotton, cacao, rubber, and banana industries in the past await the monocultures of the future.

A related factor is the rapid growth of weeds. "Mechanization may speed the clearance of weeds between the rows," Lee points out, "but hand

[1] Karl J. Pelzer, "Land Utilization in the Humid Tropics: Agriculture" *Proceedings of the Ninth Pacific Science Congress, 1957*, Vol. 20 (1958), p. 125.
[2] Pierre Gourou, *The Tropical World: Its Social and Economic Conditions and Its Future Status* (Paris, 1947; English translation, New York, 1953), p. 13.
[3] Douglas H. K. Lee, *Climate and Economic Development in the Tropics* (New York, 1957), p. 34.

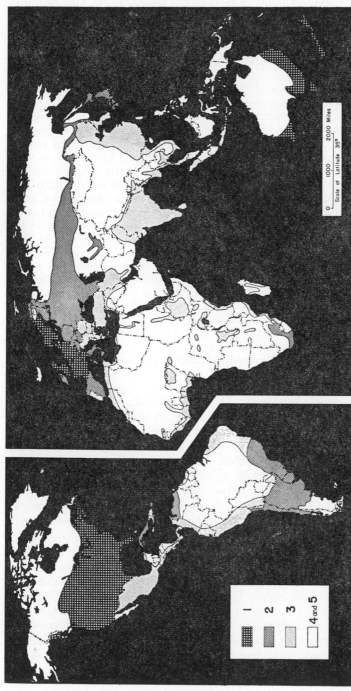

Figure 11.1. Kinds and Levels of Economic Development. (1) High level of productivity, predominantly exchange economy; (2) intermediate level of productivity, generally of exchange economy but with large sectors of subsistence economy in most cases; (3) low level of productivity, commonly of predominantly subsistence economy but in some cases largely in exchange economy; (4) almost completely subsistence economy, at a low level of productivity; and (5) largely undeveloped for production, with no distinction as to kind or level of the economy that does exist. (4) and (5) are not distinguished from each other on this map. SOURCE: Richard Hartshorne, "Geography and Economic Growth," in Norton Ginsberg (ed.), *Essays on Geography and Economic Development* (Chicago, 1960), p. 22. Reprinted by permission of the Department of Geography, University of Chicago.)

work is necessary to clear them away between plants. In the cultivation of rice the flooding and transplanting of the paddies serves to control weeds, which would soon take over the area if cultivation by United States methods were attempted in the true tropics."

With regard to the use of fertilizers, he concludes: [4]

The replacement of lost minerals and nitrogenous compounds by the addition of fertilizers is a solution which comes readily to the mind of present-day Western man; but such a program is fraught with difficulties in many tropical regions. In the first place, factory-produced fertilizers are expensive and are often beyond the means of the country concerned, even without the added cost of transportation. Second, the use of fertilizers presupposes a knowledge of what substances are deficient in the soil, the relative acidity of the soil, and the specific requirements of the particular crop. Whereas these facts may be fairly well known for temperate situations, they are very poorly known for tropical areas. Finally, it hardly appears sensible to pour in fertilizer each year, only to have it go out to sea with the next rain. Some control must be introduced over the annual loss by leaching before artificial replenishment can be viewed with equanimity.

The time may come when fertilizers will be economically justified, but in many areas that time is not yet. There is perhaps more point to the utilization of green manure, especially where the manuring crop fixes atmospheric nitrogen; yet it cannot be blithely assumed that legumes will automatically do this. Both the species and the conditions must be right before the nitrogen-fixing bacteria can operate. Animal wastes may be used, although in many areas the diet of the animal is so poor that the excreta have very little value as manure. In some areas, such as India, it is considered more important to dry the dung for fuel than to apply it to the fields.

Turning to livestock production, Dr. Lee shows that the average output per animal of milk and wool is much lower in underdeveloped than in advanced countries. A part of the explanation for this low productivity is "that tropical grasses and other forage plants, even when abundant, are frequently lacking in nutritive value. In many instances, poor nutrition constitutes a major cause of low animal productivity in the tropics." Accordingly, raising livestock productivity may require importation of feeds, or development of new natural feeds, which may be very difficult in tropical conditions. Heat as such has bad effects on appetite, and "everything man asks of his animals—more meat, more milk, more eggs, more work—involves a greater production of heat." [5] Also, animals as well as plants are more subject to disease and pests in tropical countries.

Professor Gourou also points out that the tropics "are not eminently favourable" to raising livestock. Disease is one factor, difficulty of preserving animal products is another, but most important "is the fact that tropic pasturage of average quality is not good food value." [6] Livestock as well as men are victims of the unhealthiness of the tropics. As yet less progress has been made in raising the levels of health of livestock in the

[4] *Ibid.*, pp. 35, 38.
[5] *Ibid.*, p. 67.
[6] Gourou, *op. cit.*, p. 53.

tropics to that of other parts of the world than is the case with human beings.

Here, then, is one of the vicious circles so common in any analysis of underdevelopment; underdevelopment yields low agricultural productivity, yields malnutrition, yields low productivity, yields underdevelopment.

Climate and Human Behavior

Before the Second World War it could be said that the tropics were unhealthful. "Most of the diseases of temperate lands," Gourou wrote at that time, "are rife in hot, wet countries, whilst certain terrible endemic and epidemic tropical diseases are unknown in our latitude." [7] This statement is much less clearly true today. The malaria to which Gourou attached so much importance as a killer of men is now being brought under control in a good many tropical countries. The same may be said of yellow fever, bubonic plague, and other tropical diseases.

Professor Gourou also cites some evidence that even before the war bad health was not inevitable in the tropics. "The Europeans in the Panama Canal Zone are in a splendid health and the annual death rate is only 6.36 per 1,000." Similarly, in northern Queensland "the coastal strip is really hot and rainy; yet on it pure whites cultivate sugar cane with their own hands. The exclusive white population of the sugar belt amounted to 251,000 in 1939, and the people are in perfect health." [8]

The direct impact of climate on human beings seems to be the least important of the various effects of tropical climate on productivity. An Australian Health Department booklet says: [9]

In tropical Australia . . . there is practically no circumstance which can be laid hold of as representing a definite disability to the white race other than those faulty circumstances of social environment which are inseparable from the opening up of a new country for the purpose of primary production. First-generation, second-generation, and third-generation Queenslanders are performing their life work and following their ordinary avocations as they could in temperate climates, and there is at present no indication that the strain of tropical life is an actual one, or that the outlook for these people is anything but hopeful.

Dr. Lee summarizes his own evidence with regard to the effect of tropical climates on humans in these undramatic terms: [10]

There is a general tendency to answer questions about possible levels of activity in the tropics in a gloomy fashion and to cite past performances in support. But what has been, is not necessarily what has to be—a Roman soldier stationed in Britain would no doubt have been skeptical about the future productivity of

[7] Gourou, *op. cit.*
[8] *Ibid.*, pp. 115–16.
[9] Quoted by Lee, *op. cit.*, p. 9.
[10] *Ibid.*, p. 100.

the barbarous inhabitants in so vile a climate; and many a colonial governor has recorded grave disapproval of areas which are now highly successful. Conversely, there have been flourishing empires in areas that are truly tropical (e.g., Southeast Asia) and intense activity can be found in more than one tropical area (e.g., Venezuela).

This conclusion confirms the observations of the present writer. The attitude toward work, leisure, and income in Australia seems much the same from subtropical Darwin, where summer heat is more intense than in most equatorial countries, to chilly Hobart, with its ten-month-long winter and cool summers. Nor is there any significant difference in attitudes or productivity between Indonesians living at sea level and those living in the invigorating climate 4,000 feet up in the mountains. In the Philippines, the mountain people have remained the most primitive in the country.

These observations are of very considerable importance. In geographic terms, it appears that the comparative advantage of advanced countries is greater in agriculture than it is in industry. Technology can be transported; soil and climate cannot. In very few of the underdeveloped countries is there any hope for achieving levels of man-hour productivity in agriculture comparable to those of the advanced countries. At the same time there seems no reason why many underdeveloped countries should not be just as efficient as the advanced countries in some industries. So long as the majority of its people are engaged in unproductive agriculture, a country is bound to remain poor. We need, then, to explain why the majority of people in the underdeveloped countries have remained in small-scale agriculture instead of moving into occupations where their productivity is higher.

Dr. Lee is much more sanguine with respect to the possibilities of industrial development in tropical climates than he is about agriculture. He quotes Australia as an example: [11]

As a youth in Australia, the author frequently heard it said that the country's climate was unsuitable for weaving textiles or manufacturing steel; at a more mature age he learned that it was also supposed to affect the quality of the beer. Some years later he witnessed considerable success attending both the textile and the steel industry and came to believe that the principal effect of climate upon brewing was through the thirst induced in the inhabitants.

In general, he sees in the field of industry none of the barriers to development in the tropics that he outlines for the agricultural sector.

In previous chapters we have been able to establish very definite and important influences of tropical climate upon crop production, animal husbandry, and the general sweep of human welfare and productivity; and in discussing palliative measures we have had to refer to various nonclimatic factors which may affect the success or practicability of those measures. This was possible without losing sight of the main topic—the role of climate. But when it comes to a

[11] *Ibid.*, p. 136.

discussion of industry, the evidence for direct and important climatic effects is somewhat insubstantial, and a consideration of nonclimatic influences is apt to develop into a full-fledged discussion of the socio-economic forces necessary to the process of industrialization.

He does point out that at present the supply of labor is a serious problem, but here the possibilities of overcoming the difficulty seem relatively good.[12]

The supply of labor may present an equally difficult problem. A superabundance of extremely poor people does not necessarily provide a work force. Undernourishment, disease, lack of education, lack of ambition, or ingrained custom, singly or in combination, may make of the apparent plenitude a veritable mirage. Public health measures and education may, in time, rectify the position, but they must be paid for and presumably treated as an investment in future productivity.

Tropical conditions may impede industrialization indirectly. People living in temperate zones tend to think of the tropics as "fertile" and imagine both luxuriant growth and dense populations. In fact, however, relatively few tropical countries are densely populated. On the eve of World War II the hot and wet regions outside Asia had only 8 per cent of the world's population on 28 per cent of the usable area. The average density was only 2.2 persons per square mile. As Gourou points out, sparsely populated countries do not provide favorable opportunities for industrialization because of the limited size of the domestic market. In his view, it is countries like Indonesia, densely populated yet still at the agricultural stage, which "are obviously by far the most ready for industrialization." Moreover, he says the tropical climate does not impose any special barriers to industrialization.

Gourou does mention another geographic barrier to development in Asia and Africa, which has nothing to do with soil or climate: [13]

Tropic lands suffer from the drawback of being divided into three sections completely separated by broad oceans. Between them, and even between tropical Asia and equatorial Africa, cultural relations have been very difficult and consequently very slight. Agricultural methods are not easily communicated except within the climate in which they originate, nor do they spread, except along parallels of latitude. Hence, isolated from one another by the outline of the continents, the tropical lands in each land-mass have developed independently. These conditions were not very favourable to the progress of civilization. On the other hand, the temperate lands of Europe, Asia, and Africa as a whole offered by their cohesion far greater possibilities of cultural exchange and mutual fertilization of ideas.

Improvements in transport and communications, however, make this factor much less of a handicap today than it was in the past. Gourou con-

[12] *Ibid.*, pp. 146, 147.
[13] Gourou, *op. cit.*, p. 141.

cludes that modern civilization opens many other prospects for tropical lands. The endemic diseases can be controlled, and the country made healthful "so long as the work of improving the condition of health is accompanied by complete utilization of the land, for the conquest of disease must keep pace with the control of nature."

Natural Resources

The geographers themselves, and particularly the economic geographers, have been exceedingly chary of tracing differences in levels of development to differences in the resource base. In the first place, "natural resources" are not easy to define or to measure. If we wished to correlate levels of development with inventories of natural resources, Dr. Norton Ginsburg of the University of Chicago points out that: [14]

It would mean developing common denominators for such varied resources as hydroelectric energy, soils, drainage, growing season, etc. Since these vary in significance from society to society, from place to place, and from time to time, the development of such indices may prove insurmountably difficult.

This does not mean that we can afford to neglect natural resources in considering the economic realities or potentialities of a given country, despite the example of Switzerland which is called on interminably to illustrate the essential insignificance of the resource endowment to the development of a given region. The fact that orchids technically can be grown in greenhouses in Antarctica does not mean that hothouse agriculture is going to play a significant role in the development of that continent, although under presently unforeseeable circumstances, it might. At our present stage of knowledge, comparisons simply cannot be made between indices to natural resources and per capita indices to attained or potential economic growth, since the former do not yet exist and the latter need to be further refined. All that can be attempted, perhaps, are relatively imprecise and qualitative evaluations of the relations between natural resources available at any one time to any one region and the various other elements which together bear upon the course of economic development. Such evaluations, however, demand some explanation of these several elements and their interrelations.

Ginsburg isolates five factors determining the level of economic development: cultural configurations, technology, capital, labor, and natural resources. These five factors, he says, are intertwined:

It is clear that the course of economic growth is singularly complex and the factors which enter into it are mutually interdependent. It is not correct to say, as some cultural anthropologists might, that indigenous cultural configurations alone determine the nature of economic growth; nor can one support the geographical determinist, if such there be, who would maintain that the nature of the physical environment (or the resource base) directs the course of economic progress. All elements move together, often disjointedly and arrhythmically like a man on crutches, but, in sum, in one direction.

[14] Norton Ginsburg, "Natural Resources and Economic Development," *Annals of the Association of American Geographers,* September, 1957, pp. 197–212.

When Is a Resource Not a Resource?

The whole question of the role of the resource endowment in economic development is further complicated by two other facts: a resource that has not been discovered, or that is known to exist but is not accessible at a cost making its exploitation worthwhile, is not a resource in the economic sense; and if resources outside the country are readily accessible, through international trade, their absence from a particular country is of little consequence. In short, what is not a "natural resource" in a particular time and place may become one with capital accumulation, population growth, improved labor skills, or technological change. Given such interdependence, says Ginsburg, natural resources become ". . . a concept as elusive and dynamic as any of the other four. To the geographer, natural resources in their broadest sense include all the freely given material phenomena of nature within the zone of men's activities, at present a zone extending about twelve miles above the surface of the earth and about four miles below it, plus the additional nonmaterial quality of situation or location."

But "freely given" is itself a sticky concept, as Ginsburg notes:

If a given resource is not accessible, it cannot be described as "freely given," since it cannot be exploited without investment of "capital" in one of its several forms. The qualification may be extended to almost all resources, since they must be acted upon in order to become useful to men. It follows that many resources, as they come into use, are no more "natural" than they are "cultural." Is a long-fertilized, irrigated, and cultivated soil or a planted stand of Japanese cedar "natural?" Only to a degree, of course. We can conceive, therefore, of a classification of resources based upon their degree of "naturalness" in which classification would take place perhaps according to the amount of capital required to make them available.

Considerations such as these impel geographer Richard Hartshorne to ask, "Is economic growth everywhere possible?" [15] He answers his own question:

Lack of material factors, whether temporary or permanent, does not in itself preclude economic growth, since all these are available elsewhere and can be imported provided the country can produce currently, or subsequent to development, sufficient surpluses of other products needed elsewhere.

However, he adds:

To conclude that all regions of the world capable of supporting populations are capable of economic growth far above present levels is not to say that all regions can or need to develop all of the particular industries found in particular countries of presently high development. The proximity or remoteness of particular natural resources will continue to determine the feasibility of location of certain industries.

[15] Richard Hartshorne, "Geography and Economic Growth," in Norton Ginsburg (ed.), *Essays on Geography and Economic Development* (Chicago, 1960), pp. 18–19.

Importance of Diversity of Resources

Geographers sense, without being able to provide a complete theoretical model to explain it, that the diversity of resources, as well as the quantity, is important for development. The most advanced countries have been in some sense "rich" in natural resources, not only in having "a lot" of resources but also in having varied resources. In the United States in particular, population movements and technological advance have been accompanied by the discovery somewhere in the country of new resources important in each new phase of development. On the other hand, no country dependent on a single natural resource—the oil countries and Chile being obvious examples—has yet become highly developed. As Ginsburg puts it, "Resources tend to complement each other, to be linked in a chain of utilization patterns and of productive processes in which the production of one demands the production or availability of others."

Importance of Geographic Spread of Resources

It is the present writer's very strong hunch, developed in a book-length essay elsewhere, that not only diversity but also geographic spread of resources is important for development.[16] Of two countries with the "same" resource endowment per head—however measured—the country with resources spread throughout its length and breadth has a better chance of development than the one in which known resources are concentrated in one part of the country. The theory is related to Hansen's concept of the role of an ever-moving frontier in the generation and regeneration of entrepreneurial activity; the demonstration of the thesis rests on comparative economic history.

Regional Integration and National Development

Historically, the United States has been more successful in achieving regional integration of its economy than any other country comparable in size and geographic diversity. During the period 1840–60 the changes in relative per capita income among major regions were small and diverse, but because of the stagnation in the southern regions the over-all tendency was centrifugal—that is, the gaps in per capita income among regions tended to increase. Between 1860 and 1880 the movements were more marked, and the general trend more clearly centrifugal, partly because of the addition of the Rocky Mountain and Pacific Coast regions at very high initial levels of per capita income, and partly because of the continuing lag of the Southeast and Southwest behind the Northeast, Middle Atlantic, and West North Central regions. From 1880 to 1920, however, there was a strong centripetal tendency in regional incomes per capita. From 1920 to 1930 the over-all tendency was mildly centrifugal; the Southeast and Southwest did not share proportionately in the boom of the 1920's.

[16] Benjamin Higgins, *Regional Interactions, the Frontier, and Economic Growth,* Submission to the Canadian Royal Commission on Bilingualism and Biculturalism, Ottawa, 1966.

From 1930 to 1950 the trend was strongly centripetal. Indeed, for this period there is an almost perfect inverse rank correlation among regions—and even among states—between the levels of per capita income in 1930 and rates of increase of per capita income since. The Southeast was the poorest region in 1930 but enjoyed the most rapid rate of growth in the following two decades. The Southwest was second lowest in 1930, but had the second highest rate of growth between 1930 and 1950. The regions that were richest in 1930, on the other hand, had relatively slow rates of growth in the following two decades.

During the 1950's the picture was mixed, with relatively small differences in rates of growth in per capita income among regions. The Southeast continued to enjoy the highest rate of growth of all regions during this decade, but growth in the Southwest slowed to approximately the national average. Given the differences in levels of income in 1950, spreads in real per capita income among regions increased during the decade. The over-all tendency might be described as mildly centrifugal. The same is true for 1960–64.

The whole history of interregional relations in the United States resembles a colossal game of "follow the leader," in which one region after another takes a turn at being a leader. "Backwash effects" of the opening of new regions on the older ones have never for long outweighed the "spread effects"; somehow or other, lagging regions have always been converted into leading regions again. It is almost as though Adam Smith's "invisible hand" were operating in the American economy in a fashion never envisioned by Adam Smith himself. A consequence of this tendency for centripetal movements to appear and reappear is that the United States has eliminated the vast regional differences in per capita income that still plague other large, regionalized countries of recent settlement.

In 1880, for example, the United States average level of per capita incomes was about double that of the South (poorest region) and about 165 per cent that of the Southwest (the second poorest region). By 1960 the United States average was only 43 per cent above the South—still the poorest region—and only 116 per cent of the Southwest, still the second poorest region. In 1880, the Far West, then the richest region, had a per capita income more than four times that of the South and 384 per cent of the personal income per capita in the Southwest. By 1960, the Far West—still the richest region—had a per capita personal income only 70 per cent above that of the South, and only 138 per cent above that of the Southwest.

How has the United States avoided the extremes of regional disintegration common to underdeveloped countries? The argument is that the process of regional integration has consisted in wave after wave of frontier development in one part of the country after another, until finally old frontiers have become new frontiers again.[17] By the same token, the

[17] The term "frontier" is not used here in a geographic sense, such as an area with two to six people per square mile. It means rather an area of net immigration associated with utilization of new resources, establishment of new industries, and urbanization resulting from these industries. The concept of frontier receives fuller treatment below.

absence of a frontier of the United States variety helps to explain regional disintegration and relatively low standards of living in other countries, particularly in such large, highly regionalized, underdeveloped countries as Brazil, India, Mexico, Chile, Colombia, Indonesia, and Libya.

For some 350 years the United States enjoyed more or less continuous frontier development. Between 1890 and 1900, and again between 1910 and 1940, the process slowed down. The latter retardation contributed to the Great Depression of the 1930's. Since 1940, frontier development has been accelerated again, but instead of taking the form of an essentially westward movement, it has been dispersed. This acceleration of frontier development, in turn, has contributed to the relatively limited fluctuations of income and employment maintained since World War II, as compared to the interwar period.

This record of centuries-long frontier development is itself unmatched by any other country—with the possible exception of the Soviet Union and eastern Europe. Moreover, in contrast to most other countries, the "back-wash" effects on older regions of rapid growth of a new region have never for long outweighed the "spread effects." Lagging regions have somehow always become leading regions again. The regeneration of the Southeast took longest, but that region is now the most rapidly growing in the country. There has never been in the United States anything quite like the empty center of Australia or the chronically lagging regions of the Maritimes and the prairies of Canada, let alone the stagnant South in Italy and Mexico or the retrogressive North and Northwest in Brazil. In the United States, population growth, frontier development, and resource discovery have moved together, amplifying the effects of each on economic growth. Both flattened out between the wars and both have accelerated since.

Moreover, the American frontier has been a "small man's frontier," providing continuously changing "lands of opportunity" for men with little or no capital. This unique American experience with frontier development has given content to the "log-cabin-to-riches" legend, and has given rise to a confidence in free private enterprise, both as an avenue for individual self-expression and as a device for national economic development, which does not exist and which might be misplaced in countries where the nature of the frontier has been totally different.

No other country has enjoyed quite this pattern of interregional relations. The Industrial Revolution in Europe was not accompanied by such mass movements of population and frontier development. By the time the Industrial Revolution came along, most of the centers of European population had already been established, and while there were differences in rates of growth, urbanization took place simultaneously throughout most of Europe. Even in neighboring Canada, which shares so much of the American cultural heritage and history, the picture is very different. In Canada there has been a single shift of industry away from the Maritime Provinces, where it began, to Ontario and Quebec, and more recently to British Columbia; but there has been little industrialization or urbanization in the Canadian Midwest. The whole vast stretch from Toronto to Vancouver is still essentially empty. Even now, with the petroleum discoveries in Alberta, the impact of the postwar oil and iron booms seems to be felt more in Toronto and Montreal than in cities nearer the actual mining operations. Urban development has been confined to a narrow strip within a few hundred miles of the United States border, and there are only three large cities in all—one in Quebec, one in Ontario, and one in British Columbia. Moreover, Canada shows none of the marked centripetal tendency that has marked the growth of regional incomes in the United States during the last three decades.

When we come to Australia, the contrast with the United States is even more striking. The opening up of the Australian center led to no urbanization in the interior, but rather to population growth in the handful of cities on the coast, particularly in the two great metropolitan centers of Melbourne and Sydney. Moreover, the Australian frontier, such as it was, was always a "rich man's frontier." The Gold Rush lasted barely a decade as a small man's operation; after that it was a matter of corporate enterprise crushing quartz. In any case, the mineral discoveries in Australia were almost in the backyards of the great cities. The center itself is dead, consisting of unattractive desert. Frontier development in Australian consisted of "rich squatters" acquiring huge tracts of land, hiring a very small labor force, and running large numbers of animals. As noted in Chapter 7, this sort of development created employment opportunities in the suburbs of Melbourne and Sydney but not in the center of the coutry.

The tendency for Australians to look to their government to provide both development and welfare is a reflection of the nature of the frontier. The "log-cabin-to-riches" legend never played any role in Australia because there was never any foundation for it. From the beginning, social overhead capital had to be provided by public enterprise; the land in the interior could not even be given away. There was no chance of building railroads through private enterprise and land grants, as in the United States. Even water had to be provided by public enterprise.

Colin Clark's indices of man-year productivity, measured in his International units, show productivity in Australian above that of the United States, and also rising more rapidly than in the United States, up to the last decade of the nineteenth century. There was then a marked tapering off of growth in the 1890's, whereas the growth of the United States was accelerated so that the curves of man-year output crossed. Still more striking is the apparent stagnation of Australian income after 1925. It was at about this time that the good land was fully occupied, necessitating a structural change in the Australian economy if the growing population was to be absorbed without an actual decline in per capita output and income. As the Australian industrial base was less favorable than the base for the pastoral industries, the maintenance of early rates of growth proved to be impossible.

The contrast between the United States and other countries is of course particularly striking in the case of such highly disintegrated economies as Brazil, Mexico, and Italy, where regional dualism is a major feature of the economic situation. These cases are outlined in Part VI.

It would appear, then, that the pattern of resource endowment acts on the rate and level of economic development in subtle ways. The sheer volume or value of natural resources in relation to population—and the rate of resource discovery in relation to population growth—is not the whole story. A diverse and spatially diffused resource base permits continuous frontier development, keeping alive the spirit of enterprise. It also permits a "ratchet effect" to set in, development of one region generating spread effects to another, this development in turn accelerating growth in a third region, until finally spread effects are generated back to the region starting the process.

Conclusions

It would appear that the nature of tropical soil and climate has something to do with underdevelopment, but it does not begin to explain the differences in rate and level of development from country to country. With regard to the resource base in general, we can do no better than to turn to Ginsburg's summary: [18]

1. The possession of a sizable and diversified natural resource endowment is a major advantage to any country embarking upon a period of rapid economic growth. Diversification may be less important than the dimensions of one or more resources, if their reserves are large enough and long-run demand is steady and strong.

2. Resources need not be situated within the confines of the country undergoing development, but they must be accessible. Accessibility implies transportation, and transportation in part implies imports, both of which demand accumulations of capital with which to obtain materials from extra-national or discontinuous resource endowments.

3. One of the major means for capital accumulation is an abundance of easily exploitable natural resources (Saudi Arabia, South Africa, Venezuela).

4. In no sense, however, are natural resources responsible for development and economic growth; they possess no deterministic power. However, "they possess latent utility and are part of an over-all regional capability."

5. They also may set limits upon the approaches to natural resource planning and development. If a given raw material necessary for some phase of industrialization is not located *in situ* and is unavailable due to tariff barriers or high transportation costs, modification of that phase is likely. Or, if rapid rises in agricultural, forest, or mineral production are possible, they may strongly influence the system of priorities and scale of operations which will characterize a total developmental effort or history.

6. Even if abundant, natural resources will not determine the *kinds of uses* to which they will be put. Their availability in agriculture particularly, however, may influence critically the shift from agricultural to non-agricultural employment.

7. The significance and functions of natural resources in economic development will differ markedly with the stages in the developmental process. Under normal circumstances the role of the resource endowment is most important in the earlier stages of economic development, when it acts as a means for

[18] Ginsburg, "Natural Resources . . ." *op. cit.*, pp. 211–212.

capital accumulation and an accelerator for economic growth if abundant, and as a depressant upon that growth if niggardly.

8. Similarly, the significance of indigenous resources is much less to the highly developed countries with their discontinuous world hinterlands and larger supplies of capital, skilled labor, technology, and entrepreneurial experience, than to the relatively lesser developed regions frequently characterized by scarcities of all these factors.

9. Any comprehensive program for economic development demands the development of a sophisticated inventory of resource endowments, an appraisal of present systems of resource utilization, an analysis of cultural and physical obstacles to resource development, and an estimate of resource potentials, taking into account conflicting uses and demands for given resources and the probable role of technological change over periods of time.

12 Cultural Determinism

If economics is "what economists do," as Jacob Viner once remarked, it is clear that the scope of economics has broadened considerably in recent decades. The renewed interest in the causes of wealth or poverty of nations has taken economists into strange fields as well as strange lands. Thus we find economists today writing about the relationship between ideology and entrepreneurial activity, the importance of literacy for "development-mindedness" and "technology-mindedness," the effect of family structure on economic motivation, the relationship of childhood training to personality traits and creativity, and the like. True, some sturdy institutionalists—such as Clarence Ayres and John Gambs—maintained a steadfast interest in such questions throughout recent decades, despite the jeers of "standard" economists, jeers in which the present writer joined.[1] Twenty years ago the majority of the economics profession tended to regard interdisciplinary social scientists as the "lunatic fringe." Today, however, no one questions the right of social scientists such as Everett Hagen, Bert Hoselitz, Arthur Lewis, and J. K. Galbraith to the label "economist"; cross-disciplinary inquiries show signs of becoming "standard economics." Moreover, practitioners of other social science disciplines are invading the field of economic development, such as psychologists James Abegglen and David McClelland, political scientist Karl Deutsch, sociologists Wilbert Moore and Daniel Lerner, anthropologists Richard Adams, Charles Erasmus, Clifford Geertz, and John Gillin. The borderlines between social sciences are becoming blurred today, just as yesterday the dividing lines

[1] Benjamin Higgins, *What Do Economists Know?* (Melbourne, 1950).

between natural sciences became increasingly indistinct. Interdisciplinary and cross-disciplinary effort is becoming the rule, and it is increasingly difficult to say where "economics" ends and other disciplines begin.[2]

The Scope of Economics

According to the classic definition of Lord Robbins, economics is "the study of human behaviour as a relationship between a multiplicity of ends and scarce means that have alternative uses." Even with a broad interpretation of this definition to include all aspects of allocation of scarce resources, whether or not the allocation takes place through an organized market and with the intermediation of money, economic analysis is still limited to operational questions of resource allocation.[3] If we limit economics in this fashion, will anything significant for economic development be overlooked?

Political Development

It is obvious that economic development will not take place in countries where the political power elite is resolutely opposed to it. Development requires not only entrepreneurship but an interplay of creative entrepreneurial activity and encouragement of such activity by the political power elite.[4] Nonetheless, it is important to put the political factor in its rightful place in the analysis of social change and economic development. Many people, especially in Latin America, reduce "social aspects of economic growth" to the concentration of political power in the hands of a relatively small and conservative elite group. Economic development is indeed difficult (although not completely impossible) where the country is ruled by a landed aristocracy with deeply embedded feudal attitudes, strongly

[2] Cf. Jose Medina Echavarria and Benjamin Higgins, *Social Aspects of Economic Development in Latin America*, Vol. II (Paris: UNESCO, 1963).

[3] Very few truly non-monetary societies exist, and the number of people living in them is an insignificant fraction of the population of developing areas. Sometimes societies seem more "non-monetary" than they really are because credit is more important than cash—as in advanced countries. There is, however, a question regarding the quantitative importance of the non-market sectors, as Cyril Belshaw has pointed out (*Traditional Exchange and Modern Markets*, Englewood Cliffs, N.J., 1965, chap. 1 and pp. 75–78 and 86). Where the non-market sector is important there is certainly no reason to exclude it from economic analysis. After all, the economics of barter and even "Crusoe" (self-sufficiency) economics have been in the literature for nearly a century. Anthropologist Ralph Linton maintains that "non-monetary economies" are quantitatively unimportant in the economic development problem. "Fortunately for any plans which we may have for encouraging economic growth, China, Southeast Asia, Islamic cultures of the Near East, India, and, often ignored, the high native civilizations of West Africa, are all thoroughly familiar with trade, credit, banking, and private property. In the Islamic countries in particular, one is struck by the resemblance of these patterns to those of medieval Europe. China also seems familiar to an American in these respects. India avowedly has a different value system from the rest, but anyone who has done business there will recognize that indifference to economic gains is largely limited to ascetics." Ralph Linton, "Cultural and Personality Factors Affecting Economic Growth," in David E. Novack and Robert Lekachman, *Development and Society, the Dynamics of Social Change* (New York, 1964), p. 196.

[4] Cf. Clifford Geertz, *Agricultural Involution in Java* (Berkeley, 1963), Foreword by Benjamin Higgins.

opposed to industrialization, mass education, and technological change. In such countries a prerequisite for successful economic development may be to "get the rascals out." The socio-cultural factors that will lead to the necessary changes in the political system are a subject of great interest. Here is one aspect of economic development, at least, which economists have not dared to tackle professionally. Even pure Marxist economics has no real recipe for fomenting revolution; rather, it predicts revolution as the inevitable outcome of subjugation of the masses. For the most part, economists lay no claim to professional expertise in the field of "getting the rascals out."

Moreover, it is clear that economic development, whether defined as rising per capita income or more broadly as rising levels of living, can occur within a wide range of political systems. Economists have largely abandoned the search for Utopia, the unique system with harmoniously integrated political, social, and economic institutions that would automatically guarantee an optimal economic situation, or a maximum rate of growth. Dictatorships, military regimes of various kinds, Soviet-style Communism with highly centralized decision-making, Yugoslav-style Communism with highly decentralized decision-making, various mixtures of public and private enterprise within parliamentary democracies—even, it would seem from prewar Japanese experience, an essentially feudal regime committed to industrialization—all are capable of producing high rates of economic growth.[5] The political elite, of course, is not always united in its attitudes toward economic and social development policy. Moreover, the socio-cultural framework influences the political process in at least two ways. It helps to determine who gets political power, and—perhaps even more important—it affects the views of those in power as to just what is feasible by way of economic and social reform. "Reform" governments that prove too timid to introduce truly effective reforms are all too familiar a phenomenon in developing countries.

There is, no doubt, some form of political organization that will provide the maximum rate of economic growth for each country at each point of time, given its economic situation and its socio-cultural framework. The determination of the optimal political system from the standpoint of economic growth is a fascinating and perhaps even an important exercise.[6] As stated in an UNESCO Report, "Political structures, like other social structures, can be subjected to dispassionate analysis."[7] But even if we had an impeccable political theory of economic development, we could not expect that political regimes of the wrong complexion would volun-

[5] Cf. James C. Abegglen, The Japanese Factory (Glencoe, Ill., 1963); and "The Relationship Between Economic and Social Programming in Latin America," in Social Aspects of Economic Development in Latin America, Vol. I (Paris, 1963).

[6] See the chapters by Gino Germani and Florestan Fernandes in Social Aspects of Economic Development in Latin America, Vol. I (Paris: UNESCO, 1963).

[7] UNESCO, Social Prerequisites to Economic Growth, Report of an Expert Working Group (Kyrenia, Cyprus, April 17–26, 1963), p. 23. There is, of course, a difference between the politics of economic development and political development. For a discussion of the latter, see John D. Montgomery and William J. Siffin (eds.), Approaches to Development: Politics, Administration and Change (New York, 1966).

tarily retire from power if confronted with nothing stronger than in-exorable logic.

In the rest of this chapter we shall abstract from the purely political factor in economic development, not because the political factor is unimportant but because social scientists have little to say about it. In any case there are enough countries where the political power elite does want economic development to keep economists busy for some time to come. Clearcut successes in these countries will help to bring about political change in other countries where the dominant groups are opposed to the measures needed for raising levels of living.

Boeke and Socio-cultural Dualism

J. H. Boeke's [8] "dualistic theory" is of special interest and importance because of his experience as a Netherlands East Indies civil servant and his subsequent years of reflection as professor of Eastern economics at Leiden University. Although his theory was based largely on Indonesian experience, Boeke thought that it had general application. The reason for his choice of title for his last book, which was mainly an amalgamation of two earlier studies of the Indonesian economy was his [9]

... conviction that the economic problems of Indonesia are typical for a large and important part of the world, that therefore an analysis of these problems may be illuminating for many similar countries and that the experience gained in several decades of economic colonial policy may serve as a guide to the host of inexperienced planners for the well-being of that part of the world that has not yet conformed to their western ideals.

An analysis based largely on Indonesian experience may prove to have less general application than Boeke believed; but as one of the few prewar attempts at a general theory of underdeveloped areas Boeke's theory enjoyed considerable vogue.[10]

The Theory

Dr. Boeke gives the following formal definition of a dual society: [11]

Social dualism is the clashing of an imported social system with an indigenous social system of another style. Most frequently the imported social system is

[8] J. H. Boeke, *Economics and Economic Policy of Dual Societies* (New York, 1953), cited as Boeke, *Economics;* "Three Forms of Disintegration in Dual Societies," lecture given in the course on Cooperative Education of the International Labor Office, Asian Cooperative Field Mission, October, 1953, and published in *Indonesië*, Vol. VII, No. 4 (April, 1954), cited as Boeke, "Three Forms"; and "Western Influence on the Growth of Eastern Population," *Economia Internazionale*, Vol. VIII, No. 2 (May, 1914), cited as Boeke, "Western Influence."

[9] Boeke, *Economics*, p. vi.

[10] Also to the degree that Boeke reflected attitudes of the Netherlands East Indies government, his ideas are of considerable historical interest. For evidence that the whole structure of government in the Netherlands Indies rested on a theory of "dualism," see Rupert Emerson, *Malaysia* (New York, 1937), especially pp. 420–25.

[11] Boeke, *Economics*, p. 4.

high capitalism. But it may be socialism or communism just as well, or a blending of them.

This dualism, he says, is a "form of *disintegration*, [which] came into existence with the appearance of capitalism in pre-capitalistic countries." [12] The invading force is capitalism, but it is not colonialism. Colonialism is "a dust-bin term"; both it and "the antithesis native-foreign" are "objectionable," and [13]

... it is to be hoped that with the obtaining of national sovereignty the true character of economic dualism will be acknowledged sincerely and logically, for its negation is decidedly not to the interest of the small man.

On the other hand, "dualistic" is for Boeke virtually synonymous with "Eastern." Dualism arises from a clash between East and West; Boeke quotes in this context Rudyard Kipling's famous phrase, "East is East and West is West and never the twain shall meet." Boeke contends that "we may use the term 'eastern economics' instead of 'dualistic' economics because both terms cover the same situation, to wit, the situation that is typical for the countries in South and East Asia." [14]

A dualistic economy has several characteristic features. One of these is "limited needs," in sharp contrast with the "unlimited needs" of a Western society. Accordingly,[15]

... anyone expecting western reactions will meet with frequent surprises. When the price of coconut is high, the chances are that less of the commodities will be offered for sale; when wages are raised the manager of the estate risks that less work will be done; if three acres are enough to supply the needs of the household a cultivator will not till six; when rubber prices fall the owner of a grove may decide to tap more intensively, whereas high prices may mean that he leaves a larger or smaller portion of his tappable trees untapped.

In other words, the Eastern economy, in contrast to the Western, is characterized by backward-sloping supply curves of effort and risk-taking. Such needs as there are in Eastern societies are social rather than economic. It is what the community thinks of commodities that gives them their value: [16]

If the Madurese values his bull ten times as much as his cow, this is not because the former is ten times as useful to him in his business as the latter, but because the bull increases his prestige at the bull races.

A closely related feature, in Boeke's view, is the almost complete absence of profit seeking in an Eastern society. Speculative profits are attractive to the Oriental, but "these profits lack every element of that regularity and

[12] Boeke, "Three Forms," p. 282.
[13] Boeke, *Economics*, p. 20.
[14] *Ibid.*, p. 12.
[15] *Ibid.*, p. 40.
[16] *Ibid.*, pp. 37–38.

continuity which characterizes the idea of income." [17] Similarly, there is no professional trading in the Eastern village community. Eastern industry is characterized by "aversion to capital," in the sense of "conscious dislike of investing capital and of the risks attending this," only slight interest in finish and accuracy, lack of business qualities, failure to come up to even the minimum requirements of standard and sample, lack of elasticity of supply, lack of organization and of discipline and corrective local specialization. All this is said to be in sharp contrast to the industry of the Westernized, capitalistic sector of underdeveloped areas. The Oriental is, unfortunately, totally lacking in organizing power where modern Western enterprises are concerned. Where Western industry is dominated by common-sense reason, Eastern society is molded by "fatalism and resignation." [18]

Because of these great differences between Eastern and Western economies, Western economic theory is totally inapplicable to underdeveloped areas. "We shall do well," Boeke sternly admonishes, "not to try to transplant the tender, delicate hothouse plants of western theory to tropical soil, where an early death awaits them." [19] Western economic theory, he says, is based on unlimited wants, a money economy, and many-sided corporative organizations, none of which exists in Eastern societies. Western theory is designed to explain capitalistic society, whereas the Eastern village is precapitalistic. He is particularly critical of any effort to explain the allocation of resources or the distribution of income in terms of marginal productivity theory, mainly because of the great immobility of resources in an Eastern society.

Policy Implications

This picture of the nature of underdeveloped areas led Boeke to pessimistic views on policy. In general, his conclusion is that the kindest thing the Western world can do for underdeveloped areas is to leave them alone; any effort to develop them along Western lines can only hasten their retrogression and decay. Perhaps Boeke's strongest statement of this conclusion was his last one. We cannot reverse the process of social disintegration in dual societies, he said, "because it is not possible to transform the operating forces into the opposite of what they are. The contrast is too all-inclusive, it goes too deep. We shall have to accept dualism as an irretrievable fact." [20] The acceptance of social and economic dualism leads to two policy conclusions: "first that as a rule one policy for the whole country is not possible, and second that what is beneficial for one section of society may be harmful for the other." [21]

Even in agriculture, efforts to bring about improvement in methods are likely to cause retrogression instead, especially if "mental attitudes" of farmers are not changed in the process. The culture of the village com-

[17] Ibid., p. 41.
[18] Ibid., pp. 101–102, 106.
[19] Ibid., p. 143.
[20] Boeke, "Three Forms," p. 289.
[21] Ibid., p. 289.

munity, Boeke said is "perfectly adapted to the environment"; and the methods of Eastern agriculture "could hardly be improved upon." [22] The existing agricultural system is a result of adaptation and is not at a low stage of development.

Dr. Boeke doubted the ability of the Javanese cultivator to grow new crops. Nor did he think that Indonesians could [23]

assume part of the work of the western enterprises, the agricultural part, so as to allow entrepreneurs to devote their energies exclusively to the industrial aspect of the business. This would mean that what is now one united concern, one business, what is being nursed and developed in serried areas, uniformly raised, scientifically guarded and improved, qualified on the basis of the knowledge of market requirements, promoted by means of cheap and plentiful capital, brought into immediate contact with industrial processing, would begin to disintegrate and retrogress at all these points. The present organization of these enterprises is the product of a long history, and handing over cultivation of these products to the petty native peasant would mean a return to an arrangement in the main abandoned as inefficient.

As for industry, "Eastern business will always present a very different appearance from western, even in cases where the two are concerned in the production of the same commodity." Technological progress along Western lines is impossible. "There is no question of the eastern producer adapting himself to the western example technologically, economically or socially." Indeed, if Eastern enterprises endeavor to imitate Western methods, they will merely lose their competitive qualities.[24]

Similarly, Boeke did not believe that there is anything government can do about the unemployment of underdeveloped areas. He distinguishes five kinds of unemployment: seasonal, casual, unemployment of regular laborers, unemployment of urban white-collar workers, and unemployment among Eurasians (he does not specifically mention disguised unemployment). All five kinds of unemployment, Boeke said, "are beyond the reach of government help," because dealing with them "would entail a financial burden far beyond the government's means." [25]

Economic development of any kind is hampered by limited wants. Either an increase in supply of foodstuffs, or industrialization, will lead to a glutting of markets, a fall in prices, and havoc. Even the transmigration program, on which the Indonesian government has placed so much hope for economic development, is worse than useless, according to Boeke. It only transplants Java's population problem to the Outer Islands, while Java itself is worse off than before.[26]

Any effort on the part of the West to improve these harassing conditions by training Indonesian leaders can only hasten decay: [27]

[22] Boeke, *Economics*, p. 31.
[23] *Ibid.*, pp. 193–94.
[24] *Ibid.*, p. 103.
[25] *Ibid.*, pp. 318–19.
[26] *Ibid.*, pp. 187, 182–83.
[27] *Ibid.*, p. 39.

In my opinion, here the western influence tends to divert the attention of the leading classes from their own society to the new and promising western power. The masses, however, unable to follow their leaders on their western way, thus lose the dynamic developing element in their culture. Eastern culture in this way comes to a standstill, and stagnation means decline.

In the field of international relations as well, the outlook for the under-developed areas is dismal. For,[28]

after the Second World War disintegrating forces have asserted themselves and binding forces have grown weaker in the international field as well. I am alluding to the formation of new sovereign nations and to the decline of the uniting influence of colonial and imperial powers on all the dual countries.

Boeke had little to suggest by way of positive policy, as a substitute for the "technical- and capital-assistance" approach which he deplores. However, his idea seems to be that any industrialization or agricultural improvement must be "a slow process," small-scale, and adapted to a "dualistic" framework.

The conclusion to which these arguments about industrialization as well as about agricultural reforms lead us can be no other than the one already expressed, to wit, that social-economic dualism, far from being considered as a passing phase the termination of which may be hastened considerably by a western policy of integration, must be accepted as a permanent characteristic of a large number of important countries, permanent at least within a measurable distance of time. [We must have a] dichotomy of social-economic policy, which is fundamentally different according to the social groups at which it is aimed.[29]

What this policy means in concrete terms is not spelled out. "I will expose no plans," said Boeke, except to stress the need for "village restoration." This restoration will not take place through a revival of the rural gentry, but must "follow more democratic ways." New leaders must spring from "the small folk themselves," and must be accompanied by "a strong feeling of local social responsibility in the people themselves." Just how all this is to be accomplished Boeke did not say; but the sphere of action must be small, the time slow, and the goal won by "faith, charity, and patience, angelic patience." [30]

Appraisal of the Theory

As prologue to any critical appraisal of the Boeke theory, three things should be said. The first is that the late Professor Boeke was one of those devoted and highly trained Netherlands East Indies civil servants who went to Indonesia during the period of the "ethical policy," determined to help raise the standard of welfare of Indonesians. During the period

[28] Boeke, "Three Forms," p. 294.
[29] *Ibid.*, p. 293.
[30] Boeke, "Western Influence," pp. 366–69.

from 1900 to 1930, when the "ethical policy" was pursued, the Dutch had a scientific—even scholarly—approach to their colonial policy. N.E.I. civil servants arrived in Indonesia with a special degree in Oriental studies, speaking the Indonesian language and well-versed in Indonesian history and culture. In that period, a genuine, albeit limited, effort was made to improve the lot of Indonesians. The effort failed. There was even doubt as to whether the Javanese standard of living was not lower in 1930 than it had been two generations earlier. In 1940 the last of a series of Royal Commissions to look into the condition of the Indonesian people was appointed—the so-called Coolie Budget Commission. Boeke himself had cried out in despair,[31]

But the only popular response to all these nostrums is an increase in numbers, while foreign capitalists and foreign energy take out of native hands a rapidly increasing share of native activities.

　　Thus Boeke's defeatism must be explained in large measure by the failure of the "ethical policy" in Indonesia. Undoubtedly, there is an element of "hen-and-egg" in the relationship between this failure and sociological dualism. For the dualistic theory did not spring full-blown from the head of Dr. Boeke: similar views can be found in the earlier Dutch literature, some of them lineal descendants of German theories about the "primitive and civilized mind." To some degree the theory of sociological dualism informed Dutch colonial practices, even under the "ethical policy." The conception of what was appropriate for Indonesians in the way of education, training, and industrialization was very limited; the "ethical policy" was far indeed from the contemporary concept of "the big push," discussed below. In the light of present-day theories of development, one might argue from the strength of hindsight that the "ethical policy" was foredoomed to failure. Be all that as it may, it remains true that the Boeke theory must be explained partly in terms of Indonesian history during Boeke's lifetime.

　　The second point is that there can be no question about the phenomenon of dualism; it is one of the distinguishing features of underdeveloped countries. Virtually all of them have two clearly differentiated sectors: one confined mainly to peasant agriculture and handicrafts or very small industry, and the trading activities associated with them; the other consisting of plantations, mines, petroleum fields and refineries, large-scale industries, and the transport and trading activities associated with these operations. Levels of technique, productivity, and income are low in the first sector and high in the second. Overcoming this dualism is a major task of economic development policy.

　　However, it is our view that Boeke looked in the wrong place for his *explanation* of dualism. He thought it had to do with the nature of the society, if not actually of the people themselves. As we will see below, dualism is more readily explained in economic and technological terms;

[31] Boeke, "Het Zakelijke en het Persoonlijke Element in de Koloniale Welvaarts-politiek," *Koloniale Studien*, April, 1927.

and this explanation withstands scrutiny better than Boeke's sociological explanation. It is well that such is the case; for if Boeke were right, all our efforts to produce a take-off into sustained growth in underdeveloped countries through vigorous development programs supported by technical and capital assistance from the West would be in vain.

The third point is that Boeke did not speak for Dutch scholars as a group. On the contrary, some Dutch social scientists, including some of Boeke's own students, were severely critical of Boeke's theories. Indeed, most of the criticisms made by the present writer have been made in the Dutch literature by one social scientist or another.[32]

The Facts

In examining this gloomy analysis of the prospects for underdeveloped areas, let us first consider Boeke's presentation of the facts regarding Eastern society.

Let us begin with his argument about "limited wants" and backward-sloping supply curves of effort and risk-taking. There is an all-important difference between saying that the people of underdeveloped countries really cannot envisage a standard of living higher than their own, or that they could think of no satisfactory way of spending increases in income, and saying that they see no simple way of raising their standard of living by their own efforts or enterprise. The last of these statements is to some extent true, and the reasons for it receive attention below. The first two are definitely not true. In most Asian countries, both the marginal propensity to consume and the marginal propensity to import are high. Wants of the villagers, far from being limited, are so many and varied that any "windfall," occurring initially through increased exports, is quickly spent on imported semiluxuries unless vigorous import and exchange controls are applied to prevent it. Far up the great rivers of Kalimantan (Borneo), hundreds of miles into the jungle, good rubber prices result in a spate of orders for bicycles, mattresses, watches, fountain pens, and the like. *Sampans* in the remotest canals are loaded with Australian tinned milk and American tinned soup. The same is true of the Outer Islands as well. Indeed, the limitless wants of the Indonesian people confront the authorities concerned with import and foreign exchange controls with their major problem. To turn these wants into a wellspring of economic growth, the people must be shown the connection between satisfaction of their wants and their own willingness to work, save, and take risks—a difficult but not impossible task.[33]

Considering the growing number of enterprises efficiently organized and operated by Orientals, along Western lines, it is difficult to share Boeke's pessimism regarding possibilities of technological progress in

[32] See for example the collection of essays in A. van Marle (ed.), *Indonesian Economics: The Concept of Dualism in Theory and Policy* (The Hague, 1961).

[33] This point is made, in different terms, by Professor D. H. Burger, "Boeke's Dualisme," *Indonesië*, Vol. VII, No. 3 (January, 1954). See also chap. IX, "Technical Assistance to Underdeveloped Areas," in Lyle W. Shannon, *Underdeveloped Areas* (New York, 1957).

Eastern industry. Boeke's characterization of Oriental casual labor as "unorganized, passive, silent, casual" would be acceptable to very few of the employers in Asia who have to deal with contemporary trade unions, especially those where communist influence is strongest.[34] Similarly, it is hard to reconcile Boeke's isolation of "repugnance to alienation from the village community" with the continued growth of the large cities in Asia. Urban life of the larger cities, with its cinemas, cafés, shops, libraries, and sports events, has proved attractive to villagers who get a taste of it; the result is congestion, inadequate community facilities, and unemployment in the larger cities. It is also hard to reconcile Boeke's insistence on the inefficiency of native agriculture, as compared with Western agriculture, with the postwar growth of smallholders' exports, in Indonesia, Malaya, Nigeria, and elsewhere.

Again, Boeke's insistence on the difficulty of persuading Javanese people to leave their villages, in order to move to the Outer Islands, is contradicted by the files of the Department of Transmigration in Indonesia which hold two million applications for removal under the transmigration scheme.

At times, Boeke's "facts" seem to conflict with each other. For example, at one point he emphasizes the immobility of labor;[35] at another, he states that wages cannot be raised by industrialization, because[36]

... as soon as, for instance, a new mill is opened or an irrigation work is constructed, from all sides wage laborers, colonists, traders, and partisans rush in, if need be from hundreds of miles away, to seize this opportunity to supplement their scanty means of living.

The latter of these two contrasting pictures conforms more closely to the results of field studies conducted by the M.I.T. Indonesia Project.[37] Plantation owners often complained of the difficulty of maintaining a labor force, in the light of an infinitesimal increase in wage rates on neighboring plantations or in neighboring factories. The drain of trained Chinese workers from the bauxite and tin mines, in response to more attractive wage offers from Red China, became a major problem during the 1950's. Again, at one point Boeke explained the impossibility of significant expansion of smallholder agriculture.[38] Yet earlier, he complained of the N.E.I. government's difficulty in forcing smallholders to grow less rubber

[34] Boeke, *Economics*, pp. 144, 145. At one point, Boeke seems even to deny the possibiltiy of growth of labor organizations. Because of the nature of agricultural enterprises, which are scattered and more likely to support each other in their common interests than to compete, every effort at organization could be nullified, Boeke argues. The fact is, however, that it is precisely in plantation agriculture that the Indonesian trade-union movement is strongest.

[35] Boeke, *Economics*, pp. 143–45.

[36] *Ibid.*, p. 177.

[37] C. Geertz, *Modjokuto: Religions in Java*, February, 1958; H. Geertz, *Modjokuto: Town and Village Life in Java*, 1957; A. Dewey, *Modjokuto: The Market*, August, 1957; M.I.T., CIS (mimeographed).

[38] Boeke, *Economics*, pp. 214–16.

during the 1930's; imposition of what amounted to "penal" export duties resulted instead in an increase in productivity of native smallholders.[39] This experience seems to suggest that expansion of smallholders' agriculture is a matter of finding the right incentive system.

The observations of other economists who have enjoyed the opportunity for studying economic behavior in underdeveloped countries for themselves confirm the view that economic incentives are at least as powerful there as in advanced countries. Thus Arthur Lewis, speaking of the assumption made by colonizers in Africa that "wants were limited" and that accordingly compulsion would be necessary to obtain an adequate supply of labor, says: [40]

These compulsions (except slavery) are still to be found in one or the other of the African colonies of all the European powers, but they are not so necessary now as they were formerly thought to be. For imitation has done its work. The Africans have acquired new wants, and are willing to work to satisfy them without compulsion.

Regarding the degree to which people of underdeveloped countries are aware of opportunities for making profits and willing to seize them, he writes: [41]

It is . . . hard to get the farmers in tropical countries to work as many hours as industrial workers in temperate countries, but this does not prevent them from seizing opportunities to use better seeds, or fertilizers, or to plant more profitable crops. It has not prevented the Gold Coast farmer—who is said, no doubt erroneously, to be one of the laziest farmers in the world—from switching from subsistence production to creating the largest cocoa industry in the world, over a short space of time; or prevented the farmers of Uganda or of Indonesia from taking enthusiastically to cotton and to rubber respectively.

Similarly, Peter Bauer speaks of the "great readiness to migrate, especially to the rubber and tea estates in Malaya and Ceylon," and "their prompt reaction to changes in economic conditions." "There is available a great volume of evidence [which] illustrates prompt and sensitive responses to small differences in prices." Even something so "deeply rooted in tribal custom as bride prices" varies appreciably with economic conditions.[42]

Similarly, Bauer and Yamey deny that the wants of peasants are fixed or static [43] and present many examples of economic responsiveness. "Observation of behavior in many different parts of the underdeveloped world suggests strongly that most producers are aware of current opportunities open to them, and are also anxious to use the information that they seek

[39] *Ibid.*, pp. 124–26.
[40] Arthur Lewis, *The Theory of Economic Growth* (London, 1955), p. 39.
[41] *Ibid.*, p. 41.
[42] P. T. Bauer, *Economic Analysis and Policy in Underdeveloped Countries* (Durham, N.C., 1957), pp. 21–24.
[43] P. T. Bauer, and B. S. Yamey, *The Economics of Underdeveloped Countries* (London and Cambridge, 1957), pp. 86–93.

out or is conveyed to them." In Cyprus "even comparatively small changes in price ratios bring about large changes in the conversion and disposal of produce." "The ready response of many East African cotton growers to price differences was recognized in an unusual context by an official commission of inquiry into the Uganda cotton growing industry in 1948. . . . It is well known that Africans in various territories are keen and discriminating buyers even though many of them are illiterate. Nor is entrepreneurship lacking in underdeveloped countries." They quote Professor Tax to the effect that "the Indian is perhaps above all else an entrepreneur, a businessman, always looking for new means of turning a penny." Bauer and Yamey are even doubtful as to whether the technological differences are as great as sometimes supposed. The technique which is most efficient in advanced countries is—unfortunately—likely to be most efficient in underdeveloped countries as well, because the more mechanized techniques are not only labor saving but also capital saving.[44]

Is "Dualism" an Eastern Phenomenon?

Some degree of "dualism" certainly exists in underdeveloped areas. Is dualism a special feature of Eastern countries? Merely to raise the question is to answer it. Boeke himself suggests at one point that dualism exists in other underdeveloped areas, including those of Latin America and Africa, as well as those of the Orient. But there is perhaps no country in which "dualism" is more striking than in Italy, with its industrialized and progressive north, and its agricultural and stagnant south. Indeed, one could go further, and argue that some degree of dualism exists in virtually every economy. Even the most advanced countries, such as Canada and the United States, have areas in which techniques lag behind those of the most advanced sectors, and in which standards of economic and social welfare are correspondingly low. Notable examples are the rural sections of the Province of Quebec, rural areas in the Southern hills and northern New England hills, and Mexican communities in Texas, Arizona, and New Mexico. Most economies can be divided into distinct regions, with different degrees of technological advance.

Many of the specific characteristics of the "Eastern" society described by Boeke seem to the present writer to be attributable to Western societies as well. The preference for speculative profits over long-term investment in productive enterprise appears wherever chronic inflation exists or threatens. Such attitudes prevail in Greece today as they did in Germany, France, Austria, and Italy after World War I. And surely the "conscious dislike of investing capital and of the risk attending this" prevails everywhere. A famous American financier has said, "nothing is so shy as a million dollars"; Western economists have recently developed a whole field of analysis relating to "liquidity-preference" and "safety-preference" to take account of the reluctance of investors the world over to accept risk or illiquidity, and their strong preference for keeping their capital in safe and liquid form. Only the prospect of large and fairly safe profits has

[44] *Ibid.,* pp. 105, 123.

called forth the large volume of investment that has resulted in the rapid development of the now advanced countries. Growth breeds growth, stagnation breeds stagnation, in any economy. As for valuing goods according to prestige conferred, rather than direct use-value, what Western society is free from such behavior? Veblen made such behavior a vital aspect of his analysis of American society, and gave it his famous label, "conspicuous consumption."

Similarly, Boeke's distinction between Eastern societies, especially Indonesia, where "export is the great objective," and Western countries, where export "is only the means which makes import possible"—a distinction which Boeke regards of "essential importance"—is hard to understand in view of the popularity of protectionist policies in most countries in recent decades. It is true, of course, that Dutch colonial policy was directed toward expanding exports, and was not much concerned with increasing imports for Indonesians. British policy in India, on the other hand, was very much concerned with expanding imports of British manufactures.

Dr. Boeke also speaks of absenteeism of regular laborers as "undoubtedly in part an expression of the very general pre-capitalistic phenomenon of desiring a large number of holidays." But employers in the United States or Canada in the early part of World War II, or in Australia since the war, would be quick to deny that absenteeism is no problem in the capitalist world. The same is true of the "backward-sloping supply curve of effort," which was all too evident in Australia during the immediate postwar period, and which began to appear at that time in certain industries, such as coal mining, even in the United States. It is the present writer's contention that this "backward-sloping supply curve" is not exclusively a feature of Eastern societies, but appears in any society which stagnates (or slows down) long enough to weaken the "demonstration effect," provided by people moving from one standard of living to another, as a result of their own extra effort, directed specifically toward earning additional income.[45]

---

[45] The truth may well be that, in a static world, supply curves of effort and risk-taking are normally backward sloping. Where no other changes are taking place, most people would probably like some additional leisure, or some additional safety and liquidity, when rates of pay for effort and risk-taking are increased, so that the extra leisure, safety, and liquidity can be had without a reduction in material standard of living. Can anyone doubt that most academicians would offer fewer man-hours for sale each year if basic university salaries were doubled and nothing else changed? The assumption of more and more outside work by members of university faculties really represents a movement along the backward-sloping portions of their supply curves in response to a cut in real wage rates through inflation. In dynamic societies the *illusion* of upward-sloping supply curves has been created by continuous *shifts* to the right of both demand curves and supply curves, in response to population growth, resource discoveries, and technological progress, as illustrated in Figure 12–1. The increase in demand prices has been *accompanied* by increases in supply; but if the increased demand prices had been offered with all other things remaining unchanged, the result would probably have been a contraction of supply.

For a discussion of response of labor to various incentives in various underdeveloped countries, with special reference to Mexico, see Wilbert E. Moore, *Industrialization*

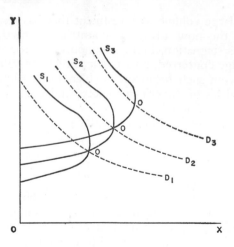

Figure 12–1

Again, Boeke's contrast between colonization in the Western world, where "people on their own initiative and at their own cost leave their country for abroad to better their living conditions" and Eastern migration policy which "means propagating migration from overcrowded regions with financial help from the government" seems to overlook the very large role that private and public assistance played in the migration from Europe to the New World. Dr. Boeke also remarked that in Indonesia "when recruiting new colonists, the attraction exerted by the large, well-known colonies was needed, where relations and friends from the village awaited the newcomer." Surely immigrants always needed some pressures at home to make them move, and surely migrants always preferred to move to places where they could join their own kin; hence the concentration of Scandinavians and Germans in the states of Wisconsin and Minnesota, and of Dutchmen in New York. Also, internal migration in Western countries as well as Eastern may require active government intervention. Consider, for example, the efforts of the British government to relocate industry, of the Australian government to decentralize industry, and the endeavors of the Quebec government to colonize its northern territories.

Similarly, Boeke's contrast between urban growth in Western and in Eastern societies does not ring true in the ears of the present writer. In dual societies, Boeke contends, urban development proceeds at the cost of rural life. In East and West alike, so far as one can judge from available data, urbanization is accompanied by an absolute growth, but relative

and Labor (Ithaca, N.Y., 1951). In the Mexican villages where intensive field work was carried out, Moore found that there was less resistance to a move from peasant agriculture to factory work in the more purely agricultural and isolated villages than in semisuburban villages with easier access to the city.

decline, in the rural population; although in countries where the birth rate has not fallen, the relative fall in rural population and income may not stick. If Boeke means that urbanization has yet to bring true economic progress in Eastern countries, he is, of course, right; but that is because urbanization in the East has not brought the same degree of industrialization, nor the same decline in birth rates. In short, "urban growth" has not been "urban development."

Is Western Social Theory Applicable to Underdeveloped Areas?

If dualism is not primarily the product of a clash of two irreconcilable cultures, its existence is not in itself a barrier to application of Western social theory to underdeveloped areas. Sectoral differences are a challenge to economic theorists, but one that can be met.

The question of usefulness of Western theory is an important one; clearly, the possibility of effective prescriptions for economic and social policy in underdeveloped areas by Western social scientists depends on the degree to which the tools of analysis, in the use of which the Western social scientist is an expert, can be applied in underdeveloped countries.

When Boeke spoke of "the tender, delicate hothouse plants of western theory" he seems to have had in mind the neoclassical theory of a generation ago. All his examples of "inapplicability" of Western theory refer to conflicts between his observations and simple neoclassical theory of value and distribution, with pure competition and "normal" schedules. He referred to no non-Dutch economist more recent than Schumpeter, and even in Schumpeter's case his references were to his theory of economic development, which first appeared before World War I. Most economists would contend that the economic theory of Alfred Marshall was only limited applicability in the Western world as well; and the inability to derive policy conclusions for underdeveloped areas on the basis of neoclassical theory alone hardly constitutes a proof that contemporary Western economic theory is useless in the East.

In order to demonstrate that Western theory is not so handicapped in explaining phenomena in dualistic economies as Boeke suggested, let us examine two of his examples. Marginal productivity theory, Boeke contended, provides no explanation of differences in rents charged for land leased to Westerners in Indonesia: Instead, the rent depends on "the scarcity of money in the region concerned."[46]

This case is not unfamiliar in orthodox Western economic analysis. There is not free competition for land in Indonesia and more than one product is involved in estimating the value of marginal product. It is, indeed, a case of monopsony plus joint production, not the simplest model, but one which exists in the Western world and one which can be analyzed with familiar tools. Moreover, there is nothing peculiarly "Eastern" about dependence of rents on "the landowner's need of money." *Supply* price will always depend on "the scarcity of money," as well as on the relative scarcity of the resource in question; it is only the demand

---

[46] Boeke, *Economics*, pp. 133–36.

schedule that is determined by value of marginal product. If, on the other hand, Boeke argued that rents paid by Western enterprise depend *solely* on the amount of money in the hands of native landowners, as some of his statements suggest, he takes us beyond the limits of credibility. Is the demand for land really infinitely elastic? Is the demand price for land really *totally* unrelated to the income that can be earned from it? At another point [47] he suggests that it is the amount of money in the hands of buyers that determines price of land. Clearly, the demand price for land will depend on how much money buyers have, in the West or in the East; there is no inconsistency with Western theory in that.

Let us next examine Boeke's argument that wage differentials cannot be explained in terms of Western marginal productivity theory. First, Dr. Boeke stated, the profitableness of various forms of culture varies so much that it is impossible to generalize about "the marginal productivity of native agriculture." Moreover, he argued, "marginal productivity presupposes the existence of a real labor market, that is to say mobility of labor. None of these is to be found in native agriculture: the vessels do not communicate, the liquid is thick and slow moving." [48] As we have already indicated, Dr. Boeke himself provided some evidence that *landless* labor is actually highly mobile; all landowners, working their own land, are highly immobile in the Western world as well. In any case, use of the concept of marginal productivity as one aspect of wage analysis is not precluded because of immobility. Even Marshall recognized the existence of "noncompeting groups," among which marginal productivity need not be equalized. Finally, Boeke asks, "How can we make the theory of marginal productivity accord with the phenomenon of wages for the same kind of work varying so greatly at the same time of the year in neighboring localities?" Clearly, the application of marginal productivity theory does not require that wages should be equalized throughout an economy. Immobility of labor, both geographic and occupational, is a common phenomenon everywhere. Indeed, it may be questioned whether occupational mobility is not greater in underdeveloped areas, where trade unionism is thus far less widespread, than it is in the advanced countries. Moreover, contemporary Western economic theory does not contend that wages must equal marginal productivity of labor. It recognizes a host of market situations, with relative degrees of monopoly and monopsony power, on the part of labor and of employers, and with wages varying from marginal productivity accordingly.[49]

Finally, the theory underlying monetary and fiscal policy—is a very

[47] *Ibid.*, p. 133.

[48] Boeke, *Economics*, pp. 142–43.

[49] Cf. John T. Dunlop and Benjamin Higgins, "Bargaining Power and Market Structures," *Journal of Political Economy*, February, 1942. For evidence that Western economists no longer stress "marginal productivity" in the effort to explain the wage structures of the real world, see Lloyd G. Reynolds, *The Structure of Labor Markets* (New York, 1951); and John T. Dunlop, *Wage Determination under Trade Unions* (New York, 1944). Lest some reader fear that such analysis would not apply where there is no *organized* labor market, let me hasten to add that a "market" in this sense exists wherever there is a wage, in money or in kind—even for the self-employed.

useful tool indeed when formulating such policies for underdeveloped areas. Perhaps, since the monetary and fiscal institutions are largely (though not wholly) Western, Boeke would not disagree on this point.

The Achieving Society

One of the few psychologists who has devoted himself to problems of economic development is David C. McClelland of Harvard. His book, *The Achieving Society*, is concerned with interactions among social organization, individual behavior, and economic development. "In its most general terms," he says, "the hypothesis states that a society with a generally high level of *n*-achievement will produce more energetic entrepreneurs who, in turn, produce more rapid economic development." [50] The book tries "to isolate certain psychological factors and to demonstrate rigorously by quantitative scientific methods that these factors are *generally* important in economic development." [51] He admits that "the psychologist has been of little help to date" in the understanding of economic development, but he feels that recent improvements in techniques for measuring motivation permit the application of psychology to "a problem of real interest to economists and sociologists." [52]

The Concept of *n*-Achievement

To begin with, says Professor McClelland, we must gain some understanding of what is meant by "achievement motivation." Because the concept is technical, we may let McClelland speak for himself:

The "achievement motive" is ordinarily measured by performing a "content analysis" on imaginative thought. The scoring criteria for the "content analysis" were derived by comparing the thought processes of people under the influence of achievement motivation with the thought processes of people not under its influence. "Thought processes" were sampled by asking subjects to write imaginative stories to pictures. It was found that they introduced more ideas of a certain kind into their stories when their motivation to achieve—to do well— was aroused than when it was not aroused. An objective coding definition has been worked out for detecting these "ideas" with high agreement among different observers. Nearly all of the "ideas" can be classified under the heading of "desiring to do well" or "competing with a standard of excellence." This then became the scoring definition for a variable which was named technically *n*-achievement to distinguish it from other common-sense measures of achievement motivation such as one would get from how well a person said he was trying. The *n*-achievement score for an individual is simply a sum of the number of instances of achievement "ideas" or images and their subtypes, and the score for a group of individuals is some measure of central tendency (the average, the mode) of the scores of individuals who make up the group. In this way it can be determined, for example, that the average *n*-achievement of a group of teen-age German boys is slightly but significantly lower than the

[50] David C. McClelland, *The Achieving Society* (Princeton, N.J., 1962), p. 205.
[51] *Ibid.*, p. ix.
[52] *Ibid.*, pp. 18–19.

average *n*-achievement of a carefully matched group of American boys, or that American boys from lower class backgrounds have lower average *n*-achievement than boys from middle class backgrounds.

McClelland goes on to say that by now psychologists know a good deal about the characteristics of people with high *n*-achievement. They work harder at laboratory tasks, learn faster, do better work in high school than others with the same IQ, and "seem to do their best work when it counts for their record and not when other special incentives are introduced such as pressure from the outside to do well, money prizes, or time off from work." They are more resistant to social pressure, choose experts rather than friends as partners in their work activities, and like risky occupations, performing better under longer odds, and choosing moderate risks over either safe or speculative ones. Finally—and perhaps most important in terms of social policy—they come from "families in which there has been stress on early self-reliance and mastery."

The Method

Professor McClelland is critical of the "armchair theorizing" of economists, and considers it a great merit of his own methodology that it is "rigorously empirical." As indicated above, McClelland began by testing college students in the United States, using thematic apperception tests (TAT) in which the subjects were shown pictures and asked to tell stories based on them. In making comparisons of some countries with others and in following the course of *n-ach* (the abbreviation *n-ach* is sometimes used for *n*-achievement) through long periods of time, this direct approach to individuals could not always be used. As a consequence, McClelland writes: [53]

Three general types of research have been carried out: the first deals with *group* measures of *n*-achievement and other psychological variables in relation to over-all rates of economic development, the second, with *individual* measures of motives, interest, values and performances of both mothers and sons in various countries, the third with the motives and other behaviors of actual business entrepreneurs.

Where the TAT could not be used, other "imaginative products" such as folk tales or stories in primary-school readers were taken "as rough indexes of the level of *n*-achievement and other variables in the country."

Folk tales were used to measure *n-ach* in a number of preliterate Indian cultures, and the levels of *n-ach* were then compared with the number of full-time entrepreneurs in the society. A "significant relationship" was found; in the 22 high-*n-ach* cultures, 74 per cent of them had at least some full-time entrepreneurs, whereas only 35 per cent of the 21 low-*n-ach* cultures had full-time entrepreneurs. Also 58 per cent of the high-*n-ach* cultures had above-median technology, and only 45 per cent of the low-*n-ach* cultures had above-median technology.

To compare levels of *n-ach* among contemporary nations, an effort was

[53] *Ibid.*, p. 57.

made "to collect twenty-one stories for each of two time periods (around 1925 and around 1950) from all of the nations in the world." However, the team was able to find satisfactory sets of stories in the school books of only twenty-three countries for the early period 1920–29, and for forty countries in the later period (1946–55). The stories from each country appeared to be consistently high or low in n-achievement.

To test the validity of this measure, the ranks obtained by scoring stories in school readers were compared with those obtained by direct testing of individuals for a smaller number of countries. Here inconsistencies appeared. For example, scores for India and the Lebanon were identical for the readers, but Indian students at the University of Madras scored significantly higher than Lebanese students at the University of Beirut. The inconsistencies, concludes McClelland, "raised some interesting questions as to just what the readers are measuring." Nothing daunted, however, McClelland pressed on with his study; for, he said, the proof of the pudding is in the eating. The question is, "Do they enable us to predict which countries will develop more rapidly economically?" By "predict" he means discover a significant correlation in the past.

Here is one example of what McClelland seems to mean by "rigorous empirical method." Awkward results are ignored, and only convenient ones retained. If the two measures of n-ach fail to fit each other, while both correlate with "economic development," either one measure must be abandoned, or else there are two, and not one, kinds of motivation that may lead to or cause economic development. The argument here comes uncomfortably close to saying, "We don't know what is measured by scoring school readers by our methods, but if the thing so measured correlates with economic development, we will call it n-achievement and argue that high levels of n-achievement cause high rates of economic growth."

Despite McClelland's claims to "rigorous empiricism" it would seem that a good deal of personal judgment goes into the evaluation of stories: [54]

The code for n-achievement includes a number of subcategories which are summed to get an over-all score. It is first decided whether a story contains any achievement imagery ("concern with a standard of excellence") and then, if it does, whether it also contains additional ideas connected with the achievement sequence, such as a stated wish to succeed, obstacles to achievement, or means of gaining an achievement goal.

Measuring Development

McClelland expresses some misgivings about using figures of per capita income to compare levels of economic development, and expresses his preference for electric power produced as an alternative. This figure, he argues, comes closer to a measure of technological progress, which is the core of development, and permits the use of the same simple unit—kilowatt hours—for all countries. He recognizes the need to correct for basic

[54] *Ibid.,* p. 103.

power resources in the form of coal reserves and usable water power per capita, but does not do so. He does retain Colin Clark's "International units" of national income per capita as an independent measure of development. The electricity production figures give some curious results—for example, Canada was twice as "developed" as the United States in 1929, and advanced much more between 1929 and 1950. McClelland does not seem to be well acquainted with the literature and techniques of national accounting; he might be less confident of the superiority of any single production figure over the measurement of total productivity as an index of technological progress if he were. However, for large numbers of countries, electricity production per capita correlates highly with per capita income in any case, and little harm is done by using both figures together.

To measure the relative amount of development over the period 1925–50 McClelland does not take the actual figures for electricity production (or national income per capita in International units) but deviations from "expected" growth as determined by a regression line relating growth to initial level of electricity production or income per capita. This complication is introduced, apparently, because absolute amounts cannot be used (obviously the United States is likely to have a bigger absolute increase in per capita electricity production than Mexico) and because McClelland distrusts percentages. The lower the base the easier it is to achieve a given percentage increase.

It is not clear, however, that McClelland has thought through the implications of his alternative measure. Maintaining above-average growth may be much more difficult for a country that is already advanced than for one that is below average in the initial year. It is not just a question of arithmetic, but of the differences in the "technological lag" and in the opportunities for overcoming it. In fact, McClelland recognizes that countries like Canada and Norway could not have been expected to maintain their high growth of electricity production because of "saturation"; he adjusts the regression weights accordingly. But once started on such adjustments, why stop there? Why not adjust for other factors likely to make a difference in growth rates? Is there not some "armchair theorizing" behind this manipulation of the data?

McClelland concludes from his results that "the readers do not appear to have been such a poor method of estimating *n*-achievement level in 1925 after all"; that is, he finds a significant correlation between his measures of *n-ach* and his measure of development; 75 per cent of the above-average, *n-ach* countries were "overachievers" in electricity production, whereas only 25 per cent of the below-average-*n-ach* countries were "overachievers." Note again the methodological implications of this statement: It says in effect that anything correlating significantly with economic development is acceptable as a measure of *n*-achievement. Methodologically this statement means that Professor McClelland has decided *in advance* that *n*-achievement is the cause of (or at least is closely associated with) economic development. Thus the rate of economic development itself becomes a measure of the level of *n*-achievement in the preceding period, meaning by *n*-achievement here anything that correlates significantly (not necessarily highly) with economic development—i.e., with expansion of electricity production. The dangers in this approach are obvious. Other variables—copper consumption, say—might correlate more highly with electricity production than McClelland's school-reader *n-ach*. Does that mean we must encourage copper consumption to assure economic growth? Unless McClelland can establish a clear-cut measure of *n*-achievement that can be used for international comparisons, the validity of which can be tested independently of economic growth itself, and then establish a logical connection (as well as an empirical one) between *n-ach* and development and show that this variable is more closely associated with economic development than other variables, which have a clear causal relationship with development, McClelland's basic hypothesis must be regarded as "not proven."

McClelland, however, seems pleased with his results: [55]

In conclusion, if we look back over the diverse findings reported in this chapter, they confirm our general hypothesis to a surprising extent, considering the many sources of error that could affect our measures. A concern for achievement as expressed in imaginative literature—folk tales and stories for children— is associated in modern times with a more rapid rate of economic development.

Achieving Societies in the Past

Turning to ancient Greece, McClelland was of course unable to find school readers, but his concept of empirical research seems to be very broad. He used plays and poetry instead. Measuring economic development in ancient Greece also presents problems; data on electricity production are naturally scant, and Colin Clark has not got round to measuring income in International units for the pre-Christian period. McClelland therefore measures development in terms of millions of square miles of trading area. He then compares *n*-achievement with development thus defined and concludes, "The hypothesis is confirmed: a high level of achievement motivation precedes economic growth, a lower level of achievement motivation precedes economic decline."

But what is confirmed? Quite apart from the *post hoc ergo propter hoc* fallacy involved in McClelland's conclusion, what his data actually show is that in ancient Greece *n-ach* as he measures it declined continuously from 700 to 200 B.C., rapidly for the first three centuries and less rapidly for the next two. Economic development as measured, however, continued very rapidly from 600 to 400 B.C., and then fell off sharply. In short, economic development continued at a fast pace for 250 years after *n*-achievement started to fall rapidly, and declined only after *n*-achievement began falling less rapidly. What exactly is the causal connection supposed to be? What sort of lag between a change in the level of *n*-achievement and the rate of development is to be expected? Factors that require 250 years to be effective are not likely to interest the planning boards of developing countries very much.

[55] *Ibid.*, p. 105.

McClelland also finds "independent evidence" with regard to ancient Greece. Other psychological studies have indicated a relationship between the level of *n*-achievement of individuals and the form of individual "doodles." McClelland relates the design of "doodles" to changes in the designs on Grecian urns, and in this manner measures once again changes in the level of *n-ach* in Grecian society from one era to another. He finds that the signs of high *n*-achievement are most frequent in the period of growth and significantly less frequent in the period of climax. What his results actually show, however, is that *n-ach* as measured by designs on vases declined throughout eight centuries, making it a little difficult to explain the rise and fall of Greek trade in these terms alone.

Nevertheless, encouraged by this "success" with Greek vases, McClelland goes on to apply the same method to the ancient Incas of Peru. Not having trading area figures, he shifts to measuring development by the volume of public building. The level of *n*-achievement, as measured by designs on pottery, declined fairly rapidly for six centuries, more slowly for two more, rose rapidly for five centuries, and dropped drastically between 550 and 700 A.D. The volume of public building rose rapidly during the nine centuries of declining *n-ach* and rose more slowly through the five centuries of rising *n-ach*, which would seem to cast doubt on the thesis. But McClelland feels that his thesis is borne out by these data too, because "two high levels of *n*-achievement are followed by marked cultural growth, and two low levels are followed by conquest by outside civilizations." Are we then to shift to military success as the measure of development?

n-Achievement and Entrepreneurship

The next step in establishing the chain of causation is to show that high levels of *n*-achievement are associated with entrepreneurial endeavor. In general, McClelland does this by establishing that people with high *n-ach* like taking moderate risks: "They should have personality characteristics which should lead them to 'blossom' under conditions of moderate uncertainty where their efforts or skills can make a difference in the outcome." [56] The sort of proof he offers is that high-*n-ach* children like to stand a moderate distance from the peg when tossing rings, whereas low-*n-ach* children like to stand close or far away. In studying *n-ach* in relation to managerial success, he found that with a certain amount of reshuffling of data he could show a tendency for the high-*n-ach* individuals to earn high salaries in small companies. In large companies, however, it was quite clear that the highest *n-ach* individuals earned salaries in the middle range, with lower *n-ach* managers both above and below them on the salary scale. So confident is the author of his thesis, however, that he is willing to believe that high salaries associated with relatively low-*n-ach* probably reflect inherited influence or personal charm, or something else other than entrepreneurial drive.

[56] *Ibid.,* p. 211.

Sources of n-Achievement

If *n-ach* is to be a policy variable in promoting economic growth, we must know its origins. Not surprisingly, McClelland finds the source of *n*-achievement mainly in family environment and childhood training. Mothers with moderate levels of *n-ach* of their own are most likely to produce sons with high *n-ach*; "the mother with too high a level of *n*-achievement may make too early demands on her son, or she may be too interested in her own success to be interested in her son's."[57] Similarly, moderate pressure to become self-reliant works best. "Early mastery training promotes high *n*-achievement, *provided* it does not reflect generalized restrictiveness, authoritarianism, or 'rejection' by the parents. . . . Or, to look at it another way, the boy can be put on his own either too early, as in the predominantly lower-class early caretaking families, or too late, as in the predominantly middle-class families that expect achievement and independence quite late." [58] (Does this mean that upper-class families are likely to remain upper-class, contrary to the "shirt-sleeves to shirt-sleeves" legend?)

Policy Implications

The Max Weber thesis concerning the rise of capitalism, McClelland says at the outset of his final chapter, "can now be understood as a special case, by no means limited to Protestantism, of a general increase in *n*-achievement produced by an ideological change." What is required to launch a similar process in traditional societies today is increased "other-directedness and market morality." Once the need for a new orientation is "clearly and unequivocally accepted," the rest is easy and follows the ordinary prescriptions of the economic development planner—communications, transport, electricity, newspapers, "even public speeches." But resistance to modernization is likely to be massive, and can best be overcome by equally massive ideological campaigns of the sort brought by Communism in our day and by religious movements in the past. Apart from inducing change, such ideological movements provide "an important source of emotional security for people who are rendered rootless and unhappy by the disruption of traditional ways of doing things."

An informed public opinion will help. So will emancipation of women. Much can be taught by properly directed group play. "Drawing individuals out of their homes into *centers of employment* appears more likely to break up traditional value patterns"—creation of "sociological pôles de croissance," we might say. But McClelland is not over-sanguine about what can be done by education alone; the crucial years for creation of high levels of *n-ach* are probably those between the ages of five and ten. Nursery schools might help. But on the whole, "a government or an outside agency apparently cannot do much to stimulate an increase in national *n*-achievement levels." Consequently, development planners will

[57] *Ibid.*, p. 349.
[58] *Ibid.*, p. 345.

do well to concentrate on utilizing existing n-achievement resources more efficiently. McClelland mentions rural industrialization, subcontracting to local firms, and creation of industrial estates as useful devices.

All this sounds rather discouraging; but McClelland is eager to disassociate himself from the pessimism of the Hagen theory of social change, to which we turn in the next section. "Neither Hagen nor his theory" he writes "has much to offer those working with the Burmese or the Sioux, except to tell them to be patient. In two or three generations their clients may pass through retreatism into the innovative, economically active phase. Who knows? I strongly suspect that in the Burmese case the Communists will have a chance to prove that it needn't take so long, for they 'naively' reject Freudian pessimism and espouse a Skinnerian optimism about the infinite educability of human beings through ideological reform." [59]

Evaluation of the McClelland Thesis

McClelland's work is obviously bold, imaginative, and entertaining. But it is hard to see what there is about his loosely related series of psychological experiments and statistical tests that makes his methodology more "rigorously empirical" than the cautious work of the econometricians—work of which McClelland seems largely unaware.[60] Econometricians like to have a tight, logically consistent theoretical model, mathematically expressed, to begin with. When putting numbers into such a model they like their regression coefficients to be high—not just within the range of statistical significance—and they like the regression coefficients for the

[59] David C. McClelland, "A Psychological Approach to Economic Development," *Economic Development and Cultural Change,* April, 1964, p. 324.

[60] It is clear, too, that McClelland has not always understood the economics he has read. One should not chide a psychologist for not being an economist—except when he claims to write better economics than the economists. For example, he describes the use of the "profit motive" in economic analysis as a "typical oversimplification of rational or armchair psychology." Not that entrepreneurs have no interest in profitability, but they are not interested in money as such. The interest in profit can now be understood, he says, "not in terms of the naive psychology of the 'profit motive' but in terms of a need for Achievement which is interested in profitability precisely because it gives definite knowledge of how competent one is." Of course this is exactly the way economists have viewed the "profit motive," even if the term "n-achievement" was not used. It has long been clear that money as such was not the objective, and that from the psychological point of view profits were important mainly as a measure of success. It is just not true that non-Marxist as well as Marxist economists pictured capitalists as "driven by greed," as McClelland would have it. The "profit motive" was never thought of as a "motive" in the psychological sense; the expression was simply a shorthand for the formal assumption that other things being equal, men who are involved in policy-making for enterprises will try to set prices, determine the product mix, choose plant locations, and type of equipment, etc., so as to increase rather than decrease the profitability of the firm. Among the "other things" kept "equal" in this assumption was the cost in time and energy to the entrepreneur himself of alternative policies. Recently Robin Marris and some other economists, observing the lengths to which the managerial revolution has gone, have suggested that a more useful assumption may be that entrepreneurs try to maximize the rate of growth of the firm rather than its profitability to the shareholders; but this change in assumption does not reflect a new view of the basic psychological motivation of entrepreneurs, but rather reflects recognition of a change in the economic power-structure.

variables given causal significance to be substantially higher than those for variables that are rejected as causal factors. Some of McClelland's correlations, even if within the bounds of statistical significance, would seem frighteningly low to most econometricians, and when these are strung together in a chain where every link is weak, the causal connection between the variables at each end of the chain seems very weak indeed.

If McClelland is telling us once again that societies conducive to the generation of effective entrepreneurship are likely to have more rapid development than societies that are not, he is not adding much to our knowledge. To make a real contribution he must be able to identify *n*-achievement clearly as an independent variable, measure it in a uniform manner permitting interspatial and intertemporal comparisons, show precisely that there is a stronger link between this variable and entrepreneurship than there is between entrepreneurship and other variables, and tell us how to create or direct *n*-achievement in operational terms. His book, stimulating as it is, falls far short of meeting these criteria.

The Theory of Social Change

The most ambitious effort to date to construct a general theory of development based on a nexus of sociological, anthropological, and psychological factors is Professor Everett Hagen's.[61] According to its author, the book "examines the factors which cause a traditional society to become one in which economic growth is occurring. . . . [It] attempts to contribute to knowledge of the process of economic growth, and in doing so to make some additions to the content of social theory, and suggests some changes in its method of analysis." This effort requires integration of "the three major social sciences": anthropology, sociology, and psychology —especially psychoanalysis. The book is in the grand tradition of theories of entrepreneurship, along the lines of Weber, Tawney, and Schumpeter, but is if anything even more interdisciplinary than these. Hagen's debt to David McClelland, with his concepts of "need-achievement," "need-aggression," and the like is substantial, and one that Hagen is happy to acknowledge, even if McClelland declines the honor.[62] His other debt is to those theories of entrepreneurship, such as Schumpeter's, which have run in terms of the emergence of entrepreneurial activity from a fairly clearly defined and relatively small group, constituting a socially deviant, subdominant, or threatened elite.

The book has its genesis in the dissatisfaction Hagen felt with his own discipline while serving as economic advisor in Burma; Part I of the book

---

[61] Everett E. Hagen, *The Theory of Social Change: How Economic Growth Begins* (Homewood, Ill., 1962).

[62] In his review of Hagen, McClelland writes, "Psychological analysis of this type requires a far greater discipline, a far greater concern for operational precision and the laws of parsimony than Professor Hagen shows, if it is not to be laughed out of court." Hagen's dynamics, he says, "leaves at least this clinical psychologist breathless." McClelland, *op. cit.*, pp. 320–24.

is devoted to showing the inadequacy of standard economic models as an explanation of economic growth.[63] Hagen concludes that "economic growth theory has rather little to offer towards an explanation of economic growth, and that broader social and psychological considerations are pertinent." More discouraging is his view that "The transition to economic growth, one may reasonably conclude from these several examples, typically occupies a period of several generations." [64] He begins his analysis by setting up an idealized form of peasant society which he then contrasts with the industrialized society in order to isolate its distinguishing characteristics. Hagen's "village," and also his "peasant" and his "elite," are highly idealized concepts, at least as abstract as Adam Smith's "economic man." Hagen is, of course, well aware that his model is an abstraction and a generalization.[65] The question is, as Hagen rightly points out, not whether the model is abstract but whether it is useful in increasing our understanding of the problem and process under investigation. In any case, his claims for his model are considerable: [66]

The following chapters then evolve, piece by piece, a fully defined model of society, a model which stresses the chain of causation from social structure through parental behavior to childhood environment and then that from childhood environment through personality to social change.

Hagen occasionally gives way to excessive particularism in his idealized image of the village society. He says, for example, "The typical house consists of one room. Except in cold country, the floor is the dirt of the ground." Hagen must know that in Indonesian villages, for example, houses have more than one room and the bamboo floor is usually raised above the ground. There are a number of tropical regions where the soil and climate dictate that houses should be built on stilts. Of what use are such details when not even generally applicable?

In general, the picture he gives of village society does less than full justice to the level of civilization achieved in peasant societies, particularly in Asia. He refers to the "tank which will hold the village water supply"; one thinks immediately of the medieval "tanks" in Ceylon, which were in fact small lakes and the foundation of rather impressive irrigation systems. It would seem more useful to stress the lack of any significant difference in the degree of technological advance in Europe and Asia, at least up to the time when the Portuguese arrived in Asia at the begin-

[63] Parts II and III, which constitute about half of the book, present Hagen's own general theory of economic development and social change, in terms of socio-cultural patterns and their impact on personality traits. Parts IV and V are devoted to case studies designed to document the general theory, in England, Japan, Colombia, Burma, and the Sioux reservations.

[64] Hagen, *op. cit.*, p. 22.

[65] In his Appendix II, in which he criticizes the Rostow stage theory of development, Hagen recognizes the Rostow model as a "heroic simplification," and then adds, correctly, the "this is not a defect, but rather a quality of any fairly general theory. My own model of society and personality involves simplications no less drastic."

[66] *Ibid.*, p. 8.

ning of the sixteenth century, than to stress the differences today. Attention is then properly focussed on the interaction of events taking place in Europe and Asia after that time, in the manner of Clifford Geertz' book, *Agricultural Involution in Java*.

Hagen can, of course, argue that the more advanced villages of Southeast Asia are no longer "traditional" in his sense; his reasoning is always uncomfortably close to circularity.[67] But their departure from "traditionalism" in this sense does not prevent many of these villages from being stagnant in terms of per capita income and occupational structure.

Hagen's main thesis can be assembled from a number of his summary statements. To understand why some traditional societies enter into economic growth sooner than others, he maintains, we must understand the internal structure and functioning of these societies; both the barriers to growth and the causes of growth seem to be largely internal rather than external. The traditional society is dual or triple, consisting of the "peasantry and other simple folk, the elite classes, and, on one side, the trader-financier." This traditional society leads to a particular type of uncreative and non-innovational individual behavior. A member of a traditional society is uncreative because he sees the world as an arbitrary place rather than one subject to analysis and control. His unconscious processes are both inaccessible and uncreative. Interpersonal relations are solved on the basis of "ascriptive authority"; and people avoid anxiety by resort to authority. However, out of traditional society emerge some creative individuals, particularly the "anxious innovator." His childhood training has been such that he "anticipates success" each time he tries to achieve later in life, but "because success is not a foregone conclusion, he forever feels a need to try another task and reassure himself."

Technological change is difficult in traditional society. Who will introduce it? The urban craftsman does not have the capital and cannot obtain the credit for such a venture because bankers "do not customarily look upon him as worthy of credit except on a pawnshop basis." A member of the elite, on the other hand, would not set up a modernized textile enterprise because it would be demeaning himself. In a peasant society, large-scale enterprise can be introduced only by foreigners. An isolated deviant with the necessary need-autonomy, need-achievement, and creative imagination will be hemmed in by social pressures tending against cumulative innovation and change. Here Hagen seems almost to be saying that traditional society does not change because its nature is such as to be resistant to change; economic development takes place where the socio-cultural conditions are appropriate for it, and cannot take place otherwise.

Because traditional society is so resistant to change, the forces that disrupt it must be powerful ones. The change comes about if and when members of some one social group perceive that their purposes and values are not respected by groups in the society whom they respect and whose esteem they value. Such social disaffection is most readily apparent when

[67] As McClelland puts it, "Professor Hagen is playing 'heads I win; tails you lose.' Any case can be made to fit his hypothesis so long as it remains so flexible." *Op. cit.*, p. 323.

a group migrates to a new society. However, there are only four types of
events that result in withdrawal of status: a change in the power structure,
derogation of institutional activity without change in the power structure,
contradiction among status symbols, and non-acceptance of expected
status on migration to a new society.

Hagen proceeds to an analysis in terms of Merton's typology of modes
of individual adaptation: conformity, innovation, ritualism, retreatism,
and rebellion. Retreatism, Hagen believes, is the typical reaction to withdrawal of status. The retreatist person, he says, "is not free of rage." On
the contrary, "his rage is intense," but held in leash, with occasional outbursts. However, retreatist parents give rise to creative children; and the
Hagen gives a number of cases in point.

Hagen then goes on to argue that growth in the size of the market or a
more rapid rate of capital accumulation is relevant only in the sense that
"the more favorable these economic circumstances are, the more readily
change in personality may bring about continuing technological progress."
However, he insists that where the socio-cultural environment is appropriate and an innovational effort is present, an expanding market is created
almost automatically. Similarly, under these conditions, the ratio of savings
and investment to income will rise more or less automatically. True, if
economic conditions change for the better, at the same time that personality traits become more favorable, the impetus for growth is increased.
But the change in personality is empirically more important, and it is
therefore more convenient to treat the economic situation as a datum or
parameter.

Hagen's long economic history of England seems to add little to our
knowledge; it merely translates well-known facts into his particular
jargon. For example, in the War of 1642 "the king was supported by most
of the titled nobles, Catholics, Anglican clergy, gentry, especially the
greater gentry, and peasantry, who because of their high need-submission
tend in almost every society to remain loyal to the traditional regime. . . ."
On what kind of empirical observation is such a statement based?

Just how much Hagen's gigantic intellectual efforts have advanced our
knowledge of the process of economic development is an open question,
particularly if by "knowledge" we mean understanding of a kind that
provides guidance to policy decisions. In a general way we have known
for a long time that culture patterns and personality traits are important
in determining the rate of economic development and cultural change.
Hagen's discussion of "the impotence of the peasant" is reminiscent of
Boeke's observations on "the voiceless East." And it is to be doubted that
such statements as, "the creative individual is not necessarily a happy man
who faces problems with pure pleasure," or "the individual with conflicting needs may be paralyzed, or he may oscillate between contradictory
actions," are really contributions to knowledge. Hagen's appendix on
"toilet training" recalls a remark made many years ago by Ronald
Walker: Suppose one learns that the tightness or easiness of money
reflects the anal eroticism of bankers, what exactly does one do about it?

It is hard to see what is left for the economic adviser if this sort of theory of growth is accepted. Indeed Hagen (together with the remaining "old-fashioned" anthropologists) may well be pleased to see economists kept at home until somehow or other the socio-cultural stage in one country after another is set for economic development—by which time, presumably their advice will hardly be necessary anyhow.

The Evidence[68]

Let us examine one of Hagen's more extensive attempts at factual support for his thesis: the case of Colombia. He begins with a brief summary of economic growth since the middle of the nineteenth century, and then asks, "Why did growth begin?" The reasons usually given for economic growth, he replies, were not operative in Colombia. The economy grew, not because of foreign capital inflow, or contact with foreign technology, or construction of social overhead capital, or large and growing markets, but despite the absence of all these factors. His conclusion is that continuing growth was launched by a particular group of Colombians: the people of Antioquia. It was they who provided the entrepreneurial leadership. Hagen states the general conditions that led to the emergence of the Antioqueño as the entrepreneur: [69]

Under some human motivation or other, a group must come to perceive it to be both possible and good to undertake acts of capital investment. . . . What appears to be required . . . is not merely an appropriate value system but two further conditions: first, the new élite must feel itself denied the conventional routes to prestige and power by the traditional less acquisitive society of which it is a part; second, the traditional society must be sufficiently flexible (or weak) to permit its members to seek material advance (or political power) as a route upwards alternative to conformity.

To support the contention that Antioqueños hold a more than proportionate share of entrepreneurial positions in the country, Hagen conducted some statistical tests, using telephone directories and lists of executives compiled by the National Association of Industrialists. In trying to discover the reasons for the Antioqueños fitting the role of the "sub-dominant élite," he discovers four possible determinants:

1. Ancestral background. (Probably Basque.)

2. Mining experience. (Although much gold was taken out of the Antioquia area during the first years of the Spanish occupation the supply was soon exhausted. Since neither Indians nor Negro slaves were available, the mine owners were forced to work their own claims. This experience may have conditioned the Antioqueño for acceptance of the role of industrialist more so than his counterpart in other sections of the country.)

3. Loss of foreign trade. (Before the turn of the century, several events

[68] This section shamelessly plagiarizes a term paper prepared for my seminar at the University of California by William Long.
[69] Hagen, *op. cit.*, p. 378.

led to the loss of profitable foreign trade. In Cali and Bogotá, the other main regions of the economy, displaced commercialists turned to land ownership and real estate speculation. However, in Antioquia, land was less productive and therefore provided less opportunity for profitable investment. The displaced commercialists in that region turned to industry, the only other avenue open to them.)

4. Withdrawal of status respect. (Colombians among the elite of other regions of the country looked down on those from Antioquia, primarily because they stooped so low as to actually get their hands dirty in working. The conclusion is that "the Antioqueños reacted gradually over a period of several centuries to withdrawal of status respect, and that this reaction and its impact on their personalities form an important strand in the explanation of the economic growth of Colombia." [70]

Hagen places primary emphasis on the withdrawal of status respect. To prove that Antioqueños are better entrepreneurs than other Colombians, he administered the Thematic Apperception Test (TAT) to a group of twenty business leaders in Antioquia. In these tests, the subject is shown a series of pictures, depicting people in various situations subject to differing interpretations. The interpretations given to the pictures enable the examiner to draw conclusions about the subject's basic psychological make-up.

In order to have a control group, Hagen administered the same test to a group of community leaders in the city of Popayán, the capital city of the Department of Cauca. The two sets of results consistently revealed a remarkable difference in the basic make-up of the two types of leaders. In commenting on these results, Hagen remarks: "It should be emphasized that what is portrayed is not a difference in personality between all Antioqueños and all Popayanese or other Colombians. The Antioqueños selected were those most apt to have creative personalities. *So, however, were the Popayanese, for they were community leaders.*" [71]

What then does this test prove? Hagen was looking for indicators of relative levels of creativity. His hypothesis was that this level would be different for entrepreneurs from Antioquia and for those from other parts of the country. Why then choose "community leaders" from Popayán as his control group? Why not business men from Bogotá, or Cali, or Barranquilla? Popayán is known as the city that is the most conservative, most resistant to technological change, and most leisure-oriented of all cities of its size in Colombia. In short, Hagen's choice of control group makes his test worthless.

Can we find no more satisfactory explanation of regional development differentials in Colombia? In its *Analyses and Projections of Economic Development*, the Economic Commission for Latin America divides the nation into five regions: [72]

[70] *Ibid.*
[71] *Ibid.*, p. 369. (Italics added).
[72] Economic Commission for Latin America, *Analyses and Projections of Economic Development: III—The Economic Development of Colombia* (United Nations, Department of Economic and Social Affairs, 1957), p. 285.

1. North (Barranquilla).
2. West Central (Medellin).
3. East Central (Bucaramanga).
4. Southeast (Bogotá).
5. South (Cali).

In 1960, the five central cities of these regions were the largest in Colombia. The United States Government publication, *Investment in Colombia* (1957),[73] gives only four regions: West, North, Southeast, and South. Each classification has its advantages and disadvantages, but in each the west or west central covers roughly the same area and constitutes the "rich region."

What is there about the west or west central region (here called Antioquia) that it should be more progressive than the others? Two sets of historical developments differentiate Antioquia from the other regions. The first relates to coffee and the second to manufacturing.

The advantage of Antioquia in the production of coffee seems to be the single most important factor in the relatively rapid economic growth of the region, explaining in large measure both the subsequent industrialization and the development of entrepreneurship. Coffee was introduced to Colombia in 1808 via Venezuela, and was first cultivated in Cucuta. It spread a little later to Bucaramanga. Later still it spread to the areas bordering the Mag River. It seems that the first planting in Caldas was at Pereira, in 1886. At some time in the 1880's, coffee became the leading Colombian export, and it has retained that position ever since. By 1900, Antioquia and Caldas were exporting over half of all coffee exported from the country, and they have continued to do ever since.

The dominance of the Antioquia region in the production of coffee is mainly due to three factors: first, the type of soil found in the region is superior for coffee; second, the relative proportion of coffee-producing land in the region is high; and third, transportation facilities are better. James J. Parsons has this to say about the influence of volcanic activity on coffee production in Colombia: [74]

The fertile slopes of the Cerro Bravo were the forcing-bed of western Colombia's modern coffee economy. . . . this Mellizos-Cerro Bravo volcanic zone has been the primary geographic factor in the development of the Antioqueño settlement pattern and the coffee economy of Antioquia and Caldas . . .

Caldas, much more than any other department, has received the benefits of volcanic ash deposits.

Caldas, which produces almost one-third of Colombia's coffee, is the smallest of the sixteen departments. It has the smallest number of producing coffee trees per hectare. But, in total area under cultivation, total production, yield per producing tree, and income per hectare, it is first in

[73] Office of International Trade, *Investment in Colombia* (Washington, 1957), pp. 61–67.
[74] James J. Parsons, *Antiqueño Colonization in Western Colombia* (Berkeley and Los Angeles, 1949), pp. 39–40.

the nation. It is also first in proportion of total trees that are yielding trees, and in man-hours per hectare. Yet in income per man-hour, Caldas is sixth in the nation, below the national average. It seems that Caldas' dominance in coffee production is due solely to natural conditions, not to farmers' greater initiative. A similar story could be told for the department of Antioquia, where income per man-hour is eighth in the nation.

Caldas has a unique position also in regard to topography. The *arabica* coffee grown in Colombia grows at altitudes between 3,000 and 6,000 feet.[75] Over 90 per cent of coffee in Colombia is grown in the altitude range 3,280 to 6,560 feet. Caldas has a higher percentage of coffee-producing land, at appropriate altitudes, than any of the other departments.

The transportation network in the region is far from natural. Coffee became the leading export *for the nation* before it was grown extensively in the Antioquia region. When it was discovered that the region had the natural advantages listed above, it was in the nation's interest to facilitate production there. The solution was to build a railroad into the interior of the region. The first line, from Medellín to Puerto Berrio (on the Magdalena) was started in 1874 by the government of Antioquia. It was not completed until 1929, but as each section was finished it found immediate use.

In 1926, after about fifteen years of indecision as to the best solution to the problem, an English firm was contracted to construct a tunnel through the Quiebra. This project accounts for much of the foreign capital inflow of 1925–29. Of total public investment in these years over one-half was in the department of Antioquia. The tunnel was completed in 1929, and Medellín then had a direct link to the Magdalena River. A similar story could be told for the highway system.

Once the transport system was built for coffee it was available for manufacturing as well. The ECLA study on the economic development of Colombia, commenting on the general development of industry in Colombia, gives a list of reasons for the establishment of the first manufacturing nucleus in the department of Antioquia: [76]

1. It was one of the largest population centers and had a relatively high income.

2. It was the principal coffee-producing center. It received the major share of the benefits of export earnings. Therefore it had the greatest opportunities for financing manufacturing investment.

3. The limited amount of coffee-producing land led to investment in non-agricultural activities.

4. Because it was the coffee-exporting center it had many advantages with respect to the means of communication, for priority was given to facilities for the transportation of coffee. Of public investment made in the late twenties, over half of it was in Antioquia. Internal transport costs

[75] William H. Ukers, *All About Coffee* (New York, 1935), pp. 134–35.
[76] Economic Commission for Latin America, *op. cit.*, p. 262.

from the coast for imported end products were still sufficiently high to form a natural protection for local industries.

5. A greater available capacity for the production of electric energy.

Are we not justified in concluding that the causal sequence runs from coffee to transportation facilities to manufacturing? Antioquia's advantages in these areas have been to a large extent "natural," and have been effectively supplemented by public investment and foreign investment in the infrastructure. At the very least, such familiar explanations of Antioquia's more rapid growth seem just as plausible as Hagen's explanation in terms of personality traits.[77]

What seems to be needed is not the Hagen-style model, which relies wholly on socio-cultural and psychological factors to explain social change and economic growth, but rather a model in which strategic "economic" and "non-economic" variables are combined. Hagen comes closest to this sort of model in discussing the interactions of personality change, capital accumulation, and growth of markets. But even there he relegates the purely economic factors to a minor role.

The need for interdisciplinary research in the field of economic conditions is now recognized by all practitioners in the field. There still is doubt, however, as to whether the most effective kind of interdisciplinary work consists of teamwork among specialists in the various disciplines, or efforts by individual scholars to combine in their own mind facets of all the related disciplines. It may well be, as Professor Max Millikan suggests in his Foreword to Hagen's book, that rare beings such as Everett Hagen, "at home in each of a number of usually rather isolated ivory towers . . . make possible a degree of communication amongst [various disciplines] that would [be] much more difficult in his absence." But such rare beings are not our only hope; there remains the possibility of interdisciplinary teamwork. The integration need not be achieved in a single mind. Social scientists (other than economists) with a policy-oriented, operational interest in economic development are still rare; but when and where they can be found and assembled for a joint attack on development problems, this seems to be a better solution to cross-disciplinary problems.

The Anthropologist's Viewpoint

Today it is not the anthropologists or sociologists who are claiming that the socio-cultural characteristics of underdeveloped countries (or "peasant societies") are insuperable barriers to economic growth. In the conclusion of his comparative study of entrepreneurship in east-central Java and Bali, Clifford Geertz says: [78]

[77] With regard to Hagen's empirical evidence, David McClelland says, "He has nowhere shown conclusively that loss of respect *preceded* ideological change or even entrepreneurial behavior. On the contrary, there is some evidence that disrespect sometimes accompanied or followed being successful in business, as in the case of the Antioqueños." *Op. cit.,* p. 323.

[78] Clifford Geertz, *Peddlers and Princes; Social Development and Economic Change in Two Indonesian Towns* (Chicago, 1963), pp. 144–45.

The issue, properly stated however, is not whether each and every aspect of society must change or nothing but the economy itself must change in the process of economic rationalization; for clearly neither of these extreme positions is defensible. Rather it is: what must change and what need not?

Professor Geertz' studies lead him to the conclusion that a wide range of cultures is capable of generating entrepreneurship and economic growth. The problem is to recognize in each culture those forces which are conducive to growth and those which are not: [79]

From a narrowly economic point of view development takes the same general form always and everywhere; it consists of a progressively more rational employment of scarce means toward the achievement of specified material ends. But from the sociological point of view it is not clear that such a basic and obvious similarity of form exists, that the changes in religious outlook, class structure, family organization and so on are identical from one developing society to another. In any case, the employment of highly generalized dichotomous concepts of holistic types, to describe the broader processes in the light of our still confused and uncertain understanding of them and of their inter-relations with the much better conceptualized processes of economic rationalization would seem premature.

On the basis of his own studies, Geertz is willing to risk only six generalizations: (1) Innovative economic leadership (entrepreneurship) occurs in a fairly well-defined and socially homogeneous group; (2) This innovative group has crystallized out of a larger traditional group which has a very long history of extravillage status and interlocal orientation; (3) The larger group out of which the innovative group is emerging is one that is at present experiencing a fairly radical change in its relationships with the wider society of which it is a part; (4) On the ideological level the innovative group conceives of itself as the main vehicle of religious moral excellence within a generally wayward, unenlightened, or heedless community; (5) The major innovations and innovational problems the entrepreneurs face are organizational rather than technical, and (6) The function of the entrepreneur in such transitional but pretake-off societies is mainly to adapt customarily established means to novel ends.

These generalizations are not inconsistent with the Hagen thesis, but their implications for policy, and the prognosis that one might base on them, are very different indeed. With respect to Indonesia in particular, Geertz' conclusion is not that drastic changes in the social organization or culture patterns are a prerequisite to economic development; it is rather that economic development planning should take due account of the differences in these factors from one part of the country to another, and should not stifle the internal dynamics of individual cultures by trying to force every society within Indonesia into the same developmental mold. "To say that Indonesian development must in great part be consciously planned," Geertz writes, "is not to say that such planning should

[79] *Ibid.*, p. 145.

take place in deliberate ignorance of the very domestic social and cultural processes which it is supposedly concerned to transform. . . . For successful developmental planning within an at least partially democratic framework it is necessary that programs and policies be designed to encourage, support, and intensify processes of economic rationalization such as those described for Modjokuto and Tabanan as they appear throughout the whole of the country, and that government-sponsored enterprise be keyed in with that arising autochthonously in the general population." [80]

Anthropologist Charles Eramus is even more insistent on the dominance of economic factors in economic development, and the possibilities for adapting cultures to the needs of economic growth. He lays great stress on the significance of the "demonstration effect" in inducing technological change. As an example of successful intervention he describes the terracing to prevent erosion in the Bío-Bío River in Chile. The terraces, he says, survived "a downpour of flood proportions," which caused much damage to neighboring fields which were not terraced. This demonstration led to many requests for similar assistance, and to the ultimate establishment of a soil conservation department in the Ministry of Agriculture.[81]

Similarly, the introduction into Bolivia of Cuban yellow corn, which is quick-growing and weevil-resistant, led to the introduction of this strain by one-third of all the farmers in the area within two years. Again, the mosaic-resistant sugarcane in Colombia and Costa Rica, and the disease-resistant Kennebec potatoes substantially replaced local varieties within three years after their introduction by foreign technical assistance experts. According to Erasmus, the motivation was economic in the simplest and purest form. Depending on the level of living of the farmers concerned, "in some cases the motivation of the farmers of Bolivia, Colombia and Costa Rica was to increase survival margins, and in other cases to increase conspicuous consumption." [82] For an economic development planner, it is not of great importance which of these two motives is in operation; all that is necessary is to be sure that people want to increase their real incomes.

Erasmus also contrasts the success of penicillin injection against yaws in Colombia with the failure of water purification in Ecuador. People must either have a high level of knowledge and literacy so that they can understand what is being attempted, or the demonstration effect must be clear. "People choose new alternatives or controls," Erasmus maintains, "when frequency interpretations make possible a clear connection with reward." Although the language is slightly different, this statement is precisely the kind of assumption about human behavior that underlies ordinary economic analysis.

Erasmus also points out that failure of pilot projects is sometimes attributed to cultural resistance when, in fact, the explanation is purely technical. He describes as an example the failure of irrigation systems introduced in Mexico. The refusal of the local population to use appar-

[80] *Ibid.,* p. 156.
[81] Charles Erasmus, *Man Takes Control* (Minneapolis, 1961).
[82] *Ibid.,* pp. 23–25.

ently superior techniques was not so much due to cultural resistance, he argues, but to relevant technical factors which were overlooked by the Western "expert." The system consisted of scraping the topsoil into the dikes, which washed away during the floods, leaving the soil denuded. In any case, the summer rains came too late to get a crop in before the frost.

Erasmus cites cases where hybrid corn was rejected by Mexicans and American Indians; despite the higher yield per acre, it was unacceptable because "it makes poor tortillas." The rejection of the higher-yield corn cannot be regarded as "non-economic"; in the absence of a market for corn surplus, the yield was really lower with the hybrid corn because it produced less in the way of satisfaction for the farmers. The same is true of cassava and rice in Indonesia; the caloric content per acre is higher if cassava is grown than if rice is grown, but cassava is regarded as inferior food to which the Javanese resort only under conditions of severe hardship. Thus, in true economic terms, the yields are lower when the land is put under cassava.

An example from the present writer's own experience is the slaughter of the cattle, provided to farmers in the pilot-zone regional development project in Greece as the basis for building up a dairy herd. The cattle were killed and eaten not because there was cultural resistance to dairy farming but because the transportation connections of the pilot zone with the outside world were so poor, and consequently the price of feed so high and the price of dairy products so low, that there was really no incentive to build up dairy herds.[83]

Erasmus also mentions the case of soybeans in Colombia, which were abandoned except in those cases where margarine factories were established, thus providing a market for a surplus. There is nothing "economic" in eating highly nutritious but unpleasant food.

In his conclusions, Erasmus denies that there is any serious cultural lag that delays or retards technological change:

I agree, of course, that society must continually adjust to its technological changes, but it does not lag far behind them waiting for students of society to find a short-cut to Utopia. . . . For the sake of argument a better case might be made for technological . . . rather than social . . . lag in the world today.

By technological lag he means the lag of productivity behind advanced ideas of social welfare. Where low-income peoples have difficulty in accepting new technologies, Erasmus maintains, "the lag is really between the felt needs of the host group and those of the donors of technology." But "where we are faced with rising expectations—that is, with helping people satisfy needs they already feel—social conditions will no longer be a major concern for the lag will be primarily technological." [84]

Regarding the development problem as essentially economic and technological, Erasmus takes a dim view of community development: [85]

[83] For a full discussion of the pilot zone experiment, see Chap. 32.
[84] *Ibid.*, p. 312.
[85] *Ibid.*, p. 320.

I am opposed to the notion that construction projects are Quixotic and extravagant compared to the inexpensive, self-help projects through which people are supposedly taught to help themselves by their own bootstraps. The ideas that we can advance underdeveloped areas by small changes promoted by ingenuous, Messianic technician-inventors, the like of which I seldom encountered in the flesh, and all at little cost to themselves, is wishful fantasy.

His studies, coupled with his own experience with technical assistance missions in Latin American countries, lead Erasmus to conclude that "technical assistance is most likely to be successful when it works with market-oriented goals among people producing for the market."

Finally, Erasmus concludes that sociologists and anthropologists can be of greatest value in helping to select areas ripe for development through projects that involve investment in "positive controls rather than persuasion." In short, there is no escape from the "big push" on the economic front.

The "Revisits"

To this kind of evidence we can add the results of the increasingly frequent "revisits" by anthropologists to areas studied earlier, which have since been subject to some major outside shock. The import of these "revisits" is that cultural change can come with great rapidity, and apparently with little suffering on the part of the peoples ivolved, where the magnitude of the outside shock is great enough. Most famous of the revisits, perhaps, is Margaret Mead's description of the transformation of Manus' society as a consequence of the occupation of the island by American troops during World War II.[86] The demonstration effect of having on the island a number of American GI's considerably in excess of the local population resulted in the Manus' culture jumping 2,000 years in ten. Why should not a well-construed economic development program have a similar effect?

In appraising the significance of her revisit to the Manus, Margaret Mead characterizes the anthropology of the first four decades of the twentieth century. In this period, she says, anthropologists were concerned with demonstrating that the human race was one, and that the various races of mankind were specializations without measurable differences in their capacity as groups of individuals to take on any civilizations; that each people has a shared, learned way of life, or "culture"; and that this culture should be respected, in the same way that individual human beings should each be respected. This approach led consciously or unconsciously to an attitude among anthropologists that regarded rapid cultural change as something imposed on a society from outside. However, "Now our old sense that all change was one-sided and came from a misuse of power suffered a new transformation. All change was now seen as terribly difficult and against the real will of the people, who only thought they wanted

[86] Margaret Mead, *New Lives for Old* (New York, 1956). See also Daniel Lerner, *The Passing of Traditional Society: Modernizing the Middle East.* (Glencoe, Ill., 1958).

tractors because they were symbols of Western superiority but who really hated regular hours, clocks, machines, hospitals, the dictates of nutritionists, sitting still in school, and learning to think in realistic Western terms." [87] (The present writer is tempted to add—like any Western child!)

The experience of the Manus, Dr. Mead concludes, "points up the completeness with which the people may want to change rather than merely submit to being changed." She also suggests that the interest in preserving aspects of the traditional culture may really lie with the Westerner who is somewhat concerned with other cultures, rather than with the people of that society itself. It is necessary to offer people all aspects of a new civilization if it is to be attractive, and not just bits and pieces: [88]

The first groups of women who are admitted to some male occupation perform astonishingly well, learn faster than the norm for men, while women who enter the same occupation after it has been defined as something done by men and women will show no such conspicuous superiority. Throwing off colonial yokes, which have included definition as second class human beings, has the same releasing effect on members of former colonial status.

The study of the Manus suggests the importance of a "Gestalt" approach: "It is easier to shift from being a South Sea Islander to being a New Yorker—as I have seen Samoans do—than to shift from being a perfectly adjusted traditional South Sea Islander to a partly civilized, partly accultured South Sea Islander." Each human culture, like each language, is a whole, and is capable of being learned. The term "learned" is the keynote; where culture is learned, it can be changed by re-education.

Nor does Dr. Mead feel that rapid change is necessarily painful. On the contrary, she maintains that rapid change may well be less upsetting than gradual change.

The Manus experience shows [89]

that rapid change is not only possible, but may actually be very desirable, that instead of advocating slow partial changes we should advocate that a people who choose to practice a new technology, or enter into drastically new kinds of economic relationships, will do this more easily if they live in different houses, wear different clothes, and eat different, or differently cooked, food. . . . The alternative to the culture which has existed so long and changed so slowly that every item of behavior is part of a pattern and so perfect that it seems that it must have sprung complete from the head of Jove, is seen to be not the culture in which necessary and wanted change is artificially slowed down and retarded, but rather the culture in which—if there is to be purposeful change, by an Ataturk . . . an enterprising Maharajah, or the agriculture extension department—the whole pattern is transformed at once, with as little reminder of the past as possible to slow down the new learning, or to make that learning incomplete and maladaptive.

[87] Margaret Mead, "From the Stone Age to the Twentieth Century," in Novack and Lekachman, *op. cit.*, p. 201.

[88] *Ibid.*, p. 203.

[89] *Ibid.*, pp. 204–205.

The Backward Bending Supply Curve of Effort

Perhaps no presumed characteristic of primitive or peasant societies has been more frequently cited as a barrier to development than "limited wants" or the "backward bending supply curve of effort." Thus J. L. Sadie, for example, is impressed by the socio-cultural resistances to economic change among the South African Bantus. They are community-centered rather than individualistic, he says, and abundance of material things plays no role in their philosophy. One would like to know whether the Bantus had ever been presented with a picture of a life fundamentally different from the one they have, and capable of achievement by their own efforts. In any case, Sadie concludes that: [90]

There is much to be gained and many misconceptions can be avoided, if the economic problem of an underdeveloped community of the type described above is framed, not in terms of the vicious circle of poverty, Malthusian pressure or inadequate capital formation, etc., but in terms of the strategic factors of an ultimate character, namely its social and psychological inertia.

The basic mistake here is in assuming that there is a difference between these two approaches. Obviously, the vicious circle of poverty, Malthusian pressure, and inadequate capital formation are the products of that very social and psychological inertia to which Sadie refers. If the leaders of the society were in a position to assure adequate capital formation, offsetting Malthusian pressure and breaking the vicious circle of poverty, the socio- and psychological inertia would have disappeared among the leaders, and would soon disappear among the people.

At another point, however, Sadie buttresses the conclusion of Margaret Mead: [91]

Economic development of an underdeveloped people by themselves is not compatible with the maintenance of their traditional customs and mores. A break with the latter is a prerequisite to economic progress. What is needed is a revolution in the totality of social, cultural and religious institutions and habits, and thus in their psychological attitude, their philosophy and way of life.

As pointed out above,[92] there is little doubt that supply curves of effort turn backward at some point in all societies. The question is only at what level of income the turn comes, and what it takes to "unbend" the curves.

As Ralph Linton puts it,[93]

... there are two factors effecting economic growth; all societies and most individuals welcome improvement in their economic condition, as long as such improvements do not involve more trouble than they are worth, that is, neces-

[90] J. L. Sadie, "The Social Anthropology of Economic Underdevelopment," in Novack and Lekachman, *op. cit.*, pp. 218–19.
[91] *Ibid.*
[92] Chapter 12, p. 237.
[93] Linton, *op. cit.*, p. 193.

sitate too many changes in established behavior patterns and controvert too many accepted values. . . . Where a society no longer tries to improve economic conditions, this attitude can be traced to a series of past failures and frustrations . . .

Where the supply curves of effort turn backward at a level of living as low as that of the Bantus, the question might well be raised as to whether or not they are really "underdeveloped." Can a society that has everything it wants be regarded as underdeveloped? The question is perhaps more relevant if applied to somewhat higher civilizations—Bali, for example—a civilization in which people meet their basic needs for food, clothing, and shelter on the basis of some twenty hours of work a week, leaving them free to devote the rest of their time to their highly refined arts, their social life, their philosophy, and their religion—might be regarded as the pinnacle of development. The question is, of course, whether such traditional cultures, even when so dynamic within their own framework as the Balinese, can be preserved in the face of population pressure without technological progress and structural change. If the outside observer has *clear proof* that the existing culture, no matter how satisfactory to its adherents, will break down because productivity is not rising as fast as population, then the outsider may be morally obliged to recommend the drastic change in the cultural system that Dr. Sadie feels is necessary. In the absence of such a gloomy prognosis, why not leave satisfied people alone? There are more than enough dissatisfied people to keep social scientists busy.

Another point that should perhaps be made is that when we speak of changing the "culture" we do not mean abandoning those refinements of sensate culture that we so much admire in some of the older civilizations, such as the Balinese. Some increase in the working week may indeed be required; but the painting, the sculpture, the music, and the dance need not be abandoned as industrialization proceeds under the leadership of the Balinese sultans. More people love Bach, medieval painting, and architecture today than before the Industrial Revolution in Europe.

To conclude this section, let us quote the Minutes of the UNESCO Round-Table Conference on Social Prerequisites of Industrialization: [94] "There are no social prerequisites that must be fulfilled *first* in order that economic development may take place *afterward*."

Economic Development Without Cultural Change

One more piece of evidence is of importance here—James Abegglen's conclusion that the industrialization of Japan took place essentially within the framework of feudal society. The industrialization of Japan, Abegglen argues, took place through the transfer of the feudal system from farm to factory. The discipline entailed in the feudal system was used as the very vehicle of industrialization: [95]

[94] Raymond Firth, *General Working Paper*, UNESCO Expert Working Group on Social Prerequisites to Economic Growth, UNESCO/SS/SP/WP 22 March 1963.
[95] James Abegglen, *op. cit.*, pp. 129, 131, 134.

If a single conclusion were to be drawn from this study it would be that the development of industrial Japan has taken place with much less change from the kinds of social organization and social relations of preindustrial or non-industrial Japan than would be expected from the Western model of the growth of an industrial society. . . . At repeated points in the study of the factory, parallels to an essentially feudal system of organization may be seen—not, to be sure, a replication of the feudal loyalties, commitments, rewards, and methods of leadership but a rephrasing of them in the setting of modern industry. . . . It would seem from this study, then, that the very success of the Japanese experience with industrialization may well have been a function of the fact that, far from undergoing a total revolution in social structure or social relationships, the hard core of Japan's system of social relationships remained intact, allowing an orderly transition to industrialization continuous with her earlier social forms.

Here the argument seems to be that profound cultural change is not always necessary in order to achieve technological change and economic development.

Conclusions

If we add up the evidence provided by the "non-economists," we seem to arrive at the following set of conclusions:

1. Virtually any society or culture is capable of economic development. The problem is to recognize within the culture those dynamic elements that contribute most to rising productivity and incomes. Efforts to force all societies into the same mold are likely to retard rather than accelerate economic growth in developing countries as a group. (Geertz, Belshaw, Moore.)

2. It is not even certain that drastic cultural change is always necessary for the combination of capital accumulation, technological progress, structural change, and acquisition of skills that are the essence of economic development. In at least one important case—the grandest success story of them all, Japan—industrialization seems to have taken place by utilizing the existing institutions and value systems of feudalism. (Abegglen.)

3. Where, however, cultural stability is incompatible with rapid economic growth, the culture will adapt readily and painlessly enough to an economic "big push," particularly if the big push includes, as it should, a maximum effort on the educational front. It is, of course, useful to understand the culture in order to accelerate and ease the transition, but rapid and complete cultural change is likely to be less traumatic than gradual and partial change. (Mead, Belshaw.)

Thus we end up with a "big push" doctrine in the socio-cultural field as well as in the economic field.[96] There is nothing we know *for certain* that would suggest to us that a "big push," including massive efforts at education and re-education, will fail, or that it will be particularly painful to a society. On the other hand, there is a good deal of evidence that gradualism will fail, and that it will be very painful indeed in a great many

[96] For more on the economic aspects of the "big-push doctrine," see Chap. 15.

developing countries. On the evidence we have, we have no choice but to recommend a "big push" on all fronts.

All this does not mean that economists should stop studying anthropology, sociology, psychology, and political science. Clearly the maximum domestic effort, absorptive capacity, and the scale of the necessary "big push" are all affected by socio-cultural factors. The chances of success will vary considerably from one society to another, and the chances of success within any one country will be greater if the planners and politicians understand and heed the society and culture with which they are working. The determination of priorities, and the pattern of incentives offered, the decision-making groups to which alternatives are posed and the way in which they are posed, all these should be influenced by the nature of the society. There should be sociologists, anthropologists, and psychologists on the planning team. It does mean, however, that development economists should fight tooth and nail any line of argument that might result in a reversion to gradualism as a basis for development policy.

The difficult cases, of course, will be the countries at so low a level of economic and social development that the maximum domestic effort and total absorptive capacity are both below the "big push" or minimum effort needed to guarantee a rate of growth of income higher than the rate of population growth. Here technical assistance and education will be the major requirements, and the supply of properly trained teachers may be the ultimate bottleneck. Perhaps the whole debate about socio-cultural "obstacles" to economic development really boils down to that; education in its broad sense is an essential component of the development process, and some countries may not be able to mount the necessary "big push" in the field of education without a good deal of outside help.

13 | Colonialism and the "Backwash" Effects of Foreign Trade

As Professor Ragnar Nurkse was fond of pointing out, the great Alfred Marshall pronounced that "the causes which determine the economic progress of nations belong to the study of international trade." Nurkse himself remarks rightly that "in the middle of the twentieth century this may seem to us a curious statement." Marshall may have been perfectly well justified in speaking of "the splendid markets which the old world has offered to the new," when referring to the countries of recent settlement in the nineteenth century;[1] and Malthus and Mill may have been right in regarding expansion of international trade as a safety valve, postponing stagnation in advanced countries, in nineteenth-century Europe. But it can hardly be said that international trade has been a major cause of economic growth for the developing countries of the mid-twentieth century. On the contrary, balance of payments problems are frequently cited as a major deterrent to economic development. Recently, some economists have gone so far as to argue that international trade, far from encouraging growth of underdeveloped countries, has actually retarded it by accentuating the dualistic nature of the economy. In these countries, conditions are such that "backwash" (unfavorable) effects outweigh "spread" (stimulating) effects.

[1] Alfred Marshall, *Principles of Economics* (London, 1920), pp. 91, 668; Ragnar Nurkse, *Equilibrium and Growth in the World Economy* (Cambridge, Mass., 1961), p. 242. Nurkse refers to the contrasting impact of foreign trade in the nineteenth and twentieth centuries at several points in this volume. See also his chapter in Howard Ellis and Henry Wallich (eds.), *Economic Development for Latin America* (New York, 1961).

The failure of foreign trade to serve as an "engine of growth" (to use D. H. Robertson's phrase) is usually traced to one or more of four factors.[2] First, it is contended that there is a long-run tendency for the *terms* of trade to turn against producers of raw materials and foodstuffs, a tendency which in effect diminishes the resources available for development of underdeveloped countries. Second, it is argued that exports of developing countries are excessively concentrated in one or a few commodities and that commercial policies of advanced countries should be designed to help underdeveloped countries diversify their exports. Third, it is pointed out that markets for major exports of developing countries are extremely unstable and that development programs are continuously jeopardized by the instability and uncertainty of foreign exchange earnings. Fourth, it is contended that long-run trends in patterns of consumption lead to a deteriorating *balance* of trade for underdeveloped countries. These unfavorable or "backwash" effects of international trade are sometimes associated with the colonial heritage of underdeveloped countries.

The Myint Model

Professor Hla Myint proposes the following model: [3]

1. The country starts its period of expansion, resulting from its being opened up to economic relations with the outside world, "with a fairly sparse population in relation to its potential natural resources."

2. Its natural resources are then developed in the direction of a few specialized lines of primary production for export. This development is generally carried out by foreign private enterprise, assisted by government policy, and limited by the expansion of the world market for the export goods.

3. The native inhabitants of the country enjoy legal equality with other people in their economic relations, including the right to own any type of property and to enter into any type of occupation. (In some colonial countries this assumption did not hold, but it is all the more interesting that the Myint model does not *need* discrimination against native people to show the tendency toward technological dualism.) In such a model, Professor Myint points out, "The disequalizing factors must be considered as operating not only between the backward and the advanced countries as aggregate units, but also between the backward and advanced groups of peoples within the same backward country itself." The usual "country A and B" approach "is seriously inadequate for our purpose." Disaggregation, at least to the extent of recognizing the two major sectors, is necessary if we are to obtain useful results.

Myint suggests that before the underdeveloped countries were "opened up," they were "primitive or medieval stationary states governed by habits and customs. Their people might have lived near the 'minimum subsistence

[2] D. H. Robertson, "The Future of International Trade," in *Essays in Monetary Theory* (London, 1940), p. 214.

[3] Hla Myint, "An Interpretation of Economic Backwardness," *Oxford Economic Papers*, Vol. VI, No. 2 (June, 1954), p. 146.

level,' but that standard, according to their own lights, did not appear too wretched or inadequate. Thus in spite of low productivity and lack of economic progress, there was no problem of economic discontent and frustration: wants and activities were on the whole adapted to each other and the people were in equilibrium with their environment."

He then moves on to the second stage. "Particularly in the second half of the nineteenth century," when "these stationary backward societies were opened up to the outside economic forces. . . . Measures for economic development then consisted mainly in attempts to persuade or force the backward people into the new ways of life represented by the money economy—for example, by stimulating their demand for imports and by taxing them so that they were obliged to turn to cash crops or work in the newly opened mines and plantations." [4] The yardstick of development of such countries was their export and taxable capacity. However, the "opening up" process drew increasing numbers of the native peoples into a new elite, in which the values of Western society were increasingly accepted. This gave rise to "a sense of economic discontent and maladjustment." It was in this third stage that the political problems associated with underdeveloped countries appeared.

The form of development in such dualistic economies was not such as to require a high degree of specialization among the native peoples: [5]

In spite of the striking specialization of the inanimate productive equipment and of the individuals from the economically advanced groups of people who manage and control them, there is really very little specialization beyond a natural adaptability to the tropical climate, among the backward peoples in their roles as unskilled labourers or peasant producers. . . . Thus all the specialization required for the export market seems to have been done by the other co-operating factors, the whole production structure being built around the supply of cheap undifferentiated labour. . . . Even where a new cash crop is introduced, the essence of its success as a *peasant* crop depends on the fact that it does not represent a radical departure from the existing techniques of production (e.g., yams and cocoa in West Africa).

Indeed, Professor Myint goes so far as to suggest that the process of specialization of a backward economy for the export market is most rapid and successful when it leaves the backward peoples in their unspecialized roles as unskilled laborers and peasant producers using traditional methods of production.

Dual or Plural?

Myint also draws attention to another characteristic of the dualistic— or more properly in this context, plural—economy which has been noted by other observers as well; viz., very often even the middlemen between the big European concerns and the indigenous population are foreigners. He mentions the Indians and Chinese in Southeast Asia, Indians in East

[4] *Ibid.*, pp. 149, 150.
[5] *Ibid.*, p. 153.

Africa, Syrians and "Coast Africans" in West Africa, and so on. He might also have mentioned the Indians in his own country of Burma. These middlemen collect produce from peasant farmers, distribute imported articles to the local consumers, and act as moneylenders.[6] They operate as a buffer between the indigenous population and the advanced Western society, thus depriving the former of "the educating and stimulating effect of a direct contact." Even skilled labor was brought in from abroad. Professor Knowles has said that in the British Empire of the nineteenth century there were three "mother countries": the United Kingdom, India, and China. Immigrant labor from India and China was deliberately introduced into Southeast Asia, Fiji, the West Indies, and part of East and South Africa.

True, some opportunities for acquiring skills occurred on the plantations and mines, but these were diluted by the high labor turnover. Backward peoples are not used to the discipline of the mines and plantations. They keep one foot in their traditional tribal and village economies and look upon the wage labor "not as a continuous permanent employment but as a temporary or periodical expedient to earn a certain sum of money." Thus, "even after many decades of rapid economic development following the opening-up process, the peoples of many backward countries still remain almost as ignorant and unused to the ways of modern economic life as they were before."

The middleman of the Asian type, selling consumers' goods, advancing seed and simple tools on a sharecropping basis, and lending money, was by no means unknown to the West. In the American South or the Canadian prairies, such middlemen were also buffers between the small farmers and the advancing technology of the big cities. The difference is that at a certain point it paid Western middlemen as a class to take over the land altogether, to foreclose on their tardy debtors, and to amalgamate small holdings into units large enough to permit large-scale, extensive, mechanized, and commercial agriculture. From there on the advance of technology spread to agriculture as well as to industry.

The question is, then, why this process did not occur in underdeveloped countries. Why have the middlemen in Asia and Africa continued to squeeze the peasant rather than maneuver him into a position where they could foreclose on peasant land? The answer is that in Europe and the New World a time came when manpower was obviously scarce in the agricultural sector, making it profitable for individual farmers to increase the size of their holdings and to use more capital-intensive methods. The barrier to agricultural improvement in the underdeveloped countries has been that labor never became scarce in the rural sector. The "population explosion," brought by industrial investment in the capital-intensive sec-

---

[6] It is said in the Philippines, for example, that the growth of a particular village depended entirely on the resources of the local Chinese, for it was his resources that determined the size of the cash crops of which they could dispose. Moreover, there is a continuous draining-off process. The Chinese who becomes successful in the village does not stay there but moves on to a city, installing in his village store a relative whose talents are less striking than his own.

tor, meant that there was an adequate supply, and later a superabundance, of labor in the peasant agriculture sector. Thus in Asia and Africa the middleman has continued to play his traditional role, directing his efforts to maximizing his share of the output obtainable through labor-intensive methods, rather than endeavoring to get the peasant off the land, so as to cultivate it himself by more land-and-capital-intensive methods.

Backwash versus Spread Effects

Professor Myint goes on to explain why the growth of foreign trade failed to bring over-all economic growth in Asian and African countries. For these countries did experience some development. During the nineteenth and twentieth centuries, their export sectors expanded very rapidly, as Table 13–1 clearly shows. The value of Indonesian exports grew over

TABLE 13–1
Value of Total Exports, Indonesia and Malaya

Indonesia		Malaya	
Year	Total value, billion florins	Year	Total value, billion Straits dollars
1870	....	1906	0.293
1880	0.175	1912	.357
1890	.175	1920	.879
1900	.258	1925	1.282
1913	.671	1929	.925
1920	2.228	1932	.323
1925	1.801	1937	.897
1929	1.443	1947	1.295
1930	1.140	1950	3.961
1932	.541	1951	5.991
1937	.990	1952	3.795
1940	0.939	1953	2.897

SOURCE: G. C. Allen and Audrey G. Donnithorne, *Western Enterprise in Indonesia and Malaya* (New York, 1957), pp. 291, 293.

tenfold between 1880 and 1920; Malayan exports increased nearly fourteenfold between 1906 and 1950. Other countries show similarly dramatic growth of exports; in Burma, exports grew by 5 per cent per year between 1870 and 1900, and Thailand enjoyed a comparable rate of expansion. Moreover, as Myint points out, capital was not especially scarce in the export sector of underdeveloped countries: "The foreign firms in the export sectors were normally able to borrow capital on equal terms with firms of comparable credit worthiness in the advanced countries." [7] Why did the growth in value of exports have no multiplier effects on per capita incomes in the rest of the economy?

[7] Hla Myint, "The Gains from International Trade and the Backward Countries," *Review of Economic Studies*, Vol. XXII, No. 2.

Myint lists these factors operating against spread effects: the high turn-over of labor, workers' willingness to accept very low wages, the convic-tion among employers that the supply curve of labor was backward sloping, and the general lack of industrial skills, which made entrepreneurs feel that it was difficult to recruit an adequate labor force. Wages were not considered low relative to estimates of efficiency. "The attempt to switch over from the cheap labor policy to a policy of higher wages and more intensive use of labor usually involved taking decisions about 'lumpy investments' both in the form of plant and machinery and in the form of camps and villages where it was necessary to change over from a casual to a permanent labor force."

Professor Myint stresses the reluctance of European entrepreneurs to make heavy investments of a kind which would require a large supply of skilled workers, and their preference for simple labor-intensive techniques which left labor productivity low and afforded few training facilities. The same factors also provided an incentive for a shift to wholly capital-intensive techniques, requiring relatively few skilled workers where such methods were technically possible. Consequently, we find on the same plantation labor-and-land-intensive methods, of a sort that give little generalized traning, in the agricultural side of the operation, combined with capital-intensive techniques in the processing part of the operation. The intermediate kind of technique, requiring fairly large numbers of workers in skilled occupations was shunned by entrepreneurs in under-developed countries; and it is these intermediate techniques that provide the best means of training large numbers of workers.

Finally, Professor Myint explains the lack of spread effects from de-velopment of the export sector by an appeal to the concept of "non-competing groups": [8]

Thus it may be possible to find an analogue of non-competing groups in the foreign and domestic sectors of the backward countries which contributes to a lack of secondary rounds of activities. This leads us to the second argument, that the dynamic gains from specialization in industry are likely to be greater because it has a greater "educative" effect on the people of the country than agriculture. Here it must be admitted that in contrast to the tremendous stim-ulus to further economic development enjoyed by the advanced countries, international trade seems to have had very little educative effect on the people of backward countries except in the development of new wants. Apart from the introduction of modern transport, it is difficult to observe any revolution-ary changes in their methods of production and efficiency both in the peasant and in the non-peasant sectors. The peasants specialize for international trade simply by going on producing traditional crops by traditional methods or new crops which can be readily produced by traditional methods.

In a more recent article, Myint shows that, although the "comparative cost" doctrine of the classical theory of international trade is largely in-applicable in underdeveloped countries, the relatively neglected "vent for

[8] *Ibid.*, p. 140.

surplus" aspect of this theory is very useful.[9] The "vent for surplus" was J. S. Mill's term for the idea—at least as old as Adam Smith—that expansion of foreign trade, by widening the market and permitting more division of labor, accelerates economic growth. The comparative cost doctrine assumes full employment of labor and resources before the country enters into international trade. The vent for surplus theory assumes more realistically that "a previously isolated country about to enter into international trade possesses a surplus productive capacity." Exports can be raised without reducing domestic production. Similarly, whereas comparative cost theory assumes a high degree of internal mobility of factors of production and a high elasticity of demand for commodities, the vent for surplus theory assumes—again more realistically—inelastic domestic demand for the exportable commodity "and/or a considerable degree of internal immobility and specificness of resources."

The contribution of Western enterprise to colonial development was mainly improvements in transport and communications and discoveries of new mineral resources. Investment of this kind adds to total resources but does not necessarily make existing resources more productive. The contribution of Western enterprise to the domestic (peasant) export sector was to act as middlemen between the peasant and the world market and to stimulate the peasants' demand for imports, thus unbending some backward-sloping supply curves.

The expansion of the export sector was possible without a decline in domestic production because of the labor surplus: [10]

This surplus labour existed, not because of a shortage of co-operating factors, but because in the subsistence economies, with poor transport and little specialization in production, each self-sufficient economic unit could not find any market outlet to dispose of its potential surplus output, and had therefore no incentive to produce more than its own requirements. Here, then, we have the archetypal form of Smith's "unproductive" labour locked up in a semi-idle state in the underdeveloped economy of a country isolated from outside economic contacts. In most peasant economies this surplus labour was mobilised, however, not by the spread of the money-wage system of employment, but by peasant economic units with their complement of "family" labour moving *en bloc* into the money economy and export production.

The existence of a labor surplus, unfortunately, did not lead to the use of labor-intensive methods in the export sector. Instead population pressure led to highly labor-intensive and unproductive employment in the rural sector. "Indeed," says Professor Myint, "we may say that these countries remain underdeveloped precisely because they have not succeeded in building up a labour-intensive export trade to cope with their growing population."

Thus population pressure "inflicts a double loss: first, through simple

[9] Hla Myint, "The 'Classical theory' of International Trade and the Underdeveloped Countries," *The Economic Journal*, June, 1958, pp. 321, 322.
[10] *Ibid.*, pp. 328, 331, 332.

diminishing returns, and secondly, by diverting resources from more to less productive use." Instead of growing rubber or sugar, where his comparative advantage is greater, and importing rice, the Javanese peasant still grows rice. Nor will mere removal of restrictions solve the problem. Given "the combination of population pressure, large pockets of subsistence economy and traditional methods of production which can no longer be made more labour-intensive," only "a more vigorous policy of state interference" is likely to be successful. In the Javanese case, this vigorous policy would include "removal of her surplus population either to thinly populated Outer Islands or to industries within Java and a vigorous export-drive policy supplemented by bulk purchase and subsidies on the imported rice."

Myint closes this article with a highly pertinent word of caution to policy makers in underdeveloped countries. The "export-bias" doctrine outlined above, distorted by "the strong feelings of economic nationalism and anti-colonialism in the underdeveloped countries" can become "very mischievous," supporting the view that to go on producing raw materials for export is tantamount to preserving a "colonial" pattern of trade. Correctly interpreted, the doctrine means only that the export sector was artificially expanded relative to the domestic sector; it does not mean that the export sector is absolutely too large. Thus nationalistic governments fail to give enough support to peasant exports and concentrate too much on industrial development. Three home truths remain important: foreign aid is unlikely to relieve underdeveloped countries of the necessity of earning most of the foreign exchange needed for development; the only way to earn more foreign exchange in the short run is by expanding traditional exports; therefore, "export-drive policies" are very important.

Professor Myrdal and the "Backwash Effect"

Gunnar Myrdal carries the argument further than Myint. Because of "circular causation" and backwash effects, Myrdal contends, trade between underdeveloped and advanced countries, far from tending toward equality of marginal productivity and incomes, results in a tendency away from equilibrium, a vicious spiral bringing increasing discrepancies between productivity of advanced and underdeveloped countries.[11] The basic idea rather resembles Harrod's theory of cumulative movements away from equilibrium, but Myrdal's concept is broader, including social as well as economic aspects of equilibrium.

The idea I want to expound in this book [Professor Myrdal writes] is that . . . in the normal case there is no such tendency towards automatic self-stabilization in the social system. The system is not by itself moving towards any sort of balance between forces, but is constantly on the move away from such a situation. In the normal case a change does not call forth countervailing changes but, instead, supporting changes, which move the system in the same direction as the

[11] Gunnar Myrdal, *Economic Theory and Under-developed Regions* (London, 1957), pp. 13, 28, 29.

first change but much further. Because of such circular causation a social process tends to become cumulative and often to gather speed at an accelerating rate.

Myrdal begins his analysis with the tendency toward regional inequalities in a single country. The growing communities will exert a strong agglomerative pull, accelerating their rate of growth and bringing increasing stagnation or decline in other parts of the country. No offsetting forces arise to prevent the acceleration of this shift of economic activity from decadent to progressive regions. Any accident or shock giving a momentary advantage to one region can start this chain of disparate growth movements. Among such shifts in the relative advantages of regions of a country, Professor Myrdal singles out "a change in the terms of trade of a community or a region" as one factor which has historically played this role.

Demographic factors will rank among the aggravating forces, he says, since the poorer regions will have relatively high fertility. This factor, together with net inmmigration from the decadent regions, makes the age distribution in these regions unfavorable. The poverty in rural regions of Europe during the long period of net immigration to industrial centers and to the United States, "has a main explanation in the unfavorable age distribution there, caused by migration and in part also by higher fertility rates."

The expansion of trade only aggravates the process. "The freeing and widening of the markets will often confer such competitive advantages on the industries in already established centres of expansion, which usually work under conditions of increasing returns, that even the handicrafts and industries existing earlier in the other regions are thwarted." As a dramatic example of the growth of regional disparities following liberation of trade, Myrdal cites the expansion of the north and retrogression of the south of Italy following political unification in 1860. For one thing, regions "not touched by the expansionary momentum could not afford to keep up a good road system and all their other public utilities would be inferior." [12]

True, expansion in one region also has spread effects as well as backwash effects; the growth of industrial cities, for example, should create a demand both for agricultural raw materials and for consumers' goods. There is, however, no reason for equilibrium between backwash and spread effects. The preceding analysis offers some reason to assume that the backwash effects will be predominant. The spread effects could outweigh the backwash effects only if income and employment in the leading sectors grew relative to that of the laggard sector, as they did in the now advanced countries. In underdeveloped countries, however, the historical pattern of growth has been such that spread effects were weak. The rural sector (as defined above) did not produce the raw materials for the expanding industrial sector, nor did the expanding industrial sector rely heavily on the rural sector for foodstuffs. (Rice was not the major item in the food

[12] *Ibid.*, p. 29.

budgets of the British, Dutch, or Spanish in their colonies.) Thus the growth of the industrial sector did not much expand the market for cash crops of the rural sector.

Myrdal reports two striking correlations which were discovered in the studies of the Economic Commission for Europe: first, regional disparities are greater in poor countries than in rich ones; and second, the disparities are increasing in poor countries and decreasing in rich ones. "A large part of the explanation for these two broad correlations," he says, "may be found in the important fact that the higher the level of economic development that a country has already attained, the stronger the spread effects will usually be."

National policy strengthened these inherent tendencies toward integration in advanced countries and leading and lagging sectors in underdeveloped ones. The poorer countries, and especially those which were colonies, had no effective policies for national integration, of the sort that were introduced in the more highly developed countries.

Generally speaking, on a low level of economic development with relatively weak spread effects, the competitive forces in the markets will, by circular causation, constantly be tending towards regional inequalities, while the inequalities themselves will be holding back economic development, and at the same time weakening the power basis for egalitarian policies. A higher level of development will strengthen the spread effects and tend to hamper the drift towards regional inequalities; this will sustain economic development, and at the same time create more favourable conditions for policies directed at decreasing regional inequalities still further.

Thus, it is entirely possible for international trade to have "strong backwash effects on the underdeveloped countries." [13] The present pattern of production in underdeveloped countries reflects these backwash effects rather than true comparative advantage. Instead of increasing production of primary goods for export, the true advantage of these countries may lie in improving the productivity of the rural sector and in developing manufactures. Capital cannot be expected to flow to underdeveloped countries simply because capital is relatively scarce there. On the contrary, in the absence of exchange controls capital would flow out of the underdeveloped countries to those more advanced (and more rapidly advancing). Furthermore international adjustment through migration is no longer possible.

The present pattern of production in underdeveloped countries also reflects the past policies of the colonial powers, which often "took special measures to hamper the growth of indigenous industry." Since "cumulative social processes holding it down in stagnation or regression" remain, the colonial heritage cannot be dispelled merely by political independence. For "colonialism meant primarily not only a strengthening of all the forces in markets which anyhow were working towards internal and international inequalities. It built itself into, and gave an extra impetus and a peculiar character to, the circular causation of the cumulative process." [14]

[13] *Ibid.*, pp. 34, 41, 51.
[14] *Ibid.*, p. 60.

The evidence seems to support Myrdal in this contention. In some measure, the failure of investment in the export sector to have "multiplier effects" on domestic incomes in Asian-African countries and in Europe does reflect colonial policy. In advanced countries investment directed toward production of raw materials for export stimulated expansion of the secondary and tertiary sectors of the economy. In most Asian and African countries colonial policy was directed toward promoting the expansion of those sectors in the metropolis, not in the colony. Most financing, transporting, storing, insuring, and processing of industrial raw materials occurred *outside* the colonial country. Here again, we see the importance of differentiating between a *country*, as a geographic entity, and an *economy* as a nexus of interrelated prices and decisions.

In his final pages, Myrdal calls for a new theory of international trade as applied to underdeveloped countries; he deplores the tendency of the International Monetary Fund and GATT to apply outmoded theory because they "tend continuously to be permeated by the ideological elements which I have referred to as the predilections of economic theory, and which have had a particularly strong influence on the theory of international trade." [15]

The Terms of Trade

Recently, certain economists have argued that one of the difficulties faced by underdeveloped countries is a long-run tendency for the terms of trade to turn against them. By "terms of trade" is meant the ratio of export prices to import prices; they should not be confused with balance of trade, volume of trade, stability of markets, or balance of payments. The argument regarding *terms of trade* has had particular vogue in Latin America.

The debate on terms of trade of underdeveloped countries really began with the report of the First Session of the Subcommission on Economic Development of the UN Economic and Employment Commission. This report stated that the purpose of borrowing abroad to finance economic development would be defeated unless the lending countries took measures to make capital goods available for export at reasonable prices. The report observed that the recent rise in prices of capital goods had made the task of economic development more difficult, and requested "a careful study of the prices of capital goods and of the relative trends of such prices and of prices of primary products." In response to this request, a study of "Relative Prices of Exports and Imports of Under-developed Countries" was published in December, 1949.[16]

The major findings of this report are presented in Table 13–2. The index of the ratio of prices of primary products to those of manufactured commodities shows a declining trend, from 147 for the period 1876–80 to

---

[15] *Ibid.*, p. 155.
[16] UN Department of Economic Affairs, "Relative Prices of Exports and Imports of Under-developed Countries," New York, December, 1949.

TABLE 13–2

Selected Unit Value Ratios, 1876–1948

(1938 = 100)

| Period | Primary to manufactured commodities in world trade* (1) | United Kingdom imports to exports | |
		Current year weights† (2)	Board of Trade index (3)
1876–1880	147	163	...
1881–1885	145	167	...
1886–1890	137	157	...
1891–1895	133	147	...
1896–1900	135	142	...
1901–1905	132	138	...
1906–1910	133	140	...
1911–1913	137	140	...
1913	137	137	143
1921	94	93	101
1922	103	102	109
1923	114	107	111
1924	121	122	117
1925	123	125	120
1926	121	119	117
1927	125	122	117
1928	121	123	120
1929	118	122	120
1930	105	112	109
1931	93	102	99
1932	89	102	99
1933	89	98	96
1934	96	101	99
1935	98	103	100
1936	102	107	103
1937	108	107	109
1938	100	100	100
1946	...	...	108
1947	...	...	116
1948	...	...	117

* Based on League of Nations, *Industrialization and Foreign Trade* (Geneva, 1945). Represents major trading countries and others.

† Based on W. Schlote, "Entwicklung and Strukturwandlungen des englischen Aussenhandels von 1700 bis zur Gegenwart," *Probleme der Weltwirtschaft*, No. 62 (Jena, 1938).

SOURCE: UN Department of Economic Affairs, "Relative Prices of Exports and Imports of Under-developed Countries," December, 1949.

100 in 1938. The report also gives figures for the United Kingdom which show a fall in the relative prices of British imports (mostly raw materials and foodstuffs) to the prices of British exports (mostly manufactured goods). The ratio of American imports of primary goods to American imports of finished manufactures between 1913 and 1948 shows a similar tendency, declining from an index of 141 in 1913 to 108 in 1948.

The report also presents a table listing countries whose terms of trade have improved, worsened, or remained unchanged between 1938 and 1946–47. This table is reproduced here as Table 13–3. No conclusions can be drawn from this table alone. The terms of trade of some countries were better in 1946 and 1947 than before the war, some were worse, some were unchanged. Of course, the short period covered in this table does not tell very much about long-term trends. At best, the figures suggest that the trend indicated in Table 13–2, may have been reversed since World War II.

The report states the general principle that "a favorable change in terms of trade," allows a given quantity of exports to buy more imports and so releases resources for development. But in conclusion, the report warns

TABLE 13–3

Changes in Postwar Terms of Trade of Certain Underdeveloped Countries, Compared with Prewar

	Terms of trade of underdeveloped area		
Region and Country	*Improved*	*No change**	*Worsened*
Central America, including			
Mexico and Caribbean area (17)	8	2	7
Bahamas	X	..	..
Barbados	..	..	X
British Honduras	..	..	X
Costa Rica	X	..	..
Cuba	X	..	..
United Kingdom	X	..	..
United States	X	..	..
Dominican Republic	X	..	..
Grenada	X	..	..
Guadeloupe	..	X	..
Guatemala	X	..	..
Haiti	X	..	..
United States	X	..	..
Jamaica	..	..	X
Martinique	..	X	..
Mexico	X	..	..
Nicaragua	..	..	X
Puerto Rico	..	..	X
St. Vincent	..	..	X
Trinidad and Tobago	..	..	X
South America (11)	4	2	5
Argentina	X	..	..

TABLE 13–3 *(continued)*

Region and Country	Terms of trade of underdeveloped area		
	Improved	No change*	Worsened
Bolivia	..	..	X
Brazil	X	..	..
United Kingdom	X	..	..
United States	X	..	..
British Guiana	..	..	X
Chile	..	..	X
Colombia	X	..	..
Ecuador	X	..	..
French Guiana	..	..	X
Peru	..	X	..
Surinam	..	..	X
Venezuela	..	X	..
United States	X	..	..
Europe† (1)	1	..	..
Eastern Europe	X	..	..
Africa (8)	3	1	4
Belgian Congo	X	..	..
French Equatorial Africa	..	..	X
French West Africa	X	..	..
Gold Coast	..	..	X
Kenya and Uganda	..	..	X
Madagascar	..	..	X
Sierra Leone‡	..	..	X
Tanganyika	..	X	..
Asia (7)	3	1	3
Burma			
United Kingdom	X	..	..
China			
United States	..	..	X
Lebanon and Syria	..	X	..
India and Pakistan‡§	..	..	X
Iran¶	..	..	X
Turkey			
United States	X	..	..
Total (44)	19	6	19

* Or inconclusive data.
† Eastern Europe–Western Europe.
‡ Preware composition of trade considered representative.
§ Favorable change in trade with United States; unfavorable change in trade with United Kingdom.
¶ Result obtained on broad commodity classification considered representative.
SOURCE: UN Department of Economic Affairs, "Relative Prices of Exports and Imports of Under-developed Countries," December, 1949.

that the terms of trade constitute "only one factor—and not generally the most important single factor—in determining national income and funds available for economic development." To illustrate this point the authors cite cocoa prices:

A good illustration of this is provided by the post-war rise in the price of cocoa. As has been indicated in some of the preceding tables, cocoa prices showed a marked increase; hence under-developed countries which concentrated on cocoa in their exports tended to have favourable changes in their terms of trade. This "favourable" change, however, is partly due to a virus disease, the "swollen shoot disease," affecting the Gold Coast, at present the major producing area. The disease reduced supplies and thus tended to raise prices. It is evident that this is not a favourable change for Gold Coast. It merely means that the rise in the price of supplies due to the virus disease, tended to offset to some degree—perhaps only to a slight degree—the unfavourable development by which it was caused.

The Prebisch-Singer Thesis

The argument that economic development of Latin American countries is impeded by a tendency for long-run deterioration of terms of trade of raw-materials-producing countries has acquired added importance because of the support given to this thesis by Dr. Raul Prebisch, former Director General of the Economic Commission for Latin America, and by Dr. Hans Singer, Special Assistant to the Director of the Department of Economic and Social Affairs of the United Nations. The thesis has aroused a great deal of controversy regarding both the supporting facts and the theory. It is not denied, of course, that some underdeveloped countries have on occasion suffered declining terms of trade, nor that such a situation inhibits economic development while it lasts. The criticism has been directed toward the effort to elevate to the status of "law" the thesis that producers of primary products *inevitably* suffer declining terms of trade.

The theoretical explanation for the presumed historically deteriorating terms of trade of underdeveloped countries rests partly on "Engel's Law": in most countries the proportion of income spent on food falls as incomes rise. This argument, obviously, applies only to food and not to all products of the primary sector. There is also empirical evidence that income-elasticities of demand for other products of the primary sector are low; but we cannot proceed directly from this fact to a conclusion that their prices will fall relative to prices of industrial goods. We need to know something as well about both the price and income-elasticities of supply, about relative rates of technological progress in the two sectors, and about relative degrees of monopoly power and how these are changing. It is frequently argued that price-elasticity of supply of primary products is low; falling prices do not result in a prompt and substantial reduction of output as they do for industrial products. However, if the problem arises simply from a long-run reduction of demand for products of underdeveloped countries, which cannot be prevented by any feasible price reduction, the only possible solution is to reduce output of these products.

It may well be that monopoly power is greater in most fields of industry than it is in most fields of agriculture. But this fact alone would not bring a long-run trend toward deteriorating terms of trade of agricultural countries; only if the *degree* of monopoly power were increasing in industry, while agriculture remained purely competitive and rates of technological progress are the same in both sectors, would there be a *con-*

tinuous rise in prices of industrial products relative to agricultural prices. If technological progress is more rapid in industry than in the primary sector, so that costs are falling relatively more rapidly in industry, the difference in trend with regard to monopoly power would have to be enough to offset this tendency. It would be difficult to prove that there is an inherent tendency for the degree of monopoly power in industry to increase at such a rate.

Occasionally the argument is put in terms of the monopoly power of labor rather than monopoly power of the industrialists themselves. With equal increases in productivity, it is contended, wages will rise less in the "peripheral" (developing) countries, where there is a labor surplus, than they will in the "metropolitan" (advanced) countries where rapid industrialization creates labor scarcity. It is not contended, however, that the result is a squeeze on profits in the metropolitan countries; entrepreneurs defend themselves by raising prices. Nor is it contended that bargaining power of unions, or monopoly power of firms, is higher in export industries of metropolitan countries than in other industries of those countries. Such could hardly be the case, for in world markets exporters compete with producers in other countries as well as their own.

It will readily be apparent that when cast in this form the argument has many similarities to the "cost-push" doctrine of inflation. It is subject to the same limitations. What is there about a negotiated increase in wages, followed by a rise in administered prices, that guarantees a sufficient expansion of the money flow to absorb the same or higher output at higher prices? Perhaps credit will be expanded to finance the enlarged payrolls and greater cost of inventories; perhaps higher wages and prices will lead to economizing on reserves, resulting in a higher velocity of circulation. More likely, governments committed to high levels of employment and economic growth will step in with easy money and budget deficits if the initial wage-price increases begin to cause unemployment and reduced output. Thus government policy provides the "demand-pull" to make the "cost-push" effective.

Here, however, we are in completely different analytical territory. For now the "declining terms of trade" argument takes the following form: because governments of advanced countries, committed to full employment and rapid growth, are required to support the "cost-push" generated by trade unions and monopolistic entrepreneurs, whereas unions and industrialists in peripheral countries have less power, inflation will be more rapid in metropolitan countries than in peripheral ones. Since demand for both imports and exports of advanced countries is inelastic, while supply of exports of peripheral countries is also inelastic, the result is declining terms of trade for the peripheral countries. But this argument simply does not stand up to the facts; inflation in metropolitan countries has not been more severe than in peripheral ones. If anything, the reverse is the case. And if inflation were more rapid in advanced countries, the solution would lie in appreciation of the currencies of the peripheral ones. This is the exact opposite of what has been happening.

Objections have also been raised to the facts presented to support the thesis. In the first place, it is pointed out that terms of trade measured by prices in the metropolitan countries do not take account of the great reductions in cost of transport, which reduce the price in the metropolitan countries but not the price paid to the producer in the peripheral ones. It is also argued that technological progress in manufacturing has taken the form of great improvement in quality rather than price reductions, so that relative prices do not properly reflect the gains from trade of peripheral countries. (This argument might properly be objected to on the grounds that what constitutes improved quality from the standpoint of people in advanced countries may be less important to people in underdeveloped ones—changes in automobile styles, for example.)

Questions have also been raised as to what the historical picture actually shows. A recent review of the available data has been provided by Professor Theodore Morgan of the University of Wisconsin.[17] His analysis of the data for seven countries indicates no uniform pattern. Thus he found that in the United Kingdom between 1801 and 1953 (and particularly between 1801 and 1870) the ratio of prices of agricultural products to manufactured products improved; but from 1880 to 1953, the ratio fell drastically. In the United States there was a major improvement in terms of trade of primary goods throughout the whole period 1787 to 1953. In India, there was a rise, a fall, and then a rise again, between 1861 and 1953. In Japan there was a gentle rise between 1873 and 1930, and then a major fall. In New Zealand, from 1861 to 1952 there was a marked improvement in terms of trade of primary products, with, however, violent fluctuations. In the Union of South Africa, in the relatively short period 1910 to 1952 there was a fall, a rise, and a fall in terms of trade of primary products. Brazil showed varying fluctuations between 1901 and 1950, with terms of trade of primary products rising, falling, rising, falling, and rising again.

The whole question of the role of trends in terms of trade in Latin American development was thoroughly discussed at the Rio de Janeiro meetings of the International Economic Association in 1957.[18] Professor Gottfried Haberler led the attack against the thesis. Haberler began by asking whether deteriorating terms of trade are always bad. He pointed out that "a change in the terms of trade resulting from a shift in the countries' own offer curve cannot be unambiguously said to be good or bad according to the direction of the change, even if full employment is maintained continuously"; and "the optimum terms of trade which maximize welfare is not the highest price of exports in terms of imports which a country could possibly attain." The statistical difficulties, and particularly the difficulty of taking account of changes in product-mix and in quality were briefly summarized. He expressed his preference for the concept of "capacity to import," developed by the Economic Commission for Latin America, "as a measure of gains in trade or an indicator of welfare change." But "the relations between the terms of trade and economic welfare are

[17] Theodore Morgan, "The Long-Run Terms of Trade Between Agriculture and Manufacturing," *Economic Development and Cultural Change,* October, 1959.

[18] Howard Ellis and Henry Wallich, *Economic Development for Latin America* (New York, 1961).

intricate," and the more knowledge that the terms of trade for a country or a group of countries have changed in a certain way over a period of time is of precious little importance unless it is combined with other types of information."

He pointed out that the economic structure and particularly the composition of exports vary a great deal from one underdeveloped country to another. Considering only Latin American countries, he says, "It would be a very strange coincidence indeed, if in the long run, the commodity terms of trade, let alone the factual terms of trade, moved parallel for coffee countries, mining countries, petroleum exporters and exporters of wheat, wool, and fats." Moreover, "the dissimilarity of the trade structure of developed countries is hardly less pronounced than that of under-developed countries."

In discussing Haberler's paper, Dr. Helio Schlittler-Silva pointed out that in point of fact the terms of trade of Latin America deteriorated between 1870 and 1940 for both minerals and tropical products, and with respect to both the United Kingdom and the United States. Thus he was "not convinced by Professor Haberler's argument on this point." Howard Ellis, on the other hand, agreed with Haberler that "on any sober and objective basis . . . many other lines of activity and policy are vastly more important for raising per capita income than operations directed toward influencing the terms of trade." Ragnar Nurske also maintained that there has been a tendency "to exaggerate both the actual extent and the economic significance of changes in the terms of trade."

Concentration

There is no denying that exports of developing countries are highly concentrated. In 1958 coffee accounted for 55 per cent of the exports of Brazil, cocoa beans another 7 per cent. Coffee also accounted for 77 per cent of Colombia's exports, 76 per cent of Guatemala's exports, and 72 per cent of El Salvador's exports. Sugar was 80 per cent of the value of Cuban exports. Bananas were 58 per cent of Panama's exports. Tin ore represented 55 per cent of the export value of Bolivia, copper 62.5 per cent of Chile's exports. And in Venezuela, petroleum was 91 per cent of exports and coffee another 5 per cent. Virtually all Latin American countries present the same picture of one to half-a-dozen commodities accounting for well over half the total value of exports. Nor has the situation improved in the last two decades. Clearly, where these exports are also a significant share of the national income, the economic position of these economies is much affected by fluctuations in demand for or supply of these key commodities.

Some Latin American economists have proceeded directly from these facts to the contention that greater diversification of exports is a prerequisite to their further development. However, a considerable degree of economic development is possible without dramatic changes in the general composition of foreign trade. Canada has the second highest standard of living in the world; yet the general composition of Canada's foreign trade shows only limited change. In 1870, 32.9 per cent of Canadian exports consisted of raw materials, 38.5 per cent of partly manufactured goods, and 28.6 per cent of fully or chiefly manufactured goods. In 1953, the allocation of exports among these three broad categories was 32.2, 28.9, and 38.9 per cent. With respect to imports, in 1870, 7.5 per cent of Canada's imports represented partly manufactured goods, 74.9 per cent fully or chiefly manufactured goods, and 17.6 per cent raw materials. In 1953, these percentages also showed relatively little change: 5.0, 76.5, and 18.5.

In the course of three generations, Canada moved toward further processing of its own agricultural and forest products; but in 1953, as in 1870, the farms and forests were the major sources of Canadian exports. Yet the economy as a whole shows the same general structural change that took place in the United States and other countries enjoying rapid growth during that period. The proportion of the labor force engaged in primary production fell from about 55 per cent to 20.7 per cent over the period. Agriculture alone accounted for half of total employment in 1870, and only 17 per cent in 1953. The proportion in manufacturing rose from 13.1 to 26.1 per cent, construction dropped, and the proportion in the tertiary sector increased from 17.0 to 46.2 per cent.

What seems to be needed for economic growth is diversification of *production*, rather than diversification of exports. However, whereas Canada added new commodities as incomes rose, in Latin American countries it may be a matter of replacing imports with domestic production. If that is done, and incomes of importing countries grow steadily, continued concentration in *exports* may make very good sense. At the same time, it is worth noting that Canada's exports were never quite so concentrated as they now are in some Latin American countries.

Others have argued that the concentration of exports leads to instability. This argument, however, rests on experience of a kind that should not be repeated. Interwar fluctuations were generated from *both* the demand side and the supply side. A major factor in world market fluctuations was the business cycle in the United States and in other advanced countries. The extreme instability of the American economy tended to spread outward to other countries, particularly producers of raw materials and foodstuffs. Clearly, this picture will be greatly changed if the current stress on steady growth in advanced countries leads to successful policies for achieving it.

Diversification of output may indeed be necessary, not for stabilization but to permit economic growth. If a country wants to increase its output at a faster rate than the world market is expanding, it cannot be content with retaining its share in world markets and leaving its structure of production unchanged. Industrialization becomes a virtual necessity. Some countries may also need to find new exports to replace present ones—which is a different thing from diversification of exports. Even plantation products, where soil and climate advantages are most clear-cut, face doubtful futures because of increasing competition from synthetics. At best, plantation products can expect a gradual decline in their share of the world markets. Such a development is not incompatible with absolute growth of plantation production, but it does imply a falling share of plantation output in national production, if the country is to raise its income at a faster rate than world markets expand. If productivity in plantations keeps pace with productivity in industry—and if it does not, it is likely to lose out even more rapidly to competing synthetics—the share of plantations in national employment will also fall. Industrialization appears to be the only solution. But all this is a way of saying that economic development requires economic development.

Instability

There have been violent fluctuations in both the prices and the volume of exports of Latin American countries. This instability, combined with the concentration of exports already noted, has resulted in violent fluctuations in foreign exchange earnings and consequently in the ability to import. It is quite clear that these fluctuations are an impediment to economic growth. Long-range programming of developmental investment is well-nigh impossible under the circumstances. The problem is aggravated by the fact that, in contrast with industrialized countries where the balance and terms of trade tend to improve in depression, in Latin American countries output, exports, terms of trade, and balance of trade tend to deteriorate together.

The Economic Survey of Latin America for 1960 describes the recent situation as follows: [19]

Commodity prices in 1958–59 and in 1960 remained at the lowest level for the last decade. A cursory examination of world primary commodity trends shows that eleven of the main commodities were being quoted at considerably lower prices than in 1950. Only in the case of three items—copper, tin and crude petroleum—did the level of prices continue to be slightly above the 1950 level, although market conditions tended to deteriorate steadily. Despite this decline in prices, the total value of Latin American exports in 1959 was 22 per cent more than in 1950. This gives an idea of the production effort made by Latin America to overcome that unfavourable circumstance. It should be observed, however, that the main effort was made between 1951 and 1957, since the value of total sales abroad decreased slowly from 1957 onwards, with the exception of 1960, when a slight recovery was recorded. This circumstance, combined with others, explains why Latin American imports had to be cut in 1958 and 1959. The contraction took place in sixteen countries in 1958 and in fourteen in 1959. Nevertheless, the deficit on current account was 1,300 million dollars in the former year and led to a drain of 700 million on reserves. Although the deficit was not as big in 1959, it still amounted to about 500 million, and reserves went down by 100 million dollars.

In 1958, a Panel of Experts set up by the contracting parties to the General Agreement on Tariff and Trade (GATT) found that although the general price level of primary products was more stable since World War II than it had been during the interwar period, instability was still a problem, and the dissimilarity in price changes in individual commodities was still a factor in the instability of terms of trade of particular countries.

[19] Economic Commission for Latin America, *Economic Survey of Latin America, 1960* (New York, 1961), pp. vi–vii.

Although price and volume tended to move in the same direction for both manufactured and primary products, the volume and price changes of manufactured goods were largely of the same magnitude, whereas the fluctuations in value of exports of primary products reflected price changes more than changes in volume.

The commodity composition of exports from the less-developed countries shows a drastic change since prewar days. The volume of petroleum exports rose nearly sixfold between 1928 and 1955; the volume of agricultural raw materials, tropical foodstuffs, and minerals was about 40 per cent higher, whereas non-tropical foodstuffs suffered a 15 per cent decline in volume. Moreover, the volume of imports of underdeveloped countries had risen much more than the volume of the exports in the period between 1945 and 1957.

The Panel reiterated the conclusion that exports of underdeveloped countries are much affected by the internal policies of the advanced ones. While denying any clear-cut necessity for the terms of trade to move against underdeveloped countries in the long run, the Panel felt that it would be unwise to count upon any improvement in the terms of trade of the non-industrial countries to raise their ability to purchase imports.

Trends in Demand

Even if the "terms of trade" argument does not stand up as a general principle, there can be no doubt that a number of Latin American countries are hampered in their economic growth by balance of payments difficulties. The economically advanced countries are more than ever each others' best customers, and primary producing countries do not benefit from expansion of world markets to the same degree as industrialized countries. The income-elasticity of demand for major exports of a number of Latin American countries seems to be low. Demand for all raw materials has lagged far behind the increase in output of the United States. The demand for imports into Latin American countries tends to rise more than the demand for their exports as world incomes rise. The demand for manufactures is income-elastic, the demand for many primary products is income-inelastic. The faster increase in value of imports as compared with exports has resulted in a reversal of the trade *balance* of underdeveloped countries in general. In 1928 these countries had an export surplus of $1.7 billion, some 16 per cent for their export proceeds. In 1957 they had an import surplus of $3.4 billion, 11 per cent of the value of their export. In addition, the share of the less-advanced countries (semi-industrialized and non-industrialized) in world trade declined during the postwar period. As the UN Department of Economic and Social Affairs has pointed out:

. . . in order to maintain international economic balance, the relative rates of growth in the two groups of countries would have to be in inverse proportion to the relative degrees of responsiveness of the demand for imports to changes in income. Should the income elasticity of import demand—the term used to designate the responsiveness of import demand to changes in income—be twice as high in under-developed as in developed countries, then the under-developed countries would have to grow at half the rate of the developed countries in order to keep their trade in balance. Should the under-developed countries, on the other hand, seek to expand at the same rate as the developed countries, they would then be faced with a permanent and growing deficit in their balance of payments; their imports would expand faster than their exports in direct proportion to the relative import elasticities of demand of under-developed and developed countries. With an import elasticity twice as high as that of the developed countries for their exports, the under-developed countries would find their imports increasing at twice the rate of their exports. The resulting trade gap would be permanent and it would grow not only in absolute, but even in percentage terms.[20]

The GATT Panel also concluded that "technological changes so far have been most unfavorable to the demand for primary products, mainly because the impact of newly invented synthetic materials seems to exceed substantially that of new uses of minerals and other primary products." [21]

Terms of Trade of the Rural Sector

Although there is much room for doubt as to the logical necessity of the terms of trade of underdeveloped *countries* turning against them, the case for deteriorating terms of trade of the *rural sectors* of such countries seems clear. Imagine, for example, a typical underdeveloped country exporting, say, petroleum and plantation products; importing textiles, other consumer durables, and luxury foodstuffs; producing rice, fish, and handicraft products in the rural sector, and trading in these. Favorable developments in the industrialized sector (improved techniques, higher world market prices) will not increase the demand for the output of the rural sector. Indeed, in so far as the rise in income of the industrialized sector is shared by domestic workers, the demand for output of the rural sector may even fall, as these workers substitute "superior" imported consumers' goods for home-produced ones. On the other hand, any favorable development in the rural sector will increase the demand for industrial products imported into that sector (either from outside the country or from the industrial sector of the same country) and *reduce* the demand for output of the rural sector.

It is even possible that "Giffen's paradox" may operate. The favorable income-effect of a fall in rice prices, following upon increased yields, may be so strong that the demand for rice *falls* and demand for more "luxurious" imports (into the sector) increases. A large share of the incomes of everyone in the rural sector (including even the rice growers) is spent on rice. When rice is cheaper, they can afford to substitute other foodstuffs and manufactured goods which they consider superior. Thus improvements in rice culture benefit the rest of the world more than they do the rice-growing rural sector itself.

Moreover, when we confine our argument to the rural sector of under-

---

[20] UN Department of Economic Affairs, *World Economic Survey, 1958*, p. 8.
[21] Trends in International Trade: General Agreement on Tariffs and Trade, *A Report of a Panel of Exports* (Geneva, 1958), p. 8.

developed countries, the differences in bargaining power between people in such sectors and workers in industrialized countries is more obvious. As Myint puts it: [22]

> The backward peoples have to contend with three types of monopolistic forces: in their role as unskilled labor they have to face the big foreign mining and plantation concerns who are monopolistic buyers of their labour; in their role as peasant producers they have to face a small group of exporting and processing firms who are monopolistic buyers of their crop; and in their role as consumers of imported commodities they have to face the same group of firms who are the monopolistic sellers or distributors of these commodities.

In advanced countries such tendencies toward monopolistic exploitation are offset by the development of "countervailing power," to use Professor Galbraith's term. No such countervailing power emerged in the under-developed countries before their achievement of independence. Even now workers and peasants have a long way to go before their organization will give them really effective bargaining power. As Myint says, "The first lesson is that some sources of countervailing power, like the co-operative societies, themselves need a fairly high degree of business-like behaviour and 'economic advance' and can only be fostered very slowly in the backward countries. The second lesson is that it is easier to redistribute existing income than to redistribute and stimulate economic activity by the use of countervailing power." Moreover, he points out, countervailing power is sometimes sought in the preservation of traditional social institutions, which do not provide equivalent bargaining power in an economic sense.

The deterioration of the terms of trade of the rural sector in its relations with the industrial sector of the same country must, of course, be reflected in the terms of trade of the *rural sector* with the rest of the world. Obviously, it is the latter which is important to most of the people in the country, since the great majority derives its income from the rural sector. In advanced countries, the primary sector accounts for a small share of income and employment and agricultural productivity is several times as high as in the rural sector of underdeveloped countries. It seems very likely, then, that there has been—and is still—a trend toward deteriorating terms of trade between the rural sector of underdeveloped countries and the rest of the world.

The Case for Multiple Exchange Rates

It is the present author's belief that in many underdeveloped countries multiple exchange rates are both a convenient way of curtailing unwanted expenditure and the most appropriate foreign exchange policy.

Let us first remind ourselves of the purpose of a foreign exchange rate. It is to equilibrate the balance of payments in the long run, protecting the

[22] Hla Myint, "An Interpretation of Economic Backwardness," *Oxford Economic Papers*, Vol. VI, No. 2, June, 1954.

minimum reserves which are needed to meet inevitable short-run fluctuations in the balance of trade, but at the same time permitting a satisfactory rate of economic development and the achievement of other objectives of economic policy. In somewhat imprecise terms, we might say that the exchange rate should equate the man-hour costs of goods and services entering into international or interregional trade. An exchange rate may be said to be too high if it leads to a chronic deficit in the balance of trade, with consequent retardation of economic growth, unemployment, and the like. An exchange rate may be said to be too low if it leads to a chronic surplus in foreign trade, with accumulation of reserves and inflationary pressure as a consequence.

In highly regionalized economies no single rate may accomplish this task. Two examples from the author's experience illustrate this point. When the present author first arrived in the Philippines as a United Nations adviser in 1956, a bitter controversy was raging between the National Economic Council on the one hand, and the Central Bank, the International Monetary Fund and the United States Point IV Mission on the other. The NEC wished to devalue the peso from the existing rate of two to a dollar to something like the free market rate of three to the dollar; the Central Bank and its supporters were insistent on stability of the foreign exchange rate. This controversy was front-page news for nearly a year, until President Magsaysay himself stepped in and decided in favor of the Central Bank.

The United Nations was asked by the NEC to send them an adviser, no doubt in hopes that a United Nations adviser would counter the advice received from the IMF and the United States Mission and recommend devaluation. After a careful study of the existing situation, however, he came to the conclusion that devaluation to a new uniform rate would not solve the complex of problems then confronting the Philippines. On the export side, devaluation to a new uniform rate would have benefited mainly those categories of exports that good development policy would have discouraged. The volume of exports of sugar—and thus the foreign exchange earnings from sugar exports—depended almost entirely on the United States quota, which would not have been increased by devaluation. Devaluation might have helped cocoanut products and abaca (Manila hemp), provided it was not followed by countermoves on the part of the other major exporters of these products. However, the long-run prospects of both cocoanut products and abaca were dim, and far from encouraging increased planting with these commodities, good development policy required that acreage under these products should be reduced. The major use of cocoanut products is to manufacture soap, which was being displaced in the major markets of the Philippines by detergents. The major market for abaca was rope for ships, where it was being displaced by steel cables and synthetic fibers. At best there would have been a considerable lag between improvement of the peso price for these commodities and an increase in the physical supply and thus in foreign exchange earnings. But more important was the consideration that long-range development policy required reductions rather than increases in acreage under these products. A few exports, such as forest products, might have been helped in the European market by devaluation to a new uniform rate, but the impact on the over-all balance of payments position would have been very small.

On the import side a good job was already being done to the system of foreign exchange control. Luxury imports were being restricted to a level far below what would have obtained in a free market, and imports of raw materials and capital goods needed for development were encouraged. With income and wealth so highly concentrated as it then was in the Philippines (some 60 per cent of national income going into dividends, interests, and rents and with a great deal of concentration within this income group), the demand for luxury imports was price-inelastic. A devaluation, even to three pesos to the dollar, accompanied by relaxation of exchange control, would certainly have resulted in an increased allocation of foreign exchange to luxury imports. It would probably also have been accompanied by considerable capital outflow. At the same time, an across-the-board devaluation would have raised the peso cost of imported necessities and of raw materials and capital equipment for development. There would have been pressure for wage increases, which were already lagging, and the dissatisfaction among peasants, already menacing the political stability of the country, would have been further aggravated.

Inflationary pressure was already gathering pace in the Philippines, and devaluation would have added fuel to the flames. The competitive advantage for Philippine exports through devaluation could have been quickly wiped out by internal inflation.

In short, it was doubtful whether any single foreign exchange rate would have created equilibrium in a free market for foreign exchange. Under these circumstances, what seemed to be called for was a simple two-rate system. Exports which ought to be encouraged, and whose competitive position could be significantly improved by devaluation, such as forest products, should have had a relief from the clearly overvalued official rate for the peso. For exports which one wishes to discourage as a matter of long-run development policy, the official rate might be maintained. The higher rate could be applied to luxury imports one wished to discourage, whereas the official rate could be maintained for imports of necessities and of raw materials and equipment needed for development. In due course the Philippines shifted to such a simple multiple rate system, and it has worked well.

The other example is Indonesia. Indonesia provides a case of economic disintegration even more marked than one finds in the case of Brazil. For in Indonesia there is virtually no economic relationship between the lagging traditional sector and region, consisting roughly of peasant agriculture and small industry in Java, and the leading modern sector region, consisting of the plantations, mines, and petroleum industry in the Outer Islands, especially Sumatra, Kalimantan, and Sulawesi. The modern sector does not provide an important market for the products of the traditional sector; the rice and other foodstuffs grown and textiles manufactured in Java are consumed in Java. Nor does Java constitute an important market for the rubber, petroleum, bauxite, tin, etc., produced in the Outer Islands. (Although local consumption of petroleum products is becoming increasingly important as a consequence of artificially low prices maintained by the government.) The traditional sector of Java generates no capital flow to the modern sector, nor does capital flow from the modern sector to the peasant economy in Java, although rates of interest on rural credit are much higher than rates of return on investment on rubber or petroleum. There is some movement of people from Java to the Outer Islands, but this is a tiny fraction of the annual population growth in Java.

The relationship of both the modern and the traditional sector to the outside world is more important than the interregional trade. The Outer Islands have a handsome export surplus, Java a distressing import surplus. This imbalance was one of the factors behind the Civil War in 1958. In short, these two distinct sectors and regions, although politically part of the same country, are really two distinct economies. The relationship of the Outer Islands to the United States and Europe is more important than their relationship to Java. No single foreign exchange rate for the Indonesian rupiah could have brought equilibrium in both regions. The export economy did quite well under the official rate of exchange, whereas imports into (and capital flow from) Java were such that at one time the free market rate reached a level more than ten times the official rate. This problem was met—and for a time at least solved—by a four-way multiple rate system, with import surcharges varying from zero to 400 per cent, and with advance payments of foreign exchange.

The argument for a uniform exchange rate is based on the assumption that the economy is integrated, with quick response to any regional differences in prices or wage rates, with prompt flows of people and capital and goods to take advantage of any temporary regional differentials, flows that will themselves quickly eliminate the differentials. In fact, however, underdeveloped countries bear no resemblance to these hypothetical integrated economies. In the case of Indonesia, there is less economic relationship between the two major regions than there is, let us say, between France and Germany or even between France and England. But no one insists that every country in Europe should have the same rate of exchange in terms of dollars—at least not yet.

The arguments against multiple exchange rates are partly economic and partly political. The economic argument is that multiple exchange rates introduce a distortion into the price structure and thus lead to misallocation of resources. In reply to this argument, the first point to be made is that *any* kind of government policy "distorts" the price structure and alters the distribution of resources. One might think in terms of a hierarchy of degrees of interference with the market in accordance with the instrument chosen. As far as international trade is concerned, tariffs may be regarded as the least interventionist of measures, for once a tariff is set, the actual volume of imports of particular goods, the allocation of foreign exchange among them, and the total volume of imports are left to the market. Quotas are more interventionist, because the physical volume of the import is determined independently of the market. Even under a quota system, however, the prices of imports and the amounts of foreign exchange spent on them are determined on the market. Under foreign exchange control, the amount of foreign exchange spent on particular imports is independent of the market.

It must be remembered, however, that if one had sufficient knowledge of the demand and supply curves for particular commodities, one could achieve exactly the same allocation of resources through the use of tariffs or quotas—or for that matter, through the use of sales taxes or tax-and-subsidy systems—as are obtained through any system of exchange control. Indeed the merit of exchange control, as compared to the other devices, is precisely that one needs less knowledge of demand and supply curves in order to achieve the target allocation of foreign exchange among categories of goods than would be needed with the other devices.

Secondly, the argument that multiple exchange rates are bad because they distort the price structure implicitly assumes that the pre-existing price structure and the resulting allocation of resources are optimal. Nothing could be further from the truth. Most underdeveloped countries have inherited a colonial economic structure that is very far from optimal for an independent nation. The market structure and resource allocation have been further distorted by monopolies and monopsonies of various kinds, and by misguided government policy. Most underdeveloped countries face a serious task of offsetting the existing accumulation of distortions in price structure and resource allocation, and an astute policy of multiple exchange rates can be a weapon for this purpose. In the view of the present author, the emotion evident in the opposition to multiple exchange rates arises mainly from the simple fact that multiple exchange rates are a more recent form of intervention than tariffs or taxes. Just as an old tax is a good tax, so an old policy is a good policy, and a new one is bad.

On the political side, it is argued that multiple exchange rate systems provide too much discretionary power to the administrators of the system and open the door to corruption. There is no doubt—to recall the now hackneyed phrase of Lord Acton—that power corrupts and absolute power corrupts absolutely. But this principle does not apply uniquely to multiple exchange rates; it applies to every aspect of government policy. It is a matter of discovering in each country what forms of government intervention are likely to be most effective from the administrative point of view. In the Lebanon, for example, evasion of personal income tax approximates 90 per cent of tax liability, and no aspect of government administration seems to offer such opportunity for corruption as the administration of the income tax. Many businessmen there admitted to the author that the bribes they paid to the tax inspectors exceeded the taxes they paid to the government; a typical pattern would be that a man with a tax liability of £100,000 would pay £10,000 in taxes and £15,000 to the tax inspector.

On the other hand, it should be remembered that the argument *for* the use of multiple exchange rates rather than other instruments of policy for the achievement of development objectives is also a purely administrative one. As pointed out above, with sufficient knowledge of the operation of the economy, anything that can be accomplished by multiple exchange rates can also be achieved with taxes or tariffs. It is a fact that many governments of underdeveloped countries have tighter control over the economy at the point of application for foreign exchange than at any other point in the circular flow. It is this fact, and this fact alone, that justifies the use of exchange control, including multiple rates, rather than other measures. In countries where control is not as tight over allocation of foreign exchange as it is, for example, in the administration of the tariff system or the tax system, the case of multiple rates is much weaker.

Also, the use of multiple exchange rates to eliminate *regional* imbalance depends on the pattern of regional trade. Multiple exchange rates were a highly appropriate instrument in Indonesia, because interregional trade was insignificant in comparison with international trade. Where the reverse is the case, although there may be an argument for multiple exchange rates in terms of sectoral or industrial imbalance, the argument cannot be made in terms of regional imbalance. For it is not possible to establish widely different foreign exchange rates for different regions in the same country. The differences in foreign exchange prices in, say, Recife and Rio cannot be much greater than the cost of transport between the two Brazilian cities. One can approximate wide *regional* differences in effective foreign exchange rates only by differentiating among commodities entering into international trade. Thus a multiple exchange rate system can discriminate substantially among regions only to the extent that the commodity pattern of trade is very different from one region to another, and where trade between regions is relatively unimportant.

One should neither embrace nor reject multiple exchange rates as a matter of faith; the decision to embrace or reject—like all decisions to embrace or reject—should be made only after careful consideration of the consequences.

The United Nations Conference on Trade and Development

The special problems of underdeveloped countries with regard to foreign trade formed the agenda for the United Nations Conference on Trade and Development (UNCTAD), held at Geneva in the summer of 1964. Some 2,000 delegates from 120 member nations participated in the meetings. Raul Prebisch served as Secretary General, and his background document set the tone for the Conference.[23] This document presented the need for a new approach to the trade problems of developing countries in striking fashion. During the decade of the fifties the trade of underdeveloped countries expanded only half as fast as that of the advanced countries of the West and one-third as fast as that of the Communist countries. As one would expect, the Prebisch document also stressed the point that during this decade the terms of trade of developing countries had deteriorated. The balance of trade has also become increasingly adverse; imports have grown faster than exports. In a decade during which

[23] Raul Prebisch, *Towards a New Trade Policy for Development* (UN 64 II B. 4).

total world trade doubled, the share of underdeveloped countries shrank from one-third to one-fifth.

Foreign aid and investment has helped, but not much. The total net inflow of foreign capital—public and private—between 1950 and 1961 was only $47 billion. Deducting remittances of profits and interest reduces the figure to $26 billion. Deducting also the $13 billion lost through reduced purchasing power of exports from developing countries leaves a mere $13 billion. In short, the net gain through aid-and-trade was a little over $1 billion per year—an average of about $16 million per year for each of the seventy-five less-developed countries. Such figures hardly sound relevant to national economies at all; they sound more like reports of individual corporations.

The delegates to UNCTAD were divided into five major committees to discuss five sets of problems: international commodity agreements; trade in manufactures and semi-manufactures; financing expansion of international trade; institutional arrangements; international trade and its significance for economic development. Little concrete progress was made with any of these sets of problems. The advanced countries as a group were on the whole opposed to any extension of commodity agreements. Discussion of compensatory financing schemes was inhibited by the fact that in February 1963 the International Monetary Fund had offered to permit increased drawings by nations suffering temporary losses of export earnings, and the system was as yet largely untried. Efforts to obtain preferential treatment for industrial exports of developing countries were thwarted by the fears regarding impact on employment in the advanced countries. Perhaps the major concrete outcome of UNCTAD was its establishment as a permanent organ of the United Nations. Conferences are to be held at least once every three years, a fifty-five-nation trade and development board was created, and a secretariat established. The new organization is charged with responsibility to "promote international trade, especially with a view to accelerating economic development."

As one observer put it: [24]

The results of the 1964 United Nations Conference on Trade and Development can only be described as disappointing. Much was anticipated of these meetings: the outcome fell far short of expectations. The modest results are undoubtedly unsatisfactory to the developing countries who viewed the conference as the most important single event for them since the founding of the U.N. Dismayed also must be the statesmen and citizens, unfortunately few, of the industrialized nations who realize the moral and economic necessity of new rules of the game in international trade.

The foreign trade problems of underdeveloped countries must certainly continue to be classified as "unsolved." Indeed, there seems to be no real solution for them except economic development itself—the vicious circle again.

[24] Joseph C. Mills, "The Geneva Trade Conference: Success or Failure?" *The Canadian Banker*, Winter, 1964.

14 | Interactions of Modern and Traditional Sectors

Almost from the beginning of economists' interest in economic fluctuations there was a strong suspicion that the key lay somewhere in the interactions among savings, investment, and consumption, but it took generations of thought before these relationships were sorted out in a form permitting useful recommendations for policy. So today there is an equally strong suspicion that the key to underdevelopment lies somewhere in the interactions between the modern or industrial sector of the economy and the traditional or agricultural sector. A number of two-sector models have been produced to analyze these interactions. It could hardly be said that these models are as successful in providing a foundation for development policy as the savings-consumption-investment models have become for suggesting stabilization policies for advanced countries; however, progress has been made and some insight has been gained. This chapter outlines some of the more important of such two-sector models.

Technological Dualism and the Population Explosion

In many underdeveloped countries the initial favorable impact of industrial investment (including investment in plantations as well as in mines, petroleum, etc.) was swamped by population growth, in a way that did not occur in the currently advanced countries. In most countries, an initial increase in population growth seems to have followed the first wave of rapid industrialization. In the advanced countries of the West, however, the rise in *per capita* income continued long enough to bring subsequent drops in fertility rates and to permit economic growth to be sustained. The question is why the process in underdeveloped countries was different.

When the colonial powers first came into contact with countries of Asia and Africa, the populations of the latter were apparently not much higher, relative to natural resources, than those of European lands. In the case of Asia, moreover, there is little evidence that the level of technology was markedly below that of Europe in the sixteenth century. India, Indonesia, and China had firearms, navigation instruments, modes of land and water transport, techniques of manufacture and agriculture, and educational systems that compared favorably with Europe's best. We have small evidence that the standard of living of either rich or poor was significantly lower in Asian than in European countries at that time. Like the European countries, the Asian lands were actively engaged in international trade. The sixteenth-century picture would have given little basis for forecasting that in 400 years *per capita* incomes in Europe would be several times as high as in Asia.

During the seventeenth and eighteenth centuries, when the relationship of the colonial powers to Asian and African peoples was mainly a trading one, the countries of Europe seem to have made more progress toward establishing the preconditions for take-off than did those of Asia. In particular, during this period Europe benefited from improvements in agricultural methods and increased transport facilities. Even at the beginning of the nineteenth century, however, populations of many Asian countries were still small relative to resources, and prospects for economic growth would still have been good. By the end of that century, population growth in such countries as Indonesia, India, Japan, and the Philippines was already so high that launching a steady rise in *per capita* incomes had become a difficult problem.

Industrial Investment and Population Growth

The major impact of nineteenth-century industrial investment on rates of population growth probably came through the accompanying reduction in mortality rates. As the colonial powers shifted from trading to settlement, in order to exploit more effectively their new interest in plantations and mines (and later in petroleum), they followed policies that tended to reduce death rates. By maintaining internal law and order the colonial powers hampered the freedom of the native peoples to kill each other. Secondly, when Westerners settled in the country they became more interested in public health. In protecting themselves from malaria, typhoid, plague, and other diseases, they reduced the incidence of these diseases among the native peoples as well. Improved transport lessened the impact of famine. A fourth effect was an initial rise in *per capita* incomes even of native peoples. This improvement in living standards permitted—if it did not cause—a more rapid rise in the size of the population. Educational standards also rose, which may have had an indirect effect on mortality rates.

In some countries, industrial investment may have offered incentives for raising larger families. In Indonesia especially, after the shift from trading

to the "culture system," which involved compulsory deliveries of plantation products to the colonial authorities, the easiest way for the people
to maintain their standards of living and leisure, while meeting the levy
of the colonial government, was to have more children, occupy more land,
and devote a larger proportion of the land to irrigated rice culture, as
distinct from the slash-and-burn shifting agriculture. Something similar
may be true of other countries. Harvey Leibenstein, who has devoted
much study to demographic aspects of economic growth, is quite ready
to generalize on this relationship and to argue that initial rises in *per
capita* income will tend on balance to bring initial increases in the "demand
for children."

We saw in Chapter 2 that a crucial factor in the course of *per capita*
income is the length of the lag between the drop in mortality rates in the
early stages of industrialization and the subsequent drop in fertility rates.
The population explosions of Asian countries reflect a longer lag between
the initial drop in mortality rates and subsequent drop in fertility rates
than occurred in European countries or in the New World. No one
knows for certain why this longer lag appeared. Some evidence suggests
that the drop in fertility rates in Europe and the New World was a concomitant of urbanization. Development in Asia and Africa, centered as it
was on plantations, mines, oil fields, and exports of raw materials, brought
more *industrialization* than *urbanization;* hence the checks on family size
enforced by the urban industrialization of Europe and the New World
operated less effectively in the underdeveloped countries. Eventually fertility rates did drop in most Asian countries, but in some that drop came
too late to prevent serious population pressure from arising before planned
economic development began.

Colonial policy may, at least in part, account for the difference in the
demographic patterns in the Asian-African countries and in Europe.
Initial investment in Europe and the New World was also directed in
large measure toward agricultural improvement, mining, and production
of raw materials for export. In advanced countries, this investment gave
rise to subsequent marked expansion of the secondary and tertiary sectors
of the economy. Colonial policy in most of the Asian countries did not
permit development of the secondary and tertiary sectors in the colonies
themselves. Where domestic entrepreneurship appeared in the "Western"
sector, it was usually discouraged. For example, when the development of
the sugar plantations and refineries in the mid-nineteenth century in Java
led to a shift from rice cultivation to sugar planting on the part of Javanese
landowners, the Netherlands East Indies government sought to nip this
local industrialization in the bud by imposing a regulation forbidding the
sugar refineries to buy cane from native growers. Since the Javanese did
not have the capital or the technical skills for large refineries, they had to
be content with simple refining methods, producing brown sugar for the
local market. Similarly, when smallholders' rubber became an active
competitor of plantation rubber, the N.E.I. administration imposed a discriminatory tax on smallholders' rubber (in this case without much
success). Thus the secondary and tertiary sectors associated with industrial

investment in the colonies developed in the metropolitan countries rather than in the Asian and African countries themselves. The financing, transporting, storing, insuring, and processing of industrial raw materials took place mainly *outside* the colonial country.

Industrialization which is confined to the production of raw materials does not lead to urbanization. Indeed, it can proceed very far without seriously disrupting the pattern of village life led by most of the people. One may conjecture that the disastrously long lag between the initial drop in mortality rates and the subsequent drop in fertility rates is associated with the peculiar form of industrialization in underdeveloped countries, a form which did not bring with it rapid urbanization.

One may doubt whether the reverse process, urbanization without industrialization, such as has taken place in a number of developing countries since the war, can be expected to have the same effect on fertility rates as the combination of industrialization and urbanization in Europe during the eighteenth and nineteenth centuries. The growth of Calcutta, Bombay, Tokyo, Manila, and Djakarta since World War II reflects the "pull" of employment opportunities in industry less than the "push" of dwindling opportunities for advancement in rural society. There is, of course, no assurance that this kind of urbanization will affect fertility rates in the same way Western urbanization did.

Some sociologists and anthropologists might ask whether there would be any reason for expecting twentieth-century Asian society to behave like eighteenth-century European society even if economic conditions were similar. Two points might be made in reply. First, as a policy prescription no one would recommend urbanization as such; it is industrialization and urbanization together that hold the hope for rising per capita income. Secondly, we have some evidence that even in Asian cities fertility rates tend to fall below those of rural areas in the same country. For one thing, the extended family system tends to break down under urban conditions; indeed, the wish to escape the responsibilities of the extended family system is one of the motives for ambitious young people moving from country to city.

Technological Dualism

If the industrial investment which launched the "population explosions" in Asia, Africa, and Latin America had provided opportunities for productive employment for the whole of the population increase, per capita incomes could still have risen. But industrialization in the form common to underdeveloped countries did not provide a proportionate increase in job opportunities. Analysis of production functions and factor endowment in an economy with two sectors, two factors of production, and two goods, is enlightening in this regard. Although such a model is necessarily simplified, it approximates reality closely enough to provide significant results. The two sectors are the industrial sector (plantations, mines, oil fields, refineries, etc.) and a rural sector engaged in production of foodstuffs and in handicrafts or very small industries. The first of these sectors is capital-intensive. Moreover, it either is characterized in fact by relatively fixed technical coefficients (fixed proportions in which factors of production must be combined), or is assumed by entrepreneurs to be so. The effect on employment patterns is much the same in either case. The other sector has variable technical coefficients; that is, the products could be produced with a wide range of factor proportions. The two factors of production are labor on the one hand and capital, including improved land, on the other. The two products are industrial raw materials for export and necessities for domestic consumption.

Figure 14–1 represents the production function in the industrial sector.

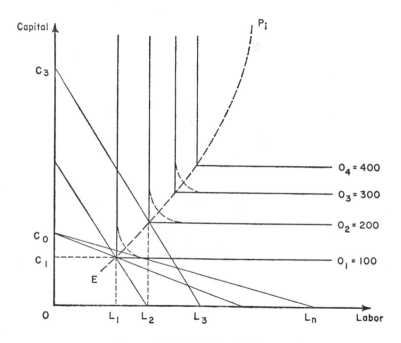

Figure 14–1. The Industrial Sector

Units of capital are measured on the vertical axis, labor on the horizontal axis. Each curve is an *isoquant* representing combinations of labor and capital producing the same output (sometimes called an "isopod"). As we move away from the origin from curve O_1 to curves O_2, O_3, etc., we move up the "hill" of production to higher and higher levels of output. The diagram is thus a kind of contour map.

The solid curves are drawn to conform to the case of "fixed technical coefficients." In this case labor and capital must be combined in fixed proportions to get any output at all. Output can be increased only by increasing the amounts used of *both* factors so as to maintain these proportions. (Some production processes, such as petroleum refining, actually come very close to having fixed technical coefficients.) The production process in this sector is also capital-intensive; relatively large amounts of capital and relatively small amounts of labor are used. Thus to produce an output of O_1 the industrial sector will use OC_1 units of capital and OL_1 units of labor. If OL_2 units are available, the excess labor supply will have no effect on production techniques, and L_1L_2 units of labor will simply remain unemployed, or must seek employment in the other sector, no matter what the relation of wage rates to capital costs. As more capital becomes available through time, more labor will be employed and output will be expanded. The line EP_i is the expansion path of this industrial sector. However, employment increases relatively little as investment and output in the industrial sector expand along this path.

Perhaps technical coefficients are actually less fixed than entrepreneurs think. If managers and technicians, used to particular methods of production in Western countries which they accept without question as superior, do not look for alternative techniques more suited to the factor endowment, the effect is the same as if coefficients were technologically fixed. The dotted portions of the isopods in Figure 14–1 indicate a situation in which there is actually some flexibility in factor-proportions. It can readily be seen that *small* changes in factor endowments (and in relative prices of factors of production) would not bring marked changes in technique even if entrepreneurs learned that the production function was like the dotted lines rather than the solid ones. But for very large differences in factor endowment (and prices), such as that represented by the line C_oL_n, a more labor-intensive technique would be used if its existence were recognized by the decision makers.

Figure 14–2 represents the production function for the rural sector. Here coefficients are variable: a wide range of techniques and of combinations of labor and capital will give the same output. Accordingly the proportions actually used will be adjusted to the factor endowment (and to the consequent relative prices of labor and capital). In this context capital includes improved land.

Now let us imagine that we begin with production at O_1 in each sector. Then capital begins to flow into the industrial sector, mostly from abroad. The industrial sector expands along EP_i. But we have already seen that this industrialization generates a population explosion. In some countries and some periods, the percentage rate of population increase considerably exceeded the rate at which capital was accumulated in the industrial sector. Because of the actual or accepted fixed technical coefficients in that sector, employment opportunities did not occur at the same rate as that at which the population grew. Far from bringing a shift of population from the rural to the industrial sector, industrialization, after its first impact, may even have brought a relative *decline* in the proportion of total employment in that sector.

Thus the increased population had to seek a livelihood in the other, variable-coefficient sector. At the beginning of the expansion process, no factor of production was relatively abundant or scarce in this sector. For

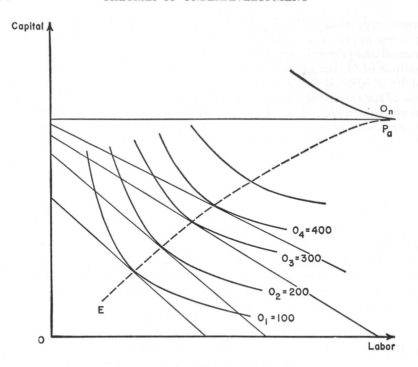

Figure 14–2. The Agricultural Sector

a while, the response to population growth was to bring additional land under cultivation, so as to keep the ratio of labor to land relatively constant; since other forms of capital were not available in any quantity to this sector, the amount of land that could be effectively worked by one family was in any case limited. Thus for a while the "optimal" combination of labor and capital (mostly improved land) could be maintained, as output rose from O_1 to O_3. Eventually, good land tended to become scarce. The ratio of labor to capital available in that sector rose steadily, and since technical coefficients were variable, techniques in that sector became increasingly labor-intensive. For example, irrigated rice culture was substituted for shifting dry rice culture. Finally the point was reached at output O_n where all available land was already cultivated by highly labor-intensive techniques and the marginal productivity of labor fell below zero even with the most labor-intensive techniques available; with continuing population growth, disguised unemployment began to appear.

Under these conditions there was *no incentive* for groups of individual farmers or small enterprises to make marginal and unrelated investments of capital in the labor-intensive sector, even if they had capital to invest. Nor had they any reason to introduce labor-saving innovations, even if they knew about them and could finance them. And as yet there is no technology designed to raise output per man-hour without also raising the ratio of capital to labor. Labor *as a group* had no incentive to increase its efforts, since the labor supply was already redundant. Thus methods remained labor-intensive and levels of technique, man-hour productivity, and economic and social welfare remained low.

This tendency toward "disguised unemployment" in the rural sector is enhanced if technological progress takes a form favoring the capital-intensive sector. There can be little doubt that this process is what in fact occurred. Indeed, during the last two centuries little or no technological progress has occurred in peasant agriculture and handicrafts, while technological progress in the plantations, mining, and petroleum sector has been rapid. The tendency toward disguised unemployment in the rural sector will also be aggravated if wage rates are kept artificially high by trade-union activities or by government policy. Industrial wage rates that are high relative to productivity provide an incentive for the introduction of labor-saving devices and consequently diminish still further the capacity of the industrialized sector to absorb the population growth.

Esther Boserup suggests that diminishing average returns to labor may set in before land is used really intensively. Shifting agriculture, she suggests, may be quite efficient in terms of manpower productivity; given the possibility of varying periods of fallow, the distinction between cultivated and uncultivated land virtually disappears. We should think in terms of a continuum of types of land use, ranging from still virgin land which is never cropped, through land cropped at shorter and shorter intervals, to land where a new crop is planted as soon as the last one is harvested. The shift to more intensive agriculture as population pressure mounts may bring a decline in man-year productivity even while some land is still under shifting cultivation. Conversely the return from intensive to shifting agriculture in parts of Latin America where population has declined is not retrogression, but a rational adaptation to the factor endowment.[1]

Conclusions

Putting together the theory of the population explosion with the theory of technological dualism we obtain a deeper understanding of some of the "characteristics" of underdeveloped countries. We saw in Chapter 1 there that the proportion of the total labor force in agriculture is virtually a measure of the degree of underdevelopment; the more people in agriculture, the more underdeveloped the country. Yet we also saw that it is precisely in agriculture that the spread in man-year productivity is greatest as between advanced and underdeveloped countries. In the industrial sector, techniques are often advanced and productivity is high; in agriculture, techniques are labor-intensive and simple and productivity is abysmally low. Why does labor not shift from the rural to the industrial sector, from low-yield to high-yield occupations, in accordance with orthodox theory?

[1] Esther Boserup, *The Conditions of Agricultural Growth* (London and Chicago, 1965).

The same sort of question arises with respect to capital. According to orthodox theory, the marginal productivity of capital ought to be higher in the rural sector, where the ratio of labor to capital is high, than in the industrial sector, where it is low. There is evidence that returns to capital actually are higher in the rural sector than in the industrial sector. George Rosen, on the basis of his extensive knowledge of the Indian economy, concludes that an important factor delaying the development of indigenous industry has been the high returns on investment in agricultural credit.[2] Interest rates on loans in the rural sector range from 16 to 100 per cent; in addition, the rural capitalist, who usually makes loans on a sharecropping basis, is frequently in a position to earn a handsome profit on speculative investment in stocks of food crops. It is easy to see why the rural capitalist is not attracted to industrial investment. But why does not industrial capital flow into agriculture, if returns there are really so much higher than on the plantations and in the mines and oil fields?

Here is the most vicious of all the vicious circles encountered in a theory of underdevelopment. Labor does not flow into the industrial sector because the supply of capital to that sector is limited—each investment project in an underdeveloped country competes against projects the world over in the international capital market—and technical coefficients are fixed, or thought to be so. The supply of domestic capital to the rural sector is also limited. It is not directed toward improving techniques, because although the elasticity of substitution of labor for capital may be high, the elasticity of substitution of capital for *land* is low. Relatively small amounts of investment in tools, simple irrigation, seed selection, and fertilizer could bring the *marginal* productivity of capital down to zero, given the present ratio of labor to land. It may well be that in some underdeveloped countries the marginal productivity of both labor and capital is close to zero in the rural sector.

The only way to overcome the redundancy of labor in the rural sector is to increase the supply of the scarce factor. But the *immediately* scarce factor is land. The only way to raise the marginal productivity of capital is to increase the ratio of land to labor a great deal. The production function is highly discontinuous in this respect. Increasing the size of the typical family farm from 2 acres to 3 will not raise the marginal productivity of capital very much. The size must be raised to 20 or 200 acres so that mechanization becomes profitable. With high population densities such increases in size of holding can be attained only by luring people out of peasant agriculture into the industrial sector. For *this* kind of program, however, capital becomes the scarce factor once again. It requires heavy investment in *both* the industrial and agricultural sectors. Neither agricultural improvements on the present holdings nor industrialization will, by itself, break through this particular vicious circle. Industrialization without an agricultural revolution brought the underdeveloped countries where they are.

The failure of foreign capital to flow into peasant agriculture must be

[2] George Rosen, "Capital Markets and Underdeveloped Economies: A Theoretical Frame-Hypothesis for Empirical Research," M.I.T., CENIS, May, 1958.

explained in somewhat different terms. The industrial and rural sectors are not part of the same "economy" in the ordinary sense. Geographically, the plantations, mines, and oil fields are in the same country, but economically they may be more closely tied to the metropolitan country providing the capital, technical knowledge, and managerial skill than to the underdeveloped country in which the operation is located. The men who launch, organize, finance, and manage these enterprises—even when they are urbanites of the country itself—know little of peasant agriculture and village life. The rural capitalist relies for his success on his personal and firsthand knowledge of the villagers with whom he deals; he lends to them, sells to them, and buys from them. This is knowledge of a sort the foreign or urban capitalist does not have and does not wish to acquire. As for a wholesale shift to mechanized commercial agriculture, it is not an operation to be carried out on a piecemeal private enterprise basis.

Indeed here is one of the major reasons for government intervention in the development process. Once countries are in the situation analyzed in this chapter, only a unified and large-scale program involving more rapid industrialization and bold schemes for agricultural improvement can launch cumulative growth. In short, a "big push" is necessary.

Unlimited Supplies of Labor?

W. Arthur Lewis begins his well-known article on "Economic Development with Unlimited Supplies of Labour" by asserting that many underdeveloped countries conform to the Classical model, in which the supply of labor is perfectly elastic at current wage rates.[3] The "widow's cruse" of workers consists of existing farmers, casual workers, petty traders, domestic retainers, and additions to the labor force through population growth. As his conclusions rest on this basic observation, let us begin by examining the premise itself.

Some observers, including the present writer, have pointed out that the optimism concerning development by absorption of disguised unemployment from agriculture was unfounded. It is not possible to transfer large numbers of workers permanently and full time from peasant agriculture to industry without a drop in agricultural output, for during planting and harvesting seasons, which together amount to several weeks per year, the entire labor force is occupied. It may even be necessary to bring back members of the village who have gone off to take casual jobs in the industrial sector. Reorganization of agriculture and a shift to relatively extensive and mechanized techniques could release large numbers of workers from agriculture, to be sure, but that requires a certain amount of investment in the agricultural sector itself. Some observers have suggested that disguised unemployment has moved from country to city, and cite as evidence the host of petty retailers. But even the urban peddler, with three empty bottles in one basket and two right shoes in the other, may be performing a real service, and so may be truly employed, if there

[3] W. Arthur Lewis, "Economic Development with Unlimited Supplies of Labour," *The Manchester School of Economic and Social Studies*, May, 1954.

are customers with left shoes and customers who want empty bottles. Thus, in the static sense, it may be questioned whether supply curves of labor to the industrial sector are perfectly elastic.

If one puts the whole growth process in time, however, as one must to get meaningful results, the Lewis model accords with reality in many underdeveloped countries, as far as *unskilled* labor is concerned. The Lewis argument does not require disguised unemployment. It requires three conditions: that the wage rate in the industrial sector be above the marginal productivity of labor in the rural sector by a small but fixed amount; that investment in the industrial sector be not absolutely large relative to population growth; and that costs of training the necessary numbers of skilled workers be constant through time. The first condition seems to be met in many countries. If the "population multiplier" operates, population growth being accelerated by the very process of industrialization, the second condition is automatically guaranteed. But even if industrial investment does not actually accelerate population growth, the second condition can be met if employment in the industrial sector is a small proportion of the total and population growth is fairly high. Suppose, for example, that the labor force is twenty million, that four million are employed in the industrial sector, that the capital-job ratio in that sector is $2,000 per man, and that the total labor force grows at the rate of 2 per cent per year. To employ the total increase in the labor force in the industrial sector would require net investment of $800 million next year, or 10 per cent of the total stock of capital. Net investment on this scale would double the stock of capital in about seven years, a rate of growth beyond the wildest dreams of most underdeveloped countries. Thus for all practical purposes the supply of unskilled labor to the industrial sector can be treated as perfectly elastic, whereas in the rural sector it is already redundant, in the sense that marginal productivity there is below the subsistence standard of living.

Of course, the industrial employers are interested in skilled labor too. Lewis argues that labor skills are only a "quasi-bottleneck"; if you have unskilled workers, you can convert them into skilled ones.

In the short run, the need to train or import skilled workers may not alter the argument very much; if the cost of training or importing is constant, the elasticity of supply of skilled labor can still be infinite. As we have seen, it is possible that the cost of training or importing technicians may be high enough to induce entrepreneurs to use capital-intensive techniques in those parts of their operation where skill is necessary, but this fact does not change the argument either, unless these costs are rising. The Lewis thesis is of dubious validity even for unskilled workers, if we think in purely static terms, however; and if we think in terms of long-run supply through time, the relevant question about the supply of skills is whether the cost of training or importing is rising through time. The answer will depend on the nature of technological progress; if it is of a sort that reduces both the capital-labor ratio and the capital-output ratio simultaneously, the Lewis thesis may hold for skilled labor as well as for unskilled.

Now if we accept the thesis, the process of growth will look like Figure 14–3. Here $\bar{w}$ is the productivity per man-hour in peasant agriculture, and w is the conventional wage in the industrial sector. The marginal productivity of labor in industry is $M_1 M_1$, which permits the capitalist to earn a surplus, $AM_1 s$. When he invests this surplus—perhaps improving techniques at the same time—the curve of marginal productivity shifts to $M_2 M_2$ and so on. Industrial employment grows from N_1 to N_2, N_3, etc. The per capita income of workers and peasants remains unchanged, and the entire benefits of development accrue to capitalists. Lewis suggests three ways in which the process might be halted: if the expansion of the industrial sector is rapid enough to reduce the absolute population in the

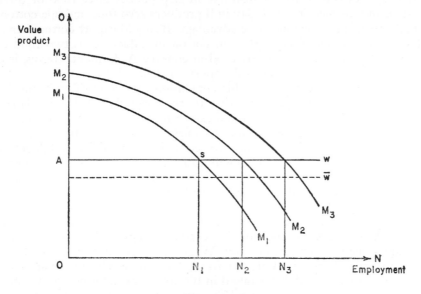

Figure 14–3

rural sector, raising the man-hour productivity in that sector, and so raising $\bar{w}$ and w (this will not happen if the population multiplier is operating); if technological progress in the rural sector raises productivity there, and so raises $\bar{w}$ and w; or if the terms of trade turn against the industrial sector with rising prices of food and raw materials, and so bring a rise in $\bar{w}$ and w (this is the Classical model). The achievement of balanced growth and generally higher living standards requires that the process *must* be halted by either method 1 or method 2, while, at the same time, measures are taken to continue investment in the industrial sector.

Lewis applies his analysis to the impact of international trade. First, he shows that technological progress in the export sector of underdeveloped countries helps only the workers of advanced countries. Suppose one man-day of labor in the advanced country, A, produces three food or three steel, whereas in the underdeveloped country, B, it produces one food or one rubber. The rates of exchange will then be one food equals one steel equals one rubber. Now assume that productivity in rubber growing trebles. Then one steel will buy three rubber. But the wage in B is still equal to one food (plus the conventional surplus in the industrial sector) because the supply of labor to the rubber industry is unlimited. Thus foreign investment in the industrial sector of B can provide only additional employment and perhaps some tax revenues; in itself it cannot raise per capita incomes.

Now assume a man-day in A produces three food or three cotton manufactures, whereas a man-day in B produces two food or one cotton manufactures. The *marginal* man-day in A produces three food or three cotton, and the *marginal* man-day in B produces zero food and one cotton. On the principle of comparative advantage, B should export cotton manufactures and import food. But w in cotton manufactures is two food in country B; and w is three to six food in country A. In money terms, it is cheaper for B to export food and import cotton.

Lewis seems to be correct in his conclusion that countries with inadequate agricultural resources relative to their population (India, Japan, Egypt, the United Kingdom) should export manufactures and import agricultural products. It is impossible to imagine India as a truly efficient agricultural country, but it is easy to see India as an efficient producer of steel and textiles. This kind of misallocation of resources occurs in many underdeveloped countries. The implication is that planning must be based on "shadow prices" as they would prevail after a drastic structural change has been achieved.

Finally, Lewis indicates a way out of the vicious circle. Suppose a man-day in A produces five food or five cotton textiles, and a man-day in B produces one food or three cotton. Wages in B are one food, and B will export textiles. Wages in A are five food; A gets all the benefit from trade. Now suppose productivity is raised in B's cotton-manufacturing industry. The wage in B is unchanged, and the entire benefit goes to A, as before. But if productivity is raised in B's food production, B's wage will rise. Then cotton prices will also rise, to the benefit of B and the disadvantage of A. Thus economic development requires raising productivity per man-day—not per acre—in the peasant agriculture sector. Given the rates of population growth in that sector, raising productivity per man-day almost certainly requires—sooner or later—a shift to more extensive and more mechanized agriculture.

One final point may be noted. The current nationalist policies, with their emphasis on training and upgrading domestic labor and their limitations on immigration of skilled workers, managers, and technicians, may mean that skilled workers will be a more serious bottleneck to future expansion than they have been in the past. It is a question whether techniques of training, as well as of production, can be improved sufficiently to keep training costs per unit of *output*, at least, from rising as industry expands.

Development of the Labor Surplus Economy

One of the most ambitious efforts at a theory of underdevelopment to appear in recent years is that of John Fei and Gustav Ranis.[4] It does not pretend to complete generality: "It is the purpose of this book," the authors state in their preface, "to present a theory of development relevant to the typical labor surplus type of underdeveloped economy and to extract some policy conclusions from it." It is time, they say, to "venture beyond the customary eclectic survey of growth problems and ideas and towards the evolution of a particular theory aimed at a particular type of economy." In their view, efforts at a completely general theory are less likely to be fruitful, in our present state of knowledge, than "attempts to generalize from specific country experience." The theory presented in their book, accordingly, is limited to "a particular type of underdeveloped economy, the labor surplus type." It is clear, however, that the authors consider this type of economy common enough; and the theoretical construction they build to analyze this kind of economy is one of the most elaborate yet to be presented in the whole field of economic development.

The Basic Model

The fundamental features of the labor surplus economy, on which the entire analysis rests, are as follows: (1) The supply of land is sharply limited. (2) There is a "constant institutional wage" in the industrial sector. The supply of labor is perfectly elastic to the industrial sector at this wage, which is taken to be slightly above the real wage in the agricultural sector, as in W. Arthur Lewis's "unlimited supply of labor" model. Workers do not have to be "bid away" from the agricultural sector through raising wage rates above current levels, at least in the initial stages of industrialization. (3) Labor is redundant in the agricultural sector. There exists some number of workers in the agricultural sector with zero marginal productivity, who can be transferred—completely, permanently, and full time—without investment in the agricultural sector and without a fall in agricultural output. (4) There are "well-behaved" isoquants in the industrial sector. This assumption is fundamental to the analysis. Any number of workers whatsoever can be absorbed into the industrial sector, with no additions to the stock of capital in that sector, and without innovations, by resorting to known techniques which are increasingly labor-intensive. (5) For this reason, innovation in the industrial sector as such leads to a transfer of workers to the industrial sector. Innovations of any kind raise the marginal physical productivity of labor, and employment will accordingly increase until the marginal physical productivity of labor is once again reduced to the critical minimum wage. The increase in employment depends on the "intensity" of the innovation (the magnitude of the increase in labor productivity) and on its capital-using or labor-using bias. As in the Classical model, innovation seems to be

[4] John C. H. Fei and Gustav Ranis, *Development of the Labor Surplus Economy: Theory and Policy* (Homewood, Ill., 1964).

largely limited to the industrial sector. (6) The transfer of labor to the industrial sector is limited by the size of the agricultural surplus. If the attempt to shift workers from agriculture to industry results in a shift of the terms of trade against the industrial sector, industrial money wage rates must be raised, thus limiting the increase in employment. (7) Capital accumulation as such also increases employment in the industrial sector. The transfer of the agricultural surplus to the industrial sector is easiest if there are "dualistic landlords," who operate in both sectors and invest agricultural profits in industry. (Indeed, it is so much easier if dualistic landlords exist that it is not quite clear from the book how it is to be accomplished otherwise.)

The basic diagram of the Fei-Ranis model is reproduced in Figure 14–4. Both the upper and the lower parts of the diagram apply to the industrial sector of the economy. Each part shows one cross section of the production function: the upper part presents the usual isoquants (or isopods), the curves showing combinations of labor and capital that will produce the same output, with output rising as we move from Q_0 to Q_1 to Q_2; and the lower part is the usual curve of marginal productivity of labor, showing additions to total output as more units of labor are combined with a fixed stock of capital (and land). As the stock of capital is increased from K_0 to K_1 to K_2 in the upper figure, the marginal productivity curve in the lower figure shifts from M_0 to M_1 to M_2, etc. To maximize profits (the shaded area bounded by the marginal productivity curve and the supply curve of labor), employment will be extended to the point where the marginal productivity is equal to the real wage rate. With a capital stock of K_0, this point is reached with employment of L_0. As the stock of capital is increased to K_1, K_2, etc., employment will rise to L_1, L_2, etc., taking us along the expansion path in the upper diagram.

Up to the point L_2 additional labor can be attracted into the industrial sector as a constant real wage. But beyond that point the real wage rate must be raised in order to lure more labor away from the rural sector, either because labor becomes scarce in agriculture or costs of food rise or both. Beyond this "turning point" capital accumulation in the industrial sector must proceed at an ever-faster rate if employment in that sector is to continue expanding at the same rate—or something else must happen to shift the marginal productivity curves upward and to the right.

The various factors influencing the rate of labor absorption into the industrial sector are pulled together in the fundamental equation,

$$\pi L = \pi K + \frac{B_L + J}{\epsilon_{LL}}$$

The dependent variable "πL," is the rate of labor absorption, most easily thought of as the percentage rate of growth of industrial employment through time. The term "πK" is the rate of capital accumulation through time. "B_L" is the degree of labor-using bias, or deviation from "neutrality," of innovations. Completely neutral innovations would leave the ratio of capital to labor unchanged; the more innovations deviate from neutrality in this sense, in the direction of raising the labor-capital ratio, the higher

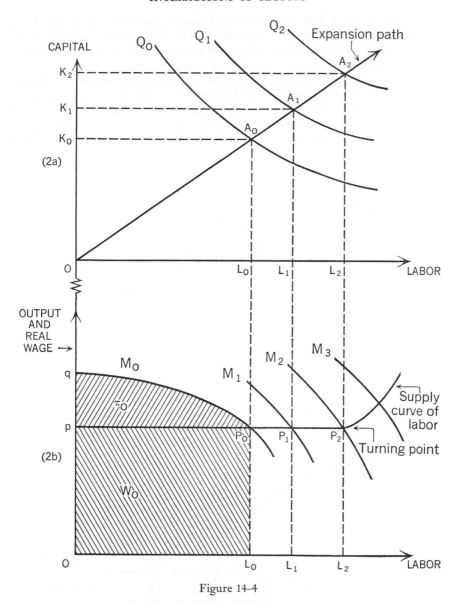

Figure 14-4

is B_L. "J" is the "intensity of innovation," or "the fractional increase in output due entirely to the passage of one unit of time, holding both capital and labor constant." In simpler language, it is the rate at which productivity is raised through time by technological progress, and may be thought of as the rate at which the marginal productivity curve of labor is shifted upward and to the right through innovations. ϵ_{LL} is the rate at which the marginal productivity of labor falls as the ratio of labor to capital is raised. Thus the equation states the truism that the rate of growth of industrial employment depends on the rate at which marginal pro-

312   THEORIES OF UNDERDEVELOPMENT

ductivity of labor falls with increased employment (other things being equal), on the rate of capital accumulation in the industrial sector, on the extent to which innovations release or absorb labor, and on the rate at which productivity is raised by technological progress.

The concepts and their interactions are illustrated further in Figure 14–5, which is an elaboration of Figure 14–4. We have added a curve showing the shift in the curve of marginal productivity of labor that would constitute a "neutral" innovation, with which actual shifts may be compared. We begin with a stock of capital K_1 and employment L_1. Then

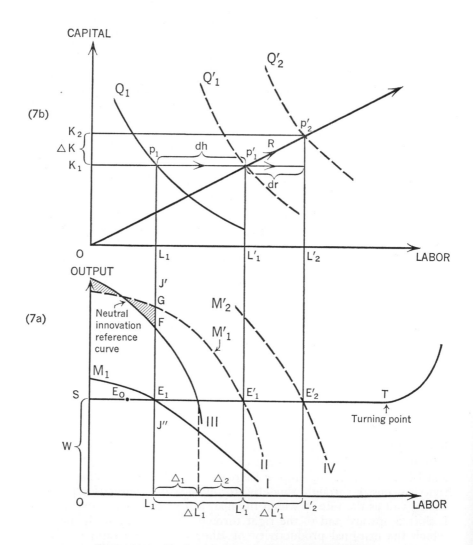

Figure 14–5. Production Contour Map Industrial Sector

technological progress raises the marginal productivity of labor to the dotted curve M'_1. Because the innovation is labor-absorbing in character, employment rises to L'_1 even without any capital accumulation. In the upper diagram this shift is shown by redrawing Q_1 and Q'_1. If in addition the stock of capital is increased to $\bar{K}_2$, the equilibrium position shifts to E'_2 and employment increases to L'_2.

Reiterating the fundamental equation in terms of this diagram, the authors state that the rate of labor absorption depends partly on the rate of capital accumulation, whereas the absorption due to innovations alone, with fixed capital stock, depends in turn on three factors:

1. The "height" of point F relative to point E_1, representing the intensity of the innovation, that is, how much the original production contour has been blown up.

2. The "height" of point G relative to point F, representing the degree of labor-using bias of the innovation.

3. The "steepness" or "flatness" of the M'_1 curve representing the relative strength or weakness of the law of diminishing returns to labor. (The "flatter" M'_1 the further to the right equilibrium point E'_1.)

Successful economic development requires "structural change" in the sense of growth of industrial employment more rapid than the growth of total employment. This condition can be expressed as a "critical minimum effort criterion" derived from the basic equation above, letting "π_P" stand for the rate of growth of total employment through time:

$$\pi_P < \pi_L = \pi_K + \frac{B_L + J}{\epsilon_{LL}}$$

Thus for "success" we need capital accumulation, technological progress in the modern sector, preferably of a labor-absorbing type, and improvement in agricultural productivity, to prevent excessive increases in the industrial real wage which would slow down the relative transfer of labor from the traditional agricultural to the modern industrial sector.

From this model the authors derive a simple and not very original formula for launching economic development. First, the total agricultural surplus should be raised; and then there should be as much investment and capital-saving (labor-absorbing) innovation in the industrial sector as possible. "Our analysis indicates," the authors conclude, "that besides accumulating as much capital as possible [either domestically or via foreign aid] the economy should seek innovations of as high intensity as possible and, given intensity, subject to as high a labor-using bias as possible." No one could quarrel with this formula; the problem is to arrange its application in particular cases.

Major Questions of Fact

The validity and applicability of the model, of course, depends on the extent to which the basic assumptions conform to reality. The authors would no doubt agree that all developing countries are not fundamentally short of land; slash-and-burn agriculture still exists in a number of developing countries, including Brazil and Thailand. More serious questions arise regarding the "redundancy of labor." The question of "disguised underemployment" or "redundancy of labor" is a complex one that has given rise to a substantial literature, some of which will be considered below. This literature is ignored by Fei and Ranis, who simply state the existence of redundant labor as though it were a well-known fact. As already suggested, however, the truth is that redundant labor of the kind assumed by the authors is probably non-existent; Dr. Yong Sam Cho, whose study is outlined in the following section, found none in Korea. Even in so densely populated an area as Java there are still labor shortages in planting and harvest seasons. The same is true of small and rapidly industrializing countries like Greece. What one finds is not chronic underemployment, but extreme seasonal variations, combined with work-sharing devices and short hours during the off-seasons.

Fei and Ranis fail to make the all-important distinction, on which Cho's analysis rests so heavily, between marginal productivity in terms of numbers of workers, and marginal productivity in terms of hours per worker. The work-sharing devices typical of Asian countries are such, and the hours so short, that the marginal productivity of individual workers is not zero. Labor is "redundant" only in the sense that if real wages could be raised so as to permit more *hours* of work to be undertaken per man, the same agricultural output could be produced for smaller *numbers* of people. Moreover, not all of those who could be released, even in this sense, are actually available at the "constant institutional wage"; only those who are, in Cho's terms, "marginal men" in both economic and social terms are thus available. No country has a "reserve army" of agricultural workers, completely unemployed, who can be transferred the year around with no rise in industrial wages, no investment in the agricultural sector, and no drop in agricultural output.

In particular the assumption that any number of workers can be combined with a fixed stock of capital is unrealistic and misleading. We have seen above that it is a good deal more useful, in explaining how underdevelopment and technological dualism have appeared, to make the reverse assumption of fixed technical coefficients in the industrial sector. Of the two extreme assumptions, the latter explains a wider range of reality. If, for example, the modern sector consists mainly of rubber plantations, tin and bauxite mines, and petroleum fields and refineries, how is one to combine an unlimited number of workers with a fixed stock of capital in these industries, and still achieve enough increase in output to justify the increase in employment? Much depends on the particular product-mix in the actual modern industrial sector of the country concerned.

Historically, innovations in the modern sector have been labor-saving to a substantial degree. Fei and Ranis seem to regard this fact as a matter for regret, if not actually a sign of perverseness on the part of entrepreneurs and government authorities concerned with industrial investment. Throughout their analysis, they miss the fundamental point that innovations can be both labor-saving and capital-saving, and still be labor-absorbing and capital-absorbing during the gestation period. In the United States even the railroad, certainly a heavy absorber of capital and a significant creator of employment during the period of railroad construction in the nineteenth century, was both labor-saving and capital-saving once in place; both labor costs and capital costs per ton-mile were lower in railway freight trains than in wagon trains. If investment is maintained on a high and increasing level, employment can go on increasing even if each successive individual innovation is labor-saving, in the sense that it reduces labor costs and increases output per man-hour. If at the same time the ratio of capital to labor goes up, this incidental result seems little reason for concern.

Fei and Ranis also overlook the fundamental fact that a good many small-scale and labor-intensive activities have high capital-output ratios. They seem to take it for granted that if the capital-labor ratio is reduced the capital-output ratio will be reduced as well. The limited results of research undertaken thus far, however, suggest that over a very wide range of industrial activity the reverse is the case. One of the many "vicious circles" with which "the road to development is paved" is this one: underdeveloped countries cannot afford "labor-intensive" techniques, in the sense of low capital-labor ratios, because they are too expensive in terms of capital—they have high capital-output ratios. This fact is surely at least one part of the explanation of the famous "Leontief paradox," the discovery that through its international trade the United States exports labor and imports capital.

As for their "dualistic landlords," these no doubt existed in Japan, and they exist today in the Philippines and to some degree in the Brazilian State of São Paulo. But they do not exist everywhere, and they are not easy to create where they do not exist. The alternative, of course, is for the state itself to play the role of "dualistic landlord," shifting agricultural surpluses to the industrial sector. But that is precisely what all governments interested in development are trying to do, and it is precisely what proves to be so difficult from a political and administrative point of view.

Success and Failure

Fei and Ranis apply their theory to cases of success and failure. In the "success story," an original rise in the total agricultural surplus raises the real income of industrial workers, thus "shaking loose" labor from agriculture, and as an impact effect, raising the return to investment in industry relative to investment in agriculture. Indeed the return to investment in agriculture actually falls initially. Thus the dualistic landlord shifts capital from agriculture to industry. As employment in the industrial sector rises, the marginal productivity of labor industry falls, and eventually the industrial real wage returns to the customary institutional wage. The terms of trade shift back to agriculture again, and the incentive to raise total agricultural surplus further is restored. Thus a new cycle of development begins and the process becomes cumulative.

In the failure case, there is no rise in the marketable technical total agricultural surplus. Thus the effort to expand the industrial sector entails a continuous worsening of the terms of trade of the industrial sector and a rise in the industrial real wage. This rise in the industrial real wage in turn leads to the introduction of labor-saving innovations in the industrial sector, thus choking off the increase in industrial employment.

Once again, this case of "failure" seems oversimplified and does not fit the cases of "failure" most familiar to this writer. It overlooks, for example, the fact that the product of the industrial sector is frequently sold in the world market, whereas the product of the agricultural sector is sold in the domestic market. Indonesia is as clear-cut a case of failure as one could find, but there is no evidence of improving terms of trade between the agricultural and industrial sectors of Indonesia itself; indeed, the evidence suggests just the reverse. What has happened in Indonesia is that because of the very low elasticity of substitution of labor for capital in the industrial sector, the capital-intensive nature of the most efficient technology in that sector (efficient in terms of capital-output ratios), the limitation of technological progress of the industrial sector, and the nature of the technological progress, the absorption of labor into the industrial sector—despite rapid expansion of that sector—never kept pace with population growth in the country as a whole. When World War II began, only 7 per cent of the labor force had been absorbed into the modern sector. The other 93 per cent of a large and rapidly growing population had to find a livelihood in the traditional sector, where their productivity was inevitably low.

Population growth is a factor that seems not to enter into the Fei-Ranis model. Despite the complexity of the diagrams, and the emphasis on innovation, the whole analysis remains essentially neoclassical and static.

The analysis includes two case studies, Japan as a "success story" and India as a failure. Japan's success is attributed mainly to a rapid rate of innovation, initially of a capital-saving and labor-absorbing nature. About 80 per cent of the total growth of the industrial labor force is attributed to such innovation, capital accumulation accounting for the other 20 per cent. According to the figures presented, the capital-labor ratio actually fell in Japan between 1888 and World War I, and this fact is given high marks in explaining the success of Japan. Japan also succeeded in reducing the absolute size of its agricultural labor force after 1898.

On the other hand, in India there was a "premature deepening" of capital, with an increase in the capital-labor ratio throughout the whole period, 1949–60. The industrial labor force grew very slowly, and the agricultural labor force continued to increase. Thus India has yet to reach a critical minimum effort.

The authors summarize the comparison as follows:

The contrast between these two historical cases is unmistakably clear. Continuous capital shallowing in Japanese industry between 1888 and the end of World War I is evidence that Japan made maximum use of her abundant factor, surplus agricultural labor, while adopting labor using (or, at least, not very labor-saving) innovations. The continuously positive labor absorption due to innovations corroborates this finding. India, on the other hand, seems to have resorted to very labor saving innovations from the very beginning of her development effort, thus yielding to the temptation of an increasingly capital-intensive industrial structure and neglecting the potentialities of a maximum utilization of her abundant, and rapidly growing, surplus agricultural labor force.

This statement of the contrast between Japan and India is a distortion of the facts. Has India stubbornly and misguidedly refused to use capital-cheap, labor-intensive techniques? On the contrary, the second Indian Five-Year Plan states clearly that if it is a choice between employment and income, employment should be given preference; and a good deal of experimentation and research has been conducted in India with small-scale, labor-intensive activities. The point is that these proved to be too expensive in terms of capital—as stated above; the products and technologies with the low capital-labor ratios turned out to have high capital-output ratios. Moreover, the statement ignores both the difference between the choice of technology and the choice of product-mix, and the difference between launching industrialization in 1888 and launching it in 1949. It seems likely that the change in the product-mix had more to do with the drop in capital-labor ratios in Japan than any ingenious and insistent use of labor-using, capital-saving innovations. Industrialization on the basis of toys and silk scarves is not a process that other countries can follow, launching their industrialization today.[5] For some countries, comparative advantage forces them into industries where the most efficient technology —efficient even in terms of capital-output ratios—is one that is highly capital-intensive.

In any case, the figures themselves are suspect. The authors have elected to use a depreciation rate of 20 per cent in calculating the rate of capital accumulation in Japan. For the kind of industrialization that was taking place, and for the rate at which new plants and equipment were being built up, this rate of depreciation is surely too high. Obviously, selection of a lower depreciation rate would assign a greater role to capital accumulation in the explanation of Japan's growth, and a smaller one to innovations. Moreover, the estimate of the stock of capital excluded land. Even with a realistic "shadow price" for improved rice land (which could be rather high) the capital-labor ratio for the economy as a whole no doubt rose in Japan during the first phase of industrialization. The impression left by Fei and Ranis that growth can be achieved with relatively little capital accumulation, provided only that decision-makers are diligent in introducing innovations of a labor-saving nature, is quite misleading. Of course, there is no reason to suppose that the "residual factor" was not high in Japan as elsewhere; but the "residual factor" does not operate by itself; it needs capital accumulation and resource discovery to make it operate. There are still no primrose paths to prosperity.

In any case, the model does not lend to fundamentally new prescriptions for policy. Government action to create the preconditions of growth, to

[5] The Japanese "success story" is outlined in Part VI, Case Studies.

provide the necessary social overhead facilities and infant-industry protection, to give the economy the necessary psychological impetus and thus supplement the contribution of the dualistic landlords, these policy conclusions would be obtained without the authors' very laborious analysis.

General Appraisal

These flaws do not completely destroy the Fei-Ranis model. It contains elements of fundamental truth, and with modifications can still cast light on the problem of underdevelopment. The rate of structural change (relative growth of industrial as compared to agricultural employment) is indeed a fundamental aspect of the development process. The rate of such structural change is surely limited by the degree of success in raising agricultural output. The rate of capital accumulation in the modern (and traditional) sector, the pace and nature of technological progress, and the speed with which the marginal productivity of labor falls with increased industrial employment are obviously important factors in the outcome. But the whole process of launching and sustaining economic development in countries with a large volume of low-productivity employment in a traditional agricultural sector is a good deal more complex than the Fei-Ranis analysis would suggest.

Does Disguised Unemployment Exist?

The extent to which "disguised unemployment" exists in underdeveloped countries, and the degree to which it offers a source of "free" increases in our gross national product, is one of the major questions that recur in the literature on development of underdeveloped countries. At the beginning of his thoughtful book, Dr. Yong Sam Cho states that his objectives are "to examine the most respected concepts in theories on surplus labor in underdeveloped agricultural economies, particularly in the literature on 'disguised unemployment' and to point out their flaws." [6] He also endeavors to measure surplus labor in rural Korea.

Dr. Cho notes the vagueness and ambiguities in current concepts of disguised unemployment: the amount of capital stock available is "more or less" fixed; population growth reduces the marginal productivity of employed labor "to zero or to near zero (or even to a negative value)." His own basic definition, however, is also subject to ambiguities. "In my analysis," he says, "such limited changes (as reshuffling of workers, replacing one person with another, etc.) are purposely assumed to be compatible with the *ceteris paribus* assumption. However, the following changes are considered to be incompatible with the assumption: a decrease in total farm output; an increase in capital (monetary or real); the introduction of new technologies, including the adoption of improved seeds or new crops; the diversification of agriculture to compensate for its seasonal nature; and the consolidation of scattered and fragmented land hold-

[6] Yong Sam Cho, *Disguised Unemployment in Underdeveloped Areas, With Special Reference to South Korean Agriculture* (Berkeley, 1963).

ings. A change in social institutions is, of course, not compatible with the *ceteris paribus* assumption." With these restrictions, it is a little hard to envisage what the "limited changes" compatible with the *ceteris paribus* assumption may be.

Dr. Cho reminds us that the term "disguised unemployment" was first applied by Joan Robinson to those workers in advanced countries during the Great Depression who were driven into such occupations as selling matchboxes in the Strand, where their productivity was much lower than in the occupations they had left. Dr. Cho complains that Mrs. Robinson's definition is unusable because the distinction between regular and inferior occupations is not clear-cut. This observation is no doubt correct for underdeveloped countries, but within Mrs. Robinson's context the distinction between "inferior" and "regular" occupation was not so difficult.

Dr. Cho points out early in the book that the problem of manpower utilization in underdeveloped agricultural countries is not cyclical or chronic unemployment, but underemployment reflected in the willingness of agricultural workers, who do not have regular employment during the whole year, to work at existing wage rates. This so-called structural underemployment, he says correctly, "is no more than open (and visible) unemployment which arises from seasonal variations of agricultural operation." "The position taken by Alfredo and Ifigenia de Navarrete on this point," he says, "is no different from saying that disguised underemployment in underdeveloped agricultural countries is the same as open unemployment in economically advanced countries. To claim that hidden (or disguised) unemployment *are* identical is absurd." [7]

Nurkse's definition of disguised unemployment is clear enough: the agricultural population that can be removed from the land with unchanged agricultural techniques and without reducing agricultural output. Nurkse believed that "a large part of the population engaged in agriculture" fell into this category. Such is not the case: as Cho rightly points out, "Almost every point in Nurkse's analysis fails to be congruent with the facts." Very few countries indeed have surplus agricultural population in this sense.

Rosenstein-Rodan avoids this particular trap, defining disguised underemployment as the amount of idle work force, in terms of man-equivalent hours, that exists at the peak of the agricultural operation. Rosenstein-Rodan's "removable disguised underemployment" consists of workers who are employed less than fifty-one days per year (or less than two calendar months). [8] "Fractional disguised underemployment" consists of people who are partially employed for more than fifty-one days during the year. The latter, says Rosenstein-Rodan, are not removable. Thus Rosenstein-Rodan's underemployed are not "disguised" but are visible, chronic idle labor. Cho also maintains that even the fractional disguised

[7] Alfredo and Ifigenia de Navarrete, "Underemployment in Underdeveloped Economies," in A. N. Agarwala and S. P. Singh (Eds.), *The Economics of Underdevelopment* (Bombay, 1958), pp. 342–43.

[8] P. N. Rosenstein-Rodan, "Disguised Unemployment and Underemployment in Agriculture," *Monthly Bulletin of Agricultural Economics and Statistics*, VI (July-August, 1957).

underemployment could be utilized for economic development projects in and near the villages; in this sense these are also removable.

Dr. Harvey Leibenstein has still another concept of disguised unemployment: with additional resources or means of creating additional employment opportunities of the right kind, more effort could be obtained from the existing labor force. This type of unemployment is due to the seasonal nature of the production process in agriculture. Thus, says Liebenstein, agricultural labor suffers from disguised unemployment in the same sense that taxi drivers do. Leibenstein might have added "directors of companies," who may work only a few hours a week, and would be capable of putting in more hours if need be, although their incomes are very high. Cho rejects this concept too as essentially useless and misleading.[9]

For some obscure reason, Dr. Cho also rejects the effort of K. N. Raj to associate disguised unemployment with the social organization.[10] According to Cho, this attempt "adds further confusion," overlooking the fact that visible idle labor resulting from technical and institutional conditions exists in various types of social organizations. Yet Cho himself regards the "tradition-directed society" as a major part of the explanation of the existence of disguised underemployment. Certainly, there can be no doubt that work-spreading devices do exist in village societies where there is a redundance of labor.

Disguised Unemployment or Low-Productivity Employment?

Having shown the welter of confusion surrounding the concept of disguised unemployment, Dr. Cho might well have concluded, as does the report of the ILO Expert Group on *Employment Objectives in Economic Development*, that the whole concept was a nuisance and better eradicated from the literature altogether. As K. N. Raj pointed out during the discussions of the ILO Expert Group, all concepts of disguised unemployment really reduce to "employed unemployed." The nature of the problem is made much clearer if so-called disguised unemployment is referred to simply as low-productivity employment.

The Cho Model

Although Dr. Cho's concept and measure of disguised unemployment are not free from the shortcomings inherent in the concept itself, his analysis makes a fundamental contribution to the understanding of underdevelopment. The basic idea is that the number of hours of work provided by individual workers is a function of the level of wages. His analysis relates to societies where agricultural incomes are so low that only an increase in agricultural wage rates will permit the increase in caloric intake necessary for a man to work additional hours. Cho maintains that in such countries we may even have "disguised employment," in the sense that the caloric intake is too low for the number of hours work put forth,

[9] Harvey Leibenstein, *Economic Backwardness and Economic Growth: Studies in the Theory of Economic Development* (New York, 1960), pp. 62–66.

[10] K. N. Raj, *Employment Aspects of Planning in Underdeveloped Economies* (Cairo, 1957), pp. 4–5.

resulting in malnutrition and excessive fatigue. It is clear, therefore, that the whole analysis applies only to the poorer countries of Asia, Africa, and Latin America; many countries commonly regarded as underdeveloped would not be included.

Cho introduces the concept of a "marginal individual" who is "poised in uncertainty between two or more apparently different social worlds." These are people on the farms wondering if they should go to the city, and people who have gone to the city wondering if they should go back to the village. The economically marginal individuals are those who are tempted by a higher level of living in another occupation. To be considered withdrawable surplus labor, Cho insists, individuals must be marginal in both the economic and the social sense.

Cho next defines a "technical wage" as the minimum wage needed to sustain an employed worker, in a biological sense. In Cho's analysis the supply of labor is divided into the number of hours per worker, dependent on the wage level, and on the number of workers.

Another fundamental feature of Cho's model is that the position and shape of the marginal productivity curve of labor is also a function of the wage rate. His marginal productivity curves refer only to the number of workers. With a higher wage rate, each man works more hours. Therefore the marginal productivity curve starts higher, but falls more rapidly, the higher the wage rate. In Cho's own words, "This higher marginal productivity declines more rapidly because, given a total output to be produced, the aggregate number of workers required to accomplish the task decreases as the wage rate rises (or increases as the wage rate falls)." [11] The restriction of "a total output to be produced" may seem an excessive one, although it is a part of the Cho analysis that a given output must be produced to provide the biologically minimum wage for the number of hours of work expended, plus a margin for necessary saving. The analysis could be made more general, however, if instead of fixing total output, he simply fixed the total land supply. In a good many Asian societies, the assumption that the supply of land is fixed is realistic enough.

In a "capitalistic" system, the entrepreneur will choose a wage level that will maximize the ratio of the number of hours of work offered to the wage bill, thus maximizing output per unit of wage paid, or minimizing wages per hour. Under those conditions there can be only open unemployment representing the difference between the number of workers willing to work at that wage, for the number of hours that are biologically possible at that wage, and the number of workers the employer wishes to engage.

In a traditional society, however, a system of work-sharing is in effect, so that all workers are absorbed. Limitations are imposed on the level of total output-and-consumption by the necessity of providing savings (in the form of seed, for example) for next year's cultivation. The argument here seems to be that an increase in output requires an increase in consumption, and at some point the increase in consumption needed for additional hours of work for each member of the labor force exceeds the increase in output

[11] Cho, *op. cit.*, p. 41.

obtained by the increase in hours. We are confronted here with a question of fact. It is doubtful whether, even in so densely populated an area as Java, for example, caloric intake ever rises faster than output, as the number of hours of work per day increases, within the range of positive marginal productivity for numbers of workers. It may be a more accurate description of what takes place to say that the marginal productivity of labor really does fall to zero, in the sense that more workers added to the fixed amount of land can bring no increase in total output, except of course during the planting and harvesting seasons. (Seasonal underemployment is common to agriculture everywhere—including large-scale wheat farming in Canada or sheep grazing in Australia.)

Dr. Cho's argument, in any case, is that in traditional societies the wage level is set so that the supply of labor hours is restricted to a point where the marginal productivity of labor is still positive, with all members of the labor force employed. In this equilibrium position there is surplus labor (and zero marginal productivity) only in the sense that the numbers of workers could be reduced and their hours increased by raising the wage rate (leaving the wages bill unchanged) if the social system did not require work-sharing among all members of the labor force. But this surplus is effective, and thus true disguised underemployment exists only if some of the workers are "marginal" in both the economic and social sense.

Cho's fundamental diagram is reproduced in Figure 14–6. On the horizontal axis the number of hours worked per day (or week) by each

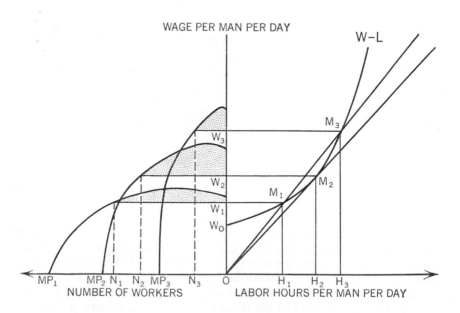

Figure 14–6. Wage-productivity relationship of wage labor.

man is measured to the right of the origin, and the number of workers engaged is measured to the left of the origin. On the vertical axis is measured the daily (or weekly) wage per man. The slope of the straight lines through the origin measures the wage per hour—wages per man-day divided by hours worked per man-day. At point H_2, for example, the number of hours worked per man is OH_2, the wage per man is H_2M_2 and the hourly wage is H_2M_2/OH_2. The W-L curve shows the relationship between the number of hours worked by each man and the wage rate per man-day (week). As the wage per day (week) rises from OW_0 to OW_1 to OW_2 the hours worked per day (week) rises from zero to OH_1 to OH_2, etc.

In the left-hand portion of the diagram is shown the marginal productivity of additional workers (with fixed land and capital) at different levels of wages per man-day (week). At the low wage OW_1 the marginal productivity starts low and falls slowly, as shown by curve MP_1. The reason is that each man can work only a few hours per day (or week) at that low wage, and adding more men adds little more output but also little more in the way of effective labor to be combined with the fixed stock of land and capital. At the higher wage per day (week) OW_2, the marginal productivity starts higher but falls more rapidly, because each man adds a larger number of man-hours, as shown by MP_2. With a still higher wage rate OW_3, the marginal productivity curve is MP_3.

Under "capitalistic" conditions employers will seek to maximize profits, which requires minimizing the ratio of wages per man-hour to output per man-hour. This equilibrium position will be achieved with a wage per day (week) of OW_2, and a work day (week) of OH_2 hours and employment of ON_2 workers. In this position the straight line through the origin, showing wages per hour, is just tangent to the W-L curve showing hours per man. It therefore represents the lowest possible *hourly* wage, expressed in terms of wage per man-day (or man-week). The level of employment will be ON_2 even if the number of workers is larger. If, for example, the labor force is ON_1, unemployment will be N_1N_2 and the presence of unemployment cannot reduce the wage rate. Profits are shown by the shaded areas in the left-hand portion of the diagram and are maximized at the wage W_2.

In the tradition-directed society, on the other hand, the institution of work-sharing and income-sharing prevails, and wholly unemployed *persons* are not permitted. The solution is to lower the daily (weekly) wage rate to W_1, which reduces the hours worked per day (week) to OH_1 but shifts the marginal productivity curve to MP_1 and permits a level of employment ON_1. Output and income of those employed is reduced, and the phenomenon of low-productivity employment appears. Profits will be lower. It cannot be said from the diagram alone whether or not total output will be less; it depends on the production functions. If we liked, we might define N_1N_2 as the volume of disguised unemployment, equal to the amount of open unemployment that would appear in a "capitalistic," profit-maximizing society. Dr. Cho does not choose to do so, because we do not yet know whether or not N_1N_2 workers are actually "marginal" and transferable.

In his conclusions, Dr. Cho states his position as follows: "Marginal men are those who are most susceptible to making new adjustments in situations of change, owing to their marginal economic and social situations. Therefore, only the idle labor of marginal men may be considered as true surplus labor which can be removed from the land without creating problems. Self-supporting family workers are not socially marginal individuals because they are steeped in tradition and, by and large, prefer the security, the personal dignity, and the lack of imposed pressures which accompany land ownership and self employment." [12] Dr. Cho reiterates that if there is chronic open unemployment, in the sense of excess labor over and above the peak requirements, it can be withdrawn without difficulty; but if there is only seasonal unemployment, then permanent removal of the unemployed is impossible. Thus in estimating the numbers of workers who can be removed, seasonal unemployment must be sharply differentiated from chronic unemployment. "In the tradition-directed society, in which open unemployment is not acceptable, underemployment is characteristic, and the system of earnings is based on the practice of sharing. We have deduced in our model that the openly unemployed under the hypothetical capitalistic society would be true surplus labor (of the technical type), but that current underemployment under the traditional social arrangement is not true surplus labor (of the technical type)." Finally, "Technical underemployment is true (or removable) surplus labor when it is chronic, but tradition-directed underemployment is not true surplus labor even when it is chronic under the *ceteris-paribus* assumption." [13]

Underemployment in Korea

Having cleared away the concept and analysis of disguised underemployment, Dr. Cho proceeds to measure the amount of surplus labor in the South Korean economy. This measurement first requires a statement of statistical sources and concepts. Active population, for example, is defined as those persons between fifteen and fifty-nine years of age. The estimated work year is 280 days for men and 268 for women. Cho has some difficulty in deciding what is a normal work day, but ends by accepting "the rigid Western standard of eight hours a day." The labor force participation rates are similarly estimated, and also the amount of labor available. Dr. Cho assumes a labor participation rate of 1.0 for all male farm workers in the fifteen to fifty-nine age range and 0.6 for female workers in the same age range.

On this basis he reaches the following conclusions: First, there is much seasonal variation in employment in Korean agriculture; second, there are shortages of family labor in the peak agricultural seasons—there is no chronic underemployment, only seasonal underemployment; third, self-supporting family workers suffer relatively more underemployment than

[12] *Ibid.*, p. 141.
[13] *Ibid.*, pp. 49–50.

attached wage workers. About 32 per cent of the total labor time available annually is unutilized, but disguised unemployment in the sense of chronic idle labor does not exist. Approximately 62 per cent of the unutilized labor (or about 19 per cent of the total labor available) represents tradition-directed underemployment. Technical underemployment is approximately 12 per cent of the total labor available, or 38 per cent of total unutilized labor.

Cho rejects Nurkse's scheme for transferring surplus labor to the industrial sector as inapplicable in the Korean context. "It is impossible to withdraw any labor permanently if, as in Korea, there could be an actual seasonal shortage of labor. Only if the labor shortage during peak seasons were eliminated would there be any chronic underemployment that could be permanently withdrawn." He suggests that this objective might be achieved by providing more and better food during these peak months, so that farm workers could work longer hours during these peak seasons. He also recommends that subsidies to promote agricultural production should be allocated to a fund for community capital improvement projects, rather than being given to individual farm households. He further recommends that some of the rent paid to absentee landlords should be retained for rural capital projects. He prefers a land property tax to an income tax on incentive grounds. He believes that this development program "would not only put to work unutilized labor in much-needed rural capital improvement projects, but could also pave the way to the gradual dissolution of those traditions and institutions that contribute so heavily to the economic stagnation of a typical underdeveloped world community."

The proposal for using surplus labor in the off-season for development work projects in the neighborhood of the same villages is, of course, not new; as far as it goes is beyond reproach. The really important conclusion, however, is that disguised unemployment or underemployment in rural areas does not provide the basis for an "up by the bootstraps" approach to economic development. Releasing any significant number of workers permanently from rural areas will require capital investment in the agricultural sector, to raise productivity and permit (in Cho's model) longer hours to replace larger numbers, while at the same time investment is made in the industrial sector to provide alternative job opportunities. Thus, we are led once again to the "big push" as the sole recipe for launching sustained economic growth.

The Agricultural Lag

All this is not to say that increases in agricultural productivity are unimportant in the development process. On the contrary, increasing concern is being expressed among development economists regarding the "agricultural lag." This lag is particularly striking in Latin America. Agricultural productivity is low in all developing countries, almost by definition; but in some countries the low output per man-year reflects overcrowding on the land, a phenomenon which is still relatively rare in Latin America. In Latin America more than any developing region, perhaps, the gap between actual and potential agricultural productivity, with existing population densities in agriculture, seems needlessly large. Moving large numbers of people from rural to urban occupations requires an increase in the supply of foodstuffs and agricultural raw materials to the industrial, urban sector. If these increased requirements for food and agricultural raw materials are not met by increased domestic production, they must be met by imports, increasing the burden on the industrial sector. Any country that ignores agricultural improvement in the course of economic development does so at its peril, as one socialist country after another has learned. In short, industrialization and agricultural improvement are not alternative roads to economic development, but are completely complementary.

15 | Balanced versus Unbalanced Growth

The last few years have brought a concentrated attack on "gradualism" and "incrementalism" as an approach to economic development policy. Any such approach is foredoomed to failure, the argument goes: by its very nature, the development process is a series of discontinuous "jumps." The functional relationships among the causal factors in economic growth are full of "lumps" and "discontinuities"; hence a minimum effort or "big push" is needed to overcome the original inertia of the stagnant economy and start it moving toward higher levels of productivity and income. To explain this basic concept, economists often resort to analogy. Leaning on a stalled car with gradually increasing weight will not get it started, for it needs a big push.

Essentially, all the arguments in support of the "big push" are related to the old idea of "external economies": benefits which accrue to the society as a whole, or to some members of it, in a fashion that does not bring a direct return to the investor concerned.[1] The basic concept is thus an old one. What is new is the importance attached to it in theories of development.

[1] This somewhat loose and general definition of external economies has been chosen deliberately over the more rigorous definitions available in the literature. For economic development the important consideration is that certain investments are clearly "profitable" for the society as a whole, but are unprofitable to the individual private investor because the institutional framework does not permit him to charge a price for the by-product benefits his investment brings. It has not seemed worthwhile to digress here on the history of ideas about external economies or to try to unravel the contemporary discussion of the concept.

Rosenstein-Rodan and the Three Indivisibilities

One of the earliest and most often cited statements of the importance of discontinuities, or external economies, in economic development was Paul N. Rosenstein-Rodan's article published in 1943.[2] In this early statement, Rosenstein-Rodan stressed the limitations imposed by the size of the market. More recently, he has restated his argument in terms of "three indivisibilities." [3] The stress upon external economies, Rosenstein-Rodan argues, is a major mark of the difference between static theory and a theory of growth. In static theory, external economies are relatively unimportant. But in a theory of development,

. . . external economies abound because given the inherent imperfection of the investment market, imperfect knowledge and risks, pecuniary and technological external economies have a similarly disturbing effect on the path towards equilibrium. While the distinction between pecuniary and technological external economies becomes practically irrelevant in the theory of growth, three different kinds of indivisibilities and external economies may be distinguished.
   1) Indivisibilities in the production function especially the indivisibility of supply of Social Overhead Capital (lumpiness of "capital").
   2) "Indivisibility" of Demand (complementarity of demand).
   3) "Indivisibility" (kink in the) "Supply of Savings."
[Because of these indivisibilities] Proceeding "bit by bit" will not add up in its effects to the sum total of the single bits. A minimum quantum of investment is a necessary (though not sufficient) condition of success. This is in a nutshell the contention of the theory of the big push.

Thus in contradiction to traditional static equilibrium theory, development theory maintains that nature does make jumps (*natura facit saltus*). Why the difference? Because development theory is more realistic in taking account of indivisibilities and "non-appropriabilities" in the production functions, because a growth theory must examine the *path* to equilibrium and not just the equilibrium conditions, and because in underdeveloped countries, markets—especially investment markets—are more imperfect than in developed countries.

Indivisibilities in the Production Function (Lumpiness of Capital)

Social overhead capital (power, transport, communications, housing, etc.) is the most important instance of indivisibility and external economies on the supply side. Its most important products "are investment opportunities created in other industries." Moreover, they usually require "a great minimum size," so that "excess capacity will be unavoidable over the initial period in underdeveloped countries." Social overhead capital is irreversible in time. It must precede other directly productive investment.

[2] P. N. Rosenstein-Rodan, "Industrialization of Eastern and Southeastern Europe," *The Economic Journal*, 1943.
[3] P. N. Rosenstein-Rodan, *Notes on the Theory of the "Big Push,"* M.I.T., CIS, March, 1957.

Its services cannot be imported. Investments in the "infrastructure"—to use another common term for social overhead capital—have a high minimum durability, a long gestation period, and a minimal "industry mix" of several different kinds of public utilities.

Indivisibility of Demand

The indivisibility of demand was stressed in Rosenstein-Rodan's original article and later given wider publicity by Professor Ragnar Nurkse.[4] The basic idea is that investment decisions are interdependent, and individual investment projects have high risk because of uncertainty as to whether their product will find a market. Rosenstein-Rodan uses an example which has by now become famous:

Let us restate our old example, at first for a closed economy. If a hundred workers who were in disguised employment (i.e., with marginal productivity of their labor equal to zero) in an underdeveloped country were put into a shoe factory, their wages would constitute additional income. If the newly employed workers spent all of their additional income on shoes they produce, the shoe factory would find a market and would succeed. In fact, however, they would not spend all of their additional income on shoes; there is no "easy" solution of creating in this way an additional market. The risk of not finding a market reduces the incentive to invest—the shoe factory investment project will probably be abandoned. Let us vary the example: instead of a hundred (unemployed) workers in one shoe factory, let us put ten thousand workers in say one hundred factories (and farms) who between them will produce the bulk of such (wage) goods on which the newly employed workers will spend their wages. What was not true in the case of one single shoe factory will become true for the complementary system of one hundred factories (and farms). The new producers would be each others' customers and would verify Say's Law by creating an additional market. The complementarity of demand would reduce the risk of not finding a market. Reducing such interdependent risks increases naturally the incentive to invest.

Rosenstein-Rodan also points out that a minimum quantum of investment is needed to produce a "bundle" of wage goods on which additionally employed workers can spend their income. In general, unless there is assurance that the necessary complementary investments will occur, any single investment project may be considered too risky to be undertaken at all. There is, in other words, an indivisibility in the *decision-making* process. The present writer would be inclined to stress this indivisibility, perhaps more than Rosenstein-Rodan does. Allocation of capital on the basis of individual estimates of short-run returns on various marginal investment projects is the very process by which underdeveloped countries got where they are. The basic reason for government action to promote development is that each of a set of individual private investment decisions may seem unattractive in itself, whereas a large-scale investment program undertaken as a unit may yield substantial increases in national income.

[4] Ragnar Nurske, *Problems of Capital Formation in Underdeveloped Countries* (Oxford, 1953).

True, the government may be able to arrange for this lump-sum investment to be made by groups of private entrepreneurs; whether it should be done this way or through public investment is a matter of administrative convenience, not of economics. But the needed investment is unlikely to take place without government intervention in the decision-making process.

Rosenstein-Rodan makes a related point in referring to the "psychological indivisibilities" involved in development. "Isolated and small efforts may not add up to a sufficient impact on growth," he maintains, and "an atmosphere of development effervescence may also arise only with a minimum speed or size of investment."

Finally, Rosenstein-Rodan agrees with the writers discussed in Chapter 13 that international trade is not always a means of avoiding the necessity of a "big push." International trade may reduce the range of fields in which the big push is required; some of the needed wage goods, for example, can be imported. But the history of the nineteenth century is evidence enough that trade does not eliminate the need altogether.

The Low-level Equilibrium Trap

A similar theory has been developed by Richard R. Nelson. Since Nelson's version of the theory is presented in an article, it is already highly compressed and hence difficult to summarize. Readers who find this summary too sketchy to be persuasive should turn to the original article.[5]

Nelson uses an essentially simple model with three equations. First, there is an income determination equation. This is fundamentally the same as the "production function" which kept recurring in the various models in Part II: income depends on the stock of capital, the size of the population, and the level of technique. (The labor force is assumed to bear a constant relationship to the size of the population.) Second, net investment consists of savings-created capital plus additions to the amount of land under cultivation. The savings-created portion is roughly the same as investment in the industrial sector; it represents additions to stock of tools and equipment. No such investment will take place until income rises above the subsistence level, after which it rises with per capita income. The amount of new land brought under cultivation tends to increase with the population, but cultivating fresh areas becomes more difficult as good land becomes scarce. There is a "floor" to disinvestment; "one cannot eat torn-up railroad track no matter how hungry one gets." Finally, there is a population growth equation:

In areas with low per capita incomes short-run changes in the rate of population growth are caused by changes in the death rate, and changes in the death rate are caused by changes in the level of per capita income. Yet once per capita income reaches a level well above subsistence requirements, further in-

[5] R. R. Nelson, "A Theory of the Low-Level Equilibrium Trap," *American Economic Review*, December, 1956, pp. 894–908.

creases in per capita income have a negligible effect on the death rate. The result is a curve of population growth similar in shape to the dP/P curves [in Figure 15-1. The sharp break] is artificial but simplifies exposition . . . A shift in income distribution towards greater equality (or improved medical technique) shifts the function to the left along the Y/P axis.

With these three sets of relationships it is easy to see that an economy may be "trapped" at a low level of income, as illustrated in Figure 15–1.

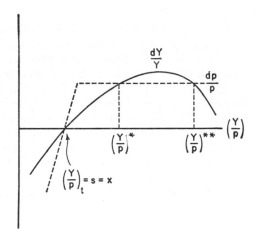

Figure 15–1

It is necessary only for the rate of increase in population, dP/P, to exceed the rate of increase in income, dY/Y, at a level of national income close to subsistence. For the intersection of the dY/Y and dP/P curves at a level of per capita income, Y/P, equal to S provides a stable equilibrium at that level. Any tendency for income to rise leads to a more rapid increase in population, forcing the economy back to S.

The conditions "conducive to trapping," Nelson points out, are (1) a high correlation between the level of per capita income and the rate of population growth; (2) a low propensity to direct additional per capita income to increasing per capita investment; (3) scarcity of uncultivated arable land; and (4) inefficient production methods. Clearly, in a good many underdeveloped countries, these conditions have been met in the past.

Getting out of the trap requires increasing the rate of growth of income to levels higher than the rate of increase in population. The surest way to do this—returning to Leibenstein—is to promote rates of growth of national income in excess of 3 per cent per year. If a jump can be made to the point, Y/P^*, sustained growth will take place, without further government action, until the high level, Y/P^{**}, is reached.

Balanced Growth

In presenting his version of the minimum effort thesis, Ragnar Nurkse advocates "a frontal attack . . . a wave of capital investments in a number of different industries," which he calls "balanced growth." [6] Hans Singer and Albert Hirschman have criticized Nurkse's formulation; they insist that what is needed is not balanced growth but a strategy of judiciously unbalanced growth.

The Nurkse Thesis

Nurkse's basic argument resembles Rosenstein-Rodan's; indeed he cites Rodan's famous example of the shoe factory to support his case. Low real income, Nurkse says, "is a reflection of low productivity, which in turn is due largely to lack of capital. The lack of capital is a result of the small capacity to save, and so the circle is complete." The inducement to invest, in turn, is limited by the size of the market—a "modern variant" of Adam Smith's dictum that "the division of labour is limited by the extent of the market." But a crucial determinant of the size of the market is productivity; capacity to buy means capacity to produce. And productivity "depends largely, though by no means entirely, on the degree to which capital is used in production. . . . But, for any individual entrepreneur, the use of capital is inhibited, to start with, by the small size of the market." Another vicious circle.

How to escape? We cannot count on individual investment decisions to do the trick. "Even though in economically backward areas Say's Law may be valid in the sense that there is no deflationary gap, it never is valid in the sense that the output of any single industry, newly set up with capital equipment, can create its own demand." Technical discontinuities call for "jumps" in the rate of output, but "the small and inelastic demand in a low-income country tends to make such jumps risky, if not altogether unpromising."

Thus the only way out of the dilemma is "more or less synchronized application of capital to a wide range of different industries. Here is an escape from the deadlock; here the result is an over-all enlargement of the market. . . . Most industries catering for mass consumption are complementary in the sense that they provide a market for, and thus support, each other. . . . The case for 'balanced growth' rests on the need for a 'balanced diet.' "

This is the essence of Nurkse's argument. Two subsidiary points might be noted in passing. First, Nurkse contends (correctly, in the opinion of the present writer) that the choice between public and private enterprise for achieving the required bundle of investment is mainly a matter of administrative expediency. Second, Nurkse joins the growing list of "development economists" who deny that international trade provides an automatic escape from the limitations of the domestic market: "To push exports of primary commodities in the face of an inelastic and more or

[6] Nurkse, *op. cit.*, chap. I; see also, p. 5.

less stationary demand would not be a promising line of long-run development." He makes a case for building up import-replacing industries behind a tariff wall and points out that the *ultimate* result need not be a reduction in imports—even of goods first receiving protection. He cites Canada for illustration: there "textile manufacturing was one of the first industries to develop, with the aid of tariff protection from 1879 on; yet Canada to-day is one of the world's biggest importers of textile manufactures." [7]

The Singer Critique

Hans Singer has expressed grave doubts about the applicability of this thesis. To understand the problem of balanced growth, Singer asserts, "we have to construct some kind of fundamental structural picture—model if you like—of an underdeveloped country." [8] He defines an underdeveloped country as one with 70 to 90 per cent of the employed population in agriculture, and adds, "Arthur Lewis has defined the process of economic growth as one of transforming a country from a 5 percent saver to a 15 percent saver. We can, with equal justice, define the process as one of transforming a country from an 80 percent farmer to 15 percent farmer." The high proportion of population in farming is another of the vicious circles: it reflects low productivity. "The low level of productivity in farming decrees that the bulk of the people must be in farming in order to feed and clothe themselves, and that they have little to spare over and above their own needs." By writ of Engel's law, a high percentage of low incomes is spent on food and essential clothing, and the demand for other things is "limited to a very small percentage of a very small income." There is thus only a tiny market for these other things and investment in producing them is not attractive. Underdeveloped countries are also, as a rule, net exporters of agricultural goods and net importers of other products.

To make matters worse, productivity in agriculture is significantly lower than productivity in the small industrial sector. "In fact for a surprising number of countries figures come remarkably close to a constant relation of the form, $A = 2/3\ N$, where 'A' is output per employed person in agriculture and 'N' is output per employed person in the economy as a whole." From this fact follows an arithmetic law "of considerable political and emotional significance: if an 80 percent farmer economy produces only two thirds of its national per capita average in the agricultural sector, the differential between the agricultural sector and the non-agricultural sector will be much larger than will be the case in a 15 percent farmer economy (i.e., a typical advanced economy) which also produces two thirds of its

[7] *Ibid.*, pp. 10, 11, 22. In putting his argument in this unqualified manner, Nurkse opens himself to Haberler's criticisms of the arguments regarding deteriorating terms of trade. Not *all* primary products face an inelastic demand; there is good reason to believe that the demand for natural rubber or petroleum would prove highly elastic in face of significant price reductions. There is still less reason to believe that demand for such products remains "more or less stationary" in an expanding world market.

[8] Hans Singer, "The Concept of Balanced Growth and Economic Development: Theory and Facts," University of Texas Conference on Economic Development, April, 1958, pp. 4, 6.

national average in the agricultural sector. In fact, in the underdeveloped country output per worker outside agriculture compared with agricultural output per worker would be in the ratio of 3:1." Thus a transformation from mainly agriculture to mainly non-agriculture is not only an essential part of the development process, but this structural change also has a "multiplier effect." "As the levels of productivity and of real demand and markets rise, the structural change from an 80 percent farmer economy towards a 15 percent farmer economy, made possible by this rise, will in its turn generate forces which will themselves tend to raise productivity and real incomes." This hen-and-egg riddle, Singer maintains, is "the starting point of the doctrine of balanced growth." The doctrine might be expressed by paraphrasing a metaphor coined in a different context: "100 flowers may grow where a single flower would wither away for lack of nourishment."

Singer agrees that the slogan, "stop thinking piecemeal and start thinking big" is sound advice for underdeveloped countries, but he also feels that there are "several areas of doubt" about the balanced growth theory in its Rodan-Nurkse form. First, if that is interpreted to counsel underdeveloped countries to embark on large and varied packages of *industrial* investment, with no attention to agricultural productivity, it can lead to trouble. Engel's law "certainly does *not* say that the demand for food does not increase at all" when incomes rise, especially when incomes rise from the low levels existing in underdeveloped countries. The big push in industry may have to be accompanied by a big push in agriculture as well, if the country is not to run short of foodstuffs and agricultural raw materials during the transition to an industrialized society that could perhaps obtain these goods in exchange for industrial exports. Once this fact is admitted, the balanced growth doctrine sounds more like the orthodox theory that "structural change must rest on a foundation of raising productivity within the existing structure . . . until real incomes have risen to a level which justifies structural change."

But when we start talking about varied investment packages for industry and "major additional blocks of investment in agriculture" at the same time, we run into serious doubts about the capacity of underdeveloped countries to follow the balanced growth path. Singer quotes Marcus Fleming: "whereas the balanced growth doctrine assumes that the relationship between industries is for the most part complementary, the limitation of factor supply assures that the relationship is for the most part competitive." [9] Singer adds: "the resources required for carrying out the policy of balanced growth . . . are of such an order of magnitude that a country disposing of such resources would in fact not be underdeveloped." The doctrine is premature rather than wrong, Singer concludes; it is applicable to a subsequent stage of sustained growth rather than to the breaking of a deadlock. For *launching* growth "it may well be better development strategy to concentrate available resources on types of investment which help to make the economic system more elastic, more capable

[9] Marcus Fleming, "External Economies and the Doctrine of Balanced Growth," *The Economic Journal*, June, 1958.

of expansion under the stimulus of expanded markets and expanding demand." [10] He instances investment in social overhead capital and removal of specific bottlenecks as examples of such "strategic" investments.

The fundamental trouble with the balanced growth doctrine, Singer concludes, is its failure to come to grips with the true problem of underdeveloped countries, the shortage of resources. "Think Big" is sound advice to underdeveloped countries but "Act Big," is unwise counsel if it spurs them to effort to do more than their resources permit.

One final point of Singer's will serve as a bridge to our next section. The balanced growth doctrine, he says, assumes that an underdeveloped country starts from scratch. In reality, every underdeveloped country starts from a position that reflects previous investment decisions and previous development. Thus at any point of time there are highly desirable investment programs which are not in themselves balanced investment packages, but which represent unbalanced investment to complement existing imbalance. And once such an investment is made, a new imbalance is likely to appear which will require still another "balancing" investment, and so on. Is this not a perfectly good way to develop?

Hirschman's Strategy of Unbalance

Albert Hirschman, at any rate, thinks that it is. He carries Singer's idea further, and contends that *deliberate unbalancing* of the economy, in accordance with a predesigned strategy, is the *best* way to achieve economic growth.[11]

On many points, Hirschman agrees with both Nurkse and Singer. He does not deny the need for a big push. On the contrary, he argues that "ability to invest" is the one serious bottleneck in underdeveloped countries; he readily agrees that ability to invest depends mainly on how much investment has already been made. "The ability to invest," he says, "is acquired and increased primarily by practice; and the amount of practice depends in fact on the size of the modern sector of the economy. In other words, an economy secretes abilities, skills, and attitudes needed for further development roughly in proportion to the size of the sector where these attitudes are being inculcated." He stresses the "complementarity" among investments no less than Nurkse, maintaining that it is of much greater importance in underdeveloped than in advanced countries. He also agrees that analysis based on static assumptions can be very misleading when applied to underdeveloped countries. Thus he says of Aubrey's argument, that industrialization should take the form of small industries in small towns in order to economize on overhead capital outlays,[12]

This position is of course entirely valid on the assumption that the supply of capital is fixed. But if we drop this assumption and let ourselves be guided by

[10] Singer, *op. cit.*, p. 10.
[11] Albert Hirschman, *The Strategy of Economic Development* (New Haven, 1958), p. 36.
[12] H. Aubrey, "Small Industry in Economic Development," *Social Research*, September, 1951.

the rule that during a prolonged phase the essence of development strategy consists in maximizing induced decision-making, then we would favor rather than oppose the establishment of industries in cities precisely because it compels additional or complementary capital formation that otherwise might never have taken place. Obviously, what we are opposing here is not the principle of husbanding capital in general but a policy which in the name of this principle would reduce the stimuli and pressures toward additional capital formation that might emanate from the investments of a given period. Such a policy would . . . "economize" on capital *formation* rather than on capital!

Hirschman also agrees with Singer that application of the balanced growth theory "requires huge amounts of precisely those abilities which we have identified as likely to be very limited in supply in underdeveloped countries." Indeed he quotes an earlier statement of Singer's: "The advantages of multiple development may make interesting reading for economists, but they are gloomy news indeed for the underdeveloped countries." [13] He characterizes the balanced growth doctrine as "the application to underdevelopment of a therapy originally devised for an underemployment situation." In an advanced country during depression, "the industries, machines, managers, and workers, as well as the consumption habits" are all present; in underdeveloped countries "this is obviously not so."

But if we need a big push to get an underdeveloped country off dead center, while at the same time such a country cannot manage simultaneously a balanced "investment package" in industry and the needed investment in agricultural improvements, what are we to do? Hirschman answers: undertake a big push in strategically selected industries or sectors of the economy. After all, he points out, the industrialized countries did not get where they are through "balanced" growth. True, if you compare the economy of the United States in 1950 with the situation in 1850 you will find that many things have grown; but not everything grew at the same rate throughout the whole century. Development has proceeded "with growth being communicated from the leading sectors of the economy to the followers, from one industry to another, from one firm to another." [14] Having concluded that the market mechanism will not guarantee growth in the now underdeveloped countries, we need not take "the defeatist view that growth has to be balanced from the start or cannot take place at all."

One of the shortcomings of traditional theory as a basis for development policy is the underlying assumption that the profitability of different investment projects is independent of the order in which they are undertaken. In fact, Hirschman maintains, such need not be the case. He gives the following example: suppose there are two projects, M and N, requiring equal amounts of capital and yielding 10 per cent and 8 per cent, respectively. Suppose further that the interest rate stands at 9 per cent. If invest-

[13] Hans Singer, "Economic Progress in Underdeveloped Countries." Cf. Hirschman, *op. cit.*, chap. III.
[14] Hirschman, *op. cit.*, pp. 62–63.

ment is left to the market, only project M will be undertaken. Once it is in operation the return on project N rises to 10 per cent and so it, too, is launched. But it could perfectly well be, Hirschman argues, that if N had been undertaken first, despite the temporary loss in terms of market considerations, the return on M would rise to 14 per cent. Thus investors as a group—or the society as a whole—would be better off if they reversed the process that would result from independent market decisions. Moreover, the subsequent rate of growth would be faster; for once N was in place M would be rushed to completion, and in the next period other investments would become profitable because M was in operation, and so on. Hirschman admits that this example is artificial, but states that it embodies "a number of concepts that are recurring throughout this essay: the difference between 'permissive' and 'compulsive' sequences, the possible rationality of violating 'first things first' norms and the fact that the difficulty of taking a development decision is not necessarily proportional to the amount of capital it requires."

Hirschman analyzes these concepts in more systematic fashion with respect to the relationship between "directly productive activities," *DPA*, and social overhead capital, *SOC*. For this purpose he makes use of a special kind of diagram, reproduced here as Figure 15–2. Costs of new investment in *SOC* are measured on the horizontal axis, and costs of related output of *DPA* on the vertical axis. At the far right, *SOC* is plentiful and costs of

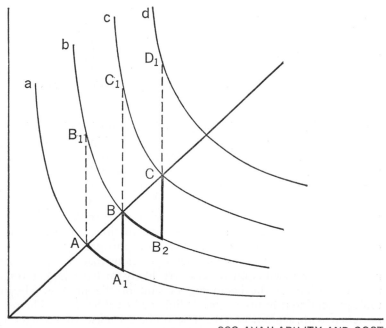

Figure 15–2

DPA accordingly low. As we move left, costs for any given output of *DPA* rise, first slowly, then more rapidly. For convenience the curves are drawn so that the 45° line through the origin connects the optimal points on the curves. Thus "this line expresses the ideal of balanced growth of *DPA* and *SOC:* a bit of each at each step no doubt would result in the greatest economy of the country's resources."

The trouble is that "poor countries cannot always afford to be economical." The real scarcity, in Hirschman's view, is not the resources themselves "but the ability to bring them into play." To illustrate this principle, he makes the simplifying assumption that *SOC* and *DPA* cannot be expanded simultaneously, because of this limited ability to utilize resources. Thus the planning problem is to determine the *sequence* of expansion that will maximize *induced* decision making.

We might start either by expanding *SOC* or by expanding *DPA*. If we adopt the first course the economy will follow the heavy line AA_1BB_2C. We begin by increasing *SOC* from A to A_1, which induces increased *DPA* until balance is restored at B, with the whole economy on a higher level of output. We then increase *SOC* further—and can afford to do so because of the higher gross national product already achieved—to B_2; *DPA* follows to point C. Hirschman calls this process "development via excess capacity (of *SOC*)." If we take the other route we follow the dotted line AB_1BC_1C. We begin by increasing *DPA* to B_1; balance requires increasing *SOC* to B. Then *DPA* is expanded further to C_1, and *SOC* has to move to C to catch up. This route is labeled "development via shortage (of *SOC*)."

Either method of unbalanced growth yields an "extra dividend" of "induced, easy-to-take, or compelled decisions resulting in additional investment and output." Balanced growth (of *SOC* and *DPA*) is not only unattainable in most underdeveloped countries, it may not even be desirable. The rate of growth is likely to be faster with chronic imbalance, precisely because of the "incentives and pressures" it sets up.

Linkage

Having demonstrated the virtues of strategic imbalance, however, we are left with the problem of discovering what kind of imbalance is likely to be most effective. Any particular investment project may have both "forward linkage" (may encourage investment in subsequent stages of production) and "backward linkage" (may encourage investment in earlier stages of production). The task is to find the projects with the greatest *total* linkage. The projects with the greatest linkage will vary from country to country and from time to time, and can be discovered only by empirical studies of the "input-output matrix" variety.

Hirschman thinks that on balance operations that are somewhere in the middle of the production process are likely to have higher total linkage than operations at the beginning or end of the process. He presents a table presenting measurements of "linkage" (Table 15–1). The results must be taken with a grain of salt. The highest backward linkage appears in grain mill products, and one can hardly regard wheat and rice production as being "induced" by the existence of wheat and rice mills. Hirschman

TABLE 15–1

Average Degree of Interdependence of Economic Sectors in Italy, Japan, and and the United States

Sector	Interdependence through purchases* from other sectors (backward linkage)	Interdependence through sales† to other sectors (forward linkage)
1. "Intermediate manufacture" (backward and forward linkage both high):		
Iron and steel	66	78
Non-ferrous metals	61	81
Paper and products	57	78
Petroleum products	65	68
Coal products	63	67
Chemicals	60	69
Textiles	67	57
Rubber products	51	48
Printing and publishing	49	46
2. "Final manufacture" (backward linkage high, forward linkage low):		
Grain mill products	89	42
Leather and products	66	37
Lumber and wood products	61	38
Apparel	69	12
Transport equipment	60	20
Machinery	51	28
Non-metallic mineral products	47	30
Processed foods	61	15
Shipbuilding	58	14
Miscellaneous industries	43	20
3. "Intermediate primary production" (forward linkage high, backward linkage low):		
Metal mining	21	93
Petroleum and natural gas	15	97
Coal mining	23	87
Agriculture and forestry	31	72
Electric power	27	59
Non-metallic minerals	17	52
4. "Final primary production" (backward and forward linkage both low):		
Fishing	24	36
Transport	31	26
Services	19	34
Trade	16	17

* Percentage ratio of interindustry purchases to total production.
† Percentage ratio of interindustry sales to total demand.
SOURCE: Albert O. Hirschman, *Strategy of Economic Development* (New Haven, 1958).

points out that the highest aggregate linkage occurs for iron and steel, and suggests that perhaps underdeveloped countries are not so foolish or prestige-motivated as some critics have suggested in insisting on having iron and steel mills. Perhaps; but perhaps not. Interindustry tables of the sort shown in Table 15–1 do not really measure "linkage." The only meaningful concept of linkage would be investment-decisions up or down the line, which are prompted by creation of a particular industry. The fact that iron and steel plants, once in existence, buy a great deal from some industries and sell a great deal to others is no guarantee that setting up an iron and steel mill in "Esperanza" will lead to investment either in iron mines or in automobile production in that country.

This analysis leads Hirschman to suggest one more way of characterizing underdeveloped countries; they are countries "weak in interdependence and linkage." A ranking of countries in terms of the proportion of inter-sectoral transactions to total output would probably show a high correlation with both per capita output and proportion of population in manufacturing. Agriculture, especially peasant agriculture, is short on linkage effects. Primary production is low in backward linkage effects by definition; but agriculture and mining are low in forward linkage too. Here is the intuitive source of "the grudge against the 'enclave' type of development," for output of mines, oil wells, and plantations can "slip out of a country without leaving much trace in the rest of the economy." Similarly, "enclave" development in industries providing "finishing touches" may add little to gross national product or to employment.

However, Hirschman draws a distinction between the long-run effects of enclave export industries and of enclave import industries, a distinction which is of interest in the light of our discussion in Chapter 13 of the impact of foreign trade on development. Enclave export industries, he says, have great difficulty in breaking out of the enclave situation and producing "forward linkage" effects within the country. Such need not be the case with enclave import industries; "much of the recent economic history of some rapidly developing underdeveloped countries can be written in terms of industrialization working its way backward from the 'final touches' stage to domestic production of intermediate, and finally to that of basic, industrial materials." He mentions Brazil, Colombia, and Mexico as examples. He might also have included Japan.

He extends this argument to support of the case for protection or subsidization of import-replacing industries, at the right stage of development. Too early encouragement of import-replacers, he points out, may retard economic growth by depriving the country of the "backward" linkage provided by large-scale imports. And backward linkage is more reliable than forward linkage. There is some reason to believe that investment will take place in any industry where demand reaches a certain "threshold." While that threshold is being reached, it is good policy to leave the market to importers. But "it would be absurd to set up any model that would presume to indicate which kind of metal-fabricating industries would come into existence at what point of time in the wake of the establishment of a basic iron and steel industry." Forward linkage should be regarded as "an important and powerful reinforcement to backward linkage" rather than as "an independent inducement mechanism."

Thus Hirschman envisages a kind of "jacking up" process for the economy, using import industries for their backward linkage effects, and then jumping into the production of the import itself when the market reaches a sufficiently large size. When the "threshold" is reached, protection or sibsidies to import-replacing industries becomes good policy. The process of starting with final touches has brought a good deal of industrialization to underdeveloped countries, but "much is to be said for biting off as large pieces of value added at a time as the underdeveloped country can possibly digest."

When the whole process is put into an appropriately dynamic context, Hirschman concludes, we are led to a principle that could never be derived from traditional theory: countries tend to develop a comparative advantage in the articles they *import*. "If a country does not produce commodities A and B and if it is importing A in more rapidly increasing volume than B, then it is likely to undertake domestic production of A long before that of B and is acting quite rationally in doing so."

Thus foreign trade policy should go through clearly defined stages with respect to any one industry. In the "prenatal" stage "the opposite of the infant industry treatment is called for." It might even be advisable to restrict *other* imports, to build up an artificial market for the commodity "whose eventual domestic production is to be fostered." [15] Infant industry protection should be given only *after* the threshold is reached and a new industry has been established. Tax concessions are an "apt instrument" for such protection.

Balanced or Unbalanced Growth?

On the whole it is unfortunate that the concept of "balanced growth" was ever introduced into the literature of economic development. "Balance" sounds like something "good" in itself. Perhaps our earliest childhood fears are of losing our balance; as adults we tend to like "balanced" people and "balanced" budgets and "balanced" growth. Thus the emphasis on "balance" enables various people to make special pleas for their pet projects or programs within the development budget. Agricultural experts plead for "balanced" agricultural and industrial development, hoping to offset what they consider to be an excessive emphasis on industrialization. People interested in education and public health plead for "balanced" social and economic development, hoping thereby to increase the budgets for health and education. But there is no acceptable concept of "balance" that can be stated *a priori;* what constitutes the proper "balance" among sectors can be determined only after careful analysis. It is too bad that Nurkse did not make his last statement on balanced growth first; it might have saved a good deal of misunderstanding. For in his definitive statement on the subject, Nurkse says clearly that the concept applies only to directly pro-

[15] *Ibid.*, p. 122.

ductive investment and not to the social overhead sector. It applies strictly only to a closed economy, and applies at all only if export markets for major products are not expanding fast enough. It is an essay in development with unlimited supplies of capital. It is an application of the "classical law of markets," that supply creates its own demand. In short, it says that were foreign trade is not "an engine of growth" we cannot concentrate investment in one or a few industries, because the markets created thereby will be inadequate. We need investment on a broad front all at once. Given lumpiness in production functions, it means we need a lot of investment all at once; the "balanced growth" doctrine is another version of "the big push." [16]

In the years following the publication of Keynes' *General Theory*, economists wasted a great deal of time and energy debating the question, "Is savings always equal to investment, or is the difference between savings and investment the determinant of changes in income and employment?" The difference of opinion turned out to rest on nothing more fundamental than definitions of the basic concept; when the distinction was made between *ex ante* (planned) and *ex post* (realized) savings and investment, it became clear that the difference between *ex ante* savings and investment was indeed equal to (not really the cause of) the change in income from one period to the next, whereas *ex post* savings and investment were not merely equal but identical. The way was then cleared for the next step, which was to stop talking about *ex ante* and *ex post* altogether and to talk instead about savings, consumption, and investment functions. Let us hope that the controversy over "balanced versus unbalanced growth" can be solved in the same manner but with less loss of energy. It is important to distinguish between balanced growth as a technique of development and a goal; even Hirschman's zigzag growth must have some kind of "balance" as the ultimate aim. One might, that is, deliberately create *ex ante* imbalances in order to produce subsequent *ex post* balance at a higher level of per capita income. Once we recognize that we are not dealing with an "either-or" proposition, we can stop talking about balanced and unbalanced growth altogether, and talk instead about functional relationships among the major sectors and regions of an economy.[17]

[16] Ragnar Nurkse, *Equilibrium and Growth in the World Economy* (Cambridge, Mass., 1961).

[17] For further discussion of the issues raised in this chapter, see Paul Streeton, "Unbalanced Growth," *Oxford Economic Papers*, June, 1959; Tibor Scitovsky, "Growth: Balanced or Unbalanced," in Moses Abramovitz (ed.), *Allocation of Economic Resources* (Stanford, 1959); and Allyn Young, "Increasing Returns and Economic Progress," *Economic Journal*, December, 1928.

16 | A Synthesis of Theories of Underdevelopment

In this chapter we shall endeavor to weave together the major elements of a theory of underdevelopment presented in the five previous chapters, together with some of the wisdom distilled from the general theories outlined in Part II.

Despite the amount of intensive on-the-spot study of underdeveloped countries during the last few years, our chief problem in attempting a synthesis of theories of underdevelopment is still empirical. We do not need elaborate econometric models before we can explain the behavior of underdeveloped economies or prescribe policies. But we do need to know what the strategic functional relations are and we need to know their general shapes. Unfortunately, we are not yet very sure of either of these things. What we have provided in the five previous chapters is a kind of analytical economic history of underdeveloped countries. We have pointed to some strategic relationships which have prevailed in the past. Dare we project them into the future? Let us review briefly the contents of those chapters.

Chapter 14 dealt with the relationship of population growth to industrial development. We showed that in the now underdeveloped countries, investment was made in plantations, mining, petroleum, etc., for the export market, in a way which brought little or no structural change in the economy. It brought rising rates of population growth, but no "built-in habit of technological change," to peasant society.

Concentration of investment in the export sector, combined with population growth, led to increasingly apparent technological dualism. The industrial sector actually was, or was believed to be, capital-intensive and fixed-technical-coefficient in its techniques. It did not provide jobs proportionate to the rate of capital accumulation in that sector. The increased population had to seek employment in the variable-coefficient rural sector. Techniques in that sector therefore became increasingly labor-intensive, and once good land gave out, disguised unemployment began to appear. The shortage of skilled labor, and the effective shortage of unskilled labor where real wages were too low to permit hard and efficient work, aggravated the tendency toward introduction of labor-saving devices in the industrial sector. If population growth is itself a function of the capital-labor ratio (directly or indirectly), there must be a discontinuous jump to a considerably higher ratio of capital to labor if steady growth is to be launched and maintained. Myint points out the barriers to specialization in the rural sector and the vicious circle that develops in this respect. With no specialization, no improvement in skills occurred. Also, the high labor turnover in the industrial sector meant that little effective training was accomplished even there.

In Chapter 13 we outlined some of the reasons why the expansion of foreign trade did not bring generally rising living standards to underdeveloped countries. Myint shows that the rural sector of these countries was confronted by monopolies and monopsonies, without the capacity for developing effective countervailing power of the sort that there is in advanced countries. Wages remained low; techniques were of a kind requiring either little skill or very few workers. Thus industrialization in the export sector had no educative or "spread" effects.

Myrdal goes further, arguing that the world economy is characterized, not by general tendencies toward equilibrium or adjustment to initial changes, but by circular causation, leading to vicious spirals which carry the world economy farther and farther away from an equilibrium position. He demonstrates the tendency both toward regional inequalities in single countries and toward increasing disparities in productivity between advanced and underdeveloped countries. Among the factors which may launch such disparate growth tendencies are shifts in terms of trade; he implies that shifts in the terms of trade in favor of now advanced countries, and against the underdeveloped ones, was one of the factors which resulted in the increasing spread between productivity and standards of living in the two groups of countries.

Far from alleviating these discrepancies, foreign trade tends to aggravate them, especially under conditions of colonial administration in the underdeveloped countries. The colonial heritage is not dispelled by independence alone. Even now, were it not for exchange controls, underdeveloped countries would be exporting rather than importing capital. The marginal productivity of capital is not higher in underdeveloped than in advanced countries, despite the relative scarcity of capital in the former. Only a discontinuous jump to a much higher level of investment, which would have to be made simultaneously in the industrial and agricultural sectors, would create conditions in which the relative scarcity of capital already accumulated could be translated into a higher return on new investment.

Arthur Lewis, on the basis of similar but more systematic analysis, concludes that because the supply of unskilled labor to the industrial sector was virtually unlimited, the "marginal calculus" of individual entrepreneurs became a less and less accurate guide to a socially optimal allocation of resources. Many underdeveloped countries now have a pattern of production just the opposite of what *true* comparative advantage would dictate; they produce agricultural output inefficiently when they could be producing industrial goods efficiently—and exporting them to pay for agricultural imports.

Finally, we saw in Chapter 13 that the terms of trade never moved in favor of the indigenous economy. The statement applies most clearly with respect to internal terms of trade between the rural and the industrial sector of the same country, but it also applies in some measure to terms of trade between underdeveloped countries as a whole and advanced countries as a whole.

Rosenstein-Rodan shows the need for a "big push," because of indivisibilities in the production function (especially with respect to social overhead capital), demand, and the supply of savings. The "low-level equilibrium trap" or "minimum effort" thesis leads to three major conclusions

1. If population growth is an increasing function of investment, there is a constant tendency for *per capita* income to revert to a minimum level at which both population growth and capital accumulation are equal to zero. Rising income can continue so long as investment is taking place in the industrial sector and new land is available in the rural sector to absorb the rising population. Once new land gives out, *per capita* income must revert to the minimum level.

2. Only concentration of a large number of entrepreneurs on productive (positive-sum) investments will confirm the profit expectations of individual entrepreneurs. If only a few entrepreneurs are willing to engage in such investments, the rate of growth of the society as a whole is likely to be such that profit expectations will be disappointed, and those few entrepreneurs will revert to unproductive (zero-sum) activities.

3. The configuration of income-raising and income-decreasing factors in underdeveloped countries may be such that only a discontinuous jump to considerably higher levels of capital accumulation will bring the economy into the zone of steady growth.

Nurkse argues for "balanced growth" to get over the hurdle of indivisibility of demand in a closed economy. Singer points out that few underdeveloped countries can manage a big push in industry and agriculture at once without foreign capital. He urges concentration on investment of a "bottleneck-breaking" sort. Hirschman goes further, favoring deliberate unbalancing of the economy to maximize the "linkage" effects of investment.

Scope and Method

Before attempting a diagrammatic synthesis of these theories, let us note their implications for the scope and method of a theory of underdevelopment. The scope and method of an economics of underdeveloped areas must differ from that of traditional economics for several reasons:

1. Some strategic functions are discontinuous. The discontinuities may take either of two forms. If *A* is a function of *B*, instead of a smooth curve relating the two variables, there may be a sudden jump in the value of *B* at a critical value of *A;* or the functions may have sharp points. Both the first and second derivatives may have positive signs within one range of *A* and negative signs in another value of *A*. These discontinuities are particularly important in the relationship between capital accumulation and output, in the supply of labor effort, the supply of risk-taking, in decision making, and in production functions.[1]

2. In underdeveloped countries, intersectoral and interregional relations, instead of being a frill to be superimposed on a more or less complete system, are the very core of the analytical framework.[2]

3. Cumulative movements *away from* dynamic equilibrium, or from balanced and steady growth, are typical of underdeveloped countries.[3]

4. In a theory of economic development, population growth and technological progress cannot be treated as exogenous variables, but must be worked into the system. Technological progress, in this context, includes resource discoveries and the spread of managerial, technical, and entrepreneurial skills. The relationship between these factors and economic growth is circular and must be treated as such; that is, population growth and technological progress cannot be treated only as factors *influencing* the rate of growth; the system must include the factors which determine them in turn. This is unfortunate, since we know relatively little about the causes of technological progress and population growth, but by leav-

[1] It is probably true that there are discontinuities in the strategic functions for advanced countries as well; but they are of relatively minor importance. For advanced countries the assumption of continuity gives a reasonably good approximation to reality, and the differential calculus is a useful tool. In underdeveloped countries, on the contrary, the discontinuities are fundamental, and the use of differential calculus can give quite wrong results. Difference equations may help, but a system of mathematics especially designed to take care of discontinuous functions might be more helpful still.

[2] This fact was well understood by the Classical economists, who were always concerned with relations between the agricultural and industrial sectors of the economy. Intersectoral relations played a more explicit role in the Marxist analysis. Specialists like Boeke were groping toward such a framework in their theory of "dualism," but were misled by the feeling that sectoral discrepancies were based on sociological factors, whereas in fact they can be explained in purely economic and technical terms. An important part of the intersectoral relation is the relationship between shifts in location of industry and economic growth, a relationship which has been pointed out by Professor Burton Keirstead in his *Theory of Economic Change* (Toronto, 1948) but which he has not yet worked into a systematic theory of growth.

[3] Cumulative movement away from stable equilibrium is not unknown in advanced countries; but in advanced countries these cumulative movements are important mainly for the theory of fluctuations, where they are limited by a "floor" and a "ceiling," as in the Hicks model of the trade cycle. Where we are concerned with *trends,* however, there are no such limits, at least within very long periods. Trends in the terms and balance of trade, regional discrepancies in productivity, and the like, can continue for decades, even generations. It is this kind of destructive cumulative movement that development policy must endeavor to halt. On this point, see also Albert O. Hirschman, "Investment Policies and Dualism in Underdeveloped Countries," *The American Economic Review,* September, 1957.

ing them out we produce theories which are not solid foundations for policy recommendations.

5. "Psychological individualism" is of limited use as a method of analysis—not because "people are different" in underdeveloped countries, but because so many of the important decisions are group rather than individual decisions. What may be bad policy for each one of a thousand entrepreneurs may be good policy for the thousand entrepreneurs together; what is unattractive to an individual worker may be very attractive to a trade union or to a village. (This is one aspect of point 1 above.)

6. The analytical framework must be a general equilibrium system, not a partial equilibrium one. It is the *conjuncture* of forces causing economic growth that is important, and no one of them alone will have the same effect as it does in conjunction with others. The system is bound to be rather complicated; it is doubtful whether the method of "successive approximations" will give the right answers. Dealing with the whole system at once enormously increases the intellectual difficulty of handling the problem.

7. The whole process must be put into time; the shape of functions at a point of time is less important than their shape through time.

8. Considering the enormous complexity of the problem and the overweening importance of the empirical framework, we may be wise to abandon the "purist" approach suggested by the writer on an earlier occasion [4] and to content ourselves with the relatively "sloppy methods of the physicists." [5] That is, instead of insisting on having explanations that are *both necessary and sufficient*, we might adopt explanations that are merely *sufficient*, until they prove inconsistent with other theories or with observations. This method has, after all, worked well for the physicists. At this stage of our efforts to find a general theory of development, any *refutable hypothesis* is well worth stating. Let us be bold in statement rather than wait until we can set forth *irrefutable* hypotheses (axioms), which are quite likely to be fruitless anyhow. If this approach is adopted, much time and energy must be devoted to empirical testing.

A Diagrammatic Synthesis

Our diagrammatic synthesis of the theories of underdevelopment in this part falls far short of fulfilling all these conditions for a wholly satisfactory theory of underdevelopment. One reason for this failure, of course, is that development is a multi-dimensional problem, and there is a limit to the number of variables that can be presented in one diagram. However, the writer freely confesses that simple ignorance, not the limitation of diagrammatic techniques, prevents him from presenting a definitive theory of underdevelopment. Our real problem is lack of the necessary factual knowledge about some of the basic relationships involved in the growth

[4] Benjamin Higgins, *What Do Economists Know?* (Melbourne, 1951), chap. I, and especially p. 27.

[5] To my knowledge, this expression was first used by Professor Kenneth Boulding in a seminar at McGill University.

process—particularly those relating to population growth, entrepreneurial motivation, political, social, and cultural prerequisites, and the like. Nevertheless, it is the writer's belief that some simple diagrams based on the contents of the previous three chapters, will help us to understand the problem of underdevelopment and to formulate policies for dealing it.[6]

Let us begin by treating the economy as a unit; we shall divide the economy into sectors later. In Figure 16–1 we measure per capita income, Y/N, on the horizontal axis, and various percentages on the vertical axis.

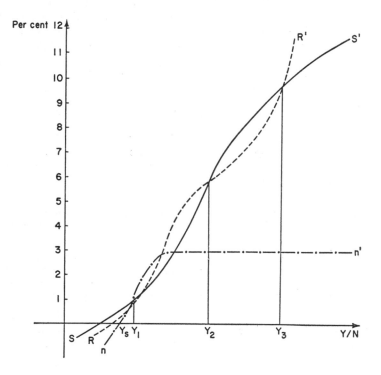

Figure 16–1

The curve n-n' shows percentage rates of population growth (as a function of per capital income). For income below the subsistence level, population declines. Once above this level, it rises rapidly until it hits the "ceiling" of the "biological maximum," which may be put at about 3 per cent. (Some countries have growth rates higher than this, but these presumably reflect unusual age distributions that cannot be indefinitely maintained.)

The curve ss' represents aggregate net savings, measured in per cent of

[6] In the working out of these diagrams, the author has had invaluable assistance from Professor Trevor Swan.

national income, as a function of per capita income. It will also be negative for very low levels of income. Experience with low-income societies suggests, however, that some net savings will appear even at levels of income at which population does not grow. Savings will reach a maximum proportion of income, at some very high level of per capita income, in the neighborhood of 15 per cent.

We are now in a position to derive a "capital requirements" curve, RR', showing the amounts of capital, in per cent of national income, needed to achieve the corresponding level of per capita income. To explain the shape of this curve, we must resort once again to some simple mathematics. We can write:

$$R = \frac{\frac{Q}{N} \cdot \Delta N}{Y} \tag{1}$$

That is, required investment, to maintain a constant per capita income with a given amount of population growth, ΔN, is equal to the stock of capital, Q, divided by the population, N, and multiplied by the increase in population. To express this requirement as a percentage of income, Y, we divide through by Y.

We can rewrite Equation (1) as follows:

$$R = \frac{Q}{Y} \cdot \frac{\Delta N}{N} \quad \text{or for convenience,}$$

$$\text{letting } n = \frac{N}{\Delta N} \qquad R = \frac{Q \cdot n}{Y} \tag{2}$$

Now we have the equation in a familiar form, similar in meaning to Harrod's "capital requirements for a natural rate of growth," except that we are expressing requirements in terms of capital per head and allowing for a constant rate of technological progress. The term Q/Y is the capital-output ratio, n is the rate of population growth, and $Q/Y \cdot n$ is the rate of increase in capital required to maintain per capita income constant.

We know something about the relation of the capital-output ratio to per capita income and to the amount of capital per head, which helps to specify the shape of this capital requirements curve. Poor countries are largely agricultural; in such countries the capital-output ratio is low, say, 1:1. However, the marginal (incremental) capital-output ratio is higher than the average. In order to raise per capita income from subsistence levels, without accelerating technological progress, either agricultural techniques must become more capital using (irrigated rather than shifting agriculture) or labor must be transferred from agriculture to industry. Either process will raise capital-output ratios. As industrialization proceeds and really high levels of income are reached, the capital-output ratio will rise less steeply and will taper off at, say, 3:1. On the other hand the capital-output ratio will rise as the stock of capital per head increases;

this is just good old-fashioned diminishing returns to investment. If good land is exhausted, the capital-output ratio may rise sharply as the amount of capital per head is increased.

The shape of the capital requirements curve will depend on these two relationships. For the slope of the curve

$$R = \frac{Q}{Y} \cdot n \quad \text{or} \quad \left[\frac{d}{d(Y/N)} \cdot \left(\frac{Q}{Y} \cdot n \right) \right]$$

is $\frac{Q}{Y} \cdot n' + n \cdot \frac{Q'}{Y}$

In order to translate this expression into words, let us coin two new technical terms. Let us call the rate at which the required capital per head rises with per capita income "the marginal capital requirement." This is the expression Q'/Y. Let us call the rate at which population growth rises as per capita income goes up "the marginal propensity to populate." This is the expression n'. Then we have this proposition: capital requirements (for the maintenance of per capita income) are (the capital-output ratio) times (the marginal propensity to populate) plus (the rate of population growth) times (marginal capital requirements).

For very low levels of per capita income, both the rate of population growth and the marginal rate of capital accumulation will be low; n will be very small and the shape of the capital requirements curve will be governed by the marginal propensity to populate and the capital-output ratio, $Q \cdot n'/Y$. Since $Q \cdot n'/Y$ is in the neighborhood of unity the curve will start out with a shape similar to that of the population curve itself. As needs for social overhead capital are met, the capital-output ratio will taper off and the capital requirements curve will do the same.[7]

At some higher level of per capita income, population growth hits the ceiling; n' becomes zero. Thus $Q/Y \cdot n'$ is also zero. On the other hand the rate of population growth, n, is high. Thus for higher levels of income the shape of the R curve will be governed by the effect of capital accumulation on the capital-output ratio. Accordingly, capital requirements will tend to rise more steeply again.

Technological progress reduces per capita capital requirements. Exhaustion of good land (decreasing returns) raises them. With very low levels of population growth and high rates of capital accumulation, such as may occur in a "mature economy," labor may become the scarce factor, and returns to investment may diminish on that account. Even in an underdeveloped country, a sufficiently big push could run into bottlenecks other than capital (skilled labor, entrepreneurship), which could raise the capital-output ratio to very high levels.

Where will the R curve cut the horizontal axis? It must do so *at least* as far to the right as Y_s; for with a shrinking population, *both* technological progress *and* increasing returns tend to reduce capital requirements

[7] Professor Trevor Swan has shown, in an unpublished paper presented to an M.I.T. seminar, that so long as the elasticity of substitution of capital for labor, is somewhere between 0.5 and 1.0, as it really has to be, the R curve wil have an S shape.

for a given per capita income. In fact, R must cut the s curve at a level of per capita income where technological progress and diminishing returns just offset each other (which might be at zero rates for both, if land is plentiful). This point is likely to occur at a level of per capita income somewhat above the zero savings or zero population growth levels.

Thus the R curve will have the shape and position of RR'_1 in Figure 16–1.

At a level of per capita income Y_1, the R and S curves cross. This is a Classical equilibrium position. The rate of capital accumulation is just enough to maintain per capita income slightly above the subsistence level with a modest rate of population growth. This is the "low-level equilibrium trap." The position is stable; any "marginal" move toward higher per capita incomes will be thwarted by capital requirements which exceed savings. On the other hand, to the left of Y_1 savings exceed capital requirements. If "Say's law" holds and inducements to invest are sufficient to make sure that all *ex ante* savings are offset by investment, per capita income will grow to Y_1.

The high-level income Y_3 is also stable, but Y_2 is unstable. In order to assure growth to Y_3, a "minimum effort" is required to provide capital (and everything else) enough to raise income above Y_2.

Figure 16–2 starts with the same situation as in Figure 16–1. We have eliminated the population growth curve, since we need it only to derive the curve of capital requirements, and we do not want to clutter the diagram unnecessarily. We are now applying the diagram to the rural sector of the economy. The savings curve is a little flatter, since the range of per capita incomes on the x axis is lower. Let us imagine that investment is taking place in the industrial sector, which does not raise productivity in the agricultural sector, but brings a population explosion in the manner described in Chapter 14. The population explosion will show in the diagram by a shift of the capital requirements curve upward and to the left, to RR'_2. The immediate impact will be a slight decline in per capita income in the rural sector. If the population responds by improving techniques (by shifting from "slash and burn agriculture" to irrigated agriculture, for example), the R curve may shift back to R_1, and income may return to the previous positions.

With the capital requirements curve, RR_2, a stable equilibrium position is established at the rather low per capita income of Y_3. A considerable increase in investment is needed to get even to that level; but truly high levels of income, such as Y_4, are *impossible*, unless technical progress takes place or population growth tapers off again. It is even possible that the population explosion will shift the capital requirements curve to R'_4; in this case no escape from the low-level equilibrium trap is possible until techniques improve or population growth tapers off. Otherwise no "effort" is big enough.

Now let us suppose that the "Hirschman effect" sets in; the problems posed by population pressure lead to accelerated technological progress, and a large-scale program of agricultural improvement is launched. A "built-in habit of technical progress" becomes characteristic of the rural

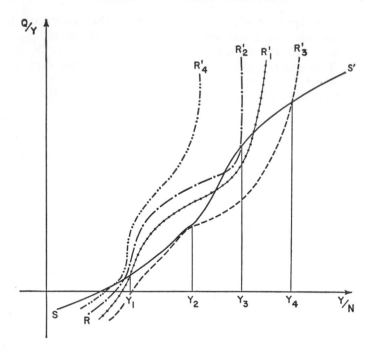

Figure 16–2

sector, the "Hagen effect" takes place and the rate of population growth falls. With luck, we may succeed in shifting the capital requirements curve to the position RR'_3. Now the equilibrium position, Y_2, is unstable in an upward direction. Any favorable event bringing an initial increase in per capita income will start the economy on its way to the high-level income Y_4.

   Moreover, the society does not really have the choice between staying in position Y_3 or making the effort to move to still higher levels of income. At this level of income, the rate of technological progress is high enough for the moment to offset the higher rate of population growth generated by the first wave of industrialization. But as good land begins to give out, diminishing returns will operate more and more strongly; accelerated technological progress, or restrictions on the size of families, will be needed just to keep per capita income from falling. Without acceleration of technological progress or reduced population growth, the RR'_2 curve will shift to the left toward RR'_4 and incomes will revert to the subsistence level. With the labor-intensive techniques typical of small-scale peasant agriculture the opportunities for technological improvement are extremely limited. The optimal combination of seed, fertilizer, irrigation, and tools for small family holdings can be reached with relatively little investment of capital, and once attained, the marginal productivity of capital drops to zero. The discontinuous jump to more extensive and more mechanized agriculture can be postponed while this optimal combination is being reached, but it must be made sooner or later. Unless really significant increases in man-year output can still be obtained in other ways, there is a strong case for making the jump sooner rather than later.

It should be noted, however, that although this position is stable in the Classical sense, it may be unstable in the Keynesian sense. That is, savings exceed capital requirements at this level of income. We must make sure that actual investment *exceeds* requirements, so as to offset savings; otherwise, the situation will be deflationary, and private investment will tend to fall off. Investment in excess of requirements for growth is not likely to be forthcoming without an active government policy.

So we see that in the case of the rural sector, the big push cannot be confined to the sort of policy implied in moving *along* the curves. The capital requirements curve must be *shifted*. For some countries such a shift may be possible through seed selection, fertilizer, etc., on present holdings. Sooner or later, however, it will require a transition to mechanized agriculture, while the rate of population growth in the rural sector is reduced by attracting peasants into industrial employment.

Figure 16–3 applies to the industrial sector. Where capital for investment in the industrial sector is provided mainly from abroad, some savings will be provided to this sector even at very low levels of domestic per capita income. The contribution of domestic savings to total capital formation is limited, and the savings curve will therefore be somewhat flatter than in Figure 16–1. [8] Industrial investment is less likely to encounter diminishing returns than agricultural investment, because of the "unlimited supply of labor" to this sector, and because the availability of additional land is somewhat less important to the industrial sector than it is to the rural sector. Finally, population growth within the industrial sector will be closely related to capital accumulation; it is limited by the amount of *employment* provided through investment in these capital-intensive, fixed-technical-coefficient operations. Capital-output ratios will start high, because of the need to provide social overhead capital. As industrial investment proceeds, however, the capital-output ratio in this sector will fall. At levels of investment where bottlenecks appear, it will rise again. Thus at the beginning of industrial expansion both the *marginal* propensity to populate and *marginal* capital requirements will be high. The rate of population growth and the capital-output ratio will also be high. Capital requirements will rise steeply for initial increases in per capita income in this sector. As higher per capita incomes are reached, the marginal propensity to populate will decline; indeed it will approximate the rate of increase in the stock of capital, technical coefficients being relatively fixed. Capital-output ratios will also taper off.

[8] This case would fit Indonesia, Libya, prewar India, and other former colonies. For countries where most of the capital is provided internally, such as Japan or postwar Philippines, the ratio of savings to income would rise somewhat more steeply with income.

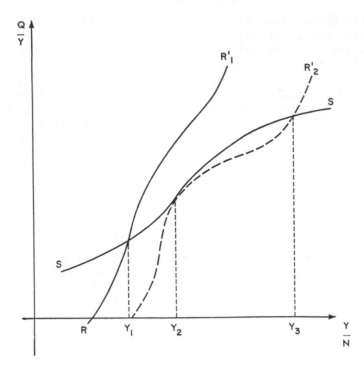

Figure 16–3

Since, under our assumptions, demographic factors in the industrial sector affect mainly the rate of population growth in the rural sector, there is no reason for either a "population explosion" or a subsequent drop in the rate of population growth. On the other hand, not only does the rate of technological progress start relatively high in the industrial sector, but it tends to increase periodically as new innovations and "clusters of followers" appear. After each new wave of innovations, it is true, the rate of increase in technological progress will fall off. Thus some sort of "cobweb" will tend to develop, the R' curve first shifting to the right and causing a rise in per capita income, and then shifting to the left and causing incomes to drop. If there is also induced investment related to the rate of increase in per capita income, it is easy to see that a cyclical fluctuation in income (and employment) will result. Here, however, we are concerned with the long-run movement; the important consideration is that the long-run movement of the RR' curve is to the right—at least so long as the supply of Schumpeterian New Men is increasing. One of these rightward shifts will bring the RR' curve to the position RR'_2. Now the equilibrium position, Y_2 is unstable upward. Any favorable event will start the economy merrily on its road to Y_3. Thus progress to high levels of per capita income in the industrial sector is virtually assured.

If the development of the rural sector follows the course indicated in Figure 16–2 without a big push in that sector itself, while the industrial sector follows the course of Figure 16–3, it is clear that per capita output and income in the two sectors must diverge, with an ever-widening gap.

Effect of Foreign Trade and Investment

Now let us assume that we have a closed economy with two sectors of production, one agricultural and one industrial. If these sectors are to be considered part of the *same* economy, in the ordinary sense of the term "economy," there must be some transferability of both labor and capital between sectors, and the two sectors must trade with each other. Under these conditions, there is a strong possibility that the barter terms of trade will turn against the industrial sector and in favor of the agricultural sector as development proceeds—as the British terms of trade deteriorated in the integrated world economy of the early nineteenth century. For per capita output and income will be rising considerably faster in the industrial than in the agricultural sector. The rate of technological progress will be much higher in the industrial sector. The size of population will, of course, be much higher in the rural sector, but the rate of population growth within the sectors will be somewhat the same, since both are related to the rate of industrial investment. Thus the supply of industrial products will increase much more rapidly than the supply of agricultural products. Prices of manufactured goods will tend to fall relative to prices of agricultural goods. Capital requirement curves will shift up in industry, down in agriculture. Growth rates will be accelerated in agriculture, decelerated in industry.

There will also be a tendency for capital to move from the industrial sector to the rural sector. For the marginal productivity of capital will tend to be falling (at each point of time) in the industrial sector; it can be prevented from doing so only by accelerated technological progress or cessation of growth. Indeed, if technical coefficients are really fixed, the *marginal* productivity of capital at each point of time will be zero.

In the rural sector, on the other hand, the marginal productivity of capital is high; capital is scarce, labor abundant. So long as there is land to be brought to cultivation or converted to more efficient techniques the rate of return on agricultural investment will be handsome. As we saw in Chapter 13, peasants can pay extremely high interest rates to money-lenders and still survive. In some countries returns in the rural sector may be high enough to attract large lumps of capital investment in a shift to extensive, mechanized agriculture, thus providing the needed minimum effort in agriculture, as was the case in the Southern United States.

If on the other hand there is no significant amount of trade between the two sectors, and if there is no capital movement between the two sectors, this transition will not take place. Where underdeveloped countries are engaged in foreign trade, this pattern often appears. The industrial sector produces for export, whereas the rural sector sells virtually nothing to the export sector. Under these circumstances there is no reason for the terms of trade to turn in favor of the rural sector. Indeed, if incomes in the rest of the world are rising more rapidly than in the rural sector, the terms of trade may turn *against* the rural sector, as we saw in Chapter 13. Expansion of the industrial export sector may merely attract those villagers with high n-achievement, aggravating the tendency toward stagnation in the rural sector.

Moreover, foreign capital does not flow into the rural sector because marginal returns are higher there. The high interest rates earned by the moneylenders, we have seen, are based on personal knowledge of and contact with the villagers which foreign capitalists—and even native urbanites—do not have. In any case, this sort of money-making is often distasteful to the foreign or urban entrepreneur. If an economy which already has these two distinct sectors moves from a closed economy to one engaged in foreign trade, the spread between the levels of production and income between the two sectors may be greater than if there were no foreign trade. The RR' curves tend to shift continuously to the right in the industrial sector, and continuously to the left in the rural sector. It will take considerable ingenuity in peasant agriculture just to keep incomes from falling, while *average* incomes in the industrial sector tend to rise continuously.

To complete the analysis, we would need a third sector: advanced countries. If it is true that the terms of trade of the industrial sector with the rest of the world tend to deteriorate through time, the rightward shift of the RR' curves in that sector would be retarded, and it might even be reversed. In addition, the international flow of capital would be redirected toward the expanding economies of the advanced countries. In that case the influx of capital even to the industrial sector may be insufficient to maintain incomes in that sector. The SS' curve in Figure 16–3 may shift downward while the RR' curve shifts to the left, until SS' is above RR' except for one point of tangency. The underdeveloped country is then in a precarious position indeed; any unfavorable shock will send incomes in the industrial sector plunging downward toward Y_1.

Introducing Indivisibilities

Now let us introduce the indivisibilities with respect to supply of capital which were discussed in Chapter 15. These would result in discontinuities in the curve relating the capital-output ratio to per capita income. These discontinuities would be reflected in turn in the capital requirements curve, RR'. Capital requirements would rise steeply over a certain range of increases in per capita income, particularly when social overhead capital is being provided, and then would fall abruptly to considerably lower levels. The provision of transport facilities, power, and the like, involves the biggest discontinuities of this kind, but other discontinuities appear at various levels of per capita income. As very high levels of per capita income are reached, however, the discontinuities are less noticeable. In advanced countries, the required "lumps" of new investment are small

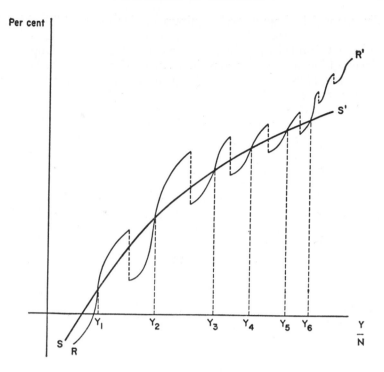

Figure 16–4

relative to the existing stock of capital. Thus the capital requirements curve assumes a "saw-toothed" aspect, as in Figure 16–4. The "teeth" become smaller as per capita income rises, and for very high levels of per capita income, a smooth capital requirements curve is a reasonably good approximation to reality.

The dotted portions of the curve have no economic meaning; equilibrium is possible only on the rising portions of the curve.

It is apparent that with such a saw-toothed capital requirements curve there may be a whole series of income traps at various levels of per capita income. The intersections of the savings curve with the capital requirements curve provide stable equilibrium at the levels of Y_2, Y_3, and Y_4 as well as at Y_1. In the real world, these "traps" would appear as bottlenecks in the supply of capital, or in supply of other factors of production. For example, a shortage of skilled labor may require a shift to a more completely mechanized system of production; lack of trained managers or technicians may lead to inefficient use of capital.

Is there any reason why the R curve should remain in the neighborhood of the S curve after the initial intersection? Since income equals spending, and actual investment varies with spending, actual investment will not long diverge widely from capital requirements for any established level of income. If it is not profitable to invest as much as is required, and unless any deficiency is filled by public investment, income must drop. And at stable levels of income, savings equal investment, if trade and the budget are also in balance. Thus the capital requirements curve could not remain long in a position far removed from the savings curve. Such being the case, a series of "traps" is virtually certain with discontinuities in the capital supply. Sustained growth may require a whole series of planned minimum efforts. But as per capita income rises, each successive "push" gets easier and is more likely to be produced by individual market decisions without government intervention.

Indivisibilities of demand would introduce a different kind of break in the RR' curve. When we take account of effective demand, we must think of capital-output ratios in terms of goods and services produced and sold; production will not continue long if there is no market. The indivisibilities of demand stressed by Rosenstein-Rodan and Nurkse mean that over certain ranges investment can take place without raising "output" in the sense of goods and services produced and sold. Over these ranges, then, the marginal capital requirements become infinite—which really means that over these ranges the capital requirements curve is non-existent. We can depict these ranges by horizontal dotted sections, added to the vertical dotted sections introduced by lumpiness of the production function. Thus we end up with an RR' curve like that in Figure 16-5.

Given kinks in the savings function, such as illustrated by the curve SS' in Figure 16-5, there could be a whole series of "traps" even with a perfectly smooth capital requirements curve. With discontinuities in both curves, a multiplicity of equilibrium points can occur. Only those levels of income at which solid savings and capital requirements curves intersect have real meaning; only they could be equilibrium points. Only the levels of income that constitute such points are shown in the diagram. We can see at once that the minimum effort for a further rise in per capita income becomes smaller, relative to the existing income and stock of capital, as income rises. At very high levels of income, growth has the appearance of being practically continuous.

Development Past and Present

We can use a diagram of this kind to illustrate some of the differences between the task confronting underdeveloped countries today and the situation of the now advanced countries in the eighteenth and early nineteenth centuries. The "population explosion" in Europe and the New World was never quite so explosive as it has been in some Asian, African, and Latin American countries. Moreover, the upsurge of population growth came *after* a marked acceleration of the rate of technological progress in both the agricultural and industrial sectors, and it was owing mainly to economic improvement. With the urbanization that Western industrialization brought with it, fertility rates declined after a lag of two or

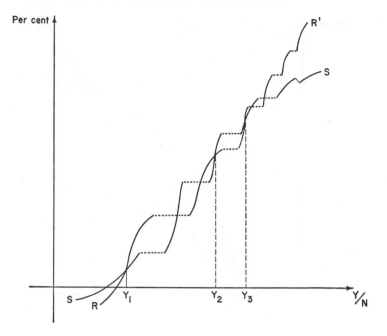

Figure 16–5

three generations. Expansion started when the resource-population relationship was relatively favorable, and in most of the advanced countries it is doubtful whether either the level of population or the rate of population growth was ever above the optimum for any length of time. Moreover, as we saw in Chapter 10, at the beginning of the Industrial Revolution the level of the zero population growth income was high enough to permit a significant amount of saving.

Thus, in contrast to the situation of underdeveloped countries as illustrated in Figures 16–1 to 16–4, the now advanced countries at the beginning of their expansion were in a position more like that shown in Figure 16–6. The position of the RR' curve reflects the relatively slow rate of population growth and the relatively high accompanying rate of technological progress. The position of the savings curve reflects the relatively high initial levels of income. Whereas the underdeveloped countries need a big push followed by lesser pushes, no big push is needed for countries in the situation depicted in Figure 16–6. Income can expand steadily (except for minor fluctuations of the sort that characterized nineteenth-century business cycles). Moreover, the RR' curve moved steadily to the right, with accelerated technological progress, and particularly after the drop in fertility rates. For these countries, continuous and cumulative growth was fairly easy.

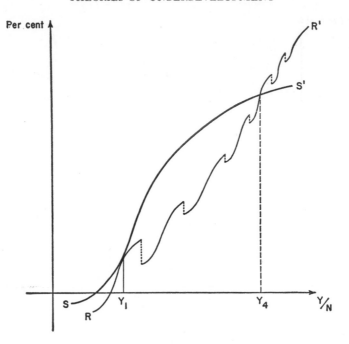

Figure 16–6

Conclusions

We could go on proposing various models and translating them into terms of these diagrams, but we have now covered the main points made in the preceding five chapters. From the reformulation in this chapter, it should be clear that traditional marginal analysis, however useful it may be as a first approximation to understanding advanced economies, can be very misleading for underdeveloped ones. When such factors as population growth and technological progress are made an integral part of the analysis, instead of being left out altogether as in traditional equilibrium theory, and when the relevant discontinuities are introduced, our analysis can lead us to policy conclusions exactly the reverse of what orthodox equilibrium theory might suggest. Some of the policy conclusions implicit in our analysis have been noted in passing. We have now reached the point where we must turn explicitly to questions of development policy.

PART V || Policies

17 | The Welfare Economics of Growth

Thus far, we have merely been trying to answer the question, "What *causes* development or underdevelopment?" We have not asked whether or not development in this sense is a "good thing." Now that we are about to discuss policy, however, we had better face the issues: does economic development always bring an increase in social welfare? How can one tell whether it does or not?

Traditional welfare economics, we have seen, takes preferences as given; it is concerned with using the market, patching it, or replacing it, in such a way as to provide maximum scope for satisfaction of wants through freely expressed individual choices. True, traditional welfare economics has never quite resolved the problem of deciding how income should be distributed. Some economists have thrown in the sponge and admitted the need for a basic value judgment on the ethics of income distribution, although they grace the value judgment with the term "welfare function." Others have tried to rescue *Wertfreiheit* (that is, freedom from value judgments) by arguing that an economic change is clearly "good" if it does not cause a "bad" redistribution of income and if the potential losers could not profitably bribe the potential gainers to oppose it. It is also true that such inconvenient possibilities as increasing returns to scale, discontinuities, and kinks, are awkward to handle. Nevertheless, once given a "welfare function" as a basis for income distribution, it is possible to evaluate any current policy proposal in terms of *marginal* rates of substitution between goods and services, and technical possibilities of production as indicated by *marginal* productivities of various factors of production in various uses.[1] The "best" policy is the one that will allocate resources so as to maximize the aggregate satisfaction of the community through the consumption of goods, services, and leisure, with *given* resources, techniques, institutions, and tastes.

We could, of course, state the objective of economic development policy in analogous terms: viz., to maximize the *rate of increase* in this flow of goods, services, and leisure through time. Several writers, indeed, have stated the aim of economic development policy in these terms. Arthur Lewis begins his book by stating his *credo:*[2]

The subject matter of this book is the growth of output per head of population. . . . The definition of output we leave to the theorists of national income. . . . The definition, however, must relate to goods and services—"economic" output, in the old fashioned meaning of "economic"—and not to some such concept as welfare, satisfaction or happiness. It is possible that a person becomes less happy in the process of acquiring greater command over goods and services. . . . This book is not, however, an essay on whether people ought to have or to want more goods and services; its concern is merely with the processes by which more goods and services become available. The author believes that it is good to have more goods and services, but the analysis of the book does not in any way depend upon this belief.

Having thus set himself free to analyze the factors which will maximize the rate of growth of output, however, Lewis adds an appendix to his book in which he explains why he thinks economic growth is desirable. "The advantage of economic growth," he says there, "is not that wealth increases happiness, but that it increases the range of human choice. It is very hard to correlate wealth and happiness." For "what distinguishes men from pigs is that men have greater control over their environment; not that they are more happy. And on this test, economic growth is greatly to be desired." It gives us the freedom to choose greater leisure. It permits cultivation of the arts and sciences. "Art, music, the study of philosophy itself" can be afforded "only as economic growth permits [a society] to spare increasing numbers from the basic task of growing food." More people hear the work of the best composers, and see the work of the best painters, in the present day than in the times of Mozart or Bach, Rembrandt or El Greco.[3]

Similarly, Bauer and Yamey open their discussion of the role of government in economic development by stating that "We believe that the widening of the range of effective choice is the most valuable single objective of economic development as well as the best single criterion of its attainment."[4]

[1] For an excellent and relatively readable summary of contemporary welfare economics, see Francis M. Bator, "The Simple Analytics of Welfare Maximization," *The American Economic Review,* March, 1957.
[2] W. Arthur Lewis, *The Theory of Economic Growth* (London, 1955), pp. 9–10.
[3] *Ibid.,* pp. 420–22.
[4] P. T. Bauer and B. S. Yamey, *The Economics of Underdeveloped Countries* (London, 1957).

The present writer shares these beliefs. But to say that we believe in economic development does not really solve the problem; development policy is still left on a very different footing from that of traditional welfare economics. Is it the best we can do?

Observation tells us that practically everyone wants a higher standard of living, in the sense of "command over more goods, services, and leisure." We can also observe that practically everyone is willing to make *some* sacrifice in order to have a higher standard of living. Welfare economics tries to balance the satisfaction of these wants with the sacrifices "at the margin"; each individual is supposed to equalize the marginal rates of substitution among goods and services, between goods and services and leisure, and between income now and income later. But our whole analysis of the development problem, especially in poor and stagnant countries, led us to the conclusion that *current market choices are a very unreliable guide to development policy*. We have seen that if people are to get over the hump to sustained economic growth they have to "want" it in a way quite different from "wanting" goods and services, in the sense of being willing to pay for them. They may have to work harder and better, save more, and restrict family size even if there is no clear "marginal" increase in their real incomes in the immediate future. They may have to become technology-minded, acquire higher levels of training and skills, shift from agriculture to industry and from country to city, acquire high *n*-achievement, accept changes in institutions and social organization, acquire new tastes—perhaps even a new "way of life"—although many of the people involved in this process of "economic development and cultural change" may not like it at all. For let us be clear on one point; if the pattern of individual preferences was such as to produce economic growth, we would have it now. The present situation in underdeveloped countries is the result of *somebody's* decisions. And no government can launch economic growth where it does not exist without "interfering in the market" in a sense quite different from the intervention involved in the nostrums of welfare economics. We have seen that launching a takeoff is *not* merely "patching the market." Even raising the ratio of effective savings and investment to national income to finance a "minimum effort" involves an element of intervention; it would not occur through market forces alone.

We could, of course, treat the development of underdeveloped countries as an item of Western national policy. Professors Millikan and Rostow, in their *Proposal* argue that *our* way of life is more secure in a world of "mature democracies" than it is when we are surrounded by poverty-stricken countries with unstable governments.[5]

If economic development is part of *our* national policy, of course, whether or not people "want" it is a purely technical question. "Absorptive capacity" will be lower in countries that do not want development, and "technical assistance" might have to be directed toward changing the culture and instilling new wants. We might decide, as a matter of efficiency, to concentrate our aid in countries where absorptive capacity is

[5] Max F. Millikan and W. W. Rostow, *A Proposal: Key to an Effective Foreign Policy* (New York, 1957).

higher and the task easier. In countries peculiarly important to our security, however, it may be unwise to frame policy in terms of economic efficiency alone.

If we think only in terms of our own national policy, however, we would be rash to go as far as Gunnar Myrdal and set as our goal "the reduction of the gap between per capita incomes of the United States and Canada and those of underdeveloped countries." [6] Reducing the gap may not prove possible, and if the goal of development policy is to assure our own national security, promising the impossible is not likely to be an effective means to this end. Aiding foreign countries with their development programs will no doubt bring their *per capita* incomes closer to those now enjoyed in advanced countries, but the incomes of advanced countries will meanwhile have risen to new heights. In all likelihood they will rise by bigger amounts than most underdeveloped countries. Even in Latin America, where present incomes and growth rates are relatively high, a level of per capita income *one-third of the United States level* may prove unattainable in the foreseeable future.[7]

The present writer has his own "welfare function" in this regard. *Redistribution* of income among *advanced* nations may not be very important, just as redistribution of income among individuals is not very important in advanced countries. What is important and possible in both cases is to *eliminate poverty*. The amount of income redistribution actually achieved by the modern welfare state is relatively small. But where *poverty* has been eliminated by economic and social policy, as in Australia and in lesser degree in the United States or Canada, the presence of a few rich people is not very serious, and redistribution from rich to less rich would not raise incomes of the less rich very much. In the same way, if there were no poor countries, the presence of a few rich ones would not be a menace to world peace and prosperity.

The writer's own "welfare function" is such, however, that he would be sorry to see his profession abandon the attempt to formulate development policies that will give the people of underdeveloped countries what *they* want. Markets may be poor guides, but we still have the polls. Where representative governments have made economic development a major national goal, we can accept it as a policy goal, too. In these cases, the two possible approaches are reconciled in large measure, for absorptive capacity *is* higher where governments are determined to achieve higher living standards for their people. As economists, we can then suggest measures to promote growth; if the governments pursue these measures and the people do not like them, the people can toss the government out. If that happens, the economists may get tossed out, too, unless they can suggest development policies more to people's liking. This approach will give economists plenty to do, for many representative governments are com-

[6] Gunnar Myrdal, *op. cit.*

[7] Cf. UN Department of Economic and Social Affairs, *Analyses and Projections of Economic Development: A Study Prepared by the Economic Commission for Latin America:* I. "An Introduction to the Technique of Programming" (New York, 1955), p. 11.

mitted to economic development.

The foreign technical assistance "expert" who remains long enough in the field typically goes through three stages. Too often his first reaction is, "Everything here is different from at home; that is terrible, we must change everything." As he lives and travels in these countries, however, he begins to appreciate their culture, civilization, values, and way of life. At this stage the reaction often is, "Why should we force on these happy people the frictions and neuroses of our Western society?" In the third stage, attained after still further experience with underdeveloped countries, the "expert" comes to realize that the question "to develop or not to develop" is not one for the West to answer. Most underdeveloped countries today are determined to achieve higher standards of living, and the events of the last twenty years have injected into their bodies politic the dynamics of economic and social change. Our task is to help these countries to attain their economic goals within a political and social framework that remains democratic.

The present writer would also like to see some of the tenets of traditional welfare theory retained in development policy. Development is for people, and the current wants of people should not be ignored for the sake of raising per capita output in the future. For example, leisure should be respected. Output per capita can be increased, within limits, by the simple device of lengthening the working week; but such an increase in per capita output is not necessarily economic progress. Whether it is or not depends upon how the people concerned value the extra flow of goods and services on the one hand and the loss of leisure on the other. There are problems here; if we are to have growth at all, the choice between a higher material standard of living and more leisure must be made to some degree collectively; it cannot be left to each individual, as it is in traditional welfare economics. There are discontinuities and complementarities in the function relating hours of work to output, and the decisions of various individuals and groups are interrelated. These problems, however, are not peculiar to underdeveloped countries.

Similarly, production can be increased by increasing the proportion of the active labor force to the total population. Part of the increases in output achieved by the belligerent countries during World War II resulted from drawing into employment young people who would otherwise have been in school, older people who had reached the normal retirement age, and housewives who would normally have been fully occupied in their homes. One may doubt whether such increases in output can properly be considered "economic development." At least the people themselves should make their own choice between more goods and services, and more leisure in the form of higher school-leaving ages, lower retirement ages, and freedom of housewives from responsibilities outside their homes.

In sum, the choice between higher material standards of living and more leisure is one that the people themselves should make. The economist's role stops with indicating the nature of the choice to be made. However, the choice cannot be made by each individual separately. Achieving a "minimum effort" requires collective decisions by extended family units, villages, trade unions, employers' assocations, or even by the people as a whole through their government.

The choice between a higher level of current consumption and a more rapid rate of economic progress is also one to be made by the people concerned. Here, too, discontinuities appear. Half a railway is useless; power plants, blast furnaces, or refineries below a certain size are too inefficient to be worth constructing; even irrigation projects below a certain scale may not be worthwhile. A certain minimum volume of saving is necessary before significant economic progress can be made. In large measure, the choice between much or little sacrifice of current consumption for a higher standard of living in the future is the choice between a slow or rapid rate of economic progress. This choice, like the choice between material income and leisure, must be made collectively.

As productivity rises it may be translated into a higher level of per capita income or into a larger number of children per member of the labor force. This choice also is for the people themselves to make, and it, too, cannot be left entirely to individuals, since the wishes of some individuals or groups can be thwarted by the decisions of others. A humanitarian society does not permit children to starve; and if some people have more children than they can support, the rest of the community will take care of them through private charity or through the government. In this manner, the income which would otherwise have gone toward swelling the stream of saving and accelerating the rate of economic progress will go instead toward supporting a larger population, in defiance of the wishes of those who prefer smaller families and more rapid progress. Unless income per capita reaches a certain level, the stream of savings cannot rise to the point where an underdeveloped economy is able to finance the whole of its further economic progress from its own resources, without outside assistance in the form of loans or grants. If the population grows so fast that increases in productivity do not bring the country closer to that level of per capita income, the economy will never get "over the hump" to the point where it can finance its own economic development alone and unaided.

Although economic development policy seeks to raise per capita production as quickly as possible, it is not a matter of indifference how this increased output is attained. The limitations imposed by the people's desire for leisure, by their wish to have large families, and their reluctance to sacrifice current consumption for the sake of a higher standard of living in the future, should be considered. Per capita income can be raised if people work harder and longer, if they save larger shares of their income and so release resources for investment projects, and if they restrict the size of their families; but increases in output achieved in these ways are assuredly "progress" only if the gains outweigh the sacrifices in the view of the people concerned.

We shall define the over-all goal of economic development, then, as raising per capita productivity as much as possible over some long-run "perspective planning" period, and spreading the consequent improvements of welfare among all major groups and regions; in the process, due weight should be given to people's wishes regarding the choice between goods and services or leisure, between more income now and more income later, and between a higher per capita income and larger families, expressed as collective choices made by the smallest group whose decisions can be effective in promoting development.

The Ethics of Development

This concept of development may still be too narrow; it still skirts some fundamental questions of social ethics. It is well for the econometricians to push the methodology of economics as far as possible in the direction of that of the natural sciences; but when we come to development it is also well for us to remember that one of the ancestors of modern economics is moral philosophy. As Denis Goulet points out in his book on *The Ethics of Development*,[8] "development" in the ultimate sense cannot be regarded merely as industrialization or modernization, nor even simply as the increase in productivity, as suggested above. We might paraphrase Lord Keynes' toast to the Royal Economic Society, quoted at the beginning of Chapter 1; the general rise in productivity is not development, but the possibility of development. Goulet argues that the concept of development is best expressed in the phrase "the human ascent," the ascent of all men in their quintessence of humanity, including the economic, biological, psychological, social, cultural, ideological, spiritual, mystical, and transcendental dimensions.

Who, Goulet asks, is the ultimate "developer"? The hydraulic engineer who controls the waters of the Nile? The economist who designs a brilliant new tax system? The WHO official who eliminates malaria? The planner, the politician? The answer, Goulet rightly maintains, is that none of these by himself is the developer; development is the result of the interplay of these and many other kinds of activity. He insists—and the present writer would agree—that the philosopher needs to be added to the development team; without a clear concept of the philosophy of development, the team becomes "a simple *ad hoc* mission."

Similarly, the distinguished French economist, planner, and philosopher Father Louis-Joseph Lebret, founder of *Économie et Humanisme* and of the *Institut de Récherches et de Formation en vue de Développement*, warns against identifying the "ultimate success" with high levels of consumption.[9] The "most triumphant" civilizations, on the plane of humanity and perhaps also of power, have been somewhat austere. Nonetheless, the late Father Lebret was no less insistent on the need to abolish poverty than the present writer. Deficiencies in standards of food, clothing, and shelter must be eliminated; for this, both agricultural improvement and industrialization are necessary, as well as generalized education, better technical training, increased saving and investment. And all this will require planning.

[8] Denis Goulet, *La Ethica del Desarollo* (Madrid, 1965).
[9] L. J. Lebret, *Dynamique concret du développement* (Paris, 1961), pp. 63–64.

Decision Functions and Shadow Prices

The next three chapters are concerned with planning, and the discussion of planning begins with the decision function. There is also some analysis of the use of shadow prices in planning. Before leaving the broader philosophical questions raised in this chapter, it may be useful to say a word about the philosophical foundations of decision functions and shadow pricing. In the traditional welfare economics, *Wertfreiheit* was the goal. "Revealed preferences" in the marketplace were accepted at face value; whether people preferred bibles or beer, the economist did not question the ethics of the choice. He was concerned only with obtaining an optimal allocation of resources that would give people as much as possible of what *they* want, whatever it might be.

The welfare economics of growth retains a species of *Wertfreiheit;* the economist or the planner tries not to introduce his own value judgments. But having discovered the inadequacies of the free market as a device for discovering what people want, let alone a mechanism for assuring them what they want, the economist now reverts to the "decision function"— that is, to "revealed preferences" which emerge through the political process, rather than through the market. The economist or development planner states that he will not introduce his own preferences, but will accept objectives laid down by "the government," with the belief—or at least the hope—that "the government" will be responsible to the people and responsive to their wishes.

Similarly, "shadow prices" or "accounting prices" are sometimes introduced into the planning process to make calculations and establish priorities where the market prices are "clearly inadequate" as a guide. Here we may distinguish two philosophically different types of shadow price. Sometimes a market price is "clearly inadequate" as a guide to policy because of imperfections of the market, exercise of monopoly power of various kinds, discontinuities, external economies, linkage effects, or previous misguided government intervention. In this case the economist can use well-worn tools of analysis to try to figure out what the market price would be under more "ideal" conditions (pure competition and perfect divisibility, let us say) and insert this calculated price into the planning models. Some value judgments are hidden in this process, but at least the economist knows more or less what he is doing. The other kind of shadow price involves a decision that some good or service (or some cost) is intrinsically "worth more" (or less) than the market price because individual decisions do not reflect the collective welfare. On these grounds, education and public health are subsidized in most countries, and housing, transport, and other services in many. This subsidization implies placing a "shadow price" above the market price to assure a supply greater than would be forthcoming in a completely free market.

It is clear that we are here on completely different grounds from those involved in accepting the "revealed preferences" of the marketplace. Who is to determine "shadow prices" in the second sense? The economist or planner has no special knowledge enabling him to determine *ultimate* values. He may demonstrate all the interconnections between education and other aspects of development, try to measure costs in terms of other objectives sacrificed, and the like; but he cannot bring any professional expertise to bear on the question "Is education intrinsically worth more or less than health?" Once again the government must make the ultimate decisions, hopefully in the interests of the people. But it is clear that the power to determine shadow prices is an important political power; and the power to determine the decision function is even more important. We spent more than a century studying the workings of the market before deciding that it was inadequate as a sole guide to policy; if we are to replace the market with the polling booth—or any other device for forming governments—as the source of "revealed preferences," it is time someone started equally serious study of the political process in various countries, to determine just how effective the political process is in discovering what people want in the way of "development."

Sometimes it is quite clear that governments in power are not reflecting the wishes of the people in either their "decision functions" or their choice of "shadow prices." What does the economist or development planner do then? This question is a profoundly moral one to which no satisfactory answer can be given. It was discussed at length in a conference on problems of development planning in Southeast Asia, held at the East-West Center in Honolulu in February, 1965. Out of the discussion of this question came the following hierarchy of situations, each of which calls for a different response from the development planner: [10]

1. A government with strong popular support, placing economic development high on its priority list, establishes a "decision-function" with priorities reasonably well quantified and expressed in terms of measurable economic objectives—income, employment, balance of payments, distribution of income among groups and regions, etc. This situation is "bliss" for the development planner and he can work along familiar lines.

2. The same government adds to its list of development objectives certain goals that until recently, at any rate, were considered "non-economic"; levels of literacy and general education, standards of public health, national security, prestige items, etc. Here the task of the development planner is a little more complicated, mainly because it is difficult to determine the appropriate accounting prices for education, health, national security, and the like. Conceptually, however, the planner's situation is no different in this case from the first one. It is a matter of measuring costs and benefits, determining opportunity costs, complementarities and linkages, etc. and the same tools of analysis can be used.

3. Through sheer incompetence the politicians, while sincerely aiming at national welfare, fail to see planning as a problem of resource allocation and continue to insist on mutually incompatible goals, making systematic preparation and implementation of plans impossible. The planner then has two essential choices. He may stay on the job and do his best to educate the politicians, or he may resign and try to educate the general public to the need of replacing the government.

[10] Benjamin Higgins, "Dominant Problems in Southeast Asian Planning: a Western View," *The Philippine Economic Journal*, Vol. IV, No. 2, 1965, pp. 434–36.

4. The politicians are pursuing goals which, in the opinion of the planners, are contrary to the national welfare, not through ignorance but through genuine lack of concern for it. They may be concerned simply with staying in power, or getting rich, or preserving the privileges of a privileged class, or acquiring new territory not worth the cost of getting it or using it, etc. In this case the planner as a technician can have no function. As a citizen, he has a responsibility to help "get the rascals out"; and as a citizen, not as a planner, he must decide whether he can be more effective boring from within or attacking from without. Nothing in economic science, and little in the other social sciences, is of much help to him here.

18 Planning and Programming Economic Development

Achieving rapid rates of economic development in any country requires astute government policy—including, in some cases, a policy of letting well enough alone. Today the usefulness of planning and programming development is universally recognized. Tastes regarding the form and extent of governmental management of the economy vary widely, from the highly centralized control of a socialist system in the USSR and Poland, through the more decentralized and otherwise modified socialist systems of Yugoslavia and Egypt, to the almost libertine systems of free private enterprise in the Lebanon, the Philippines, and Thailand. Yet all of these countries go through the motions of preparing development plans and programs; it is considered slightly disreputable not to do so. Moreover, if planning and programming are to be effective, the basic techniques must be essentially the same no matter what the form of economic and political organization.

Planning, Programming, and Politics

In some Latin American countries there is a body of public opinion that regards "economic development planning" or "developmentalism" as a political ideology in itself. Economists, on the other hand, tend to regard planning or programming of economic development as essentially non-political. The political limitations within which an economic development plan must be prepared are taken as data, restraints on the scope and nature of development policies, which must be taken into account in formulating plans and programs.

From a purely economic viewpoint there is a whole hierarchy of degrees of government intervention, all of which are consistent with the preparation of some kind of economic and political development program. There are two main criteria for judging the degree of government intervention: the relative size of the public sector, and the extent and tightness of control over the private sector. In terms of degree of intervention in the private sector, one might rank development policies in the following order. (1) Reliance on monetary and fiscal policy alone. Accelerating development may be difficult in some countries if government intervention is so limited, but it would still be possible to construct an economic development program utilizing nothing but public investment plus monetary and fiscal policy designed to encourage and direct private investment. (2) Reliance on monetary and fiscal policy *plus* foreign trade policy. Tariffs and quotas can be used to influence the pattern of private investment, to encourage investment in import-replacing industries, and the like. (3) Reliance on monetary and fiscal policy *plus* foreign trade policy *plus* exchange control. From a purely economic viewpoint there is little difference between controlling the pattern of trade through tariffs, quotas, sales taxes, etc., and exchange control. From a political viewpoint, however, exchange control is usually regarded as involving more "dirigisme" than tariffs or quotas—perhaps because exchange control is a more recent invention. With this combination of instruments, a country could exert powerful effects on the pace and pattern of economic development. (4) All the foregoing *plus* direct controls. With this degree of intervention, a country would have in effect a "war economy," but with economic development rather than winning a war as the objective. The direct controls might include price controls, rationing, wage fixing, licensing of investment, control of new capital issues, manpower allocation, etc.

One may also have a hierarchy with regard to the relative size of the public sector, extending from 1 per cent to 100 per cent of national income or investment. As a matter of record, successful economic development has occurred with a ratio of public investment to the total investment ranging from about 10 to perhaps 35 per cent, and from, say, 70 to 100 per cent. As yet, there is no clear case on record of successful economic development with a ratio of public to total investment between, say, 40 per cent and 60 percent. Incentive systems seem to work best in predominantly socialist or predominantly private enterprise economies. On the other hand, World War II economies of the United States, the United Kingdom, Canada, and Australia all had ratios of government expenditures to national income in the neighborhood of 50 per cent, and they were successful in the achievement of their objectives. If the electorate wants development as much as the people in these countries wanted victory during the war, it should be possible to operate similarly mixed "disequilibrium" economies for longer periods.

It is clear that economic development can occur within a wide range of political systems. Economists have largely abandoned the search for Utopia, the unique system with harmoniously integrated political, social, and economic institutions which would automatically guarantee an optimal economic situation, or a maximum rate of growth. Dictatorships, military regimes of various kinds, Soviet-style Communism with highly centralized decision-making, Yugoslav-style Communism with highly decentralized decision-making, various mixtures of public and private enterprise within parliamentary democracies—even, it would seem from prewar Japanese experience, an essentially feudal regime committed to industrialization—all are capable of producing high rates of economic growth. As suggested above, there is no doubt some form of political organization that will provide the maximum rate of economic growth for each country at each point of time, given its economic situation and its socio-cultural framework. But generating high rates of growth is mainly a matter of making and implementing the right decisions within whatever economic and political framework is preferred.

Plans, Programs, Policies

In the literature of economic development, one finds references to economic development planning, economic development programming, economic development projects, and economic development policies. Our first step toward an understanding of the techniques involved must be to define our terms.

One basic manual produced under United Nations auspices defines Project, Program, and Plan as follows: [1]

A *Project* is the smallest unit of investment activity to be considered in the course of programming. It will, as a rule, be a technically coherent undertaking which has to be carried out by a private or public agency and which can be carried out, technically speaking, independently of other projects. Examples of projects are the building of a factory, the construction of a bridge or a road, the reclamation of a piece of land. A *Programme* is a coordinated set of projects. They will be located in the same country or in some smaller geographical unit (state, province, region, municipality). They will also be started in some specified period, which may be a year, a five-year span, or some other period. The degree of coordination in other respects may vary but the projects will have been considered by some authority with a view to coordinating them. An Investment *Plan*, in this context, is something arrived at "from above," through calculations referring either to the whole economy or to certain sectors in certain areas. It is not constructed by combining projects, but derived from the broad development aims set.

Elaborating on these concepts, we may define an economic development plan as a document setting forth over-all targets for economic and social development. These will usually include a target rate of increase in total production, given the estimated (or possibly planned) rate of population growth. Given the total output, targets may be established for the division of this output among various sectors in the economy. Where statistics are available in sufficient quantity and of sufficiently high quality, a target input-output matrix may be worked out. Usually these targets are set at

[1] United Nations, Economic Commission for Asia and the Far East, *Programming Techniques for Economic Development* (Bangkok, 1960), Chapter IV.

least ten years in advance, and such a long-range plan is frequently called a "perspective plan."

Programming begins with projections of economic quantities. These will typically start with the projection of such aggregates as national income, gross national product, total consumption, total investment, total employment and unemployment, total imports and exports, and the like. The program will then proceed to allocate these aggregates among various sectors, regions, and perhaps individual industries in the economy. These projections will then be examined for mutual consistency, and for consistency with the targets laid down in the plan. The comparison of projections with the targets will suggest criteria to be applied in the selection of public investment projects. The preparation of these projects is in turn part of the process of programming. Usually precise implementation programs are limited to fairly short periods, two or three years.

Finally, the comparison of sectoral projections with plans will suggest certain policies. We may define policies as governmental measures undertaken to effect private decisions. These may be monetary, fiscal, foreign trade, or similar measures, wage and price controls, regulation of monopolies, and the like.

The Decision Function

Not so many years ago, economists used to think that it was possible to design a set of economic policies that would maximize economic welfare through pure economic analysis alone. We have been forced to abandon that position and to admit that economic analysis by itself does not permit anyone to say with assurance what policies are "best." The invention of the "decision function" (also called the "welfare function" and the "objective function") is a response to the recognition that basic decisions must be made by somebody else before economic policy analysis can begin. However, the people to whom the basic decisions are handed over—the politicians—are not always in a position to make sound judgments without help from technicians. There is need for continuous interaction between the technicians—especially the planners—and the people who have ultimate responsibility for political judgment.

Let us note briefly the objectives that are usually set forth in development plans and programs. All plans include some target for raising per capita income. Most include also some target with respect to employment and unemployment. Many have separate targets with respect to the balance of payments. It is really illogical to have a separate target for the balance of payments, since the balance of payments is important only because of its effects on income and employment; but balance of payments pressures are so common and so severe among underdeveloped countries that there is some justification for setting up separate targets regarding the external position of the economy.

Quite a few plans also include separate targets for income distribution—distribution not only among individuals and groups, but also among regions. Goals stated in the form of reduced gaps in productivity and income among major regions in the country are finding their way into development plans more and more frequently. Some countries also have explicit goals with regard to the structure of the economy, particularly with regard to the relative role of public and private enterprise. India and Burma, for example, want to move toward a socialist state. The Philippines and Brazil, at the other end of the scale, want to restrict the role of government and to maintain as much as possible of free private enterprise. Indonesia has chosen "socialism à la Indonesia" and "guided democracy." Every society obviously has the right to decide what sort of economic and social organization it wants. If a particular form of economic organization, whatever it may be, is important in the eyes of the people and the leaders of the country, independently of its contribution to achievement of other goals, it should be included as part of the over-all development plan and assigned a proper weight.

Some countries have views with regard to foreign aid and investment. Indonesia, for example, has expressed reservations regarding reliance on foreign capital from any source. Again, it is any country's right to limit foreign aid or investment. If there are restraints of this kind, which limit what may be done within the plan, they should be stated explicitly.

These, then, are the common goals. Other "objectives" belong logically under the heading of "shadow prices" rather than under the heading of goals as such. For example, many development plans include some reference to "social development": education, public health, public housing, social welfare, and land tenure. But education, public health, improved housing, and social security are not really separate goals in themselves, but are a part of national income. These particular items are (or at least may be) both capital goods and consumers' goods; they contribute to raising productivity as well as providing direct satisfactions. Other objectives, such as national defense, national prestige (reflected in beautiful capital cities, sports stadiums, etc.), preservation of traditional culture, and the like are essentially consumers' goods. It does not follow that their priority is necessarily low; it is a matter of determining the appropriate "shadow prices" at which they are to be included in the national income.

Conflicts among Goals

Planning also involves assigning weights to objectives so as to make it possible to resolve conflicts among objectives. For example, over some range of increase in developmental investment, income and employment will increase together. Within this range no conflict between income and employment arises. But just as surely, at some level of investment a conflict between further increases in income and further increases in employment will appear. The universe seems to have been constructed to make things difficult for development planners. One of the ways in which development is difficult is that over a very wide range of productive activity, the techniques with the high labor-capital ratios also have high capital-output ratios. Here is one of the many paradoxes in this baffling field of development; labor-intensive techniques may be something which only

advanced countries can afford. Underdeveloped countries sometimes cannot afford labor-intensive techniques because they are too expensive in
terms of output per unit of capital.

Income, Employment, Choice of Product Mix and Technology

Unemployment and underemployment, as well as low man-hour productivity, are major characteristics of less-developed economies. Low-
income countries, unfortunately, face a possible conflict between maximization of output and maximization of employment. In many of them,
capital is scarce and unskilled labor is redundant; they cannot afford to
waste capital. To make matters worse, there is evidence that over a wide
range of products the techniques which utilize a high ratio of labor capital
(or land) also involve a low ratio of output to capital (or land). In other
words, underdeveloped countries may be unable to adjust their techniques
to their factor endowments by adopting labor-intensive techniques; the
most efficient organization of production in many fields may be capital-
intensive. Technical coefficients (proportions in which factors of production are used) may be subject to little variation without a sharp rise in the
capital-output ratio. Moreover, technological progress of an essentially
labor-saving nature, while raising man-hour productivity, may also raise
the level of unemployment in face of a rapidly growing labor force. In
considering the contribution of science and technology to raising productivity, therefore, the possible adverse effect on employment must also
be taken into account.

Technological displacement is at least as old as the Industrial Revolution,
and misgivings about the impact of scientific and technological progress
on employment are equally old. Over the centuries fear of mass technological unemployment largely disappeared in the now advanced
countries, although automation has revived this fear since World War II.
There are, however, some important differences between the situation of
less-developed countries today and that of Europe, North America, or
Australasia on the eve of their industrial revolutions. Per capita incomes
were relatively high, capital accumulation correspondingly easier. Ideology
and social structures were more favorable to capital accumulation. Population-resource ratios were more favorable. Rates of population growth
were lower. Expansion of world trade served as an "engine for growth" in
a fashion unlikely to be repeated in the next few decades. Most important
for the present discussion, the now advanced countries did not launch the
process of transforming essentially agricultural into essentially industrial
economies with a large backlog of unemployment and underemployment
to absorb. Taken together, these factors mean that solving simultaneously
the problems of low productivity and income on the one hand, and unemployment and underemployment on the other, will require substantially
higher ratios of investment to income in the now underdeveloped countries
than those which did the job for the now advanced ones. As stated by the
ILO Expert Group on employment objectives in economic development,[2]

[2] International Labour Office, *Employment Objectives in Economic Development*,
Report of a Meeting of Experts (Geneva, 1966), p. 49.

Incautious application of the experience of the more advanced countries is likely to result in an under-estimation of capital requirements for employment creation. In the early phases of their development few countries in Western Europe faced the problem of absorbing such large numbers of underemployed and unemployed as exist today in some underdeveloped countries where, in addition to high rates of growth of the labour force, there have been for some decades very high rates of displacement of labour from agriculture and traditional industries. . . .

Rates of investment which were adequate to absorb the supplies of labour in various countries in the past may be wholly inadequate to meet the master problems of the present day.

Income Targets versus Employment Targets

Development plans and programs which may seem quite satisfactory in terms of targets set for rates of growth of per capita income may fail to bring acceptable reductions in under- or unemployment. Indeed, casting development plans in terms of income creation alone can result in the mere projection of past trends with respect to employment and unemployment.

Brazil and Mexico, which have enjoyed high over-all rates of growth since World War II without solving their employment problems, are cases in point. Even countries that have adopted employment-oriented plans, such as India and Italy, have found their plans too modest for the task. The Second Five-Year Plan in India made employment creation its primary objective; indeed, it made it clear that if a conflict arose between maximizing output and maximizing employment, the latter goal should have priority. Yet the rise in non-agricultural employment, estimated at 6.5 million, was less than half of the increase in the labor force in the same period; the bulk of the additional workers had to seek a livelihood in the already overcrowded agricultural sector. To quote the noted Indian economist K. N. Raj: [3]

Not only has the place of development up to now been inadequate to cope with the growth of the working force resulting from the rise in population but, what is a more serious aspect of this failure, there has been no great success in mobilising idle labour in order to accelerate the tempo of development.

The Italian Ten-Year Plan (1955–65), frequently referred to as the Vanoni Plan, laid particular stress on employment creation in the south. It was hoped that gaps in per capita income as between north and south could thus be narrowed. During its first five years, the Plan was successful in raising national income at an average rate of 5.5 per cent, slightly above target. It was also successful in establishing equilibrium in the balance of payments. However, investment continued to be concentrated in the north as before; while the percentage rate of growth of per capita income in the south was raised to about the same level as in the north, the gap in absolute levels of per capita income continued to increase. More important for present purposes, even Italy's concentrated effort succeeded only in

[3] K. N. Raj, "Appendix I:C, India," in ILO, *loc. cit.*, pp. 167–68.

cutting unemployment in half, and even this accomplishment was possible only because net emigration from the country almost equalled the decline in unemployment.[4]

Technological Progress, Employment, and Dualism

The large-scale migration to cities since World War II has transported some share of the underemployment, unemployment, and low productivity from a rural to an urban setting. Nevertheless, in most underdeveloped countries it is still the agricultural sector in which these problems are most acute. To some degree, then, the conflict between maximizing income and maximizing employment appears as a conflict between the wish to take advantage of the superior productivity of investment in the modern sector or leading region and the wish to create employment in the traditional sector or lagging region. The powerful agglomerative pull of leading regions usually reflects genuine advantages in terms of availability of training and skills, social overhead capital, access to raw materials, finance, and markets. In many—if not most—cases, additional investment in the already progressing sector and region will add more to national income than an equal amount of investment in the stagnant or retrogressing region. In terms of raising national income, the case for active intervention by government to shift investment from leading to lagging regions must rest on certain rather special conditions: there must exist in the lagging region large-scale, "lumpy" investments of a kind not now attractive (under existing policies) to private enterprise; the investment projects must be of a kind that can be executed efficiently with relatively labor-intensive methods (where the elasticity of substitution of labor for capital is high); and output-capital ratios must be higher for those undertakings than for any investment of equal size in the leading region. It is a question whether such cases appear very frequently.

It is also a question whether employment as such is ever a legitimate aim of public policy. No doubt it is good for morale to do a certain amount of work; but most people would happily accept more "underemployment" if their incomes were substantially raised at the same time. The ideal policy would maximize income and then distribute both income and leisure equitably among individuals, groups, and regions. Unfortunately it is not always possible—technically, administratively, and politically—to adopt this ideal policy; sometimes satisfactory incomes for the unemployed or underemployed in the lagging sector or region can be provided only through more or less full-time employment, with a capital outlay that would produce substantially more output if it were utilized to create fewer jobs in the modern sector or leading region.

Product Mix versus Choice of Technology

The amount of employment created by a given volume of investment depends in part on the product mix and partly on the technology chosen to produce the various goods and services in the product mix. At first

[4] See Chap. 31.

blush, it would seem that underdeveloped countries, where capital is scarce and unskilled labor redundant, can keep the aggregate capital-output ratio down, without undue loss of efficiency, more easily through choice of product mix than through choice of technology. If it is difficult to produce a wide range of commodities efficiently with labor-intensive methods, cannot developing countries specialize in those products where efficiency is possible with a relatively high labor-capital ratio? The answer, unfortunately, is "not always." The country's resource pattern may be such that its comparative advantage in international trade may lie in industries that require relatively capital-intensive techniques—oil, tin, bauxite, copper, and plantation agriculture, for example. The balance of payments situation may be one strongly favoring the development of import-replacing industries of a capital-intensive nature. The subtle factor of "linkage" —stimulation of investment in other fields by initial investment in one field—may be higher for heavy, large-scale, capital-intensive industries than for light, small-scale, or labor-intensive industries. Acquisition of fundamental technical and managerial skills, "technology mindedness" and "development mindedness," may be more closely associated with modern technology of a capital-intensive nature than with old-fashioned technology of a labor-intensive type.

Very little research has been done on the choice of technology for particular undertakings. The complexity of the analysis that must be undertaken before one can be sure which technique is best has been admirably set forth by the Indian economist A. K. Sen.[5] In addition to the capital-output ratios for the whole range of available techniques, one needs to have information regarding labor costs at present and probable future wage rates, working capital requirements (quality and price of the project with different techniques), managerial costs, surplus available for reinvestment, impact on the balance of payments, linkage effects, and even—since the time-pattern of expansion of output will be different for different techniques—communal time-preference functions. Applying his analytical framework as best he could with the data available, Sen came to the conclusion that "the case for hand looms or for power looms is much less straightforward than the Hand Loom Board of India on the one hand and the Millowners' association of Bombay on the other seem to suggest." [6] His calculations show that the Banaras hand loom has a higher output-capital ratio; but the rate of surplus is so much higher with the non-automatic power loom that with reinvestment of the surplus, total output with the power loom will surpass that of the hand loom within six years. The basic data are shown in Table 18–1. Dr. Sen is much more definite regarding the Ambar Charkha spinning wheel: "As a technological possibility, the Ambar Charkha seems to offer very little." [7]

Dhar and Lydall present Indian data (Tables 18–2 and 18–2a) which suggest a general tendency for output-capital ratios to rise with the size of the factory. The Netherlands Economics Institute has gathered statis-

[5] A. K. Sen, *Choice of Techniques* (Oxford, 1960).
[6] *Ibid.*, p. 114.
[7] *Ibid.*, p. 119.

TABLE 18-1

Alternative Techniques in Indian Cotton-Weaving Industry and Some of Their Economic Implications*

Technique	Capital cost per loom (Rs.)	Output per loom per day (yds.)	Net value added per loom per year (Rs.)	Output-capital coefficient	Labor required per loom per day (no.)	Rates of profit per loom per year (expressed as percentage of capital cost) at daily wages of:				
						Rs. 1	Rs. 2	Rs. 3	Rs. 4	Rs. 5
Fly-shuttle handloom	30–50	6	450	9.0	1	150	Neg.	Neg.	Neg.	Neg.
"Banaras" semiautomatic handloom	200	20	1,500	7.5	1	600	450	300	150	0
Cottage power loom	1,500	30	2,250	1.5	1	130	110	90	70	50
Factory non-automatic power loom	4,000	80	6,000	1.5	1	143	135	128	120	113
Automatic power loom	10,000	80	6,000	0.6	⅛	60	59	59	59	58

SOURCE: K. N. Raj, "Employment and Unemployment in the Indian Economy: Problems of Classification, Measurement and Policy," in *Economic Development and Cultural Change*, April, 1959, p. 276.

* The estimates are based on the assumption that (1) the number of working days per year is 300; and (2) the net value added per yard is Rs. 1/4 and is the same for all techniques. The second of these assumptions means, in effect, assuming that (1) costs of depreciation and replacement are the same for all techniques; (2) the input of raw materials required per unit of output is the same for all techniques; and (3) despite the different quantities of raw cotton required, in the aggregate, under different techniques (due to differences in the total volume of output), costs of production of raw cotton do not differ.

TABLE 18-2

Output-Capital Ratios in Different Sizes of Factory in India, 1956,
According to Census Data*

| Industry | Average daily number of employees | | | | |
	20–49	50–99	100–249	250–499	500 and over
Wheat flour	0.23	0.44	0.35	0.80	..
Rice milling	0.32	0.34	0.30	(0.24)†	..
Vegetable oils	0.20	0.24	0.22	0.30	(0.31)
Soap	0.13	0.18	0.55	(0.09)	0.71
Tanning	0.28	0.39	0.38	0.55	(0.32)
Cotton textiles (spin-ning and weaving)	0.24	0.50	0.23	0.41	0.63
Woolen textiles	0.14	0.34	0.16	0.34	0.51
Bicycles	0.51	0.58	0.39	0.51	0.49
Electric fans	0.36	0.33	0.53	0.41	0.30

* Output = annual net value added. Capital = net fixed capital at book value plus stocks and cash, at end of year. The book values of fixed capital are based on historical costs.

† Figures in parentheses relate to one factory only.

SOURCE: *Census of Indian Manufactures, 1956.* From P. N. Dhar and H. F. Lydall, *The Role of Small Enterprises in Indian Economic Development* (New York, 1960).

tics for several manufacturing industries in the United States, Mexico, Colombia, and India which indicate a wide range of possible capital-labor ratios in these industries, but except for cotton textiles and bakery products the capital cost per job is high in all countries—above $2,000.[8] A United Nations study for France, India, Poland, and the USSR shows a relatively narrow range of capital-output ratios, with a much wider range of capital-labor ratios, resulting in almost equal costs per cubic meter-kilometer for a combined operation of excavation, transport, and compaction.[9] On the whole, however, both the quantity and quality of such data are inadequate for any general conclusions about the potential use of labor-intensive technology.

More important, there has yet to be any large-scale, systematic scientific and engineering research into the possibilities of *new* techniques which, hopefully, may have both low capital-labor ratios and low capital-output ratios. Such research has been concentrated to date in advanced countries where capital is relatively abundant and labor relatively scarce, so that labor-saving innovations are unhesitatingly accepted as "progress." The need for organized research into possibilities of an efficient but labor-intensive technology has frequently been noted. The ILO Expert Group on Employment Objectives calls for international action for promotion of

[8] Netherlands Economic Institute, Division for Balanced Economic Growth, *Capital-Labour Ratios in Certain Industries in Some Countries*, A Progress Report (The Hague, December, 1955).

[9] United Nations, "Capital Intensity and Costs in Earthmoving Operations," in *Industrialization and Productivity*, Bulletin No. 3 (March, 1960), p. 13.

TABLE 18–2a

Output-Capital Ratios* in Small and Large Factories in India According to Certain Plans

Product	Small factory (not more than 50 employed—one-shift basis)	Large factory (50 or more employed)	
		Present shift basis	"Desirable" shift basis
Fruit and vegetable preservation	0.25	0.30	0.42
Leather footwear	0.33	0.52	0.68
Cycle tires and tubes	0.46	0.61†	0.61
Superphosphate	0.28	0.45†	0.45‡
Matches	0.29	0.87	1.10
Sanitary wares and related products	0.53	0.35	0.54
Steel furniture	0.54	0.48	0.66
Tin containers	0.47	0.48	0.66
Bolts and nuts	0.50	0.48	0.66
Sewing machines	0.57	0.97†	0.97‡
PVC insulated cables	0.26	0.55	0.67
Storage batteries	0.54	0.57	0.73
Radio sets	0.52	0.56	0.72
Refrigerators	0.68	0.32	0.47
Bicycles	0.46	0.57	0.71

* Output = annual gross value added. Capital = initial outlay on fixed and working capital, including required cash balance.
Note: The data in this table are forecasts, not results.
† Three shifts. All the other figures are one shift.
‡ Three shifts. All the other figures are two shifts.
SOURCE: The estimates for the small factories were originally derived from certain "model schemes" prepared by the Small-Scale Industry Organization; those for the large factories are taken from various sources, but primarily from information collected by the development wing of the Ministry of Commerce and Industry regarding plans for expansion by large-scale units in the private sector. From P. N. Dhar and H. F. Lydall, *The Role of Small Enterprise in Indian Economic Development* (New York, 1960).

experimental research "to develop and disseminate technologies best suited to the conditions of underdeveloped countries, patricularly in view of their need to raise the level of employment associated with any given level of employment."

Technology and Programming

As long as the supply of capital to underdeveloped countries is limited, incomes are low, and underemployment and unemployment prevail, the only solution seems to be to assign priorities for projects within a development program according to contribution to national income, until most of the investment budget is exhausted, but to save some of the budget for useful projects that can be carried out with highly labor-intensive methods. Suppose, for example, that a Planning Board is confronted with the following group of projects:

Project	Capital-Labor Ratio ($)	Capital-Output Ratio
A	10,000	2:1
B	8,000	2.2:1
C	6,000	2.5:1
..	..	..
..	..	..
..	..	..
..	..	..
..	..	..
I	2,500	2.8:1
J	2,000	3.0:1
..	..	..
..	..	..
..	..	..
N	500	4.0:1

Suppose further that the total investment budget is such that only projects "A" through "I" and one more project can be undertaken. The Planning Board would then be well advised to include Project "N" rather than Project "J" (or "K," "L," or "M,"), in order to make a significant contribution to employment-creation, despite the fact that the total contribution to national income over the perspective planning period (it is in this sense that the term "output" should be measured if capital-output ratios are to be used for assigning priorities) is less. In most underdeveloped countries there are opportunities for substantial amounts of employment-creation in this fashion without serious sacrifices in gross national product-opportunities which are not being exploited to the full. Multiple shifts, irrigation and construction works, community development projects, afforestation, village housing, fisheries, and land reform all offer possibilities.

In deciding whether or not such projects are worthwhile, care must be taken to account for labor utilized at social costs rather than money costs. The social costs consist only of any necessary increase in consumption of former unemployed or underemployed who are given work or more work. If their marginal contribution to gross national product exceeds this amount—which is usually very small—it pays to employ them (or to employ them more fully) even though law requires the payment of a money wage higher than this marginal contribution.

Need for Weighting Objectives

Confronted with this basic conflict it becomes necessary to put weights on income and employment as objectives. The planner must measure as well as he can the relative cost of increased income and increased employment—how much income must be sacrificed in order to add one permanent job. If we must sacrifice some national income in order to add one man-year of employment, is it worth it or not? The answer requires a political judgment. Somebody else—not the planner—has to decide whether a loss of national income of $600 to raise employment by one man-year is too high or not. The planner's role is simply to point up the question in as precise a form as possible and to quantify the alternatives as much as possible, so that the final political judgment can be as refined, as accurate, and as wise as possible.

Redistribution of Income

A conflict may also arise between greater equality of income distribution and a higher level of per capita income. In many underdeveloped countries, in contrast to most advanced ones, it is probably possible to redistribute income a good deal, and still add to the rate of investment and thus to the level of income and the rate of growth of income. We ought not to apply without question the experience of advanced countries, where it appears that the rich save and invest more than the poor, and where savings and investment out of profits are considerably higher than savings and investment out of wages. In some underdeveloped countries, the marginal propensity to consume out of high incomes is very high. Countries like the Philippines or Chile, with very unequal income distributions, have low ratios of private savings and investment to income. In such countries, redistribution of income from rich to middle income groups, moving the upper income groups along the backward-sloping portion of their supply curves of risk-taking and effort, and creating a mass market for durable consumers' goods, could increase investment and bring higher rate of growth. Nevertheless, it is still true that in any country a point will be reached where greater equality of income distribution will mean a lower level of investment and a lower rate of economic growth.

The problem is to find the optimal distribution of income, not in the old sense of maximizing welfare or satisfaction (which is really meaningless), but in the sense of maximizing growth. More important is to find the optimal rate of redistribution of income, through time, that will maximize investment and growth through time. But there is still a choice to make between achieving equality more rapidly and achieving a high income more rapidly. This choice is another the planners cannot make themselves. They can put price tags on the alternatives and quantify the decisions, but the decisions must be made through the political process.

The same is true of public versus private enterprise. Some rates of nationalization of private enterprise may retard economic growth, at least in the short run; some rates of "unscrambling the omelette"—denationalizing already nationalized industries—may also slow down the rate of growth. The planner's job is to isolate the conflicts and to determine the opportunity costs of a more rapid rate of nationalization (or slower rate of nationalization) and so on.

Choosing the Growth Path

The most difficult task of all in this first phase of development programming is to choose the growth path. Ideally, we would design our program so as to maximize the present value of a composite index, expressing all goals: income, employment, income distribution, balance of payments, cultural values, etc. We would maximize the present value of the stream of benefits in terms of this composite index of goals. Unfortunately we do not have the data or the knowledge to do so.

Some people have sought an escape from this dilemma in "turnpike theorems." (This term is a somewhat confusing one for people outside of North America who may not realize that the "turnpike" is the road on which you can travel fastest.) Turnpike theorems are theories of maximum growth rates. A simple turnpike theorem is shown in Figure 18–1. The

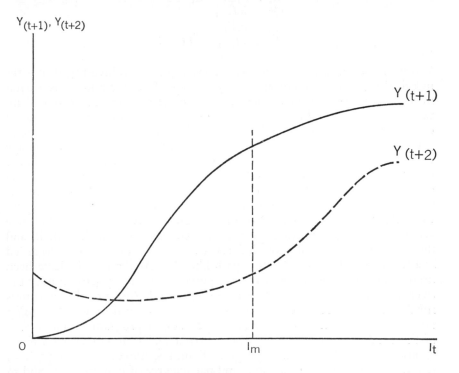

Figure 18-1

model assumes a technologically fixed relationship between investment in the present period and the increase of income in the next period, divided between total production and consumption. There is a maximum growth rate where these two curves are parallel to each other; there the gap between current consumption and current production, and so the rate of capital accumulation, is maximized. This is a highly oversimplified turnpike theorem, but it gives an idea of what is mean by the concept.

In any case, even sophisticated turnpike theorems are of limited use. It is no doubt true, as Professor Radner has proved, that at the limit any turnpike theorem leads to proportional growth. The American economy— and probably only the American economy—is reaching the point at which proportional growth makes sense. But it has taken several hundred years to get to that point. The significant decision which confronts the planner and the politician is not what the maximum growth path will be when you get there, but how rapidly and by what path the economy should approach the "turnpike." It may take a long time to get on to the turn-pike; there are many detours and bad roads on the way.

The diagram is derived from the following equations:

$$S_t = Y_{t-1} - C_t$$
$$Y_t = a.I_{t-1}$$
$$C_t = c.Y_{t-1}$$
$$I_t = b.I_{t-1} + d.C_{t-1}$$

Where S is savings, Y is income, C is consumption, I is investment, c is the marginal propensity to consume, a is the capital-output ratio, b is a parameter relating current investment to past investment (carrying out of investment plans) and d is a parameter relating current investment to recent consmuption (the Harrod "relation"). The subscripts denote time-periods.

One growth path that makes little or no sense is a constant percentage rate of growth. Yet this is the growth path most frequently found in the literature and in actual plans. There is no logic in having a constant percentage rate of growth from now to infinity. Let us assume, for example, that we have a perspective plan with a horizon of twenty years. In Figure 18–2, Path A is a "turnpike" from year 20 on. We can have the same *average* rate of growth through the next twenty years with Path B, and then have a high rate of growth forever after. This may also be regarded as a turnpike. Or we may have a path like "C." As these paths have been drawn, they all give the same average percentage rate of growth over the twenty years of one perspective planning period. And yet the prognosis for the economy from year 20 onward is clearly very different depending on whether we choose program A, program B, or program C. The future of this economy is clearly much better from the twentieth year on if we choose program B. Choosing program B means, however, a big push—a relatively slow growth of income, and particularly of consumption, and so greater sacrifice in the early years, in order to have higher income later. Path C gives the least sacrifice in the early years, but the lowest income in the later ones. Path A is in between.

If these are the three technologically and economically feasible growth paths, the society must choose among them. Nothing in economic analysis by itself would tell us which is the "best" plan. (We used to think that some market-determined interest rate was a measure of "community time-preference"—the interest rate of gilt-edged bonds, perhaps. We now

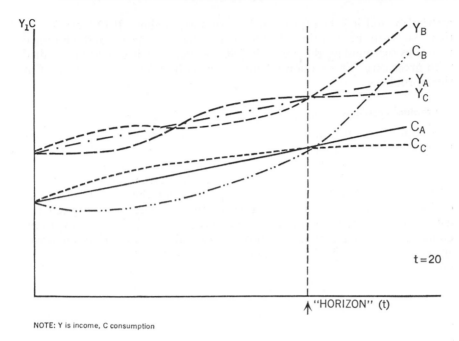

NOTE: Y is income, C consumption

Figure 18–2

realize that the interest rate on bonds is the result of decisions in the central bank and similar institutional factors. Unless, indeed, these decisions accurately reflect the community time-preference, there may be very little relationship between any interest rate in the whole structure and the actual valuation of income now as compared to income later by the society as a whole.) We cannot avoid making a judgment as to community time-preference, but this judgment has to be a political one. No planner is in the position to make that decision by himself. He can, however, point out the problem, put price tags on it, and quantify it so that the final judgment is made on the basis of the most complete information and understanding possible.

Estimating Capital Requirements: The Incremental Capital-Output Ratio

Once the growth path is selected, the next question is, "How much total investment is needed to produce target increases in per capita income?" Answering this question requires determining the relationship between investment, I, and the consequent increase in income, Y. This relationship, $I/\Delta Y$, is the incremental capital-output ratio (ICOR) that has been introduced in earlier chapters. Some ICOR is always implicit in any development plan, and it is helpful to make assumptions about ICOR explicit so that they can be scrutinized. However, the conceptual and empirical problems surrounding the use of ICOR are such that it should be handled with great care. This section is concerned with an exposition of some of these problems.

Conceptual Problems

Measuring ICOR for any given country involves obtaining conceptually comparable estimates of capital stock for at least two different dates, income estimates for the same dates, and calculating the ratio between the increments in capital stock and in income. The dates must be far enough apart in time so that the probable margin of error in the estimate of capital or income at each date is small relative to the increment between the dates. Unfortunately, such long income series are available for only a few countries. Measurements of the aggregate capital stock of various countries are even less easily obtained, and are none too accurate. Consequently the number of countries for which estimates of ICOR can be made without assurance that the statistical margin of error does not make the conclusions doubtful, is rather small.

Where long series of income and wealth are lacking there is a strong temptation to derive ICOR from national income statistics available over short periods. However, an ICOR derived from a short period in the past is not really what is wanted as a basis for projecting capital requirements. To determine the capital requirements of a given income target, one needs a figure (preferably one for each major sector of the economy) approximating an average relation between additions to the stock of capital and increases in national income over some period in the future. The use of an average over five previous years is justified only if those five years are part of a much longer period, so that there is a solid basis for assuming that the average for the five years is an approximation to a ratio that is stable in the long run, and if the planning period will not be significantly different from the last five years. If, for example, the previous five years represents the completion of a reconstruction period, while the plan explicitly provides for a long-run structural change, a projection of the ICOR in the recent past can be dangerous. Moreover, over short periods, the net investment figures in the national accounts are seldom an accurate measure of actual increases in the stock of productive capital. The net investment is usually derived from gross investment and a depreciation figure that is based on an accounting concept, rather than an estimate of the actual depletion of the stock of productive capital.

ICOR and Priorities

Further problems arise if, as a result of using ICOR for determining total capital requirements, planners slip into the error of using ICOR also as a factor in determining priorities. What should be compared in choosing among investment projects is not their ICOR's, but their contributions to income during a crucial period.

	Investment A	Investment B
Initial investment	100	100
Annual output	40	20
Investment life (years)	4	20
Annual straight-line depreciation	25	5
Total output over investment life	160	400
Capital-output ratio	2.5	5.0

The total output over the life span of Investment B is 400 as against 160 for Investment A. The capital-output ratios, on the other hand, are 5.0 and 2.5, respecively. In each case, annual output net of depreciation is 15. Which investment yields the greater increase in national output?

Overlooking any costs other than that of the investment, the output streams may be reduced to comparability by means of discounting. Given a rate of interest, it is possible to assign a present value to the income streams of $40 for four years and $20 for twenty years. Assuming an interest rate of 5 per cent, the present values would be $142 and $249, respectively. Thus Investment A is "worth" $142 in output and Investment B is worth $249. The choice would clearly favor Investment B and the fact that the capital-output ratio is less "favorable" is irrelevant.

Statistical Problems

The use in any country of ICOR's derived from experience in other countries where statistics are more complete also has its dangers. The work done on ICOR at the M.I.T. Center for International Studies turned up only five countries whose statistics could be considered complete enough to give a reasonable approximation of a long-run ICOR (see Table 18–3). With the possible exception of Japan, all these countries are highly developed, and Japan is much more industrialized than other countries in Asia. The range of ICOR among these five countries is itself very wide: from 3 in the United States to 7.4 in The Netherlands. It would be difficult to decide from these figures what would be an appropriate ICOR for any particular underdeveloped country.

Moreover, the averages for individual countries hide wide fluctuations in the figures from one year to another, or even from one decade to another. For the United States, ICOR varies from 4.8 for the decade 1899 to 1919 to 1.9 for the decade 1919 to 1929. For Britain the figure ranges from 8.4 for the decade 1885 to 1895 to 0.4 for the period 1905 to 1909. Much wider fluctuations occur from year to year.

In addition to the long series for the five countries with reasonably reliable data, there are figures over fairly long periods for five other countries which are subject to a greater margin of error. These show a range of ICOR from 3.9 to 7.5. For underdeveloped countries, figures are available only for short periods. These show a range from 1.8 for Czechoslovakia to 2.5 for Poland.

There is also a very wide range of ICOR from one sector to another of the same economy. For the United States, for which the sectoral figures are by far the most complete, the highest sectoral ICOR's are more than

TABLE 18-3

ICOR for Various Countries and Periods

	Period	ICOR
Long periods, reasonably reliable data:		
United States	1879–1953	2.3:1 (3.0)*
Japan	1924–1939	4.7:1*
Denmark	1924–1939	3.5:1
The Netherlands	1900–1952	7.4:1
Sweden	1896–1929	3.5:1
Long periods, unsatisfactory data:		
Canada	1895–1920	4.2:1
	1895–1929†	2.7:1
United Kingdom	1865–1933	5.9:1
Australia	1913–1938	3.9:1
France	1852–1913	7.4:1
Italy	1861–1895	4.5:1
	1891–1938†	7.5:1
Underdeveloped countries: short (plan) periods:		
Czechoslovakia	1948–1953	3.3
Poland	1950–1955	2.0
Hungary	1950–1954	3.2
Bulgaria	1949–1953	1.2
Yugoslavia	1947–1951	2.2

* Reproducible capital only.
† Different basis.

100 times as high as the lowest one (Table 18–4). For India, the range is from 1 to 5; but these are for broad sectors rather than for individual industries. Even with this range of structural variation, it is apparent that the aggregate ICOR will depend a good deal on the investment structure in the development plan, and that it will change as the structure of investment changes in the course of economic development.

The effect on estimates of capital requirements of relatively small errors in ICOR estimates is borne out by an arithmetic example. Assuming an investment coefficient of 0.1 (that is, that net investment is 10 per cent of net national income), one obtains the following results:

ICOR	Rate of Growth (per cent)
3.0	3.3
1.8	5.5
4.2	2.4

There is some indication that ICOR falls with the achievement of high levels of industrialization (Table 18–5). This tendency is explained by the necessity of making heavy investments in social capital (housing, transport

TABLE 18–4

ICOR's for Various Sectors

Country and sector	ICOR
United States: *	
Trade and services	0.1 or less
Manufacturing	1.3–2.0
Housing and public utilities	10 or more
India: †	
Calculations:	
Cement	3.0–3.5
Pulp and paper	3.5–4.0
Iron and steel	3.5–4.0
Agriculture	1.0
Estimates:	
Small industries	2.0
Factories	3.0
Mining	4.0
Communications and transport	5.0

* U.S. Department of State, "Intelligence Report No. 7670" (Washington, D.C., 1958).
† M.I.T., India Project.

facilities, public utilities, schools, hospitals, etc.) in the early phases of development, together with the very high ICOR for such investments.

The "Main Sectors" Approach

Planning in terms of "main sectors" is at best a poor substitute for the establishment of priorities for individual projects as parts of whole programs. The contribution of any one project clearly depends on all the other projects with which it is combined. (In Libya the Italians decided just before World War II to build a railroad across the coastal strip from Tripoli to Tunis. For unknown reasons they began by building the terminals and that is as far as they got. So Libya had handsome stations

TABLE 18–5

ICOR and Stage of Development

Country	Period I	ICOR	Period II	ICOR
United States	1889–1929	3.0	1929–53	1.8
Japan	1900–1924	6.0	1924–39	4.7
Denmark	1864–1909	4.5	1909–39	2.0
Canada	1895–1920	4.2	1920–29	2.0*
Mexico	1940–45	1.54	1946–50	2.75
Czechoslovakia	1947–48	1.4	1949–50	1.8
Bulgaria	1947–48	0.9	1949–52	1.9
Hungary	1940–49	0.7	1949–52	2.4

* Rough estimate.

out in the desert but no railroad.) [10] If there are "n" projects, there are n ($n-1$) programs—that is, n ($n-1$) collections of projects. If there are 1,000 possible projects there are 999,000 programs to evaluate. If programs are assembled in this way, the sectoral allocation of the development budget comes out as a by-product. The projects to be included in industry, in agriculture, transport, education, etc., are determined by their contribution to "welfare" as defined by the decision function.

Dangers in the "Balanced Growth" Concept

Any preconception as to what constitutes sectoral "balance" is likely to lead planners astray. It is time that the controversy over balanced versus unbalanced growth should be buried forever. The father of the concept was Ragnar Nurkse; as shown in Chapter 15, his last statements on balanced growth provide a clear picture of its importance (or unimportance) in his own mind. By the time all the necessary qualifications are made, the balanced growth doctrine is reduced to a rather simple statement; if we wish to sell increased output for a profit, we cannot concentrate investments in one or a few industries, because the marginal propensity to consume their products would be too small relative to the income generated. Thus the balanced growth doctrine is really another facet of the "big push" argument. It says we must have investment on a broad front all at once; given lumpiness and discontinuities in the production function, it means we must have a great deal of investment all at once. We should not *start* with any preconception as to what constitutes an appropriate "balance" between industry and agriculture, or between economic and social development. The "balance" must come out of the whole process of assigning priorities to projects, within the context of general programs, and in terms of the decision function.

Input-output Analysis

While the mathematics can be cumbersome if the number of sectors included is large, conceptually an input-output or interindustry matrix is simple enough. It merely shows the interrelationships among all the industrial sectors in an economy, broken down into as many categories as statistics and computing facilities permit, in terms of purchases of each industry from all others and sales of each industry to all others. Tables 18–6 and 18–6a show fairly simple input-output matrices for two Asian countries. Such matrices provide a "*tableau économique*," to use Quesnay's term, a picture of the flows of goods and money through the economy at a point of time. When one has such pictures for two or more years, it may also be possible to project the relationships to some future "target" year of the development plan.

An input-output table is a useful tool for economic development plan-

---

[10] Actually the productivity of the stations was not zero, since they were used by smugglers to conduct barter trade. When I asked the British administrators, who were still there at that time, why they permitted this open violation of the law, they replied, "It makes our statistics so much better. Otherwise we wouldn't know what is crossing the border."

ning—even, some planners insist, if no actual figures are available and only "x's" can be put in some of the boxes. It serves to remind planners of the interrelationships among expansion of some sectors and expansion of others, and thus prevents failure to provide for simultaneous growth of all industries which must by their nature grow together. Since one sector is imports (in a complete matrix), it can also warn planners of the import implications, and consequent needs for foreign exchange, of a particular development program.

At the same time, input-output matrices must be used with care. Input-output analysis is a useful exercise but it is not a substitute for cost-benefit analysis of projects as parts of programs. An input-output matrix—even a projected input-output matrix—is not a plan. Unless the matrix is very big, the parameters do not represent technologically fixed relationships. On the contrary, even with a one-hundred-by-one hundred box, say, the "parameters" may cloak important policy decisions. There is a wide range of technologically possible relationships among the components. The product mix and the technology can be varied within limits. As shown above, the choice of technology and product mix are among the major decisions in the planning process. The presence of a foreign trade sector gives a wide range of choice as to what goes into the product mix; and in developing countries, a major question is what *new* commodities to produce and what *new* techniques to use.

Linear Programming

Linear programming is a mathematical procedure designed to simplify the problem of finding optimal solutions when more than one objective is involved. Programming economic development clearly belongs to the category of problems requiring allocation of scarce means among several objectives; consequently, it is also clear that linear programming is a useful tool in the process. Essentially, linear programming is a method of reducing such problems to sets of linear equations that can be solved relatively easily. By itself, however, linear programming can neither determine goals nor provide the basic technical and economic data needed to put numbers into the equations; it is far from being the whole of the planning process and is no substitute for the other essential operations in the process. Readers wishing to acquaint themselves with the technique should refer to one of the textbooks on the subject.[11]

Econometric Projections

A development plan, even in centrally controlled countries such as Russia, is always a mixture of agenda for government action and forecast. Even to determine what government actions are needed to attain established goals it is necessary to forecast what would happen without them. In countries such as France and Japan, where central government plan-

[11] See, for example, Robert Dorfman, Paul A. Samuelson and Robert M. Solow, *Linear Programming and Economic Analysis* (New York, Toronto, and London, 1958); and United Nations, *Programming Techniques for Economic Development, op. cit.*, chap. V.

TABLE 18-6. Japan: Abridged Input-Output Table, 1960*

(billion yen, producers' prices)

From \ To	Agriculture	Food processing industry	Textiles	Manufacturing	Transport and electricity	Construction and service industries	Mining	Sub-total	Consumption expenditure	Gross domestic fixed capital formation and increase in stock	Less exports of goods and services	Sub-total	Total output
Agriculture	500	1,609	341	543	..	33	14	3,039	586	114	61	761	3,138
Food processing industry	127	550	6	42	..	2	..	728	2,928	86	61	3,075	3,629
Textiles	35	2	728	269	6	54	2	1,096	472	52	302	827	1,957
Manufacturing	261	287	297	710	393	2,302	43	10,688	1,123	2,106	907	4,136	13,951
Transport and electricity	32	76	44	523	107	338	33	1,152	624	20	144	789	2,030
Construction and service industries	80	223	101	786	131	1,176	33	2,530	5,251	3,058	153	8,462	11,108
Mining	1	13	6	608	83	94	7	812	14	−1	1	14	393
Sub-total	1,036	2,760	1,524	9,875	720	4,000	132	20,045	11,000	5,436	1,628	18,064	36,105
Wages and profits	1,839	358	360	3,205	817	5,613	205	12,396	..	..	..	..	..
Capital consumption allowance	210	47	44	408	350	700	34	1,793	..	..	..	..	..
Indirect tax and subsidies	47	481	11	173	92	259	10	1,072	..	..	..	..	..
Others	7	33	18	182	51	436	12	739	..	..	..	..	..
Total output	3,138	3,629	1,957	13,951	2,030	11,008	393	36,105	..	..	..	..	..

* *Note:* Distributed figures in row "Unallocated" according to weight of each industry regrouped.

Agriculture: General crops, industrial crops, livestock for textile industry, other livestock, forestry, fisheries.

Food processing industry: Slaughter, meat and dairy, rice and flour milling, marine food products, other food products, beverages, tobacco.

Textiles: Natural fiber spinning, chemical fiber spinning, other spinning.

Manufacturing: Belongings, lumber and wood products, furniture, paper, pulp and paper products, printing and publishing, leather, rubber, basic and intermediate chemicals, oils, fats and final chemicals, petroleum products, coal products, ceramic, stone and clay products, iron and steel primary products, steel casting, forging and hot-rolled products, non-ferrous primary products, metal products, general machineries, electric machineries, automobiles, other transport equipments, precision machineries, other manufacturing.

Transport and electricity: Electricity, railroad, road transport, other transport.

Construction and service industries: Housing, non-housing, public works, other works, gas, water and sanitary works, commerce, real estate, communication, banking and insurance, official business, public services, other services.

Mining: Coal, iron ore, non-ferrous metal ore, crude oil and natural gas, other mining.

SOURCE: "1960 Interindustry Economic Tables," Government of Japan, Toyko, Japan, 1964. From United Nations, *Economic Survey of Asia and the Far East, 1964* (Bangkok, 1965), p. 34.

TABLE 18-6a. India: Abridged Input-Output Table, 1960/61* (ten million rupees, 1959/60 producers' prices)

From \ To	Agriculture	Food industry	Textiles	Chemical fertilizer	Transport and electricity	Manufacturing and mining	Construction	Sub-total	Consumption	Gross fixed capital formation	Net exports	Output
Agriculture	604.7	795.0	371.0	..	11.0	143.1	68.9	1,993.7	5,412.6	83.6	−113.0	7,577.0
Food industry	55.0	48.4	5.6	..	..	12.9	..	121.9	1,072.2	102.3	26.6	1,323.0
Textiles	3.9	6.6	25.3	0.9	0.4	18.8	..	55.9	713.9	10.8	144.8	930.0
Chemical fertilizer	30.3	..	..	..	..	..	..	30.3	..	1.3	−10.7	20.7
Transport and electricity	8.0	5.8	25.5	0.3	13.4	37.0	..	90.0	302.9	175.5	−68.7	1,164.0
Manufacturing and mining	49.4	22.2	62.2	5.5	264.1	555.4	630.4	1,589.2	687.2	499.6	−631.2	2,164.1
Construction	..	..	..	..	..	..	..	..	104.0	1,360.0	..	1,617.0
Sub-total	751.3	878.0	489.6	6.7	288.9	767.2	699.3	3,881.0	8,292.8	2,233.1	−652.2	14,795.8
Value added	6,752.0	271.2	325.6	9.2	750.1	905.5	636.6	9,650.2	860.0	..	..	13,734.3†
Margin	44.4	67.4	36.8	1.7	31.6	201.2	281.1	664.2	4,646.8	276.0	164.8	..
Value of output	7,577.0	1,323.0	930.0	20.7	1,164.0	2,164.1	1,677.0	14,795.8	13,984.9	2,509.1	−457.6	..

* Note: Agriculture: Plantations, animal husbandry, food grains, other agriculture, forestry products and rubber.
Food industry: Food industries.
Textiles: Cotton and other textiles, and jute textiles.
Chemical fertilizer: Chemical fertilizers.
Transport and electricity: Transport equipment, motor transport, railways and electricity.
Manufacturing and mining: Electric equipment, non-electrical equipment, iron and steel, iron ore, cement, other minerals, leather and leather products, glass, wooden and non-metalic mineral products, petroleum products, crude oil, rubber products, chemicals and coal.
Construction: Construction, urban and industrial, and construction, rural. SOURCE: "Interindustry Transactions (India), 1960/61," Planning Commission, India. From United Nations, Economic Survey of Asia and the Far East, 1964 (Bangkok, 1965), p. 35.
† Gross value added.

ning is largely limited to so-called indicative planning, forecasting is a major part of the planning operation. There, the major contribution of central government planning is to improve the accuracy of private forecasting, by making careful econometric and policy-determined projections for major sectors of the economy as a whole, encouraging increased private investment by reducing uncertainty. In any country it is a good idea to look ahead, on the basis of the best available knowledge regarding quantitative relationships among strategic variables, and to see what troubles or deviations from targets may lie ahead in the absence of appropriate government measures to prevent them. An example of such projections is provided in Chapter 34 in the case study of Libya. Once again, it should be stressed that econometric projections in themselves are not a development plan.[12]

Toward "Workable Planning"

Having discovered that pure competition is impossible and probably undesirable, but still believing that some monopolies are bad, economists have been seeking a concept of "workable competition" as a basis for policy. Similarly, having decided not to leave economic development to the free operation of an uninhibited market, and recognizing that many of the theoretically refined planning techniques are not yet usable, we need something in between. Planning in practice should be based strongly on theory, but should be possible with the empirical knowledge we have, and with the political and administrative framework within which planners must operate.

The partial interindustry analysis of Jan Tinbergen is a good example of "workable planning." In effect he suggests a partial priority formula operation and a partial input-output analysis, thus reducing the total number of computations. He divides the economy into "national" and "international" sectors.[13] National goods must be produced within the economy. The railroad from Rio to São Paulo cannot be constructed in the United States; it has to be in Brazil. Haircuts have to be produced in the country itself; they cannot be stockpiled. Thus there are certain goods and services that must be produced within the country, and others that can be imported or exported. The so-called international goods may not actually enter into international trade, but they are international in the sense that they *could* enter into international trade. In other words, Tinbergen says, in effect, "Let us apply a priority formula to the international goods, because there we have a choice whether to produce them within

[12] For a detailed exposition of the techniques of econometric projection, see Daniel B. Suits, *The Theory and Application of Econometric Models* (Athens, 1963); and United Nations, *Problems of Long-term Economic Projections* (New York, 1963), and *Review of Long-term Economic Projections for Selected Countries in the ECAFE Region* (Bangkok, 1964). See also the various projections made for its member countries by the UN Economic Commission for Latin America.

[13] See, for example, Jan Tinbergen and H. C. Bos, *Mathematical Models of Economic Growth* (New York, 1962), especially chaps. 1 and 7; and Jan Tinbergen, *Selected Papers* (Amsterdam, 1959). Perhaps the best "Manual of Workable Planning" available thus far is Arthur W. Lewis, *Development Planning: the Essentials of Economic Policy* (New York, 1966).

the economy or not. Then an interindustry analysis can be tacked on to these goods and services to determine the need for complementary national goods."

Priority Formulas

Some planners would avoid the use of priority formulas because of data difficulties. But if indeed the purpose of a development program is to contribute to the growth of income and employment, improve the balance of payments, improve the income distribution, etc., the only way to put together development programs is to estimate the contribution of each project, within each possible program, to the achievement of these objectives. The decision function itself determines the priority formula.

Let us consider two priority formulas: the Philippines formula, which is made interesting by the fact that it was used by the Philippines government for several years; and a relatively simple formula which the present author worked out for the National Planning Board in Ceylon.

The Philippines Formula

The demand for a priority formula in the Philippines came from President Magsaysay. At that time, the responsibility for approval or disapproval of investment projects was divided among several government agencies. There was no coordination among them and the criteria applied varied from one agency to another. The National Economic Council, as a kind of super-planning organization, had responsibility for general approval or disapproval of investment projects within the development programs. It was possible for a particular proposal to be approved by the National Economic Council and be granted credit by the Bureau of Industrial Research, but then be refused foreign exchange by the Central Bank or refused tax concessions by the Department of Finance. As this situation was obviously unsatisfactory, it was decided to work out a single set of criteria which would be applied by all government agencies concerned with approving or disapproving proposed investment projects.

The following formula was then devised:

$IP = R_1 + R_2 + R_3 + R_4$
IP = industrial priority
R_1 = the net contribution of the project to national income
R_2 = the impact on the balance of payments
R_3 = a measure of the degree of domestic raw materials used in the project
R_4 = the impact on employment

R_1 = can be expanded to $R_1 = \dfrac{E(w + r + i + p)}{K}$

where w = wages and salaries
i = interest paid on capital
r = rent for land and buildings

p = profits
K = total investment of the project
E = the essentiality factor

Hence $w + r + i + p$ is the total output of the project.

In the case of the interest rate, a shadow price was used: the ceiling allowed was 6 per cent regardless of the actual interest rate paid.

K was defined as the total investment of the project. It is to be hoped, however, that the government did not use this definition in practice. If the total amount of investment in a project were used as the denominator, projects requiring expensive but highly durable equipment (such as railroads) would always be low priority. What should be compared is *annual* output with *annual* capital costs or total capital costs with total contribution to national income over the entire life of the asset. To compare annual output with total investment in a project is to bias the whole development program toward quick-yielding projects, such as merchandising operations, and away from highly durable plant and equipment which take a number of years to repay the original investment. Let us therefore define K as annual capital costs, to be compared with the increase in total annual output due to the project.

E is a multiplier or "essentiality factor." Note that if we consider only the total income payments (total income payments equal total value of output), the formula measures only gross returns to investment. If we used only this criterion, in other words, we would alter the patterns of investment which would emerge from a freely operating market only to the extent that $p/w + r + i$ varies from one industry to another.

The essentiality factor, however, used as a multiplier, alters the pattern of investment a great deal. By the same token it is the essentiality factor which really determines the priority ratings. The essentiality multiplier ranges from 0.5 to 2.5. For example, a project with a 2.5 essentiality multiplier is one whose output is largely exported or used by other industries, one which has a significant impact on investment in other industries, or one which mainly uses domestically produced capital or other goods. If the product is to be exported partly in semifinished form, it gets an essentiality rating of 2 instead of 2.5. Thus the "essentiality" category in which the project is placed virtually decides what R_1 adds up to. The projects are selected when the essentiality ratings are assigned.

Finally, products largely exported in raw form, not processed within the economy, get an essentiality rating of only 0.5. Thus the E is a vague attempt to measure "linkage" effects. But the 500 per cent spread between the lowest multiplier and the highest multiplier means that the fundamental decision has already been taken when the essentiality factor is assigned. The subsequent calculation of R is almost irrelevant to the outcome.

The second component of the industrial priority rating (R_2) can be expanded

$$R_2 = \frac{FE\ s/e - FEc}{K}$$

Here FEs/e (foreign exchange saved or earned less the foreign exchange cost—(FEc), is related to the annual capital cost (K).

The third factor (R_3) was

$$R_3 = \frac{0.5 \cdot rmd/rmt \cdot rmd}{K}$$

where rmd = the value of domestic raw materials used and rmt corresponds to the value of total raw materials in an investment project. Note that the extent to which domestic materials were used influences the value of R_2 so that the inclusion of R_3 results in some double counting. The effect of double counting is diluted, however, by taking only half of the value of domestic raw materials used $(0.5 \times rmd)$ as a ratio to total raw materials used (rmt). This figure is then multiplied by the total amount of domestic raw materials used and then divided by the annual capital cost of the project. Thus the weight of R_3 in the priority formula is small.

The final component of the priority formula measured the employment effect.

$$R_4 = \frac{1d \cdot 2,000}{K}$$

In this formula $1d$ represents the number of domestic workers employed by the project, while the 2,000 is the legal minimum wage for unskilled workers in the country. Here is another shadow price; all workers are valued at the rate applicable to the unskilled workers, irrespective of their actual wage rate. The R_4 formula, therefore, favored those projects which absorbed large numbers of *unskilled* workers, which alone were in excess supply.

The adjustments that could be suggested for this formula are then:

a) to redefine K as annual capital costs
b) to eliminate the essentiality factor
c) to eliminate R_3 to avoid double counting
d) to allow for difference in profit margins.

With these modifications this formula could be used with some success to choose projects.

A Simplified Formula

The Philippines formula is still rather complex. The present author has worked out a much simpler one for the Ceylon government, though he is not convinced that it is the best possible formula nor even that it is better than a modified Philippine one. But it is easier to use.

In Ceylon there was a clear-cut policy statement laying down the overall objectives of development policy. The Budget Speech of the Minister of Finance stated that the objectives were to raise per capita income, to increase employment, and to improve the balance of payments position, in that order. The priority formula should then consist of:

R_1 = the output effect
R_2 = the employment effect
R_3 = balance of payment effect

R_1 was measured through applying the ratio $\dfrac{Ic}{\Delta Y}$, where Ic is the annual

capital cost and ΔY the increase in annual output. For example, let us assume that the incremental capital-output ratio for a project is 2:1, and that the life of the project is ten years; in this case the value of this ratio would be 2/10 or 0.2. All projects could then be grouped within certain ranges of ratios. For example, category 1 would consist of projects whose ratio varied from 0.1 to 0.19, category 2 of projects with a ratio of 0.2 to 0.29, etc. The lowest category of projects would have a ratio of 0.9 to 1.0; a project whose annual output does not cover its annual capital cost should never be undertaken regardless of the employment it creates or the foreign exchange it saves or earns.

The employment effect (R_2) could be measured by dividing the annual capital cost (Ic) by the increase in employment (ΔN): ($R_2 = \dfrac{Ic}{\Delta N}$). In this instance, too, projects could be grouped, starting with projects whose capital-job ratio is $500 or below, the second category being $501 to $1,000, and the lowest group those with a ratio above $10,000, which is extremely capital-intensive.

The balance of payments effect of a project could be calculated by relating the annual capital costs of a project to the increase in exports less the increase in imports. $R_3 = \dfrac{(X\text{-}F)}{Ic}$, where

X = increase in exports
F = increase in imports and
Ic = annual capital costs.

The best projects from the balance of payments viewpoint would be those which would save or earn more foreign exchange than their capital cost; the second group might be those with ratios of 0.9 to 0.99, and so on down to those which save no foreign exchange at all.

If, under the components (R_1, R_2, R_3,) of the priority formula, there are 10 groups, there would be 1,000 possible categories for the classification of projects. For the final steps two possible methods could be considered. The first would be to rank individual projects by all three criteria. The top priority projects would be those that fall into the top rank on all three criteria. Then since an increase in income has the highest priority, projects in the first, second, and third groups of R_1 may be selected, after which those in the first two groups of R_2 and R_3, followed by those in the fourth group of R_1, and so on.

Class	R_1 (Ic/Y)	R_2 (Ic/N)	R_3 $\dfrac{X\text{-}F}{Ic}$
A	0.1–0.19	$500	1.0
B	0.2–0.29	$500–$1,000	0.8–0.99
:	. .	.	.
:			
N	. .	.	.
.	. .	.	.
N	0.9–1.0	$10,000	0

Top priority projects would be "Class A" on all criteria.
Next would be the A, B, Bs, to A, D, Ds.
Then   B, B, Bs, to B, D, Ds.
Then   C, A, As, to C, D, Ds.
Then   D, A, As to D, D, Ds, etc.

The order chosen should reflect the weights attached to the various objectives.

Another possibility would be to add up for each project the actual increase in income, the increase in employment valued at the minimum wage, plus the net foreign exchange earning generated per $1,000 invested in a project. These amounts could also be weighted. However, this approach gives a spurious impression of precision of measurement which could be misleading. A project adding up to $100,000 might be included and one adding up to $99,999 excluded. Our measures are not that accurate, and the exercise of judgment is still a necessary part of the planning process.

We could also add other criteria if there are other stipulated objectives. For example, an R_4 might be added for location; projects in the favored (lagging) region might be classified as "A" under R_4, those in the leading region as "C" and those in other regions as "B." Similarly, those making income distribution more equal might be "A," those making it more unequal "C," and those leaving it unchanged "B."

A Final Point

One final point that is too little understood: once a priority formula, reflecting a decision function, has been established, all types of investment projects, without exception, should be subjected to it. Education, public health, housing, social welfare programs, land reform—everything— should be evaluated in terms of their contribution to national objectives. It would be nonsense to evaluate them in any other terms. All these aspects of development are in fact subjected to some kind of cost-benefit analysis; none of them gets the whole development budget. Such being the case, it it better to make the cost-benefit analysis explicit, objective, quantitative, and consistent with the rest of the plan.

19 | Planning Social Development —I. Education

The day will no doubt arrive when the distinction between "economic" and "social" development will disappear from the literature. As pointed out by the United Nations Bureau of Social Affairs, "the separation between the social and the economic is often an artifact of academic analysis and Government departmentalization." [1] The remark applies to the United Nations itself; the Division of Social Affairs is responsible for education, public health, housing, and social security. It is hard to see what makes these fields "social" while others are "economic." Clearly, all of them come within the scope of contemporary economics: all of them involve questions of resource allocation, and all are subject to cost-benefit studies and to economic analysis. True, they may have aspects which fall outside the scope of economics, even with the broad definition of "economics" adopted in Chapter 12 above. The programming of education so as to produce the system of values and quality of civilization that is desired, for example, is much more difficult than making sure that manpower requirements are met. Economic analysis is of little use for such purposes. But once the goals are established and technical data accumulated, economics takes over in establishing the appropriate programs and budgets. Measures for improving education, health, housing, land reform, and social security can and should be written into the development program, and their shares of the development budget should be determined by some sort of cost-benefit analysis.

Indeed, there is no real distinction in this respect between education or

[1] UN Department of Economic and Social Affairs, *Report on the World Social Situation* (New York, 1961), p. 23.

health on the one hand and transportation or power on the other. All development projects have both "economic" and "non-economic" aspects, a fact that is too little understood. This common confusion was well illustrated by some discussion at the UNESCO-ECAFE Conference on Investment and Education held at Bangkok in April, 1964. Most delegates recognized that pursuit of ambitious goals for education would at some point confront planners with the necessity of considering the opportunity costs of still further expansion of the education program. Concern was expressed, however, regarding the great difficulties of measuring returns to education, particularly in such intangible forms as "bringing the peoples of underdeveloped countries abreast of the times" and "providing equality of opportunity." The economists maintained in reply that this concern reflected an unwarranted mixture of sectors with projects. The benefits of "education" (or perhaps "universal primary education") as a single unit are compared with the benefits of a power plant, a road, or an irrigation project. The legitimate comparison is "education" versus "transport and communications" or "rural electrification"; or alternatively, a "bridge" versus a "school building" or "a primary school teacher."

The returns to other investments are just as intangible and as immeasurable as those to education or health. Improved transport and communications, for example, may in some contexts make a greater contribution to "bringing people abreast of the times" and "providing equality of opportunity" than construction of school buildings. At Bangkok, the present writer cited the case of some stranded Greek villages, with no schools and virtually no contact with the outside world, separated by a mile-deep gorge from a small town which happened to have high-quality schools with room for more students and a generally high cultural level. The town also had communications with the rest of the world. By constructing a *téléphérique* across the gorge—a transportation project—the villages "were brought abreast of the times." Similarly, the returns to rural electrification might be described as bringing the people of remote villages into contact with modern technology, permitting them to read at night, linking them with the outside world through radio, television, the cinema, etc. Conversely it would be possible to value returns to a particular education project in terms of fees and tuition that are paid to private institutions for such educational services, plus an estimated value of indirect effects, as is done in traditional cost-benefit analysis for power or transport projects.

The term "social" tends to be applied in fields where the political decision was made long ago to abandon the pure market criterion for allocation of resources. In contemporary economic jargon, these are fields in which it is generally agreed that a "shadow price" higher than the market price should be established, so that the supply of services in that field will be greater than would be forthcoming if the prices of the services covered their cost. However, this criterion will scarcely do as a means of distinguishing "social" from "economic." In various underdeveloped countries one can find transport, power, housing, basic foodstuffs—even refined petroleum products—being provided to consumers below cost, as a deliberate act of government policy. Do all these items belong in the "social" sphere?

Economic analysis is just as important as a basis for determining the optimal resource allocation when "shadow prices" are used as it is when market prices are accepted. The burgeoning literature on economics of education and the birth of an economics of public health are evidence of this fact. The purpose of economic analysis is to achieve the resource allocation which is optimal in the light of *whatever* goals a society may have; there is no "optimum" independent of the decision-function. Economists are perhaps to blame for the widespread association of "economic" with "profitable" and "uneconomic" with "unprofitable"; but in fact economics is by no means limited to activities where prices cover costs.

There has been a tendency among practitioners in the fields of education, public health, etc., to insist that they are dealing with "human rights" or non-material values which are somehow superior to the "crass materialistic concerns of the economist," and so not subject to economic analysis. This attitude, as educators have recently discovered, is based on a misapprehension of what economic analysis is and does.[2] If society places high values on health and education, the economist is as much concerned as anyone—and perhaps more concerned than most—to make sure that these values are reflected in the allocation of resources. But no one—not even Ministers of Education or Health—would maintain that the entire development budget should go to education or to health. There has to be a cut-off point, and a cut-off point implies some kind of cost-benefit analysis. If a cost-benefit analysis is to be made, the only logical thing to do is to apply the same priority formula to so-called social development projects as to all the others. The formula itself should reflect all the goals of development, and all goods and services should be valued at appropriate accounting prices.

Many economists would agree with the educators that everyone has a

[2] A typical example of this kind of misconception is provided by Lewis Perinbam, Secretary of the Canadian National Commission for UNESCO, in a speech to the Western Canada Conference on "The Challenge of World Development" in August, 1963:

"It is clear . . . that education has a decisive role to play in developing these countries. However, the requirements of economic development should not be over-riding in the educational system of a country. Building a new society is not like building a factory or a workshop—its future will depend on the quality of its people. Education must be regarded, therefore, as a human right which is an end in itself. It is good even if it does not pay and it stands on its own without reference to costs or returns. Its chief purpose is to develop the human personality so that men may achieve their spiritual, intellectual and material potentialities, preserve and transmit a society's values and to enable men to understand the world in which they live. Only an education system based on humanistic values and sound social purposes can develop human resources effectively."

"We have here (1) The confusion of 'economic' with 'profitable' and the feeling that educators must resist an 'economic' approach because education 'does not pay for itself.' (2) The assumption that education is concerned with 'quality' and so a quantitative approach is inappropriate (is the 'quality' of a factory or workshop a matter of indifference?). (3) The suggestion that there is a conflict between 'spiritual, intellectual' considerations and any consideration of 'costs or returns.'"

"right" to some education. However, since it is the economist's special task to consider all aspects of human welfare simultaneously, and to endeavor to determine the allocation of scarce resources which would maximize human welfare, he has to take into account other "rights" as well. Some of these "rights" were stressed even at the UN Conference on Education and Economic and Social Development in Latin America: the right to medical services; the right to adequate nutrition; the right to minimum standards of housing; the right to employment; the right to leisure and to recreation facilities that permit rewarding use of leisure. All these "rights" taken together may add up to a "right" to an income higher than the average for underdeveloped countries. In short, such "rights" really amount to a "right" to economic development. They are not in the same category as such constitutional rights as freedom of speech and press which have no economic cost. While recognizing the enormous importance of education, both as an end in itself and an instrument of economic development, it is the economist's task to find ways of determining the proper "cut-off" point for investment in education (or health) where returns to further investment in education (or health) fall below returns to investment in other fields.[3]

Similarly, as we have seen, economic analysis can be applied to the problem of determining the "absorptive capacity" of an underdeveloped country; and such questions as the quality of the civil service and the supply of

[3] Some of the most basic problems are non-economic, in the sense that resource allocation is a minor aspect of them. Perhaps most important of these in the field of development is the establishment of the "decision-function" or "objective-function" itself. The determination of fundamental objectives and values, deciding whether income is more important than employment, or education worth more than health, or national security more important than preserving traditional culture, etc., is a matter first of all of social and moral philosophy. The basic question here is, "Who is to decide?" If the answer is "the people themselves" then other questions, essentially non-economic, arise: How can we best find out what the people want? What are the relative merits of the polling booth and the marketplace for revealing preferences? Should we dispense with the legislative branch of government and rely on a referendum-a-day and electric voting machines and computers? Who then will have the political power to frame the questions? There is also the range of political questions suggested in Chapter 12. What kind of political organization is likely to function best, given the objectives, in a particular country at a particular time? When improving the system requires dislodging an entrenched elite, how can revolution best be fomented and guided?

There are certain highly important social institutions that are essentially costless: freedom of speech, freedom of the press, freedom of assembly, various civil rights. How can the libel law be designed to preserve freedom of speech and press while preventing irresponsible and dangerous use of these freedoms? (This question occupied a fair share of the time and energy of the Ministry of Planning in Brazil in 1964 and is also a problem in the Philippines.) Should freedom of assembly be permitted to the point of causing traffic jams? Danger of riots?

There is the problem of the quality of civilization to be produced and the design of the education system to produce it. There is the question of interrelationships between social class structure and political power. There is a host of operational questions: what is the optimal size of a school class for various subjects, how to establish priorities in health programs, what is the optimal size of a farm for various products and conditions? How can 100,000 policemen best be deployed to maintain order?

skilled managers will certainly enter into such analysis. We cannot classify a lack of managers, trained civil servants, and engineers, or even generally low standards of education and public health, or a bad land-tenure system, as "social" obstacles to economic development. They are economic obstacles, and they can be removed by economic measures within the framework of an economic development program.

For the purposes of this chapter and the next, however, we shall accept —despite our reservations—the United Nations concept of "social" development. In this chapter we shall deal with education. In the next chapter we shall discuss public health, land reform, social security, and community development.

"Balanced" Economic and Social Development

The emphasis on "balanced growth" has led, among other things, to a plea for "balanced" economic and social development. This plea reflects the feeling in some Ministries of Health, Education, Housing, etc., that their fields were being neglected in development plans and budgets, because Ministers of Finance and Planning considered them to be "non-economic," something that could be "afforded" only after "economic" development had proceeded further. In the early years of the development drive there may even have been some basis for this feeling. Now, however, it is recognized that these programs make an important contribution to productivity as well as being desirable in their own right. It is also recognized that the concept of "balance" has no more precision here than it has anywhere else in the development field. As the Economic Commission for Asia and the Far East has put it: [4]

. . . the concept of balance in the sense of acting simultaneously on all the factors involved is likely to be useless in practice. That is quite true, but perhaps it would be well to pursue this a little further. It may be impossible to act simultaneously all along the line, upon all the factors involved, but it is not impossible—and indeed essential—to consider simultaneously all the factors involved. This, in fact, is the essence of development programming, and underlies nearly all available techniques. The principle of integrated economic and social development would, then, mean that social and economic factors should all be looked at, that we should try to form a picture of all direct, and indirect costs, and all direct and indirect benefits of given programmes, and that, in deciding our final expenditure programme, we should apply the same kind of criteria to the two types, social and economic, without any preconceived priority according to the "social" or "economic" label. This course will be greatly facilitated if we could think less in terms of categories of expenditure, and more in terms of important development problems to be solved. It would be difficult to think of any underdeveloped country in which, on listing the 6 or 8 major problems to be solved, one would not find that in each of these problems both social expenditure and social policies and economic expenditure and economic policies would have to be applied simultaneously."

[4] ECAFE, Problems of Social and Economic Development in the Countries of Asia and the Far East (E./CN.11/OPWP.5/4.2/Rev.), 1963, p. 8.

Education and Economic Development

For three centuries economists have emphasized the importance of "human investment." Jean Bodin maintained that *"Il n'est richesse que d'hommes,"* and William Petty attempted to measure the value of human capital, and showed that returns to investment in human capital are very high.[1] In line with this view, economists have stressed the need to devote more public funds to education.

The reasons for this enthusiasm have varied from one economist to another. Adam Smith attached little importance to education as a means of raising productivity. The rise in productivity would come from technological progress and increasing division of labor. But education is important to offset the "stultifying effects" of increasing specialization. The workingman's dexterity at his particular trade, Adam Smith believed, is acquired at the expense of his "intellectual, social and martial virtues." Education is necessary to prevent degeneration of the working classes. Smith also believed that education contributes to social and political stability. "The more they are instructed, the less likely they are to delusions of enthusiasm and superstition, which, among ignorant nations, frequently occasion the most dreadful disorders. An instructed and intelligent people, besides, are always more decent and orderly than an ignorant and stupid one."

Malthus agreed with Adam Smith that an educated people would be less prey to "inflammatory writings," but was more interested in the greater foresight accompanying increased education, which he felt would lead to more effective family planning. Whereas poor relief tended simply to aggravate the misery of the working classes, education is "perhaps" the only means in our power of really raising their condition. Senior, too, emphasized the relationship between education and foresight, but in his case it was an increased propensity to save, rather than family planning, that he expected to accompany the improved foresight. Senior also believed, however, that compulsory education would tend to check population growth.

With McCulloch, emphasis on education as a form of human capital entered the economics literature. He would include the "dexterity, skill and intelligence of the masses of the people," in this measurement of national capital. John Stuart Mill agreed with Malthus and Senior that education would help to check population growth, and favored both universal elementary education and equal educational opportunities for women. Alfred Marshall also regarded education as a "national investment," and argued that there are "few practical problems in which the economist has a more direct interest than those relating to the principles on which the expense of the education of children should be divided between the state and the parents." According to Marshall, "the wisdom of expending public and private funds on education is not to be measured by its direct fruits alone. It will be profitable as a mere investment, to give the

[1] Cf. Thank Khoi Le, *Le Rendement de l'Education*, UNESCO, (WS/1962.121), January, 1963.

masses of the people much greater opportunities to get the start for bringing out their latent abilities. And the economic value of one industrial genius is sufficient to cover the expenses of the education of a whole town." Pigou, similarly, insisted that education is an investment "yielding a rate of return in extra product which would much exceed the normal rate of interest on capital invested in machinery and plants."

Karl Marx pleaded for a type of training which would give more flexibility to labor's skills. True to his general theory of capitalistic development, he argued that the increase in productivity accompanying training, while merely a means of maintaining profits in a capitalistic society, would become the means of raising living standards in a socialist one.

When in Doubt, Educate

Today the conviction among economic development planners that "investment in human resources" yields particularly high returns is so strong that there is a maxim among them, "when in doubt, educate." Development planners tend to feel that when they are confronted with seemingly impossible problems of establishing priorities and allocating development resources, they can never make a mistake by putting a lot of money into education—meaning here not only formal education, but all aspects of training as well, including adult education, literacy campaigns, vocational and technical training, agricultural extension work, and the like.

But while economists are sure that returns to education are high, they are much less sure as to how to go about measuring returns to investment in education, so as to permit a comparison with returns to other kinds of developmental investment and determine the proper "cut-off point." Some Ministries of Education seem content to continue with the traditional demographic approach: "The children are there, they've got to be educated," as one Asian Minister of Education once outlined his "programming techniques" to the author. Efforts have been made to derive returns to education from income differentials. Others have tried to measure returns in aggregative form, as a residual after all other factors causing economic growth have been accounted for. Others still, regarding themselves as more "practical," would limit the planning of education to making sure that manpower requirements are met. The econometricians have had their say, suggesting a direct mathematical relationship between education and national income. Some defeatists would abandon the effort to measure returns directly, and rely on certain "norms" to determine the proper size of the education budget. Others, more defeatist still, deny the usefulness of any attempt to measure something so amorphous as returns to education.

The Necessity of a Cost-Benefit Approach

The simple truth is, however, that there is no way of avoiding a cost-benefit approach to the planning and programming of education, or of any other aspect of "social development." An implicit cost-benefit comparison is always involved whenever the cut-off point is determined. Deciding not to spend another million *esperitos* on education means deciding that for, the same cost, higher returns—in whatever form or however measured—can be obtained in some other way. Much confusion has been introduced into the discussion by presenting the manpower approach, or the residual factor approach, or "norms," or econometric models, as an *alternative* to cost-benefit analysis. Logically all these approaches are just different ways of getting at returns. The manpower approach accepts meeting skill requirements as a satisfactory approximation to maximizing returns. The residual factor approach, as already indicated, attempts to measure returns in the aggregate, for the economy as a whole. "Norms" in the form of percentages of GNP or total government expenditures to be spent on education reflect a strong hunch that until these norms are met we can be certain that returns to investment in education will be higher than on any other form of investment. Since an implicit cost-benefit analysis is always involved, there is much to be said for making it explicit, and as accurately quantified as possible. As Professor John Kendrick has pointed out: [2]

In my own statement I indicated some of the difficulties involved in estimating and projecting rates of return and there are many. But to me it is clear that (a) theoretically, the correct investment mix can be determined by equating the marginal efficiency of investment with the marginal cost of funds; and, as a corollary, (b) much more work should be undertaken to estimate past and prospective rates of return on various types of investment.

Education as a Factor of Production..

A theoretically perfect approach would be to treat education as both an input and an output in the "input-output matrix" of the economy as a whole. The value of education as an end in itself, quite apart from its contribution to increasing output of other goods and services, would be treated as a part of a national income. In addition, investment in education would be considered, together with inputs of labor, raw materials, and capital equipment in the production of other goods and services. Both in choosing the product mix (the amounts of all goods and services to be produced) and in choosing the appropriate technology for producing each good and service in the product mix, education inputs would be considered along with inputs of other factors of production. Textiles, for example, can be produced with more or less "education-intensive" techniques, higher degrees of skill being substituted for more raw materials, capital equipment, or unskilled labor, just as the technique may be more or less capital-intensive. Similarly, some products are inherently more "education-intensive" (petrochemicals) than others (rice). Consequently, required education inputs should be considered simultaneously with all other costs in determining returns to investment in various kinds of education, and in comparing returns on investment in education with returns on other forms of investment. The total size of the education budget will then be established by expanding investment in education until returns on further investment in education fall below the returns on other forms of invest-

[2] John W. Kendrick, "Comments," in John Vaizey (ed.), *The Residual Factor and Economic Growth* (Paris: OECD, 1964), pp. 216–17.

ment. This is just another way of saying that the education budget would be determined by a "cost-benefit" approach.

Measuring Costs

No serious problems arise with regard to measuring costs of education.[3] Teachers' salaries, supplies, equipment, etc., can be included as costs in terms of actual expenditures. Some complications arise in distributing the cost of buildings throughout the life of the building, but these are the same for education as for other sectors of a development program. More serious difficulties arise in determining the opportunity cost of keeping children in school rather than releasing them to the labor force, but these problems are not insoluble. For the United States, Professor Theodore W. Schultz of the University of Chicago estimates earnings foregone at 43 per cent of total costs of education in 1956. For secondary and higher education he puts the figure at 60 per cent. Professor Rudolph Blitz of Vanderbilt University gives still higher estimates. Preliminary calculations for Mexico in 1957 gave figures of 61 per cent for secondary education and 59 per cent for higher education. For Chile in 1959 the estimates were 74 per cent and 46 per cent.

There is some reason to doubt the validity of these calculations for countries with substantial unemployment and underemployment, especially where "educated unemployed" are already a problem. Vaizey questions the procedure even for advanced countries: [4]

It is doubtful whether this exercise is justified. The inclusion of income foregone opens the gate to a flood of approximations which would take the concept of national income away from its origin as an estimation of the measurable flows of the economy; if income foregone is added to education costs it must also be added to other sectors of the economy (notably housewives, mothers, unpaid sitters-in, voluntary work of all sorts); and it is doubtful whether any more useful purpose is served by a statistical exercise of this kind, than could be achieved merely by observing the numbers of people engaged in education.

Problems in Measuring Returns

The real difficulties, however, arise in the effort to measure returns to investment in education. The returns to an additional unit of investment of a certain type (one pupil-year of primary education, for example) consist of the value of this unit of education as a "consumer good," plus the increase in total output of the economy that it yields, directly and indirectly. It is not the fact that education is both a capital and a consumer good that gives rise to the difficulties. This ambivalence occurs with other forms of investment as well. A town hall may be used for dances on Saturday night; the toll bridge may be beautiful to look at; the farmer may use his truck or the taxi driver his car to take his family to the beach on

[3] Cf. Friedrich Edding, "Estimating Costs of Educational Requirements," in Herbert Parnes (ed.), *Planning Education for Economic and Social Development* (Paris: OECD, 1963), pp. 233–45.
[4] John Vaizey, *The Economics of Education* (London, 1962), p. 43.

Sunday. In Kalimantan (Borneo) Indonesia, students in the agricultural school use the school tractors to take their girls to the movies in the evenings. Conceptually, there is no difficulty in measuring both the direct returns from education and the increase in output of other goods and services which it permits. The real difficulty is that with the techniques and data presently available neither direct nor indirect returns can be measured with any precision.

The Income Approach

In default of such a theoretically perfect approach, various approximations to it have been suggested. One of these is to assume that differences in personal incomes are a close approximation to differences in individual contribution to gross national social product, and to correlate personal incomes with the amount and kind of education received by individuals. It is also assumed that differences in lifetime earnings are the result of differences in educational background. Putting these two assumptions together, a rough measure of the contribution to total social product of additional pupil-years of education of various kinds can be obtained. Professor Schultz was a pioneer in the use of this method. He estimates returns on investment in education in the United States measured by differences in lifetime earnings associated with amounts of education received at 78 per cent for the fifth to eighth years of elementary school, and 23 per cent for four years of high school or four or more years of higher education.

There are two obvious defects in this approach. One is that income is not a perfect measure of contribution to total output. Questions of monopoly power, parasitism, and special privilege arise. These affect income directly, and since they are also associated with the amount of education received, they raise average returns to education above marginal returns. The other is that differences in income do not result from differences in educational background alone, but also from native ability (intelligence) and special privilege.

An interesting effort to isolate the contribution of education as such to national output, while taking account of the impact on income of intelligence and privilege, has been undertaken by Professor John Chipman of the University of Minnesota. Like Professor Schultz, Chipman first assumes that income is an approximation to productivity; but his method is a refinement of the Schultz approach, since it includes a device for measuring the effect of privilege on income as well. Income of any individual is treated as a function of the last grade of school attended, the age of the person, the type of training received, his wealth or social status (privilege) and his innate intelligence. Income, age, and education received are obtained from questionnaires. The relationship between the privilege and intelligence factors is approximated by the ratio of enrollment at any grade of school to the total population in the corresponding age group (dropout rates), obtained from education statistics. The underlying rationale is simple: children drop out of school either because they do not have the intelligence to continue or because they lack the social status that would enable them to continue anyway. Those who remain in school are either intelligent or privileged, or both. This variable also takes account of the difference between income and productivity, to the degree that such differences are also a reflection of the relationship of privilege to intelligence. That is, the method involves an underlying assumption that the same kind of relationship of intelligence to privilege which makes income diverge from productivity also determines the ability of a student to survive to an additional year of schooling. In other words, it assumes that the kind of privilege which enables an unintelligent student to obtain more education than other children of equal intelligence will later enable him to obtain an income which is high in relation to his intelligence and training. In many societies these two kinds of privilege are indeed closely correlated.

It should be noted that the relative importance of education, intelligence, and privilege is not determined in advance, but is determined econometrically for each country from the data pertinent to that country. The present writer's view is that the Chipman method would be worth trying in a number of countries to see how it works. If it turned out that the high regression coefficient was between income and the proxy variable measuring intelligence and privilege, one might feel inclined to abandon this approach, since the dropout rate is only an approximation to the true causal factors. But if it turned out that the high regression was between income and education, it would appear that we were on the road to an accurate measure of returns. It should be noted, however, that it would still be necessary to allow somehow for the complementarity between the productivity of one individual and the level of education of people around him.

It may be that the effect of social privilege and intelligence (as factors operating independently of education received) is not very great anyhow. The evidence available is very limited, but it suggests that we may worry too much about other factors in income determination. A study conducted in Minnesota showed that standardization of incomes for father's occupation (an approximation to social privilege) left 93 per cent of the income differential between high school graduates and college graduates, and 90 per cent of the differential between high school graduates and those with "some college," "to be attributed to education and inter-related factors." [5] The same study showed that standardization for IQ left 97 per cent of the differential between high school and college graduates and 102 per cent of the difference between high school and "some college" groups (implying that a higher IQ slightly reduced incomes of those with "some college") to be explained by level of education alone. Minnesota is not the world and much more work along these lines needs to be done; meanwhile we can take heart from these limited results.

One of the most difficult problems in using the income approach to measure returns to investment in education is to determine the proper discount factor. We cannot simply add up lifetime incomes and compare

[5] "Appendix to Edward F. Denison's Reply," in John Vaizey (ed.), *op. cit.*, pp. 92–95.

them, for, as Mary Jean Bowman points out, "the time patterns of cost and incomes associated with one or another level of educational attainment will be quite different." [6] Because of time-preference (and also, for that matter, liquidity- and safety-preference) people will be far from indifferent as to which pattern is chosen—unless, as Professor Harry Johnson has pointed out to the author, the time-pattern of earnings can be offset by recourse to the capital market. Consequently the usual procedure is to compare present value of costs and lifetime incomes, using an "appropriate" interest rate to discount future values. But what is the "appropriate" rate, either for an individual or for a community as a whole? In the end, as Miss Bowman says, the choice of any "external" rate is "inevitably quite arbitrary"; yet at the same time "what rate is chosen can substantially alter the rankings of computed present values among educational alternatives yielding income flows with differing shapes to their time paths." [7]

Some of these difficulties are avoided by using instead an "internal rate of return"; that is, the rate which would equate the present value of extra income earned with the extra cost of additional education—college versus high school, for example. This rate of return can then be compared with returns on alternative investments, and if it is higher, the extra education will be worthwhile. There are, however, still deficiencies in this method. One would have to add some estimate of the value of education as a consumers' good to the returns, and some estimate of the effect of educating one person on the productivity of others—as in any "income" approach. In addition, even the use of "internal" rates of return ignores the fact that liquidity and safety, as well as time pattern, vary from one kind of investment to another, and consequently equal rates of return are not equally attractive from either an individual or a social point of view. Education, for example, is a highly illiquid asset from either a personal or social viewpoint; the investment in it can be "liquidated" only by using it over the years. It is also a somewhat risky investment, particularly in the absence of an accurate forecast of future manpower requirements; the value of investing in petroleum engineers in the past may have little to do with their value in the future, either in a country which formerly had no oil and then made significant discoveries or in a country which once had oil but has exhausted its reserves. (There are limitations on migration.) There is also a risk of death and incapacitation (which is calculable for large numbers of students). For developing countries there is a very considerable risk of loss through emigration. For these and other reasons, expanding investment in each category of education precisely to the point where the internal rate of return is no longer higher than any other would not guarantee an optimal volume or pattern of education.

Table 19-1 shows the results of some efforts to measure returns to investment in education from income differentials. In calculating "total returns," public as well as private outlays on education are taken into account. In the case of Mexico there is an adjustment for "social privilege"

[6] Mary Jean Bowman, "The Requirements of the Labor-market and the Education Explosion," *Yearbook of Education 1965.*
[7] *Ibid.*

TABLE 19–1

Rates of Return to Investments in Education

(A) Hansen: All Males, United States, 1949

Educational Attainment Increment	Total Direct Rates	Private Rates	
		Without Tax Adjustment	*Adjusted for Income Tax*
Grades 3–6	14.5	—	—
Grades 7–8	29.2	—	—
Secondary (9–12)	11.4	15.3	14.5
Higher (13–16)	10.2	11.6	10.1

(B) Mincer: United States, 1939, 1949, and 1958   (C) Harberger: Hyderabad, India

Educational Attainment Increment	Total Direct Returns			Total Direct Returns
	1939 Urban White Male Wage and Salary Workers	*1949 All Males*	*1958 All Males*	*Male Wage and Salary Workers, 1956*
Grades 5–8	20.9	22.2	19.3	—
Secondary	12.5	11.8	15.1	10.0–11.9
Higher	11.0	10.6	11.5	16.3–16.9

(D) Carnoy: Mexican Urban Wage and Salary Workers, Three Cities, 1963

Educational Attainment Increment	Total Direct Returns		Private Returns	
	Unadjusted	*Adjusted for Parental Occupation*	*Unadjusted*	*Adjusted for Parental Occupation*
2–4	17.3	12.8	21.1	15.2
5–6	37.5	34.5	48.6	44.9
7–8	23.4	20.6	36.5	31.0
9–11	14.2	12.3	17.4	15.2
12–13	12.4	11.4	15.8	14.6
14–16	29.5	31.5	36.7	39.5

SOURCES:
(A) W. Lee Hansen, "Rates of Return to Investment in Schooling," *Journal of Political Economy* Vol. LXXI, No. 2, (April, 1963), tables, 3, 4, and 5, pp. 134–36.
(B) Jacob Mincer, "On-the-Job Training: Costs, Returns, and Some Implications," *Journal of Political Economy*, (Supplement on Investment in Human Beings), October, 1962, pp. 76–8, tables A5, A6, and A7.
(C) Arnold Harberger, "Investment in Man versus Investment in Machines: The Case of India." Paper prepared for the Conference on Education and Economic Development, sponsored by the Social Science Research Council and the Comparative Education Center of the University of Chicago (Chicago, 1963).
(D) Martin Carnoy, "The Cost and Return to Schooling in Mexico," (Ph.D. dissertation, University of Chicago, 1964), Table 26, p. 64.

through parental occupation. It will be noted that the returns to the final years of a particular level, such as primary school, are very high in both the United States (grades 7–8) and Mexico (grades 5–6). It may be questioned whether the personal gains involved in not being officially classified as a "dropout" really have any social equivalent; it is hard to believe that the social returns to the final years of elementary school are so much higher than social returns to the first years of secondary school.

Miss Bowman, in commenting on these data, makes several pertinent observations. First, she says, they cast doubt on "the spreading dogma that the highest priority educational need in virtually all except the most advanced countries today is at the secondary level." Second, the Mexican data provide evidence, so far unexplained, that coming from a family of high occupational status reduces, rather than increases, the effects on income of a given amount of education. For what they are worth, these data strengthen the conclusion of the previous section that we may be worrying too much about the effect of "social privilege" on incomes—apart, that is, from the effect of social privilege on the amount of education particular individuals receive. The Harberger data for India (see Table 19–1) were designed for comparison with returns to investment in physical capital. Even with liberal upward adjustments for returns to education, his highest rates of return for college and postgraduate study were 16.9 per cent, while returns to physical capital ranged from 17.2 to 26.1 per cent. These data raise questions as to whether or not it is true that returns to investment in education in the less-developed countries are *always* higher than returns to investment in physical capital. They suggest the need for capital accumulation in physical and human form to proceed together. One reason for the success of the United States in raising productivity has been "a fairly stable equilibrium situation as between investments in education and in physical capital . . . investments in human and physical capital have moved along in easy step with each other and will presumably continue to do so." [8]

Income versus Rate-of-Return

Some writers have confused the issue by arguing as though the simple income approach were the same thing as a cost-benefit approach, treating the limitations on the simple income approach as limitations on all efforts to measure returns to investment in education. Thus C. Arnold Anderson and Miss Bowman, in comparing the "rate-of-return" analysis with "the more pervasive methods of manpower planning," list two common criticisms of the former which also apply to the latter and three which are false: [9]

1. Ignores the non-economic benefits of education.   } apply also to
2. Catches only direct but not indirect returns.   } manpower approach

[8] *Ibid.*

[9] C. Arnold Anderson and Mary Jean Bowman, "Theoretical Considerations in Educational Planning," in Don Adams (ed.), *Educational Planning* (Syracuse, 1964), pp. 28–29.

3. Assumes pure competition. (False: can correct for effects of monopoly.)

4. Impractical because the necessary data are not available. (Circular reasoning. Data no more difficult to obtain than those needed for manpower planning. Lacking because few people interested in using rate-of-return for planning.)

5. Ignores income effects of ability, motivation, family status correlated with schooling. (Not statistically insurmountable.)

Anderson and Bowman, while correct in showing the invalidity of the last three criticisms of the rate-of-return approach, are in error in suggesting that the manpower approach and rate-of-return approach are on a par with regard to the first two. These criticisms apply to the manpower approach but *not* to a broad rate-of-return approach. A shadow price for "non-economic" (income) benefits of education can be established and the value of education at these shadow prices can be included in returns. Similarly, an effort can be made to measure indirect returns (especially the increase in one group's productivity through working with other people who are educated) as well as direct returns.

Anderson and Bowman go on to state what seem to them more fundamental weaknesses of the "rate-of-return" method.

1. It does not incorporate systematic assessment of linkages between educational and economic developments over time.

Answer: This criticism applies only to the method of using age-income data at one point of time to measure differences in life income streams; it does not apply to rate-of-return approach as such.

2. The central decisions with respect to educational policy necessarily involve lump changes; marginal analysis is inappropriate.

Answer: True—but the comment applies equally to all other aspects of economic development planning. One must compare the returns to various "lumps" of expenditure with their costs.

3. Rates of return at a point of time can suggest only a direction of change, not a magnitude.

Answer: This is also true of all development investment decisions.

4. Market prices, with or without an incomes policy, are faulty indices of productivity, and administered prices (wages, salaries) do not measure productivity at all.

Here Anderson and Bowman provide the answer themselves: use shadow prices for both cost and return estimates.

Herbert S. Parnes falls into the same trap. The "returns-to-education approach," he says, has "a certain elemental appeal," but fails to take account of "non-economic benefits," ignores the contribution through raising the general level of understanding, attributes all differences in income to education, and accepts income as a measure of social product.[10] Once again, these comments apply to the narrow income-differential approach, not to the rate-of-return approach as such.

[10] Herbert S. Parnes, "Assessing the Educational Needs of a Nation," in Don Adams, *op. cit.*, p. 53.

The Manpower Approach [11]

The manpower planning approach is based on the assumption that the main link of education with economic development is through the knowledge and skills it produces in the labor force. It implies that if the educational system produces qualified people in the right numbers and places, the major part of the economic and social contribution of education planning is achieved. It is recognized, of course, that the educational system must also provide for people, such as housewives not in the labor force; but it regards projections of manpower needs as basic to educational planning.

Four difficulties limit the usefulness of this approach. First, forecasts of manpower needs can seldom be made with any reliability beyond short-term periods of five to eight years. The time perspective required by educational planning as a whole is fifteen to twenty years, though it is possible to influence the supply already in the "pipeline" over shorter periods. Secondly, the educational component of different occupations changes with technological progress and the rise of educational standards. Thirdly, the occupational needs of the economy are not the whole of society's needs for education. An addition has to be made for women and girls who do not work, and for the supplementary amount of education which a country requires to fulfill its cultural, political, and social goals. Some educators would also wish to assure that educational output will grow faster than demand to the degree required to stimulate growth, without creating problems of unemployment. The educational plan must also provide for turnover of employment and continuous adjustment between the educational system and the socio-economic environment. Full account must be taken of the "wastage" involved in various educational systems as well as students switching in mid-stream, students' and parents' preferences, locational disequilibrium of supply and demand, and adjustments required by technological change.

These necessary additions mean that a great deal of "guesstimating" is involved as in the case of the other methods in producing educational targets.

The narrow manpower approach is imperfect for other reasons. It leaves out of account the value of education as a "consumers' good." More important, the product mix itself should not be determined irrespective of educational requirements for production of various goods and services. The composition of the target product mix, and of the investment program undertaken to achieve it, must depend in part on the relative cost of the various types of educational programs needed. In short, investment in education and in all other sectors of the development program should be determined mutually.

Anderson and Bowman have some fundamental criticisms of the manpower approach at the conceptual level, which have nothing to do with the purely statistical problems of forecasting.[12]

1. It assumes near-zero *ex ante* elasticities of demand for skills (*ex ante* near-zero skill substitution).

[11] See also Herbert Parnes (ed.), *op. cit.*, Part Two, "The Manpower Approach to Educational Planning."
[12] Anderson and Bowman, *op. cit.*, p. 22.

Since levels of national income are forecast, and the impact of rising incomes on demand for various goods and services (and so for various skills) is explicitly taken into account, the reference here is presumably to price-elasticity of demand rather than income-elasticity of demand. The point is an important one, however. In the past relative shortages of particular skills have led to relatively high prices of those skills; and entrepreneurs have reacted where possible by substituting other factors of production for scarce skills, or by changing the product mix so as to reduce the requirements of scarce skills. It is by no means apparent that this sort of adjustment has been harmful; why not allow for similar adjustment in the future, rather than taking both the product mix and the factor proportions as determined solely by the level of per capita income, whatever the price-cost structure?

2. The period of specialized training in several of the more critical skills is taken to be long.

This point is also fundamental. The manpower approach assumes that skill requirements are a proper basis for determining the amount and pattern of investment in the educational *system*. At the present stage of development of most developing countries, however, it is probable that rigorous application of a manpower approach by itself would lead to much less formal education than is currently desired even in the least ambitious among them. There is a good deal of evidence that most of the skills required by development programs over the next decade or so can be produced by on-the-job training, more or less independently of the formal school system. A survey in Saõ Paulo, which has probably seen a more rapid rate of industrialization during the past two decades than any similar subdivision of a developing country, revealed that in the opinion of employers there skilled labor had never been a serious bottleneck. A combination of on-the-job training and vocational schools, originally set up by the enterprises themselves to produce higher level skills, sufficed to meet all skill requirements within three months to a year, even when the intake consisted in large measure of illiterate peasants.

Stanislav Strumulin gives some figures from Russian experience which suggest that one year of primary education increases a worker's productivity on the average by 30 per cent, while one year's apprenticeship raises productivity by only 12 per cent to 16 per cent. Since the cost of one year of formal education is likely to be higher than the cost of a year's apprenticeship, and since even an apprentice is likely to produce something, these figures might mean that one year's formal education is not worthwhile from a manpower viewpoint. Strumulin also reports that after four years' primary education a worker's "output and wages" are 79 per cent higher than those of a "first-category" worker with no schooling; and after seven years' schooling "an office worker's qualifications may be as much as 235 per cent above the lowest level." However this statement says only that men with more formal schooling get higher-grade jobs; it tells us nothing about the relative costs and returns of formal schooling versus on-the-job training for *particular* jobs.

H. M. Phillips presents some figures (Table 19–2) also taken from

TABLE 19–2

Rise in Efficiency (in work units) Per Year

Year	Training on the Job without Schooling	Schooling and Training
First	0.16	0.30
Second	0.16	0.23
Third	0.14	0.15
Fourth	0.13	0.11
Fifth	0.11	0.08
Sixth	0.08	0.04
	0.77	0.91

SOURCE: UNESCO, *Economic and Social Aspects of Educational Planning*, p. 24.

Strumulin.[13]

Unfortunately we are not told how many years of schooling are involved in these figures; but such as they are, the figures raise grave doubts as to the advantages of formal schooling for meeting manpower requirements. After six years on the job the worker with no schooling has increased his efficiency 71 per cent, while the worker with schooling has raised his productivity 91 per cent. If many years of formal schooling underlie these figures it certainly would not pay to provide schooling from a narrow manpower viewpoint alone.

Nearly all developing countries have set their sights on universal primary school education within a decade or so. It would be impossible to justify these targets from a manpower viewpoint alone; but that does not mean that the targets are not justified. Even from the standpoint of productivity, it is possible that a higher level of general education will bring a more rapid rate of technological progress and cultural change in any society.

3. It assumes that a long lead time is needed to provide the personnel and facilities to train new manpower cohorts.

This assumption also is "unproven." It may prove possible to adapt training methods and equipment quickly to changing needs.

4. Production coefficients in the formation of each type of manpower are taken to be highly fixed. Actually an educational system (including its technical and vocational training components) may be able to shift quickly from producing one set of skills to producing another.

5. It assumes that the pace of change in manpower requirements is rapid and irregular, requiring decisions on investment in education that are both "lumpy" and long-term.

6. It implicitly assumes (although few manpower planners claim it) a high degree of accuracy in long-term forecasting.

It does not seem therefore, that either conceptually or in terms of practicality the manpower approach has any clear advantage over a more straightforward kind of cost-benefit analysis. At the same time, it is well to remember that limitations of the manpower approach *by itself* do not

[13] Stanislav Strumulin, "The Economics of Education in the U.S.S.R.," *Economic and Social Aspects of Educational Planning* (Paris: UNESCO, 1964), p. 71.

mean that it may not be a useful exercise in conjunction with other types of analysis. Certainly it makes no sense to ignore manpower requirements altogether, as some educational planning has done in the past.

The "Econometric Approach"

The method suggested by Professors Tinbergen, Bos, and Correa is to relate the stock of educated people, and the flow of children and students completing education at the different levels, directly to the national output of goods and services without passing through the intervening stage of making manpower forecasts. It is possible to set up a series of linear equations which relate the stock of persons who have completed a given level of education, and the number of students at each level, to the aggregate volume of production. These equations will show how the structure of the educational system should change with different growth rates of the economy. One difficulty in this method is that assumptions have to be made about teacher-student ratios and about the adequacy of the relation of the education "mix" to the product "mix" at the base from which the projection is made. If these assumptions are incorrectly made, they will invalidate the conclusions. Further, the differences of rates of growth in the different economic sectors, and increases of productivity, need to be included; the range of assumptions as to the technical coefficients is very wide.[14]

A further difficulty common to both the manpower planning and the Tinbergen-Correa "input-output" approach is the assumption that a given output requires a *fixed* volume of manpower with *fixed* amounts of education and training. The fact is, however, that considerable latitude exists for substitution of capital for manpower in general, and for substituting additional education and training for man-hours. A given output may be produced with a small number of highly trained workers or a larger number of less trained workers. It may even be possible, through automation, to produce it with a smaller number of less highly trained workers. In short, the choice of technology, and its implications for education, is a major aspect of development programming; so is the choice between more education and training and less employment, or less education and training and more employment in each sector.

The broader the categories of output, and the broader the definition of educational inputs, the less fixed are the relations between them and the wider the area of choice. In some of the underdeveloped countries, limitations in data, skilled mathematical statisticians, and computing facilities would not permit computation and projection of relationships among a large number of output categories and a large number of education projects. In such cases, the choice of parameters to be used for projection—a choice which is a policy decision and not a matter of statistical analysis alone—is more important than the projection as such.

The basic Tinbergen model has been neatly summarized by A. K. Sen: [15] The basic model used involves six equations. There are two scarce commodities

[14] For a brief outline of Tinbergen's approach, see Herbert Parnes (ed.), *op. cit.*, chap. XVI.
[15] A. K. Sen, "Comments on the Paper by Messrs. Tinbergen and Bos," in John Vaizey (ed.), *op. cit.*, pp. 188–89. The Tinbergen equations are:

represented by N^2 and N^3 (leaving out the time subscripts), which in this model stand for "the total stock of people with a secondary education" and "those with a third level education." The first is required to produce national income and the relationship is assumed to be a proportional one (see equation 1). The second is needed partly to produce the national income, partly to produce people with secondary education, and partly to produce more of their own kind, i.e., people with third-level education. These requirements in commodity-production and in the two types of teaching are taken to be proportional to the products produced (see equation 6). The rest of the equations relate to stocks and flows of the two items referred to above. Equation (2) says that this period's stock of men with a secondary education is equal to the previous period's stock of such men, minus that part of the previous period's stock who died or retired, plus the new entrants into this field. Death and retirement claim a fixed proportion of the stock of educated people each period. Equation (5) says the same thing about third-level educated men. Equation (3) shows that those who received secondary education in the previous period minus those of them who are going in for third-level education, equals the number of new entrants in the stock of people with secondary education. Finally, equation (4) points out that those who received third-level education in the previous period constitute the new entrants into stock of third-level educated man-power in this period.

This proposed method has, understandably, called forth a good deal of criticism. Herbert Parnes considers "the chief limitation of the model" to be "its basic assumption that the correlation between the educational structure of the labor force . . . and the volume of output means that the former is a necessary condition for the latter. It may well be that the causal relationship, at least in part, is the reverse of the one postulated." [16] Thomas Balogh is much more brutal. "What Professors Tinbergen and Bos do," he maintains, "is to assume the answers, and then put them into a simple mathematical form." He severely questions the basic assumptions: that secondary education lasts six years; that secondary school-leavers do not teach in primary schools, but that a proportion of college graduates do teach in secondary schools ("the primary schools do not seem to absorb any educated persons—they presumably do not need teachers"); that higher education also lasts six years. Balogh insists that "all these implausible assumptions cannot be said to amount to serious investigation of the first problem. Their treatment of the rest is no less cavalier." [17]

(1) $N^2_t = V^2 U_t$
(2) $N^2_t = (1 - \lambda^2) N^2_{t-1} + m^2_t$
(3) $m^2_t = n^2_{t-1} - n^3_t$
(4) $m^3_t = n^3_{t-1}$
(5) $N^3_t = (1 - \lambda^3) N^3_{t-1} + m^3_t$
(6) $N^3_t = V^3 U_t + \pi^2 n^2_t + \pi^3 n^3_t$ where V is the total income of the country, N^2 the labor force with secondary education, N^3 the labor force with third-level education, m^2 those who have entered the labor force N^2 within the previous 6 years, m^3 those who have entered the labor force N^3 within the previous 6 years, n^2 the number of students in secondary education, n^3 the number of students in third-level education.

[16] Herbert Parnes (ed.), *op. cit.*, p. 54.
[17] Thomas Balogh, "Comments on the Paper by Messrs. Tinbergen and Bos," in John Vaizey (ed.), *op. cit.*, p. 180.

Tinbergen, Correa, and Bos are of course well aware that their simplifying assumptions will not hold in all countries. The real difficulty is that in order to make the parameters of their models bear anything like the constant relationship to levels of income assumed in the models, we would need data of a kind not available even in the most advanced countries, let alone in underdeveloped ones. We would need national income broken down into something like the Department of Commerce "two digit" classifications—cotton textiles, synthetic textiles, silk textiles, woolen textiles, say—on the one hand, and equally fine divisions of the educational output on the other—chemical engineers, petroleum engineers, civil engineers, mechanical engineers. We would need similarly detailed breakdowns for all industries and all levels of skill. We would then be *approaching* fixed relationships between the level and composition of total output and the level and composition of educational inputs; but even then the relationships would not really be fixed, but would be subject to variation by policy decisions based on cost-benefit considerations.

A. K. Sen suggests that a more refined version of the Tinbergen-Bos-Correa approach might give us some hint of the *minimal* requirements of education; other factors of production are not *infinitely* substitutable for education. The model does not tell us much about the optimal level and pattern of education. Even for determining the minimal requirements, Sen argues, four fundamental adjustments would be necessary: [18]

1. The assumption of "radioactive" depreciation must be dropped. Even for machinery the assumption that physical depreciation is directly proportionate to the stock, so that mortality is independent of age, is dubious; for the stock of human capital it is "totally inapplicable."

2. "Learning by doing" (as distinct from formal education) must be introduced into the model.

3. The educational coefficients should be the minimal, not the actual ones.

4. Allowance should be made for the possibility of reducing the number of years of schooling in each stage.

The "Residual Factor" Approach

Available data and techniques do not as yet permit the determination of an educational program by comparing various educational projects with each other and with projects in other sectors, in terms of total returns to investment in these projects. For the time being some less complicated method must be used to decide the appropriate size of the education program. The "residual factor" analysis suggests one alternative approach. The essence of this approach is to compare increases in inputs of labor and capital with the expansion of gross national product over a long period. Such measurements have been made for the United States and some European and Latin American countries. They indicate that the increase in inputs has been small in comparison with the growth of the gross national

---

[18] A. K. Sen, *op. cit.*, p. 197.

product, indicating that the bulk of improvements in production and levels of living is due to a "residual factor." Some enthusiasts have been willing to assume that this "residual factor" is "education" in the broad sense, including all kinds of technical training, and including also the technological progress that comes from investment in education.

The original estimate for the United States by Robert Solow showed that only 10 per cent of the growth of American output between 1900 and 1960 could be explained by the increase in inputs of physical and human resources, leaving 90 per cent to be explained by the "residual factor." A study of manufacturing alone by B. Massel produced similar results. Odd Aukrust found that about two-thirds of the growth in Norway between 1900 and 1955 could be attributed to the residual factor. In the United Kingdom a study by Reddaway and Smith for a much shorter period, 1948 to 1954, indicated that three-quarters of the increase in manufacturing output must be explained by the residual. Professor T. W. Schultz made some analysis of agricultural sectors only, and obtained the following figures for the share of increased output due to the residual factor: United States (1910–14 to 1945–49), 83 per cent; Argentina (1912–14 to 1945–49), 62 per cent; Brazil (1925–29 to 1945–49), 45 per cent; and Mexico (1925–29 to 1945–49), 50 per cent. [19]

The Denison Variant

Perhaps the boldest attempt to date to break down sources of economic growth has been made by Edward F. Denison. His main results for the United States are shown in Table 19–3. Denison distinguishes the increase in amount of education from the "advance of knowledge" as such. The former factor accounted for 23 per cent of the total growth of output in the United States since 1929 and the latter factor for 20 per cent. If we consider the "advance of knowledge" as part of the contribution of education in the broad sense, we could say that Denison's calculations attribute 43 per cent of past growth in the United States to "education." This figure is still small in comparison to some other estimates of the "residual factor," but the difference is to be explained by Denison's efforts to isolate other sources of growth besides increased inputs of labor and capital and the "residual." For example, Denison assumes that 10 per cent of the increase in output can be attributed to economies of scale. The increase in inputs of land, labor, and capital by themselves explain only 30 per cent of the increase in output; if everything else is regarded as the "residual factor," as in some of the other studies, then Denison's results are not so different from the others. It might be noted that in Denison's calculations "advance

[19] Robert Solow, "Technical Change and the Aggregate Production Function," *The Review of Economics and Statistics,* Vol. XXIX, No. 3 (August, 1957). B. Massel, "Capital Formation's Technological Change in U.S. Manufacturing," *The Review of Economics and Statistics,* Vol. XLII, No. 2 (August, 1960). O. Aukrust, "Investment and Economic Growth," *Productivity Measurement Review,* No. 16, 1959, pp. 35–50. W. B. Reddaway and A. D. Smith, "Progress in British Manufacturing Industries in the Period 1949–1954," *Economic Journal,* March, 1960. T. S. Schultz, "Economic Prospects of Primary Products," in Howard S. Ellis (ed.), *Economic Development for Latin America* (London, Macmillan), 1961, chap. 11, pp. 308–31.

of knowledge" is the true residual; other factors, including education, are measured or "guesstimated."

As Denison is the first to admit, a good deal of "guesstimating" is involved. For example, it is "guesstimated" that 40 per cent of wage differentials can be explained by factors other than formal schooling. When all allowances are made, however, Denison's figures leave us with the conclusion that education has been an important factor in the economic growth of the United States.

Great care must be exercised, nonetheless, in applying the results of such studies to educational policy. The fact that expansion of the education system in the United States and other countries has made a substantial contribution to growth in the past, when capital accumulation, resource discovery, scientific research, and engineering advance were all going on together does not mean that less-developed countries can now count on the same sort of aggregative returns to investment in the formal education system alone. There is a high degree of complementarity among all these factors; and marginal returns to investment in education could be brought to zero quickly enough if the other sources of growth are not present as well. Capital accumulation, in particular, is a vehicle for the application of advances in knowledge. Even improvements in labor skills are largely a matter of learning to use new and better tools and equipment, rather than increased dexterity in use of old ones. In his criticism of Denison's work, J. Sandee of the Central Planning Bureau in The Hague says, "my main difference with Denison is that his technological progress is 'disembodied,' while I believe most of it to be 'embodied' in new plant and equipment. . . . The believer in 'embodied' progress usually finds at least twice the yield deduced by the classical Cobb-Douglas cum disembodied trend analyst, because he considers the whole 'residual' (and also some of Denison's other effects) as the result of new investment." [20]

Some critics have questioned the use of the Cobb-Douglas production function for such purposes at all. The Cobb-Douglas production function is linear and homogeneous, so that if inputs of both labor and capital are doubled, output will double too; and the marginal product of each factor, multiplied by the number of units of that factor and added together, equals the total product. The specific Cobb-Douglas function attributed three-quarters of the total output to labor and one-quarter to capital. As Professor Erik Lundberg points out: [21]

The main defence of the use of a marginal productivity concept of a production function, both for time series and country comparison analysis, is that it is a straightforward and common-sense method that yields results—and that simple alternatives are very difficult to find. The relative importance of the input-factors (the weights) is given by the shares in national income (being exponentials of the production function). The great explanatory importance

[20] J. Sandee, "Comments on Mr. Edward F. Denison's Paper," in John Vaizey (ed.), op. cit., p. 74.

[21] Erik Lundberg, "Comments on Mr. Edward F. Denison's Paper," in John Vaizey (ed.), op. cit., pp. 68–69

TABLE 19-3

Sources of Growth of Real National Income of the United States

Source of Growth	Share of National Income (per cent distribution)		Growth Rate (per cent per year)		Contribution to Growth Rate of Real National Income (percentage points)		Contribution to Growth Rate of Real National Income (per person employed)	
	1909–29	1929–57	1909–29	1929–57	1909–29	1929–57	1909–29	1929–57
1. Real national income	100.0	100.0*	2.82†	2.93	2.82	2.93	1.22	1.60
2. Increase in total inputs, adjusted	..	..	2.24	1.99	2.26	2.00	0.66	0.67
3. Adjustment	..	..	−0.09	−0.11	..	..	..	..
4. Increase in total inputs, unadjusted	..	..	2.33	2.10	..	..	..	..
5. Labor, adjusted for quality change	68.9	73.0	2.30	2.16	1.53	1.57	0.42	0.57
6. Employment and hours	..	..	1.62	1.08	1.11	0.80	0.00	−0.20
7. Employment	..	..	1.58	1.31	1.11	1.00	..	..
8. Effect of shorter hours on quality of a man-year's work	..	..	0.03	−0.23	0.00	−0.20	0.00	−0.20
9. Annual hours	..	..	−0.34	−0.73	−0.23	−0.53	−0.23	−0.53
10. Effect of shorter hours on quality of a man-hour's work	..	..	0.38	0.50	0.23	0.33	0.23	0.33
11. Education	..	..	0.56	0.93	0.35	0.67	0.35	0.67
12. Increased experience and better utilization of women workers	..	..	0.10	0.15	0.06	0.11	0.06	0.11

13. Changes in age-sex composition of labor force	..	..	0.01	−0.01	0.01	−0.01	0.01	−0.01
14. Land	7.7	4.5	0.00	0.00	0.00	0.00	−0.11	−0.05
15. Capital	23.4	22.5	3.16	1.88	0.73	0.43	0.35	0.15
16. Non-farm residential structures	3.7	3.1	3.49	1.46	0.13	0.05	0.07	0.01
17. Other structures and equipment	14.6	15.0	2.93	1.85	0.41	0.28	0.17	0.10
18. Inventories	4.8	3.9	3.31	1.90	0.16	0.08	0.08	0.03
19. United States-owned assets abroad	0.6	0.7	4.20	1.97	0.02	0.02	0.02	0.01
20. Foreign assets in United States (an offset)	0.3	0.2	−1.85	1.37	0.01	0.00	0.01	0.00
21. Increase in output per unit of input	..	..	0.56	0.92	0.56	0.93	0.56	0.93
22. Restrictions against optimum use of resources	..	..	..	..	n.e.	−0.07	n.e.	−0.07
23. Reduced waste of labor in agriculture	..	..	..	..	n.e.	0.02	n.e.	0.02
24. Industry shift from agriculture	..	..	..	..	n.e.	0.05	n.e.	0.05
25. Advance of knowledge	..	..	..	..	n.e.	0.58	n.e.	0.58
26. Change in lag in application of knowledge	..	..	..	..	n.e.	0.01	n.e.	0.01
27. Economies of scale-independent growth of local markets	..	..	..	..	n.e.	0.07	n.e.	0.07
28. Economies of scale-growth of national market	..	..	..	..	0.28	0.27	0.28	0.27

*For 1930–40 and 1942–46 interpolated distributions rather than the actual distributions for these dates were used. Estimates are 1929–58 averages.

†This rate, like that for 1929–57, derives from Department of Commerce estimates. Estimates by John W. Kendrick, based on adjustment to Department of Commerce concepts of estimates by Simon Kuznets yield a growth rate of 3.17, which would result in a figure for output per unit of input (line 21) of 0.91.

n.e. = Not estimated.

SOURCE: John Vaizey, (ed.), op. cit.

that Denison can attribute to education, in fact, depends on the big share of labor income, 70–75 per cent. The low share of capital, 20–25 per cent, gives this factor its subordinate position and instead permits more room for the residual.

In any case, Lundberg argues, a static equilibrium concept like the production function is a dubious instrument for analysis of the dynamics of growth. He also suggests that if the gross investment rather than the net investment ratio is used, the role of investment can be made to look much bigger.

Some economists go further still and deny the usefulness of marginal productivity analysis for any problem whatsoever. Nicholas Kaldor of Cambridge University maintains that the marginal productivity theory is valid only on the highly unrealistic assumptions of perfect competition and absence of external economies of scale, and denies that factor shares have any relationship whatsoever to marginal productivity. Professor Harry Johnson, however, considers such extreme views to be a peculiarity of the Cambridge school, "a stubborn refusal to face analytical issues and resolve them, whereas a proper application of marginal productivity theory could clarify matters considerably." He refers rather scornfully to "light blue economics" (following Dennis Robertson, who once referred to a controversy between Hungarian-born Oxford economist Balogh and Hungarian-born Cambridge economist Kaldor as "the dark blue Danube vs. the light blue Danube") which discerns "a spurious conflict between the view that people are educated because they are rich and the view that people are rich because they are educated, whereas marginal productivity theory leads me to discern an imperfection in the capital market that requires correction by social policy." [22]

Whatever imperfections there may be in the "residual factor" approach to measuring returns to investment in education, something like this approach—to the degree that economic analysis has any influence on educational planning at all—underlies the ambitious targets that have been laid down by the Ministers of Education, and for the most part later accepted by governments, in a series of UNESCO conferences in the Asian, African, and Latin American regions. Virtually all developing countries are committed to universal primary school education within a very few years, and to expanding and improving secondary and higher education as well. To a large degree these ambitious programs are based on the conviction that for the next decade at least the returns to investment in education will be very high, and that there is little danger of investing "too much" in education.

Indeed they assume that it is virtually impossible to spend too much on education, provided it is efficiently programmed so as to assure an optimal allocation of educational resources among various uses, provided restraint is exercised in school building programs, and provided that educational standards are maintained or improved while opportunities for technologi-

[22] Harry G. Johnson, "Comments on Mr. John Vaizey's Paper," in John Vaizey (ed.), *op. cit.*, pp. 226–27.

cal advance in education are seized. Considering the physical limitations on rapid expansion of education systems (especially the shortage of well-trained teachers), this assumption is probably correct in a broad aggregative sense in most developing countries at the present time. But it may not be true of all kinds of education in all underdeveloped countries, and it may soon cease to be so in the aggregate in some of them. In some Latin American countries the education problem is already more qualitative than quantitative. Nor does the "residual factor" approach tell us how to design an educational system in any detail. It provides a reason for confidence in pushing ahead with ambitious education programs, but we will need a much sharper tool for effective educational planning.

Use of "Norms"

From a logical point of view the use of "norms" to determine the appropriate size and pattern of the education budget is a primitive form of "econometric" approach. That is, it involves looking at advanced countries in the past and saying, "high income countries seem to spend about 5 per cent of their gross national product, or 25 per cent of their aggregate governmental budgets, or "x" per cent of total public investment, on education. Therefore if developing countries want to have high incomes too they must do the same." Obviously, there is even less justification for confidence in this approach than there is in the case of the much more sophisticated Tinbergen-Bos-Correa econometric approach. The range of any one of these norms from one country to another is enormous, and the differences do not correlate highly with differences in per capita incomes. Nor do changes in these ratios in particular countries correlate closely with changes in per capita incomes in the same countries. (Even if they did, it could mean simply that the demand for education rises with incomes).

Let us look first at the ratio of public expenditures on education to total public expenditures. There happen to be fairly good data for this ratio for Latin American countries. The range for Latin American countries in 1957 was from 4.4 per cent to 22.4 per cent, and in 1960 from 9.2 to 27 per cent. The change for individual countries in these three years was much greater than the rise in incomes. It increased from 7.1 per cent to 11.7 per cent for Columbia, from 9.4 to 15.6 per cent for Honduras and from 4.4 to 9.2 per cent for Venezuela. In any case, private expenditures on education should obviously be taken into account, and the ratio of private to public expenditures on education varies greatly from one country to another. Use of this norm makes the education budget dependent on the ratio of total expenditures to national income, a ratio which also varies widely among developing countries. According to available data in recent years the ratio of public expenditures to national income in Latin America ranged from 7.8 per cent to 35.4 per cent.

Turning to ratios of public expenditure for education to national income, in 1964 these showed a range within the Latin American region from less than 0.15 to over 5 per cent. There is, moreover, a major caveat to be entered here. The number of children to be educated relative to population is much higher in developing than in advanced countries, and the cost of education is also higher relative to incomes. Teacher-student ratios, opportunity, are—rightly or wrongly—not lower in less-developed countries than they are in advanced ones (see Table 19–4). For equal effectiveness it may be that a greater proportion of GNP needs to be

TABLE 19–4

Teacher-Pupil Ratios in a Number of Countries
for Primary and General Secondary Schools

Country				
		Teacher-Pupil Ratio		
	Year	Primary Education	Year	General Secondary Education
Africa				
Egypt	1959	0.03	1959	0.07
Liberia	1959	0.03	1959	0.08
Morocco	1960	0.02	1957	0.04
Nigeria	1958	0.03	1958	0.05
Sudan	1959	0.02	1959	0.05
America, North				
Canada	1959	0.04	1959	0.05
United States	1958	0.03	1958	0.06
America, South				
Argentina	1959	0.04	1959	0.14
Brazil	1960	0.03	1960	0.07
Colombia	1959	0.03	1959	0.08
Paraguay	1960	0.04	1959	0.14
Venezuela	1959	0.03	1959	0.06
Asia				
India	1958	0.02	1958	0.03
Indonesia	1959	0.03	1959	0.04
Iraq	1959	0.03	1959	0.03
Japan	1960	0.03	1960	0.04
Thailand	1959	0.03	1959	0.04
Europe				
France	1958	0.04	1958	0.03
Greece	1958	0.02	1958	0.03
Netherlands	1959	0.03	1959	0.05
Norway	1959	0.05	1959	0.07
United Kingdom	1958	0.03	1958	0.05

SOURCE: UNESCO, *Basic Facts and Figures*, 1961; UNESCO, *World Survey of Education*, 1961.

devoted to education in developing countries than in Europe and North America.

The proportion of GNP spent on education will also be affected by the age composition of the population. Another variant strongly influencing the ratios is the relationship of per capita teachers' salaries to per capita income, as the country differences are wide and the great proportion of educational cost is made up of teachers' remuneration.

Ultimately, however, the trouble with "norms" is that they do not tell us what we want to know. In the course of the series of UNESCO conferences a figure of 4 to 5 per cent of GNP has somehow come to be accepted as an appropriate target for expenditure on education. There seems to be no particular reason for this figure except that a number of advanced countries do spend about this amount. Japan spends more, however, and Peru spends nearly twice as large a share of national income (publicly) as France. The same percentage figure obviously means very different things, in terms of either quantity or quality of education, from one country to another.

Moreover, concentration on any such norm means ignoring the flexibility which exists with regard to education policy because of the elasticity of substitution of other factors of production for education. Some fascinating figures, reproduced in Table 19–5, bear evidence to this fact. In terms

TABLE 19–5

Educational Coefficients and Capital Coefficients:
An Intercountry Comparison

Country	Secondary-Educated Ratio*	Third-Level-Educated Ratio*	Capital-Output Ratio
Venezuela (1950)	1.5	0.45	2.1
France (1954)	3.3	0.9	4.0
Italy (1951)	5.0	2.2	3.6
Canada (1951)	5.0	1.2	5.4
Brazil (1950)	5.7	1.1	2.9
United States (1950)	6.3	1.4	5.0
Costa Rica (1950)	7.5	2.0	not available
Colombia (1950)	8.2	1.0	4.2
India (1955)	10.7	2.6	2.1

* These ratios are millions of people to national income in billions of dollars, multiplied by 100.

SOURCE: John Vaizey (ed.), The Residual Factor and Economic Growth, op. cit., p. 193.

of either the ratio of secondary-school-educated manpower or of university-trained manpower to national income, India turns out to have a good deal more "education-intensive" system of production than the United States, Canada, or France. So does Costa Rica; and at the secondary school level, so does Colombia. The capital-output ratio, however, is higher in the United States and Canada; these two countries are successfully substituting capital for education, India is—less successfully—substituting education for capital. These figures do not, of course, mean that India and Costa Rica are spending "too much" on education; they do mean that the size of the education program cannot effectively be determined solely by the ratio of outlays on education to national income.

The Traditional Approach

The method still in most general use in Ministries of Education simply projects educational needs in terms of the demand for education at the different levels on the basis of population increase, age distribution, the prospective rise of national income, long-term social goals, and estimated consumers' preferences for education. Among such goals and preferences are universal literacy, universal compulsory primary education, the progress of the country's culture and religious life, etc. This traditional approach works reasonably well in high-income countries, although even in these, concern over flagging rates of growth and ever keener competition in export markets, space, and defense is leading to increased emphasis on the contribution of education to scientific and technological progress. For underdeveloped countries the approach is clearly inadequate. It assumes implicitly that the existing pattern of education will meet the needs of economic development, if only the system is expanded as the school-age population grows. There is virtually no developing country in which this assumption holds.

The Thirteen Steps

UNESCO is currently stressing a "rule-of-thumb" integrated manpower and educational planning approach. This method can be set out in a series of thirteen steps, starting with population growth and the economic perspective and adding other key factors progressively as follows: [23]

1. Projection of future size and age composition of the population.

2. Determining the social minimum standards of education (e.g. universal primary school education by year "x").

3. Assessment of the economic perspective over a period of 15–20 years.

4. Translation of the demands of the economy and its structural changes into manpower terms.

5. Establishment of the educational component of the manpower needs thus disclosed.

6. (a) Additions of education for consumption and social purposes (to the extent not already covered by "4") in accordance with cultural, political and social goals, including adult education, literacy campaigns, etc.

   (b) Additions to cover turnover, switches of students in mid-stream, students' preferences, friction between the educational system and the environment (economic, social and locational).

   (c) Education in excess of demand, on the grounds that in this field "supply creates demand" and accelerates progress.

7. Analysis of quantitative changes required on the supply side, in terms of existing educational system and its logistics, and the constraints on its expansion arising from the nature of the form of education (feasibility of creation of different educational pyramids in specific time periods, time taken for teacher training, etc.).

[23] Cf. H. M. Phillips, "Education and Development," UNESCO, *op. cit.*, pp. 32–37.

8. Detailed assessment of curriculum, teacher training and building needs, etc.

9. Further qualitative appraisal of the education system in terms of social mobility, selection of talent, etc.

10. Establishment of the comparative cost and efficiency of different technologies of education. The results of these last two steps will have to be "fed back" into earlier steps.

11. Translation into financial cost and comparison with financial resources.

12. Co-ordination with other social programs and with the economic development plan.

13. Analysis of the incentives or other measures required to guide pupils into particular studies.

Conclusions on Planning Education

Although an improvement over the traditional approach, these "steps" are clearly makeshift. In the final analysis no approach is defensible on rational grounds except cost-benefit analysis, because there can be no rational justification for expanding investment in education unless it will bring more benefit for a given cost than any other investment. Not even the most enthusiastic educator will argue that education should be expanded even if it brings less benefit to society than something else to be had for the same social cost. Thus while imperfect alternatives for precise measurement of costs and benefits must still be used at present, we should at the same time encourage efforts to refine cost-benefit analysis. On balance the income approach is the most helpful one for measuring returns to investment in education. It entails problems, as we have seen; but we know precisely what the problems are, and conceptually they are all soluble. Let us therefore press on with attempts to measure the difference between social product and personal income, to measure indirect returns, and to determine the relative importance of the amount and kind of education and of other factors in determining personal income.

Foreign Aid and Education

The United States and other donor countries, the World Bank and the International Development Association are all providing small amounts of capital assistance for education projects. It is clear, however, that the role of foreign capital in the field of education is limited for the simple reason that the scarce resources needed to expand education programs are normally supplied through domestic rather than foreign channels. Ultimately, the question is the same: to what extent can the supply of trained teachers, classroom space, textbooks, and laboratory equipment, etc., be built up through the expenditure of foreign exchange provided by external assistance?

First of all, it is apparent that schoolteachers cannot be provided from abroad to any significant extent. Certainly technical assistance programs can provide limited numbers of foreign teachers in special fields where the need is particularly pressing, and where the supply in other countries is relatively abundant. It must be recognized, however, that all advanced countries, as well as underdeveloped ones, face a shortage of teaching personnel over the next ten years; and the relative cost of providing large numbers of teachers from abroad makes such an approach impossible. Similarly, the extent to which teachers can be provided to students from underdeveloped countries by sending these students abroad is severely limited. Schools in many advanced countries are crowded to capacity, and the number of foreign students that can be accepted, even at university level, is severely restricted. The limitations on provisions of textbooks and laboratory equipment from countries with a different language, culture, and technology are obvious. As for the classroom space, most countries have adequate supplies of building materials appropriate for construction of schools, and it is doubtful that it would be appropriate over-all development policy to allocate any significant proportion of foreign aid budgets to the purchase abroad of building materials or equipment for the construction of schools.

It is clear enough from some of the statements regarding external financing of education that those interested in expanding educational programs, and particularly ministers of education, really have in mind increased allocations in domestic currency, to acquire human and physical resources domestically available, while the foreign exchange is utilized for other projects within the over-all economic and social development program. Certainly, in so far as expansion of the education program requires the attraction of human and physical resources from other fields of activity, thus reducing the output of other goods and services and adding to inflationary pressure, increased foreign exchange may be used to import raw materials and equipment for other projects, or even to import final consumers' goods, thus offsetting inflationary pressure. In this way, any harmful effects of expanding the educational program may be offset. However, it should be noted that in this event there is absolutely no significance in first attaching foreign assistance to educational programs. The ultimate result is exactly the same if the external assistance is provided against the economic and social development program as a whole, and in that event there is less likelihood of misallocation of the actual foreign exchange provided. Ministries of education seldom have particular expertise in over-all economic and social development programming, and accordingly it is preferable that foreign exchange which will not, in fact, be utilized for educational purposes should not be allocated to ministries of education.

Capital Assistance for Education

Technical assistance requests should be geared to the output of the educational system and should be adjusted to changes in that output. Just as no country need aim at complete self-sufficiency in goods, no country need aim at complete self-sufficiency in skills. At the same time, a healthy economy must be capable of meeting the bulk of its own needs. By the same token, one of the major policy issues in the field of technical assistance is the division of scarce resources between supplementing the outflow of the "education industry" and adding to its "stock of capital."

THE EDUCATION INDUSTRY [24]

The economic policy decisions entailed in programming education, and the relation of technical assistance to it, can be illustrated by the application of some simple principles of production theory. The product of the education industry consists of trained and educated people. For planning purposes, this industry, like any other, must be judged in terms of the efficiency of its operation in furthering all the goals of development, including higher levels of education as a goal in its own right as well as the contribution made by education to the achievement of other objectives.

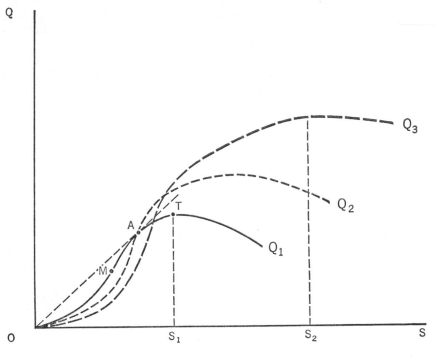

Figure 19-1

Figure 19-1 shows the familiar "total product curve" applied to the "education industry." Output is measured on the vertical axis. Output is measured in terms of numbers of students passing examinations of a given standard, weighted in accordance with the number of years of training, and perhaps by type of training and "grade." For primary school students,

[24] Educators should feel no compunction in treating the field of education as an "industry" for analytical purposes; the publishing industry, after all, produces bibles, poetry, and scientific books as well as comic books and pornography, and the entertainment industry produces Shakespearean plays as well as stripteases.

total student-years of training is probably a close enough approximation to true social product. For higher education one may wish to assign different weights to various types of product (engineers versus classical scholars) and to students of different quality (first-class honors versus bare pass) in accordance with studies of manpower requirements and the priorities established in the over-all development program.[25]

On the horizontal axis are measured inputs of the "variable factor of production"; that is, intake of beginning students. The "fixed factor of production" consists of classrooms with trained teachers in them. In practice it is the supply of properly trained teachers that is likely to be the major bottleneck in efforts to accelerate the expansion of the educational system in most developing countries.

The curve of total returns might be expected to assume a normal "growth curve" shape. Returns in terms of numbers of students passing examinations of given standards can be expected to increase at an increasing rate, as intake of pupils rises, up to a certain point (M, or the point of diminishing marginal returns, in the diagram). Beyond this point, returns will rise at a decreasing rate, become zero (at point T) and then fall. The point of maximum returns per pupil taken into the system is at point A, the point of diminishing average returns. Up to point A, the marginal returns to the fixed factor (classrooms with trained teachers in them) are actually negative. That is, the effort to use all the classrooms and teachers with so few students means that the pupils are forever on the move from one classroom and teacher to another with little time to sit down and learn something. If the supply of students were really so small, it would be more efficient to release some of the teachers and rooms to other uses. Few underdeveloped countries indeed are in this happy position.

Beyond T, the marginal returns to additional intake of students are negative. Classrooms become so crowded and the student-teacher ratio so high that the numbers passing examinations of fixed standards actually fall as more students are admitted. It is more than likely that most underdeveloped countries find themselves in this unfortunate situation.

Efficient operation of the education system requires that with the given stock of educational capital the number of students admitted should be somewhere between A and T. If the objective of national education policy is to produce "education," in the sense of numbers of students passing examinations of appropriate standards (and properly weighted by type and level of examination and quality of performance), as distinct from an objective of simply *having children in school*, there would never be any justification for taking in more students than St. If the actual supply of school-age children in the hypothetical country of Esperanza is S_2 there is no choice but to leave some children uneducated.

Obviously the fixed factor is much scarcer for universities than for secondary schools, and scarcer for secondary schools than for primary schools. That is, the amount of training needed to teach effectively in

[25] If educational standards are raised, the weights must be adjusted. Otherwise the numbers passing might indicate a drop in "educational output" when effective output was actually increasing.

universities is greater than for secondary schools and (probably) greater for secondary schools than for primary schools. (The actual teaching task may be more difficult at the elementary level, but in good secondary schools teachers are required to have some degree of specialization in subject matter—a masters degree in some educational systems—in addition to teacher training). At any one point of time, the curve Q_1 may apply to universities, Q_2 to secondary schools, and Q_3 to elementary schools. Assuming that the entire population of school-age children is divided equally among the three levels, so that the supply is S_2 in each category, Esperanza will be able to provide universal primary school education, can admit about half of the current supply of secondary school students, but only a small fraction of the supply of students of university age.

To reduce the number of diagrams we can also think of the curves Q_1, Q_2, and Q_3 as referring to the same level of education at different points of time. We begin with the stock of educational capital represented by Q_1. We can admit only S_1 students, at the maximum, but the supply is S_2. Thus $S_1 - S_2$ students must be left uneducated. However, either through adding to the stock of teachers by training them, or by obtaining teachers through technical assistance programs, we can shift to curve Q_2 and then to Q_3. The number of pupils that can be absorbed thus increases to S_2 and then to S_3. Meanwhile, of course, the supply of students will also increase as population grows. If we rely solely on the output of teacher-training institutes, it is even possible that the supply of school-age children will grow faster than the absorptive capacity of the educational system. If such is the case the argument for recruiting teachers through technical assistance programs (or sending students abroad) is very strong. The rate at which the supply of teachers can be expanded depends on the "stock of capital" in the "stage of production" earlier in the whole process—the capacity of teacher-training institutes. It also depends on the extent to which the output of the educational system can be turned back into the educational system. The educational system is one of the major consumers of its own product, and deciding whether to turn back a large proportion of the output into the system itself, permitting rapid accumulation of educational capital and a sharp increase in educational output at some later date, or whether to release a larger share of its output to the directly productive occupations, with a slower buildup of educational capacity, is one of the most difficult problems of programming education. Technical assistance, of course, can be used to supplement the supply of skills in the directly productive occupations while the output of the national education system is used to expand the educational system itself.

THE OPTIMAL INTAKE OF STUDENTS

It would always be inefficient to admit more students to the education system than St on the appropriate curve of total returns; but it does not follow that this number of students should always be admitted. The optimal intake must be between Sa and St, but where in this range is optimal depends on the relative costs of providing "capital" and of supplying raw materials (admitting students). For this kind of analysis the other cross section of the production function, shown in Figure 19–2, is more useful. Here we are measuring the stock of capital (Q) on the vertical axis and the intake of students (S_i) on the horizontal axis. Each curve shows combinations of capital and raw materials that will produce an identical output. As we move up the "hill" of output (the curves, or isoquants, are analogous to contour lines on a map) from O_1 to O_2 to O_3, we move to higher and higher levels of output. The straight lines represent transformation curves, or curves of opportunity cost, and reflect

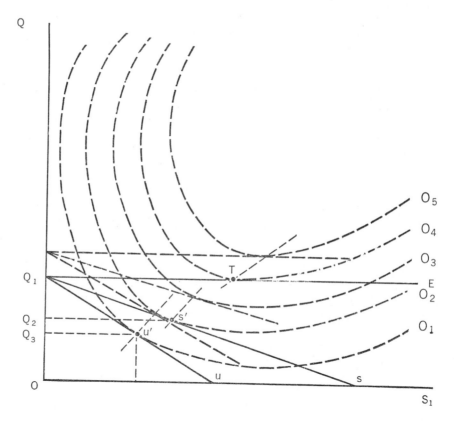

Figure 19–2

factor endowment. With a given budget (in terms of social value of product foregone) we could "buy," according to line Q_iu, OQ_1 capital or Ou students. That is, with a given sacrifice of gross national product, we could provide either OQ_1 units of capital (well-staffed classrooms) or Ou students, or any combination of teacher-classrooms and student intake along the line. The optimal combination is at point U'; here the educational output is maximized for a given "budget."

In Figure 19–2 the line Q_1E refers to elementary education, Q_1S to secondary education, and Q_1u to university education. If the school year is adjusted to the requirements of the planting and harvesting seasons, there need be no loss of income involved in having children in school rather than in the fields; and even in developing countries children of primary school age are not usually (and should not be) in the factories. Thus, for primary school the intake of students is pushed to point T, the point of diminishing total returns, exactly identical to the point T in the earlier diagrams. That is, the existing stock of educational capital at the primary school level should be used to capacity. In secondary schools, however, some students are in an age group that puts them definitely into the labor force, and some income is foregone by having them in school rather than serving as full-time workers in factories or fields. Thus, in the secondary schools the optimal intake is at point S' where some of the existing educational capacity is not used. If, as a result of past mistakes in planning, Q capital exists and cannot be used for anything but education, some excess capacity must be accepted. Of course, if the educational capacity can be shifted quickly and costlessly to other uses, the excess capacity would be eliminated by reducing the stock of educational capital to Q_2. In universities the income foregone by having students in school is clearly higher; the optimal combination is at point U'.

It should be noted that the "budget" used here for analytical purposes is different from the purely financial budget of the minister of education. Even if the outlays of the ministry of education measure exactly the alternative income foregone by devoting resources to production of classrooms, teachers, textbooks, etc. (which is in itself rather unlikely), the financial budget seldom if ever includes estimates of, let alone payments in compensation for, income foregone by having children in school rather than in the labor force. But if such costs are present they must be considered in educational planning.

As we move through time, the supply of students increases, and the stock of educational capital grows as teacher-training institutes turn out graduates. Once the commitment is made to train a certain number of teachers, the "opportunity cost" budget rises less than the financial budget. That is, while trained teachers are always useful elsewhere in the economy, once trained they are presumably more productive in the classroom than elsewhere. If they are not, a mistake has been made in the programming of teacher training, and the stock of education capital has been expanded too fast and investment in other developmental sectors has been correspondingly squeezed. From what we know of the returns to investment in education, however, it is highly unlikely that investment in education would yield lower returns than investment in other sectors if the expansion path in Figure 19–2 were a straight line; that is, unless the stock of teachers was expanded at least as fast as the supply of students. In most countries an expansion path that becomes convex downward at some point would clearly be justified; that is, once the whole supply of qualified students has been absorbed at present student-teacher ratios, some reduction in student-teacher ratios, or upgrading of teacher training, or both, would be justified. In virtually no case would an expansion path that is concave downward, representing rising student-teacher ratios or declining standards of teacher training or both, be called for. (For lack of clear evidence regarding economies or diseconomies of scale in the "education industry" we are assuming that the isoquants are parallel to each other, so that the expansion path depends on changes in the "factor endowment" alone.)

The argument concerning technical assistance is, of course, the same no matter which cross section of the production function is considered. Technical assistance to the education industry raises the stock of educational capital more than opportunity costs (the foreign experts could, of course, be used elsewhere in the economy too, so that even if there are no financial costs to the host country, opportunity costs would still be above zero). The opportunity cost curves therefore shift slightly downward and flatten out, increasing the optimal intake of students. Alternatively, technical assistance can be used to meet requirements for skills elsewhere in the economy, permitting a larger proportion of the output of the domestic education industry to be turned back into the education industry itself. Again, capital assistance is of little direct use (unless used to hire foreign personnel, in which case it is really a form of technical assistance). The same arguments hold here as those made in discussing the other cross section: capital assistance may act as a "carrot" to induce governments to expand local currency budgets for education, while foreign exchange is used for other stabilization and development purposes.

The Expansion Path

Any society may choose within limits between more education and more of other components of national income. Investment in education can always be extended beyond the point where it will add still further to productivity, measured in terms of other goods and services. But education is also valued as a consumers' good in its own right; an optimal education program will accordingly involve more investment in education than would maximize output of other goods and services. The planning problem is to determine the optimal time-path of investment in education, taking into account both its "capital good" and its "consumers' good" aspects.

In Figure 19–3 investment in education in the current year is measured on the horizontal axis and related gross national product (including education as a consumers' good) on the vertical axis. The impact of education (particularly formal education) on productivity in the same year is limited. A point is soon reached where diverting more resources to the education industry will reduce output of other goods and services in the current year. Eventually the decline in value of output of other goods and services will exceed the increase in value of educational output as a consumers' good. The curve of GNP then falls as investment in education is increased.

However, the full impact of education on productivity is felt only after a lag. An increase in investment in education this year (and in subsequent years) will raise productivity more in four years than in one, and will raise it more in eight years than in four. Thus, the point of diminishing total returns to current investment in education will be reached at higher

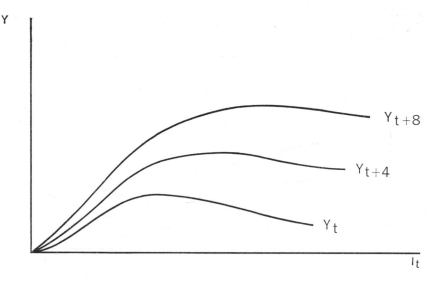

Figure 19–3

and higher figures as we look further and further into the future. A point of diminishing total returns will always be reached, no matter how far we look into the future. Other kinds of capital accumulation besides education also operate with a time lag; as more investment in education takes place, investment in other forms of capital with long gestation periods or high durability must fall. Moreover, increased investment in education this year frequently carries with it a commitment to expanded outlays on education in subsequent years, if the benefits are not to be lost. If the higher investment takes the form of buildings, equipment, textbooks, and the like, a once-over increase may be effective for some years to come; but if it takes the form of an increase in the number of teachers or in the intake of students, the higher outlays must continue for some years to have their full effect.

In Figure 19–4 the community indifference curves for education as a consumers' good and other items in national income are shown. The "other GNP" should be regarded as an appropriately discounted stream of income, up to the "horizon year" of the perspective plan. "Education" is an appropriately weighted and discounted stream of pupil-years. Since it is possible for people to be subjected to too much education, even from the standpoint of welfare or satisfaction, the indifference curves would turn away from the base axis at some point. It is presumably not possible to get too much of "everything else," and the indifference curves would move asymptotically to the vertical axis.

The transformation curves of "other income" into "education" are shown as solid lines. Over some range, education and other income rise together. This portion of the curves can be ignored; it would be senseless to stop expansion of the education industry before reaching the point

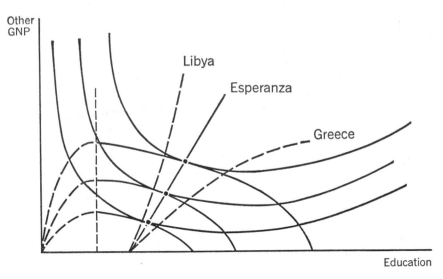

Figure 19–4

where output of "everything else" declines as a result. As the available budget for developmental investment increases, the society may have more of both education and other income in proportions indicated by the transformation (opportunity cost) curves.

In most developing countries the income elasticity of demand for education is presumably above unity; in any case, countries do in fact tend to spend a larger share of income on education as income rises. On the other hand the opportunity costs of education, in terms of other income, probably rise once a certain level of education has been reached. (More empirical research could usefully be done on this question.) The expansion path will be the outcome of these two opposing tendencies. For any particular country as we move from now into the future, moving through time as we proceed along the path, the shape of the expansion path will also depend on the initial position regarding level of per capita income and education. In resource-rich and education-poor countries like Libya the expansion path may be concave upward; it may simply be impossible to expand the education industry as fast as income rises—at least without more technical assistance than is politically acceptable. In education-rich but resource-poor countries like Greece it may be concave downward, while in a "normal" developing country like the mythical Esperanza (and probably only mythical developing countries are normal) the path may approximate a straight line.

20 | Planning Social Development —II. Other Aspects

We dealt at length in Chapter 19 with the planning and programming of education because of the obvious link between education and development, the tremendous volume of recent literature on the subject, and the importance attached to education by governments of developing countries. By the same token we shall deal much more briefly with the other categories of "social development." In no other field of social development —public health, housing, social security, land reform—is there any persuasive evidence that generally increased investment will bring clear-cut gains in per capita income. The literature dealing with the relationships of such investment to development is relatively scant. The "economics of public health" is in its infancy whereas the "economics of education" is already in its adolescence. The bulk of the literature on the economics of housing and social security is still directed toward problems of stabilization in advanced countries rather than development of underdeveloped ones. The subject of land reform can arouse political and emotional reactions, but its importance for economic development is not clearly established. For all these reasons there is not the same thorough commitment on the part of governments to expanded programs in these fields.

Programming Science and Technology in Relation to Economic Development

The latest arrival on the social development planning scene is the "science and technology sector." Both UNESCO and OECD are heavily engaged in efforts to define an appropriate methodology for programming scientific and technical research so as to meet the requirements of economic development. At first blush, the idea of "programming" scientific advance seems strange; we are accustomed to think of "scientific discovery" as something that occurs in an unplanned and unpredictable fashion to the genius in his laboratory. A little reflection, however, makes it clear that the areas in which scientific advances are made today tend to be those in which significant research expenditures are made. Few resources are more scarce than highly trained scientific and technical personnel, and research apparatus and equipment are also scarce. Why should they not be allocated in accordance with the over-all objectives of a development plan, together with the educational resources to which they are so closely related? As pointed out in a recent OECD publication, "Among the Member Governments of OECD the concept of a Science Policy has made its appearance, replacing an older idea that science is a purely cultural activity which should be supported but which should not be expected to yield much in the way of definable returns." [5]

To promote the systematic programming of scientific and technical reland, Italy, Spain, and Turkey. As described by OECD, the method now in use consists in first making a complete inventory of scientific and technical resources; undertaking an economic analysis to determine priorities for research; formulating programs for allocating scientific and technical research resources in each of the high-priority fields; and the construction of a detailed program for the deployment of all scientific and technical resources, appropriately subdivided among the three major fields of basic research, applied research, and development. Attention is also paid to the establishment of institutions to carry on the work of programming science and technology in relation to economic development.

Social Security

Social security programs, including old age pensions, unemployment insurance, health insurance, etc., have received less thorough analytical treatment than any other aspect of development. Many underdeveloped countries are introducing such facets of the "welfare state." Some observers question whether they can afford it, pointing out that social security programs were introduced in advanced countries only after a high level of productivity had already been reached. Others, recalling the debates of the 1930's in advanced countries, point out that such programs involve mere transfer payments and do not absorb resources, and so impose no additional strain on the economy. It is doubtful, however, whether this argument can be sustained where developing countries are concerned. It is still true, of course, that old age pensions involve a mere redistribution of income from young to old, health insurance from well to sick, unemployment insurance from employed to unemployed. In the poorer developing countries, however, even the office space and educated personnel needed

---

[5] "Relating Science and Technology to Economic Development," *OECD Observer*, April, 1965, p. 8. See also OECD, *Science, Economic Growth, and Government Policy*, Paris 1963.

to administer such programs may make a serious drain on scarce resources. One might also question the need for such programs in societies where the village organization, together with the extended family system, already provides a rather complete and sophisticated social security system. The incentive effects are hard to appraise. Such programs may generate enthusiasm for other parts of a government's program; they may dilute incentives to work harder and better, or save more voluntarily, to meet the contingencies of unemployment, ill health, and old age. Until a good deal of careful empirical research has been done we are not in a position to say.

The Role of Community Development

Community development is a "grab-bag" term to denote integration of development efforts at the community level, especially in education, health, transport and communications, and agriculture, plus efforts to give villagers a sense of participation in development programs—what the French call "*animation social.*" A more or less official United Nations definition is as follows: [6]

The term community development has come into international usage to denote the processes by which the efforts of the people themselves are united with those of government authorities, to improve the economic, social and cultural conditions of communities, to integrate these communities into the life of the nations, and to enable them to contribute fully to national progress. This complex of processes is then made up of two essential elements: the participation by the people themselves in efforts to improve their level of living with as much reliance as possible on their own initiative; and the provision of technical and other services in ways which encourage initiative, self-help and mutual help and make these more effective.

It is apparent that there is a close relationship between community development, as an approach to economic development, and the "up by the bootstraps" approach. The governments of several underdeveloped countries, discouraged by the magnitudes of the capital requirements suggested by applying ICORs to traditional programs, have seized on community development as a less costly, and perhaps more socially "moral" path. It is of some importance, therefore, to consider the potentialities and limitations of community development as an instrument for promoting sustained economic growth.

If the theory outlined in Chapter 16 is correct, any policy designed simply to keep people on the land is anti-developmental. Any such policy must fall instead into one of two categories: (a) it may be a policy designed to establish the preconditions for take-off, or (b) it may come under the heading of rural social work.

[6] Twentieth Report of the Administrative Committee on Coordination to the Economic and Social Council, E/2931, Annex III, paragraphs 1, 2; commended in Economic and Social Council resolution 663 D (XXIV). Quoted in United Nations, *International Survey of Programmes of Social Development* (New York, 1959), p. 156.

Establishing Preconditions

It is possible that in some underdeveloped countries resources are so limited that it is impossible to plan realistically for a take-off in the near future. In that event, there may be a case for concentrating on raising agricultural productivity in the short run, so as to produce the surpluses that can be recaptured to finance the next phase of economic growth. If this route to a take-off is the only one open to a particular country, no argument can be made against it. However, it is a route that can easily lead instead to further stagnation. For raising agricultural productivity as part of a program for establishing preconditions for a take-off means preventing the increase in agricultural output from improving rural living standards; otherwise, it may merely freeze the existing structure. With further population growth, no permanent gains may be attained even in rural welfare. Yet recapturing initial gains in agriculture to finance further development is politically very difficult.

The "up by the bootstraps" approach has succeeded in the past only where severe sacrifices have been forced on the masses of the people, to provide a basis for capital accumulation. The "up by the bootstraps" approach proposed for underdeveloped areas today may not require reductions in the standard of living to start the development process, but it does mean that the initial increases in output must be denied to the people, in order to provide an export surplus to finance further expansion. An integral part of the scheme is increased taxation for farmers, first to compel them to produce as much as before although they have fewer mouths to feed, and secondly to drain off the increase in output and income as the development projects have their effect. This increase in taxation, and consequent prevention of initial improvements in living standards is necessary, not only to provide an export surplus, but also to prevent the increased productivity from being converted into increased leisure or a more rapid rate of population growth rather than into increased output. Given the tax structures and general political situations of most underdeveloped countries, it is highly questionable whether small increases in *per capita* income, obtainable through improvements in techniques with the present structure of the economy, can be recaptured in their entirety.

Rural Social Work

If it is felt that development is impossible, there may be a case on purely humanitarian grounds for doing everything possible to alleviate the misery of people living in the peasant agriculture and handicrafts sector. A good deal of what has actually been done by community development programs would seem to fall into this category. Moreover, a good deal of the urban community development now being recommended to supplement rural community development would also have to be characterized as urban social work rather than economic development. There is of course nothing wrong with endeavoring to improve levels of social welfare; but we should be perfectly clear when we are engaging in social welfare programs and when we are assisting countries with their economic development.

Costs and Benefits of Community Development

Can the social work aspects of community development be carried out without absorbing scarce resources? The basic idea of community development is to use resources that would otherwise remain idle. If, in fact, no scarce resources are used, community development programs may not retard development, even if they are exclusively of the social work variety. There is of course some danger that raising levels of social welfare will accelerate population growth once more; nothing in our demographic knowledge suggests that it would not, unless a deliberate effort is made to introduce family planning along with improved public health. If population growth is accelerated, community development may make a later take-off all the more difficult. In that case, community development would be directly opposed to economic development.

Unfortunately, however, community development does absorb some scarce resources. In so far as community development programs remain part of the technical assistance provided by Western countries, they absorb budget funds, reducing the amounts available for other foreign aid projects. They utilize technical *expertise* from the Western countries which is scarce even in these countries. The same is true of administrative personnel in aid-giving countries. Community development also uses at least some budget funds and capital goods of underdeveloped countries, no matter how simple the community development projects may be. Most serious, they absorb the extremely scarce administrative and technical capacities of personnel in the underdeveloped country.

There is thus a real danger that expansion of community development programs may actually retard community development. The extent to which they do so will depend on the extent to which community development takes the social work form, improving levels of rural welfare and making it more attractive for people to stay where they are.

Could community development programs be designed to *accelerate* the removal of people from agriculture? It would be useful to review community development projects in these terms. Which of them could properly be considered projects designed to get people off the land? The improvement of transport facilities, which permit a higher degree of specialization and increased contrast between rural and urban centers, might accelerate the flow of people from the rural to the industrial sector. General education may provide the basis for acquisition of industrial skills. Community development programs might give more weight to the kind of training which will either produce industrial skills directly or permit their more rapid acquisition on the job. Health programs may improve the industrial work capacity of people now living in rural areas. The same is true of increases in agricultural productivity which permit rising levels of nutrition combined with reduction of the numbers of people on the land.

Thus the theory in Chapter 16 does not constitute an argument against community development as such, but only against community development projects of a kind designed to make life more attractive in the villages, as opposed to projects designed to facilitate a flow of people from the rural to the industrial sector. Economic development requires *both* agricultural improvement and more rapid industrialization. In a word, it means vastly increased levels of investment, which in turn means increased foreign aid.

Land Reform

Few aspects of economic and social development have aroused more violent emotions than the question of land reform. As Dr. Edmundo Flores, Professor of Agricultural Economics at the National University of Mexico, puts it: "Land reform is a revolutionary measure which passes power, prosperity, and status from one group of the community to another. To have an adequate understanding of land reform, its political, sociological, and economic aspects must be studied." [7] Land reform is a particularly vital issue in Latin America, and fundamental changes in patterns of land tenure have been included among the objectives of The Alliance for Progress in the Charter of Punta del Este. Usually the term "land reform" conveys the concept of breaking up large estates and dividing them among small farmers—"the soil to the tiller." Agricultural economists are quick to point out that in many developing countries, splinter holdings and scattered fragmented holdings are at least as great a problem as concentration of land ownership in few hands; they would encompass action to reassemble *minifundia* into farms of efficient size, as well as subdivision of *latifundia*, in the concept of land reform. Some go further still and include such measures as agricultural credit, agricultural extension programs, and the like. Sometimes the term "agrarian reform" is used to cover this broader concept of land tenure policy. Dr. Flores, however, is very insistent that programs for raising agricultural productivity with existing patterns of land ownership should not be confused with true land reform. "Land reform should not be confused with the introduction of efficiency in farming by means of hybrid seeds, extension services, or the like. These measures, necessary as they are, do not basically alter income distribution or the social and economic structure. Efforts to increase efficiency must be applied *after* land reform takes place, not instead of it." [8]

The controversy regarding land reform refers partly to its general importance in the whole process of development and partly to the relationship between size of farm and efficiency of agricultural production. Those who attach great importance to land reform usually stress the broader social and political considerations more than the direct impact on agricultural productivity as such. Professor Bert F. Hoselitz belongs to this group. "We need not detain ourselves long" said Professor Hoselitz, "over a consideration for the reasons for stagnation in some Latin American countries. The economies of these countries continued to function along traditional lines; the social structure and system of landholding having remained vir-

[7] Edmundo Flores, "The Economics of Land Reform," Paper for the Eighth Regional FAO Conference, Viña del Mar, March, 1965.
[8] *Ibid.*

tually unchanged from the colonial and post-colonial period, industrialization and trade having gained only a limited foothold, and the middle classes having remained weak and without influence." [9]

There can be no quarrel about the facts of concentration of land ownership in Latin America. T. F. Carrol states that approximately 3 to 6 per cent of the farm units in Latin America cover from 60 to 70 per cent of the total cultivated land area. On the other hand, 70 per cent of the farmers own only 10 per cent of the land.[10] The data in Table 20-1 are from his study.

TABLE 20–1
Estimated Percentage Distribution of Land Holdings
in Latin America, around 1950

Size of Farm (hectares)	Per Cent of Farms	Per Cent of Land Area
0–20	72.6	3.7
20–100	18.0	8.4
100–1,000	7.90	23.0
Over 1,000	1.5	64.9
Total	100.0	100.0

Professor Lambert and Dr. Borges stress the social rather than the economic aspects of the land tenure system in Latin America. "It is not easy," Professor Lambert points out, "to assess the economic value of large estates in Latin America, for some of them have an extremely low output, while others are highly productive. However, when an attempt is made, under an economic development policy, to divide up a large estate, it often proves necessary to restore some of its features in other farms." From a social point of view, however, Professor Lambert is in no doubt about the destructive influence of the *latifundia*: [11]

They are a sort of screen which keeps one part of the country untouched by the social changes taking place in the other; it tends to split the country into small egocentric societies which paralyse initiative, are often wasteful of manpower, and engender a state of underemployment, and over against a progressive society, perpetuate retarded communities, whose privilege is to reject all change in return for continued poverty.

Borges bluntly terms the regime of *latifundia* "abominable;" it maintains a high concentration of rural property in few hands, and condemns the vast majority of farmers to work inferior lands offering *per capita* returns

[9] Bert F. Hoselitz, "Economic Growth in Latin America," paper to the First International Conference of Economic History, Stockholm, 1960, p. 94.

[10] T. F. Carrol, "The Land Reform Issue in Latin America," in Albert O. Hirschman, *Latin American Issues* (New York, 1961), p. 165.

[11] Jacques Lambert, "Requirements for Rapid Economic and Social Development," in Egbert de Vries (ed.), *Social Aspects of Economic Development in Latin America* (Paris: UNESCO, 1963), Vol. I.

that are "ridiculous." [12] This system, he says, provides no opportunity for those who work the land, and no stimuli for investment, leads to a type of economy essentially precapitalistic, hampers the growth of activity, and is incompatible with large-scale industrialization. Kahl, on the other hand, is concerned with the obverse of this kind of land tenure problem: the "splinter holdings" which are all that are available to so many Latin American families.[13] In the district of Minas Gerais, which, he says, provides an excellent picture of rural Brazil, the illiterate farmers

. . . work as paid labourers for large landowners, as sharecroppers, or as sub-sistence farmers on their own tiny plots of land and often the same man holds two or three of these positions simultaneously. The standard work tool is the hoe and not the plough; the methods of cultivation have not changed much in two hundred years . . .

Each tenant family, he points out, is an independent unit, and even if the land is owned in large tracts by an extensive family or by men who them-selves live and work in towns, it is divided into small sections, and each one is farmed quite independently of the other. Thus some Latin American countries seem to have combined the social evils of *latifundia* with the economic inefficiency of *minifundia*.[14]

It does not follow, however, that splitting up large estates is the appro-priate land policy in every Latin American country, let alone a panacea for economic development—as experience with the Mexican *ejidos* clearly shows. In the first place, it is important to distinguish the political and social aims of land reform from the purely economic objectives. With re-spect to the former, two things may be said. First, in at least some Latin American countries, such as Mexico and Brazil, industrialization has in itself loosened the hold of large landowners on social status and political power—and where the old landowner class merges with the new industrial one, as in Chile, it is doubtful whether dividing up the land would alter the socio-political situation very much. Second, a government willing and able to carry through a program of redistribution of land can redistribute wealth and power in other ways—an effective progressive income tax, or a progressive land or capital tax, combined with vigorous industrialization and social development programs, for example.

Solving the social and political problems in other ways would leave each government free to determine the optimal size of farm for each type of agricultural enterprise in the country, and then seek to establish tenure in parcels of optimum size, so as to maximize man-year productivity in vari-ous fields of agriculture. In some cases this policy might call for breaking up large estates; in others, such as Greece, where fragmentation has gone to extremes, it would mean reassembly of holdings or increasing the aver-

---

[12] Unpublished paper presented to the United Nations Conference on Social Aspects of Economic Development in Latin America, Mexico City, 1960.
[13] Essays prepared for the United Nations Conference on Social Aspects of Economic Development, Mexico City, December, 1960.
[14] *Ibid.*

age size of farms or both. Reassembly (*remembrement*) can be done by swapping pieces of land among owners into contiguous plots; increasing the average size frequently requires reducing the number of farms.

Those who have reservations about land reform as a panacea are usually thinking in terms such as these, and would stress a broad attack on the problems of the agricultural lag, of which changes in land tenure would be a part, but only a part. Professor Raul Branco, for example, thinking of his own country of Brazil and other Latin American countries, points out that plantations are usually a highly efficient form of agricultural organization, heavily capitalized, and responsible for the bulk of agricultural exports. Breaking them up into smaller units might result in a decrease in production.[15] He points out that in Mexico the immediate result of land reform was a decline in the production of staples, and that it took more than two decades for the total output of corn, wheat, beans, and rice to regain its 1920 level. The appropriation of large estates by peasants in Bolivia in 1952 reduced production by one-third.

Dr. Flores, on the other hand, is very skeptical of the concept of "optimum size of farm," feeling that the concept may be used to justify traditional patterns of land holding and thus delay economic and social progress. So many factors influence the optimal size of unit, he says, that the actual optimum will "oscillate widely and continuously." [16] No doubt; but the difficulties in establishing the precise optimum for a particular crop in a given country at a particular time does not mean that there is no such optimum. Dr. Flores, in his policy recommendations, does provide for a *politically* determined minimal unit to be left to present landowners; but he maintains that successful land reform requires expropriation of all land above this minimum without immediate compensation (otherwise no redistribution of wealth is involved), it must proceed rapidly and massively, and it must be accompanied by vigorous development policies both within the agricultural sector and elsewhere.

Dr. Flores distinguishes among three types of land reform: those in already industrialized countries, such as Japan; those in countries with ready access to foreign exchange, through grants or strong exports, like Taiwan and Venezuela; and those in countries with severe shortages of capital, like Mexico. In Japan the land reform beginning in 1947 increased the share of owner-operated land from 54 per cent of the cultivable total to 92 per cent. It transferred technology and capital from the industrial to the agricultural sector, raised agricultural productivity, and expanded the market for industrial products. In Taiwan the landlords were compensated, partly by shares in government enterprises and partly in commodity bonus. The peasants, in turn, bought the land on easy terms. American aid made this type of reform possible. In Venezuela too the land was paid for at market prices, in cash up to about $6,000 and in bonds above that. When the reform began in 1958 some 2 per cent of the landowners owned 80 per cent of the land. The plan was to grant land to 350,000 families over a ten-year

[15] Raul Branco, "Land Reform: The Answer to Latin American Agricultural Development?", for publication in *The World Economic Review*.
[16] Edmundo Flores, *op. cit.*, p. 4.

period, but because of the high cost of the compensation paid, only 63,000 families had been resettled by 1964. Dr. Flores obviously considers the land reform in Mexico a success, even if it reduced agricultural output for the time being. Together with the expropriation of oil fields and nationalization of public utilities, he believes, land reform set the stage for the subsequent rapid growth.

In broad outline, it is clear that the approach to land reform as part of the over-all development program must be the same as for any other sector of it. A "shadow price" must be attached to the social, political, and indirect economic benefits accruing from the land reform measures. To this sum must be added (or subtracted) the net impact on agricultural output itself over the perspective planning period. The net benefits must then be compared with the costs of the program, including the opportunity costs entailed in allocating scarce administrative, scientific, and technical skills to the program. The program should then be expanded until the cost-benefit ratio falls below that of other programs or projects using the same scarce resources.

HOUSING

The Charter of Punta del Este includes, as the ninth objective of the Alliance for Progress, augmented construction of low-cost housing for the lower income groups and reduction of the housing shortage in Latin America. Housing is generally substandard in Asia and Africa as well. There can be no doubt that improved housing is an important component of rising living standards. There are also good reasons for singling out housing for special attention not accorded to other components of the normal budget of low income families: the large proportion of income devoted to this single item; the relative lack of technological progress and consequent continued high cost in the field of housing as compared to other major items of consumption; the importance of housing standards, in terms of health and aesthetics, for the whole community, irrespective of income group; the role of the construction industry as an employer, and the opportunities it offers for converting a notoriously unstable sector of the economy into one which can be used to offset fluctuations in income and employment generated elsewhere in the economy.

On the other hand, while it is reasonable to expect some association between housing conditions and health, the direct relationship between housing standards and productivity must be regarded as essentially unproven. It would not be surprising if such a relationship exists; but meanwhile, the case for a vigorous housing policy is strong enough without making unsupported proclamations that better housing will also accelerate the expansion of output of other goods and services. The relationship of housing to urbanization and city planning is discussed in the next chapter.

Public Health

We have left public health to the end because of all the major components of "social development" health programs alone are a double-edged sword. There may be some doubt about the contribution of housing and social security programs to increased productivity, but few would argue that such programs in themselves (as distinct from what they cost in scarce resources) might *retard* economic development. Because of the link between health programs and death rates, however, a good many people have wondered whether indiscriminate expansion of public health activities may not do more harm than good.

If either the level or rate of growth of population is above optimum, the effect of investment in public health on the rate of economic growth is ambivalent. For under these circumstances, a decline in death rates, in and of itself, will lower the rate of increase in per capita income—unless we attach high shadow prices to people as such, as part of national income. As noted in Chapter 2, experience since World War II has shown that with vigorous public health campaigns death rates in almost any country can be reduced to levels comparable to those of advanced countries. If birth rates do not quickly follow, very high rates of population growth can result. It may then prove extremely difficult to produce rates of technological progress and capital formation that will permit significant rates of increase in per capita income. Moreover, public health programs tend to be particularly effective in reducing infant mortality rates and extending life expectancy, thus raising the proportion of unproductive to productive population.

One must, however, distinguish between two kinds of improvement in health. The elimination of debilitating diseases which do not kill (or which kill slowly), such as malaria and dysentery, may raise productivity much more than population, thus increasing per capita income. The elimination of diseases from which one either recovers or dies quickly—such as yellow fever or bubonic plague—will raise population without much increase in productivity. In most cases investment in public health will bring both kinds of improvement, so that even where levels of rates or growth of population are above optimum the effects of health programs on economic development are uncertain.

One must also ask whether, for example, productivity per man-year is really higher without malaria than with it. Where labor is redundant, the effect of eliminating malaria from a village may be only to increase the degree of underemployment and work-spreading. What is certainly true, however, is that elimination of debilitating diseases results in more efficient use of caloric intake, permitting an increase in the number of hours worked per week on a given diet, and facilitating the production of an agricultural surplus.

There are also sharp differences in the costs of dealing with various types of health problem. Yaws can be cured with a single injection. Intestinal parasites are cheap to control. Malaria is easily controlled up to a point, after which costs rise steeply. In general, costs of improving public health seem to be fairly constant up to some point and then rise sharply. Facts such as these suggest that the field of public health is one in which cost-benefit analysis could yield very useful results.

As in the other sectors of "social development" the benefits must include the value of "health" as a consumers' good, at an appropriate shadow price. Here the task is, if anything, even more difficult than it is in the field of education. Should one attach a higher shadow price to saving children from leukemia than to saving middle-aged men from lung cancer? The medical profession in general dislikes facing questions such as these, feeling that nothing less than complete "health" is an acceptable goal. There is, in fact, a common approach to programming public health which is analogous to a "the children are there, they have to be educated" approach in the field of education: "if people are sick, they have to be cured; and if they are well, they have to be protected from illness." But clearly this approach will not do; in health as in education, the budget and the development program must have a cut-off point, and a cut-off point implies a cost-benefit comparison of some kind.

The public health profession, and particularly the World Health Organization, has become hypersensitive to allegations that they may be "doing more harm than good," and has responded with a defense of their position. They have also, however, taken a harder look at their own planning and programming and have moved a long way in the direction of establishing priorities in their field. The paper presented by WHO to the Expert Group on Social Development Planning (Bangkok, 1963) and prepared by Sir John A. Charles, K.C.B., M.D., F.R.C.P., D.P.H., is a good example of recent WHO thinking on the subject. In one respect, Dr. Charles says, "the economist is a little open to criticism." True, some attention has been given recently to "the economic value of a man." The benefit of saving young people until they can enter the labor force and repay the investment in them during their early years, and the losses entailed in preventable disability and absence from work, is recognized. "But even now there are economists," he continues, "who, without any suggestion of inhumanity, complain that the successful achievements of the health services make the task of the planner more difficult. They have in mind the resultant population increase, and the consequential questions of finding employment and food which can arise." [17]

Yet the methods by which the economist and the health planner approach their problems are essentially the same, Dr. Charles maintains. Both begin with an inventory of facts pertinent to the present situation, and then proceed to analyze these facts, and through a process of "successive approximations," come up with a plan for dealing with the high-priority problems. Plans should be flexible enough to permit readjustment in the light of experience gained in implementation. The health planner is "more pragmatic and rather less academic" than the economist, Sir John adds, because he must not only undertake step-by-step planning but also deal with emergencies when they arise. (Here, however, he introduces a distinction without a difference; the economist too must deal with "emergencies"— balance of payments crises, accelerating inflation, crop failures—that arise in the course of implementing a plan.)

To show that public health officers are becoming concerned with plans

[17] WHO, "National Health Planning with Some Observations on the Relation to Economic Development" (SDP/Working Paper No. 3), March, 1963, pp. 6–7.

and programs, Sir John quotes the conclusions of the Report of the Expert Committee on Public Health Administration—Planning Public Health Services: [18]

(a) that emphasis be placed on prevention (though this should not prevent the concurrent introduction or development of both curative and preventive health services);

(b) that provision be made for services to people engaged in productive work—and that there may even be a differentiation between the claims of various types of productive labor—e.g. heavy as contrasted with light industry;

(c) that provision be made for services to vulnerable groups (e.g. mothers and children);

(d) that the services provided affect the health of the maximum number of the people; and

(e) that provision be made for improvement of the nutritional standard of the population.

The *Second World Health Situation Report* [19] presented results of a questionnaire on unresolved health problems. The replies indicated three main groups of countries:

1. Those with virtually no residual problems.

2. Those with a relatively small number of problems, which however differed materially between the developed and developing countries.

3. Those with a large number of problems, a list of ten or twelve such problems frequently being given.

The first group consisted entirely of developed countries. According to Dr. Charles, "certain of the residual problems quoted seemed almost trivial, though no doubt locally they were both troublesome and potentially dangerous as, for example, hydatidosis in dogs." The third group included among its members many of the developing countries. Their health problems "might seem complex and almost overwhelming." The second group included both developed and emerging countries, many of the latter having partially organized health services with useful statistics.

A typical advanced country would list its health problems, in descending order of importance, as cancer, the care of the aged, chronic and degenerative disease, mental illness, and accidents. For the majority of the emerging countries (mostly in the tropical zone), the outstanding problems were, in order of descending importance, malaria, tuberculosis, biharziasis, nutritional deficiencies, and environmental defects. Next came leprosy, yaws, and certain other endemic diseases, maternal and child health, "and—remarkable in its relative infrequency as a stated problem—shortage of personnel and material."

While this approach suggests the need for planning in the public health field, including the establishment of priorities, the implicit goal is still that of maximizing the level of *health* (however measured) rather than that of maximizing general *welfare*. It ignores the effect of health programs on the

[18] *WHO, Technical Reports,* Series No. 246.
[19] *Official Records of the World Health Organization, No. 22.*

rate of population growth except as the latter in turn affects health. It over-looks the impact of health programs on productivity, directly through the increase in numbers and indirectly through the change in age structure. An economic (that is, general welfare) approach to public health planning, on the other hand, would first try to measure direct returns, in terms of reduced number of man-days lost through illness and increase in life-expectancy (up to the point where life expectancy exceeds the working life, when direct returns become negative). It would then add a "consumers' good" component, as a shadow price for "health" as such. Probably one should have one shadow price for continued "health" of already healthy persons, and a whole set of shadow prices for cures of various diseases and disabilities. Finally, an attempt would be made to measure complementarities between health and other sectors of the development program. It is obvious, for example, that there is a complementarity between returns to investment in education and investment in public health. Once a man is trained it becomes more than ever important to keep him alive and well; the more the investment in education the higher the returns to investment in public health. The reverse is also true, since public health outlays increase life expectancy.

Curative versus Preventive Medicine [20]

One of the basic problems confronting the public health planners is determining the proper division of public health funds between curative and preventive medicine. Human beings are incurable procrastinators; they tend to attach higher value to being cured when sick than to being kept well. The pressures on the medical profession to engage in curative activities are strong. But it is generally recognized that preventive programs are cheaper. In per capita terms it is much easier to prevent diseases than it is to cure them. Here lies the dilemma which confronts the health planners. Should we "get the most for our money" by concentrating mainly on preventive work, at the risk of losing public support for the program? Or should resources be concentrated in curative efforts that are more likely to meet with widespread acceptance and appreciation?

A recent study lists five "current concepts of prevention:" [21]

Good health habits. It notes that this idea is as old as civilization, and refers to such things as sufficient sleep, exercise, proper diet, etc.
Environmental sanitation. Refers to controlling the environment through sewage disposal, water purification, pasteurization of milk, etc.
Communicable disease control. Vaccination against smallpox, diphtheria, etc. as well as T.B. x-rays are common examples of this conception. Here the cooperation of the public is essential since something must be done *to* individual people.
Health education and promotion. Recently it has been recognized that "the

[20] This section leans heavily on work done for the author by Murray Milner, Jr.
[21] Odin Anderson and George Rosen, *An Examination of the Concept of Preventive Medicine*, New York, Health Information Foundation, Research Series No. 12.

facts" are not enough to motivate people; their values and habits must be taken into account—and often changed—before the facts can have much impact.

Health services for the individual. This seems to be somewhat of a residual category, but refers mainly to the personal health service, e.g. regular health examinations required to recognize and prevent chronic diseases such as arthritis, cancer, and cardiovascular diseases.

Curative medicine refers to clinical treatment of sick individuals. Obviously the two types of effort are not mutually exclusive and at points blend into one another. Nonetheless there is a clear-cut distinction in focus and emphasis.

Are preventive programs cheap as is usually assumed? The available data do not allow a clear-cut answer, but there are some figures worth considering. Winslow notes that: [22]

In Great Britain it has been estimated that the cost of preventive services for the year 1949–50, after deducting fees etc. paid by the public, was £67,500,000. The all-inclusive National Health Service cost for the same period was £425,200,000, more than six times as much, giving an average cost of £8.6 per capita per year.

A survey of Ceylon, Chile, Czechoslovakia, Israel, Sweden, and the United States showed that none of these countries spent as much as 5 per cent of its *total current operating expenditures for health* on preventive efforts as such.[23] The highest figure 4.6 per cent, was for Chile. The lowest, 0.8 per cent, was for the United States. Winslow's figure of 5 per cent of the national income as the probable cost of curative and preventive efforts combined was confirmed by the UN study.

The report also indicates the relative amounts spent per capita for health services for each country. Ceylon is the lowest, $5.60 per year, while the United States is the highest, $133.70 per year. There is much less difference in the amounts spent on preventive efforts. Czechoslovakia is highest with $2.30 [24] annually while Ceylon spends $0.20 annually. The difference in expenditure on preventive work is even less if the Czechoslovakian figure is ignored, since the next highest figure is $1.00 per person for Israel and the United States. These and other relevant figures are presented in Table 20–2. In addition, the crude birth and death rates for each of the six countries have been supplied. It is interesting to note that Ceylon, with the lowest per capita outlays on health, has a lower crude death rate than any of

[22] C. E. A. Winslow, *The Cost of Sickness and the Price of Health*, WHO Monograph Series No. 7 (Geneva, 1951), p. 69.

[23] Brian Abel-Smith, *Paying for Health Services*, WHO Public Health Paper No. 17 (Geneva, 1963). All percentage figures quoted in this section are the percentage of the current operating expenditures, governmental and private, for the year studied.

[24] The high Czechoslovakian figure may be due to an artificial exchange rate. The conversions were based on the "official rate," while conversion ratios for other currencies were noted as "selling rate," "free rate," or "tourist rate."

Table 20-2

Comparison of Expenditures for Health Services, and Recent Birth and Death Rates in Six Countries

Country and Year on Which Data Were Based	Ceylon 1957/58		Chile 1959		Czechoslovakia 1958		Israel 1959/60		Sweden 1956		United States 1957/58	
Local Currency and Conversion Rate per U.S. $	Rs. 4.765 (selling rate)		Esc. 1.053 (free rate)		Ksc. 7.20 (official rate)		£ 2.16 (tourist rate)		K 5.175 (selling rate)			
	(millions)	%	(millions)	%	(millions)	%	(millions)	%	(millions)	%	(millions)	%
(1) I. Gross national expenditure	Rs. 5,725		Esc. 4,115		Ksc. ...		£14,176		K 49,106		$441,249	
(2) A. Expenditures on health* (2) as % of (1)	247	4.3	71†	‡	7,152	...	250	5.3	2,414	4.9	23,173	5.3
(3) 1. Capital development	12.1		...		546.4		25.0		205		825	
(4) 2. Current operating	234.6		71.7		6,605.4		225.3		2,209		22,358§	
(5) a. Personal health (curative)¶	221.4	94.4	64.5	90.0	6,027.6	91.5	212.7	94.4	2,123	96.2	21,604	96.6
(6) b. Public health (preventive)	9.6	4.1	4.6	6.4	224.7	3.4	4.2	1.9	30	1.3	172	0.8
(7) c. Teaching and research	3.6	1.5	2.6	3.6	353.1	4.9	8.4	3.7	56	2.5	582	2.6

(8) II. Expenditure *per head* (U.S. $)	$ 5.6	$ ‡	$ 75.7	$ 56.0	$ 63.7	$ 133.7
(9) A. Capital development	0.3	...	5.6	5.6	5.4	4.8
(10) B. Current operating	5.3	9.6	68.1	50.4	58.3	128.9
(11) 1. Personal health (curative)	5.0	8.6	62.3	47.6	56.1	124.5
(12) 2. Public health (preventive)	0.2	0.6	2.3	1.0	0.8	1.0
(13) 3. Teaching and research	0.1	0.4	3.3	1.8	1.4	3.4
(14) Crude birth rate	36.6	34.8	15.8	25.8	13.9	22.4
(15) Crude death rate	8.6	12.2	9.5	5.7	10.0	9.5

* All expenditures, government (all levels) and private, capital and operating.

† Includes only current operating expenses.

‡ Inapplicable.

§ In one place (Table No. 9) this figure is given as $22,348, but this is probably a misprint.

¶ These categories were defined in such a way as to be *roughly* equivalent to curative and preventive.

... Indicates data not available.

SOURCE: Tables 5, 9, and 12, Brian Abel-Smith, *Paying for Health Services*, WHO Public Health Paper No. 17 (Geneva, 1963), and UN Department of Economic and Social Affairs, *Provisional Report on World Population Prospects*, 1964. (The figures cited are the most recent given (all after 1960) in the latter report.)

the six countries except Israel. Death rates in Israel are lowest of all, although per capita outlays for health are second from the bottom. Age structure, of course, affects the crude death rate figures but nonetheless these figures raise questions about the efficiency of health planning.

21 | Urbanization and Regional Planning

In its Report on Social Development in Latin America, for the May, 1963, meeting of the Economic Commission for Latin America, the ECLA Secretariat stated:

The most striking aspect of the social structure of the majority of the Latin American countries is the rapidity of their urbanization process—a seemingly hopeful circumstance, in apparent contradiction with the agricultural bottle-neck. . . . Is it not precisely the big city, that is, figuratively speaking, the vehicle of modernity?

Urbanization is, of course, not confined to Latin America, nor to recent decades. On the contrary, urbanization and economic development have been closely related ever since the Industrial Revolution of the seventeenth and eighteenth centuries. As shown in Table 21-1, between 1800 and 1950, the share of the world population living in cities of 5,000 and more increased from 3 per cent to 29.8 per cent. The proportion of the population in cities over 20,000 in the same period rose from 2.4 to 20.9 per cent, and the percentage of the population in cities of 100,000 and more grew from 1.7 to 13.1.

If one accepts the 20,000 size as the definition of "urban," the urban population in 1850 was 2.3 times that of 1800, the 1900 urban population was 2.9 times that of 1850, and the 1950 urban population 3.4 times that of 1900. On the other hand, says the Economic Commission for Latin America, "the striking fact remains that growth in the world's rural population has changed little in the course of time despite marked acceleration in the

TABLE 21-1

World's Urban Population Compared with World's Total Population,
1800-1950

Year	World Population (millions)	5,000 and Over		20,000 and Over		100,000 and Over	
		Population (millions)	Percentage of World Population	Population (millions)	Percentage of World Population	Population (millions)	Percentage of World Population
1800	906	27.2	3.0	21.7	2.4	15.6	1.7
1850	1,171	74.9	6.4	50.4	4.3	27.5	2.3
1900	1,608	218.7	13.6	147.9	9.2	88.6	5.5
1950	2,400	716.7	29.8	502.2	20.9	313.7	13.1

SOURCE: UN Economic and Social Council, *Preliminary Study of the Demographic Situation in Latin America*, (E/CN.12/604), April 23, 1961, p. 31.

growth of the world's total population." [1]

In countries like Canada, The Netherlands, and Sweden, ECLA points out, the population in each of four size-groups of cities (5 to 20,000; 20,000 to 100,000; 100,000 to 500,000; and 500,000 or more) is much the same. In India and Turkey, on the other hand, there are more people in small towns than in the big cities. However, in Latin America, and particularly in Argentina, Brazil, and Chile, considerably more people live in the large cities than in the next size-class of cities. Moreover, the large towns are growing faster than the small ones. Thus the urban population structure in Latin America is "top-heavy" and tending to become more so.

Urbanization, Industrialization, and Economic Development

Is this pattern of urban growth to be welcomed, or is it to be deplored? One can find strongly voiced opinions on both sides of this question. We know, of course, that industrialization, economic development, and urbanization have gone together in the past. Is there really an inseparable link between each of these three trends, or could a more astute policy give us economic development without industrialization, or industrialization without urbanization—assuming that such a pattern of growth would somehow be preferable to what is now observed in developing countries?

Industrialization and Economic Development

As was pointed out in Chapter 1, the statistical relationship between rising per capita income and a declining proposition of the labor force in agriculture is very close indeed. Economic development in the past has consisted very largely of transferring population from low-productivity agriculture to much higher productivity industrial occupations, thus re-

[1] Economic Commission for Latin America, *Preliminary Study of the Demographic Situation in Latin America* (E/CN.12/604), April 23, 1961, p. 31.

ducing population pressure on the land and permitting agricultural improvement in the form of conversion to large-scale mechanized agriculture at the same time. Even regional differences in producticity and income within the same country are largely a reflection of differences in the occupational structure among regions, and particularly of differences in the share of the labor force engaged in agriculture. The well-known convergence of per capita income among major regions in the United States is a direct result of a convergence of occupational structure; there remains no truly agricultural region in the United States. By the same token, the failure to produce convergence of productivity and income among regions in countries such as Brazil, Mexico, and Italy reflects failure to produce convergence of occupational structures in the major regions. Economic development without industrialization in this sense is hard to imagine.

Industrialization without Urbanization?

Is there an equally close relationship between industrialization and urbaniaztion? Once again we face a problem of definition, this time complicated by differences in statistical practice among various countries. "Urban" is variously defined to include centers of more than 2,000, more than 5,000, or more than 20,000. From a socio-cultural point of view, perhaps even the *lowest* of these figures is too high. A Balinese village like Ubud, with its palace, its market, its temples, its art school, and its performances of dance, theater, and music, is in some ways very urbane indeed. Where possible and convenient, however, we shall use the term "urban" to mean centers with a population of more than 20,000.

It might be well to clear away one misunderstanding at the outset. A connection between industrialization and urbanization does not require that industries be established in cities. It could happen (although it is fairly rare) that the actual factories are built in the countryside, with the services connected with them concentrated in the cities; but even then, industrialization and urbanization will proceed side by side. Thus Professor Bert F. Hoselitz is evading the issue when he says, "Although industrialization and urbanization go usually hand in hand, there is no necessary connection between the two processes. Industries can be and have been established in rural districts, and cities have grown up without large industrial plants." [2]

The same is true of Heberle when he says, ". . . industrialization and urbanization should not be considered as identical processes . . . cities have been in existence before industrialization and not all cities are highly industrialized." [3]

Why should we expect urbanization and industrialization to go together? It is unnecessary to belabor this question here. The tendency toward agglomeration of services in cities, the economies of scale involved in urban growth, and the external economies created for other activities by each new enterprise or service established in one town are too well known

[2] Bert F. Hoselitz, "The City, The Factory, and Economic Growth," *The American Economic Review*, May, 1955, pp. 166-84.
[3] Quoted in Leo F. Schnore, "The Statistical Measurement of Urbanization and Economic Development," *Land Economics*, August 1961, p. 230.

to need repetition. However, one point is perhaps too little stressed in the literature: the simple fact that highly trained people of the kind needed for middle and high positions in either the public or the private sector like to live in or near cities. In short, the kind of people needed to launch and maintain a process of industrialization have urbane taste. The ludicrous spectacle of cabinet members in Brazil solemnly boarding their planes on Tuesday morning to fly to Brasilia for a cabinet meeting, and flying joyously back to Rio de Janeiro on Tuesday evening, is evidence enough of the difficulties involved in moving such people even from large cities to small ones. The painfully slow growth of Canberra since its establishment in 1920 provides further support for this argument.

The Economic Commission for Latin America has provided some data on urbanization and industrialization in Latin American and European countries (see Tables 21–2 and 21–3). Urbanization is defined as living in

TABLE 21–2

Indices of Urbanization and Industrialization for Selected
Latin American Countries, in the Latest Census Year

Country	Census Year	Indices of	
		Urban-ization*	Industrial-ization†
Argentina	1947	48.3	26.9
Chile	1952	42.8	24.2
Ecuador	1950	17.8	17.8
Venezuela	1950	31.0	15.6
Paraguay	1950	15.2	15.5
Bolivia	1950	19.7	15.4
Colombia	1951	22.3	14.6
Peru	1940	13.9	13.2
Brazil	1950	20.2	12.6

* Percentage of total population in places of 20,000 or more inhabitants.
† Percentage of economically active males engaged in manufacturing, construction, gas, and electricity.
SOURCE: Official census data.

cities of more than 20,000 inhabitants. Industrialization is defined alternatively as the proportion of the active male labor force engaged in manufacturing, construction, gas and electricity, or a percentage of the total labor force working as salaried employees or wage earners in manufacturing alone. A glance at these tables shows that the rank correlation is fairly high, although the ratio of the industrialization index to the urbanization index varies a good deal. The number of cases here (particularly the number of cases in Latin America itself) is too small to provide a rank correlation of any high degree of reliability. Broadening the definition of "industrialization" would no doubt improve the correlations.

TABLE 21–3

Urbanization and Structure of Employment

Country	Census Year	Urbanization Index*	Industrial Employment†	Second Index as a Percentage of the First
Latin American Countries:				
Argentina	1947	48.3	17.3(1)	36
Venezuela	1950	31.0	7.1(5)	23
Mexico	1950	24.0	8.4(3)	35
Puerto Rico	1950	27.1	16.2(2)	60
Bolivia	1950	14.0	3.8(6)	27
Costa Rica	1950	10.9	8.2(4)	75
Haiti	1950	5.4	2.0(7)	37
European Countries:				
Great Britain	1951	67.7	38.6(1)	56
Western Germany	1950	45.3	27.6(4)	61
Austria	1951	39.8	21.5(5)	54
Sweden	1950	34.5	28.7(3)	83
France	1946	31.4	18.9(6)	60
Switzerland	1950	31.2	33.4(2)	107
Finland	1950	24.0	18.4(7)	77

* Percentage of total population in places of 20,000 or more inhabitants.
† Percentage of total active labor force working as salaried employees or wage earners in manufacturing.
SOURCE: Adapted from Table 16, UN Economic and Social Council, *Preliminary Study of the Demographic Situation in Latin America*, (E/CN.12/604), April 23, 1961, p. 55.

In the present context—and assuming that industrialization is desired as an inevitable concomitant of economic development, but that urbanization for some reason or other is not, the question to ask is whether an act of policy could retard the rate of urbanization without retarding the rate of industrialization and thus of economic development? Alternative versions of this question might be, "What is the optimal size of a city from the standpoint of economic development?" or "Could we have economic development based on small industries located in small towns?"

The present author has not done research on the optimal size of a city. But in 1949, in an article somewhat pompously entitled "Towards a Science of Community Planning," he wrote: [4]

Urban centers grow up largely because people want to be "close to" a variety of facilities—business and professional contacts, educational institutions, recreation and cultural facilities requiring participation of large numbers of people,

[4] Benjamin Higgins, "Towards a Science of Community Planning," *Journal of the American Institute of Planners*, Fall, 1949, p. 9.

specialized shops—and to other people with similar tastes. "Close to" is obviously not a matter of mere distance but of travel time. Three miles of congested city streets may remove people farther from the points they want to reach than ten miles of open highway. Thus one of the major objectives of city planning must be minimum travel time. The city planner must try to provide effective proximity to places of work, recreation, education, and residence. If such proximity cannot be provided the city ceases to function as a city and becomes an inconveniently arranged collection of specialized communities. (The Standard-Vacuum Company's move from the Wall Street area to Westchester County and back to mid-Manhattan is an illustration of the frustrations that arise when a city ceases to perform its functions effectively.) A city of "optimal size" must be big enough to be urbane in its range of activities and small enough to provide effective proximity to these activities for its residents, with the available techniques of city planning and transportation.

With respect to decentralization of industrial activities through reliance on small industries that can be grouped together in correspondingly small towns, there is more that can be said. As we have already seen, over a very wide range of industrial activity, small enterprises cannot be afforded by developing countries, because they are too expensive in terms of capital. Small industries, with relatively low capital-labor ratios frequently turn out to have high capital-output ratios. On the other hand, large-scale industries do not necessarily require large cities. Any country wishing to do so could probably achieve some decentralization by moving industry and related services from large cities (such as Rio and Melbourne) to middle-sized cities (such as Brasília and Canberra). We have not yet asked the question, "Why should anyone wish to do so?"

Urbanization without Industrialization?

While it would appear that significant industrialization is not possible without some accompanying urbanization (although metropolitanization may not be absolutely necessary), it is less clear that urbanization is impossible without industrialization. There is substantial evidence that during recent decades the pace of urbanization has been faster than the corresponding rate of industrialization would require, especially in Latin America. This imbalance takes the form of urban unemployment, urban underemployment, and low-productivity employment in cities. Through the process of urbanization, in Latin America as in Asia and the Middle East, there has been a transfer of these three aspects of underdevelopment from the countryside to the city.

Raymond Firth tells the story of some Trobriand islanders who, observing the high standard of living among American soldiers occupying their island, rearranged their villages with a rectangular street pattern, threw away their ceremonial regalia, and marched up and down the streets with sticks looking like rifles, hoping thereby to achieve economic development.[5] There is nothing about the fact or form of growth of cities that

[5] R. W. Firth, "Social Changes in the Western Pacific," *Quarterly Bulletin, South Pacific Commission* (Novmen), October, 1953, p. 27.

guarantees rising levels of income. The *1957 United Nations Report on the World Social Situation* made this observation: [6]

Open unemployment is not a serious problem in most of the Latin American countries, either among the permanent city population or the migrants (Cuba and Puerto Rico, in which a high proportion of the labour force depends on seasonal plantation work, are the known exceptions). However . . . with the probable exceptions of Argentina and southern Brazil, the growth of the cities "has multiplied considerably the unsalaried sector of the urban lower class; poor artisans, shopkeepers on a small scale or with semi-permanent places of business, ambulatory pedlars and workers many of whom have occupations that constitute incredibly poorly paid forms of underemployment. As in other less-developed regions, there has been a transfer of rural underemployment to the cities, where it may be statistically concealed under "services" or "activities not defined."

The comparison of the figures for Latin America and Europe in Table 20–3 (and particularly the ratio of industrialization to urbanization) leads the Economic Commission for Latin America to state, "Not only are Latin American countries less industrialized than European countries are, or were, at similar levels of urbanization, but the increase in Latin America's urbanization—as distinct from Europe, North America, or the Soviet Union—was not accompanied by commensurate increase in industrialization." [7] The Commission adds, "Unfortunately, as is well known, services that are unsolicited or are only in small demand are being performed in Latin America by a low class of urban workers so numerous that their earnings are not far superior to those of beggars." The Commission concluded that in Latin America urbanization has outrun employment opportunities outside of the agricultural sector. They accordingly recommend measures to improve conditions in the rural areas, including provision of rural employment, increasing rural productivity and purchasing power, improving education, housing, and health in rural societies, and a wider dispersal of industries.

The conditions noted in the late 1950's have been aggravated since. The report on social development, presented to the Tenth Session of the Economic Commission for Latin America at Mar del Plata, Argentina, in May, 1963, after pointing to the continuing rapid urbanization in Latin America, contains the following comment: [8]

A rapid urbanization process should imply the presence of conditions similar to conditions found elsewhere. In other words, there should presumably be that continuum between the urban and rural sectors which is typical of the

[6] United Nations, "Urbanization in Latin America," *Report on the World Social Situation* (E/CN.5/324/Rev. 1; ST/SOA/33), p. 181. The quotation included in this passage is from José E. Oturriaga, *La Estructura Social y Cultural de México* (Mexico, D.F., Fondo de Cultura Económica, 1951), p. 40.

[7] Economic Commission for Latin America, *op. cit.*, p. 56.

[8] Economic Commission for Latin America, *Social Development in Latin America* (E/CN.12/660), April, 1964.

great industrial countries of our time. In Latin America, however, no such continuum exists, but a complete rupture. No smooth, straight-forward transmission line—where distances are naturally a bridge—but the ragged series of abrupt switch-overs, jumps and hiatuses. May there not be a flaw in the prevailing theory with respect to the urbanization process? How is it possible to account for the steady expansion of the larger towns alongside a stationary agricultural productivity?

Dualism may even be increasingly aggravated in Latin America because of the increasing discrepancy between urban and rural development. The old type of organization of work known as the *hacienda*, says the Commission, "holds out against the rationalization and modernization called for today. It is a survival of the past that hinders quick and easy adaptation to the demands of modern industry." Thus the rapidity of urbanization in Latin America reflects the "expulsion" of the agricultural population as much as the attractions of job opportunities in the cities. One would think, says the Commission, that the "rapid expansion of the larger towns is attributable to the concurrent establishment of thriving industrial activities in the urban areas concerned. But the correlation is so tenuous—quite irrespective of its probable causal links—that it has become a matter of controversy. The Commission is careful to add, however, that "the suggestion in the preceding paragraph is not that there has been no widespread modernizing effort—the rationalization process has been an effective operation as everywhere—but that the degree of modernization achieved has not been sufficient.

In short, the solution may not be to retard the movement to the cities by making conditions more attractive in the countryside—a policy which is in itself anti-developmental—but rather to accelerate the rate of industrialization and consequently the rate of employment-creation outside the agricultural sector. As pointed out by the Bureau of Social Affairs of the United Nations on another occasion, in presenting their paper to the Joint Conference with UNESCO, ILO, and the OAS on urbanization problems in Latin America, "This paper takes it for granted that the cities will continue to grow and that a policy of preventing further urbanization would not be realistic." The Bureau adds, "Such an outlook, however, does not imply disregard of the numerous warnings that have been made on the over-rapid and unbalanced character of Latin American city growth at present. It may well be desirable to slow down the rate of urbanization and to divert from the capital cities to provincial towns as much as possible of the stream of internal migrants." [9]

It is clear that the phenomena of technological and regional dualism are closely related to the urbanization process. Much of the modern sector tends to be concentrated in cities, although it would be a mistake to identify the modern sector with urban areas completely. The modern sector includes capital-intensive, large-scale, mechanized agriculture and modern mining. What is true, however, is that growth of the modern sector and of the urban sector are closely correlated. In small countries

[9] Phillip M. Hauser (ed.), *Urbanization in Latin America* (New York, 1961), p. 294.

like those of Central America, the modern sector and leading region tend to consist of the capital city and its hinterland. Even in larger countries, one finds technological and regional dualism *within* both the rich and poor regions. Thus within the Brazilian northeast and Amazonia much of such modern sectors as there are can be found in the large cities of Recife and Belém. The solution, however, is not to delay urbanization but to accelerate it, and so to empty the countryside of low-productivity farmers.

"Evils" of Urbanization?

We have mentioned one undesirable by-product of the urbanization process in Latin America: the transfer of unemployment, underemployment, and low-productivity employment from farm to city. The solution to the problem is accelerated economic growth. But growth alone will not solve other undesirable by-products of urbanization. The main purpose of urban concentration (being "near to" a variety of activities) is increasingly frustrated through the growing difficulties of traffic circulation in the very large cities. The solution to this and a host of related problems is improved city planning, perhaps combined with an improved "national urban policy," which might involve a higher degree of decentralization of the industrialization process.

There is a tendency on the part of the general public, and even on the part of some social scientists to associate urbanization with other undesirable by-products as well: crime, juvenile delinquency, broken families, slums, disease, and the like. It is extremely doubtful whether, in fact, cities are any worse in terms of these social evils than the countryside, and with a national urban policy combined with effective city planning and more rapid economic development, there is no reason for the experiences of the early phase of the Industrial Revolution of Europe to be repeated in other countries. As the present author pointed out on another occasion: [10]

Perhaps the earliest association of social factors with economic development was concern over the "evil consequences" of industrialization in Europe. In the late nineteenth century, the United Nations Bureau of Social Affairs points out, "the goal of social policy was to protect the weak and the poor against further exploitation or to achieve a radical redistribution of wealth in the name of social justice." With this approach, "industrialization was widely seen as a negative retrogressive influence from a social welfare point of view. Deep concern arose over social ills that were observed in rapidly growing industrial and urban centres—unhealthy working conditions, starvation wages, child labour, disruption of family life, overcrowding, filth and sordidness in slums, delinquency and corruption of youth." Some of these attitudes still prevail. The Bureau considers them anachronistic, for today social scientists no longer believe that "such social ills are a necessary consequence of industrialization. Many of them simply represent evils of urban poverty and overcrowding that appear quite independently of growth; they often result from a transfer through migrants of rural destitution to an urban setting where it

[10] José M. Echavarría and Benjamin Higgins, *Social Aspects of Economic Development in Latin America*, Vol. II (Paris: UNESCO, 1963), pp. 182–83.

becomes more conspicuous. What is needed in these cases is not less industrialization."

There can be no doubt that the levels of education are higher in the cities than in the rural areas. Indeed, so difficult is the problem of bringing universal primary school education to the remoter rural regions that the Ministry of Éducation in Brazil, for example, has simply despaired of meeting the targets laid down for all Latin American countries in the UNESCO-ECLA "Charter of Santiago" of 1962.[11]

It is also clear that health conditions are on balance better in the cities because of the greater availability of medical services and the greater ease of controlling epidemic diseases. The effects on fertility are less clear. According to the United Nations Bureau of Social Affairs, "Perhaps the most striking feature of the data is the absence of any systematic relationship between degree of urbanization and level of fertility, although the most urbanized country—Argentina—has the lowest fertility period." [12] The report goes on, however, to speculate about the fertility ratio in terms of children of zero to four years of age per 1,000 women of child-bearing age and probable differences between the single and non-single fertility ratios. This speculation leads the United Nations Bureau of Social Affairs to say: "In general, therefore, it may be said that, within the limitations of the data, in this region the fertility of the urban population is uniformly below that of the total population." [13] On the other hand, an analysis of the census and of the national sample survey in India, "failed to show any significant rural-urban differentials in fertility"; although Indian experience obviously cannot be projected to Latin America, the data in this case were certainly better than those available for most Latin American countries.

A more recent statement of the United Nations Bureau of Social Affairs also casts doubt on the relationship between urbanization and fertility. Among countries with gross reproduction rates higher than 2.0, the Bureau says: "Little consistent association can be found between the levels of these rates and indices of the degree of urbanization." On the whole, it must be said that there is no conclusive evidence that urbanization is bringing with it high hopes for early curtailment of the population explosion. In this respect, at least, the experience of Europe during the Industrial Revolution is not yet being repeated in Latin America. The Bureau adds: "The implication of these findings is that fertility levels in the developing countries are determined to a large extent by cultural traits that have not been greatly affected by the social and economic changes of the modern era." [14]

[11] J. Roberto Moreira, *Social Aspects of Economic Development in Latin America*, Vol. I (Paris: UNESCO, 1963), and *Programa de Acao Economica do Governo, 1964–1966*, chap. XXI.

[12] Hauser, *op. cit.*, pp. 103, 104.

[13] United Nations, *Economic Bulletin for Asia and the Far East*, June, 1959, p. 8.

[14] United Nations, *1963 Report on the World Social Situation*, p. 17.

Housing and Physical Planning

Perhaps the most obvious drain on development potential through urbanization—and especially through urbanization and excessive industrialization—is the increased requirement for housing, and the complications of physical planning. When people move from village to city, they do not bring their houses with them, and in an urban environment, the construction of satisfactory housing through traditional "mutual help" methods is sometimes more difficult. The differences in housing standards among the *favelas, jacales, villas miserias,* and the villages can be exaggerated, and the concern over the urban slums may reflect nothing more basic than the fact that they are a good deal more visible to high-income persons and foreigners than the villages are. Yet there can be no doubt that in some basic sense housing is less far below acceptable standards in the villages of many developing countries than it is for the lowest income groups in the cities. In any case, housing costs are likely to be somewhat higher, since free building materials are not so readily available as they are in some rural communities.

Certainly the movement from farm to city has aggravated the housing shortage in underdeveloped countries, and perhaps in Latin American countries in particular.

Housing and Economic Development

One of the most difficult problems confronting the development planner is to determine the appropriate standards for housing. When the present author was attached to the United States Housing Authority, he was prepared to argue that improved housing raised productivity, reduced the incidence of disease, crime, and juvenile delinquency, and made people Live Right, Think Right, and Vote Right. The simple truth is, however, that the evidence for this kind of argument is awfully thin. It is true that the average incomes of slum dwellers went up after they moved into public housing projects—but the move took place during the recovery from the Great Depression, when the incomes of those remaining in the slums went up too. It does appear that in the United States the provision of family housing has some tendency to reduce labor turnover. But just how good must housing be in each country to hold a labor force where it is needed? The difficulty is that high-standard urban housing has a higher incremental capital-output ratio than almost any other major investment sector—higher even than petroleum, railroads, or iron and steel. The opportunity costs of providing such housing are accordingly very high.

The Economic Commission for Asia and the Far East (ECAFE) in grappling with this problem, suggests as a general principle that "in the lowest-income countries, the case for higher investment priority to housing and urban services is greater than in higher-income countries. The lowest-income countries are those which lack the satisfactory requirements or the fundamental minimum in housing and related services." [15] Unfortunately, the same statement applies to education, health, transport, power, nutrition, and every other item in the gross national income. ECAFE goes on to list eight requirements for investment programs in housing and urban services: objective housing needs must be ascertained; economical but satisfactory housing standards must be adopted; non-monetary resources in labor and materials should be mobilized; personal monetary savings should be mobilized for homes; the efficiency of the building industry should be improved; investment in housing and urban services should be controlled to serve sound social and economic objectives; there should be a clear, properly defined statement of national housing policy and program; and housing and urban services should be adequately staffed. Most of these "requirements" apply equally well to any other sector of an over-all economic and social development program.

The basic difficulty in programming housing and related urban services as a part of economic development is the same as in the field of education; housing is both a capital and a consumers' good. Some quantity and quality of housing (and related services) are necessary to maximize productivity of the labor force; or better, there is an "optimal" supply of housing where the marginal cost of more or better housing is an important component of personal income and so of individual welfare. One cannot determine appropriate housing standards by effects on productivity alone, any more than one can determine appropriate standards of public health or education in this manner.

One can, however, say that the minimal requirement for housing and urban services is that the "optimum" equating marginal costs with marginal output should be reached. Beyond that, unless a clear decision is made to redistribute income from rich to poor *in the form of housing* (which means, in effect, that the planners and politicians do not trust people to decide for themselves how they should spend an increased income or what they should sacrifice when income is reduced by public policy), housing should be as good as people are willing to pay for at cost. The "cost" is, however, subject to control by public policy to some extent; if labor and materials are allocated to other uses, housing costs will rise. One might, for example, leave housing to the market after determining what is the minimal use of strategic materials consistent with health and safety—which is more or less what was done in the United States War Production Board during the war.

The difficult questions are, "Should housing standards be higher than that, even if other programs have to be cut down to provide materials and skilled labor to the housing industry?" and "Should lower income groups be provided with housing below cost?" Answering "yes" to the second question, let us note once again, means making the decision that planners and politicians are wiser than people, and that people must be prevented from spending on something else increased income that "ought" to be spent for housing. If there are opportunities for cost reduction through

[15] United Nations, *Economic Bulletin for Asia and the Far East,* September, 1963, p. 59.

public housing, these could be seized, and the units rented at cost, the lower income groups receiving a generalized subsidy in the form of family allowances, for example. The United States Housing Authority really made housing cheaper by making available to tenants the low rates of interest and long terms at which the Federal Government was then able to borrow. It was "subsidized" only in relation to the unnecessarily high financing costs of private housing.

In our latest economics jargon we could say that programming housing requires putting a "shadow price" on it as a consumers' good for various income groups, and adding the shadow price to the increase in other output produced by more and better housing, and comparing the sum with costs of providing more and better housing. The problem is statistical rather than conceptual, and a great deal more empirical research is needed as a foundation for such policy decisions.

Meanwhile, looking at Table 21–4 we can see that the Latin American

TABLE 21–4

Dwelling Construction as Percentage of Gross Domestic Product

Gross Domestic Product Per Capita	Annual Average Rate of Population Increase During 1953–59		
	Under 1 Per Cent	1 to 2 Per Cent	Over 2 Per Cent
$1,000 or more	Denmark 2.8 Norway 4.2 United Kingdom 2.7	United States 4.5	
$300–$1,000	Greece 5.1 Italy 6.1 Malta 4.2	Argentina 4.1 Jamaica 3.0 Netherlands 5.0 Puerto Rico 5.0	Chile 3.3 Mauritius 3.5 Venezuela 3.2
Under $300	Portugal 3.2	Japan 2.0 Kenya 3.5 Korea, Republic of 1.8 Nigeria 4.6 Tanganyika 4.7	British Guiana 3.5 China (Taiwan) 1.8 Colombia 2.7 Ecuador 2.2 Honduras 3.9 Mexico 2.4

SOURCE: United Nations, *Economic Bulletin for Asia and the Far East* (September, 1963), p. 60.

countries included are, for the most part, spending a smaller proportion of national income on housing than countries in other regions in the same income category, even though the rate of population growth is lower in the other countries than it is in Latin America. For what they are worth, these figures suggest that Latin America may be spending too little on housing, but more study is needed for a firm conclusion.

Regional Planning

The resurgence of interest in regional economics has been accompanied by a growing literature on and widening interest in regional planning. In part, this interest reflects a belated realization that interregional relationships are a fundamental factor in the level and rates of growth of national income and employment. The literature, however, is still more concerned with "regional planning" than with "regional science."

The term regional planning may mean any of three different things:

1. It may mean planning for a region (city, state or province, group of states, depressed area, river valley, metropolitan region, etc.) as a separate economy. Regional planning in this sense implies that there is some authority that has regulatory and fiscal powers for the geographic unit in question. It is, of course, possible to prepare "plans" for regions, such as the United States Southwest, for which no discrete authority exists, in the hopes that federal, state, and local governments will take account of such plans in framing their own policies. However, regional planning in this sense is a somewhat fruitless undertaking unless there is some governmental authority or group of authorities that can give effect to the plan.

2. Regional p'anning may mean testing the consistency of regional plans (including plans for states, cities, distressed areas, metropolitan cities, etc.) with each other and with the national plan. If the constitution allocates certain powers to regional governments, and if these governments have budgets of their own, it is important at some stage in the over-all planning process to make certain that the two or three levels of government are not preparing plans that conflict with each other. Ideally, the aggregation of regional plans would add up to an over-all allocation of land, labor, and capital for the economy as a whole that would be identical with the allocation required by the national plan.

3. Regional planning may mean putting "space-tags" on projects in the national plan, with two objectives in mind: (a) to assure the best possible location of industry, and (b) to reduce gaps in productivity and income among various regions in the country. (It may well turn out that these two objectives are mutually inconsistent, beyond a certain margin of total development investment.)

Planning for a Region

When constructing a plan for a subnational geographic unit considered as a separate economy it is possible, and perhaps even desirable, to carry through all the exercises involved in national development planning. It is unusual for data at the regional level to be as abundant and as good as those for the nation, but one can try to do the best job possible with the data available. A regional plan should begin with surveys of natural and human resources. It may be worthwhile constructing social accounts for the region. These may be refined to the point of constructing an input-output matrix of whatever degree of complexity is possible with reasonable accuracy. The income-output matrix could be projected in terms of the desired product mix in a target year.

Linear programming techniques could be used to assure consistency in detailed objectives of the plan. Incremental capital-output ratios and incremental capital-employment ratios could be applied to the regional development budget, in order to forecast its impact on output and employment. An industrial complex analysis may be undertaken, to assist in decisions regarding the location of industries within the region. In assigning priorities, cost-benefit analyses may be undertaken, or priority formulas applied. One may choose to apply a regional multiplier to the investment budget in order to determine its inflationary impact within the region and its effect on regional balance of payments. Such analysis may suggest the proper tax policies of governments operating effectively in the region. One may even endeavor to measure the "regional linkage" effects of projects undertaken within the region.[16]

As far as such operations are concerned, there are no obvious differences in techniques between regional planning and national planning. As a matter of practice, however, it would appear that as the geographic unit becomes smaller, the relative role of physical planning (or land-use planning) in the over-all p'anning process becomes greater and greater. The same is true of the design aspects of planning.

At this stage, we might say that this kind of regional planning has four features that distinguish it from national development planning.

1. The differences in availability of data, and the consequent differences in statistical ingenuity required, are so great as to constitute almost a difference in kind. The procedures for empirical analysis inevitably take different forms at the national and regional levels.

2. For any country the external sector is a bigger proportion of individual regional economies than it is for the national economy. The "balance of payments" aspects of development require even greater attention for regions than they do for the whole nation.

3. The mobility of resources, and especially of labor, is greater within any country than the mobility between countries. Study of migration and capital flows is consequently a more essential component of regional planning than of national development planning.

4. As national development planning runs mainly in terms of capital use, and city planning mainly in terms of land use, regional planning provides a kind of "no-man's-'and" where the two approaches meet. Some integration of economic and physical planning at the regional level is therefore essential.

5. The branch of economic theory underlying regional planning (location theory) is in a particularly unsatisfactory state, providing only limited guidance for policy formation.

It is perfectly clear that in any of the concepts of regional planning listed above, the design aspect has almost totally disappeared. There will,

[16] See for example, Walter Isard and John H. Cumberland, (eds.), *Regional Economic Planning, Techniques for Analysis for Less Developed Areas* (Paris, 1961), p. 64. See also Walter Isard and others, *Methods of Regional Analysis; An Introduction to Regional Science*, especially chaps. 6 and 9.

of course, be problems of the routing and design of highways, the design of multiple-purpose river valley projects, irrigation schemes, and the like. However, when it comes to regional planning, the special training of the architect and the engineer really becomes important only in the implementation phase and has little to do with the actual plan preparation. Of course the planners may need to consult architects and engineers on the physical and design problems involved in the regional plan, but the process of planning itself, as already indicated, is mainly one of decision-making with respect to resource allocation.

Determining the Consistency of Regional and National Plans

Most of the exercises that should be undertaken to assure consistency of regional plans with each other and with the national plan boil down to good common sense.[17] For example, a project may seem unjustified if only the regional market, expanded in accordance with the plan, together with existing markets in other parts of the country are taken into account; but it may seem highly desirable when the development plans of other parts of the country are considered. Professor Walter Isard illustrates this with the case of a modern glass plant. A careful analysis shows that the regional markets, taking into account the growth of regional income and employment generated by the plan, together with existing exports from the region, would be inadequate to absorb the output of a modern glass plant. But when the growth of exports due to execution of other regional plans was added, the glass plant was clearly worthwhile. Professor Isard goes on to point out that consideration of the impact of plans of other regions and of the national development plan as a whole is an important factor in deciding the appropriate size of plants to be constructed in any one region.

There is also a quite different line of approach to integration of regional and national plans. The execution of national development plans may carry with it a good many undesirable by-products which necessitate action at the regional level to prevent or offset them. (We are still including cities, metropolitan regions, distressed areas, etc., as "regions.") These undesirable by-products may include slums, urban blight, traffic congestion, increased crime and delinquency, housing shortages in some areas combined with an excess supply of housing in others, overcrowded schools in some districts and lack of schools in others, and the like.

Producing a "Ratchet" Effect

There can be little doubt that the third concept of regional planning (reducing regional gaps) is the most important one. Maximizing spread effects among regions, while reducing regional gaps, must be the main aim of regional development policy. Economic development means eliminating the poor or lagging sectors and taking full advantage of the leading sectors or "growing points," maximizing the "spread effect" of growth where it occurs, and overcoming the tendency for productivity of "leading" and

---

[17] These are outlined in the ECAFE report, *op. cit.*, chap. VI. For other suggestions see Isard and Cumberland, *op. cit.*, especially chap. 1.

"lagging" sectors and rich and poor regions to pull farther and farther apart. An economic development plan must be defined in terms of inter-sectoral, and so interregional, relations. In short, a development plan is necessarily concerned with interspatial relationships and urban-rural relations.

Integration of Economic and Physical Planning

Both economic and physical planning are needed at all levels of govern-ment, and integration of "land-use planning" with "capital-use planning" is essential.[18] The neglect until very recently of the spatial aspects of eco-nomic development is all the more unfortunate because it is gradually being realized that the spatial relationships are the very core of the devel-opment problem. There are almost no "underdeveloped countries." There are only underdeveloped areas, and an underdeveloped country is one in which the underdeveloped areas are a large proportion of the total economy.

On the other side of the coin, the addition of economic development planning to the responsibilities of government makes it all the more essential for physical planners to know exactly what it is that they are doing that is different from what any other government officials or advisers are doing and which activity requires special training geared to it. In the Western democracies, in which physical planning grew up, for a long time little conflict arose from the growing scope of physical planning because no other planning was being undertaken. In many underdeveloped countries, on the other hand, the central government has assumed wide responsibilities for promoting economic development. There can be no doubt that location of industry, land-use patterns, and rural-urban rela-tionships are essential parts of a national development plan. Indeed, the rural-urban pattern is the very core of the economic development prob-lem. Consequently, in countries doing both physical planning and develop-ment planning the overlap between the current concept of physical planning in the West and the new task of development planners is readily apparent.

Frequently the two major sectors in dualistic economies appear as a contrast between one or a few large and growing cities and the surround-ing countryside—Djakarta, Surabaya, and Indonesia; Delhi, Calcutta, and India; Manila and the Philippines; San Juan and Puerto Rico; Harcourt and Nigeria; Mexico City, Monterey, and Mexico; Tripoli and Libya—the examples can be extended to virtually every underdeveloped country.

It is clear that there must be a two-way street between city and regional planners and national development planners. Drafts of city and regional plans should be among the data studied by national development planners. The national development plans should then be submitted in draft to city and regional planners so that their impact on the city or

[18] Cf. C. Haar, Benjamin Higgins, and L. Rodwin, "Economic and Physical Planning: Co-ordination in Developing Areas," *Journal of the American Institute of Planners,* October, 1958.

region can be analyzed. The analyses of the city and regional planners should, in turn, be made available to the national planners, and utilized in revising the draft national plan in preparation of the final one. National development plans, once in final form, should immediately be available to city and regional planners so that they, in turn, can make their final plans accordingly. This whole process is one of solving a set of simultaneous equations and therefore it should be continuous.

Some Longer-Run Problems

Such administrative devices can help to meet the immediate problem of determining national urban policies, as a minimal basis for integrating national development plans with city and regional plans. The real problem of integration, however, is more deep-seated. In the long run it is doubtful whether mere exchange of views and information among planners and planning authorities at different levels of government will produce truly integrated planning. There must also be greater uniformity of approach and methodology than now exists in the fields of physical planning on the one hand and national development planning on the other.

National development planning is generally considered to be one facet of economic policy. It is designed primarily to maximize per capita income over the perspective planning period within the limits imposed by other goals of economic policy. Economic development planning tends to be "market-oriented" to a large degree. A development plan calls for direct government intervention where the market does not work and cannot be made to work. The first job of the development planner is to find out, by empirical and theoretical analysis, how the market is operating and the places and ways in which it is yielding unsatisfactory results. Next, the possibilities of making the market work better through monetary, fiscal, foreign exchange, and similar policies (perhaps including anti-monopoly legislation) should be explored fully. If there are still important aspects of the economic development process that are not taken care of, the economic planner may suggest direct controls over the private sector or expansion of the public investment sector.

The over-all approach to development planning is "economic," in the sense that the market process and ways of influencing it are the core of the planning process. Engineering, sociological, and other data are fed into the analytical machinery, but the analytical tools are essentially those of the economist.

It is true that economic development requires discontinuous and large-scale change in the structure of the economy, as distinct from comparison of marginal returns on isolated investment decisions. It is also true that economic theory as it now exists does not provide a reliable guide for decisions when such discontinuous jumps are needed. Nevertheless, even in socialist countries, development planning is still largely a matter of "patching the market," however big the patches may be.

Perhaps the chief contribution of economics to general knowledge has been the construction of a method for testing social policies by objective and quantitative means. The broad goals of city and regional planning, however, are usually stated in some such terms as "an efficient and harmonious environment." As stated, such goals are subjective and immeasurable. Could "thermometers" be developed to measure—indirectly—"efficiency and harmony" in the environment? If so, it would be possible to use a method in physical planning that would make integration with national policy a good deal easier and more effective. It would then be possible to analyze the market process, isolating the defects in it in terms of these quantitative indicators of efficiency and harmony. Next the planner could decide, on the basis of empirical and theoretical analysis, what can be done to remove these defects by indirect policies (taxation, credit policy, etc.). Finally, analysis could be undertaken to isolate those remaining defects in the market operation which could best be removed by public investment in unprofitable impulse sectors, and those which could best be handled by direct controls of private investment, such as zoning, licensing, legal master plans, and the like. All this analysis should be conducted in terms of quantifiable functional relationships, the derivatives of which would be related unequivocally to the *direction* of change in degree of "harmony and efficiency."

In other words, the first requirement for the development of a national urban policy, as a guide to inclusion of land-use aspects of development in the development plans, is an analysis of what is happening now. Most underdeveloped countries show a disturbing tendency toward agglomeration, conurbation, and the like. Why have these trends appeared since World War II? Is it a healthy or an unhealthy development? What objections are there to permitting the pattern of land use to develop "naturally"? These questions deserve much more study than they have yet received. Conditions seem to vary from one country to another. For example, the UNESCO studies suggest that in India people move from partial employment in rural areas to total unemployment in the cities. In Indonesia, on the other hand, it seems that unemployment among inmigrants is lower in the capital city of Djakarta than it was in the rural areas from which they came.

At the same time, national development planning must pay much more attention to spatial aspects of development than it has to date. A national development plan should include a map as well as an investment budget—as a city plan should include a budget as well as a map. Most development planners are not trained to think in land-use or spatial terms. It is not merely a matter of analyzing location of industry, but also of taking account of the physical interrelationships of the projects included in a development plan.

Training Planners

What all this means with respect to training depends on how much teamwork can be expected at the national and local level. If we could be sure that every city planning organization would include professional economists, public-opinion poll specialists, engineers, sociologists, and architects, as well as "city planners," and if national development teams would include all these disciplines and also agriculturalists, geologists, etc., then city and regional planners could be trained primarily to test proposed plans in terms of their physical balance—their contribution to "harmony and efficiency in the environment" as indicated by quantitative analysis. But such teamwork is probably more than we can hope for in every case. Accordingly, it would seem safer to make sure that city planners are capable of conducting economic analysis and that development planners can conduct physical analysis. If we accept these capabilities as part of our training goal, the organization of courses in both city planning and development planning will need substantial revision.

22 | Inflation and Economic Development

Most underdeveloped countries have experienced inflation during recent decades. Particularly violent inflations have taken place in some Latin American countries since World War II. In some cases, the inflation seems to have been justified as a lubricant to economic growth. In others it appears that rampant inflation has disrupted the economy and retarded economic development. This whole experience has given rise to considerable controversy about the relationship between inflation and economic growth, especially in Latin America.

Structuralist versus Fiscalist Explanations

In Latin America, in particular, the controversy about inflation and growth is related to the controversy between "structuralists" and "fiscalists." The issues in this controversy have been well summarized and analyzed by Dr. Roberto Campos.[1] The disturbing element in the more extreme structuralist arguments is the reiterated suggestion that inflation in Latin America is associated with the structure of Latin American foreign trade, and thus in some vague way the fault of foreigners rather than of Latin Americans. Nowhere does the "structuralist" view appear in more extreme form than in the document presented to the Ninth Session of the Economic Commission for Latin America in Santiago in

[1] Roberto de Oliveira Campos, "Economic Development and Inflation, with Special Reference to Latin America," in OECD, *Development Plans and Programs* (Paris, 1964), pp. 127–48.

May, 1961.[2] Here it is argued that if "the national product is growing quickly, as it may have to if the rate of increase of the population is high," there will also be

a fast expansion in demand, especially for some types of goods and services . . . for in underdeveloped economies such as those in Latin America, these rises in demand may create problems. Of course they can be accommodated, if exports are rising fast enough. Foreign exchange supplies will then permit imports of durables . . . to increase, and allow equipment for electricity genera-tion and for transport services to be purchased overseas. It will similarly be possible to ease other shortages that arise during the inevitably somewhat un-even process of growth.[3]

Again, "If exports rise rapidly enough, as they did in Venezuela for many years, the economy can grow quickly without serious danger of inflation, even though labour and capital are immobile, enterprise is de-ficient, and the government lacks an adequate policy." [4]

As stated, the argument that more rapid expansion of exports permits more rapid economic growth without danger of inflation is simply wrong. An increase in exports that is not offset by an increase in savings, taxes, or imports is in itself inflationary. It expands the money supply and reduces the supply of goods available in the whole market. Of course, if the exports are entirely offset by imports of consumers' goods, there is little or no increase in inflationary pressure, although in accordance with the Haavelmo "unit multiplier theory," even a balanced expansion of foreign trade is in itself inflationary.[5] If increased foreign exchange earnings are used to import capital goods of a superior type to replace existing capital equipment, the net effect might conceivably be anti-inflationary as a con-sequence of the increased flow of final goods and services. But if growth is limited to what is possible through replacement of existing capital goods with better ones as they wear out, the rate of economic development will certainly not be very fast.

The structuralist argument, however, is different from either of these cases. It is that developmental investment is inhibited by lack of certain raw materials and equipment which must be imported. The expansion of exports permits breaking bottlenecks by importing strategic items of equipment and raw materials. Thus even if exports are completely bal-anced by imports, growth will be faster because the level of investment can be higher than it would be without the growth of exports. But it is obvious that an increase in exports that is just offset by an increase in imports but that permits an increase in investment is inflationary unless

[2] Economic and Social Council, "Inflation and Growth: A Summary of Experience in Latin America" (E/CN.12/563), April 12, 1961. (In passing, it is interesting that nowhere in this document is there a comparison of rates of growth with rates of inflation in various Latin American countries.)

[3] *Ibid.*, p. 6.

[4] *Ibid.*, p. 8.

[5] Trygve Haavelmo, "Multiplier Effects of a Balanced Budget," *Econometrica*, December, 1945, pp. 311-18.

savings and taxes are also increased. There is nothing about expanded foreign trade that permits increased developmental investment to take place, without inflation, while avoiding any need for increased savings and higher taxes. The argument that growth of exports is needed for economic development is perfectly valid, but we cannot properly argue that the limited market for exports is at once a fact inhibiting growth and a factor causing inflation.

Forced Savings

Advocates of inflation as a stimulant to economic growth sometimes cast their argument in terms of "forced saving." If the people of a society will not voluntarily save enough to finance economic development, the argument goes, they can be "forced" to do so through an inflationary process which creates a spread between increases in money incomes and in real incomes. The concept of "forced savings" belongs to that era of confusion in the theory of savings and investment which was mentioned in Chapter 15 above. "Forced savings" in this context are simply the difference between ex-ante and ex-post savings, or the increase in money income during an income period. It is a question whether "forced savings" should be called savings at all; "forced savings" are not a means of financing investment, they are a measure of inflation.

It is true, of course, that if resources are mobilized for developmental investment, without any offset in the form of voluntary savings, tax payments, or imports, prices will rise. The rise in real standards of living will then be slower than the rise in money income. In this sense the community is "forced" to save. But, which groups within the community bear the brunt of this lag in real incomes behind money increases? Not the speculators, certainly; not the wage earners, supported as they are by strong trade unions. And as Dr. Eugenio Gudin, dean of Brazilian economists, has pointed out, the rentiers have virtually disappeared anyhow; it is not they who suffer from inflation. Those who suffer are people with relatively fixed incomes, such as teachers, scientists, civil servants, the armed forces and the like. It may be questioned whether the incentive effects of deprivation of such members of the middle income groups are conducive to accelerated economic growth.

There is even some reason to doubt that inflation *as such* can be counted upon to reduce aggregate consumption significantly. H. S. Odeh, in his study of the impact of inflation on the level of economic activity,[6] first establishes the "relative change in income hypothesis," expressed as $C'' = r_0 + r_1 (Y'')$, where C'' and Y'' are the relative change in money consumption and in money income, respectively, and r_0 and r_1 are constants. Testing the hypothesis against Brazilian and Chilean experience, he obtained high correlation coefficients in both cases. He concluded that in these countries, for the period studied, inflation did not exert a significant influence on consumption demand. In passing, it may be noted that

[6] H. S. Odeh, *The Impact of Inflation on the Level of Economic Activity* (Rotterdam, 1963).

Odeh also concluded that inflation had a negative effect on investment in Chile, whereas the more moderate inflation in Brazil between 1939 and 1956 had a favorable effect on investment. This conclusion was borne out by both the single-equation and model approaches utilized.

A Look at the Record

The determination of the net gains and losses from inflation would be easier if experience of various countries indicated a clear relationship between the degree of inflation and the rate of economic growth. Unfortunately no such uniformity appears. The data in Table 22–1 relate to relatively long periods for Latin American countries. Table 22–2 covers a

TABLE 22–1

The Relationship Between Inflation* and Economic Growth†
in Latin America, 1945–1959

Country	Growth Rate (% per year)	Annual Average Increase in Cost of Living (index points)	Currency Units per U.S. Dollar			
			1945	1951	1959	
Venezuela	5.9	4	3	3	3	
Dominican Republic	4.6	2	1	1	1	High Growth Countries
Nicaragua	4.2	1	6	7	7	
El Salvador	4.0	5	3	3	3	
Brazil	3.9	57	20	20	202	
Ecuador	3.4	13	14	17	17	
Costa Rica	3.4	5	6	7	7	Moderate Growth Countries
Mexico	2.9	16	5	9	12	
Uruguay	2.3	27	2	2	11	
Colombia	2.1	26	1	15	28	
Peru	2.1	26	7	15	28	
Cuba	1.5	2	1	1	1	
Honduras	0.9	3	2	2	2	
Paraguay	0.9	381	3	32	128	
Panama	0.7	1	1	1	1	Low Growth Countries
Chile	0.6	340	32	93	1,052	
Guatemala	0.6	5	1	1	1	
Argentina	0.4	185	5	14	83	
Haiti	0.3	..	5	5	5	
Bolivia	−0.8	1,257	64	247	11,885	

* Measured in currency units per U.S. dollars at end of the year. It should be noted that the dollar was itself devalued by 42 per cent in terms of its gold parity in January, 1934. Free market rates are used where applicable and available. This table gives only a general indication of movements in exchange rates.

† Cumulative annual increase in per capita product.

Computed from statistics published by the Economic Commission for Latin America.

larger number of underdeveloped countries for the 1950's. The Latin America data provide examples of every conceivable combination: monetary stability with high rates of growth; monetary stability with stagnation; inflation with rapid growth; and inflation with stagnation. Thus Brazil experienced considerable inflation between 1929 and 1940, and violent inflation between 1951 and 1959; but its rate of growth in real per capita income has been very high. The Mexican experience is similar, except that the inflation between 1951 and 1959 was very much less than in Brazil, and the rate of economic growth is also somewhat lower. On the other hand, Chile and Bolivia experienced much more violent inflations, with no economic growth between 1945 and 1958. In these countries, inflation did not serve as a lubricant to economic development; on the contrary there were slight declines in per capita income in the postwar years in Bolivia, and stagnation in Chile. Argentina provides another example of a country with considerable inflation combined with stagnation or even decline. The approximate total number of non-industrialized, non-Communist-Bloc countries for which c or w is available was eighty-six. The total number of such countries for which the increase in prices was 3 per cent or more, sustained over at least five years in the period 1950–61 was twenty-four. The distribution of these twenty-four countries according to rate of inflation is shown in Table 22–3, on page 490.

The prevention of inflation is no guarantee of economic development either. Cuba, for example, had a completely stable currency throughout the whole period of 1929 to 1959, yet Cuba suffered a decline in per capita income during the period following World War II. Haiti also had a stable currency throughout the whole period, but had a very slow rate of economic growth. Panama and Honduras had stability of the foreign exchange value of their currency, but rates of growth which, though higher than in Haiti, were very much lower than in Brazil or Mexico. Nor is stability of the currency always a deterrent to rapid economic development. Venezuela, too, enjoyed currency stability throughout most of the period, and had the highest rate of growth since World War II of all Latin American countries. Nicaragua also enjoyed monetary stability, with the second highest rate of growth in per capita income since World War II. Guatemala and El Salvador had somewhat lower but still respectable rates of growth, combined with monetary stability.

In Table 22–3, the figures for the 1950's also show a wide range of experience. The hyperinflationary group includes countries with declining rates of growth, as well as two countries which rank among those with the highest rates of growth of all. The high inflationary group, on the other hand, shows more cluster around moderate rates of growth. The moderate inflationary group, again, shows an extreme diversity of growth rates, from −1.4 to 8.5 per cent. Finally, the monetarily stable countries show a range of growth rates from −1.9 to 4.6.

In grouping countries as they are in Table 22–3, there would seem to be some suggestion that moderate inflation produces the highest rates of growth; however, this conclusion cannot be taken too seriously, in view of the extreme variance among the data. It does appear that net growth

TABLE 22–2
Inflation in Non-industrialized Countries, 1950–1961

Pace of Inflation and Country		Period*	% ▲ Prices† No. of Years	Index‡
Hyperinflationary (over 15 per cent increase per year)	Argentina	56a–61	75.2	w
	Bolivia	50 –60a	947.7	c
	Brazil	50 –61	66.6	w
	Chile	50 –61	194.0	w
	Indonesia	50 –58a	30.4	imports
	Laos	50 –60a	29.6	c
	Paraguay	50 –60a	187.0	w
	Taiwan	50 –61	29.5	w
	Uruguay	50 –61	42.9	c
(No instances in the 10–15 per cent range)				
High Inflationary (7–10 per cent increase per year)	Bolivia	57 –62	12.2	c
	Cambodia	51 –60a	12.1	c
	Colombia	50 –61	12.3	w
	Ivory Coast	55a–61	10.0	c
	Korea	55a–61	15.5	w
	Peru	50 –61	15.2	w
	Turkey	50 –61	15.5	w
	Vietnam	50 –58b	11.2	w
Moderate Inflationary (3–7 per cent per year)	Algeria	55b–60b	6.8	w
	Cameroun	53a–61	5.1	c
	Central African Republic	56a–61	9.6	c
	Cyprus	50 –59b	7.2	c
	India	55b–61	6.1	w
	Jamaica	56b–61	4.8	c
	Lebanon	54b–60b	4.6	c
	Madagascar	53a–61	3.5	c
	Mexico	50 –61	8.4	w
	Morocco	54b–61	5.4	w
	New Caledonia	55a–60a	6.8	c
	Nigeria	53a–60a	4.4	c
	Philippines	55b–61	3.8	w
	Fed. Rhodesia and Nyasaland	50 –61	3.8	c
	Senegal	54b–61	7.0	c
	Tanganyika	50 –59b	4.6	c
	Thailand	50 –58b	8.6	c
	Uganda	51a–61	4.0	c

* 1950-61 was selected as the period for consideration. Variations in the terminal dates are explained either by the lack of data or by the span of reasonably sustained inflation (obviously, a subjective element in the compilation). If the former, the date is marked "a," if the latter "b." Only those inflationary trends reasonably sustained over five years or more are considered.

is possible with widely varying degrees of inflation. The important thing, in other words, is to assure that the developmental investment is undertaken. Possibly some of the countries with high rates of growth and inflation could have had still higher rates of growth with less inflation; the data alone cannot tell us. It is also interesting to note that during the 1950's no country produced rates of price increase averaging between 10 and 15 per cent. These figures in themselves suggest a kind of "watershed" beyond which high inflation turns rapidly and discontinuously into hyperinflation. Further empirical analysis is necessary before we can derive from experience the precise relationship between rates of inflation and rates of economic growth.

Meanwhile, the widely varying experience with inflation and economic growth suggests that we must look elsewhere than at the monetary situation for an explanation of differences in growth rates. The record suggests that inflation may be either a good or a bad thing, depending on the way in which inflation is generated and on what other things are happening at the same time. An inflation which is the price of successful execution of a large volume of development investment may be worthwhile—although even in such cases the question may be raised as to whether economic growth might not have been still more rapid had inflation been better controlled. Inflation produced by deficit financing of current expenditures or careless extension of bank credit is likely to hamper economic growth.

Both experience and recent economic analysis suggest that there is for any country at any time an "optimal" pattern of inflation. It may well be that the structural change in production required for economic growth is more easily brought about when wage and price incentives are used to encourage a transfer of resources from the traditional sector to the modern sector—at least up to the point where unemployment and excess capacity have been eliminated. Professor Bronfenbrenner expresses this argument in terms of the "money illusion." [7]

A slow inflation or even a rapid one in its early stages induces labourers to work more intensively for real incomes which are no higher and which may be lower than their previous level. To a lesser extent owners of land and capital may be induced to put their property to work intensively in the same way when money incomes rise.

On the other hand, once inflation has taken place at such a pace and for so long a period as to be built into the expectations of entrepreneurs, further inflation tends to aggravate the tendency, already excessively

† This column shows the percentage increment in the price index between the terminal dates, divided by the number of years in the period. The first column expresses the group range in average annual percentage increments.

‡ w = general wholesale price index (this was used whenever available). c = consumers' goods price index.

SOURCE: Computed from price indices in various issues of the United Nations *Monthly Bulletin of Statistics*.

[7] See Martin Bronfenbrenner, "The High Cost of Economic Development," *Land Economics*, August, 1953.

TABLE 22–3
Inflation and Real Per Capita Growth in Non-industrialized Countries
1950–1961

Pace of Inflation and Country*		Growth Rate Per Capital	Annual Period (per cent)	Group‡ Average (per cent)
Hyperinflationary Group	Argentina	57–62	−0.9	
	Brazil	50–61	3.0	
	Chile	51–61	0.7	
	Indonesia	52–58	2.2	1.5
	Paraguay	51–59	−0.4	
	Taiwan	51–61	4.2	
High Inflationary Group	Cambodia	52–58	1.6	
	Colombia	50–61	1.6	
	Korea	54–59	2.8	
	Turkey	50–61	0.1	1.7
	Peru	50–61	2.0	
	Bolivia	57–62	1.9	
Moderate Inflationary Group	Algeria	54–58	8.5	
	Cyprus	50–59	2.1	
	India	57–62	2.3	
	Jamaica	54–58	6.9	
	Lebanon	56–61	1.7	
	Mexico	50–61	1.6	
	Morocco	54–58	−1.4	2.8
	Nigeria	51–56	−0.3	
	Philippines	53–61	1.8	
	Rhodesia-Nyasaland	55–59	4.1	
	Thailand	52–59	3.0	
No sustained inflationary trend, or inflation under 3 per cent per year	Burma	54–59	3.6	
	Ceylon	51–59	0.4	
	Congo	51–58	2.5	
	Costa Rica	50–61	1.6	
	El Salvador	51–58	2.0	
	Fed. of Malaya	56–59	−0.2	
	Guatemala	51–59	1.8	
	Honduras	51–57	0.4	
	Iran	57–62	2.7	
	Nicaragua	56–61	−0.4	1.5
	Pakistan	50–61	0.0	
	Panama	56–61	3.0	
	Puerto Rico	51–59	4.6	
	Syria	54–59	−1.9	
	Tunisia	51–57	1.1	
	U.A.R.	57–62	1.5	
	Venezuela	53–61	3.3	

*Countries include only those for which per capita growth rates were available. The stable group comprises all those for which price-income data were found.

strong in underdeveloped countries, for investors to prefer quick profits on trading and speculation to long-run investment in productive enterprises. When this happens, inflation becomes a deterrent to further economic growth. It is also true, of course, that inflation tends to affect different income groups differently, disturbing the income distribution, very often in ways that increase the inequalities existing in society. In terms of direct social objectives as well as in terms of economic development as such, inflation can become an obstacle to the goals of policy.

The question is, of course, what the optimal pattern of inflation is. The answer depends on reactions of individual workers, consumers, and investors in particular societies at particular times. How strong is the "money illusion" in particular countries? At what point do continuously rising price levels deflect investment from productive enterprises to speculation and trade? What are the important differences in reactions to continuous inflation and sporadic price increases followed by stability? How does the process differ when wages lead prices rather than lagging behind? These are questions which cannot be fully answered by economic analysis of the ordinary kind.[8] Socio-psychological studies are needed as well.

The distinction between an optimal *rate* and an optimal *pattern* is a simple but important one. Any rate of steady price increase—even a modest increase of ½ per cent per month—will become a built-in factor in expectations of investors, and lead to the misallocation of new investment toward land, buildings, speculation in inventories, and short-run trading operations, and away from long-run productive enterprises, of the sort indicated above. A safe and sure return of even 7 or 8 per cent per year may prove more attractive than the more risky long-run returns involved in investment in manufacturing, mining, or large-scale agricultural enterprises. Thus the problem is to discover means of utilizing the wage-price incentives to achieve rapid transformation of the economy when necessary, without permitting investors to become confident of continuing price increases.

Although it is difficult to say precisely what the optimal pattern of inflation would be, there is reason to believe that it would take the form of a "step function," with short periods of fairly rapid price increase alternating with long periods of price stability. Capital requirements for economic development may follow a "saw-toothed" pattern, with capital requirements rising sharply as bottlenecks appear at the beginning of each new phase of economic growth. Economic development is a matter of successive "big pushes," although each "push" may seem smaller, as the stock of capital and national income grows. At various stages in the growth

† Periods determined by the availability of data, although every attempt was made to have them conform to those used in Table 22–2.

‡ Simple arithmetic average of growth rates for each group.

SOURCES: UN *Monthly Bulletin of Statistics; UN Yearbook of National Account Statistics,* 1960, 1961; Unpublished data issued by the United States Agency for International Development.

[8] Some of them are handled by Nicholas Kaldor in his essay on "Inflation and Economic Development," *Revista Brasileira de Economia,* March, 1957, pp. 55–82.

of any economy, however, a point is reached where movement to still higher levels of per capita income requires investment in new fields, which will sharply raise capital requirements until this necessary capital is in place. For example, in the early stages of development, investment in roads and harbors may be necessary; later, railroads and power may be required. Still later an iron and steel industry, and later still petrochemicals and electronics, may become necessary. Indeed, need for transport facilities, power, and public utilities appear sporadically with each new phase of economic growth. These periods of rapidly rising capital requirements may correspond to the periods during which price increases should be permitted to facilitate the attraction of labor and capital from low-productivity traditional occupations to the higher productivity new uses. When the new capital is in place and begins to produce, not only are further price increases unnecessary, but the prevention of inflation is relatively easy because of the expansion of output of final goods and services. In this phase, price increases are likely to do more harm than good by distorting investment in the fashion already described.

The "War Finance" Approach

The wartime experience of such advanced countries as Australia, Canada, the United Kingdom, and the United States may hold valuable lessons for countries now embarking on a "big push" with respect to economic development. For the wartime problem in those countries, like the development problem, was essentially one of achieving rapid large-scale transformation of the economy, involving rapid and substantial re-allocation of resources. Indeed, the reallocation of resources involved was much greater in the fighting of a major war than is required for economic development. When the war effort was at its peak, all of the above-named countries were devoting more than half of the gross national product to the war effort. Yet all of these countries succeeded in preventing inflation throughout the final years of the war.

The Canadian experience is of particular interest because there was a more conscious use of the price mechanism in the early years to accelerate transformation of the economy, combined with highly successful price stabilization in the latter years of the war. Canada, like the other advanced countries, entered World War II with unemployment and excess capacity. So long as these prevailed, it was felt that the wage-price incentives could be utilized to attract labor or capital into the war economy without danger of runaway inflation. Between August, 1939, when the war began, and December, 1941, the cost of living index rose by 19 per cent. By that time, unemployment and excess capacity had disappeared and the war economy had been created. At this point, therefore, the Canadian government threw into the battle against inflation a whole battery of powerful measures; extremely high income tax rates, high-pressure war loan campaigns, price ceilings, rationing, subsidies, licensing of investment, and the like. In this fashion the government was able to stabilize the cost of living index until the end of the war. Reconstruction from war to peace also took place on a rising price level, while price increases have been relatively modest since.

There was never any question of limiting the war effort for fear of creating inflationary pressure. The amount of government expenditures for war that would have been possible with existing saving functions, tax structures, and other policies, without generating inflation was probably not more than half of what was actually undertaken. But none of the belligerent governments said to themselves, "Well, unfortunately, we will have to lose the war, because we cannot undertake a war effort big enough to win without generating inflation, and we just can't have inflation." Similarly, if a careful analysis in "Esperanza" indicated that investment of 16 per cent of national income was needed for steady and widespread economic growth, while a similarly thorough analysis indicated that investment in excess of 12 per cent of national income would generate serious inflationary pressure under existing conditions, it would be foolish to say, "Well, it looks as though Esperanza cannot have development, because the investment needed for development will bring inflation, and we can't have inflation."

The appropriate policy for developing countries would be the same as that pursued by the belligerent countries during the war: to undertake the public investment and encourage the private investment needed to achieve the major objective, and to use every possible means to mop up excess purchasing power when it appeared that price increases were impeding rather than facilitating the achievement of these objectives.

There is an enormous difference between this "war finance" approach, which first makes sure that the developmental investment takes place and then does what is possible to offset undesirable inflationary effects, and a policy of straightforward monetary expansion, through easy money and deficit financing of current expenditures, in hopes that the price increases themselves will generate developmental investment. The latter approach almost never works, whereas the former almost always does.

In short, it is time we stopped talking about inflation as a "good thing" or a "bad thing." It may be good under some circumstances and bad under others. The problem is to discover precisely the pattern of price movements that will maximize economic growth in particular countries at particular times.[9]

The Probability Approach to Inflation and Stability [10]

Once the "war finance" approach to financing economic development is accepted, the way is cleared for the consideration of the optimal pattern

[9] Cf. Geoffrey Maynard, "Inflation and Economic Growth," in Eastin Nelson (ed.), *Economic Growth* (Austin, Texas, 1960); Raymond Mikesell, "Inflation and Growth: Observations from Latin America," in Paul L. Kleinsorge (ed.), *Public Finance and Welfare: Essays in Honor of C. Ward Macy* (University of Oregon, 1966); Markos Mamalakis, "Growth as a Cause of Inflation," Center Paper No. 81 (New Haven, 1966); and Werner Baer and Isaac Kerstenetsky, *Inflation and Growth in Latin America* (Homewood, Ill., 1964).

[10] This section leans heavily on a term paper prepared for my Economic Development Seminar at the University of California, "Taking Risks with Inflationary Financing," by Paul S. Armington.

of inflation in terms of probabilities of loss and gain. For any country at each point of time there is some maximum taxable capacity, a ratio of tax collections to national income that will maximize the growth of national income over some planning period. The maximum taxable capacity depends partly on the pattern of taxation and also on the pattern of expenditure. People are willing to pay higher taxes to guarantee national security than they will in peacetime, and they may be willing to pay higher taxes for economic development than for financing of routine government activities. Let us suppose, however, that an underdeveloped country—Esperanza—has reached its maximum taxable capacity and that the over-all level of public and private investment is still too low to guarantee achievement of income and employment targets over the planning period. Let us also assume that no additional foreign aid is in sight. The decision faced by the government is then, "Shall we add additional projects to our development program, in order to move closer to our income and employment targets, recognizing that the addition of one more project will bring some degree of inflation? That is, there will be some level of investment that will be completely non-inflationary with tax revenues at their maximum level. Taking the "unit-multiplier" into account, if the tax capacity budget represents an expansion of total spending, it is possible that complete avoidance of inflationary effects may require a budget surplus—that is, a level of investment somewhat below capacity tax revenues. Now the problem reduces to estimating the degree of inflation that would be generated by adding another project, and comparing any net loss of income and employment over the planning period with the increase in income and employment contributed by the project. Within some range, of course, it is possible that the income incentives accompanying inflation would have a favorable effect. Within this range no problem arises; clearly the development budget should be expended as long as both the direct impact of the project undertaken and the impact on price movements are favorable. In

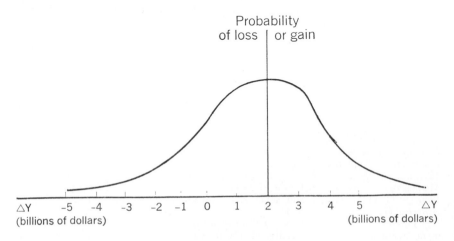

Figure 22–1. Z-Distribution

other words, investment should always be pushed to the point where the degree of inflation is optimal; but it may be desirable to push it beyond that point, if the loss involved in postponing investment projects exceeds the loss involved in an excessive rate of price increase.

None of the quantities involved in this decision can be calculated with complete accuracy. We are therefore confronted with a series of probabilities. For example, let us suppose that moving down through our priority list of projects, we reach the optimal rate of inflation with Project "P." Now suppose that the probability distribution for Project "Q" (which we shall call the "Z" distribution) appears as in Figure 22–1. For an individual investor, the decision whether or not to undertake Project Q would depend not only on this probability distribution, but also on individual safety preference. For a nation, accordingly, some concept of safety preference would have to be built into the decision function. How does a nation compare a small risk of 1 per cent loss and reasonable probability of a 1 per cent gain versus a smaller probability of a 10 per cent loss and a small probability of a 20 per cent gain, for example? In any case, some rule regarding the minimum probability would have to be established as a basis for deciding whether or not to add projects to the development budget.

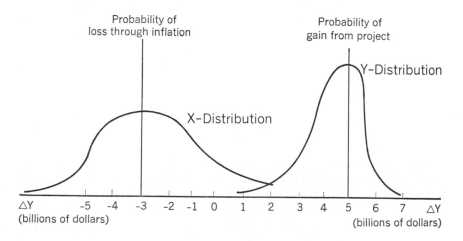

Figure 22–2. X- and Y-Distribution

The Z distribution is the sum of two other distributions: the probability distribution of income losses due to the resulting rate of inflation, and the probability distribution of gains from the project itself. Let us call these two distributions "X" and "Y," respectively. They might look like Figure 22–2: the maximum likelihood loss from the degree of inflation involved in undertaking Project Q is $3 billion. The maximum likelihood gain, which is regarded as independent of the degree of inflation, is $5 billion. The most probable net result is, therefore, a gain of $2 billion, as shown in Figure 22–1.

In Figure 22–2, the variance of estimated losses is greater than that of the gains. The reason is that the estimate of net loss depends in turn on two other estimates: the degree of inflation that would result, and the estimates of positive and negative effects. The variance of estimated gains, on the other hand, reflects only such difficulties as there may be in estimating the capital-output ratio (and capital-employment ratio, etc.) of the investment project. In some cases the degree of certainty attaching to estimates of the impact of a particular project may be high enough to warrant showing the Y distribution as a vertical line. In this case we can dispense with the Z distribution as in Figure 22–3. The shaded area in this figure indicates the probability (rather low) of making a net loss.

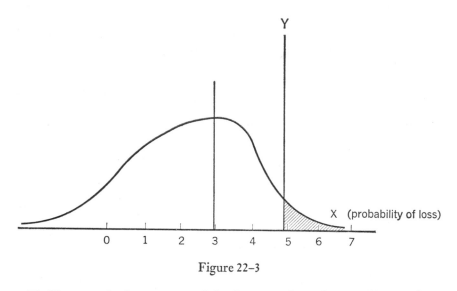

Figure 22–3

To illustrate the importance of the "community safety preference function," consider two Z distributions, as shown in Figures 22–4 and 22–5. It would take a rather peculiar safety preference function to make the Project Q undesirable under the conditions shown in Figure 22–4, but a "normal" safety preference function might lead to the rejection of Project Q under the conditions of Figure 22–5. The political situation might require the government to "play safe."

The importance of the degree of certainty or uncertainty attaching to the outcome of a project should be clear from the foregoing analysis. A major factor in the decision regarding Project Q is the variance of the Z distribution, which is the sum of the variances of the X and Y distributions (plus the covariance of X and Y if these are not independent). Thus, the greater the certainty with which we can predict the impact of the project on income and employment, the more attractive it becomes in terms of a given function. The more certain is the positive effect of an investment project, the less risky is inflationary financing of it.

There is also, of course, uncertainty as to the precise degree of inflation

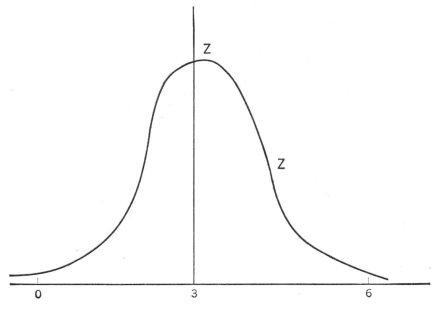

Figure 22–4

that the deficit financing of a particular project will involve. We really
have a family of X distributions, as shown in Figure 22–6. The range of
possibilities here is from a net loss of 6 (0—6) to a net gain of 11 (6+5).

If it is decided to undertake Project Q, we move on down the priority
list to Project "R." In terms of a given priority formula (here considered
to consist only of the impact on income and employment) the fact that R
has a lower priority means that its Y distribution will lie to the left of that
of Project Q. The probability of inflation is, of course, also increased, moving the X distribution to the right. Thus the attractiveness of each successive project declines, in terms of the national safety preference function,
and ultimately we will reach a margin where an additional project will not
seem worthwhile, in view of its relatively small return and the relatively
high risks of unfavorable effects of inflation.

With a given propensity to save and a given initial income, up to some
level of investment the undertaking of additional projects would clearly
have a positive effect on income, both from the direct yield of the project,
and from its multiplier effects as the deflationary gap is filled. Positive
effects may continue for some increases in investment after the deflationary
gap is converted into an inflationary one. Since projects are not infinitely
divisible, but have a certain size, the curve of maximum likelihood increase
in income as a function of investment would be a step function, beginning
positive and ending negative, as shown in Figure 22–7.

In Figure 22–8 we have safety preference curves (solid lines) with the

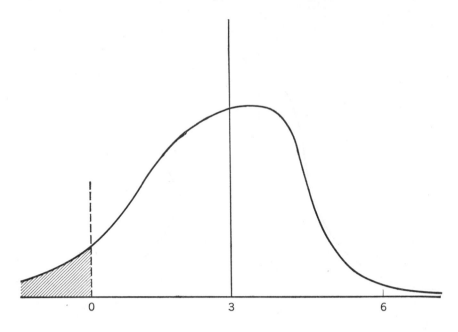

Figure 22–5

expected direct yield to be obtained from the investment projects as such on the base axis, and the risk of negative effects through inflation on the vertical axis.[11] Each project would be a point on the plane. The dotted curves show the boundary of lowest-risk highest-yield projects. To begin with, nearly all projects would lie within the southeast quadrant; that is, all of them would have a positive direct yield, and up to the point where the deflationary gap is filled, and some distance beyond, the risk of unfavorable effects on income through inflation would be negative. Some particular project would touch the highest safety preference curve (have the highest yield and make the maximum contribution to filling the deflationary gap) and that project would be undertaken. As soon as that project is added, all other projects shift their position. They would shift somewhat upward, as the deflationary gap is filled, and might shift in either direction along the horizontal axis, depending on the impact on their direct yield of the completion of the top priority project. The boundary lines would shift upward. This process would continue until the highest priority project was just tangent to the safety-preference curve through the origin: here it is a matter of indifference to the society whether the last project is undertaken or not. At that point the development program would be completed.

[11] Strictly speaking both "yield" and "risk" are distillations of three-dimensional figures of the kind shown in the present author's article "A Diagramatic Analysis of the Supply of Loan Funds," *Econometrica*, July-October, 1941.

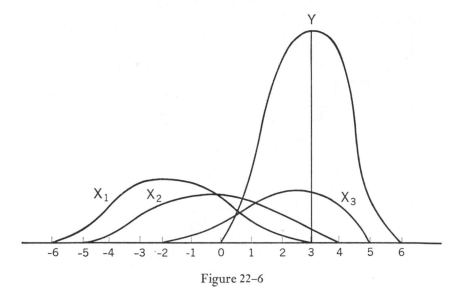

Figure 22–6

Simultaneous Inflation and Unemployment

Neither the neoclassical nor the Keynesian model adequately explains the simultaneous appearance of increasing unemployment and underemployment and of rising price indices. In the neoclassical model the phenomenon might appear in the short run through a rise in costs unaccompanied by an increase in demand. In the long run the unemployment would tend to disappear through a drop in wage rates relative to labor productivity and the substitution of labor for capital. However, in the short run the rise in prices and unemployment would be accompanied by a reduction in output as well. The inflations that have taken place since World War II, however, have not been accompanied by reductions in output. On the contrary, in nearly all countries total output and total employment have increased; demand curves as well as cost curves have shifted upward and to the right. In the Keynesian model, either effective supply exceeds effective demand, leading to unemployment and falling prices, accompanied by reduced output; or effective demand exceeds effective supply, leading to increased output and employment, and ultimately to rising prices when full employment is reached.

Most efforts to explain simultaneous inflation and unemployment have run in terms of the cost-push. The process begins with a rise in cost, resulting from trade union pressure for wage increases, or from rising prices of raw materials and capital goods through import substitution. Monopolistic enterprises pass on these increases in cost by raising administered prices. Adherents of the cost-push doctrine, however, have the responsibility of showing how an initial increase in cost results automatically in the increased money flow needed to take a growing volume of goods and services off the market at ever higher prices. There are indeed two ways in

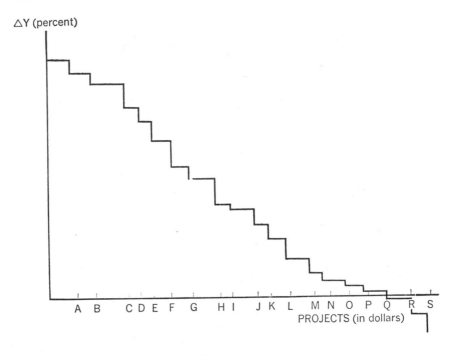

Figure 22–7

which negotiated increases in wages, or rising prices of raw materials and capital equipment, may increase the money flow; by leading to economies in the use of reserves (increasing the velocity of circulation of money) or by leading to increased demand for credit to finance payrolls, inventories, and equipment at the higher price level. A banker, however, may well wonder if his clients' credit-worthiness has gone up simply because their costs have risen, and idle reserves can be activated only once. Quantitatively, the increase in velocity and in credit extension needed to permit a given percentage increase in costs without a reduction in sales and output is unlikely to occur automatically in response to the price increases themselves. It seems quite clear that what has in fact happened is that governments committed to acceleration of economic development and to full employment have periodically provided the demand pull to make the cost push effective. The "classical medicine" for excessive wage or price demands—a reduction in sales, output, and employment—has not been applied because governments, fearful of retardation of growth or unemployment, have pursued expansionary policies on balance.

Even when the demand pull is added to the cost push, however, some further explanation is needed to show how an expanding economy can be accompanied by increasing unemployment. It is the present writer's belief that the answer lies in large measure in the phenomenon of technological and regional dualism. Investment is concentrated in the modern sector and leading region. The technology in the new field of investment is highly

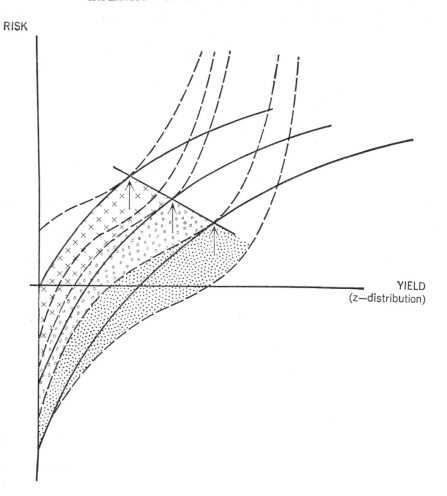

Figure 22–8

capital-intensive, and both capital-output ratios and capital-job ratios (technical coefficients) are either fixed in fact or considered to be so. There is a good deal of evidence accumulating that in fact the techniques with the high capital-labor ratios are so much more efficient in terms of capital-output ratios than others, that enterprises in the modern sector have little range of choice of technology. They are virtually compelled to use the more efficient capital-intensive methods. Add a type of technological progress that is highly labor-saving and a rapid growth of the labor force, and simultaneous inflation and unemployment become easy to explain. The monetary effects of increased investment are diffused fairly rapidly throughout the economy; the employment effects are concentrated in the modern sector and leading region. Even there, given the relatively fixed technical coefficients, the level of investment, which is high enough to generate inflationary pressures, may be insufficient to absorb the growth of the labor force, let alone permit a net outmigration from traditional sector and lagging region.

The following model, while essentially illustrative, was originally worked out to approximate the situation in Brazil in 1961. Equation (1) is a generalized multiplier equation:

$$Y = \frac{1}{\Delta S / \Delta Y + \Delta T / \Delta Y + F / \Delta Y} \Delta (I + E + X) \qquad (1)$$

where Y is national income, S is savings, T is tax payments, F is imports, I is investment, E is government expenditures on goods and services, and X is exports. In the Brazilian case, it seemed reasonable to assume at that time that $\frac{\Delta F}{\Delta Y}$ is equal to zero, and $\frac{\Delta F}{\Delta X}$ is equal to one. That is, without an increase in foreign exchange earnings, no increase in imports would be or could be permitted. On the other hand, there was no intention of accumulating foreign exchange reserves indefinitely. Increased foreign exchange earnings would be allocated for import. Thus the "unit multiplier" could be applied to exports:

$$\frac{1}{\dfrac{\Delta F}{\Delta X}} \cdot \Delta X = 1 \cdot \Delta X = \Delta X$$

The only exception to this relationship would be that in which increases in imports were offset immediately and completely by reductions in domestic consumptions (imported goods being preferred when available), thus leading to an increase in savings. We may also assume that $\Delta E = \Delta T$ (the government is not concerned with eliminating or even reducing its deficits) and therefore $\Delta E / \Delta Y = \Delta T / \Delta Y$. At that time, investment was running at about 10 per cent of national income: $Y = 10 \times I$. Let us put Y at 1,000. Then $I = 100$. Let us also assume that taxes are 20 per cent of national income, and that the marginal rate of tax payments equals the average rate. We then have

$$\Delta Y = \frac{1}{0.10 + 0.2} \cdot (\Delta I + 0.2Y) = \frac{1}{0.3} \cdot (100 + 200) = 1,000$$

$\Delta Y = 10 \cdot \Delta I$. On the other hand $\quad \Delta O = \Delta a \cdot Q + a \cdot \Delta Q$
$$= \Delta a \cdot Q + a \cdot \quad I.$$

Where Q is the stock (quantity) of capital and a the output-capital ratio. The incremental capital-output ratio in the country had been running between 2.5:1 and 3:1. Considering the structural change that was taking place, with increasing industrialization and the need for increased outlays in transport and power, it seemed likely that the incremental capital-output ratio would tend toward the upper end of this range for new investments. We also assume that the average capital-output ratio, including land as part of capital, would be lower, perhaps 2:1. Thus $Q = 2Y$.

The target of government policy was taken as maintaining the rate of increase in per capita income at 3 per cent. With population growing at 2.5 per cent per year, the required growth of national income as a whole was 5.5 per cent. Thus $I = 19 \cdot \Delta I; \dfrac{\Delta I}{I} = \dfrac{\Delta Y}{Y} = 5.5$ per cent; $\dfrac{100}{5.5} = 19.$

For purposes of illustration we might also assume that Δa is 1 per cent of Q. Technological progress, which made the existing stock of capital 1 per cent more productive each year, would be a fairly rapid rate, permitting some "catching up" of the underdeveloped country with the more advanced ones. We thus have $\Delta O = (0.01 \times 12) I + 0.3I = 0.42I$. Since $I = 19 \cdot \Delta I, \Delta O = 7.98 \, \Delta I$, or rounding off, $8 \, \Delta I$. We thus have $\Delta O = 8 \, \Delta I$, and $\Delta Y = 10 \, \Delta I$. $\Delta P = \Delta (Y/O) = \dfrac{O \cdot \Delta Y + Y \cdot \Delta O}{O^2}$. Beginning with $Y = O$ at current prices, we will clearly have a chronic inflationary gap under these circumstances.

Now let $n = N/Q$, where n is the job-capital ratio and N the total level of employment. Thus $N = n \cdot Q$ and $\Delta N = \Delta n \cdot Q + n \cdot I$. Let L equal labor force. Unemployment $U = L\text{-}N$, $\Delta U = \Delta L - \Delta N = \Delta L - (\Delta n \cdot Q + n \cdot I)$. In Brazil at that time, the labor force seemed to be growing at about 750,000 per year. In addition, it was planned to remove some 250,000 workers per year from the overpopulated areas in the neighborhood of Recife. Thus, to absorb the increase in the labor force, and create new jobs for the particularly low productivity workers of the Brazilian northeast, would require reducing unemployment only in so far as the persons resettled under the program were among the unemployed, rather than among the low productivity employed. If the capital-job ratio were $3,300, investment of 16 per cent of income (then running at about $10 billion) would be $3.3 billion. In other words, even with investment of 16 per cent of income, unemployment would tend to grow unless the capital-job ratio were below $3,300. Considering that for the ECAFE region as a whole the capital-employment ratio has been estimated at $2,500, it seems likely that investment in the modern sector and leading region of Brazil has a capital-job ratio well above $3,300. Thus, under these circumstances, a ratio of investment to national income that would create considerable inflationary pressure might nonetheless be accompanied by increasing unemployment.

Given this kind of sectoral and regional disintegration, no simple aggregative monetary and fiscal policies of the central government will suffice to eliminate both inflation and unemployment. What is required is not a unified national policy, but a carefully differentiated policy from region to region and sector to sector. It may even be necessary to have anti-inflationary policies in one region and anti-deflationary policies in another.

23 | Measures to Increase Savings

How far can voluntary domestic savings go toward meeting capital requirements where the rate of net investment must be doubled or trebled as part of the "minimum effort" needed for take-off?

In underdeveloped countries, the rate of voluntary saving is low, and existing institutions are not very successful in mobilizing such savings as there are. Most people have incomes so low that virtually all current income must be spent to maintain a subsistence level of consumption. However, there is considerable disparity in income levels among income recipients. Some groups, at least, receive real incomes high enough for a comfortable, even luxurious, standard of living and substantial savings as well. Prewar studies of income distribution in Indonesia showed significant inequalities.[1] In Japan, unequal distribution of income contributed greatly to financing developmental investment after the initial wave of government investment.[2] In an economy still in the stage of establishing preconditions for development, however, upper-income groups often assign considerable prestige value to conspicuous consumption. This propensity seems to be reinforced by what Ragnar Nurkse calls the "demonstration effect": people at all levels of income try to emulate standards of consumption in economically advanced societies.[3] Thus in the Philippines, despite great disparities in income and wealth, the rate of saving and investment is very

[1] J. J. Polak, *The National Income of the Netherlands Indies, 1921–1939* (New York, n.d.), pp. 64–66.
[2] William W. Lockwood, *The Economic Development of Japan* (Princeton, N.J., 1954), pp. 278-80.
[3] Ragnar Nurkse, *Problems of Capital Formation in Underdeveloped Countries* (Oxford, 1953), pp. 57–70.

low relative to national income.[4]

Moreover, the saving of the upper-income groups in these countries is seldom channeled into developmental investment. High rates of return on short-term loans to consumers, farmers, and traders, and speculative gains from hoarding goods attract capital into these channels instead. Pawnshops, the landlord who lends to tenants during the growing season on a share-cropping basis, the village moneylender, divert the savings of one group to financing consumer expenditures of others. Since the total supply of savings is low and consumption demands for credit are urgent, rates of return may be as high as 50 to 100 per cent per annum for consumer and trade credit while longer-term investments yield considerably less.

If voluntary savings from upper-income groups are to contribute to financing developmental investment, therefore, they must be mobilized by institutions capable of making them available to investors rather than con-sumers. Of course, this process means enforcing general reductions in consumption. If real income is growing, it is necessary only to restrict consumption to existing levels. The role of voluntary saving is therefore no different from taxation in effect upon consumption.

The political and social reawakening in many underdeveloped countries since the war inclines them toward the welfare state and a more egalitarian distribution of real income. Fiscal redistribution of income, social legisla-tion, and labor union activities backed by government policy, all tend to reduce inequalities in income distribution. Such redistribution usually does little to raise the real incomes in the lower ranges, even where higher in-comes have been significantly reduced. This process tends to reduce net saving.

Arthur Lewis has argued that the ratio of voluntary savings to national income is a function, not just of inequality of income distribution, but of inequality of a particular kind.[5] He maintains that voluntary savings have become a significantly large share of national income only where inequal-ity of income distribution is such that entrepreneurial profits are a rela-tively large share of national income. If unequal distribution of income exists and the society's upper incomes accrue to landlords or to traders, Lewis believes that there is little change of providing significant amounts of voluntary savings to finance investment. Profits, interest, and rental incomes as a whole are a much smaller share of national income in some underdeveloped economies than is general in advanced economies.

A study comparing these distributive shares as a percentage of national income in Indonesia (1938) and the United States (1951) seems to confirm this hypothesis. Profits, interest, and rental incomes represented about 24½ per cent of national income in the United States, but only 11 per cent in Indonesia.[6] On the other hand, in the Philippines it is clear that

[4] Cf. Benjamin Higgins, *Final Report to the Government of the Philippines* (New York, 1957).

[5] Arthur Lewis, *The Theory of Economic Growth* (Homewood, Ill., 1955), pp. 225–44.

[6] Charles Wolf, Jr., "Economic Development and Reform in South and Southeast Asia," *Far Eastern Quarterly*, XII (1952), pp. 29–30.

the share of entrepreneurial and property income is extraordinarily high, some 56 per cent, and still savings and investment are low. It should be emphasized, however, that this may not contradict Lewis' hypothesis since not all of these high incomes are true "capitalistic profits." Many of them reflect positions of privilege and power rather than returns to entrepreneurial endeavor.

In sum, the social and political context of some newly independent countries is hostile to the accumulation of capitalistic profits of the kind that played an important role in financing economic growth in the West. Both voluntary savings and private investment are likely to be less important in these countries than they were in the development of the now advanced ones. Nevertheless, savings have an important role to play in restricting consumption during the early stages of economic growth. Taxes are never popular, and there is much to be said for encouraging people in underdeveloped areas to save a larger share of their incomes voluntarily. Mobilization of small savings from the agricultural sector might permit more rapid development, if this sector cannot be reached by taxation. Voluntary savings amounting to only 2 or 3 per cent of national income might well prove to be the critical margin in permitting a take-off.

The literature on development of underdeveloped areas has several suggestions for increasing the supply of domestic loan funds. These suggestions are of unequal merit; let us review them.

Savings versus Credit

In assessing such proposals, it is essential to distinguish between savings and credit; the former is anti-inflationary, the latter is inflationary. Credit may be necessary for expansion in some fields, especially small agriculture and small industry. But the expansion of credit is in itself inflationary. Moreover, few underdeveloped countries lack credit institutions; some of them already have *too many*. Consider Indonesia, for example. Before the recent amalgamation of the larger government banks, there were the Bank Indonesia, the Bank Industri Negara, the Bank Negara, the Bank Umum Nasional, the Bank Rakjat Indonesia, the Housing Development Corporation, the *desa* banks, the post office savings system, the government pawnshops, and the credit activities of various ministries. In addition, there are private banks: the former large foreign commercial banks, which have been nationalized, and the many small Indonesian commercial banks. Carrying out an integrated monetary policy is almost impossible with such a plethora of institutions. And this sort of situation is all too common among underdeveloped countries.

To assure adequate credit control by the central bank, banking legislation should have the following features:

1. All banks should be licensed under national law.

2. All banks should be required to have a reasonably high minimum capital. Small banks complicate the problem of monetary control and weaken the banking system. It is much sounder to have a small number of strong commercial banks (preferably not more than ten) with head offices

in one center and branches scattered throughout the country, as in Australia, Canada, and England. In this way the whole country can be served, the risks of bank failure are minimized, funds can be moved easily in response to regional shifts in demand for credit, and at the same time an integrated monetary and fiscal policy becomes feasible and a disciplined banking system can gradually be built up.

3. The banks should be required to hold minimum reserves in the form of notes of or deposits with the central bank, subject to change by regulation.

4. In the absence of rediscounting or a broad open market, the central bank should have authority to control the volume of money in other ways. For example, it might be empowered to set a ceiling on deposits beyond which 100 per cent reserves in special reserve-privilege treasury notes are required. This system permits individual banks to expand, at the expense of others, by bidding away reserve-privilege notes from the less active banks. It also provides a ready market for government securities and so provides the foundations of open market policy. The interest rates paid on the bills can be low, not above 1 per cent.

5. The central bank should also have authority to impose selective credit controls, e.g., restrictions on consumer credit, loans for speculative purposes, for unessential construction, etc. Selective controls have recently proved quite successful in the United States, the United Kingdom, and Canada, and are an essential part of the tool kit for encouraging development and restraining inflation.

6. As a general rule the banks should be restrained from trading and from providing long-term capital. They should not be permitted to lend more than a certain proportion of their total assets to one client.

7. The banks should, however, be permitted to make term loans (one to five years) to finance purchases of equipment.

8. The number of financial institutions should be kept as small as possible. Special institutions for financing agriculture and small business should be brought within the system, and should be subject to control by the central bank.

It is sometimes argued that new financial institutions are needed to "channel" savings more effectively. Savings should be directed toward lending institutions, it is contended, so that they provide the basis for effective extension of credit, rather than being held as cash hoards or invested in jewels, gold, and the like. This argument in this form rests on a misunderstanding. The act of saving is essentially an act of restraint from current consumption; holding cash or buying jewelry (if it is already in the country) is as much saving as putting money into a bank. If the authorities can be assured that money withdrawn from circulation into cash hoards will remain in hoards, they can extend credit for development projects to an equal amount without inflationary effect; the net result will be exactly the same as if the money had been brought into the bank for deposit in the first place. True, money in hoards may be "hot," in the sense that it may suddenly be spent, requiring credit contraction if inflation is to be avoided. But the same situation would arise from any increase in velocity of circulation of existing deposits and notes in circulation; all money in existence is in a sense "hoarded" whenever it is not actually being spent. At most, the control of the authorities over the money supply is slightly greater if savings are channeled into credit institutions, rather than being held in cash hoards, jewelry, or the like.

There is, of course, some difference in the effects of hoarding, depending on the forms it takes. Hoarding currency, or holding unused bank balances, is clearly deflationary. If hoarding takes the form of buying jewelry or precious metals already in the country, the effect is to raise the price of these commodities while reducing inflationary pressure on other prices, permitting an increase in development spending without any rise in the general price level. Indeed, it is not even certain that the prices of jewelry will rise. In some countries, such as Libya, there are dealers in the silver bracelets commonly used to store wealth, who are essentially bankers performing a species of "counterspeculation" function. They buy and sell, by weight, within narrow margins. They "hoard" when the market is "dishoarding," and vice versa.

If hoarding takes the form of importing jewelry or precious metals, the effect is wholly anti-inflationary, but such hoarding is less anti-inflationary than use of equivalent amounts of foreign exchange for imports of consumers' goods to be sold in local markets. From the standpoint of economic development, it is obvious that a much greater contribution would be made by using the foreign exchange to finance needed raw materials and equipment.

If hoarding takes the form of buying land, with a consequent rise in land values, there may be repercussions on prices of agricultural products. However, since *demand* for final products is *reduced* by the process of bidding up land prices, the net effect is still likely to be deflationary on balance, unless the land is actually withdrawn from use.

Hoarding in the form of holding livestock rather than slaughtering, a practice common in arid zones in good rainfall years, is clearly inflationary. Such practices might be regarded as "investment in inventories," rather than hoarding, but they perform much the same function as accumulation of liquid assets in advanced countries.

Thus it is not apparent that channeling savings into financial institutions adds significantly to the amount of development that can be undertaken without inflation. Perhaps use of savings institutions will develop the savings habit and so raise the ratio of savings to income, but this result is not certain. Nor is it clear that monetization of the economy will increase productivity. There is no obvious and significant difference between the motivation to work and to save between peasants living in a partly non-monetary economy, and that of workers on plantations receiving most of their income in a money wage. It is hard to discern any sharp differences in average or marginal propensities to save between peasants and government employees whose entire income is in money. Monetary economies are usually richer than non-monetary ones; but the casual connection is *from* low production *to* poverty *to* a non-monetary economy, not vice versa. Monetization will follow an increase in productivity, but there is no assurance that an increase in productivity will follow monetization. Indeed a mere increase in money supply might be used to finance increased hoarding of goods. In Indonesia, a temporary reduction of the money supply during 1953, which was felt with particular intensity in rural areas, was very successful in forcing dishoarding of goods.

Sometimes the case is made for new financial institutions in terms of high interest rates that now prevail. Interest rates in some underdeveloped countries, especially for certain categories of agricultural loans, are no doubt extremely high. However, these interest rates do not always reflect insufficient monetization of the rural sector or even a lack of credit facilities. Sometimes high interest rates charged by moneylenders exist side by side with low interest rates from government credit institutions in the same locality. The peasant often prefers to borrow at high rates from a moneylender rather than meet the formal requirements of a government lending agency. The high interest rates may reflect accurately the risk of the loan. Moreover, there is a question whether the lower interest rates which can be provided by the government agency represent a real increase in the supply of investible funds or mere monetary expansion. If it is the latter, the gains through such "monetization" will be small indeed.

Proliferation of savings and credit institutions, then, is no substitute for a genuine increase in savings. This is not to say that new and specialized institutions, such as agricultural banks or housing agencies, may not play a useful role in economic development under certain conditions. Sometimes existing financial organizations do a poor job of allocating credit because of the prejudices and limited experience of their personnel. Managers of large commercial banks may underestimate the productivity of small loans to agriculture or may exaggerate the risk attached. In these circumstances, specialized institutions to finance agriculture, with personnel experienced in and sympathetic to this field of endeavor, may be needed to make sure that small farmers get their proper share of total available capital funds. Such organizations can also do a useful job of training, linking "extension work" to loans.

Finally, in such fields as housing and small business, specialized institutions can often operate more flexibly than the more hidebound existing agencies. For example, a case can sometimes be made for giving loans in kind, that is, for a policy of deliberate demonetization of the rural sector. Arab members of the United Nations Working Party on Fiscal Policy in Libya were quite insistent that agricultural credit should be given in kind; if it were given in money, they contended, the farmers would merely buy themselves additional wives.

Government Borrowing

The effects of government borrowing on the spending stream depend on where and how government loans are raised. When virtually all loan funds come directly or indirectly from the central bank, as in Indonesia or the Philippines, the result is highly inflationary. The process is all the more inflationary if commercial banks hold legal reserves in notes or deposits of the central bank; it then increases the flow of money directly and also permits credit expansion by the banks. Borrowing directly or indirectly from the commercial banks is very little better.

Selling securities to the general public is more likely to have neutralizing effects on expenditure of the funds; if the securities are bought with income that would otherwise be spent, whether on consumers' goods or on capital goods, the government borrowing is thoroughly anti-inflationary. If, on the other hand, the offer by the government of safe, liquid securities yielding an attractive return merely diverts savings from other liquid assets, such as currency or savings accounts, government borrowing has little anti-inflationary effect. Generally speaking, the farther down the income scale the government succeeds in placing securities, the more likely it is that the purchase of securities will displace spending, rather than other forms of saving, and the more anti-inflationary the borrowing is likely to be.

It has been suggested that governments of underdeveloped countries should attach special features to their obligations, designed to make them attractive to potential savers. Maturities and interest rates should be patterned as much as possible to fit current savings habits. Government securities should be easily liquidated, perhaps by providing a ready market in the central bank. Issues might be constantly available "on tap" in the central bank and its branches, and always salable to the bank at preannounced prices. In order to provide an inducement to keep securities rather than cashing them, interest rates might be made to rise as the obligation approaches maturity. Where legal or religious bans on "usury" are a deterrent to purchase of interest-bearing securities (not a problem in most countries), the securities might bear no stipulated interest but might appreciate in value as they approach maturity. Some countries have found it useful to introduce lottery features in connection with their public obligations. Government securities may be more attractive if attached to particular projects, such as assisting land ownership for small farmers (important where feudal systems of land ownership are widespread), housing, or development projects.

All such devices are worth trying. It is doubtful whether any very large flow of savings will be stimulated in the near future by such measures alone, but there is no reason for not doing whatever is possible in this way.

Other tailor-made features of government securities may be more effective. There is still a shortage of *credit* (as distinct from credit facilities) in most rural areas, while at the same time some of the more prosperous traders and farmers have occasional surpluses of cash. Perhaps they could be persuaded to buy securities if they were assured that they would always be accepted as collateral for loans from an agricultural or small business loan bank. Of course, this system would bring a net increase in savings only to the extent that the securities were *not* used as a basis for borrowing. Another feature that might be attractive is tax payment privileges; that is, a guarantee that the securities would always be acceptable at face value for payment of taxes. This guarantee would be a partial assurance against the risk of depreciation of the internal value of the securities through inflation.

Some writers have suggested that tax exemption be granted to investors in bonds; but this feature is useful only if it encourages the growth of savings habits, so that later on savings will continue even if the tax exemption feature is dropped. Paying taxes is at least as effective as saving in preventing inflation from arising out of development spending—perhaps more so, since as pointed out above, the man who has accumulated savings may feel justified in spending a larger share of current income. Perhaps the feature that would be most attractive of all, especially to foreigners, would be a guarantee that principal and interest would be maintained at face value in gold or dollars. This guarantee would be a safeguard against devaluation of the currency, fear of which is a major deterrent to investment in some government securities.

Marketing Boards

In a number of African countries, government marketing boards have been used as an instrument for compulsory saving by paying growers prices below the world market level. The present writer has no direct experience with such boards.[7] Peter Bauer, who has, is not enthusiastic about them. He does not deny that "the heavy accumulation of surpluses by the boards . . . raises total savings" where "the level of capital is very low." [8] But he maintains that the boards reduce private saving, and in his view this result entails "disadvantages beyond the obvious and substantial adverse effect on the level of supply and on individual incentive to produce." It retards the growth of the personal saving habit in countries where this habit is just getting established, as shown for example by the "great increase and improvement of building, especially house-building, for Africans" in Nigeria and the Gold Coast.[9] To Bauer it seems "paradoxical" to pay producers less than half the market price and then send around teams to encourage increased production, as the Nigerian Marketing Board has done.

Conclusions

In general, our answer to the question asked at the beginning of this chapter seems to be, "Not very far." It is highly unlikely that measures to increase voluntary domestic savings alone—or even measures for voluntary and compulsory savings together—can provide all the financial resources needed for development of underdeveloped countries. At the same time, there is no reason to eschew measures which hold promise of bringing

[7] The Indonesian *Jajasan Copra* is not a good test case for judging the effectiveness of marketing boards in increasing aggregate savings and investment. Squeezing out profits from copra growing was not a purpose pursued vigorously or continuously, and in recent years, much of the copra export was smuggled directly to Singapore, bypassing the Copra Foundation altogether.
[8] P. T. Bauer, *West African Trade* (Cambridge, 1954), p. 313.
[9] *Ibid.*, p. 314.

some increase in the flow of savings. There can be no doubt that the ratio of savings to income varies enormously from one underdeveloped country to another, and the differences reflect variations in policy to some extent at least.

24 Tax Policies

Domestic financing of economic development requires increased total savings (including taxes) and investment (public and private). When total output remains relatively constant over time, an economy can generate a higher level of total saving only by reducing its existing level of consumption. If previously idle factors of production can be brought into use, of course, investment can take place without either a reduction in consumption or inflation. Where such excess capacity is insufficient for a minimum effort, where voluntary savings are inadequate, and where foreign aid is not sought or offered in sufficient quantities, the launching of a take-off may require "collective thrift" through taxation.[1]

Taxes versus Savings

Which is better, taxes or savings? There is no simple or general answer to this question. The main purpose of either, from the standpoint of development finance, is to permit increased public and private investment without inflation. Taxes which are paid at the expense of savings rather than at the expense of current spending are not anti-inflationary at all. On the other hand, it has been argued that taxes not only make people poorer, but make people *feel* poorer, whereas an increase in savings, with the accompanying increase in liquid assets, makes people feel better off; consequently, the reduction in spending is likely to be greater if a certain sum is raised in taxes than if it is raised in savings. Much depends also on what

[1] This is Nurkse's apt term for savings forced by government fiscal policy. Cf. Ragnar Nurkse, *Problem of Capital Formation in Underdeveloped Countries*, p. 151.

income is most affected by an increase in savings or in tax collections. By and large, the upper-income groups tend to be savers, and the lower-income groups spenders. Thus the anti-inflationary effects of taxes or savings are likely to be greater if obtained from lower-income groups, than if the same volume of taxes or savings is obtained from the higher-income groups. The unpleasant task of limiting the consumption of the middle- and lower-income groups—and thus limiting total consumption—is probably easier *administratively* through taxes than through measures to increase savings.

Taxation: The Question of Tax Capacity

With these considerations in mind, let us consider briefly some of the major questions that arise with regard to tax financing of economic development. The first of these questions is likely to be: "How much can be collected in taxes? What is the 'taxable capacity' of underdeveloped countries? What tax burden can they bear?" There is no simple answer to this question either. Today, among businessmen, trade-union officials, government advisers, and even professional economists, from Canada to Indonesia, one hears the statement that, when tax rates reach a certain limit, further increases in tax rates will be inflationary rather than deflationary. It is the present writer's opinion that this statement is based upon a misunderstanding and that its frequent repetition in high places calls for a restatement of home truths regarding the economic effects of taxation.

The Colin Clark Argument

The statement that excessive taxation is inflationary is sometimes supported by reference to Colin Clark's article on "Public Finance and Changes in the Value of Money." [2] The basic thesis of this article is that the ceiling to tax revenues in peacetime is about 25 per cent of national income. However, Colin Clark's main argument was not economic but political. It ran, in effect: if the tax burden becomes uncomfortably high, one or another politically powerful group will bring pressure successfully and so relieve the burden. Clark's somewhat scanty data really show only that before World War I, and again between the wars, several countries collected less than 25 per cent of national income in taxes most of the time. In the "analysis" with which Clark "explains" his facts, he argues that since people do not like paying taxes, in democratic countries the government will find it difficult to impose a heavy tax burden for very long, except when the major power groups in the community are in the mood to make sacrifices, as during a war. By the same token, however, Clark's evidence and explanation, carried into the war and postwar periods, suggests that wherever these powerful groups are prepared to make sacrifices, in order to assist the government in carrying out some program entailing heavy expenditures, the tax burden can be increased. For example, if these

[2] Colin Clark, "Public Finance and Changes in the Value of Money," *Economic Journal*, December, 1945, pp. 371–89.

TAX POLICIES
515

groups consider an economic development program to be as important as war, they will accept tax burdens as great as those in wartime.

The share of income that people will be willing to pay out in taxes is by no means independent of the level and structure of government expenditures. If the ratio of government expenditures to national income rises, so that relatively more goods and services are being offered in exchange for taxes and relatively fewer are sold for prices, and if the goods and services provided by government yield satisfactions as high as those formerly bought in the market, there is no reason why people should not accept a higher ratio of taxes to income. Indeed, if no redistribution of income and no reallocation of resources were involved there is no theoretical reason why a strongly supported government should not collect 100 per cent of personal income, and pay it out again in family allowances, pensions, interest on debt, etc., without any economic effects whatsoever.

Much the same sort of argument applies here as in the discussions of the burden of national debt; if no redistribution of real income is entailed, there is no real burden and, therefore, no economic limit. There can be a "burden" for particular income groups if they suffer a net loss of real income through the fiscal process, and this burden may have an unfavorable effect on their incentive to work or to invest. There can also be a "burden" for the community as a whole, if government expenditures provide goods and services of a less satisfactory kind than would be provided by private enterprise were the same amount of income spent in the market. But this latter argument amounts only to saying that there is a limit to the extent to which a democratic government can alter the distribution of resources, in a manner reducing psychic income, without destroying the incentives to work and invest, or losing its political support, or both. This statement is axiomatic, but it provides no rationale for an "iron law" regarding the ratio of taxes to income. How much people will pay in taxes, without shifting their political support, and without working or investing less, depends on the value they place on what they get for their money.

How far short of the theoretical maximum the actual maximum is depends on the effects of the fiscal process on various groups, on the relative political power of these groups, and on the degree of enthusiasm felt by the people for the government's program. If the people of the underdeveloped countries could have the same unity of purpose with respect to development as did the people of advanced countries with respect to the war effort during World War II, the ratio of tax collections to national income, for the purpose of financing the development program, could be high. Where such unity of purpose does not exist, and where the fiscal process of collecting and spending money redistributes income from politically powerful groups to politically weak ones, the limit of taxable capacity is likely to be low.[3]

Taxable capacity also depends on the skill with which the tax system is adapted to the institutional framework. For example, it has been sug-

[3] For a more complete discussion of this point, see Benjamin Higgins, "A Note on Taxation and Inflation," *Canadian Journal of Economics and Political Science,* August, 1953.

gested that the experience of mainland China, Taiwan, and Korea indicates that higher levels of agricultural taxation are possible if taxes are collected in grain rather than in money. By collecting taxes in kind, the government performs marketing functions which increase the ability of producers to dispose of their surplus output and so raises their taxable capacity.

The question of taxable capacity is therefore related to the question of incentives. Current income may not be a satisfactory indication of taxable capacity because the imposition of the tax may itself provide an incentive for increasing production and income. This situation is said to prevail in a number of Latin American countries, where potentially fertile land is allowed to go unused by big landlords. Considerations such as these influenced a mission from the International Bank for Reconstruction and Development to recommend to the government of Colombia that land be taxed in terms of potential rather than actual yield.[4]

Moreover, in underdeveloped countries there is more difference than in advanced ones between taxes that can be *imposed* and taxes than can be *collected*. It is generally agreed that tax revenues in underdeveloped countries could be substantially increased, without increase in tax rates, by improved tax administration and enforcement. Part of the explanation may be found in the large proportion of income earned in agriculture. The assessment of agricultural income, especially in relatively primitive economies where bookkeeping is virtually unknown within the agricultural sphere, is extraordinarily complex and provides opportunities for both laxity and corruption. Sometimes it is easier for local government officials to collect taxes in full than it is for central government officials, who may be regarded as interlopers in the outlying regions of a country. In general, collections could be improved by encouragement to, or where feasible an insistence upon, proper accounting. The organization of marketing cooperatives may help a government collect taxes in the agricultural sector. Each government of underdeveloped countries must assess these factors for itself.

Taxation and Inflation

We have stated above that the main purpose of collecting more taxes is to permit increased government spending without inflation. Some recent literature, however, has suggested that taxation may aggravate rather than alleviate inflationary pressures. Since this controversy has direct bearing on the problem of financing development in underdeveloped countries, a brief discussion of this question is in order.

Some of the confusion about the effects of tax increases in an inflationary period springs from failure to distinguish the effects of collecting taxes from the effects of collecting and spending them. Those who maintain that increases in taxation have obviously been inflationary, merely because prices have risen even where taxes were high enough to balance budgets, clearly fail to take account of the "Haavelmo proposition." Haavelmo has

[4] H. P. Wald and J. N. Froomkin (eds.), *Papers and Proceedings of the Conference on Agricultural Taxation and Economic Development* (Cambridge, Mass., 1954), p. 17.

demonstrated that, even without any redistribution of income from savers to spenders, a balanced budget is in itself inflationary. It adds to monetary income an amount just equal to the amount of government spending and under conditions of full employment, any addition to money incomes is in itself inflationary.

Although the Haavelmo proposition is by now widely accepted, the simple corollary that a budget must produce a surplus to be "neutral" has not received enough attention. A much simplified version of the Haavelmo argument would be as follows: let Y be national income, E be government expenditures, T, tax revenues, and c, the marginal propensity to consume. The expansionary effects of government expenditures (on goods and services) will then be

$$\Delta Y = \Delta E \ (1 + c + c^2 + c^3 + \ldots + c^n)$$

Since taxes are not an income generator and influence the level of national income only through their effects on spending in the period following their collection, the deflationary effects of collecting taxes will be

$$- \Delta Y = \Delta T \ (0 + c + c^2 + c^3 + \ldots + c^n)$$

Thus if E equals T, the net effect of the budget, $E - T$, is to raise national income by the amount of E (or T). This argument ignores the effects of taxation on investment, but since it is based on the assumption that no redistribution of income takes place through the fiscal process and since net income is increased, there is no reason why investment should be influenced very much one way or the other. If there is any effect, it will presumably aggravate the inflationary pressure. Of course, if the fiscal process redistributes income from savers to spenders, the effects through the multiplier process will be still more inflationary, but the effects on investment may then be deflationary.

The somewhat startling corollary of the Haavelmo proposition is that, if a budget is to be "neutral," the ratio of government expenditures (on goods and services) to tax revenues cannot exceed the marginal propensity to consume. That is, if the marginal propensity to consume is two-thirds, the ratio of government expenditures to tax revenues cannot exceed two-thirds. Put in another way, "neutrality" in the budget requires a ratio of budget surplus to total revenues of one minus the marginal propensity to consume. With a marginal propensity to consume of two-thirds, the budget surplus must be equal to one-third of total tax revenues if the budget is to be neutral. Given a marginal propensity to consume of four-fifths, which may be more realistic for some countries, a neutral budget would be one in which the ratio of government expenditures to tax revenues is four-fifths, and in which the budget surplus is one-fifth of total revenues.[5]

[5] In this discussion "national income" means net national income at market prices, and not personal or disposable income. Consequently, the appropriate marginal propensity to consume to use in making an estimate of the budget surplus necessary to prevent inflationary effects from government spending should be the marginal propensity to consume out of national income, and not out of personal income or out of disposable income. For the less developed countries, a marginal propensity to

This corollary of the Haavelmo proposition can be easily proved by putting figures into the above equation. Let us suppose, for example, that government expenditures are 10 (billion dollars or rupiahs) and that the marginal propsensity to consume is four-fifths, giving a multiplier of five. In order for the budget to be neutral, assuming no redistribution of income and thus no effects on investments through the fiscal process, tax revenues must be 12.5 billion and the budget surplus must be 2.5 billion. Substituting these figures in the above equations, it will be seen that the increase in income generated by government expenditures will be 50 billion, and that the reductions in national income generated by collection of taxes will be 50 billion. Thus, on the assumption made, the whole process of collecting taxes and spending them on goods and services will have no effect on the level of national income. With a marginal propensity to consume out of national income of three-fourths, government spending of 10 billion would require tax revenues of 13.3 billion, or a budget surplus of 3.3 billion. With a marginal propensity to consume of two-thirds, a budget of 10 billion would require tax revenue of 15 billion and a budget surplus of 5 billion if the budget is to be neutral.

The limitations of this analysis must be borne in mind. It ignores the effects on investment of the announcement of a particular tax policy, and it ignores the effects of any redistribution of income through the fiscal process. It also ignores the effects on incentives of a change in the composition of national income as a result of extension of government activity. Limited as it is, however, the Haavelmo proposition, with the corollary outlined above, teaches a valuable lesson. The fact that some countries have succeeded in balancing their budgets, or even in producing small surpluses, is no reason to expect that the fiscal policy of these countries should have succeeded in checking inflation, especially when there was strong expansionary pressure from credit-financed private investment or from increasing exports. Budget surpluses in most countries have been far too small to prevent the net effect of the fiscal process alone from being inflationary. Indeed, it seems unlikely that any country in the world has been courageous enough to follow a "neutral" fiscal policy during the postwar period. True neutrality would have required budget surpluses and taxes far higher than most governments were strong enough to impose.

High taxes combined with equally high government expenditures are certainly inflationary. The inflationary component of a large budget is the expenditure side, however, not the tax side. If, in the simple equations presented above, expenditures remain at the stipulated levels, while no taxes

consume out of national income of four-fifths may be fairly realistic. In advanced countries, however, a marginal propensity to consume closer to three-fourths or even two-thirds would probably be more realistic. In that case, a neutral budget would be one in which the budget surplus is equal to one-fourth or one-third of total tax revenues.

For a systematic presentation of the requirements for "neutral" budgetary policy in somewhat more complex cases, see Haskell P. Wald, "Fiscal Policy, Military Preparedness, and Postwar Inflation," in Arthur Smithies and J. Keith Butters (eds.), *Readings in Fiscal Policy* (Homewood, Ill., 1955).

are collected at all, it is obvious that the net inflationary effects of government fiscal policy will be far greater than if budgets are balanced. The collection of taxes, in itself, reduces national income (spending) by a multiple of the amount of taxes collected, a multiple that is one less than the multiplier operating on government expenditures. For clear thinking about tax policy, it is essential to distinguish the effects of collecting taxes from the effects of collecting *and spending* them. In what follows we shall assume that the level of government expenditures is a datum and concentrate our attention on the effects of collecting taxes as such.

Other Objectives of Tax Policy

Offsetting the inflationary effects of development spending is not the only matter of concern in collecting taxes or encouraging savings. A government must consider the effect of its monetary and fiscal policies on incentives, on the allocation of resources, and on the distribution of income. Administrative problems must also be taken into account.

The collection of taxes may destroy the incentives which are the very mainsprings of economic growth. Taxes which fall on the wage earner may diminish the incentive to work harder and better; taxes which fall on profits of enterprise or on the higher-income groups may undermine the incentive to save and to make investments in new (and hence risky) enterprises. Taxes on output or income of farmers may reduce the incentive to improve agricultural techniques. Somehow the tax system must be devised so as to provide the necessary offset to the inflationary effects of development spending without destroying these incentives.

An incentive problem may also arise with regard to saving. Providing credit for private ventures associated with the development program—such as use of fertilizers or improved tools and the establishment of new industries—is the exact opposite of saving and is in itself inflationary. Yet the provision of such credit may be one of the most effective incentives to these development projects, and failure to provide adequate credit facilities may be a major barrier to expansion. Reconciling the need to provide incentives and the need to prevent inflation is thus a problem of credit policy as well as of tax policy.

Any pattern of government expenditure and taxes affects the relative attractiveness of various occupations and various uses of capital. It will therefore have an effect on the allocation of resources. Unless careful consideration is given to this effect, it may be haphazard or positively disadvantageous. The method chosen to finance a development program should affect the resource allocation in a manner tending to promote, rather than to retard, economic development. Also, the fiscal system should be carefully scrutinized to see whether it may create or strengthen monopoly positions, thus leading to misallocation of resources, and whether it may discourage desirable enterprises or encourage undesirable ones.

The fiscal pattern will also affect the distribution of the fruits of economic development among various individuals and groups. The determination of an "optimal" distribution of income is a matter for the social philosopher rather than the economic development planner; but one must take into account the generally accepted view that greater equality of income distribution is preferable to greater inequality, other things being equal. Where two fiscal systems are equally effective in promoting economic development, but one leads to greater equality of income distribution and the other to greater inequality, the former system would be considered preferable by most people. Thus consideration of the effect of financing economic development on income distribution is a part of the process of planning economic development.

Taxation: The Question of Structure

In nearly all underdeveloped countries some attention should be given to the problem of tax structure. Sometimes the tax system incorporates a large number of "nuisance taxes" which yield very little revenue, which are administratively expensive, and which are an annoyance to the taxpayer. This was true, for example, of the slaughter tax and the "statistical tax" in Indonesia, which were introduced by the Dutch authorities for reasons long since forgotten. Similar items exist in the tax structure of a good many countries. Removal of such nuisance taxes is one of the relatively easy steps toward tax reform.

Foreign "experts" are often struck by the difference between the overall structure of taxes in underdeveloped countries and in advanced countries. As a general rule underdeveloped countries rely much more heavily on indirect taxes, such as sales taxes, import duties, and the like, and much less heavily on such direct taxes as income and inheritance taxes, than do advanced countries. At first blush this relatively heavy dependence on indirect taxes strikes the foreign observer as highly "regressive." Here, however, caution must be exercised. It is often quite impossible to increase the share of tax revenues from income tax merely by increasing income tax rates. Indeed some of the underdeveloped countries already have income tax structures which are heavier and more steeply progressive than those of more highly developed areas. Moreover, the governments of some underdeveloped countries have learned how to build a high degree of progressivity into their indirect tax systems, which may provide a more effective way of relating tax collections to income than an increase in income tax rates. With the institutional framework and administrative system existing in some underdeveloped countries, income taxes are too easily avoided. Finally, with incomes so low and with supply curves of labor and capital turning backward at such low levels of income, unfavorable "incentive" effects may occur at much lower ratios of income tax to income than in advanced countries.

As a long-run policy, increased reliance on income taxes, as administration and compliance improve, should no doubt be a goal of most underdeveloped countries. Meanwhile, however, astute uses of indirect taxes are to be recommended.

Inheritance taxes, on the other hand, could probably be introduced more quickly, from the purely administrative point of view, than extension of income taxes. The problem here is more apt to be political, since in many underdeveloped countries large property owners, who would be most strongly opposed to inheritance taxes, still wield considerable political power. Similarly, corporation income taxes if not noticeably higher than in other countries are a good source of revenue for underdeveloped countries. Many corporations are likely to be foreign, reducing the political problem, and they must keep accurate accounts.

In countries so largely agricultural, some use of land taxes would appear to be inevitable if the anti-inflationary potential of taxation is to be fully realized and if an equitable distribution of the tax burden is to be achieved. From the standpoint of equity, and perhaps also from the standpoint of yield, some gearing of land tax assessment to the output of the land taxed is desirable. From an incentive viewpoint, on the other hand, a lump-sum tax, which is not related to current output, is preferable. This point is discussed more fully below under the heading of "Incentive Taxes."

Because of the relative ease of control over goods passing international borders and the relative completeness of records of goods moving in international trade, many underdeveloped countries have found it desirable to rely heavily on import taxes and export duties as sources of revenue. As already suggested, it is not too difficult to introduce into such taxes on foreign trade a degree of progressivity, which removes from them any serious disadvantages from the standpoint of equity. Nor need they constitute a more serious interference with the volume and structure of trade than any other kind of tax system.[6] The major disadvantage of this type of tax is its instability. Since many underdeveloped countries are primarily producers, exporting foodstuffs, agricultural raw materials, and industrial raw materials, and importing manufactured goods, the volume, balance, and terms of trade tend to move together. Revenues tend to be buoyant during periods of world depression. Export duties are particularly unsatisfactory from this point of view, for in their case, there may be a conflict between measures necessary to improve a budgetary situation and measures necessary to improve the balance of payments. In order to close budgetary gaps in periods of falling export prices, export duties should be raised. But an increase in export levies, in conjunction with falling world market prices of exports, could prove so discouraging to exporters as seriously to diminish the volume, adding further to the difficulties of earning foreign exchange. If the level of money income is closely related to exports, however, and the traditional sector is too poor to tax, no change in tax structure can divorce revenues from the vagaries of the export market.

Local Government Finance

An important aspect of tax structure is the allocation of tax functions among different levels of government. Few underdeveloped countries are wholly free of problems regarding the financial relationships between cen-

[6] Cf. E. M. Bernstein, "Some Aspects of Multiple Exchange Rates"; and B. H. Higgins, "The Rationale of Import Surcharges," *Economics and Finance in Indonesia* (*Ekonomi dan Keuangan Indonesia*), May, 1953.

POLICIES

522

tral and local governments. The precise nature of the problem, of course, varies from country to country. Financial questions are related to responsibility for planning and executing development projects and so to the general division of powers among central and local governments. On the one hand are countries with federal constitutions, such as India and Brazil, where central government officials sometimes feel inhibited in the planning, financing, and execution of development projects by the constitutional powers specifically allocated to the provinces. In unitary countries like Indonesia and the Philippines on the other hand, complaints are sometimes heard in areas remote from the capital that financial powers are too heavily concentrated in the hands of the central government.

Each underdeveloped country must seek its own optimum mix between central and local contributions. Each has certain advantages which cannot readily be transferred from one level of government to the other. Central fiscal devices, for example, are appropriate to levy taxation upon major components of national income which are generated in a particular geographic area or sector of the economy. The taxation of income arising from foreign trade provides one example. Local fiscal processes, on the other hand, are necessarily decentralized in impact and can best be designed to reach income arising from scattered geographic areas. They appear to have special advantages for the direct mobilization of unemployed or partially unemployed resources in many occupations traditional to the underdeveloped economy.

A few generalizations can be made. First, if the rural people who constitute the bulk of the population in most underdeveloped countries are to understand the process of economic development, some projects must be carried out at the local level, so as to demonstrate the relationship between investment and rising standards of living. Only local projects with clear "demonstration effects" will engender widespread support for the over-all program of economic development. If a wholehearted effort is to be made to increase domestic financial resources for economic development, widespread popular support for the plan is essential. As already indicated, taxable capacity itself is not unrelated to the degree of enthusiasm for the program of expenditures. There is much to be said for having a substantial portion of the development program planned, financed, and executed at the local government level.

Second, taxes which are likely to be unpopular, or difficult to administer from a distance, are in general more suitable for local governments. In particular, taxes which require much administrative discretion, such as those involving assessment of land values, surmise income taxes, and the like, are as a rule better administered by local government officials who are known to the taxpayers and who are considered to represent them. Against this clear advantage is the danger that personal favoritism and discrimination may be greater if taxes of this kind are administered by local officials, who are subject to more or less continuous pressures, than if they are administered from the center. On balance, in the early stages of a development program, the advantage would seem to lie with local administration of such taxes.

By the same token, taxes which are collected in a form difficult to measure precisely, such as labor services or taxes in kind, are probably more easily administered at the local level. Experience with "community self-help programs" indicates that a substantial volume of resources for economic development can be obtained in the form of labor, if the development projects are organized and executed by local governments for the immediate benefit of the local citizenry.

Incentive Taxes

The literature on public finance in advanced countries has devoted a good deal of attention to "incentive taxation." However important the incentive aspects of taxation may be in advanced countries, their importance in underdeveloped countries is clearly much greater; it is easier to sustain a process of steady growth than it is to initiate it. The purpose of incentive taxation is to stimulate an increase in the flow of labor or managerial effort, or of savings and investment, or to improve the allocation of capital, land, labor, and entrepreneurship.

The term "incentive taxation" has been used with some ambiguity. Indeed it might refer to any of six kinds of tax measures. The term is sometimes used erroneously to mean reductions in tax rates, which are designed to provide incentives for increased effort or risk-taking. In some circumstances, general tax reductions may indeed provide an incentive to increased productivity, but the circumstances under which a general reduction in tax rates would raise the flow of goods by more than it raises the flow of spending are rare. General tax cuts are usually inflationary, and incentive taxation in this sense must be eschewed by most underdeveloped countries.

Secondly, the term may be applied to selective tax reductions, designed to improve the balance of prospective gains and prospective losses on new investment, without necessarily reducing the total tax burden on taxpayers as a group. An example of this kind of incentive measure is the averaging of profits for tax purposes over a number of years, to improve the prospects of average profits after tax, for investment subject to violent fluctuations in demand for its product. The averaging of profits for tax purposes is especially important in such risky fields as mining, petroleum, rubber plantations, and the like, which have a long production cycle and are subject to substantial fluctuations in prices.

Another example of this kind of incentive taxation is the exemption of new investment from taxes for a certain number of years. Investment in new industries always carries more risk than expansion of old ones, and expansion of old ones is more risky than mere replacement. Moreover, there is some reason to suppose that the "chain reaction" effects on the pace of economic development are greater for new investment than for expansion of existing industries. Agricultural taxes which impose lower rates for increases in output than for "normal" returns, thus reducing the risk attached to improvements in agricultural techniques, might also be included under this heading.

Exempting new investment from taxes is a policy to be handled with care; it should be introduced only where it is quite certain to encourage investment that would not otherwise take place. An example of injudicious application of this policy was to be found in the Philippines during the 1950's, when a very wide range of enterprises was classified as "new and essential" and accorded tax freedom, with no very clear stimulus to private net investment, which remained about 5 per cent of national income. Complete tax freedom is an enormous concession to make and unnecessary for industries that prove profitable in the early years of their lives.

Third, tax rates might be increased or reduced selectively, in such a way as to control either the allocation or the timing of investment. One such system of incentive taxation, which has been used with considerable success in Canada and which was recommended in the Five-Year Economic and Social Development Plan in the Philippines, is "accelerated" and "postponed" depreciation. In general, the principle of accelerated depreciation, introduced by the Canadian government at the end of 1944, permits more rapid write-off of plant and equipment for tax purposes. Initially, the privilege of accelerated depreciation was allowed to industries which were converting from wartime to peacetime uses. With the outbreak of war in Korea, the accelerated depreciation privilege was allowed to defense industries and to industries significant for Canada's basic development. The principle of postponed or deferred depreciation introduced into the 1951 budget meant that except for the defense or developmental industries which the government wished to encourage, the right to charge capital costs against income for tax purposes was postponed, in this case for four years.

Fourth, incentive taxes may be imposed not with the purpose of collecting them, but to persuade people to take certain action to avoid them. In this category would be included taxes on hoarding, whether goods or of money. In underdeveloped countries, speculative hoarding of goods is likely to be the more serious problem. By imposing a penal tax on inventories held in excess of some stipulated "normal," the prospective profitability of such speculation can be removed and goods forced into the market, diminishing the inflationary pressure from development spending.[7] Occasionally hoarding of money also becomes a problem, especially if it occurs side by side with hoarding of goods.

Sometimes tax proposals are linked with proposals for subsidies. For example, it would be possible to provide a subsidy for investments of a kind which the government wishes to encourage, and then impose a lump-sum or percentage tax on profits, so as to recoup the subsidy plus any "supernormal" profits remaining when the desired scale of production is reached. The subsidy would encourage production of the desired kind, and a lump-sum or percentage tax on profits cannot be "shifted;" that is, it cannot be avoided by reducing output and raising price. In short, the subsidies serve to expand output in the desired direction, and the recapturing of the subsidy through a lump-sum or percentage tax on profits will not be

_____

[7] The administration of such a system is described in detail in Chap. 25.

a deterrent to this expansion. The Italian government has utilized subsidies in somewhat this manner, to encourage land reclamation.[8]

Fifth, there are incentive taxes which compel increases in output by the taxpayer, to enable him to meet the assessment. In this category are the poll tax or head tax and lump-sum taxes on land.

It is a long-standing proposition in the literature of public finance that a head tax or poll tax is desirable from the standpoint of incentive, because it is unrelated to the volume of output or to the level of income earned. The tax is not reduced if productivity is diminished nor is it increased if output is raised. In underdeveloped countries, where a larger number of workers, farmers, or entrepreneurs may be operating slightly above the level at which their supply curves turn backward, the case for the poll tax is even stronger; for by reducing income net of tax, more effort or risk-taking is called forth; output must be increased to meet the tax while maintaining "customary normal" standards of living. Unfortunately, in underdeveloped countries this "customary normal" may be close to the subsistence level, a fact which calls forth opposition to the poll tax for such countries. If the tax is too high, so that incomes net of tax are reduced below levels where satisfactory nutrition is maintained, or where the standard of living is so low as to destroy incentives altogether, the imposition of a poll tax may reduce rather than increase output. It has been contended that the poll tax imposed in certain African countries was too high in this sense, disrupting tribal life, and forcing large numbers of people to migrate to cities.[9]

In this connection, however, a distinction might be made between the use of poll taxes to recapture initial increase in income, resulting from the development program, and taxes which constitute a net reduction of income from current levels. As has already been indicated, it may be necessary in some situations to tax away initial increases in income, in order to prevent initial improvements in productivity from being dissipated in accelerated population growth or in increased leisure. Also, if a development program which concentrates on agricultural improvement in the first phase is to provide self-financing for subsequent phases of development, the initial increases in income must be recaptured, in order to increase exports or reduce imports of consumers' goods and thus obtain the necessary foreign exchange to pay for the raw materials and equipment needed for further development. If the general economic situation makes such an austere fiscal policy necessary, a poll tax has much to recommend it, since it would even provide an incentive for increased production, in the event that the tax reduced income below the "customary normal" without endangering health or efficiency. If such a "development tax" is accompanied by a progressive income tax, a progressive sales tax, or a progressive land tax, it is less objectionable from a social welfare viewpoint.

[8] For an analysis of tax and subsidy schemes, and of the tax on "profits in excess of a fair return on utilized capacity," see Benjamin Higgins, "Postwar Tax Policy," in Carl Shoup and Richard Musgrave (eds.), *Readings in Public Finance* (New York, 1959).

[9] Wald and Froomkin, *op. cit.*, p. 26.

A variety of lump-sum tax, of more importance in agricultural countries than a head tax, is a lump-sum tax on land. Like the poll tax, a lump-sum land tax imposes no penalties on increased production and, if farmers are operating on the backward-sloping portions of their supply curves, may even stimulate increased production. In order to diminish the regressiveness of such a tax, it could be defined as a lump-sum tax *per acre*, so that larger landowners would pay proportionately more in total tax. In addition, the tax rate could vary according to the type of product, so that the more productive land would bear a higher rate of tax. If it is desired to use the tax as an incentive for shifting to more desired types of products (exports, for example), the ratio of tax to potential value output per acre could be made to decline, if production is shifted to high-priority products. The Indonesian system of differential rates of export duty for smallholders and plantation operators, which are designed to encourage expansion of smallholders' production, shows some recognition of this principle, although an export tax at any level provides some disincentive to increased output. Several countries, however, including South Korea, Yugoslavia, and the Soviet Union, fix land taxes on the basis of a standard assessment, related to the "normal" productive capacity of the land, so that increases in output do not bring any increase in tax. Similarly, Australia and New Zealand impose land taxes on *unimproved* land values, to avoid barriers to land improvement. New Zealand grants liberal depreciation allowances under its income tax law for land improvements of a developmental type.

A quite different approach, designed for countries where large areas are withheld from cultivation, or cultivated incompletely or inefficiently, by large-scale landlords, is to gear the lump-sum tax to the *potential* output, rather than to the *actual* output of the land in question. Several Latin American countries, including Panama and Brazil, have taxes of this nature.[10]

Sixth, taxes may be classified as incentive taxes, because they are directly linked to government expenditures which have a popular appeal.

The use of lump-sum taxes of the poll tax type is less likely to encounter resistance, and is more likely to have favorable incentive effects, if it is linked to specific services provided by the government, or to specific development projects. Such a system was suggested to the Libyan government by the United Nations Mission of Technical Assistance to that country.[11]

In countries where there is widespread support for development as such, *any* new tax might be more favorably received, if it were labeled a "development tax" and publicized as a measure needed to facilitate the development program.

Finally, taxes may be designed to provide special incentives for saving. One such tax is a compulsory contribution to a provident fund, which has

[10] For a more complete discussion of incentive taxation in agriculture, see Wald and Froomkin, *op. cit.*, Part III, chap. III.
[11] Cf. Benjamin Higgins, "The Economic and Social Development of Libya," United Nations Mission of Technical Assistance to Libya, (A/AC.32/TA.16), July 1, 1952, p. 68.

been successfully utilized in Singapore. Deductions from payrolls are justified in terms of the need to build up reserves to meet old age pensions, unemployment insurance, sickness benefits, and the like. While such a system is reaching "maturity" current contributions will exceed benefits, increasing the total revenues of the government and adding to the effective savings of the economy.

A more general measure to stimulate savings is a "spending tax." In an underdeveloped country, spending rather than income should be taxed; saving should be encouraged, and the part of income that is saved should be left tax-free as much as possible. Various devices might be used to convert the income tax into a tax on spending. For example, as already suggested, the portion of income invested in new plant equipment and housing, held idle in savings deposits, used to pay insurance premiums, or to purchase securities issued to finance industrial expansion, might be wholly or partly deductible from taxable income. The tax legislation of advanced countries offers precedents for all these kinds of deductions.

Under appropriate conditions, a general sales tax is a close approximation to a spending tax. Some progression is possible in a general sales tax; rates on luxury items can be much higher than on necessities. Basic foodstuffs might be entirely exempt.

Some countries with wide disparities between the standards of living at the top and bottom of the income scale and with administrative difficulties in preventing income tax evasion have resorted to a "surmise income tax," which is also, in effect, a tax on luxury spending. The estimate of taxable income is revised upward in the light of conspicuous consumption of such items as large houses, many servants, expensive cars, foreign travel, and the like. This system is open to abuse because of the large amount of discretion that must be accorded to the officials estimating income for tax purposes. Nevertheless, it is worthy of serious consideration in countries where estimates of income can seldom be checked by reference to account books and where it is desirable to limit luxury spending. At the end of his tax policy mission to the Lebanon in 1960, the author recommended a "progressive" tariff structure as the most effective way of tapping higher incomes. Income tax evasion was general, the administration of customs duties was honest and efficient, and luxuries were mainly imported. In the tax field there is more than one way to skin a cat.

25 A Self-enforcing Incentive Tax System for Underdeveloped Countries

Few underdeveloped countries are in a position to enforce rigorously tax systems of the kind that have become orthodox in advanced countries. Yet it is essential for underdeveloped countries to increase tax revenues, so as to permit increased investment in development projects without disruptive inflation. If possible, tax increases should be of a kind that does not destroy incentives for private undertakings of a developmental nature. Thus the construction of a tax system which by its very nature cannot be evaded, and which nevertheless gives due weight to incentive features, is of particular importance for underdeveloped countries.

This chapter attempts to formulate such a system. The integrated system and even some of its components are so designed that efforts to evade one tax will automatically involve the taxpayer in other tax liabilities so great that evasion is not worthwhile. In short, the system makes it pay to be honest about taxes. At the same time, it has built-in incentive aspects that should contribute to economic growth.

The system might be easier to administer in advanced countries, but where bookkeeping systems are complete and accurate and tax observance prevails, and where accordingly loss of revenue through tax evasion is a small fraction of tax liability, a self-enforcing system may not pay. It is likely to prove somewhat more expensive to operate than traditional income tax systems, and the added costs might outweigh the added collections. Where evasion is the rule rather than the exception, on the other hand, the improvement in tax collections under the self-enforcing system presented here will far outweigh any added cost of operating it.

Kaldor's "Tax Reform"

Various components of the system were developed by the author in the course of advisory missions in Libya, Indonesia, and the Philippines. The idea of a completely closed system, however, came from reading Nicholas Kaldor's book on *Indian Tax Reform*. In the course of a visit to the University of Bombay and the Indian Planning Commission, Kaldor proposed to the government of India a tax system built around a progressive tax on total consumer outlays. The system has subsequently been elaborated in a book.[1] Its main features are as follows:

1. A personal income tax at rates ranging from zero to 45 per cent. Income is defined for tax purposes so as to include all capital gains.

2. A tax on all assets (wealth) ranging from 0.3 to 1.5 per cent, with an exemption for some small minimum holdings.

3. An expenditures tax ranging from 25 to 300 per cent according to the total amount of consumer spending by a family unit, with an exemption for some small minimum amount of expenditure.

4. A gift tax varying from 15 to 80 per cent according to the total value of gifts made in the tax period.

5. To assist in enforcement, Kaldor suggests compulsory auditing of accounts.

6. To check on total spending, income, and wealth every one of the one million taxpayers would be assigned a code number, which would be entered on all documents arising out of capital transactions.

This system goes a long way in the direction of self-enforcement, but it is not a closed system. As Kaldor himself admits, it will not prevent evasion if both parties to a transaction gain by concealing or understating it. In his system the seller of an asset does gain from reporting the sale, offsetting the gain to the buyer from hiding it or understating it. But in the case of goods, both buyer and seller gain from concealment or understatement; the buyer reduces his expenditures tax thereby and the seller his income tax. Ultimately Kaldor relies for enforcement on his compulsory auditing and the difficulty of hiding assets.

An Integrated Self-enforcing Tax System

Although Kaldor's own system is not completely self-enforcing, it provided the present writer with the "missing link." By adding to Kaldor's expenditure and assets taxes a penal tax on excess inventories and a turnover tax, it is possible to devise a closed system, so that anyone failing to report one taxable transaction will either find himself paying more under another tax, or having the transaction reported by the other party to it, because the other party can reduce his tax liability by honest reporting.

The essential components of this integrated system are as follows:

1. A personal income tax of, say, 20 per cent on incomes above, say, $400
2. A flat-rate corporation income tax of, say, 20 per cent

[1] Nicholas Kaldor, *Indian Tax Reform* (Delhi, Ministry of Finance, 1956).

3. A general sales or turnover tax of, say 2 per cent
4. A tax on all assets:
   a) Cash, say, 4 to 8 per cent according to amount (with exemption for x per cent of reported income)
   b) Bonds, say, 3 to 5 per cent according to amount held
   c) Equities, say, 2 to 3 per cent
   d) Productive assets (plant and equipment, land in an "appropriate" use), 1 to 2 per cent
   e) Normal inventories, 2 per cent
5. An excess inventories tax of, say, 40 per cent
6. An expenditures tax of, say, 6 to 20 per cent according to amount for individuals subject to income tax

Enforcement

Income for tax purposes is defined as profits (dividends, interest, rents, entrepreneurial gains) plus "capital gains" (increase in value of total assets held, less purchases of new assets plus wages and salaries. In symbols, $Y_t = R + G + W$.

The expenditure tax will apply for income tax payers to all consumption, C. National income may be defined as $Y = R + W = C + I$. (I is "investment" in the sense of all purchases of assets.) Also, by definition $G = \Delta A - I$, where A is total assets. Thus taxable income is $Y_t = C + I + (\Delta A - I = C + \Delta A$.

The question is then whether any taxable transaction is *worth* hiding or underreporting by both parties, and whether in that case it *can* be hidden or underreported without leading to an increase in tax on other transactions for at least one of the parties.

Wages and salaries paid out will of course be reported by employers as costs, in order to keep down income taxes. If there is any likelihood that some employers may overreport wages and salaries paid, and split the tax savings with employees, exemptions could be set very low so as to remove any difference in *marginal* tax between employers and employees, or a payroll tax could be added to the system.

Profits are equal to gross sales less costs. Sales will tend to be reported by sellers to avoid excess inventory taxes, which will always be higher than sales taxes plus income taxes on the same volume of goods. Wage and salary earners in the lower brackets whose incomes are fully reported will also have an incentive to report sales to them (expenditures for them) since the tax on *their* expenditures will be lower than the assets tax on cash that will otherwise be ascribed to them. That is, income less reported expenditures will be automatically calculated as an increase in assets held; in the absence of reported purchases of other assets, it will be assumed that the assets are held in cash; and this accumulation of cash will also represent an increase in total net worth, and so a capital gain, since no investment has been reported.

Capital gains, in other words, are a residual:

$$G = \Delta A - I = Y_t - (C + I)$$

Purchases of capital goods, I, will be reported by buyers as costs (depreciation for income tax purposes is geared to purchases of capital goods) to avoid the higher assets tax on cash and a tax on capital gains. They will be reported by the sellers to avoid excess inventory taxes. Sales or expenditures, C, will be reported by sellers to avoid excess inventory taxes and by buyers in the lower brackets to avoid taxes on cash balances and capital gains. Buyers in high-income, low-spending brackets will also find it worthwhile reporting consumer spending, rather than adding to their imputed capital gains, which are part of taxable income, and paying the assets tax on imputed increases in cash as well.

Will not taxpayers eager to hoard goods report fictitious sales to avoid the excess inventory tax? It would hardly pay. The seller would have to pay income and turnover tax on the fictitious sale. The buyer must pay the expenditure tax if the transaction involves consumers' goods and capital gains plus assets taxes if the transaction involves assets. If the fictitious buyer is himself a dealer, he puts himself in the position of being liable to excess inventories tax if he makes many fictitious purchases. Moreover, a dealer who reports purchases but no sales would soon arouse suspicion.

The main point, however, is that revelation of *any* transaction in a chain provides the key to the whole chain. There is always someone along the line who will gain by reporting the transaction, exposing any taxpayers who have sought to conceal transactions.

It is true that it will pay both a buyer and a seller to hide a transaction if both have stocks below normal, so that both the sale and purchase for replenishment of inventories can be concealed without penalty. If sales are concealed but purchases for replenishment are reported by either party, the would-be tax evader would soon find himself in an excess inventory bracket. It would be extremely difficult to hide transactions all down the line; at some stage some buyer or seller will *want* to report the transaction to save himself taxes. In the case of imports the whole process would have to begin with smuggling, and in the case of exports it would have to end with smuggling. For most commodities accumulation of inventories could be discovered by physical checks, thus laying bare a whole series of illegal transactions. For all practical purposes, evasion becomes impossible under such an integrated tax system.

Under this system, then, taxes can be profitably evaded by all parties to a transaction only by:

1. Buying goods or assets without reporting or detection and later selling without reporting or detection

2. Reporting false sales (to avoid inventory tax) and later selling without reporting or detection

Method 1 does not apply to imports, unless smuggled, since the initial purchase is recorded on customs slips and import licenses. In the case of large-scale home producers of goods for export, books are usually orderly, and since failure to report sales would be a violation of income tax laws, the risk of detection would be great. Unreported purchases by wholesalers or final exporters from small producers outside the income tax system can be policed by sample physical checks; most export items are too bulky to be hidden in large quantities. As an additional check, however, godowns might be required to report on goods in storage, say, once a quarter, subject to a heavy fine for false information. Some document is always involved in storing goods; the godowns could be required to send a copy to the statistical authorities. Moreover, sellers would have to compensate low-income buyers for the difference between expenditures tax and tax on cash assets, to persuade them not to report the transaction. They would have to compensate high-income buyers for the imputed income tax on capital gains plus tax on cash assets. Enforcement could be tightened by sample checks on bank statements, to disclose false reporting of increases in bank balances.

A retailer may consider it worthwhile reporting fictitious sales, and paying income and sales tax on them, if he can then hold goods for a price rise without paying inventory tax and later sell without reporting sales when actually made. (It would seldom be considered worthwhile to pay income, sales, and expenditures tax twice on the same sale, on the *chance* that the price rise would more than offset the double taxation.) It might even be considered worthwhile for a wholesaler to make an agreement with retailers to report such fictitious sales and share the profits. However, making unreported sales would involve all the usual problems of income tax evasion, plus the problem of physically hiding goods while held for future (unreported) sale. Moreover, if any firm shows a sharp drop in reported sales from one period to another, a clue is provided for investigation; and it would be very difficult for any firm to expand *actual* sales enough to keep *reported* sales on the same level, while adding *unreported* sales of unreported stocks held over from the previous period.

An ingenious device for assuring the reporting of final sales has been suggested by Professor Albert Hart of Columbia University, who hit upon it in the course of a tax policy mission to Chile. Let the government take over the operation of retail "stamp" systems, including the redemption centers. Stamps would be issued to buyers against all sales, and the stamps would be redeemable only at the government redemption centers. To prevent forgery of stamps, the code number of each retailer could be put on the stamps issued to him by the government. From the stamps redeemed the government would have a precise measure of the sales of each retailer.

Professor Carey Brown of M.I.T. has pointed out to the author that in advanced countries the most common form of income tax evasion is one not adequately cared for in the above system: charging as an expense something that is really consumption. "Expense accounts" of various kinds are the most obvious case of such evasion, but there are others. A grocer's wife takes food from the shelves of the shop for family use, reducing sales but not costs; a farmer consumes his own crop but charges full costs against income, or uses farmhands as domestic servants. In most underdeveloped countries, it will be a long time before tax enforcement is rigorous enough for this kind of evasion to become particularly troublesome. In most of them, the trouble now is that people with high incomes do not pay taxes at all. It is doubtful whether evasion of the sort that bothers Professor Brown would be very significant in underdeveloped countries, under the system outlined above. If the grocer's wife takes too much from the shelves, the grocer will get caught on excess inventory tax. Most peasants are not in the tax-paying brackets anyway. In the case of the smallholders or plantation operators, the problem is the same as it is for Texas ranchers, and water-tight enforcement would take some policing, perhaps on a sample basis. In any case, the system proposed here does not make this kind of evasion more serious than under the usual kind of income tax, and it makes it at least somewhat more difficult to do undetected.

Administration

A key feature of the system is that computations of tax liability would be made by the statistical office, rather than through the internal revenue service. The tax authorities would be left only the simpler task of collecting the tax after each taxpayer's liability had been clearly established. Each income-tax payer would have a code number, as under the Kaldor proposal; each taxpayer would have a card on which his income, expenditures, and assets would be recorded; and whenever a document arising out of a transaction reached the statistical office the appropriate entries would be made by machine on the cards of the taxpayers involved. Needless to say, the system would bring as a by-product a considerable improvement in economic statistics, permitting more ready and more accurate computation of national income, production, sales, inventories, input-output matrices, etc. The computations required are by no means beyond the capacity of modern electronic computers, and the cost involved would be a tiny fraction of the improvement in tax collections.[2]

The Tax on Excess Inventories

The most unfamiliar of the taxes in the system is the tax on excess inventories; let us, therefore, consider its administration in more detail. As originally conceived, this tax was designed for incentive rather than enforcement purposes. During 1952 and 1953 the Indonesian Ministry of Finance was concerned with the hoarding of goods, especially goods entering into foreign trade, which was then believed to be taking place on a large scale. Over a period of several months, discussions took place within the government over the possibility of forcing these hoards into the market through a penal tax on excess inventories. In designing such a tax the author worked in close cooperation with Dr. Nathan Keyfitz of the University of Chicago, who was then Expert on General Statistics, for the Indonesian National Planning Bureau. As the proposal was studied more carefully, it was recognized that the introduction of an excess inventory tax administered through the Central Office of Statistics, together with the income and turnover taxes, would afford opportunities for improved administration of the whole tax system. It became apparent that conceptually simple extensions of existing statistical operations would permit the government to follow the flow of goods through every stage of the

[2] In order to avoid the cost of doing the same bookkeeping twice, the government could make quarterly computations for firms requesting this service, in exchange for a reasonable fee which would reduce the net cost to the government.

economy, providing the basis for a completely efficient system of income, sales, and excess inventory taxes. These extensions also seemed fairly easy from the technical and administrative point of view, except for two "open ends" in the flow of goods:

1. Original purchases of goods from small-scale producers for sale in the home market or for export

2. Final sales to consumers

Except for rice, purchases of home produce from small producers for resale in the home market were not of great importance, and rice sales were already subject to government control. Under the incomplete system then proposed, purchases from small producers for export and final sales of imports would have required policing; these deficiencies disappear in the integrated system outlined above.

Let us consider the general nature of the fact-gathering task. The following sources of information were already available to the statistical services in Indonesia and would be available in many underdeveloped countries:

1. *Imports:* licenses issued, exchange certificates issued, customs slips issued, income tax returns. These were available for each importer and each class of import. There were also data on bank credits issued to importers.

2. *Exports:* estate production, smallholders' rubber production, copra production

   a) Reports by district governments on production

   b) Export licenses, by exporter and by product

   c) Income tax returns

3. *Rice production for home market:* district government reports, sundry production figures for various commodities

Essentially, the additional material required was as follows:

1. *Importers*

   a) Estimate of *stocks* at starting date (questionnaire plus physical check)

   b) One copy of each invoice of *sales by importers* to be provided to statistical services

   c) One copy of each invoice of *sales by wholesalers* to retailers

   d) If feasible, *sales slips* of *retailers*

2. *Exporters*

   a) Estimate of *stocks* at starting date (questionnaire plus physical check)

   b) Invoices of *sales by producers* to wholesalers (or exporters)

   c) Invoice of *sales by wholesalers* to exporters

3. *Producers for home market*

   a) Estimate of *stocks* at starting date

   b) Invoices of *sales by producers* to wholesalers

   c) Invoices of *sales by wholesalers* to retailers

   d) *Sales slips* of *retailers*

With these materials and an appropriate system of coding and cards, it would be technically possible to compute, for any period after the starting date, the average stocks, sales, and incomes of every firm. Each firm would be considered to hold the goods in stock, and to be liable for any excess inventories tax, until their sale was confirmed by the purchaser. At that time, the seller must pay any sales tax for which he is liable, and the invoices would be held in his income tax file. Thus with this information in the hands of the government, it would be impossible for any firm to evade any one of the three taxes.

THE PROBLEM OF MARKUP

There is one major conceptual problem. If excess inventories are to be defined in terms of a ratio of the value of sales to the value of stocks, which is the simplest approach, account must somehow be taken of the markup at each turnover. A simple subtraction of value of sales from value of stocks would not measure the value of stocks still held.

It would of course be impossible to take account of the markup in defining a "normal" turnover. If the "normal" turnover is four times per year, and the markup is 12.5 per cent, then the "normal" ratio of sales to stocks is 4.5. However, in an inflationary situation, an entrepreneur may build up a "normal" ratio of sales to stocks by holding goods for a price rise, which is precisely the kind of action the tax is designed to discourage.

The problem is avoided, of course, by defining normal turnover in physical terms. There is then no conceptual or technical problem; given the statistical material itemized above, physical turnover is measurable for every entrepreneur. However, for firms dealing in a wide range of commodities, separate computations for each item would be very time-consuming, and the simplest "index" of the physical volume of sales is total value.

One possibility would be to determine maximum markup for each category of goods, and to value *sales* at the actual price for income and sales tax purposes, while revaluing them *at the maximum markup level* for inventory tax purposes. In evaluating the stocks of the *purchaser*, moreover, the *actual* purchase price would be used. In this way a price control system can be built into the tax system. The incentive to hold goods for higher prices is reduced, because of the penal tax on excess inventories, whereas the purchaser has an added incentive to resist price increases, since he must dispose of his stock at still higher prices to make a profit, and his chances of building up a sufficient value of sales at *ceiling* prices to offset his purchases at *actual* prices, and so avoid excess inventories tax, diminish as his purchase price increases.

The best compromise might be to use physical volume for exporters, who usually deal in a small range of goods and whose markup is limited by world market conditions, and to declare maximum markups for imports.

ASSESSING THE TAX

As already indicated, the tax will be defined as

$$T = \frac{R}{100} \cdot x$$

where T = tax, R = the rate of tax, and x = excess inventories. We define x as $A - N$, where A is actual average inventories over a period, $P_1 - P_6$, and N is normal inventories. In turn, N is defined as $S_A/N = O_N$, where S_A is actual sales and O_N is normal turnover as laid down for the category of goods involved.

Let $S_A = 1,000$ and $O_N = 4$
Then $N = 250$

If $A = 350$, $T = \dfrac{R}{100} = (350-250)$

If $R = 100$, the tax will be 100

The period of averaging stocks should be long enough to cover erratic or seasonal fluctuations in demand and supply, but short enough to avoid serious inflationary effects through hoarding of stocks in one part of the period for sale in a later part. The best system would probably be to average each quarter a moving average of stocks for two quarters. Suppose $N = 100$, and actual end-of-quarter stocks are as follows:

Quarter:	III	IV	I	II	III	IV
Stocks	0	0	200	200	0	0
Average	0	0	100	200	100	0
x	0	0	0	100	0	0

The firm then becomes liable for excess inventory tax of 100 as a penalty for hoarding through the second quarter of the second year.

If this system involves too much computation, two averages over nine months might suffice.

Quarter:	I	II	III	IV
Stock	0	200	200	0
A ⎰3 ⎱ N ⎰quarters⎱			133.3 100.0	133.3 100.0
x			33.3	33.3

The firm is, therefore, liable to excess inventory tax of 66.6

The actual computation need not be made more than once a year, at the same time that income tax is assessed. Excess inventory taxes can then be assessed, and paid along with income tax.

For defining N, four categories of goods, or six at the most, would suffice. Few goods turn over, on the average, more than six times a year, and few less than once. In the author's opinion all goods could be divided into four classes, with turnovers of once a quarter, once every three quarters, and once a year.

The cost of such computation for Indonesia was estimated by Dr. Keyfitz at 1 or 2 million rupiahs per year, say, $100,000 as a maximum, using a reasonably realistic foreign exchange rate for conversion. The improvement in income and sales tax collection which the system would bring would run into hundreds of millions of rupiahs. Moreover, by forcing goods out of hoards into the home market, the tax will make a significant contribution to price stabilization and so save money for the government; each 1 per cent rise in the price level costs the Indonesian government some 150 mi'lion rupiahs. Compared to such saving and the increased revenues it could bring, the cost of the proposed tax system is insignificant.

Incentive Features

This system already has built-in incentive features. For any taxpayer, with a given income, the total tax burden on that income will be minimized by maximizing the share of income spent on productive equipment. The next most favorable use of income is purchase of equities, which assists others in financing expansion of plant and equipment. The national debt becomes more or less self-liquidating; the tax on bonds is about equal to the interest paid on them. Speculative investment in inventories becomes unprofitable.

In two respects, the objectives of self-enforcement and provision of tax incentives do conflict with each other. The first relates to the treatment of cash balances. In setting out the self-enforcement system above, we defined capital gains as income less consumer spending plus purchases of assets. With this definition, income held as cash is taxed twice, once as earned income and once as capital gains. The "capital gains" tax is needed to make it pay to report transactions in assets. A penalty tax on cash holdings is needed, since only in this way can it be made profitable to taxpayers to report their consumer expenditures. Holdings of cash balances, and especially holdings of currency, which in most underdeveloped countries exceed bank deposits, are the hardest thing to check in the whole chain of transactions. The simplest way of assuring that taxpayers will not underreport expenditures and hold undisclosed stocks of currency is to treat increases in cash balances as a residual, and include them in income as capital gains. This device more or less forces the honest taxpayer to buy securities— treasury bills, say—rather than hold his liquid reserves in cash, in order to avoid the double taxation on cash balances. Purchase and sales of securities, or physical assets, are relatively easy to check, and must be reported by both parties to the transaction.

From an incentive viewpoint, however, the double taxation of cash balances is somewhat severe. In the generally inflationary situation common to underdeveloped countries, holding cash balances is not a particularly serious economic sin; there is no reason for providing a powerful disincentive to cash holdings. True, there are some advantages in having people hold reserves in the form of government securities rather than cash. A market for government securities is built up, broadening the scope of central bank open market policy. It may also make deficit financing less purely inflationary. As people become used to the idea that government securities provide a safe and liquid means of holding wealth, the propensity to save might actually be raised. Moreover, the government authorities have somewhat more control over sudden liquidation of government securities for spending purposes than they do over sudden activation of idle deposits. Cash balances held for speculative purposes are subject to sudden and sharp increases in velocity of circulation which complicate the problems of monetary policy; sudden liquidation of government securities by the general public is possible only if the monetary authorities provide a sufficient market for them. Thus the authorities have a tighter control over the spending stream where reserves are held in the form of securities rather than cash.

Nevertheless, these advantages scarcely warrant the punitive treatment of cash accumulation implicit in the self-enforcement system. Accordingly, it might be desirable to define capital gains so that only increases in cash above some reasonable percentage of declared income would be included.

The other conflict is more serious. From a self-enforcement standpoint, it is convenient to have the tax rate on consumer spending lower than the tax rate on imputed increases in cash balances, so that it will pay to report consumer spending. From an incentive viewpoint, on the other hand, the tax rate on consumer spending should be higher than the rate on any kind of saving. We want taxpayers to report consumer spending, but we want them to save rather than consume.

There seems to be no way of escaping this dilemma completely. However, what we really want taxpayers to do in underdeveloped countries is not just to save, but to save and invest. By buying assets (other than excess inventories) the taxpayer can reduce his marginal tax rate below what he would pay on consumer outlays. It would of course pay to underreport consumer expenditures and overreport purchases of assets; but the document recording the sale of an asset requires two names, and the seller named in a false transaction would be liable for capital gains tax on the imputed increase in *his* cash balances, unless he also reported false purchases and the tax on them—and also the taxes for which the "seller" in the false transaction would be liable. Thus collusion to disguise consumer spending as an assets-transaction would not pay.

A simple way of adding to the incentive effects is to apply the penalty rate on excess inventories to land held idle or put to relatively unproductive or "inappropriate" uses. Land use can be controlled by defining the "appropriate" uses in various areas according to the development plan. Holding land idle for speculative purposes becomes unprofitable. Truly powerful incentive effects can be introduced, however, by adding a tax on "profits in excess of a fair return on utilized capacity" and a tax-and-transfer system for foreign investors.

The former tax has been outlined in detail in an earlier article, and will not be repeated in detail here.[3] The basic idea is simple; capacity is defined for tax purposes in terms of output, and a "fair return" is allowed on the proportion of capacity actually utilized, which may be above or below 100 per cent. For example, if a plant is worth $1,000,000 and capacity is defined as 100,000 units per year, the enterprise will be allowed a return of, say, 20 per cent of $500,000 if it produces 50,000 units, and 20 per cent of $1,500,000 if it produces 150,000 units. Taxes will be 100 per cent of the profits in excess of these amounts. Thus the amount of profits an enterprise

[3] Higgins, "Postwar Tax Policy," Part I, *Canadian Journal of Economics and Political Science*, August, 1943.

can earn and keep depends solely on production. There is accordingly a powerful incentive to expand output up to approximately the purely competitive equilibrium position, and to introduce innovations reducing the capital-output ratio.

A Tax-and-Transfer System for Foreign Investors

The system of business taxes and regulation of profits transfers presented in this section was originally devised to fit within a general policy framework laid down by the Indonesian government. At the time, the government wished to attract foreign capital, but was reluctant to allow unlimited transfers from profits for four main reasons: profits higher than 15 per cent or 20 per cent after tax were considered unjustly high, representing exploitation of Indonesian resources and workers; it was considered desirable to block profits in excess of 15 per cent or 20 per cent in order to provide capital for expansion of Indonesian industry and agriculture; it was feared that in the absence of such limits, the privilege of transferring profits would be used to transfer capital, imposing a serious drain on foreign exchange reserves; and it was feared that without limits on transfers, the transfer of excessively high profits would in itself result in serious losses of foreign exchange reserves.

The original context of the proposed system was therefore specifically Indonesian, but the conditions which informed that system prevail in other underdeveloped areas: difficulty in achieving an appropriately anti-inflationary budget, and a consequent need to make every reasonable use of business taxes as a source of revenue, without unduly hampering private investment for development purposes; an unfavorable balance of payments, and consequent need to conserve foreign exchange reserves and, if possible, to attract foreign capital; inadequate domestic savings and taxes (actual or realistically potential) to finance economic development, providing a still more pressing need for foreign capital; strong nationalist sentiment, expressed as opposition to "exploitation" of domestic labor and resources by foreigners through earning and transferring large profits; and, finally, a shortage of trained and competent personnel to administer the tax and foreign exchange control systems, and a consequent need for simplicity in tax and foreign exchange measures.

Fundamentally, the proposed system consists of evaluating capital by discounting returns at an appropriate rate of interest, taking account of the complexity of the managerial problem, and the degree of risk, involved in the enterprise. According to economic theory, the value of an asset is the discounted sum of anticipated future returns on it, or in other words, the sum of the "present values" of annual earnings over the life of the asset. For purposes of tax administration, for firms with an earnings record extending over several years, valuation might more simply be based upon a moving average of returns over, say, five years. The government could permit each firm itself to state what it considers a "fair rate of return" in its field of enterprise. The regular corporation income tax would be kept fairly low (say 20 per cent) but a supertax would be imposed on companies wishing transfer privileges, varying *inversely* with the rate of return selected as "normal." The formula suggested below is gross earnings minus estimated "normal" net earnings times 20 per cent minus the selected "normal" percentage. If an enterprise overstates past earnings in order to build up a high capital value as a basis for estimating transferable profits, it will become liable to additional corporation income taxes and penalties for tax evasion in the past. If it overstates its "normal" rate of return, in order to avoid the supertaxes, its earnings will be capitalized at a high rate of discount, and transferable profits (and depreciation allowances) will be reduced.

Considering this tax in isolation, there is one way in which an enterprise could escape the pincers: by selecting a very low "normal" rate of return (say 2 per cent) which would give it a high capital value for transfer purposes. If earnings do not increase, they will escape supertax even though the return on actual capital investment may be high. Moreover, all profits net of tax could be transferred.

In the integrated system outlined above, the loophole is closed by the general tax on all assets, which destroys the tax advantage of overvaluation of capital. The firm might be allowed to estimate for itself the number of years over which earnings are to be projected in determining capital value. It would then be required to amortize its plant for tax purposes over the same period. The firm itself might be allowed to determine how amortization would be spread over the lifetime of its plant; but when the period is up, the enterprise would of course be allowed no further deductions of depreciation. If a firm overestimates the life of existing plant in order to build up a high capital value for transfer purposes, it would not be allowed foreign exchange for replacement in excess of depreciation allowances accumulated. The government might reserve the option of buying out any firm which is fully amortized by the firm's own definition, or which requires foreign exchange for replacement in excess of its own estimates for tax purposes, for the amount of its accumulated depreciation allowances. Thus no firm could benefit by giving false information about the probable life of its plant.

If depreciation allowances were used for actual replacement, the value of capital, and so transferable profits, would remain unchanged unless earnings rise. If a firm brings in capital in excess of depreciation allowances, the excess could be added to capital value. Transferable profits, and permissible replacement or withdrawal, would increase accordingly.

Capitalization of *past* earnings would be unfair to firms with poor earnings records which can legitimately expect higher rates of return in the future. Such firms may justly contend that the true value of their plant is greater than the sum of present values of average *past* annual earnings, over the expected life of the plant. Such firms might be permitted to estimate their *future* capacity for production and sales, as well as their "normal" rate of return. In this case, however, they would be allowed to transfer only the stipulated percentage of their "utilized" capacity. For example, capital might be valued at $1,000,000 on the assumption that future output will average 100,000 units per year, and that output can be sold at present prices, and that a normal return for such enterprises is, say, 10 per cent.

No allowances should be made for price increases since this would be an invitation to speculation and to exploitation of monopoly power. If output turns out to be only 50,000 units, the firm would be allowed to transfer, not 15 per cent on $1,000,000, but only 15 per cent on the amount of plant "utilized," that is, $500,000. In calculating tax liabilities and permissible withdrawals for replacement, depreciation would likewise be permitted only on "utilized capacity." In this case, too, the supertax would be applied to earnings in excess of a "normal" rate of return on "utilized capacity." Under this system, it would not pay firms to overestimate future sales in order to obtain a high capital valuation for transfer purposes.

Firms might be given the option of capitalizing past earnings and applying the appropriate rates to the resulting capital value when estimating transferable profits and excess profits tax, or of capitalizing estimated future earnings (that is, estimated output times present prices) and having depreciation, transferable profits, and excess profits tax calculated on the basis of "utilized capacity." Indeed, they might be allowed to average over *any* five-year period that includes the current year. Only firms confident of their ability to produce and sell more in the future than in the past would choose to capitalize on the basis of future earnings alone. If firms demonstrate an ability to produce and sell more at current prices, they should be rewarded. The whole system then provides an incentive to improve techniques, lower costs, and expand output, and at the same time it destroys the incentive for monopoly restriction or for hoarding.

To provide protection against internal inflation or devaluation of the currency, foreign firms might be permitted to keep their accounts (including taxes, of course) in terms of foreign currencies invested.

Enterprises such as plantations which may suffer wide fluctuations in earnings over very long periods might be allowed to choose a longer averaging period, providing that the replacement period is at least as long. As indicated above, if a firm chooses an excessively long period for averaging and amortization, its depreciation allowances for tax purposes will be very low, and its taxes accordingly high. It will also be a long time before the firm benefits fully from a shift to a higher level of earnings.

This business tax system has several advantages which in themselves would constitute a major tax reform:

1. Unlike the usual progressive corporation income tax, it does not penalize size as such. The *rate* of tax on large profits is the same as on small profits. Taxing size, as such, has never been good economic policy; a small firm with a tidy little monopoly, or a group of traders who have cornered a market on a minor item, may earn 100 per cent return on their capital, whereas a large firm may earn only 5 per cent. The British plantations in Indonesia apparently earned only 2.5 per cent average over recent decades; the oil companies in turn earned 5 to 10 per cent. If the intent is to encourage *new national* firms, these may be exempt from tax for, say, three years, or allowed accelerated depreciation. If it seems desirable to help struggling small firms, profits up to a certain amount might be totally exempt. But large firms are often efficient firms and should not be penalized merely for being big.

2. Since the tax system does not penalize size, neither does it penalize

growth. Doubling earnings does not increase the *rate* of tax. The disincentive to expansion involved in a progressive tax structure is avoided. Indeed, if capital is valued according to output, as suggested above, the tax system encourages expansion. Transfers and tax deductions both rise with output. No penalty attaches to earnings of 30 to 40 per cent, before tax, through efficiency or innovation. Indeed, *higher* rates of return can be earned, and the balance after taxes transferred, provided increased earnings come through increased *output*, and not through monopoly restrictions.

3. At the same time, the system has a built-in tax on very high *rates* of earning. Suppose a firm is actually earning 100 per cent. It will not nominate a rate above 20 per cent, even if permitted to do so; otherwise its taxes will rise (through reduced depreciation allowances) and transfers will fall. At 20 per cent, its capital value will, of course, be valued above cost. But as profits the firm can transfer only 15 per cent of "capital." The balance of its profits (before depreciation) can be transferred only as repatriation or for actual replacement. If transferred as repatriation, its entire capital will be regarded as withdrawn after five years and no more transfers of any kind would be permitted. If used for replacement, the firm must invest much more than the plant is worth. In other words, it must build up its *actual* capital to the *estimated* capital, if it wishes to go on transferring the *same* amount. It gets no reward for reinvesting. But the alternatives are to repatriate, and so give up a profitable enterprise, or have its profits blocked in the underdeveloped country. As suggested above, any temptation to set normal rates of profit too *low* could be removed by a progressive tax on assets.

4. The proposed system provides an incentive for long-term investment in productive enterprise rather than in trading ventures which have a quick turnover. The supertax,[4]

E_g = Gross earnings (total receipts less operating costs)
E_n = Net earnings (gross earnings less taxes)
E'_n = Estimated net earnings
E_T = Transferable profits
E_d = Net earnings after depreciation
D = Depreciation
R = Estimated "normal" rate of return
V = Value of capital
E_R = "Normal" earnings (i.e., $E_R = VR$)
T_n = Normal tax, defined as $\frac{40}{100}$ of $(E_g - D)$
T_x = Supertax, defined as $(E_g - E_R) \cdot (20\% - R\%)$
T_T = Total tax
P = Period of replacement

$$T_x = (E_g - E_R) \cdot (20\% - R\%),$$

is also $T_x = (E_g - VR) \cdot (20\% - R\%)$. If E_g and R are given, then $T_x = t(V)$, with $dTx/dV < 0$. But $V = V(P)$ with $dV/dP > 0$. Thus $dTx/dP = dV/dP \cdot dTx/dV < 0$. That is, the supertax falls as the period of investment increases.

5. The system contains a built-in reward for ploughing back profits. By

[4] The following symbols are used.

choosing a high rate of "normal" return, 20 per cent, a firm can reduce its tax burden, at the cost of having some profits blocked. These profits can be invested domestically. Thus the system results in lower taxes for firms choosing to plough back profits in domestic investment. This effect could be enhanced by reducing the normal tax to, say, 35 per cent and raising the supertax rate to $(25 - R)/100$. If loss of revenue were no problem, there would be advantages in these rates, which bring the system close to "a tax on profits in excess of normal returns on utilized capacity."

6. The only "discrimination" in the system is the imposition of a super-tax on firms wishing foreign exchange transfer facilities. In a situation which requires conservation of foreign exchange, such "discrimination" is perfectly valid. Indeed, the proposed system provides an incentive for firms, nominally "foreign" but actually domestic, not to register as foreign firms in order to avoid the supertax.

7. If it is considered undesirable to discriminate, domestic firms can be brought within the system. Choosing the 20 per cent rate of "normal" return, to eliminate the supertax, would reduce their capital value, and so their allowable depreciation, for normal tax purposes. If it seems advisable to strengthen this effect a flat-rate deduction for all firms of x per cent of capital might be allowed and offset by a higher normal tax rate. This modification would also strengthen the built-in incentive to undertake long-period productive investment. Other sanctions on undervaluing capital might be imposed on domestic firms. Foreign exchange allocations for imported raw materials and equipment, or permissible bank indebtedness, might be geared to capital value.

8. Indeed, its flexibility is one of the great attractions of the system. By minor modifications, the government can make the system operate in almost any way that it likes.

9. Another great attraction is that most of the work of administration, and most of the decisions, become the responsibility of the firms themselves. The administrative work of the tax authorities is no more complex than with the present tax system. Only figures of output, sales, and costs need be checked by the tax authorities, and these figures usually require checking to administer existing tax systems. The computation of tax and transfer rights involves only the simplest kind of arithmetic. The tax forms utilized can be just as simple as those commonly in use, perhaps simpler.

Conclusion

It is more than possible that the tax system presented here still has loopholes and presents administrative difficulties which have been overlooked by the author. It is his belief, however, that any loopholes others may find could be plugged and the administrative problems overcome. Discussion must begin somewhere, and it is as a starting point for discussion that the system outlined above is presented. The problem of finance is fundamental to the whole problem of developing underdeveloped areas. The tax system outlined here seems to the author to have enormous advantages; if it could be worked out in practical form, it would go a long way toward overcoming financial barriers to economic development.

26 || Stabilization Policies

Of all the branches of traditional economics, those most readily applicable to underdeveloped countries are monetary, fiscal, and foreign exchange policies aimed at stabilizing the economy. Even here, however, certain differences between the causes of economic fluctuation in advanced and in underdeveloped countries call for caution in applying these policies to underdeveloped countries.

Beneath the prescriptions of contemporary monetary and fiscal policy lies a theory of economic fluctuations which assumes that the major cause of fluctuations is the instability of private investment. Private investment is treated as depending in some way on the rate of increase in national income or spending. This relationship is called the "accelerator." Consumer spending, in turn, depends on level of investment and the size of the "multiplier," which is determined by the "marginal propensity to consume." An accelerated rate of increase in spending generates additional investment, and additional investment generates an increase in spending. However, the nature of the relationship between consumer spending and income is such that each round of increase in income caused by an initial increase in investment brings forth a smaller increase in consumer spending. There is a built-in tendency for the expansion of consumer spending to taper off. When it does, investment tends to fall; when investment falls, consumption will fall too. Here is the genesis of the downswing. Interactions of "accelerator" and "multiplier" cause fluctuations in income and employment.[1]

[1] This statement is, of course, highly simplified, but we cannot go into detail here on the theory of business cycles in advanced countries. For a good recent statement, see Kenneth E. Boulding, *Economic Analysis, Volume II: Macroeconomics*, New York, 1966.

In relatively few underdeveloped countries, however, are fluctuations in private investment in response to changes in domestic spending the major factor in economic fluctuations. The instability of underdeveloped economies can usually be traced to one of two factors: fluctuations in output as a consequence of variations in rainfall, and variations in demand for exports. Instability of these kinds requires policies of a different sort from those needed to offset fluctuations in private investment.

Fluctuations in Arid Zone Countries

There are hundreds of millions of people in the world whose incomes depend primarily on the amount of rainfall in the growing season. In the arid zone the rainfall cycle can be the major factor in fluctuations in output, income, and employment.

The similarity of the configuration of rainfall cycles to that of the "Juglar," seven-to-eleven-year cycle in advanced countries has long since been noted by economists. W. Stanley Jevons drew attention to this correlation in his paper for the British Association in 1875, and elaborated on it in his *Investigations in Currency and Finance* some decades later.[2] A more refined presentation of the rainfall cycle theory of economic fluctuations was presented by Henry Ludwell Moore.[3] Economists in advanced countries have discarded these theories as naïve and totally inapplicable to the fluctuations in advanced countries. In view of the violence of economic fluctuations in underdeveloped arid zone countries, however, and of the obvious relationship of these fluctuations to rainfall cycles, it may be time to review these theories in relationship to the stabilization problems of such countries.

Jevons seemed to feel that his theory stood or fell according to the closeness of the correlation between sunspot cycles and economic fluctuations. Thus in his *Investigations in Currency and Finance*, he wrote:[4]

While writing my 1875 paper for the British Association I was much embarrassed by the fact that the commercial fluctuations could with difficulty be reconciled with a period of 11.1 years. If, indeed, we start from 1825, and add 11.1 years time after time, we get 1836.1, 1847.2, 1858.3, 1869.4, 1880.5, which shows a gradually increasing discrepancy from 1837, 1847, 1857, 1866 (and now 1878), the true dates of the crises. To explain this discrepancy I went so far as to form the rather fanciful hypothesis that the commercial world might be a body so mentally constituted, as Mr. John Mill must hold, as to be capable of vibrating in a period of ten years, so that it would every now and then be thrown into oscillation by physical causes having a period of eleven years. The subsequent publication, however, of Mr. J. A. Broun's inquiries, tending to show that the solar period is 10.45 years, not 11.1 [*Nature*, vol. xvi,

[2] Cf. W. Stanley Jevons, "The Causes of Unemployment," *The Contemporary Review*, LCV, LCVI (1909), pp. 548-65; 67-89; and W. Stanley Jevons, *Investigations in Currency and Finance* (London, 1909).

[3] Henry Ludwell Moore, *Economic Cycles: Their Law and Cause* (New York, 1914), and *Generating Economic Cycles* (New York, 1923).

[4] W. Stanley Jevons, *op. cit.*, p. 206.

p. 63], placed the matter in a very different light, and removed the difficulties. Thus, if we take Mr. John Mill's "Synopsis of Six Commercial Panics in the Present Century," and rejecting 1866 as an instance of a premature panic, count from 1815 to 1857, we find that four credit cycles, occupying forty-two years, give an average duration of 10.5 years, which is a remarkably close approximation to Mr. Broun's solar period.

As economists, we need not be concerned about possible association between rainfall cycles and sunspots. We may take rainfall cycles as given and ask whether and how fluctuations in rainfall generate fluctuations in income and employment. Jevons' own theoretical framework was very simple. Concerned as he was with fluctuations in his own country, he argued that drought in the colonies led to famine there and consequent reduction of imports of British manufactured goods, especially textiles, with repercussions on the economy of the mother country.[5]

Probably, however, we ought not to attribute the decennial fluctuation wholly to Indian trade. It is quite possible that tropical Africa, America, the West Indies, and even the Levant are affected by the same meteorological influences which occasion the famines in India. Thus it is the nations which trade most largely to those parts of the world, *and which give long credits to their customers*, which suffer most from these crises. Holland was most easily affected a century ago; England is most deeply affected now; France usually participates, together with some of the German trading towns. But I am not aware that these decennial crises extend in equal severity to such countries as Austria, Hungary, Switzerland, Italy and Russia, which have comparatively little foreign trade. Even when they are affected, it may be indirectly through sympathy with the great commercial nations. . . .

Here again some may jest at the folly of those who theorise about such incongruous things as the cotton-mills of Manchester and the paddy-fields of Hindostan. But to those who look a little below the surface the connection is obvious. Cheapness of food leaves the poor Hindu ryot a small margin of earnings, which he can spend on new clothes; and a small margin multiplied by the vast population of British India, not to mention China, produces a marked change in the demand for Lancashire goods.

Although Moore's analysis was somewhat more sophisticated, he, too, attached primary importance to statistical correlations; his elaboration of Jevons' theory was mainly on the statistical side. Moore's main argument was that rainfall cycles bring fluctuations in yields of raw materials, which in turn bring fluctuations in their prices. Bad rainfall means high raw materials prices, which in turn squeeze profits of manufacturers and lead to a decline in industrial investment and a general downswing. Band harvests may also result in an increase in real wages (given great flexibility of money wages) and a consequent drop in profits and investment. Moore was satisfied that, with the introduction of appropriate leads and lags, this explanation of fluctuations fitted the facts.

Much more study should be devoted to the process by which such fluc-

[5] *Ibid.*, pp. 212, 215.

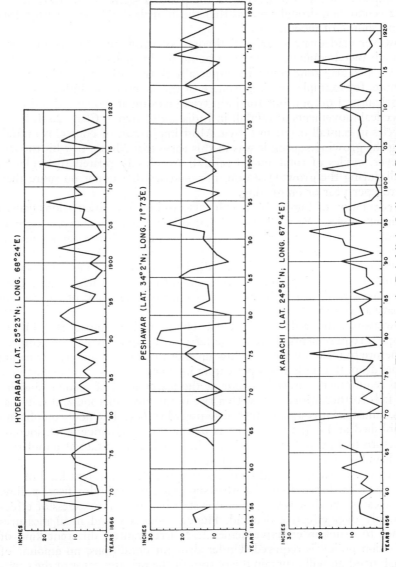

Chart 26-1. Fluctuations in Rainfall in India and Pakistan.

SOURCE: *World Weather Records*, Smithsonian Institution Miscellaneous Publications, Vol CV, No. 79.

tuations are generated; nevertheless, there can be no doubt of the violence of fluctuations in income and employment in arid zone countries nor of their relation to rainfall cycles. The impact effect is clear and direct: no harvest, no work for the rural population, and perhaps even no seed for them to plant for the next harvest. In the pastoral sector of the Libyan and similar economies, drought means that the animals die, leaving pastoralists with no source of income.

However inadequate a "rainfall theory" of economic fluctuations may be for advanced countries, there can be no doubt of its importance in underdeveloped arid zone countries, especially those without petroleum. We may note, for example, the importance of the monsoon in India, not only for agricultural output, but for industrial investment. Some indication of the cyclical movements of rainfall in India are shown in Chart 26–1. Similar cycles in rainfall occur in Libya. Most important, of course, is rainfall during the growing season; it was in this form that Moore cast his theory. However, cycles of total annual rainfall are closely related to cycles in rainfall during the growing season, in countries that count on more than one crop per year or on grazing.

An adaptation of Figure 26–1, will serve to illustrate fluctuations caused by rainfall cycles. We shall assume that this is a poor country, caught in the low-income trap. We shall ignore the upper, high per capita income portions of the curves. We start with equilibrium at Y_1. There is little technological progress and also little diminishing returns, because population growth is small; high fertility rates are offset by high death rates. Thus the *investment* curve will be affected mainly by the stock of capital and will have a negative slope like I_1.

Now assume that a drought occurs. The immediate impact is a shift of the capital requirements curve to the left; more capital would be required than before to maintain the same low level of per capita income. Per capita incomes drop. But with lower per capita incomes, savings also fall; the new capital requirements exceed savings at the lower level of income, and income falls further. Moreover, with a rise in the costs of food and raw materials, industrial investment shifts downward to I_2I_2. The new equilibrium is established at Y_2. If this income is below the subsistence level, income may return to Y_1 through starvation, which reduces the rate of population growth and so reduces capital requirements.

When cycles are generated from the supply side, a different kind of stabilization policy is required from that suggested by orthodox fiscal policy. In these cases, the downswing does not start because of an excess of effective supply over effective demand. Hence, monetary and fiscal measures designed to maintain effective demand are irrelevant; a different kind of stabilization policy is required. Under drought conditions, no amount of internal spending will maintain the output of the private sector of the economy. A major problem in a drought period in such countries is simply to maintain the physical supplies of foodstuffs. For aggregate demand may exceed aggregate supply, and if supplies are not made good by imports or sales from stocks, unemployment and inflation can occur side by side.

In Libya this constellation of problems was met by the establishment of

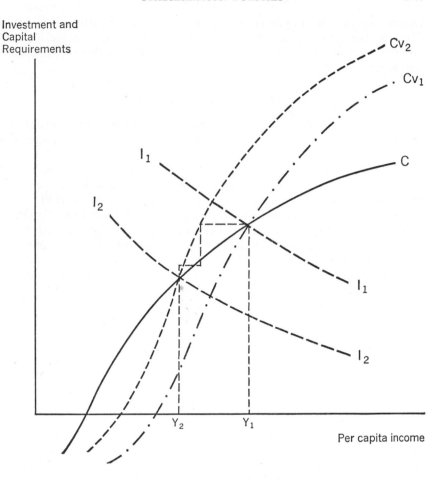

Figure 26-1

the Libyan Public Development and Stabilization Agency. This Agency had a dual purpose: (1) the stockpiling of barley (the staple food in Libya) and the accumulation of foreign exchange reserves in high rainfall years to permit sales from stocks and imports (if needed) in drought years; and (2) the planning and execution of a development program. The Agency received its funds (directly or indirectly) in the form of grants from foreign governments. Thus the foreign exchange needed to expand development spending while maintaining the legal 100 per cent reserves in foreign exchange against the currency was provided automatically. In drought years, the development program can be speeded up to provide money incomes and employment. Barley can be sold against these money incomes from stocks and, if necessary, from imports as well. Accelerated development spending in itself increases the money supply but the required reserves are automatically provided. As the barley stocks are sold the money supply is

reduced again, releasing foreign exchange reserves for further increases in
development spending or for imports. Thus food, money income, and jobs
are provided simultaneously in a manner consistent with maintenance of
stability.[6]

Fluctuations in Exports

Underdeveloped countries outside the arid zone are unstable mainly because of their orientation toward exports, often combined with concentration on a very small range of raw materials and foodstuffs. In recent
decades the markets for these exports have been extremely unstable. This
importance and instability of exports is the main factor which, through the
action of the "multiplier" and "accelerator," causes fluctuations in income
and employment. According to a report of the Economic Commission for
Asia and the Far East, "It has . . . been estimated on a global basis that a
change of only five per cent in average export prices is approximately
equivalent to the entire annual flow of private and public capital and government grants to underdeveloped countries." [7] Yet during the nine-year
period 1948 to 1956 the actual fluctuation *averaged* 10 to 15 per cent for
Thailand rice, for Ceylon tea, for Indonesian and Malayan tin, and Philippines abacá. For Burmese rice, Philippines copra, and Pakistan jute the
range was 15 to 20 per cent. Rubber prices showed an average fluctuation
of 30 per cent. Volume of exports from these countries showed similar
fluctuations in the same directions, adding up to very substantial fluctuations in export earnings.

Variations in income and employment through changes in demand for
exports in underdeveloped countries differ in four ways from fluctuations
generated in this fashion in more advanced countries. First, a larger proportion of the unemployment resulting from a contraction of exports may
be disguised, taking the form of an increase in the number of supernumer-
aries in agriculture. Second, in some of these countries a large reduction in
physical exports cannot be offset by reduced physical imports without
causing extreme hardship. Third, the secondary "super-multiplier" effects
of a contraction in foreign trade are likely to be less pronounced in underdeveloped than in advanced countries. Underdeveloped economies are less
interdependent than advanced ones and the repercussions of changes in income in one sector on employment in another are not as marked. A substantial proportion of the population may be largely outside the market
economy, living close to a subsistence, self-sufficiency level, with a large
share of trade taking barter form. The accelerator, the chief destabilizer of
advanced economies, plays a relatively small role in the less industrialized
ones. Cyclical unemployment therefore tends to be more localized and to
spread less quickly and less comprehensively than in a complex, interdependent, multistage, industrialized economy.

Finally, if the export industries are in foreign hands and profits are usu-

[6] The Agency has since disappeared and Libya's situation has changed. See Chap. 34.
[7] United Nations, *Economic Survey of Asia and the Far East* (New York, 1957),
p. 114.

ally transferred, the domestic income is relatively unaffected by fluctuations in exports; the main impact will be on profits transfers, which are not strictly part of the domestic income. Repercussions may be felt through the government budget because of the close tie between revenues and the volume of exports in such economies. As we shall demonstrate more fully below, most of these countries are in a position to offset fluctuations in exports by internal measures. If government expenditures are maintained in the face of a drop in tax revenues, while, despite a drop in exports, imports are maintained from reserves built up during goods years, domestic income and employment can be kept quite stable in spite of fluctuations in the world market. Since the export sector is often relatively capital-intensive, it represents a smaller share of *employment* than of national income. This makes stabilization easier in such countries than in advanced ones which are similarly export-oriented; the prevention of widespread unemployment does not require shifting of a large share of the labor force from export industries to others.

An International Commodity Stabilization Authority?

Some underdeveloped countries—in particular those such as Indonesia, Brazil, Burma, and Thailand, whose national incomes depend a good deal on export markets for raw materials and foodstuffs—have recently expressed the view that they would need little in the way of foreign capital assistance if they could get a "fair" and stable price for their major exports. An international agency, perhaps under United Nations auspices, might be set up to perform a "buffer stock" and price stabilization function, holding surpluses in years of excess production and disposing of them in years in which demand exceeds supply at the fixed "fair" price.

In the past, some underdeveloped countries have suffered substantially from violent fluctuations in prices of raw materials and foodstuffs. It is also true that if prices of their exports were maintained at the levels reached, let us say, at the peak of the Korean War boom, they could finance their own development program—if they would. But here is the rub: people in underdeveloped countries, no less than in advanced ones, tend to think of the "fair" price as the highest price in the memory of living man. Yet if prices were maintained at peak levels, the danger is that an international stabilization authority would find itself accumulatng continually increasing stockpiles. Moreover, distinguishing cyclical reductions in demand, which will be compensated before long by a cyclical increase, from long-run downward trends, is difficult enough, statistically and analytically, for any group of objective experts. How much more difficult such a distinction will be if deep-seated political considerations are also involved. Suppose, for example, that careful study shows clearly that the cost of production of synthetic rubber has a downward trend, while its range of use is expanding. Will an international stabilization authority have the courage to insist that in the light of this trend the fixed price of natural rubber must be gradually reduced? If it has not, the result will be that countries producing natural rubber will go on producing it for the authority's stockpile, instead of undertaking the structural reorganization of their economies that the situation demands.

One particular scheme has been seriously discussed at international conferences. The International Monetary Fund, an international agency with considerable prestige, in consultation with experts from the major exporting and importing countries, would undertake responsibility for studies aimed at examining the long-run trend in prices of major exports of underdeveloped countries. The Fund and the Governments involved would then agree on an appropriate price for some years in the future, revised as frequently as seemed desirable. If the world market demand for this commodity falls, prices fall below the agreed "trend" price, and the volume of sales falls even at the lower price, the governments concerned would undertake stock-piling as a matter of domestic policy, and make whatever payment to the producers they wish, from their own buffer funds. However, to support this operation and permit imports to continue on a normal basis without hampering development programs, the IMF would permit drawing on its reserves, up to a stipulated percentage of the value of these stockpiles at the predetermined "normal" price. Some increase in the total reserves of the IMF might be necessary for the undertaking of this scheme.

The system has several advantages. It makes the judgments regarding the price trend a matter for joint domestic and international action. It leaves a wide range of discretion to the governments of the countries concerned as to the degree to which they want to enter into buffer stock and buffer fund policies. At the same time, it provides them with international support for the execution of any such policy they may undertake.

The elimination of violent swings in the prices of raw materials and foodstuffs through an international agency could contribute a good deal to the development of underdeveloped areas. It would permit them to prepare and undertake development plans with some assurance that a collapse of the market for their major exports would not prevent their being carried out. The proposal has its dangers, however; if such an agency is established it should not be expected to shore up economies of underdeveloped areas, which have become shaky through failure to adapt to clear-cut and irreversible long-run trends.

Stability and Diversification

Some governments have justified restrictive trade practices on the grounds that diversification of their economies is needed for stabilization purposes.

As a rule, the argument for diversification has been put just the wrong way around. Its function is *not* primarily to stabilize an economy. The argument for diversification as a means of reducing instability arose during a period when the extreme instability of the American economy tended to spread outward to other countries, particularly producers of raw materials and foodstuffs. But let us assume that the United States succeeds in its own brave hopes for steady growth. Let us also imagine that underdeveloped countries diversify to the point of becoming self-sufficient, in investment as well as in production. The main determinant of income and employment in these countries would then be domestic investment. Since some of this investment would be in risky enterprises, domestic investment could be very unstable indeed, and consequently the economy as a whole might be subject to severe fluctuations. If these economies were relatively open, while the American economy was stable, international trade would tend to damp economic fluctuations. Rising national income (inflation) would lead to diminished exports and increased imports, thus checking the boom. Conversely, deflation would lead to rising exports and reduced imports, damping the downswing. This whole question is one which needs reexamination when the assumption that the dominant economy is unstable is replaced by the assumption that it is stable and growing.

The main purpose of diversification is not stabilization but to permit economic growth. If a country wants to increase its output at a faster rate than the world market is expanding, it cannot be content with retaining its share in world markets. Industrialization is then a virtual necessity. Even plantation products, where soil and climate advantages are most clear-cut, face doubtful futures because of increasing competition from synthetics. At best, plantation products can expect a gradual decline in their *share* of the world markets. Such a development is not incompatible with absolute growth of plantation production, but it does imply a falling share of plantation output in national production, if the country is to raise its income at a faster rate than world markets expand. If productivity in plantations keeps pace with productivity in industry—and if it does not, it is likely to lose out even more rapidly to competing synthetics—the share of plantations in national employment will also fall. Industrialization appears to be the only solution.

In short, it is not merely that balanced growth is better than unbalanced growth; rather, these countries must have balanced growth in order to have growth at all. These countries must have an agricultural as well as an industrial revolution. Myrdal quotes Tarlok Singh: "Industrial expansion without agricultural reorganization will leave the bulk of the people in a state of poverty. In other words, we can plan against mass poverty only if we set out to create the conditions of a rapidly expanding and efficient economy both in agriculture and in industry."[8] Myrdal adds, "In most underdeveloped countries improvement of productivity in agriculture is, furthermore, an essential pre-condition for industrialization."

Stability and Commercial Policy

The unbalanced economies of underdeveloped countries do, of course, require special commercial policies. The classical dicta with regard to free trade were based on a kind of marginal analysis which is quite inappropriate where the problem is one of inducing large discontinuous jumps to a completely new structure and level of employment and output. Indeed,

[8] Gunnar Myrdal, *An International Economy: Problems and Prospects* (New York, 1956), p. 206.

given the degree of misallocation of resources already existing in under-developed countries, relative to what could be achieved through such a big push, it may well be that any "distortion" of the price-cost structure through government intervention would bring an improvement. Certainly a properly planned intervention will improve rather than worsen the re-source allocation of underdeveloped countries.

Myrdal is lukewarm about cooperation among underdeveloped countries with respect to foreign trade. Although he does not deny that such coop-eration may be useful, he feels that "the scope for such a cooperation is naturally limited, as almost by definition partnership is more natural between underdeveloped and developed countries than between underde-veloped countries by themselves." This statement seems somewhat in-consistent with Myrdal's insistence that underdeveloped countries be permitted, and indeed urged, to industrialize and shift to a more extensive and mechanized agriculture. It does not follow that there are no limits to the desirable degree of self-sufficiency nor that cooperation among under-developed countries is less natural than with advanced ones. Regional plan-ning among countries in Asia and Africa is long overdue. Industrialization is not tantamount to every country's endeavoring to produce everything, and some integration of national plans to avoid costly overlapping is surely desirable.

Meanwhile, import-replacers are the most hopeful avenue for industrial development. Both the price elasticity and the income elasticity of demand for agricultural products are very low, whereas agricultural countries have a high marginal propensity to import. Consequently, if underdeveloped countries are not to run into serious drains on their foreign exchange bal-ances through their efforts to develop, they must find either new exports or import-replacers. The latter is clearly easier.

The "precarious balance" in which underdeveloped countries find them-selves, with the danger that large-scale development investment will lead to both inflation and a drain on foreign exchange, is an added reason for import controls. Of all kinds of possible import restrictions, multiple ex-change rates come closer to being "a free trader's dream." Recent Indone-sian experience would seem to support this contention; in 1956, thanks to higher advance payments and import surcharges, it was possible to let the market govern foreign exchange allocations and grant virtually all applica-tions for import licenses.[9]

If economic development plans are successful, import restrictions do not involve a decline in total imports of underdeveloped countries. They imply rather a shift in the composition of imports and limiting the *increase* in im-ports as national income rises.

Monetary Policy

Since few underdeveloped countries have highly developed systems of commercial credit or capital markets, it is customary to discount monetary

[9] This experience is analyzed more fully in Benjamin Higgins, *Economic Stabiliza-tion and Development in Indonesia* (New York, 1957).

policy as a stabilization device in these countries. If we include in "monetary policy" all government measures to increase or decrease the money supply through the banking system, however, there is some evidence that monetary policy can be very effective. Efforts at stabilization in Indonesia are a case in point.[10] One of the most interesting aspects of Indonesia's economic policy between 1950 and 1958 was the success of the measures undertaken to reduce the money supply during the two periods when Dr. Sumitro was Minister of Finance. This experience corroborates the evidence provided by the failure of the "cheap money" policies in the United Kingdom, the United States, Canada, and Australia, during the postwar period. This failure, and the consequent reversal of policy by one after the other of these countries, showed that an anti-inflationary fiscal policy is likely to be ineffective unless it is supported by an anti-inflationary monetary policy. The Indonesian story is even more dramatic. It suggests that, where political and administrative barriers prevent the pursuit of the fiscal policy appropriate in an inflationary situation, powerful anti-inflationary forces may be generated by monetary policy alone.

The methods used by the Indonesian government to check monetary expansion were unorthodox in terms of central bank policy of advanced countries. Quantitative and qualitative controls that have become standard central bank policy in advanced countries were not available to the Indonesian government. The revised statutes of the Java Bank, setting it up as a full-fledged central bank with the new name of the Bank of Indonesia, under the control of a monetary board, and with sweeping general powers for monetary control, did not come into force until July, 1953. Even with these statutes in effect, control through ordinary central bank policy was virtually impossible. The Bank of Indonesia statutes were not supported by general banking legislation governing the activities of the commercial banks until 1957. The largest of these were branches of foreign banks whose reserves were held abroad; hence they could not be controlled by ordinary measures to increase or decrease the quantity of commercial bank reserves. There was no "open market" in Indonesia, and the commercial banks did not follow the practice of rediscounting commercial paper with the central bank. Accordingly, during the period in question it was necessary to resort to a species of monetary "gadgetry" designed to fit the institutional framework.

On the whole the "gadgets" worked well. The most effective of them was probably the system of advance payments for foreign exchange. Under this system importers, instead of waiting to take up foreign exchange grants when goods arrived in Indonesian ports, were compelled to make rupiah payments when the foreign exchange license was granted. They also had to pay in advance any "import surcharges" (special duties) to which they would become liable. The 40 per cent advance payments, at their peak at the end of 1952, withdrew nearly 600 million rupiahs from the money supply. The 40 per cent and 75 per cent advance payments combined, at their peak in mid-1953, reduced the money supply by close

[10] For a more detailed exposition of these measures, see *ibid.*

to a billion rupiahs, or by about 15 per cent. During 1955 the net prepayments of importers rose no less than 2 billion rupiahs, or some 17 per cent of the money supply. To some extent, these reductions in money supply may have been offset by financing of importers by wholesalers, or, in the case of standardized commodities such as bicycles, by consumers. To the degree that this financing by wholesalers or consumers represented use of otherwise idle currency or deposits, it meant an increase in velocity of circulation of money which would offset in some measure the reduction in money supply. On balance, however, there can be no doubt that the system of advance payments was a powerful offset to forces tending to increase the money supply. Perhaps the most convincing evidence of the effectiveness of these policies was the reduction in the black market price of the rupiah, despite the strong pressures tending to raise the price of gold and foreign exchange in the black market. The system of advance payments was admirably supplemented by a "gentleman's agreement" with the banks limiting credit to importers, and by a prohibition of transfers of profits by firms indebted to banks, which compelled liquidation of bank loans by foreign firms.

The Indonesian experience supports some of the recent developments in the pure theory of interest, particularly the writings of G. L. S. Shackle. These studies suggest that variations in interest rates influence two kinds of investment decisions: those pertaining to investment in inventories, and those pertaining to investment in long-run projects of a relatively safe nature. These types of investment predominate in a number of underdeveloped countries. Manufacturing, which is characterized by investment in equipment with rapid but uncertain rates of obsolescence, is relatively unimportant in these countries. Investment in inventories, and investment in such long-range projects as rubber and copra plantations, petroleum, and mines, are the major alternatives. Under present circumstances, the latter type of investment may not be considered particularly "safe" in some underdeveloped countries, including Indonesia. Moreover, interest rates in foreign capital markets may be more important than interest rates in the country where the operation takes place. However, the policy regarding transfers of profits probably persuaded foreign companies to obtain working capital abroad rather than through the Indonesian banking system, which in itself was an anti-inflationary move since it permitted a larger volume of imports with a given balance of payments deficit. Certainly the Indonesian "tight money" policy succeeded in forcing goods out of speculative hoards into the market, which is a particularly desirable kind of anti-inflationary move.

To be sure, the monetary measures in Indonesia were all of a type which has only a once-over effect. The impact on money supply of the system of advance down payments dwindles as the lag between application for foreign exchange and sale of imports in Indonesia disappears. The gentleman's agreement imposes a ceiling on, but does not reduce, credit to importers. Similarly, the limit on transfer of profits by firms indebted to banks loses its effect once those debts have been liquidated. Improving fiscal policy was no easier, and offsetting inadequate fiscal policy by ingenious monetary policy was more difficult, for the succeeding government than it had been for the Wilopo government. In 1957, Indonesia finally introduced reserve requirements for banks, partly in cash and partly in treasury bills. By controlling the supply of treasury bills, the central bank has a more orthodox influence on bank reserves.

In general, we may conclude that underdeveloped countries may need monetary measures of a sort tailor-made for their own institutional framework, but that such measures can be an effective instrument of economic stabilization.

Anticyclical Timing of Public Developmental Investment

In the past, economic development has been a powerful destabilizing factor. The theories presented in Chapters 4, 5, and 6 show some of the reasons why. Proper planning, however, can convert *public* investment for development into a stabilizing device. The chronic structural unemployment of the sort common in underdeveloped countries requires steady expansion of investment, public and private. Where *cyclical* unemployment also exists as a consequence of fluctuations in exports and related private investment, it can be offset by timing the expansion of public investment inversely with these fluctuations.

The process of bringing forward public investment projects in order to offset cyclical unemployment has been called "telescoping." Telescoping does not mean diverting physical or fiscal resources to make-work projects; it means only offsetting the temporarily low level of private investment and exports with worthwhile public projects already included in the development plan because of their high priority ratings. Nor does it mean inflation, since the increased public investment merely replaces private investment. As private investment recovers, the public investment sector can be contracted simply by not starting new projects as earlier ones are completed. The development plan should include a reserve of useful projects at the regional and local levels which can be used to absorb cyclical unemployment if necessary. Experience in other countries indicates that the relatively small and labor-intensive projects typically undertaken by regional and local governments have greater flexibility than the heavier construction projects normally undertaken by the central government. Regional and local projects will meet this requirement. The Philippine approach to development planning, with annual revision and addition of another year's projects to replace the projects already completed, permits adjustments more easily than a fixed-period plan.

The problems of timing public investment to help maintain full employment are not intrinsically different in underdeveloped and advanced countries. The present writer has dealt with these problems at some length in an earlier publication, and so will not repeat the discussion in any detail here.[11] It may be worthwhile to point out, however, that underdeveloped

[11] Benjamin Higgins, *Public Investment and Full Employment* (Montreal, 1946), especially Part III.

countries with ambitious development programs including a substantial volume of public investment are in a better position to use public investment as a stabilizing device than are most advanced countries. For such countries should always have a reserve of highly useful public works that can be brought forward whenever private spending falls. Moreover, a large proportion of the projects should be of the small-scale, labor-intensive type that permits greatest flexibility.

In both underdeveloped and advanced countries there is a widespread, but essentially erroneous, idea that public investment is a less flexible instrument of employment policy than variable taxes or transfer payments (such as unemployment insurance). Yet even American experience illustrates the great flexibility of public works on the expansion side. The Civil Works Administration had men at work ten days after it was created, had 814,000 workers on its payroll on the first payday. By the week following, this figure had been doubled and a month later the agency was providing jobs for nearly four million men.[12] The worst that could be said of this remarkable record is that not all the projects were of high priority, but this deficiency reflects lack of advance planning, not lack of flexibility. On the contraction side, the chief requirement for flexibility is a sufficient sprinkling of small-scale projects that can be finished within a few months. Here again the CWA record is impressive; employment was cut from 4.2 million at the end of January, 1934, to 2 million at the end of March, when the operation was transferred to the FERA.

The flexibility of an employment policy has economic, legal and administrative, and technical aspects. The economic aspects consist of the rate at which income and employment can be varied with a given fiscal cost, in the absence of legal, administrative, or technical barriers. On economic grounds, public expenditures on goods and services ("public investment") are clearly *more* flexible than taxes or transfer payments, for the simple reason that variations in public investment affect income and employment in the same income period as that in which action is taken, whereas variable taxes and variable transfer payments affect income and employment only after a lag.[13] Moreover, the marginal propensity to consume is likely to be higher for public investment than for taxes, since the great bulk of public investment goes into wage incomes, whereas a large share of almost any kind of taxes comes out of non-wage incomes. Transfer payments of the family allowance or unemployment insurance type also go mainly to wage incomes. Moreover, the relevant income period itself will tend to be shorter for variable public investment than for variable taxes, since the average lag between receipt and re-spending of income is much shorter for wage than for non-wage incomes. When all these factors are taken into account, it is apparent that, on purely economic grounds, a policy of varying public investment would be more flexible than a policy of variable transfer payments, and a good deal more flexible than variable taxes. This argument, of course, holds a fortiori when unemployment is concentrated

---

[12] Cf. *ibid.*, chap. IX.
[13] This proposition is the basis of the "balanced budget multiplier" theorem.

in particular industries or regions.

By the same token, reliance on variable tax rates and transfer payments for the achievement of a flexible employment policy will necessitate more accurate forecasting than a program which also includes variable public investment. To have expansionary (or deflationary) effects starting at the same time as would be produced by increases (or decreases) of public investment, the decision to reduce (or increase) taxes must be made at least one income period sooner. It should be noted also that the sort of built-in flexibility that is achieved with stable tax rates can be obtained in a public investment policy merely by assuring that public investment falls less than other components of national income. Automatic rules for variations in tax rates would be more effective, especially if coupled with automatically varying or even stable transfer payments. (In Canada such a policy exists in part through the family allowance program.) However, automatic rules for variable expenditures are just as easily formulated. No rule could be more simple than one requiring the government to take onto its payroll any worker discharged by private enterprise. The truth in the proposal to achieve flexibility through tax policy alone is simply that if the budget is big enough, a substantial compensatory effect can be achieved by varying taxes while keeping expenditures stable.

The chief legal and administrative requirements for flexibility of any type of employment policy are two: there must be departments at all relevant levels of government with legal powers to take all necessary steps without delay, including powers to collect or spend funds; and these departments must be going concerns with efficient personnel. These requirements can be met for any type of policy, and the achievement of complete flexibility of any policy requires the concession of a wider range of independent decision to the executive branch of government.

More specifically, the requirements for a flexible tax policy are that the executive branch of government must have power to vary taxes; that channels must be established for giving notice of tax changes or issuing forms and instructions, and so forth; and that some inducements must be available to persuade regional and local governments to integrate their tax policies with the central policy. Requirements for a flexible public investment policy are a fully planned reserve of useful projects, power of the executive branch to subsidize acceleration of central, regional, and local public investment programs, advance acquisition of sites or sweeping powers of condemnation, and reliance on government force-account work or advance letting of contracts with an "escalator clause."

The technical barriers to a variable tax policy or a variable transfer payment consist mainly of paper work and are not very important. The technical problems in a public investment program consist mainly of the engineering limitations on the speed with which projects can be started and finished. A program heavily weighted with relatively small-scale projects, which reach peak employment quickly and have an average duration of about six months, would involve no serious technical barriers to flexibility. Within two months of starting the expansion, some projects would mature each month. Within six months, some 15 to 20 per cent of the total program would mature each month. Consequently, the program as a whole could be rapidly contracted merely by failing to replace maturing projects with new ones. If large projects of long duration are launched in a downswing of private investment, they should be of a sort that has social priority so high that prompt completion is desirable even under prosperity conditions.

Thus, on economic grounds, public investment is most flexible, transfer payments are next most flexible, and tax policy is least flexible. On legal and administrative grounds, all types of policy could be made equally flexible. On technical grounds, public investment presents the greatest problems, but these can be overcome.

In underdeveloped countries, however, there may be an incompatibility between stability and growth of a more subtle form. Maximizing the rate of economic growth requires an *optimal sequence* of projects. This optimal sequence may require undertaking projects in a different order from the one that would be most efficient in terms of telescoping. Where such a conflict arises, the society must choose between greater stability and more rapid development.

27 || Foreign Investment

Few questions of economic development policy arouse such deep emotions or generate such wide differences of opinion as the role of foreign private investment. Some writers, mainly in the advanced "private enterprise" countries, see foreign investment in underdeveloped countries as the one real hope for abolishing poverty. Others, mostly in newly independent countries, see it as the chief instrument of "economic imperialism," the device by which the former colonial powers wish to retain control over the economies of the ex-colonies. Even in advanced countries, however, there are scholars who argue that the developing countries are better off without foreign investment, and some go so far as to maintain that the developing countries not only should forget about new foreign investment but should expropriate the foreign investments they already have.

The Cost of Foreign Investment

The argument against foreign investment on economic grounds is based on the cost of servicing foreign debt relative to the benefits it brings. Professor Wendell C. Gordon, for example, has shown that even in the United States, the cost of servicing foreign debt exceeded new net capital inflow from about 1830 on.[1] Foreign investment may also delay the development of domestic cadres of managers, scientists, and technicians. On these grounds Professor Gordon believes that developing countries would do better to proceed on their own. However, we are confronted here with a question of fact; the relationship of cost of debt service to net capital in-

[1] Wendell C. Gordon, "Foreign Investment," *University of Houston Business Review*, Fall, 1962.

flow is not the only element involved in appraising the contribution of foreign enterprise—nor even that plus the impact on long-run supply of skills. The question is whether in the United States, for example, the railways and the canals could have been built at all, at the time they were constructed, without British capital and high-level skills. The debt incurred was serviced out of the much higher level of income which the imported capital and skills helped to produce. The question cannot, unfortunately, be answered with precision; no one can say what would have happened to the rate of economic growth in the United States (or anywhere else) if no foreign investment had taken place.

The Case for Expropriation

The economic argument for expropriating existing foreign enterprises also rests, obviously, on the high cost of servicing foreign private indebtedness (including transfers of profits) and the stimulus expropriation provides to the development of domestic skills. Large-scale expropriation has taken place in several developing countries—Mexico, Iran, Egypt, Indonesia, Brazil—with varying degrees of success. It seems to have worked well in Mexico. In Indonesia, it seems to have delayed a take-off.

Using arithmetic models based on reasonable assumptions as to quantitative relationships and behavior patterns, Bronfenbrenner shows that economic growth can be significantly accelerated by expropriation "in societies whose income distributions include high property shares which are not ploughed back into economic development."[2] In his examples, property income is set at 15 per cent of national income. The initial flow of savings is set at 5 per cent of national income, but developmental investment is only 2 per cent of national income, yielding a 1.7 per cent annual increase in national income. With restraint on consumption, development investment jumps immediately to 10 per cent of national income and the rate of growth to about 2.5 per cent. With some immediate increase in consumption permitted, development investment rises to 5 per cent and the growth rate to about 1.9 per cent.

Obviously, unilateral action by the government of an underdeveloped area to confiscate foreign properties would undermine that country's relations with the outside world and would probably destroy temporarily any hopes of obtaining new capital assistance. Transfer of foreign enterprises to domestic ownership might be arranged on a multilateral basis, however, and this could be the form that foreign aid takes. The United Nations, or one of its Specialized Agencies, or some other organization engaged in capital assistance to underdeveloped areas, might undertake to compensate foreign investors in underdeveloped areas in their own currencies. Ownership of these enterprises could then be transferred to nationals of those underdeveloped countries without loss to the original investors. The effect would be to enrich those countries, in the form of free foreign exchange, by the amount of profits and depreciation now being transferred to foreign

[2] Martin Bronfenbrenner, "The Appeal of Confiscation in Economic Development," *Economic Development and Cultural Changes*, April, 1955, pp. 201-18.

investors. This foreign exchange, and its domestic currency counterpart, could then be used to finance economic development.

This approach has some serious limitations. First, there are relatively few underdeveloped countries where the additional financial resources that could be made available for economic development through confiscation would be sufficient to do the job. There would of course be substantial differences in this respect from one country to another; in countries where foreign enterprises comprise a large share of the economy and plough back little of their earnings within the country this limitation would not apply.

Secondly, the necessary technical and managerial personnel for operating such enterprises is often not available among nationals of underdeveloped countries. Obtaining them on a salary basis may not be easy if combined with confiscation, even when the confiscation takes place through international agreement.

Thirdly, the confiscation approach is essentially "isolationist" in character. From many points of view, an approach involving elements of "partnership" between the underdeveloped countries and the advanced ones is more attractive; it seems better designed to produce an integrated international economy.

The Case for Foreign Investment

Some of the arguments made for foreign investment, on the other hand, have been somewhat incautious. Sometimes they come dangerously close to saying only, "Foreign investment took place in Esperanza and development took place afterward, so foreign investment is the road to future development as well;" and sometimes, too, they seem to say, "What worked in the United States should work anywhere."

Western Enterprise in Indonesia and Malaysia

An example of the former approach is Allen and Donnithorne's study [3] of the impact of Western enterprise on development in Indonesia and Malaya. Allen and Donnithorne seem to accept as a foregone conclusion the tenet that Western enterprise *must* have raised per capita incomes of the native peoples. By 1940, in Indonesia, "The standard of life of the native population was still low; but the vastly increased numbers certainly enjoyed a higher consumption per head than the tiny population of the early nineteenth century. . . . In Malaya the transformation had been equally striking. A savage and empty land had been peopled. . . . In the early 1950's the population of Malaya enjoyed a higher level of income per head than any other country in East Asia. For these accomplishments Westerners can take most of the credit. . . ."

[3] G. C. Allen and Audrey G. Donnithorne, *Western Enterprise in Indonesia and Malaya* (London, 1957). See also, G. C. Allen and Audrey G. Donnithorne, *Western Enterprise in Far Eastern Economic Development: China and Japan* (London, 1954), pp. 264–65. For a more detailed discussion of the first-named, see Benjamin Higgins, "Western Enterprise and Economic Development of Southeast Asia," *Pacific Affairs*, March, 1958.

This judgment on the contribution of Western enterprise to economic development leads the authors to an implicit policy conclusion: for further development, what such countries need is more Western enterprise. They leave the impression that "the outlook is bleak"—especially for Indonesia—because the climate is no longer favorable for Western enterprise. They suggest that what Indonesia and Malaya need for their further development is "more of the same." But the fact is that Western enterprise did not develop those countries, in the sense in which their governments now use the term "develop." Western enterprise was limited to land-and-capital-intensive ventures providing incomes and employment for only a small fraction of the population. Western enterprise generated a "population explosion" for which there was no offsetting growth of employment opportunities in the technologically advanced, high-productivity sector. There was not enough capital for high productivity in the peasant agriculture sector where most of the rapidly growing population had to seek a livelihood. In that sector, incomes remained close to subsistence levels.

As a result of the efforts and ingenuity of Western enterprise, in 1937 Malaya had some $455 million, and Indonesia some $2.24 billion, invested in plantations, mines, oil fields and refineries, commerce and finance. Western enterprises had made substantial profits, and as Allen and Donnithorne demonstrate, had shown admirable flexibility in adapting themselves to changing conditions so as to produce a respectable profits record. The Malayan population had grown from a few hundred thousand at the beginning of the nineteenth century to some six million in 1940, the Indonesian population from some five million to seventy million. For the period 1952–54 (no comparisons can be made for earlier years) per capita net national product was about $310 in Malaya and about $90 in Indonesia. Malaya was more highly developed than Indonesia in terms of the structure of the economy, with less than half the national income originating in agriculture as compared to nearly two-thirds in Indonesia.

These differences in results demand explanation. Even more important than the differences, however, is the fundamental similarity in outcome: all this investment and enterprise left most of the people poor in both countries. Satisfactory figures are not available, but it would appear that peasant per capita income in both countries is in the $40–$60 (annually) range prevalent throughout Asia, with Malaya (which has a somewhat smaller proportion of peasants in the total population) somewhat closer to the upper end of this range than Indonesia.[4] No Asian government could contemplate another century of development that produced such meager results as the last one. For it is not at all "certain" that per capita consumption of the *native* population rose during the period under review. Obviously, taking national income and dividing it by total population tells little about living standards of the masses of the people, even where reliable figures are available. Probably per capita consumption did rise in Malaya. In Indonesia there seems to have been an initial rise followed by a fall. The Dutch

[4] There seems to be some kind of "iron law" of peasant income. Yields seem to vary inversely with size of holding, so as to keep income per family much the same in all Asian peasant societies.

have on the whole taken pride in their performance in Indonesia, but few Dutch writers or politicians have claimed that Indonesian living standards "certainly" rose under their rule. On the contrary, Dutch scholars and administrators have periodically voiced their misgivings and have frequently expressed concern over the declining living standards of the Indonesians, especially on the island of Java.

The theories of underdevelopment presented in Part 4 explain why foreign investment in plantations, mines, oil fields, and commerce did not bring rising living standards to the peoples of underdeveloped countries. These theories certainly do not show that further foreign investment in these countries is undesirable. On the contrary, there can be little doubt that foreign enterprise still has a substantial role to play in the development of underdeveloped areas. Countries like Indonesia and Malaya lack the capital and the technical and managerial skills for further development. Providing these resources through foreign aid programs is difficult and seldom completely satisfactory. But foreign enterprise must adapt itself to the needs of national economic development; it cannot be just "more of the same." Industrial investment of a capital-intensive nature will not do the job alone; the problem of low productivity in agriculture must be attacked directly, and some capital must be directed into the peasant agriculture sector to permit more mechanized and larger-scale farming. In short, foreign investment must be encouraged, but within a framework of national development planning, not laissez faire.

United States Enterprise in Brazil

An example of the second kind of uncritical praise for foreign investment is the study by a group of scholars from Michigan State University of United States business in Brazil.[5] The authors begin by announcing that the predominant United States presence in Latin America today is not the United States government but American private enterprise. The statement is based on field work conducted in Brazil only; a survey was made of the operations, attitudes, and problems of forty-seven American firms in that country.

Since World War II, the United States has become much the most important source of foreign capital for Brazil, with West Germany in second place. The typical evolution of American firms in Brazil is (1) the use of a Brazilian distributor for American products, (2) the sale of American products through the firm's own distribution organization in Brazil, (3) licensing of a Brazilian firm to manufacture some or all of the parent firm's products, (4) establishment of assembly operations in Brazil, and finally (5) complete integration. American firms have been encouraged to expect higher profits on their Brazilian returns. Since 1950 the number of American firms has increased from 236 to more than 600. With increasing restrictions on imports, these firms ultimately face the choice between

[5] Claude McMillan, Jr., and Richard F. Gonzales (with Leo Erickson), *International Enterprise in a Developing Economy, A Study of U.S. Business in Brazil* (Lansing, Mich., 1964).

abandoning their Brazilian markets or producing within the country. In implementing the decision to produce in Brazil, the entrepreneur-promoter has played a strategic role. With the growth of United States manufacturing concerns has come a parallel growth of American banking, accounting, legal, and consulting services.

The major obstacles to American investment in Brazil have been import restrictions, control of capital movements, red tape and delay in government agencies, labor legislation, shortage of skills, inadequate transport and communications, underdeveloped capital and money markets, left-wing nationalism, and rampant inflation. One might question the last of these factors. As previously mentioned, the present writer's impression (shared by the World Bank Mission) was that until 1963, inflation was not clearly an obstacle to economic growth or investment in Brazil: the entire institutional framework was adapted to it in such a way that the economy operated on a sort of "real value" basis. Indeed, the present government's efforts to curb inflation met with strong opposition from some elements of the business community. It may be, however, that American enterprises, less accustomed to operating under chronic inflation than their Brazilian counterparts, did find inflation a problem. The Michigan State study goes on to say that investments were made despite these obstacles, and "those U.S. firms who have invested and are operating in Brazil today regard these impediments largely as nuisances."

The study devotes considerable space to and exhibits much concern for the image of United States enterprise in Brazil. It repeats the story of the International Monetary Fund's insistence in 1959 on Brazil's "putting its fiscal house in order," which led to breaking off negotiations with IMF and identification of United States as the villain in the piece, the IMF being regarded in Brazil as a mere instrument of U.S. policy. A survey of public opinion showed that Brazilians typically believe that American firms are making huge profits and exploiting Brazilians. Some United States managers, the authors report, have been shocked to learn that their "missionary crusade" in Brazil has not been appreciated. In sum, the authors state, "while it is apparent that the image of U.S. enterprise in Brazil is generally good, and probably better than in other of the less developed nations of the world, animosity smoulders."

American executives in Brazil are younger and better educated than those in the United States. Brazilians are usually passed by in favor of such Americans for top management positions. The American executive in Brazil tends to pattern his operations after those of the parent company. American managers in Brazil are good employers and more ready to deal with organized labor than their Brazilian counterparts. Whatever the explicit complaint of Brazilian employees of American companies, the real basis of dissatisfaction is likely to be the higher salaries paid to foreign personnel and the reservation of top management jobs for Americans. As far as the general public is concerned, a major problem is the unwillingness of Brazilians to "turn over their rich natural resources" to foreigners. This attitude has been vividly expressed in the case of M. A. Hanna Company, an international mining company interested in developing Brazil's iron industry. Reluctance to make conditions attractive to foreign firms has left Brazil with only 1 per cent of the world's iron ore market, although it has one-third of the world's known iron ore reserves.

Unfortunately an otherwise interesting and solid study is marred by gratuitous conclusions, not based on the author's own research. "The real obstacles," they say, "which limit optimum beneficial exploitation of U.S. enterprise in Latin America, are: (1) ignorance of the character of modern, international corporate enterprise; (2) ignorance of the incompetence of government to initiate or accelerate economic growth through central planning." Brazil's early industrial development under government guarantees and tax exemptions, etc., they say, did not initiate sustained industrial growth. The inability of governments to deal effectively with the totality of economic development has been fully documented, they add, and in rapidly developing societies, the vast majority of decisions are made by private managerial leadership. Western Europe is cited as a case in point. But the reconstruction of western Europe was a very different affair from the promotion and continuation of economic growth in Latin America today. It may be true that "private business is society's most ideologically neutral institution, its most specifically goal-directed force" in the United States at the present time; it can surely be debated whether the same may be said of Brazilian private business today.

Brazil is a country that has suffered from misdevelopment, as well as underdevelopment. Government intervention has been sporadic, unsystematic, contradictory, and based on no rational calculus of any kind. In an essentially private enterprise society (although it should not be forgotten that 60 per cent of new investment in Brazil is made by public enterprise, including Autarchias and mixed enterprises), this sort of intervention has no doubt discouraged some private investment. There can be no doubt that United States private enterprise can provide managerial and scientific skills that are badly needed in Brazil for its next phase of economic development. But the Michigan State study itself does not demonstrate that "U.S. corporate enterprise constitutes the most promising vehicle with which the United States can promote rapid development in Latin America." Brazil is not the whole of Latin America. Even in Brazil, the United States may have a greater impact on Brazilian development through encouraging and supporting the kind of enlightened economic policy which the Brazilian government pursued under Minister of Planning Campos and Finance Minister Bulhoes, than it can be making Brazil attractive for United States corporate enterprise.

The Scale of United States Foreign Investment

We saw in Chapter 10 above that in relation to the world economy the total flow of capital from the United States to other countries today is a tiny trickle in comparison with the flood of capital emanating from the United Kingdom in the nineteenth century. If United States foreign investment is to play a substantial role in the future development of the now underdeveloped countries it must be expanded greatly. As it is now, even such foreign investment as is made by Americans goes mainly to

Western Europe and Canada (see Table 27–1). Among developing countries the richer countries in Latin America are the favorites; but at the end of 1961, private investments in Western Europe exceeded those in all Latin American countries combined, and investments in Canada were

TABLE 27–1

United States Investment Position at the End of 1961 (millions of dollars)

	Total	Western Europe	Canada	Latin America
United States assets and investments abroad (including government)	77,331	21,189	19,229	14,374
Private investments	55,517	12,737	19,224	11,579
Long-term	48,927	11,340	18,040	9,565
Direct	34,684	7,655	11,804	8,166
Portfolio and other	14,243	3,685	6,236	1,599
Short-term	6,590	1,397	1,184	1,814

SOURCE: U.S. Department of Commerce.

nearly double those in Latin America. Safety, liquidity, and profit rates combine to make nearby Canada and well-understood Western Europe attractive to American investors. There is a notion abroad that because underdevelopd countries are "short of capital," investment there must be more profitable than in advanced countries. The reverse is closer to the truth. For example, in 1958–59, returns on United States manufacturing investment abroad were only 8.1 per cent for Latin America, whereas they were 13.8 per cent for European Common Market countries combined and 13.9 per cent for the European Free Trade Area.

Encouragement of Private Foreign Investment

Many people in underdeveloped countries still believe that a huge flood of foreign capital is waiting to inundate those lands if the gates are opened. Nothing could be further from the truth. Currently there is a *world* shortage of capital. Even countries with high standards of living, such as Canada and Australia, still find it necessary to borrow abroad to finance their economic development. The most highly developed country of all, the United States, offers investors earnings above 10 per cent on the highest-grade industrial securities. Far from being a matter of "permitting" foreign capital to enter under restrictive conditions, it is a matter of competing for capital against other countries in both the highly developed and the less developed categories.

In countries recently emerged from colonial status, the general public must learn the difference between "colonialism" and foreign investment. Foreign investment in a sovereign country, with its own corporation, tax, and monetary legislation, foreign exchange control, etc., is a totally different thing from investment in colonies by citizens of a colonial power.

Certainly, big business tends to exert an influence on government policy in any country where it exists; but this fact is no less true when the big business is owned by nationals than when it is owned by foreigners, and the foreigners are often easier to handle, just because they are foreigners with less influence on the electorate, than nationals would be.

The United Nations Economic Commission for Asia and the Far East has summarized very well the requirements of foreign investors regarding investment in less-developed countries—the requirements that must be met if any significant volume of foreign capital is to be attracted to these countries: [6]

The question of encouraging private foreign investments in the countries of the [ECAFE] region has recently assumed very great importance. The prospective investor, however, wants to be sure about the climate for foreign investments in the receiving countries. The elements that constitute a favourable climate from his point of view may be briefly indicated as follows:

(1) Political stability and freedom from external aggression.
(2) Security of life and property.
(3) Availability of opportunities for earning profits.
(4) Prompt payment of fair compensation and its remittance to the country of origin in the event of compulsory acquisition of a foreign enterprise.
(5) Facilities for the remittance of profits, dividends, interest, etc.
(6) Facilities for the immigration and employment of foreign technical and administrative personnel.
(7) A system of taxation that does not impose a crushing burden on private enterprise.
(8) Freedom from double taxation.
(9) Absence of vexatious controls.
(10) Non-discriminatory treatment of foreigners in the administration of controls.
(11) Absence of competition of state-owned enterprises with private capital.
(12) A general spirit of friendliness for foreign investors.

Guarantees for Foreign Investors

What measures can be suggested for meeting the twelve requirements listed above, without sacrificing any degree of sovereignty and without compromising the government's freedom with respect to economic policy?

1 and 2. The question of international security and political stability is of course outside an economist's field of competence. Internal security is also a non-economic question. Insurance provisions might help. The governments might consider setting up their own insurance organizations for the purpose or, lacking experience and personnel for such a task, might enter into discussions with foreign insurance firms. It might pay to give some subsidy in local currency to insurance companies assuming the risks of loss of life and property of foreigners, if such subsidies would help to

[6] United Nations Economic Commission for Asia and the Far East, Committee on Industry and Trade, Second Session, "Foreign Investment Laws and Regulations in the ECAFE Region," (Bangkok, March, 1950), pp. 4-5.

bring significant amounts of foreign exchange into the country. Of course, foreigners would want only policies with benefits payable in foreign currency, but any insurance company will have local currency expenses, so a local currency subsidy would be acceptable to them. Alternatively, the government of the lending countries might expand the scope of insurance of approved foreign investment.

3. No special policy is necessary to provide opportunities for profitable investment; in some fields, they certainly exist. Governments might provide information to foreign business and industrial organizations regarding investment opportunities, however, and they might undertake to provide the complementary public utilities, public works, and community services needed to permit new enterprises to operate, attract personnel, and market products.

4. With regard to nationalization, there are two possible approaches: First, to guarantee that no nationalization shall take place until initial and supplementary investments have been recouped, and a reasonable aggregate profit on the investment has been earned. The only obvious objection to this approach is need for a government to put up with an inefficient foreign firm indefinitely, just because its rate of earnings is low and accordingly it requires a very long time to accumulate the stipulated aggregate profit. In such cases, the foreign investor would usually be willing to sell out for a reasonable price. Secondly, to promise prior consultation and notice, plus "fair compensation," to be determined in cases of dispute by the International Court of Justice at The Hague. Some combination of these two provisions might be worked out, the first to apply in general, and the second to be resorted to in special and unusual circumstances, which might be itemized.

5. If foreign capital is to be attracted in significant quantities, freedom of transfer of profits (net of tax) must be accorded, including transfer of depreciation allowances if the foreign investor wishes to withdraw his capital gradually over a period of time. Also, facilities should be provided for the transfer of ownership from one foreigner to another, subject to approval of the authorities. The only restrictions on transfers should be on transfer of proceeds of sales of assets for local currency.

6. Direct investment (which is the only form likely to be attractive to foreigners in the near future) will not take place unless the foreign firms can bring their own managers and technicians.[7] No restrictions, other than those essential to security, should be imposed on immigration of such personnel; on the contrary, every facility should be afforded to assist such immigration. Indeed, except for diplomatic status, skilled personnel of foreign firms should be accorded the same sort of treatment as experts brought in under the UN Technical Assistance program; assistance should be provided in obtaining passage and visas, in finding suitable living accommodations, etc.

Foreign firms should, however, take on some obligations with respect to training local staff. Perhaps amounts spent on training local staff might be

[7] Cf. paper by Everett Hagen, "The Problem of Management in an Underdeveloped Economy," M.I.T., CIS, October 18, 1954 (Document Control #C/54–18).

made deductible from tax, instead of from taxable income.

7. The tax problem is most complex of all and cannot be analyzed fully here. Some of the problems regarding taxation apply equally to foreign and to domestic firms. However, some major points may be made:

a) The regulations governing foreign investment should promise identical treatment with respect to taxes of foreign and domestic firms and their personnel; there must certainly be no discrimination against foreign firms.

b) The governments might also promise prior consultation of foreign investors when tax legislation clearly injurious to their interests is under discussion.

c) Some tax concessions might be made to encourage investment. A difficulty here is that concessions on personal and company income tax may be of no use, because they would merely mean that foreign firms and their staffs would pay more taxes in their own countries. However, it would be possible and helpful to exempt new firms, or new investments of existing ones, from export and import taxes for a limited period.

d) Income taxes present a special problem, since the rates are often higher in the underdeveloped country, on salaries which are at customary levels for managerial and technical personnel, than they would be in the lending countries. That is, when translated into local currency at official rates, a normal salary in United States or Canadian dollars for a production manager, say, would put him into a higher tax bracket than he would be in at home, with the same salary. Thus exemption from income tax for a limited period would be significant for many foreign investors. Another possibility would be to permit the employers to pay income tax, in order to attract efficient staff, and allow the firm to deduct such income tax payments on behalf of staff from tax liability, instead of from taxable income. Any such privilege should then be accorded also to new investments of domestic firms, to avoid discrimination. It is unlikely that such a scheme would reduce revenues of the government; by bringing a larger proportion of employees into the range of accurate bookkeeping, it might very well improve personal income tax collections so much that it would more than offset the loss on corporation income tax.

In general, care must be taken not to drive out existing firms by giving new firms competitive advantages. Potential foreign investors will get their impressions of possibilities in underdeveloped countries mainly from the reports of foreign firms already operating in the country. Also, experienced firms are likely to contribute more to development than inexperienced ones.

e) Certain types of "incentive tax schemes," which might be applied to investment in general, would be of special interest to foreign investors. These include:

(1) Averaging profits for tax purposes over a longer period, say, ten years
(2) Liberal provisions for accelerated depreciation on new investments of a type, or made at a time or place, designated by the government
(3) Permitting profits used for new investment of a kind, or made at a time or in a place, approved by the government, to be deducted from taxable income

Certain less-developed countries, such as India and Pakistan, have already taken steps of this kind.

8. Double taxation must certainly be avoided, and the governments should sign treaties concerning double taxation with all the countries likely to provide significant amounts of capital.

9. The question of controls is a sore point among foreign businessmen and investors. Many of the controls which irritate foreign investors are not essential to the achievement of the government's true policy objectives. Existing controls should be thoroughly reviewed to distinguish the essential from the nonessential.

10. Foreign investors should be guaranteed treatment regarding controls identical to that accorded to nationals.

11. An outright guarantee that no publicly owned enterprise would compete in the same field would leave the door open to monopolistic exploitation by foreign firms. It should be given, therefore, only in conjunction with some provision for control of monopolistic exploitation.

12. A "general spirit of friendliness" is not something that can be written into regulations but public information could be so phrased as to indicate such a spirit, where it exists.

No government, of course, can undertake not to devalue its currency; a situation might conceivably arise in which devaluation was necessary. The guarantees regarding nationaliatzion might be stated in terms of the currency of the investors' home countries; that is, the Canadian investor would be assured of no nationalization until he had got back his capital plus reasonable cumulative profits, in terms of Canadian dollars. Apart from this assurance, the only other possibility would be some sort of insurance against loss through devaluation. Perhaps the lending countries could be induced to provide such insurance, along the lines of the Canadian Export Credits Guarantees Corporation or the Mutual Security Administration's guarantee program. Permitting foreign firms to do their accounting in the currencies they initially invest would also help.

Again, no government could guarantee foreign investors against labor difficulties. The governments might, however, improve the arbitration machinery and publicize this improvement abroad. They might also embark on a campaign, similar to that undertaken by the Labor government in the United Kingdom after 1946, to teach organized labor its responsibilities toward the nation, and to teach workers that only through increased output can they gain a higher standard of living for themselves. Publicity abroad could then be given to this campaign as well.

Raising labor productivity through training and improved equipment is of course a long-run approach. Meanwhile, for export industries facing genuine difficulties because of high labor costs and falling prices, some system of wage subsidies might be worked out. Such subsidies should accrue in the first instance to the employer, to permit him to cover the gap between current wage rates and value productivity per man-hour. For social and political reasons, there would have to be an accompanying benefit for workers, but it should not take a form that would permit workers to maintain a customary normal standard of living while working less hard or less well. It might, for example, take the form of a government contribution to an employer-managed old age pension fund, or an employer-managed health scheme, or something of the sort, with the government contributions exceeding the actual cost to the employer.

Handling foreign investment problems so as to offer every possible inducement to foreign investors, while protecting vital national rights, requires a special high-level organization, which might be called the Foreign Investment Board. The Board would need a secretariat, which might be called the Foreign Investment Bureau. This Bureau would be comprised of technicians and experts, who would be responsible for administering policy regarding foreign investment, along the general lines laid down by the government. The logical place for this Bureau would be either in the central bank, or in the development planning agency.

It would be helpful if this "F.I.B." had on its staff one or two foreign experts, provided under one of the technical assistance programs, who could "talk the language" of foreign investors, not merely in the sense of knowing English, French, or German, but in the sense of knowing what attitudes and worries they have, and what various words mean to them. These experts should have experience with capital markets abroad. It would also be desirable for the F.I.B. to have a representative attached to the embassy in each country likely to furnish significant amounts of capital, to provide information to potential investors. The F.I.B. might also prepare prospectuses of particular investment possibilities, for distribution among potential investors abroad.

In order to make it unnecessary for the F.I.B. to deal separately with hundreds of small foreign firms, parallel organization of foreign investors should be encouraged. This organization might retain legal counsel and possibly a small research staff, and contributions to the expenses of the organization might be made deductible from taxable income. The organization could then deal with the F.I.B. on matters of taxation, import regulations, foreign exchange regulations, etc., of interest to all foreign investors. Large-scale foreign investors, such as oil companies, would of course retain their right to deal directly with the Board, or even directly with the government in the case of very large interests.

Increasing the flow of private capital to underdeveloped countries will probably require a recasting of economic policies in both underdeveloped and advanced countries. Professor Gunnar Myrdal has suggested that ways should be found of inducing the international capital market itself to play its proper role in channeling capital from countries where it is relatively abundant to those where it is scarce. He points out that financial institutions are no longer permitted to pursue shortsighted and selfish profit-maximizing policies so far as their domestic operations are concerned. On the contrary, they have been compelled to serve the interests of national policy, including improvements in income distribution, maintenance of full employment without inflation, and the like. The problem now, Myrdal argues, is to make these institutions play a similar role internationally, promoting the aims of agreed international policy.

To the present writer two things seem essential to any such policy.

First, capital must be provided in bigger lumps than private organizations have hitherto found feasible. As shown earlier, in underdeveloped countries it often happens that each of a series of one hundred $1,000,000 loans would be rejected on banking principles, whereas a single investment of $100 million may be very worthwhile indeed. Some means must be found to persuade private institutions to make loans of this order.

Institutional rearrangements would be necessary on the marketing side as well. The major benefits derived from such large-scale investments are often in the form of "external economies," rather than direct returns through sale of the immediate product. Consequently, if such large units of investment are to be made attractive to private enterprise, methods must be found to permit either the borrower or the lender to cash in on the external economies as well as on the direct returns. These two requirements probably involve collective action by groups of financial institutions, and we may need to recast our thinking about the merits and demerits of "combination" in the field of finance.

The problem of inducing a larger volume of international capital movements, however, is not merely one of increasing the *supply* of international capital; in some of the countries that need it most, it is also a matter of increasing the *demand*. Nationalist revolutions and the recent emergence from colonialism, especially in the neutralist countries that count most in this context, have left an aftermath of suspicion of foreign enterprise. In some of these countries there is a firm resolve not to allow "foreign-monopoly-capitalist-imperialists" to gain access to the country's "rich natural resources." Yet as we have seen above, direct investment in resource development is often the most attractive form of investment to foreigners.

One solution to this dilemma is the "management contract." Where there is a large domestic market for an existing product, a contract can sometimes be arranged to set up a national company, with management hired from a foreign company producing the product. The new national company is granted licenses to import from the foreign "managing" concern in certain amounts and for certain periods. During this time the new company, with technical and managerial advice from the foreign firm, builds a local plant to produce the same commodity. The foreign firm might continue to operate the new plant until the host country can take over. In the case of exports for which there is no significant domestic market, the foreign managing firm must set up a plant immediately, which is not quite such an attractive proposition as a rule. However, the arrangement can involve handsome profits for the foreign concern even if they are disguised as management fees. Some management contracts between Latin American countries and foreign oil companies have actually proved more profitable to the companies than the usual "fifty-fifty" arrangement. At the same time, the arrangement has the great advantage that the *ownership* is national from start to finish. Tax concessions for investment in underdeveloped countries and special insurance arrangements as sketched earlier in this chapter might also help to promote a flow of capital to underdeveloped countries.

28 | Foreign Aid

Even with the most liberal policies toward private foreign investors in developing countries—in lending and borrowing countries alike—the flow of private capital will not fill the gap between capital requirements for development and potential domestic investment. A substantial role will remain for loans and grants from governments, commonly called foreign aid. By the same token, international transfers of human resources through government channels, whether bilateral or multilateral, will be needed to supplement technical assistance through the private sector. The controversy over foreign aid has been much more in the public eye than any controversy over policy regarding foreign investment, and thinking about it has been considerably more confused. We shall begin, therefore, with a brief review of the "theory" of foreign aid—such as it is—and then turn to a description of foreign aid programs.

Theory of Foreign Aid

There is very little really sophisticated literature on the theory of foreign aid, and it could hardly be claimed that foreign aid programs in practice are based on such refined theories as there are. The truth is that foreign aid programs developed first on an *ad hoc* basis, and the effort to provide a logically consistent rationale came afterward.

Why Is Aid Given?

It is not even clear as to why the donor countries believe foreign aid should be provided. Moral obligation to help the poor, the threat to national security entailed in the widening gap between rich and poor nations, the desire to win allies, and the possibilities of expanding world trade have all been cited as reasons for helping the underdeveloped countries with their development programs.

In his Inaugural Address, President Kennedy stressed the moral obligation to help less prosperous peoples:

To those peoples in the huts and villages of half the globe struggling to break the bonds of mass misery, we pledge our best efforts to help them to help themselves, for whatever period is required—not because the Communists may be doing it, not because we seek their votes, but because it is right. If a free society cannot help the many who are poor, it cannot save the few who are rich.

Most statements of the objectives of foreign economic policy are general and vague. There is no lack of such statements: speeches by presidents, secretaries of state, and foreign policy administrators; the documents arising out of work of the Draper Committee; [1] the various submissions to the Special Senate Committee of the United States Senate to Study the Foreign Aid Program; [2] the more recent submissions to the Senate Committee on Foreign Relations; [3] and statements by independent research organizations and scholars. [4] Nearly all these statements have a common stamp. For the purposes of an earlier study, [5] the present writer summarized the essence of these statements as follows:

1. The major aim of American foreign economic policy is to accelerate economic growth in underdeveloped countries, on the grounds that poverty-stricken nations are a threat to the security, peace, and freedom of the American people. In addition, however, it is desired to demonstrate to the underdeveloped countries and to the world that high rates of growth can be achieved within a non-Communist economic framework and with a democratic political system. The political objective, in other words, is to achieve the economic goals in a fashion that will contribute to the growth of representative, responsible, and independent governments, which are not hostile to the West, and which can be expected either to remain neutral or to support the United States in a major war. It may also be—although

[1] See especially, The President's Committee to Study the United States Military Assistance Program, *Letter to the President of the United States and the Committee's Third Interim Report* (Washington, D. C., July 13, 1959).

[2] See for example, Center for International Studies, M.I.T., *The Objectives of United States Economic Assistance Programs*. A study prepared at the request of the Special Committee to Study the Foreign Aid Program, United States Senate No. 1 (Washington, D.C., 1957).

[3] See for example, Council on Foreign Relations, *Basic Aims of United States Foreign Policy*. A study prepared at the request of the Committee on Foreign Relations, United States Senate (Washington, D.C., November 25, 1959).

[4] See, for example, Max F. Millikan and Walt W. Rostow, *A Proposal: Key to an Effective Foreign Policy* (New York, 1957); Harland Cleveland, *The Theory and Practice of Foreign Aid*, a paper prepared for the special studies project of the Rockefeller Brothers Fund (November 1, 1956), pp. 31–32.

[5] Benjamin Higgins, *The United Nations and U.S. Foreign Economic Policy* (Glencoe, Ill., 1963).

this is a question for analysis—that stagnation elsewhere in the world may become a drag on the economic development of the United States itself.

2. A secondary objective is to assist in economic stabilization of other countries, on the grounds that economic instability hampers development and is a threat to security, peace, and freedom. Instability elsewhere may also aggravate the problem of maintaining steady growth in the American economy, although this too is a question for analysis.

In formulating the political objective, we avoided any blunt statement that United States foreign economic policy is designed "to combat Communism." The United States has given aid to both Yugoslavia and Poland. It would presumably be contrary to American principles to "combat Communism" in countries where it is clear that the majority of the people support a Communist government, and where the government is representative of the people, responsible to its wishes, and independent of foreign domination.

We also avoided stating the economic goal as "closing the gap between the levels of per capita incomes in the United States and other countries." It is extremely unlikely that this aim could be accomplished in less than a century, if ever. Since the United States starts from a level of per capita income so much higher than that of underdeveloped countries, growth *rates* would have to be several times as high in underdeveloped countries as in the United States, if the absolute difference between American incomes and their incomes is to be reduced. The technical difficulties involved in generating such a process are enormous, and for the advanced countries to promise the impossible would in the end prove contrary to their interests. Moreover, we argued, just as in any one country the presence of a few rich people is not a very serious matter if no one is poor, the fact that some nations are richer than others is not very serious if there are no poor nations. The economic goal is to eliminate poverty everywhere, rather than to "close the gap" between American and foreign incomes.

We also rejected the idea that the aim of foreign economic policy is to "buy friends." Friendship cannot be bought; the motto most clearly established by foreign aid experience would seem to be, "the feeding hand shall be bitten."

France continues to provide more bilateral assistance, relative to gross national product, than any other country. The bulk of French aid goes to French colonies and territories, the rest goes almost entirely to ex-colonies. In France, therefore, the question is not only "Why aid?" but also "Why aid concentrated in these few countries?" The most thorough review of French foreign aid policy to date is the Jeanneney Report.[6] The report attaches little importance to any economic gains from aid. The basis for the relatively generous aid program is simply the necessity of cooperation with underdeveloped countries for the purpose of "human solidarity." There is also a responsibility for the spreading of French civilization and keeping

[6] Ministère d'État Chargé de la Réforme Administrative, *La Politique de Coopération avec les Pays en Voie de Développement,* Rapport de la Commission d'Étude instituée par le Décret du 12 mars 1963, remis au Gouvernement le 18 juillet 1963.

alive the French tongue as an international language. Finally, France must join other Western powers in preventing the emergence of a bloc of developing countries hostile to the West. The Report recommended broadening the geographic scope of French aid, but felt that French-speaking Africa should continue to enjoy priority. France's revolutionary tradition gives her special advantages in dealing with developing countries, the Report argues.

The United Kingdom also provides most of its assistance to colonies or ex-colonies. A White Paper of September, 1963, pointed out that half the increase in British aid between 1957–58 and 1961–62 went to colonial territories. Most of the rest of the increase went to independent Commonwealth countries; aid to other countries and contributions to multilateral programs both remained small. The White Paper had little to say about why aid is given; the British people feel a responsibility for development of the remaining colonies and a continuing responsibility toward independent Commonwealth countries. Having helped these countries to political independence, "it is a natural and fitting continuation of the earlier relationship that we should now assist them in their efforts to achieve balanced and self-sustaining economies." [7]

The German approach to foreign aid policy seems even more simple. As Goran Ohlin puts it, "No strategic or security considerations are given much weight, and no historic ties of any importance have guided the direction of aid. . . . Repeatedly, the present Minister for Economic Cooperation, Herr Scheel, has described it as 'welfare policy on an international scale.' " [8] Japan stresses the diplomatic aspects of aid. The Prime Minister stated to the Diet in October, 1963,[9]

It is quite natural that Japan should extend assistance to other countries as she herself has attained such remarkable economic growth, and Japan must also make a greater effort to establish friendly relations of solidarity with Asian countries, bearing in mind the necessity for stability and peace in all of Asia.

In the smaller countries, like Norway, Sweden, Belgium, Italy, and Canada, the expectations of diplomatic gains from aid are somewhat diluted; the major motives seem to be a feeling that all advanced countries share the responsibility of helping the poor ones and a general desire to be "in on the act."

The Role of Capital Assistance in Economic Development

In the complex process of interacting economic, social, and political forces which brings economic development, what contribution can capital assistance make? It is quite clear that capital assistance cannot begin to do the job alone. At the same time, the availability or absence of foreign aid of the right kinds and in the right amounts might make the difference be-

[7] Goran Ohlin, *Foreign Aid Policies Reconsidered* (Paris: OECD, 1966), p. 16.
[8] *Ibid.*, p. 39.
[9] *Ibid.*, p. 49.

tween success or failure of a country's own efforts to launch a process of
sustained economic growth.

Capital Assistance and Absorptive Capacity [10]

The most obvious thing that foreign aid can do is to fill the gap between
capital requirements for a take-off into sustained growth and domestic
capacity for savings and investment. There is no use in providing a country
with more capital than it can effectively use. On the other hand, an ideal
international economic policy would see to it that all countries were able
to invest annually an amount equal to their "absorptive capacities." They
would then be able to maximize income over a long-run planning period,
given the supplies of factors of production other than capital, and the institutional, political, and economic framework. Capital assistance would
be "on tap" in such quantities that lack of capital would never cause a
bottleneck in the economic development of any country.

We can imagine that the planning authorities estimate the net contribution to national income, direct and indirect, from now to infinity, resulting
from the addition of successive blocks of investment to the total investment
program planned for the next five years.[11] The additional blocks of investment for which estimates of contribution to income are made should be big
enough to take care of the relevant discontinuities, economic, political, and
social, in the development process of the country concerned. In calculating
the contribution to the national income of a particular extra "block" of
investment, allowance must be made, of course, for maintaining the capital
stock at its new, higher level thereafter. We shall call the addition to income of each successive block of investment the "marginal contribution"
of investment, to distinguish it from the "marginal productivity" of capital
in its ordinary meaning, and also from "marginal efficiency." The marginal
contribution includes *all the changes* that would accompany a substantial
addition to the developmental investment program.

Definition of Absorptive Capacity

We can then define absorptive capacity as the amount of investment that
can be undertaken, within a five-year program, without reducing the marginal contribution of the last "block" of capital below "x." In other words,
it is the amount that can be undertaken without raising the incremental
capital-output ratio of the last block of investment, or marginal ICOR,
above $1/x$.[12] In this context we are concerned with investment over a five-

[10] A somewhat longer and somewhat more technical version of the analysis presented in this section can be found in: Benjamin Higgins, "Assistance étrangère et
capacité d'absorption," *Développement et Civilisations*, October–December, 1960,
pp. 28–43. See also P. N. Rosenstein-Rodan, *International Aid for Underdeveloped
Countries*, CENIS, January, 1961.

[11] In practice, projections of income would probably not be carried beyond twenty
to twenty-five years; but if an appropriate discount factor is applied, additions to
income in the next generation will not be a very important consideration—thus the
difference between the theoretically perfect projection to infinity and projection
for twenty years would not be great.

[12] See Figure 28–1.

to-ten-year planning period and the resulting increase in income over a very long period—twenty years or more.

The question is, then, how high do we put x?

One could make a strong case for putting x equal to zero. Absorptive capacity would then be the total amount of capital that could be invested during the planning period and still add something to future income. Putting it the other way round, it is the amount that can be invested without raising the marginal ICOR to infinity. In most countries the real obstacles to acceleration of growth are lack of entrepreneurship, inefficiency of public and private administration, and shortage of technicians and skilled workers, lack of commitment of government and people to economic development, resistance to social change, and the like. As the investment budget is increased, a point is reached where the inadequate supplies of these other factors of production will reduce the "marginal contribution" of additional investment sharply to zero. Given the discontinuities in the supply of new capital (one cannot build half a railroad or half a power plant), it is doubtful whether the amount of investment that would raise the marginal ICOR to infinity would be very different from the amount that would raise it to, say, 30:1.

If foreign capital assistance is provided in the form of hard loans carrying a rate of interest of Y per cent, it seems clear that x should not be set lower than Y. That is, investment financed by foreign aid should not be carried beyond the point where the addition to national income offsets the increase in the cost of servicing the debt.

An operational manual of the United States Agency for International Development suggests that in determining the cost-benefit ratio of projects proposed for AID support an interest rate of 3.5 per cent should be applied to the foreign component of the cost; for the domestic component local interest rates should be used, or if no accurate local rate can be isolated a "shadow price" of 6 per cent should be applied.[13] Dr. John H. Adler, commenting on this suggestion, maintains that its economic rationale is doubtful. The use of a different rate of return on foreign and on domestic capital, he argues, presupposes that:

(a) a project suitable for partial financing by foreign aid with a rate of return at or above the cut-off rate cannot be developed because (b) the supply of co-operant factors cannot be increased in the short run, but (c) the undertaking of the project itself will somehow stimulate the supply of deficient co-operant factors, and (d) that this cannot be brought forth by any other method, such as import or technical assistance.

Dr. Adler agrees, of course, that certain projects can increase the flow of domestic resources and thus raise rates of return above initial levels. In such cases it may be justified to accept the lower rate of return in the first place. But it is justified only if the internal rate of return over the entire life of the project is above the "cut-off rate." "In that event," he insists,

[13] AID, *Benefit-Cost Evaluations as Applied to AID Financed Water or Related Land-Use Projects*, Supplement No. 1 to Feasibility Studies, 1964.

"the project itself is 'good' and what is bad, or inadequate, is the cost-benefit analysis which does not permit systematic and rational determination of the rate of return allowing for the lapse of time." [14] Adler accordingly favors a single "acceptable rate of return applied to total capital;" but he does not tell us very precisely how the "acceptable rate of return" is to be established.

What about the gestation period? Is it a matter of indifference how long it takes before increases in income start to accrue? If the capital is costless to the receiving country, it is a matter of indifference—not in assigning priorities to projects, when a discount factor *should* be applied to future income, but in deciding on the *total amount* of investment to be undertaken. If the capital involves a future debt service, of course, the addition to income must be compared with this debt service. The rate of capital accumulation should be pushed to the point where the increase in income *net* of debt service is zero. But no interest rate prevailing *within* the underdeveloped countries themselves seems pertinent as long as the capital comes from abroad and represents savings performed *outside* the economy. The marginal contribution of additional investment within the economy is certainly relevant, but there is no *internal* "cost of capital" with which this rate might meaningfully be compared.[15]

It may be, of course, that different time-paths of income yield different *total* income, from now to infinity, with the same total investment over the *next* five years but differing allocations between saving and consumption in subsequent five-year plans. This fact raises the problem of the country's "welfare function" regarding income now and income later. Ultimately, such decisions must be made by the government; no purely economic analysis can provide an answer as to what time-path is "optimal." [16] The selection of a discount factor, of course, is essentially a determination of the optimal time-path of income.

If a substantial proportion of capital assistance is to take the form of loans, perhaps the best definition of x would be the rate of interest at which the aid-giving government can borrow. This interest rate provides a rough measure of the value to the people in donor countries of this marginal use of savings. Clearly, this interest rate is a highly institutionalized phenomenon and depends a good deal on the monetary and fiscal policies currently pursued by the governments of donor countries. Nevertheless, this measure is probably as good as any available. Let us therefore define "absorptive capacity" as the amount of investment that can be undertaken, over a five-year planning period beginning from the present, without reducing the addition to perpetual national income below 3 per cent. Or, putting it once more the other way around, absorptive capacity is the amount of in-

[14] John H. Adler, *Absorptive Capacity: The Concept and Its Determinants*, Brookings Institution Staff Paper, June, 1965.

[15] There is, of course, no relationship between money rates of interest in donor countries and real rates of return in recipient countries. It is really hard to justify anything but soft loans or grants, and thus an x between zero and 2 or 3 per cent.

[16] Cf. ECAFE, *Report of the Expert Group on Development Programming Techniques*, Bangkok, 1960.

vestment that can be undertaken in five years without the marginal ICOR rising above 30:1.

It has been suggested to me that the concept of absorptive capacity involves a time limit on the period during which aid must be continued. This idea has some validity but must be applied with care. When should a country stop borrowing? Canada was a net borrowing nation for nearly a century after confederation. It became a net lending nation during World War II, and is now expanding rapidly as a net borrowing country once more. Could it possibly be argued that Canada's recourse to international capital markets to finance recurrent phases of development indicates that the capital inflow between 1880 and 1910 was too high?

It could perhaps be said that if the amount of foreign aid is so great that at the end of a twenty-year planning period further capital inflows are necessary merely to maintain per capita income, "absorptive capacity" has been exceeded in the interim. It is easy enough to spot countries where this situation has prevailed: Korea, Vietnam, Libya, etc. Foreign aid is itself part of per capita income, and if it can be counted on to increase steadily, there may be no limit to "absorptive capacity" in this distorted sense.

However, our definition really takes care of this problem. It involves a comparison of the addition to the stock of capital with the addition to national income in perpetuity which it produces. Military aid with no offsetting increase in domestic savings, or support to current consumption, involves no addition to the stock of capital and no permanent addition to national income. The ICOR involved is infinite, and it cannot be justified at all on economic policy grounds. In short, such assistance falls outside the scope of foreign economic policy, and so is outside the scope of this essay.

The "Maximum Effort" Level of Investment

There is some level of domestic investment which represents a "maximum effort." "Effort" is partly a matter of saving and investing more, and partly a matter of working harder or better; but both can be expressed in terms of investment inputs.

It is possible for the level of investment to be too low, not only in the sense that the rate of growth is lower than need be, but in the sense that it requires no fundamental policy decisions, no changes in attitudes or behavior patterns, no acquisitions of skills or improvements in technique, no improvement in business or public administration, etc. All these things, once in motion, tend to have a cumulative effect on *future* growth. On the other hand, it is possible for a country to try to invest too much. Some degree of austerity may so destroy incentives that growth is retarded rather than accelerated. Obviously, no country should try to invest more from its own resources than it can absorb.

As a rule, the maximum domestic effort will be below absorptive capacity for several reasons:

1. It is usually necessary to feed and clothe a growing population either through production of consumers' goods at home or production of exports to finance imports of food and textiles.

2. The sacrifice entailed may go beyond what is indicated by the domestic welfare function, destroying incentives, and reducing output, capital accumulation, and welfare below potential levels.

3. The structures of inherited capital (and future comparative advantage) may be such that certain increases in production of consumers' goods are necessary in the near future, if excess capacity is to be avoided. In other words, some existing capital, of a kind that should be reproduced, or some types of new capital recommended by future comparative advantage, may be specific to the production of exports or consumers' goods.

An ideal international policy, then, would be one which guaranteed that foreign capital would always fill any gap between absorptive capacity and the maximum domestic effort, provided domestic investment is actually equal to the latter. Subtracting the amount of foreign private investment that is acceptable and forthcoming from the gap, we obtain the amount of foreign capital assistance to be provided to each country.

The increase in total aid involved in applying this criterion would probably not be very great. It would, however, mean considerable geographic redistribution of foreign aid. As things are now, some countries are clearly getting more than enough to fill the gap between absorptive capacity and maximum domestic effort. If this criterion were universally understood and recognized as being wholly without political strings, its application could greatly improve the atmosphere in which foreign aid programs are administered.

It is unlikely that absorptive capacity will exceed maximum domestic effort by very much in most countries. A big gap will occur only where the supply of skills of all sorts is unusually high relative to the current level of income, as in India.

If a country needs capital assistance, by definition its maximum domestic effort is below the "minimum effort" required for a take-off into sustained growth. If the country is worthy of capital assistance, on the other hand, it must have an absorptive capacity which is at least equal to this minimum effort. The really difficult cases are those in which *both* absorptive capacity and the maximum domestic effort are below the minimum effort required. In these cases, foreign economic assistance must be concentrated on technical assistance, designed to raise both the maximum domestic effort and absorptive capacity by training workers, managers, public administrators, and technicians, and providing expertise directly in the short run.

Other Approaches

W. Arthur Lewis suggests in effect providing foreign aid as a reward for increasing the domestic effort. He would make aid equal to the growth in the ratio of savings (S) to gross domestic product (GDP) over three years:

$$\text{Aid} = S_1/GDP_1 - S_4/GDP_4$$

If total public and private capital formation from domestic sources is 24 per cent of GDP last year while three years earlier it was 22 per cent, aid for next year would be 2 per cent of *GDP*. The necessary computations would be made annually on agreed definitions by an international team of national income statisticians. Lewis regards his proposal as "just about the simplest self-policing aid formula that one could devise." [17]

Simple it may be; but it is hard to fathom the rationale, except in terms of the Protestant ethic—to him who hath shall be given, virtue is its own reward, waste not want not, make what you can and save what you can. Rigorous application of the formula would mean that a country that has just struck oil, like Libya, with more capital than can be used effectively already, would stand high on the list for aid in per capita terms because she could hardly help a rapid increase in the ratio of developmental investment to *GDP*. But a country in trouble, like India during the Second Plan, finding itself unable to sustain its rate of domestic investment because of bad harvests, collapse of world markets, or other disasters, would suffer a cut in its foreign aid as well. A more flexible method of deciding whether, under existing conditions, a country is making a maximum domestic effort or not, with aid provided in amounts equal to the difference between that maximum and absorptive capacity, seems much better designed to achieve the objectives of international economic policy.

John C. H. Fei and Douglas S. Paauw raise a somewhat different question: [18] assuming that the objective of international economic policy is to bring all countries to a situation of self-sustained growth, where the per capita marginal savings ratio (PMSR) is high enough in itself to permit target growth rates to be achieved indefinitely, how many years of gap-filling aid will be needed before this type of "bliss" is achieved? The question was answered for thirty-one countries for which data were available for the key variables: initial savings ratio, PMSR, capital-output ratio, rate of population growth, and target rates of growth. The results were rather startling. Among the thirty-one countries, Yugoslavia alone had already reached "bliss." In seven other countries, a policy such as that recommended above of filling the gap between domestic effort and requirements for reaching targets (assuming the targets accurately reflect absorptive capacity) would produce self-sustained growth, where no further aid would be needed, in due course. Mexico, for example, is only four years away from "bliss" and the Philippines only six; but with the present parameters Colombia will need sixteen years to achieve self-sustained growth, Greece will need seventeen years, and Taiwan thirty-two years. The other twenty-three countries, with the values ascribed to the key variables, will never reach bliss at all; aid requirements will continue to increase forever. This group of countries includes Argentina, Brazil, Chile, India, Indonesia, and Burma, among others. No African country in the sample can attain "bliss."

[17] W. Arthur Lewis, "Allocating Foreign Aid to Promote Self-sustained Economic Growth," in Theodore Geiger and Leo M. Solomon (eds.), *Motivations and Methods in Development and Foreign Aid*, Proceedings in the Sixth World Conference of the Society for International Development (Washington, D.C., March, 1964).

[18] John C. H. Fei and Douglas S. Paauw, "Foreign Assistance and Self-Help: A Reappraisal of Development Finance," *Review of Economics and Statistics*, August, 1965, pp. 251–67.

The eight "successful" countries divide again into two subgroups. Some are already on a "glide path;" foreign aid can fall monotonically to the termination date. Others belong to the "hump scale" group, where aid must increase for some time before starting its slide down the "glide path."

In the "successful" cases, aid should be provided to fill the gap. In the others, international economic policy must be directed toward reducing the gap—in our terms, toward raising both the maximum domestic effort and absorptive capacity. Here technical assistance can play an important role.

Technical Assistance

In the short space of fifteen years attitudes toward the contribution of technical cooperation to economic development have gone full circle. When President Truman announced his "Point Four" program in 1949, much was expected from simple transfer of know-how from technologically advanced to technologically retarded countries. The attitude was well expressed at the time by American Under Secretary of State Webb: [19]

It is important to us and to the rest of the world that people in these areas realize that, through perseverance, hard work, and a little assistance, they can develop the means of taking care of their material needs and at the same time can preserve and strengthen their individual freedoms.

Technical assistance in agriculture was expected to be particularly productive, bringing back "one hundred fold" the modest outlays required, according to Secretary of Agriculture Charles Brannan.[20]

As time went by and the bilateral and multilateral technical assistance programs failed to produce spectacular results in developing countries, while understanding of the development process accumulated and the large-scale capital assistance under the Marshall Plan brought impressive increases in productivity in Europe, emphasis shifted for a while to industrialization and to massive transfers of capital. But with new disappointments and still deeper understanding of the complexities of economic development, it was recognized that the capacity of developing countries to absorb capital effectively was sharply limited by shortages of skills both in technical and scientific activities, and in everyday application of manpower in the productive process. Consequently, emphasis is shifting back to technical assistance. This time, however, no quick miracles are expected from the "expert" who will simply tell people in developing countries what to do, and return home leaving a permanent advance in technology behind him. It is recognized that significant technological change can take place only if the requisite skills are widely and deeply infused in the people of the developing countries, and that this infusion is a matter of a long, slow, and painful process of training, retraining, education, and re-education.

[19] Charles Wolf, Jr., *Foreign Aid: Theory and Practice in Southern Asia* (Princeton, 1960), p. 59.
[20] *Ibid.,* p. 63.

Stocks and Flows

At any point of time there are certain numbers of people in a country with a given type of skill. Others are in the "pipeline" of the educational system, including in this context all types of training as well as formal education—agricultural extension, training-within-industry, technical and vocational training, adult literacy campaigns, and the like. Over the long-run perspective planning period, a certain flow of skills can be expected from the "pipeline." There will also be net reductions in the flow through death, retirement, and emigration. Technical assistance may be directed toward both an immediate increase in the flow of skills, by providing "experts" who will do operating jobs, and toward swelling the future flow by adding to facilities and building institutions for education and training.

International Trade in Human Resources

A clearer picture of technical assistance as an aspect of economic and social development may be obtained by drawing analogies between trade in skills and trade in commodities. In the first place, just as no country, whatever its stage of development, is expected to be exclusively an exporter or exclusively an importer of goods, or even of capital, so no country should be expected to be exclusively an exporter or an importer of human resources. All countries can be expected to be both exporters and importers. However, the pattern of international trade, the terms of trade, the balance of trade, and the over-all balance of payments are all-important aspects of a country's economic situation.

The composition of international trade in skills should reflect comparative economic advantage. Even developing countries with over-all shortages of skilled manpower have surpluses of certain types of skill, sometimes at a very high level, as indicated by the presence of the "educated unemployed." Until the developing countries with such surpluses reach the level of development that permits them to absorb all of their own trained people, it makes very good sense to export surplus skills to countries with shortages of the same categories of trained personnel, whether through organized technical assistance programs or in some other fashion. To some degree, the existence of surplus skills reflects past inadequacies in the educational system, in the sense of failure to adapt it to the occupational needs of the country at each stage of its development. However, there may be a case for continuing to produce skills for export. Greece, for example, might continue to turn out archaeologists, ancient historians, and scholars of Greek literature and language in excess of its own immediate needs.

TERMS OF TRADE IN HUMAN RESOURCES

Of particular importance to developing countries are the terms of trade —whether in commodities or in skills. It is by no means clear that the terms of trade in skills of developing countries have been universally favorable, in the sense that the average cost, in man-years of training, of people coming into the country is higher than that of people going out. Unfortunately, among the emigrants from developing countries are some of the most highly educated people, and they are not always in the categories with surpluses at home. Consequently, the terms of trade in skills are not as favorable for developing countries as they might be.

BALANCE OF TRADE IN HUMAN RESOURCES

It is sometimes said that the optimal balance of payments situation for a developing country is an import surplus offset by a net capital inflow. An analogy can be obtained for human resources if we think of trained adults as "capital goods" and the educational system as the basic stock of capital. We could then say that the optimal "balance of payments" situation for a developing country is an import surplus on human resources account (in terms of *value* rather than *volume*) offset by a "net capital inflow" in the form of educational facilities. The latter can be accomplished either by foreign-financed fellowships to train students abroad, or by the development of the domestic educational and training facilities through foreign aid.

When cast in terms such as these it is clear that technical assistance is one part—an important one—of a much broader spectrum. It is apparent, for example, that technical assistance policy cannot properly be formulated independently from the international exchange of human resources through the private sector. Information regarding import and export of skills by private institutions should be available continuously to the authorities, to assist them in formulating technical assistance policy.

Beyond such additions to the standard statistical services there is the broader issue of "carrots and sticks" that governments may wish to employ in order to direct international trade in skills within the private sector, toward the attainment of policy goals. The whole apparatus of tariffs, quotas, export and import subsidies, and multiple exchange rates can be applied to human resources as well as to commodities. A policy of permitting the Greek Center for Economic Research or the University of Libya to pay salaries well above civil service scales in order to attract highly trained and talented expatriate Libyans and foreigners might be regarded as an import subsidy or a dual exchange rate.

Technical Assistance and Capital Formation

It is also clear that technical assistance policy cannot be formulated independently of capital inflow. Both the amount and the type of technical assistance required depend on the amount and kind of new capital formation taking place. Most developing countries are in need of structural change, not only in the sense of relatively rapid growth of employment outside agriculture, but also in the sense of increases in scale and a shift to a more productive technology in both the agricultural and industrial sectors. Technical assistance can help to bring about this structural change, but without capital formation it can accomplish relatively little.

Allocating Scarce Technical Assistance Resources

By the very nature of things, government technical cooperation programs—bilateral and multilateral combined—cannot fill more than a part of the gap between skill requirements and skill supplies. There are first of all limitations on the supply side. These limitations are not primarily financial; the real limitation on the supply side is more physical than fiscal. No country has a superabundance of those skills which are most in demand in developing countries. Trained teachers at all levels, highly trained engineers, natural scientists, agricultural experts of all kinds, economists, skilled and experienced managers—these are in short supply even in the most advanced countries. The language problem is often a barrier to the transmittal of skills.

There are also sharp limitations on the demand side. The people of any country will become understandably concerned when the number of foreign "experts" in strategic activities of the country surpasses a certain figure. This is particularly true of experts supplied by foreign governments. Perfectly reasonable resentment on the part of young and well-trained personnel within the country will develop if jobs are turned over to foreigners which, in the view of nationals of the country, could perfectly well be done by nationals. There is a clear recognition on the part of the recipient countries that having too many foreign experts around may delay rather than accelerate the acquisition of skills by nationals, even if, when left to themselves, the nationals have to learn by the painful process of trial and error. Foreign experts can absorb an unconscionable share of the time and energy of hard-pressed, high-level officials. Moreover, as technical assistance programs are organized, foreign experts are far from free to the recipient country. Even if no formal counterpart contribution is required, there are usually demands for housing, office space, transport, supplies, and counterpart personnel. Providing these complements to technical assistance can become a real burden on the host country. When the number of foreign teachers surpasses some level, people begin worrying about ideological influences, as in the case of Egyptian teachers in Libya. There is also a limit to the usefulness of training abroad. This process may take important people away from key jobs. Study abroad for ordinary students may also lead to excessive drains, especially if it is on a large scale and unduly prolonged, or if it leads to permanent emigration. Absorptive capacity for technical assistance, as well as capital assistance, has its limits.

Interactions of Technical and Capital Assistance

It is clear that technical and capital assistance are closely interrelated. Almost any technical assistance program involves some plant and equipment, and a good many of them (technical training, agricultural extension) imply a subsequent change in the structure of capital if the technical assistance is to be put to good effect. Conversely, capital assistance, leading to the establishment of new enterprises and introduction of new techniques, nearly always involves a need for new skills, especially in the pre-investment and construction phase, some of which might be provided directly or indirectly through technical cooperation. The success or failure of technical cooperation depends a great deal on the capital assistance with which it is combined, and integration of the two is one of the most important aspects of the planning of foreign aid.

Absorptive capacity is limited by the supply of technical, managerial, scientific, entrepreneurial, and labor skills; by the willingness to accept the risks of investment in durable productive capacity; by the supply of natural resources; by the stability of the government, its commitment to development goals, the honesty and efficiency of the civil service, the quality and scope of the educational system, the appropriateness of development plans and stabilization policies, and the like. The maximum domestic effort is affected by these factors, and also by the commitment of the population to the goals of development, their savings and consumption habits, attitudes toward work and leisure, confidence in their government, etc. It is clear, therefore, that well-conceived technical assistance programs can raise both absorptive capacity and maximum domestic effort. Indeed, within the context of an ideal international foreign aid program, it could be said that the function of technical assistance is to do just that.[21]

In Figure 28–1 the returns to developmental investment in terms of the

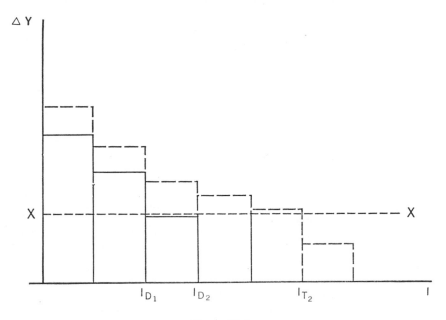

Figure 28–1

permanent increase in national income it produces are measured on the vertical axis and investment during a planning period on the horizontal axis. The rate of return x is the minimum that is acceptable to donor countries as a basis for capital assistance. Absorptive capacity for aid is there-

[21] These ideas are presented in more detail in the present author's article, "Assistance étrangère, et capacité d'absorption," *Développement et Civilisations*, Octobre–Décembre 1960, as well as in Benjamin Higgins, *United Nations and U.S. Foreign Economic Policy* (Homewood, Ill.), 1962.

fore the difference between the maximum domestic effort and the total investment that brings returns down to x.

To begin with, the domestic maximum effort is I_{D1}. At that level of investment, returns are already down to x; there is no absorptive capacity for capital assistance. An infusion of technical assistance, however, will shift the maximum domestic effort to I_{D2} and at the same time raise the whole curve of returns to the dotted line, increasing the yield on small development programs a little and the yield on larger programs a good deal.[22] Returns fall to x only at the level of total investment I_{T2}. Absorptive capacity is $I_{T2} - I_{D2}$, and capital assistance should be available in this amount. With these concepts we can classify countries in terms of their present position regarding foreign aid and indicate some "stages of growth" through which all countries will hopefully pass. At the bottom of the scale are countries where both the maximum domestic effort (I_{Ymde}) and absorptive capacity (I_{Yac}) are below the level of the "big push," the ratio of investment to current national income needed to assure growth of national income in excess of population growth ($I_{/Ybp}$): $I_{/Yac} \lessgtr I_{Ymde} < I_{/Ybp}$.

Libya before the oil discoveries or Yemen today might be in this category. The situation in Libya today is $I_{/Yac} < I_{/Ybp} < I_{Ymde}$. In both of these situations there is no justification for capital assistance, but a massive technical assistance program is indicated. How quickly absorptive capacity can be raised depends on how much technical assistance is available and acceptable. If any country is willing to see its government, as well as all managerial, entrepreneurial, scientific, and technical positions, taken over by foreigners, and if such skilled personnel is available in unlimited quantities, absorptive capacity can be raised very high and very fast. Thus if capital assistance were truly on tap (or domestic capital abundant, as in the oil countries), it would be the flow of technical assistance that would determine the rate of growth of very poor countries. In countries like Libya and Kuwait where capital is abundant and human skills scarce, this is precisely the situation.

Class Two countries would be those where $I_{/Yac} > I_{/Ybp} > I_{/Ymde}$. Here both technical and capital assistance would be provided.

In Class Three countries $I_{/Yac} > I_{/Ymde} > I_{/Ybp}$. These countries would receive only capital assistance.

Finally, there are countries where $I_{/Ymde} \gtrless I_{/Yac} \gtrless I_{/Ybp}$. These countries are no longer underdeveloped and should receive no foreign aid of any kind.

Foreign Aid in Practice

Since World War II a host of organizations has been engaged in assisting the war-devastated or underdeveloped countries with their reconstruction, stabilization, and development.

[22] It is true that some types of technical assistance, such as research and OPEX-style (Operation and Executive Personnel) administration projects, may raise the yield of even small development programs a good deal.

First there are the members of the United Nations family: the International Bank for Reconstruction and Development; the International Finance Corporation, the International Development Association; the Technical Assistance Organization; the Food and Agriculture Organization; the International Labor Organization; the World Health Organization; the United Nations Children's Fund; the UN Korean Reconstruction Agency, the UN Relief and Work Agency for Palestine Refugees; the International Civil Aviation Organization, and the World Health Organization.[23] There are United States Government agencies: the Agency for International Development, the Export-Import Bank, the Commodity Credit Corporation, and others. These are non-governmental organizations like the Rockefeller, Carnegie, and Ford Foundations, and the International Development Corporation. Others are governmental but limited in membership by some geographic criterion such as the Colombo Plan and the Organization of American States. The Soviet Union, China, Czechoslovakia, the United Kingdom, France, West Germany, Canada, Australia, New Zealand, Sweden, Norway, Japan and Switzerland all have their own bilateral aid programs.

The International Monetary Fund and the International Bank for Reconstruction and Development

In July, 1944, representatives of forty-four nations assembled at Bretton Woods, New Hampshire, and after three weeks of discussion, agreed on the Articles for the International Monetary Fund (IMF) and the International Bank for Reconstruction and Development (IBRD). Ten years later, when the delegates of these two organizations met in Washington for their annual conference, the membership had increased to more than fifty countries, including a good many of those considered "underdeveloped." By that time, the Bank had been in actual operation for more than eight years, the Fund for more than seven. At this tenth anniversary meeting, however, the representatives of underdeveloped countries expressed dissatisfaction with the contribution the two institutions had made to solution of their problems. The attitude with respect to the Fund was typified by some remarks of Dr. Sjafruddin, Governor of the Bank of Indonesia. Dr. Sjafruddin pointed to the peculiar problems of underdeveloped areas, and argued that they need special treatment: [24]

I hope not to be misunderstood. What I am pleading for on behalf of the underdeveloped countries is not a privilege from the Fund but a fair treatment, which is not always identical with equal treatment. Aid is good for those who can get it. Trade is good for those who are in a strong bargaining position. But the only thing which underdeveloped countries request is a fair treatment, a fair share of the world's income, based on a good understanding of our needs,

[23] We shall use the term "United Nations" to refer to this entire "family," unless a distinction between the UN proper and the specialized agencies, regional commissions, etc., is explicitly made.

[24] From the statement by the Hon. Sjafruddin Prawiranegara, Governor for Indonesia, at the discussion of the Fund's Annual Report, September 27, 1954. (Press Release No. 41.)

not from the viewpoint of bare commercialism, but from that of human ideal-ism. This may not be quite in line with the ideas of our founding fathers, something of which I am not quite sure, but certainly quite in line with the ideas of our Father who created us.

The attitude of delegates from underdeveloped countries toward the Bank was well expressed by Mr. Cuaderno, Governor of the Philippines: [25]

Four years ago, at the Paris meeting in 1950, I took occasion to urge the Bank, since the other areas of the world had already received ample aid from it, to give due consideration to the needs of Asia and the Far East. At that time I warned: "The need of the Far East for such a program is great and merits increased attention from the Bank. . . . Time is of the essence and the time is now."

If, however, there is no disposition on the part of the influential members of the Bank to do this, then I believe that they should give their support to the desire of the underdeveloped countries to establish institutions which would enable them to accelerate their economic development. I refer to the proposed U.N. agencies already alluded to by several of the distinguished Governors here, namely, the Special Fund for Economic Development and the Interna-tional Finance Corporation. If the need for such agencies was great in 1950, it is critical now, and the free world can ignore it only at the risk of its own survival. I would urge, therefore, the fullest support of all member countries for the formation of these agencies.

The Bretton Woods organizations were not set up with the primary aim of assisting in the development of underdeveloped areas. The chief purpose of the Fund was "to promote exchange stability, to maintain orderly ex-change arrangements among members, and to avoid competitive exchange depreciation." The purpose of the Bank included assistance in developing less-developed countries, but at the time of Bretton Woods, the recon-struction of war-devastated areas was uppermost in the minds of the delegates. Thus although the Bank and Fund had not done very much to solve the financial problems of underdeveloped countries, it was perhaps a little unfair to criticize them on this score; they were not set up to do so.

By 1965 the IBRD was "meeting needs" of underdeveloped countries rather better. During the fiscal year 1965, 12.3 per cent of World Bank loans went to Africa; some 39 per cent went to Asia and the Middle East; about 29 per cent went to underdeveloped countries in Europe; and 21 per cent to the Western Hemisphere (Latin America).

This shift in the pattern of lending by the Bank has not completely mollified the governments of underdeveloped countries. In the case of the IMF, relations with the Latin American countries probably reached an all-time low during 1959. It was argued that the Fund was bringing undue pressure on the governments of Latin American countries, with respect to their domestic monetary, fiscal, and foreign exchange policies. As for the

[25] Statement at the closing session, ninth annual meeting, International Monetary Fund and International Bank for Reconstruction and Development, Washington, D.C., September 29, 1954. See *Guideposts to Economic Stability and Progress* (Manila, 1955), pp. 57–59.

Bank, spokesmen for underdeveloped countries still argue that the conditions it imposes on loans are too onerous to meet the needs of underdeveloped countries, and the total amounts involved are obviously too small to meet the capital requirements of all underdeveloped countries. Interest rates on IBRD loans have been high; there has been little of the soft loan in the Bank's operations. From the beginning, the Bank has been handicapped by the need to establish itself in the private capital market. It has therefore tended to stress good, solid, self-liquidating *projects* of a kind that would seem respectable to private investors. An occasional gesture has been made in the direction of a "program approach" (providing loans against a whole development program), as in the case of its support to the Italian Ten-Year Plan. However, the Bank's activities are still guided primarily by a "project approach." There has been continuous pressure for the establishment of a new United Nations agency, which would give grants or make loans on less onerous terms.

The Special Fund and IDA

The continuing dissatisfaction with the nature and scale of lending by the IBRD was expressed in support for the "SUNFED" proposal. The Special United Nations Fund for Economic Development would have been a new agency making outright grants to underdeveloped countries. The pressure for SUNFED had two results. First, in October, 1958, the United Nations Special Fund was established by the General Assembly. Its budget of $26 million in its first year (1959) obviously could not make any significant contribution to capital requirements. It was decided to limit its function to the financing of surveys, which might lead to capital assistance from other sources.

THE INTERNATIONAL DEVELOPMENT ASSOCIATION

The International Development Association (IDA) was proposed by the United States delegate to the Bank and Fund meetings in September, 1959. The purposes of IDA are defined as follows: "To promote economic development, increase productivity and thus raise standards of living in less developed areas of the world included within the Association's membership, and particularly by providing finance to meet their important developmental requirements on terms which are more flexible and bear less heavily on the balance of payments than does a conventional loan, thereby furthering the development objectives of the International Bank for Reconstruction and Development and supplementing its activities."

It came into being on September 26, 1960; by June 30, 1965, it had assets of $1.6 billion. The allocation of IDA subscriptions is more or less the same as the distribution of subscriptions to the capital of the IBRD; the United States is the largest contributor, the United Kingdom is second. In contrast to the majority of United Nations organizations, where voting is on a "one country, one vote" basis, voting rights in the IDA are roughly proportionate to subscriptions, as in the IBRD. IDA provides both soft loans and grants. Of total outstanding credits of $1,085.5 million on June 30, 1965, almost 75 per cent were in Asia and the Middle East, about 11 per cent in Africa, about 9 per cent in Latin America, and under 6 per cent in Europe.

THE INTERNATIONAL FINANCE CORPORATION

The International Finance Corporation (IFC) was established as a subsidiary of the World Bank in July, 1956. There is a question as to whether or not it should be regarded as a "foreign aid agency." It was set up "to promote the growth of productive private enterprise, particularly in less-developed countries." It makes hard loans, usually on medium terms, at interest rates of 5 to 10 per cent, and participates in equity capital. Over the first nine years of its operation its cumulative total of commitments reached a mere $137 million. New commitments for the year 1964–65 amounted to only $26 million—$15 million in loans and $11 million in equity participation. More than half of its commitments have been concentrated in twelve countries in Latin America. Asia and the Middle East account for 22 per cent of total commitments and Africa for 12 per cent.

THE INTER-AMERICAN DEVELOPMENT BANK

The Inter-American Development Bank (IDB) is essentially a creature of the Organization of American States but is an autonomous inter-American organization. In terms of capital resources it is comparable in size to IDA, but its operations are limited to members of the OAS. The United States provides some 40 per cent of the total capital, the balance being subscribed by the Latin American republics themselves. Under an interesting system of allocating voting rights, each member has 135 votes plus 1 vote for each share of capital stock held. Thus the United States has only about one-third of the total voting power. The IDB provides technical as well as capital assistance.

THE ORGANIZATION FOR ECONOMIC COOPERATION AND DEVELOPMENT

In 1961 the Organization for European Economic Cooperation (OEEC), which had been established to assist in the administration and planning of the Marshall Plan program for European reconstruction, was converted into the Organization for Economic Cooperation and Development (OECD). Its present members are the United States, Canada, the advanced countries of western Europe, and the "developing" countries of Spain, Portugal, Italy, Greece, Turkey, and Yugoslavia. The OECD provides technical assistance to its own "developing countries," particularly in the fields of regional planning and education. It has no funds for capital assistance of its own, but it plays an important coordinating role as a "donors' club." The "confrontation" technique, in which a recipient country and its major donors meet together to review development plans and problems, has proved an important step toward coordination of foreign aid and a big step toward "multilateralization of bilateral aid." The Development Assistance Committee of OECD has also been instrumental in promoting the device of the aid "consortium," through which various donor countries group together to assist a particular recipient country.

Technical Assistance

In addition to the capital assistance provided through the IBRD, the United Nations provides technical assistance through eight participating organizations: the United Nations Bureau of Technical Assistance Operations and seven specialized agencies, the International Labor Organization (ILO), the Food and Agriculture Organization (FAO), the United Nations Educational, Scientific, and Cultural Organization (UNESCO), the International Telecommunications Union (ITU), the International Civil Aviation Organization (ICAO), the World Health Organization (WHO), and the World Meteorological Organization (WMO). Part of these technical assistance operations is financed through the budgets of the organizations themselves, as provided to them directly by member governments; this is referred to as the regular program. The great bulk of the technical assistance of the UN and its specialized agencies, however, is provided through the Expanded Program of Technical Assistance (EPTA) which began in 1953. For the two-year program of 1960–62 expenditures of about $85 million (total) were planned. The United Nations program is on a very small scale as compared to United States technical cooperation under the (AID) program.

In 1959 a new division of the UN technical assistance program was established, Operational and Executive Personnel (OPEX). Under this program UN experts became actual operating officials of the host government. The host government pays the regular salary established for nationals in the same post and the UN pays a supplement to bring the total up to the salary established for UN experts.

THE REGIONAL COMMISSIONS

An important aspect of the United Nations' operations in the economic field is the work of the regional commissions. They include the Economic Commission for Asia and the Far East (ECAFE), established March 28, 1947; the Economic Commission for Europe (ECE), established March 28, 1947; the Economic Commission for Latin America (ECLA), established February 25, 1948; and the Economic Commission for Africa (ECA), established April 29, 1958.

Bilateral Assistance

We cannot take space here to provide details of all the bilateral programs that are in operation. We shall therefore concentrate on the program of the United States, which is much the biggest, and that of the USSR, which has special interest in terms of international relations. Some comparative figures for France, the United Kingdom, and other donor countries are provided in Tables 28–1, 28–2, and 28–3. It will be noted that while the United States provides three to four times as much total aid as France and five to nine times as much as the United Kingdom, in terms of the share of gross national product devoted to aid the United States lags far behind France and somewhat behind Belgium, and is only slightly ahead of the United Kingdom (1961 figures). Canada occupies an igno-

596 POLICIES

TABLE 28–1

The Nature of Capital Contribution to Underdeveloped Countries by Major (Capitalist) Contributors (million U.S. dollars)

Country and Nature of Aid	1960	1961	1962
United States: total	3,193	3,736	3,874
Official donations	1,275	1,472	1,538
Official loans	997	1,316	1,559
Private capital	921	948	777
France: total	1,146	1,052	1,148
Official donations	625	654	775
Official loans	181	80	104
Private capital	340	319	269
United Kingdom: total	681	667	438
Official donations	170	231	249
Official loans	155	196	166
Private capital	356	240	24

SOURCE: United Nations, *International Flow of Long-term and Official Donations 1961–62.* Table 4.

TABLE 28–2

Official Aid (Gifts and Loans) as Percentage of Gross Domestic Product in 1961 (including multilateral contributions)

Country	Percentage of GDP
France	1.50
Belgium	0.73
United States	0.67
United Kingdom	0.59
Netherlands	0.56
Western Germany*	0.53
Australia†	0.46
Japan	0.45
Italy	0.19
Norway	0.19
Canada	0.17

SOURCE: United Nations, *World Economic Survey 1963.*
* Figure for 1962.
† Figure for 1962/3.
The Australian figure calculated on the basis of data in *Vernon Report* M. 25., and the *Australian National Accounts.*

minious position at the bottom of the list; but in recent years the Canadian figures have been somewhat higher, at least in terms of commitments (see Appendix Table II). In October, 1966, the Canadian government announced to the UN General Assembly its intention to raise its annual

TABLE 28–3

Distribution of Official Bilateral Loan Commitments
According to Interest Rates in 1962
(percentages)

Interest Rates	West Germany	France	Italy	Japan	United Kingdom	United States	Total
0–1%	..	..	..	..	8	58	39
Over 1–3%	..	28	..	..	..	2	3
Over 3–5%	54	30	19	..	1	13	17
Over 5–6%	40	27	4	40	33	27	29
6% or more	6	16	77	60	58	..	13

SOURCE: United Nations, *World Economic Survey 1963*. Table 8.4.

foreign aid commitments to 1 per cent of GNP. The United States provides a higher share of its loans at low interest rates than the other
countries shown.

THE EXPORT-IMPORT BANK

The Export-Import Bank of Washington, popularly known as the Eximbank, is the oldest of the agencies providing capital assistance to underdeveloped countries. Throughout its early years, the Export-Import Bank
was handicapped by an uncertain future, since Congress tended to regard
it as an institution designed for a narrow emergency purpose. It came into
being because the recognition of the USSR by the United States in 1934
was expected to lead to a sharp increase in trade between the two countries, and it was felt that special financing would be necessary to take
advantage of these new trade opportunities.

It is only in recent years that a high proportion of loans has gone to
underdeveloped countries. Up to June 30, 1954, of total new credits
authorized amounting to $6.6 billion, only $995 million had gone to Asian
countries and $2,192 million to Latin America. Moreover, of these loans
to Latin America, the great bulk had gone to the relatively advanced Latin
American countries. Brazil alone had accounted for $842 million, Mexico
another $321 million, Chile $155 million, and Argentina $224 million.

By the end of 1956, the picture had already changed substantially. Of
total credits authorized as of that date amounting of $8,362 million, $1,372
million had been allocated to Asia and $2,939 million to Latin American
countries. Brazil, Mexico, Chile, and Argentina were still the chief bene-
ficiaries among Latin American countries, but by the end of 1956, some
of the less prosperous Latin American countries had obtained substantial
loans. Peru, for example, had by then received credit authorization
amounting to $165.7 million, Cuba $116.6 million, and Colombia $103.8
million.

By June of 1960, the shift toward underdeveloped countries was still
more marked. Even such dubious risks as Indonesia had received $263
million, and the Philippines $194 million. Brazil's figure had reached $1,345

million, Argentina's $518 million, Mexico's $621 million, and Peru's $252 million. Of total authorized net credits of $10.7 billion, 36.9 per cent had gone to Latin America, 20.4 per cent to Asia, and 2.6 per cent to Africa. During recent years, the Export-Import Bank has made a marked shift away from the finance of foreign trade, as such, to capital assistance to underdeveloped countries. While the credits are extended for American exports, they permit a higher rate of capital formation in the borrowing countries, at least in the short run.

THE MUTUAL SECURITY PROGRAM

In his inaugural address of January 20, 1949, President Truman made his famous "Fourth Point," which has provided the foundation for American foreign aid policy ever since:

We must embark on a bold new program for making the benefits of our scientific advances and industrial progress available for the improvement and growth of underdeveloped areas.

The principles laid down in Point Four led to the establishment of the Technical Cooperation Administration in October, 1950, and the passage of the Mutual Security Act of 1951. The Mutual Security Act provided for military assistance, capital assistance for defense support and for economic development, as well as for technical assistance. The Technical Cooperation Administration was to have responsibility for the latter, but TCA was brought under the Director of Mutual Security. A Mutual Security Agency was set up to administer the other types of assistance. In 1953, military assistance remained the responsibility of the Department of Defense, but a Foreign Operations Administration (FOA) was established to administer the economic development and defense support appropriations, to direct the operations of the Military Assistance Program, and also to direct the activities of TCA. Under the Mutual Security Act of 1954, FOA was abolished in turn and replaced by the International Cooperation Administration (ICA). Military assistance then became entirely the responsibility of the Department of Defense. Economic aid and technical cooperation were handled by ICA. In 1957, the Development Loan Fund was established to administer capital assistance.

THE AGENCY FOR INTERNATIONAL DEVELOPMENT

In November, 1961, the Kennedy Administration reorganized the foreign aid program once more. Economic assistance of all kinds was brought together in the Agency for International Development (AID). The new agency was established within the State Department, under a director who has the status of Under Secretary of State and reports directly to the Secretary of State and the President.

As may be seen from Chart 28–1, up to 1953 the economic assistance provided by AID and its predecessor agencies was heavily concentrated in Europe. As European reconstruction was completed, interest shifted to the Far East. Toward the end of the 1950's Latin America attracted increasing attention, and in the present decade a growing proportion of aid funds has

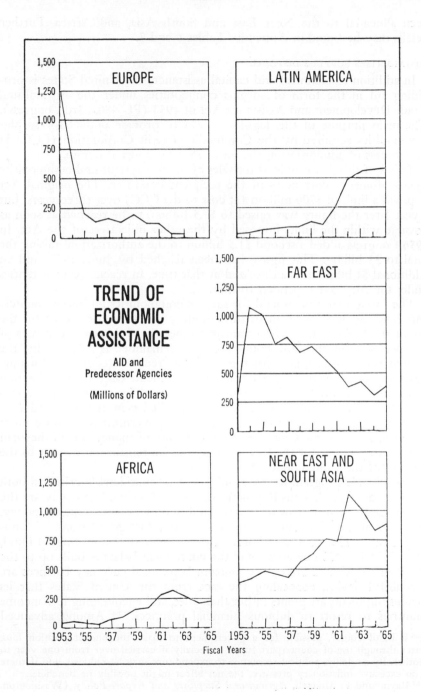

Chart 28-1

SOURCE: Agency for International Development.

been allocated to the Near East and South Asia, and Africa. Further details may be found in Appendix Tables 6 and 7.

COMMODITIES SURPLUS DISPOSAL

In addition to technical and capital assistance, the United States is providing aid in the form of surplus commodities under the Agricultural Trade Development and Assistance Act of 1954 (PL–480, 83rd Congress). The main purpose of this legislation was to provide outlets for surplus commodities acquired by the Commodity Credit Corporation (CCC) in the process of administering the Farm Price Support Program.

Title I of this Act provided for sales of surplus agricultural commodities against domestic currencies of the recipient countries. The original Act imposed a limit of $700 million (at cost to the CCC) over three years; but a year later the figure was raised to $1.5 billion, to be reached as soon as possible within the limits imposed by the other objectives of the Act. In 1956 Congress added a second $1.5 billion to the authorization, raising the total to $3 billion. This figure had been reached by June, 1957, and an additional $1 billion was authorized at that time. In recent years, activities under the Act have expanded further.

The foreign currencies paid for surplus commodities go into a counterpart fund. Some 30 per cent of this counterpart has been reserved for the use of the United States Government, to meet local currency expenses of its operations in the host countries. The remainder is released by the United States Government for the use of the recipient countries, for purposes approved by the United States Government. Only a small fraction of the amounts available have actually been used by the recipient countries. No country with a government-controlled central bank need ever be short of domestic currency, and the host governments see little point in consulting with the United States for the use of money which they can just as easily create for themselves. The balance remains on deposit to the account of the United States.[26]

The PL–480 program has been subjected to considerable criticism both at home and abroad. Thus Raymond F. Mikesell writes, "Not only are the foreign disposal programs of questionable soundness for domestic policy, but some of them have proved harmful to our foreign relations." [27] Similarly, Paul G. Hoffman, now Director of the United Nations Special Fund, says of the PL–480 operations and the consequent balances built up to the credit of the United States, "At bottom large local currency balances are a doubtful device, concealing the fact from the United States that its surplus shipments are grants rather than sales, and encouraging low income countries to resort to dubious financial practices." [28] Among advanced

[26] It is, of course, possible for a government to make the budget position *look* better through use of counterpart funds, especially if carried over from one year to another. By so doing, political resistance to expenditure may be reduced, and if there is no excessive inflationary pressure, the net effect might possibly be beneficial.

[27] Raymvond F. Mikesell, *Agricultural Surpluses and Export Policy* (Washington, D.C., 1958), p. 1.

[28] Paul G. Hoffman, *100 Countries: One and One-Quarter Billion People* (Washington, D.C., 1960), p. 32.

countries, the strongest complaints have come from the Canadian government. In September, 1957, the Prime Minister himself publicly complained of the effect of the United States' surplus commodity disposal on the world market for wheat.[29]

An optimal international division of labor, *after* the underdeveloped countries have made their transition to industrialization, may involve even greater exports of American agricultural goods to now underdeveloped countries. Once the transition is over and the now underdeveloped countries are able to finance imports of agricultural goods through export of industrial products (and assuming that United States commercial policy is such as to encourage this development), the underdeveloped countries will be able to buy increased quantities of American agricultural exports at normal market prices. Taking these factors into account, a case can be made for continuing the program under international auspices. On the other hand, as we have seen, inadequate supplies of food and raw materials can be a serious bottleneck for countries endeavoring to launch a take-off into sustained economic growth. A case can also be made for continuing the farm-price-support program, with its corollary of surplus commodity disposal, in terms of seeking a long-run optimal geographic division of labor. The United States is an extraordinarily efficient agricultural country, and is likely to remain so. Many of the underdeveloped countries, on the other hand, are very inefficient agricultural countries, and raising agricultural productivity per man-year to anything approaching American levels is close to impossible.

THE SOVIET BLOC

The Soviet Bloc has been providing both technical assistance and loans. The loans have been "tied" to expenditure in Soviet Bloc countries, and like Eximbank loans, are usually granted to finance exports of particular kinds of equipment. They are also "tied" in the additional sense that the recipient country must obtain material and equipment through the state-trading organization responsible for them. Interest rates on Soviet Bloc loans have been considerably lower than on United States or IBRD loans; it is difficult to say whether the prices set for the equipment provided included a built-in interest rate which is actually higher than the standard 2 to 2.5 per cent stipulated for these loans. Repayments are usually in twelve annual installments, sometimes with an initial period of grace of eight years. The aid is usually "without strings"; no economic and political conditions are imposed other than the formal conditions of the loan (or technical assistance) and the requirement that proceeds must be spent within the Soviet Bloc. The "line-of-credit" approach gives the Soviet Bloc a means of assuring financial support over several years, thus avoiding the problems of annual budgeting that still plague the United States program.

Soviet Bloc aid to non-Communist countries is much more concentrated geographically than either United States or United Nations aid. In late

[29] John Diefenbaker, "Address to the Anglo-Canadian American Convocation at Dartmouth University," Canadian Embassy Press Series, September 7, 1957.

1958 the Soviets had 2,800 technical assistance experts and 1,200 military experts in only seventeen countries. Most of these were in the uncommitted countries of Asia, Africa, and the Middle East.[30] Capital assistance was even more concentrated. Up to the middle of 1959, Egypt was the greatest beneficiary, both in terms of amounts offered and amounts actually drawn. Adding the aid to Syria, the United Arab Republic accounted for nearly one-third of the total credits extended. Asian neutralist countries account for most of the balance of Soviet Bloc capital assistance. In terms of economic assistance offered or delivered, India was ahead even of Egypt in mid-1959. Although the United States has provided aid to both Yugoslavia and Poland, the Soviet Bloc has yet to provide aid to any country that is openly allied with the West.

Although Russian aid has been a significant factor in the total aid picture, and is becoming more so, it has nonetheless been small in comparison with aid from OECD countries. In 1963 it was only 4.7 per cent of the total flow of official resources from OECD countries. Western countries *other* than the United States have provided more economic assistance to underdeveloped countries than the amount of Soviet credits actually utilized. Chinese aid has been about 10 per cent of the Sino-Soviet total, and has been mainly in the form of interest-free loans.

The enormous gap between credits offered and credits utilized (Table 28–5) is partly the result of the Soviet practice of providing lines-of-credit to be drawn on over several years, and partly a result of administrative delays in both donor and recipient countries. It may also, however, reflect

TABLE 28–4

Aid of Communist Countries to Underdeveloped Countries; Commitments
(millions of U.S. dollars, national currencies converted
at the official rates of exchange)

Donor	Total Aid Between 1954–1959	1960	1961	1962
Bulgaria	..	1	23	..
China (mainland)	145	106	51	51
Czechoslovakia	210	99	208	1
Eastern Germany	29	..	71	6
Hungary	..	32	124	..
Poland	54	71	86	88
USSR	1,880	584	555	233
Total* all donor countries	2,327	893	1,168	444

SOURCE: United Nations, *International Flow of Long-term Capital and Official Donations 1960–1962.* Table 19.

* The figures in the original source do not add up to this total presumably because "others" have been left out as being unimportant.

[30] U.S. Department of State, *The Communist Economic Threat* (Publication No. 6777), March, 1959, p. 12.

TABLE 28-5
Economic Assistance of the Sino-Soviet Bloc to the
Developing Countries 1954–1963
(in millions of U.S. dollars)

Year	Commitments	Disbursements
1954	11	1
1955	149	3
1956	608	107
1957	227	87
1958	556	205
1959	894	161
1960	1,165	186
1961	957	294
1962	507	391
1963	319	425
Cumulative total	5,393	1,860

SOURCE: OECD Statistics, Goran Ohlin, Foreign Aid Policies Reconsidered (Paris: OECD, 1966), p. 52.

reluctance even in neutralist countries to accept large amounts of Soviet Bloc assistance if other sources are available.

Conclusions

The gap between the theory and practice of foreign aid remains large, both in terms of amounts of aid available and in terms of its allocation among countries and uses. Elsewhere the present writer has suggested in some detail a reorganization of international assistance, the essential features of which are further internationalization, making the International Development Association what the name implies and channeling all aid through it, both bilateral and multilateral; extension of the OECD "confrontation" and the Colombo Plan "consultative assembly" devices to include all donor and all recipient countries; and greater use of the UN Regional Commissions.[31] There is clearly room for improvement. Goran Ohlin, at the conclusion of his study of foreign aid, pleads for a "code of development assistance":[32]

If development assistance is to remain a prominent international institution for many decades to come, it will require a code of behaviour not only for donors but for all those involved, a code which needs for its emergence not only a basis in joint interests but a clear understanding of the functions and potential contributions of foreign resources.

Yet when one considers what an extraordinary and novel concept it is that rich nations have a responsibility to help poor nations become rich too, the remarkable feature of the foreign aid effort is not its deficiencies, but the fact that it has continued so long and made such apparent progress.

[31] Higgins, op. cit., Chap. 8.
[32] Ohlin, op. cit., p. 100.

29 || Population Policy

In Part 4 we saw that getting out of the low-income trap and staying out requires accelerated technological progress, retardation of population growth, or both. We have already indicated that in the past these two developments have had some tendency to come together; conditions of rapid technical change have also been conducive to declining fertility. The possibility must be faced, however, that in some countries *no* feasible rate of technological progress will guarantee sustained economic progress, unless the rate of population growth drops. In these countries, a positive population policy may prove to be an essential part of over-all planning for economic development.

The cold diagrammatic analysis of Part 4 may destroy for the reader any sense of the intense human and social problems involved in the very concept of "population policy." Let us consider what a reknowned anthropologist had to say: [1]

In summary, every society would like to improve its economic position, and every society is capable of learning to operate the machines and follow the scientific procedures which might lead to such improvement. Let us turn now to the cultural and social factors which may operate to inhibit or retard economic growth.

The first and perhaps most important of these is unrestricted breeding. This is no more and no less natural than other features of human behavior. It is

[1] Ralph Linton, "Cultural and Personality Factors Affecting Economic Growth," in Berthold F. Hoselitz (ed.), *The Progress of Underdeveloped Areas*, Harris Foundation Lectures (Chicago, 1952) pp. 79–80.

intimately wrapped up with the society's culture, and birth control is infinitely older and more widely distributed than the use of rubber.

Economic development itself may bring falling birth rates as well as falling death rates. Industrialization may cut the birth rate through the operation of such factors as urbanization, the breaking up of peasant society, general education, higher school-leaving ages (especially for girls), and a "built-in habit of technological progress." Yet such indirect effects on birth rates may be too little and come too late to prevent a long postponement of take-off in some underdeveloped countries.

Hagen's "Common Sense of Population"

Everett Hagen takes issue with "Neo-Malthusians" who persist in regarding population pressure as a barrier to economic development, chiding them for excessive gloom.

Hagen states his main point as follows: [2]

The Malthusian thesis suggests that as income rises, the rate of population growth will rise until it reaches the maximum biological growth rate of, say, 3 per cent per year. Only by exceeding this maximum rate of population growth can growth in aggregate output beat population and continue to raise per capita income until it reaches a level high enough to induce new modes of behavior. Indeed, the forecast that population growth if not checked by deliberate action will prevent improvement in human welfare is the heart of the Malthusian message. But while the population of the West has grown, in not a single country has the expected rate of population growth occurred. There is no *single* case of continuing growth in aggregate output of even 1.5 per cent per year, in which population growth has matched it and prevented continuing rise in per capita income. This fact, and not that of growth in world population, may be the fact of recent world history most important for population theory.

This thesis is a projection of the historical record in thirteen countries in Europe and the New World. Hagen's "explanation" of the taperingoff of population growth in these countries is simply that in societies where technological advance becomes habitual, and where significant initial improvements in standards of living are obtained, a "standard of living effect" takes place, bringing a reduction in fertility rates. He outlines this sequence in the following terms:

Let us now make the further assumption that a standard-of-living effect occurs at any level of income above the subsistence level, if this level of income is sustained for a minimum period (say the period from early infancy to parenthood). There is no reason in logic to assume any specific floor of per capita income, below which the standard-of-living effect does not operate. . . .

The tremendously important conclusion follows that technological progress,

[2] Everett E. Hagen, "The Common Sense of Population" (CENIS Document C/58-14), p. 20. See also his "Population and Economic Growth," *American Economic Review*, June, 1959, pp. 310–27.

at any rate above a certain minimum rate, will cause a standard-of-living effect, i.e., will check population growth. First, by raising per capita income, technological progress causes a fall in the death rate, and an accelerated rate of population growth. Then, because continuing technological progress holds per capita income above subsistence, the birth rate falls and with it the rate of population growth. Per capita income therefore rises further; the death rate falls further; and so on, until death and birth rates have reached their minimum levels.

Some Questions of Fact

In appraising this population theory we must first consider the facts on which it is based. Let us note at the outset that by "continuing growth in aggregate output" Hagen has in mind growth sustained for two or three generations.

"The decline in death rate in England," Hagen writes, "probably began some decades before 1800 and elsewhere in Western Europe at latest not many decades after 1800. Throughout Western Europe and Britain the decline in birth rate seemed to have begun only in late 1870s or 1880s. Not until the 1920s has birth rate fallen to a minimum." Thus the interval between the initial fall in death rate and the subsequent fall in birth rate is a matter of fifty to seventy years. He is prepared to admit that during Malthus' own lifetime (1766–1834) there was no clear increase in English per capita output; during the first seventy years or so of industrial revolution, population growth may have prevented the rise in per capita income. The whole ring of the Hagen thesis sounds very different if it is maintained, not that underdeveloped countries need not worry about population pressure, but only that there is reason to hope that *if* they succeed in maintaining expansion of per capita output for fifty or seventy years, there will *then* follow a drop in fertility rate which will permit continuing increase in per capita incomes.

Hagen shows some reluctance to accept figures which do not fit his thesis. Thus he considers the result of studies by Phyllis Deane, showing that between 1770 and the end of the Napoleonic Wars English population grew faster than real income, "difficult to accept."

His tendency to shy away from inconvenient facts is also apparent in his discussion of the Chinese case. The fact that mainland China had in 1953 a population of 582 million, and a rate of population growth of 2 per cent a year, he says, suggests that long-run rapid population growth occurred in China which would contradict his generalizations. But he considers "an estimate of the population growth rate derived from a single census" too flimsy to be evidence "either for or against the thesis presented here." Similarly, he recognizes that "in Ceylon, Malaya, Mexico, Venezuela, Ecuador, and several Central American countries in the Carribean area . . . the rate of population growth has been about 3 per cent in recent years." He might have added the Philippines and some African countries. These cases he dismisses by saying "we do not know how long this rate of increase may continue." He thinks, wishfully, that because the rate of drop in the *death* rate in these countries has been more rapid than it was in western Europe and in England, "one may hope that the lag (between the drop in death rate and the subsequent drop in fertility rate) may be correspondingly short." One may indeed *hope* so, but there is little reason to forecast any such relationship. And, as Hagen himself points out, "if in countries already densely populated rapid population growth continues for even one generation results may be tragic."

Some Questions of Causation

From the analytical point of view the main weakness of Hagen's statement of his thesis is his failure to take account of the dualistic character of most underdeveloped economies. A great deal of technological progress can take place in the industrial sector of an underdeveloped country without raising per capita incomes in the rural sector, let alone bringing a built-in habit of technological progress in that sector. If then, as we maintain, technological progress in the industrial sector brings a spurt of population growth, while nothing happens in the rural sector to bring the subsequent drop in fertility rates Hagen postulates, it can indeed happen that the initial spurt of growth in per capita income is subsequently swamped by population growth.

This process is particularly clear in Indonesia, which Hagen chooses to treat as a "limiting case." The process can be traced more easily in Indonesia than in other countries where population growth is now at very high levels, merely because industrialization started earlier there than in other Asian and African countries. The "population explosion" began in Java after 1820, with the introduction of the "culture system" and the first sugar plantations. Why should the Philippines, African countries, and other countries having current rates of population growth near 3 per cent follow the European rather than the Indonesian pattern?

Hagen charges that economists who attach significance to the Indonesian experience have "a misconception" which "arises, not out of empirical research but from the assumption that since men desire to maximize income and examples of improved techniques of West have been available, per capita income should have risen in low income countries, and its failure to rise must be due to some barrier such as population growth." But Hagen himself generalizes from skimpy empirical research. He misses completely the essential point of Indonesian experience. "The official estimates of population in the Netherland Indies," he says, "indicate population increase at a rate above 1.5 per cent per year from 1870 to 1900 and from 1920 to 1930." He suggests that these data may overstate population increase because of progressive improvement in census coverage; or that the population increase was due to introduction of public health measures; "or, more probably, the disruption of the culture by the Dutch created an intense need to strive for emotional security by sexual activity for increase in progeny."

Actually, the Dutch disrupted Indonesian culture very little—certainly far less than any other colonial power disrupted the culture of the native people. It was official policy of N.E.I. administrators *not* to disrupt the local culture any more than they could help. The system of "indirect rule" through local sultans was well designed to carry out this conservative policy. Public health measures and the establishment of law and order, as we have seen above, did indeed bring a drop in death rates. The culture system may have provided the positive incentive for increase in the size of family.

The main point, however, is that the over-all rate of population increase in the Netherlands Indies of 1.8 per cent is almost as meaningless an average as, say, the average rate of population growth in England and India. Under Dutch rule there was probably less contact among the islands constituting the Indonesian archipelago than there had been in the days of the *Madjapahit* empire. The *significant* fact is that the "population explosion" followed the Dutch settlers, beginning in central and east central Java, where Dutch settlement first assumed significant proportions with the development of sugar plantations; proceeding to other parts of Java; and after 1870, as the Dutch began their mining and plantation operations in the Outer Islands, appearing there. The rates of population growth in the areas immediately affected by Dutch settlement and industrialization reached figures very close to Leibenstein's "biological maximum" of 3 per cent.[3] Between 1920 and 1930 the population growth on Java and Madura had dropped from a peak decennial increase of 2.7 per cent to 1.7 per cent, but in Sumatra the rate was 2.7 per cent and in Borneo 2.8 per cent. Much the same pattern can be observed in the Philippines, where industrialization started relatively recently and where the current rate of population growth is between 2.2 and 2.9 per cent, as suggested by a recent sample survey. For from being a "limiting case," the Indonesian experience, viewed in this light, is a grim warning of what may happen in other under-developed countries as industrialization takes place.

With regard to India and China, where populations are large but rates of growth slow, Professor Hagen says that population growth "obviously has not prevented increase in output from raising national income. . . . Per capita income has failed to rise in such countries—because the technological ferment necessary for a rate of growth in output above a minimum rate has not occurred." Maybe. But this is merely a complicated way of saying that where nothing happens, nothing happens. Indian and Chinese experience to date certainly does not entitle us to advise these countries not to worry lest improvements in public health and nutrition bring population pressure that will retard economic growth.

The figures presented by Hagen could be just as well used to support an alternative thesis; viz., that the drop of fertility rates in Europe was an accompaniment of Western style urbanization. Those figures could equally well support the thesis that "population growth occurs when per capita income in excess of $100 is reached, and the subsequent drop in fertility rates comes only when per capita incomes in excess of $200 are reached." This interpretation would leave many underdeveloped countries with the colossal task of surpassing *initial* rates of increase in population growth as they move into the region of per capita incomes above $100 but below

[3] Harvey Leibenstein, *Theory of Economic-demongraphic Development* (Princeton, N.J., 1954).

$200. As pointed out in Chapter 9, the now underdeveloped countries start their process of economic development from much lower levels of per capita income than the currently advanced countries enjoyed in 1800. Other economic, social, technological, and political differences conjoin to make it less easy for present underdeveloped countries to achieve rates of growth that will assure rising per capita incomes, in face of the possible increases in rates of population growth. Considering his usual caution in forecasting for Asian, African, and Latin American societies response to given economic situations similar to those we expect in the West, it is surprising that Hagen is so ready to project into these societies Western experience with so complex a matter as population growth.

Although we have reservations about both the facts and theories presented in Hagen's "Common Sense," we can nevertheless accept his final conclusion: [4]

. . . density of population relative to natural resources presumably implies a steep slope of diminishing marginal returns to labor, since the curve of returns is concave downward.

Finally, for any given level of techniques, per capita income will be lower in a densely populated country than in a less densely populated one. (This is true by definition. If it is not true, the country is not appropriately termed densely populated.) *Cet. par.*, the densely populated country will never catch the less densely populated ones in per capita income. Further, because of the difference in factor proportions, its relative progress may be slower, and not only the absolute but the relative gap between it and the less densely populated countries may increase.

Population Pressure as a Stimulant to Growth

In our discussion of the Hansen thesis in Chapter 7 we argued that population growth is less likely to encourage autonomous investment in underdeveloped countries than in advances ones. Where labor is already redundant, growth of the labor force is not needed to permit the optimal combination of labor and capital to be maintained while capital accumulation takes place. Also there is less assurance that increased numbers will be accompanied by increased effective demand for housing, transport facilities, and public utilities. Albert Hirschman, however, suggests that even in underdeveloped countries population pressure may, if it is not so severe as to be demoralizing, provide the stimulus needed to improve production techniques. Once having discovered the ability to raise living standards by their own efforts, people will continue to make such efforts and sustained economic growth will result.[5]

The argument is a little like the more sweeping generalizations of the historian Arnold Toynbee: civilizations progress as a consequence of "response" to some "challenge." Societies where customary ways of life can be maintained without effort and nothing happens to disrupt the traditional

[4] Hagen, *op. cit.*, pp. 35–36.
[5] Albert O. Hirschman, *The Strategy of Economic Development* (New Haven, 1958).

economic and social organization are unlikely to progress. Societies confronted with a situation so serious that a universal feeling of hopelessness sets in will not progress either. But where there is both a challenge and a recognized means of dealing with it economic and social advance will ensue.

Hirschman starts from Duesenberry's "fundamental psychological postulate" that people resist any lowering of their living standards and try to prevent it if possible. Duesenberry applied his postulate to savings-consumption patterns during a cyclical downswing in advanced countries: when incomes drop people squeeze their savings in order to maintain their consumption patterns. But if people do that, asks Hirschman, why should they not also resist having their incomes squeezed by population growth? He sets forth two propositions of his own: "that population pressure on living standards will lead to counterpressure, i.e., to activity designed to maintain or restore the traditional standard of living of the community"; and "that the activity undertaken by the community in resisting a decline in its standard of living causes an increase in its ability to control its environment and to organize itself for development."

Of course, Hirschman adds, population growth can provide the stimulus for sustained growth only if there is some slack to be taken up in the economy. Also, a strong reaction is more likely "if the population increase comes as a sudden shock."
"Creeping" population pressure is less likely to result in a successful effort to overcome it than "a dramatic decline in mortality rates" and a consequent population "explosion." Thus Hirschman's argument lends some support to Hagen's suggestion that where drops in mortality rates have been particularly rapid the lag until fertility rates are reduced may be correspondingly short.

Hirschman also believes that action is more likely to be stimulated if population growth is combined with increased urbanization; or if the consequent growth in domestic market and labor force carries the country across "minimum production thresholds in a number of important industries;" or if the original increase affects mainly the upper classes.

Hirschman "certainly does not conclude that underdeveloped countries should institute a generous system of family allowances." For "population pressures are a clumsy and cruel stimulant to development" and "underdeveloped countries are today abundantly supplied with this stimulant." But he does conclude that "if a country is able to offset, be it even partially at first, the effect of the population increase, then we may have confidence that, through the learning acquired in this process, it will be able to do progressively better in marshalling its productive forces for development so that eventually output growth will overtake population growth."

In short, a "population explosion" is one form of "shock" which may move a country off dead center and start it on the path to economic development. There can of course be no denial that it *may* have this effect, and there is good reason to believe that in Europe and the New World in the nineteenth century, and perhaps in Australia since World War II, it *did* have this effect. But it *need not* have this effect, and in a good many underdeveloped countries it *did* not, because of the special conditions that accompanied the population explosions, analyzed above under the heading of "technological dualism."

Dr. Nathan Keyfitz, a demographer and sociologist with a great breadth and depth of experience in developing countries, is very skeptical of Hirschamn's prescription. He declares himself to be pessimistic about the chances of general population pressure arousing the necessary action toward development, if only because a population explosion can lower per capita incomes (in comparison to what they would otherwise be) by only 3 per cent per year or so. Such a process, he says, "is too gradual for people to have a point from which to take a stand." He does see some possibility of reaction to the "shock treatment" involved in having the number of entrants into the labor force double within a few years, because of earlier drops in infant mortality rates and a consequent rapid increase in numbers in the critical age group. But he is less certain as to what the reaction to the presence of an "essentially unemployed younger generation" may be.[6] Persuading a country to accelerate population growth in order to shock it into taking steps to launch economic development is a little like setting fire in a slum area in order to persuade the residents of the benefits of fireproof construction.

Family Planning

It seems likely, therefore, that in a good many underdeveloped countries some form of family planning will be needed if early "take-off into sustained economic growth" is to be achieved. But is family planning socially and culturally acceptable in all these countries, or will efforts to promote birth control run into unyielding obstacles in the form of religious or ideological opposition?

Two statements may be made at the outset in reply to this question. First, what once looked like religious or ideological opposition to birth control has frequently turned out, on closer study, to be the product of poverty and ignorance. Women in poor societies, in particular, are usually eager to limit the size of their families, provided a cheap, simple, and reliable device is available. Second, there is no clear correlation between predominant religion and birth rates among countries. Canada and the United States, which are predominantly Protestant, have had birth rates in recent years well above those of predominantly Roman Catholic Argentina, Austria, Belgium, France, and Italy. Birth rates in Australia and New Zealand, also predominantly Protestant, have been higher than in European Catholic countries. Birth rates in the Catholic province of Quebec are below those of the rest of the country, which is mainly Protesant. Birth rates in Spanish North Africa are below those of Spain, which in turn are below those of vehemently Protestant Northern Ireland. Before World War II several Catholic countries had stagnant or even declining populations. Conversely, it is worth noting that Asian religions as such do not prohibit family plan-

[6] Nathan Keyfitz, "Age Distribution as a Challenge to Development," *The American Journal of Sociology*, May, 1965, pp. 659–68.

ning. Thus, what international comparisons seem to show, rather than any clear religious or cultural influence on birth rates, is an economic influence; birth rates tend to be high in very rich and very poor countries, and to be relatively low in middle-income countries.

There is also a clear relationship between high birth rates and high infant mortality rates. Some poor families have large numbers of children in order to assure the survival of a few. As infant mortality rates fall and parents become aware of the increased probability that their children will survive to maturity, this cause of high birth rates can be expected to disappear, as it has in societies that have experienced rapidly falling infant mortality rates in the past.

The Medical History of Contraception

Dr. Norman B. Himes' *Medical History of Contraception* remains the major work in its field. As Dr. Alan F. Guttmacher writes in his preface to the new edition, "It is a classic—complete, accurate, scholarly, and well-written." [7] Its major lesson is clear and simple: contraception is as old as human society, and every culture, no matter how ancient, how primitive, or how modern, has permitted, if not actually encouraged, contraception in one form or another. In ancient, medieval, and primitive societies there was much ignorance on the subject, and the same society frequently mixed methods that were rational and effective with others that were crude and still others that were essentially magical in nature.

The *Atjehnese* provide an example of the use of rational and magical methods, side by side. One of the former was "a black mass in the form of a pill, which the natives were accustomed to introduce into the vagina before coitus, and which was supposed to prevent impregnation. Upon examination, this black mass was found to contain a large quantity of tannic acid. Quite possibly these natives had, by trial and error, hit upon a vaginal suppository sound in principle." For "tannic acid ranks very high as a spermicide—much higher than lactic acid, which is the supposed active agent in jellies applied to vaginal diaphragms in the modern birth-control clinics."

In summary, Himes writes: "Contraceptive practices were rare among preliterate peoples when compared with abortion and infanticide, the chief primitive substitutes for conception control." *Coitus interruptus* is quite general in Africa, and also in Sumatra. Both magical and rational contraceptive devices are found. "But so far as the most common indications for contraception are concerned, we find them not only in modern societies but in primitive. The desire for control is neither time nor space bound. It is a universal characteristic of social life."

Himes summarizes Asian experience as follows: "The antiquity of some of the Chinese and Sanskrit texts and the age of certain practices are often obscure. None the less, it is clear that even in Oriental cultures, which have stressed family solidarity and ancestor worship rather than scrambling, self-maximizing individualism, the *desire* for prevention is old. So likewise

[7] Norman E. Himes, *A Medical History of Contraception* (Gamut Press, 1963).

are some of the techniques." With regard to Islam, he says, "While the work of Islamic physicians on conception control is not as brilliant as that of Soranos or Aetios, it is, none the less, work of distinction. Their techniques were, considering the small accumulation of medical knowledge in those days, often reasonable and more or less workable."

As a final conclusion on European experience, he says "What is new is not the desire for prevention, but effective, harmless means of achieving it on a grand scale. The older effective techniques were never until recently democratically diffused; and even that process is still going on."

On the other hand, as Dr. Guttmacher also points out in his preface, there have been important changes and innovations in this field since 1935, when Himes wrote his book. Some advance has been made on the American legal front. Among underdeveloped countries, says Dr. Guttmacher, some governments have taken a "strong, positive governmentally supported policy toward the restriction of population growth," including Japan, India, Pakistan, Puerto Rico, Singapore, Egypt, Korea, and Taiwan. Partial support to birth control programs is given by the governments of Ceylon, Hong Kong, and Malaya. Communist China has followed a vaccillating line with regard to population policy. In 1957 there was an "active governmental attempt to introduce birth control by billboard advertisements, radio, and public lectures. However, the clinics which were opened closed ten months later and the effort was abandoned." In 1962, however, a law was passed making the minimum age for marriage for the wife twenty-three, and birth control clinics were reestablished.

The Protestant Church has taken a strong stand in favor of family planning. Both the Reform and Conservative wings of the Jewish faith also "approve the use of contraceptives without any serious qualifications." Pope Pius XI approved the rhythm method in 1930, and approved family planning "for a long time, and even for the duration of marriage, if there are serious reasons, such as those often provided in the so-called indications of the medical, eugenical, economic and social order." (This would seem to cover just about every conceivable reason for birth control.) According to Guttmacher, "there seems to be confusion about the Catholic Church's position in regard to physiologic contraception, 'the pill.' Liberal Catholics seem hopeful that the Church will find theological grounds to accept it as a contraceptive."

Speaking generally, it would appear that on ideological grounds the barriers to family planning as a part of over-all development policy have been overcome in many, if not most, developing countries. The remaining problems seem to be mainly technical, educational, and administrative— as is the case with so many aspects of the development problem.

The trend with respect to population policy is well illustrated by an article written by B. L. Raina, Director General of the Family Planning Institute in India.[8] He first quotes figures for the family planning budgets in the series of Indian Five-Year Plans: Plan I, 1.45 million rupees; Plan II, 21.56 million rupees; Plan III, 270 million rupees; Plan IV, an estimated

[8] B. L. Raina, "Possible Effects of Public Policy Measures on Fertility in India," *Family Planning News*, December, 1965.

950 million rupees. The Indian family planning program is attacking on all fronts at once. In the field of contraception, it is using voluntary sterilization, intra-uterine contraceptives, mechanical and chemical contraceptives, coitus interruptus and the rhythm method, and oral contraceptives. It is also attacking through social factors: raising the age of women at marriage, improving the status of women, introducing old age security programs, compulsory education of children and elimination of child labor, and the like. According to Dr. Raina, "The net effects are showing themselves up." Fertility rates in the upper classes are clearly falling. Urban birth rates are lower than in the surrounding countryside. In country districts where the program has been in operation for five to seven years, birth rates show a falling trend. Sales of contraceptives are rising. All the evidence suggests that India is starting to follow the road of Japan to declining rates of population growth. And few countries indeed present more formidable barriers to successful family planning than India did at the beginning of the First Five-Year Plan.

In a recent article, Göran Ohlin argues that the "complete change of mood" towards limiting family size, together with the intra-uterine device (IUD), constitute a turning point in population history.[9]

[9] Göran Ohlin, "A Turning Point in Population History," *The OECD Observer, Special Issue on Development Aid*, Sept. 1966, pp. 35–39.

PART **VI** | Case Studies

30 | Three Success Stories

Japan: the Lone Graduate

In contemporary economic history, Japan provides the most spectacular success story. It is the only country in recent decades to have "graduated" from the ranks of developing countries into the fortunate group of advanced countries. One hundred years ago Japan was clearly an underdeveloped country. Today Japan has joined the "donors club" as a member of OECD. The structure of its economy, the extent of its industrialization, and even the level of per capita income now qualify Japan as an advanced country.

During the period 1879–1964 (Table 30–1) Japan's rate of growth of per capita income was probably already the highest among major countries of the world. During the decade of 1955–64 there can be no doubt that Japan reached rates of economic growth unprecedented in the history of any country at any time. In the postwar period, Yugoslavia, Venezuela, the USSR and its satellites, and West Germany are its closest rivals; the comparison differs somewhat with beginning and ending dates. But there can be no doubt that the Japanese experience in recent years has been phenomenal and unique.

The Meiji Restoration

The beginnings of Japanese industrial growth are usually traced to the Meiji Restoration of 1868. At that time, the Tokugawa Shogunate was deposed after more than two and one-half centuries of power. Angus Maddison traces the Meiji Restoration to "reactive nationalism of the type of

618   CASE STUDIES

TABLE 30–1

Comparative Long-term Growth Performance

Country	Years	Annual average compound rates		
		GNP	Popu-lation	GNP per head
Japan	1879–1964	3.9	1.2	2.7
United States	1871–1964	3.6	1.7	1.9
Canada	1870–1964	3.5	1.7	1.8
Argentina	1902–1964	3.5	2.5	1.0
Mexico	1895–1963	3.3	1.7	1.6
Australia	1870–1963	2.9	2.0	0.9
USSR	1870–1963	2.9	1.0	1.9
Denmark	1870–1964	2.9	1.0	1.9
Germany	1871–1964	2.8	1.0	1.8
Sweden	1870–1964	2.8	0.7	2.1
Switzerland	1890–1964	2.6	0.9	1.7
Norway	1871–1964	2.6	0.8	1.8
Netherlands	1870–1964	2.4	1.3	1.1
Belgium	1870–1964	2.1	0.6	1.5
Italy	1870–1964	2.0	0.7	1.3
United Kingdom	1870–1964	1.9	0.7	1.2
France	1870–1964	1.7	0.2	1.5
India	1870–1964	1.4	0.7	0.7

SOURCE: Angus Maddison, "Japanese Economic Performance," *Banca Nazionale del Lavoro, Quarterly Review*, December, 1965, p. 4.

Ataturk in Turkey or Nasser in Egypt." [1] During the 1850's the threat of foreign domination appeared off Japanese shores in the person of Commodore Perry, demanding extraterritorial landing and trading rights. The French, British, Russians, and Dutch appeared shortly after. The Japanese leaders recognized that maintaining independence would require a stronger Japan, and that strengthening Japan would in turn require rapid industrialization. According to Maddison, "the reaction to the threat of foreign domination was much sharper than in China because of the presence of a very large class of educated but functionless military men who were much more sensitive to the foreign technical challenge than the scholar gentry of China who had a sense of innate superiority to the West." [2] A land reform of 1873 translated feudal property rights into titles to land for landowners and customary tenants, without (according to James Abegglen) changing the social or political power structure very much.[3] Heavy land taxes were imposed, which were used, among other things, for the establishment of government enterprises in the fields of banking, insurance, shipping, and manufacturing. The proportion of land held by tenants rose from 37 per cent in 1883 to 46 per cent in 1914, with cultivation of small plots (less

[1] Angus Maddison, "Japanese Economic Performance," *Banca Nazionale del Lavoro, Quarterly Review*, December, 1965, p. 9.
[2] *Ibid.*, p. 9.
[3] Cf. Chap. 12.

than one hectare) remaining typical of Japanese agriculture. From 1882 on, the government disinvested itself of most of its enterprises, selling them off at a low price to private enterprise. Private enterprise was also encouraged by subsidies and other privileges. Government ships were given away to private lines. Government and business worked hand in hand, and industrialization was organized through large corporations (Zaibatsu) with strong monopoly positions. During the period 1879 to 1913, gross national produce grew at the rate of 3.3 per cent per year. Agricultural output probably grew at a higher rate than this, while industrial output grew at more than 7 per cent per year, the services sector expanding more slowly.[4]

Angus Maddison, on the basis of his review of the literature and his own observations, attributes the success of the Japanese development policy prior to World War I to four major factors: (1) commitment of the government to the promotion of economic development, through institutional reform, plus drastic fiscal and monetary measures; (2) efforts of the government to transfer and develop a technology suitable to Japanese conditions; (3) the opening of a hitherto closed economy to the benefits of international trade; (4) a savings ratio (during this period in Japan one savings ratio while commendably high, was no higher than it is in many developing countries today). Thus the relatively high rate of growth has to be explained in terms of a comparatively low incremental capital-output ratio rather than in terms of a high investment ratio. To this extent, at least, the observations of Ranis and Fei would appear to be correct.[5]

In contrast to the Socialist countries in the periods following World War I, industrialization in Japan was not impaired by neglect of agriculture. On the contrary, the technological advance and increase of productivity were particularly striking in the agricultural sector. Here productivity per man year grew by 3.6 per cent a year for thirty-five years, although fixed investment was no more than 4 per cent of gross agricultural product. Agriculture provided 40 per cent of the increase in the output between 1878 and 1913. It supplied the bulk of government revenue, most of the savings of the economy, half the foreign exchange requirement, fed an increasing population on rising standards, and permitted the increase in the labor supplies to be absorbed by other sectors.

JAPANESE DEVELOPMENT 1913–1938

During the inter-war period, when Europe and North America suffered various combinations of inflation, stagnation, and unemployment, culminating in the Great Depression of the 1930's which all of them shared, Japan not only managed to avoid stagnation but actually accelerated her economic growth. During the whole period 1913–38 Japanese gross national product grew at the rate of 4.4 per cent per year. Expansion of exports was facilitated by a drastic depreciation of the yen.

[4] These figures come from K. Ohkawa and H. Rosovsky, "Economic Fluctuations in Prewar Japan: A Preliminary Analysis of Cycles and Long Swings," *Hitotsubashi Journal of Economics,* October, 1962; K. Ohkawa, *The Growth Rate of the Japanese Economy Since 1878,* (Tokyo, 1957), and Henry Rosovsky, *Capital Formation in Japan, 1860–1940* (Glencoe, Ill., 1961).
[5] See Chap. 14.

The Silk Industry as a Leading Sector [6]

In the early years of the Meiji Restoration the silk industry was a leading sector, both in terms of exports and in terms of total production. The expansion of the Japanese silk industry was stimulated, at least in part, by a European disaster which provided a windfall for Japan. During the 1860's, the silkworm industries of Italy and France were decimated by disease. Japan was able to step into this breach and exploit it to the full. Between 1868 and 1913, both silk production and silk export expanded rapidly, and they continued to expand until the Great Depression. Even during the 1930's the value of Japanese silk exports fell very little. During the late 1920's, raw silk exports were almost 40 per cent of the Japanese total. For the decade prior to 1940, Japan was the world's greatest producer and exporter of raw silk (Table 30-2).

TABLE 30-2

Production and Exports of Raw Silk

(1934–38 average in thousands of pounds)

Country	Production	Exports
Japan	95,368	66,633
China	22,046	8,741
Italy	5,833	5,044
USSR	4,226	114
Others	17,011	10,959
Total	144,484	91,491

SOURCE: Foreign Capital Research Society, *Japanese Industry After the War* (Tokyo, 1950), p. 86.

These facts have induced some observers to explain Japan's success during the late nineteenth and early twentieth centuries in terms of an "up by the bootstraps" theory, based on silk. The combination of circumstances which permitted the rapid expansion of the Japanese silk industry, the argument goes, provided surpluses of savings and manpower which could be transferred to the growing industrial sector; it also earned the foreign exchange to finance imports of capital goods for the growing industrial sector.

The latter part of this theory, at least, does not stand up. For the most part the increased foreign exchange earnings were not used to finance imports of capital goods but were used rather to import military equipment, consumers' goods, and ships. As shown in Table 30-3, the import of non-military capital goods (other than ships) did indeed expand very rapidly between 1870 and World War I; but at no point was the import of non-military capital-equipment a significant proportion of total imports. At their peak in the years 1908-12, such imports constituted less than 8 per cent of the total.

[6] This section makes uninhibited use of a paper prepared for the author by Julien E. de Sloovere.

Table 30-3

Supply of Non-military Producers' Durables* from Abroad and Their Share in Imports, 1868–1902

	(1) Import of non-military producers' durables other than vessels (1,000 yen)	(2) Export of non-military producers' durables other than vessels (1,000 yen)	(3) Balance between (1) and (2) (1,000 yen)	(4) Total imports	(5) (1) ÷ (4) (percentage)	(6) (3) ÷ (4) (percentage)
1868–1872	75	..	75	22,662	0.33	0.33
1873–1877	478	..	478	26,586	1.80	1.80
1878–1882	546	2	544	32,618	1.67	1.67
1883–1887	709	34	675	32,789	2.16	2.06
1888–1892	3,409	52	3,357	69,508	4.90	4.83
1893–1897	9,349	109	9,240	145,195	6.44	6.36
1898–1902	13,312	431	12,881	267,932	4.97	4.81
1903–1907	23,730	1,623	22,107	524,137	4.53	4.22
1908–1912	33,953	3,394	30,559	432,001	7.86	7.07

* Statistics on producers' durables are those compiled by Shigeru Ishiwata from Dainihon Gaikoku Bōeki Nempō.
SOURCE: Shigeru Ishiwata, "Senzen No Nihon Ni Okeru Shihon Stock Suikei, 1868–1940" (unpublished discussion paper in the Hitotsubashi Rockefeller Project, D-27), pp. 26–29, and Nihon Bōeki Seiran (Tokyo, 1935), pp. 2 and 663. Cited in: M. Miyamoto, Y. Sakudo, and Y. Yasuba, "Growth in Pre-industrial Japan," The Journal of Economic History, December, 1965, p. 555.

The contribution of the silk industry to Japanese growth seems to have been somewhat different from what is implied in this excessively simple "up by the bootstraps" theory. It did add substantially to the income of small farmers, as well as to large landowners. It did indeed permit an increase in savings, and a transfer of capital to the industrial sector, by both these groups. It also provided the base for an expanded production of consumers' goods for the domestic market; consumer spending as well as savings went up with the additional agricultural income. The whole process was assisted by a steady rise in the prices of silk during the early years of the expansion of the Japanese industry.

Silk seems also to have provided a challenge to Japanese society in the form of a need for technological advance. In the American market, which quickly became the most important for Japan, the silk textile industry was already highly automated by 1870. It therefore required silk yarn of standard size and of reliable strength and elasticity. In the beginning the silk industry of Japan was unable to meet these requirements; but with the incentive provided by the large American market, and with the scientific and technical progress which was already being instilled through reform of the Japanese educational system, the necessary technological improvements came quickly enough. It is at least possible that technological progress in the silk industry had spread effects to the rate of technological improvement in other parts of the economy.

In the late nineteenth century, Japanese productivity in sericulture (measured in terms of five-year averages of cocoon yield per ten grams of silkworm eggs) was well below that of Italy and France. By the end of World War II Japanese productivity had caught up with French, and a few years later it surpassed that of both Italy and France. Meanwhile daily wages in sericulture were nearly twice as high in Italy as in Japan, and in France they were higher still. These facts enabled Japan to undersell her major competitors, and at the same time to enjoy a larger profit margin.

One thing at least is certain; Japan is a case of an initial "one export country" which succeeded in diversifying. As may be seen from Table 30–4, the share of raw silk exports in the total declined from nearly 41 per cent for the years 1876–80 to 24.6 per cent in the years 1916–20. During

TABLE 30–4

Raw Silk Exports as a Percentage of Total Value
of Exports, 1876–1958

Year	Percentage	Year	Percentage
1876–1880	40.7	1924–1931	39.6
1886–1890	40.0	1934–1936	11.1
1896–1900	29.4	1950–1953	1.7
1906–1910	30.0	1956–1958	1.3
1916–1920	24.6		

SOURCE: Karl Hax, *Japan, Wirtschaftsmacht des Fernen Ostens* (Köln, 1961), p. 261, table 112.

the following few years, it rose again, less because the silk industry expanded than because exports of other commodities declined. However, in the mid-thirties the figure had already fallen to 11.1 per cent, and since World War II, with the development of synthetic fibers, raw silk exports have become an insignificant fraction of the total.

The rapid change in the structure of Japanese foreign trade is indicated by Table 30–5. Exports of food and raw materials show a steady and rapid

TABLE 30–5

Changes in the Commodity of Foreign Trade, 1868–1956
(in per cent of total)

Years	Food	Raw materials	Semi-manufactured raw materials	Finished manufactures	Miscellaneous
Commodity composition of exports					
1868–1872	32.2	23.2	40.8	1.9	1.9
1898–1902	12.0	11.3	47.2	26.7	2.8
1933–1937	7.9	4.3	26.2	58.7	2.9
1953–1956	8.2	3.4	25.9	62.0	0.5
Commodity composition of imports					
1868–1872	29.0	4.1	20.2	44.5	2.2
1898–1902	22.9	31.4	16.3	28.0	1.3
1933–1937	7.9	60.0	20.1	11.3	0.7
1953–1956	26.7	50.4	10.7	12.1	0.1

SOURCE: Computed from Nippon Tokei Kenkyusho (Japan Statistical Research Institute), *Nihonkeizai-Tokeishu* (Statistics on Japanese Economy), Tokyo, 1958. From Miyohei Shinohara, *Growth and Cycles in the Japanese Economy* (Tokyo, 1962), p. 55.

decline from 1868–72 to 1953–56. Exports of semi-manufactured raw materials were also a dwindling proportion of the total, while remaining fairly important. The exports of finished manufactures, on the other hand, expanded from a mere 1.9 per cent of the total in 1868–72 to 62 per cent of the total in 1953–56. The composition of imports shows the reverse trend. Imports of foodstuffs declined rapidly from 1868–72 to 1933–37; while they increased again during the reconstruction period following World War II, they remained below the figures of the early industrialization phase. Imports of raw materials, on the other hand, expanded significantly. Imports of semi-manufactured raw materials have been cut in half (as a share of the total), while imports of finished manufactures, in percentage terms, were scarcely more than a quarter of what they were in 1868–72.

This experience has led Professor K. Akamatsu to speak of the "Gankokeitai" pattern of economic development. The "Gankokeitai" is the inverse and overlapping V-shaped pattern in which wild geese fly in Japan. This pattern is reproduced in Figure 30–1. In the first stage of development, imports of consumers' goods increased, but decreased during a sec-

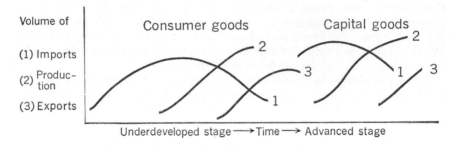

Figure 30–1

SOURCE: Miyohei Shinohara, *Growth and Cycles in the Japanese Economy* (Tokyo, 1962), p. 58.

ond phase in which production of consumers' goods expanded rapidly; later still, exports began. At a more advanced stage of development the same pattern is repeated for capital goods.

Professor Miyohei Shinohara reaches the following conclusions with regard to the role of exports in Japanese development: (1) Both in the prewar and in the postwar period the rate of expansion of Japanese exports was among the highest in the world. (2) In the nineteenth century a combination of factors served to expand foreign trade, including the speculative decline in the relative price of silver under the silver standard, reparations from China after the final Japanese war, the silkworm diseases in Europe, and the like. (3) In the present century the drastic deterioration in the terms of trade between 1910 and 1920 and again in the 1930's contributed to the expansion of the volume of foreign trade. (4) The expansion of exports resulting from deterioration of terms of trade contributed to domestic economic expansion through the multiplier process, and through the increased use of imported raw materials. (5) A combination of advanced technology and cheap labor contributed to the rapid expansion of textile exports. (6) The commodity composition of foreign trade shifted toward processing from the beginning of the Meiji period, and during the first decade of this century a turning point was reached when cotton textiles began to be exported rather than imported.

It is interesting to note that in sharp contrast to the Prebisch thesis, Shinohara includes the deteriorating terms of trade, and the consequent expansion in volume of exports, among the causes of Japan's rapid growth during the nineteenth century. There is also a suggestion here of a different kind of "ratchet" effect. Declining terms of trade in one period may lead to an expansion of exports; when later the terms of trade improve, with industrial export capacity already greatly expanded, the consequent rise in incomes gives fresh vigor to the expansion process. According to Shinohara, during the Great Depression, "Japan was the country which suffered the severest deterioration in the terms of trade, whose export prices declined most drastically, and whose volume of exports showed the greatest expansion when exports of many countries fell steeply." [7]

Other Factors Contributing to Prewar Growth

The industrialization of Japan in the nineteenth century was also facilitated by what we would now call a program of technical assistance. Early in the Meiji period the government sent people abroad to study in European countries and invited foreign technicians to assist in the organization of modern armed forces, a new legal system, a public health service, a police force, and an improved public administration. Foreign scientists were brought to the new Imperial University in Tokyo and were employed in newly established research institutions. Angus Maddison points out that whereas in 1872 there were only 385 foreigners in the government service, the cumulative total of foreigners brought in during the period 1876–95 was 3,916. He also reports that the Japanese were willing to pay average salaries ten times as high as were paid to their Japanese equivalent—here again, the analogy with contemporary technical assistance programs is clear.[8]

Of great importance in the Japanese "take-off" were improvements in the educational system. The Ministry of Education was established in 1871 and in the following year a law governing the operation of the school system was put into effect. The educational reform was a combination of increasing the proportion of school-age children attending school and a redirection of education toward the requirements of economic development. The proportion of children of elementary school age attending school increased from 28 per cent in 1873 to 46 per cent in 1886. As Maddison points out, this was a relatively slow expansion of primary education in comparison to the more ambitious programs in developing countries today; but by the same token the "wastefully high drop-out rates currently so characteristic of education in developing countries, where many children attend school for only one or two years and do not acquire literacy" was avoided.

Japan avoided the mistake made by virtually all of the Socialist countries (and some others as well) of neglecting the agricultural sector. On the contrary, special efforts were made to find an appropriate agricultural technique and to diffuse it throughout the agricultural sector of the economy. In the beginning, the government apparently sought to introduce the extensive and mechanized agricultural techniques of the United States and the United Kingdom. While these techniques proved appropriate in some recently opened areas, it was soon apparent that they were not suitable for the small farms that still constituted the bulk of Japanese agriculture. Consequently attention was diverted to increasing the productivity of small farms. Technical assistance was switched from British and American to German and Dutch technicians, who helped to develop new chemicals and fertilizers suitable to Japanese conditions. Seed selection was also an impor-

[7] Miyohei Shinohara, *Growth and Cycles in the Japanese Economy* (Tokyo, 1962), p. 66.
[8] Angus Maddison, *op. cit.*, pp. 24–25.

tant part of the program. Livestock was greatly improved.

Japan also recognized from the beginning the importance of spending money on research and development. In 1962 Japan was spending about the same proportion of gross national product on research and development as were Germany and France, with a much smaller share of these expenditures being allocated to military objectives. In 1959 the number of scientists and engineers engaged in civilan research was double that of the United Kingdom, more than three times that of Germany, and almost four times that of France. Japan was also quite willing to make use of foreign capital to meet the recurrent deficits in the balance of payments as rapid industrialization proceeded.

That the investment ratio was not the major factor in Japan's "take-off" is clear from the figures presented in Table 30–6. It was not until after

TABLE 30–6

Gross Investment Ratio in Japan 1887–1962

Years	Gross domestic capital formation as a proportion of GNP	Non-residential* capital formation as a proportion of GNP
1887–1916†	10.8	9.0
1917–1936†	16.1	14.8
1955–1962	33.2	30.2

* Residential construction on farms is included for prewar years.

† 1887–1936 from H. Rosovsky, *Capital Formation in Japan 1860–1940* (Glencoe, Ill., 1961), pp. 2, 9 and 24. The figures exclude military investment. The Rosovsky figures are 5-year moving averages. Recent unpublished European Productivity Agency estimates show a lower fixed investment rate for 1917–36, of 15.2 per cent. 1955–62 from unpublished estimates of the E.P.A. incorporating latest revision in GNP figures. Rations are in current prices.

SOURCE: Angus Maddison, "Japanese Economic Performance," *Banca Nazionale del Lavoro, Quarterly Review*, December, 1965, p. 9.

World War I that the investment ratio in Japan reached levels associated with "take-off into sustained economic growth." On the other hand, it is clear that Japan enjoyed a relatively low incremental gross capital-output ratio (Table 30–6a). This in turn was a reflection of the product mix on the one hand and of the structure of wages on the other, which permitted full exploitation of relatively labor-intensive but less efficient techniques.

Economic Growth in the Postwar Period

Japanese development since World War II may be divided into two phases: a period of reconstruction, ending around 1955, and a period,

TABLE 30–6a

Incremental Gross Capital-Output Ratios in Japan
1887–1963*

Years	Ratio of total capital formation to GNP growth	Ratio of non-residential capital formation to GNP growth
1887–1917	3.0	2.5
1917–1936	4.5	4.1
1955–1963	3.2	2.9

* Investment ratios from preceding table. GNP growth from sources cited in Table 30–1.
SOURCE: Augus Maddison, "Japanese Economic Performance," *Banca Nazionale del Lavoro, Quarterly Review,* December, 1965, p. 9.

termed by Maddison the phase of "explosive growth," from 1955 to the present time.

Shinohara lays particular stress on the reconstruction character of the high rate of growth of per capita product in Japan in the first decade after the war. He has analyzed the relationship between the losses of industrial production between 1938 and 1948 on the one hand and the growth of industrial production in percentage terms between 1948 and 1956. There is a marked relationship between these two factors. Countries such as the United States and Canada, where industrial production in 1948 was about double its 1938 level, enjoyed relatively little further expansion of industrial output during the period 1948–56. Japan, on the other hand, having suffered the greatest contraction of industrial production during the war years, also enjoyed much the highest rate of expansion during the 1948–56 period. West Germany, the other defeated country, had the second largest decline in industrial output between 1938 and 1948, and the second highest increase between 1948 and 1956, except for Rumania and Poland.

Low incremental capital-output ratios and consequent high rates of economic growth, as we have seen, are relatively easy to obtain during a period of reconstruction. In the case of Japan, however, the end of the reconstruction period, instead of leading to a tapering off of growth, as many Japanese economists and politicians expected it to do, was followed by a still higher rate of increase in per capita product. It is this period of "explosive growth" which needs particular explanation. Dr. Shinohara tends to stress the "dualistic wage structure." As may be seen from Table 30–7, wage differentials for different sizes of firms are much greater in Japan than in the United Kingdom or the United States.

The capital intensity, as would be expected, tends to increase with the size of firm, as may be seen in Table 30–8. However, in contrast to the experience in some other countries, the capital-output ratio (output measured in value added), is fairly constant for firms with up to 300 employees, after which it rises fairly steeply. Similarly, the ratio of wages and salaries

TABLE 30–7

Wages and Productivity per Worker in Manufacturing Firms in Japan,
United Kingdom, and United States

(Average wage and productivity in firms with 1,000 employees and above = 100)

Size of firm by number of employees	Wage differentials			Productivity differentials (value added per employee)		
	Japan (1957)	United Kingdom (1949)	United States (1947)	Japan (1957)	United Kingdom (1949)	United States (1947)
1,000 and above	100	100	100	100	100	100
1–3 (1–9)	36	..	65*	17	..	108*
4–9 (5–9)	40	..	73*	23	..	90*
10–19 (11–24)	44	84*	79	30	90*	89
20–49 (25–49)	48	83*	84	36	92*	93
50–99	52	84	86	46	94	91
100–199 (100–249)	56	85	86	53	96	102*
200–499 (250–499)	66	86	88*	68	97	104*
500–999	76	89	90	85	98	105

* Indicates that the figures refer to the size of firms shown in parentheses.

SOURCES: Japan—Smaller Enterprise Agency, *Chushokigyo Kihonchosa* (Basic Survey on Small Enterprise), 1957; United Kingdom and United States—respective Censuses of Manufactures. From Miyohei Shinohara, *Growth and Cycles in the Japanese Economy* (Tokyo, 1962), p. 18.

to value added, while somewhat higher for middle-sized firms than for others, and higher again for very large firms, does not vary as greatly with size of firm as one might expect.

What all this means is that the Japanese have found ways of adapting their production methods to the wage structure and to the size of firms. For example, Japan has made much more use of second-hand machinery, which it could afford to use when combined with cheap labor, than have other countries where relatively uniform wage rates tend to apply throughout the economy. In short, the wide wage differentials mean that Japan is able to exploit any elasticity of substitution of labor for capital that may exist. Thus the effective range of choice of technology is much wider than in other industrialized countries. Shinohara points out that during the 1950's big, medium-sized, and small firms expanded simultaneously, no group developing at the expense of others.

OTHER CAUSES OF RAPID POSTWAR GROWTH

There is substantial agreement among observers of the Japanese economy as to the major reasons for the spectacular performance of the Japanese economy between 1955 and 1964. One of these, the wide wage differentials and adaptation of the product mix and structure of production and choice of technology to it has already been mentioned. Others that are generally recognized include the following. (1) The investment ratio was extraordinarily high. While the prewar growth was largely a matter of low

TABLE 30–8

Capital Intensity, Capital Coefficient, Share Distribution of Value Added by Size of Manufacturing Firms—1957

Size of firms (employees)	Number of firms	Value added per man (1,000 yen)	Capital intensity (1,000 yen)	Capital-value added ratio	Wages per man (1,000 yen)	Wages and salaries—value added (per cent)
1–9	300,374	186	69	0.371	114	34.6
10–29	77,644	289	78	0.270	136	44.5
30–49	13,332	348	91	0.261	146	42.1
50–99	8,460	420	120	0.285	157	38.1
100–199	3,146	492	166	0.337	172	35.7
200–299	981	564	209	0.371	187	33.6
300–499	645	696	309	0.445	205	29.9
500–999	441	780	408	0.523	230	29.6
1,000–1,999	222	922	589	0.639	259	28.7
2,000–4,999	135	1,078	687	0.669	301	28.3
5,000–9,999	46	866	558	0.729	287	37.8
10,000 and over	28	897	651	0.727	329	37.1
Total	405,424	516	289	0.560	194	34.4

SOURCE: Recompiled from the original data of the *Chūshō-kigyō Sōgō Kihon-Chōsa* (Comprehensive Basic Survey of Small-Medium Enterprises), 1957. Economic Planning Agency, Economic Research Institute, *Shihonkōzō to Kigyō-kan Kakusa* (Capital Structure and Interfirm Differential), Ministry of Finance, Printing Office, Study Series 6, (Tokyo, 1960), p. 71.

incremental capital-output ratios, during the postwar period Japan has had both a relatively high investment ratio and an incremental capital-output ratio which has continued to be low in comparison to other countries. For the decade 1955–64 the ratio of gross investment to gross national product reached the extraordinarily high level of 33 per cent. (2) Demographic factors were favorable; the declining rate of population growth had not yet had much effect on the age structure; and in this period the labor participation rate rose, because the labor force grew more rapidly than the total population. (3) A high level of effective demand permitted rapid and drastic shift of labor from low-productivity to high-productivity occupations. (4) The world market situation provided opportunities for rapid growth of exports, and the flexibility of the Japanese economy enabled Japan to take advantage of this situation. (5) Military defeat had its compensations: Japanese military spending has been a much smaller fraction of gross national product than in most industrialized countries. Demilitarization has freed not only capital but also high-level manpower for use elsewhere. (6) Japan has continued to make a major effort on the educational front. For example, the stock of engineers in Japan increased threefold during the decade of the 1950's—an achievement, as Maddison points out, paralleled only by the USSR. (7) The domestic supply of capital goods was increased, resulting partly, no doubt, from the reconversion of war plants to peace-time uses. (8) Not only capital but also technology was absorbed from abroad; while Japanese technology was advanced in comparison to most developing countries, there was nonetheless some technological lag in Japan behind the most advanced countries, and the postwar environment, with American occupation and American economic aid, was one that provided opportunities for eliminating this lag. (9) Institutional reforms were made, especially the replacement of monopolistic structures of private enterprise with a highly competitive system. One ought also to mention an outburst of indigenous entrepreneurship, although the explanation for its appearance is not easy to provide.

The Role of Government in Japanese Postwar Development

The above list of causes of Japan's rapid growth since 1955 makes no mention of government policies, let alone of government planning. It remains to appraise the impact of government plans and policies on the recent development of Japan.

ECONOMIC FLUCTUATIONS AND STABILIZATION POLICY

During the first long phase of Japanese development from 1870 to 1913 the Japanese economy was a highly unstable one. The Japanese cycles were more violent than those in other countries, whether measured in terms of the maximum cyclical fall in real gross national product from peak to trough, or in terms of the percentage of years below peak levels of gross national product. During the inter-war period the Japanese economy was somewhat more stable than that of the advanced countries of North America and Europe. During the period of explosive growth there have been no years in which gross national product actually fell; the "cycle," if such a term may be used, occurred only in rates of growth. However, in terms of maximum cyclical fall from peak to trough in industrial output, using quarterly data, the Japanese economy was once again more unstable than that of other industrialized countries during the period 1956–64.

Shinohara gives considerable weight to a twenty-year "Kuznets cycle" as a facet of Japanese development. During the upswing of this long cycle, he says, the Japanese expanded their investment "at an extraordinary tempo," bringing a sharp rise in the investment ratio. This investment boom leads both to overcapacity and balance of payments problems, resulting in a situation in which wage cuts, price deflations, and deteriorations in the terms of trade must ensue.[9] In the postwar period, a "Kitchin" (3- to 4-year) cycle of business activity appears, as well as inventory cycles and a "Juglar" (7- to 11-year) cycle in the ratio of output of producers' durable goods to gross national product.

The cyclical experience raises questions as to whether or not either the prewar or the postwar cycles are a factor in the rapid growth in Japan, and whether stabilization efforts might have retarded economic growth. Everett Hagen, at least, feels that growth might well have been even higher if monetary and fiscal policy had not been designed to put a stop to the boom every so often: [10]

There is no reason to think that the cyclical behavior is associated with the rapid advance; in the main the cycles were due to the fact that periodically Japan felt she was threatened with a foreign exchange crisis and the Central Bank imposed severe restrictions in order to curtail activity and so to curtail imports. Then, when foreign exchange reserves improved, they relaxed credit and the economy expanded again. Essentially, it was as simple as that, and there is no reason to think growth was any faster than it would have been without the cyclical ups and downs.

THE IMPACT OF PLANNING

The economic development of Japan between 1870 and World War II took place through government design, with the government working hand in hand with big business, but without any formal plans as we now know them. Since World War II Japan has followed the fashion of the day and prepared a series of official plans. The Economic Stabilization Board was set up in 1946; it became the Economic Deliberation Board in 1952 and the Economic Planning Agency two years later. A Three-Year Economic Plan was prepared in 1952 and a Five-Year Plan for Economic Self-Support in 1955. Naturally enough, the major objective of the first of these plans was postwar reconstruction. The Economic Self-Support Plan of 1955 aimed mainly at becoming independent of American aid and at providing a sufficient number of job opportunities to absorb the increase in the labor force and reduce underemployment.

In 1959 the famous "income-doubling plan" was introduced. This plan

[9] Shinohara, *op. cit.*, p. ii (see also Part II, Cycles).
[10] OECD, Studies in Development, *Development Plans and Programmes* (Paris, 1964), p. 65.

aims at doubling national income in ten years, implying an annual rate of growth of 7 per cent. Subsidiary targets are the building up of social overhead capital, which has lagged behind the booming private sector seriously enough to have become a bottleneck; further industrialization, especially in heavy and chemical industries; export promotion (the target for expansion of exports is 10 per cent per year); investment in human resources, and advance of science and technology; and a mitigation of dualism and the achievement of social stability.

According to Dr. Saburo Okita of the Economic Planning Agency,[11] this latest plan has several features which, while present in earlier plans, were less distinct than in the income-doubling plan. First, it emphasizes long-range structural change. Second, it divides the entire economy into public and private sectors. Third, it emphasizes long-run policies. Fourth, it stresses imbalances or differentials in incomes among different groups, between large and small enterprises, and among regions. Fifth is the emphasis upon investment in human resources.

What influence have these plans had? As may be seen from Table 30–9 and 30–9a, the actual growth of the Japanese economy in the postwar period has been consistently higher than the plan targets. Under these con-

TABLE 30–9

A Comparison between Actual and Planned Levels of National Income
(in billion yen)

Year	Actual*	Plan I	Plan II	Plan III	Plan IV	Plan V	Plan VI
1947	968	968					
1948	1,962	1,142	1,962				
1949	2,737	1,279	2,197	2,737			
1950	3,382	1,416	2,374	3,110			
1951	4,525	1,565	2,550	3,573			
1952	5,085	1,671	2,727	3,761			
1953	5,748		2,923	3,964			
1954	6,022				6,022		
1955	6,719				↓		
1956	7,628					7,628	
1957	8,286				6,937		
1958	8,519				↓		
1959	10,037						
1960	11,904				8,072		11,904
1961	14,118					↓	12,995
1962						11,129	14,191

* Figures for actual national income are given in *National Income Report,* Economic Planning Agency, and the planned series are adjusted to a level of starting year or the base year, in order to give a comparability.

SOURCE: OECD, Studies in Development, *Development Plans and Programs* (Paris, 1964), p. 61.

[11] Saburo Okita and Isamu Miyazaki, "The Impact of Planning on Economic Growth in Japan," in OECD, *op. cit.,* pp. 41–66.

TABLE 30–9a

A Comparison of the Growth Rate of GNP in Real Terms

Year	Actual*	Plan I	Plan II	Plan III	Plan IV	Plan V	Plan VI
1947							
1948	17.2	17.0					
1949	15.7	12.0	12.0				
1950	12.2	10.7	8.0				
1951	13.5	10.5	7.4	4.3			
1952	10.5	8.0	6.9	5.3			
1953	8.4		7.2	5.4			
1954	3.3						
1955	10.3				4.8		
1956	9.0				4.8		
1957	7.9				4.9	6.5	
1958	3.2				5.2	6.5	
1959	17.9				5.2	6.5	
1960	13.2				5.2	6.5	9.1
1961	14.0					6.5	9.1

* The series of actual rate of growth are reported in *National Income Report,* Economic Planning Agency, and the planned series are compiled from each report of the plans.

SOURCE: OECD, Studies in Development, *Development Plans and Programs* (Paris, 1964), p. 61.

ditions, what is the meaning of a plan? Dr. Shinohara puts it this way: "Once a plan was announced, firms always behave assuming that the plan's target is a minimum line below which the firms could not but be defeated in the cutthroat competition with other firms. Therefore, firms try to expand their investment beyond the target prescribed by the plan in order to exend their market share."[12]

Dr. Okita points out that the Japanese economic system is not a centrally planned one, but a predominantly private enterprise economy. Businessmen speak of "excessive competition." The economic plans, he says, have reflected the basic features of government business relations in the country. The direct responsibility for making and implementing plans rests primarily with the private sector. The actual government planning, he adds, was more for achieving balance in economic growth than for stimulating more rapid growth. Similarly, Dr. Miyazaki of the Economic Planning Agency states that national plans provide guideposts for the decisions of private entrepreneurs and outline what the government policy will be.[13] In the main, the effect of planning in Japan seems to be primarily the same as it is in France; it increases the degree of certainty for private entrepreneurs, improves their own forecasting, and instills in them a basic confidence in the future on which their own investment plans can be based.

As Everett Hagen pointed out, the Economic Planning Agency had little

[12] Shinohara, *op. cit.,* p. iii.
[13] Isamu Miyuzaki, "Introductory Statement," in OECD, *op. cit.,* pp. 55–60.

to do with the real investment decisions. The actual planning was done by an unofficial group of private industrialists, representatives of the Ministry of Finance and of the Ministry of International Trade and Industry, and of the Central Bank and the Mortgage Bank. "These men," he stated, "got together without any public statement or discussion, or any reports. They decided that electricity was important, and so their Government lent a lot of money to the private electrical companies at a time when it was important to expand electricity. They did the same thing for some other industries in the early 1950's." [14]

The present writer, in the same discussions, suggested that for a country where there are a good many "Schumpeterian entrepreneurs" and these have a high marginal propensity to save, the distribution of income between wages and salaries on the one hand and returns to fixed factors on the other is very conducive to a high ratio of national savings to income; the share of fixed factors is high and increasing.[15] Mr. Miyazaki's example of the steel industry suggests a simple model to explain the constant lag of plans behind performance. Letting "k" stand for the ordinary Keynesian multiplier, $\overline{Y}$ for the forecast level of income, Y for actual income and I for investment, Japanese investment behavior suggests the following relationship:

$$I_t = 1/k \cdot \overline{Y}_{t+1} + 0.02 Y_{t-1}$$
$$\Delta I_t = 1/k \cdot \Delta \overline{Y}_{t+1} + 0.02 \Delta Y_{t-1}$$
$$\Delta Y_t = k \cdot \Delta I_t = k \cdot 1/k \Delta \overline{Y}_{t+1} + 0.02 \Delta Y_{t-1}$$
$$= \Delta \overline{Y}_{t+1} + 0.02 \Delta Y_{t-1}$$

That is, investment decisions take into account not only the projected increases in income in the plan, but also past rates of growth of actual income. This equation not only gives a constant lag of projected behind actual growth of income but also a tendency toward cumulative movements.

Even the "income-doubling plan" has proved insufficiently ambitious. In the first three years of the plan, actual growth averaged 11 per cent as against the plan target of 7 or 8 per cent. So a new medium-term plan for 1964–68 was introduced, revising targets upward still once again. This plan was not approved until January, 1965, and it introduces a new note. There is now a feeling in Japan that purely "economic" growth has gone fast enough; the new plan projects a growth of 8.1 per cent per year to 1968, lower than recent actual growth rates. But it also stresses the need for a shift in emphasis toward social development, including education, public health, housing, and social welfare.

Conclusion

If Japan continues to perform for a few years more as it has in the past four decades, it will reach a point at which its gross national product is second only to that of the United States among non-Communist countries.

[14] OECD, op. cit., p. 65.
[15] Ibid., p. 66.

Japan already is the world's third largest steel producer, and among the world's five largest in several other branches of industry.[16] As the London *Economist* stated in its article on Japan in September, 1962, "The growth of the Japanese economy in the past ten years has been one of the most extraordinary economic stories of all time."

What is Japan's secret? It seems to be the same for over-all economic growth as it is for the "Japanese method" of rice cultivation: both are simply a matter of doing everything right. A high ratio of savings and investment to national income; a careful adaptation of product mix and technology to factor endowment; large expenditure on research and application of its results to technological improvements; expansion of education and its direction toward needs of development; eager acceptance of technical assistance, foreign aid, and foreign private investment; development-minded governments willing to plan economic development with the help of highly qualified technicians, but still more willing to cooperate with and encourage private entrepreneurship. Any country willing and able to produce all these things can develop quickly too.

Mexico: the Happy Marriage

Not long ago the prestigious London *Economist* referred to Mexico as "the Japan of the Western Hemisphere." In terms of degree of industrialization or levels of living thus far attained this designation may be a bit generous; Mexico still has a long way to go to reach the stage of development already achieved by Japan. In terms of the rate of transformation of the economy in recent decades, however, or in terms of prospects for the future, the analogy is well drawn. A typical underdeveloped agricultural country at the turn of the century, Mexico is now well on the road to becoming an industrialized nation. Much of this transformation has taken place in the last four decades. It is in large measure the result of conscious policy and is the fruit of an unusually happy marriage between vigorous private enterprise and government initiative, guidance, and control.

The revolution

Mexicans like to speak of their continuing revolution. The revolution is usually dated from 1910, when the dictator Porfirio Diaz was overthrown after nearly forty years in power. The war of independence, however, began a full century earlier, and in some respects the Mexican revolution began then. In other respects the revolution of 1917, which resulted in the introduction of the present Constitution, or the revolution of 1938 when foreign enterprises were nationalized, were sharper breaks from the past than the revolution of 1910. Indeed the history of Mexico for the last one hundred and fifty years is better described as a continuous and fairly steady change than as a series of isolated and cataclysmic upheavals. The successive "revolutions" modified the power structure rather than reversing it. Perhaps the blood shed along the path to progress war-

[16] Cf. Saburo Okita, "Japan's Seventh Inning Stretch," *Columbia Journal of World Business,* Winter, 1966, pp. 123–30.

rants the use of the term "revolution" to describe Mexican history in the early part of this century; but "bloody evolution" might be a more accurate label. Yet the concept of revolution has been a major ingredient in the Mexican success story; it has permitted steady and systematic progress with enough political continuity for economic development policies by surrounding the whole operation with a revolutionary atmosphere.

It may be that the Diaz regime itself established "preconditions" for a "take-off into sustained growth." Howard F. Cline gives Diaz credit for bringing Mexico "into the modern world, laying the foundations for its present advances in that sphere but at a social and political cost such that the Mexican people finally rose in revolt. . . ." [17] In any case the events following 1910 unleashed energies that have been successfully harnessed and directed into developmental channels. Eastin Nelson writes: [18]

Institutionally Mexico is a product of her revolution. . . . Eighty per cent of the people lived on the land when the French occupation of Spain made the first revolution possible (1810). . . . Diaz is said to have alienated 135 million acres of the public domain. . . . The poverty of the Mexican people and the attitude of the government with respect to land made it easy for foreigners to acquire vast tracts of land which they would hold speculatively at little cost. . . . Ninety-eight per cent of the mines were in the hands of Americans by 1911. Banks with Spanish, French and English capital developed between 1865 and 1900. But they were not at the service of the Mexican peasantry. Each such bank had a few large landowners as clients and dealt with big business borrowers, preferably exporters. . . . General social conditions are believed to have been worse by 1910 than a century earlier. . . . Once Diaz was challenged (by landed gentry in remote Coahuila) it appeared that there were men all over Mexico ready to enter the breach.

Before the revolution, Mexico was just another example of a poor and stagnant country: [19]

Mexico lay in the apparently closed circle of poverty resulting from the narrowness of the local market, lack of big social capital, lack of savings, monopolistic advantages possessed by foreign enterprises exploiting local natural resources and from many other hindrances to economic growth. [After the revolution,] having been dormant for many decades, living on the basis of a settled peasant agriculture, the basic concern of Mexicans was to set the national economy into a self-sustaining growth process.

The "pillars" of the Mexican development program were agrarian reform, public investment in social overhead capital, expropriation of foreign-owned railroads and oil properties, labor legislation, education in technical training, and the development of a domestic system of banking

[17] Howard F. Cline, *Mexico: Revolution to Evolution, 1940–1960* (London, 1962), p. 20.
[18] Eastin Nelson, *The Economic Potential of Mexico, 1970–1975* (Santa Barbara: TEMPO, 1959), pp. 9–10.
[19] Alfredo Navarrete, "Mexico's Growth: Prospects and Problems," in Eastin Nelson (ed.), *op. cit.*

and credit institutions. The agrarian reform abolished the feudal system of land ownership, with its "self-contained isolated units and absentee holdings," and redistributed the land in a manner permitting modernization of techniques. Improved farming methods, irrigation, extension work, and better farm implements helped to raise agricultural productivity.

The land reform was no small affair. Eastin Nelson estimates that one-quarter of all farmland and about half of cultivated land was taken from one owner and given to another. Whatever the impact of the *ejido* system on agricultural productivity, there can be no doubt that the administration of a land reform on this scale, with the power and irrigation projects and agricultural extension services that followed, was a factor in the growth of the bureaucracy which has contributed so much to Mexican development. As Nelson puts it, "it is small wonder that Mexico has developed a strong executive government." [20]

TABLE 30–10

Foreign Direct Investment in Mexico by Fields, 1938–1957

Type of investment	1938	1946	1954	1957
Agriculture	3.0	5.4	6.1	20.2
Mining	115.6	143.2	162.9	211.2
Petroleum	1.2	0.8	17.6	18.4
Manufacturing	23.8	105.4	278.3	413.3
Construction	..	2.2	10.5	16.1
Electricity	126.0	133.0	189.2	230.7
Commerce	14.2	42.8	116.2	218.3
Transportation	126.4	128.2	47.9	63.5
Others	1.2	3.8	5.5	8.3
Total	411.4	564.8	834.3	1,200.0

SOURCE: Banco de Mexico, *Informe Añual*, various issues.

The expropriation of foreign-owned petroleum and railroad investments in 1937–38 led to an international boycott of Mexico in protest. Contrary to expectations, and indeed contrary to the objectives of the boycott, it served as a further impetus to Mexican development. For the boycott compelled the Mexicans to make a redoubled effort to manage their productive assets themselves. "A hard-working type of new local managers for the railroads and oil industries," says Dr. Navarrete, "as well as national entrepreneurs interested in agricultural and industrial investments in the home market, started to develop." Once the Mexican economy began to move and new opportunities for profitable investment appeared, foreign capital flowed back into the country, accelerating the rate of economic expansion.

The educational effort included a literacy campaign, agricultural extension work, reorganization of the University of Mexico so as to provide training more suited to the needs of developing countries, and establishment of a National Polytechnic Institute to provide technicians. A Na-

[20] As may be seen from Table 30-10 in 1957 the only important sector in which foreign investment was not well above the 1938 level was transport.

tional School of Economics was also established, and courses provided in business administration to swell the supply of managers for new enterprises.

Measures in the field of credit and finance included the establishment of the Central Bank in 1925, a national bank for agricultural credit in 1926, and the establishment of the *Nacional Financiera* in 1934 to serve as an industrial bank, development corporation, and investment company. In the early stages of development, the government was responsible for a large share of development finance. Public investment in the "infrastructure" included railroads, highways, power, and housing.

World War II gave the final fillip to Mexico's "take-off." There was considerable excess capacity in industry at the beginning of the war, which permitted substantial increases in output without much new industrial investment. For example, output of textiles increased by an average of 6.6 per cent per year during the war, with almost negligible new investment. Industrial production as a whole grew by 9.4 per cent per year on the average, with relatively little new investment. In general, investment during the period 1939–50 was concentrated in high-yield projects. "Investment could be concentrated in 1939–50 on projects yielding high returns quickly because large numbers of public facilities already existed which were not being used to capacity. The railroads, ports, communication systems, power plants, and community works have all taken on additional loads particularly in the first half of the period." [21] Nearly half the total investment in this period was in agriculture, petroleum, mining, industry, and motor vehicles, and "within each of these fields, projects were available which required only small expenditure to yield the exceptional results." Moreover, only a small part of the investment in this period went into maintenance or replacement. For example, less than 2 per cent of the investment in public irrigation went into maintenance and only 14 per cent of the investment in highways went into repair and maintenance. "Newness of much of the Mexican capital stock kept repair and replacement cost low, but under-maintenance was also partly responsible." Thus investments for maintenance and replacement and repairs are likely to be much higher in the future.

Economic Growth

The result of this constellation of policies, measures, and events has been an extraordinarily high rate of growth, accompanied by an equally rapid structural change. Between 1939 and 1945, total output increased at an average rate of 8 per cent per year. Since then the rate of growth has tapered off somewhat, to an average rate of about 6 per cent per year. Since the population is growing by some 3 per cent per year, (and possibly even more in recent years), these figures correspond to an annual growth of per capita income of about 5 per cent during the war years and about 3 per cent since.[22] Gross national product grew from 15.9 billion

[21] International Bank for Reconstruction and Development, Combined Mexican Working Party, *The Economic Development of Mexico* (Baltimore, 1953), p. 17.
[22] Cf. Victor Urquidi, *The Challenge of Development in Latin America*, (New York, 1964).

pesos (at 1950 prices) to 84.7 billion in 1963. Thus Mexico is one of the
few countries in Latin America to have achieved the target rates of growth
laid down by the Alliance for Progress. In 1960, it is true, the Mexican per
capita income of $336 was still slightly below the Latin American average;
but by now it is somewhat above the average for the region (see Table
30–11).

TABLE 30–11
Gross National Product
(millions of pesos)

Year	GNP
1951	51,800
1952	58,300
1953	56,300
1954	66,478
1955	84,000
1956	94,000
1957	103,000
1958	114,000
1959	122,000
1960	134,000
1961	141,000
1962*	150,000
1963†	159,000
1964†	169,000
1965†	180,000

* *Anuario 1961–62.*
† Estimated projection at 6 per cent annual
growth average rate.
SOURCE: Mexico, *Anuario 1960–1961*, p. 627.

In 1930 some 70 per cent of the labor force was engaged in agriculture,
producing only 21.6 per cent of the gross national product (Table 30–12).
By 1959 less than 56 per cent of the labor force was in agriculture, but it
was still producing nearly 23 per cent of GNP, indicating a significant
increase in man-year productivity. By 1962 agriculture's share in GNP
was down to 20 per cent, with a further decline in agriculture's share of
total employment. By 1966 Mexico was presumably over the watershed
with respect to the employment structure, with more than half the labor
force engaged outside of agriculture. The share of mining in GNP shows a
marked decline between 1930 and 1962. Construction also shows some decline, but is subject to such violent fluctuations that trends are hard to
discern. All other sectors show expansion, especially marked for manufacturing and petroleum.

Individual time series show even more dramatic expansion. Between 1934
and 1963 the amount of irrigated land increased twentyfold; the highway
network thirteenfold; petroleum production nearly fourfold. In 1956 gross
consumption of energy was nearly three times the 1934–38 average; gaso-

TABLE 30-12

Sectors of the Mexican Economy, 1930–1962

(Per cent of national income or national product [100 per cent])

Sectors	1930	1935	1940	1939–45	1945	1950	1951–54	1957	1960	1962
Agriculture	21.6	17.6	14.5	19.9	17.2	21.5	19.8	24.2	20.4	20.0
Secondary activities										
Mining	13.2	14.9	12.7	3.0	7.8		2.5		2.2	2.0
Petroleum	2.6	3.2	2.3	1.4	1.1		1.4		4.5	5.0
Manufacturing	12.8	16.3	24.2	17.6	25.2		16.1		25.6	26.0
Sub-total	28.6	34.4	39.2	22.0	34.1	28.8	20.0	27.1	32.3	33.0
Tertiary activities										
Commerce	18.6	21.2	20.7	28.0	24.8		29.1		20.9	21.0
Construction	6.7	6.2	6.4	1.9	6.2		1.8		3.5	
Electric power				0.5			0.5		1.3	1.0
Others	24.5	20.6	19.2	27.7	17.7		28.8		21.6	25.0
Sub-total	49.8	48.0	46.3	58.1	48.7	49.7	60.2	48.7	47.3	47.0

SOURCES: Howard F. Cline, *Mexico: Revolution to Evolution*, (London, 1962), p. 256; *Mexico 1963 Facts, Figures, Trends*, Banco Nacional de Commercio Exterior (Mexico, 1963), pp. 90, 95.

line consumption was nearly nine times the 1934 average; crude steel consumption was over four times the level of the mid-1930's. Crude steel production in 1957 was more than eight times the 1934–39 average; beer production rose 600 per cent from the middle thirties to 1957.

Between 1939 and 1956, agricultural output increased two and a half times. The increase can be broken down as follows: 40 per cent was the result of bringing new land under cultivation; 35 per cent resulted from a shift to more productive crops; and 25 per cent was due to improved yields. Between 1949 and 1955, gross investment in agriculture increased by 148 per cent, three-fourths of this amount representing private investment. Increased use of fertilizers and mechanization contributed to the rise in agricultural output. Particularly dramatic has been the expansion of cotton output, which in 1955 was six times the 1939 figure, making Mexico the world's second biggest exporter. Coffee output has nearly doubled, and coffee is now Mexico's second most important export. At the same time Mexico has achieved near self-sufficiency in foodstuffs. The fish catch increased at an average annual rate of 13 per cent between 1940 and 1949, while the shrimp catch increased more than threefold in that same period.

Businessmen and Bureaucrats

Behind the burgeoning Mexican economy is an unusually smooth-working and harmonious partnership between the government bureaucracy and the business, industrial, and financial community. The Mexican recipe is hard to reduce to a formula precise enough for application in other countries, but one ingredient is certainly the extraordinarily high level of competence of the bureaucracy itself, and its pragmatic approach to economic policy. Behind the facade of "revolution" is a healthy commitment to a philosophy of *ad hocery*. In Professor Nelson's felicitous phrasing, "The revolution itself, a protest in no small degree against the aping by Mexicans of the classical liberalism of the eighteenth century revolutions and its failure of 'too little and too late,' has tended to make the career bureaucrat the idea man, the man of initiative and imagination, the reader of books, the writer of books." [23] The genuine commitment to economic development runs through the bureaucracy to the President himself. Two-thirds of President Gustavo Diaz Ordaz' first Presidential report, of September, 1965, is concerned with economic development; and he reaffirms what he regards as the generally accepted view that the State must assume responsibility as the principal stimulator of economic growth. The power of the bureaucracy is greatly extended by the fact that both the labor movement and the *ejidos* are "held in tutelage by the bureaucracy." [24]

But if government provides the leadership, certainly private enterprise is at its heels. The bureaucracy has had no wish to crush the spirit of entrepreneurship in the interests of equality. "The men of the revolution have never advocated absolute equality, but rather have attempted to erect minimum guarantees and to effectuate economic development. In many respects Mexico is almost anarchical in the freedom to acquire riches which it accords men." [25] Profits of 15 to 25 per cent are the rule. Some writers distinguish between those members of the business and industrial elite who were members of the dispossessed landlord class or closely allied to that class, and the New Group more closely allied with the revolution. Sanford A. Mosk writes: [26]

The New Group is composed of owners of small manufacturing plants. . . . (They) came into being during the second world war and . . . do not have good relations with the principal financial institutions in Mexico. . . . Their feeling of insecurity has led them to seek alliance with other groups in the general economy such as agriculture and labor . . .

Others, too, wonder about the kind of society Mexico is creating. Daniel Cosio Villegas, President of the Collegio de México and a leading Latin American intellectual, wonders whether the new "robber barons" are better than the old: [27]

The new captains of industry and bank magnates end by forming not mere pressure groups, but actual oligarchies, which in the Latin American social scene have superseded the erstwhile landowning oligarchy. Between the old

[23] Nelson, *op. cit.*, p. 15.
[24] *Ibid.*, p. 16.
[25] Nelson, *op. cit.*, p. 17.
[26] Sanford A. Mosk, *The Industrial Revolution in Mexico* (Berkeley, 1950), pp. 21–24.
[27] Daniel Cosio Villegas, "Programmed economic development and political organization," in Egbert de Vries and Jose Medina Echvarria (eds.), *Social Aspects of Economic Development in Latin America*, Vol. I (Paris: UNESCO, 1963), pp. 250–51.

and the new there are, however, two very important differences, one political and the other social. The old landowning oligarchy . . . openly seized political power and certainly availed themselves of it to promote their own interests; but at the same time they did assume the attendant responsibilities. The new industrial and banking oligarchy wishes to influence governmental decisions, and actually does so, but without shouldering the responsibilities that such decisions necessarily involve. The social difference is no less important. In the course of time the old landowning oligarchy reformed itself from within; its members acquired culture and good taste, learned to understand general problems which had nothing to do with the farming of their land, and were therefore able to indulge in the luxury of becoming patrons of the arts and letters. The new oligarchy is still unduly crude and coarse, smacks unmistakably of money because it thinks of nothing else, and does not seem to understand anything that has no direct bearing on its business affairs.

Cosio wonders, therefore, whether the government's system of incentives to private enterprise has not created a caste of *nouveaux riches* under cover of promoting economic growth. In any case, there can be no doubt that it has succeeded in doing the latter.

The Financial Institutions [28]

The "happy marriage" of bureaucrats and entrepreneurs is perhaps best illustrated by the important group of enterprises whose ownership is divided between the public and private sectors, but whose control is public. This group includes the Central Bank itself and most of the other major public financial institutions.[29] These institutions are regulated by the Finance Minister (Secretaría de Hacienda y Crédito Público) and the two commissions under his general supervision, the National Securities Commission (Comision Nacional de Valores) and the National Banking Commission (Comision Nacional Bancaria). The former regulates new private securities issues, authorizes registration on the various securities exchanges, has the power to set rates of interest, etc., while the latter is the supervisory agency for technical aspects of bank operation, such as reverse requirements, and the proper categorization of various assets and liabilities.[30]

BANCO DE MÉXICO

The Banco de México was established in 1925 to bring order into a chaotic monetary situation. It is the nation's central bank, and as such provides the base for the entire monetary and credit system. At the end of 1962 the Banco de México had assets of 16.1 billion pesos, and the other national institutions 26.0 billion—a total of 42.1 billion. At the same time, all private banks combined had an asset total of 35.3 billion pesos.[31]

During the first years of its operation, the Banco de México concen-

[28] This section draws heavily on a paper prepared for the author by Sterling Drumwright.
[29] Raymond Vernon (ed.), *Public Policy and Private Enterprise in Mexico* (Cambridge, Mass.), p. 114.
[30] *Ibid.*, p. 115.
[31] Banco de México, *Informe Anual, 1962* (pub. 1963), pp. 90–93.

trated on reconstructing the nation's banking system. This involved acting (through branches) as an ordinary commercial bank as well as using its powers of rediscount and issue. In 1932, having successfully filled some of the gaps and deficiencies in the private financial sector, a reorganization enabled the bank to limit its functions to those ordinarily undertaken by central banks. In 1941 the *Ley Organica* of the Banco de México was revised to give the bank's authorities initiative to formulate a monetary, credit, and foreign exchange policy suitable for the changing economic requirements of the nation.[32]

Despite its extensive responsibilities the Banco de México is by no means an "independent" central bank.[33] It operates within the policies established for it by the federal government and all important monetary actions of the Bank are subject to the veto of the Finance Minister. The Bank is expected always to place the financial needs of the public sector above whatever specifically monetary goals it may be pursuing; it nonetheless enjoys a status not shared by other public-sector entities, and exerts a significant independent influence on economic policy.[34]

Since the revision of its organic law in 1941 the Bank has shown much more interest in promoting industrial growth in the Mexican economy. To this end it has substantially increased its own direct investments in the national economy. Raymond Vernon notes: [35]

As the government has become more and more committed to economic growth as a goal, the central bank has become more and more the keystone of a banking system whose intended orientation is the financing of growth. As the definition of a policy for growth has become more complex, so the task of the Banco de México has become more intricate and demanding.

Nacional Financiera

Next to the Banco de México, the Nacional Financiera is without question the most important financial institution in Mexico. Created in 1934, Nacional Financiera is a "public sector" entity. Although it draws capital and directors from both the public and private sectors, the organization's organic law has seen to it that the public sector dominates in both respects. There are two classes of capital stock representing ownership in the Nacional Financiera. The first, Series "A" stock, is held by the federal government. The second, Series "B" stock, is held by the "general public." The stipulation that Series "A" stock outstanding must always exceed Series "B" stock ensures the public nature of Nacional Financiera.

No financial institution in Mexico has contributed more to the economic growth of that country than Nacional Financiera (NAFIN). There are

[32] Banco de México, *Vigesima Asamblea General Ordinaria de Accionistas* (Mexico, D.F.: Editorial Cultura, 1942), pp. 20–21.

[33] William Patton Glade, *The Role of Government Enterprise in the Economic Development of Underdeveloped Regions: Mexico—a Case Study*, Doctoral Dissertation, The University of Texas, 1955, pp. 190–91.

[34] Vernon, *op. cit.*, p. 116.

[35] *Ibid.*, p. 117.

many specialized public sector banks in the country designed to give aid to particular areas of the economy (and these will subsequently be given brief treatment), but none of these banks approach Nacional Financiera in either scope or volume.[36]

As of mid-1961, it [Nacional Financiera] was creditor, investor, or guarantor for 533 business enterprises of all kinds; it held stocks in 60 industrial firms; and it was majority stockholder in 13 firms producing steel, textiles, motion pictures, plywood, paper, fertilizers, electrical energy, sugar, lumber, and refrigerated meats. At the end of 1961 . . . Nacional Financiera's loans were nearly half as large as those of all private credit institutions, and they accounted for more than one-third of total lending by Mexico's public credit institutions. Long-term loans by NAFIN were considerably greater than those of the private lending agencies taken together.

Table 30–13 presents the sources and uses of Nacional Financiera's resources at three different points in time during an eight-year period. The portion of resources labeled "non-equity securities" consists of *titulos financieros* (a form of bond) and *certificados de participación* (a security giving participation in the variable income from a common fund, but treated as a bond).

The increasing proportion of foreign loans to NAFIN reflects NAFIN's success with such organizations as the International Bank for Research and Development and the International Monetary Fund.

Table 30–13 also shows the increasing emphasis on the development of the infrastructure and encouraging import substitution. This emphasis is noted by Calvin P. Blair: [37]

There have been five administrations during NAFIN's lifetime, but NAFIN's history may be divided into three periods. The first is an experimental period, 1934–1940, corresponding to the regime of Lázaro Cárdenas, during which time NAFIN tried out in incipient form every role it was later to play and one or two which it was to discard. The second, 1941–1947, is a period of uninhibited industrial promotion deriving largely out of the stimuli provided by World War II and corresponding roughly to the administration of Manuel Avila Camacho. After 1947, an entrenched and successful NAFIN served three administrations as agent for developing the infrastructure and promoting import substitution.

NAFIN has not limited itself to loans; it has also assumed the role of majority and minority stockholder, bondholder, and guarantor. Direct loans have accounted for anywhere from 35 to 50 per cent of amounts outstanding at year's end, security investments for 12 to 17 per cent, guarantees of credit extended by other lending institutions for 25 to 40 per cent, guarantees of mortgage bonds for 2 to 6 per cent, and loans from trust funds for 4 to 7 per cent.[38]

Its ventures into the realm of ownership have periodically aroused the

[36] *Ibid.,* p. 194.
[37] *Ibid.,* p. 205.
[38] *Ibid.,* p. 231.

TABLE 30–13

Sources and Uses of Nacional Financiera Funds

Origins and recipients	Millions of pesos			Per cent of total		
	1953	1958	1961	1953	1958	1961
Origins of resources						
Total	4,742	8,949	15,361	100.0	100.0	100.0
Foreign loans to NAFIN	1,097	2,020	5,318	23.1	22.6	34.6
NAFIN'S non-equity securities	1,400	1,833	2,910	29.5	20.5	18.9
Capital and reserves	206	482	812	4.4	5.4	5.4
Guarantees and endorsements by NAFIN	933	3,550	5,164	20.9	39.7	33.6
Trust funds	583	720	1,062	12.3	8.0	6.9
Other	464	344	95	9.8	3.8	0.6
Recipients of financing						
Total	4,742	8,949	15,361	100.0	100.0	100.0
Infrastructure	2,240	4,349	9,414	47.2	48.6	61.3
Electricity	817	1,698	4,198	17.2	19.0	27.3
Transportation and communication	1,015	2,364	2,632	21.4	26.4	17.2
Irrigation and other works	408	286	2,583	8.6	3.2	16.8
Basic industry	586	1,252	1,872	12.4	14.0	12.2
Petroleum and coal	298	548	1,014	6.3	6.1	6.6
Iron and steel	259	654	795	5.5	7.3	5.2
Cement and other construction materials	29	49	63	0.6	0.6	0.4
Other manufacturing	707	2,315	2,740	14.9	25.9	17.8
Food and beverages	309	430	490	6.5	4.8	3.2
Textiles and clothing	123	179	143	2.6	2.0	0.9
Paper and products	44	325	378	0.9	3.6	2.5
Chemicals and fertilizers	106	324	435	2.3	3.6	2.8
Transport equipment	7	641	780	0.1	7.2	5.1
Other	118	416	515	2.5	4.7	3.3
Other activities	1,210	1,033	1,335	25.5	11.5	8.7

SOURCE: Raymond Vernon (ed.), *Public Policy and Private Enterprise in Mexico*, (Cambridge, Mass.), p. 224.

anxiety and hostility of certain components of the private sector. Such opposition together with close government supervision has restricted the role of NAFIN in encouraging economic growth and development through such means. Nevertheless, as Blair has noted: [39]

Nacional Financiera has clearly been something more than just another source of finance capital. It has advised, promoted, invested in and directed business enterprises often enough to be identified as a genuine entrepreneurial agent.

[39] *Ibid.*, p. 232.

OTHER PUBLIC SECTOR INSTITUTIONS

As William Glade has pointed out, the highly imaginative and inventive use of Mexican banks as agencies of an economic policy has also helped to accelerate industrialization. He attributes this success to the fact that the salient characteristic of the Mexican banking-financial system is the federal government's domination of the capital market.[40]

1. *Banco Nacional Hipotecario Urbano y de Obras Publicas.* One of several important specialized development banks, this institution is concentrated in the area of construction and industry and particularly in the area of state and municipal public works and low-cost housing development. In addition to promoting and directing the investment of capital in public works, services, and housing projects, it also makes financial, technical, and legal studies related to such projects and works.

2. *Banco Nacional de Comercio Exterior.* This bank deals mainly in short-term credits designed to stimulate exports, especially agricultural exports. Its credit is provided on a highly selective basis, and its capacity for intervention in areas of commerce often gives it the air of a governmental agency of economic control rather than a bank.

3. *Banco Nacional de Crédito Agrícola.* Created in 1926 in an attempt to aid in the establishment of a national system of agricultural credit, the primary functions of this institution are the making of *avío*, *refaccionario*, collateral, and long-term real property loans. The *avío* (crop), and *refaccionario* (investment) loans are by far the most important kinds of credit which this bank extends. The former have been used primarily in the financing of basic foodstuffs such as cotton, corn, wheat, beans, and rice. The latter have promoted agricultural expansion and development by opening new lands to cultivation, providing for irrigation by drilling water wells and installing pumping equipment, and increasing the mechanization of agriculture. In providing such financial assistance, this bank works both directly and indirectly through other institutions such as credit societies, credit unions, etc.

4. *Banco Nacional de Crédito Ejidal.* The Cárdenas regime, as part of its intensified program of land reform and support of the *ejidos*, set up this special bank to provide financial support for this agricultural institution which, it was then hoped, would become the bulwark and cornerstone of the Mexican society and economy.[41] The powers of the bank are almost as broadly stated as those of the other agricultural bank, but because of the basically weak position of the *ejidos* (especially at the time the Banco Nacional de Crédito Ejidal was formed), this institution has been forced to accept more responsibility than has the Banco Nacional de Crédito Agrícola; they range from supervising local *ejido* credit societies to guaranteeing the mortgages of these groups and acting as their purchasing agent. In a great many of the cases, this bank administers the market of *ejido* crops as well as their finance production and selection.

5. *Patronato del Ahorro Nacional.* This is one example of several insti-

[40] Glade, *op. cit.*, p. 160.
[41] *Ibid.*, p. 210.

tutions in the Mexican financial structure designed specifically to encourage savings. It was established in 1946 to sell savings bonds to the general public. Its attempts to promote these securities have included a lottery feature designed to appeal to the national propensity for games of chance. The funds so obtained have been used by the *Patronato* in various public works projects.

CONTINUING PROBLEMS

With this spectacular economic growth, what problems remain for Mexico? In the first place, the benefits of economic growth have not been equally spread, either among income groups or among regions. As Dr. Navarrete puts it, "Mexicans are aware that their principal task is to reduce widespread poverty through relatively high rates of economic growth over a sustained period." [42] A national average income of $350, although higher than in most Asian countries, is still low as compared even with the more advanced European countries, let alone the United States or Canada. Moreover, this average figure conceals great differences in personal income between upper and lower classes. It also conceals regional differences. As the Combined Mexican Working Party puts it: [43]

. . . agricultural development between 1939 and 1950 was confined chiefly to the northern states of Mexico and to some tropical and semitropical regions where there was scope for irrigation and expansion of cultivation. In the south-central plain, traditionally the most important agricultural part of the country, development has been slow. In this region where all the arable land is used and where only limited possibility exists for irrigation, increased production could be achieved only by improving farming methods.

The "North-South" Problem in Mexico

The Mexican case of "regional dualism" is slightly more complicated than the Brazilian or Italian one. [44] In general, one can draw a line across the country just south of the capital city, and say that the developed region lies to the north of the line and the underdeveloped region to the south. However, the geographic split is somewhat less clear-cut than in the other two countries. Quintana Roo far to the south has a higher level of per capita income, and a higher industrial output per capita, than some of the states farther north. The Federal District and the states bordering the United States are most advanced; but some of the states in between belong to the middle rather than the upper ranks. Nonetheless, one can in general describe the north as the leading region and the south as the lagging region.

The percentage gap in per capita incomes by states is even greater than in Brazil or Italy: in 1960 the richest state had a per capita income nearly twelve times that of the poorest state. If the Mexican states were grouped

[42] *Ibid.*, p. 14.
[43] International Bank for Reconstruction and Development, Combined Mexican Working Party, *Economic Development of Mexico* (Washington, D.C., 1959), pp. 4–5.
[44] See Chap. 32 for a discussion of Italy and Brazil.

by major regions—the six states on the United States border, say, and all
the states south of Mexico City—the differences in per capita regional incomes would be of the same order of magnitude as in Brazil.

In terms of percentage rates of change there is a more clear-cut centripetal tendency in per capita income by states than in Brazil. Between 1940
and 1960 the poor states, as a group, had higher rates of growth than the
rich states as a group. The richest state of all—Baja California del Norte—
actually suffered a decline in per capita output in two decades, while the
poorest, Oaxaca, enjoyed an increase of 163 per cent. It may well be that
Mexico is "over the hump" as far as regional disintegration is concerned.
However, the Mexican picture should not be painted in too bright colors.
Some rich states still have higher growth rates than some poor states; and
because of the enormous difference in the base levels of per capita output,
it will in any case be fifty years or more before the absolute gaps between
the richer states and the poorer ones begin to narrow.

A FACTOR ANALYSIS

In a paper presented to the first Latin American Conference on Regional
Science, Dr. Mary MeGee applies factor analysis to the problem of differential growth of the Mexican states.[45] Dr. MeGee sets the stage for her
analysis with the following statement regarding the interaction of regional
and national economic development:

Economic growth is generally the result of some steady movement which
originates in one quasi-isolated region of the national economy and which is
largely brought about by an innovating group, who are making a gradual
transition from a livestock and agricultural society to an industrial and commercial one. From this core, growth becomes intensified on the one hand, but
also serves as a nucleus for the spread of industry, commerce, and improved
agricultural practices elsewhere. In terms of Mexico, this growth began in the
North, more specifically in Monterrey, becoming not only intensified there in
terms of eventually setting up agglomeration economies, but also having external impacts on border areas and later to the Central Plateau, including
Mexico City, which unlike capital cities in most underdeveloped countries,
was never completely the nation's primate city.

Industrialization in Mexico was delayed by Spanish colonial policy.
When independence was attained, the industrial sector was limited to relatively small-scale sugar mills, tanneries, flour mills, hand-woven textiles,
and candle, soap, and beverage factories, mostly in the north. The loss of
Texas diminished Mexico's natural resources, and created spatial shifts in
trade patterns and urban growth, which on balance accelerated development in the north. The War between the States accelerated this tendency,
since the Mexican north replaced New England and the mid-Atlantic states
in supplying munitions and cotton textiles to the Confederacy. The first
Mexican railroads were built in the north, during the 1880's.

Dr. MeGee's statistical analysis includes four factors: irrigation and

[45] Mary MeGee, "Social and Economic Factors in the Differential Growth of
Mexican States," *Regional Science, Special Issue*, September, pp. 144–79.

energy, accounting for 15 per cent of the total variance; energy and urbanization, comprising 9 per cent of the variance; chemical production,
accounting for 8 per cent of the variance, and education and capital expenditures, comprising some 7.5 per cent of the variance. These factors were
derived from a matrix of ninety-eight social and economic variables for
each of the twenty-nine Mexican states, two territories, and the capital district for the year 1960. She finds the central region to be most developed in
terms of all factors, with the north second. Her figures indicate that since
World War II the north has lost to the central plateau region, as the result
of new concentration of industry and development of power resources
there. At the same time, her analysis indicates a simultaneous tendency toward decentralization, with new industries developing in the peripheral
regions. The Gulf and South Pacific regions seem to be fairly highly developed in terms of the first two factors, in which energy production plays
a major role.

The primary sector is sharing in the economic development of Mexico,
as production for export replaces subsistence agriculture. Dr. MeGee finds
that: [46]

. . . all three sectors of the economy [primary, secondary, and tertiary] are
being activated, though primary activities are the most important, at least in
terms of the variance comprised by the first two factors in particular. . . . Mexican economic development which was originally concentrated in the North
and secondarily in the Central Region has on the one hand become more
intensified in the Central Plateau, and on the other has decentralized with
growth being accelerated in every region of the country—along the border
and the Pacific North, and the South Pacific state of [Chiapas] and the Gulf
States of Vera Cruz and Tabasco."

Dr. MeGee recognizes the limitations of her study; only 38.27 per cent
of the total variance is accounted for by the factors included in her analysis.
However, her conclusions would seem to be consistent with more general
observations of recent developments in the Mexican economy.

THE UNIVERSITY OF TEXAS SURVEY

In the summer of 1962 a team of research economists from the University of Texas, under the direction of Professor Eastin Nelson, conducted
their own analysis of regional data in Mexico. Mistrusting the national income figures (with some justice, in view of the subsequent drastic revisions
of those figures), the team worked with data of minimum wage rates and a
weighted index of per capita consumption of meat and sugar as an approximation to per capita incomes. They also calculated the minimum real daily
wage rates by states; but as may be seen in Tables 30–14 and 30–15, the
adjustment for differences in price movements among states has no significant effect on rank orders of states by level of minimum daily wage. Comparing the figures for 1960 with those of 1938–41, we see that the three
states at the top of the list were the same in both years: Baja California,

[46] MeGee, *op. cit.*, p. 156.

TABLE 30-14

Weighted Average Minimum Daily Wage in States of Mexico*
(current pesos)

Region†	States	1938-41	Rank 1938-41	1942-44	1945-49	1950-54	1955-59	1960	Rank 1960
C	Aguascalientes	1.43	12	1.85	2.97	4.78	7.81	9.20	17
NP	Baja Calif.	3.06	1	3.82	5.53	9.38	14.67	17.22	1
G	Campeche	2.00	5	2.47	4.16	5.48	7.42	7.66	24
SP	Chiapas	1.13	23	1.14	1.71	3.55	4.31	5.55	31
N	Chihuahua	1.71	9	2.10	3.31	5.92	9.74	11.78	6
N	Coahuila	1.71	8	2.07	2.74	5.18	9.35	10.34	9
SP	Colima	1.40	13	1.85	3.24	4.78	8.39	11.74	7
C	Distrito Federal	2.45	3	2.99	4.44	6.82	11.42	14.48	3
N	Durango	1.38	14	1.47	2.04	4.23	7.13	8.87	20
C	Guanajuato	1.07	27	1.07	1.97	4.32	6.27	7.53	25
SP	Guerrero	1.02	29	1.10	2.11	3.93	5.58	6.17	29
C	Hidalgo	1.08	25	1.09	2.61	3.10	4.91	7.01	26
C	Jalisco	1.07	26	1.43	2.86	4.46	6.92	8.74	21
C	México	1.28	19	1.06	1.81	3.34	6.99	10.00	12
C	Michoacán	1.00	31	1.16	1.61	4.77	8.44	9.97	13

C	Morelos	1.15	21/22	1.45	2.86	5.01	8.73	13.30	5
NP	Nayarit	1.35	15/16	1.88	3.38	4.51	7.09	8.26	22
N	Nuevo León	1.29	18	1.58	1.91	3.94	7.14	9.34	15/16
SP	Oaxaca	1.26	20	1.65	2.23	3.25	4.93	6.20	27
C	Puebla	1.34	17	1.35	2.30	4.79	8.06	10.09	11
C	Querétaro	1.01	30	1.01	1.68	3.01	4.82	5.78	30
G	Quintana Roo	3.00	2	3.59	5.00	7.47	12.75	15.00	2
N	San Luis Potosí	1.15	21/22	1.35	2.48	3.42	5.11	6.97	28
NP	Sinaloa	1.55	11	1.76	2.53	4.66	8.09	9.39	14
NP	Sonora	1.84	6	2.29	4.00	6.37	13.35	14.12	4
G	Tabasco	1.65	10	1.66	2.67	5.95	7.45	9.13	19
N	Tamaulipas	1.35	15/16	1.59	1.79	4.54	7.42	9.34	15/16
C	Tlaxcala	1.04	28	1.35	2.29	3.79	6.73	9.16	18
G	Veracruz	1.81	7	1.99	3.25	4.80	8.03	11.06	8
G	Yucatan	2.10	4	2.07	2.10	4.73	8.67	10.30	10
N	Zacatecas	1.09	24	1.38	2.39	3.77	5.80	7.99	23

SOURCES: Average Minimum Wages in Mexico: 1938–39 through 1944–45, Anuario Estadistico 1943–45; 1946–47, Compendio Estadistico 1951; 1948–49 through 1956–57, Anuario Estadistico 1951–52, 1955–56, 1958–59; 1958–59 and 1960–61, Compendio Estadistico 1960.
*Weights used were the proportions of urban and rural populations to the total population. Source of urban and rural population data: Compendio Estadistico, 1960, Table 9, pp. 14–15; Compendio Estadistico, 1947, Table 11, pp. 41–42.
C = Central; G = Gulf of Mexico; N = Northern; NP = Northern Pacific; SP = Southern Pacific.

TABLE 30–15

Weighted Average *Real* Minimum Daily Wage in States of Mexico

(1953 pesos)

States	1938–41	1942–44	1945–49	1950–54	1955–59	1960
Aguascalientes	6.38	5.24	4.67	5.04	5.67	5.69
Baja Calif.	13.67	10.82	8.69	9.88	10.65	10.65
Campeche	8.93	7.00	6.54	5.77	5.39	4.74
Chiapas	5.04	3.23	2.69	3.74	3.13	3.43
Chihuahua	7.63	5.95	5.20	6.24	7.07	7.29
Coahuila	7.63	5.86	4.31	5.46	6.79	6.39
Colima	6.25	5.24	5.09	5.04	6.09	7.00
Distrito Federal	10.94	8.47	6.98	7.19	8.29	8.95
Durango	6.16	4.16	3.21	4.46	5.18	5.49
Guanajuato	4.77	3.03	3.10	4.55	4.55	4.65
Guerrero	4.55	3.12	3.32	4.14	4.05	3.82
Hidalgo	4.82	3.09	4.10	3.27	3.57	4.34
Jalisco	4.77	4.05	4.50	4.70	5.03	5.41
México	5.71	3.00	2.85	3.52	5.08	6.18
Michoacán	4.46	3.29	2.53	5.03	6.13	6.17
Morelos	5.13	4.11	4.50	5.28	6.34	8.23
Nayarit	6.03	5.33	5.31	4.75	5.15	5.11
Nuevo León	5.76	4.48	3.00	4.15	5.19	5.78
Oaxaca	5.63	4.67	3.50	3.42	3.58	3.83
Puebla	5.98	3.82	3.62	5.05	5.85	6.24
Querétaro	4.51	2.86	2.64	3.17	3.50	3.57
Quintana Roo	13.39	10.17	7.86	7.87	9.26	9.28
San Luis Potosí	5.13	3.82	3.90	3.60	3.71	4.31
Sinaloa	6.92	4.99	3.98	4.91	5.88	5.81
Sonora	8.21	6.49	6.29	6.71	9.69	8.79
Tabasco	7.37	4.70	4.20	6.27	5.41	5.65
Tamaulipas	6.03	4.50	2.81	4.78	5.39	5.78
Tlaxcala	4.64	3.82	3.60	3.99	4.89	5.66
Veracruz	8.08	5.64	5.11	5.06	5.80	6.84
Yucatan	9.38	5.86	3.30	4.90	6.30	6.37
Zacatecas	4.87	3.91	3.76	3.97	4.21	4.94

SOURCE: Average Minimum Wages in Mexico: 1938-39 through 1944–45, *Anuario Estadistico 1943–45;* 1946–47, *Compendio Estadistico 1951;* 1948–49 through 1956–57, *Anuario Estadistico 1951–52, 1955–56, 1958–59;* 1958–59 and 1960–61, *Compendio Estadistico 1960.*

Current wages adjusted by use of cost-of-living index of workers in Mexico City.

Quintana Roo, and the Federal District, in that order. There is more change at the other end of the scale. Chiapas fell from twenty-third to thirty-first, while Michaocán, which was at the bottom of the list in 1938–41, moved up to sixteenth in 1960. In the latter year, Chiapas, which had been twenty-third in 1938–41 was at the bottom of the list. Querétaro, however, occupied the second lowest position in both years. The percentage spread between highest and lowest shows little change over the whole period. In the middle ranks, there were dramatic shifts. Thus Campeche fell from fifth to twenty-fifth during the period, and *Morelos* rose from twentieth to fifth.

Generally speaking, the high wage areas in both years were in the north, the Gulf states and territories, and the Federal District, while the low-wage states were mainly in the central and southwest areas.

Turning to the figures of per capita consumption of meat and sugar (Table 30–16) which are probably a better indication of general living levels, we see that in 1938–41 the regional pattern is very clear. At the top of the list is the Destrito Federal. Next come five northern states. From there to the mid-point we have three more northern states, the three peninsula districts (Yucatan, Campeche, and Quintana Roo), and Morelos, which is virtually an extension of the Destrito Federal. In 1945–49, relatively little change had taken place in the regional pattern of consumption. The Federal District and the northern states were still at the top, with the three peninsular areas still in the upper half; Morelos had slipped from tenth to seventeenth place and Jalisco had come up from sixteenth to thirteenth place. The states grouped at the bottom of the list were also essentially the same in both periods.

The 1960 figures, however, reflect some postwar convergence, mainly in the form of a reduced gap between the richest and the national average. Between 1938–41 and 1945–49, there was actually a widening of the gap, chiefly in the form of great differences between consumption in the poorest states and the national average. World War II itself brought no clear-cut convergence. However, there has been steady convergence since World War II. Particularly striking is the rise of two of the peninsular areas, Yucatán and Campeche, to second and third place after the Destrito Federal. We then get the usual group of northern states in the next places, but Quintana Roo has slipped to twenty-fifth place. Querétaro has fallen from third to ninth place and Coahuila from ninth to fifteenth. At the very bottom, the list remains much the same as in 1938–41, although the order is somewhat changed.

The high per capita consumption in the peninsular areas (two states and one territory) has somewhat different meaning from comparable figures in other parts of the country, since these are thinly settled, virtually frontier areas.

These studies provide additional evidence that Mexico is "over the hump" as far as regional discrepancies are concerned. The problem area remains the mountainous states in the center of the country, together with Chiapas far to the south. These are not, however, thickly settled states, and consequently the problem of regional dualism is not as intractable in Mexico as it is in Brazil.

India: Pilgrim's Progress

India is clearly one of the two most important nations in Asia. In terms of population it stands second only to its neighbor, China, also an underdeveloped country seeking higher living standards, although by a different route. Since India has chosen the democratic system and China the Com-

TABLE 30-16

Indices of Per Capita Consumption of Meat and Sugar (1953 Pesos) by States in Terms of National Aggregate for Mexico for Period 1938–41 to 1960

(national aggregate = 100)*

Region	Rank	States	1938–41	Rank	States	1942–44	Rank	States	1945–49	Region
C	1	Distrito Federal	287	1	Distrito Federal	301	1	Distrito Federal	280	C
NP	2	Baja Calif.	265	2	Baja Calif.	234	2	Baja Calif.	242	NP
SP	3	Colima	181	3	Nuevo León	170	3	Nuevo León	172	N
NP	4	Sonora	171	4	Tamaulipas	157	4	Sonora	168	NP
N	5	Tamaulipas	162	5	Sonora	153	5	Sinaloa	153	NP
N	6	Nuevo León	156	6	Colima	145	6	Tamaulipas	149	N
G	7	Campeche	146	7	Coahuila	141	7	Coahuila	142	N
C	8	Aguascalientes	140	8	Sinaloa	141	8	Campeche	140	G
N	9	Coahuila	140	9	Aguascalientes	132	9	Aguascalientes	137	C
C	10	Morelos	129	10	Chihuahua	116	10	Chihuahua	115	N
G	11	Yucatán	123	11	Yucatán	114	11	Yucatán	114	G
NP	12	Sinaloa	121	12	Campeche	109	12	Colima	109	SP
N	13	Chihuahua	114	13	Quintana Roo	104	13	Jalisco	101	C

	No.	State	Value	No.	State	Value	No.	State	Value	
NP	14	Nayarit	113	14	Jalisco	95	14	Quintana Roo	100	G
G	15	Quintana Roo	107	15	Nayarit	94	15	Nayarit	91	NP
C	16	Jalisco	95	16	Morelos	90	16	Guanajuato	88	C
C	17	Guanajuato	83	17	Guanajuato	88	17	Morelos	84	C
N	18	Durango	77	18	Durango	81	18	Durango	77	N
G	19	Veracruz	74	19	Tabasco	73	19	Tabasco	77	G
N	20	San Luis Potosí	71	20	Veracruz	68	20	Veracruz	71	G
G	21	Tabasco	68	21	San Luis Potosí	62	21	Michoacán	56	C
C	22	Michoacán	63	22	Puebla	56	22	San Luis Potosí	52	N
C	23	Puebla	62	23	Michoacán	55	23	Querétaro	51	C
C	24	Hidalgo	62	24	Zacatecas	47	24	Zacatecas	46	N
SP	25	Chiapas	57	25	Querétaro	46	25	México	45	C
N	26	Zacatecas	52	26	Hidalgo	43	26	Puebla	43	C
C	27	Querétaro	51	27	México	36	27	Guerrero	29	SP
C	28	Tlaxcala	47	28	Chiapas	36	28	Hidalgo	37	C
C	29	México	44	29	Tlaxcala	36	29	Chiapas	31	SP
C	30	Oaxaca	38	30	Guerrero	26	30	Tlaxcala	24	C
SP	31	Guerrero	35	31	Oaxaca	25	31	Oaxaca	18	SP

* Per capita consumption for the nation as a whole equated to 100.
C = Central; G = Gulf of Mexico; N = Northern; NP = Northern Pacific; SP = Southern Pacific.

munist one, the whole world watches with keenest interest the race between these two countries. India takes on added interest because it was one of the first countries to embark on a formal development plan. Indeed, in 1966 India was already at the end of its Third Five-Year Plan.

The Indian leaders who framed the First Five-Year Plan were well aware of the immensity of the task they had undertaken. In setting forth the objectives of the Plan, they wrote: [47]

The central objective of planning in India at the present stage is to initiate a process of development which will raise living standards and open out to the people new opportunities for a richer and more varied life. . . . The urge to economic and social change under present conditions comes from the fact of poverty and of inequalities in income, wealth and opportunity. The elimination of poverty cannot, obviously, be achieved merely by redistributing existing wealth. Nor can a programme aiming only at raising production remove existing inequalities. . . . A process of all-round and orderly development, such as is indicated above, must inevitably take time to come into full fruition. Large-scale changes in modes of production, in commercial and industrial organization and in the institutional framework of corporate life cannot be seen through within a brief period of four or five years.

. . . The task of organizing a democracy for rapid and co-ordinated advance along several lines is one of special difficulty. The party in power has not only to carry public opinion with it; it has to get the active cooperation of all sections. . . . But, it must be emphasized that for democratic planning to succeed, it will have to energize the entire community and to place before it a goal of endeavour which will call forth all its latent creative urges. . . . Under the Constitution, India is organized as a federation, in which the Central Government and the Governments of States have their assigned spheres of action. . . . A planned economy aiming at the realization of larger social objectives entails a vast increase in governmental functions. For these to be discharged efficiently, appropriate local, regional and functional organizations have to be built up and strengthened.

A country with so much vitality and determination among its leaders— in both the public and private sectors of the economy—was inaccurately described as "stagnant," even in the early 1950's. Yet if one looked only at the main economic aggregates one would have been inclined to put India into the "poor and stagnant" category. At that time per capita income was only $60 per year and had risen very slowly in recent ears. The proportion of national income derived from agriculture (at constant factor cost) remained within a fraction of 49 per cent between 1950 and 1954 and was just under 48 per cent in 1955–56. The proportion derived from manufacturing, mining, and public utilities remained just under 17 per cent, despite considerable industrial investment.

Actually India had been static in terms of structure for some decades. Industrialization was not new to India. A modern textile industry was established a century ago and a modern steel industry over fifty years ago. Both of these industries were efficient, low-cost organizations which en-

[47] Government of India, Planning Commission, *The First Five-Year Plan* (New Delhi, December, 1952), Vol. I, pp. 1–6.

joyed healthy expansion, but their establishment did nothing to transform the Indian economy. Similarly, India benefited from early completion of transcontinental railways; and it has a banking system and capital market that other underdeveloped countries might well envy. Yet modern industry was not more significant as a source of income in 1951 than it was in 1921, and perhaps even earlier. These are the facts which impelled the distinguished Indian economist, V. K. R. V. Rao, to refer to his country as "a static economy in progress." [48]

The handicaps in Indian agriculture are indicated by the spread between the share of income and the share of employment in agriculture, a spread that is even bigger than in other underdeveloped countries. In the mid-fifties over 80 per cent of the population was rural, yet only 48 per cent of the national income was produced in the rural sector. Much of India is arid, much of the soil is poor; increasing acreage and raising yields per hectare both require substantial investment.

The disappointing record of agriculture after the unusually good monsoon years in the mid-1950's was a stiff blow to Indian hopes and expectations. For although the long-run prospects of Indian agriculture are less bright than the outlook for industry, as long as three-fourths of the active population is engaged in agriculture, increases in agricultural output must be obtained, to sustain increases in population and permit some labor to be shifted to industry. India may eventually be able to finance food imports with industrial exports, but that day is not yet. Meanwhile, as Professor Hoselitz puts it: [49]

Indian agriculture still operates within such a narrow margin in comparison with minimum food requirements for health and survival of its population, that inclement weather, an unfavorable monsoon, or some major disaster, like an inundation, leads to wide-spread famine in large parts of the country. In these situations scarce foreign exchange must be used for food imports, and this affects adversely imports of capital vitality needed for industrial development.

Professors Vakil and Brahmananda make the point in even stronger terms. In underdeveloped countries like India, they argue, the concept of capital as a stock of wage goods available to support labor in investment activities is still valid: [50]

We have maintained that unemployment in underdeveloped countries is due solely to the prevalence of the wage-goods gap. It is the inability of the economy to provide in the short-period the required surplus of wage-goods necessary in order that the disguised unemployment can be employed in investment, that inhibits expansion in employment and in investment.

[48] Rao introduced the expression "static economy in progress" in an article, "Changes in India's National Income," *Capital*, December 6, 1954, Supplement, pp. 15–17. See also, chap. V, "A Static Economy in Progress," of Wilfred Malenbaum, *Prospects for Indian Development* (Glencoe, Ill., 1962).
[49] Bert F. Hoselitz, "The Prospects for Indian Economic Growth," in Eastin Nelson, *op. cit.*, pp. 15–16.
[50] Chandulal Nagindas Vakil and P. R. Brahmananda, *Planning for an Expanding Economy* (Bombay, 1956), p. 23.

The Plans

In its *Review of the First Five-Year Plan,* the Planning Commission listed the pressing problems confronting the country in 1951. There were acute shortages of raw materials and foodstuffs; in 1951, 4.7 million tons of food grains had to be imported. Industrial production was below capacity. The transport system was in bad shape. Millions of displaced persons poured over the border from Pakistan. The Korean War and a bad harvest created inflationary pressure. Coordination of central and state government operations had yet to be achieved. The balance of payments on current account was unfavorable. In these conditions, the First Plan set itself two main targets: to correct "the disequilibrium in the economy caused by the War and the partition of the country"; and "to initiate simultaneously a process of all-around balanced development which would ensure a rising national income and a steady improvement in living standards over a period." [51]

THE FIRST PLAN

In the opening chapter of the First Five-Year Plan, the Planning Commission raised two basic questions: "What increase in per capita income can we reasonably hope to attain over a given period of years? What rate of capital formation will be required to achieve it?" The Commission stressed the fact that the Indian people were confronted here with a "definite problem of choice—a choice between, on the one hand a small or moderate increase in the standard of living in the near future but with only relatively small additions to capital equipment and hence no marked and sustained upward trend; and, on the other, a substantially higher standard of living for the next generation at the cost of continued austerity and privation to the present generation in the interests of rapid capital formation." The Commission assumed that the "weight will incline towards the second alternative."

The Commission went on to state two basic assumptions: that population growth would continue at the rate of 1.25 per cent annually, and that the incremental capital-output ratio (ICOR) would start at 3:1 and rise gradually to about 4:1.

Targets On the basis of these assumptions, the Commission chose modest targets for its plans. It hoped to double per capita national income in one generation, but expected to do no more than lay the groundwork for this expansion during the first five-year period. Although recognizing that rapidly expanding economies had invested (net) 12 per cent to 15 per cent of the national income the Commission did not consider it feasible during the first five years to do more than to raise net investment in India from 5 per cent to 6.75 per cent of national income. It was contemplated, however, that this increase in investment would occur at an increasing rate, so that by the end of the first five-year period, 50 per cent of

[51] Government of India Planning Commission, *Review of the First Five-Year Plan* (Delhi, May, 1957), p. 1.

additional income could be saved and invested and that "by 1967–68 the annual saving would amount to no less than 20 per cent of the aggregate national income—a rate which it would not be necessary to exceed."

The Commission also stated as objectives of the Plan, reduction in inequalities of income and wealth, and reduction of the rate of population growth to about 1 per cent per year.

Public and Private Investment   To accomplish these objectives, the Indian government depended primarily on public investment. With respect to the private sector, the Commission pointed out that the state "cannot determine absolutely the investment of the savings of private individuals and corporations; it can only influence their investment by offering facilities and incentives to encourage their flow into certain channels while discouraging or even prohibiting them from being drawn off into others." For encouraging and directing private investment the Commission recommended credit controls, fiscal policy, licensing, and, if necessary, price controls.[52]

Deficit Finance   In the light of subsequent developments the Commission's statement with regard to deficit financing is of some interest:

The dangers of "creating" money are sufficiently well known. Such a course means the depreciation of the existing currency and consequent inflation of prices and, if carried beyond certain limits, may completely undermine public confidence in the currency with catastrophic results. Deficit financing can be countenanced only if there is an assurance of steady supplies of the essential commodities of consumption. The injection of increased purchasing power into the system is apt to lead to increased demand for basic commodities and, if their supply cannot be expanded quickly, their prices rise and push up the cost of living. It will thus be apparent that the scope for deficit financing is intimately bound up with the policy of controls.

Results Under the First Plan   The budget for the First Plan and the actual outlays under it are compared in Table 30–17. It will be noted that the emphasis in the First Plan was on agriculture (including community development and irrigation) and transport. Power projects received a substantial allocation (especially railways) and social services were not neglected. Very little was allocated for industry and mining. The percentage distribution of actual outlays conformed closely to the Plan, except that investment in large-scale industry and mining was even less than planned, and investment in railways even more. There was, however, an over-all shortfall of about 15 per cent in actual outlays.

This developmental investment brought useful but not dramatic increases in output. As may be seen from Table 30–18, national income at constant prices rose 17.5 per cent and per capita income 10.5 per cent. Despite the emphasis on agriculture, it was mining, manufacturing, and transport that showed the biggest percentage expansion. Favorable monsoons were an important factor in the increase in agricultural output.

[52] Government of India Planning Commission, *First Five-Year Plan*, pp. 15, 21–22, 32–33.

TABLE 30–17

Allocations and Outlay under the First Five-Year Plan by
Major Heads of Development

Allocation	Total plan provision (including adjustments)		Outlay, 1951–56	
	Rs. crores	Per cent	Rs. crores	Per cent
Agriculture and community development	354	14.9	299	14.8
Irrigation and power	647	27.2	585	29.1
Industries and mining	188	7.9	100	5.0
Transport and communications	571	24.0	532	26.4
Social services	532	22.4	423	21.0
Miscellaneous	86	3.6	74	3.7
Total	2,378	100.0	2,013	100.0

SOURCE: Government of India Planning Commission, *Review of the First Five-Year Plan* (New Delhi, May, 1957), pp. 2–3.

The feared inflation did not develop. Deficit financing (which in Indian parlance means borrowing from the banking system) accounted for 21 per cent of the government expenditures under the Plan, and market borrowings another 10 per cent; deficits in the ordinary sense were therefore nearly one-third of the total outlays. Taxation, together with surpluses of the state-owned railways, provided only 38 per cent of the

TABLE 30–18

Increases in Output under the First Five-Year Plan

Category of output	Percentage increase
Agriculture, etc.	14.7
Mining, manufacturing, and small enterprise	18.2
Commerce, transport, and communications	18.6
Net domestic product at factor cost	17.5
Per capita net output	10.5
Population	6.6

SOURCE: Government of India, *Review of the First Five-Year Plan* (New Delhi, 1957), pp. 7–8.

needed funds. Yet prices fell and unemployment grew during the Plan period—facts which greatly influenced attitudes toward the scale and financing of the Second Plan. The reasons for the coexistence of deficit finance, deflation, and growing unemployment seem to have been the favorable monsoons, foreign aid which permitted an import surplus, and investment of a kind that provided more output than jobs. Some Indian officials, however, apparently translated the experience under the First Plan into a proof of excessive pessimism on the part of others who warned of the dangers of inflation and unduly ambitious plans.

Professor Malenbaum offers this appraisal of the results of the First Plan: [53]

Without playing down an Indian achievement without parallel among free world nations, it is true that circumstances surrounding the Indian effort were unusually favourable. Notable, of course, was the weather—with excellent monsoons, at least after the first two years of the Plan. The international political and economic environment was such that India could obtain assistance from abroad, beyond what she actually used during the First Plan. The First Plan years did not involve reductions in current consumption levels, or even unpleasant choices about what to do with increased incomes. True, government did want more tax revenues than it collected, but at the same time people were prepared to lend, especially to government, more than seemed to be demanded. The economy actually suffered somewhat from deflationary pressures.

THE SECOND FIVE-YEAR PLAN

Early in 1956, the Indian Planning Commission released its Second Five-Year Plan. The Commission noted that participation in preparation of the Plan had been much broader than in the case of the First Five-Year Plan. "The enthusiasm and the widespread participation which have gone into the making of the Second Five-Year Plan" said the Commission, "are the best augury for its fulfillment." [54] The assistance of the Indian Statistical Institute, under the direction of Professor Mahalanobis, and of the Commission's panel of economists, was especially mentioned.

The Mahalanobis "Framework" Indeed the final plan followed closely the draft prepared by the Statistical Institute, as approved by its panel of economists, although it was somewhat less ambitious in its income targets and less optimistic with regard to the capital-output ratio. In the preface to this "Plan framework," public attention was called to the decision of the National Development Council that "the widest possible publicity be given to the draft outline so as to facilitate a discussion on the overall objectives of the plan and the means of obtaining them." The substantial success of the First Five-Year Plan "has laid the foundations for a bolder plan in the second five-year period." Although it was recognized that complete control over the private sector of a mixed economy was impossible, the achievement of balanced growth required conformity of the activities of the private sector to the program of production "in a general way." [55]

The First Five-Year Plan was regarded as unsatisfactory in terms of employment creation; unemployment was still increasing, especially in

[53] Wilfred Malenbaum, "Some Political Aspects of Economic Development," *World Politics*, April, 1958.

[54] Government of India Planning Commission, *Second Five-Year Plan* (New Delhi, 1956), p. 3.

[55] *Ibid.*, p. 8.

urban areas. Agricultural prices were declining. Thus despite modest deficit financing for the First Plan, the trend within the economy had remained deflationary. Accordingly, the draft plan called for more vigorous development and a more expansionary approach for the Second Five-Year Plan. In particular, "a large increase in employment opportunities must be regarded as the principal objective—the Kingpin—of the second plan." [56] The Plan recognized that maximizing employment might conflict with maximizing output, especially where cottage industries were concerned; accordingly, it was felt that development of basic industries should not result in destruction of the small-scale industries that provided opportunities for employment.

Objectives of the Second Plan   For the second phase of planning, the Commission itemized four principal objectives:

(a) a sizeable increase in national income so as to raise the level of living in the country;
(b) rapid industrialization, with particular emphasis on the development of basic and heavy industries;
(c) a large expansion of employment opportunities; and
(d) reduction of inequalities in income and wealth and a more even distribution of economic power.

The Commission added that a low standard of living, underemployment, and maldistribution of income are all symptoms of "the basic underdevelopment which characterizes an economy depending mainly on agriculture." Rapid industrialization was thus the core of the new plan.

Much more attention was directed toward the problem of employment creation in the Second Plan than in the First. "The question of increasing employment opportunities," stated the Commission, "cannot be viewed separately from the programs of investment envisaged in the plan"; [57] for there was general agreement that "the Second Five-Year Plan should have a distinct employment bias." [58] Employment creation was to be designed to reduce existing unemployment in the urban and rural areas, to absorb an increase in the labor force of about two million persons per year, and to lessen underemployment in rural and household occupations.

Comparison with the First Plan   The increase in plan outlay and the changes in its composition are indicated by Table 30–19. Over-all expenditures under the Second Plan were more than doubled. The most striking changes in composition were the increased investment in industry and mining and the reduced investment in irrigation and power (especially irrigation). The actual capital-output ratio under the First Plan was calculated at 1.8:1, somewhat better than anticipated. Making allowance for the favorable monsoons and the shift in structure of investment, the ICOR for the Second Plan was set at 2.3:1; it was estimated that in the course of subse-

[56] *Ibid.*, p. 66.
[57] *Ibid.*, pp. 7, 8.
[58] *Ibid.*, p. 41; see also Table 1, p. 43.

TABLE 30–19

Distribution of Plan Outlay by Major Heads of Development

Allocation	First Five-Year Plan		Second Five-Year Plan	
	Total provision, rs. crores	Per cent	Total provision, rs. crores	Per cent
Agriculture and community development	357	15.1	568	11.8
Irrigation and power	661	28.1	913	19.0
Industries and mining	179	7.6	890	18.5
Transport and communications	557	23.6	1,385	28.9
Social services	533	22.6	945	19.7
Miscellaneous	69	3.0	99	2.1
Total	2,356	100.0	4,800	100.0

source: Government of India Planning Commission, *Second Five-Year Plan* (New Delhi, 1956), pp. 51–52.

quent Plans it would rise to 2.6, 3.4, and 3.7. The long-run expectations with regard to increase in investment were scaled down. The target was an increase from 7 per cent of national income in 1955–56 to 11 per cent in 1960–61. Instead of reaching 20 per cent by 1968–69 as originally hoped, it would rise to 16 per cent by 1970–71.

The Plan document noted the lack of change in occupational structure in the past, stating that, although immigration to cities may have resulted in some decline in agriculture's share of total employment, "the change is unlikely so far to have been of any noteworthy character." The objective was to keep increases in agricultural employment to a minimum. However, the targets set up for structural change were still very modest: to reduce the proportion of agricultural employment to 60 per cent of the total by 1975–76. At the same time, the Plan undertook to protect cottage industry, while stressing the need to find new products and develop new techniques in this sector of the economy.

As may be seen from Table 30–20, the new Plan relied much more heavily on deficit finance in the public sector than the first did. Of the entire budget, 4,800 crores of rupees, tax revenue was to provide only 800, and of this more than half was hopefully assigned to "new taxes." The "other budgetary sources" might be regarded as anti-inflationary sources of finance, but these added only 450 crores of rupees. The bulk of the program was to be covered by what was actually called deficit financing, borrowings from the public that might or might not be inflationary in effect, external resources, and an unspecified "gap."

Results Under the Plan   The Second Plan was hardly more than a few months old when it became apparent that it was heading for trouble. The chief symptom of trouble was the loss of foreign exchange, during the First

TABLE 30–20

Financing the Public Sector, Second Five-Year Plan

Source of funds	Amount, crores of rupees
Surplus from current revenue	800
At existing (1955–56) rates	350
Additional taxation	450
Borrowings from the public	1,200
Other budgetary sources	400
Railways' contribution	150
Provident funds, etc.	250
Resources to be raised externally	800
Deficit financing	1,200
Gap—to be covered by additional measures to raise domestic resources	400
Total	4,800

SOURCE: Government of India, *Second Five-Year Plan* (New Delhi, 1956), pp. 77–78.

Plan year, India lost $600 million in reserves (including drawings on the International Monetary Fund that may have to be repaid before the end of the Plan period)—50 per cent more than was contemplated for the entire Plan. The deficit on current account in 1956–57 amounted to 332 crores of rupees, more than double the estimate in the Plan. Imports were nearly 200 crores above estimates, exports more than 60 crores below estimates; net income on invisibles was somewhat better than expected. The consequent foreign exchange crisis was met in the first instance by drawings on the IMF equal to 50 per cent of the Indian quota and by import restrictions. It was soon recognized, however, that the implications were much more serious. Without greatly increased foreign aid, the Second Plan would have had to be abandoned. At best, it might have been possible to finish the "hard core" projects.

It should be emphasized that, for the most part, this drain on foreign exchange was not the result of any unhealthy trend in the Indian economy. On the contrary, it reflected unexpectedly vigorous expansion, particularly in the private sector. During 1956–57, private imports of capital goods were nearly 50 per cent higher than in the preceding year and nearly 25 per cent above Plan estimates. Capital goods imports on public account were more than double the 1955–56 level, but somewhat below Plan estimates. Raw material imports showed relatively little expansion over the previous year. Food imports were three and a half times the 1955–56 level and more than double the Plan estimate. In part, this increase indicated failure to maintain expansion of food production, but since much of this increase represented United States commodity surplus disposal, it did not impose an immediate drain on Indian foreign exchange. Another part of the drain was due to unexpectedly large outlays for defense.

The foreign exchange crisis was not the only fly in the Indian ointment. Perhaps more serious was the failure of the investment undertaken to produce the predicted increase in output; the estimates of the capital-output ratio proved too optimistic. Disappointments have occurred even in the field of community development, where much effort was concentrated and a special Ministry established. Here was an approach to increased agricultural productivity that seemed tailor-made for India's traditional village pattern in mobilizing mass effort; yet continuous application of effort, personnel, and funds from the central government proved necessary to achieve continuous improvement.[59]

Planning and Performance   To what extent can the imperfections in performance under the Plan be traced to imperfections in the planning process? To answer this question we must first take a look at the manner in which the Second Plan was put together. The Introduction to *The Second Five-Year Plan* says,[60]

The Plan which is now presented to government for submission to parliament is a result of the labours of large numbers of persons in the Central Government, in the States at various levels and leaders of thought and opinion in every part of the country. In its preparation, men and women from all walks of life have given generously of their time and experience.

Certainly a sincere effort was made to base the Second Plan on "planning from below." As early as April, 1954, the Planning Commission asked the state governments to encourage the preparation of district and even village plans. Discussions took place between the states and the districts and between the states and the central government to iron out differences in conception of the Plan. Analysis and coordination was the task of the secretariat of the Planning Commission, which had the advice of a panel of economists. Malenbaum doubts "that there is any conceptual device, statistical tool or theoretical argument known to economists anywhere which has not in some way been used, or been mentioned, in the two Five-Year Plans." [61]

However, as Malenbaum also points out, "a flow from the bottom can scarcely exist where more than 80 per cent of the population is illiterate, where an even larger number may be only remotely concerned with the need for a development plan or program to say nothing of a land where higher authority is traditionally accepted." [62] He gives India credit for "retaining the semblance of this multiple interchange" but said bluntly in 1956 that at that time planning was still from top to bottom. The Deputy Chairman of the Planning Commission, the Minister of Planning, the Finance Minister, and the Statistical Adviser all played extremely important roles, but most important was the Chairman of the Planning

[59] Cf. Malenbaum, *op. cit.*, p. 385.
[60] Government of India Planning Commission, *op. cit.*, p. xiv.
[61] Malenbaum, "Who Does the Planning?" (Paper presented to the Seminar on Leadership and Political Institutions in India, University of California, August, 1956).
[62] *Ibid.*, p. 4.

Commission, the Prime Minister himself. Nehru, Malenbaum added, "is clearly India's top politician," and "progress on the Plan . . . is an excellent political point of contact with the people," a fact that Nehru clearly understood. In a Plan which left so much to individual and group initiative, it was necessary to know much more about motivation, especially in the rural sector, so as to decide what measures were most likely to bring the actions implicit in the Plan. "The structure and dynamics of Indian economic life . . . are only beginning to become known." [63] The excessive optimism with respect to the capital-output ratio was one example of inadequate study of actual conditions in the country.

A closely related point was the failure of the Plan to make full allowance for and use of the dynamism of Indian private enterprise. The point here was technical, not ideological; if the dynamism could be diverted to the public sector in accordance with Indian social philosophy, well and good; if not, failure to encourage it where it existed would have meant a slower rate of growth than would otherwise have been possible. The balance of public and private enterprise underlying the Second Plan, together with the lack of measures to change the structure of the economy, turned out to be quite unrealistic. Malenbaum thinks that the lack of realism was particularly apparent with regard to agriculture and small enterprise. In the First Plan, the balance of public to private investment in agriculture and irrigation was roughly 1:1; in the Second Plan it was about 2½:1, 800 crores of rupees, public and 300 crores of rupees, private. How was this shift in balance to be achieved? What reason had the planners to assume that such an increase in public investment would not encourage a proportionate increase in private investment—considering, for example, that the Italian planners made precisely the reverse assumption?

Indeed, another flaw in the planning process was a general failure to think in terms of implementation and control as well as in terms of setting targets.

The truth is that despite the emphasis on planning and the announced socialist philosophy (which really means a social welfare philosophy) India is one of the least regulated economies in the world. Professor Galbraith points out that [64]

. . . by almost any test, the economy of India is less responsive to public guidance and direction than that of the United States. Indeed it is one of the world's least controlled or "planned" economies. In the United States the several levels of government dispose of about 20 per cent of the total production (or $434 billions in 1957). In India the corresponding figure is not over 10 per cent. By this test—the size of state activity in relation to all activity— more than twice as much of the American economy is managed or planned by government as is the case in India. . . . In the aggregate there can be little doubt that ours is both much the more manageable and the more managed economy. India has, in fact, superimposed a smallish socialized sector atop what, no doubt, is the world's greatest example of functioning anarchy.

[63] *Ibid.*
[64] J. K. Galbraith, "Rival Economic Theories in India," *Foreign Affairs*, July, 1958.

Perhaps the basic trouble with the Second Plan was that it was an admixture of physical planning and economic planning, of ideology and *ad hocery*, reflecting the basic splits in Indian society as a whole. The Indian government was committed to democracy and to socialism, to preserving traditional values and to getting on with the job of development, to raising productivity and to avoiding technological unemployment,[65] to steadfast independence and refusal of political commitments, and to use of foreign aid in development. India's neutralism, like Indonesia's, reflected the strength of opposing viewpoints within the society rather than complete political unity. The election of a Communist government in the state of Kerala and a Communist mayor in Bombay, the strength of the Communist party elsewhere in the country, the restiveness within the Congress party itself, the success of Communist China—all meant that left-wing viewpoints could not be ignored. Yet majority opinion was still anti-Communist. The Plan tried to please both sides, incorporating some Russian style physical target planning and some Western style economic planning, with neither being completely carried through. The physical planning was not carried as far as input-output analysis, although the facilities of the excellent Statistical Institute would have permitted that to be done. Had full use been made of these facilities, the foreign exchange crisis and inflationary pressure could have been predicted. The same is true if economic planning had been carried through in terms of the usual sort of multiplier analysis. Indeed, such predictions were made by a number of private economists.[66]

The mixture of incomplete physical planning with incomplete economic analysis reflected the personalities involved in the planning process as well as the political differences in the country as a whole. Both the Statistical Adviser and the then Minister of Finance, as well as the Minister of Planning, were trained originally as natural scientists, and tended toward a physical planning approach. The top staff of the Planning Commission Secretariat, together with the panel of economists, leaned toward an economic policy approach to development. Apparently, in the preparation of the Second Plan, the influence of the former group outweighed that of the latter, but the Plan reflected the ideas of both groups without completely coordinating them.

Was the Second Plan "Too Ambitious"? The Indian experience with the Second Plan illustrates the necessity of "planning big," in order to assure a take-off into sustained growth, while not planning more than available resources permit so that the economy runs into serious loss of foreign exchange or inflation or both. In terms of what was needed to

[65] "Mr. Nehru can talk about the greater appropriateness of energy from cowdung than from atomic fission at India's present stage of progress; Indian political and governmental leaders can give abundant lip service to Gandhian proclivity for rural and handicraft activities. But the effective force is one for rapid modernization, for a quick transition to the industry and power in the U.S. and the U.S.S.R. prototypes." Malenbaum, *op. cit.*, chap. III.

[66] See for example the articles on the Second Plan in the *Quarterly Economic Report* of the Indian Institute of Public Opinion, especially Vol. I, No. 3, 4, 8, 1955.

provide a "big push," bring the required structural change, produce simultaneous agricultural improvement and industrialization, and assure increases
in productivity that would significantly outrun population growth, the
Second Plan was certainly too small. In Malenbaum's view, the necessity
for the Indian leadership to show results that would not be so obviously
at a disadvantage in comparison with China as to shift public opinion further
to the left, plus the fact that over the First Plan national income actually
did grow by 17 per cent or 18 per cent, "meant that over-all targets for
1961 could not have been significantly smaller than the 25 per cent increase
actually established." Malenbaum also hold that "given the drive and ex-
citement of the process of a transformation from stagnation to growth, the
resource potential of India and especially the knowledge and ability of Indian business and governmental leadership, such targets were not unreasonable." [67]

On the other hand, it is clear in retrospect that India planned beyond its
actual capacity, given the amount of foreign aid that was then forthcoming and the limited measures for mobilizing and directing India's own
saving and investment potential.

Table 30–21 presents a comparison of plans with performance for the
first two Five-Year Plans. It will be noted that up to 1955–56, marking the
end of the First Five Year Plan and the beginning of the Second, the
growth of national income was above target. The planned increase was 11
to 12 per cent, and the actual increase was more than 18 per cent. It should
also be noted, however, that the overfulfillment was most evident in the
services and trade sectors in agriculture as well as in mining and manufacturing. Despite the favorable monsoons, the actual increase in output
was only very slightly above targets. In the second year of the Second
Five-Year Plan, however, the growth of the Indian economy fell below
the planned target. It had not recovered by the end of the Second Five-
Year Plan. In the Second Five-Year Plan only the services sector expanded
more than was planned; all other sectors were below planned targets.
In manufacturing, the mining sector, in particular, was well below the
planned target.

THE THIRD FIVE-YEAR PLAN

The Third Five-Year Plan for 1961–66 involved no sharp changes in the
structure of investment. The proportion of total investment allocated to
agriculture, community development, and irrigation on the one hand, and
the proportions allocated to power, large industry, and mining on the
other, were slightly increased. Small industries remained about the same
proportion of the investment budget as in the Second Plan. Transportation and communications and social services were both reduced to a smaller
proportion of the total, while nonetheless increasing in absolute amount of
investment outlays. The Third Plan was approximately 50 per cent bigger
in terms of total expenditures (at constant prices) than the Second Plan:
$21,843 million as compared to $14,175 million. The Third Plan postulated

[67] Malenbaum, *op. cit.*, chap. II.

TABLE 30–21

Growth in National Income, Plan and Performance
1950/51–1960/61
(million dollars)

	Plan*		Actual†	
	Income (1948/49 prices)	Ratio (1950/51 = 100)	Income (1948/49 prices)	Ratio (1950/51 = 100)
1950/51	18,900	100.0	18,560	100.0
1951/52	19,320	102.1	19,100	102.9
1952/53	19,740	104.4	19,870	107.0
1953/54	20,160	106.7	21,060	113.4
1954/55	20,580	109.0	21,590	116.0
1955/56	{21,000 / 22,010	111.5} / 116.5}	22,010	118.4
1956/57	23,100	122.3	23,200	125.0
1957/58	24,190	128.1	22,870	123.2
1958/59	25,280	133.9	24,465	131.8
1959/60	26,380	139.7	[24,700]	[133.1]
1960/61	27,480	145.5	[26,300]	[141.7]

* Plan figures: Data for 1950/51 and the first figure for 1955/56 are as given in the *First Five Year Plan*, pp. 20–21; interim years are interpolated. The *Second Five Year Plan* presents projections in terms of 1952/53 prices only (p. 11). The starting point, 1955/56, is taken at Rs. 10,800 crores ($22,680 million), which is the figure for that year in 1952/53 prices. In 1948/49 prices, it is Rs. 10,480 crores ($22,010 million). The 1960/61 estimate assumes the same real growth as in the plan (p. 11) interim years are interpolated.

† Actual figures: Data through 1959/60 are from G.O.I., *Estimates of National Income*, March, 1961. Figures for 1960/61 are "quick estimates" released by the Government of India on August 21, 1961.

SOURCE: Wilfred Malenbaum, *Prospects for Indian Development* (Glencoe, Ill., 1962), p. 209.

an increase in agricultural production of 30 per cent, of industrial output of 70 per cent, and of national income as a whole of 30 per cent.

In addition to the economic difficulties which retarded the rate of India's growth during the earlier plans, during the Third Plan period there were international political difficulties as well. The invasion of India by China necessitated a sharp increase in defense expenditures. As pointed out in the *Mid-Term Appraisal*, "in reviewing recent developments, it has to be remembered that for over a year the Third Plan has been implemented against the background of a serious threat to national security and a continuing emergency that has brought new burdens and responsibilities." [68]

While the Third Plan placed its major emphasis on agriculture, seasonal conditions were unfavorable during the first two years of the Plan, and expansion of output fell below target.

[68] Government of India, Planning Commission, *The Third Plan, Mid-Term Appraisal* (New Delhi, November, 1963), p. 1.

The Employment Problem   The difficulty in creating sufficient new jobs
to absorb the increase in the labor force, reduce unemployment and underemployment, and permit some transfer out of agriculture continues to be
the bugbear of the Indian planners. The Second Plan started with a backlog
of unemployment in the neighborhood of 5.3 million and the expectation
that the labor force would grow by some 10 million during the period of
the Plan. There was no expectation that the economy could absorb 15.3
million workers during the five years of the Second Plan. However the
Second Plan did aim at preventing an increase in unemployment. Even this
modest goal was not attained; the Third Five-Year Plan started with a backlog of unemployment of some 7.5 to 8 million. While continuing to stress
the importance of providing employment, the Third Plan could not see
any possibility of reducing the backlog of unemployment; it hoped only to
prevent an increase, absorbing the entire increase in the labor force. The
expansion of the labor force was expected to be about 15 million. The Plan
was expected to provide about 14 million jobs, 10.5 of which would be outside of agriculture.[69] Thus even the plan foresaw some increase in unemployment.

Dr. A. Vaidyanathan felt that even this view of the employment
prospect was overly optimist.[70] First, he doubted whether any significant
increase in genuine employment was possible in the agricultural sector.
He also felt that the estimates of increase in non-agricultural employment
were overly optimistic. His pessimistic view is based on his doubts concerning the projected capital-output ratio in the Third Plan of 2.5 to 1 for
the Plan as a whole, and 2:1 for industry and mining. He points out that
the actual experience in the Second Plan was an over-all capital-output
ratio of 3:1 and in industry and mining of 3.3:1.

The introduction to the Plan framework for the Third Plan reiterated
the objective of achieving a "socialist pattern of society." However, it
went on to say that the socialist pattern in India does not mean that all
economic initiative must rest with the State. On the contrary, an important role in national development continues to be assigned to private
enterprise. The "socialist pattern" does, however, place special emphasis
on small producers, cooperatives, agriculture, and medium and small-scale
industry. The specific aim of the Third Plan was to increase the investment ratio from 11 per cent at the end of the Second Plan to 14 per cent
at the end of the Third. Income was to rise at 5 per cent a year.

It was hoped to achieve self-sufficiency in food gains while increasing
agricultural production so as to meet requirements of industry and export.
It was also planned to expand basic industries like steel, fuel, and power,
and to expand the capital goods industry, so that within ten years most
of the requirements for further industrialization could be met from the
country's own resources. As already mentioned, expansion of employment
opportunities was a major objective. The Third Plan also added, and gave
special emphasis to, the new objective of reduction of inequalities in

[69] See B. N. Datar, "Employment in the Third Plan," in Government of India,
Ministry of Information and Broadcasting, *Problems in the Third Plan*, pp. 130–32.
[70] *Ibid.*

income and wealth and a more even distribution of economic power.

Prime Minister Nehru, in presenting the Third Plan, stressed the continuity with the Second and the First. The Second Plan, he pointed out, was nearly twice as big as the first one, and the Third Plan would be much bigger again. The objectives remained substantially the same. Nehru regarded the first two Plans as modest successes. "The record of the first two Plans, even though sometimes criticized," he said, "is a fairly remarkable record of achievement. It did not, in some matters, come up to what we wanted it to be, but it is, nevertheless, a very creditable record, whether it is transport, communications, steel, fuel, power, scientific and technological research. In fact the whole of the Indian economy has arrived at the threshold of accelerated growth."

Family planning was already given some emphasis in the Second Plan, but it was emphasized still further in the Third. The draft outline of the Plan stated, "The objective of stabilizing the population has certainly to be regarded as an essential element in a strategy of development." The Plan accepts a projection of a Central Statistical Organization which assumes that the birth rate will fall from 39.6 to 32.9 during 1966–71 and to 27.3 during 1971–76. However, as pointed out by Chandrasekran, reductions in the birth rate of 20 per cent during a five-year period and of 33 per cent during a ten-year period "are unprecedented in any part of the world in the early stages of birth-rate decline." [71]

Results Under the Third Plan During the Third Five-Year Plan India ran into inflationary pressures for the first time. During the first three years of the Plan the money supply expanded by 31 per cent, which was considerably more than the increase in total production. The Plan itself explains much of the expansion of the money supply. Expenditures within the Plan increased sharply from 1,100 crores of rupees in 1961–62 to 1,700 crores of rupees in 1963–64 and 1,984 crores of rupees in 1964–65. Despite the large volume of foreign aid, the balance of payments has been under continuous pressure. India has drawn on the International Monetary Fund to the extent of 131 crores of rupees, but nonetheless her foreign exchange reserves have fallen. The foreign exchange reserves had already fallen from 785 crores of rupees to 186 crores of rupees during the Second Five-Year Plan, and they continued to fall the first two years of the Third Plan. During 1963–64 the balance of payments improved somewhat, but during 1965 the reserves fell once again. The ratio of taxes to income has expanded significantly, from about 9.6 per cent at the end of the Second Plan to 13 or 14 per cent in mid-1965, and private voluntary savings have also risen. Nonetheless, the continuing deficit financing of the Plan led to continuing increases in the Indian price level. Private investments as well as government spending for the Plan have risen significantly during the Third Plan.

Indian Planning Techniques

Having started on systematic five-year planning rather earlier than other

[71] Chandrasekran, "Strategy of the Third Plan," in *Problems in the Third Plan, op. cit.*

developing countries, India has acquired a reputation for highly sophisticated planning which is in fact undeserved. From a technical point of view the planning methods are simple and straightforward. The emphasis is on attaining a broad measure of public support, based on widespread discussion and "planning from below" rather than on application of the most advanced planning techniques. The process breaks down into three major branches: long-term or perspective planning; five-year planning (which has had the most publicity); and annual planning. Dr. F. R. Sen characterizes the perspective plan as "a long-term plan for all sectors of the economy, and is a combined exercise by economists technicians, and administrators." [72] The economists and statisticians first make long-run projections of resources and requirements over a fifteen- to twenty-year period, and analyze the intersectoral relationships in an endeavor to discover the pattern that will provide optimal results. These sectoral projections are then worked out in more detail with the technicians in each sector. The Five-Year Plan is then formulated as the first phase of the perspective Plan. Essentially, says Dr. Sen, the Five-Year Plan is a budget for the national economy for a period of five years, but for operational purposes five years is too long; it has therefore to be broken down into annual plans, which are expressed in the national economic budget for each year.

As pointed out by Professor R. S. Eckaus to the Universities-National Bureau Conference on Planning Economic Development, "Indian planning is an open process." Much of the controversy and debate accompanying the preparations of Plans are public, and the calculations, projections, and assumptions of the professional planners "are not only sensitive but responsive to criticism and suggestions from a wide variety of national and international sources. From original formulations through successive modifications to parliamentary presentation, plan making has evolved as a responsive democratic political process." [73]

EVOLUTION OF PLANNING

The First Five-Year Plan was more a projection than a Plan. It was based on a simple growth model of the Harrod-Domar variety, with a constant ratio of savings to income and a constant capital-output ratio. The marginal propensity to save was assumed to be above the average propensity to save, implying a diminishing reliance on foreign assistance as the economy grew. While the plan had policy implications with respect to fiscal and foreign exchange policy, there was little in it that could be rigorously controlled. Even the sectoral breakdown of the development program was incomplete.

The basic model used by the Planning Commission remained the same

---

[72] F. R. Sen, "Planning Technique in India," *Problems in the Third Plan, op. cit.*, p. 105.

[73] R. S. Eckaus, "Planning in India," paper for the NBER-Universities Conference on Economic Planning (November, 1964), mimeographed, p. 1. The Proceedings of the conference are to be published by the National Bureau of Economic Research.

in the Second Five-Year Plan with "an optimistic extrapolation of the First Plan experience" superimposed. In addition, however, the Second Plan is believed to have been greatly affected by the four-sector model drawn up by Dr. Mahalanobis. As has been pointed out, this model began with income and employment targets and indicated the investment ratio, together with its allocation among four major sectors, which would be required to achieve these targets. A curious feature of the model was that it ignored foreign trade altogether; it may be partly for this reason that India ran so quickly into balance of payments problems during the execution of the Second Plan.

Both theoretical models, underlying the Second Plan, Eckaus maintains, "were too limited in scope to indicate the most desirable allocation of resources among inter-dependent sectors. Their sectoral distinction was too gross; no attempt was made to find optimal allocations; dynamic inter-relations were not taken into account and the targets were defined in highly aggregated terms." [74] Once again the plan that was implemented was a collection of projects, not too well integrated with each other, plus a set of fiscal and foreign exchange policies which once again were not too well integrated with the investment budget. "To the extent that coordination and scheduling was achieved," Eckaus and Lefeber observe, "it was through the screening procedures of the inter-ministerial committees and working groups that met with Planning Commission representatives." They point out too that "the State governments come to the Center not only as petitioners but as powerful advocates backed by substantial resources. They are determined to have a voice not only in matters affecting their local economy such as the location of new plants, but on over-all economic policy as well."

Not much refinement was introduced into the planning procedure for the Third Plan. Once again, Eckaus observes, "there were macro-economic projections which, though less explicit, were accompanied this time by a clear recognition of the alternative possible values of parameters which made, in turn, the parameters themselves a matter of policy." [75] If anything, Eckaus believes, there was less effort to use models in determining sectoral priorities than there was in the Second Plan. "Instead, the consultation and review procedures appear to have operated more intensively and the calculations of commodity balances were done more extensively, in more detail and there was greater attention given to improving the basic data." [76]

In summarizing Indian planning methods, Dr. Eckaus points out that while the Plans encompass the entire economy, including the private sector, the government really has tight control only over the public sector. Even in the public sector the Plans fall short of being "a set of blue prints." The Plans are better characterized, the author maintains, as "a general statement of government intentions as to its own programs as well with respect to those sectoral programs open to private initiative."

[74] *Ibid.*, p. 6.
[75] *Ibid.*, p. 7.
[76] *Ibid.*, p. 7.

As far as implementation is concerned, the Plans, because of licensing requirements, can authoritatively indicate what the limits to private investment are but do not provide particular inducements for such investment decisions as are deemed necessary for the completion. Much of the basic planning in India takes the form of successive iterations, accomplished by the work of overlapping and pyramiding committees. Without questioning the superior judgment of such committees, Eckaus points out that much of their work is done "with little consideration of the specific composition of economic targets in the light of social preferences."

PERSPECTIVE PLANNING

With the preparation of the Third Five-Year Plan, long-range perspective planning became thoroughly established as a recognized part of the whole planning process. Pitambar Pant, in a paper describing the techniques used for perspective planning, begins by pointing out the necessity of a long-term view in such sectors as heavy industry, large-scale irrigation projects, transport and education, all of which have long gestation periods.[77]

There is a limit beyond which the stock of physical and human resources, particularly skilled personnel, cannot be expanded within the compass of a Five-Year Plan. The period of the perspective plan should be long enough to cover the time lags in long-maturing investments and programs and to permit an attack on basic problems. On the other hand, it should not be so long as to be rendered useless by changes in technology, or to be relevant to a period so far in the future as to be of no interest to people now living. On this basis the Indian planners have settled on a perspective plan of fifteen years, divided into shorter plans of five years each.

Once a perspective plan is prepared, a manpower plan in terms of skills and occupations can be worked out. Mr. Pant feels that such a perspective plan can play a vital role in making political democracy an effective instrument of rapid advance in developing countries. Like the late Prime Minister Nehru, Mr. Pant believes that on the whole Indian planning has been successful: "At the end of the period of the three Plans agricultural production would be higher by 80 per cent, production of organized manufacturing industry by 230 per cent and per capita income would increase by more than 35 per cent, despite a high rate of growth of population. Considering the utter stagnation of the preceding several decades this represents a considerable measure of achievement." Taking steel as an example, Dr. Pant points out that the long-range strategy implicit in the Third Plan requires an expansion of steel capacity by about two million tons a year by 1970 and three million tons a year by 1975. Thus planning for steel during the Third Plan, he says, is concerned not only with obtaining the

[77] Pitambar Pant, "Role of Perspective Planning," paper prepared for the International Conference on Comprehensive Planning, Berlin, Deutsche Stiftung Für Entwicklungsländer, 1962. Papers presented to this conference were published in Albrecht Kruse-Rodenacker, *Grundfragen der Entwicklungsplanung* (Berlin, 1965).

objective of the Third Plan but is concerned "nearly as much with advanced preparation connected with the Fourth and, to the extent necessary, the Fifth Plan." For one thing, the plans for steel require the training of some 5,000 technical persons over the next ten years.

Perspective planning in India is based on a variant of "Pareto's Law." Dr. Pant settles on a particular sector of the curve of income distribution, the relationship between the per capita income of the poorest 20 per cent of households and the aggregate income of all households. The Perspective Planning Division (of which Dr. Pant is chief) collected data on income distribution for a number of countries including Sweden, the United States, the United Kingdom, West Germany, Israel, Italy, The Netherlands, and India. For some countries they have information for different points of time. "These data show," says Dr. Pant, "that if we rank all households in a given country in ascending order of their incomes, the income of the poorest one-tenth is one to two per cent of the total income, and the second tenth three to four per cent, and the third tenth, four to five per cent of total income." Dr. Pant believes that the constancy of these relationships for several countries "quite different from each other in their social, economic and political set-up (for example, West Germany and Israel) and at different stages of development (the United States and Italy) showing such relatively high constancy, is enough support for a tentative hypothesis that if a certain given average of income is to be expected at the lower end of the scale through processes of economic development the total income would have to be raised in a more or less determinant manner."

In other words, if a target level of per capita income for the poorest 20 per cent of the households is set, the required level of gross national income is also set.

Dr. Pant concludes that the lowest 10 per cent of the Indian population cannot earn a satisfactory level of per capita income within the period of a perspective plan. These, he says, represent hard social cases, such as "persons living in isolated areas or comprising special tribal or other groups not closely economically integrated with the rest, or a transient low income group—all cases which need specific individual treatment by way of extension of measures of social security, community welfare, work programs, etc." He therefore concentrates on the second poorest 10 per cent, and establishes a target family income for them of 100 rupees per month, as the lowest level of income consistent with minimum standards of living. This amount would provide for "a modest diet, a reasonable standard of clothing and some small provisions for other items." Attaching a projection of the population to this second decile, he arrives at a figure of the total income of households in this group. Then from his variant of "Pareto's Law" he is able to establish the target level of gross national income that would provide the minimal family incomes for the second decile. This is the basic calculation of the perspective Plan. From there on, the procedure includes the determination of required levels of investment by applying capital-output ratios and sectoral subdivisions of gross national income and assuring the consistency of sectoral relationships, and the like. Five-Year Plans are then fitted into this perspective plan.

Conclusions

We have used the subtitle "Pilgrim's Progress" for this section to under-
line the fact that India has made slow and painful progress against the formidable and frequent obstacles in her path, some expected and some
unforseen. On balance, India's economic development policy must be considered a success. It is true that the rates of increase in per capita income
have not been as spectacular as in some developing countries; but in India,
with its enormous population, scant resources, and totally inadequate levels
of skills at the time of the transfer of sovereignty from Great Britain, any
increase in per capita income at all must be regarded as a success. As may
be seen from Table 30–22, (adapted from Walter C. Neale's book on

TABLE 30–22
National Income of India (at factor cost)

	Annual data			Three-year moving average	
Year	Rs. billions at constant 1948–49 prices	Index number	Year	Rs. billions at constant 1948–49 prices	Index number
1950–51	88.5	100.0			
1951–52	91.0	102.8	1950–53	91.4	100.0
1952–53	94.6	106.9	1951–54	95.3	104.3
1953–54	100.3	113.4	1952–55	99.2	108.6
1954–55	102.8	116.1	1953–56	102.6	112.4
1955–56	104.8	118.5	1954–57	105.9	115.9
1956–57	110.0	124.3	1955–58	107.9	118.2
1957–58	108.9	123.1	1956–59	111.8	122.8
1958–59	116.5	131.7	1957–60	114.7	125.6
1959–60	118.6	134.0	1958–61	120.8	132.2
1960–61	127.3	143.8	1959–62	125.5*	137.3
1961–62	130.6*	147.6	1960–63	130.5*	142.8
1962–63	133.7*	151.1	1961–64	134.6†	147.2
1963–64	139.4†	157.5			

* Preliminary.
† Provisional.
SOURCE: Walter C. Neale, *India: the Search for Unity, Democracy and Progress*
(New York, 1965), p. 82.

India), the record of Indian growth is a good deal better than that. In
1963–64, national income was 57.5 per cent above the 1950–51 level. Dr.
Neale also provides figures in the form of a three-year moving average, in
order to iron out some of the violent fluctuations that have taken place in
the Indian rate of growth. Even in these terms, the increase in income is
impressive enough. Over the decades 1951–61, per capita income rose by
16.5 per cent, or an annual cumulative rate of growth of 1.5 per cent. Perhaps even more important is the success in raising the ratio of investment
to income from 6 per cent in 1951 to 14 per cent in 1966. This achievement
is a harbinger of a more rapid rate of growth of income in the future.

India has also been extraordinarily successful in providing a framework for large-scale foreign aid. While remaining a neutralist country, India has nonetheless provided development plans, programs, and policies of a type which instill confidence in Eastern and Western donors alike. India is the only country that can with confidence write foreign aid of $1 billion per year into its official plans. While not high on a per capita basis, this is far more than any other developing country regularly receives.

31 || Indonesia: The Chronic Drop-out

Indonesia must surely be accounted the number one economic failure among the major underdeveloped countries. No other large and populous country presents the same stark picture of prolonged economic stagnation, persevering throughout centuries of colonial rule and continuing throughout a decade and a half of independence. Stagnation—in the form of virtually constant levels of per capita income or an unchanging structure of employment and production or both—is certainly not unknown among underdeveloped countries; but the Indonesian experience, in which a whole series of concepts of economic organization, first in a colony and then in an independent nation, failed to bring significant or lasting improvements in levels of living at any time, seems to be unique.

In 1966 the basic economic problems in Indonesia were still essentially the same as they were when the author arrived there as monetary and fiscal adviser to the government in 1952, or when the United States Economic Survey Team arrived in 1961—only worse. Per capita income in 1966 was probably below that of 1938. The national accounts, for whatever they are worth, showed a slightly falling per capita income in recent years. Indonesia was stagnant even in comparison with their neighbors (Tables 31–1 and 31–2). Self-sufficiency in basic foodstuffs continues to be a stated objective, but no clear improvement in rice yields has been achieved, and rice output has failed to keep pace with population growth. Per capita rice production was clearly below the 1935–39 average. The same was true of rural food production. Rice imports rose from 707 metric tons in 1958 to 1,200 metric tons in 1964. The consequent pressure on Indonesia's slim foreign exchange reserves limits imports of raw materials and spare parts (let alone

TABLE 31–1

National Income, Net National Product, and Consumption

	National Income (million rupiahs)			
	1938	1951	1952	1955
Net national income:				
At current prices	2,700	63,600	78,800	100,000†
At 1952 prices	81,221	78,000	78,800	96,400
Income per head (rupiahs)				
At 1952 prices	1,230*	1,000	1,005	1,175

Net national product by sources of origin (in per cent)			Consumption of goods and services available in Indonesia (in per cent)		
	1951	1952		1951	1952
Agriculture, fishing, and forestry	55.7	56.5	Private consumption	84.4	79.7
Mining	2.2	2.3	Government current expenditure	10.8	15.3
Industry (including cottage industry)	8.7	8.2	Gross domestic capital formation:		
Transport and communications	2.8	3.0	Private	2.6	3.0
			Government	2.2	2.0
Trade, banking, and insurance	15.2	13.4	Total	100.0	100.0
Government	5.6	6.4			
Other	9.8	10.2			
Total	100.0	100.0			

* Estimate.
† Preliminary minimum estimate.
SOURCE: *Ekonomi dan Keuangan Indonesia.*

new capital goods) and inhibits expansion elsewhere in the economy. Manufacturing still accounts for less than 10 per cent of net national product, and even this small industrial sector operates at excess capacity—in mid-1965 textile mills were operating at 5 to 10 per cent of capacity. Sugar production was still below prewar levels, even in absolute terms, and declining. Rubber production was about at prewar levels but below postwar peaks, and falling. With increasing competition from synthetic rubber and because of prolonged failure to replant with high-yield strains, rubber output seemed doomed to still further decline—and rubber has been Indonesia's major source of foreign exchange for decades. Vegetable-oil output was stagnant. Tin production was below prewar levels, and coal output was hardly one-third of prewar levels. Bauxite production was above the prewar level but well below the 1951 figure. Only petroleum production showed some buoyancy, but even that was below potential.

Meanwhile budget deficits had reached 50 per cent of government expenditures, the money supply grew from 19 billion rupiahs at the end of

TABLE 31–2

Rates of Growth (%) in GNP and Gross Value-Added
by Major Sectors, 1955–1962
(constant prices)

	Philip-pines	Burma	Indo-nesia*	Malay-sia†	Thai-land	India	Korea
I. Gross national product	4.7	3.3	2.1	4.3	7.1	3.5	4.1
II. Major sectors							
A. Primary (agriculture and mining)	1.5	3.6	2.6	3.2	2.4	3.7	1.5
B. Secondary (manufacturing and construction)	9.3	6.0	} 2.0	5.6	6.7	} 3.7	6.3
C. Social overhead (electricity and transportation)	5.5	4.2		7.4	12.7		14.4
D. Services (trade, banking, housing, administration, other services)	5.6	1.9		5.0	5.6		4.4

* 1955–59.
† 1955–1961.

SOURCES: *ECAFE Economic Survey of Asia and the Far East*, 1959 through 1963. *United Nations Yearbook of National Accounts Statistics*, 1961, 1962, and 1963. *International Financial Statistics*, Vol. 17, No. 8 (August, 1964) and Vol. 15, No. 8 (August, 1962). AID *Regional Data Books* for the Near East and South Asia and for the Far East, September, 1964, and previous issues.

1957 to 600 billion rupiahs at the end of 1964, and Indonesia presented one of the worst cases of hyperinflation in the world. The cost of living index for Djakarta, with March, 1957—February, 1958 as 100, reached 3,064 in August, 1964, and 7,595 in April, 1965—and prices had already doubled between 1950 and 1957. In December, 1965, a "new rupiah" was issued at one new to 1,000 old rupiahs—but inflation continued virtually unchecked. The balance of payments worsened accordingly and foreign debts grew to a point where servicing them was impossible without severe hardship—perhaps even starvation—for the Indonesian people. In December, 1965, the Bank of Indonesia found itself unable to pay on letters of credit. By 1966, Indonesia's total foreign debt reached $2.4 billion.

The transport system continued to deteriorate for lack of maintenance. In that island economy, shipping had become a serious bottleneck and crops rotted on the docks. Fewer miles of railroad and asphalted road were in use than before the war. Railroad capacity in East Java was estimated at 15 to 16 per cent of requirements. General disrepair of the road system took a heavy toll on the limited supply of trucks and busses, which could not be repaired for lack of parts. In Surabaja, less than one-fifth of the existing busses were in operation.

Throughout fourteen years of visiting Indonesia at various intervals, the present writer has become used to finding that conditions are less bad than they are portrayed in the foreign press or even than the statistics indicate. But in 1966 he found the situation even worse than expected. In parts of Djakarta, there were signs of genuine distress, reminiscent of Calcutta or Bombay—people with bloated stomachs and deficiency diseases, who live under sacks and pick over garbage in the streets in hopes of finding something edible. Yet the population explosion continues unabated, especially in the Outer Islands, and a shortage of land is appearing even in Sumatra. Indeed Sumatra is clearly heading the way of Java, and not too much time remains to build a modern economy there and prevent serious overpopulation.

"Eat More Mice"

During a discussion of economic conditions, an Indonesian friend of the author quoted Sukarno as having said "The people should eat less rice and eat more mice." It is some measure of the economic deterioration in Indonesia that despite long acquaintance with the country, at first blush it seemed to the writer quite reasonable that Sukarno might have made such a remark in the course of a speech. He had been trying to relieve the pressure on rice supplies by persuading people to change their diets, and while it seemed going a bit far to urge them to eat mice, it also seemed within the range of possibility. It was only some time later that it became clear that this particular Indonesian, whose original education had been partly Dutch, was actually referring to maize and giving it the Dutch pronunciation.

Yet ever since the Portuguese arrived in 1500, Indonesia has been regarded as a country rich in natural resources. Foreign interest in the country has ranged all the way from pepper to petroleum, with sugar, tea, coffee, copra, rubber, tin, and bauxite in between. At every stage of the expansion of Asian trade with Europe and America, Indonesia has been an important exporter of something; one might hope that a country so blessed by nature would afford opportunities for easy and rapid improvements in living standards.

Resources—Natural and Human

Indonesia's land area is about equal to that of the United States east of the Mississippi. In terms of transport problems or unification, stating the size of Indonesia this way is misleading, for Indonesia is comprised of a string of islands stretching from a point opposite the northern tip of Malaya almost to the northern tip of Australia—a distance considerably greater than the width of the United States at any point. The equator is the string on which these islands are strung; it cuts three of the major islands, and the whole country is within 10 degrees of it, north or south. The climate is hot and varies little from one season to another. There is more variation according to altitude, and wealthier members of the community find relief from the monotony of the coastal climate by going into the mountains which form the "spine" of most of the major islands.

The total population is about 105 million. Relative to the area of the country, the population is not so great as in some other Asian countries. The figure of total population, however, is rather meaningless, since over three-fifths of the population are crowded onto the one small island of Java. Java is consequently the most densely populated large area in the world, with nearly 1,400 people per square mile. This extreme population density is made possible by Java's rich volcanic soil and its assured rainfall, which together permit two or three crops a year throughout much of the island.

In the other islands, the soil is for the most part less fertile than in Java, and in some of them the rainfall is less certain, but Indonesia as a whole can be regarded as a fertile land. To this day, Indonesia's soil remains its most important natural resource; it admits not only near self-sufficiency in foodstuffs (of which the most important are rice, cassava, and maize) but also the great plantation industries: rubber, copra, coffee, tea, sisal, tobacco, pepper, teak, and others.

The country also has abundant hydroelectric potential in some areas and a wide variety of mineral resources. Of the latter, petroleum has become most important since the war. Tin and bauxite are also found in significant quantities. There are deposits of gold and silver, iron, coal, manganese, nickel, diamonds, copper, sulfate, lead, and zinc.

It is this wide range of natural resources that evokes the frequent reference to Indonesia as a country "rich in natural wealth." True, the quantity and quality of some of these resources are not impressive in relation to the present size of the population, and the quantity and quality of some others are not thoroughly known. The most promising source of hydroelectric power (the Asahan Valley) is not ideally located in relation to population and sources of raw materials, and other regions, with dense populations and larger supplies of raw materials, are power-poor. A growing share of petroleum output is absorbed by domestic consumption. Nonetheless, compared to other countries with similar levels of per capita income, Indonesia must be considered well off where natural wealth is concerned. "Per capita resources" is a somewhat meaningless concept, as we saw in Chapter 1. So much of the value of "natural" resources is created by human activity that an aggregate ratio of total value of natural resources to population can have only a very limited significance as an explanation of economic development. A more important question is, "Are there sufficiently diverse 'growing points' to permit 'balanced growth,' or sufficiently strong exports to permit 'unbalanced growth,' or both?" The answer to this question is surely "yes;" Indonesia has been blessed among underdeveloped countries in having always had, ever since 1500, at least one strong export to serve as "leading sector" and "focal point of growth." First it was spices, cinchona, and indigo; then it was sugar; later it was tea and coffee; later still it was tobacco, copra, sisal, and palm oil; then came rubber; and finally tin, bauxite, and petroleum. Nor did new strong exports always replace the earlier ones. In many cases the new exports were simply added on to the existing export base. Indonesia's economic history is not one of repeated "boom-and bust," like Brazil's. The export sector as a whole expanded almost without interruption, and sometimes in spectacular fashion, for four centuries. Between the two World Wars, exports constituted about one-quarter of the gross national product. After 1850 there was also a substantial inflow of foreign capital. Yet, for Indonesia, foreign trade was a feeble "engine of growth" indeed; its expansion never raised Indonesian standards of living much, if at all, above the levels already established in 1500.

A sixteenth-century observer with foresight as to future resource discoveries and technological change—and nothing else—would surely have predicted a brighter future for her than for any of her neighbors. Indonesia is not one of those countries in which there is little with which to work. Up to 1850, at least, the resource-population ratio was higher than in most countries now classified as underdeveloped. At the beginning of the nineteenth century, Indonesia's population was little bigger than Thailand's or the Philippines', and her area was very much greater. Consisting as it does of thousands of islands, with most productive activity taking place near the coasts and with numerous harbors, Indonesia also had a ready-made source of cheap transport. Moreover, its people have proven resourceful and quick to learn. Yet the ceiling of $100 annual per capita income has never been broken.

Certainly Indonesian stagnation cannot be explained in terms of the limited size of the domestic market. By 1900 Indonesia already had a population of 50 million, with about 40 million on the one relatively small island of Java and thus easily accessible from the major ports of Djakarta and Surabaja. In 1966, with a population over 100 million—still concentrated very largely on Java—Indonesia is presumably the fifth biggest country in the world in terms of population.[1] In essence, the Indonesian tragedy is a story of a repeated nipping off of a budding entrepreneurial upsurge by a political elite essentially hostile to it.

Stagnation under Colonialism

Had it not been for the delaying action of three and one-half centuries of colonial rule, an Indonesian "take-off" might have occurred long ago. When the Portuguese arrived in Indonesia at the end of the fifteenth century, they showed no marked superiority to the Indonesians in technology, labor and managerial skills, or entrepreneurial activities. Indonesians were heavily engaged in the expanding international trade of the fifteenth and sixteenth centuries. The Javanese were also "shipbuilders, seafarers, and colonizers . . . dominating the trade of the whole Archipelago, and even of the Malay peninsula and the Philippines."[2] They founded their own cannon, and were well supplied with builders, plaster workers, smiths, and carpenters. There was "a complex and elaborate centralized administrative organization" to regulate trade, and "the people as

[1] "Presumably" because intercensal estimates for Indonesia are not wholly reliable and Indonesia is hard-pressed by Japan and Pakistan in terms of total population.
[2] J. S. Furnivall, *Netherlands India: A Study of Plural Society*, (Cambridge, 1939), pp. 9–10.

a whole led a fuller life and had a larger range of activities than at any time before or since." [3] Both Asian shipping and Asian navigation techniques compared favorably with those of the Portuguese. Nor can it be demonstrated that in 1500 the standard of living of either rich or poor was significantly higher in Europe than in Indonesia. Peasants and unskilled workers lived near the subsistence level in both places. But princes, merchants, and merchant princes in Indonesia were all engaged in domestic and international economic activities, and many lived in considerable luxury.[4] There is even some evidence that Javanese literacy was higher in 1600 than in 1900.[5]

Even from a military point of view, the Portuguese superiority was never clear-cut. They were uneasy in their trading posts, and never had much more than a toehold in Indonesia. The Portuguese never really conquered the strongest sultans of Java and Sumatra, and the Atjehnese were even strong enough to make attacks on the Portuguese fortresses, turning the Portuguese into harried defenders of their own position. Indeed, it is interesting to speculate what the fate of Indonesia might have been if the Portuguese had arrived a century earlier (or the Dutch two centuries earlier) than they did. For the Europeans would then have encountered, not a disintegrated nation ruled by a host of petty sultans, but a powerful and Madjapahit empire. The "response" to the "challenge" provided by the arrival of the Europeans might then have been similar to the Japanese response to the European challenge some 350 years later; a cementing of the hold of the Madjapahit empire, as leaders in all parts of the country sought unity against the foreign aggressor, and a deliberate effort on the part of an elite-turned-entrepreneur to develop the country economically and to make it strong from a military viewpoint as well.

Having little to offer in the way of technical, managerial, or administrative skills, and having only a toehold in the remoter islands, the Portuguese did nothing to develop Indonesia. By the same token, however, they did little directly to retard Indonesian development. The Portuguese may have had an indirect influence that was unfavorable. They acted as a buffer rather than a link between Indonesia and the more rapidly progressing parts of the world. In Europe at that time the transition from feudalism to commercial capitalism was well advanced, the agricultural revolution was on its way, even the beginnings of the factory system could be observed. Had Asia carried its trade to Europe rather than the other way around, some of this process of establishing "preconditions for take-off" might have been transferred to Asia as well. As it was, whereas the fifteenth century was one of relative stagnation in Europe and Asia alike, the sixteenth century brought the first stirrings of the subsequent industrial revolution to Europe, while Asia continued to stagnate, as far as technology and productivity were concerned.

[3] J. C. van Leur, *Indonesian Trade and Society: Essays in Asian Social and Economic History* (The Hague: W. van Hoeve Limited, 1955), p. 117.
[4] Cf. van Leur, *op. cit.*, p. 138.
[5] Cf. B. Schrieke, *Indonesian Sociological Studies* (The Hague: W. van Hoeve Limited, 1955), Vol. I, p. 34.

Prince versus Peddler: Mataram versus the N.E.I. Company

The Netherlands East Indies Company did not want much in the way of land or political power in the Indies—all they wanted was profitable trade —but what they felt necessary for their trading operations they took readily enough. There were exceptions: the effort to establish a stronghold in Atjeh was no more successful than the earlier Portuguese attempt had been. Indeed, the Atjehnese were able in 1599 to attack Cornelius de Hout-man on his own ship, killing him and capturing his brother. It was not until 270 years later that the Dutch made another serious bid for control of North Sumatra.

By and large, however, the neglect of the Outer Islands throughout the period 1600–1870 reflected the fact that the Dutch were busy enough in Java and the Moluccas, rather than that the sultans of the more remote districts (daerahs) were militarily superior. The military and technical superiority of the Dutch was certainly not so great in 1600 as it was in 1800, but it served the immediate purposes of the Netherlands East Indies Company well enough. It made formal treaties with the sultans wherever convenient, but behind the formality was always the threat of force, and often actual violence. In effect, the sultans were converted into servants of the N.E.I. Company. In most cases, the "regent" of a district was the hereditary ruler, even when his cooperation had to be obtained by force.

The empire of Mataram in Central Java was the chief threat to Dutch control over Javanese trade. In a vague sort of way, Mataram inherited the glories of Madjapahit. It is possible that in the absence of Dutch power Mataram would have grown to the size of the former Madjapahit. More-over, the sultans of that day showed no reluctance to "sully their hands in trade."

One way for a "take-off" into sustained economic growth to occur is for the political elite themselves to become ardent entrepreneurs. The Susu-hunan of Mataram never commanded the military power to give reality to his ambitions, although it was not until 1755, when Mataram was split into three smaller and weaker kingdoms, that Dutch control over Central Java was fully established. It might have taken even longer had not the coastal sultans themselves risen against the oppression of Susuhunan Mangkurat I, forcing him to seek Dutch protection in 1677 in exchange for territorial concessions. Mataram was never a serious threat after that; it survived seventy-five years more under Dutch sufferance. Meanwhile, Dutch power in *other* parts of the archipelago was gradually extended.

Impact of the N.E.I. Company

The failure of Mataram to withstand the steady encroachment on its power by the Netherlands East Indies Company really meant the end—for all time—of the bid for ascendancy in Indonesia from the Javanese aristoc-racy. Thus the Javanese aristocracy, who were in themselves both power-elite and entrepreneurs before the Europeans came, and who tolerated and even encouraged trading and productive enterprises by merchants and farmers lower in the social scale, were undermined both as political leaders and as entrepreneurs by the rival traders, the Netherlands East Indies Company.

The system of forced deliveries led inevitably to control of production; expansion of output was encouraged or curtailed according to market conditions. Thus decision-making was transferred even from farmers to the N.E.I. Company, helping to snuff out whatever entrepreneurial abilities may have been still flickering in the Javanese classes below the sultans and regents.

The British Interregnum

During the Napoleonic Wars, when France occupied Holland, the British attacked "France" by seizing Java. For five years Java was under the administration of Sir Stamford Raffles, the brilliant British colonial administrator who later established Singapore as the major port in Southeast Asia. Raffles' effort to replace the system of forced deliveries by a system of land taxes (or rents) and to replace indirect rule through the feudal aristocracy by a more modern colonial administration has been the subject of a good deal of controversy. In any case, the experiment was so short-lived that the impact on Javanese development is difficult to assess.

Raffles' reforms might have generated a take-off had they been pushed for fifty years instead of five. Feudalism might have broken down, and both princes and peasants driven into the world market. The latent entrepreneurial and labor skills, which were to be disclosed and then repressed by the Dutch, might have found scope for development. We shall never know.

More interesting than Raffles' brief experiment in Java is his extension of the system of forced deliveries in Sumatra. The English administration lasted a good deal longer in Sumatra than in Java (until 1824, when the British holdings in the area around Benkulen were exchanged for Singapore). The impact of British administration was accordingly greater there. Since the system pursued by Raffles in South Sumatra was not very different from the culture system later introduced into Java by the Dutch, its effect on labor and enterprise was much the same.

In one respect, the British administration in South Sumatra was even more oppressive of domestic enterprise than the culture system in Java: enforcement of the Company's policy was turned over, not to the local chiefs nor even to Europeans, but to imported Buginese officers.

This system of forced civilization and indirect rule, enforced through the Buginese, was introduced *only* in South Sumatra. The Dutch became interested in Sumatra only after the culture system was already dying out. Thus Raffles did for enterprise and skills in South Sumatra what Van den Bosch did for Java. It is no accident that this area of Sumatra is the only one which has not produced political and economic leaders proportionate to its population, and which is distinctly lacking in local enterprise and skills. The Menangkabau farther to the north are famous as exporters of both political leaders and entrepreneurs. The same is true of the Bataks in the Lake Toba region. The people of the Benkulen region (lampongs) have no such reputation. Differences in resource patterns may have something to do with this striking contrast, but the difference between South Sumatra and the Menangkabau area in this respect is not great enough to provide the whole explanation of it. The explanation must be sought mainly in socio-cultural history; and when speaking in these terms, the demoralization of the local aristocracy, the crushing of individual initiative, the elimination of free choice of occupation and land use, the conversion of peasants into coolies, and the consequent destruction of labor incentives and enterprise under the British administration form a large element of any such explanation.

The Culture System

In 1830 Van den Bosch became Governor of the Indies, and in the course of his first year in office, the Dutch king sent him a secret instruction setting a target for exports of five guilders per capita. This instruction was the immediate incentive for Van den Bosch's culture system. Its main feature was the replacement of the Raffles' land-rent system with the old system of forced deliveries, still operative in the Preanger and apparently more productive than the land-rent system. Indeed, Van den Bosch defended the system as a return to traditions which Raffles had ruthlessly violated. The reservation of one-fifth of their land for their sovereign—or compulsory labor for one-fifth of the year in the case of the landless—was traditional, he maintained. Henceforth any village reserving one-fifth of its land for cultivation of designated export crops would be exempt from land rent. The produce might be bought at a low fixed price, or simply taken as a kind of tax; it was then shipped to Holland by the Netherlands Trading Company (NHM) where it was sold for handsome profits. With the culture system, the cultivator's freedom to choose the use of the land devoted to the "sovereign" was abolished altogether.

There is evidence that in practice the share of the land taken over for forced cultivation exceeded one-fifth of the total, and that the share of value product taken was even larger, in the areas where the system operated.

The culture system carried one step further the process of converting the Javanese aristocracy into low-grade N.E.I. civil servants. The use of the existing feudal structure to force increased production on an unwilling people reflected no Dutch respect for the aristocracy, but rather the lack of it, and a willingness to utilize the feudal system, not because it was admired, but because it was convenient and profitable. Moreover, there is no evidence that the individual Dutchmen who were responsible for administering the culture system were a great improvement over those who served the Netherlands East Indies Company. For the most part, the Javanese aristocrats must have considered their masters inferior to themselves in everything but brute force; and being compelled to serve people for whom you have no admiration can be demoralizing indeed.

The Liberal System

After 1850 the culture system gradually gave way to private enterprise, and particularly to large-scale corporate enterprise. The simple fact that

The Netherlands economy was expanding under private enterprise while the Indonesian economy was stagnant under the culture system had much to do with the demand for change in the Indies. Private interests saw opportunities for profits in the Indies and became increasingly resentful of governmental barriers to earning them. This late nineteenth-century pattern of organization is usually referred to as the "liberal" system; but it was liberal only in the nineteenth-century sense of being anti-governmental. It was monopolistic from start to finish—and highly monopsonistic in the Indonesian market. It left less freedom of choice of occupation to Indonesians than ever, and excluded them from the decision-making process even more completely than the culture system had done.

Sugar was one of the first industries to make the change. Even in 1830 the necessary investment for efficient operation of a sugar plantation and mill was larger than could easily be provided on an indivdual enterprise basis. Until 1870, sugar was still produced under government contract; in that year there were 100 factories, mostly in European hands, the rest still Chinese. From 1870 on, the government gradually disappeared from the marketing as well as from the production of sugar. Coffee too shifted over to large-scale plantation enterprise. Tobacco planting in Java began in 1859. Mr. Birnie's pioneering effort grew to an enterprise, with a European staff of 60 and 500 Indonesian *mandurs* (foremen) supervising 35,000 peasants. The really big tobacco plantations, however, were established later in Deli in North Sumatra. The export of rubber, which was to become the most important plantation product, did not really start until the first decade of the present century. The major rubber enterprises were established on Sumatra. Tin mining is as old as Indonesian history, but it became a major enterprise only with the Billiton discoveries in 1851. The big expansion of tin production came in the late decades of the nineteenth century and the early decades of the twentieth. Petroleum production began in the 1890's, but the rapid growth of the oil industry is also an affair of the present century. Bauxite production became important only in the 1930's.

All these enterprises had three common features: they had access to the capital markets of Europe and America; they were land-hungry and labor-hungry; and they had no room for Indonesian enterprise and little room for Indonesian skills. Their relations with the local population were directed mainly toward obtaining the use of the necessary land and assuring a large and continuously available supply of unskilled labor. Their impact on Indonesian society differed from that of the culture system much less than the opponents of the culture system had imagined. Indeed, the main effect of the transition to the "liberal" system was to spread and intensify the disintegration of Indonesian society started by the culture system.

The "demonstration effect" that introduction of Western enterprise might have had was deliberately destroyed by Dutch policy. The most flagrant of the measures to destroy Javanese enterprise in sugar came later, with the law of 1920 forbidding the purchase of native-grown sugar by the mills.[6] Since the Javanese entrepreneurs lacked capital to install modern

---

[6] Cf. *Encyclopedie Van Nederlands Indie*, Vol. 6, p. 885.

refineries of their own, this law meant that the market for native-grown sugar was confined to small, crude mills refining brown sugar for the home market.

In a sense, the trouble with the modern industrial undertakings (including plantations) was that they were always on too small a scale to have a decisive impact on the Indonesian way of life. They never succeeded in absorbing a significant proportion of the labor force—let alone reducing the relative importance of the traditional peasant agricultural sector. The population explosion launched by the culture system was given new impetus by the growth of corporate enterprise. All the factors operating under the culture system were reinforced by the "liberal" era. Corporate enterprise required still more Dutch settlement than the culture system had done. Efforts to improve public health became more systematic and widespread, and law and order became even more imperative. The transport system was enlarged and improved, and after 1900 was built up in the Outer Islands as well as in Java.

Because of the high rate of population growth and the capital-intensive nature of the modern enterprises, the number of jobs provided in the modern sector was never more than a fraction of the total increase in the labor force. The total amount of new capital investment in the modern sector was in any case not very large up to 1900, when petroleum, mining, and rubber became really significant. At no time did more than 7 per cent of the labor force find employment in the modern sector.

Even rice production failed to expand as fast as population, as the good land gave out and virtually all of it suitable for *sawah* (irrigated rice culture) was converted to that form of cultivation. The rents paid to Indonesian landowners by plantations in 1900 were lower—even in florins, let alone in purchasing power—than the government had paid under the culture system. Apparently wages were lower too.

The Doctrine of the "Little Push": the "Ethical System"

By the end of the nineteenth century the liberals had become Liberals, well entrenched as the leading political party, responsible for policy in the Netherlands East Indies and so the butt of criticism of that policy. By 1900 there was plenty of such criticism. In the Indies themselves concern over the plight of the Indonesians seems to have been mingled with the "drain theory" and the concept of a "debt of honor"—the idea that Holland should restore to Indonesia the capital drained off through profits transfers under the culture system. It was also linked with a desire of Dutchmen in the Indies for greater local autonomy. Such, at least, was the tenor of the articles and editorials in the Semerang newspaper, *De Locomotief*.[7]

The result of this outcry against "Liberalism" was increased emphasis on technical assistance in the administration of the Indies. During the period from 1900 to 1930, when the "ethical policy" was pursued, the

---

[7] Cf. Robert van Niel, *The Emergence of the Modern Indonesian Elite* (The Hague, 1960), p. 8.

Dutch had a scientific—even scholarly—approach to their colonial policy. N.E.I. civil servants arrived in Indonesia with a special degree in oriental studies, speaking the Indonesian language, and well versed in Indonesian history and culture. Many of these civil servants were genuinely devoted to the cause of raising Indonesian living standards, as well as being highly trained. One of these was J. H. Boeke, whose name is so inseparably linked with the theory of cultural dualism.[8]

This very dualism, however, was the undoing of the ethical system. There is no doubt that the Indonesian economy was a highly dualistic one at the time the ethical policy was launched. Much Dutch social theory, however, explained this dualism in sociological terms and regarded it as immutable, rather than recognizing it as the *result* of Dutch policy during the preceding three centuries.

Since many Dutch officials regarded Indonesia as incapable of development along western lines—and in the case of Boeke, felt that any such efforts would serve to hasten the disintegration of traditional society without replacing it with any other unified social system—their concept of an economic development program was limited in the extreme. The *perintah halus*—gentle pressure—was, indeed, the very opposite to the "big push" in either economic or social terms. It was limited to a bit of agricultural extension work, a bit of rural credit, an unsuccessful attempt to relieve population pressure on Java by moving people to empty Sumatra, and a very little bit of education. There were, however, modest efforts to educate the aristocracy. The Chiefs Schools were reorganized in 1900 to bring them closer to the pattern of the European secondary schools, and were renamed Schools for Training Native Administrators. To make it easier for boys in aristocratic families to obtain European educations, the European Primary Schools were opened to select Indonesians. Van Niel reports that in the early twentieth century, nonetheless, "the presence of an Indonesian at a European secondary school was rare."[9] A few scions of noble families found their way to the Netherlands for higher education. The School for Training Native Doctors was established in 1902. In 1907 there were only 135,555 Indonesian pupils in Java, and 132,385 in the outer islands.[10] Even in 1930, there were only 1,656,244 Indonesians in the lower grades of the elementary schools, a mere 15,716 in vocational schools, and only 178 Indonesians in universities.[11]

Meanwhile, of course, the population growth proceeded unchecked. Public health measures seemed to be more successful than any others, successful, that is, in reducing death rates. Whether or not the result was an improvement in Indonesian welfare is doubtful at best. Even Boeke asked, "How is the economic situation improved if the chance is created for two natives to lead a miserable existence whereas there was earlier only a chance for one"?[12] Since the development efforts under the ethical

[8] See Chapter 14, below.
[9] R. van Niel, *op. cit.*, p. 47.
[10] Furnival, *op. cit.*, p. 316.
[11] *Ibid.*, p. 377.
[12] Boeke, *Staathuishondkunde*, pp. 137–138.

policy were so modest in scale, they did little to raise productivity in the traditional sector. The net result was that per capita income remained more or less unchanged, and may even have fallen. At any rate, the impression was widespread among the Dutch officials themselves that at least the Javanese standard of living was falling. Already in 1901, Queen Wilhelmina announced in her speech from the throne the government's intention to inquire into the *minderewelvaart* (declining welfare) of the Javanese people.

It was at this time that Idenburg, also an N.E.I. engineer, was appointed colonial minister; and in 1902 he in turn appointed three experts, including Van de Venter, to look into economic conditions in Java. This was the first of a series of Royal Commissions to investigate living standards in Indonesia. In the years immediately following World War I, inflation led again to a clear-cut decline in real wages, and in 1930 a Labor Commission "for the determination of legal minimum wages for employees in Java and Madura" was appointed to investigate the situation. The Commission noted "general underpayment" of coolies, and unanimously advocated a minimum wage-rate. No steps were taken to implement this recommendation. It is interesting to note that the Commission recommended a minimum wage based on minimal biological requirements, and suggested prison rations as a standard. This proposal drew attacks even from so liberal a critic as Meijer Ranneft, who pointed out that if the whole of the Javanese population were to be fed prison rations, about forty percent of the island's rice requirements would then have to be imported. It was this sort of experience which led Boeke to cry out in despair,[13]

. . . but the only popular response to all these nostrums is an increase in numbers, while foreign capitalists and foreign energy take out of native hands a rapidly increasing share of native activity.

In 1939, still another Royal Commission was appointed, the so-called Coolie Budget Commission, to look into "living conditions of plantation workers and peasants on Java." In general, the situation at that time was that money wage-rates had fallen at least as much as prices during the downswing of the Great Depression, but had failed to follow prices back up again. This careful study indicated that virtually all classes of Indonesian workers and peasants were inadequately nourished, and that peasant families were somewhat better off than workers and plantation workers living off the plantation, and about the same as factory workers living off the plantation.[14]

[13] J. S. Boeke, "Het Zakerijke en Het Persoonlijke Element in de Koloniale Welvaartspolitiek," *Koloniale Studien*, April 1927.
[14] A somewhat later study made for the Center for International Studies, MIT, by G. Tergast ("Improving the Economic Foundations of Peasant Agriculture on Java and Madeira," unpublished manuscript quoted in Geertz, *The Social Context of Economic Change*, pp. 44–45) shows that between 1900 and 1940 rice production on Java failed to keep pace with the increase in population. Nutritional standards were maintained by increasing the cultivation of other foodstuffs in rotation with rice, and on

Perhaps even more important, the "ethical system," with its bevies of enthusiastic do-gooders in the civil service, completed the process of demoralizing the Javanese aristocracy. For under the ethical policy, Dutch officials felt it to be part of their job to protect the Indonesians from their own chiefs. The French geographer Bousquet describes the situation as follows:[15]

At this time they (the officials) resigned themselves to relinquishing their position as agricultural supervisors but not as officials. Since their original usefulness had disappeared, they cast about for some new means of making themselves useful. Now there began to take shape the protective system for the Javanese, those meek people who nowadays are called the little folk (de kleine man). I do not wish to be misunderstood. This noble attitude which does so much honor to the Dutch was not born of self-interest or even of hypocrisy, but it produced a very natural change of feeling. . . . This new departure had surprising results. The Dutch fell passionately in love with their work and allowed their enthusiasm to lead them farther than they had foreseen. . . . They superseded native chiefs, whom they distrusted, and natives, whom they considered inept. They transferred the entire load to their shoulders: public affairs, private matters—all was grist to their mill.

Bousquet also quotes Shouck Hurgronje:[16]

"One of my friends, an Assistant Resident, stationed on an outlying island, was temporarily transferred to Java. After he had been in Java for some time, I asked him for his impressions. 'I rather felt,' he said, 'that we are going too far in trying to regulate everything, but I never dreamed that there could be an administrative tyranny such as I have found here. All that is now lacking is an order instructing the natives at what hour they must do their daily duty.' "

He also cites Meijer Ranneft, who had expressed concern about the implications of the Report of the 1930 Commission, as also expressing concern about the "illegal" nature of the policy of "gentle compulsion" under the ethical system. The difficulty was, according to Ranneft, that orders were given to native chiefs, who in turn were required to execute these commands. The commands were given orally, and thus the person affected was unable to test their legality:[17]

The situation thus created, which is maintained with or without popular consent, is dependent upon the enforcement of a system of constraint through fear of punishment. In other words, the native knows that he must do something distasteful, or, contrariwise must refrain from doing something pleasant, be-

---

dry land. In 1900, the per capita foodstuff production was about 110 kilograms of rice, 20 kilograms of tubers, and 3 kilograms of pulses. By 1940 this had become 85 kilograms of rice, 40 kilograms of maize, 180 kilograms of tubers, and about 10 kilograms of pulses. According to Tergast, the caloric contents of these two product-mixes was about the same, leaving per capita consumption below 2,000 calories for both dates.

[15] G. H. Bousquet, A French View of the Netherlands Indies (London and New York, 1940), p. 51.
[16] Ibid., p. 52.
[17] Ibid., pp. 54–55.

cause if he does otherwise he is threatened with something even worse. When compulsion is illegal, it can be enforced only by the means of illegal punishments, and these are far more common than might be supposed.

Thus Dutch colonial policy failed to bring economic development to Indonesia even when, at long last, it aimed to do so. The developmental effort under the ethical system was too little and too late to be effective in raising levels of living of the Indonesian people.

Impact of the Great Depression

The Great Depression of the 1930's had a mixed effect on Indonesian development. On the one hand, there is some evidence that if the sugar boom had lasted longer it would eventually have had a Westernizing effect on Javanese society despite the efforts of the Dutch to prevent it. In any case the dramatic collapse of the export market for sugar destroyed any possibility that sugar would become a "leading sector" for a generalized take-off into sustained economic growth for Indonesia. On the other hand, the very speed and extent of the destruction of Dutch manufacturing and trading enterprises seem to have opened opportunities for venturesome Indonesians to enter the market—and once again Indonesians responded to these opportunities. A third effect of the Great Depression was a shift from a relatively free to a highly regulated economy. This influence was to be a lasting one; for it was the regulated and not the free economy that the Indonesians inherited from the Dutch, and the tendency of governments of independent Indonesia has been to add new regulations without removing the old ones.

Stagnation after Independence

The Japanese occupied Indonesia in 1940. In August, 1945, as the Japanese were withdrawing, Sukarno issued the Declaration of Independence. After five years of intermittent fighting, Holland transferred sovereignty to the new republic in December, 1949.

Enterprise and Economic Policy, 1945–1950

The confusion of economic policy with social philosophy came very early in the republican regime. At the Jogjakarta Economic Conference in 1946, Vice-President Hatta in his keynote address spoke of the abandonment of principles of individualism in favor of those of *tolong-menolong* (mutual aid) and of applying the principle of cooperation from the village outward. Land ownership, he declared, should be under government control, although he was opposed to outright confiscation of alien property. At this economic conference, no one represented the Indonesian businessman.[18]

The first years of the republic saw a new upsurge of Indonesian enterprise (salt fish, rubber, glassware, bottles, among others) and 1947 brought

[18] John O. Sutter, *Indonesias: Politics in a Changing Economy*, (Ithaca, 1959), p. 393.

some thaw toward private enterprise. At the Jogjakarta Economic Conference, Hatta had seen no role for the private entrepreneur above the level
of *tukang* (craftsman) in the future Indonesian society. By 1947, however,
"private enterprise was an accepted institution in the economic order envisaged in government policy."[19] That year saw the entry of Indonesians
into foreign trade on a large scale, and the Ten-Year Plan of 1947 envisaged a substantial role for both foreign and domestic private enterprise.

At the time of the transfer of sovereignty, anti-capitalistic views prevailed. Already there was general support for some kind of "guided economy." At that time, too, the sharp division between those who thought that
the government should completely dominate business (at least whatever
business was not organized on a cooperative basis) and those who felt that
government policy should encourage the growth of national capitalism
(Indonesian enterprises) appeared. But even those who favored the encouragement of some Indonesian enterprise condemned "capitalism" as a
system. Capitalism as a form of economic organization which could be
directed toward the general welfare, according to the prevailing attitudes
in the United Kingdom, the United States, Canada, and Australia, was an
image that simply did not appear to Indonesian leaders. "Exploitation of
man by man," "seeking the greatest possible profit," and "free fight" were
the sort of terms used to typify the capitalist system. Moreover, the concept of "liberalism" was scarcely differentiated from this kind of capitalism, and was mainly identified with a nineteenth-century "freedom to
exploit." The outlook for Indonesian entrepreneurs was therefore none too
good even at the time of the transfer of sovereignty; but it was to get better before it got worse. It might have become quite favorable had not the
attempt to remove squatters from plantation lands led to the fall of the
Wilopo Cabinet in 1953—an event that Herbert Feith rightly regards as a
turning point in Indonesian economic history.[20] The Wilopo Administration, whatever else one may think of it, had a certain shape with regard to
economic policy, especially after the "Treasury-Bank accord" of 1952,
which paved the way to close collaboration between Central Bank Governor Sjafruddin and Finance Minister Sumitro, a collaboration which produced the most effective economic policy in the whole history of the
Indonesian republic. Sjafruddin and Sumitro had a vision of a growing
economy in which the relative role of public enterprise would increase
by vigorous expansion of the public sector, not by hampering the growth
of the private sector.

Economic Policy, 1950–1960

Since Independence, all governments and all parties have expressed themselves in favor of "converting the colonial economy into a national economy," but the concept of a "national economy" differed from party to
party and from leader to leader. All parties pay lip service to the national

[19] *Ibid.*, p. 433.
[20] Herbert Feith, *The Wilopo Cabinet, 1952–53, A Turning Point in Post-Revolutionary Indonesia* (Ithaca, 1958).

goal of "organizing the economy along cooperative lines" which was written into the Provisional Constitution; but this goal also lacked clear definition. For some leaders it meant an extension to national economic policy of the principles of rice-roots village democracy—*gotong rojong, kerdja sama, ramah tamah*, and *musjawarat desa*;[21] but what this would mean in terms of specific development projects, or monetary, fiscal, and foreign exchange policies was never spelled out. For other leaders, the "cooperative society" was defined in the 1930's—European-fashion—as the "middle way" between Communism and unbridled monopoly-capitalism. For them the extension of the cooperative way to the national economy meant quite simply organizing more and bigger cooperatives—credit cooperatives, producers' cooperatives, marketing cooperatives. They seemed to take it for granted that the European cooperative and Indonesian village communalism were the same thing in spirit. The idea that a cooperative can be as ruthlessly exploitive in intent as a corporation, if not more so, seems to have occurred to few Indonesian leaders.[22]

Thus, while there was no agreement on concrete social goals there was agreement that Indonesia was not to be developed on "capitalist" lines. Rugged individualism, free competition, and private enterprise had few enthusiastic backers. They were associated in the minds of most Indonesians with imperialism, colonialism, materialism, and a ruthlessly exploitive, ferociously competitive, "devil-take-the-hindmost" approach to social organization. Indonesians did not want such "capitalism," but were divided as to what they *did* want. Similarly, while everyone agreed that the political system was to be "democratic," they also agreed that it was not to be democratic in the ordinary "Western" sense. No one but the Communists wanted a "People's Democracy." It was to be an "Indonesian" democracy, reflecting the spirit of *gotong rojong* and *musjawarat desa*, and rejecting—as Sukarno put it—"the principle that 50 per cent plus one is right." There was, however, no agreement as to what "Indonesian" democracy would be. Meanwhile, it was felt that "as the twig is bent so is the tree inclined." No new institutions should be set up that might prejudice the final outcome.

The paralysis resulting from this disunity and political instability, and disappointment over the consequent failure of Independence to bring prosperity, aggravated the growing discontent in the Outer Islands. The conflict between the Outer Islands and Djakarta culminated in February, 1958, with the declaration of a revolutionary government (P.R.R.I.) with headquarters in South Sumatra. The rebel leaders wanted Indonesia to develop on non-Communist lines, with increased regional and local autonomy. They proposed a return to a federal constitution. They also urged building on the "growing points and leading sectors" in the Outer Islands in order to launch an effective economic development program and eliminating from the central government corruption, incompetence,

---

[21] Roughly, mutual assistance, working together, a family-like society, and search for unanimity.

[22] For a further discussion of this point, see Benjamin Higgins, "Hatta and Co-operatives: The Middle Way for Indonesia?" *The Annals*, July, 1958.

and abuse of party politics. The rebellion was quickly crushed. Success in quelling the rebels' main force further enhanced the army's growing prestige and the political influence of Chief-of-Staff Nasution and others in the army command. The army had a civilian organization throughout much of the country, and the diumvirate "Sukarno-Nasution" had replaced the old diumvirate "Sukarno-Hatta" in shaping the course of political events.

Return to the 1945 Constitution

In July, 1959, with continued unrest in the country, and deadlock in both the Parliament and the Constituent Assembly, President Sukarno decreed a return to the 1945 Constitution. Sukarno thus became the chief executive, at once President and Prime Minister. Like the American President, he could not be removed from office by failure to obtain support in the legislature, the Chamber of Representatives. The Chamber was half appointed, half elected from an approved slate; in any case, it could largely be bypassed under the regulations governing the then prevailing state of war and siege regulations. The People's Consultative Assembly had only one mandatory task: to meet once in five years and choose a new President. The President was advised by a National Planning Council of seventy-six men, and a Supreme Advisory Council of forty-four, both appointed by himself to represent "functional groups" (armed forces, labor, peasants, youth, women, religious groups, etc.) and the regions. There was a small Inner Cabinet of eleven men, headed by former Prime Minister Djuanda as First Minister and Minister of Finance. Each department had one or more junior ministers. The Cabinet as a whole was expected to be an executive rather than a policy-making body. Indeed, a Presidential decree of August 26, 1959, converting the ministries into departments, stated that the ministers were not in full charge of their departments but would be "assisted" by saffs "comprising civil and military personnel."

While Sukarno was the strongest single person in the new government, there was a species of system of checks and balances. There were two main forces: Sukarno, with his extreme nationalist and Communist support; and the army, with its direct representation in the Cabinet, in the two Councils, the Chamber, and the People's Assembly, and with its elaborate grass-roots organization (army-youth corps, army-women corps, army-peasant corps, army-worker corps, etc.), its "observers" in strategic offices of the civil service, and its hold on administration of plantations and other former Dutch enterprises. The "regions," while rather nebulous in organization, constituted a third force. They were represented directly in the two Councils and in the Assembly and were still represented to some degree through the Masjumi (Moslem) and PSI (Socialist) parties, although these parties no longer had any direct influence on the government since they had officially been dissolved. Finally, there were moderate nationalists in the Cabinet, with some popular support but no organization.

Constitutional reform in the direction of "democracy with leadership" was probably necessary to give Indonesia a stable, non-Communist govern-

ment. At that stage ordinary parliamentary democracy could only mean
rule by Java, since Java has two-thirds of the electorate. The only way in
which Java could have provided the required coalescence of entrepreneur
and elite would have been through further growth of the Communist
Party and the establishment of a Communist regime.

The Plans

Indonesia's First Five-Year Plan covered the years 1956–60. It was a very
modest plan, largely a projection of what the ministries were already
doing. But even this plan was not fulfilled. In connection with the August
17th celebrations in 1959—the first under the new system of "guided
democracy"—the National Planning Bureau issued a report on progress
under the Plan. It would be more accurate to say that the Bureau made a
"lack-of-progress" report; in most fields performance fell far short of the
modest targets laid down in the Plan. The Bureau explained the shortfall in
terms of the conflict with The Netherlands in 1957, the rebellion in 1958,
continuing budget deficits and consequent increases in prices, and shortages
of foreign exchange.[23]

In mid-1959, only forty-two of the ninety-two pilot industrial projects
were completed; thirty were not even started. By the end of 1958, only
five of the projected sixty-one new central power plants had been completed. The large Djatiluhur power project was still in the second of the
projected three stages; the still larger Asahan project in North Sumatra
had not been started at all. The proposed iron and steel plant was still
under discussion. The total mileage of roads was essentially unchanged,
although the number of vehicles using them quadrupled between 1950 and
1957. Nor was there clear evidence that the over-all condition of the roads
had improved during the Plan period; some roads were better, others were
worse. Repair and extension of railways were delayed by the rebellion and
general insecurity; total mileage was unchanged, maintenance fell off. On
balance, it seems likely that the railroads deteriorated between 1955 and
1959. Total rolling stock remained more or less unchanged, although the
number of passenger carriages declined. The number of passengers carried
increased slightly, but the total freight carried dropped about 15 per cent.
A good deal of work was completed on harbors, but coastal shipping was
clearly less adequate in 1959 than in 1955; the Bureau reported that by the
end of 1958 40 to 50 per cent of the shortages resulting from withdrawal
of the Dutch (KPM) ships had been replaced. Both tonnage and passengers
through Indonesian harbors declined. Some new aircraft were purchased,
but in 1958 Garuda Indonesian Airways carried fewer passengers and less
freight than in 1955.

Even in agriculture the picture was mixed, with no clear evidence of
over-all progress. Rice imports increased from 261 million tons in 1954 and
128 million in 1955 to 563 million in 1957, and 681 million tons in 1958.
For the first four months of 1959 the imports were running still higher

[23] The Bank of Indonesia, in its report for 1958-59, put somewhat more stress on
the recession in the United States and its repercussions on exports.

than in the previous year. Harvested areas under food crops barely kept pace with population growth, and there were no important changes in yields per acre. Principal foodstuffs available per capita from domestic production actually declined during the period of the first Plan, so that maintaining food supplies made increasing inroads into foreign exchange earnings. For a country with Indonesia's industrial potential, this development was not necessarily unhealthy in itself—but the Plan called for self-sufficiency in foodstuffs, and there was not enough expansion of the industrial export sector to justify the increase in food imports.

Indeed, not one of the traditional plantation products had regained pre-war levels of planted area by 1959. Rubber output increased despite the drop in acreage, because the replanting done between 1946 and 1950 was done with higher-yield strains. For all other major estate crops, output as well as acreage was still well below prewar levels. Even for rubber, both estate and smallholders' exports reached a peak physical volume in 1954, while the value of total rubber exports was at its peak in 1955. Even when allowance is made for smuggling, copra exports showed a decline in value during the Plan period. The same was true of tin. Only the expansion of petroleum exports prevented foreign exchange earnings from falling more drastically than they did; and in 1958, with the growing domestic market for refined products and disruption through the rebellion, even petroleum exports fell in value.

The National Planning Bureau estimates showed national income at constant prices substantially lower in 1958 than in 1957, and their estimates for 1959, while showing recovery from 1958, remained lower than in 1957. The component of national income showing the biggest drop between 1957 and 1958 was private consumption, which dropped by 17 billion rupiahs at 1957 prices. Private investment dropped almost a billion, government investment by almost 2 billion, and "desa (village) investment" by 300 million. Government consumption also dropped by 2 billion. Gross investment as a percentage of gross national product fell from 6.2 per cent in 1957 to 5.1 per cent in 1958, and was expected to recover only to 5.6 per cent in 1959. Meanwhile, the Indonesian population was growing at a rate of about one and a half million persons per year. The National Planning Bureau estimates showed 1952 per capita income below that of 1938; since 1958 per capita income was below 1952 at constant prices, one must conclude that in 1958 per capita incomes in Indonesia remained lower than they had been twenty years before.

Among the new institutions established under Sukarno's konsepsi (concept) in July, 1959, was the Dewan Perantjang Nasional, or National Development Council, called DEPERNAS for short. It was charged by the President with the task of preparing an economic development plan in the shortest possible time, keeping in mind the evolving concept of "Indonesian socialism." The council was composed of seventy-four political appointees under the chairmanship of poet and historian Yamin, with M. Hatusoit, a former secretary-general of education, as its secretary-general. The council met for the first time in August, 1959, and a year later presented a draft Eight-Year Plan nearly 5,000 pages long to the President.

The Eight-Year Plan is not merely a design for economic development; it also seeks to crystallize the concept of Indonesian democracy and to define the sort of society the Plan is expected to produce. The spirit of the Plan is well indicated by its division into 8 parts, 17 volumes, and 1,945 paragraphs, to symbolize the Proclamation of Independence on August 17, 1945. The Indonesian national identity, the Plan states, is to be sought in the traditional culture—the songs, the dance, the *wayang* (traditional theater) the literature. The goal must be "a just and prosperous society based on the Pantja Sila," the five pillars of Indonesian social and political philosophy—nationalism, internationalism, democracy, social justice, and belief in God. It must also be a "family-like society," reproducing at the national level the spirit of village organization.

The Plan also summarizes the principles of Indonesian socialism as follows:

1. Emphasis on the production of consumers' goods.
2. Better distribution of daily necessities.
3. Use of agriculture and industry to produce foreign-exchange-earning finished goods.
4. Use of imports to create increased employment opportunities and to produce foreign exchange-saving goods.
5. Development of basic industries.

Somewhat more concretely, the Plan states that Indonesian socialism should guarantee every citizen adequate food, clothing, and shelter; appropriate public health and education facilities; support in old age; and freedom to develop his spiritual and cultural life.

The Eight-Year Plan is a "project plan." The council relied mainly on the work of the ministries to provide them with proposed projects, and many of the unfulfilled projects of the old Five-Year Plan were carried over into the new one. The scale is determined by a social welfare judgment that with present living conditions Indonesia cannot invest more than 13 per cent of its national income. It was this judgment, together with a rough estimate of the present level of national income, that gave the figure of 240 billion rupiahs as the planned investment over the eight-year period. This figure applies to the A projects which constitute the Plan proper; these A projects are to be financed from the yield of the B projects, mainly foreign investments in the export industries, and the capture of foreign exchange now lost by smuggling of exports.

THE A PROJECTS

The A projects are designed to improve the standard of living of the Indonesian people, and are divided into several sections: culture, education, research, social welfare, government, defense, food, clothing, industry, pharmaceutical goods, communications, and distribution.

The mental and spiritual sector involves forty-three educational projects and nine cultural ones, accounting for 7.4 per cent of the total budget. Among the latter is expansion of the National Museum and National Art

Gallery. The section on education recommends that scientific and technical education be encouraged, while emphasis on humanities in secondary schools and training in law or economics in universities should be discouraged.

Research, the second sector in the Plan, is to be centered in seven institutes. Only 1.1 per cent of the budget is allocated to this sector. The eleven welfare projects account for 2.58 per cent. An interesting feature of the government sector (1.51 per cent) is the explicit abandonment of the ambitious resettlement projects that played so large a role in discussions of development during the early days of the National Planning Bureau. The 12.5 per cent of the budget for special development includes national security, and the 4.7 per cent for finance includes tourism. The allocation of 25.16 per cent of the budget to distribution seems high until one realizes that this sector includes transport and communications.

By far the biggest chunk of the development budget, however—45.02 per cent—is allocated to production. In this sector there are eighty-eight industrial projects, eight foodstuffs projects, seven clothing projects, and six pharmaceutical projects. On the whole, these projects seem well conceived, although managerial and marketing problems associated with them receive too little attention.

THE B PROJECTS

The B projects, which are planned to provide the capital to finance the A projects, are the big export industries—the plantation industries, including rubber and copra, oil, timber, fisheries, tin, and aluminum, which were reviewed for the Five-Year Plan. The Eight-Year Plan adds tourism to the list.

The foreign oil companies alone are expected to yield $1.5 billion over the period—at least five times as much as they have invested in rehabilitation, expansion, and modernization of their facilities since World War II —and to provide $1,180 millions in revenue to the government from their earnings. Foreign timber enterprises are expected to yield $52 million to the government (scaled down from an initial estimate of $1,455 million), fisheries $12.5 million (scaled down from an original $4,000 million), and aluminum $11.5 million. Tourism plus increased output of tin and aluminum are expected to yield $71.5 million. Stopping the smuggling of exports of rubber and copra should bring in $396 million, according to the Council. Smuggling is to be stopped by making it unprofitable; that is, by stabilizing the rupiah and eliminating the spread between official and black-market prices of foreign exchange.

The most serious weakness of the Plan was its vagueness with regard to financing. The total of the estimated revenues from the B projects, $2,462.5 million, does not even meet the estimated foreign-exchange costs of the plan in full. Converted into rupiahs at official rates of exchange, it is less than half the total projected costs. Yet there is no specific provision for meeting the balance. The Indonesian plan is unique in making no provision for domestic financing of any kind; no effort will be made to increase either voluntary savings or tax revenues, because the Indonesian population is poor, and any restrictions on consumption would not be "in accordance with the humanitarian principles of our society." If there is to be no additional taxation or saving—and no drastic reduction in current government expenditures—the difference can be met internally only by inflationary deficit finance, a policy totally inconsistent with the scheme to make smuggling of exports unattractive.

The Default of Economic Leadership

Indonesia's lack of progress since Independence, and particularly since 1959, might be summed up by the one word "Sukarno"; but to be fair, "government indecisiveness" must be added. When the author first went to Indonesia as financial adviser to the government in 1952, unconscionable amounts of time and energy were devoted to ideological debate. What was the precise meaning of Indonesian socialism? How was the ideal of *ramah tamah* (the family-like society) to be extended to the national level? How was *gotong royong* (the spirit of mutual assistance) to be translated into cooperatives? Meanwhile the seeds of present economic difficulties sprouted and grew. Some leaders were aware of the mounting problems and knew well enough how to deal with them, but in the "debating-society" political atmosphere of the fifties nothing could be done.

The hopeless indecisiveness of Indonesia's parliamentary democracy led to Sukarno's introduction of his *konsepsi—his* concept of Indonesian democracy in 1959. Unfortunately, Sukarno's "guided democracy" turned out to be mainly misguided nationalism and a misguided economy; Sukarno deflected the country's resources and energies into quarrels over West Irian and Malaysia. He did not grasp the country's urgent need for economic development; his 1966 statement that he would root out the people responsible for inflation and shoot them epitomizes his approach. His concept of economic policy was to find the miscreants who were depriving the Indonesian people of their natural prosperity and to liquidate them. On these grounds he expropriated and exiled the Dutch, drove the Chinese out of business, deliberately bankrupted Indonesian entrepreneurs, and later forced out the British and Americans. There may have been some rough justice behind some of these moves, but they left the country with no effective economic leadership at any level. Most of the nation's economists were either exiled, in jail, or excluded from all government policy-making positions.

Not one trained economist was retained in a position of influence or power within the government. There were well-trained Indonesian economists in the universities and a few in the civil service, but their advice was not sought on important policy questions. They were associated in the minds of Sukarno and other government leaders with the anti-Sukarno faction, largely because many of them were students or colleagues of Sumitro who became Minister of Economic Affairs in the rebel "government."

The monetary reforms of August, 1959, illustrate very well the kind of ill-considered palliative that characterized economic policy during the Sukarno regime. With rising inflationary pressure and a soaring black-market rate for the rupiah, with reserves having dwindled to less than three months' normal imports, it was clear that something had to be done. The measures called for by the situation were ruthless pruning of unnecessary government expenditures; more rigorous tax enforcement and introduction of new taxes, particularly some kind of land tax (which might have been called a "development tax" to withdraw some of the sting); encouragement of export industries—including petroleum—and import-replacing industries; assignment of greater financial powers and development responsibilities to the regions to permit more rapid growth of export industries; and careful studies to determine an official rate of exchange that could be made to stick if these complementary measures were carried out. None of these things was done. Instead, the official rate of the rupiah was reestablished at 45 to the dollar *without* the complementary measures to make this rate stick; notes of 500- and 1,000-rupiah denominations were devalued by 90 per cent; and deposits of over 25,000 rupiahs were devalued by 90 per cent although government securities were given to depositors with a face-value equal to the amount of deposits cancelled by the government.

Thus the measures constituted a capital levy, plus a forced loan, of a highly discriminatory sort. The government justified its move on the grounds that people holding considerable sums of notes of large denomination were speculators and black-marketeers anyhow. There was little evidence to support this contention. Over two-thirds of the total money supply consisted of currency, and many holders of large notes were legitimate businessmen—those very entrepreneurs who were responsible for such economic development as Indonesia enjoyed under the First Five-Year Plan. This sudden destruction of their working capital could not have failed to impede their further expansion. The replacement of deposits with government securities was also a partial expropriation of the working capital of Indonesian enterprises; the market value of the securities was less than face value, and efforts to replenish working capital by liquidating government bonds involved the holders in substantial losses; even if no losses were suffered, the measure was not anti-inflationary. To hold cash balances is no great sin in an underdeveloped country—it is more virtuous than spending them on scarce commodities. A similar measure was undertaken in 1950 and thus will be feared in the future. Consequently, the people will tend to spend rather than hold cash, velocity of circulation will rise, and the anti-inflationary effects of the reform will be short-lived—as they were in 1950. The only merit of the measure was a purely political one—there was no strong, organized, and articulate group to oppose it.

The antagonism toward both foreign and domestic capital, and particularly the destruction of much of indigenous Indonesian entrepreneurship which characterizes the period of Sukarno's "guided democracy," apparently cannot be attributed to the influence of the Indonesian Communist Party (PKI) on the President. The PKI program was to maintain the agrarian economy on a basis of "private ownership of peasants of the land"; it insisted that "economically the national capitalists should, moreover be developed . . . protection and facilities must be granted to the national capitalists."[24] There is reason to believe that it was Sukarno himself who feared the rise of national capitalism, not so much on ideological grounds as because he was afraid that a thoroughly entrenched class of Indonesian entrepreneurs, on whom a large number of workers might depend for employment, would have constituted a political force with which he did not wish to contend. The fact that Sjafruddin, ex-Prime Minister Natsir, Sumitro, and the other leaders of the rebellion in 1957–58 were precisely those who showed more sympathy toward the development of private enterprise when they were in positions of power no doubt strengthened the President's opposition to capitalism in any form.

The most disturbing feature of the monetary reform of August, 1959, was the accompanying evidence that it was *deliberately* designed to discourage private *enterprise*. In his 1959 Independence Day address and subsequent speeches, President Sukarno reiterated his antagonism toward "national capitalism," referring to it as "vulture capitalism" and warning against the dangers of "liberalism" which he identified with exploitation of the many by the few. He stressed the necessity of sticking to the socialist, cooperative path and insisted that a guided democracy must have a "guided economy." Similarly, in a June, 1959, speech, Acting President Sartono criticized Indonesian governments for allowing the economy to remain "capitalistic" instead of transforming it into a "socialist" state according to the 1945 Constitution. The "transfer of power from white [Dutch] and yellow [Japanese] hands to brown [Indonesian] hands" is not enough, for "fundamentally our economic system has remained capitalistic and not socialistic as it should be."[25]

Economic growth can take place through public enterprise as well as through private enterprise, but there is a vast difference between public ownership and control and public enterprise. True enterprise has been conspicuously lacking in the public sector of the Indonesian economy. Many Indonesian leaders have strong views as to the things they are *against*, but few of them have clear, pragmatic ideas of what they are *for*. "Guided democracy," "converting the colonial economy into a national economy," "organizing the national economy on a cooperative basis," "avoiding the evils of national capitalism," and similar popular slogans provide no guidance as to the kind of economic *system* Indonesia is to have, let alone concrete answers to specific economic policy questions. The ideology most needed in Indonesia is *ad hoc-ery*, analyzing problems and dealing with them, one at a time—the one most seldom encountered Economic leadership has yet to appear in central government circles. There is a good deal of potential economic leadership in the private sector, as we have seen; but the Sukarno regime had a strong bias against encouraging it, and all the available entrepreneurial talent could not be pushed or lured into the procrustean bed of government enterprise.

---

[24] Juan Justus van der Kroef, "Indonesia's Unfinished Revolution," *United Asia*, Vol. XII, No. 6, 1960, p. 486.
[25] *Antara News Bulletin* (New York), June 23, 1959.

Now Indonesia seems to have outlived some of these growing pains. Since the Suharto take-over in February, 1966, Sukarno has been in eclipse. The new Suharto Administration is development-minded, and is giving able men a chance. Sultan Hamengku Buwono IX, now charged with major responsibilities for economic development, has been in ten cabinets and recognizes the importance of making use of the professional economists around him. Indonesia has a group of bright and able younger economists with the best training that leading European and American universities can provide, and the wit to avoid the pitfalls of their predecessors. "The economic leaders of the fifties were brilliant, but they were too 'Western' to be effective," one of these young economists commented to the author. "They failed to translate economic policy proposals into language reflecting Indonesian attitudes and values. We see just as clearly the need for pragmatic policies, but we also see the possibility of dressing up *ad hoc* policies in traditional costume, with a liberal sprinkling of 'good words'—like *gotong-rojong, ramah, tamah,* and *musjawarat desa*" (mutual assistance, the family-like society, and village discussion).

Conclusions

The reason for Indonesia's spectacular failure should now be clear: no regime, from the Netherlands East Indies Company through Sukarno's guided democracy, provided the combination of "big push," economic leadership, and a political framework encouraging to the exercise of entrepreneurship, which is needed for a "take-off" into economic development. Under the Dutch colonial regime a series of "development systems" were tried: private trading monopoly and forced deliveries; public trading monopoly and forced deliveries; free private enterprise with large-scale corporative undertakings; limited planning with modest technical assistance. They succeeded only in launching and sustaining the population explosion and destroying indigenous entrepreneurship, while building a modern sector that was really part of the Dutch economy, and never big enough to permit a decline in the share of a rapidly growing Indonesian population which was forced to seek a livelihood in the traditional sector. After Independence came a period of parliamentary democracy with debate but no decisions on fundamental questions of economic development policy. The result was stagnation of per capita output and gathering inflation. Finally came Sukarno's "guided economy," in which Dutch, Chinese, other foreign, and eventually Indonesian private entrepreneurship was destroyed, without being replaced by effective public enterprise and without developmental investment of "big push" proportions.

We know that rapid growth can take place with public entrepreneurship—or better, economic leadership—as well as with private. But it cannot take place without entrepreneurship or economic leadership of some kind. At this time, the new Suharto-Nasution regime had just announced its streamlined Cabinet. The confrontation of Malaysia had been dropped. There was evidence that at long last Indonesian natural and human resources would be directed toward economic development within some systematic plan. A consortium was being formed to provide substantial foreign aid. There was reason to hope that the new regime would provide, after centuries of postponement, the conjuncture of entrepreneurial endeavor and political power elite favorable to the exercise of entrepreneurial talent which would permit Indonesia to realize her economic potential.

32 | The North-South Problem: Italy and Brazil

Stephen Potter, in his book *Lifesmanship*, describes the proper gambit for the man who uses the Foreign Travel Ploy to dominate the dinner-table conversation: wait until he pauses for breath, and then, no matter what he has been saying about whatever country, interject, "But not in the south!" Although regional differences are pronounced in nearly all countries, wide and growing gaps among major regions are one of the most important distinguishing characteristics of developing countries. Albert C. Hirschman has labeled this widespread phenomenon of regional dualism "the north-south problem." An increasing number of development plans include reduction of regional gaps as a major objective; some also include specific measures for attaining this goal. In this chapter we analyze the two classic cases of "the north-south problem" and the efforts to deal with it: Italy and Brazil.

Italy: Trials of Union

It may seem surprising to find Italy, a European power which has made a distinguished contribution to Western civilization almost continuously throughout 2,500 years, included in the category of developing countries. If Italy consisted only of Rome and everything north of Rome, the level of per capita income and the degree of industrialization would indeed preclude use of the term "underdeveloped" to describe the region. But Italy also contains the poor and lagging south, where incomes are below the Mexican average and little industrialization has taken place. Since 1880 the north has had a vigorous and varied industrialization. Indeed the north provides a good example of rapid take-off into sustained growth. Why did the development of the north fail to carry the south along with it?

Italy as a whole got off to a late start in its industrialization. As Professor Gerschenkron puts it: [1]

It is obvious that in the decades following its political unification Italy's economy remained very backward in relation not only to that of England, but also to the economies of industrially advancing countries on the continent of Europe. Whatever gauge one may choose for the purposes of comparison, be it qualitative descriptions of technological equipment, organizational efficiency, and labor skills in individual enterprises; or scattered quantitative data on relative productivity in certain branches of industry, or the numbers of persons employed in industry; or the density of the country's railroad network; or the standards of literacy of its population, the same conclusion will result. It is true that there were very large differences in this respect among the individual regions of the Peninsula; but according to Pantaleoni's computations, which—subject to a considerable margin of error as they are—probably give a correct idea of the order of magnitudes involved, the private per capita wealth of the richest and most advanced areas in North Italy in the second half of the eighties was still very much below one half of the contemporaneous figure for France as a whole.

After 1880, however, Italy had a rapid increase in industrial production. It came in two waves, one from 1881 to 1888, and the second from 1896 to 1908.

TABLE 32–1
Annual Average Rates of Growth of Italian Industrial Output
for 1881–1913 and Subperiods*

Period	Percentage change
1881–1888	4.6 (Moderate growth)
1888–1896	0.3 (Stagnation)
1896–1908	6.7 (Very rapid growth)
1908–1913	2.4 (Reduced rate of growth)
1881–1913	3.8 (Moderate growth)

* Computed on the assumption of a geometric rate of growth between the first and the last years of the specified periods.
SOURCE: Gerschenkron, "Notes on the Rate of Industrial Growth in Italy, 1881–1913," *The Journal of Economic History*, December, 1955, p. 364.

Professor Gerschenkron says of these data: [2]

One point seems to emerge with sufficient clarity from the data contained in the preceding tabulations: Italy did have its period of a big industrial push.

[1] Alexander Gerschenkron, "Notes on the Rate of Industrial Growth in Italy, 1881–1913," *The Journal of Economic History*, December, 1955, p. 360.
[2] Gerschenkron, *op. cit.*, p. 364.

While there may be some question concerning the exact choice of the initial and terminal years for the individual subperiods, it seems appropriate to locate the period of the great push between the years 1896 and 1908. Before 1896 lay the years of a laborious return from the low of 1892 to the level of 1888. After 1908, the rates of growth of all the index industries but one were greatly reduced.

Industrialization in northern Italy was resumed after World War I, until interrupted by the Great Depression. Some expansion took place in the late thirties, but the war brought retrogression. A new upsurge began about 1952.

The *Mezzogiorno* (Southern Italy, including Abruzzi, Molise, Campania, Basilicata, and Calabria on the mainland and the islands of Sicily and Sardinia), however, has not shared in this expansion. One may dispute the propriety of regarding Italy as an underdeveloped *country*, but there can be no doubt that the *Mezzogiorno* is an underdeveloped *area*. For the Italian south displays nearly all the characteristics of underdeveloped countries. The dramatic discrepancy between the economic development of the south and the rest of Italy after unification in 1860 has been stated in trenchant terms by SVIMEZ (the Association for the Industrial Development of Southern Italy): [3]

Between 1861 and 1936 (first and last census years) the population of Southern Italy, if we consider the 1861 frontiers, rose from 9.8 to 15.4 millions showing an increase of 5.6 millions. During the same period the natural increase in the population (births minus deaths) was 9.4 millions. There was consequently a real exodus of 3.8 million persons (to Northern Italy or abroad), equal to more than 40 per cent of the natural increase. In the rest of Italy 3.1 million persons emigrated, equal to 22 per cent of the natural increase.

Of the 5.6 million inhabitants that remained in Southern Italy, only 200,000 were able to find employment there in 75 years; the economically active population (of over ten years of age) rose in fact from 5.6 millions in 1861 to 5.8 in 1936.

Of the remaining 5.4 millions, 4.1 millions increased the size of the inactive (unproductive) population, while the other 1.3 millions represent the increase in the population under ten years of age. This alarming expansion of the inactive population was due partly to social progress (increase in the number of children over ten receiving compulsory schooling, in the number of civil pensioners, etc.), but mainly to the fact that the economic activities of the South were not sufficient to give employment to an appreciable part of the growing population during three-quarters of a century. More or less the same number of economically active persons had to provide a livelihood for 4.2 million inactive persons in 1861 and for 9.6 millions in 1936. On an average, therefore, every occupied person had to provide for 0.75 inactive persons in 1861 and for 1.66 in 1936.

Despite the low income available, Southern Italy brought up and gave a livelihood till the attainment of working age to 40 per cent of the natural increase in the population (3.8 millions), which then emigrated abroad or to the North.

[3] SVIMEZ, Survey of Southern Italian Economy (Rome, 1950), p. 17.

At some point in the period between 1861 and 1936, the south seems to have actually retrogressed. During that period the number of industrial units decreased by 250,000. "Industrial progress in Southern Italy," says the SVIMEZ report, "seems to have limited itself to converting the home worker and craftsman of 1886 into a factory worker, reducing thereby the total amount of occupation." With the decline in the capacity of productive apparatus to provide new jobs, emigration to the north and to foreign countries increased.

The lack of development in the *Mezzogiorno* showed up as a greater volume of disguised unemployment in the south, rather than as a greater share of the *population* engaged in agriculture there. In 1936, the proportion of the total population in agriculture in the Italian south was only slightly higher than in the north, and was slightly lower than in central Italy. However, the proportion of the *economically active* population engaged in agriculture in southern Italy was 57 per cent, as against 42 per cent in northern Italy. As may be seen from Table 32–2, the relative backwardness of the occupational structure in the south was even more apparent in 1952. Furthermore, these averages mask discrepancies among major regions within the *Mezzogiorno*. Thus in 1936, the proportion of active population engaged in agriculture in Abruzzi and Molise was 74.5 per cent, and in Basilicata 75.4 per cent.

The relative backwardness of the *Mezzogiorno* is also shown in demographic figures. Before the war the birth rate in the south was 2.88 per cent, as compared to 2.05 per cent in the rest of Italy. The death rate was 1.58 per cent compared to 1.29 per cent, giving a natural rate of population growth of 1.3 per cent in the south and .76 per cent in the rest of the country. Since the war, the death rate in the south has fallen to a figure very close to that of the rest of the country, while the birth rate remains nearly as high as before the war. As a consequence, the *natural* rate of population growth in the south has increased, whereas in the rest of the country it has declined.

The average level of education is also lower in the south than in the rest of the country: [4]

The most serious and decisive shortcoming in Southern Italy, inasmuch as it affects all later development, is the fact that in the elementary schools only 30 per cent of the children (as against 53 per cent in the rest of Italy) take the modest elementary degree, while only 10 per cent (18 per cent in the rest of Italy) finish the secondary schools. In reality, with the extension of compulsory schooling to the age of 14, this should be the limit reached by all who are subject to this compulsion and should therefore be attained by two-thirds of each school generation (after allowance for children who die, fall ill or prove refractory to schooling), instead of by 10 per cent as is actually the case.

Thus it goes; almost any measure that might be applied shows the relative poverty and lack of development of the south. The south lags behind in social overhead capital: with 39.7 per cent of the country's area and

[4] SVIMEZ, *op. cit.*, p. 17.

36.5 per cent of its population in 1945, the *Mezzogiorno* had only 11.4 per cent of Italy's communal roads; in 1931, 56.1 per cent of the southern population lived in overcrowded houses (more than two people per room) as compared to 21.8 per cent in the north; the south accounted for only 10.4 per cent of the total electricity production in 1935–38, and only 8.1 per cent in 1948.

Productivity as well as production is lower in the south than in the north. Yields per hectare of wheat, maize, and potatoes were less than half of what they were in northern Italy during 1948. The south had less than half the number of livestock in the north. Only 21 per cent of the industrial establishments, and only 12.1 per cent of the establishments with motor power, were in the south in the years 1937–39. Moreover, the southern establishments were smaller, with an average of only 2.4 persons per establishment, as compared to 5.2 per cent in the north.

When did this disparate movement between the economies of the Italian north and south begin? There was no such marked difference between north and south at the time of unification, as Table 32–2 suggests. There have been suggestions that unification itself was responsible for the growing gaps in output and income. More recent studies, however, indicate that the seeds of disproportionate growth had already been planted before the unification of Italy. True, the structure of employment in 1861 seems to have been much the same in north and south (Table 32–2); but

TABLE 32–2

Composition of the Working Population in 1861, 1936, and 1952
(percentage)

Occupation	1861			1936			1952			Workers (millions)
	North	South	Italy	North	South	Italy	North	South	Italy	
Agriculture	57.3	57.2	57.2	44.0	56.9	48.1	36.6	52.3	41.6	7.97
Industry, transport, and communication	25.8	30.4	27.6	36.8	27.6	33.9	40.2	28.3	36.4	6.971
Other activities	16.9	12.4	15.2	19.2	15.5	18.0	23.2	19.4	22.0	4.241
Total	100.0	100.0	100.0	100.0	100.0	100.0	100.0	100.0	100.0	19.182

SOURCE: I. M. D. Little and P. N. Rosenstein-Rodan, *Nuclear Power and Italy's Energy Position* (Washington, D.C., 1957), p. 15.

a closer look shows that significant differences already existed. For example, at the time of unification, the north was better endowed with social overhead capital, especially transport facilities. As Eckaus puts it, "railways, outside the North and Center were virtually a *curiosium*."[5] The

[5] Richard S. Eckaus, "The North-South Differential in Italian Economic Development," *Journal of Economic History*, September, 1961, p. 288. See also Ettore Massa-

difference in number of livestock per capita noted above was already apparent in the years 1855 to 1860. And the production of silk—the most important industry at that time—was almost totally a northern enterprise; nearly 80 per cent of the total production occurred in the northern provinces. True, sulphur, the most important Italian mineral product at the time, came almost entirely from Sicily; but "its export earning ability should not be overestimated." Two-thirds of the iron ores were mined on the island of Elba in the north, and employment in metal-using industries was much lower in the south than in the north.

When the discrepancy in the economic development of north and south began is less important, however, than the fact that it exists now. Dr. P. N. Rosenstein-Rodan, director of the M.I.T. Italy Project, emphasizes the fact that "the problem of the South is not just the regional one —it is a problem for Italy as a whole." [6] The Italian Ten-Year Plan (1955–64) was naturally directed mainly toward increasing employment and productivity in the south; primary stress was laid on the creation of employment opportunities:

A survey of Italian economic developments over the past few years and especially since 1950, when real income per head had approximately regained the pre-war level, reveals one particularly striking feature. Despite the very considerable progress made in the direction of increased production and higher national income, the Ministry of Labour figure of registered unemployment has remained undiminished at about 2 million.

During the four years 1951–54 national income in real terms showed an average annual rate of growth of just over 5 per cent, rising (in terms of constant prices) from 8,570 billion Lire in 1950 to 10,450 billion Lire in 1954.

This rate was achieved under conditions of monetary stability and is amongst the highest on record in Italian economic history.

A measure of the effort made by Italy in order to realise this high rate of expansion is given by the investment figures for the same period. The average annual rate of growth in gross investment between 1950 and 1954 was 6.6 per cent, the absolute figure rising from 1,808 billion Lire in 1950 to 2,350 billion

cesi, "Regional Economic Development Policies in Italy," in U.S. Department of Commerce, *Area Development Policies in Britain and the Countries of the Common Market*, Washington, D.C., 1965. Dr. Massacesi says (pp. 224–225):

"A consideration of utmost importance to an understanding of regional economic differences in Italy is the fact that national unity was achieved only a century ago, and that before unification Italy was divided into seven national states of extremely diverse size and political and economic institutions. The fusion of these systems into a unified economy took long to achieve and has had continuing effects on relative regional development. Each national state was a more or less closed economic system. For example, the railroad network, then a most important determinant of economic development, was extremely unequal in density from state to state, and communications between states were not continuous."

It is Dr. Massacesi's view that the tariff concessions made in 1887 to industry and to grain producers had "a very damaging impact on the Mezzogiorno." The northern manufacturers had a secure market in the south, while the south experienced difficulty in exporting the products of its diversified agricutlure."

[6] P. N. Rosenstein-Rodan, "Programming in Theory and in Italian Practice," in *Investment Criteria and Economic Growth* (Cambridge, Mass., 1955).

Lire (at constant prices) in 1954; and the annual average rate of growth of net investment was over 7 per cent, the absolute figure rising from 1,135 billion Lire to 1,500 billion Lire. Over the four-year period 1951–54 gross investment absorbed about 21 per cent of gross national income, and net investment more than 14 per cent of net national income. These proportions are very high, especially in view of the low level of Italy's national income. A still better measure of the effort made since 1950 is given by the "marginal" saving ratios: over 26 per cent of the increment in gross national income, and about 20 per cent of the increment in net income was devoted to investment purposes.

The other problem emphasized in the Ten-Year Plan was the chronic balance of payments deficit:

A second factor to keep in mind is the large volume of foreign funds that were made available to the Italian economy. During the period 1951–54 the average deficit in the balance of payments on current account was of the order of 200 billion Lire a year. The foreign financial assistance, mostly consisting of outright grants, by which this deficit was covered, was unquestionably a very important factor helping toward the expansion of economic activity during those years.

Thus the development problem in Italy might be defined as raising productivity and employment in the south, while at the same time sustaining growth in the rest of the country and solving balance of payments problems.

The problem of the south, we saw, is not merely regional; it is a problem for Italy as a whole. Dr. Rosenstein-Rodan cites four economic reasons and one social reason for giving development of the *Mezzogiorno* priority in the over-all Italian development plan: [7]

(1) Lower wages in the South are not a sufficient incentive for investment. Without a changed economic framework, the long-run flow of investment would become smaller and the bulk of it would continue to flow to the North. We might then see in the 1960's 40 million people concentrated in the North and only 10 million in the South. Expensive new housing and other not directly productive capital investment would have to be provided in the North—while the already existing social overhead capital assets in the South, which need only a slight extension, far from being increased, would not even be maintained at the present level. The over-concentration in the North might produce an economic congestion, i.e., diminishing returns (though this is far from certain). It would then be very costly to reverse the process. The end result might be an economic loss to the whole of Italy.

(2) Undeveloped land and unused manpower can be used in the South. Employing workers on the land increases income without drawing on scarce resources by using manpower which could not otherwise be used. In the process manpower will get some training while doing work it is used to.

(3) The development program in the South produces great extra-regional external economies by giving contracts to the North. An industrialization program in the North, on the other hand, could hardly use any of the Southern

[7] Rosenstein-Rodan, *op. cit.*, pp. 28–29.

resources. It would thus only aggravate the existing disparity between the two areas and be ultimately checked by not creating a sufficient new effective demand.

(4) Programming requires a great deal of effort and organization besides capital. No preliminary work on investment and projects has been done for the North, while several years programming work has been accomplished for the South. While there are single projects in the North of Italy which might be directly more profitable, they are too few to provide a minimum quantum capable of generating enough momentum to create a new economic structure in Italy.

(5) Social case: without a development program in the South a social explosion would upset not only the South but the whole Italian economy.

The stagnation of the *Mezzogiorno* is reflected in the aggregate level of unemployment and the balance of payments position of the Italian economy as a whole. As pointed out in the ten-year program ("Vanoni Plan") itself, the over-all picture with respect to growth of national income was quite impressive for the immediate pre-Plan years: [8]

. . . During the four-year period from 1951 to 1954, national income in real terms increased at an annual rate of just over 5 per cent—from 8,570 billion lire in 1950 to 10,450 billion lire in 1954 (constant prices). This rate of expansion was achieved under conditions of substantially stable prices and it is among the highest recorded in Italian economic history.

Investment was running at high levels; gross investment amounted to 21 per cent of national income, net investment to more than 14 per cent. The marginal savings rate reached 26.5 per cent of the increase in gross national income. Of this investment, public investment accounted for about 30 per cent. However, the rise in national income resulted from rising productivity rather than rising employment, and continued growth was hampered by lack of foreign exchange. Dr. Pasquale Saraceno, Secretary General of the Association for the Industrial Development of Southern Italy pointed out that "the impressive postwar development, which had brought industrial production in 1954 to almost twice the pre-war level, was leaving largely unsolved the big structural problems that had characterised the Italian economic scene ever since the time—almost a century ago—of the country's political unification." [9]

The Vanoni Plan

For these reasons the Italian plan was essentially employment-oriented. It began with an estimate of the increase in the labor supply, as shown in Table 32–3. It then established as a target the elimination of unemployment, including disguised unemployment, during the plan period, while

---

[8] SVIMEZ, *Outline of Development of Income and Employment in Italy in the Ten-Year Period 1955–64*, January, 1955, p. 1.

[9] Pasquale Saraceno, "The Vanoni Plan in its Third Year: Results and Perspectives," lecture delivered to the Economic Development Institute, International Bank for Reconstruction and Development (Washington, D.C., October 27, 1957), pp. 1–2.

TABLE 32–3

Labor Supply as Estimated for the Period 1955–64
(thousands of workers)

Additional labor supply from natural increase 1955–64		2,000
Labor supply from other sources:		
Agriculture		
Unemployment in 1954	400	
Underemployment	900*	
	1,300	
minus frictional unemployment in 1964	250	1,050
Non-agricultural sectors		
Unemployment in 1954	1,400	
Technological unemployment	800†	
	2,200	
minus frictional unemployment in 1964	450	1,750
		4,800
minus emigration 1955–64		800
Total labor supply 1955–64		4,000

* Including such small technological unemployment as can be foreseen in agriculture.
† Including such underemployed as are believed to exist especially in the handicraft and tertiary sectors.
SOURCE: SVIMEZ, *Outline of Development of Income and Employment in Italy in the Ten-Year Period 1955–64* (Rome, 1955).

absorbing the current growth of the labor force. Allowing for technological displacement, frictional unemployment, and emigration, the conclusion was reached that expansion of the economy must provide four million new jobs. The required rate of growth was then projected to various sectors of the economy by use of input-output matrices.

The planning team eschewed employment creation by retarding technological progress, pointing out that higher productivity was essential to any solution of Italy's economic problems. At the same time, the team faced squarely the possibility that in the Italian economy full employment and maximum national income may be mutually inconsistent unless and until a new labor-intensive, but nonetheless efficient, technology is discovered. Dr. Rosenstein-Rodan has put the problem in the following terms: [10]

Under variable coefficients of production even small changes in wage-rates would lead to different factor proportions and to higher employment, without a fall in Real National Income. Under rigidly fixed coefficients of production even large changes in wage-rates may not lead to an appreciable increase in employment without a fall in Real National Income. Under "discontinuously variable" coefficients of production large changes in wages may be required to increase employment; the reduction in wages may, however, affect the income-and-price-elasticities of demand in such a way that the higher employment-

[10] P. N. Rosenstein-Rodan, "Factor Proportions in the Italian Economy," M.I.T., CIS, December, 1953.

output may represent a smaller value than the previous output-combination. . . .

The Italian economy consists presumably of three sectors: (1) a small one with fixed coefficients, (2) a large one with "discontinuously variable" co-efficients, (3) a small one with variable coefficients of production. The last sector may be too small to eliminate technological unemployment although it helps to reduce it. International Trade has an effect similar to an extension of the "variable coefficients" sector; it reduces but does not eliminate the divergence between the maximum-value and the full-employment output.

There still remained the question as to the best method for eliminating unemployment and absorbing the increase in labor supply. Rosenstein-Rodan has indicated that three courses of action were considered: [11]

The *first* might be a large-scale industrialization program in the North. The advantages of increasing an existing industrial system rather than creating a new one are obvious. Many difficulties stand, however, in the way of this solution. There would be considerable uncertainty regarding markets for the newly-produced industrial product. An industrialization program in the North would mainly benefit the North and not the South, apart from some migration outlet to the North. More houses would have to be built in the North for the immigrants while existing houses can be used to a large extent in the South thus saving a proportion of capital required for development. The development of Southern Italy on the other hand would place many contracts for the industries in the North and thus benefit the North as well as the South; investment in the South produces many more extraregional external economies.

The *second* way of implementing an investment program might be an industrialization program in the South. Again, however, the same or even greater difficulties than in the North would obtain in the South. There would be uncertainty in finding proper markets for the new industrial products greater even than in the North because of the smaller size of the existing market. There would be additional difficulties in transforming Southern Italian peasants into industrial workers, a task which cannot be completely achieved within a few years.

A *third* way has been chosen: a large-scale development of agrarian resources and social overhead capital, which is to create an additional market, a changed economic structure which would attract a flow of private capital sufficient to secure a higher standard of living in the South and a more balanced economy for Italy as a whole. The increase in output will find established markets at home and markets abroad for exports in which the comparative advantage is clearly in favor of Italy. It is a pre-industrialization program foregoing somewhat higher profits in the short run, which might be obtainable by investments elsewhere, for the sake of securing more profits in the longer run. Both the direct and indirect profits accruing from the must be taken into account, as well as new investment opportunities created, although the latter may only emerge after the first phase of the program has been successfully achieved.

Mere expansion, without structural change, is not enough; in the stagnant south, a discontinuous change in structure is a necessary adjunct of development, and must be provided for in the plan.[12] For this purpose,

[11] *Ibid.,* pp. 27–28.
[12] "The decision to develop the South of Italy by a ten-year $1.6 billion public investment program initiated a structural change which no market decision would

and also to provide the basic stimulus for balanced growth in the private sector, the plan included government development projects in three "impulse sectors": agriculture, public utilities, and public works. Thus the public investment aspect of the plan involved both "sectoral planning" and "project planning."

Detailed planning in Italy was confined to public investment in those "impulse sectors" and in housing. In the rest of the economy a projection was made on the basis of a rather thorough input-output analysis (Table 32–4). This analysis, together with multiplier analysis, also yielded esti-

TABLE 32–4

Composition of the Assumed Increase in Income 1955–64
(rounded figures)

Income	Billion lire	Percentages
Income produced by 3,200,000 additional workers in non-agricultural sectors, with average productivity of the ten-year period (Lire 900 thousand multiplied by 3.2 million)	2,900	44.2
Increase in net agricultural product	550	8.4
Income increase from better utilization of residual idle capacity	600	9.2
	4,050	61.8
National income, increasing at an annual rate of 5 per cent, is expected to rise in the ten years by	6,550	100.0
Hence increase of income to be achieved through higher productivity of workers employed in non-agricultural sectors	2,500	38.2

SOURCE: SVIMEZ, *Outline of Development of Income and Employment in Italy in the Ten-Year Period 1955–64* (Rome, 1955), p. 10.

mates of foreign exchange requirements for the achievement of development targets. The foreign exchange drain was also one of the considerations in assigning priorities to particular projects. The other major variables in the priority formula were the ratio of value added to capital requirements

---

ever have reached." P. N. Rosenstein-Rodan, "Programming in Theory and in Italian Practice," in *Investment Criteria and Economic Growth* (Cambridge, Mass., 1955), p. 26. Dr. Vera Lutz distinguishes between two periods in policy regarding the Mezzogiorno. During the first "cycle" of policy, roughly from 1947 to 1957, the emphasis was on fiscal relief, special credit facilities, and other incentives to private enterprise, combined with the establishment of the *Cassa per il Mezzogiorno* to make investments in the social overhead sector. The second cycle started with the Law on Provisions for the Mezzogiorno in July, 1957. This Law broadened the scope of activities, providing for new forms of government aid, including outright grants towards the capital costs of private industrial enterprises as well as new kinds of public investment. This Law was supplemented by two others of July, 1959, providing new incentives for medium and small industries. (Vera Lutz, *Italy: A Study of Economic Development* [London, 1962], p. 101.) *op. cit.*, p. 162.

and the ratio of cost of domestic factors to capital requirements (a negative weight). The heaviest weight was attached to the foreign exchange requirement because analysis proved foreign exchange to be the major limiting factor in determining the total scale of the plan. The net inflationary impact was also been calculated from household data and multiplier analysis, but the danger of inflation proved less serious a limitation than the need to protect foreign exchange reserve.[13]

The housing sector was treated as the balance wheel in the economy. The three impulse sectors were "in large part closely connected with the planned process of expansion of productive capacity." For them more or less steady growth was needed. "As regards housing, by contrast, Government action is influenced up to a certain level by urgent social needs, which must be met in any event; beyond that level, the housing programme can be regarded as a further possible stimulus to the process of expansion of demand." Unlike other investment, housing does not add to productive capacity or to permanent employment. Thus it can become the basis of flexible action, to offset fluctuations in other kinds of investment in the economy.

In the field of agriculture, emphasis was placed on reclamation and land reform. The investment program for agriculture is shown in Table 32–5.

TABLE 32–5
Breakdown of Net Investment in Agriculture, 1955–64

Type of investment	Billion lire	Per cent
Land reclamation projects	543	16
Transformation (irrigation and dry) and mountain improvement projects	1,004	29
Land reform	522	15
Mechanization	313	9
Other investment (livestock, inventories, etc.)	385	11
Facilities for produce sorting and preservation	300	9
Technical assistance and vocational training	400	11
Total	3,467	100

The plan also called for 3,210 billion lire investment in provision of additional electric power, 700 billion in electrification and improvement of railroads, 450 billion for aqueducts, and 300 billion each for natural gas and telephones. The public works program includes 1,150 billion lire for roads, 790 billion for river and mountain improvement, 220 billion for schools, and 650 billion for hospitals, sewers, airports, and other works.

[13] The multiplier analysis established the following relationships:
The marginal propensity to consume domestic goods $C = 0.45$
The marginal propensity to import $I = 0.20$
The marginal propensity to tax $T = 0.26$
The marginal propensity to save $s = 0.09$
The multiplier $k = \dfrac{1}{1 - c} = \dfrac{1}{1 - 0.45} = 1.8$

Altogether, the program covered public investments of 11,237 billion lire.
These investments themselves were not expected to add much to
permanent employment:

> . . . the role of the impulse programmes consists, not so much in the direct
> effect on employment, as (a) in the utilisation of natural resources (agricul-
> tural and sources of power); (b) in the creation of environmental conditions
> and external economies essential to development; (c) in the impulse given via
> the multiplier to the general process of expansion.

Employment creation, then, was expected to come mainly from the private
investment that would be generated by the program. The estimated
capital-job ratios for three major sectors are shown in Table 32–6. Trans-

TABLE 32–6

Capital Directly Needed for the Creation of New Jobs

Branches	Number of jobs	Capital required per job, million lire	Total capital required, billion lire
Industries with heavy capital requirements	100,000	10.0	1,000
Other industries and the handicraft sector	1,500,000	1.5	2,200
Tertiary activities	1,600,000	1.0	1,600
Total	3,200,000	1.5	4,800

SOURCE: SVIMEZ, *Outline of Development of Income and Employment in Italy in
the Ten-Year Period 1955–64* (Rome, 1955), pp. 18, 30.

lated into dollars, they come to about $16,000 per job in heavy industry,
$2,500 in small industries and handicrafts, $1,600 in tertiary activities, and
$2,500 for the over-all program. These figures, of course, cannot be used
in other countries without adjustment for differences in costs. However,
it is likely that *capital* costs would be higher in still less developed countries than they would be in Italy. These calculations should dispel any
easy optimism regarding the cost of bringing about structural change in
underdeveloped economies.

The ten-year program did not include detailed recommendations for
financing. Instead, sources of financing for investment in 1952–54 were
presented, and a case was made for confining detailed financial plans to the
first four years covered by the program.

If the goals of the Vanoni Plan were achieved, said Saraceno, the north
"ought to present in 1964 the characteristics typical of a highly industrial-
ised country with only 18 per cent of its gross income deriving from
agriculture and as much as 45 per cent deriving from industrial activity."
But the structural change in the south was the main goal of the Plan.
"Thus, while in 1954, 43 per cent of the income of the South was derived
from agriculture, and 57 per cent from industrial and tertiary activities

combined, in 1964—assuming that the employment aims of the 'Plan' were reached—the proportion of income derived from industry and services would have to have risen to 76 percent." [14]

Considering the strength of the "backwash effects" on the south of economic development in the north, it might be regarded as a notable achievement to equalize rates of growth in the two regions, especially since the agricultural south has shared less in the world boom than the industrialized north and has suffered bad crop years. But the Italian planners were not content with this result. They had aimed at growth rates in the south double those in the north, and they were determined to find the means of producing faster development in the south than in the north.

The balance of payments position improved under the Plan, but the nature of this improvement was not without its worrisome features. The income-elasticity of demand for imported capital goods proved much higher than expected, despite the high level of development of the Italian machine industries in the north. Indeed each 1 per cent increase in gross national product brought a 2 per cent increase in industrial imports. The income elasticity of demand for imports in general proved higher still. Under these conditions, the growth of national income might well have been accompanied by a worsening of the balance of payments position but for three developments in the world market that were no part of the Plan: the world-wide boom in investment resulted in expanded exports of Italian engineering products, which are marginal sellers in the world market, enjoying good sales in such a boom but losing their market quickly in a world recession; the Italian terms of trade improved; and there was a net inflow of foreign capital (including repatriation of Italian capital).

In one respect, the difficulties that arose during the first years of the Vanoni Plan are similar to those that arose under the Second Five-Year Plan in India; in part, they reflect the unexpected vigor of the private investment sector. It was recognized that a private investment boom in the north would not in itself solve the problems of the south. It was also recognized that it was impossible simultaneously to give the private investment boom its head, expand public investment in the "impulse sectors" through deficit finance, and maintain monetary stability. It was decided "not to hinder the spontaneous expansion of productive activity" and "to keep down the budget deficit by keeping down public expenditure."

The Plan provided various incentives to encourage private enterprises to locate in the south. These included a ten-year exemption from income tax and related taxes; a 50 per cent reduction of the turnover tax on machinery and materials; exemption from customs duties on imported machinery and materials; "soft loans" for expansion of existing plants or establishment of new ones. In addition, there were loan guarantees, state participation in the share capital of new industries, outright grants as contributions to construction costs, and preferential rates on state railways for materials and

[14] Saraceno, *op. cit.*, p. 3.
[15] *Ibid.*, pp. 9–10.

supplies. Government agencies were required to place one-fifth of their orders with southern firms, apart from "normal" orders which southern enterprises could obtain on a competitive basis. Government-owned enterprises were also established in the region.

Results under the Plan

The results obtained under the Vanoni Plan were rather disappointing for the south. The over-all rate of growth of the Italian economy was high. The percentage rate of growth of per capita income in the south was slightly higher, so that the percentage difference between per capita incomes in the north and the south was somewhat reduced. The absolute gap, however, remained essentially unchanged. Even this limited success would not have been possible without the net emigration from the south to the north and to other countries; although birth rates continued higher in the south than in the north and death rates were much the same, the share of the south in the total population fell because of emigration. Unfortunately, the continuing emigration carried with it a "brain drain"; it was the more enterprising and better trained men who left for the north.

Considering the problems faced, preventing a further increase in the rift between the "two Italies" might be regarded as a species of triumph; but the south was left a poor and underdeveloped region at the end of the Plan. As one recent observer puts it,[16]

Notwithstanding the efforts of the Cassa and other well-intentioned government agencies over the last twelve years, the economic problems which for so long have plagued Southern Italy remain unsolved. There are still nearly one million unemployed (and maybe more, were all underemployed accounted for) and the vast majority continues to live in abject poverty.

In agriculture, underemployment continued to be a serious problem. A SVIMEZ survey of 1960 indicated that one-third of the agricultural labor force was employed for less than 100 days and only 28 per cent worked more than 150 days per year.[17] The south's share of irrigated land, use of tractors and fertilizers, ownership of livestock, and other indices of agricultural development remained lower than the region's share of agricultural population. The number of tractors in the region increased from 11,000 to 39,287 between 1951 and 1960, but not all of these were used and to some degree their introduction merely added to technological unemployment. Productivity per agricultural worker rose at an average of only 1.1 per cent per year during the 1950's. Schachter speaks of "the spectacle of from ten to fifteen peasants walking behind a tractor, with no definite purpose in mind other than that of 'killing time.' "[18] With productivity still low, levels of living are still low too. A sample survey in the early

[16] Gustav Schachter, The Italian South: Economic Development in Mediterranean Europe (New York, 1965), p. 193.

[17] G. de Rossi and G. E. Marciani, "L'Agricoltura Meridionale," Il Veltro, December, 1962, p. 1030.

[18] Schachter, op. cit., p. 185.

1960's showed that 32 per cent of the families in Calabria and Basilicata never ate meat and another 35 per cent ate meat only rarely. For wine the figures were 24 per cent and 47 per cent, for oil 53 per cent and 34 per cent, and for sugar 37 per cent and 44 per cent.[19]

The obstacles to agricultural development in the harsh physical environment of the south were clear at the outset. More disappointing was the failure to transform southern industry. The incentives to private enterprise proved inadequate. According to Schachter, "Northern industrialists interviewed in 1962 claimed that these subsidies actually amounted to very little and too much red tape is involved." [20] The typical industrial establishment in the south remained pitifully small. A 1961 industrial census showed that manufacturing enterprises in the south averaged three employees per establishment. Even in construction and utilities the average number of employees was only twelve per establishment. Between 1951–53 and 1959–61, the total increase in net income generated by the industrial sector (including manufacturing, trade, credit, insurance, and transportation) was only $50 per capita. The south's share in industrial output actually declined slightly, from 17.8 per cent to 17.2 per cent, between 1951 and 1961. Industrial employment increased much less than the labor force. Employment remained concentrated in "first-stage" industries, such as food processing, wood products, textiles, stone and glass products, etc.[21]

Lessons from Italian Experience

1. The need for powerful measures to counteract forces leading to disparate rates of growth in different regions and sectors of an economy, and the need for a flexible approach to development planning are the chief lessons to be learned from Italian experience.

2. In the Italian plan, we see underlined the relationship between public and private investment. The Italian planners counted heavily on public investment in the "impulse sectors" to generate the private investment needed to attain employment and output targets.

3. Another important lesson from Italian experience is that planning for full employment need not mean resorting to make-work projects or waste of resources. The employment target determines the *scale* of the program; it does not determine priorities. Priorities for particular projects are still determined according to their contribution to the long-run growth of per capita income. Maximizing the rate of increase in national income requires the absorption of unemployment up to the point where, with the given

[19] *Ibid.*, p. 94.
[20] *Ibid.*, p. 181.
[21] Allan Rodgers, "Regional Industrial Development with Reference to Southern Italy," in Norton Ginsburg (ed.), *Essays on Geography and Economic Development, op. cit.*, p. 162.

The continuing lag in the Mezzogiorno is reflected in the slower rates of structural change in the southern region. For the country as a whole, the share of the population working in agriculture fell from about 40 per cent in 1951 to less than 30 per cent in 1961. In the north, the corresponding figures are 34 per cent for 1951 and 23 per cent in 1961. In the south, however, the share of the labour force engaged in agriculture was still 52 per cent in 1951 and 45 per cent in 1961. (Ettore Massacesi, *op. cit.*, p. 231.)

supply of capital and foreign exchange, further increases in employment would necessitate choosing more labor-intensive techniques or projects, even if they contribute less to national income than other projects or techniques that are more capital-intensive. Only at this point does a conflict arise between maximizing output and maximizing employment at a particular point of time. At this point, as we have already stated, the choice becomes a matter of social policy. Given a supply of capital and foreign exchange equal to their absorptive capacity, most underdeveloped countries can go a long way toward reducing unemployment, open and disguised (dynamic), before being confronted with this choice.

Brazil: Boom-and-Bust Development in a Regionalized Economy

Professor Henry William Spiegel begins his well-known book on Brazil with the sentence, "There is no other tropical country in the world where Western civilization has flowered more richly than in Brazil." [22] This fact alone would make Brazil one of the most interesting of the Latin American republics. It is also much the biggest of them, both in area and in population, and has much to work with in the way of natural resources. Since World War II Brazil has enjoyed rates of increase in per capita income which clearly entitle her to the label "developing," although the level of living and economic structure of Brazil are such that the country obviously still belongs in the "underdeveloped" category.

Some international comparisons will serve to locate Brazil on the scale of economic development and to "bracket" the Brazilian economy. First, in terms of the rate of growth measured in the usual way (increase in per capita income), postwar Brazil ranks in the upper class but not among the elite. With a rate of growth of real per capita gross domestic product of 3 per cent between 1947 and 1961, Brazil was a fast-developing country in comparison with the United States, Canada, and Australia, or to most countries in Latin America, Asia, or Africa; but it lagged well behind such stars in the development firmament as Japan, Venezuela, West Germany, Italy, Greece, USSR, Yugoslavia, and Poland. Brazil had no strong export comparable to Venezuela's oil nor did Brazil share in the opportunities for achieving low capital-output ratios through reconstruction of war-damaged productive facilities such as existed in some other high-growth countries. All things considered, Brazil's rate of growth since World War II was highly respectable. It was not as high as it might have been if development policy had been better designed, but even the target rates of growth in many development plans are no higher than those actually achieved in Brazil. However, the rate of growth fell considerably during the years 1961–63, with per capita income actually declining in the last of these years. Even if earlier rates of growth might have been acceptable as targets, the recent rates were not. (See Table 32–7.)

This growth of per capita income took place with limited structural change. In the last two decades structural change has been much faster in

22 Henry William Spiegel, *The Brazilian Economy* (Philadelphia, 1949), p. 1.

TABLE 32-7
Average Annual Rate of Growth
(in per cent)

Period	Real gross domestic product	Real gross domestic product per capita
1947–52	5.4	3.5
1953–56	4.9	1.8
1957–61	6.9	3.8
1947–61	5.8	3.0
1962	5.4	2.2
1963	1.4	1.8

SOURCE: Instituto Brasileiro de Economia, Fundacão Getulio Vargas.

both Australia and Canada than in Brazil, although these countries were already much further advanced at the beginning of the period. In 1947, 26.9 per cent of net domestic product was produced in the agricultural sector. In 1950, 58 per cent of the total employment was in this sector. Industry (the secondary sector) accounted for 21.4 per cent of income (1947) and 16 per cent of employment (1950), while the tertiary sector (services) produced 51.7 per cent of income and provided 26 per cent of employment. In 1960, the relative share of the agricultural sector was 28.2 per cent in terms of income and 49.2 per cent in terms of employment, while the industrial sector had increased to 25.8 per cent of income and 18.6 per cent of employment. The tertiary sector declined to 46 per cent of income but was 32.1 per cent of employment. (See Tables 32–8, 32–9 and 32–9a.) Estimates for 1963 show agriculture still accounting for 27.4 per cent of income, while industry showed little change (27.9 per cent) and the tertiary sector had declined further to 44.7 per cent. Within the tertiary sector, commerce and services account for the decline; government, rents, transport, and finance have all risen.

In terms of level of per capita income in 1963, Brazil might be regarded as lower middle class. The existence of multiple and variable exchange rates makes the translation of Brazilian per capita incomes into dollars somewhat difficult, but it was somewhere around the $300 range. Thus Brazil is clearly above the class of genuinely poverty-stricken countries, with per capita incomes below $100, such as India, Burma, Pakistan, Indonesia, and Bolivia. It is somewhat better off than other aspirants to the lower-middle ranks such as Ceylon, the Philippines, Paraguay, and Egypt. It is roughly comparable to Malaya, Mexico, Lebanon, Turkey, or Portugal, but is clearly less prosperous in the aggregate than Venezuela, Argentina, Israel, Chile, or Italy.

The Agricultural Lag

All underdeveloped countries, we have seen, suffer from a lagging peasant agriculture sector. In many of these countries, the basic problem

TABLE 32-8

Index and Annual Change of the Real Product by Sectors

(Base: 1949 = 100)

(1947/1963)

Year	Agriculture		Industry		Commerce		Transportation and Communication		Government		Services		Rents		Total Product	
	Index	Annual Change	Index	Annual Change	Index	Annual Change	Index	Annual Change	Index	Annual Change	Index	Annual Change	Index	Annual Change	Index	Annual Change
1947	9.5	..	81.4	..	81.4	..	79.5	..	93.3	..	94.2	..	93.2	..	86.5	1.8
1948	95.7	6.9	90.6	11.3	96.2	18.2	92.3	16.1	97.6	2.4	97.1	3.0	96.4	3.6	94.7	9.5
1949	100.0	4.5	100.0	10.0	100.0	4.0	100.0	8.3	100.0	2.4	100.0	3.0	100.0	3.6	100.0	5.6
1950	101.5	1.5	111.4	11.4	104.1	4.1	108.0	8.0	102.4	2.4	103.5	3.0	103.5	3.6	105.0	5.0
1951	102.2	0.7	118.5	6.4	117.9	13.3	118.8	10.0	104.9	2.4	107.1	3.0	107.1	3.6	110.4	5.1
1952	111.5	9.1	124.4	5.0	122.5	3.9	126.4	6.4	107.4	2.4	111.0	3.0	111.0	3.6	116.6	5.6
1953	111.7	0.2	135.2	3.7	119.0	−22.9	137.8	9.0	110.0	2.4	115.1	3.0	115.1	3.6	120.3	3.2
1954	120.5	7.9	146.7	8.5	136.7	14.9	147.7	7.2	112.6	2.4	119.3	3.0	119.3	3.6	129.6	7.7
1955	129.8	7.7	162.3	10.6	143.5	5.0	152.4	3.2	115.4	2.4	123.7	3.0	123.7	3.6	138.4	6.8
1956	126.7	2.4	173.5	6.9	142.7	−0.6	157.5	3.3	118.1	2.4	128.2	3.0	128.2	3.6	141.0	1.9
1957	138.5	9.3	183.2	5.6	160.2	12.3	166.9	6.0	121.0	2.4	132.9	3.0	132.9	3.6	150.7	6.9
1958	141.3	2.0	213.2	16.4	171.1	6.8	176.7	5.9	123.9	2.4	137.8	3.0	137.8	3.6	160.7	6.6
1959	148.8	5.3	240.7	12.9	186.9	9.2	183.7	6.8	126.9	2.4	142.8	3.0	142.8	3.6	172.5	7.3
1960	156.1	4.9	264.8	10.0	197.8	5.8	219.1	16.1	130.0	2.4	148.0	3.0	148.0	3.6	184.0	6.7
1961*	167.9	7.6	293.4	10.8	209.8	6.1	240.0	9.5	133.1	2.4	153.2	3.0	153.2	3.6	197.4	7.3
1962*	177.1	5.5	316.0	7.7	217.8	3.8	256.2	6.8	136.3	2.4	158.8	3.0	158.8	3.6	208.0	5.4
1963*	177.3	0.1	316.7	0.2	220.7	1.3	272.2	6.2	139.9	2.4	164.6	3.0	164.6	3.6	210.9	1.4

* Provisional data

SOURCE: Instituto Brasileiro de Economia, Fundacão Getulio Vargas.

TABLE 32–9
Employment of Economically Active Population by Sector
(1950)

Employment	(1000)	%
Agriculture, forestry, hunting and fishing, and extractive industries	10,369,906	60.6
Manufacturing, electricity, gas, water and sanitary services, and construction	2,231,205	13.0
Commerce	1,073,997	6.4
Transport, storage, and communication	697,089	4.1
Services	2,698,491	15.8
Other activities	46,674	0.3
Total	17,117,362	100.0

SOURCE: Yearbook of Labour Statistics, 1963, International Labour Office.

TABLE 32–9a
Employment—Economically Active Population
(1940–1960)

Employment	1940 (1000)	% of total	1950 (1000)	% of total	1960* (1000)	% of total
Agriculture	9,448	67.8	9,960	57.8	11,795	49.2
Industry	1,792	12.9	2,749	15.9	4,459	18.6
Others	2,689	19.3	4,535	26.3	7,701	32.1
Total	13,929	100.0	17,244	100.0	23,955	100.0

* Estimated.
SOURCE: U.S. Agency for International Development (Brazil) *Statistical Tables Relating to Northeast Brazil* (Recipe, 1963), Table 18.

is overcrowding on the land. Brazil, on the other hand, seems to suffer from an agricultural lag in the sense that productivity is needlessly low, even with the existing pattern of land tenure. Certainly the picture for agriculture is a good deal less satisfactory than for industry. There is even some doubt as to whether or not the production of foodstuffs has kept pace with population growth. A calculation of the Brazilian Ministry of Agriculture suggested that per capita food consumption had actually declined between the depression year of 1933 and the relatively prosperous year of 1946. However, the ECLA calculations show a volume of agricultural production during 1945 to 1949 which was 55.8 per cent higher than that from 1925 to 1929, as compared to a population growth of 46.9 per cent between the 1925 to 1929 average and 1949. In any case, it is quite clear that agricultural output has not expanded as fast. The expansion of agricultural income in recent years has been much slower than for other industries.[23]

[23] See George Wythe, "Brazil: Trends in Industrial Development," (p. 35, especially), and Preston E. James, "Brazilian Agricultural Development," (pp. 78–102),

Demographic Factors

At the beginning of 1967 Brazil had a presumed population of about 85 million people. Brazil is therefore one of the six or seven largest countries in the world in terms of population as well as area. Considering Brazil's vast empty spaces, little of which can be dismissed as completely useless in terms of agricultural or potential mineral resources, there is no clear evidence that the population is above optimum. That is, with the given level of techniques, the existing pattern of tastes, the given world market for exports, it could not be said with assurance that a reduction in the total population would in itself inevitably raise per capita income. On the contrary, the size of the internal market, combined with the rate of increase in national income, provides opportunities for a wide range of profitable investment and for "balanced growth" of the Nurkse type—opportunities which many smaller countries lack. The level and distribution of income, moreover, bring a high income elasticity of demand for a good many manufactured goods.

Brazil has one of the highest rates of population growth in the world, about 3.2 per cent annually during the 1950's and probably somewhat higher today. In the present phase of Brazilian development, when much of the new investment must be allocated to such capital-intensive sectors as transport, power, housing, and heavy industry, this rate of population growth imposes a severe strain on the Brazilian capacity to save and invest.

The rate of population growth may well be above optimum. That is, the rate of increase in per capita income might be higher if the rate of growth in population were lower. Population growth can be a favorable factor in raising per capita income if the rate of capital accumulation is so high that population growth is needed to permit continued use of the optimal combinations of capital to labor throughout the economy; or if the increase in population is translated into an immediate and proportionate increase in effective demand. It is not clear that either of these conditions prevails in Brazil. On the contrary, the pressure of population growth imposes a heavy burden on the economy in terms of investment requirements. This statement is particularly true of the poorer regions, where natural rates of population growth are high and the ratio of savings to income is relatively low.

The distribution of fertility by sectors and regions is unfortunate. Birth rates are higher in the rural areas and poorer states than they are in the richer and more urbanized states. It is true that death rates are also higher in the more rural and poorer areas, but this difference in death rates does not entirely offset the differences in fertility rates. The recorded rates of population growth are lower in the poorer regions than in the richer ones, because of migration from the former to the latter. However, the higher fertility of the poorer regions, combined with improved public health everywhere, aggravates the problem of transferring people from

in Simon Kuznets (ed.), *Economic Growth: Brazil, India, Japan* (Durham, N.C., 1955); and *Programa de Acão do Governo, 1964–66*, EPEA (November, 1964), chap. XVII.

low-productivity agricultural employment and urban underemployment in the poorer regions to high-productivity occupations, whether in the modern sector of the same region or in the richer regions.

The main problems with regard to human resources, however, are two: an age distribution that imposes a severe burden on the active labor force, and an inadequate educational system. These two factors are interrelated, and reinforce each other.

As may be seen from the Appendix Table, in comparison with other countries, Brazil has a very high proportion of its population in the 0 to 4 age bracket, a high proportion in the 5 to 14 and 15 to 19 brackets, and a very low proportion in the most productive age group ranging from 20 to 64. Brazil is not, however, afflicted with the high proportion of aged people characteristic of the populations of the more advanced countries.

No country which is classified as "developed" in the Appendix Table, has so high a proportion of its population in the 0 to 4 year range, as Brazil. Indeed, in this respect Brazil resembles the poorer countries of Africa and Asia; even in Latin America, only relatively poor countries such as Peru have comparable figures for the proportion of infants in their population. Generally speaking, the same is true of the 5 to 14 and 15 to 19 age groups, although here Brazil's relative disadvantage is more striking. The differences in numbers in the lower age brackets are of course mirrored in the relatively small proportion of the population in the more productive age groups. Of all countries listed in this table, only Morrocco, Pakistan, and the Philippines have as small a proportion of their populations in the more productive age brackets.

This situation is reflected in a low labor force participation rate. As may be seen from the Appendix Table, with only 33 per cent of its population in the labor force, Brazil is more unfortunate in this respect than any of the major groups of countries in the table taken as a whole. It is far below the developed countries of the OECD (43.2 per cent), still further below the Communist countries (46.2 to 54.5 per cent), somewhat below Asia and Africa (40 and 39.3 per cent), and slightly below the Latin America average (34.5 per cent). Indeed, of the individual countries listed, only Ceylon, Vietnam, and Mexico are worse off than Brazil on this criterion.

The Educational Lag

Brazil has a serious problem of education. It is not only a matter of improving literacy of the masses, but also a matter of adapting higher education to the needs of a developing economy. Slavery lasted till 1888 in Brazil, and the tradition of a slave economy, in which the labor force is expected to provide only unskilled work, dies hard. Industrialization, however, requires a highly trained labor force, for which literacy is a necessary but not a sufficient condition. Higher education, instead of being "an ornament for the ruling classes," must become "an instrument for action in daily life." [24] A part of the educational reform required involves opening

[24] L. A. Costa Pinto, "Economic Development in Brazil: A General View of its Sociological Implications" in *Information*, Paris (International Research Office on Social Implications of Technological Change), July, 1959.

the educational system to all classes in society. The traditional system of providing free elementary and university education, while secondary education remains very expensive, is a recipe for preserving higher education as a device whereby the privileged classes protect their privileges. In part, too, Brazilian education suffers from early independence combined with continuing cultural ties with Portugal, which was not a leading center for management, science, and engineering in the nineteenth and twentieth centuries, but rather is itself an underedeveloped country. With a per capita income three times as high, Brazil is less able than India to turn out the managers, technicians, scientists, economists, and others needed for development.

Boom-and-Bust Pattern of Growth

The failure of economic development in Brazil to bring even moderately high levels of living to the Brazilian people as a whole is related to the well-known boom-and-bust pattern of this development. Each era of Brazilian development has had its own special growing point—sugar, livestock, minerals, rubber, coffee, and manufacturing. However, until recently each of these sources of growth has produced a limited period of expanding activity, followed by stagnation or decline, with only limited impact on the rest of the country. The sugar industry in the northeast—the first focal point of growth in Brazil—is now a problem industry, hardly able to hold its own in competition with sugar produced in other regions of Brazil and elsewhere in the world, while the world market fails to expand with world income. The livestock industry, similarly, now lags behind rather than leading the growth of national income as a whole. The mineral boom has passed, leaving ghost towns in its wake. The most spectacular of all boom-and-busts was the short rubber bubble, which has left behind a small high-cost industry, unable to meet even domestic requirements, and empty opera houses. Coffee today remains the major export, but it too has become a problem commodity rather than a generator of growth for the economy as a whole. The new industrial development is more hopeful but will bear watching for symptoms of the pattern of development that has been characteristic of Brazil in the past.

In comparison with the other large countries of recent settlement (Canada, the United States, and Australia), what is striking about Brazil is the failure of each successive wave of development, each based on a new commodity, to generate "spread effects," so essential to the widespread diffusion of high rates of growth among all sectors and regions of a country, with development in one sector and region encouraging growth in another, that growth in turn providing a basis for new expansion in the sector and region which started the process. Except for a modest contribution of capital and entrepreneurship from the coffee sector to the recent industrial development, each new wave of growth has been almost entirely discrete. There has been very little transfer of profits and skills of the "leading sector" of one era and area to the "leading sector" of the next. The outcome is regional disintegration and "hollow frontiers," in contrast to the movements into the inferior of Canada and particularly of the United States.

In Brazil the most recent phase of frontier development has transported the modern sector almost intact from the east coast to the far west, leaving nothing but empty space in between. Frontier cities like Campo Grande and Corumbá bear little resemblance to the "frontier towns" of the recent North American past. Their quality is not noticeably different from that of cities of comparable size near the east coast. Yet they are separated from the east coast centers by hundreds of miles of almost wholly unsettled territory. The problems of transport, communication, and power transmission resulting from this kind of frontier development are immediately apparent.

Limited Role of Foreign Trade

In Brazil, foreign trade has been an "engine of growth" of very low horsepower rating. Most of the profits and much of the expertise generated by the successive waves of development were transferred abroad, particularly in the early phase of Brazilian development. More recently much of the profits has gone into luxury consumption rather than into investments in other sectors. The terms of trade, if not clearly deteriorating over the long run, have certainly been submitted to disturbing fluctuations. Since the war there have been periods when the capacity to import, and thus the capacity to finance development, declined seriously (Table 32–10). The index of terms of trade (1953 = 100) ranged from 44 in 1948 to 134 in 1954, falling to 85 in 1963.

During the postwar period of rapid growth, exports may even have played a negative role; the index of quantum of exports (1953 = 100) fell from 131 in 1948 to 114 in 1962. As a result, Brazil has emerged in the mid-twentieth century with one of the lowest ratios of exports and imports to national income of all underdeveloped countries. In this respect, indeed, Brazil is closer to the United States than to typical underdeveloped countries. While this fact may be welcomed as a source of strength in the Brazilian economy, providing as it does opportunities for growth that are independent of the world market, it is also a source of weakness; expansion of imports probably cannot be avoided if high rates of development of the Brazilian economy are to be resumed. In terms of the efficiency of resource allocation Brazil is probably already more self-sufficient than it should be. To finance import requirements for growth, Brazil must find new strong exports.

In recent decades the structure of Brazilian exports shows little change. The share of particular commodities in total exports has fluctuated substantially, with changes in world market and crop conditions, but the general pattern has remained essentially unchanged over the last three decades. Coffee, while less important than in 1925–29 when it constituted 71.7 per cent of the value of exports, remains by far the most important export, accounting for 53 per cent of total exports in 1962. Cotton showed radical changes in importance from one period to another, rising from 2.1 per cent in 1925–29 to 18.6 per cent in 1935–39, falling to 2.7 per cent in 1957–59, and recovering to 9.2 per cent in 1962. Cocoa ranged from 3.5 per cent in 1925–29 to 5.6 per cent in 1957–59 and dropped to 2 per cent in 1962.

TABLE 32–10

Terms of Trade, Purchasing Power of Exports, and Quantum Index

Year	"Quantum" of exports		Terms of trade 1953 = 100 (B)	Purchasing power of exports	
	1953 prices (A)	Index 1953 = 100		1953 prices (C)	Index 1953 = 100
1947	1.961	127	45	882	57
1948	2.005	130	44	883	57
1949	1.803	117	53	956	62
1950	1.562	99	93	1.453	94
1951	1.686	110	95	1.602	104
1952	1.375	89	90	1.237	80
1953	1.539	100	100	1.539	100
1954	1.331	87	134	1.784	116
1955	1.526	99	118	1.801	117
1956	1.665	108	113	1.882	122
1957	1.530	99	117	1.790	116
1958	1.480	96	119	1.761	114
1959	1.806	117	109	1.969	128
1960	1.813	118	101	1.831	119
1961	1.976	128	97	1.917	125
1962	1.816	118	84	1.522	99
1963*	2.045	133	85	1.607	110

(1) $C = \dfrac{A \times B}{100}$

* Provisional data.

SOURCE: "*Conjuntura Economica*," Fundação Getulio Vargas.

Sugar showed some recovery in relative significance, from 0.4 per cent in 1925–29 to 3.2 per cent in 1962, with the development of the south-central plantations. Tobacco remained relatively constant, in the neighborhood of 2 per cent during the whole period. Rubber exports were still of some importance in the late 1920's when they constituted 2.9 per cent of the total, but they have since dwindled to insignificance. Pine wood showed more steady growth from 0.4 per cent to 3.2 per cent and iron ore, a relatively late arrival on the export scene, grew in importance from 3.3 per cent of the value of exports in 1957–59 to 5.7 per cent in 1962. Thus in 1962 Brazil remained dependent on coffee and a small range of other agricultural products and raw materials for its foreign exchange earnings.

Much the same may be said for the geographical pattern of Brazilian exports. The dependence on the United States market has scarcely changed. In 1925–29, 45.3 per cent of the value of Brazilian exports went to the United States, and in 1962 the figure was still 40 per cent. Exports to Germany also remained unchanged at 9.1 per cent over the whole period. Exports to France showed a fairly steady decline in importance, from 10.3 per cent in 1925–29 to 3.4 per cent in 1962. The Latin American market remained relatively unimportant for Brazil. Even Argentina, a relatively advanced and nearby country, took only 6 per cent of Brazilian exports in 1925–29 and 4 per cent in 1962. Neighboring Uruguay is even less important as a market for Brazilian commodities.

The import structure showed somewhat more change. Food, drink, and tobacco, which accounted for 14.9 per cent of the value of imports in 1938–39, still constituted 13.5 per cent in 1961. However, the industrialization of Brazil has been reflected to some degree in the sharp decline in the role of manufactured consumers' goods, from 10.9 per cent in 1938–39 to 1.5 per cent in 1961. Raw materials (other than fuel, lubricants, and coal and petroleum derivatives, which increased from 13.1 per cent to 18.8 per cent) fell from 30 per cent to 26.3 per cent. Capital goods exports showed an increase in relative importance from 29.9 per cent to 39.8 per cent.

The decline in the role of exports in Brazilian economic growth is indicated in the falling ratio of agricultural exports to domestic income, from 10.5 per cent in 1947 to 5.7 per cent in 1960 (in current prices), or at constant prices, from 14.9 per cent in 1947 to 6.1 per cent in 1961. As a proportion of total agricultural output, exports declined from 43 per cent in 1947 to 23.3 per cent in 1961 (current prices).

This experience is shared by most of the individual major exports. Thus the ratio of exports to total coffee production fell from 101.4 per cent in 1948 to 48.8 per cent in 1960. For cocoa the equivalent figures were 87.1 per cent and 62 per cent, for cotton 21.2 per cent and 7.8 per cent, for rubber 23.3 per cent and 16.1 per cent, and for tobacco 27.2 per cent and 23.5 per cent. On the other hand, in iron ore, production grew from 36.2 per cent to 54.9 per cent. Exports were an insignificant share of sugar production in both 1948 and 1960—0.5 per cent and 1.3 per cent, respectively.

Brazil's share of the world market for its major exports has declined. In 1934–38 Brazil enjoyed 52.8 per cent of the world market for coffee; in 1961 the figure had fallen to 37.6 per cent. For cocoa, the figures were 16.5 per cent and 10.2 per cent. In tobacco and cotton, Brazil had held its own in the world market, but its share is not large (5.8 per cent and 6.3 per cent, respectively). Brazil has increased its share in the world sugar market, but the proportion remains low, only 4.3 per cent in 1961.

The Balance of Payments Problem

While the role of foreign trade is small, Brazil, like other underdeveloped countries, is limited in its future economic growth by its balance of payment problems. It would not be correct to call Brazil a "one-crop" country, but it is very nearly a one-export country. The other significant exports, as well as coffee, are subject both to fluctuations in world market prices and to uncertainties with respect to long-run demand. The United States has been the major market for Brazilian exports for some decades, absorbing between 34 and 57 per cent of total Brazilian exports, with no very clear-cut trend. In terms of total expenditures on Brazilian exports, the trend is clearly upward. What is more impressive, however, is the enormous fluctuation in the value of American imports from Brazil, which in three and one-half decades varied from $82.1 million in 1932 to $910.6

million in 1951. Under these circumstances, it is not surprising that the
Brazilian government has occasionally suggested to the United States that
it introduce or support international measures for commodity stabilization.

The rapid growth of Brazil between 1944 and 1954 was permitted by a
strong coffee market with low inventories, such that occasional acute
shortages resulted in sharp increases in price. Indeed, the value of exports
in general increased substantially during this period. However, by 1956,
the threat of a chronic world surplus of coffee had reappeared. The small
Brazilian crop of 1956–57, which was decidedly smaller than the two previous years, brought only a moderate and temporary increase in coffee
prices. The value of exports of cotton and cocoa were lower, expenditures
on services were higher. Only the net inflow of capital, of which official
capital played an increasingly important role, permitted Brazil to maintain
its imports of goods and services in the face of the declining value of its
imports.

Chronic Inflation

Inflation is a traditional way of life in Brazil. In the sixteenth century,
inflation in Spain and Portugal reached such proportions that some economic historians termed it "the price revolution;" the colonies shared in
the process. Brazil itself has experienced secular inflation since the first
days of independence. Prior to World War II, however, the problem of
inflation did not assume alarming proportions. Cumulative and accelerating
increases in prices and depreciation of the foreign exchange value of the
cruzerio really appeared only in 1959. Then inflation gathered pace and
for the first time showed signs of getting out of hand. In the first quarter
of 1964 the price rise reached the rate of 25 per cent, which, had it continued throughout the year, would have brought aggregate price increases
of 144 per cent, or even more when the tendency toward acceleration is
taken into account. When the Castello Branco government came to power
in April, 1964, Brazil was on the verge of hyperinflation. Inflation had
reached proportions that not only brought balance of payments disequilibrium but endangered economic growth itself. In these circumstances, as
stated in the government's Action Program for 1964–66, no other item
was so urgent as the curbing of inflation.

Regional Dualism

Brazil is one of the countries where "technological dualism" results also
in "regional dualism." The sharply differentiated sectors overlap with
differentiated regions. The modern sector consists of the south, whereas
the traditional sector consists of the north and the northeast. Undeveloped
or lagging regions do not matter so much if, as in Australia, few people
live in them. But in Brazil nearly 30 per cent of the population now lives in
the northeast, another 6 per cent in the north. Adding the population employed in the pockets of low productivity within the southern region, it
may be said that nearly half of the Brazilian population is still engaged in
the traditional sector. Moreover, the spreads in per capita income between
the traditional and modern sector are enormous—of the order of 400 per

cent—and are not clearly diminishing. No such differentials exist in the other three large countries of recent settlement (United States, Canada, and Australia). Indeed, there is no traditional sector or region left in them. There may be a few farmers struggling on submarginal land, but the great bulk of the population lives and works in high-productivity industry and agriculture.

Even more than Italy, then, Brazil may be regarded as a classic case of a country where technological dualism takes the form of regional dualism. The over-all growth of the economy still leaves half the population in poverty and shows little sign of significantly improving the lot of this submerged half of the population. The development has been concentrated in certain sectors and regions, leaving the rest of the country virtually untouched. The State of São Paulo might be regarded as having already emerged from the category of underdeveloped regions, with a per capita income of nearly $400, two-thirds of its population urban, one-third of its income produced in the industrial sector, and only 23.5 per cent of its income produced in the agricultural sector, where productivity is, in any case, relatively high. The State of São Paulo has many of the characteristics of a middle-ranking European country. At the other end of the scale is Piauí with a per capita income of barely $60, only 24 per cent of its population in the urban area, and the bulk of labor force still engaged in agriculture, mostly of a rather rudimentary and small-scale type.[25]

During the decade of the fifties the northeast region as a whole had a per capita income of less than half the national average and less than one-quarter of the level for the south-central region (São Paulo, Guanabara, and Paraná). In the northeast nearly half of total production and nearly two-thirds of employment are accounted for by the agricultural sector, as compared with about one-third and about 40 per cent for the rest of the country (Tables 32–11 and 32–24). It is true that vestiges of the traditional sector can be found even in the advanced regions of Brazil; poverty exists among landless agricultural workers, among small farmers, fishermen, and unskilled industrial workers, even in the south and south-central regions. On the other hand, elements of the modern sector have appeared in the north and northeast, notably in recent industrial development in Recife and Salvador.[26] Nonetheless, the striking contrast between the north and northeast on the one hand and the south and south-central regions on the other have been noted by all students of the Brazilian economic and social structure.

Unfortunately in Brazil the poor regions are quite heavily populated. With over 24 million people in the northeast and over three million in the north, these poor regions account for more than one-third of the total Brazilian population. Adding the pockets of poverty in other regions, it is clear that at least half of the Brazilian population is living under unacceptable conditions. In this respect, Brazil is perhaps less unfortunate than Indonesia, which has two-thirds of its population—a number of people

[25] In 1960, per capita income in Piauí was only sixteen percent of that of São Paulo.
[26] "Northeast" is here defined to coincide with the area under SUDENE (Superentendencia para Desinvolvimento do Nordeste) jurisdiction and so includes Bahia.

TABLE 32–11*

Regional Distribution of the Brazilian Population
and National Income

Region	Population, percentage				
	1947	1949	1957	1959	1960
North*	4	4	3	3	3
Northeast	25	24	24	25	24
East	36	36	35	35	34
South	32	33	34	34	35
Middle west†	3	3	4	3	4
Total	100	100	100	100	100

Region	National income, percentage				
	1947	1949	1957	1959	1960
North	2	2	2	2	2
Northeast	11	11	10	10	11
East	37	37	36	36	34
South	48	48	50	50	51
Middle west	2	2	2	2	2
Total	100	100	100	100	100

* In the table, Bahia and Sergipe are included in the "east." If they were included in the northeast, as they are by SUDENE, the figures would indicate a slight decline in the region's share of national income between 1947 and 1960. The share of total population in the SUDENE "northeast" fell from 34.7% in 1950 to 31.6% in 1960.

† North includes the states of Amazonas and Para; Middle west, the states of Mato Grosso and Goias.

SOURCE: Adapted from Werner Baer, *Industrialization and Economic Development in Brazil* (Homewood, Ill., 1965), p. 169.

almost equal to the total population of Brazil—crowded onto the small island of Java. There are nonetheless some common characteristics. In the sugar area around Recife, current population growth sustained for another generation would produce a population density comparable to that of Java today. In Brazil, as in Indonesia, people tend to remain in relatively high rainfall areas, where employment opportunities were at one time better than elsewhere, despite subsequent changes in economic and social conditions. Good land with assured rainfall is already suffering from overcrowding, with population densities in the coastal areas near Recife as high as 300 per square kilometer—one generation of growth at current rates would create a problem of population pressure in the coastal areas of the Brazilian northeast as bad as the one that now prevails in Java. It has been estimated that in order to guarantee a minimum per capita income of even $100 per year in this area it will be necessary to move 7.5 million people out of it.

In Indonesia, as in Brazil, sugar was the first really important export product, and the population explosion in both countries was launched by development of the sugar industry. However, the population explosion to date has gone less far in Brazil than in Indonesia, relative to the available land and other resources. Moreover, in Brazil, industrial investment in the modern sector (and rich region) has been relatively high. Thus at the end of the Dutch colonial period (1949) only 7 per cent of the Indonesian labor force had been drawn into the modern sector. In Brazil perhaps half of the labor force might be regarded as being employed in the modern sector. Moreover, in Brazil the dualism is less sharp; there is a sizable sector of middle-sized operations with reasonably high productivity both in industry and agriculture, which provides a kind of bridge connecting the traditional to the modern sector.

The Indonesian modern sector and leading region has been almost entirely export-oriented. It is therefore submitted to the vagaries of the world market. The principal growing points during the period 1890–1930 can no longer be counted on to provide the impetus for growth on the economy as a whole. While the same may be said of coffee, in Brazil only 6 or 7 per cent of national income derives from foreign trade (either as export or import). Much of the modern sector consists of new industrial enterprises, producing mainly for the domestic market but providing the base for new export industries, as the scale of their operations grows and their efficiency is raised.

On the other hand, Brazil is worse off, in terms of the proportion of population struggling for a living in the traditional sector and lagging regions, than many other underdeveloped countries, such as Argentina, Chile, or the Philippines. With respect to urban growth, Brazil resembles the underdeveloped countries of Asia rather than any of the three large advanced economies of the New World; that is, urbanization is outrunning industrialization.

In one sense it might be said that Brazil lags behind Asia. For in Brazil, we have seen, the population explosion is largely an affair of this century, whereas in such Asian countries as Indonesia the population explosion began early in the nineteenth century. Java, for example, had only four million people when large-scale organized agriculture for export first began, in 1830; by 1900 the population had reached 40 million. Brazil is still in the stage in which Indonesia found itself 100 years ago. The growth of population in the traditional sector can still be met to some degree by the occupation of new land, and to some degree by shifting from slash-and-burn agriculture to stable agriculture. But if this process is allowed to continue for another generation Brazil may well find itself in the situation of some Asian countries, in which all the really fertile land is occupied and converted to stable agriculture, with the typical size of farm too small to yield a satisfactory standard of living, and the population still growing. In Brazil there is yet time to avoid the almost hopeless situation which exists in a region like Java, but the time is limited.

If the whole country were as highly developed as the south, let alone the southeast and central regions and if the recent high rates of growth still prevailed, there would be little reason to be concerned about Brazilian development problems. But this is far from the case. Poverty and squalor in the shanty towns of the northeastern cities rival those of the poorest Asian cities, and in the rural areas conditions are even worse.

Even more distressing is the fact that postwar rates of growth—even percentage rates, let alone absolute rates—are no higher in the northeast than in the country as a whole. With such enormous differences in the base incomes, it would take decades of faster percentage growth in the poorer districts before the gap in levels of per capita income would begin to close, and more decades before the gap would disappear; but in Brazil this process of diminishing gaps has scarcely started.

The overlap of regions and sectors is not perfect. There are elements of the modern sector in Amazonia and the northeast—such as the new industries in Recife. And there are pockets of extreme poverty in the south, such as the fishing villages near Rio and São Paulo and the tenants on *latifundia* in Rio Grande do Sul; but the proportion of the labor force employed in the modern sector in the north, and the proportion employed in the traditional sector in the south, is very small. In general, the north-south division is very sharp.

The Northeast: a Poor and Lagging Region

Of all regions in Brazil the northeast has attracted the greatest attention, partly because it is the poorest region and yet has 30 per cent of the total population, partly because of the publicity it has received—largely for political reasons, and partly because of the dynamic leadership and vigorous activity of the agency established for its development, SUDENE. Preston E. James likens the northeast to New England, although a closer comparison might be made with the Atlantic Provinces of Canada, since the northeast has yet to have a clear-cut resurgence: [27]

The Northeast plays a part in Brazilian national life which resembles that played by New England in the national structure of the United States. Some of the first successful colonies on the coast of Brazil were planted in Bahia and Pernambuco, around the primary settlement centers of Salvador and Recife (or near-by Olinda). Bahia and Pernambuco were the most prosperous of the Portuguese colonies in America during the sugar period. Inland from the sugar-cane plantations was Brazil's traditional sertão—the backlands of the Northeast. In this setting many of the Brazilian traditions and Brazilian attitudes were first developed. Although the region in modern times is one of great poverty, the Northeast has supplied more than its share of Brazil's intellectual, artistic, and political leaders. For centuries, too, the chief product of the Northeast has been people—people who have migrated to other parts of the country where economic opportunity seemed to beckon. Workers from the Northeast panned gold in Minas Gerais, planted coffee in São Paulo, tapped rubber in the Amazon, harvested cocoa in southern Bahia. People from the Northeast are now building the great cities of Rio de Janeiro and São Paulo.

[27] Preston E. James, *Latin America* (New York, 1959), p. 409.

The northeast has been an area of "calamities." There are small areas in it where the average rainfall is very low, but where there were more than fifty years of floods or drought between 1835 and 1935. Other parts of the area show a varying tendency to recurring calamities. In "good" years, about 90 per cent of the rain in the drought area falls between December and April or early May. The rainfall for an entire month may be brought by four or five violent showers. In bad years, some localities may have no rain at all. James describes this "repeated calamity of flood and drought" as "the curse of the Sertão." These conditions have set a limit to development of the frontier. As in the more arid zones of Australia, people push into the interior beyond the margin of safe cultivation, and then return to coastal cities when disaster occurs.

The share of the northeast in Brazilian national income declined from 16.5 per cent in 1950 to 15.9 per cent in 1960. A comparison with 1947 shows much the same picture. However, a part of this relative decline represents a lower rate of population growth in the northeast than in the rest of the country. During the decade of the 1950's the per capita income of the northeast rose from 48.5 per cent of the national average to 50.6 per cent. This movement can be divided into distinct periods. From 1950 through 1954, per capita income in the northeast declined in relation to the Brazilian average; it rose through 1957 and then dropped back to its 1956 level. In 1959, per capita income in the northeast was still slightly below its 1950 level, and only in 1960 did it rise above it.[28]

Thus the period of uninterrupted relative improvement in the northeast, for which official estimates are available, is very short. Moreover, the picture is changed somewhat if account is taken of the difference in price movements in the northeast and in the rest of Brazil. During the 1950's the real per capita income of the northeast rose only 34.4 per cent compared with 65.6 per cent for the rest of Brazil. Once again, however, the northeast lagged behind the rest of Brazil between 1950 and 1955, grew somewhat more slowly than the rest of Brazil between 1955 and 1960, but grew more rapidly than the rest of Brazil between 1958 and 1960.

The big gains came in the States of Maranhão and Bahia, Maranhão registering much the biggest increase in agricultural production and Bahia the biggest increase in industrial production. The decision to move the headquarters of Petrobras to Salvador contributed substantially to the high rate of industrial growth in the State of Bahia. There is some question, however, whether Bahia belongs properly in the "northeast" for analytical purposes; its ties would seem to be with the south rather than with the rest of the northeast.

For the region as a whole, such relative gains as took place were entirely in agriculture. The northeast's share of total agricultural income in Brazil rose from 6.2 per cent in 1949 to 7.4 per cent in 1960. Its share of total Brazilian industrial income declined over the same period from 2.1 per cent to 1.9 per cent. It is worth noting that this relative gain in agriculture re-

[28] These figures are from USAID-Brazil, *Statistical Tables Relating to Northeast Brazil* (Recife, 1963), Table 19, 22, and 26.

flected a decline in agricultural output in the rest of Brazil from Cr.$428 billion in 1955 to Cr.$396 billion in 1960, as well as an increase in agricultural output in the northeast. The drop in agricultural output elsewhere in the country is the consequence of the difficulties faced in the coffee sector, and the increase in production in the northeast reflected relatively good rainfall in the last years of the decades of the 1950's. Thus all these trends are easily reversible, and it is by no means certain that the share of the northeast in Brazilian income, in per capita as well as in absolute terms, may not decline again in future years.

It is also worth noting that for the whole period 1949 to 1961, the increase in agricultural output in real terms was almost identical in the northeast and in Brazil as a whole—66.7 per cent versus 65.6 per cent. In industry, on the other hand, real income increased only 30 per cent in the northeast during this period as compared to 94.4 per cent in Brazil. There is little evidence, therefore, that the northeast is clearly "over the hump" and on the path toward convergence with Brazilian levels of output and income. Much more dramatic structural change than has taken place in the northeast is likely to be necessary before a prolonged convergence can be expected.

Only the slower rate of population growth has prevented further deterioration of even the relative position of the northeast in the Brazilian economy. During the 1940's, the annual rate of population growth in the northeast was 2.2 per cent, as compared with 2.4 per cent in the rest of Brazil; and during the 1950's, the northeast population grew at an average rate of 2.2 per cent per year, compared with 3.6 per cent for the rest of Brazil. Large-scale emigration from the northeast helps to account for this slower rate of population growth. Only the eastern region has a larger total out-migration than the northeast. It is interesting to note that the larger share of the out-migrants from the northeast go directly to the eastern region. Thus a triangular pattern of migration has been set up in Brazil, with people from the northeast moving into the plantation economy of the east and filling the jobs left vacant by easterners moving into the nearby cities of the south. As a percentage of the total population in 1950, the out-migration amounted to 6.6 per cent in the east, and 4.8 per cent in the northeast.

Urbanization is proceeding more rapidly in the rest of the country than it is in the northeast. In the rest of Brazil, the proportion of rural population in the total declined from 64.6 per cent in 1940 to 49.9 per cent in 1960; the comparable figures for the northeast are 76.6 per cent and 65.8 per cent. The share of the northeast in the total Brazilian urban population actually declined by 11.2 per cent between 1940 and 1960. It does not seem that a process of rapid structural change has yet set in in the northeast.

THE SECOND MASTER PLAN

A common failing of regional plans is an underlying assumption that the problems *of* the poor or lagging regions must be solved *in* the region. Interactions between development within the region and development in other regions and in the national economy as a whole seldom get the attention they deserve. In particular, the possibility that investment outside the region might, under some circumstances, raise income and employment within the poor region more than investment within the region itself, is seldom even considered. This failing is particularly pronounced in the SUDENE Second Master Plan for 1963–65. The document contained no analysis of interregional trade, capital movements, or even of emigration or immigration. There was no analysis of the relationship of development of the northeast to the situation in the relevant world markets. There was no attempt to measure the inflationary impact of carrying out the proposed SUDENE investment program. There was no analysis of the probable impact of the program on the balance of payments. There was no use of even such simple tools of development planning as incremental capital-output ratios and incremental capital-employment ratios, let alone more sophisticated techniques such as linear programming and input-output analysis. There was not even the most primitive attempt at cost-benefit analysis.

The plan was also too modest; it could scarcely make a dent on the problems of the northeast. Estimates made in collaboration with SUDENE officials led to the conclusion that in the densely populated coastal areas (roughly corresponding with the sugar belt) the achievement of even a minimum per capita income of $100 per year for everyone would require the removal of 7.5 million people from the area. If the ratio of members of the labor force to population is 1:3 (as it seems to be), this means that 2.5 million jobs must be created elsewhere. If this problem is to be solved over a ten-year period, this means finding 250,000 new jobs per year. Adding to this figure the annual increase in the labor force of the region, which also approaches 250,000 per year, SUDENE should be thinking in terms of creating nearly half a million new, high-productivity jobs (that is, jobs that would create per capita incomes at least as high as the present Brazilian average of $250). Yet the development program for five years was only Cr.$228 billion, less than $1 billion, or less than $200 million per year. Even with the highly conservative estimate of capital requirements for each new permanent job of $3,000 (which might be achieved through a combination of resettlement, small industries, and heavier industries either in the region itself or outside the region altogether), the creation of half a million new jobs per year would require $1.5 billion per year of new investment, as compared to the $200 million provided for in the Plan.

THE THIRD MASTER PLAN, 1966–1968

The Third Master Plan, covering the years 1966–68, shows considerably more awareness of the need to integrate the economy of the northeast with the national economy, and to take full account of the interactions among the regional, national, and world economies. Its basic objectives are to produce an annual increase in regional domestic product of 7 per cent (double the goal, in per capita terms, laid down for Latin America as a whole in the Charter of Punta del Este) and by so doing to "diminish the inequalities of income between the man of the Drought Polygon and his counterpart in the Center-South of the country," and "to promote the spatial and sectoral integration of the Northeastern economy, linking it more tightly

to the national economy." Subsidiary goals are to provide new job opportunities, to raise the growth rate in the primary sector, and to assure widespread diffusion of the benefits of development by enhancing social
mobility.

The projected scale of the regional development program is also more
realistic than that of its predecessors. It asks for an over-all budget of Cr.
$3,846 billion; at the exchange rates prevailing when the Plan was finished,
this figure was equivalent to about $2 billion. Thus the proposed program is
roughly double the scale of the Second Master Plan.

It is interesting to note among the "general guidelines" for achieving
these goals the inclusion of a public investment program designed to attract
and orient private investment, the attraction and orientation of foreign
resources, creation of an entrepreneurial mentality that will permit more
effective participation of private initiative in the development of the region, and—taking a leaf from the book of François Perroux and the French
planners—"to identify and promote the development of regional growth
poles." The authors of the Plan, in underlining major differences between
the Third and the previous two plans, point to "the utilization of a methodology which emphasizes the spatial aspects of economic activities in the
analysis and solution of regional problems." [29]

There is also a difference in the approach to the sugar problem. The
Plan notes that the sugar economy is in crisis condition but recognizes that
solving the problem is beyond the scope of SUDENE's powers, since it
requires a "radical and immediate transformation in the present structure
of the sugar industry." The Plan also demonstrates a clear recognition of
the importance for the region of its external sector. It notes an accentuated
decline of imports into the region, a rise in real world prices of major exports, and a trend in foreign exchange rates which has been favorable to
regional exporters and which has improved the terms of trade between
exporters in the northeast and the rest of the Brazilian economy, helping
to stem the tide of resource transfers from the northeast to the center-
south. The stimulus of the foreign sector has been a major factor in the
reduction of the gap between the northeast and the rest of the economy
between 1960 and 1963.

The Plan includes efforts to demonstrate through more ambitious publicity programs the advantages to investors in the center-south in making
industrial investments in the northeast. The high priority given to electric
power and transport facilities is explained by the need to incorporate
growing areas of the region into the development process and to improve
the connection with the center-south of the country.

There is therefore in the Third Plan a clear recognition of the interactions of development among areas of the region, the region and other
regions within the country, and the region with the world economy. So
far, however, knowledge as to the precise nature of these interactions is
very limited. A joint research project of the Universities of São Paulo,

[29] The quotations from the Third Master Plan are from the English translation
prepared by USAID/Brazil in Recife.

ANPES (Associacão National para Pesquisa Economica e Social), and the University of Ceará, now under way, should contribute a good deal to knowledge of relationships between development in the center-south and development in the northeast.

Amazonia: the Forgotten Region [30]

Amazonia is defined by the Superintendência do Plano de Valorizacão Econômica da Amazônia (SPVEA) [31] to include the States of Amazonas, Para, and Acre, the three territories of Rondônia, Roraima, and Amapá, plus the parts of the states of Mato Grosso north of the sixteenth parallel, and Maranhão to the west of the forty-fourth meridian. This area encompasses 59.39 per cent [32] of Brazil, but contains only three million inhabitants, or 3.6 per cent of the total Brazilian population (1964). The degree of urbanization is relatively high, reaching 87 per cent in Boa Vista, Roraima; 72 per cent in Pôrto Velho, Rondônia; 30 per cent in Rio Branco do Acre; 25 per cent in Manaus, Amazonas; and 25 per cent in Belém.[33] The distribution in 1964 of the population of Amazonia is shown in Table 32–12.
The growth rate of the regional population has declined slowly in the past sixty years, from 3.57 per cent in 1900–10 to 1.99 per cent for the period from 1950–60.[34] The population is still growing at about the same rate.

The economic history of the region is linked to the exportation of agricultural and extractive products, mainly rubber. The traditional agricultural products of the region also include *babacú*, Brazil nuts, various types of *timbó, guaraná, piacava*. The rubber boom came in the early 1900's. Nevertheless, the boom collapsed just before World War I with the introduction of Malayan-produced latex into the world market. Even today, Amazonia still ranks first in the production of many of these traditional products.

Natural latex is still being gathered and sold both domestically and abroad. The largest producer is the State of Acre, followed closely by Amazonas. Production in 1964 was 11,038 tons and 14,597 tons for each state, respectively.[35]

Realizing that the Amazon Valley and Basin is a critical area economically for the future progress and development of Brazil, the federal government decided in 1953 that a development plan must be formulated so that the region could be integrated into the national economy and contribute to the over-all progress of the nation. The producers of primary goods such as wood products, oils, gum, fibers, etc., for the industrial sector will find it more imperative that a national mobility of resources take place in order to facilitate the supply of these primary goods to the industrial com-

[30] The author had the assistance of Kent H. Smith in preparing this section.
[31] *Plano de Valorizacão Econômica da Amazônia* (Pará-Brasil, 1960), p. 3.
[32] *Loc. cit.*
[33] Werner Baer, "Regional Inequality and Economic Growth in Brazil," *Economic Development and Cultural Change*, XII, No. 3 (April, 1964), 269.
[34] Baer, *op. cit.*, 278.
[35] *Ibid.*, p. 79.

TABLE 32–12

Population of Amazonia, 1964

States and territories	Population
Rondônia	91,000
Acre	182,000
Amazonas	817,000
Roraima	35,000
Para	1,743,000
Amapá	87,000
Total	2,961,000

SOURCE: Banco do Brasil, *Relatório* (Brasília, 1965), p. 258.

plex.[36] Much of the population in the Amazon area lives close to subsistence levels. To realize social and economic progress in all of Brazil the living standards of this marginal population need to be elevated to a level where these people can enjoy full participation in the social and economic life of the nation. The Amazon region must also be populated and developed so that this vast empty area will not remain a threat to national security.

The basis for this development program lies in the Constitution of 1946 which states: "In the execution of the Economic Valorization Plan of Amazonia, the Union will apply, during at least twenty consecutive years, a specified quantity of not less than 3 per cent of its tax revenue." (Art. 199) [37] The Constitution also specifies that: "The States and Territories of that region (Amazonia), along with their respective *municipios*, will reserve for the same goal, annually, 3 per cent of their respective tax revenues. The resources of which this paragraph concerns will be applied through the Federal Government."

For almost seven years little was done to comply with this article of the Constitution. Finally, at the insistence of several northern deputies and senators, together with other northern state officials, the government under Getúlio Vargas finally set forth a plan for the development of Amazonia. Two laws were sanctioned: Law #1806 of January 6, 1953, and Decree #34.132 of October 9, 1953. The former prescribes the Economic Valorization Plan of Amazonia and creates SPVEA. The latter sets down the rules and regulations governing the functioning of the Plano de Valorizacão Econômica da Amazônia (PVEA). Law #1806 states in the first article that the purpose and objective of PVEA is: "to increase the development of the extractive and agricultural sectors, the livestock sector, the mineral sector, the industrial sector, and the trade relations." The second main objective of PVEA is the social and economic betterment of the population of this region.

[36] Cosme Ferreira Filho, "Novos Ângulos do Problema Amazônico," *Colecão Araújo Lima* (1954), p. 16.
[37] *Ibid.*, p. 223.

The law defines quite specifically the objectives to be obtained and the general areas of concentration of the Plan. Among the major goals of the Plan are: the development of a flood control system; the further processing of raw materials; development of transportation and communications; a sound energy and demographic policy; a regional system of banking; encouragement of private investment; and the maintenance of an information service.

To finance the Plan the law provides for the establishment of the *Fundo de Valorizacão Econômica da Amazônia* (FVEA). Its financial resources consist of: (1) 3 per cent of the federal tax revenue; (2) 3 per cent of the tax revenue of the states, territories, and *municípios* (a country-like unit with one main town) which are encompassed in the Amazon region; (3) income originating from services rendered by the PVEA; and (4) extra financial allocations from the Union, states, or *municípios*. The financial resources from the federal government to the FVEA must be included in the national budget. In order to ensure maximum utilization of the resources available for the economic development of Amazonia, SPVEA is granted almost complete control over all business enterprises and autonomous entities operating in the region. SPVEA maintains branch offices in Manaus and Cuiabá; the headquarters are in Belém. The Superintendent, appointed by the President of the Republic, presides over the Superintendency and the Planning Commission. The Planning Commission consists of fifteen members: six technicians from the general sectors of activity and nine representatives from the several states and territories of Amazonia. Their main obligations are to formulate projects and to draw up the budget proposal for the Plan.

Toward the end of 1953 the machinery for the execution of an economic development plan was completed. Yet in 1966 the SPVEA had not been able to implement even its first Five-Year Plan, for the simple reason that the congress had not seriously discussed it,[38] let alone ratified it. As a result, the SPVEA has had to formulate each year an "emergency plan" covering one year's operations.

The first "emergency program" in 1954 emphasized the intensification of development efforts and services already in existence. In spite of the financial resources available, the 1954 "emergency program" had little impact on the social and economic structure of the region. Regional income and *per capita* income stayed at the same levels.[39]

The figures in Table 32–13 indicate significant structural change, but they reflect stagnation in agriculture rather than vigorous growth in other sectors.

The agricultural sector in Amazonia is weak because the farmers still rely on the traditional products, such as jute, chestnuts, rubber, etc., despite limited markets. Prior to the SPVEA no attempt had been made to diversify or to introduce modern techniques. One of SPVEA's agricultural

[38] *Ministério Extraordinário para Coordinação dos Organismos Regionais, Superintendencia do Plano de Valorizacão Econômica da Amazônia, Programa de Emergência para 1965*, (1961), 1.

[39] Ferreira Filho, *op. cit.*, p. 231.

TABLE 32–13

Structure of the Amazonia Economy

North	Income of region %		National production in north %
	1947	1958	1958
Agriculture	29.1	16.5	2.0
Commerce	18.4	16.5	2.7
Industry (manufacturing)	23.5	26.2	2.4
Transportation and communication	8.4	7.7	7.9
Interim financing	1.0	1.3	2.3
Rents	1.1	1.7	1.0
Government	7.4	10.1	0.8
Services	10.9	10.2	1.9

SOURCE: *Revista Brasileira de Economia*, Marco, 1960.

projects has been extension of rural credits to small producers for the acquisition of agricultural implements and for the organization of producers' cooperatives. Interest rates have been extremely low (2 to 4 per cent *per annum*), considering the chronic inflation.[40]

Another major SPVEA project has been dealing with the revitalization of rubber production on an organized basis. Total Brazilian production amounted to 36,915 tons in 1964 in comparison with 30,814 tons in 1962.[41] Rubber plantations are being created on a small property basis to supplement the somewhat haphazard gathering of wild rubber.[42]

Transport and communication have needed improvement for many years. The late 1950's brought a new attitude on the part of the federal government and SPVEA with respect to the expansion of the highway and road system in the region, in an effort to connect the north with the south and the east of Brazil. The attention of SPVEA was focused on the construction of the Belém-Brasília highway (BR-14). It was completed in 1960 and has a total length of about 2,275 km. The average speed of construction was about 2 km. a day.[43] To aid in the planning and construction of BR-14 a subcommission of Rodobrás (the federal road-building company) was placed under SPVEA's control.

Other roads being constructed now will also facilitate the economic integration of Brazil's diverse regions. Among those still being constructed are: the Brasília-Rio Branco do Acre road; the Macapá-Oiapoque road in Amapá; and several others. The funds for the construction of these roads and highways, in the Amazon region, originate with the federal govern-

[40] "Planejamento transforma a Amazônia," Separata de *O Observador econômico e financeiro*, XXIII, 275 (Janeiro, 1959), p. 17.
[41] Instituto Brasileira de Geografia e Estatistica, *Anuário Estatístico*, 1965, *op. cit.*, p. 78.
[42] "Planejamento, etc.," *op. cit.*, p. 28.
[43] *Ibid.*, p. 6.

ment. Table 32–14 shows the extent of the road network of each region of Brazil and each region's percentage of the national road system.

Water and air transportation are also beginning to play an important role in the development of the region. SPVEA has aided in the formation of shipping companies in Amapá, Goiás, Mato Grosso, Roraima, and Rondônia. SPVEA also invested CR.$37,400,000 in renovating and constructing port installations along the Amazon River.[44]

TABLE 32–14

Road Network

Region	Length in km.			% in relation to the total		
	1961	1962	1963	1961	1962	1963
North	6,502	7,514	7,534	1.3	1.5	1.4
Northeast	79,763	79,699	79,862	16.0	15.3	14.8
East	115,798	141,438	141,322	23.2	27.2	26.2
South	241,358	246,175	259,847	48.3	47.4	48.3
Center-west	56,129	44,626	50,214	11.2	8.6	9.3
Total	499,550	519,452	538,779	100.0	100.0	100.0

SOURCE: Banco do Brasil, *Relatório* (Brasília, 1965), p. 168.

SPVEA has granted subsidies to such airlines as Cruzerio do Sul and Paraense so that they may render more adequate air service to towns and villages in the region that would otherwise have little or no communication with the outside world. Also installations such as airports, hangars, and paved runways have been built with SPVEA's aid.

A third important sector in the economic development of the region is livestock for regional as well as for extraregional consumption. Ten per cent of SPVEA's budget is to be used for the development and expansion of the livestock sector. Yet little progress has been made. The number of head of livestock in Amazonia has increased substantially since 1950, but it is still small, even on a per capita basis, when compared with the rest of Brazil. Table 32–15 gives the statistics for the years 1962 and 1963.

Industrialization, the fourth sector of economic activity, has been one of the primary goals of SPVEA's programs for the economic development of the region. The plan for the development of a manufacturing industrial complex in Amazonia should, in the early stages of development, be based on the raw materials existing in the region and on the expansion of the small industries already established there. Many projects for the initiation of new industries have been summitted to the SPVEA and have been approved, but have not been undertaken due to lack of funds. Among the projects proposed are: (1) the installation of two cellulose and paper factories in Pará and Amazonas; (2) the construction of two cement plants; (3) the establishment of several sawmills; (4) the complete renovation of

[44] "Planejamento, etc.," *op. cit.,* p. 37.

TABLE 32–15

Number of Head and Value of Livestock, Amazonia and Brazil,
1962 and 1963

1962	Amazonas		Brazil	
	1,000 head	Cr. $1,000	1,000 head	Cr. $1,000
Cattle	201	4,131,582	79,078	1,473,510,906
Horses	15	258,012	8,692	87,987,783
Asses	1	21,121	2,393	10,802,949
Mules	6	133,044	4,421	69,949,190
Pigs	414	1,751,644	52,941	284,212,863
Sheep	42	66,018	19,718	45,486,932
Goats	34	48,562	12,397	18,753,101
Total	826	6,409,983	179,640	1,990,703,624

1963	Amazonas		Brazil	
	1,000 head	Cr. $1,000	1,000 head	Cr. $1,000
Cattle	233	8,256,725	79,855	2,378,622,297
Horses	18	509,244	8,903	142,464,075
Asses	1	35,808	2,552	17,743,279
Mules	6	235,437	4,586	112,961,305
Pigs	478	3,407,340	55,990	525,203,622
Sheep	47	123,491	21,033	76,123,589
Goats	43	104,389	13,210	33,700,602
Total	713	12,672,434	186,129	3,286,858,769

SOURCE: *Anuario Estatistico Do Brasil,* 1962, 1963, 1964.

the textile industry in Maranhão.[45] Some local industrialization projects have been undertaken such as the construction of a cold-storage plant in Rondônia, the installation of a packaged-food industry in Goiás, and a fish-processing industry in Belém.[46]

Besides taking the initiative in the establishment of new industries in the region, SPVEA also provides credits and participates in "mixed capital" enterprises already established in the region. Occasionally, SPVEA cooperates with other public entities, such as the Banco do Estado de Amazonas, the Cia. de Forca e Luz do Pará, and the Papel Amazonas S.A.[47]

SPVEA also subsidizes private enterprises, such as the Cia. de Petróleo do Amazonas, the Emprêsa de Navegacão Acreana, Ltda., the Servicos Aéreos Cruzeiro do Sul, and the Servico de Navegacão de Amazônia.[48]

Mining and mineral extraction is increasingly important in the economic composition of the Amazon region. The area within Amazonia that has benefited the most from mineral extractions has been Amapá, where just recently a large manganese deposit was discovered. At present, it is being

[45] Gabriel Hermes, "Amazônia e a Unidade Nacional," *O Observador Econômico e Financeiro,* XXI, (Julho, 1956), p. 42.
[46] "Planejamento, etc.," *op. cit.,* p. 38.
[47] *Ibid.,* p. 21.
[48] *Ibid.,* p. 24.

exploited by the Bethlehem Steel Corporation under the terms of an agreement made with the Brazilian government. The importance of the mining concern has led to the construction of Amapá's first railroad, between Macapá and the mining site. Recent development of manganese output is shown in Table 32–16.

TABLE 32–16
Manganese Production in Brazil
(in 1,000 tons)

	1961	1962	1963
Amapá	775	951	1,084 (86.3% of total production)
Minas Gerais	181	165	82
Mato Grosso	46	37	61
Bahia	8	7	28
Amazonas	6	..	..
Brazil	1,016	1,160	1,255

SOURCE: "Planejamento transforma a Amazônia," Separata de *O Observador econômico e financeiro*, XXIII, 275 (Janeiro, 1959), p. 24.

Since 1962, the largest mineral export of Rondônia is tin. Production in Rondônia now exceeds 50 per cent of the national production (see Table 32–17).

TABLE 32–17
National Production of Tin
(in tons)

	Rondôrua	Amapá	Mato Grosso	Goiás	Others	Total production
1959	18	93	508	..	2	621
1960	49	85	312	2,188	1	2,635
1961	35	62	344	540	4	985
1962	678	62	337	162	..	1,239
1963	1,038	16	437	462	..	1,953

SOURCE: "Planejamento transforma a Amazônia," Separata de *O Observador econômico e financeiro*, XXIII, 275 (Janeiro, 1959), p. 154.

A few electrification projects have been completed and subsidies or credits have been granted to "mixed capital" electric companies for the restoration and improvement of their systems. Among those companies which have also received SPVEA aid from SPVEA are municipal water and sewage departments. These scattered programs and projects have not added up to significant over-all regional development integration and structural reform.

The funds allotted by the congress to various ministries for application in Amazonia have been considerably reduced over the years. The congress has maintained that funds for the operations of the different federal ministries in Amazonia should now come from the funds granted to FVEA since all the tasks carried out by the ministries and SPVEA involve, at least indirectly, economic development. This action on the part of the congress has led to increased deficiencies in the amount and quality of work done by the *reparticóes públicas,* and they have had to obtain their financial resources from FVEA, thus reducing considerably the amount of working capital available for the development projects of SPVEA.

The region is actually exporting more capital in the form of federal taxes than it is receiving from the federal government in the form of appropriations for the economic "valorization" of the region.

TABLE 32–18

Years	Federal tax collections (Cr. $1,000.00)	Federal allotments for the valorization of the area (Cr. $1,000.00)	Balance
1957	1,488,628,000	1,831,009,375	+ 342,381,375
1958	1,825,548,000	2,184,093,501	+ 358,545,501
1959	2,558,118,000	3,059,931,825	+ 501,813,825
1960	3,705,253,000	4,205,458,644	+ 500,205,644
1961	5,197,912,000	3,885,416,469	−1,312,495,531
1962	8,193,332,000	4,349,493,326	−3,843,828,674
	22,968,781,000	19,515,403,140	−3,453,377,860

SOURCE: *Ministério Extraordinário para Coordinacão dos Organismos Regionais, Superintendencia do Plano de Valorizacão Econômica da Amazônia, Programa de Emergência para 1965,* (1964), p. 4.

In the period from 1957 to 1960, for each cruzeiro collected in taxes in the region, 1.20 to 1.30 centavos were returned to the region in the form of "valorization" payments to FVEA. In the years 1961 and 1962, however, for each cruzeiro allocated to the FVEA, the federal government collected 1.80 to 1.90 cruzeiros in taxes. In effect, the financial resources invested in the region by the federal government during the first four years were repaid, with interest, in the form of taxes, during the last two years.

The region also has an unfavorable balance of trade with the rest of the country, which more than offsets the export surplus to the rest of the world (see Table 32–19).

The region's foreign commerce (Table 32–20), while not insignificant, was only 1.6 per cent in weight and 1.9 per cent in value of the total amount of Brazilian foreign commerce in 1956. It is therefore less than proportional to population.

Amazonia's share of national income for the period 1956–60 ranged from 2.1 per cent to 2.4 per cent. Meanwhile the south of Brazil retained 50 per cent of the total national income. Amazonia's share in the national income has not increased significantly during the last ten years even though the "valorization plan" has been legally in effect since 1953.

TABLE 32-19
Trade with Other Regions of Brazil

Years	Exportation (Cr. $1,000)	Importation (Cr. $1,000)	Balance
1956	5,542,491	7,455,545	− 1,913,054
1957	6,776,097	8,367,640	− 1,591,543
1958	7,853,423	11,619,334	− 3,765,911
1959	10,070,287	15,127,422	− 5,057,135
1960	14,941,269	20,198,271	− 5,257,002
	45,183,567	62,768,212	−17,584,645

SOURCE: *Ministério Extraordinário para Coordinacão dos Organismos Regionais, Superintendência do Plano de Valorizacão Econômica da Amazônia, Programa de Emergência para 1965*, (1964), p. 5.

TABLE 32-20
Amazonia's Foreign Commerce

Years	Exportation (Cr. $1,000)	Importation (Cr. $1,000)	Balance
1956	1,128,182	1,081,993	+ 46,189
1957	2,380,995	1,617,310	+ 763,685
1958	3,071,129	1,309,472	+ 1,761,657
1959	4,653,326	2,037,513	+ 2,615,813
1960	8,021,024	2,494,527	+ 5,526,497
	19,254,656	8,540,815	+10,713,841

SOURCE: *Ministério Extraordinário para Coordinacão dos Organismos Regionais, Superintêndencia do Plano de Valorizacão Econômica da Amazônia, Programa de Emergência para 1965*, (1964), p. 6.

Since the First Five-Year Plan has yet to be approved by congress, another "emergency program" was formulated in 1964, as in the previous years, as an attempt to prevent further deterioration of the economic position of the region and to initiate the beginning of a truly effective development program.

The 1964 emergency program was designed to diagnose and correct the basic causes of the deplorable economic position of the region; previous plans had aimed at improving economically important facilities already in existence.[49] The factors considered in formulating the plan included: (1) the economic disequilibrium among the regions of Brazil; (2) the federal government's attitude toward the distribution of resources for economic development; (3) the lack of growth or increased productivity in the region; and (4) SPVEA's investment policy.

The Emergency Plan for 1965 had eleven specific objectives: (1) investments in electric energy; (2) a rational system of transportation, mainly by highways; (3) improvement of sanitary conditions by increas-

[49] *Ibid.*, p. 9.

ing the water supply and the sewage system; (4) the intensification of livestock production for human consumption; (5) mechanization of agriculture and storage facilities for agricultural products; (6) encouragement and coordination of industrial investments which will make use of the natural resources of the region; (7) intensification of economic research; (8) educational improvements; (9) intensification of mineral explorations and development; (10) reformation of the administrative system of the SPVEA; (11) unification and coordination of investment planning.

The total appropriation requested for this emergency program was CR.$23,212 million, divided as follows:

Cr. $1,000

Agricultural production and storage	Cr.$2,230,000.
Animal production	1,800,000.
Rural credit, etc.	3,770,000.
Energy	4,400,000.
Transportation and communications	2,600,000.
Industry and commerce	5,000,000.
Education and culture	412,171.
Health	3,000,000.
Total	23,212,171.

SOURCE: *Ministério Extraordinario para Coordinacão dos Organismos Regionais, Superintendência do Plano de Valorizacão Econômica da Amazônia, Programa de Emergência para 1965*, (1964), pp. 11–12.

The program itself contains virtually no economic analysis and no effort to indicate interactions among various projects or sectors. It is "project planning" of the simplest kind. Under each heading (power, transport, health, etc.) a "justification" is offered, but the justification is presented in terms of technical feasibility and simple cost-benefit analysis. For example the "justification" for the energy program is that Amazonia is potentially rich in hydroelectric power—about 4,500,000 horsepower—but is currently producing only 0.1 per cent of this potential. A list of individual projects is added, with no indication of how the extra capacity will be used.

The results of the Emergency Plan for 1965 were not available at the time of writing.

One of the principal reasons why the PVEA has made so little progress in the task of developing Amazonia has been lack of financial resources to carry out the program and its projects.

The relationship between the constitutionally authorized allotment to SPVEA and actual allocations has been discussed by Dr. Octávio Mendonca. In the course of ten years (January, 1954 to July, 1964) CR.$70,683 million were allocated to the FVEA. But due to the government attempts at "economy," the allocations to the FVEA were reduced by CR.$21,028 million or 29.75 per cent of the total. Of the remaining CR.$49,654 million, CR.$9,975 million were never handed over to the

FVEA. Consequently, only about CR.$39.7 billions, or 56.13 per cent of the original CR.$70 billion were actually received by the SPVEA.[50]

The criteria by which the appropriations for PVEA are derived are constantly different and diverse. Sometimes the basis for the estimation of future tax receipts is taken from the budget proposal for the coming year, sometimes from the current year, and sometimes from the previous year.

During the discussion of the 1965 budget, for example, the 3 per cent of the total federal tax revenue which is allotted to the PVEA was calculated from the total federal tax revenue for the year 1963. Consequently, PVEA's appropriations are always two years in arrears, a serious matter when inflation is as violent as it has been in Brazil. Moreover, as stated above, a substantial proportion of FVEA's appropriations must be applied to the maintenance of federal entities operating in the region, rather than to economic development plans as specified by the law. The Ministries of Health and of Education, the Special Service of Public Health (SESP), and the Malaria Service are but a few examples of the federal entities operating in the region which depend on financial resources from SPVEA in order to keep functioning.

The manner in which payments are made to the SPVEA also hampers the continuity of the projects and programs. The payments are made on a monthly basis but they are not always paid in equal amounts.[51] This policy has resulted in distortions and reductions of the original appropriation. For example, in 1955, only 40 per cent of the authorized appropriation was ever received by SPVEA, and half of the 40 per cent received had to be utilized in supporting the work of the federal entities in the region. The Minister of Finance exercises complete control over the spending of financial appropriations approved by congress for the FVEA. For reasons unknown to the author, not one full appropriation for any one fiscal year has ever been granted to the FVEA.

Amazonia has lacked the large-scale integrated investments that could change the character of the regional economy. The isolated, single projects that have been realized have done little to raise the level of productivity of the region as a whole. The federal government and its agencies have not shown any genuine interest in the promotion of development. The federal government has been more concerned with promoting, aiding, and protecting the continued growth and advancement of the industrial and agricultural complex in the south, and in rehabilitating the northeast. Development of the south has more immediate impact on the economy as a whole, and the powerful politicians of the south can exert more pressure on the government.

Table 32–21 indicates the share of credits received by each geographical region from the Agricultural and Industrial Department of the *Banco do Brazil* for the years 1963 and 1964.

In 1965 Amazonia received 5 per cent of the total amount of loans

---

[50] Speech by Dr. Octávio Mendonca, Manaus, 1964.
[51] Gabriel Hermes, *op. cit.,* p. 39.

TABLE 32–21

Percentages of Loans Conceded

	1963		1964	
	No. of loans	Value	No. of loans	Value
North	0.8	0.8	0.9	0.7
Northeast	29.1	20.1	28.6	17.0
East	27.1	18.5	24.7	15.1
South	36.3	53.1	38.7	58.3
Center-west	6.5	7.5	7.1	8.9
Brazil	100.0	100.0	100.0	100.0

SOURCE: *Relatório*, Banco do Brasil (Brasilia, 1965), p. 37.

granted, while the south obtained 90 per cent of the total.[52] Thus the Amazon region is losing out to other regions of the country. The proportion of credits extended to the north is decreasing in all sectors. The state and territorial governments of the region have also failed to contribute their legal share of financial resources to the FVEA, which amounts to 3 per cent of their respective tax revenues.

There has also been a decline in the share of state government outlays allocated for development projects. This fact adds even more to the tendency toward the economic stagnation of the region.

BANCO DE CREDITO DA AMAZONIA

The BCA was originally established to finance rubber production and to encourage increased rubber output. It also financed the rubber trade. In 1963, however, its functions were extended to the financing of development in general; it became in effect a regional development bank on the same general lines as the Banco do Nordeste. The Bank obtains capital from the United States government, the Brazilian government, and private investors. As part of the Brazilian government contribution, the Bank receives automatically and by law 10 per cent of the 3 per cent of federal revenues accorded to SPVEA.

At the end of 1964, when visited by the author, the Bank had yet to adapt its operations to its new functions. According to the directors, when the new law became effective in 1963 they had no personnel with experience and training suitable for a regional development bank; the senior officials were for the most part experts in the production, financing, and marketing of rubber. The administration remained essentially as it was before; and for this reason little effective integration of the Bank's operations with regional development planning had as yet been accomplished. One of the directors expressed doubts as to whether the Bank was hindering or helping development, because of its traditional methods of operation. He maintained that the Bank's operations tend to maintain an existing

[52] Gabriel Hermes, *op. cit.*, p. 37.

social structure in a fashion that may well be anti-developmental.

Because of the confusion of the administration regarding the Bank's functions, the directors maintained, research also lags. Research tended to be directed toward day-to-day administrative problems rather than toward fundamental requirements for development of the region. The research section had made a series of specific studies but had carried out no systematic research. The Bank has no resources for general studies; these were left to the university.

The Bank is engaged mainly in providing rural credit, and its plans are submitted to the Ministry of Rural Credit. The 1963 Report of the Bank lists five major activities: financing the production, sale, and purchase of rubber throughout the country; promotion (*fomento*) of agricultural-livestock and agricultural-industrial activities; promotion of manufacturing, mining, and general economic activities; technical and capital assistance to rural activities through the expansion of the cooperative system in the region; discounts, deposit covers, and other banking services for the commercial banks; and serving as a regional development bank, in accordance with Law No. 4.216 of May 6, 1963, extending to Amazonia the benefits of Article 34 of Law 3.995 of December 14, 1961, for SUDENE.

The Report refers to four main sources of funds for its operations: (1) Fund for Promotion of Production (10 per cent of the annual grants through Article 199 of the Constitution allocating 3 per cent of federal revenues to SPVEA); (2) Fund for the Promotion of Production of Rubber, comprising 10 per cent of the value of rubber imported into Brazil plus 10 per cent of national production of synthetic rubber consumed in the local market; (3) funds provided by the federal government, through Certificates of Rediscount (*Carteira de Redescontos*) of the Bank of Brazil and in other forms; (4) the Bank's own disposable resources and other funds made specifically available for this purpose. The application of these resources is made in accordance with an agreement with SPVEA, designed to assure the execution of a unified program.

The Report also notes that under the 1963 law the Bank should become a genuine regional development bank, a "Banco da Amazonia" rather than a "Banco de Credito da Amazonia."

The South

The rich regions of the center and south are not so rich that they have no desire to grow richer. All of the south-central and southern states have their own development planning organizations. When visited in 1961, the Planning Commission of the State of São Paulo—the richest state of all—was probably the most sophisticated planning organization in the country. In 1964–65, one of the most vigorous planning groups was concerned with the development of the region comprising the three states of the extreme south—the "Extremo Sul." These three states—Rio Grande do Sul, Santa Catarina, and Paraná—while less advanced than São Paulo or Guanabara, have together a per capita income well above the national average. Recent and rapid industrialization superimposed on an efficient agricultural sector is the basic reason.

Regional Planning in the South

The Conselho de Desenvolvimento do Extremo Sul (Codesul) and the Banco Regional de Desenvolvimento do Extremo Sul were established more or less simultaneously,[53] the former on June 15, 1961, and the latter on August 21, 1961. The agreements setting up the two institutions were signed in Curitiba by the three governors concerned. Codesul consists of the three governors, three representatives of the Union appointed by the president, three representatives designated by the states, the director-president of the regional bank, and an executive secretary. Its terms of reference require Codesul to raise the socio-economic level of the region, study its problems, and propose solutions; to establish the broad lines of policy for regional development, in harmony with national plans and in coordination with state planning organs; to supervise and suggest adequate measures for interregional and foreign trade so as to permit the proper retention and determination within the region of the returns to the labor of the local populations, as a positive factor in regional development. The research department of Codesul has carried out a series of studies, some very detailed, such as one on family income and expenditures in Curitiba and one on the primary sector of Santa Catarina.

The Bank is required by its statutes to cooperate with the *Conselho* in the economic programming of the region, in the systemization of an economic policy for the region, in the study of economic policy measures, and examination of current economic trends. The Bank's headquarters are in Pôrto Allegre with branches in Curitiba and Florianópolis. The initial capital of the Bank was Cr.$120 million; but each of the three states is required to allocate 1 per cent of annual tax revenues to the Bank, and the Bank may receive other grants or loans from the states.

Recent Trends in Regional Development

Is the present tendency with respect to regional discrepancies in productivity and income in Brazil centrifugal or centripetal? It is not altogether easy to tell. The statistics are limited in time, scope, and quality, while at the same time both the Brazilian economy as a whole and the regional subeconomies are subject to violent fluctuations. On balance, there is some slight preponderance of evidence to suggest that Brazil may have reached a stage of convergence, as far as percentage differences in income and output are concerned; but the evidence is far from convincing or clear (Tables 32–11 and 32–22 to 32–22c).

Up to 1964 (after which no data were available at time of writing), there was no clear sign of improvement in the regional distribution of income in Brazil. When income is broken down by states it can be seen that in both Amazonas and Pará the per capita income fell in relation to the national average (Table 32–23). The relative per capita income of Maranhão and Ceará was almost constant, Piauí and Pernambuco declined

[53] Council for Development of the Extreme South and Regional Development Bank of the Extreme South.

TABLE 32–22

Regional Distribution of Gross Domestic Product

Region	Year, percentage	
	1950	1960
North	2.25	2.20
Northeast	16.33	15.90
M.G. and E. Santo*	12.04	10.75
East central	51.55	50.48
South	15.87	18.22
Middle west	1,96	2.49
Brazil	100.00	100.00

* Minas Gerais and Espirito Santo.
SOURCE: Fundacão Getulio Vargas.

TABLE 32–22a

Regional Distribution of Income Generated in Agriculture

Region	Year, percentage					
	1950	1960	1961	1962	1963	1964
North	1.67	2.03	2.45	1.67	1.81	1.55
Northeast	20.26	22.14	21.42	23.56	23.78	23.75
M.G. and E. Santo *	18.48	15.45	14.01	14.92	13.16	15.04
East central	33.98	27.52	28.28	25.08	27.18	24.75
South	22.29	28.18	27.74	27.87	27.41	27.14
Middle west	3.32	4.68	6.10	6.90	6.66	7.77
Brazil	100.00	100.00	100.00	100.00	100.00	100.00

* Minas Gerais and Espirito Santo.
SOURCE: Fundacão Getulio Vargas.

TABLE 32–22b

Regional Distribution of Income Generated in Industry

Region	Year, percentage					
	1950	1960	1961	1962	1963	1964
North	2.86	2.30	..	1.76	1.28	1.43
Northeast	10.34	8.24	..	6.91	5.08	6.30
M.G. and E. Santo*	8.22	8.09	..	7.15	6.67	6.98
East central	65.19	68.22	..	71.66	76.22	74.16
South	12.60	12.30	..	11.88	10.33	10.39
Middle west	0.79	0.85	..	0.64	0.47	0.74
Brazil	100.00	100.00	..	100.00	100.00	100.00

* Minas Gerais and Espirito Santo.
SOURCE: Fundacão Getulio Vargas.

TABLE 32–22c
Regional Distribution of Population

Region	Year, percentage	
	1950	1960
North	3.55	3.67
Northeast	34.7	31.6
M.G. and E. Santo*	16.5	15.5
East central	26.6	27.7
South	15.1	16.7
Middle west	3.36	4.24
Brazil	100.00	100.00

* Minas Gerais and Espirito Santo.
SOURCE: *Anuario Estatistico.*
Note: Estimates of the Demographic Sector of the Office of Applied Economic Research in the Ministry of Planning indicate that from 1960 to 1964 the percentage population distribution of various regions remained roughly stable.

in relation to the national average, and the other northeastern states registered slight relative gains. In the south, Paraná showed a sharp gain and the other states loses relative to national per capita income (these are the states with the heaviest net immigration), Goiás registered a relative gain, while Mato Grosso just held its own on the national scale.

The pattern of structural change reveals a similar picture. In the northeast the share of income generated in the agricultural sector actually increased between 1947 and 1960, and the share from commerce, industry, and services declined (Table 32–24). The north did enjoy modest development in terms of structure of income, but half the decline in the share of agriculture is accounted for by the increased share of government. The east, too, shows relatively little structural change. The south, with its high-productivity agriculture oriented to the export market, did not generate any decline in the share of agriculture, but industry gained on both commerce and services. In the middle west the share of agriculture actually increased.

In terms of foreign trade, the north and northeast both suffered a decline in relative shares between 1947 and 1960. The east enjoyed an increase in the share of exports but a decline in share of imports; in the south this pattern was reversed. The share of the middle west in foreign trade is insignificant. It is also of interest that the northeast has a large and increasing import surplus from the center-south (Tables 32–25 and 32–26).

Preliminary figures for 1960–64 indicate higher growth rates for the northeast than for the country as a whole. However, this convergence was partly the result of retarded growth elsewhere in the economy (in 1963 national per capita income actually fell) and partly to a favorable

TABLE 32–23

Per Capita Income by States

(per cent of national average)

States	1947	1953	1956	1957	1958	1959	1960
Amazonas	94	67	76	78	72	66	68
Pará	65	54	61	60	54	53	56
Maranhão	33	33	31	31	31	34	34
Piauí	37	25	25	28	26	28	29
Ceará	44	33	37	41	30	41	45
Rio Grande do Norte	53	41	46	48	40	52	57
Paraíba	43	37	41	42	38	46	54
Pernambuco	63	55	53	61	62	61	60
Alagoas	46	41	43	48	50	49	51
Sergipe	53	50	50	54	55	56	55
Bahia	53	46	46	48	50	51	56
Minas Gerais	77	80	81	82	75	75	71
Espirito Santo	67	83	80	76	66	65	64
Rio de Janeiro	100	101	107	97	96	95	95
Guanabara*	330	308	316	308	321	311	291
Paraná	103	121	94	98	105	110	111
São Paulo	184	192	181	176	179	176	178
Santa Catarina	101	90	89	87	89	86	90
Rio Grande do Sul	122	120	130	125	118	116	120
Mato Grosso	79	114	110	84	94	71	78
Goias	46	65	59	54	54	57	55
National average per capita gross domestic product in U.S. dollars	225†	257	279	298	312	321	340

* Formerly the Federal District.

† For 1948.

SOURCE: Werner Baer, *Industrialization and Economic Development in Brazil* (Homewood, Ill., 1965), p. 170.

swing in the rainfall cycle of the northeast. The experience of these years can hardly be accepted as clear evidence of a break in trend.

Summary*

In the most advanced region, the east-central (São Paulo, Guanabara, and the State of Rio de Janeiro), the ratio between per capita income and the national average remained roughly the same throughout the period 1950–64. The heavy concentration of industrial production in this region continued and even increased. On the other hand, per capita agricultural production grew more slowly than the national average. It would appear that this region has increasingly been importing foodstuffs from the rapidly growing agricultural regions of the south and middle west.

Per capita income in the south (Rio Grande do Sul, Paraná, and Santa

* The author wishes to express his gratitude to Dr. Orlando Menezes of the Brazilian Ministry of Planning for his assistance in bringing this section up to date.

TABLE 32–24
The Structure of Brazil's Regional Economies
(percent of income of region)

Year	North	North-east	East	South	Middle west
1947					
Agriculture	29	37	25	33	49
Commerce	18	21	18	14	13
Industry*	24	13	17	22	10
Services	11	16	17	13	13
Transport and communications	8	5	8	8	6
Financial intermed.	1	1	3	2	1
Rents	1	1	3	3	1
Government	8	6	9	5	7
Total	100	100	100	100	100
1960					
Agriculture	25	47	26	33	60
Commerce	17	15	15	10	6
Industry*	26	11	21	27	8
Services	11	12	12	10	8
Transport and communications	8	6	8	7	6
Financial intermed.	2	2	3	3	3
Rents	1	1	4	4	2
Government	10	6	11	5	7
Total	100	100	100	100	100
1960 (Per cent of total production in sector)					Total
Agriculture	2	15	27	51	5	100
Commerce	3	13	40	42	2	100
Industry*	2	5	32	60	1	100
Services	2	12	38	47	3	100
Transport and communications	2	9	40	47	2	100
Financial intermed.	1	5	39	53	2	100
Rents	1	4	35	59	1	100
Government	3	8	48	39	2	100

* Includes manufacturing industry, public utilities, and construction.
SOURCE: Werner Baer, *Industrialization and Economic Development in Brazil*
(Homewood, Ill., 1965), p. 171.

Catarina) remained roughly proportional to that of the east. Since the
former is not much below the latter, the fact that this gap was not reduced
cannot be considered of serious import. In per capita agricultural production, the south grew much faster than the east or the nation as a whole.

Minas Gerais and Espirito Santo—geographically a sub-region of the
east but with a considerably lower per capita income and a different
economic character—failed to narrow the gap between them and the east.
The same is true of industrial production. The rapid growth of a single

TABLE 32–25

A. Foreign Trade of Northeastern Brazil

Year	Exports	Imports	Balance
1948	197.6	93.2	104.4
1949	133.0	100.3	32.7
1950	174.1	86.9	87.2
1951	197.6	166.4	31.2
1952	114.5	173.3	−58.8
1953	169.6	95.3	74.3
1954	235.4	86.9	148.5
1955	238.5	86.2	152.3
1956	163.9	97.7	66.2
1957	212.1	131.9	80.2
1958	246.1	94.4	151.7
1959	216.1	79.3	136.8
1960	247.7	85.3	162.4

B. Regional Percentage Distribution
of Exports and Imports

Region	Exports		Imports	
	1947	1960	1947	1960
North	2.4	1.7	1.3	1.2
Northeast	9.8	7.7	6.4	4.5
East	22.2	39.2	42.6	33.9
South	65.6	48.3	49.6	60.3
Middle west	0.1	0.3	..	..

SOURCE: Werner Baer, *Industrialization and Economic Development in Brazil* (Homewood, Ill., 1965), p. 175.

resource-oriented industry group (iron ore and the iron and steel industry) offset the relative stagnation of others. In agriculture the region lost ground relatively, undoubtedly because much of it is topographically unfavorable.

The great gap in per capita income separating the northeast from the east-central was slightly reduced in 1950–60. However, the growth was practically all due to agriculture and, more particularly, due to the accident that the world market for Brazilian sugar suddenly became favorable —for the time being—because of the elimination of Cuban sugar from the United States market. In industry the northeast continued to lose ground relatively through 1964, despite SUDENE's investments and incentives which were aimed principally at industrial expansion. However, there are some indications that its efforts will be successful in reversing this trend in the near future.

The expansion of the middle west's economic frontier, starting from a low level, has proceeded rapidly. Population has grown much more rapidly than in any other region, but agricultural production has grown even

TABLE 32–26

Value of Northeastern Trade with the Center-South
(in millions of cruzeiros)

Year	Exports	Imports	Balance
1948	4,069	5,541	−1,472
1949	4,579	6,630	−2,051
1950	5,349	7,141	−1,792
1951	6,843	8,298	−1,455
1952	6,687	8,159	−1,472
1953	7,975	10,792	−2,817
1954	10,804	12,871	−2,067
1955	13,495	16,477	−2,982
1956	19,845	19,692	153
1957	17,892	21,078	−3,186
1958	16,878	22,732	−5,854
1959	21,857	26,699	−4,842

SOURCE: Werner Baer, *Industrialization and Economic Development in Brazil* (Homewood, Ill., 1965), p. 176.

faster. Agricultural output per capita has grown rapidly relative to the national average. A part of this production has been destined for the new market created by the construction of Brasilia, but most of it has been absorbed by the advanced east.

1950–1960 VERSUS 1960–1964

Additional light is cast on regional trends by breaking up the period 1950–1964 into two sub-periods, 1950–1960 and 1960–1964.

Advanced Areas
East Central
1) 1950–1960. Per capita GDP and per capita industrial production remained roughly constant in proportion to the national average. Concentration of industry within the region was already great in 1950, and continued at about the same level through 1960. On the other hand, the ratio of per capita agriculture production to national per capita agricultural production declined by about 25 per cent, leaving the figure for the region about equal to that of the nation as a whole.

2) 1960–1964. The ratio of per capita industrial output to per capita national industrial output rose by another 10 per cent, marking a new high in concentration. On the other hand, the ratio of per capita agricultural production to national per capita agricultural production fell by a further 10 per cent. The regional figure is now below the national level.
South
1) 1950–1960. The ratio of per capita GDP to national per capita GDP remained roughly constant. The ratio of per capita industrial output to national per capita industrial output decreased by about 10 per cent. On the other hand, the ratio of per capita agricultural output to national per capita output increased by about 15 per cent. In absolute terms, the south

was by far the fastest growing agricultural region of the country. While export products—notably coffee in north Paraná—one would guess that this region also became an important supplier of foodstuffs to the industrial east region. In the latter, as noted, growth of agricultural production was relatively slow.

2) 1960–1964. The ratio of per capita industrial production to national industrial production declined at a faster rate—by about 20 per cent— while the ratio for agricultural production remained roughly stable. One would deduce from the preceding that the corresponding ratio for per capita GDP showed an appreciable decline.

Backward Regions
Minas Gerais and Espirito Santo
1) 1950–1960. The proportion of per capita GDP to national per capita GDP remained roughly stable. The same was true of the corresponding ratio for industrial output per capita. (No doubt, rapid growth of the iron and steel industry offset the mediocre growth of other industries.) The corresponding ratio for agricultural production showed a decline of 10 per cent. This is not surprising, as much of this area is too mountainous to be of much value for agriculture.

2) 1960–1964. The ratio of per capita agricultural and industrial production to the corresponding national figures remained roughly stable.
Northeast
1) 1950–1960. The ratio of per capita GDP to the national figure increased by nearly 10 per cent. However, this appears to have been the result of an accidental factor, of limited and temporary effect, rather than of stimuli provided by SUDENE. For industry, which is the chief beneficiary of the actions of this institution (whether the actions affect industry directly or the infrastructure) showed a decline of 10 per cent in production per capita relative to the corresponding national figure. (Of course northeast industrial production per capita showed a substantial absolute increase. To this extent, SUDENE action many have been effective; it may have stimulated a greater absolute increase—that is, prevented a larger relative decline—than would otherwise have occurred.)

On the other hand, the ratio of per capita agricultural production to the corresponding national figure showed about a 10 per cent increase. While more detailed examination of this sector has not been undertaken, it is probable that much of the growth was in sugar production—due to the accidental factor (as earlier mentioned) of the elimination of Cuba from the United States market. This hypothesis becomes more plausible when it is noted that natural conditions in most of the northeast are unfavorable for production of foodstuffs even for the local market. On the other hand, the northeast does enjoy naturally favorable conditions for two export crops— cotton and sisal—whose output probably grew appreciably.

2) 1960–1964. The ratio of northeast per capita industrial production to the national figure declined still further—by the substantial figure of more than 20 per cent. On the other hand, some fragmentary data from SUDENE indicate that industrial investment has grown more rapidly in

the northeast than in the center in the last two years or so. If so, these investments have not yet fructified; but it would indicate that the relative production trends should be reversed in the coming few years.

Middle West Frontier (*Goias and Mato Grosso*)

1) 1950–1960. In terms of population, this frontier area has been by far the fastest growing region of the nation. Its population increased by about 25 per cent more than the percentage increase for the nation during this period; the ratio of per capita GDP to national per capita GDP (the former being appreciably lower) remained roughly stable. The corresponding ratio for industrial production declined by more than 15 per cent. For agricultural production it increased by about 15 per cent.

2) 1960–1964. Population growth accelerated further as compared to 1950–1960. A preliminary estimate of population increase indicates that it was 25 per cent above the national percentage population increase; that is, a relative increase about equal to that of 1950–1960 was accomplished in a much shorter space of time. The decline of *relative* industrial production accelerated still further; that is, it failed to keep pace with the rapid population growth. But the ratio of per capita agricultural production to the corresponding national figure increased. In other words, regional agriculture grew at a very rapid rate indeed—much faster than even the rapid rate of population growth.

The construction of Brasilia is no doubt largely responsible for the rapid growth of the region, and especially for the acceleration in growth since 1960. However, the fact that the construction of Brasilia was completed only in 1960, and the growth of the livestock sector for supply of meat to the Rio-São Paulo market, would indicate that the relatively rapid growth had begun well before construction of Brasilia. There is no doubt that rapid development of this agricultural frontier has occurred spontaneously and that it will continue to grow—especially now that Brasilia has been built—even if the government should not adopt other measures to stimulate regional development. Agriculture has been and will continue to be the mainspring of the region's economy, apart from the effects of the creation of Brasilia.

These conclusions would be indicated even by *a priori* consideration of the natural conditions of the region, which are favorable to agriculture, and of its reasonable proximity to the markets of the more highly developed east region. Data provide definite confirmation of what has actually occurred. For example, in 1950 the region's agricultural production was only twice that of the larger north region (practically coterminous with the Amazon basin). In 1964 it was about five times the north's agricultural production. In 1950 the middle-west's agricultural production was only 10 per cent that of the east. In 1964 it was nearly 30 per cent of the east's —and the latter is an advanced region not only industrially, but also agriculturally.

The *North* (*Amazonia*)

1960–1964 saw in Amazonia an acceleration of the relative decline of 1950–60. Indeed, in the decade of the fifties, the north's share of agricultural production increased somewhat more than the region's share of population; but Amazonia's share of GDP declined and the region's share of industrial production declined substantially. In the later period, the north's share of industrial output declined even more drastically, and the share of agricultural output also fell a good deal.

Conclusion on Regional Integration

In sum, it appears that Brazil has not yet broken the back of her "North-South" problem, and without much more effective regional development policies in future, the disturbing discrepancies among regions are likely to remain for a long time to come.

33 | "Pôles de Croissance" versus "Zones Pilotes": Lessons of Greek Experience

Introduction

In recent years French theory and practice of economic planning has attracted considerable attention. In the light of French success with reconstruction and development, this attention is not difficult to understand. It is also easy to understand that French planning experts, called to assist the governments of underdeveloped countries with their development planning, have drawn on French theory and experience wherever it seemed applicable. By the same token, in areas where French culture, language, and literature are prevalent—as in the Canadian province of Quebec and in some Mediterranean countries—French ideas regarding planning exert considerable influence.

In this chapter we are concerned with one major aspect of French planning—regional development planning—as it was applied in a particular test case. This case was the *zone pilote* (pilot zone or "trial and demonstration area") in Greece. Obviously, Greek regional development planning has not been wholly "French" in either its theory or its practice; the Greek authorities themselves bear ultimate responsibility for plans and their implementation, and other foreign influences than French have made themselves felt. Nevertheless, during the period covered by this chapter the Greek planning officials were themselves greatly influenced by French concepts and administration of planning, and the predominant influence brought to bear by foreign experts was also French.[1]

[1] This chapter is a by-product of a mission undertaken for OECD on evaluation of technical assistance to Greece. The author wishes to express his obligation to

It could also be argued that the test case was in itself rather small and unimportant. Nevertheless, it represented a substantial effort on the part of Greek officials and foreign experts, and the lessons to be derived from the experience—especially as to the dangers involved in confusing a *zone pilote* with a *pôle de croissance* (focal point of growth), can be useful for other countries or regions interested in applying these concepts in their own planning.

Pôles de Croissance

The more important concept, on which there is substantial literature, is the *pôle de croissance*. The term originated with Professor François Perroux, but the concept has been elaborated by other French economists, notably Jacques de Boudeville and Joseph Lajugie.[2] The basic idea is that economic development never takes place at a uniform rate throughout an economy but tends to concentrate on a limited number of "nodes" or "focal points" (perhaps only one), from which "spread effects" are generated to the rest of the economy.

The *pôle de croissance* in Perroux' thinking is associated with his concept of "domination" of one national, regional, or local economy over others. Thus the United Kingdom in the nineteenth century and the United States in the twentieth are regarded as "dominant economies" and "focal points of growth" for the world economy. Similarly a particular industrial city may dominate a region and at the same time generate growth in the region as a whole through the spread effects of its own growth. The *pôle de croissance* is, in turn, an aggregation of "propulsive economic units"—key industries or leading sectors (*unités économiques motrices*). The interactions can be expressed in the form of an interindustry matrix with both "upstream" and "downstream" effects (backward and forward linkage, in Hirschman's terms) emanating from the collection of key industries, located spatially at the *pôle de croissance*.[3] Growth is inherently unbalanced or desequilibrating; here too, Perroux and his colleagues anticipated some of Hirschman's ideas. A "key industry" must be responsible for a major part—say 60 per cent—of the output of its products within the economy where its effects are felt. Indeed, a "propulsive industry" must be large, it must be fast-growing, and it must generate substantial spread

---

members of the Regional Service in Greece and of the OECD. In particular, he wishes to express his appreciation for the help of Mr. Giulio Fossi, of OECD, whose unique experience with both the Sardinia and Epirus projects makes him a gold mine of information on the subject. It should be clear, however, that the analysis and views presented are those of the author alone and do not commit anyone else connected with regional planning in Greece to the same interpretation and conclusion.

[2] See, for example, François Perroux, "Note sur la notion de pôle de croissance," *Economie appliquée*, Nos. 1-2, January–June, 1955; Jacques de Boudeville, *Les espaces e'conomiques* (Paris, 1961); and Joseph Lajugie, "L'Expérience francaise de planification," *Rivista internazionale di Scienzi economiche e commerciali*, May, 1965, pp. 432-453.

[3] Cf. H. Aujac, "La hiérarchie des industries dans un tableau des échanges interindustrielles et ses conséquences dans la mise en oeuvre d'un plan national décentralisé," *Revue économique* XI, May, 1960, pp. 169-238.

effects. The French literature uses the term "Perroux effects" to refer to structural change involving horizontal production increases, in contradistinction to the "Keynes effect" (multiplier).

Perroux has a rather complicated concept of "economic space," defined in terms of sets of economic relationships. He distinguishes three kinds of "abstract economic space": space defined by a plan, space as a field of economic forces, and space as a homogeneous aggregate. Boudeville picks up the concept of "planning space" and converts it into "program regions," which in practice is close to the concept of a "pilot zone" or—as the Quebec government prefers to call it—a "pilot region." Whereas in Perroux' discussion it is left a little uncertain as to whether or not "economic space" can be defined geographically, Boudeville is more definite that economic space "is the application of a mathematical space on or in a geographic space." [4]

Originally the concept of *pôle de croissance* and its refinements were an explanation of development and underdevelopment in the past; but it has come to be thought of as an instrument of policy. Since growth proceeds through the appearance of *pôles de croissance*, in regions where no growth is occurring it is necessary to create *pôles de croissance* by active intervention.

The "Zone Pilote"

The *zone pilote* is a less sophisticated concept and is the subject of relatively little literature. It is an operating unit rather than a tool of analysis and policy. Basically, it means just what the words imply; a geographic area selected for an experimental application of planning techniques and development programs and policies, in hopes that success with the initial program will lead to effective implementation of similar programs in other areas—modified, perhaps, in the light of experience with the pilot zone. A part of the concept is the integration of government services in pursuit of agreed common targets within the selected geographic area. In France itself, the concept has gradually given way to the concept of "program regions," of which there are now twenty-one in the country. The "program region," accordingly, is a sizable area, in contrast to the pilot zone in Greece. Even so, the system has been subjected to criticism on the grounds that the "program regions" are too small. Within the regions, the policy prescribed is really broader than development planning; it is called *aménagement du territoire*, a virtually untranslatable term, imperfectly rendered by "area planning and management." [5]

---

[4] Cf. François Perroux, "Economic Space: Theory and Applications," *Quarterly Journal of Economics*, February, 1950; Jacques de Boudeville, "Les notions d'espace et d'intégration," paper presented to the International Congress for Town and Regional Planning, Basel, September, 1965; "L'économie régionale, espace opérationnel, *Cahiers de l'Institut de Science Économique Appliquée*, Serie L, No. 3.

[5] Cf. Philippe Lamour, *L'aménagement du territoire* (Paris, 1964). For a critical analysis of the theory and practice of French regional planning, see the forthcoming book by Professor Niles Hansen, *Resource Allocation in a Regional Economy: The Case of France*. On the French "program regions," see Jacques de Boudeville, *Les programmes économiques* (Paris, 1963), especially p. 87; Pierre Bouchet, "La compta-

The Greek Economy[6]

Greece is on the borderline between the underdeveloped and the more advanced countries, but, on balance, still belongs in the former category. Greece is not desperately poor. The health of its people is good, with a life expectation of 66 years compared with 70 in the United States, 50 in Brazil, or 27 in Mali. It has one doctor for every 800 inhabitants compared with one in 1,000 in France, one in 5,000 in India, and one in 77,000 in Mali. Nutrition is reasonable, at 2,900 calories per person a day. Primary education is available to all, and only 18 per cent of the population over 10 years of age is illiterate. Total output grew at a rate of 6 per cent a year from 1951 to 1961 and output per employed person at 5.1 per cent—in both cases faster than any OECD country, except Germany and Japan. Greece has also had relative price stability since 1953.

On the other hand, real GNP per head is only a third of that in Germany and half of that in Italy, and the growth rate contains a large element of recovery, as prewar GNP per head was only restored in 1956. Half of the labor force is still in agriculture, and natural resources are negligible. Unemployment is 6.5 per cent of the labor force, and there is large-scale seasonal unemployment in agriculture. The country is spread over a vast area, and a great deal of it consists of islands or mountainous regions. Only a quarter of the land is cultivated. Regional differentials in productivity and per capita income are dramatic. Greece has experienced large-scale emigration which has eased the problem of unemployment but has drawn off many intellectuals and much entrepreneurial talent. Commodity exports are largely agricultural and are stagnating through inelastic demand and falling prices, and Greece has to meet the challenge of joining the Common Market and eliminating its rather high tariffs over the next twenty years. Exports cover only 40 per cent of imports. A favorable balance on invisibles meets a good part of the trade deficit because of large earnings from shipping, tourism, and emigrant remittances, but a sound long-term position will require a big expansion of manufactured exports which are now only 9 per cent of the total.

Thus Greece has major problems of industrialization and export promotion, and the Greek government has heavy responsibilities for spreading modern technology. In this it is faced with major problems.

A major obstacle to the absorption of modern technology is the small scale of enterprise in both agriculture and industry. Successive land reform measures have practically abolished large-scale land ownership. The average area per family farm is about 8 acres, but the average farm is split

bilité économique et son usage," *Économie appliquée*, January, 1961, p. 80. See also François Perroux, *L'économie du XXᵉ siècle* (Paris, 1961); "La firme motrice dans un région et la région motrice," *Cahiers de l'Institut de Science Économique Applilquée*, Serie AD, No. 1 (March, 1961).

[6] This section draws on background work done for *Foreign Skills and Technical Assistance in Greek Economic Development*, by Angus Maddison, Alexander Staurrianopoulos, and Benjamin Higgins (Paris: OECD, 1966).

into six or seven separate plots.[7] Farm fragmentation is worse in Greece than in any other European country. The majority of the labor force in manufacturing is employed in low-productivity small-scale plants. The size of enterprises is smaller in Greece even than in most developing countries. Only 27 per cent of Greek manufacturing employment is in firms with more than fifty employees, whereas in Brazil the proportion is 66 per cent, and in Japan it is about 50 per cent. Furthermore, the size of the domestic market is an obstacle to Greek industrialization as it is a country of only 8.5 million people with rather poor transport facilities and low incomes. This means that it will be difficult to get industries operating at the optimum scale unless Greece can develop exports of manufactured goods.

Structure of the Economy

In 1961, agriculture accounted for 53 per cent of the total labor force and 31 per cent of total output; industry employed 14 per cent of the labor force and accounted for 22 per cent of total output; the remaining 33 per cent were engaged in the rest of the economy, which produced 47 per cent of total output. The fastest-growing sectors have been industry and construction, but services have expanded fairly rapidly as well. Agriculture grew rapidly in the early 1950's, but slowed down thereafter. Total employment increased at less than 1 per cent a year, and the biggest increases were in mining and construction and services. Employment in agriculture and manufacturing increased less than the average.

In 1961, agricultural output per man/year was 60 per cent of the national average, manufacturing 135 per cent, and services 146 per cent. An indication of relative productivity in Greece may be obtained by comparison with the average for the European Economic Community. In 1959, gross value added per person employed in the agricultural sector was $500 for Greece and $1,360 for the EEC countries. In industry Greek output per man was $1,100, as compared with $2,920 for the EEC countries. In services, Greek output per man was $1,200, while the average for all EEC countries was $2,580.[8] Thus, Greek productivity levels were about one-third of those of the EEC in all three sectors.

From 1951 to 1961, output per man grew at 5.1 per cent a year in the economy as a whole, 4.3 per cent in agriculture, 6.7 per cent in industry, and 4.1 per cent in services. Apart from the growth in each sector, the structural shifts were favorable to productivity growth.

The increase of productivity in Greek industry and services was higher than in any other OECD country, and agricultural productivity grew faster than in Belgium, Denmark, France, Germany, The Netherlands, Canada, and the United States.

UNEMPLOYMENT

Unemployment remains a serious problem in Greece. The census of

[7] The figures refer to 1950 and are derived from K. Thompson, *Farm Fragmentation in Greece* (Athens, 1963), p. 29.

[8] See Industrial Development Corporation, *Situation Générale de l'Industrie en Grèce* (Athens, 1962), p. 15.

TABLE 33-1

Changes in Employment and Productivity 1951–1961

	Output	Compound Annual Per Cent Changes	
		Employment	Product per man/year
Agriculture	4.7	0.4	4.3
Industry	8.9	2.0	6.7
Services	5.3	1.1	4.1
Total	6.0	0.9	5.1

SOURCE: S. Geronimakis, *"Postwar Economic Growth in Greece 1950–61,"* Corfu paper of I.A.R.I.W.

1961 reported 239,000 people out of work, or 6.5 per cent of the labor force. This figure does not include underemployment in agriculture. Concepts and measures of underemployment and disguised unemployment in agriculture vary considerably. The Ministry of Coordination has estimated surplus labor in agriculture at 400,000. A Bank of Greece estimate runs as high as 750,000. Such estimates, however, are based on annual averages which are not disaggregated into seasonal or monthly terms. A more recent study of the Center of Economic Research [9] suggests that during the peak load periods, there is actually a shortage of available agricultural labor. The unemployed are nearly all people with poor skills, although some university graduates are also unemployed. The 1961 census in Greece counted an extremely high proportion of women in agriculture in comparison with the conventions adopted in other Mediterranean countries (except Turkey). According to the census, there were 1,188,500 men and 769,500 women in agriculture, whereas in 1951 the census recorded 1,152,000 men and only 215,000 women. The censuses, therefore, need adjustment before comparisons are made.

Regional Structure

The problem of regional disequilibrium in Greece is bigger than in any other European country. Considering that the country is so small, the regional differentials in productivity and income are dramatic. The leading region comprises central Greece and Euboea, with Athens as its center, and the lagging region consists of the rest of the country. Per capita income of the leading region was 33 per cent above the national average in 1958. All of the 10 subregions, which together constitute the lagging region, have per capita incomes below the national average. However, these subregions vary considerably among themselves. Per capita incomes range from 97 per cent of the national average for Macedonia, to 52 per cent for Epirus. Within each of the regions, there are areas much poorer

[9] A. A. Pepelasis and P. A. Yotopoulos, *Surplus Labor in Greek Agriculture* (Athens: Center of Economic Research, 1962).

than others. According to Professor Papandreou: [10]

The per capita income of Athens is probably 5 times the per capita income of mountain communities. Thus, while Athens enjoys a standard of living comparable, say, to that of Italy, the standard of living of mountain communities is closer to that of Asiatic countries. Such evidence as is available on personal distribution points to a highly skewed income distribution. Thus, participation in the growth of the last decade has been highly unequal, both from a personal and from a regional point of view.

Wide discrepancies in productivity and income from one region of a country to another are frequently associated with large countries, such as Brazil or India. Such countries are big enough to have significant differences in soil, climate, mineral and power resources among regions, together with serious problems of transport and communications arising from sheer distance, which limit mobility of labor and capital. However, regional disintegration can also occur in small countries that are resource-poor, and where industrial activity and services are concentrated in the capital city and its environs, creating a general difference in productivity and income between the region around the capital city and the rest of the country. Greece belongs to this group of countries, along with the Lebanon, Libya, Tunisia, and some Central American countries. In Greece, the regional pattern is further differentiated by micro-climates, an uneven distribution of the limited power and mineral resources, and the general division into mountain areas and coastal plains. In the 1950's, government policy largely ignored this problem. As a result, there was no clear strategy for the technical assistance projects for regional development carried out by OECD and FAO. This is also one of the rare fields in which Greek statistics are deficient and need further development.

There was some tendency for convergence of regional income levels between 1954 and 1958, but this was not true in Epirus, which substantially increased its relative poverty, nor was it true of the Aegean Islands. The situation in 1962 is shown in Table 33–2.

History of Greek Regional Planning

Planning for regional development is of relatively recent origin in Greece. It was not until 1957 that the Greek government took formal steps to launch a process of systematic regional planning. The government decided to participate in the European Productivity Agency (EPA) project for the creation of "trial and demonstration areas." This Greek venture followed on the heels of a similar project in Sardinia, undertaken by the EPA on the request of the Italian government. Thus the decision to establish a trial and demonstration area in Greece represented an acceptance by the Greek government of a program already established by

[10] Andreas Papandreou, *A Strategy for Greek Economic Development* (Athens: Center of Economic Research, 1962), p. 25.

TABLE 33-2

Per Capita Gross Domestic Product, by Regions, 1962

Region	Per Capita Gross Domestic Product (dollars)	Index	
		National Average = 100	Attica = 100
Attica	627	156.3	100.0
Rest of Central Greece	307	76.6	49.0
Peloponnesos	355	80.6	56.7
Macedonia	297	74.1	47.4
Thessaly	228	56.9	36.4
Thrace	371	92.6	59.2
Epirus	287	71.6	45.7
Crete	265	66.0	42.2
Aegean Islands	274	68.4	43.7
Ionian Islands	232	57.7	36.9
National Average	401	100.0	64.0

SOURCE: Center of Planning and Economic Research, *Schedion Programmatos Economikis Anaptyxeos tis Hellados, 1966-1970* (Draft of the Economic Deveolpment Plan of Greece, 1966-1970), Athens: 1965, p. 174.

EPA/OEEC,[11] and the Greek team was in a position to benefit from the earlier experience in Sardinia.

After an initial exploratory mission provided by the EPA/OEEC, the poor and lagging province of Epirus was chosen for the first regional development planning operation. A "trial and demonstration area" or pilot zone was selected within the region of Epirus, consisting of the districts of Konitsa, Zagori, and Paracalamos. The EPA mission recommended that

[11] In 1956, the Italian government elaborated a development scheme covering the period 1954-64. A special program for the development of southern Italy had been launched in 1950 and a special agency, the *Cassa per il Mezzogiorno*, had been established to implement it. A comprehensive regional development program was to be elaborated for the whole of Sardinia. The OEEC and the Italian government then decided to use the island to experiment with new and more effective methods of technical assistance, designed to secure more popular participation. The results of the experiment were to be applied subsequently to the whole of southern Italy and to other European regions having similar characteristics. Those responsible for setting up the trial and demonstration area in Sardinia found that no comprehensive development program had been elaborated, and that there was no specific regional investment program to which technical assistance could be directly related. The "pilot project" for Sardinia was started nevertheless, as the regional development program was in the process of being elaborated and was to be ready "very soon." The pilot area was 170,000 hectares, including forty-one communes, with a total population of 110,000 inhabitants. It had been selected as approximately representative of the rest of the island (28 percent was plains, with a section having irrigation possibilities, 45 percent was hills and 27 percent mountains). The OEEC was accorded responsibility for the management of the pilot area through an international committee. (The OEEC became OECD on September 30, 1961. See Chapter 28 for a brief account of the agency's operations.)

the two operations be undertaken simultaneously: the elaboration of a general plan for the economic development of the Epirus region; and the setting up of a trial and demonstration area "which would constitute a kind of trial and practical application laboratory for the regional plan." The general idea was to raise productivity and the living level in the zone enough to demonstrate the possibilities for developing the whole region of Epirus. In the eyes of members of the local populations and some local Greek officials, the experiment was an alternative to depopulation of the region by emigration.

The "Epirus Project" was started in 1958, financed from Greek government funds, on the basis of a program elaborated by a National Committee for Epirus, comprising representatives of the various public and semi-public Greek organizations, under the general sponsorship of the Ministry of Coordination. Program implementation was entrusted to a special project staff (about forty-five persons, most of them in the field), in cooperation with all the competent government services, and under the guidance of an executive committee located in Jannina (the chief town of Epirus).

In contrast to the Sardinia project where foreign experts accounted for a large proportion of the total effort, the technical assistance contribution in Epirus was a small fraction of the total investment of human and capital resources, in accordance with the wishes of the Greek government.

Regional Planning and OECD Reports

The initial report of the OECD team included an inventory of the natural resources and the economic and demographic situation of the region, an indication of the basic elements of a regional plan, and a suggestion of the methods to be applied in the elaboration and execution of the regional plan. This initial report also included suggestions for immediate action to be undertaken in the first trial and demonstration zone.

With regard to the fundamental elements of the regional plan, this first report indicated some priorities with regard to investment in the region. It regarded as particularly essential the establishment of transport and communications facilities for the region, the extension of electrification, some irrigation and flood control works, some land reform, and reorientation of agricultural activities in the three "natural sectors" of the region: in the irrigated sector, intensive cultivation of fruits and vegetables and production of beets and other fodder for livestock; in the foothills, the progressive replacement of sheep and goats with cattle; and in the mountain areas the expansion of forestry. It also suggested the development of pig husbandry, with strains adapted to the conditions of the region, improved marketing facilities, progressive industrialization of the region through the creation of establishments to process agricultural products, better transport facilities (especially roads) and the development of tourism. The importance of education, including vocational training and the popularization of technological progress, was also emphasized.

During 1959 the Greek government obtained the assistance of a team of economists from the Italian organization Svimez, which had the major responsibility for preparing plans for the Italian south. The national development plan prepared by this team was submitted to the Central Committee, and to the international experts, at a meeting held in Athens in June, 1960, for application at the regional level.

The activities of the EPA/OEEC in the field of regional planning resulted in the inclusion in the 1960–1964 *Five-year Programme for the Economic Development of Greece* of a brief section on regional development policy. The chapter on regional development in the national plan was very short and presented no data. Meanwhile, experts concerned with both the Epirus Development Plan and with the trial and demonstration area had to work without any guidance in the form of a regionally disaggregated national plan. However, the national plan did commit the Greek government to a policy of regional development that would reduce the gaps in productivity and income among regions. It stated that:

The regional development effort has been directed towards an integrated growth of the less-developed regions of the country. Epirus was chosen as the first region for such an intervention. The effort undertaken by the Government, within the present programme, to eliminate the obstacles which hinder a balanced growth, among the regions of the country, is directed, on the one hand, towards furthering the development of immediately productive activities, and on the other, towards securing the formation of the required fixed social capital in the various areas.

By the time the five-year program was prepared, it had been decided to extend regional development activities to western Peloponnesus. Some time later, Crete was added as a third area for a concentrated effort in regional development.

Actual operations began in the trial and demonstration area considerably before the implementation of any formal, comprehensive plan for the region as a whole. The planning and execution of projects for the trial and demonstration area benefited from technical assistance from UNESCO as well as from OEEC (later OECD).

While the general planning for the whole of Epirus was still continuing, public investments were already being undertaken in the pilot zone. In 1960, in the first report of the experts of the European Productivity Agency (OEEC), the team felt able to write:

The work accomplished by the trial and demonstration area since its origin is remarkable, as much in its orientation as in the results obtained on the spot. We can congratulate without reservation the executive committee which has assumed the responsibility, as well as its Director, and the combination of services and agencies which have collaborated in the success of this undertaking.

The report takes note of various kinds of investment made in the infrastructure, both physical and human. In the field of transport and communications, the report states:

The zone has established its programme of road communications and the chronological order for their undertaking, completed studies of several hundred kilometers of roads and particularly difficult traces, and had launched by the 1st June, 1960, the opening of several dozen kilometers of mountain routes destined to "free" the villages of Zagori, until now deprived of any other means of communication than donkey paths.

In the field of energy, the zone had installed some power lines and created some new centers of energy production, while electrifying several dozen villages. In the fields of irrigation and sanitation, the zone had surveyed and executed the irrigation of several hundred hectares on the plains of Konitsa, as well as at Sitaria, Castania, and Pighis. It had made studies for the irrigation of 3,000 hectares in the district of Paracalamos-Doliana, and this project was under way under the auspices of the agricultural services. Irrigation surveys of seventy-five mountain villages had also been made. By the end of 1960 fourteen of these had been completed, twenty-six more were expected to be finished in 1961, and the remaining thirty-five during 1962. In the field of education, the zone had reformed and modernized the agricultural school at Konitsa, organized an extension service for the whole of the zone, constituted in the various communities agricultural associations for technological progress, and created twenty-two adult education centers with help from UNESCO. OECD helped to develop modern methods of education in the centers by providing a visual-aid specialist. In the field of agriculture, the zone authorities had organized the preparation of the soil and the reorientation of cultivation in the Konitsa plain, in view of the expected irrigation. They also made some installations and demonstrations of the effects of irrigation. In the whole zone, technological progress for fruit trees, horticulture, and animal husbandry was encouraged.

It was recognized from the outset, by both foreign experts and Greek authorities, that preparation of plans for the trial and demonstration project was handicapped by the lack of any plan for the region as a whole, and by the lack of a national development plan broken down by regions. Given the difficulties of area planning in the absence of regional planning, the interest of the Greek authorities seems to have shifted gradually away from the trial and development area as such to planning for Epirus as a whole. The preliminary five-year program for the region was approved in April, 1960. This plan, however, consisted essentially of aggregative projections, similar in nature to those in the five-year program for the country as a whole. The Greek authorities apparently felt that it was important to translate this program into sets of specific projects as quickly as possible. The result was some dilution of the more purely demonstration aspect of work in the *zone pilote*. Instead of serving as an example, it would become only one element in the general scheme.

Some of the foreign experts lamented the tendency to extend to other areas in the Epirus region the kind of activities that had already been undertaken in the trial and demonstration area. The common features of projects for the area and for the Epirus region as a whole, they pointed

out, accentuated the tendency to extend to all comparable areas in the
region the activities then underway in the demonstration area. They
recommended that such extensions should be limited to cases of necessity
so that trial and demonstration activities could remain chiefly concentrated
on the area. They felt that the pilot zone should always show more
progress than the neighboring areas so as to demonstrate clearly the
effectiveness of the methods adopted.

A year later, however, the foreign experts expressed some reservations
about the trial and demonstration project. Epirus, they agreed, was not a
sufficiently self-contained unit for work in a trial and demonstration area
to have full effect, or to be of any use at all in certain fields, such as
industrialization or tourism. However, they did feel that the pilot zone
could continue to serve as a laboratory for the development of the region
in many spheres.

Results in the Pilot Zone

Gross capital formation in the zone during the years 1957 to 1961
amounted to 165.7 million drachmas, or about 125 per cent of the average
gross domestic product during the period. In other words, gross investment
averaged about 25 per cent of gross domestic product during these years.
There was a rapid acceleration of the rate of investment from slightly less
than 8 million drachmas in 1957 to 60.2 million drachmas in 1961. In the
latter year, gross investment was about 45 per cent of gross domestic
income. Thus more than a sevenfold increase in investment yielded only
an 8 per cent increase in income.

Taking the aggregate increase in income over the whole period in
comparison with aggregate capital formation, the incremental capital-
output ratio was about 16 to 1. Some 70 per cent of total investment went
into the agricultural sector, and two-thirds of total investment was public.
For an investment program with this pattern, an average incremental
capital-output ratio of 16 to 1 must surely be one of the highest on
record.

The Agricultural Bank itself extended credits in the zone on a considerable scale (see Table 33–3). Indeed, credits extended to twelve
villages in the zone (by the Delvinaki branch) were more than thirteen
times as much as credits to thirty-eight villages in the same area but outside
the zone.

The trial and demonstration project did not stop the flow of emigrants
from the region. Between 1956 and 1960, the total labor force of the zone
fell from 18,435 to 16,102. Man-year productivity, therefore, rose more
than total income. There was little structural change; 87 per cent of the
active population was engaged in primary production in 1956 (agriculture,
animal breeding, and forestry), 87 per cent in 1956 and 84 per cent in
1960. There had been a modest increase in the numbers engaged in
cottage and handicraft industries and transport, and a significant increase
in the number employed on construction projects—from an estimated 645
to 1,658. This increase reflects the direct impact on construction employ-

TABLE 33–3

Loans and Grants Given by the Agricultural Bank,
Branch of Delvinaki, during the Period 1957–1962
(in drachmas)

	Pilot zone*	Outside the zone†
Agricultural construction	1,269,770	150,000
Improved stock (cows)	1,200,000	150,000
Horticultural and flower cultivation	75,683	
Beehives	39,778	
Milk containers	300,000	
Equipment for cheese factories	750,000	
Subsidies for agricultural construction	280,392	
(Interest support)	63,125	
Total	3,978,748	300,000

* Twelve villages are included in the pilot zone.
† Thirty-eight villages are included in the area outside the pilot zone.
SOURCE: Agricultural Bank, Delvinaki.

ment of public investment in the zone. On the other hand, there had been a decline in numbers engaged in services. The gross income of the zone had increased by 8 per cent at constant prices between 1956 and 1961. The income in the primary sector where most people were engaged increased only by 7 per cent over the five years. Gross income originating from other sectors than agriculture increased by 12 per cent. Crop production increased by slightly less than 3 per cent in terms of value, livestock production by 9 per cent, forestry production by 11 per cent.

Levels of Living

Total consumption in the area increased more than production, because of emigrant remittances and because the presence in the region of rather large-scale governmental activities provided opportunities for increases in consumption in excess of the local increase in production.

Emigrant remittances were the major factor. The total value of checks cashed through the Post Office Savings Bank in the zone increased from 8.9 million drachmas in 1956 to 13.1 million drachmas in 1961. Foreign checks, however, increased from a mere 16,000 drachmas in 1956 to 2.8 million drachmas in 1961. There was also a substantial increase in the total volume of deposits in the branches of the Agricultural Bank and Post Office Savings Bank in the zone, presumably also largely as a result of emigrant remittances, but possibly as a result of increased public activities in the region as well.

The increase in real income was reflected in a higher level of living. An improvement in the pattern of food consumption is indicated by a 17 per cent decline in consumption of wheat, accompanied by a 70 per cent increase in fish consumption. Other items such as coffee, sugar, olive oil, etc., also showed significant increases. It appears, however, that a part of the explanation of the increase in meat consumption is that the farmers slaughtered and ate cows provided to them by the Regional Service as a basis for building up a herd. The numbers of cows provided were not sufficient to make a significant difference in family output; the cost of feed was excessively high; milk prices were low in comparison; and the difficulties of marketing from that isolated spot virtually insuperable. Also of interest is the remarkable increase in wine consumption—44 per cent over four years. Neighboring villages, starting from a level of per capita wine consumption slightly more than half that of the zone in the best years, suffered a decline in wine consumption in the four following years. It is possible that the larger numbers of persons coming from outside the region to do work in connection with the development plan may account for some part of this increase of wine consumption.

No great change took place in housing conditions over these years. The water supply improved, in the sense that water flow to the villages was increased, but in terms of actual installations of water pipes and taps in individual houses, the improvement was much less marked. In the field of power, the major result was the electrification of eleven villages. There has been a significant increase in the number of radio sets (although less than in neighboring Pogoni) and in subscriptions to newspapers. Here again, we find a reflection of the increase in income, over and above the increase in output, resulting from emigrant remittances and expenditures on the project. Thus in a period when investment was concentrated in the public sector, the main improvements in living level have come through purely private channels.

Comparison with Pogoni

It is of interest to compare these results with developments in the neighboring region of Pogoni, where no such trial and demonstration project was taking place. There, the increase in gross value of crop production over the same period was 3 per cent, while livestock production increased by 45 per cent and forestry production by nearly 10 per cent. Total income in Pogoni rose by 21.3 per cent, as compared to 8 per cent for the demonstration zone. Taking gross agricultural income alone, which is more nearly comparable, the increase in the demonstration zone was 7.1 per cent, while in Pogoni it was 13.4 per cent.

POGONI AS A "CONTROL" AREA

The selection of an appropriate area for comparison with the pilot zone similar enough in character to the zone to be an effective "control" and, at the same time, statistically manageable, is no simple task. In the first place, the zone itself has a range of conditions that is hard to reproduce in any nearby area of similar size. Paracalamos, with its relatively fertile plain, has land that is 23.2 per cent arable, while 40.3 per cent is in pasture and 30.4 per cent under forest. Arid and mountainous Zagori has only 3.3 per cent of its land arable, with 38.6 per cent in pasture and 52 per cent under forest. Few other areas can reproduce the special circumstances of

Paracalamos. For the zone as a whole, 6.7 per cent of the area is arable, 41.2 per cent is pasture, and 44.2 per cent of the area is forest. Pogoni was selected, mainly on statistical grounds, because its pattern of land use is similar to the average for the zone: 8 per cent arable, 64.9 per cent pasture, and 20.9 per cent forest.

From the statistical and administrative point of view as well, the pilot zone is a somewhat awkward unit. The entire Nomos is divided into four prefectures: Dodona, with its center at Jannina; Konitsa, with its center at Konitsa; Metzovo, with its center at Metzovo; and Pogoni, with its center at Delvinaki. The zone, however, is an aggregation of villages cutting across the borders of prefectures. The zone includes 72 of the 236 villages in Dodona, all of the 40 villages in Konitsa, and none of the villages in Metzovo. Pogoni has 32 villages.

While recognizing the difficulties of finding any better "control" zone, some caution is required in interpreting the comparison between Pogoni and the pilot zone. From almost any point of view, Pogoni has a very special and peculiar economy. Basically, Pogoni is a less-productive area than the zone. However, because of a long tradition of emigration and emigrant remittances, the actual levels of living in Pogoni have been relatively high. Before the war, Pogoni lived almost entirely on emigrant remittances, and as far as one can judge, lived rather well. Emigration was then mainly to the United States and to other parts of Greece, particularly the Athens region. Since the war, emigrants have gone mainly to West Germany. From the small, thinly populated area of Pogoni, 1,200 emigrants have recently gone to Germany. Many emigrants come back to the village, after having accumulated some savings, and live in the village as pensioners. This process has been going on for generations and has led to a significant amount of capital accumulation in the village. This capital accumulation has permitted some improvements in agricultural methods. In the villages of the zone, on the other hand, large-scale emigration is a relatively new, postwar phenomenon.

Another factor of considerable importance is that in Pogoni, the average size of the holdings is increasing as a result of a combination of circumstances peculiar to the area. Between 1956 and 1960, the size of the flocks and herds was increasing, with 1960 as a peak year. More recently, however, the combination of rising wages for shepherds as the labor supply diminished through emigration, and rising rents of land, together with the relatively low prices for milk, wool, and meat and the difficulties of marketing with the extremely poor transportation system, has made livestock-raising unprofitable. As a consequence, the farmers are slaughtering their animals or selling them to other areas. The number of sheep declined from 75,000 in 1961 to 60,000 in 1963, while the number of goats fell from 25,000 to 15,000 in the same area. Thus, what appears in the statistics as real income is partly a species of capital consumption, as the size of flocks and herds is diminished through slaughter and sale.

It may be, however, that this trend will once again reverse itself, through the *remembrement* of land. There has been a considerable turnover in land ownership, with the number of buyers only one-third of the number of sellers, indicating that some farmers are systematically increasing the size of their holdings. Cultivation of flocks of fifty to sixty sheep (which has been the average size) is no longer profitable; but with larger herds livestock-raising may become profitable again.

The use of emigrant remittances as working capital has resulted in some increase in yields per acre. Recently, the farmers have been keeping their lambs instead of killing them as they had done in the last two or three years. The need for some cash to make the voyage to Germany has contributed to the decumulation of flocks. The Agricultural Bank has made loans—1.5 million drachmas in a single year—for the purchase of land. In the zone, however, this kind of process of *remembrement* is not yet taking place because emigration is on a relatively small scale and the possibilities of aggregating land holdings are much fewer. The credits extended by the Agricultural Bank in Pogoni for all purposes are a small fraction of those in the zone.

It is also clear that incomes in Pogoni are affected by central government activities in the central village, which indeed has some of the aspects of a small town. The central town of Pogoni is the headquarters for an entire district, with the district offices of the Agricultural Bank, Ministry of Agriculture, and the like. This fact has resulted in construction of new office buildings, housing, etc. By the same token, Delvinaki has some importance as a market. All these factors could easily have contributed to the increase in the income of Pogoni during the years 1956 to 1961, in a way that makes it not strictly comparable with the neighboring areas in the pilot zone. Konitsa, the central town of Konitsa, has some of the characteristics of Delvinaki, but has considerably less of the aspect of a "provincial capital."

Evaluation of the Trial and Demonstration Project

Investment was high in the zone only in comparison to the rather low per capita income (about $138 per year on the average for the period). The average annual investment amounted to only $30 per head, which would be a low figure in an advanced country. It should also be noted that the investment is calculated in financial terms, and not all of this capital expenditure accrued as income in the region. Surveys of experts, equipment purchased from outside the region, etc., are included in the investment figures but do not constitute part of the regional income.

It must also be said that the trial and demonstration area did at least introduce the idea of regional planning to the Greek government and the Greek people. It has resulted in the establishment of an organization for regional planning which may bring better results in Epirus as a whole, or in the other two regions where the Regional Service is now operating, Peloponnesus and Crete.

Even when such allowances are made, however, the project must be accounted a failure in terms of its demonstration effect. It is, of course, possible that the investment will result in more significant increases in income sometime in the future, as roads and power lines are completed, irrigation systems connected with farms, and the like. But a demonstration effect cannot be obtained through the publication of statistics showing improvement over a twenty-year period. A demonstration project, by definition, must bring visible and rapid results.

It appears that the zone was selected because it was a kind of "stratified sample" of all the representative conditions of the entire region of Epirus. It has some districts on the plains, some mountainous areas, and some other areas in-between. It was hoped that on the plains, at least, quick results could have been obtained through irrigation. However, the regions seem to have been badly chosen from other points of view. The area is extraordinarily isolated. Albania lies to the north, with a closed frontier. To the east are high mountains. The only communication is south to Jannina and then to the west. However, even the connections with Jannina are very poor, for the roads are inadequate.

It also appears that the investment plan was implemented too slowly. Road plans were not well organized, and in 1964 the region was still not properly connected with either east or west. When the area was visited by the writer at that time, there were many half-finished roads, power lines, and irrigation channels. The Regional Service was apparently unable to resist completely the pressures of local politics, with the result that many projects were launched simultaneously throughout the zone instead of having a few projects in selected villages that could be fairly quickly completed. Also, the composition of the team of experts—without any reflection whatsoever on their individual competence—seems to have been badly designed. There was no regional survey that would indicate what might be the most promising field of development. In particular, there was no effort to assemble the relevant statistics before launching the development program. The missions made by economists or agricultural economists were much too short to be truly effective. Finally, as is now recognized, the planning and execution of development for the zone was insufficiently coordinated with plans for the region and for the nation as a whole.

The district of Zagori, except for the wooded areas on the other side of the mountain range, is clearly hopeless from the standpoint of increases in basic production. Zagori has depended largely on emigrant remittances, and remote villages high in the mountains have astonishingly high levels of living (especially in terms of housing) in relation to the infertility of the surrounding countryside. The constant ebb and flow of emigrants has not only brought an inflow of financial resources, but of culture and civilization as well. One village with 150 people high in the mountains, with practically no roads, completely isolated, has produced 27 teachers plus a number of doctors and engineers, etc. The doctors and other professional personnel formerly worked for a clientele across the Albanian border. Zagori is a region where the possibilities of tourism are considerable, but the project did little to promote it. The landscape is overwhelmingly beautiful, the villages are charming, with a great deal of excess capacity in high-standard housing. The summer climate is close to ideal, and there are such points of interest as early fifteenth-century monasteries, seventeenth-century churches, and the like. In one or two villages there are already arrangements for taking care of tourists in the homes of residents. The houses are spacious, well-designed, spotlessly clean, and attractive. The residents of these villages count heavily on the completion of the improved road as a means of increasing their incomes.

Peloponnesus

The second Regional Service to be established was in Peloponnesus with headquarters at Patras. An agreement was reached between the Greek government and the UN Special Fund for the provision of a team of foreign experts to assist in the preparation of an economic development program for West Peloponnesus. Indeed, it appears that the initiative for the project came from the FAO itself, and that in effect FAO "sold" the project both to the Special Fund and to the Greek government. The project was related to the FAO Mediterranean Regional Project, and in Rome, at least, was viewed as a larger scale "trial and demonstration" project. It differed from the Epirus pilot zone, however, not only in the size of the unit but also in its quality; instead of seeking a "representative" region, FAO chose one that is relatively prosperous and has relatively good prospects for development. The contract was granted to the Food and Agricultural Organization, a fact which resulted in a heavy weighting of agricultural specialists in the team.

Four major problems plagued the operations of the West Peloponnesus team. First was the manner of its original organization. As suggested above, the choice of the Food and Agricultural Organization as the contractor for the Special Fund Project in West Peloponnesus resulted in a bias toward agricultural surveys and a plan emphasizing agricultural improvement. In effect, the decision to turn over the contract to FAO meant a prior decision that the future of the region lies in the direction of agricultural improvement.

Secondly, the East-West division of the region handicapped the functioning of the team. The line demarcating the region is essentially a rainfall and vegetation line, and reflects the agricultural bias in the original planning of the project. In terms of movements of the labor force and of markets, the division of the region in accordance with this vegetation line is extremely inconvenient. For some purposes, the group was compelled to redefine their region, so as to incorporate complete statistical units. This problem was aggravated, during the life of the project, by extension of the responsibilities of the Regional Service in Patras to cover Southwest Epirus, thus increasing the discrepancy in the definition of the "region" by the two teams.

Third, the FAO team was not well-integrated with other planning organizations. For example, the plans prepared for the port of Patras apparently counted on the port serving as a major outlet for citrus fruits; the view of the FAO team, however, was that the region was not well-suited to the production of citrus fruits. There was little consultation between the Technecon team charged with planning the transport development for the region and the FAO-Special Fund team. More serious was the inadequacy of the cooperation between the regional service and the

FAO team in the same area. The fact that the Regional Service plans were for the whole of Peloponnesus and the Special Fund team only for West Peloponnesus complicated the problems of collaboration between the two groups.

Partly because of the difference in the area covered, partly because of physical separation of the two offices, partly because the Greek government was unable to provide a complete set of counterparts, and partly for other reasons the work of the FAO team was never satisfactorily coordinated with that of the Regional Service at Patras. Each group went its own way, did its own work, prepared its own plans. This situation was able to continue because there was no organization in the central government that could assure integration of the work of the two teams.

The Regional Service for Peloponnesus constructed its plans on the assumption that 70,000 people now engaged in agriculture in Peloponnesus would be moved out of agriculture by 1974; only in this way can the target of doubling per capita income in agriculture by that year be attained. This target is modest enough; it would mean that farm incomes would be 85 per cent of those of unskilled workers in Patras industry, instead of 60 per cent as they are today. Once again, therefore, the real problem is to find alternative occupations for the surplus agricultural population, while the size of holdings is increased and technology and product mix changed in agriculture. The Special Fund program, however, could provide only limited help in the determination of where and how these new jobs might be created, and no guidance on this matter was provided by the central government.

The fourth and most serious problem of the Special Fund project was the lack of guidance for the Special Fund team from the Ministry of Coordination in Athens. This problem was not specific to Peloponnesus but was true of Epirus and Crete as well. The Regional Development Section of the Planning Division of the Ministry was insufficiently staffed and could not brief the Special Fund group properly. It was not able to provide even rough guidelines relating the potential of the region to the plan for the national economy as a whole. In the absence of a regional breakdown of the national plan it was impossible for the Special Fund team to translate the projections of the national plan into possible regional budgets. The disparity in the scale of technical assistance provided to West Peloponnesus and to other parts of the country also creates a serious problem for the planners in the Ministry of Coordination. They naturally want to make use of the work of so highly qualified a group as a Special Fund team, but the absence of similar teams in other parts of the country means that the Central Planning Office will have great difficulty in appraising the merits of the recommendations made by the Special Fund team relative to projects that might be proposed for other regions instead.

Crete

The Regional Service for Crete was established in October, 1962. In contrast to the method of operation in the other two regions, regional planning for Crete began with general surveys, including the building up of regional statistics to provide a profile of the region. Some difficulties were experienced in acquiring a collection of statistics adequate for this purpose, but these are being assembled.

Because Crete, like the other lagging regions, is heavily dependent on agriculture, the planners first constructed an agricultural investment program. Irrigation projects were surveyed for three (and eventually for four) districts. One of these includes 25,000 hectares, in comparison with the 30,000 now under irrigation. Completion of this one project, therefore, would nearly double the irrigated area on the island. Work was begun on a selection of sixty village centers which would serve—and perhaps eventually empty—surrounding clusters of small villages. The centers will be provided with roads, schools, water, and electrification. One of these sixty centers will be chosen as an initial "trial and demonstration area." It will be selected in the hope of providing early and significant results.

As in the case of Epirus and Peloponnesus, the agricultural experts soon discovered that there was no way of obtaining satisfactory levels of rural income without substantial emigration from the agricultural sector, on the order of 30,000 families. The real problem, therefore, was to find alternative occupations for these people. There are some processing industries, some social overhead investments, and some services that clearly belong in Crete, and can provide job opportunities. A balance of the population, however, must either leave the island or obtain work in industries deliberately established in Crete, rather than elsewhere, to provide employment in Crete. Here the team was severely handicapped both by the lack of a national policy on location of industry and migration, and by the shortages of industrial and economic expertise on their team.

Both the Regional Service and the foreign advisers gave high priority to a perspective plan for the island, setting forth the broad framework for potential development of the region. However, the foreign group felt that they could not proceed far with detailed planning for the island as a whole without more guidance from the central government regarding national plans. Instead they also chose a kind of "trial and demonstration area" for detailed planning. However, they followed the Peloponnesus rather than the Epirus example in choosing the "model village;" that is, rather than trying to assemble a "representative sample" of the whole island, they chose an area where the size of holdings is relatively large and the prospects for development are relatively good. The fragmentation problem is worst in Crete of all Greek regions, and consolidation of holdings into a model village, introduction of irrigaton, and improved pasture are major aspects of the planning for the pilot zone.

Conclusions on Greek Experience

It is of course always easier to be critical in retrospect than it is to foresee exactly what should be done. Moreover, economic development has been a particularly fast-moving field; the accumulation of knowledge regarding the problem and the process of development between 1956 and 1966 has been substantial. Not a few theorists and practitioners were willing in 1956 to resort to a counsel of despair, sometimes graced with the term "project planning," the essence of which was, "Let us get something —anything—done!" The state of knowledge in the field of regional development planning was, if anything, still worse than in the field of national development planning.

It must also be said that the Greek or foreign development economist or official, eager to launch the process of regional planning in Greece in 1956, would have been hard put to decide where to begin. Not only was there no Regional Service and no regional planning division in the central government; there was not even a national development planning division or a Center of Economic Research to which such efforts might be attached. The information that would have permitted a rational design for regional planning in Greece was lacking. Under these circumstances, and confronted with the appalling poverty of the backward areas of Epirus, it is not surprising that the sponsors of the pilot zone should have fallen back on a "get something done" approach. However, one form of progress is making mistakes and profiting by them; it would be most unfortunate if the trial and demonstration project in Epirus did not have at least this beneficial effect.

Rationale of the "Pilot Zone" Approach

Just what the sponsors felt would follow from a successful trial and demonstration project is not now altogether clear. There seems to have been some idea that the launching of "planning from below" would lead ultimately to some planning from above—the establishment of the requisite organizations for development planning at the regional and national levels. In this anticipation the sponsors were to a degree correct. There seems also to have been something of the community development idea, although in fact the majority of projects were not "community" projects in the strict sense but were rather investments by the central government. There was something of a rural social work approach—"the people are poor, they must be helped." As a "demonstration,," it was probably hoped that the project would lead to a spreading of "development-mindedness" and "technology-mindedness" among the population of the entire region, providing a psychological framework within which many things could subsequently be done.

There seems also to have been something of the *pôle de croissance* concept behind the project. However, as shown above, a focal point of growth must by definition be big enough and dynamic enough to generate spread effects to the entire region, in this case the whole of Epirus. The pilot zone project did not meet these criteria. Neither the scale nor the form of the project was such that its successful execution could be expected to generate, in itself, significant increases in investment, income, and employment throughout the Epirus region. Rising incomes in the zone would have brought only negligible increases in demand for either consumers' goods or capital goods produced elsewhere in the region. It is likely, given the pattern of income-elasticities of demand in interregional trade, that the impact of rising incomes in the zone would have been felt more in the Athens region than in other parts of Epirus; but the scale was such that the effect on the Athens region would not be noticeable.

It is possible to argue in retrospect that it is fortunate that the pilot zone was not a spectacular success; for if quick and dramatic results had been achieved, the pilot zone project would no doubt have been followed by similar experiments in neighboring areas. The misallocation of human and capital resources would thereby have been aggravated. If one looks at the Greek economy as a whole and considers the "investment in human resources" policy that is appropriate to Greek conditions and opportunities, it seems clear that Greece should aim at a slowly increasing population, combined with rapid industrialization and net migration out of the poorer agricultural regions into the industrial centers. It is equally clear that the pilot zone, with the possible exception of the subdivision Paracalamos, would be high on any list of areas selected for such reductions in total population. It would not have been necessary to compel anyone to move; the emigration was already taking place and continued despite the large investments in the zone. One of the reasons for the better success with raising per capita output and income in neighboring Pogoni was precisely the pattern of emigration, emigrant remittances, capital formation, credit extension, and land consolidation (permitting a shift to more productive agriculture, substitution of sheep for goats, etc.). With the hindsight now possible, it would seem that a similar development policy would have been more appropriate to the pilot zone as well. Indeed, as long as the population and the product mix remain essentially what they are, the pilot zone can never be anything but poor.

All this is not to say that rural electrification, improved transport, and irrigation may not make a substantial contribution to raising agricultural productivity in Greece. It is no doubt true that "most of the activities undertaken so far" in Epirus "are activities whose returns are by definition long-term," and that "the evaluation of their success can only be made over a long-term perspective."[12] But by their very nature, these are projects of a kind that must be planned and implemented on a national scale. Roads built within a small pilot zone and ending at the borders, for example, would be patently absurd. The same is true of electric transmission lines. Irrigation projects might be planned in terms of regions, but since Greece is a country in which irrigation might add to total agricultural output of all major regions, priorities for irrigation projects must be determined on the basis of a national plan.

Even the "institution-building" contribution of the project should not be exaggerated. It is true that there is now a Regional Service in Greece, and that regional planning has been extended to three areas. But it is also true that in the middle of 1964, seven years after the launching of the pilot zone project, regional planning in Greece was still in an unsatisfactory state. Except for the work done by one foreign expert provided by OECD, there was no real regional planning operation in the Ministry of Coordination in Athens at all. The regional planning division of the central government had

[12] OECD, *Regional Development and Accelerated Growth*, Paris, December, 1965, p. 40.

for all practical purposes disappeared. The three regional planning operations were proceeding with very limited contact with each other or with the central government. In Epirus the contribution of foreign experts had effectively ceased. In Peloponnesus the FAO-Special Fund team was completing its work, in essential isolation from the Regional Service of Peloponnesus as well as from the central government and the other two regional planning operations. The Crete program, with more emphasis on the "pôles de croissance" concept and less on the "*zone pilote*," and benefiting from mistakes of the earlier programs, looked more promising.

All three operations were severely handicapped by the lack of directives from the center and the absence of a national policy regarding regional development, including location of industry, emigration, and internal migration. It had become clear in each of the three regions that there was no solution to the problem of agricultural poverty except the movement of large numbers of people out of agriculture. But where were the surplus farmers to go? Only a few could be absorbed in industries clearly belonging in the regions themselves and clearly viable. Others could be absorbed by establishing industries in the region that could just as well or perhaps better be established elsewhere. But what was the government policy in this regard? No one could say, because regional planning at the national level had not proceeded to the point where government decisions on these questions could be made on sound grounds.

It had also become clear that the stated goals of the government were mutually inconsistent. A high rate of growth for the national economy, reduced emigration, and narrowing gaps in output and income among regions could not be attained simultaneously. Rates of growth in the three regions as high as those projected for the national economy could be attained only through large-scale movement out of the region—as long as locational advantages for new industries in other regions were respected. But high rates of growth in the national economy would mean continuation of the tendency for output to grow much more than employment; no conceivable rate of investment in the leading region could create employment opportunities at a rate sufficient to absorb all the people that must be moved out of agriculture in the lagging regions if growth of per capita income there were to keep pace with (let alone exceed) that of the leading region. The only solution would be continued large-scale emigration from the country as a whole. Yet even here there were limits; if emigration continued with the same pattern in terms of age-groups and skills, growth of the national economy might soon be limited by shortages of younger workers with some industrial skills.

In short, it seems safe to say that the "planning from below" approach to regional development in Greece, which started with the pilot zone and unfortunately still characterized the work in the three regions at least as late as mid-1964, delayed the finding of a solution to the problem of poverty in the lagging regions of Greece. In this respect one could even argue that the pilot project did considerable and lasting harm.

There has also been a failure to learn from experience regarding the composition of regional planning teams. In each of the three regions the approach has been to give emphasis to agricultural improvement, and accordingly to weight the team heavily with agricultural experts. In each region the agricultural experts have soon discovered that there is no way of raising agricultural productivity to adequate levels—adequate, let us say, to prevent further widening of the percentage differential between incomes of the region and of the leading region—without significant reduction in the number of farmers. No one would deny the importance of improving agricultural techniques and changing the product mix for the majority of the population that will remain in agricultural occupations for the next few years in the lagging regions; but the simple truth is that the real solution for these regions lies outside of agriculture. The expertise provided in the field of industrialization—the key to success in all three regions, whether the industrialization takes place in the region or outside it, with net emigration from the region—has been totally inadequate in relation to the expertise provided in the field of agriculture in all three regions. This fact, together wtih the lack of personnel in the central government to find an answer to the core question of where industrialization can best take place if national objectives are to be achieved, has meant that much of the work of a substantial number of highly competent Greeks and foreigners in the regional development field was largely wasted.

Greek Regional Planning Since 1964 [13]

The Greek government itself has learned a good deal from its early experiences with regional planning, and the last few years have seen some significant changes in the organization, scope, and method of Greek regional planning. The country has been divided into five regions for planning purposes: northern Greece, Thessaly, Crete, western Greece, and central and insular Greece. These regions were chosen in an effort to delineate areas which are more or less homogeneous in socio-economic structure and which are comparable in dimension, while leaving open the possibility of moving ultimately to a different division of the country if further experience suggests it. The first three of the regions listed have Regional Services of their own; western Greece has two Regional Services, one for Peloponnesus and one for Epirus. As yet no Regional Service has been set up for central and insular Greece. The National Plan for 1966–1970 adds to the objectives of raising the rate of growth of national income as a whole and strengthening the country's competitive position in the Common Market, the reduction of disparities among regions.

In terms of basic planning theory, the operation in Crete continues to be the most advanced. The comprehensive plan for 1965–1975 was completed at the end of 1964, setting forth macro-economic and sectoral targets. The next phase, lasting from July to November, 1965, was the review

[13] This section relies heavily on materials provided to the author by Bernard Wetzel, OECD regional planner in Crete. For a detailed study of development potential in Epirus, see Pan A. Yotopoulos, *Allocative Efficiency and Economic Development; A Cross Section Analysis of Epirus Farming*, Athens (Center of Economic Research), 1967.

of the plan by the Greek authorities and the selection of certain pilot projects. The third phase of preparing detailed programs for these pilot projects ended in August, 1966, when implementation began. One of the important projects is bringing into effective use the four agricultural zones selected for irrigation. Detailed plans for these zones include the determination of the kinds of production best suited to their physical conditions, the determination of the types of farm best suited for such production, and suggestion of means for developing these types of farm. The detailed program also includes some industrial projects such as a modern olive oil refinery, two factories for preparing fresh grapes, a plastics factory, and a tannery, etc. However, Bernard Wetzel, a regional planner provided by OECD to the Crete Regional Service, observes in a communication to the author that difficulties have been experienced in finding private entrepreneurs willing and able to take over projects of this kind.

Integration of national and regional plans is more complete and effective today than it was in 1964; indeed, the regional plans are regarded as part of a national strategy. A continuing weakness in Greek regional planning is the inability of regional planners to make well-informed decisions as to whether a particular development project belongs better in their region or in some other. Lacking any other device for testing the appropriateness of planning a particular project for their own region, the team in Crete compares the incremental capital output ratio for agricultural projects undertaken in Crete with the average ICOR for Greek agriculture as a whole. While recognizing the gross deficiencies of such a test, the Crete planners feel that it is better than nothing and diminishes somewhat the risks of making a mistake.

General Conclusions

Greece is, unfortunately, not the only country in which there has been confusion in the theoretical underpinnings of regional and area development policy. On the contrary, there is in most countries a reluctance to consider seriously the possibility that development in poor regions may best be promoted by investment in rich regions. There is a related reluctance to require or even encourage people to leave poor regions and migrate to rich ones. In part, perhaps, this reluctance reflects the great difficulty in obtaining precise measurements of interregional multipliers that would permit us to allocate developmental investment between rich or growing and poor or stagnant regions so as to make the maximum contribution to the achievement of national goals. In part the confusion arises from failure of governments to state clearly what the national goals are; politicians tend to hope that maximizing development of the national economy and reducing regional gaps by investment in poor regions are mutually consistent goals, and that they will never be required to say which goal is more important. The United States, with its Economic Development Administration established to help designated "distressed" areas (with express provision in the Act against encouraging out-migration), its Appalachia program and its antipoverty campaign, is no exception to the rule; area and regional development policy is designed primarily to help poor people where they are. Canada, with its Area Development Administration, Atlantic Provinces Development Board, and its Agricultural Rehabilitation and Development Agency, is in general following the same format, although Canada also assists with transport costs of people willing to move to find jobs. Even the Province of Quebec, despite its open espousal of French concepts and practices of regional planning, has come dangerously close to making the same mistake. The eastern part of Quebec, chosen as the pilot region for the regional development of the province, is perhaps the poorest and most stagnant area with similar population in the entire province. The region as a whole is as far from being a *pôle de croissance* for the provincial economy as a whole as any populated sub-region of the same size could be. However, these facts are recognized by the Quebec regional planners, and at least their recommendations encompass the establishment of "pôles de croissance" in the more dynamic towns within their pilot region, and the depopulation of the more hopeless areas. In this respect their application of French regional planning theory is much more consistent and sophisticated than was the case with the Greek pilot zone.

It should be clear from the foregoing, however, that not all the difficulty lies in the application. Much of the difficulty lies in the theory itself. Obviously, no one could quarrel with the idea of establishing *pôles de croissance* which will generate powerful spread effects to some larger region. But if the concept is to become the sharp tool of analysis and the basis for policy that Professor Perroux would like it to be, it must be a great deal more elaborate and more refined than it now is. How can we decide where *pôles de croissance* should be located, how big they must be, what key industries they should include? The Perroux theory by itself does not tell us. Nor, for that matter, does any other. Here is one more field within the general subject of economic development where models need to be specified more fully, and where a great deal more empirical knowledge is necessary before policy recommendations can be made with confidence.

34 || Cuba: The Anatomy of Revolution*

The United States has at its very doorstep one experiment in Communist-style planning for economic development. Cuba is one of the few countries to have carried through a successful revolution and to have introduced a Communist system in recent years. Even if Cuba were not so close a neighbor, and even if the prerevolutionary ties had not been so tight, the Cuban experiment would be well worth watching. Considering that Cuba lies clearly within a geographic area that has long been regarded as the United States "sphere of influence," economic development policy in Cuba is obviously of great interest and importance. Unfortunately, the period of Communist-style development planning in Cuba is so short, and the data for recent years so scant and unreliable, that nothing like a thorough evaluation of Cuba's success or failure is yet possible. We can, however, try to understand the factors which gave rise to the revolution, and obtain some picture of what the Castro regime is trying to do and how it is trying to do it. We will then have some background for evaluating new information about Cuban development as it becomes available.

An Economic Survey of Cuba

Let us imagine that we are members of a United Nations team, sent to Cuba in 1958. Our task is to conduct a general survey of the economic problems and potential of the country and to make recommendations regarding its economic stabilization and development.

* This chapter is a revised version of an essay originally prepared in collaboration with Professor Eastin Nelson.

Resources

Any such survey must begin with an analysis of basic natural and human resources. As underdeveloped countries go, we would find Cuba relatively well off in terms of the resource-population ratio. With an area of 44,217 square miles, it is certainly a small country. On the other hand, with a population of only 6.6 million, it is relatively thinly populated in comparison to other tropical areas similarly blessed as to soil and climate. (During the same period, the Indonesian island of Java, for example, with an area not very much bigger, had a population nearly ten times as great.) Most of the land is cultivable. Only a quarter of the area is mountainous; the rest consists of rolling land and gentle slopes. Cuba has an assured rainfall, 54 inches per year. The rainfall is fairly evenly distributed throughout the country and throughout the year, with about three-quarters of the total occurring during the six months of the wet season. The proximity to the ocean in all parts of the island, together with the trade winds, assures a pleasant semitropical climate with an average temperature below 80 degrees.

Cuba is a long, narrow island surrounded by some of the world's deepest waters, possessed of seven of the most generous natural bay ports and many lesser ports. Cuba is below the frost line, and the cane, therefore, has the optimum sugar content. The topsoil is, for the most part, deep and rich, adapted to mechanical cultivation on a large scale, well watered, and generally laved by cooling but balmy breezes from the sea. The soil has qualities which produce a tobacco that has made Cuban cigars famous the world over.

The latest Cuban census (1953) showed a population of 5,829,029 with an annual rate of increase of 2.1 per cent. The birth rate is apparently like that of Puerto Rico rather than like those of other Caribbean neighbors: not more than 30 per thousand. No figures are available on the work force, but the rate of population increase would suggest a participation rate midway between that of Mexico (32 per cent) and that of the United States (in excess of 41 per cent). Density per kilometer was 61. Anyone who has flown east-west over Cuba gets the impression of large cattle ranges and frequent empty spaces, with a large proportion of population in and near Havana. Obviously the country could support a much larger population with more intensive land use, with more cattle feed and more rapid turnover of the herds, less land committed to grazing, less fallowing, more fertilizers, and crop rotation.

While the resource pattern is not strikingly rich or varied, there is nonetheless plenty with which to work for a country of 6.6 million people. Most of the land is extremely fertile (volcanically renewed). The country has large deposits of iron and nickel and useful reserves of chrome, manganese, copper, limestone, marble, and clay. Cuba has no coal and very little oil; energy resources are its major deficiency. (In 1958, however, that deficiency was not very serious, because of the country's easy access by sea to Venezuela and the United States.) Cuban export products, principally sugar, enable energy resources to be obtained through foreign trade.

Three-quarters of the population are regarded as white, the remainder

Negro or mulatto. The main problem as far as human resources are concerned is the low level of education. There were few professionally trained people, except for lawyers and teachers. For example, in 1953 there were only 3,000 engineers in the whole country. There was little incentive to acquire professional training, since even with the limited numbers then available, unemployment or underemployment was all too common among lawyers, medical doctors, engineers, and architects. Illiteracy was about equal to the Latin American average, about 40 per cent. In 1953, one-quarter of the population age 10 or more had never been to school, while another quarter had attended, but had not completed, primary school. Over half of the population had abandoned their formal education at some point during the first six years of elementary schooling. About 20 per cent of those completing primary school education had gone further. A mere 1 per cent of the population over the age of 10 in that year had completed a professional school training, and less than 2 per cent had completed pre-university training. Of the total population, 0.5 per cent had completed a full five years of university education.

Moreover, there was little evidence that educational levels were rising. Indeed, a comparison of the educational structure in 1953 with that in 1923 suggests that in relation to the total population there was more primary education in 1923 than in 1953.[1] The general shortage of trained people of all kinds is suggested by the figures in Table 34–1. In 1955, only three countries in Latin America claimed lower levels of primary enrollment than Cuba. In relation to the population aged 5 to 14, primary school enrollment in Cuba was only 51 per cent, in comparison to the Latin American average of 64 per cent.[2] The trouble with Cuban education seems to have been badly administered educational programs rather than inadequate budgets. As the World Bank report of 1950 put it, "The Cuban people have not been getting their money's worth for the relatively generous amount they have been willing to spend on education."

Inadequate education and training, however, are an impediment to economic development that is fairly easily overcome. The upgrading of educational standards is a time-consuming but not overly difficult process. On the whole, the resource pattern, human and natural, was favorable to Cuban development. As one observer put it, "In Cuba there were no obstacles of a material nature that could explain the backwardness that is sometimes found in underdeveloped countries."[3]

Level of Economic and Social Development

The relatively favorable resource-population ratio was reflected in the average level of Cuban economic development. In the years immediately following World War I, per capita incomes in Cuba were already about $200 per year at current prices. In terms of the price levels of the mid-1950's, an equivalent figure would be about $400. In the early twenties,

[1] Richard Jolly, "Education," in Dudley Seers (ed.), *Cuba: The Economic and Social Revolution* (Chapel Hill, 1964), p. 168.
[2] *Ibid.*, p. 170.
[3] Max Nolff, "Industry," in Seers, *op. cit.*, p. 292.

TABLE 34–1

Occupations of the Economically Active Population, 1952
(Technical and professional persons 14 years of age and over)

Profession	Total Number
Dentists	1,934
Physicians and surgeons	6,201
Nurses, professional	1,763
Pharmacists	1,866
Teachers: college and university	3,137
secondary and vocational	2,361
primary	36,815
Engineers: civil (including architects)	1,468
mechanical, industrial, mining	309
other	449
Technicians: draftsmen	1,109
laboratory	2,021
mechanical, industrial, electrical	1,784
Chemists	1,257
Lawyers	6,560*
Surveyors	335
Agronomic engineers	294
Veterinarians	355
Other professional persons	15,891†
Total	85,909

* Includes 623 judges and magistrates.
† Includes 258 scientific specialists, 9,914 artists, writers, etc., 2,184 religious and social workers, and 3,535 others.
SOURCE: *National Census 1953*, Table 54, p. 204.
(Reproduced from Dudley Seers (ed.), *Cuba: The Economic and Social Revolution*, [Chapel Hill, 1964], p. 169.)

therefore, Cuban per capita income was at least one-third that of United States, and by present-day concepts of underdevelopment, Cuba might not have been classified as an underdeveloped country. By 1958, per capita income had risen to about $500; but meanwhile United States incomes had risen much more quickly, so that in 1958, Cuban average incomes were only about one-fifth of those of the United States. Thus in 1958, Cuba might have been regarded as on the borderline between underdeveloped and relatively advanced countries. Among Latin American countries only Venezuela, Uruguay, and Argentina had a higher per capita income.

There were, however, extremely unsatisfactory aspects of the Cuban economic and social situation, some of them typical of underdeveloped countries. Unemployment and underemployment were at very high levels. The income distribution was very unequal, so that the average provided a very misleading picture of actual levels of living of the majority of the people. As Professor Dudley Seers puts it,[4]

[4] Seers, *op. cit.*, p. 18.

About a third of the nation existed in squalor, eating rice, beans, bananas, and
root vegetables (with hardly any meat, fish, eggs, or milk), living in huts,
usually without electricity or toilet facilities, suffering from parasitic diseases
and lacking access to health services, denied education (their children receiving
only a first grade education, if that). Particularly distressing was the lot of the
Precaristas, those squatting in makeshift quarters on public lands.

In the aggregate, Cubans were not the worst fed people in Latin America. Published figures on food consumption in that country indicate that
at mid-century they consumed an average of 2,700 calories a day. This is
perhaps 400 below the caloric intake per capita in industrial countries, but
it should be remembered that industrialized countries are in the northern
or far southern temperate zones, where more calories are required than in
the tropics. The composition of the diet was less satisfactory, leaning heavily on starches and fats, with a total intake of foods of animal origin, of
about 20 per cent, about half the proportion characteristic of the United
States and most other northern countries. Meat and milk, consumed at the
rate of 33 and 90 grams daily per capita, ranked Cuba far below the standards of industrial countries, but about on a par with Brazil and Chile, well
below Argentina, Uruguay, Colombia, and Venezuela, perhaps quite near
the Latin American median.[5] The approximate character of such figures
must be admitted, as also the fact that they conceal as much as they reveal
with respect to individual welfare among the rural laborers and sharecroppers.

The problem of unemployment, underemployment, and low-productivity employment was aggravated by a rather high rate of population
growth during the latter fifties, about 2.5 per cent per year. Because of the
age structure, which was relatively young, the labor force was growing
at a somewhat faster rate.

The generally low standards of living are documented by a survey undertaken in the late 1950's of 1,000 peasant families scattered throughout
the country. This survey indicated that the per capita income of peasant
families was below $100 per year. Over two-thirds of family budgets had
to be spent for food. About one-quarter of the diet consisted of rice; beans
and root crops supplied much of the balance. Only 4 per cent of the families interviewed included meat in their standard diet; only 2 per cent had
eggs, and only 1 per cent fish.[6] Over a third of those interviewed had intestinal parasites, 31 per cent had been subject to malaria at one time or
another, 14 per cent to tuberculosis, and 13 per cent to typhus. Such medical attention as these people got had to be financed from their own slender
budgets.

A comparison of Cuban levels of development with other Latin American countries may be derived from Appendix Table 3. A third unsatisfactory aspect of the Cuban economic situation was the relative stagnation of
the Cuban economy. Cuba, while enjoying monetary stability, had one of
the lowest rates of economic growth of all the Latin American countries

[5] *Statistical Yearbook of the United Nations*, 1955, p. 298.
[6] Andrés Bianchi, "Agriculture—Prerevolution," in Seers, *op. cit.*, pp. 96, 97.

in the period following World War II (see Table 22–1). In the years immediately prior to the Castro revolution the rate of growth was slightly higher, about 4.3 per cent, giving a rise in per capita income of about 1.8 per cent.

TABLE 34–2

Long-term Changes in Population and in Apparent Consumption
of Certain Staple Goods

	Annual Average for Period			Percentage Increase	
				1905–09 to 1925–29	1925–29 to 1945–49
	1905–09	1925–29	1945–49		
Population (millions)	2.0	3.6	5.1	78	41
Apparent consumption, final products:					
Rice (thousand tons)	102.0	208.0	254.0	104	22
Wheat flour (thousand tons)	73.0	113.0	157.0	55	38
Potatoes (thousand tons)	..	104.0*	109.0	..	5
Coffee (thousand tons)	..	28.0	36.0	..	29
Beans (thousand tons)	59.0	13.9	18.1	119	40
Beer (million liters)	..	47.0	89.0	..	89
Cotton cloth (thousand tons)	7.3	8.8	9.5	20	8
Passenger transport (million passenger-kilometers)	180.0	524.0	662.0	191	26
Apparent consumption, intermediate products:					
Energy (million equivalent kwh)	1.2	3.5	3.9	192	12
Iron (thousand tons)	48.0	84.0	95.0	75	12
Cement (thousand tons)	61.0	306.0	321.0	401	5
Freight transport (million ton-kilometers	0.3	1.3	1.3	362	0

* Imports only.

SOURCE: Calculated from tables in *El Desarrollo Economico de Cuba* (ECLA E/CN. 12/218, 1951), based on *Anuarios del Comercio* and *Memorias del Banco Central*.

(Reproduced from Dudley Seers (ed.), *Cuba: The Economic and Social Revolution* [Chapel Hill, 1964], p. 14.)

For the period 1905–09 to 1925–29 there is evidence of considerable progress in Cuba (see Table 34–2). During these decades, population increased 78 per cent, while rice consumption increased 104 per cent, bean consumption 119 per cent, and passenger transport 191 per cent. True, some items of consumption, such as cotton cloth and wheat flour, showed less increase than population. On the other hand, expansion of consumption of intermediate products, such as energy (192 per cent), cement (401 per cent), and freight transport (362 per cent), was much greater than expansion of population. Among the items in this category, for which data are readily available, only iron shows a slightly smaller expansion than the population (75 per cent).

When we come to the period 1925–29 to 1945–49, on the other hand, the only item in the list which shows an expansion greater than the population is beer. In this period, population grew 41 per cent, but the consumption of rice only 22 per cent, beans 40 per cent, and passenger transport 26 per cent. The intermediate products which show more clearly the course of industrial expansion fell still further below the rate of population growth. Consumption of both energy and iron increased only 12 per cent, of cement 5 per cent, and of freight transport not at all.

Figures for agricultural production present a similar picture. Thus between 1904–10 and 1921–30, tobacco production increased from 25.1 thousand metric tons to 32.2 thousand metric tons; but in 1946–50, the figure had risen only to 33.6 thousand metric tons. Similarly, between 1931–40 and 1946–50, coffee production increased only from 29.6 to 32.2 thousand tons. Looking at the livestock herds, we see that there were fewer cattle in 1955 than in 1930, and also fewer poultry. The herds of hogs and sheep do show some increase over this period, but their total numbers were relatively small in comparison to either cattle or poultry. The production of rice does show significant expansion, but the production of beans shows a reduction, while output of henequen shows little change. During the 1950's, production of henequen, beans, and potatoes all show a reduction, with rice continuing to expand.

The Structure of Output and Employment

The structure of output and employment in 1958 also suggests that Cuba was on the borderline between the underdeveloped and relatively advanced countries. In one sense Cuba was already "over the hump," in that only 42 per cent of the labor force was still engaged in agriculture. As in most countries, whether developed or developing, productivity was relatively low in the agricultural sector, as indicated by the fact that the proportion of domestic products accounted for by the agricultural sector was only 25 per cent. Manufacturing, in contrast, accounted for 17 per cent of employment but 22 per cent of total output. Mining was relatively insignificant in both output and employment; construction and utilities accounted for 4 per cent of the jobs and 5 per cent of the product, while the services sector (private and government) provided 32 per cent of total employment and 40 per cent of the total value of domestic products.[7]

Looking at the structure of the agricultural labor force alone, we find that in 1952 73 per cent of the agricultural labor force consisted of farm laborers. Of these, 63.6 per cent of the total agricultural labor force were paid workers, 8.1 per cent were unpaid family workers, and 1.1 per cent administrators and foremen. Ranchers and farmers accounted for 27.1 per cent of the total. In terms of total farm income, sugar cane was by far the

[7] Seers, *op. cit.*, p. 21.

most important crop, providing 41.6 per cent of total farm income (1945). Livestock came second with 20.9 per cent, and tobacco third with 10.2 per cent. Cereals and beans accounted for 9.4 per cent of farm income and various products for relatively small proportions of the total.

Productivity in Cuban agriculture seems to have been low, not only in comparison with the small manufacturing sector, but also in comparison with other countries producing the same products. Thus, for example, while Cuba was and is the world's leading producer and exporter of sugar, it ranked near the bottom of the list of major sugar-cane producing countries in terms of output of sugar cane per hectare. It is true that Cuban cane had a relatively high sugar content in comparison to cane from other countries, but even after making allowances for this fact, it is clear that Cuban productivity in cane growing was not high. The cattle industry was also inefficient, taken as a whole, with little or no use of fertilizer for pasture and poor grass management. Yields per acre were also low for coffee and cacao. Rice culture, on the other hand, was relatively efficient. According to Dr. Bianchi "perhaps the principal limitation to raising the technological and organizational level of Cuban agriculture and to diversifying farm production was, however, the weakness of agricultural training research, and extension programs." [8]

Turning to the structure of foreign trade, the major weakness of the Cuban economy is immediately apparent. Sugar—scarcely a growing point in world markets—accounted for more than 80 per cent of the total value of Cuban exports in 1958. Tobacco came second, but the value of tobacco exports was less than 10 per cent that of sugar. On the import side, the weakness of the Cuban economy is indicated by the fact that in a country where over 40 per cent of the labor force was engaged in agriculture, food, drink and tobacco were the single biggest category of imports, accounting for more than one-quarter of the total in the period 1955–57. Machinery came next, and textiles third. Although Cuba manufactured and exported rum, for which it was justly famous, it was nonetheless a net importer of alcoholic beverages. Despite Cuba's fame as a tourist center, tourism produced a net drain on foreign exchange up to 1955, and even after that year the net earnings were small.

Another striking feature of the pattern of Cuban foreign trade–in 1958– was its overwhelming dependence on the United States for both exports and imports. About two-thirds of Cuban exports went to the United States, and about three-quarters of imports came from the United States. No other region—not even Latin America as a whole, the sterling area or western Europe taken as a whole—accounted for much more than one-twelfth of exports or one-ninth of imports.

From a strictly economic point of view, there is no great disadvantage in such dependence on a single market for exports and imports, provided that the market itself enjoys stable growth, without sharp shifts in taste or innovations of a kind that would displace major exports. However, the United States market has not always been so stable, and shifts in taste and

[8] Bianchi, *op. cit.,* p. 93.

technological changes have occurred which have been injurious to the exports of developing countries. It is understandable that such a situation would cause some concern.

Concern over excessive dependence on the United States was aggravated by the predominant position of United States investments in capital movements as well. In the 1950's American investment was variously estimated at from $642 million to $1 billion in this small country. The services sector accounted for over one-third of the total, while petroleum and mining and agriculture each accounted for slightly less than a third; manufacturing was relatively unimportant. There was very little increase in United States investment in Cuba between 1929 and 1958, with the result that in the latter year there was a net outflow from Cuba to the United States on capital account.

The pattern of investment, foreign and domestic, was not such as to bring rapid structural change. On the contrary, Cuba in 1958 seemed unnecessarily retarded as far as industrialization was concerned. The unequal distribution, whatever its disadvantages, provided some opportunities for industrialization that were not seized. For example, the stock of automobiles increased by more than 300 per cent between 1948 and 1958, but this expansion had little impact on employment in Cuba, even for the production of spare parts. The preferential tariff arrangements with the United States meant that American manufacturers had relatively easy access to Cuban markets, and industrialization in Cuba lagged behind that of other Latin American countries, despite relatively high levels of per capita income. During the 1950's the rate of growth in gross manufacturing product in Cuba was less than half the Latin American average and below that of any major Latin American country except Argentina. In the late 1950's, industrial production was expanding less rapidly than national income as a whole—hardly a harbinger of early take-off into sustained industrial growth. Indeed, if one compares the relationship between changes in industrial production and that of income as a whole, we find that in general, the ratio is well above unity; for underdeveloped countries generally it is close to two, while only in Cuba is the ratio less than unity.

Cuban stagnation is not easy to explain, in view of the relatively highly developed infrastructure (high, that is, in comparison to other Latin American countries) and the excess capacity that existed even in the agricultural sector. Transport and power facilities were relatively good. There was no great pressure of population on the land. There was a good deal of arable land that was not cultivated. Much of the land was cultivated with more extensive techniques than might have been necessary.

Regional Dualism

Cuba, like other countries, in the early or middle stages of development, still exhibits the phenomenon of technological dualism: a division of the economy into a modern and a traditional sector, the former consisting of modern, large-scale, capital-intensive, and high-productivity agricultural, mining, and manufacturing activities, together with various services associated with these activities; and the latter consisting of small-scale, labor-intensive, technically retarded, and low-productivity agriculture, a certain amount of small-scale manufacturing and services. As in other countries, too, there is some identification of the major sectors with major regions, the modern sector being concentrated in some parts of the country and the traditional sector in others. In countries which are relatively small in both area and population, the modern sector centers to a large degree in the capital city and other large cities, if any. Cuba is no exception. The modern sector is found in Havana itself, and to a certain extent in the other major cities such as Santiago de Cuba and Camagüey.

Cuba as a whole is far from being a highly urbanized country. In 1953, less than 60 per cent of the population lived in "urban centers," even though for purposes of the census "urban centers" were defined to include villages with fifty people or more. Yet at that time 21 per cent of the entire Cuban population lived in greater Havana. Manufacturing undertakings in particular were concentrated in the capital city. On the other hand, the concentration of the modern sector in one region may be somewhat less marked in Cuba than in many underdeveloped countries, since the sugar plantations and mills were scattered to a certain degree throughout the country, and some of the large and more efficient cattle ranches belonged to the modern sector.

Pattern of Land Holding

No account of the structure of the Cuban economy would be complete without some mention of the high degree of concentration of land ownership. As may be seen from Table 34–3, 0.5 per cent of the number of

TABLE 34–3

Cuban Farms by Size Groups, 1945

Size Groups	Farms		Area	
hectares	number	per cent	thousand hectares	per cent
0.4– 24.9	111,278	69.6	1,021.9	11.2
25.0– 99.9	35,911	22.5	1,608.0	17.7
100.0–499.9	10,433	6.5	2,193.6	24.1
500.0–999.9	1,442	0.9	992.5	10.9
1,000 and over	894	0.5	3,261.1	36.1
Total	159,958	100.0	9,077.1	100.0

* One hectare equals 2,471 acres.
SOURCE: Cuban Agricultural Census, 1946.
(Reproduced from Dudley Seers (ed.), Cuba: The Economic and Social Revolution [Chapel Hill, 1964], p. 75.)

holdings accounted for more than one-third of the total farm acreage, while less than 8 per cent of the number of farms controlled more than 70 per cent of the total acreage. At the other end of the scale were splinter holdings, with some 70 per cent of the number of farms with less than 25 per cent hectares, accounting for only 11.2 per cent of the total area in agricultural use.

The Nature of a Sugar Economy

This pattern of land holding reflects the transcendent importance of sugar in the Cuban economy; for sugar is a land-hungry and labor-hungry undertaking. It is also a type of agriculture that comes close to "mining the soil"; some rotation of sugar with other crops or fallow is necessary. Consequently, sugar companies try to own more land than is necessary in order to keep the refineries operating at capacity in any one year. In 1959, sugar mills controlled slightly less than 21 per cent of the total land area of Cuba, a decline from the nearly 27 per cent controlled by the mills two decades before. Within the sugar industry itself, land holding was highly concentrated. In May, 1959, the twenty-eight largest producers owned 1,400,000 hectares and rented another 617,300 hectares. Adding the two together, these major sugar concerns controlled nearly one-fifth of Cuban land. Yet only about half of the land actually controlled by the sugar mills was kept under sugar cane at any one time. The other half was held as a reserve, or put to lower-yield uses such as pasture for cattle grazing.

Another characteristic of sugar production is its high degree of seasonality. Planting, harvesting, and grinding together provide employment for only a few months in the year; but during these seasons, the requirement for labor is heavy indeed. During the "'dead season," employment in the sugar enterprises drops to a skeleton staff for maintenance only, together with a small amount of replanting. Not only the sugar enterprises themselves are affected. Secondary reductions in employment in transportation, shipping, etc., also occur, since these service sectors are so heavily dependent on the movement of sugar. It is estimated that at least one-fifth of the total labor force was completely unemployed between August and October, while more than half the gainfully occupied agricultural population was employed for no more than four months in the year. An indication of the disastrous effect of the dead season on living levels is that for most of the year the rural population had to give up meat, rice, beans, and coffee for plantains, roots, and cane juice. In the off-season, some of the workers drifted into cities in search of work they could not find, becoming street beggars.

The intermittent character of employment in a region so dominated by the cane harvest and grind is a source of great hardship to the rural masses. Byron White calculates that 500,000 men spend four months cutting and grinding the cane, but are largely unemployed during the remainder of the year.[9] White was still convinced as late as June, 1961, that the distortion of the Cuban countryside economy by excessive sugar and excessive idle lands held in reserve created a rather hopeless milieu for development

[9] Byron White, *Azucar Amargo* (Havana, 1955), p. 6.

planning or reform as long as the situation obtained.[10]

Another characteristic of the sugar industry is that it does not utilize the entire population or the entire land area of a region at one time, and is therefore consistent with the preservation of traditional patterns of peasant agriculture in the same region. In short, it is not calculated to bring about technological change of a kind that would have repercussions throughout the rest of the economy.

If the sugar industry provided a strong "growing point" or "leading sector" in the national economy and were a solid foundation for over-all economic and social development, it might be worth while seeking means of eliminating the undesirable impact of this industry while encouraging its growth. Unfortunately, sugar has ceased to be such a growing point in all countries where it is a major export. It suffers, perhaps as much as any commodity, from "Engel's Law"—the income elasticity of demand for sugar is very low. Consumption of sugar does not rise as incomes go up in the advanced countries which constitute the major market for sugar exports. Indeed, between the 1920's and the 1950's, when the real national income of the United States more than doubled, per capita consumption of sugar did not rise at all. During the first three decades of the century, it is true, per capita consumption did rise, suggesting that income elasticity of demand for sugar may be fairly high for lower ranges of income. If that is so, improved markets for sugar might possibly emerge as the now developing countries achieve higher levels of per capita income. On the other hand, sugar is a commodity which many countries can produce, either from cane or from beets. Not only has per capita consumption in the United States failed to rise in recent decades, but the dependence on Cuban imports has declined. Between 1906–13 and 1919–29, the share of United States consumption met by imports from Cuba rose from 44 per cent to 53 per cent; but by 1950–53, the proportion had fallen to 37 per cent.

Because of the dominant position of sugar in the Cuban economy and the high "multiplier effects" on income and employment, stagnation of the Cuban sugar industry has virtually meant stagnation of the Cuban economy as a whole.

Cuba is the world's leading sugar producer, and sugar accounts for 40 per cent of the country's total industrial production. It provides employment for one-quarter of the labor force, or for half of the active agricultural population. Sugar output provided 20 per cent of Cuba's gross national product. Its impact on the economy, however, was even greater than these figures suggest, impressive though they are. When the secondary income and employment through financing, storing, transporting, insuring, and otherwise handling sugar are brought into consideration, and the effects on the government budget, banking operations, and the multiplier effects of the respending of the income created in the sugar sector, it is clear that the Cuban economy was uncomfortably close to a monoculture.

Technological progress in the industry was so slow as to be almost non-existent. Once stagnation set in, the motive for technological improvement

[10] Byron White, "El Triunvirato de Cuba Planificada," *Revista de Ciencias Sociales* (University of Puerto Rico), June, 1961, pp. 203–13.

was diluted. With growing unemployment, trade union opposition to labor-saving devices increased. Dr. Bianchi suggests that unemployment was needlessly aggravated by misguided welfare legislation, requiring the sugar factories to pay the same minimum wage in the dead season as during the sugar harvest. Thus the incentive to develop subsidiary crops during the off-season was essentially destroyed.[11] Diversification and more intensive use of available land were essential to Cuban development, Bianchi argues: "But because of the vast area and financial resources controlled by the cattle and sugar industries, diversification on a significant scale was not possible without their cooperation. Artificially high labor costs, great concentration of land ownership, and the pull of routine and tradition made such cooperation unlikely or negligible." [12]

Finally, as we have already seen the United States dominated both the production and the marketing of sugar. In the midst of the Great Depression of the 1930's, the United States introduced a quota system for sugar, under which Cuba and other exporters to the United States received a price slightly above the world market. In 1929 Cuba had provided 52 per cent of the sugar consumed in the United States, but under the quota this share was cut back to 30 per cent. In 1939 and between 1943 and 1947, the quota system was not in operation. While the Philippines were cut off from the American market, the Cuban share in this market returned to its former peak level. When the quota system was reintroduced in 1948, however, the Philippines were once again accorded a share, and the Cuban allocation was reduced to 33 per cent. Thus, as noted above, Cuban exports of sugar to the United States were little different in the 1950's from what they had been in the 1920's. To some extent, the failure of the Cuban exports to the United States to expand was offset by the development of new markets in the 1950's, particularly in Canada, western Europe, Japan, and the Soviet Union.

Professor Lowry Nelson summarized the physical facts of sugar concentration as of 1945: [13]

Almost a third of Cuban land is owned or controlled by sugar interests, and these interests are highly concentrated in a few hands. In 1945 70 per cent of the *colonos* produced only about 10 per cent of the cane which was milled on the island.

Though most of the cane was produced by sharecroppers directly dependent on the sugar mills, there were other types of tenure. According to Lowry Nelson, 38 per cent of the *colonos* (farms) had quotas which would indicate about seven acres each in cane before World War II.[14] Professor Nelson also emphasizes that there is a great deal of land in Cuba that is either not used at all or not used intensively. Professor White cites from the *Annual Report of the Year 1957* of the United Fruit Company

[11] Bianchi, *op. cit.*, p. 88.
[12] *Ibid.*, p. 90.
[13] Lowry Nelson, *Rural Cuba* (Minneapolis, 1951).
[14] *Ibid.*, p. 115.

the statement that of the 147,770 acres owned by that company in Cuba, 50,000 acres were held in reserve, that is fallow.[15] This situation is perhaps typical of corporate landholdings or other large ownership tracts in under-developed countries, and it is obviously good business from the standpoint of the firm in the market when land is cheaper than fertilizers; of course, the very thing that makes land cheap is that the people are too poor to buy it. This policy of fallowing large tracts is not necessarily a good policy from the aggregate point of view, and it clearly limits the possibility of even commercial development of small agriculture, and even more severely puts brakes on land reform policy. It becomes one of the sore points in a country with as much rural poverty as Cuba.

But United States investments played a dominant role in sugar produc-tion as well. In 1934, when a group of American experts appointed by the Foreign Policy Association at the invitation of the Cuban President visited Cuba as "The Commission on Cuban Affairs," United States investments in Cuba were exceeded in only two countries, Canada and Germany. Of the $1.1 billion total, $600 million were in the sugar industry, and $235 million in utilities and railways. This commission concluded that "excessive foreign investment, particularly in sugar . . . stimulated an economic growth injurious to Cuban and foreigner alike."

The prospects for the sugar industry in Cuba have been well summarized by Dr. Nolff. When considering prospects for industrialization for Cuba, he says, "It becomes clear that the prospect of an increase in the production of sugar is slight, or nonexistent. In the long run, the role of this sector would hardly be very dynamic, especially with reference to employment."

An Excursion into History

At this stage in any survey mission, it is always useful to ask, "How and why did the country get into the situation in which it finds itself at present?" It will be remembered that in the context of our present hypo-thetical mission "at present" means 1958.

First of all, it is clear enough from the levels of per capita income reached in the mid-1920's that the structure of the Cuban economy was not always so inappropriate to substantial economic growth. Indeed, sugar served well enough as a growing point or leading sector for some decades. Until the end of the eighteenth century Cuban incomes depended more on tobacco than on sugar. At that time, however, the world market for Cuban sugar began to expand. With the increased mechanization of grind-ing and refining associated with the use of steam power, the number of mills increased rapidly, and sugar gradually took over as the major Cuban product. The expansion of the sugar industry was interrupted by the Ten Years' War, but resumed toward the end of the nineteenth century. Cuba's revolution against Spain came at the end of the nineteenth century, and was followed by very rapid growth of the sugar industry through sales in the United States market. It would appear that the early decades of this

[15] Byron White, "Cuba and Puerto Rico, A Case Study in Economic Development," (unpublished dissertation, The University of Texas, 1959), p. 101.

century were those of the most rapid economic development of Cuba, bringing significant rises in per capita incomes. In some respects, Cuba did better out of sugar during these years, when sugar exports could serve as a growing point, than other important sugar exporters such as Indonesia and the Philippines. Cuba's sugar boom came with considerably less population pressure than in Java and somewhat less than in the Philippines. Moreover, the population explosion in Cuba never attained the same crescendo that it did in Java.

The economic nexus between Cuba and the United States began to be serious after the War Between the States, when the Louisiana mills were destroyed, and sugar producers began to be aware that cane grown below the frost line could not only produce from five to eight years from one planting of rhizomes, but would yield a considerably higher proportion of sugar from the same tonnage of cane than sugar grown farther north. The difference in yield is perhaps as much as 50 per cent under the same refining conditions, over the best productive life of a single planting, though this varies with water and soil conditions.

Growing competition from beet sugar after 1850 led to mechanization and larger-scale operations. The Cuban industry became more capital-intensive, and American investors had the capital. Byron White, quoting from the *Anuario Azucarero de Cuba, 1953*, notes that of the 161 sugar mills in Cuba as of that year, 53 were built between 1865 and 1901; on the average, 51 mills of considerably larger capacity and more modern processes were built during the "dance of the millions" between 1902 and 1920.[16] The demonstration effect of the nexus was made apparent when after many years of low tariff and four years of no tariff, a duty of 40 per cent ad valorem was put on all foreign sugar entering the United States from September, 1894, onward until the Martí revolution was successfully launched from his political asylum in the United States.[17]

Several things went on simultaneously during the eight decades that ended about 1945: American capacity to consume sugar became progressively greater as industrialization went on; Cuba's powerful allies on the mainland of the United States assured her independence from Spain after 1898, and gradually relaxed their political suzerainty over the island; American investors tightened their hold on the investments and trade of the island republic until they participated to the extent of about 70 per cent of the imports from and exports to Cuba; and the intermeshing of the foreign investors with the Cuban elite became far advanced when, by 1945, about half the shares in the big Cuban sugar properties came to rest in the elite residential districts of Havana, while a similar proportion remained on the mainland. Meanwhile, American direct investment in the economy went on apace, and by 1953 it was estimated by Cuban sources that it totaled some $642 million.[18]

The expansion of the sugar industry in Cuba was accordingly able to outrun population growth and absorb an increasing and ultimately signifi-

[16] *Ibid.*, p. 3.
[17] *Ibid.*, p. 4.
[18] Seers, *op. cit.*, p. 13.

cant proportion of the labor force into this leading sector, and so into the modern sector of the economy. Whereas the sugar industry at one time absorbed close to a quarter of the Cuban labor force, in Indonesia at the time of the transfer of sovereignty only 7 per cent of the labor force had been absorbed into the whole modern sector, in all of its aspects. Indeed, judged by the levels of per capita income obtained, Cuba did better out of sugar than the Philippines, although population pressure in the latter country never reached the proportions that it did in Java.

On the other hand, once sugar ceased to be a solid growing point for development of less-developed countries, both Indonesia and the Philippines shifted to other products, while Cuba did not. Levels of living in Cuba seem to have stopped rising about the middle of the 1920's. Dudley Seers suggests that between 1923 and 1958 Cuba was the most stagnant country in Latin America: [19]

The stagnation was more serious and lasted longer than in any other Latin American economy—excepting perhaps the economies of one or two very small and poor nations such as Bolivia and Haiti. Although Argentina and Chile have shown rather slow growth rates since the 1920's per capita incomes have certainly significantly increased since then; while exports of these countries too have failed (in terms of purchasing power) to exceed the level of the 1920's there has been considerable expansion in other sectors.

Dr. Seers finds at least a part of the explanation of the peculiar stagnation of the Cuban economy in the trading relations of Cuba with the United States. At a time when other countries were beginning to industrialize behind a protective tariff wall, Cuba, under the United States Reciprocal Trade Agreement of 1934, was lowering import duties, limiting quantitative restrictions on imports, reducing taxes on products originating in the United States, and eschewing exchange control. A small country like Cuba would naturally have difficulty in launching new industries when its market was open to a colossus like the United States, so short a distance away by water transport.

During this same period of Cuban stagnation the optimal size of sugar enterprises was increasing. In the 1850's, Cuba had a total of 1,500 sugar factories with an annual capacity of one million metric tons. By the time of the Castro revolution the number of factories had shrunk to 161, while capacity had expanded to more than seven million tons. Expansion and concentration proceeded together between the beginning of the century and World War I.

As already indicated, whereas other sugar exporting countries shifted to other products following the crash in sugar prices during the downswing of the thirties, Cuba turned to a more open economy than ever, reducing restrictions on American imports as a quid pro quo for a sugar quota from the United States. For example, by the time World War II began, rubber, petroleum, and tin and tin ore had become more important Indonesian exports than sugar. Similarly, in the Philippines, coconut products and

[19] *Ibid.*, p. 6.

abaca had become more important than sugar by 1948. Of the major sugar exporters, Cuba alone was gripped in the vise of bitter sugar.

During the boom period in the first three decades of this century, a labor shortage appeared in sugar which led to a policy encouraging immigration. This immigration contributed to the unemployment and underemployment in the Cuban economy following the crash of the 1930's.

Comparison with Other Countries

The Cuba of 1958 invites comparison with other countries. Like Argentina, Cuba is a country that seemed on the road to affluence when it bogged down in economic stagnation, at a level of per capita income which left it on the edge of underdevelopment. The per capita income was, and is, somewhat lower than that of Argentina. But for the middle and upper classes, the result has been much the same. A country that enjoys a period of rapid economic growth, with the accompanying opportunities, at least for educated people, and then stagnates, is a country of bitterness and frustration. Political and social instability are likely to be greater in such a country than in one where no economic development has taken place.

On the other hand, the concentration of wealth and income in Cuba reminds one of Venezuela rather than Argentina. Just as the per capita income of Venezuela, estimated at $800 per year, does not convey the picture of a country where half the people are undernourished and levels of health and education are extremely low, so the per capita income figure of $400 for Cuba does not properly indicate the extent of poverty, ignorance, and ill health that prevailed in the Cuba of 1958. If one thinks of Cuba as four-fifths of an Argentina and one-half of a Venezuela, the revolution which came in 1959 should occasion no surprise.

Pre-Castro Plans and Policies

There was of course some recognition prior to Castro of the necessity for structural change, industrial development, and technological advance in Cuba. However, nothing very effective seems to have been done to achieve these objectives. There was an impressive array of agencies and institutions to promote economic growth: a Commission for National Development, a Bank for Economic and Social Development, a Bank of Agricultural and Industrial Development, a National Financing Board, an Institute for the Stabilization of Sugar, and others. Indeed, for a country of 6.5 million people, it would appear that the bureaucracy established to promote economic growth was excessive. Responsibility for achieving a resumption of increases in per capita income (if indeed these institutions were genuinely designed for that purpose) was so diffuse that no one could be held clearly responsible for the failure.

A Development Program for Cuba

Confronted with this array of problems—stagnation, inequitable distribution of wealth and income, extreme dependence on the American economy, and generally low levels of economic and social development for the majority of the people—what might have been the broad outlines of a development program to be recommended to the Cuban government in 1958?

Perhaps the first question we should settle is whether or not Cuba might have continued to expand, with a relatively unchanged structure of employment and output, as a branch of the United States economy. Rather than protecting the Cuban economy from United States exports and industrializing behind a protective tariff wall, might we not have recommended still closer integration with the United States economy, so that Cuba could have become a prosperous agricultural region, essentially within the United States economy? Surely, just because this rather small island happened to be a separate "country" from a political and geographical viewpoint, is no reason for it to strive for a high degree of self-sufficiency.

This solution, however, would have had to be rejected. We have already seen that the major product which Cuba had to sell in the United States— sugar—was one for which the income elasticity of demand, at levels of income already attained in the United States, was very low. In short, if the sugar economy had become so closely integrated with the American economy as to be essentially a part of it, it could have expected a rate of growth no higher than the rate of growth of the American population. Since this rate of growth was below that of the Cuban population, becoming a region of the United States economy while remaining a monoculture was a recipe for economic decline. It would have meant in itself a diminishing per capita income in Cuba. In any case, experience with regional development shows that even relatively small regions within a country need to industrialize if they are to achieve reasonably high levels of living for the bulk of their population. It would be difficult to find anywhere a region as big as Cuba, with a population of nearly seven million people, which had achieved levels of per capita income ranging *upward* from $400 per year (as distinct from an *average* of $400 per year) and which had more than one-third of its labor force engaged in agriculture. The story of regional development within the United States has been one of gradual convergence of occupational structures and product mixes among major regions; the long-run reduction of gaps in productivity and income among major regions has been in large measure the result of the elimination of major differences in structure among regional economies. Thus even if policy had been directed toward making Cuba essentially a region within the United States economy, diversification of agriculture and industrialization would have been primary goals of any economic development program.

The production of sugar cane, the grinding and refining of sugar, the manufacturing of sugar byproducts such as rum, would not of course need to be abandoned. However, sugar and its products could no longer be counted upon to provide the "engine of economic growth." The cattle industry might have been somewhat more promising; but here too it would not have been wise to count on grazing to provide the impetus for development of the economy as a whole. No doubt further processing of animal products would have been a part of any development program as of 1958.

It would have been necessary to diversify exports, both in terms of the commodity to be exported, and in terms of the markets to be sought. In addition, as a part of the general program of industrialization, the development of import-replacing industries would have a fundamental role. Selection of specific industries to be developed as import-replacers, perhaps behind a protective tariff wall, would of course need detailed market and engineering analysis. The manufacture of automobile parts, for replacement and repairs, and possibly the assembly of automobiles, would be one possibility. A market of nearly seven million people concentrated in as small an area as Cuba affords possibilities for the manufacture of many types of consumer durable goods.

In order to promote the necessary diversification, a system of "accounting prices" might have been introduced. We have already noted that the system of minimum wage rates aggravated the tendency toward large-scale seasonal unemployment. If any society wishes to maintain a minimum wage for all workers at all times, while marginal productivity of labor is for some people at some times higher than zero but below the minimum wage, the only sensible policy is to arrange for such workers to be employed by a system of subsidies to employers (public or private), equal to the difference between their marginal productivity and the minimum wage. The actual cost to society of such a system (which has been utilized with great success in Poland) is any increased nutritional requirements involved in having people at work instead of leaving them idle. The contribution of seasonally unemployed workers to total output could be made much higher than any such costs. There are various ways in which such subsidies could be provided. Tax concessions, pre-prepared industrial sites, long-term loans with easy repayments and low interest rates, etc., could be a beginning. However, there is no reason why any government that wished to do so should not provide a negative payroll tax—that is, an outright wage subsidy. Certainly the elimination of seasonal unemployment by provision of alternative work opportunities in the dead season would have to be a major part of any development program for Cuba.

Finally, an ambitious program of education and training, together with a public health program to eliminate diseases, would be obvious parts of any development program. As we have seen, a maxim of development planners is "when in doubt, educate"; a general upgrading of educational levels in Cuba was clearly a form of investment that would yield high returns. Moreover, Cuba seems to have been a country that was peculiarly subject to diseases of a kind that debilitate but do not kill.

The 1950 World Bank Mission to Cuba stated as major objectives of Cuban development the following: [20]

1. To make Cuba less dependent on sugar by promoting additional activities—not by curtailing sugar production.

2. To expand existing—and create new—industries producing sugar by-products or using sugar as a raw material. This objective deserves a first

[20] International Bank for Reconstruction and Development, *Report on Cuba* (Baltimore, 1951).

priority, because progress in these directions will make the sugar sector itself more stable.

3. Vigorously to promote non-sugar exports in order to reduce the emphasis of the country's exports on one product. This will help both to raise total income and employment and also to stabilize it. Among the most promising possibilities for achieving this aim are the promotion of mineral exports and the export of a variety of crude and processed food stuffs.

4. To make further progress in producing in Cuba for domestic consumption, a wide range of food stuffs, raw materials, and consumer durable goods.

Five years later, the United States Department of Commerce made essentially the same recommendations, and noted that little had been done to implement the Bank recommendations in the meantime.[21] The new Cuban government, however, is moving along the broad lines of the World Bank recommendations.

Accomplishments of the Castro Regime

It is not our purpose here to appraise the Castro regime. We have been concerned with setting forth the fundamental problems of the Cuban economy on the eve of revolution, problems that would have had to be faced, sooner or later, by any Cuban regime. However, it is worth noting that the broad framework of development policy under the Castro regime has been essentially that which any advisory mission with competence and objectivity would have been compelled to recommend to any Cuban government in 1958. As Dr. Dudley Seers puts it: [22]

The significance of Cuban experience, and its great professional interest, lies in the fact that it represents an attempt to achieve broadly the same objectives as those set out in the Charter of Punta del Este (fast growth and a more equal society) but by different means. Social change has taken place at an early state of industrialization; an ambitious educational program attempts not merely to educate the labor force of the future but to change the existing one; much of the economy has been taken over by the state, and communal incentives are stressed rather than private self-interest; industrial and agricultural development is attempted with a detailed central plan covering every sector; food is rationed and price inflation is suppressed by controls on wages and prices; the distribution of income has become much less unequal.

The Plans

Cuban planning techniques have been modeled after those of the Soviet Bloc, and thus have the virtues and shortcomings of "balance planning." The planning operation is essentially one of projecting increases in outputs of strategic commodities, and making sure that the product mix is appropriate to the target expansion of these products. The necessary inputs of capital and labor and raw materials in order to achieve the target product mix are then calculated.

[21] United States Department of Commerce, *Investment in Cuba* (Washington, 1956).
[22] Seers, *op. cit.*, p. 115.

In the beginning, the Castro regime seems to have followed an approach to planning very similar to that which had been developed by the UN Economic Commission for Latin America, using Cuban and other Latin American economists trained by ECLA. Reporting on a trip made in the spring of 1960, Leo Huberman and Paul M. Sweezy remarked: [23]

There are literally dozens of foreign individuals, mostly from Latin American countries, working in and for the government. We have met and talked at great lengths with a group of Chilian and Ecuadorian economists, all of whom had been trained and employed by ECLA at some time in the past. We can testify both to their ability as economists and to their devotion to the ideals and aims of the Cuban revolution, which they hope to help apply to their own countries in the not distant future. (Incidentally, we met neither missions nor individual experts from Soviet Bloc countries. They will doubtless come later, their numbers depending mainly on the availability of suitably trained personnel from the United States, Western Europe, and Latin America. For a variety of reasons of historical association and cultural affinity, Cuba will naturally turn to the latter areas first.)

Immediately after the revolution, UN and ECLA carried out an Expert Mission, composed of experts of a number of nationalities, under the leadership of a Mexican economist. Later, however, the government showed increasing preference for economists of established socialist sympathies. One of these was the distinguished Polish economist Michael Kalecki, one of the principal planners in his own country, who prepared a report on the first Five-Year Plan. Another was Charles Bettelheim, a well-known French Marxist.

As the planning operation in Cuba proceeded, it moved closer and closer to the Soviet Bloc model. According to Dr. Nolff, Czechoslovakia in particular served as a model for Cuban planning. The Industrial Plan, for example, includes six subdivisions. First, the Production Plan, which determines the product mix for the "consolidated enterprises" under the direct ownership and control of the Ministry of Industry; second, the Plan of Supply, which is designed to assure the flow of raw materials and equipment necessary to reach the targets in the Production Plan; the Plan for Labor and Wages, which determines the manpower requirements, fixes wages, and establishes targets for annual increases in productivity; the Expense Plan, setting forth the money outlays implicit in the Production Plan; the Finance Plan, which sets forth the monetary and fiscal measures necessary to execute the Production Plan; and finally, the Investment Plan, which determines the investment requirements, both in the expansion and modernization of existing industrial plants and in new plant and equipment. As in other Socialist countries, profits of national enterprises are a principal source of capital funds for new investment. Cuba has also received useful loans from other Socialist countries. Embarking on more ambitious industrial programs quickly revealed the shortages of skills at all levels, and led to a "big push" in the field of education and training as well.

[23] Leo Huberman and Paul M. Sweezy, *Cuba: Anatomy of a Revolution* (New York, 1960), pp. 90, 91.

The scarcity of skills at all levels has received special attention. Both the general educational system and technical training have been expanded.

Planning operations finally crystallized in the establishment of the JUCEPLAN in February, 1961. This new planning organization was charged with the responsibility for preparing a four-year plan for 1962–65, together with an annual plan for 1962. The initial targets set forth by the director of JUCEPLAN and by the Minister of Economics, Regino Boti, were ambitious. Total production was to grow by not less than 10 per cent per year, while the possibility of growth of total output in the neighborhood of 15 per cent was foreseen. Subsequently, however, these ambitious targets were replaced with more modest ones.

A published plan for 1962–65 was not available to the author, but it appears that the plan fell into two stages. In the first phase, up to 1965, the plan was essentially a "holding operation." Sugar mills and textile factories were to be repaired, with some additional capacity in such established fields as textile manufactures, foods, mining, and metal products. Hydroelectric capacity was also to be raised. Radical departures in industrial investment, however, were scheduled only for the period after 1965. Among these was the construction of a steel mill. The over-all industrial program comprised several sectors: production, especially the output of the consolidated enterprises which have been taken over by the Ministry of Industry; Supply, assuring the required flow of raw materials and equipment; Labor and Wages, determining manpower requirements for the Production Plan, fixing wages, and presumably assuring the necessary training facilities; Expenses, the cost-accounting for the Production Plan; Finance, providing the financial resources to meet these costs; and finally the Investment Plan, setting forth the capital requirements for replacement and expansion of industrial capacity.

The stated goals of Cuban development include the following objectives:

1. Expropriation of 6.2 million acres, used to grow sugar cane, graze cattle, or held idle, owned and leased by 161 sugar mills.

2. Expropriation of 65 per cent of the privately held rural land for redistribution to landless peasants. As a general rule, the maximum size of holdings is to be 990 acres. In any case no one person is supposed to hold, directly or indirectly, more than 3,320 acres. Exceptions may occasionally be made for cattle, cane, rice, and henequen. The farms distributed to landless peasants are typically 200 acres or less.

3. A prohibition of acquisition of rural land by foreigners, and also against the inheritance of land by foreigners.

4. A scientific and complementary agricultural system.

5. Elimination of unemployment.

6. The opening of new markets for Cuban exports of raw and semi-processed products, especially in eastern Europe and Asia. New sources of industrial imports are also to be sought.

7. Redistribution of income.

8. Price controls on basic commodities and other anti-flationary controls.

9. Compulsory saving for the financing of economic development.

10. Industrialization rapid enough to make Cuba's level of development comparable to that of western European economies by 1970.

Agrarian reform played a large role in the Cuban government's plans. On the whole, however, agrarian reform has proceeded in less doctrinaire fashion than in many countries, and with somewhat more attention to the necessity of raising agricultural productivity as well as eliminating the grosser inequities in land holding, and particularly the existence side by side of landless peasants and large tracts of idle land. The maximum holdings permitted are relatively generous for an avowedly Socialist country. Holdings of a thousand acres or less must be operated by the owner if his title is to be preserved. A distinction is made between expropriation with indemnification, and confiscation of properties of "counter-revolutionaries," for which no payment is to be made. For unirrigated land, 66 acres per family is considered to be the "vital minimum"—striking evidence of the absence of serious population pressure in Cuba. In Java, a holding of 10 acres for a family is regarded as great wealth. Compensation for expropriated lands is to take the form of 20-year bonds bearing 4.5 per cent interest.

A special agency, INRA, has been established to administer the land reform law. Its responsibilities, however, extend far beyond agrarian reform in the narrow sense, and include rural health, housing, education, establishment of equipment centers, statistical research, agriculture research, extension of credit, and the like. While leaving substantial scope for private ownership of land, the government has also indicated its leanings toward cooperative or collective ownership and management of agricultural enterprises. INRA has become the largest property-owner in Cuba, employing directly or indirectly more than a million workers, or about 60 per cent of the total labor force.

While stressing the need for agrarian reform, the Cuban regime has none of the starry-eyed, sentimental admiration for the peasant that has characterized some other developing countries, such as India and Indonesia. On the contrary, the Soviet Bloc model which Cuba is following has led to a relative neglect of agriculture in favor of industrialization. As may be seen from Table 34–4, about one-seventh of the 1962 development budget went into agriculture, not much more than half of the allocation for industry, only about a third more than for transport, and less than half of the allocation for basic services.

Cuba seems to be repeating the mistake of other countries that have adopted the Communist-style planning of underestimating the importance of raising agricultural output as a basis for industrialization. Minimum wages are maintained even in face of relatively bad crops. At the same time income is being redistributed to groups whose former income was so low that there is a substantial increase in demand for food as a result. As a consequence there have been food "shortages." These shortages do not seem to come primarily from failure on the production front. Indeed, the first "people's crop" in sugar was the second largest in Cuban history, nearly seven million tons.

TABLE 34–4
Government Budget for Economic Development
in 1962
(in millions of dollars)

Agriculture	112
Industry	208
Commerce	15
Communication	48
Transport	88
Basic services	233
Total	703

SOURCE: *Trimestre de Finanzas al Día*, No. 1, April, 1962.

(Reproduced from Dudley Seers (ed.), *Cuba: The Economic and Social Revolution* [Chapel Hill, 1964], p. 42.)

Dudley Seers states without hesitation that under the new regime "there has been a general improvement in the economic lot of the country workers and many peasants." [24] The existence of rationing, he maintains, does not mean that food consumption has fallen below pre-revolution levels. The rationing applies mainly to the 20 per cent of the total population living in Havana. There is some evidence that food producers are consuming more of their own product in the countryside, so that deliveries to the city are a smaller proportion of the total output.

Seers is "fairly confident" that there is less serious undernourishment than before the revolution, especially among children.[25] Bianchi states that "there is little doubt, then, that in the first half of 1961, crop output (including sugar cane) was substantially higher than before the Revolution. Indeed even with fairly pessimistic assumptions about the production of crops for which information is not available, total crop output at the end of the first period of agrarian reform must have been about 12 per cent higher than the average of the years 1957–58." [26] He presents figures which show increases in output between 1957–58 and 1961 for all major products but rice and coffee, for which there was relatively little change. On the other hand, he concludes that total agricultural output was below pre-revolutionary levels in both 1962 and 1963.[27]

INRA had an industrialization department under the direction of Che Guevara, then Castro's chief lieutenant. Guevara, well versed in Communist planning doctrine, was highly sensitive to the need of structural change and rapid industrialization, perhaps to the point of ignoring the need to increase agricultural productivity at the same time.

A part of the INRA program has been reduction of seasonal unemployment by shifting sugar workers to other tasks during the "dead season."

[24] Seers, *op. cit.*, p. 28.
[25] *Ibid.*, p. 36.
[26] *Ibid.*, p. 115.
[27] *Ibid.*, p. 156.

As a consequence, although unskilled workers receive a lower daily rate of pay than they did in the previous regime, their annual income is significantly higher. They also receive social insurance benefits, particularly old age pension. An effort has been made to use the Central Bank rediscount system for "qualitative credit control," to reduce loans for such items as purchase of automobiles and other consumer durables, jewelry, art objects, foreign securities. A campaign has been conducted to collect back taxes, which succeeded in bringing in some $80 million during the fiscal year 1959–60. The progressivity of the personal income tax has been increased, and an additional tax is imposed on income from securities. Excise taxes on liquor and luxury imports have been raised.

Energy remains the major bottleneck in Cuba's industrialization program, and there is no sign that this problem will be solved in the immediate future. For the time being, Cuba is depending on imports of petroleum from the USSR. Prior to the revolution Venezuela was the chief source of petroleum for Cuba. Domestic production meets only 10 per cent of the daily consumption. For the time being, the USSR is providing large quantities of petroleum, but the Russian tanker fleet is not large, and it is a question whether the USSR will wish to continue tying up so large a proportion of this fleet on the long run from the Black Sea to Cuba. The foreign petroleum companies engaged in refining in Cuba have refused to process Russian crude oil, and have consequently been nationalized by the Cuban government. Since the foreign companies followed the practice of using very small numbers of foreign employees, no great lack of expertise in petroleum has appeared.

The Castro government has of course nationalized other properties as well. During the fiscal year 1959–60 over half a billion dollars worth of private direct investment from the United States was taken over. During the next fiscal year some $200 million more were expropriated. All the American sugar mills have been expropriated or "intervened" and are now operated by the Cuban government. As has been so clearly shown by Professor Martin Bronfenbrenaer, there are circumstances in which nationalization may be a good policy from a narrowly economic point of view, whatever its legal and moral aspects.[28] If the reduction in profits transfers abroad is greater than any potential influx of new capital, and assuming that exports can be redirected so as to maintain total earnings, expropriation of foreign enterprises can be a means of adding to the net flow of foreign exchange.

Whatever its drawbacks, and whatever its unpleasant features, the Cuban commitment to the Communist pattern and to the Soviet Bloc provided a framework for economic development which some uncommitted countries lack. It is now clear that vigorous economic growth can take place within a wide range of political systems, given a government committed to economic development, and willing to face the political and social implications of technological advance and structural change. Where the government is strong enough to command the support of the people—whether in demo-

[28] Martin Bronfenbrenner, "The Appeal of Confiscation in Economic Development," *Economic Development and Cultural Change*, April, 1955, pp. 201–18.

cratic fashion through a party with a clear majority, as in India, or through a highly centralized government willing to use force where necessary, and responsive to the will of "the masses" as interpreted by the leader rather than to the wishes of individuals—economic development can be just that much faster.

The Cuban decision to adopt the Soviet Bloc ideology and the Soviet Bloc pattern of economic development planning has at least provided a basis for decision making, as well as a substantial inflow of technical and capital assistance. Provided these continue on a sufficient scale, there seems no reason to expect the Cuban experiment to collapse of its own weight.

There is scant statistical evidence to be had in international sources that tell us to what degree bitter sugar and fallowing land are yielding to diversification and industrialization. Such figures as are published in the United Nations Statistical Yearbook are presented in Tables 34–5 and 34–6.

TABLE 34–5

Thousands of Metric Tons of Agricultural Products

	1948–1952	1955/6	1961	1964
Rice	106	279	207	123
Cocoa (beans)	2.9	slight variations	2.5	2.0
Coffee	31.2	steady rise	37	36.0
Sugar	6,053	4,588	6,761	4,590
Tobacco	34.4	seasonal, rising	47.2	58.9
Fish catch	8.3	15.6	30.5	36.3
Cattle herd	4,079*	peak 1958—5,840*	5,025*	61/62—5,772

SOURCE: *United Nations Statistical Yearbook*, 1962, 1965.
* Expressed in thousands of head.

TABLE 34–6

Some Industrial Components*

Motor spirit	(1948) 67	(1956)139		710	(1963) 728
Distillate	(1948) 61	(1957)462	(1960) 710		(1963) 484
Residual fuel oil	(1948) 22	(1956) 86	(1960)1,654		(1963)2,222
Consumption:					
Cotton	(1954–55) 6.1	(1957/58) 8.2	(1961/62) 11.9		(1964/65) 16.3
Steel	(1953–55)183	(1956/58)266	(1961) 277		(1964) 212

SOURCE: *United Nations Statistical Yearbook*, 1962, 1965.
* Figures in thousands of metric tons.

There was an obvious and rather marked increase during the decade of the fifties in most of the lines reported, though few reach far enough into the revolution to tell us much about the impact of that movement. The series on rice, for example, indicates that the production of that cereal tripled between 1948–52 and 1961, but that a substantial amount of that increase took place by 1955. In more recent years there has been a sharp drop in rice production. Coffee production experienced a steady increase of more than 50 per cent during the decade of the fifties, and remained about the same in the early sixties. Sugar experienced ups and downs, but production was nearly three-quarters of a million tons larger by 1961 than at the beginning of the decade or for any year within the decade. Tobacco, with seasonal ups and downs, increased 50 per cent by 1961 and rose further in the next three years. The cattle herd increased from just over four million in the 1948–52 base to a peak of 5.8 million in 1958, then declined 700,000 by 1961, suggesting that more beef was consumed after the revolution, or perhaps destroyed by the military operations. Unreliability of milk production figures makes them hardly worth mentioning, but those reported almost doubled by 1957, after which no reports are available. The fish catch, though still insignificant, roughly doubled each quinquennium until 1961, and grew more slowly thereafter. The index of total food production (1952/53 to 1956/57 = 100) was 100 in 1961/62, 82 in 1963/64.

Industrial indices, sketchy as they are, suggest a higher rate of growth in that sector (see Table 34–6). The production of petroleum derivatives shows enormous increases, which must be a barometer of import substitution, but also reflects increases in production value added employment. Motor spirit and distillate production increased ten times over between 1948 and 1960 with the great bulk of the increase after 1956, but dropped in the following three years. Production of residual fuel oil increased by a multiple of about one hundred. Production of residual and distillate peaked in 1959 and declined slightly in 1960. This, of course, suggests a large new refinery rather than the impact of revolution. Industrial cotton consumption grew 275 per cent between 1958–59 and 1964–65, and is almost surely an indication of post-revolutionary expansion, during a period when world consumption was declining slightly. Steel consumption increased by about 40 per cent between 1953–55 and 1956–58, dropped to a low level in 1959, recovered in 1960, reached a new peak about 50 per cent above the earlier base in 1961, fell in 1964. This suggests that new refinery capacity swelled the 1956–58 figure, and that some other type of industrial construction has been taking place since 1959, on about the same scale.

Conclusion

The anatomy of revolution involves three steps: (1) a power transfer from one functional interest group to another; (2) a transvaluation which must talk in terms of universal values in order to furnish the *raison d'être* for the new power group; (3) a new accommodation, during which many of the old values, banished by the negative aspects of the transvaluation, will return to a position in a new value hierarchy. Cuba, in the excesses of the negative phase of transvaluation, of which the keynote is "Hate the Yankee," has for the present destroyed or banished the old dominant minority; many of them were valuable, technically and economically. At the same time it has incited a fervent loyalty in the impoverished rural mass, which may simplify the creation of a new administration and facilitate the training of a new group of technical people. Cuba has dislocated herself in trading space, alienating her trading partners of the Caribbean. This would appear to be a genuine economic loss, difficult to compensate by help from the Communist group. If the present phase of transvaluation is not followed by an accommodation—a new value synthesis which permits her to return to trade with her neighbors—she will have accepted a rather serious economic handicap.

35 | Economic Development with Unlimited Supplies of Capital: The Libyan Case

More than a decade ago, W. Arthur Lewis wrote an influential article on "Economic Development with Unlimited Supplies of Labour." [1] Despite repeated demonstrations that his assumptions do not fit the facts in most developing countries, similar models continue to be elaborated, such as the recent one by Fei and Ranis. [2] Ragnar Nurkse developed his "balanced growth" theory, on the other hand, on the assumption of an "unlimited supply of capital" and lack of strong exports. This model is perhaps even less realistic than the Lewis one; developing countries with anything approaching unlimited supplies of capital are usually in this fortunate situation precisely because they do have a strong export, such as oil. Moreover, Nurkse's advice for cases which fit his assumptions—advance on many domestic fronts at once—is cold comfort for countries like Libya and the other Middle East oil countries, where the domestic market is too small for the most efficient capital-intensive techniques to be profitably used over a large number of industrial activities. Hirschman recommends unbalanced growth; but can we be sure that expansion in one sector will generate growth in others? In view of the doubts as to the applicability of these theories, it may be worthwhile to examine in some detail an actual case in which capital has suddenly become virtually unlimited for the foreseeable future through the appearance of a strong export (oil), while

[1] W. Arthur Lewis, "Economic Development with Unlimited Supplies of Labour," *The Manchester School of Economic and Social Studies*, May, 1954.

[2] John Fei and George Ranis, *Development of the Labour Surplus Economy* (Homewood, Ill., 1964); and the present author's review of this book in *Economic Development and Cultural Change*, January, 1966. Cf. Chapter 14.

other resources remain scarce. The conclusions reached, we will find, throw some doubts on the usefulness of either the Hirschman-Lewis or Nurkse models as general theories of underdevelopment.

Few countries have undergone so sudden and drastic a transformation of their economic prospects as Libya. In 1952 Libya seemed to be an almost hopeless case: [3]

Libya's great merit as a case study is as a prototype of poor country. We need not construct *abstract* models of an economy where the bulk of the people live on a subsistence level, where per capita income is well below $50 per year, where there are no sources of power and no mineral resources, where agricultural expansion is severely limited by climatic conditions, where capital formation is zero or less, where there is no skilled labor supply and no indigenous entrepreneurship. When Libya became an independent kingdom under United Nations auspices (December, 1951) it fulfilled all these conditions. Libya is at the bottom of the range in income and resources and so provides a reference point for comparison with all other countries.

Today Libya is a prototype once again, but it is no longer a prototype of a poor country. It is rather a prototype of unbalanced growth. The average income has surpassed $450. On the basis of this single simple measure, Libya is already approaching a level comparable to that of some countries which are no longer considered underdeveloped. As in other oil countries, however, such averages can be very misleading. In terms of the levels of living of the farmers and unskilled workers, who still constitute the bulk of the population, or in terms of the levels of health and education, Libya is still clearly an underdeveloped country. Libya, like other oil-rich countries, now faces the problem of "sowing the petroleum."

Libya, 1952

When Libya became an independent nation under United Nations auspices at the end of 1951, the prospects for Libyan economic and social development were discouraging to Libyans and foreigners alike. It was taken for granted that Libya would need substantial capital assistance from abroad, and technical assistance as well. The Libyan economy seemed to offer distressingly little with which to work. The "expert" view was that for decades to come economic development of Libya must consist largely of raising productivity in agriculture, including animal husbandry. At that time over 80 per cent of the Libyan population was engaged in agriculture and animal husbandry. It seemed unlikely that this proportion would, or even should, drop significantly during the next few years. Agriculture itself faced extraordinary difficulties. For a population of only 1,200,000, Libya appeared at first blush to be a very large country—1,750,000 square kilometers. Some 95 per cent of the people were concentrated in the Tripolitanian coastal plain and in the Cyrenaican and Tripolitanian Jebel. The rest lived mainly in the strings of oases in the Fezzan.

[3] Benjamin Higgins, *Economic Development: Principles, Problems, and Policies,* 1st ed. (New York, 1959), p. 26.

Even in the occupied areas the soil was not good. The rainfall in Tripolitania and Cyrenaica was both inadequate and unreliable. The Fezzan had virtually no rainfall but had underground water near the surface. Expansion of Libyan agriculture clearly required extension of the irrigation area, but the degree to which underground water resources would permit such expansion was not clearly known.

If the prospects for rapid expansion of agriculture were not bright, the prospects for industrialization were still more limited. The basis for industrialization was almost completely lacking. Libya had no known mineral deposits big enough or rich enough to justify exploitation, except for such relatively unimportant things as natron, carnallite, and low-grade sulphur. There was no coal, no water power, and—it was thought—no oil. The labor force was largely unskilled. Any new industries would be handicapped by the distance of Libyan ports from the major European, North African, and Middle Eastern centers.

Entrepreneurship

With so little to work with, it was not surprising that vigorous indigenous entrepreneurship was rare. The Libyans themselves were almost entirely confined to agriculture of a rather primitive kind, although the Arab garden was in its way an efficient unit. About one-fifth of the population was nomadic and another fifth seminomadic. The only other important occupation of Libyans was textiles and handicrafts. Before the war, considerable numbers of Jews were engaged in trading and small enterprises, but the postwar wave of anti-Semitism resulted in the virtual disappearance of this group. By 1951 only 7,000 Jews were left in the country. Large-scale enterprises, whether in agriculture, industry, commerce, or finance, were mostly in the hands of Italians. The war brought a substantial exodus of Italians, especially from Cyrenaica, and at the time of transfer of sovereignty there were only 50,000 left, mainly in Tripolitania.

It was commonplace among observers of Libyan affairs to describe the economy as "deficitary." There were deficits in the budgets of all three provinces, and of most municipalities; the budget surplus of the federal government (with foreign grants) was expected to be exhausted by grants-in-aid to the provinces. There was a deficit in the balance of trade, whether in commodities alone or in goods and services combined, of all three provinces; this deficit was not met by net receipts from foreign investment, as it might be in an advanced country, but by the grants-in-aid, military expenditures, and investments of foreign powers. The wheat-growing experiment at Barce operated at a deficit; the tobacco-growing scheme launched at the Azienda Tabacci Italiani operated at a small deficit; most of the Italian colonization schemes operated at a deficit, perhaps because they were conceived on too grandiose a scale for the nature of the country. Fezzanese agriculture operated at a deficit. The power plant in Tripoli operated at a deficit; the railways operated at a deficit; the harbor and the gasworks at Tripoli had incurred deficits in several years of the past decade, and so on.

These separate deficits reflected the hard fact that the whole Libyan economy operated at a deficit. The country did not produce enough to maintain even its low standard of living. For four decades, these deficits were made good by foreign governments: by Italy during the thirty years when Libya was an Italian colony; from 1943 to 1952 by the administering powers (the United Kingdom in Tripolitania and Cyrenaica, France in the Fezzan); [4] and in the 1950s by foreign aid and leases of military bases.

Population and Manpower

The manpower problem in Libya took the form of inadequate skill and low productivity, rather than insufficiency of total numbers of workers. Despite the small size of the total Libyan population, there was no evidence that the country was underpopulated in relation to its natural resources and existing techniques. Moreover, judging from prewar figures, the ratio of active to total population was higher in Libya than in some other African countries, partly because about one-quarter of the children between ten and fourteen years of age were members of the labor force.

There was, moreover, a large pool of unemployment on which to draw. In the first place, there was a hard core of underemployment and low-productivity employment which probably exceeded one-third of the labor force. This unemployment was aggravated by seasonal fluctuations sometimes reaching 80 per cent of the labor force in the off-seasons. In periods of drought, a substantial volume of visible unemployment also appeared in Tripolitania and Cyrenaica. Visible unemployment may exceed half the labor force of some districts when drought is acute. In Benghazi and Tripoli, cyclical unemployment of the kind familiar in advanced countries may also be seen among industrial workers, craftsmen, dock workers, and the like. Finally, there was a substantial amount of "potential" unemployment, in the sense that simple improvements in techniques could release large numbers of workers for absorption into other occupations. Altogether, these various forms of unemployment constituted a substantial reserve of manpower, which could be tapped as economic and social development proceeds. The successive elimination of these various forms of unemployment would be only partially offset by reduced reliance on child labor as education became more widespread.

Economic Development: 1952–1958

Such development as took place under the six-year plan of 1952–58 was mainly the result of government enterprise, partly because the most important source of capital has been foreign aid granted to and administered by the Libyan government. Total foreign aid in 1954–55 ran in excess of $26,000,000 per year, or more than half the estimated national income.

In 1956, both the British and the American grants were running at even higher rates: the budgetary subvention from the United Kingdom was

[4] The Ottoman Administration apparently succeeded in collecting more in taxes than it spent within the country, but no reliable information is available concerning the relative levels of production and living standards in that period and today.

raised by £250,000 in the fiscal year 1956 and by £750,000 in the follow-ing year; American assistance reached $12,000,000 per year, of which $5,000,000 was specifically earmarked for development. The sums ear-marked for development alone exceeded 20 per cent of national income; and since all foreign aid relieves both the budget and the balance of pay-ments, the whole amount might be regarded as adding to the financial resources for development. These grants were large only in relation to the very low national income; truly large-scale projects were still not possible in Libya. But the lack of natural resources, technical and managerial skills, and entrepreneurship was even then a much more serious bottleneck than lack of capital.

Libya, 1966

At first glance, the discovery of oil in large quantities seems to have transformed the Libyan economic picture almost literally overnight. The Libyan economy of 1966 had a curious "Arabian nights" quality; cus-tomary modes of analysis of underdeveloped countries seemed irrelevant. Beneath the surface, however, lurked the same fundamental problems as were present in 1952.

Rapid Economic Growth

In the first place, the rate of growth of national income since 1960 has been fantastically high (of the order of 25 per cent per year). This rapid growth is due almost entirely to the impact of a single "leading sector." The rate of population growth is also high, possibly above 3 per cent per year; nonetheless the rate of increase in per capita incomes is several times as high as the targets set in the more ambitious development programs of other countries.

Factor Endowment

In the second place, Libya now has a very unusual pattern of factor endowment. Libya currently enjoys abundant capital and an abundant supply of foreign exchange. There is for the moment an adequate supply of unskilled labor. On the other hand, there is still a scarcity of known water resources and of known natural resources other than petroleum. Finally, there is a severe shortage of human skills.

In terms of the ordinary neoclassical analysis of factor proportions, therefore, Libya should produce commodities utilizing large amounts of capital, substantial amounts of unskilled labor, very little water or natural resources except oil, and virtually no human skills. The choice of tech-nology in the production of particular commodities should be guided by the same considerations. But where to find commodities or techniques conforming to this peculiar factor endowment?

Uncertainty

The Libyan economy is also characterized by an unusual degree of economic uncertainty. The change in the economic situation with the oil discoveries has been so drastic and discontinuous, especially where future prospects are concerned, that little in past experience is useful as a basis for policy decisions. This comment applies particularly to the evaluation of new industrial investment projects. Moreover, the new Libyan economy is very poorly "hedged." Recent growth and prospective growth in the immediate future is dependent almost entirely on the volume of production of petroleum and world market prices of this single export. Neither the value nor the price is predictable with any degree of certainty, particularly in the more remote future.

Still a Deficitary Economy

Except that the standards of living have risen substantially and the foreign governments have been replaced by foreign oil companies, Libya is a deficitary economy still. If one estimates the output of *Libyan* factors of production, including in the figure of gross national product only the strictly Libyan contribution to the value of oil production, it is clear that total consumption, public and private, exceeds this production figure. Total imports far exceed exports exclusive of oil, and this gap will increase. By 1966 Libyan imports had increased fourfold since 1957, more than twice as much as the increase in imports into such neighboring countries as Morocco, Tunisia, and the United Arab Republic. Per capita imports into Libya even in 1963 were more than four times those of the United Arab Republic or Morocco, and more than three times those of Tunisia. Meanwhile, exports of commodities other than oil have declined, mainly as a result of rising internal consumption. Exports of a few commodities, such as wool, citrus, carpets, and tomatoes increased between 1960 and 1964, but the exports of others, such as peanuts, hides and skins, castor seeds, fish, esparto grass, sponges, and almonds, fell, in some cases substantially. The budget is in deficit if oil revenues are excluded.

Sharp reductions in levels of living are socially and politically unsettling. Should an objective of economic policy be to build a Libyan economy that can eventually maintain present levels of consumption if and when petroleum reserves are exhausted, it is obvious that the structure of the economy must be drastically changed from what it was in 1966.

Creeping Inflation and Reverse Import-Replacement

The Libyan government is confronted with a dilemma concerning import policy and the checking of inflation. A liberal import policy is the easy way to offset the expansion of the money supply through the growth of petroleum exports. Under current conditions, the sales of oil are tantamount to printing money. In the absence of offsetting increases in imports, the present creeping inflation could become a galloping one. On the other hand, a liberal import policy has the effect of destroying Libyan enterprises which have already been established but are unable to compete with imports at the present time. Since the cost in Libyan factors of production is such a small fraction of the value of oil, imports are in a sense subsidized; the cost to the Libyan economy is "really" well below what is paid for them. If they had to be paid for at "full cost" in Libyan man-hours, they would be too expensive. The question arises as to whether it might not be better to subsidize Libyan enterprises having favorable long-run prospects, if only for the training facilities that such going concerns provide to the Libyan labor force.

Instability from the Supply Side

One function of the Libyan Stabilization and Development Agency established in 1952 was to time development expenditures in such a way as to counteract the violent fluctuations in income and employment generated by fluctuations in agricultural production. The basic idea was to stockpile both barley and foreign exchange reserves, so that in drought years income and employment could be provided by accelerating the development program, while food was provided and inflation prevented by selling barley from stocks. The development of the petroleum sector has not reduced the violence of the fluctuations in the agricultural economy, and the dependence on petroleum introduces a new element of instability.

The Long-Run Employment Problem

Finally, the development of the petroleum sector does not in itself solve the problems of providing high-productivity employment for the entire Libyan labor force. Indeed, because of the drift to the cities that it prompts, for the moment it has aggravated the employment problem. As will be demonstrated in more detail below, it will be difficult to generate a rate of industrialization that would absorb the entire increase in the labor force; yet if the rate of industrialization is only moderate, while unemployment in the cities is avoided, the increase in the population in the agricultural sector will be such as to make it extremely difficult to raise per capita output in that sector.[5]

Entrepreneurship

Surprisingly enough, entrepreneurship no longer seemed to be a serious bottleneck in the Libyan development situation. The oil industry and a few other large-scale enterprises were, of course, essentially foreign undertakings. Italian, Egyptian, Yugoslav, and Tunisian entrepreneurship also appeared in small and middle-sized establishments. Most impressive, however, was the upsurge of purely Libyan enterprise, not only in commerce and finance but also in manufacturing. Some of the new activities were directly related to the oil industry—oil drums, gas tanks, desert equipment, trailers, etc.—and some to rising levels of domestic consumption. Some of the most successful entrepreneurs are men of very limited formal education, but the few university graduates among the older generation have also

---

[5] The term "industrialization" here means growth of the non-agricultural sector, including services. It should be pointed out, however, that there are severe limitations to the growth of the services sector of a single economy.

found new outlets for their talents. Indeed the rapidity with which an indigenous entrepreneurial class has appeared raises grave doubts about the validity of the theories of the Weber-Hagen variety, which suggest the need for fundamental and slow-moving socio-cultural change before entrepreneurship can evolve. (Perhaps, however, Hagen would find the beginnings of change in the socio-cultural framework in Libya with the Italian invasion in the 1930's, and argue that the oil discoveries merely provided opportunities for latent entrepreneurship that was already there, although no one recognized it!)

A Projection for the Libyan Economy*

In order to clarify the problem Libya will face in her development over the next decade, some illustrative projections may be made. Two basic equations will be used for projections. The first expresses the identity that the *ex post* supply equals the demand:

Supply   = GDP + imports of goods and services
                 (GDP = gross domestic product)
Demand = Consumption of goods and services by
                 a. the private sector, i.e., households
          and
                 b. the government;
             + Gross capital formation, i.e.,
                 a. GFCF (gross fixed capital formation)
          and
                 b. net increase of stocks, including trees planted, increase
                 in the stock of livestock and stocks in the trade sector;
             + Exports of goods and services
The second equation refers to the balance of payments.
Exports − imports = Net factor payments to the rest of the world
                 (mainly transfer of net profits of oil companies)
             + Net transfers to the rest of the world (mostly
                 family remittances sent abroad by foreigners re-
                 siding in Libya)
             − New investments made by foreign companies to
                 Libya (mainly gross capital formation in the oil
                 sector)
             − Provision for depreciation of foreign assets in
                 Libya (reimbursement by Libya of capital invested
                 by foreign oil companies)
                 Thus,
Exports − imports = Net profits from oil companies and family
                 remittances
             + Depreciation of oil capital
             − Gross capital formation in the oil sector.

* This section is a slightly modified version of a projection prepared by the author's colleague on the Libyan Special Evaluation Mission, Dr. Jacques Royer.

We must also take account of possible accumulation of foreign assets from two sources:

a. If exports exceed imports plus profit transfers, an increase of foreign assets will appear as a residual.

b. Interest on Libyan assets abroad.

These two terms will be used as policy variables. Their sum will be called the net increase in foreign assets.

Substituting the difference "Exports less Imports" as expressed in Equation 2 into Equation 1 we obtain:

GDP − (net profit + oil companies and family remittances
        + depreciation of oil capital)
    = (private and public consumption
        + gross capital formation, less gross capital formation in oil sector
        + net increase of foreign assets.)

We can now subdivide both the gross domestic product and the gross capital formation into two components:

    for GDP; GDP, oil and non-oil
    for GCF: GCF, oil and non-oil

The preceding equation then reads:

    − GDP, non-oil
    + GDP, oil, less net profit, oil companies and family remittances, less depreciation, oil capital
    = private and public consumption
    + gross capital formation, non-oil
    + net increase of foreign assets.

In the accounts of oil companies, we find the following balance:

    Oil sales = GDP, oil + inputs
              = Cost + government oil revenue + net profit

It follows that:

    GDP, oil less net profit less depreciation of oil capital
    = Government oil revenue + (cost less inputs less depreciation oil capital).

Subtracting from cost inputs of raw materials and depreciation, we find the wages paid by the companies in Libya.

We then have a simple variant of Equation 1:

Resources   = [GDP, non-oil sectors
                + Government revenue paid by oil companies
                + Wages, oil (less family remittances)]
Expenditures = [Private and public consumption
                + Gross capital formation, non-oil
                + Net increase in foreign assets.]

With the oil revenue increasing from year to year, the programming problem for Libya is to determine the optimal allocation of oil revenues among three uses:

a. Gross capital formation in the non-oil sector
b. Private and public consumption
c. Net increase in foreign assets.

The government has stated that 70 per cent of the oil revenues should be allocated to development; that is, to "gross capital formation of non-oil sectors." As we have seen above, however, there are limits to the absorption of capital imposed by the lack of skills. In order to illustrate these limits, we will attempt to make a projection of the economy, until the end of the next Five-Year Plan, i.e., to 1972. This is not a *forecast*, but a means of illustrating the consequences of two basic assumptions:

a. The level of oil sales will be between 2 and 2.8 million barrels per day. The first figure, 2 million, is likely to be below the actual 1972 figures (taking into account the present level of 1.2 million and adding the expected production of the newer companies). The second, 2.8 million, is likely to be a ceiling figure, but is not extravagant.

b. The development of the non-oil economy will proceed as fast as possible without inflation. This assumption does not mean that such a rate will actually materialize; nor is it a recommendation. It would probably be better for Libya to allow herself more time for the social and physical adjustments that such a rate of growth would imply. The purpose of the projection is merely to show the possible consequences of the strain such a rate of growth would impose during the next five years.

Capital being unlimited, the growth of the non-oil economy will depend entirely on manpower and skills available. In other words, the final level of production will depend on the number of Libyan workers, the volume of foreign skills admitted, and the training effort (particularly the efficiency of agricultural extension services and the vocational training schemes) to be accomplished beetween 1965 and 1972.

To permit the economy to expand at the fastest possible rate, we will make three optimistic assumptions.

Growth of the Over-all Labor Force

Our first assumption is that the labor force will grow faster than total population, by importing foreign workers, increasing the participation rate of the active population, or having more women work in cities. In 1964, there were approximately:

140,000 males working in agriculture
214,000 males and females working outside agriculture
354,000 workers, excluding women in agriculture and 32,000 unoccupied
        workers in cities.

At a natural growth rate of 3 per cent the working population should reach a level of around 450,000 in 1972. We will assume that it reaches a level of 504,000, which implies that more than 54,000 additional workers actually join the labor force—or perhaps as much as 74,000 to 84,000, since technological unemployment is bound to appear in so fast-growing an economy.

Growth of the Agricultural Labor Force

Out of these 504,000 workers, some 170,000 males (and more women) will be assumed to work in agriculture. This figure is based on the assumption that the labor force in agriculture will grow only by 1 per cent per year, as against 4.6 per cent for the total labor force. This assumption allows for a continuation of the drift from rural areas to cities, but at a pace which will not seriously endanger agricultural production or rural life. Correspondingly, the labor force in the cities will amount to 334,000, an annual increase of 5.7 per cent—the same order of magnitude as was observed in the last few years. This is a very fast rate indeed, if judged by the accumulation of slums in the two main cities of Tripoli and Benghazi.

Increase in Productivity

Finally, as a result of a liberal policy of import of foreign skills and a vigorous training program (agricultural extension and vocational training) productivity will increase everywhere, at the following rate:

Agriculture: 4 per cent a year
Oil sector: 5 per cent a year
Industry/Transport: 3 per cent a year
Government services: 3 per cent a year.

A new non-oil, highly productive sector will be established (gas liquefaction, petrochemicals, etc.) so that the over-all rate of productivity in industry will be higher than 3 per cent, depending on the size of the latter sector. (We will allow a minimum rate of 6.7 per cent and we will see the requirements in terms of foreign skills.)

The rate of growth of productivity being assigned to the agricultural sector (4 per cent) is likely to prove impossible. However, a lower rate would not greatly alter the results, because of the small share of agricultural production in the GDP.

No increase of productivity has been allowed for private services (other than transport) or for trade. The present level of productivity is artificially high, due to the high profits and high wages in those sectors.

Projection of the GDP

In order to project the GDP, we will assume arbitrary rates of growth for exogenous sectors, the productive non-oil sectors (agriculture and industry) being considered endogenous sectors. Furthermore, two alternative levels will be tested for oil. Table 35–1 gives the targets for the

TABLE 35–1
Projection of GDP (in millions of pounds):
Exogenous sectors

Value added by:	1964	1972	Annual rate of growth (per cent)
Oil—hypothesis A	166	550	16
—hypothesis B	..	400	11
Services, rent	24	30	2.8
others	15	25	6
Trade, factor cost	27	50	8
Government services	38	65	7

exogenous sectors.

The annual rates of growth of oil output (11 and 16 per cent) correspond to the production of 2 and 2.8 million of barrels per day. A low rate of increase has been assigned to the rent of houses (2.8 per cent), implying that rents will fall with the rapid increase in number of houses being built. This assumption reflects government intentions. The "service" sector (hotels, banks, etc.) is growing rapidly (6 per cent)—though admittedly less rapidly than in the past, as a result of the policy of diverting workers toward industry. The figure for trade (8 per cent) has been selected to match the rate of growth of consumption. Finally, government services increase at 7 per cent, allowing a 10 per cent rate of growth for education and health and 6 per cent for other services. A different rate would not affect our conclusions since these services appear on both sides of the equation.

The production in *agriculture* results wholly from our assumptions on manpower and productivity. The over-all index of productivity, with a 4 per cent annual rate of growth, is 137 per cent, which means that income per farmer will increase only by 37 per cent as compared with 1964, even if productivity actually grows as fast as we are assuming. In other words, the *increase of productivity alone will not do much to reduce the income gap between farmers and city workers.* This situation calls for a policy of massive subsidies to farmers. Otherwise, rural migration would be much faster than we have assumed and rural life might be damaged forever. This is one of the important illustrations given by the model, though full particulars are not given: e.g., compare annual income per farmer, £184, i.e., £37 per capita, with average consumption figure per capita given later, i.e., 100 and above, which in turn implies £163 and above per capita in cities. This gives a ratio of 1 to 4.4 for rural-urban levels of living, against 1 to 4 now. The gap is widening.

Agricultural production was about £26 million in 1964 (a good crop year). Thus the figure for 1972 is £31 million. If productivity remained unchanged, if rural migration were faster, or even if rainfall were less in 1972, agricultural production could fall instead of increasing. In a total private consumption of £200 million, food consumption could be of the order of £80 million, as compared with basic domestic production of £31 million plus a value added in the food processing industry of £8 million at most. Thus consumption will be more than twice the production. Yet the population is growing quickly and Libyan incomes are at a level where the income elasticity of demand for food is high. Three conclusions emerge from our analysis of the agricultural sector:

The need for massive subsidies to farmers;

The widening gap between demand for and supply of food and the need for a long-term policy of increasing supply;

The growing market for food processing industries based on imports (flour mills, etc.) as well as local production.

Turning to *industry*, the total manpower available can be deducted from a manpower balance derived from the other sectors. Dividing the production figure by the productivity, we obtain the following figures:

TABLE 35–2
Number of Workers in 1972

Industry	Total		Libyans	Foreigners
Oil (A)	31,000		26,000	5,000
Oil (B)	22,000		18,500	3,500
Services and trade	107,000		102,000	5,000
Government services	83,000		80,000	3,000
Total Libyan manpower:		A	208,000	13,000
(except industry and transport)		B	200,000	11,500
Total Libyan manpower: (non-agriculture)			334,000	
Hence, by difference:				
Manpower, industry and transport		A:	126,000	
		B:	134,000	

It will be noted that in the oil sector, we have allowed for 5,000 or 3,500 foreigners in hypotheses "A and B," respectively. The figures themselves may be somewhat arbitrary, but they illustrate the fact that in the medium term, i.e., a period of eight years, no increase of productivity can be expected in the industrial sectors (especially in highly capital-intensive sectors like oil), without allowing immigration of foreign skills. This fact has been also taken into account in the other services (bank senior employees, hotel senior employees, etc.), though the rate of immigration has been set much lower in the service sector.

Having found 126,000 to 134,000 workers in the industrial sector, we will *adjust the production to these workers*—an essential feature of the model—and not impose on them, through the oil revenue and the development budget, a rate of activity derived from the 70 per cent rule or otherwise. This procedure will not only be useful for clarifying our own deductions, but it is suggested that this method (or a somewhat more refined method of manpower balance) should be the key rule of planning in Libya. If more money is forced into the industrial sector, wages will increase, inflation will take place, but—the quantity of goods and services that can be produced being rigidly defined by the manpower available and its productivity—*the only result will be that more money will be paid to get the same production.*

If the present productivity were applied to 125,000 workers, we would have an industrial output of £50 million. Since we have made the assumption that productivity will increase by 3 per cent per year (more plants, less handicrafts), we will have a production of £77 million with the same workers. As was suggested earlier, we would raise this figure further by taking into account the high increase of productivity expected from capital intensive projects. On the assumption that around £100 million will be invested during this period on this type of project (an assumption to be tested from the financing angle at a later stage), we could expect a production of £ 30 million [6] in this sector in 1972. In this case, the man-power balance will be as follows:

Hypothesis A:	Labor-intensive industry:	122,000 Libyans, 6,000 foreign skills
Hypothesis A:	Capital-intensive industry:	4,000 Libyans, 2,000 foreign skills
Hypothesis B:	Labor-intensive industry:	130,000 Libyans, 6,000 foreign skills
Hypothesis B:	Capital-intensive industry:	4,000 Libyans, 2,000 foreign skills

It will be noted that the additional production of £ 30 million is obtained by allowing 2,000 more foreign skills than in the preceding case. This is a mere illustrative figure, but it shows that *with a tight manpower domestic market, Libya can only increase production by importing more skills* (and training her own workers), on the condition (which will prove correct) that there is no financing bottleneck. We cannot say that this policy will give more jobs to Libyans, but it will give more highly paid jobs and will decrease the dependence of the economy on oil. On the other hand, the economy will be more dependent on foreign skills—which means that *the two targets, independence from oil and independence from foreign skills, contradict each other*. One of the basic issues of any plan is, therefore, to make a political choice between the two targets.

Finally, we find that by multiplying manpower by productivity, we will geet the following industrial production (millions £):

	Hypothesis	Hypothesis
Labor intensive:	74	79
Capital intensive:	30	30
Total:	104	109

Adding up production figures for all sectors we obtain the GDP:

	At factor cost		At market price	
	A	B	A	B
Oil sector:	550	400	550	400
Non-oil sector:	305	310	340	345
Total:	855	710	890	745

If we compare these figures with the 1964 GDP, we see that Hypothesis A results in an annual rate of increase of 12 per cent for the GDP, while Hypothesis B corresponds to a rate of growth of 9.7 per cent. In either case we may say that the economy is growing at full speed, far above any level so far observed in Africa. The non-oil sector progresses at a slightly slower rate, 7.8 per cent—a rate never observed in Africa. Once again, these rates are not a forecast, but are merely the outcome of our assumptions on productivity increases.

[6] Assuming a capital-output ratio of 3.3.

Gross Capital Formation and Consumption

We are now in a position to assess the gross capital formation figure. Several methods can be used to make a projection consistent with the GDP and other factors. For the capital-intensive industry, we suggested an investment of £100 million over several years preceding 1972. Assuming an upward trend in 1972, investment of this type may amount to a maximum of £40 million (as a comparison, the gas liquefaction plant may cost £60 million spread over two years, i.e., 30 million per year). With capital-output ratios of 3 for industry and 2 for other sectors, investment in these sectors can be estimated as 31 million. A third component will be an arbitrary figure for investment in agriculture, say £7 million (for so short an interval there can hardly be any rigid capital-output ratio for Libyan agriculture, since most investment will be long-term). Finally, we may assume that as much as £50 million [7] are spent on residential buildings and public works. The total fixed capital formation would be £128 million, to which we will add £6 million for increase in stocks. We thus obtain a maximum figure of £134 million as capital formation.

The next choice we have to make is the level of private consumption. This is a policy variable. A growth rate of 6 per cent per year means a doubling of per capita consumption (3 per cent annual rate) over twenty-three years. This would be considered a high target for many countries in the world. Indeed consumption per capita can hardly rise in such over-populated countries as the Maghreb group and UAR if they want to save enough for the growth of their economy. For Libya, however, 6 per cent will probably be found to be a low rate, in the sense that with the very high marginal propensity to consume, it will be difficult for the government to limit consumption to these levels. This rate would bring consumption to £200 million in 1972. It goes without saying that this rate is one of the political choices to be submitted to the National Council.

For government consumption (the current expenditures budget) we will adopt the 7 per cent rate already used for government services. This would also be a political choice. We thus obtain a current budget of £96 million, a difficult ceiling to maintain under Libyan conditions.

The Accumulation of Foreign Assets

We can now balance resources and expenditures using Equation 2:

	Hypothesis A (millions of pounds)	Hypothesis B (millions of pounds)
GDP, non-oil, market price	340	345
+ Oil revenue	307	219
+ Oil wages less remittances	20	11
+ Interest from past foreign assets	x	x
Total resources	667 + x	575 + x

[7] This figure is obtained as a residual, assuming a value added of 45 for construction and public work, or else a gross production of 76, from which 26 is deducted as civil engineering already incorporated in the first three components.

Equals:	A	B
Private consumption	200	200
+ Public consumption	96	96
+ GCF, non-oil	134	134
+ Increase, foreign assets	237 + x	145 + x
Total expenditures	667 + x	575 + x

No specific entry has been made for interest on accumulated foreign assets. We have merely entered an x on both sides of the equation.

On the expenditure side, the increase in foreign assets for the current year is a residual—the difference between total resources and the first three terms of expenditure. This is the key figure for which we have been looking all along:

a. Under assumption A (oil production, 2.8 million barrel/day), the oil revenue is £307 million, and we find an increase of foreign assets of £237 million, which means that the domestic economy has absorbed only £70 million out of £307 million, less than 23 per cent of the oil revenue.

b. In case B (oil production, 2.0 million barrel/day), the corresponding figures are £219 million for the oil revenue, £145 million for the increase of foreign assets, and only £74 million out of £219 million, i.e., 34 per cent, for the rate of domestic absorption.

In the preceding years, foreign assets will have accumulated in similar fashion. In 1972, to the enormous accumulation of foreign assets we must add the interest "x" from the preceding years. Foreign assets may easily reach a value of £50 million in case A and, say, £30 million in case B, thus bringing the total annual increase of foreign assets to £287 million and £249 million, respectively. This figure would be the equivalent of about $350 per capita, or about half a year's income. The equivalent for the United States would be net foreign investment of $350 billion per year.

Results of Projections

It is our main finding that, *under the assumptions made in the projection, the rate of accumulation of foreign assets is extremely high.* Examining the "expenditures" side of the equation, we can formulate three main consequences as follows:

a. The whole domestic investment of the country, private and public sectors together, amounts to 44 per cent of oil revenue in case A (2.8 million barrel/day) and to 62 per cent of oil revenue in case B (2 million barrel/day). Can we modify the basic assumptions of the model so as to enable the government actually to apply the constitutional rule of spending 70 per cent of oil revenue on development projects? The answer is "no." Even if productivity in industrial sectors increases by 6 per cent per year; even if the labor force grows by 4.6 per cent per year; and even if the government undertakes to finance all domestic capital formation in the country, including all residential buildings and all private plants—*the total investment will fall short of the 70 per cent constitutional rule with an oil production of 2 million barrel or above.*

b. Under such circumstances, the temptation to increase public or private consumption beyond the limits set in the model will be very great. There is, of course, the possibility of extending educational and training facilities, thus using oil revenue for "human investment." Other social schemes, such as a public health policy directed to mass preventive medicine, could also be enlarged. On the other hand, additional expenditures of this type would require basic infrastructure (school buildings, roads, dispensaries, etc.), and trained personnel. There are therefore limits to any rapid expansion of these sectors. Libya could increase private consumption much beyond the rate of 6 per cent per year through imports; but the economy then becomes more dependent on oil, not less, and exhaustion of oil reserves could lead to a drastic decline in living standards.

c. Finally, if capital formation and consumption are kept within the limits set in the model, the government must decide whether to allow oil revenue to accrue at such a high rate or conserve reserves in the ground; and it must decide how to invest accumulated foreign reserves of such magnitude.

Enlarging Investment Capacity

Could the investment capacity be enlarged beyond the limits set in the model, in order to make fuller use of oil revenue? There are formidable obstacles. First is the massive volume of foreign skills required to run such schemes; second is the possibility of finding outlets on the world market (the domestic market is too small); third is the need to adjust the infrastructure (port facilities, government agencies, banking facilities, etc.) to such a drastic mutation of the economy. We doubt very much the possibility of going much beyond the limits set in the model.

Since Libya has as yet no strong industrial base other than oil, building up an economy which can continue to grow when the oil is exhausted means finding other export industries, where Libya can compete in world markets on the basis of superior skills. The comparative advantage in skills will have to be quite marked to overcome the handicap Libya faces in terms of transport costs. Scientifically oriented industries in which transport costs are negligible like electronics and optics, come to mind. In short, to become independent of oil, Libya, whose main problem is precisely shortage of skills, must contrive to become an exporter of skills embodied in exports. Achieving such a position will require both a very liberal policy toward immigration of scientists and technicians and an enormous "big push" on the education front—which in turn will require immigration of teachers, a matter of the utmost delicacy from the political point of view.

The Importance of Technical Assistance

Capital is now virtually a "free good" in Libya, in two senses. First, the cost of foreign exchange obtained from oil in terms of Libyan factors of production is probably not more than 10 per cent of the value of the oil and probably less than 20 per cent of Libyan revenues from oil. That is, capital obtained by investing oil revenues is close to being costless to the Libyan economy as such. Second, if all oil revenues were used for formation of directly productive capital the marginal productivity of such capital would soon fall to zero and would remain there for a good many years.

The supply of skills, on the other hand, unless supplemented by technical assistance, may be regarded as virtually fixed in the short run. It can grow only so fast as the inadequate educational system produces trained personnel.

In Figure 35–1 the solid line RR' represents the minimum "return to

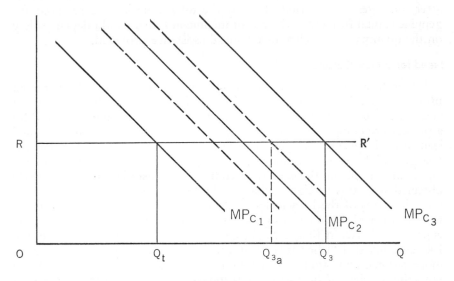

Figure 35–1

capital," equivalent in this context to the minimum wage level of the Lewis analysis. The minimum return to capital might be equivalent to the "accustomed normal rate of return," or liquidity trap level, of the Keynesian analysis. That is, both the government authorities and private investors prefer holding cash (perhaps even gold bars) to making investments on assets yielding only a very low return. Alternatively, it might be estimated at the rate of return on safe, liquid assets which could be purchased abroad with foreign exchange earnings. The curve MP_{C1} represents the marginal productivity of capital with the existing stock of human skills. If economic expansion is limited to what is possible on the basis of output of the educational system alone, this curve may shift through time in the manner indicated by the dotted lines. If the supply of human resources is supplemented by technical assistance, however, it may shift over the same time periods by the manner indicated by the solid lines. That is, technical assistance permits a more rapid rate of capital accumulation. In period three, the stock of capital can be OQ_3 with technical assistance, only OQ_{3a} without it.

Letting Y represent national income, a represent the output capital ratio, Q the stock of capital, I investment, b the ratio of capital to human resources and H the stock of human resources, we can then write,

$$Y = a \cdot Q; \quad \Delta Y = a \cdot I$$
$$Q = bH \qquad I = b \Delta H \qquad \Delta Y = a \cdot b \cdot \Delta H$$

In this simplified model the rate of growth of national income depends entirely on the rate of increase in the stock of human resources. Technical assistance which goes directly into the skilled labor force brings an immediate increase in national income. Technical assistance to the educational system or for research and surveys brings an increase in national income after some gestation period. Thus if the oil revenues were reserved for genuine capital formation, the rise of income in Libya would depend solely on the quantity and quality of technical assistance provided.

Need for a New Calculus

Under the conditions outlined above, evaluation of development projects in purely financial terms can be very misleading. The usual sort of cost-benefit analysis, in which increases in monetary income generated by a project are compared with the monetary cost associated with it, would lead to an inappropriately conservative development policy. Foreign exchange which becomes available to the Libyan government through the marketing of oil, and the capital equipment, raw materials, or skilled labor obtained with this foreign exchange, should be costed for planning purposes in terms of the Libyan factor-cost component. As indicated above, the cost to the Libyan economy, in terms of Libyan factors of production, is probably between 10 and 20 per cent of the oil revenues. Indeed, in the Libyan context a "labor theory of value" makes very good sense, and a more rational allocation in terms of man-hours, weighted in accordance with the number of hours of education associated with various types of skill. One might devise a new unit of account (a *medun*, let us say) measured in man-education-units.

If costs of possible development projects were calculated in *meduns*, with oil revenues costed in terms of *Libyan meduns*, many would be "profitable." The problem, therefore, is to choose from the wide range of "profitable" projects which should be accorded highest priority, in terms of their contribution to the development goals set forth in the decision function. Two types of opportunity cost should be calculated; first, the opportunity cost of one project, in terms of the contribution to development objectives, of alternative projects which could be undertaken at the same time; and the cost of particular projects, in terms of the contribution that could be made by projects undertaken at a later date, when the supply of human resources is more adequate. In the Libyan case, the evaluation of projects now in terms of projects later is particularly important. For Libya always has the alternatives of investing her foreign exchange obtained through oil revenues in foreign assets, or of holding oil reserves in the ground for future use. A well-construed portfolio policy, aimed at an appropriate balance of safety, liquidity, and high return might yield as much as 5 per cent on the average. At 5 per cent the value of foreign assets would double in fourteen years. The increase in the value of oil reserves in the ground is, of course, more difficult to forecast; but a part of the Libyan government's "portfolio" might be reserves of its own oil. Moreover, diverting a larger share of oil revenues to foreign investment, or a rigorous conservation policy, are the only effective ways of eliminating inflationary pressures.

One could also appraise import replacement in terms of skills. A German camera or an Italian car embodies more *meduns* of foreign labor than it costs in Libyan *meduns*, if paid for from oil revenues. The development of Libyan industries thus becomes a way of replacing foreign with domestic skills, as well as replacing foreign with domestic commodities.

Need for a "Decision Function"

In this particular situation Libya badly needs a "decision function" to which the whole planning operation can be related. Particularly important is the decision with respect to division of oil revenues between immediate improvements in economic welfare and capital accumulation. The sudden access to nationally owned wealth makes the "incomes policy" the foundation stone on which all other economic policy must be built. The path of subsidized increases in immediate welfare over the next twenty years should be plotted, and the development program designed within the restraint imposed by this path, so as to maximize the stock of capital outside the petroleum sector at the end of the perspective planning period (say twenty years).

The present indications are that per capita income will reach $1,330 by 1985, giving a national income of $4 billion with a population of three million people. On the assumption that the aggregate capital-output ratio is in the neighborhood of three to one, the development problem might then be stated as accumulating a stock of capital outside the petroleum sector amounting to £3 billion. In terms of monetary capital or foreign exchange this task is not particularly difficult; but the rate at which productive domestic capital can be accumulated depends almost entirely on the rate of accumulation of human skills. Solutions must also be found to the problem of finding markets for new industrial products, infusing into the Libyan economy a generally high level of research and technology, and the discovery of additional raw materials, either within Libya's own borders or available at low enough cost to permit establishment of new enterprises based on imported raw materials.

General Conclusions

If economic development means a combination of technological progress and capital accumulation that will raise per capita productivity, there is grave danger that Libya will retrogress rather than develop over the next twenty or thirty years. That is, it is unlikely that Libya will accumulate enough productive capital outside the oil sector, and raise productivity enough in the non-oil sectors, to offset the drawing down of oil reserves. Levels of living will of course rise, but essentially through a form of capital consumption. The problem is created, of course, by the shortage of human resources—the extremely limited supply of labor, especially of the skilled variety. From the purely economic point of view, there is probably some combination of big push in education, liberal immigration policy, astute portfolio policy, and conservation that could prevent such retrogression. Politically and administratively such a combination is probably impossible to achieve for any democratc government.

In terms of general theory of underdevelopment the main conclusion is that the importance of both shortage of capital and of the failure of Say's law can be exaggerated. The implication of the Lewis model is that if capital were as unlimited as labor, growth could go merrily on without let or hindrance. Few countries seemed closer to fulfilling the conditions of his model than Libya before the discovery of oil; but once capital was available in truly large quantities it immediately became apparent that labor, far from being unlimited, was the major bottleneck for growth. Nurkse's model implies that a country with a strong export—that is, one which is a substantial proportion of gross domestic product and whose sales expand at a rate at least as high as target rates of growth of income—should have no particular problems. Failing the strong export, it can still develop satisfactorily if it has a lot of capital and invests on a broad front all at once. Libya has both a strong export and a virtually unlimited supply of capital, but cannot really "develop" for lack of human resources. So far as the Hirschman model is concerned, the Libyan case means that "unbalanced" growth, once started, can remain unbalanced for a frighteningly long time.

Indeed, if any of the maxims of the development planner is sustained by the Libyan experience it is, "When in doubt, educate."

PART **VII** | Afterword

36 | Afterword

Scholar: But who'ere can know
      As the long days go
      That to live is happy, has found his heaven.
Industrialist: I think, my friend, that if you wish to know, as the long days go, that
      to live is happy, you must first acquire money enough for a decent life,
      and power enough to be your own master.
                    GEORGE BERNARD SHAW: *Major Barbara*
Poverty is no disgrace but it is damned annoying.
                                 SIR WILLIAM PITT

In this final chapter I wish to address a few remarks, in somewhat personal terms, to practitioners and serious students of economics. In particular, I want to raise with them the questions, "How are we doing? How much progress have we made in understanding the problem of underdevelopment in the years that have elapsed between the first and second editions of this book? Where do we go from here?"

There is perhaps some suggestion of progress in the fact that I do not now consider it worth while repeating anything that was said in the concluding chapter of the first edition. When it was written the field of development economics was still somewhat new, the literature still somewhat scant, and the number of professional economists specializing in the field still rather small. I myself was still in the stage of trying to synthesize my own experiences and ideas in the field for the first time. I was intent upon persuading colleagues and students that development economics really was a distinct and special branch of the subject, requiring radically different methods of analysis from those appropriate for other branches of the discipline. I stressed "the need to break out of the traditional molds of economic thought" when dealing with developing countries and warned that "recommendations based on misapplication of the methods of traditional equilibrium economics are likely to take us far astray." Now, however, underdevelopment is generally accepted as the most pressing problem confronting the profession, and among economists of international repute only a few mavericks have yet to acquire some experience in developing countries and to make some contribution to the literature. It is recognized, indeed, that in our new concern for the factors determining the general wealth or poverty of nations we are simply returning to the grand tradition of our field. In short, "development economics" is not a somewhat precious specialty within the broader field of economics; it *is* economics. Every scrap of knowledge of the economic process is germane to economic development—and much other knowledge as well.

We have also learned during the last decade that many of the problems so obvious in developing countries that they cannot be ignored—technological and regional dualism, for example—are still present in more subtle form in advanced ones. Failure to achieve complete economic integration helps to explain some of the knottier problems of advanced countries, such as simultaneous inflation and unemployment. Countries do not fall into two neat and easily distinguished categories, underdeveloped and advanced. Instead we have a spectrum of countries, each shading into the other in terms of economic characteristics as we go down the scale of per capita income. By the same token, we do not have one branch of economics relevant to advanced countries and another pertinent to developing ones. The points I made in the final chapter of the first edition— the need to work with discontinuous functions and multisector models, the need to deal with feedbacks rather than equilibrium tendencies and with group reactions rather than individual choices—I would still regard as important, but not as peculiar to the economics of developing countries.

For somewhat the same reasons, I would not now put so much stress on the greater reliability of the market as a guide to policy and a mechanism for achieving national goals in advanced as compared with developing countries. I am not even sure that we have a continuous spectrum in this respect. Each country needs to be analyzed separately in order to determine how and to what extent the market can be used; and there is no very obvious relationship between reliability of the market and level of development. Here, no doubt, I am influenced by my contact with "misdevelopment" in Brazil and Ceylon, both countries where "the law of supply and demand has been repealed," without any superior calculus having been put in place of "revealed preferences in the market." The result in both countries has been serious misallocation of resources. The market still tells us something about what people want and something about opportunity costs. A free market still brings some semiautomatic adjustment to change. A government that knows what it is doing can sometimes bring great improvement in resource allocation by public investment, regulation and control of the private sector, or other forms of intervention. But the market calculus is very much better than no economic calculus at all; and a government with the requisite knowledge can do anything through manipulation of market conditions that it can do by public enterprise and direct controls. In each country it is a matter of analyzing the political and administrative framework within which economic policy must be carried out, to determine the most effective mixture of implements for attaining national goals.

As for the research projects recommended in the earlier final chapter, most of them have, in fact, been carried out, if not always on an adequate scale. It must be confessed that the research helped less than I expected; the pot of golden knowledge buried at the end of the rainbow seems ever to retreat, or disappear altogether, as we approach. But the data on capital-output ratios, capital-job ratios, demographic factors, input-output matrices, linkages and the like, for which I pleaded seven years ago, have been forthcoming in subsantial quantities and have certainly helped.

The appeal to the other social sciences for help has also been heeded. Sociologists, psychologists, political scientists, anthropologists are flocking to the development field. Our danger now is not that our colleagues in the other behavioral sciences will ignore our problems, but that they will inundate us. My hope that some anthropologists would learn to use statistical shortcuts to their brand of knowledge has also been fulfilled, and that profession seems to be shifting its primary interest from primitive to peasant societies, to cultural dynamics, and to application.

Yet we seem as far from a *general* theory as ever. Indeed the flood of new knowledge seems to make generalizations of a kind useful for policy purposes in all developing countries more and more hopeless. In the concluding pages of my part of the UNESCO volume on social aspects of economic development in Latin America, I reported that one of my graduate students, oppressed by the enormity of the development problem and yearning for a "breakthrough" that would make everything simple and clear, cried out in his dissertation, "Where is our Newton?" But as I said there, I do not expect this *cri de coeur* to be followed by any quick relief. It is my view that no Newton will appear, no breakthrough will occur. Development is not that kind of problem. The three great breakthroughs in economics during the last century—the "marginal revolution" of the 1870's, culminating in the "reconstruction of the theory of value" and modern welfare economics; the theories of monopolistic and imperfect competition of the early 1930's; and the Keynesian revolution of the late 1930's—were essentially rearrangements of variables already in the analytical system, with increased emphasis on certain strategic variables so as to bring out fundamentally new conclusions.

Analysis of the process of launching or accelerating economic growth, on the other hand, requires introduction of a whole array of new variables —political, sociological, psychological, and technical. In this situation, gradual accretion of knowledge, rather than a breakthrough in the form of revealing rearrangement of old variables, is the more likely route to scientific progress. Our crying need is still for empirical knowledge about functional relationships in the process of economic and social development. Acquisition of this knowledge will require interdisciplinary teamwork among social scientists, and with natural scientists and engineers as well. Perhaps it is better to abandon the search for a generally applicable theory for a while, and concentrate on the development process in all its aspects as it occurs in particular countries.

The economists' share of this united effort should probably consist of two main kinds of operation. First, theories cast in terms of traditional variables can still be usefully subjected to further empirical testing in a variety of environments. We need not insist on our laws being "necessary and sufficient" for all times and places; we will do well to provide a basis for policy in a particular place at a particular time. Improvements in basic data, in statistical theory, and in computing devices permit us to adopt something closer to the experimental approach of the natural scientists, contenting ourselves with merely sufficient explanations, as long as they fit our observations and do not conflict with other theories that seem to explain even more.

Second, new models can be constructed in which sociological, psychological, and political variables are added to traditional economic variables as parts of a single theoretical system. At the present stage of scientific advance in this field, a good deal of useful work could be done in working out such models which are simply logically consistent and which seem "sufficient" in terms of general observations. Later, as these models are refined, they can be econometrically tested.

The Selection of Categories

Most of us, I think, are now convinced that we are not confronted with a single problem of underdevelopment, but with a range of problems mixed in various ways in different countries. No valid theory which is general enough to fit all underdeveloped countries is likely to provide adequate guidelines for development policy in all underdeveloped countries. Some kind of classification or "typology" is necessary. At a conference on problems of planning in Southeast Asia, one Malayan in the group even insisted that each region of individual countries has its own unique development problems requiring special policies. Should we then have a separate theory for each region of every country, let a thousand flowers grow? Such a conclusion would involve a contradiction of terms; the very word "theory" means selection and generalization. What we need as a basis for policy is something between a completely general theory valid to all regions of all countries and a separate theory for each region of every country. We must learn somehow to group countries in terms of some limited number of essential characteristics that are especially meaningful for diagnosis, prognosis, and prescription regarding development problems. How should they be grouped?

Role of Area Studies

Economic Factors

Area studies programs are springing up on all sides. Do geographic groupings constitute the best analytical categories? Let us look first at

Southeast Asia, the most recalcitrant of major regions. What are the important similarities among Southeast Asian countries from the economic or from the socio-cultural and political point of view? In terms of level of development as measured by per capita income there is a considerable spread between the richest and poorest of Southeast Asian countries—more than 700 per cent. This spread is somewhat smaller than the difference between the richest and poorest Latin American countries, which is about 800 per cent. The poorest countries in Southeast Asia are not markedly worse off than the poorest countries of Latin America; but there are in Southeast Asia no countries comparable to Venezuela and Argentina, which from some points of view should perhaps not be considered underdeveloped at all. Most Latin American countries and most African or Middle East countries are poorer than Malaysia. We cannot distinguish Southeast Asia in terms of levels of per capita income; the range in Southeast Asia is fairly representative of the range for most underdeveloped countries.

We could, perhaps, classify Southeast Asia in terms of rates of growth. The region has been curiously stagnant, and in some sense presents a more acute development problem than any other large geographic region. According to recent estimates by Professor L. J. Zimmerman,[1] over the entire century from 1860 to 1960 Southeast Asia had the slowest rate of growth of per capita income of all major regions (with the possible exception of Africa). In this century the region's share of world population rose from 22.3 per cent to 32.7 per cent, while the share of world income fell from 11.8 to 2.6 per cent. What is so distressing is that Southeast Asia's emergence from colonial status and its concentrated efforts at economic development since World War II have not changed this picture of relative stagnation. During the 1950's, too, it appears that growth of per capita income was lower in Southeast Asia than in other major developing regions.

Southeast Asia also has the highest proportion of its labor force still engaged in agriculture among major regions—once again with the possible exception of Africa. Nor has structural change since World War II been rapid for the region as a whole. In Vietnam and Indonesia, indeed, the share of gross national product produced in the agricultural sector actually increased from 1952–54 to 1961–63; and in no Southeast Asian country did agriculture's share of total output drop as rapidly as in already advanced Australia.[2]

Yet even with respect to these simplest of economic considerations there are significant differences among countries in Southeast Asia. Rates of growth of gross national product for the period of 1955–62 range from 2.1 per cent for Indonesia (implying a slightly falling per capita income) to 7.1 per cent for Thailand (implying a significantly rising per capita income). For the decade 1952–54 to 1961–63, the rise in per capita product

[1] L. J. Zimmerman, *Rich Lands, Poor Lands: The Widening Gap* (New York, 1965), p. 29.
[2] Economic Commission for Asia and the Far East, *Economic Survey of Asia and the Far East* (1964), p. 25.

varied from 0.6 per cent for Indonesia to 2.6 per cent for Burma, as compared with 9 per cent for Japan or 3.3 per cent for Taiwan. In short, growth rates in all Southeast Asian countries were below the 3 per cent generally regarded as a satisfactory target, but there were substantial differences among the countries of the region in this respect. Similarly, both the structure and the rate of structural change vary a good deal. It is clear that Southeast Asia does not constitute an "economic region" in the sense that all the countries in the region are more like each other than any of them is like countries in other regions, in terms of the usual indicators of economic performance.

Socio-Cultural Factors

If economic differences are impressive, do socio-cultural similarities justify lumping Southeast Asian countries together for analytical purposes? Once again the comparison with Latin America is useful. Latin America at least shares a common "Iberian" background; Spain and Portugal are probably more alike than any other pair of colonial powers—although when it comes to the use of violence to settle political disputes I am impressed by the contrast between Brazil and the Spanish American countries. There are Indian populations of varying sizes with their own languages and cultures, but the majority of the people in all countries of Latin America speak one of two closely related languages, are at least nominally Roman Catholic, and have a European culture modified by some generations of life in American frontier society in independent countries.

What are we to say of Southeast Asia regarding socio-cultural attributes? *Pasar Malay* has served as a lingua franca for trade in the area, but the language differences are more significant than the similarities. Even the European colonial powers in the region spoke at least half a dozen different languages. The Hindu-Buddhist culture plays a varying role in the different countries of the region, being expressed in the religion as well as in the arts in Ceylon, Burma, Thailand, and Indochina, persevering in the arts in Malaysia and Indonesia despite the prevalence of another religion, and having virtually disappeared in the Philippines. Indeed the Philippines always impresses me as essentially a Latin American country from this point of view; four centuries of Spain plus four decades of the United States have left a deeper imprint on the life of the people than accidents of ethnic background and geographic location.

Except for Thailand, Southeast Asian countries share the common experience of escaping from colonialism only after World War II. One might add that Thailand was something of a colony from the economic point of view—but then one would have to add also that the Philippines was hardly a colony from the economic standpoint, under either Spain or the United States. Perhaps more significant is bloodshed; the countries doing worst in the region are those that had to fight for their independence, and where nationalism accordingly takes an acute form. On the whole, however, our effort to find a common socio-cultural bond has not been very successful.

Conclusions

I would be inclined to abandon geographic groupings in favor of a typology that would be an amalgam of something like Rostow's "stages" and Roger Vekeman's "levels" of development. I would try first to determine the extent to which political prerequisites for development are present: a "responsible" government, in the sense that the government's decision function reflects the long-run wishes or welfare of the people; a commitment to economic and social development as a high-priority objective within the decision function. Second, I would try to determine the level of absorptive capacity and its relationship to the maximum domestic effort and critical minimum effort. Third, I would look at some socio-cultural factors: levels of education, demographic aspects, and the character of the dominant religion and ideology as they affect economic development. Finally, I would give considerable emphasis to the more purely economic factors: level and rate of growth of per capita income, occupational structure (perhaps above all), balance of payments, income distribution among groups and regions, degree of technological and regional dualism, and so forth. We would then end up with a considerably more sophisticated version of the typology presented in the first edition.

If geographic groupings are not convenient categories for analytical or policy purposes, what is to become of area study programs in our universities? Should the United Nations be reorganized and the Regional Commissions replaced by sections representing sectors (agriculture, industry) or concentrating on Types A, B, C, in accordance with some such composite index as is suggested above?

Obviously, as long as air fares remain as high as they are, there is always a case for decentralizing both research and operations on a geographic basis. Similarly, there is a case to be made for area studies when one or two languages and one or two religions or cultures predominate in a geographic area. Institutes of Middle East studies make sense because most of the people in the region speak Arabic and are Moslem. (On the other hand, an interest in Islam as such can lead you from Indonesia to North Africa.) The prevalence of Spanish and the similarity of Spanish and Portuguese provide a basis for Latin American studies for some time to come.

At the very least, however, the limitations of geographic groupings as analytical categories suggest the desirability of a good deal more cross-fertilization among area experts that we have had in the past. Perhaps area study programs should insist not only on thorough training in some discipline but also on some acquaintance with at least one other region for comparative purposes. I have long felt that there should be more interchange of personnel among the UN Regional Commissions, and more use generally of technical assistance experts in one region with experience in other regions. It might also be a good idea to have Latin American area specialists teaching in Africa and Asia studies programs and vice versa. Perhaps in this way we may avoid the mistake of regarding as peculiar to one region impediments to economic development that are really more general; and perhaps then we will be able to identify more precisely the reasons for the problems of each area.

Toward a Theory of Underdevelopment

Model-building is always useful, but at the present state of knowledge about underdeveloped countries fact-gathering is even more so. When we have our "typology" clearly established we can build models to fit each type. Meanwhile, as pointed out in Chapter 14, there is general recognition that the key lies somewhere in the interactions between the agricultural and industrial sectors (more or less coterminous with the traditional and modern sectors, and in many countries with poor and rich regions)—just as from the beginning of concern over economic fluctuations there was recognition that the key lay somewhere in the savings-investment-consumption interactions. But it took a long time to straighten out the theory of fluctuations and growth, and no chapter in the history of economic thought is sorrier than the "savings equals (does not equal) investment" controversy following the publication of Keynes' *General Theory*. Let us hope that we can straighten out the relationship between industrial and agricultural sectors with less waste of energy, even though the relationship is inherently more complex.

Appendix Tables

APPENDIX TABLE 1

Gross National Product per Capita, 1961 and 1964
(in U.S. Dollars)

	English-speaking and European Countries	1961	1964
Over $2,000	United States	2,790	3,242
	Canada	2,048	2,148
$1,000 to $2,000	Sweden	1,557	1,806
	Switzerland	1,555	1,799
	Australia	1,475	1,755
	New Zealand	1,470	1,611
	Belgium	1,348	1,571
	Great Britain	1,345	1,371
	Norway	1,223	1,306
	France	1,203	1,306
	Denmark	1,193	1,360
	West Germany	1,113	1,275
$500 to $1,000	Netherlands	954	1,107
	Finland	893	1,007
	Austria	830	946
	Italy	623	714
	Ireland	570	638
$250 to $500	South Africa	427	517
	Greece	383	460
	Spain*	321	
$100 to $250	Portugal	240	290
Below $100	—		

* Indicates figures not available.

The 1961 figures were adapted from P. N. Rosenstein-Rodan, "International Aid for Underdeveloped Countries," *Review of Economics and Statistics*, Vol. XLIII (1961), pp. 107–38. The 1964 figures are obtained by calculating percentage increases in official United Nations figures and applying these to the 1961 data.

APPENDIX TABLE 1 (*Continued*)

Communist Countries		1961	1964
Over $2,000	—		
$1,000 to $2,000	—		
$500 to $1,000	Soviet Union	818	973
	East Germany*	700	
	Czechoslovakia	650	650
$250 to $500	Hungary	475	551
	Bulgaria	440	580
	Poland	440	510
	Romania	440	559
	Yugoslavia	306	401
$100 to $250	Albania*	240	
	North Korea	105	127
	North Vietnam*	105	
Below $100	China	83	95

Latin America		1961	1964
Over $2,000	—		
$1,000 to $2,000	—		
$500 to $1,000	Venezuela	644	772
	Puerto Rico	643	746
	Argentina	533	533
$250 to $500	Uruguay*	449	
	Cuba*	413	
	Jamaica	357	403
	Chile	348	369
	Mexico	297	365
	Colombia	287	313
	Panama	283	314— (1962 figures)
	Costa Rica*	278	
	Brazil	268	287
	Dominican Republic*	251	
$100 to $250	Nicaragua	206	262
	El Salvador*	191	
	Guatemala	184	224

APPENDIX TABLE 1 (*Continued*)

	Latin America	1961	1964
	Honduras	180	194
	Peru	179	209
	Ecuador	159	178
	Paraguay	129	135
Below $100	Haiti*	99	
	Bolivia	87	104

	Middle East	1961	1964
Over $2,000	—		
$1,000 to $2,000	—		
$500 to $1,000	Israel	733	1,004
$250 to $500	Lebanon*	319	
$100 to $250	Turkey	222	263
	Algeria*	190	
	Syria	173	249
	Saudi Arabia*	170	
	Iraq*	161	
	Tunisia*	160	
	Egypt*	150	
	Morocco	140	164
	Jordan*	126	
	Iran*	120	
Below $100	Libya*	62	

	Asia	1961	1964
Over $2,000	—		
$1,000 to $2,000	—		
$500 to $1,000	—		

APPENDIX TABLE 1 (*Continued*)

	Asia	1961	1964
$250	Japan	383	498
to	Malaya	368	434
$500			
$100	Philippines	188	211
to	Ceylon	123	130
$250	Taiwan	116	132
	South Vietnam*	111	
	South Korea*	106	
	Thailand	101	113
Below	Indonesia*	99	
$100	Cambodia	77	88
	India	70	80
	Pakistan	62	73
	Burma	61	65
	Afghanistan*	58	
	Laos*	52	
	Nepal*	47	

	Africa	1961	1964
Over $2,000	—		
$1,000 to $2,000	—		
$500 to $1,000	—		
$250 to $500	—		
$100	Rhodesia and Nyasaland	161	176
to	Ghana*	140	
$250	Republic of Congo*	103	
Below	Kenya*	94	
$100	Liberia*	85	
	Nigeria*	84	
	Ethiopia*	76	
	Sudan*	75	
	Tanganyika*	75	
	Uganda	66	77
	Togoland*	55	

Appendix Table 2
Indices of Levels of Development

Country	Economy						Social stratification				
	Per capita income	Per capita electric consumption	Cement consumption	Newsprint consumption	Calorie intake	% labor force in agriculture	% urban population	% intermed. & senior grades of employment in secondary sectors	% labor force in primary sectors	% labor force in secondary and tertiary sectors	% employed in industry proper
Group I:											
Haiti	10	10	10	10	:	10	10	10	10	10	10
Guatemala	8	10	10	10	:	9	8	9	10	8	6
Honduras	9	10	10	10	:	10	9	10	10	10	9
Dominican Republic	8	10	7	10	:	8	9	:	:	:	6
Nicaragua	9	10	9	10	:	8	7	:	:	:	10
El Salvador	9	10	9	9	:	7	8	8	10	7	5
Group II:											
Paraguay	9	10	10	10	:	5	8	7	9	6	9
Bolivia	10	10	10	10	:	5	7	9	10	8	8
Group III:											
Peru	9	9	7	9	10	7	7	:	:	:	7
Ecuador	9	10	9	9	:	5	8	8	10	4	10
Colombia	7	8	7	9	:	5	6	5	5	5	7
Group IV:											
Brazil	7	9	9	9	7	7	7	7	10	7	3
Mexico	7	7	8	8	8	6	5	6	9	:	2

APPENDIX TABLE 2 (*Continued*)

Country	Economy						Social Stratification				
	Per capita income	Per capita electric consumption	Cement consumption	Newsprint consumption	Calorie intake	% labor force in agriculture	% urban population	% intermed. & senior grades of employment in secondary sectors	% labor force in primary sectors	% labor force in secondary and tertiary sectors	% employed in industry proper
Group V:											
Panama	7	8	5	6	..	5	6	7	10	5	5
Costa Rica	8	9	8	8	..	6	8	5	6	5	5
Venezuela	1	1	1	8	8	3	4	6	9	3	1
Cuba	5	7	6	4	..	3	5	5	10	4	3
Group VI:											
Chile	4	5	6	5	5	1	3	5	10	1	4
Uruguay	3	6	5	2	1	1	1	1	1	..	2
Argentina	2	5	6	1	1	1	3	1	1	1	2

APPENDIX TABLE 2 (*Continued*)

Country	Culture							Standard of Living				Ethnography	
	% illiteracy	% primary school enrollment	% secondary school enrollment	% university enrollment per 10,000 inhab.	Newspaper circ. as % of pop.	% radio sets	% cinema seats	Doctors per 100,000 inhab.	No. inhab. per hospital bed	Birth rate per thousand	Death rate per thousand	% foreigners	% Indians & Negroes
Group I:													
Haiti	10	10	10	10	10	10	10	10	10	10	10	10	10
Guatemala	8	10	10	10	9	10	8	10	4	9	10	10	2
Honduras	7	9	10	10	9	10	8	10	5	8	7	9	2
Dominican Republic	6	2	10	10	9	9	9	10	2	10	9	10	2
Nicaragua	7	8	10	10	6	10	4	9	3	9	8	10	6
El Salvador	7	7	9	10	8	10	8	10	3	8	9	10	2
Group II:													
Paraguay	3	2	9	8	9	8	9	7	4	8	7	8	1
Bolivia	8	7	9	9	9	8	9	9	3	8	8	10	8
Group III:													
Peru	6	6	9	8	6	7	9	9	3	8	9	..	7
Ecuador	4	5	9	9	8	10	6	9	3	8	7	10	5
Colombia	4	7	9	9	7	2	6	8	2	8	5	10	2
Group IV:													
Brazil	5	7	9	9	7	8	6	8	2	8	8	9	2
Mexico	4	5	10	8	..	7	3	8	6	7	6	10	4

APPENDIX TABLE 2 (Continued)

Country	Culture							Standard of Living				Ethnography	
	% illiteracy	% primary school enrollment	% secondary school enrollment	% university enrollment per 10,000 inhab.	Newspaper circ. as % of pop.	% radio sets	% cinema seats	Doctors per 100,000 inhab.	No. inhab. per hospital bed	Birth rate per thousand	Death rate per thousand	% foreigners	% Indians & Negroes
Group V:													
Panama	3	3	5	7	4	6	3	9	1	8	7	7	3
Costa Rica	1	3	6	8	5	8	3	8	1	8	5	8	1
Venezuela	5	6	9	9	5	6	2	7	1	8	7	8	2
Cuba	2	4	9	6	3	5	1	3	1	4	4	8	2
Group VI:													
Chile	1	2	6	6	3	7	3	7	1	6	4	10	1
Uruguay	1	3	5	5	1	1	5	4	1	1	1	1	1
Argentina	1	1	1	1	1	4	3	1	1	1	1	1	1

SOURCE: UNESCO, *Social Aspects of Economic Development in Latin America*, Vol. 1, Paris, 1963, pp. 88-89.

Appendix Table 3a
Yield of Principal Crops (100 kilograms per hectare)

Crop	World			Europe			North & Central America		
	1948/49–1952/53	1963/64	1964/65	1948/49–1952/53	1963/64	1964/65	1948/49–1952/53	1963/64	1964/65
Wheat	10.1	12.0	12.7	14.7	19.8	19.8	11.6	17.4	16.4
Rye	9.9	13.1	11.5	14.6	17.8	18.4	8.0	11.8	11.9
Barley	11.4	14.4	15.6	16.9	26.0	26.8	14.3	18.6	18.7
Oats	11.6	14.6	14.7	16.0	20.0	19.4	12.7	16.6	15.7
Maize	15.8	21.6	20.1	12.4	23.9	25.1	22.1	33.6	30.7
Millet & sorghum	5.0	7.4	7.4	8.6	16.9	20.0	12.1	25.4	24.0
Rice (paddy)	16.0	20.5	20.7	42.6	47.5	46.5	22.1	31.4	32.2
Potatoes	106.9	112.5	121.2	137.7	169.7	167.9	149.8	204.8	191.8
Sweet potatoes & yams	69.1	73.8	75.8	146.7	120.0	130.0	45.5	61.1	58.5
Cotton (lint)	2.4	3.4	3.4	1.5	3.8	4.1	3.2	5.9	6.0

APPENDIX TABLE 3a (*Continued*)

Crop	South America 1948/49–1952/53	1963/64	1964/65	Asia 1948/49–1952/53	1963/64	1964/65	Africa 1948/49–1952/53	1963/64	1964/65	Oceania 1948/49–1952/53	1963/64	1964/65
Wheat	10.7	13.3	16.3	8.2	9.0	8.6	7.1	9.1	8.0	11.3	13.6	14.0
Rye	7.4	8.3	8.5	10.0	12.6	10.4	3.8	1.6	4.4	5.0	4.0	5.0
Barley	11.3	12.9	12.3	10.2	9.8	9.6	6.5	6.6	6.7	12.1	12.8	14.0
Oats	10.6	12.2	13.0	10.4	12.3	12.4	7.1	2.0	4.9	7.1	9.1	9.1
Maize	12.4	12.4	13.6	8.0	10.5	11.5	8.5	9.9	10.8	17.5	21.1	22.2
Millet & sorghum	7.7	14.5	11.6	3.8	4.8	5.0	..	..	..	13.3	13.3	13.8
Rice (paddy)	17.2	18.8	15.3	14.0	17.8	18.3	12.4	17.1	17.8	30.0	47.1	48.6
Potatoes	52.9	60.2	70.1	80.5	91.7	..	60.6	75.0	68.1	96.7	136.7	144.0
Sweet potatoes & yams	77.4	95.0	92.6	94.3	101.2	102.4	69.1	..	..	110.0	..	..
Cotton (lint)	1.8	2.2	2.0	1.4	1.9	1.9	2.2	2.3	2.6	1.8	4.0	..

SOURCE: Food and Agriculture Organization, *Statistical Yearbook, 1964* (Rome, 1965).

APPENDIX TABLE 3b

Rice (paddy) Production (100 kilograms per hectare)

Country	1948/49– 1952/53	1962/63	1963/64	1964/65
Italy	48.5	56.0	51.2	51.6
United States	25.6	41.8	44.4	45.9
Australia	48.6	61.1	59.1	61.4
Argentina	30.5	34.1	35.2	48.6
Brazil	15.7	15.4	15.2	..
Mexico	18.0	22.7	21.9	20.7
Algeria	..	40.0	35.0	25.3
Nigeria	14.8	..	..	..
United Arab Republic	37.9	58.4	..	..
Burma	14.6	16.5	16.0	16.4
China (mainland)	21.7	..	..	..
India	11.1	13.7	15.4	16.1
Indonesia	16.1	18.3	17.4	..
Japan	42.5	52.8	52.4	51.5
Philippines	11.8	12.5	12.2	12.5
Thailand	13.1	15.0	15.9	16.0
Vietnam (Republic of)	13.6	21.0	21.0	20.2
USSR	14.5	22.6	25.6	24.3

Source: Food and Agriculture Organization, *Statistical Yearbook, 1964* (Rome, 1965).

APPENDIX TABLE 3c

Soybean Production (100 kilogram per hectare)

Country	1948/49– 1952/53	1962/63	1963/64	1964/65
Czechoslovakia	11.6	..	..	..
Italy	14.0	17.8	18.1	18.7
Yugoslavia	5.2	10.4	13.0	16.7
United States	14.3	16.3	15.6	15.3
Canada	15.9	20.2	14.8	20.3
Argentina	9.5	9.8	11.5	9.4
Brazil	13.4	9.5	8.5	..
Colombia	..	14.6	15.1	20.1
China (mainland)	8.1	7.9	8.0	..
China (Taiwan)	6.0	9.6	9.8	11.3
Indonesia	7.1	6.7	6.0	6.7
Japan	10.8	12.6	13.6	11.1
Thailand	8.0	10.6	10.6	11.4
Vietnam (Republic of)	..	7.1	7.6	6.7
USSR	4.0	4.5	..	..

Source: Food and Agriculture Organization, *Statistical Yearbook, 1964* (Rome, 1965).

APPENDIX TABLE 3d
Tobacco Production (100 kilograms per hectare)

Country	1948/49–1952/53	1962/63	1963/64	1964/65
Italy	13.4	13.0	13.4	14.7
United States	14.2	21.2	22.3	25.5
Canada	14.4	17.4	19.8	19.7
Australia	10.2	12.4	13.9	12.6
Argentina	10.4	13.4	10.4	10.8
Brazil	7.6	8.1	8.3	8.4
Chile	20.3	23.3	22.9	20.5
Mexico	10.0	12.3	13.0	13.0
Algeria	6.6	6.0	6.2	6.1
Burma	9.2	8.5	9.6	8.1
China (mainland)	11.8	..	..	..
India	7.5	8.3	8.8	8.5
Indonesia	..	4.1	4.2	..
Estates	5.5	..	..	..
Farms	4.1	..	..	..
Japan	17.3	21.9	21.6	25.9
Philippines	6.1	7.0	6.9	6.6
USSR	7.4	9.8	10.3	15.0

SOURCE: Food and Agriculture Organization, *Statistical Yearbook, 1964* (Rome, 1965).

APPENDIX TABLE 3e
Maize Production (100 kilograms per hectare)

Country	1948/49–1952/53	1962/63	1963/64	1964/65
Italy	18.4	29.1	32.9	36.6
United States	24.9	40.3	42.4	39.3
Australia	17.6	22.4	19.7	20.1
Argentina	14.8	16.5	18.0	16.8
Brazil	12.4	13.2	10.7	..
Mexico	7.5	9.4	9.5	10.9
Algeria	9.1	5.4	11.4	..
Nigeria	8.8	..	..	..
United Arab Republic	20.9	26.0	23.5	..
Burma	4.5	5.2	5.2	5.8
China (mainland)	..	..	..	..
India	6.5	9.9	9.9	9.9
Indonesia	7.6	10.2	9.4	10.8
Japan	14.2	24.6	26.7	23.3
Philippines	7.2	6.5	6.5	6.8
Thailand	9.1	20.7	23.4	21.9
Vietnam (Republic of)	12.1	10.6	10.0	12.4
USSR	13.1	16.6	13.2	..

SOURCE: Food and Agriculture Organization, *Statistical Yearbook, 1964* (Rome, 1965).

APPENDIX TABLE 3f

Wheat Production (100 kilograms per hectare)

Country	1948/49– 1952/53	1962/63	1963/64	1964/65
Czechoslovakia	19.0	24.5	24.6	22.2
France	18.3	30.7	26.6	31.5
Germany, East	26.2	31.1	30.0	31.1
Federal Republic	26.2	34.8	35.1	36.0
Greece	10.2	16.2	14.8	17.9
Italy	15.2	20.8	18.5	19.5
Lebanon	7.3	11.0	10.9	..
Poland	12.5	19.4	19.9	18.7
United Kingdom	27.2	43.5	39.1	41.4
United States	11.2	16.9	17.0	17.7
Canada	12.8	14.2	17.6	13.6
Australia	11.2	12.5	13.4	..
Argentina	11.5	14.6	15.0	18.6
Bolivia	6.1	..	..	..
Brazil	7.4	9.2	4.9	8.8
Chile	11.9	15.1	15.3	13.6
Guatemala	5.8	..	..	..
Peru	9.2	9.9	10.1	9.9
Uruguay	9.2	11.3	6.6	12.2
Algeria	6.2	8.0	7.8	5.1
Congo, Democratic Republic	8.7	..	..	..
Ethiopia	3.9	7.0	7.0	7.1
United Arab Republic	18.4	26.1	25.9	27.6
Burma	2.9	4.1	5.6	6.8
China (mainland)	6.9	..	..	..
China (Taiwan)	9.6	20.7	13.0	21.0
India	6.6	8.9	7.9	7.3
Japan	18.5	25.4	12.3	24.5
USSR	8.4	10.5	7.7	10.9

SOURCE: Food and Agriculture Organization, *Statistical Yearbook, 1964* (Rome, 1965).

APPENDIX TABLE 4
Growth of Real Product in Less-developed Countries, 1950–1964

	1960 Country Weight in the Continental Total[1]	Annual Compound Growth Rates		
		1950/55	1955/60	1960/64	1950/52 to 1962/64
Europe	100.0	7.0	5.3	7.9	6.1
Cyprus	1.1	4.6	2.7	2.6	4.0
Greece	12.0	6.5	5.0	8.5	6.4
Malta	0.5	4.8	4.7	−1.4	3.1
Spain	38.7	8.4	3.5	9.6	5.9
Turkey	21.5	6.4	5.2	4.0	4.6
Yugoslavia	26.2	5.3	8.6	8.5	7.7
Other	×	(7.0)	(5.3)	(7.9)	(6.1)
Africa[2]	100.0	4.3	4.7	4.0	4.4
North of Sahara[2]	36.5	4.0	5.8	(4.3)	(4.8)
Algeria	11.8	4.6	9.3	(1.6)	(6.1)
Morocco	7.1	3.3	0.5	3.4	2.2
Tunisia	3.1	2.7	4.5	5.8	3.9
UAR (Egypt)	14.3	4.3	6.6	(6.4)	5.6
Other	0.2	(4.0)	(5.8)	(4.3)	(4.8)
South of Sahara	63.5	4.5	4.0	3.9	4.1
Ethiopia	4.4	3.6	4.5	3.7	4.1
Ghana	5.3	4.0	3.7	3.7	4.0
Kenya	2.5	7.4	3.5	4.3	5.0
Malawi	0.5	3.8	4.5	(1.0)	(3.4)
Nigeria	10.2	5.5	3.0	4.5	4.0
Rhodesia	3.1	6.6	6.4	3.5	5.7
Sudan	4.4	4.8	5.0	4.6	5.2
Tanzania	2.2	7.2	3.0	3.3	3.2
Uganda	1.7	2.3	3.7	3.3	3.7
Zambia	2.4	1.5	8.2	3.4	4.2
Francophone countries[3]	14.6	(3.7)	(3.7)	(3.7)	(3.7)
Other	12.2	(4.5)	(4.0)	(3.9)	(4.1)
Latin America[4]	100.0	4.8	4.9	4.4	4.8
Argentina	21.4	2.9	3.2	2.0	2.9
Bolivia	0.7	1.2	1.4	4.9	1.9
Brazil	23.1	5.7	5.9	4.3	5.6
British Guiana	0.2	3.3	4.6	1.6	3.4
Chile	6.2	3.1	4.1	3.5	3.5
Colombia	6.2	5.3	4.0	4.8	4.6
Costa Rica	0.6	4.9	4.9	4.6	4.8
Dominican Republic	0.8	7.1	5.8	3.2	6.0
Ecuador	1.4	5.4	4.5	4.0	4.5
El Salvador	0.7	4.5	3.6	12.1	6.8
Guatemala	1.2	2.3	5.3	6.1	4.4
Haiti	0.5	1.5	2.3	0.7	1.5
Honduras	0.4	2.3	4.8	4.3	3.7
Jamaica	0.6	10.0	6.6	4.7	7.3

APPENDIX TABLE 4 (*Continued*)

	1960 Country Weight in the Continental Total[1]	Annual Compound Growth Rates			
		1950/55	1955/60	1960/64	1950/52 to 1962/64
Mexico	21.4	6.1	6.2	6.2	5.9
Netherlands Antilles	0.2	0.8	0.8	−1.1	0.4
Nicaragua	0.4	9.2	2.3	10.1	6.4
Panama	0.5	3.7	5.3	8.1	5.6
Paraguay	0.5	2.9	2.4	3.5	3.0
Peru	3.8	5.4	4.8	7.2	5.7
Surinam	0.1	6.2	7.8	2.8	6.1
Trinidad & Tobago	0.5	8.5	9.9	6.8	8.9
Uruguay	1.7	2.0	..	0.2	0.7
Venezuela	6.2	8.7	6.4	5.0	6.6
Other	0.7	(5.6)	(5.7)	(5.8)	(4.8)
Asia[5]	100.0	4.5	4.5	5.2	4.6
Middle East	17.1	7.5	6.2	6.7	6.7
Iran	6.2	5.0	5.9	3.8	4.8
Iraq	2.2	14.0	6.8	6.2	9.4
Israel	2.6	13.0	9.3	10.8	10.2
Jordan	0.4	2.6	11.5	11.1	8.2
Lebanon	0.7	6.4	(0.1)	(8.5)	(5.2)
Syria	0.8	4.3	2.7	11.5	5.5
Other	4.2	(7.5)	(6.2)	(6.7)	(6.7)
Other Asia[5]	82.9	4.0	4.2	4.9	4.2
Burma	2.0	7.0	5.7	2.0	5.0
Cambodia	0.8	4.5	8.3	4.0	5.7
Ceylon	1.8	4.9	3.0	2.9	3.4
China (Taiwan)	2.0	8.2	6.5	8.2	7.4
India	43.5	3.4	4.1	4.4	3.7
Korea (South)	4.4	6.7	4.2	5.6	6.1
Malaya	2.7	3.0	4.1	6.2	4.2
Pakistan	10.0	1.9	3.6	5.4	3.5
Philippines	6.0	6.9	4.5	4.7	5.4
Thailand	3.5	6.5	6.1	6.9	6.3
Vietnam (South)	2.0	4.7	2.3	5.0	3.5
Other	4.2	(4.0)	(4.2)	(4.9)	(4.2)
All Less-Developed Countries[6]		4.9	4.8	5.0	4.8

Notes to Appendix Table 4

[1] Share of GDP at market prices of component countries. For a few countries this aggregate was not available and had to be replaced by another similar aggregate. Estimates of GDP in 1960 excluding Congo (Leopoldville) and Indonesia amount to:

	$ Billion
Europe	26.4
Africa	25.2
Latin America (at purchasing power equivalents)	101.2
Asia	75.6
Oceania	0.5
All Less-Developed Countries	228.9

The figure for Latin America is not strictly comparable to the data for other continents. By using prevailing exchange rates GDP of Latin America would amount to only some $70 billion.

[2] Excluding Congo (Leopoldville).

[3] Cameroon, Central African Republic, Chad, Congo (Brazzaville), Dahomey, Gabon, Ivory Coast, Madagascar, Mali, Mauritania, Niger, Senegal, Togo, and Upper Volta.

[4] Excluding Cuba.

[5] Excluding Indonesia.

[6] According to the U.N. Yearbook of National Accounts Statistics, 1965 (Table 8B, p. 488) growth rates of less-developed countries combined were the following:

4.7 per cent for 1950/55
4.6 per cent for 1955/60
4.1 per cent for 1960/63

They are lower than the rates shown in the table because:

   i) The U.N. do not include as less-developed countries Greece, Spain, Turkey, and Yugoslavia, which have high growth rates.

  ii) The calculations give a bigger weight to Latin America, which is growing faster than average, by using purchasing power equivalents taken from ECLA sources. High growth rates registered in 1964 are responsible for the discrepancy with UN data for the last period.

To the extent possible the data have been derived from national sources. When these were not available the following sources were used: *UN National Accounts Yearbooks*, *UN Monthly Bulletin of Statistics* of June 1966, information from the French Ministry of Co-operation on Francophone Africa, the AID paper "Gross National Product, Growth Rates and Trend Data, by Region and Country" (RC. W138) of June 15, 1966, and the *AID Data Book*. For Greece, Spain, Turkey and Yugoslavia submissions to the OECD have been used also. Estimates by the Development Centre could not be avoided for a few countries, but were kept to the strict minimum.

GDP data were usually converted into US dollars by using prevailing exchange rates; in some cases the arithmetic average of rates published by the IMF had to be used. For Latin American countries recent unpublished ECLA estimates of the purchasing power of currencies provided the necessary conversion factors.

Source: OECD, *Development Assistance Efforts and Policies*, Paris, 1967.

APPENDIX TABLE 5

Crude Live-Birth Rates; Rates are the Number of Live Births
per 1,000 Population

Country	Rate		
	1920–24	1940–44	1960–64
United States	22.8	19.9	22.4
Canada	28.1	23.2	25.2
United Kingdom	21.7	15.9	18.2
Germany	23.1	17.4	17.5
Federal Republic of Germany			18.3
Italy	30.1	20.7	18.9
France	19.9	14.7	18.0
U.S.S.R.	44.4*	31.4	22.4
Greece	29.7*	18.6**	26.1
Yugoslavia	35.3	28.2**	22.0
Japan	35.0	30.1	17.2
Philippines	33.7*	32.5	27.4
Thailand	27.7	35.2	35.3
Israel	34.5	25.1	25.5
Indonesia	..	28.5	48.0
India†	46.4	39 9	38.4
Algeria	20.9	42.4	45.9
Mauritius	37.3	34.0	38.9
United Arab Republic	42.8	39.6	42.8
Mexico	31.4	44.2	46.0
Argentina	32.0	24.1	22.4
Brazil	..	43.0	40–43
Colombia	27.1	44.0	39.1
Uruguay	26.0	18.7	24.6
Venezuela	29.9	35.7	44.2
Cuba	18.9*	22.2	34.7

* 1925–29 (1920–24 data not available).
** 1945–49 (1940–44 data not available).
† India: estimated averages for 1921-31, 1940-51.
SOURCE: United Nations, *Demographic Yearbook, 1965,* New York, 1966.

APPENDIX TABLE 6

Total Official and Private Flow to Less-developed Countries and
Multilateral Agencies, 1956–65
Million U.S. Dollars

Country	1956	1957	1958	1959	1960	1961	1962	1963	1964	1965[1]
Australia[2]	(39)	(47)	(47)	(57)	(66)	(72.9)	(84.5)	(96.4)	(126.8)	143.6
Austria	4	−4	6	−1	6	20.2	31.0	5.9	21.3	47.4
Belgium	90	36	112	168	182	174.5	128.2	184.9	174.7	238.7
Canada	106	131	155	83	145	100.9	109.6	130.5	156.9	153.0
Denmark	5	2	5	21	38	33.3	14.7	(10.5)	31.8	16.0
France	1,124	1,227	1,337	1,172	1,325	1,432.3	1,407.5	1,264.6	1,381.5	1,318.6
Germany	436	545	520	799	616	834.6	632.0	589.0	690.8	705.3
Italy	134	209	155	149	303	262.4	411.9	343.2	241.8	277.2
Japan	123	118	320	195	249	387.4	295.1	278.4	303.8	485.6
Netherlands	280	147	200	264	250	213.7	143.0	147.2	128.3	224.3
Norway	9	9	3	7	10	9.9	10.9	28.7	26.7	38.2
Portugal[3]	3	2	1	17	37	43.8	40.8	51.1	61.9	30.7
Sweden	15	25	27	45	47	51.9	37.3	53.4	67.2	69.5
United Kingdom	589	957	668	844	796	900.6	727.4	694.6	907.9	923.1
United States	3,236	4,100	3,685	3,276	3,876	4,629.3	4,490.0	4,635.0	4,759.6	5,478.2
Total DAC Countries	6,193	7,551	7,241	7,096	7,947	9,167.6	8,563.9	8,513.4	9,081.0	10,149.4

[1] In order to permit totaling, certain 1964 private data have been used for Denmark.
[2] For the years 1956–1963 figures relate only to official gross flows. Figures for the years 1956–1964 are on a fiscal year basis.
[3] For the years 1956–1964, official flows only.

SOURCE: OECD, Development Assistance Efforts and Policies, Paris, 1966, p. 147.

APPENDIX TABLE 7

Summary of Growth Indicators in Selected AID-Assisted Countries, 1950–1961

Country	Time Period Covered*	Compound Annual Growth Rate (%)				Ratio of GNP in 1960–61 of		Marginal Rates	
		Population	GNP	Gross Investment	Domestic Savings	Gross Investment	Domestic Savings	Domestic Savings	Ratio of Gross Investment to Increased GNP
Argentina	1950–1961	2.0	1.5	0.1	-1.9	20.3	16.2	neg.	13.7
Brazil	1950–1961	2.5	5.5	5.7	5.2	14.9	12.1	12	3.0
Chile	1951–1961	2.6	3.3	1.8	-3.9	10.6	5.7	neg.	3.3
Colombia	1950–1961	2.8	4.4	4.4	3.3	20.9	18.4	15	2.3
Costa Rica	1950–1961	4.2	5.8	5.2	0.8	17.6	11.7	2	3.6
Cyprus	1953–1961	2.0	0.3	0	-10.6	15.6	6.3	neg.	14.9
Ghana	1955–1961	3.0	5.7	14.1	6.7	20.5	13.1	15	2.9
Greece	1950–1961	0.9	6.1	7.0	20.4	24.0	12.8	23	3.2
Guatemala	1950–1961	3.1	4.9	2.9	-2.3	11.0	6.6	neg.	2.7
Honduras	1950–1961	3.3	4.5	2.8	2.6	13.4	12.9	8	3.3
India	1950–1961	2.3	4.1	10.3	9.0	16.4	14.1	25	3.2
Israel	1950–1961	3.5	10.6	7.9	..	27.8	4.0	18	2.9
Malaya	1956–1961	3.2	3.3	1.6	8.5	10.9	17.3	39	3.7
Mexico	1950–1961	3.1	4.7	7.1	6.8	17.2	16.1	21	3.5
Nigeria	1950–1961	1.9	3.7	11.9	3.8	14.4	8.9	9	3.2

* In computing growth rates and marginal rates, two year averages from the beginning and end of the time period shown have been used as end points.

APPENDIX TABLE 7 (Continued)

Country	Time Period Covered*	Compound Annual Growth Rate (%)				Ratio of GNP in 1960–61 of		Marginal Rates	
		Population	GNP	Gross Investment	Domestic Savings	Gross Investment	Domestic Savings	Domestic Savings	Ratio of Gross Investment to Increased GNP
Pakistan	1950–1961	2.2	2.2	7.0	10.0	10.8	8.1	32	3.7
Peru	1950–1961	2.8	2.9	1.9	2.9	21.5	22.1	22	8.8
Philippines	1953–1961	3.2	5.0	6.9	5.7	9.2	6.7	8	2.0
Sudan	1956–1961	2.8	2.1	0.8	−6.3	10.4	7.6	neg.	4.7
Taiwan	1951–1961	3.5	7.7	9.7	12.5	21.9	13.5	18	2.6
Thailand	1952–1961	3.2	5.4	6.6	8.3	15.2	14.6	20	2.9
Tunisia	1950–1961	2.2	3.3	1.4	−0.3	17.5	7.2	neg.	4.7
Turkey	1950–1961	2.9	4.9	6.3	6.1	11.4	8.9	11	2.7
Venezuela	1953–1961	3.2	6.5	−2.2	1.4	18.3	23.6	6	4.5
Yugoslavia	1952–1961	1.4	9.3	11.6	13.7	37.5	31.7	40	4.0

* In computing growth rates and marginal rates, two year averages from the beginning and end of the time period shown have been used as end points.

SOURCE: U.S. Agency for International Development.

Definitions of Data Shown on Country Charts of Trends and Growth Rates
in Gross National Product, Savings, U.S. Economic Aid, etc.
(all data converted to U.S. dollar equivalents in
constant 1960 prices except as noted)

1. *Gross National Product* is GNP in market prices converted to 1960 constant prices.
2. *Net Foreign Balance*—balance on goods and services in *current prices*. No attempt was made to convert N.F.B. to a constant price basis.
3. *Gross Investment* includes changes in stocks except for Ghana and India where gross fixed investment was used.
4. *Consumption* is the residual between Available Resources (GNP plus NFB) and Gross Investment.
5. *Savings* is "domestic savings" defined to be GNP *minus* Consumption *or* Gross Investment *minus* Net Foreign Balance.
6. *U.S. Economic Aid*—consists of expenditures under the economic aid programs of A.I.D. (and its predecessor agencies) *plus* sales agreements concluded under PL 480 Title I *plus* all other economic aid (Title II and III, Ex-Im Bank and Other) on an obligation or commitment basis.
7. *Constant Per Capita Consumption*—the *current* population growth rate was applied to the consumption figure for the first year shown. Thus the "constant per capita consumption" trend line is the amount of consumption required to keep pace with population at the 1961 rate of population growth (i.e., the total consumption projects in any year to provide the same amount of per capita consumption as in the base year.)
8. *Ratios as percents shown in "inset" table:*
   (a) $\frac{\text{NFB}}{\text{Invest}}$ = Net Foreign Balance divided by Gross Investment for selected periods (2-year average).
   (b) $\frac{\text{Savings}}{\text{GNP}}$ = Domestic Savings divided by Gross National Product for selected periods (2-year average).
   (c) Marginal Savings Rate is the increment in *Domestic Savings* between the initial period (2-year average) and the final period (2-year average) divided by the similar increment for Gross National Product.
9. *Growth Rates*—These are annual rates of growth over the period computed at a *compound* rate. The growth rates were computed between the 2-year average for an initial period and the 2-year average of an ending period, generally 1950–1951 to 1960–1961. The time interval for this period was 10 years.
10. Projected data were derived by linking unreviewed figures submitted in the Country Annual Program submissions to the 1961 estimates published in S&R Regional Data Books.
11. Exchange rates used for dollar conversion in all years were the official rates existing in 1961. The exception occurred in those cases where net foreign balances were taken from International Monetary Fund publications. In these cases the IMF conversion to dollars was accepted without change.

APPENDIX TABLE 8

Average Dietary Supply of Calories as Compared with Requirements

Region and Country	Recent Level	Estimated Requirements	Percentage Difference
Far East			
Ceylon	2080	2270	− 8.3
India	2000	2250	−11.1
Japan	2230	2330	− 4.2
Philippines	1810	2230	−18.0
Middle East			
Cyprus	..	2510	
Egypt (UAR)	2670	2390	+11.7
Turkey	3110*	2440	+27.4
Africa			
French North Africa	..	2430	
Mauritius*	2370	2410	− 1.6
Union of South Africa	2820†	2440	+17.5
Latin America			
Argentina	2810	2600	+ 8.0
Brazil	2800	2450	+14.2
Chile	2410	2640	− 8.6
Mexico	2600	2490	+ 4.4
Uruguay	2970**	2570	+15.5
Europe			
Denmark	3370	2750	+22.5
France	2940‡	2550	+15.2
Greece	2940	2390	+23.0
Italy	2740	2440	+12.2
Norway	2930	2850	+ 2.8
United Kingdom	3270	2650	+23.3
North America and Oceania			
Australia	3140	2620	+19.8
United States	3100	2640	+17.4

* FAO, Yearbook 1964, Rome 1965—1960/62 level.
† 1960/61 level.
** 1961.
‡ 1957/1959.

APPENDIX TABLE 9
Indicators of Health and Education

	Percent of Population Age 15 or Over Illiterate*	Year	Number of Inhabitants per Physician†	Year
Rich				
Australia	below 5		880	1962
Canada	below 5		860	1961
United Kingdom	below 5		960	1960
United States	below 5		760	1962
Poor				
Brazil	..	..	2,500	1959
Chile	21.8	1960	1,600	1960
Colombia	..	..	2,400	1960
Egypt (UAR)	73.7	1960	..	..
India	76.0	1961	5,800	1961
Indonesia	57.1	1961	41,000	1962
Mexico	34.6	1960	1,800	1961
Venezuela	34.2	1961	1,400	1962

* UN, *Demographic Yearbook, 1963*, New York, 1964.
† UN, *Statistical Yearbook, 1964*, New York, 1965.

Value of U.S. Direct Investments Abroad[1] by Selected Countries and
(millions of dollars)

			1964[r]					
Line	Area and country	Total	Mining and smelting	Petroleum	Manufacturing	Public utilities	Trade	Other
1	All areas, total	44,386	3,569	14,334	16,931	2,020	3,688	3,844
2	Canada	13,796	1,667	3,187	6,194	471	805	1,473
3	Latin American Republics, total	8,894	1,104	3,102	2,341	568	947	832
4	Mexico	1,034	128	56	606	27	111	106
5	Panama	659	19	103	23	29	281	205
6	Other Central America and West Indies	589	31	139	46	142	26	205
7	Argentina	882	(*)	(*)	500	(*)	40	343
8	Brazil	997	40	53	668	41	153	41
9	Chile	789	500	(*)	30	(*)	20	239
10	Colombia	508	(*)	255	148	30	53	22
11	Peru	464	241	60	65	22	46	31
12	Venezuela	2,786	(*)	2,139	220	18	199	210
13	Other countries	186	7	67	35	21	18	38
14	Other Western Hemisphere	1,311	250	488	166	47	89	271
15	Europe, total	12,109	56	3,102	6,587	53	1,446	864
16	Common Market, total	5,426	13	1,523	3,139	45	528	178
17	Belgium and Luxembourg	455	(**)	66	299	1	73	16
18	France	1,446	10	286	909	22	174	46
19	Germany	2,082	(*)	577	1,326	5	117	57
20	Italy	850	(*)	350	389	2	72	37
21	Netherlands	593	(**)	244	216	16	92	25
22	Other Europe, total	6,683	43	1,579	3,448	8	918	687

[r] Revised.   [p] Preliminary.   * Combined in "Other industries."   ** Less than $500,000.
[1] The value of direct investments abroad was reduced in 1964 by $147 million, and in 1965 by $65 million, owing to valuation adjustments on companies' books, profits and losses on liquidations, or transfers to other investment categories. In particular, the value of direct investments in the public utilities industry in Brazil was reduced by $153 million as of the end of 1964 by a settlement with the Brazilian Government. The equivalent value

Industries, at Yearend 1964 and 1965

			1965ᵖ			
Total	Mining and smelt- ing	Petro- leum	Manu- factur- ing	Public utili- ties	Trade	Other
49,217	3,794	15,320	19,280	2,134	4,191	4,499
15,172	1,755	3,320	6,855	486	881	1,875
9,371	1,114	3,034	2,741	596	1,034	852
1,177	103	48	752	27	138	109
704	19	122	24	38	288	213
621	35	152	60	147	30	197
992	(*)	(*)	617	(*)	47	328
1,073	51	57	722	37	162	45
829	509	(*)	39	(*)	24	257
527	(*)	269	160	29	49	20
515	263	60	79	21	53	38
2,715	(*)	2,033	248	19	222	194
219	8	89	40	21	21	40
1,437	310	500	199	45	91	291
13,894	55	3,429	7,570	60	1,716	1,065
6,254	16	1,617	3,688	46	658	229
585	(**)	71	373	1	103	37
1,584	10	280	1,052	14	177	51
2,417	(*)	610	1,547	12	170	77
972	(*)	404	446	2	80	39
698	(**)	252	270	17	127	31
7,639	39	1,811	3,881	14	1,058	836

was added to the total for U.S. private portfolio investments included in table 14. The value of investments in
specific industries and countries is also affected by
capital flows among foreign affiliates as shown in table 9.

APPENDIX TABLE 10 (*Continued*)

Line	Area and country	Total	Mining and smelt-ing	Petro-leum	Manu-factur-ing	Public utili-ties	Trade	Other
								1964ʳ
23	Denmark	166	1	116	28	(**)	19	2
24	Norway	129	(*)	69	29	(**)	14	17
25	Spain	196	(*)	52	97	4	32	10
26	Sweden	260	(**)	157	45	(**)	49	8
27	Switzerland	948	(**)	50	158	(*)	344	395
28	United Kingdom	4,547	2	902	3,010	4	382	246
29	Other countries	438	26	233	80	—2	78	22
30	Africa, total	1,685	358	883	227	2	91	123
31	Liberia	189	(*)	(*)	(*)	(*)	16	173
32	Libya	402	(*)	(*)	(*)	(*)	3	399
33	Republic of South Africa	467	68	(*)	193	(**)	49	158
34	Other countries	628	199	357	34	6	23	9
35	Asia, total	3,112	34	2,054	556	55	225	187
36	Middle East	1,332	2	1,240	39	4	12	35
37	Far East, total	1,780	31	814	517	51	214	152
38	India	234	(*)	(*)	97	2	26	109
39	Japan	598	..	(*)	207	2	60	329
40	Philippine Republic	473	(*)	(*)	131	42	69	230
41	Other countries	474	(*)	(*)	82	5	58	329
42	Oceania, total	1,593	100	453	860	2	85	94
43	Australia	1,475	100	(*)	810	(*)	59	506
44	Other countries	117	(**)	(*)	50	(*)	25	42
45	International	1,885	..	1,064	..	821	..	..

ʳ Revised.　　ᵖ Preliminary.　　* Combined in "Other industries."　　** Less than $500,000.
SOURCE: *Survey of Current Business*, September 1966, p. 34.

				1965^p			
Total	Mining and smelt- ing	Petro- leum	Manu- factur- ing	Public utili- ties	Trade	Other
189	1	127	32	(**)	27	3
152	(*)	74	44	(**)	17	18
264	(*)	55	140	6	45	17
305	(**)	170	60	(**)	67	8
1,116	(**)	60	177	(*)	397	482
5,119	2	1,084	3,308	6	415	304
494	20	241	119	1	90	24
1,904	361	1,020	292	(**)	114	117
201	(*)	(*)	(*)	(*)	20	181
424	(*)	(*)	(*)	(*)	4	420
528	65	(*)	237	(**)	63	164
751	204	453	54	(**)	27	13
3,611	37	2,384	673	61	253	203
1,590	3	1,491	43	4	13	36
2,021	34	893	629	58	240	166
253	(*)	(*)	110	4	36	104
676	..	(*)	274	2	62	337
529	(*)	(*)	153	40	77	259
563	(*)	(*)	92	12	65	394
1,811	162	499	950	2	103	95
1,677	161	(*)	895	(*)	74	547
134	(**)	(*)	55	(*)	29	50
2,017	..	1,133	..	884	..	..

Appendix Table 10a

Direct-Investment Capital Flows and Undisturbed Subsidiary
With Major Industries for 1965

			Net capital outflows 1965ᴾ				
Line	Area and country	1964ʳ	Total	Mining and smelting	Petro- leum	Manufac- turing	Other
1	All areas, total	2,416	3,371	98	1,013	1,494	766
2	Canada	239	896	1	161	389	345
3	Latin American Republics, total	143	171	−14	−80	214	50
4	Mexico	95	100	−32	−5	115	22
5	Panama	24	11	..	7	2	2
6	Other Central America and West Indies	34	23	4	11	11	−3
7	Argentina	16	17	(*)	(*)	46	−29
8	Brazil	−36	−7	(*)	−5	2	−5
9	Chile	8	23	9	(*)	3	11
10	Colombia	28	11	(*)	13	6	−8
11	Peru	10	54	21	11	11	11
12	Venezuela	−53	−86	(*)	−98	15	−3
13	Other countries	17	25	1	21	4	(**)
14	Other Western Hemisphere	124	89	57	−5	34	3
15	Europe, total	1,368	1,432	−1	372	732	328
16	Common Market, total	807	814	(*)	135	543	135
17	Belgium and Luxembourg	75	116	..	6	65	45
18	France	139	128	(*)	−8	134	3
19	Germany	276	353	(*)	52	249	52
20	Italy	207	143	(*)	71	67	6
21	Netherlands	110	74	..	15	28	31
22	Other Europe, total	561	618	(*)	236	189	193

ʳ Revised.   ᴾ Preliminary.   * Combined in "Other industries."   ** Less than $500,000.
NOTE.—Industry detail for revised country totals of tables 10a and 10b for the years 1963 and 1964 is available from the Balance of Payments Division of the Office of Business Economics.

Earnings, by Selected Countries,

		Undistributed subsidiary earnings 1965ᵖ			
1964ʳ	Total	Mining and smelting	Petro- leum	Manufac- turing	Other
1,431	1,525	124	52	892	458
500	540	86	66	283	106
216	298	22	21	169	86
34	33	6	—3	25	5
26	42	..	13	2	26
9	11	..	2	4	5
29	87	(*)	(*)	65	22
59	84	(*)	8	53	23
13	17	(**)	(*)	5	12
11	4	(*)	—1	4	1
2	—6	(**)	—10	1	3
27	21	(*)	—2	12	11
6	5	(**)	1	—1	5
34	39	3	7	9	19
408	381	—1	—51	294	138
100	—3	(*)	—45	23	19
14	16	(**)	—1	9	9
52	32	(*)	3	34	—5
18	—42	(*)	—18	—26	2
—5	—33	(*)	—23	—14	3
21	25	..	—6	21	10
308	384	(*)	—5	271	118

APPENDIX TABLE 10a *(Continued)*

Line	Area and country	1964^r	Net capital outflows 1965^p Total	Mining and smelting	Petro- leum	Manufac- turing	Other
23	Denmark	33	19	..	13	3	3
24	Norway	2	18	(*)	5	11	1
25	Spain	35	44	(*)	2	30	12
26	Sweden	32	45	..	21	10	14
27	Switzerland	217	154	..	60	2	92
28	United Kingdom	206	324	(**)	139	116	69
29	Other countries	36	14	(*)	−5	17	2
30	Africa, total	141	160	−2	130	40	−8
31	Liberia	−7	7	(*)	(*)	(*)	7
32	Libya	70	17	(*)	(*)	(*)	17
33	Republic of South Africa	17	30	1	(*)	21	8
34	Other countries	61	105	−3	91	18	−1
35	Asia, total	224	438	1	353	56	29
36	Middle East	42	254	1	246	3	4
37	Far East, total	181	184	(**)	106	53	25
38	India	21	7	(*)	(*)	8	−1
39	Japan	78	21	..	(*)	21	(**)
40	Philippine Republic	37	31	(*)	(*)	13	18
41	Other countries	46	126	(*)	(*)	12	114
42	Oceania, total	98	142	56	41	28	17
43	Australia	125	133	55	(*)	24	54
44	Other countries	−27	9	1	(*)	4	4
45	International	80	43	..	41	..	2

^{r} Revised. ^{p} Preliminary.   * Combined in "Other industries."   ** Less than $500,000.
SOURCE: *Survey of Current Business*, September 1966, p. 34.

	Undistributed subsidiary earnings 1965ᵖ				

1964ʳ	Total	Mining and smelting	Petro-leum	Manufac-turing	Other
(**)	3	..	—3	2	4
3	5	(*)	(**)	3	3
4	15	(*)	2	9	5
4	—4	..	—8	4	(**)
113	88	..	—5	15	78
167	242	..	—1	220	23
17	34	(*)	10	18	6
42	47	4	7	20	15
—4	4	(*)	(*)	(*)	4
5	5	(*)	(*)	(*)	5
38	18	—4	(*)	17	5
3	20	8	5	3	4
74	60	3	—23	59	21
11	3	..	3	1	—1
63	58	3	—26	58	23
7	12	(*)	(*)	5	7
35	49	..	(*)	38	11
14	23	(*)	(*)	7	16
7	—27	(*)	(*)	8	—34
79	80	7	5	57	12
64	72	7	(*)	56	9
15	8	..	(*)	1	7
79	80	..	20	..	61

APPENDIX TABLE 10b

Direct-Investment Earnings and Income,[2] by Selected Countries,

			Earnings 1965[p]				
Line	Area and country	1964[r]	Total	Mining and smelting	Petro-leum	Manufac-turing	Other
1	All areas, total	5,061	5,431	571	1,825	2,019	1,017
2	Canada	1,106	1,198	198	183	606	210
3	Latin American Republics, total	1,095	1,170	206	496	269	199
4	Mexico	92	100	15	1	62	21
5	Panama	68	77	(**)	14	5	58
6	Other Central America and West Indies	36	38	10	5	5	19
7	Argentina	91	133	(*)	(*)	84	48
8	Brazil	58	102	(*)	10	64	28
9	Chile	81	83	57	(*)	6	20
10	Colombia	33	27	(*)	11	8	8
11	Peru	83	98	64	19	6	9
12	Venezuela	547	504	(*)	405	29	70
13	Other countries	6	9	(**)	−1	−1	10
14	Other Western Hemisphere	149	161	85	24	21	30
15	Europe, total	1,110	1,161	8	−42	855	341
16	Common Market, total	398	394	(*)	−32	362	63
17	Belgium and Luxembourg	53	56	(**)	3	43	10
18	France	82	79	(*)	13	65	1
19	Germany	211	217	(*)	−17	207	27
20	Italy	19	−4	(*)	−22	7	11
21	Netherlands	33	46	..	−10	41	14
22	Other Europe, total	712	767	(*)	−10	493	284

[r] Revised.   [p] Preliminary.   * Combined in "Other industries."   ** Less than $500,000.

[2] Income is the sum of dividends and interest, net *after* foreign withholding taxes, and branch profits; earnings is the sum of the U.S. share in the net earnings of subsidiaries and and branch profits; undistributed subsidiary earnings is computed as the difference between the U.S. share of net earnings of subsidiaries and the U.S. share of gross dividends (dividends *before* deduction of withholding taxes).

with Major Industries for 1965

		Income 1965ᵖ			
1964ʳ	Total	Mining and smelting	Petro-leum	Manufac-turing	Other
3,670	3,961	443	1,798	1,095	625
634	692	110	122	315	145
895	888	185	468	109	127
61	73	8	3	42	19
43	37	..	1	4	33
29	30	10	4	2	15
64	50	(*)	(*)	21	29
5	20	(*)	2	13	5
73	69	56	(*)	1	13
22	22	(*)	11	5	7
77	98	66	21	5	6
521	485	(*)	408	17	59
1	4	(**)	−2	(**)	6
116	126	82	18	15	12
654	760	8	17	532	203
275	365	(*)	18	305	43
34	35	(**)	4	30	1
27	42	(*)	9	28	5
178	236	(*)	8	205	23
23	28	(*)	(**)	21	7
13	24	..	−3	22	6
379	395	(*)	−1	227	169

NOTE.—Industry detail for revised country totals of tables 10a and 10b for the years 1963 and 1964 is available from the Balance of Payments Division of the Office of Business Economics.

APPENDIX TABLE 10b (*Continued*)

Line	Area and country	1964^r	Total	Mining and smelting	Petro-leum	Manufac-turing	Other
			Earnings 1965^p				
23	Denmark	6	6	..	−3	4	6
24	Norway	7	6	(*)	−4	4	6
25	Spain	11	25	(*)	3	12	10
26	Sweden	20	15	..	−8	6	17
27	Switzerland	151	153	..	−5	25	133
28	United Kingdom	473	498	..	−6	419	85
29	Other countries	44	65	(*)	14	22	28
30	Africa, total	346	380	61	240	42	37
31	Liberia	18	17	(*)	(*)	(*)	17
32	Libya	258	235	(*)	(*)	(*)	235
33	Republic of South Africa	87	101	34	(*)	38	29
34	Other countries	−17	28	23	−8	4	9
35	Asia, total	1,021	1,083	5	892	107	79
36	Middle East	813	826	..	816	5	4
37	Far East, total	207	257	5	76	101	76
38	India	23	30	(*)	(*)	17	12
39	Japan	54	85	..	(*)	55	30
40	Philippine Republic	47	50	(*)	(*)	16	34
41	Other countries	84	93	(*)	(*)	13	80
42	Oceania, total	142	145	8	−6	119	24
43	Australia	121	125	10	(*)	108	7
44	Other countries	21	20	−2	(*)	11	11
45	International	93	134	..	37	..	97

^{r} Revised. ^{p} Preliminary.   * Combined in "Other industries."   ** Less than $500,000.
SOURCE: *Survey of Current Business,* September 1966, p. 34.

| 1964^r | Total | Income 1965^p | | | Other |
		Mining and smelting	Petro-leum	Manufac-turing	
8	5	..	1	2	2
5	1	(*)	—4	1	3
7	10	(*)	1	3	5
16	18	..	(**)	2	17
40	68	..	(**)	10	58
276	263	..	—4	204	62
26	31	(*)	4	4	22
301	332	55	233	21	22
22	14	(*)	(*)	(*)	14
252	229	(*)	(*)	(*)	229
46	77	35	(*)	20	21
—19	11	17	—13	2	6
983	1,033	2	921	41	66
836	822	..	813	4	5
148	211	2	107	40	62
12	14	..	(*)	10	5
31	50	..	(*)	17	33
28	25	(*)	(*)	8	17
77	121	(*)	(*)	5	116
59	62	1	—11	59	12
54	52	3	(*)	50	—2
6	10	—2	(*)	9	3
27	69	..	30	..	36

APPENDIX TABLE 11

Age Structure of the Population

	Year of Reference	Percent of Total Population				
		0–4	5–14	15–19	20–64	65+
Developed O.E.C.D. Countries:						
Belgium	1960	8.1	15.4	5.9	58.6	12.0
Canada	1963	12.1	21.7	8.5	50.0	7.7
Denmark	1961	7.9	16.8	8.7	55.8	10.8
France	1962	8.6	17.6	7.0	55.0	11.8
Germany F.R.	1961	8.1	13.9	6.6	60.6	10.8
Iceland	1960	13.0	21.7	8.1	49.1	8.1
Ireland	1961	10.6	20.5	8.3	49.4	11.2
Italy	1961	8.4	16.3	7.4	58.4	9.5
Japan	1962	8.2	20.4	9.7	55.7	6.0
Luxembourg	1960	7.7	13.6	6.3	61.6	10.8
Netherlands	1962	10.0	19.1	8.9	52.7	9.3
Norway	1961	8.5	17.0	7.8	55.4	11.3
Portugal	1960	10.1	19.0	8.4	54.5	8.0
Sweden	1961	6.8	15.1	8.1	58.0	12.0
Switzerland	1962	7.4	14.6	8.3	59.0	10.7
U.K.	1962	8.2	14.7	7.5	57.7	11.9
U.S.	1963	10.9	20.1	8.2	51.5	9.3
Other Developed Countries:						
South Africa	1960	14.9	25.2	9.4	46.6	3.9
Australia	1962	10.5	19.4	8.2	53.3	8.6
Africa:						
Egypt	1960	15.9	26.8	8.3	45.5	3.5
Congo (L)	1957	16.8	22.5	6.9	48.2[1]	5.6[2]
Sudan	1963	19.0	27.7	10.7	40.5	2.1
Morocco	1960	18.6	25.6	6.2	45.7	3.9
Tanganyika	1957	17.4	25.0	10.3	45.3	2.0
Asia:						
India	1961	16.5	24.5	9.8	46.2	3.0
Indonesia	1961	17.6	24.4	8.0	47.4	2.6
Pakistan	1961	17.4	27.1	8.2	41.3[3]	6.0[4]
Philippines	1963	18.8	27.7	10.5	40.3	2.7
Thailand	1960	16.1	27.0	9.5	44.6	2.8
South Korea	1962	16.1	26.2	9.5	42.5[3]	5.7[4]
Iran	1959	17.6	26.9	7.2	44.6	3.7
Taiwan	1962	17.2	28.7	8.2	43.4	2.5
European Developing Countries:						
Spain	1960	9.9	17.5	7.9	56.4	8.3
Turkey	1960	15.3	25.8	8.3	46.8	3.6

APPENDIX TABLE 11 (*Continued*)

	Year of Reference	Percent of Total Population				
		0–4	*5–14*	*15–19*	*20–64*	*65+*
Yugoslavia	1961	10.4	20.7	7.4	55.2	6.2
Greece	1962	8.8	16.9	8.0	57.6	8.7
Latin America:						
Mexico	1960	16.5	27.7	10.1	42.2	3.5
Argentina	1961	10.4	19.4	8.5	56.5	5.2
Peru	1961	16.8	26.7	9.8	42.8	3.9
Chile	1960	15.1	24.6	9.7	46.3	4.3
Communist Countries:						
China[5]	1953	15.6	20.4	9.2	50.7	4.1
U.S.S.R.	1961	22.1[6]	10.0[7]	4.7	53.3[3]	9.9[4]
Poland	1961	11.3	22.2	6.6	53.9	6.0
Roumania	1962	8.8	19.0	7.2	57.7	7.3
Eastern Germany	1962	9.6	13.2	7.2	56.0	14.0
Bulgaria	1962	8.1	17.3	7.9	58.8	7.9
Czechoslovakia	1961	8.2	18.8	7.9	56.2	8.9
Hungary	1962	7.0	17.8	7.4	58.3	9.5
North Vietnam	1960	16.3	21.4	6.6	54.1[8]	1.6[9]

[1] Population aged 20 to 54.
[2] Population aged 55+.
[3] Population aged 20 to 59.
[4] Population aged 60+.
[5] Figures taken from *Professional Manpower and Education in Communist China*, Leo A. Orleans, p. 157.
[6] Population aged 0 to 9.
[7] Population aged 10 to 14.
[8] Population aged 20 to 69.
[9] Population aged 70+.
SOURCE: *U.N. Demographic Yearbook 1963.*

APPENDIX TABLE 12

Population and Labor Force in 1962

Mid-year

	Population (000)	Labor Force (000)	% of Population in Labor Force
Developed O.E.C.D.			
Countries	567,418	245,085	43.2
Austria	7,128	3,494	49.0
Belgium	9,221	3,679	39.9
Canada	18,570	6,734	36.3
Denmark	4,654	2,250	48.3
France	46,998	19,860	42.3
Germany (F.R.)	54,758	26,185	47.8
Iceland	182	76	41.8
Ireland	2,824	1,110	39.3
Italy	50,170	20,744	41.3
Japan	94,930	44,712	47.1
Luxembourg	320	150	46.9
Netherlands	11,806	4,519	38.3
Norway	3,638	1,518	44.6
Portugal	9,005	3,484	38.7
Sweden	7,562	3,770	49.8
Switzerland	5,610	2,633	46.9
U.K.	53,441	25,486	47.7
U.S.	186,591	74,681	40.0
European Developing			
Countries	88,000	38,460	43.7
Spain	30,817	11,831	38.4
Turkey	29,059	14,084	48.5
Yugoslavia	18,800	8,500	45.2
Greece	8,450	3,690	43.7
Other Europe	1,000		
Other Developed			
Countries	36,530	14,257	39.0
South Africa	16,655	5,929	35.6
Australia	10,705	4,303	40.2
Other[1]	9,170	4,025	43.9
Africa	254,000	99,800	39.3
Nigeria	36,500[2]	17,500	47.9
Egypt	27,300	8,200	30.0
Congo (L.)	14,800	6,300	42.4
Sudan	12,500	5,800	46.7
Morocco	12,200	3,500	28.3
Algeria	11,300	4,400	38.7
Tanganyika	9,600	3,100	31.8
Other Africa	129,800		
Asia	892,000	356,800	40.0
India	453,100	194,400	42.9

APPENDIX TABLE 12 (*Continued*)

	Population (000)	Labor Force (000)	% of Population in Labor Force
Indonesia	97,800	33,300	34.0
Pakistan	96,600	32,400	33.5
Philippines	29,300	10,800	37.0
Thailand	28,000	14,800	52.7
South Korea	26,100	9,900	38.1
Burma	23,200		
Iran	21,200	6,800	32.0
Vietnam (S.)	14,900	5,900	39.4
Taiwan	11,300	3,600	32.0
Ceylon	10,400	3,800	37.0
Other Asia	80,100		
Latin America	222,000	76,600	34.5
Brazil	75,300	24,800	33.0
Mexico	37,200	12,100	32.4
Argentina	21,400	8,700	40.6
Colombia	14,800	4,900	33.4
Peru	11,500	4,800	41.6
Other Latin America	61,800		
Oceania	4,000		
Total Developing Countries	1,460,000	574,000	39.3
Total of Countries Listed	1,182,300		
Communist Countries	1,069,400		
China	719,700		
U.S.S.R.	221,400	102,300	46.2
Poland	30,300	14,332	47.3
Eastern Germany	17,100	7,678	44.9
North Vietnam	16,600		
Czechoslovakia	13,800	6,624	48.0
North Korea	11,100		
Hungary	10,000	4,900	49.0
Bulgaria	8,000	4,360	54.5
Other	2,700		
World	3,132,348		

[1] New Zealand, Finland, West Berlin.

[2] The November 1963 census gave a population of 55.6 million compared with a 1952 census figure over 20 million lower.

SOURCES: Non O.E.C.D. developing countries from *I.L.O. Yearbook 1963*, and *Monthly Bulletin of Statistics* of U.N.; O.E.C.D. countries from O.E.C.D. *Manpower Statistics*. Communist countries derived from *Narodnoe Khoziastvo S.S.S.R. v. 1962 g.*, Moscow, p. 648. The labor force participation ratios refer to the last census year available.

Selected
Bibliography

NOTE: Articles referred to in the text are not listed here. Books referred to in the text are listed only if they have a relevance beyond the points specifically mentioned in the text.

Readers wishing a more detailed listing may consult the following specialized bibliographies:

Hazlewood, Arthur. *The Economics of Underdeveloped Areas*, London: Oxford University Press, 1954.

Meier, Gerald M., and Robert E. Baldwin. *Economic Development: Theory, History, and Policy*. New York: John Wiley & Sons, Inc., 1957. Appendices A, B, C.

Trager, Frank N. "A Selected and Annotated Bibliography on Economic Development, 1953–1957," *Economic Development and Cultural Change*, July, 1958, pp. 257–329.

GENERAL

Adelman, Irma *et al.* (eds.). *Economic Development: Analysis and Case Studies*. New York: Harper & Row, Publishers, Inc., 1962.

Adelman, Irma. *Theories of Economic Growth and Development*. Stanford, Calif.: Stanford University Press, 1961.

Agarwala, A. N. and S. P. Singh (eds.). *The Economics of Underdevelopment*. New York: Oxford University Press, 1958.

Almond, Gabriel A., and James S. Coleman (eds.). *The Politics of Developing Areas*. Princeton, N.J.: Princeton University Press, 1960.

Bruton, Henry J. *Principles of Development Economics*. Englewood Cliffs, N.J.: Prentice-Hall, Inc., 1964.

Cairncross, A. K. *Factors in Economic Development*. London: G. Allen & Unwin, 1962.

Enke, Stephen. *Economics for Development*. Englewood Cliffs, N.J.: Prentice-Hall, Inc., 1963.

Hoselitz, Berthold F. (ed.). *Theories of Economic Growth*. New York: The Free Press, 1960.

Kuznets, Simon. *Economic Growth and Structure*. New York: W. W. Norton & Company, Inc., 1965.

———. *Postwar Economic Growth*. Cambridge, Mass.: Harvard University Press, 1964.

———. *Six Lectures on Economic Growth*. New York: The Free Press, 1959, 1961.

Lewis, W. A. *The Theory of Economic Growth*. London: G. Allen & Unwin, Ltd., 1955.

Meier, Gerald (ed.). *Leading Issues in Development Economics*. New York: Oxford University Press, 1964.

Myint, Hla. *The Economics of the Developing Countries*. New York: Frederick A. Praeger, Inc., 1965.

Staley, Eugene. *The Future of Underdeveloped Areas: Political Implications of Economic Development* (rev. ed.). Harper & Row, Publishers, Inc., 1961.

PART I

Andrews, J. Russell, and Azizali F. Mohammed. *The Economy of Pakistan*. Stanford, Calif.: Stanford University Press, 1958.

Bailey, F. G. *Caste and the Economic Frontier*. Manchester: Manchester University Press, 1957.

Fine, Sherwood M. "Economic Growth in the Developing Countries," *OECD Observer, Special Issue on Development Aid*, September, 1966, pp. 23–34.

Gordon, Wendell. *The Economy of Latin America*. New York: Columbia University Press, 1950.

Hanson, Simon G. *Economic Development in Latin America*. Washington, D.C.: Inter-American Affairs Press, 1951.

The International Bank of Reconstruction and Development has published a number of economic surveys of underdeveloped countries through the John Hopkins University Press. Among these, the following may be mentioned as particularly interesting or readable: *The Economic Development of British Guiana*, 1953; *The Economic Development of Ceylon*, 1953; *The Economic Development of Guatemala*, 1951; *The Economic Development of Jordan*, 1957; *The Economic Development of Malaya*, 1955; *The Economic Development of Nigeria*, 1955; *The Economic Development of Syria*, 1955; *The Economy of Turkey*, 1951.

Kuznets, Simon, Wilbert Moore, and Joseph J. Spengler. *Economic Growth: Brazil, India, Japan*. Durham, N.C.: Duke University Press, 1955.

Lewis, W. Arthur. *The Theory of Economic Growth*. London: G. Allen & Unwin, Ltd., 1955.

Lockwood, William W. *The Economic Development of Japan*. Princeton, N.J.: Princeton University Press, 1954.

Ohlin, Göran. "A Turning Point in Population History," *OECD Observer, Special Issue on Development Aid*, September, 1966, pp. 35–39.

Schumpeter, Elizabeth B. *The Industrialization of Japan and Manchukuo*. New York: The Macmillan Company, 1940.

Shannon, Lyle W. *Underdeveloped Areas*. New York: Harper & Row, Publishers, Inc., 1957.

Staley, Eugene. *The Future of Underdeveloped Countries*. New York: Harper & Row, Publishers, Inc., 1957.

Vakil, Chandulal N., and C. N. Brahmanand. *Planning for an Expanding Economy*. Bombay: Vora, 1956.

Woytinsky, Wladimir S., and E. S. Woytinsky. *World Population and Production*. New York: The Twentieth Century Fund, Inc., 1953.

PART II

Baran, Paul. *The Political Economy of Growth*. New York: Monthly Review Press, 1957.

Baumol, William. *Economic Dynamics*. New York: The Macmillan Company, 1951.

Domar, Evsey. *Essays in the Theory of Economic Growth*. New York: Oxford University Press, 1957.

Hamberg, Daniel. *Economic Growth and Instability*. New York: W. W. Norton & Company, Inc., 1956.

Keirstead, Burton. *The Theory of Economic Change*. Toronto: The Macmillan Co. of Canada, Ltd., 1948.

Meier, Gerald M., and Robert E. Baldwin. *Economic Development: Theory, History, and Policy*. New York: John Wiley & Sons, Inc., 1957. Part 1.

Robinson, Joan. *Essay on Marxian Economics*. London: Macmillan & Co., Ltd., 1942.

Schumpeter, Joseph. *History of Economic Analysis*. New York: Oxford University Press, 1954.

Sweezy, Paul. *The Theory of Capitalist Development*. New York: Oxford University Press, 1942.

PART III

Ayres, Clarence E. *The Theory of Economic Progress*. Chapel Hill, N.C.: University of North Carolina Press, 1944.

Cairncross, Alexander K. *Home and Foreign Investment, 1870–1913*. Cambridge: Cambridge University Press, 1953.

Clark, Colin. *The Conditions of Economic Progress*. London: Macmillan & Co., Ltd., 1951.

Economic History Association. "The American West as an Underdeveloped Region," *Journal of Economic History*, XVI, No. 4 (1956), pp. 449–589.

———. "Economic Growth," *ibid*. (1947) Supplement VII.

———. "The Role of Government and Business Enterprise in the Promotion of Economic Development," *ibid*. (1950) Supplement X.

Heaton, Herbert. "Other Wests than Ours," *Journal of Economic History*, Supplement VI, 1946.

Hozelitz, B. F. (ed.). *The Progress of Underdeveloped Areas*. Chicago: University of Chicago Press, 1952.

Kuznets, Simon (ed.). *Problems in the Study of Economic Growth*. New York: National Bureau of Economic Research, Inc., 1949, especially chap. III, "Themes of Socio-Economic Growth," by Joseph J. Spengler.

Mason, Edward S. *Promoting Economic Development: United States and S. Asia*. Claremont, Calif.: 1955.

Patel, Surendra J. "The Economic Distance between Nations," *The Economic Journal*, March, 1964, pp. 119–131.

Universities–National Bureau Committee for Economic Research. *Capital For-*

mation and Economic Growth. Princeton, N.J.: Princeton University Press, 1955.

Williamson, Harold F. (ed.). *The Growth of the American Economy*. Englewood Cliffs, N.J.: Prentice-Hall, Inc., 1944.

Youngson, A. J. *Possibilities of Economic Progress* (in press, 1959).

PART IV

Ahmad, Jaleel. *Natural Resources in Low Income Countries*. Kelly-Millman, 1960.

Balogh, T. "Agricultural and Economic Development" in *Oxford Economic Papers*, February, 1961.

Braibanti, Ralph, and Joseph Spengler (eds.). *Tradition, Values, and Socio-Economic Development*. Durham, N.C.: Duke University Press, 1961.

Caves, Richard (ed.). *Trade, Growth and the Balance of Payments*. Essays in Honor of Gottfried Hubeler. Chicago: Rand McNally & Co., 1965.

Eicher, Carl, and Lawrence Witt. *Agriculture in Economic Development*. New York: McGraw-Hill Book Company, Inc., 1964.

Enke, Stephen. "Industrial Expansion through Agricultural Productivity," *Review of Economics and Statistics*, February, 1962.

Firey, Walter. *Man, Mind and Land: A Theory of Resource Use*. New York: The Free Press, 1960.

Ginsburg, N. *Atlas of Economic Development*. Chicago: University of Chicago Press, 1961.

Haavelmo, Trygve. *A Study in the Theory of Economic Evolution*. Amsterdam: North Holland Publishing Co., 1954.

Johnson, Harry G. *International Trade and Economic Growth*. Cambridge, Mass.: Harvard University Press, 1958.

——. *Money, Trade, and Economic Growth*. London: G. Allen & Unwin, Ltd., 1962.

Kimble, George. *Tropical Africa*. 2 vols. New York: The Twentieth Century Fund, Inc., 1960.

Kindleberger, Charles P. *Economic Development*. New York: McGraw-Hill Book Company, Inc., 1958.

Leibenstein, Harvey. "What Can We Expect from a Theory of Development," *Kyklos*, Vol. XIX, Fasc. I, 1966.

Lerner, Daniel (with Lucille W. Pevsner). *The Passing of Traditional Society*. New York: The Free Press, 1958.

Letiche, John. *Balance of Payments and Economic Growth*. New York: Harper & Row, Publishers, Inc., 1959.

Lewis, W. Arthur. *The Theory of Economic Growth*. London: G. Allen & Unwin, Ltd., 1955.

McClelland, David C., *et al. The Achievement Motive*. New York: Appleton-Century-Crofts, Inc., 1953.

Mead, Margaret (ed.). *Cultural Patterns and Technical Change*. Paris: UNESCO, 1953.

Mehden, Fred von de. *Politics of the Developing Nations*. Englewood Cliffs, N.J.: Prentice-Hall, Inc., 1964.

Mehta, F. "On the Theory of Raul Prebisch," *Indian Economic Journal*, January, 1957.

Moore, Wilbert E. *Industrialization and Labor*. Ithaca, N.Y.: Cornell University Press, 1951.

Myrdal, Gunnar. *Economic Theory and Underdeveloped Regions*. London: Gerald Duckworth & Co., Ltd., 1957.

Nash, Manning. *Primitive and Peasant Economic Systems*. San Francisco: Chandler Publishing Company, 1966.

Nicholls, W. H. "Industrialization, Factor Markets, and Agricultural Development," *Journal of Political Economy*, August, 1961.

Nurkse, Ragnar. *Problems of Capital Formation in Underdeveloped Countries*. Oxford: Basil Blackwell & Mott, Ltd., 1953.

Poincilit, Erhart. "The Role of Trade with Developing Countries," *OECD Observer Special Issue on Development Aid*, September, 1966, pp. 46–52.

Rostow, W. W. *The Process of Economic Growth*. New York: W. W. Norton & Company, Inc., 1952.

Schultz, T. W. *Transforming Traditional Agriculture*. New Haven: Yale University Press, 1965.

Scitovsky, Tibor. *Growth: Balanced or Unbalanced*. Stanford, Calif.: Stanford University Press, 1959.

Sen, Amartya K. "Peasants and Dualism with or without Surplus Labor," *Journal of Political Economy*, October, 1966, pp. 425–450.

Williamson, Harold F., and John A. Buttrick. *Economic Development: Principals and Patterns*. Englewood Cliffs, N.J.: Prentice-Hall, Inc., 1954.

PART V

Abraham, W. I. "Investment Estimates of Underdeveloped Countries: An Appraisal," *Journal of the American Statistical Association*, September, 1958, pp. 669–679.

Adler, John H., E. R. Schlesinger, and E. C. Olson. *Public Finance and Economic Development in Guatemala*. Stanford, Calif.: Stanford University Press, 1952, pp. xix, 282.

Allen, George C., and A. G. Donnithorne. *Western Enterprise in Far Eastern Economic Development: China and Japan*. London: G. Allen & Unwin, Ltd., 1954.

Almond, Gabriel A., and James S. Coleman (eds.). *The Politics of Developing Areas*. Princeton, N.J.: Princeton University Press, 1960.

American Assembly. *International Stability and Progress*. New York: Columbia University Graduate School of Business, June, 1957.

Baldwin, George B. *Industrial Growth in South India: Case Studies in Economic Development*. New York: The Free Press, 1959.

Baldwin, R. E. "Exchange Rate Policy and Economic Development," *Economic Development and Cultural Change*, July, 1961.

Belshaw, Horace. *Population Growth and Levels of Consumption*. London: G. Allen & Unwin, Ltd., 1956.

Benham, Frederic. *The Colombo Plan and Other Essays*. London and New York: Royal Institute of Foreign Affairs, 1956.

Bird, Richard, and Oliver Oldman (eds.). *Readings on Taxation in Developing Countries*. Baltimore: The Johns Hopkins Press, 1964.

Black, Eugene. *The Diplomacy of Economic Development*. Cambridge, Mass.: Harvard University Press, 1963.

Bonne, Alfred. *Studies in Economic Development*. London: Routledge & Kegan Paul, Ltd., 1957.

Bowman, Mary Jean. "Converging Concerns of Economists and Educators," *Comparative Education Review*, October, 1962, pp. 111–119.

Brand, W. *The Struggle for a Higher Standard of Living*. New York: The Free Press, 1958.

Chandrasekhar, George. *Population and Planned Parenthood in India*. London: G. Allen & Unwin, Ltd., 1956.

Chang Kia-Ngau. *The Inflationary Spiral: The Experience in China, 1939–1950.* New York: Technology Press, M.I.T., and John Wiley & Sons, Inc., 1958.

Conrad, Joseph W. et al. *Inflation, Growth and Employment Research Study for the Commission on Money and Credit.* Englewood Cliffs, N.J.: Prentice-Hall, Inc., 1964.

Diamond, William. *Development Blanks.* Baltimore: Johns Hopkins Press, for the Economic Development Institute, International Bank for Reconstruction and Development, 1957.

Friedman, John. "Regional Economic Policy for Developing Areas," *Papers of the Regional Science Association,* Volume 11, 1963, pp. 41–62.

Glick, Philip M. *The Administration of Technical Assistance: Growth in the Americas.* Chicago: University of Chicago Press, 1957.

Hagen, Everett E. *The Economic Development of Burma.* Washington, D.C.: National Planning Association, 1956.

Hapgood, David, and Max Millikan. *Policies for Promoting Growth.* Cambridge, Mass.: Harvard University Press, 1965.

Hicks, J. R., and U. K. Hicks. *Report on Finance and Taxation in Jamaica.* Kingston, Jamaica: Government Printer, 1955.

Higgins, Benjamin. *Indonesia's Economic Stabilization and Development.* New York: Institute of Pacific Relations, 1957.

Higgins, Benjamin, and Wilfred Malenbaum. *Financing Economic Development.* New York: Carnegie Endowment for International Peace, 1955.

Hinrichs, Harley H. *A General Theory of Tax Structure Change during Economic Development.* Cambridge, Mass.: Harvard University Press, 1966.

International Labour Office. *Employment Objectives in Economic Development.* Geneva: 1961.

Iversen, Carl. *A Report on Monetary Policy in Iraq.* Copenhagen: Ejnar Munksgaard, 1954.

Johnson, Harry G. *Economic Policies toward Less Developed Countries.* Washington: 1967.

———. "Tariffs and Economic Development: Some Theoretical Issues," *The Journal of Developmental Studies,* October, 1964, pp. 3–30.

———. "United States Policy and the Problems of Developing Countries," *The Journal of Business of the University of Chicago,* October, 1965, pp. 337–343.

———. *The World Economy at the Crossroads.* Oxford and New York: Oxford University Press, 1965.

Karefa-Smart, John. "Health and Welfare Services in Development Planning," in John Karefa-Smart (ed.) *Africa, Progress through Cooperation.* New York: Dodd, Mead & Company, 1966.

Keenleyside, H. C. "Administrative Problems of Technical Assistance Administration," *Canadian Journal of Economics and Political Science,* August, 1952, pp. 345–357.

Lewis, W. Arthur. *Development Planning.* New York: Harper & Row, Publishers, Inc., 1966.

Li, Choh-Ming. *Economic Development of Communist China: An Appraisal of the Five Years of Industrialization.* Berkeley, Calif.: University of California Press, 1958.

Marget, Arthur W. "Inflation: Some Lessons of Recent Foreign Experience," *American Economic Review,* May, 1960.

Maynard, Geoffrey. *Economic Development and the Price Level.* New York: The Macmillan Company, 1962.

Millikan, Max, and W. W. Rostow. *A Proposal: Key to an Effective Foreign Policy.* New York: Harper & Row, Publishers, 1957.

Nurkse, Ragnar, *et al.* "The Quest for a Stabilization Policy in Primary Producing Countries," *Kyklos,* XI, No. 2, 1958.

Prest, A. R. *Public Finance in Underdeveloped Countries.* New York: Frederick A. Praeger, Inc., 1962.

"Research Expenditures by Developing Countries" (Articles by MGK Menon, Mahbub in Hug, Salimuzzaman Siddign, Abdus Salam). *The Development Digest,* January, 1967, pp. 1–38.

Reuber, Grant L. *Canada's Interest in the Trade Problems of Less Developed Countries.* Montreal: Private Planning Association of Canada, 1964.

"The Role of Health Today in Economic Development," a symposium, *American Journal of Public Health,* Vol. 53, No. 3, March, 1963.

Rosen, George. *Industrial Change in India: Industrial Growth, Capital Requirements, and Technological Change, 1937–1955.* New York: The Free Press, 1958.

Rostow, W. W. *et al. The Prospects for Communist China.* New York: John Wiley & Sons, Inc., 1954.

Russell, Sir John. *World Populations and World Food Supplies.* London: G. Allen & Unwin, Ltd., 1957.

Saab, Gabriel. *The Egyptian Land Reform.* Oxford: Oxford University Press, 1967.

Schaedel, Richard P. "Land Reform Studies," *Latin American Research Review,* Vol. I, No. 1, 1965.

Schlesinger, Eugene R. *Multiple Exchange Rates and Economic Development.* Princeton, N.J.: Princeton University Press, 1952, pp. i, 76.

Schultz, Theodore W. *The Economic Organization of Agriculture.* New York: McGraw-Hill Book Company, Inc., 1953.

Tinbergen, Jan. *Shaping the World Economy.* New York: The Twentieth Century Fund, Inc., 1962.

Tsuru, S. *Essays on the Japanese Economy.* Tokyo: Kinokumiya Bookstore, Tokyo, 1958.

United Nations Department of Economic Affairs. *Domestic Financing of Economic Development.* New York: 1950, pp. vi, 231.

United Nations Department of Economic and Social Affairs. *Land Reform: Defects in Agrarian Structures as Obstacles to Economic Development.* New York: 1951.

United Nations Economic Commission for Asia and the Far East. *Mobilization of Domestic Capital in Certain Countries of Asia and the Far East.* Bangkok: 1951, pp. xii, 239.

————. *Mobilization of Domestic Capital.* Bangkok: 1953.

United Nations Economic Commission for Asia and the Far East. *Programming Techniques for Economic Development,* Bangkok: 1960.

United Nations Research Institute for Social Development. *Cost-Benefit Analysis of Social Projects: Report of a Meeting of Experts Held in Rennes, France, 27 September-2 October 1965,* Geneva: 1966.

"Urban Problems" (Articles by Anable Solow, David F. Ladin, Malcolm D. Rivicin, Catherine Bauer Wursten, Thomas Callaway). *The Development Digest,* January, 1967, pp. 1–38.

Wald, Haskell P., and J. N. Froomkin (eds.). *Agricultural Taxation and Economic Development.* Cambridge, Mass.: Harvard University Printing Office, 1954.

Wallich, Henry C., and J. H. Adler. *Public Finance in a Developing Country: El Salvador*. Cambridge, Mass.: Harvard University Press, 1951.
Weisbrod, Burton A. *Economics of Public Health*. Philadelphia: University of Pennsylvania Press, 1961.
———. "Investing in Human Capital," *The Journal of Human Resources*, Vol. 1, No. 1, Summer, 1966, pp. 6–21.
Wolf. Charles, and S. C. Sufrin. *Capital Formation and Foreign Investment in Underdeveloped Areas*. Syracuse, N.Y.: Syracuse University Press, 1955.

PART VI

AER, May 1965, *Recent Economic Exploration of India and China*.
Baer, Werner. *Industrialization and Economic Development in Brazil*. Homewood, Ill.: Richard D. Irwin, Inc., 1966.
Hansen, Niles M. "Unbalanced Growth and Regional Development," *The Western Economic Journal*, Fall, 1965, pp. 3–14.
Higgins, Benjamin and Jean. *Indonesia: The Crisis of the Millstones*. Princeton, N.J.: D. Van Nostrand Company, Inc., 1963.
Lockwood, William (ed.). *The State and Enterprise in Japanese Development*. Princeton, 1965.
Rosenstein-Rodan, Paul N. "Reflections on Regional Development," *Scritti di Economia e Statistica in memoria di Alessandro Molinari*, Milan: 1963.
Sunkel, Oswaldo. "The Structural Background of Development Problems in Latin America," *Weltwirtschaftliches Archiv*, Band 97, 1966, Heft 1.
Urquidi, Victor L. *The Challenge of Development in Latin America*. New York, 1964.

Index

Cuba *(Continued)*
  living standard, 794, 805
  occupations (1952), 793
  output, structure of, 796–98
  per capita income, 793
  population, 791–92
    changes in, long-term, 795
    pre-Castro plans and policies, 806
    regional dualism, 798–99
    resources, 791–92
  social development, level of, 792–96
    stagnation in, 798, 801, 805, 806
    sugar economy, 800–06, 807
    unemployment and underemployment, 793–94, 802, 806
Cultural change, economic development without, 264–65
Cultural determinism, 224–66
  achieving society, the, 241–49
  economics, scope of, 225
  political development, 225–27
  social change, theory of, 249–57
  socio-cultural dualism, Boeke and, 227–41

Da Gama, Vasco, 168
Davis, Kingsley, 43–44
Deane, Phyllis, 180, 185, 191, 606
Death rates, 40, 41, 459–62
  decline in, lag between decline in birth rates and, 44
  population and (1958–1963), 15
  world population and, 42
Decision function, the, 376–77
  indivisibility in, 329
  shadow prices and, 370–72
Defense Department, U.S., 598
Demand, indivisibility of, 329
Denison, Edward F., 426–27
Denison variant, education planning, 426–31
Depression of the 1930's (Great Depression), 95, 99, 101, 102, 103, 120, 132, 136, 220, 319, 473, 619, 624, 691, 693, 708, 802
Depressions, financial, 84, 99–100
Deutsch, Karl, 224
Developing countries, 30–32
  case studies of, *see* Case studies
Development Loan Fund, 598
Development tax, 525
Dhar, P. N., 381, 383, 384
Diaz, Porfirio, 635, 636
Diaz Ordaz, Gustavo, 641
Discontinuous disturbance, essence of development, 96–97
Discorsi Politici (Giuccardini), 3
Discoveries, geographical, 168–69, 170

Diseases, relationship of monoculture to, 210–12
Distribution, theory of, 56, 67
Diversification, stability and, 552–53
Djatiluhur power project, 697
Djuanda, Dr., 696
Domar, Evsey D., 117–19, 125, 155
  model of capitalist development, 117–19
Donnithorne, Audrey G., 271, 563, 564
Doody, Francis S., 88n., 93n., 96
Dualism, 87
  regional 20–21, 732–36, 798–99
  socio-cultural, Boecke and, 227–41
  sociological, 21
  technological, *see* Technological dualism
  technological progress, employment and, 380
  theory of, 69–70
Duesenberry, James S., 610

Eckaus, R. S., 672, 673, 674
Economic and Employment Commission, UN, 277
Economic and Social Affairs Department, UN, 30, 287–88
Economic Commission for Africa (ECA), 595
Economic Commission for Asia and the Far East (ECAFE), 409, 473–74, 550, 569, 595
Economic Commission for Europe (ECE), 276, 595
Economic Commission for Latin America (ECLA), 463–64, 466, 469–70, 483, 595, 725, 810
Economic development, 55, 67, 70, 86, 87, 95, 104, 147–48
  advantages of, 364–65
  balanced, *see* Balanced economic development
  balanced versus unbalanced, 327–42
    balanced growth, 332–35
    equilibrium trap, low-level, 330–31
    indivisibilities, Rosenstein-Rodan and, 328–30
    unbalance, Hirschman's strategy of, 335–41
  capitalist development versus, 106–07
  economic factors of, 188–96
    capital accumulation, 188, 189–90
    conjuncture of, importance of, 196
    population growth, 188, 190–92
    resources, discoveries of new, 188, 192–94
    technological progress, 188, 194–96
  education and, 410–35
    cost-benefit approach, necessity of, 411–12